BY THE AUTO EDITORS OF CONSUMER GUIDE®

ENCYCLOPEDIA OF AMERICAN CARS 1930~1980

50
YEARS OF AUTOMOTIVE
HISTORY

RICHARD M. LANGWORTH

BEEKMAN HOUSE
NEW YORK

Contents

Chief Contributing Author: Richard M. Langworth
Contributing Authors: Maurice D. Hendry, Jeffrey I. Godshall, Walter
  Gosden, Alden Jewell, R. Perry Zavitz
Editorial Assistant: Barbara F. Langworth
Photo Credits: Applegate & Applegate Collection, John A. Conde, Asa E.
  Hall, Richard M. Langworth, Motor Vehical Manufacturers Association,
  Richard Quinn
Cover Photos: David Gooley, Douglas J. Mitchel, Mel Winer
Book Designer: Frank E. Peiler

This edition published by:
Beekman House
A division of Crown Publishers, Inc.
One Park Avenue
New York, N.Y. 10016

ISBN: 0-517-42462-2

Acknowledgements

It would be impossible to list in this short space the numerous members of the automotive industry and the old-car avocation whose kind assistance and research over the past 25 years contributed in some way to the material in this book. We can offer them all only a general, but very sincere, thanks. We would be remiss, however, if we failed to single out those whose assistance has been particularly important:

Collections and Libraries: Henry Austin Clark, Jr. and the Long Island Automotive Museum, Southampton, New York; the late James J. Bradley and the National Automotive History Collection, Detroit Public Library, Detroit, Michigan; Randy Mason, G. Donald Adams, and the Henry Ford Museum, Greenfield Village, Dearborn, Michigan; Michael Moore and the Library of Harrah's Automobile Collection, Reno, Nevada; Briggs S. Cunningham and John Burgess of the Briggs Cunningham Automotive Museum, Costa Mesa, California; Brooks Stevens and the Brooks Stevens Automotive Museum, Mequon, Wisconsin; G.N. Georgano and the National Motor Museum, Beaulieu, Hampshire, England. The editors extend special appreciation to John A. Conde, from whose collection were drawn many photographs of 1930s models.

Editors and Publications: David Brownell, Michael Lamm, and the editors of *Special-Interest Autos* magazine, Bennington, Vermont; Donald R. Peterson and the editors of *Car Collector and Car Classics* magazine, Atlanta, Georgia; Graham Robson and the editors of *Autocar* and *Thoroughbred and Classic Car* magazines, London, England.

Individual Researchers: Pete Booz, Hudson; Alex Burr, Hudson; George E. Domer, American Bantam and Kaiser-Frazer; Jim Dunne, Buick and Pontiac; John A. Conde, American Motors; Sam Folz, Corvette; Fred K. Fox, Studebaker; Jeffrey I. Godshall, Graham, Hupmobile, Kaiser-Frazer; Walter Gosden, Cadillac; Harold Hagen, Kaiser-Frazer; Asa E. Hall, Studebaker and Avanti II; George L. Hamlin, Packard; William B. Hamlin, Tucker; Maurice D. Hendry, Cadillac and Lincoln; Rick Kopec, Shelby; Paul McLaughlin, Ford Mustang; David Newell, Chevrolet Corvair; Jan P. Norbye, Buick and Pontiac; James Petrik, Ford Thunderbird; Richard C. Ryan, Ford Thunderbird; Rich Taylor, sports cars; W. William Tilden, Willys.

Car Owners, color section: Bob Almondson, Andrew Alphonso, Vicky Bach, Jim Baldauf, Dave Bertram, Ernie Bollerud, Jim Bowersox, Tony Capua, Ben Caskey, Bill Cline, Mike Cowles, Dan Darling, Dr. James Dunkel, Ken Dyke, Warren Emerson, Doug Englin, Greg Englin, Wayne Essary, Everett Faulkner, Paul Gallo, John Hruby, Alan Jones, Bud Juneau, Len Kancer, Steve LeFevre, Ralph Leid, Mark Lopinsky, Tom Lorek, Jim Maztas, Terry McElfresh, Dennis McNamara, George Nowak, Forest Padon, Robert Peiler, John Pirochta, Chet Pollock, Roger Randolph, Vincent Rufolo, George Sampson, Larry Schaal, Richard Schick, Don Smith, Harry Soenksen, Jack Stewart, Ken Stiles, Michael Therrien, Bob Thorn, John Thorn, Carol Urban, Larry Van Horn, Charles Welsh, Bill Wertens, Gerald Wuicket, Ray Zeman.

Color Photography supplied by: David Gooley & Associates, Bud Juneau, Richard M. Langworth, Vince Manocchi, Douglas J. Mitchel.

Introduction

With this revised and expanded edition of the *Encyclopedia of American Cars*, the auto editors of CONSUMER GUIDE® magazine answer the one criticism levelled at the highly acclaimed original; namely, a desire for additional coverage. So, here it is: 50 years of Detroit history — the most momentous years in U.S. industry annals. And though it has spawned a couple of imitators since the first edition appeared, this remains the most accurate, comprehensive, incisive, and useful book of its kind for professional and hobbyist alike.

The half century detailed in these pages saw American automakers discard dead-end concepts and universally adopt the internal-combustion gasoline engine. It saw the birth of companion makes like LaSalle and the demise of all except Pontiac; the attempts by prestige marques like Packard to compete in the higher-volume market; the temporary cessation of car production during World War II, a first in the nation's history; the postwar rise and fall of the remaining independents; the advent of mergers; the growing dominance of General Motors, and Ford Motor Company's efforts to counter it; the roller-coaster ride of Chrysler Corporation; the appearance of compacts, intermediates, and ponycars; the increasing role of government in automotive design; fuel shortages and rationing; the downsizing revolution; major technological developments including front drive, turbocharging, plastics, electronics, and the science of aerodynamics; periodic challenges from foreign manufacturers; and, last but not least, extraordinary increases in the cost of buying, owning, and manufacturing cars. Through it all, however, the American car has seen little conceptual change — at least through 1977.

This half century is interesting because of its sophistication rather than any pioneering breakthroughs. It saw the golden age of the great Classics, the finest flowering of both the independents and the Big Three. At least 85 percent of the people collecting and restoring old cars today are concerned with the 1930-1980 period, and the pre-1930 antiques that once dominated the hobby have, to a large extent, long since been relegated to museums. Meanwhile, collector focus has moved forward with time and the addition of younger enthusiasts. People generally tend to be interested in the cars they remember from their youth, which explains the current high popularity of late-'60s muscle cars.

One writer has characterized the automobile's evolution as a three-part drama. In Part I (through World War I) we experimented with all manner of approaches to personal transportation, using engines running on electricity and steam as well as gasoline. In Part II (WWI through the Depression) we settled on the internal-combustion engine. In Part III (1930-1975) we simply perfected the concepts and components of Part II. One could say that we are now in a Part IV — what might be termed the Age of Efficiency — that began with GM's first downsized cars of 1977 and is still in its infancy.

At this writing it is too early for collectors to have expressed much interest in the cars of the late '70s and the '80s, although one day they undoubtedly will. Manufacturers have learned to live with goverment mandates, and the age of dull, patchwork engineering and styling responses that marked so many cars of the '70s seems to be behind us at last. American automobiles are again becoming more exciting and individual, and there's no doubt that today's Mustang SVO, Chrysler Laser and Chevrolet Camaro will have the same fascination for the next generation of enthusiasts that the Shelby Mustang, Hemi-Cuda and Camaro Z-28 have now.

In the first edition of this book we suggested that the "age of collectible cars" might actually end with 1970, but have since come to think otherwise. There were interesting cars in the '70s, a decade enthusiasts generally view as a long dry spell for Detroit, and you'll find them in these pages. The latest domestic models, many both the product and expression of fascinating new technology, are arguably the best cars built in this county since Oliver Evans of Delaware first applied for a patent on a motorized wheeled vehicle in 1775. Charles M. Jordan, Director of Design for GM, can trace his career from the heyday of Harley Earl through the upheavals of the '60s and '70s and on down to the present. We recently asked him if designing cars today is as much fun as it used to be. "It's more fun than it ever was," he replied, "because it's very satisfying working together with all the disciplines. We have the wind tunnel, we now have the ability to do all these advanced things, we're learning a lot. It is more interesting than, say, the '50s, when design was largely a matter of decoration." Obviously, the nation's oft-memorialized love affair with the automobile is alive and well, and the many recent reports of its death are, as Mark Twain said, greatly exaggerated.

Writing the first edition of this book was tremendously gratifying for those of us who comprised a vocal minority 15 years ago, trying to alert a collector body besotted with antiques and Classics to something called the "special-interest car." The tremendous response to that original work made possible this new, much larger version. We hope you enjoy it.

Genesis of an Era: The 1930s

Ironically, the automotive styling and engineering developments of 1940-75 were almost wholly the result of lessons learned during the greatest economic disaster in modern history. The Depression may have meant the end

5

for many automobile producers, but it forced the survivors to think, plan, and invent. In so doing, they altered the shape of the American automobile almost completely.

During the 1930s, the industry parted company with clumsy, unsynchronized manual transmissions; complicated sleeve-valve engines; ancient wood-and-fabric bodies; mechanical brakes; and solid front axles. In their place came synchromesh gears, semi-automatic and fully automatic transmissions, side-valve and overhead-valve engines, all-steel bodies composed of fewer and larger panels welded together, hydraulic brakes, and independent front suspension. As roads improved, buyers demanded more speed, so higher-revving engines were needed. This led to new foundry and engine-building techniques that guaranteed high-rpm reliability. Cars could then be geared higher to travel faster. The advent of automatic shiftless transmissions made it less important to gear and "cam" a car so the lazy driver could pull away from a crawl without changing out of "High." As we learned how independent front suspensions and rubber engine mounts could help absorb road shocks, we were able to design stiffer chassis, which made overall construction tighter and more solid. Compared to its 1930 forebear—an upright box on artillery wheels wheezing along on four or six small cylinders—the automobile of 1940 was a sleek torpedo on slotted steel wheels, with more room inside, a longer wheelbase, and a vibration-free, rubber-mounted engine—and it was a good 20 mph faster.

In the process of thinning out industry ranks, the Depression years largely determined the nature of the major producers as we know them today—and selected those independents strong enough to survive. Ever since its founding by W. C. Durant in 1908, General Motors had been striving for managerial and creative decentralization through its division structure. While Henry Ford ruled his strongly centralized company almost singlehandedly, the division concept put GM ahead in production during the early 1920s. Only after Henry Ford II took over his grandfather's troubled firm in 1945 did Ford begin to decentralize—and to rebuild.

Walter P. Chrysler was an old GM man, and saw the light very early on. Although Chrysler Corporation was founded in the '20s, it came of age during the '30s. Following a division structure not unlike GM's, Chrysler built the second largest car company in the nation during the decade, and it remained so until the early 1950s.

By 1940, only a few independent manufacturers were left. After the war there were just four, all with high hopes: Nash, Hudson, Packard, Studebaker. Together with newcomer Kaiser-Frazer and later joined by Crosley and Willys, the independents enjoyed as much as a 15-percent market share in the late '40s and early '50s. But it didn't last. Nash's president George Mason was the only high-ranking executive among the independents who could envision the benefits of merger. He had managed to add Hudson to his empire in 1954, thus forming American Motors, but died before he could meld in Packard and Studebaker. One by one, the other independents vanished, though Studebaker-Packard lasted longer than most. Only AMC is still hanging on, and seems destined to survive as a producer of "specialty" models not offered by the "Big Three."

The 1940s

Although classic four-square styling was largely abandoned after World War II, some of its finest expressions appeared in 1940-42: the senior Packards, the Hupp Skylark and Graham Hollywood, and the last production LaSalle. Other cars, like the sleek Fords and Mercurys of 1940, offered near-perfection in line and form. Chrysler's 1949 products, boxy and upright, symbolized that corporation's concern for ample interior space within compact exterior dimensions.

The modern V8 engine was perhaps the most significant engineering development of the decade. Of course, V8s had been around for years—at Cadillac since 1915, and at Ford since 1932. But these were relatively heavy, long-stroke, low-compression engines, known for smoothness rather than performance. In 1949, Cadillac and Oldsmobile pioneered a new generation of V8s, the forerunners of the powerplants found in most large US cars today. America's light, efficient, and powerful V8 soon became famous worldwide for its performance and reliability.

The '40s also offered traditionally designed engines for those who preferred them. Packard's magnificent 356 cubic-inch straight eight and Cadillac's 346 V8 were L-head units known for quietness and smooth operation. Both are highly prized by collectors.

Most engines of the 1940s, however, were plain side-valve inline sixes and eights that may not have been revolutionary, but were dependable and economical. The 230- and 170-cid sixes sold by Plymouth and Studebaker, respectively, served their makers well right on through the '50s, and were well-known for thriftiness. Studebaker's powerplant was a traditional winner in the Mobilgas Economy Run.

Racing was not emphasized by the industry as a whole during the '40s, but many individuals recorded performances that indicated the competition potential of certain production models. The supercharged Graham of 1940-41 was among the fastest cars powered by a conventional side-valve six. The Hudson Super Six, the Graham's postwar counterpart, could reach speeds that far exceeded what was normally expected from six cylinders. Oldsmobile and Cadillac achieved early competition success with their overhead-valve V8s. Cadillac scored an unbelieveable 10th- and 11th-place finish at the grueling 24 hours of Le Mans in 1950. Oldsmobile's fast, lightweight 88 dominated stock-car racing from 1949 through 1951.

Another extremely important engineering highlight of the '40s was the increasing use of the modern automatic transmission. Before, there had been only semi-automatics. Oldsmobile offered one in 1937, then dropped it in 1938 for Hydra-Matic—the most success-

ful completely shift-free transmission of all time. Chrysler enthusiastically marketed its Fluid Drive (which eliminated most shift motions) well into the 1950s. Ford was conservative, and stayed with the manual gearshift (both with and without overdrive) for all 1940-49 Fords and Mercurys. It offered the GM-built Hydra-Matic for the 1949 Lincoln, but did not manufacture an automatic of its own until 1951. Nash and Kaiser-Frazer stayed with stickshifts until 1950, then gave in and purchased Hydra-Matic, too.

Two independents that did strike out with automatics of their own were Packard and Studebaker. Packard's Ultramatic was the only such unit developed entirely by an independent without any help from a transmission firm. It was a smooth-shifting gearbox, but not amenable to the extra power delivered by later Packard engines. Studebaker teamed up with Detroit Gear to create a fine three-speed automatic, but it didn't arrive until 1950.

GM really had the automatic market to itself in the 1940s. Cadillac began offering Hydra-Matic in 1948; Buick debuted its Dynaflow Drive the same year. Though smooth in operation, Dynaflow was not in the same performance league as Hydra-Matic.

The '40s were years of attrition and false starts for the smaller automakers. American Bantam, Hupmobile, and Graham all ceased production well before World War II—and did not return afterward. Willys-Overland, which offered conventional passenger cars through the 1942 model year, came back after the war with an interesting line of Jeep-like vehicles. These included the unique Jeepster that appeared for 1948—the last true touring car in the American industry. The decade's best-known failure was the Tucker—a brilliant concept that nevertheless saw no more than a few dozen copies. For years, the assumption was that the Tucker had been killed—prematurely—by General Motors and its cohorts. Yet even though its admirable design caused the big manufacturers a bit of concern, it was not actually a serious threat to them. Whether the car could have been realistically produced at the price Preston Tucker claimed will probably never be known.

The 1950s

A lot of people think the cars of the '50s are responsible for the sorry state of the automotive scene today. Critics tell us they were heavy, ungainly, dumb-looking beasts with no—or at best few—redeeming virtues. Yet, they were nowhere near as uniformly bad as skeptics like to insist. In fact, several important advances were made between 1950 and 1960.

Consider, for example, torsion bar suspension, short-stroke V8s, efficient automatic transmissions, and unit construction—which we tried and liked—and air suspension, tailfins, and pushbutton transmissions—which we tried, disliked, and discarded. Notwithstanding the emphasis on chrome-laden gimmickry, the 1950s also brought some innovative new body styles such as the

two- and four-door pillarless hardtop, and the all-steel station wagon that became (for the first time in its history) more like a car than a truck.

If these years are remembered for some of the industry's worst styling excesses, they also were marked by some of the finest automotive designs of all time: the Studebaker "Loewy coupes," the Continental Mark II, the Darrin-styled Kaisers, the two-seat Thunderbirds. Finally—and this may come as a surprise—American cars of this decade are considered by many experts to have been safer than cars had ever been before. Maybe the seatbelts, padded dashes, and dished steering wheels weren't merely sales gimmicks after all.

There's something else about these automobiles that even their admirers often fail to mention, perhaps because it's so obvious. These cars have an intrinsic character—a special appeal—which the industry somehow lost in the late '60s. They were different—vastly different—from the cars of today. This was probably the last decade when a manufacturer dared sell something clearly unique, like the "Step-down" Hudson, the tiny Nash Metropolitan, or the fiberglass Woodill Wildfire. Cars of the '50s were also built differently: interiors were trimmed in comfortable mohair or genuine leather; bodies were made of heavy-gauge steel. Their makers shunned things like plastic, cardboard, and decals. While the average family car of 1950-59 probably handled as sloppily as everyone said it did, it was also built with more pure integrity than its more nimble successors. Every piece of trim met every other piece precisely where intended. Each door, trunklid, and hood closed with a resounding clunk, swinging shut on vault-like hinges. Collectors still discover rust-free examples with six-figure mileage, and interiors, paint, and mechanical components in approximately the same shape as when the car left the factory a quarter century ago. And this, despite the industry's reputation for haphazard assembly quality.

The 1960s

The '60s do not really seem that long ago, and headlines from that turbulent era are still fresh in many memories. It's not at all difficult to remember the cars: the 18-foot-long luxury hardtops, the bucket-seat sporty compacts, the personal cars, the ponycars, and the muscle cars of 1960-69. An incredible assortment of types streamed out of the factory gates in those years. There was a car for every taste and budget—anything from the $1700 Metropolitan to the $18,500 Crown Imperial limousine.

Government demands that the industry clean up exhaust emissions and make cars safer were good ideas, even if the legislation that followed was often controversial. But the mandates that took effect in the late '60s also guaranteed an end to the uninhibited experimentation that characterized the early years of the decade.

In a way, the public had as much to do with the

decline of innovation as the government. What incentive was there for automakers to develop something really new or different when buyers seemed interested mainly in performance, styling, and "pizzazz?" Consider the record. After generating high initial interest, the sophisticated Corvair was soon forgotten—long before Ralph Nader came along. Buyers yawned at the first Pontiac Tempest, not sure what to make of its all-independent suspension and rear-mounted transaxle. The Tempest sold well, but it might have done even better with a more ordinary drivetrain. In 1966, Oldsmobile introduced its radical, superbly engineered front-wheel-drive Toronado—which was consistently outsold by the conventionally designed Buick Riviera. Pontiac's overhead-cam six of 1966, an engine that offered as good a balance between economy and performance as any engine on the market, was almost completely ignored as most customers insisted on big-block V8s.

Sales records aside, there is something significant about the technological tours de force of the '60s: nearly all of them came from General Motors. There are many reasons for this. The decline of the independents after World War II (the mergers and demise of Nash and Hudson, Packard and Studebaker, plus the disappearance of Kaiser and Willys) radically altered the nature of the industry. Soon, the high-volume manufacturers discovered there were not just one or two kinds of buyers, but six or eight. The result was a raft of new sizes and concepts designed for distinct segments of the market—and new categories like compact, sporty-compact, intermediate, standard, luxury, and personal-specialty. Yet ironically, all this variety gradually blurred the distinction in price or status between makes. What had happened was that the market had subdivided after about 1955, but hadn't really expanded. This can be seen in the production figures. Chevrolet, for example, wasn't actually turning out any more cars in 1970 than it did in 1960, but it was building a far greater variety of models.

General Motors was best able to adapt to this new situation. Ford had its successes—the Mustang, the Continental Mark III, and the Torino—but they were triumphs of packaging or marketing, not technology. But GM had grown so large by the mid-'60s that it could just as easily produce either unusual, technically interesting designs like the Corvair or Toronado or boringly ordinary cars like the Chevy II or Impala.

Despite the domination of the market by GM and Ford, a few specialty manufacturers operated profitably during the '60s by appealing to small but significant groups of buyers overlooked by the industry giants. The Avanti II has continued to occupy its own market niche up to the present day, long after its parent company fell apart. The original Shelby GT-350 was little more than a re-engineered Mustang designed by a former racer who believed there was a tiny—but vocal—market for all-out performance. Checker still sold 6000 cars a year to practical folk looking for taxi-cab toughness and simplicity. Brooks Stevens found that others shared his dream of driving a "modern classic," and would buy an Excalibur.

Buyers did not always react enthusiastically to important engineering advances in the 1960s, but they did become more discriminating in their judgments of gimmicky or useless features. As the decade began, the public almost immediately started rejecting such things as tailfins, pushbutton transmissions, retractable hardtops, and chrome-encrusted super-cruisers. Rapidly, new models appeared from the likes of Pontiac, Lincoln, Dodge, and Chevrolet—cars that illustrated that good design means more than a five-pound hood ornament. The early compacts proved that the industry could still build practical cars—and that they could be designed to sell—after a generation of offering impractical ones. The sporty compacts brought home a point the Europeans had long accepted: the *best* car is not necessarily the biggest. Heading into the 1970s, it was clear that America's automotive values were slowly beginning to change. As events were to prove, the changes couldn't have been more timely.

The 1970s

In the early 1970s the industry was beset by a lengthening list of government regulations, complicated by a new set of equally stark realities resulting from the Arab oil embargo. With the sudden recognition of how interdependent the world had become, Detroit executives made key decisions that would change the nature of the American car more dramatically and more swiftly than ever before. General Motors, by then the industry's bellwether, would lead the way—and where GM went, the rest would follow. Reacting quickly to the change in consumer needs (as it always has, although naysayers insist it's the other way round), GM embarked on a daring long-term program to downsize its entire fleet. The first results appeared after the usual three-year lead time such efforts usually involve, the 1977 B- and C-body full-size models. It represented a huge gamble even for the number-one producer, for "standards" were still crucially important to profits. But it worked: the new cars were as large or larger than their predecessors on the inside yet astonishingly smaller on the outside—and up to 800 pounds lighter. More importantly, they sold well. GM went on to apply the same formula to its intermediates, specialty cars and compacts in rapid succession, while other makers rushed to follow. Meanwhile, there were advances in allied areas. Ford designer Bill Boyer told us that 96 inches is about as short as a wheelbase should be. "When you can't downsize any more," he declares, "you improve efficiency by more complicated means: aerodynamics, front drive/transverse engines." And you provide performance through turbocharging a smaller engine for "power on demand," to quote an old Kaiser slogan, rather than relying on a big V8 with a surfeit of power. This book only touches on this exciting new era, which a future edition may describe in detail. We hope so.

Qualifications and Exceptions

Even the best system of terminology and classification has its exceptions. For the Major Makes section, the intent was to include every volume manufacturer that did business in America between 1930 and 1980. Thus, makes like Marquette and Viking are listed even though both were active only briefly in the early '30s. Similarly, there is a listing for AMC, activated as a separate nameplate in 1965.

Several makes usually considered "minor" by the industry are the first exceptions. Avanti II, Checker, Duesenberg, Excalibur, and Shelby are treated as majors even though their production was a mere fraction of total industry volume. The reasoning was partly subjective, tempered by present conditions. Both the Avanti and Excalibur concerns are still in business today, and though their volume isn't likely to increase substantially, we felt any make still in production for over 10 years warranted more than a mere notation among the "minors." Shelby expired as a marque in 1970, but in some years its volume was quite considerable for a tiny company—not to mention its impact. The last is reason enough to include Duesenberg.

Canadian models are not included here, but again there is an exception: the 1965-66 Studebaker, which was nominally a Canadian product in those years. This decision was made on the grounds that Studebaker had been too much a part of the American scene in previous years to leave out its final offerings. The problem, of course, is that if these cars are listed, then Canadian Plymouths, for example, should be included, too. An argument, though perhaps lame, can be made for the 1965-66 Studebakers, because including them effectively caps a story; lumping in Canadian Plymouths would only have exceeded the basic scope of the book.

A different problem arose in deciding how to treat major models of certain makes, cars substantially different in technology or character from the marque's usual products. For improved clarity and coverage, the rear-engine Corvair and the singular Corvette have their own chapters apart from the main Chevrolet entry. Likewise, Mustang and Thunderbird are treated separately from Ford. But this led

to more exceptions. The Kaiser Darrin is not listed separately from Kaiser, for example. Another reason for treating the aforementioned models individually is that the main Chevrolet and Ford entries were already enormous. The Nash Metropolitan involved two more exceptions. Because of its individual character, it is considered distinct from other Nash models by many authorities. Yet, it was labeled a Nash until 1958, when that nameplate disappeared and Metropolitan became a make in its own right. For convenience, these cars are treated in a separate chapter following Nash. On the other hand, there was no need to do the same thing with Hudson's compact Jet, or the Valiant, officially a separate make in 1960 and a Plymouth model from 1961. Though smaller than their relatives, these cars were not, in our view, "substantially different" enough, either technically or in character, to warrant such treatment.

In other cases, we follow industry practice. For example, the 1956 Clipper has its own entry because Studebaker-Packard registered it as a separate make and created separate Clipper franchises that year. The car itself was nearly identical to the 1955 version except that it was not a Packard, strictly speaking. So, all non-1956 Clippers are found under the parent marque. Continental was a distinct Ford Motor Company make in 1956-1958, but wasn't before and hasn't been since. Although its modern-day status is vague, there was no problem separating the appropriate models from Lincoln in the period covered. The same principle applies with AMC (the make, not the corporation). The company used the Rambler nameplate exclusively from 1957 through 1965, and the '65 Ambassador and Marlin both bore the appropriate script and emblems. For 1966-67, however, these models had new "AMC" identification, and the AMX and Javelin appeared for 1968 as AMC products, not Ramblers. For 1970, the Rambler name disappeared entirely in favor of AMC. Thus, the reader will find the 1965 Marlin, for example, discussed under "Rambler," and the 1966-67 models under "AMC".

The editors were fairly groggy by the time they arrived at Willys, but unfortunately this make posed some of the most serious problems encountered. Officially, the Willys

Qualifications and Exceptions

passenger car ended after 1955 with the expiration of the domestic Aero-based models. But a steel-bodied station wagon continued to be offered through 1961 — variously called a Willys, a Kaiser Jeep, and a Jeep. From 1963 on, Jeep Corporation marketed the four-wheel-drive Wagoneer much like a passenger model and, in 1967, Kaiser-Jeep Corporation released the Jeepster 2, designed in the image of the 1948 original. Most industry sources and the collector hobby consider the 1948-51 Jeepster a passenger car, but none list the Jeep wagons, Wagoneer, or Jeepster 2, which are all defined as "trucks." Including the original Jeepster might seem to imply including these other products as well. The problem was that by leaving in those models, the book would be opened up to similar contemporary competitors like the Ford Bronco or International Scout, which were definitely beyond our scope. Ultimately, it was decided to make two more exceptions: the original Jeepster and Aero passenger cars are the only Willys models discussed.

Chapter Texts

The general text of each entry presents a detailed account of the make's history. There is, we think, sound reason for this even in a reference work. Too often, "encyclopedias" simply report statistics. But to understand what was done, it is essential to know how and why it was done and what the results were. Therefore, a cumulative total of 40 years' research has been surveyed for information on the designers, engineers, and executives who shaped these cars; the reasons why they did what they did, the alternative plans they rejected, and the successes or failures that followed. Each chapter is intended to offer a concise, yet complete, description of each major manufacturer — a basic outline for the casual user, a quick education for the uninitiated, and a solid review for the expert. In the process of writing these entries, the authors and contributors have attempted to puncture many hoary automotive legends — that the Corvair was torpedoed by Ralph Nader, for example, or that Studebaker was a victim of a plot at Ford. So much ignorance has been perpetuated by inexpert or poorly researched accounts in the past that the temptation to set down reliable facts was too great to resist.

Photographs

Selecting photographs for a work like this can be more difficult than editing text. Limited space and the great variety of cars offered by the larger companies mean it is not always possible to provide a truly representative sample for each model year over such a broad time span. While this book cannot contain the detailed photographic references of a single-make history, the most important and influential models are shown.

Unlike some other automotive encyclopedias, this one includes pictures of selected prototypes, experimentals, and show cars as well as production models — all clearly labeled as such. The reasons are the inordinate interest in such non-production designs among today's enthusiasts, and the importance of these proposals as benchmarks. While there are hundreds, even thousands, of styling studies for each model and model year among most of the major makes, there are those interesting or key design ideas that either evolved into production or were abruptly dismissed. The prototypes selected represent the industry at its best and its worst in line with the major goal of this book: to present a broad, clear, and factual account of the American automobile industry.

Tables

At the end of each chapter is a series of tables listing every model and body style offered by each make in the 1930-1980 period. Of all the elements in a book like this, charts are the most time consuming and pose the greatest problems of style and accuracy. Space naturally played a part in the choice of material shown here. The object was to provide, at a glance, the data most readers would be likely to require in a hurry: models, wheelbases, body styles, weights, prices, model year production, and engine availability. In using the tables, the reader should keep the following in mind.

Series or Model Entries

Each group of body styles is listed under a series or model heading. This indicates the factory model or series code number (where applicable), name, and wheelbase (in inches). Code numbers posed many problems. On several occasions, it was unclear whether a code applied to the series or model line as a whole, to specific body styles, or both. In instances where they were misleading or irrelevant, the code numbers were omitted. Where a code applies to both model/series and body style, the first part is shown with the model/series and the second with the body style. An example is Dodge from 1959 onward. Officially, that year's Coronet six-cylinder club sedan was designated by the factory as MD1-L21, but "MD1-L" applied to *all* Coronet sixes, and "21" only to the club sedan. The number is divided accordingly.

In the '60s, some code systems became more complex, so numbers are listed as the situation required. For 1961, for example, codes for the Dodge Lancer followed '59 practice. But the 1961 Dart Six series consisted of Seneca, Pioneer, and Phoenix sub-series. In this case, only the series number "RD3" is shown in the heading, the rest of the designation appearing alongside the corresponding body styles. In reality, a 1961 Dart Six Phoenix hardtop coupe went by the code RD3-H434; it is shown as model RD3, body style H434.

Abbreviations

For best readability, it was important to limit each entry to one line. To do this, the following standard abbreviations were adopted for the body style listings:

abbreviation	meaning
A/S	auxiliary seats
A/W	all-weather
b'ham	brougham (sedan, convertible, etc.)
bus	business as in coupe
cab	cabriolet
comm	commercial
conv cpe	two-door convertible
conv sdn	four-door convertible
cpe	coupe
CQ	closed rear roof quarters
div	division window (limousine)
fstbk	fastback ("torpedo")
form	formal, as in sedan
FQ	formal rear roof quarters
htchbk	hatchback (three/five-door)
htp cpe	two-door pillarless hardtop
htp sdn	four-door pillarless hardtop
htp wgn	pillarless station wagon
J/B	"jet back" (fastback)
lndu	landau
limo	limousine
phtn	phaeton
proto	prototype
rdstr	two-passenger roadster
R/S	rumble seat, as in roadster
sdn	sedan
sdnt	sedanette (two-door sedan)
SQ	solid rear roof quarters
spdstr	speedster
spt	sport, as in coupe
T/B	"trunkback"
tng	touring
util	utility, usually a two-door sedan
wgn	station wagon

Generally, all body styles except sports cars and very small models like American Bantam have five- or six-passenger capacity; exceptions are specified. There are also cases where it is necessary to differentiate between otherwise similar types. These abbreviations are:

P (7P, 8P, etc.)	passenger capacity
S (2S, 3S)	number of seats (wagons)
W (4W, 6W)	number of side windows
FW	fixed window

Engine abbreviations also follow a consistent pattern: block configuration is followed by the number of cylinders and, where needed, a suffix letter. The letters are as follows:

L (L6, L8, etc.)	inline or "straight"
V (V6, V8, etc.)	V-block
flat	horizontally opposed
T	turbocharged
D	diesel

Manufacturers differ widely in treating engine options. Some group both standard and extra-cost engines under the same model code; others distinguish between them and even give them separate model numbers. The charts follow the practice each manufacturer used for a given model year. The Pontiac Six and Eight, for example, were distinct models and are shown as such. Plymouth engines were usually listed as options for a given model and are combined. This difference is emphasized by spelling out and capitalizing the words "Six" and "Eight" in cases like Pontiac and by using the abbreviations "L6" and "V8" in cases like Plymouth.

Where options are combined, prices shown are for base-engine models. Production figures shown are for the total number of that model built, regardless of engine.

Weight

The column marked "wght" provides the initial advertised curb weight (not adjusted for passengers, fuel, or cargo) for each body style as listed in industry sources, usually National Automobile Dealers Association (NADA) guides. The reader may expect these to differ slightly from other published figures, because weights varied depending on equipment fitted or even the scales used.

It is important to note, however, that when more than one engine was standard for a given model, curb weights shown are *averages*, deemed necessary for maximum readability. For example, the 1955 Chevrolet Bel Air convertible weighed 3315 pounds with the six and 3285 pounds with V8. Our listed weight is the average: 3300 pounds. Usually, the choice of engine did not change curb weight by more than 100-150 pounds.

Prices

Figures shown in the "price" column are based on initial advertised prices (as delivered) according to NADA and similar sources, and represent contemporary dollars ("as-new" price). Like weights, prices varied during most model years. When more than one standard engine was available, however, prices were *not* averaged, the figure for the least expensive power unit (usually a six) being shown instead.

Model Year Production

The question most often asked about older cars—and one of the most important in a reference work about them—is "How many did they make?" The answer is not always clear-cut, and in some cases production has been a subject of research—and dispute—among automotive historians for decades. However, the figures listed are the most recent and accurate available and have been thoroughly researched and cross-checked.

Note that mainly *model year*, not calendar year, figures are used in both the tables and the text. The reason for this is that calendar year totals always include some portion of at least two model years, which creates confusion when comparing one make with another. Model year figures normally represent production of cars marketed

Qualifications and Exceptions

as the 1939, 1949, 1959, 1969, etc. models. For makes and/or years where precise model year totals were not available, registrations or calendar year figures are given and are always identified as such. These exceptions apply mainly to the early years of the '30s, before the model year concept had been universally adopted by the industry, and to low-volume independents like Duesenberg, where the idea had relatively little meaning in the context of company operations. An industy-wide production summary by model year for makes with output of 1000 units or more is found at the end of the Major Makes section.

Production received long and painstaking analysis in preparing this book. Too often, published totals have been based on company handouts that are often misleading and sometimes inaccurate. The 1953 Buick Skylark, for example, is listed by the division (and at least one other source) as the "Roadmaster Anniversary Convertible." The contradictions and false trails of factory lists were fully explored and compared to other lists from a dozen different sources. Sometimes, it was discovered that there were cars built that weren't "officially" listed; in other cases, models were listed but not actually produced.

There were a few cases where it was possible to go beyond known information by estimating, such as when a company provided only a combined total for two or three model years. Such lumping serves nobody. Where we felt confident to do so, production was proportioned over individual model years. The usual standard for these breakdowns was calendar year output in cases where it very nearly coincided with model year output (usually when a model year began in January rather than September or October).

In some instances, available factory figures included non-production models, usually styles intended for production but not produced in volume. These are retained in the charts and are clearly labeled as non-production. While not all records documented non-production models, the ones available are shown for completeness.

There were a few cases where even estimating proved impossible, or where a large group of models or body styles were lumped together. It is hoped that future editions of this book will be able to make some of these figures more specific.

Engine

Under each model year roster is a list of standard (S) and optional (O) engines and their model or series availability. Other basic information provided includes block configuration, number of cylinders, displacement (to the nearest 0.1 cubic inch), bore and stroke (to the nearest .01 inch), and SAE gross horsepower (SAE net after 1972). In cases where there was more than one standard engine, all are shown as "S."

Additions and Corrections

Much care has been taken in compiling this book to insure a high degree of accuracy. Nevertheless, additional research may yield data or conclusions other than those presented here. The publishers welcome additions and suggestions. They may be addressed to Richard M. Langworth, Box 385, Contoocook, New Hampshire 03229, or to CONSUMER GUIDE® magazine, 3841 West Oakton Street, Skokie, Illinois 60076.

—Richard M. Langworth

BOOKS

Butler, Don: *The Plymouth-DeSoto Story*
Chappell, Pat: *The Hot One, Chevrolet 1955-1957*
Consumer Guide, Editors of: *The American Sports Car; Cars of the '30s, Cars of the '40s; Cars of the '50s; Cars of the '60s; Corvette: America's Only True Sports Car; Mustang: The Original Ponycar; Ford: 1903-1984; Cadillac: Standard of Excellence*
Dammann, George: *Illustrated History of Ford, Seventy Years of Buick, Sixty Years of Chevrolet*
Dawes, Nathaniel E.: *The Packard, 1942-1962*
Deutsch, Jan G.: *Selling the People's Cadillac*
Dunne, Jim and Norbye, Jan P.: *Buick: The Postwar Years; Pontiac: The Postwar Years*
Georgano, G.N.: *The Complete Encyclopedia of Motorcars*
Heasley, Jerry: *The Production Figure Book for U.S. Cars*
Hendry, Maurice D.: *Cadillac, Lincoln*
Kopec, Rick: *The Shelby-American Guide*
Langworth, Richard M.: *Chrysler: The Postwar Years; Hudson: The Postwar Years; Kaiser-Frazer: Last Onslaught on Detroit; Oldsmobile: The First Seventy-five Years (Part 2); Personal Luxury: The Thunderbird Story; Studebaker: The Postwar Years*
Ludvigsen, Karl E.: *Corvette: America's Star-Spangled Sports Car*
MacPherson, Thomas E.: *The Dodge Story*
Martin, Terry; Bradley, James; Langworth, Richard; Weber, Don; Grayson, Stan; Yost, L. Morgan; Leslie, C.A. Jr.; Phillips, Richard; Hamlin, George; Heinmuller, Dwight: *Packard: A History of the Motorcar and the Company*
Narus, Don: *Town & Country, Chrysler's Wonderful Woodie*
Pearson, Charles T.: *The Indomitable Tin Goose*
Ritch, O'Cee: *The Lincoln Continental*
Schneider, Roy: *Cadillacs of the Forties*

PERIODICALS

Autocar, Automobile Connoisseur, Automobile Quarterly, Automotive News, Car and Driver, Car Classics, Car Collector, Cars & Parts, Mechanix Illustrated, Motor, Motor Trend, Official National Market Reports Blue and Red Books, Official N.A.D.A. Used Car Guide, Popular Mechanics, Popular Science, Road & Track, Special-Interest Autos, Sports Car Graphic, Sports Cars Illustrated, Wards Automotive Yearbook, Wards Monthly

Allstate
Sears, Roebuck & Co.
Chicago, Illinois

Theodore V. Houser, Sears vice-president for merchandising, had a seat on the board of Kaiser-Frazer. In 1949, Houser discussed with K-F the possibility of offering one of Willow Run's automobiles under the Allstate name. Sears wanted to sell a complete car, along with parts and accessories for it, at the new auto shops then opening up adjacent to its retail stores. A hookup with Kaiser-Frazer was a natural. At the time, Houser was buying Homart enamelware from Kaiser Metals Company, in which Sears held a 45-percent share.

The first Allstate proposals were simply the large 1949 K-F cars bearing different logos. Until the compact Henry J arrived for 1951, Sears remained dubious. The Henry J, however, was exactly what T. V. Houser had been looking for—a low-priced, uncomplicated, easy-to-service car.

Kaiser-Frazer president Edgar F. Kaiser managed to convince his dealers to accept a department store as a competitor, and the Allstate was announced in November 1951. It was the only new make for 1952, and the first car offered by Sears since its high-wheeler of 1912. In an apparent attempt to feel out the market with a pilot program, Sears concentrated Allstate promotion on the Southeast, although the car was available nationally through the 1952 Sears catalog.

Based strictly on the Henry J, the Allstate featured a distinctive front-end treatment by designer Alex Tremulis, special Allstate badges, and a major interior upgrading that followed Sears' practice of improving on proprietary products. K-F's interior specialist, Carleton Spencer, used quilted saran plastic combined with a coated paper fiber encapsulated in vinyl—a material he'd discovered in use on the transatlantic telegraph cable. It seemed impervious to normal wear, and was superior to the upholstery material used in most Henry Js.

The cars wore Sears-Allstate tires and tubes, bat-

1952 Deluxe two-door sedan

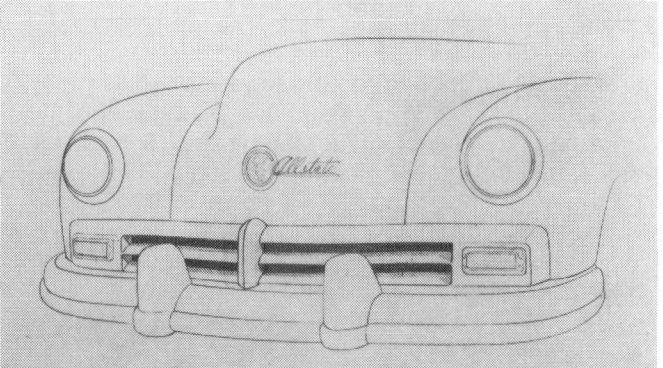

Allstate proposal based on a large K-F model

1952 Deluxe two-door sedan

1952 Deluxe interior

February 1952 proposal by Brooks Stevens for Allstate wagon

teries, and spark plugs, each with the appropriate guarantee: 18 months for the tires, 24 months for the battery, and 90 days or 4000 miles for the whole car (the standard K-F warranty). Allstates were usually fitted with trunklids and dashboard gloveboxes, items that were found less often on Henry Js. The basic and standard models lacked the opening trunk. The more expensive Deluxe Six had armrests and a horn ring, which were not available or optional on the lower-priced versions.

Sears aggressively marketed the Allstate with five trim variations (against four for the Henry J) and two different L-head engines—a six and a four. The lowest-priced 1952 Allstate (the basic Four) was priced just below the standard Henry J.

For 1953, there was little change. A full-width rubber-covered pad was added across the instrument panel, and the taillights were relocated to the rear fenders. The line was reduced to just three models—two Fours and the Six.

But the idea failed. Whether it failed because people didn't take to buying cars in department stores, or because of the narrow marketing approach in the Southeast, is difficult to determine. Both factors probably contributed. Only 1566 Allstates were built for 1952; the count was 797 when Sears canceled the project in early 1953. Exact model-by-model production figures are no longer available, so the figures shown in the tables are estimates based on reliable sources.

The Allstate's demise killed Sears' plans for future models. Among these were two proposals for a two-door station wagon, one by industrial designer Brooks Stevens, the other by Gordon Tercey of K-F Styling.

Today, Allstates are extremely rare, and are considered more desirable than comparable Henry Js because of this. In 1971, Allstate Insurance purchased one of the Sears' cars for historical purposes. In the '60s it would have been hard to convince the folks at Sears parts counters that the car had ever existed.

Allstate Specifications

1952

A2304 Four (wb 100.0)		Wght	Price	Prod
110	basic sdn 2d	2,300	1,395	200
111	std sdn 2d	2,300	1,486	500
113	Deluxe sdn 2d	2,300	1,539	200
A2404 Six (wb 100.0)				
—	basic sdn 2d	2,325	1,594	200
115	Deluxe sdn 2d	2,325	1,693	466

1952 Engines	bore×stroke	bhp	availability
L4, 134.2	3.11×4.38	68	S-Allstate Four
L6, 161.0	3.13×3.50	80	S-Allstate Six

1953

A3304 Four (wb 100.0)		Wght	Price	Prod
210	std sdn 2d	2,405	1,528	200
213	Deluxe sdn 2d	2,405	1,589	225
A3404 Six (wb 100.0)				
215	Deluxe sdn 2d	2,455	1,785	372

1953 Engines	bore×stroke	bhp	availability
L4, 134.2	3.11×4.38	68	S-Allstate Four
L6, 161.0	3.13×3.50	80	S-Allstate Six

American Austin
American Austin Car Company
Butler, Pennyslvania

When Sir Herbert Austin came to America in 1929, the well-known English manufacturer had many people excited over his plan to build cars in the USA. After a tour of the country, he announced that the American Austin would be built in Butler, Pennsylvania. Detroit shook its collective head, but Butler wasn't such a strange choice. It had access to industrial services and an eager work force, and it was close enough to east coast ports to make importing components from England quite feasible. The basic concept of the car itself seemed promising, too, and as production started in May 1930, the company claimed it had close to 200,000 orders for its new ultra-light, ultra-economical car.

The American Austin was built through 1934, and the same engine was used throughout the production run. It was an L-head four that displaced 46 cubic inches, had only two main bearings, and developed 13-14 brake horsepower at 3200 rpm. A roadster and coupe were initially offered. In 1931, a business coupe, Deluxe coupe, and 2-4 passenger cabriolet were added. Once production fired up, some of the original prices were cut, and the figures were reduced again in 1933 in an effort to boost sales.

For a while, prospects for the American Austin looked good—but only for a while: the 1930 output of 8558 units would never be exceeded. Two factors were largely responsible for lackluster reception. One was the general business decline brought on by the Depression. The other was the fact that, even in bad times, Americans didn't take to midget cars. To be sure, the American Austin was a midget. Its 75-inch wheelbase was fully 16 inches less than that of the future VW Beetle. Also, the Austin weighed only 1100-1200 pounds, and Americans were notoriously leery about light cars in those years, as many still are. It was an attractive little car, designed in part by Alexis de Sakhnoffsky, but that didn't seem to matter, and production ground to a halt in 1935.

Austins provided a welcome touch of amusement in a drab period for America. And, for a few people, they became a sort of reverse status symbol, much like the Beetle would be in the 1950s. Al Jolson, who loved cars and usually drove Packards or Lincolns, bought the first Austin coupe delivered to a private buyer. He was followed by numerous other Hollywood stars: Buster Keaton, Slim Summerville, and the "Our Gang" kiddies. Austins even starred in a movie. They were used as "steeds" for a knightly battle in Will Rogers' "A Connecticut Yankee in King Arthur's Court." It was a great scene, but it didn't help to sell Austins.

1930 Model A two-passenger coupe

1930 Model A two-passenger coupe. American Austin was based on the British Austin Seven.

American Austin Specifications

1930—8,558 built*

Model A (wb 75.0)		Wght	Price	Prod
	rdstr	1,100	445	—
	cpe 2P	1,130	465	—

1930 Engine	bore×stroke	bhp	availability
L4, 46.0	2.20×3.00	14	S-all

*Calendar year

1931—1,279 built*

Model A (wb 75.0)		Wght	Price	Prod
	rdstr	1,040	395	—
	bus cpe	1,130	330	—
	cpe 2P	1,130	395	—
	DeLuxe cpe 2P	1,130	525	—
	cabriolet 2-4P	1,175	550	—

1931 Engine	bore×stroke	bhp	availability
L4, 46.0	2.20×3.00	14	S-all

*Calendar year

1932—3,846 built*

Model A (wb 75.0)		Wght	Price	Prod
	rdstr	1,040	395	—
	bus cpe	1,130	330	—
	cpe 2P	1,130	395	—

1932 Engine	bore×stroke	bhp	availability
L4, 46.0	2.20×3.00	14	S-all

*Calendar year

1933—4,726 built*

Model 2-75 (wb 75.0)		Wght	Price	Prod
	rdstr	1,020	315	—
	bus cpe	1,100	275	—
	Special bus cpe	1,100	295	—
	cpe 2P	1,130	315	—

Model 3-75 (wb 75.0)		Wght	Price	Prod
	rdstr	1,020	365	—
	bus cpe	1,100	295	—
	cpe 2P	1,130	345	—
	DeLuxe cpe	1,130	365	—

1933 Engine	bore×stroke	bhp	availability
L4, 46.0	2.20×3.00	13	S-all

*Calendar year

1934—1,300 built (est.)

Model 375 (wb 75.0)		Wght	Price	Prod
	rdstr	1,020	365	—
	bus cpe	1,130	295	—
	cpe 2P	1,130	345	—
	DeLuxe cpe 2P	1,130	365	—

1934 Engine	bore×stroke	bhp	availability
L4, 46.0	2.20×3.00	13	S-all

* Calendar year

1935-36

Models listed in industry records, but no production.

American Bantam
**American Bantam Car Co.
Butler, Pennsylvania**

1940 convertible sedan

1939-40 Boulevard Delivery

It was in 1935 that an energetic Roy S. Evans offered to buy the down-and-out American Austin concern. He was successful, but he faced some formidable obstacles. The company owed $75,000 in back taxes and interest, and the Pullman Standard Company had a mortgage on the property for $150,000. However, the federal court with jurisdiction over the bankrupt firm felt Evans might salvage the situation and awarded him the factory for $5000 cash—only 1/2000th of its appraised valuation. Evans secured a $250 million loan from the Reconstruction Finance Corporation, and hired the necessary talent to help him create a new car.

Styling for the revised model, called the American Bantam, was assigned to Alexis de Sakhnoffsky, who had

designed the American Austin. He created a new front end marked by a smooth hood and rounded grille, and also reworked the fenders and rear deck. His bill came to only $300, and Evans was able to retool the entire line for a mere $7000.

Racing engineer Harry Miller was hired to work on the mechanicals, but his efforts were confined to a redesigned manifold. Butler's own engineers contributed most of the engine alterations. They replaced the Austin's expensive roller bearings with babbitt bearings, added full-pressure lubrication, a new three-speed transmission, Hotchkiss final drive, and Ross cam-and-lever steering. Engine displacement was unchanged, though three main bearings were used instead of two after 1939. Wheelbase remained

1940 Panel Delivery

American Bantam

1939 Foursome speedster

at 75 inches, but wheel diameter shrank from 18 to 16 inches in 1937, and to 15 inches in 1938. Also, the Bantam's frame and crossmembers were heavier than the Austin's.

For 1937, two roadsters and three coupes were offered. Several new models appeared for 1938-39, including a Speedster with a pretty "Duesenberg sweep" side panel, and the novel Boulevard Delivery. A convertible designed by Alex Tremulis and called the Riviera was added for 1939. Tremulis has recalled that this model would cruise at 75-80 mph and average 42.5 mpg, presumably at considerably lower speeds.

Bantam production continued into 1941, but even the dynamic Evans wasn't able to convince Americans of the value in his tiny package. Output was about 2000 units in 1938 and 1200 the following year. It failed to reach 1000 units for 1940-41, and ceased altogether shortly after the 1941 model year began. Bantam then concentrated on building a prototype for what ultimately became the Army Jeep, which it also manufactured during WWII. Though Bantam didn't build as many Jeeps as Ford and Willys-Overland, it does get credit for the basic design.

American Bantam Specifications

1936

Model 575 (wb 75.0)	Wght	Price	Prod
rdstr 2P	1,040	385	—
bus cpe 1P	1,130	295	—
bus cpe 2P	1,130	307	—
Standard cpe	1,130	355	—
DeLuxe cpe	1,130	385	—

1936 Engine	bore×stroke	bhp	availability
L4, 46.0	2.20×3.00	13	all

*Under 500

1937—3,500 built (est.)

Model 575 (wb 75.0)	Wght	Price	Prod
rdstr	1,100	431	—
Custom rdstr	1,100	492	—
bus cpe	1,100	385	—
cpe 2P	1,100	411	—
DeLuxe cpe 2P	1,100	431	—

1937 Engine	bore×stroke	bhp	availability
L4, 46.0	2.20×3.00	20	S-all

1938—2,000 built (est.)

Model 60 (wb 75.0)	Wght	Price	Prod
Special rdstr	1,130	449	—
rdstr	1,140	479	—
DeLuxe rdstr	1,160	525	—
bus cpe	1,230	399	—
cpe 2P	1,230	399	—
Master cpe 2P	1,250	439	—
DeLuxe cpe 2P	1,250	465	—
Foursome spdstr 4P	1,265	497	—
wgn 2d	1,434	565	—

1938 Engine	bore×stroke	bhp	availability
L4, 46.0	2.20×3.00	20	S-all

1939—1,229 built*

Model 62 (wb 75.0)	Wght	Price	Prod
rdstr	1,130	449	—
Special rdstr	1,140	479	—
DeLuxe rdstr	1,160	525	—
cpe 2P	1,230	399	—
Special cpe 2P	1,240	439	—
DeLuxe cpe 2P	1,250	469	—
Sunair cpe 2P	1,250	479	—
Foursome spdstr 4P	1,265	497	—
DeLuxe Foursome spdstr 4P	1,280	549	—
wgn 2d	1,434	565	—

1939 Engine	bore×stroke	bhp	availability
L4, 46.0	2.20×3.00	20	S-all

1940

Series 65 (wb 75.0)—800 built		Wght	Price	Prod
65	cpe	1,261	399	—
65	Master cpe	1,275	449	—
65	conv cpe	1,340	525	—
65	Master rdstr	1,211	449	—
65	conv sdn	1,296	549	—
65	wgn 2d	1,400	565	—

1940 Engine	bore×stroke	bhp	availability
L4, 50.1	2.26×3.13	22	S-all

1941

Series 65 (wb 75.0)—138 built		Wght	Price	Prod
65	cpe	1,261	399	—
65	Master cpe	1,275	449	—
65	conv cpe	1,340	525	—
65	Master rdstr	1,211	449	—
65	conv sdn	1,296	549	—
65	wgn 2d	1,400	565	—

1941 Engine	bore×stroke	bhp	availability
L4, 50.1	2.26×3.13	22	S-all

*Calendar year figures

AMC American Motors Corp.
Kenosha, Wisconsin

American Motors first marketed cars with the AMC label in 1966, when the "Rambler" prefix for the Ambassador and Marlin was dropped. In 1968, the Rebel lost its Rambler name too, and the new AMX and Javelin were added to the company's stable. The Rambler nameplate appeared for the last time in 1969 on the final edition of the Rambler American design that had appeared in 1964. In 1970, this was replaced by the Hornet and Gremlin.

The top-of-the-line 1966 Ambassador was a facelifted version of the redesigned 1965 Rambler Ambassador. It was one of the better efforts from the studios of Richard A. Teague, AMC vice-president for styling. A graceful-looking car, it rode a wheelbase four inches longer than the 1964 Ambassador's. A special model for '66 was the elegantly appointed DPL hardtop, which had reclining bucket seats, fold-down center armrests, pile carpeting, and an extensive list of accessories. Officially, the DPL was a model in its own right, not an Ambassador. It became the Ambassador DPL in 1967.

Ranked below the DPL were the regular Ambassador sedans, wagons, hardtops, and one convertible, available in the 880 and 990 series. All were offered with the long-running "Typhoon" 232-cid six, or with a choice of two optional V8 engines, in 287- and 327-cid sizes. Only the 270-bhp 327 V8 required premium gasoline.

Although most Ambassadors were ordered with automatic transmission, a few were equipped with a three-speed manual transmission or AMC's "Twin Stick" overdrive. A four-speed synchromesh gearbox was also marketed for the Ambassador 990 and DPL.

The big Ambassador evolved nicely through the late '60s. For 1967, wheelbase was lengthened and semi-fastback styling with slightly rounder body contours was adopted. In 1968, the hood was refined and a new model sequence appeared: Ambassador, Ambassador DPL, and Ambassador SST. New frontal styling, which included a sculptured hood, plastic grille, and horizontal quad headlights, arrived in 1969. The 1970 version was restyled with new rear fenders and taillamps on sedans and hardtops, and new roof panels and taillamps on wagons. By 1969, the Ambassador's wheelbase had grown to 122 inches, and air conditioning was standard.

AMC made an unsuccessful try at the booming personal-car market with the radically styled 1965 Rambler Marlin, renamed AMC Marlin for 1966-67. Styled by Teague, the Marlin was a huge fastback based on the intermediate Rambler Classic chassis of '65–'66 and borrowing some of its front-end sheetmetal. It featured rakishly shaped rear side windows and C-pillar styling. The '66 model was changed only slightly. It had a new

1966 Ambassador DPL hardtop coupe

1967 Ambassador DPL hardtop coupe

1966 Ambassador 990 convertible

1966 Ambassador 990 station wagon

1967 Marlin fastback coupe

1967 Marlin fastback coupe

1968 Rebel SST convertible

1968 Javelin fastback coupe

grille, a sway bar was adopted for six-cylinder models, and an optional black vinyl-covered roof treatment was offered. The 1967 Marlin was the last of the line. It was fully restyled and a much more handsome car because of its longer wheelbase shared with that year's Ambassador. Measuring 6.5 inches longer than 1965-66 Marlins, it was perhaps the nicest-looking of the three. But it remained a very low-production item. Fewer than 5000 and 3000 Marlins were built for 1966 and 1967, respectively. Marlin offered some sports car features (optional four-speed transmission, tachometer, bucket seats, and engines ranging up to 280 bhp), but it lacked a sports car's taut, precise handling and small, efficient size.

A more successful innovation was the 1968 Javelin, a ponycar in the Mustang image. It was beautifully shaped and exciting. More important, it was successful: over 56,000 units were built that year, helping AMC recover from a four-year sales slump. With its standard 232 six, the Javelin cruised at 80 mph; with the optional 290 V8, it could do 100 mph. The Javelin's optional "Go Package" included a 343 V8 with four-barrel carburetor, dual exhausts, power front disc brakes, heavy-duty suspension, and wide tires. So equipped, the car would run from 0 to 60 mph in eight seconds, and approach 120 mph maximum. The Javelin was roomier, larger, and longer than its Mustang, Camaro, and Barracuda rivals. Its styling was cleaner, too.

The Javelin was facelifted for 1969 with a slightly altered grille. In 1970, it received a "twin-venturi" grille, revised wheel covers, and a new hood with simulated air scoops. Sales were not as impressive in 1969-70 as they were in 1968 because of additional competition in the ponycar market—notably a sleek new Camaro.

An exciting mid-1968 introduction was the AMX, a

two-seat coupe based on the Javelin bodyshell and riding a special shorter wheelbase. AMC introduced a new 390-cid V8 for the AMX with 315 bhp and 425 foot-pounds of torque. It included a forged-steel crankshaft and connecting rods. The standard engine was a 290 V8, and the 343 was available as an option. The AMX's

1968 Javelin SST fastback coupe

1968 Javelin fastback coupe

1968 AMX two-seat fastback coupe

1968 Rebel SST convertible

1968 Ambassador SST four-door sedan

1968 Rebel SST hardtop coupe

1968 Ambassador SST hardtop coupe

1969 Rebel SST hardtop coupe

tight suspension, comprehensive instrumentation, bucket seats, and optional four-speed gearbox made it a genuine sports car, and it did well in competition. As with the Marlin, the AMX's best styling came in its last year. The 1970 models were smoothly integrated and looked the part of a serious sports car. Production was, however, much lower than management had expected. The car never sold well, and production for all three years failed to top 20,000 units. As good as it was, American Motors was probably the wrong company to sell a performance car like the AMX. (The company has revived the AMX name from time to time for its sporty models in the 1970s.)

Another new AMC make for 1968 was the Rebel, introduced the year before as a Rambler model taking over from the Classic. Rebel was AMC's intermediate with a 114-inch wheelbase. A variety of six-cylinder and V8 engines was offered. Prices were competitive, starting at around $2500. Sedans, hardtops, wagons, and a convertible were available in three series. Rebel was the only AMC line to offer a convertible in 1968, but few were built: only 377 in the 550 series and another 823 in SST guise. In fact, these would be AMC's last convertibles. The 1969 lineup was trimmed to two series—basic and SST. A wider track and a new grille, plus a restyled rear deck and taillights, were the only changes of note.

For 1970, Rebel sedans and hardtops were lengthened two inches to accommodate redesigned roof panels and rear fenders, and new taillights appeared. In addition to the basic and SST series, AMC again went after the performance crowd with "The Machine"—a

1969 Ambassador SST four-door sedan

1970 Javelin fastback coupe

1969 Javelin SST fastback coupe

1970 Hornet two-door sedan

1970 AMX two-seat fastback coupe

1970 Gremlin two-door sedan

Rebel with a difference. This car packed the company's most potent V8, a four-speed Hurst-linkage transmission, and a 3.54:1 rear axle ratio. The two-door hardtop body featured a Ram-Air hood scoop, a special red-white-and-blue paint treatment, and 15-inch mag wheels with raised-white-letter tires. An 8000-rpm tachometer, dual exhausts, low-back-pressure mufflers, and a definite front-end rake completed this expensive package. Although The Machine certainly had a performance image, the racing honors went to the Javelin. Mark Donohue drove a Javelin SST to the Trans-Am championship that year.

American Motors spent $40 million, a million man-hours, and three years to design its new compact for 1970. The car was dubbed Hornet, the first time that time-honored name had been seen since the last Hudsons in 1957. Entirely new from the ground up, the Hornet came as a two- or four-door sedan on a 108-inch wheelbase, and both six and V8 engines were available. Hornet sales for the year were 92,458—a strong showing that helped the company's sagging finances. But on the whole, Kenosha still lost money that year—$58.2 million on sales of over $1 billion.

In April 1970, another new model arrived, intriguingly named the Gremlin. As the first "subcompact" introduced by an American automaker it sold well, and over 26,000 moved out before the short model year ended in mid-1970. The Gremlin carried AMC's most economical six-cylinder engine and attractive prices. Its styling was based on the Hornet's. Ahead of the B-pillar, the two cars were quite similar, but the Gremlin had a truncated rear end. Overall, the car's appearance was controver-

sial. Stylist Teague insisted the Gremlin's unorthodox design was the only way to go. "Nobody would have paid it any attention if it had looked like one of the Big Three," he said.

With the Hornet and Gremlin, AMC began to turn away from being a "full-line" automaker competing toe-to-toe with the Big Three, and instead moved back to being a specialty producer of compacts and subcompacts. But the transition took a long time, and it wasn't until model year 1979 that AMC fully returned to the formula it had found so profitable in the late '50s and early '60s. By the time the switch was made, however, it was almost too late. In a way, it was strange that tiny AMC would have ever tried to match the giants almost model for model, but Roy Abernethy and even his market-wise successor, Roy D. Chapin, Jr., were somehow persuaded by the board to pursue the course abandoned long before by the messianic George Romney.

An important development in the corporate move toward more specialized products was the February 1970 acquisition of Kaiser-Jeep Corporation in Toledo, which instantly made AMC the nation's leading builder of four-wheel-drive vehicles. This was relatively uncharted territory, but Jeep's long experience in the field would ultimately prove valuable for AMC, and would indeed find its way into the firm's passenger-car line.

Though it took nearly a decade to complete, AMC's market reorientation was evident as early as 1971. The jazzy Rebel Machine and the interesting but slow-selling AMX two-seater were dropped, while the AMX name was applied to the new top-line version of the Javelin. The ponycar was given heavy—and not altogether successful—sheetmetal surgery on a one-inch longer wheelbase, though its basic bodyshell was much as before. The revised styling featured crisper contours and pronounced bulges over the front wheel openings, the latter likely aping Corvette. Inside was a reworked dash curved inward at the center *a la* Pontiac's then-current Grand Prix, and intended to bring minor controls closer to the driver. Javelin stumbled along in this form through 1974, a vestige of past sales tactics, but production never broke 30,000 units for any model year, reflecting the steady decline in ponycar demand generally after 1970. When Javelin was quietly killed, AMC decided against a direct replacement, which was reasonable considering the only such cars still selling in decent numbers at that time were GM's F-body Chevrolet Camaro/Pontiac Firebird. Even so, Javelin remained faithful to the cause, and the big 401-cid V8 was optionally available right up to the end.

Another AMC nameplate disappeared after 1974: the Ambassador. Continued with only minor trim and equipment changes in its final years, the firm's full-size entry was ultimately done in by lack of interest. Sales had never been high to begin with, and although its aging design was more sensible in some ways than that of its Big Three rivals, the Ambassador's lack of change increasingly weighed against it in this period. The crowning blow was probably the Arab oil embargo of 1973-74, which triggered the country's first energy crisis and temporarily crippled

1970 Rebel SST hardtop coupe

1970 Ambassador DPL four-door sedan

1971 Javelin AMX fastback coupe

1971 Hornet Sportabout wagon

1971 Hornet SC/360 two-door sedan

1971 Hornet SST four-door sedan

1971 Javelin SST fastback coupe

1971 Matador hardtop coupe

1971 Matador wagon

1971 Ambassador Brougham hardtop coupe

1972 Gremlin X two-door sedan

sales of all full-size models.

Another holdover fared only slightly better. This was the Matador, appearing for 1971 as the renamed and restyled successor to the intermediate Rebel, and basically a continuation of its original 1967 design. Offered in the same three body styles through 1973, the Matador was pretty ordinary stuff and failed to generate much showroom traffic. In later years, AMC tacitly acknowledged this line's near invisibility with a series of humorous TV commercials that asked "What's a Matador?" Few buyers apparently cared. An attempt to inject some pizzazz into the Matador's staid image arrived for 1974, when the notchback hardtop coupe was replaced by a completely different pillared fastback two-door that AMC boldly announced it would campaign in NASCAR racing. Chief designer Teague gave it smooth,

curvaceous looks, announced by an unusual front end in which the hood was shaped to form the upper portions of huge headlamp cavities. Despite special designer interiors—a marketing ploy favored by AMC at the time—and sporty options like the "X" package, the fastback provided only temporary relief, and Matador sales remained underwhelming. Like the Ambassador, the intermediate suffered further in the aftermath of the fuel shortage. By 1978, it had become quite passé—even the coupes, which had been progressively hoked up in the intervening years—so it was adios, Matador.

One "sow's ear" design decision that Teague made into the proverbial silk purse was the subcompact Gremlin, generally AMC's number-two seller after the compact Hornet. The company kept interest alive in this 96-inch-

1972 Matador hardtop coupe

1972 Hornet Sportabout wagon "Gucci"

1972 Javelin fastback coupe "Pierre Cardin"

1972 Ambassador Brougham hardtop coupe

1972 Ambassador Brougham wagon

1972 Ambassador SST four-door sedan

wheelbase squirt by offering several special models such as the "Gremlin X" and "Levis" versions. The "X" option typically comprised special tape striping, black-painted grille, slotted wheels, wider tires, custom bucket-seat interior, sports steering wheel, and other interior dressup items. Originally priced at about $300, this package has potential to make Gremlins so equipped minor collectors' items. Arguably more collectible is the special Levis edition, which arrived for 1973. Here, seats and door panels were done up in a spun nylon fabric—complete with copper rivets—that looked just like the genuine denim of Levi Strauss, which happily collaborated on the project, even allowing the use of its distinctive red jeans label for instant identification. The Levis Gremlin was probably the most winsome and interesting of this line, and if anybody is

collecting Gremlins by the year 2000, this model may well be the popularity leader.

Gremlin vanished for 1979, but it lived on in the Spirit, essentially the same car with smoother, more conventional styling. Joining the familiar chopped-tail two-door sedan was a slick new three-door coupe bearing a particularly graceful superstructure for such a short wheelbase. Both body styles were offered in three trim levels, and the AMX tag was revived for 1980 on a special "paint-on performance" hatchback. Power was supplied by a standard Pontiac-built four or AMC's own long-lived straight six. A heavy emphasis on quality meant the Spirit was generally better assembled than the Gremlin, if not always its Big Three rivals. But '60s-style specifications showed up the car's advanced design age. And while the standard four

1973 Javelin SST "Pierre Cardin" fastback coupe

1974 Ambassador Brougham four-door sedan

was fairly thrifty, it had very little urge; the optional six was quicker, but predictably much thirstier.

Shortly before Teague transformed Gremlin into Spirit, he similarly reworked the Hornet into the Concord, which bowed for 1978. Reflecting the company's limited new-model development funds, this compact was not all that different from its predecessor structurally or mechanically,

but it was better finished, had a more "important" look to it and, like other AMC models, benefited from the urgent stress on workmanship prompted by the growing success of Japanese imports. Concord was AMC's volume seller from the time it appeared. By 1980 it boasted a thriftier standard engine, cleaner appearance, more comfort and convenience extras and a broader rust protection warranty.

1973 Hornet X hatchback coupe

1974 Javelin AMX fastback coupe

1973 Ambassador Brougham hardtop coupe

1974 Matador X fastback coupe

1974 Gremlin "Levi's" two-door sedan

1974 Matador X fastback coupe

1975 Hornet DL four-door sedan

1976 Matador Brougham fastback coupe

We should not overlook two Hornet developments earlier in the '70s. One was the SC/360, a short-lived performance version of the two-door sedan offered only for 1971. As its name suggests, it packed AMC's 360-cid small-block V8, rated at 245 bhp with standard two-barrel carb or 285 bhp with the extra-cost four-pot induction. Acceleration was quite vivid, and a large functional hood

scoop, heavy-duty handling package, styled steel wheels, fat tires, and tape striping were all standard. Optional was a four-speed manual gearbox complete with Hurst linkage. But as had so often been the case before, AMC was a day late and a dollar short: only 784 were built, making this one of the rarest production models of the decade and something of a collector's item today. A more practical

1975 Matador Brougham five-door wagon

1976 Hornet Sportabout five-door wagon

1976 Gremlin X two-door sedan

1976 Matador Brougham four-door sedan

1976 Pacer DL three-door hatchback sedan

1977 Pacer DL three-door wagon

1977 Hornet AMX hatchback coupe

1977 Hornet AMX hatchback coupe

1977 Gremlin X two-door sedan

1977 Matador coupe

1978 Gremlin X "Levi's" two-door sedan

1978 Concord two-door sedan

innovation was Teague's lovely Hornet hatchback coupe, a 1973 addition. It offered vast load space, and could be quite sporty with the optional "X" package. Unhappily, needless styling gimmickry rendered some versions quite tacky by the time the Concord came in, and the hatchback was axed after '79. There was also a special AMX model based on this bodyshell, a limited-run 1977-78 offering.

The Concord spawned a novel offshoot for 1980, an intriguing and bold product for a small automaker. This was the four-wheel-drive Eagle, which revived a name that AMC owned through its Jeep buy-out and, with it, the dregs of Willys-Overland. The concept was a natural for a firm with AMC's particular and limited resources, a combination of the Concord body/chassis and a full-time 4wd system called Quadra-Trac. This employed a transfer case that apportioned driving torque between front and rear wheels via a slip-limiting silicone compound. The Eagle

was neither strictly car nor truck, but rather a specialty vehicle with some of the appeal of both.

Initially, Eagle was offered in the Concord's three body styles, built on a nominally longer wheelbase. Its ride height was greater than Concord's, too, thanks to larger tires and the need for extra ground clearance for the twin differentials. The drivetrain consisted of the firm's well-known 258-cid six mated to Torque Command (actually Chrysler's Torqueflite) three-speed automatic transmission. Power steering and brakes and all-season radial tires were standard. The Eagle flew with prominent (and necessary) wheel arch flares made of color-keyed Krayton plastic, and there was a Sport package option with black extensions and other trim, plus Goodyear Tiempo tires and "4x4" badges. Purposely designed with car-like qualities, the Eagle drove and felt much like any Concord. The reason was that AMC didn't intend it for really rough off-

1978 Matador Barcelona coupe

1979 Spirit Limited hatchback coupe

1979 Spirit AMX hatchback coupe

1980 Spirit DL two-door sedan

1979 Concord Limited wagon

1980 Pacer DL three-door hatchback sedan

road use, pitching it instead on the safety advantages of 4wd traction for everyday driving, particularly for buyers in the snowbelt states. A full range of luxury and convenience features was listed, but there was no V8 option in the interest of fuel economy— and the government's corporate average fuel economy (CAFE) mandates. For 1981, AMC would extend the Pontiac-built four to this line, and also introduced a brace of short-wheelbase "Eaglets" based on the Gremlin/Spirit platform. The latter lasted only a couple of years, but the larger models are still with us.

American Motors' major disappointment during the '70s was the Pacer, announced in 1975 as "the wide small car." A reply to Chevrolet's Vega and Ford's Pinto in the domestic subcompact stakes, it was conceived around the lightweight Wankel engine then being developed by GM and ultimately shelved. Designer Teague penned distinctive lines with acres of glass, a short nose (made possible

by the compact engine), and a hatchback body almost as wide as it was long. Unhappily, cancellation of the GM project forced AMC into patchwork engineering alterations that seriously compromised the original concept. For example, the doors ended up large and heavy, with broad inner panels that stole valuable inches of elbow room. While the rotary would have provided decent performance and fuel economy, AMC had no choice but to shoehorn its relatively weighty six into the Pacer, to the detriment of both as well as handling. And the glassy body was not only needlessly heavy for a subcompact but frankly odd to many eyes. By 1979, sales were only 10,000 or so per year despite the later addition of a V-8 option and a wagon body style, and Pacer was unceremoniously dumped after 1980.

An aging product line that didn't generate sufficient sales for funding development of more modern replacements proved an increasingly vicious cycle for AMC as

1980 Concord DL four-door sedan

1980 Eagle Sport five-door wagon

the '70s wore on. For example, the "all-new" Eagle owed much to the Concord, which in turn dated from the (by then) decade-old Hornet. Mounting losses were aggravated at decade's end by a deep national recession that cut sales further, and AMC soon found itself the object of a takeover bid by Renault of France, which acquired a controlling interest in the firm by 1982. Thus was born

what some have called "Franco-American Motors." Today, a much modernized Kenosha factory turns out U.S. versions of certain Renault models, plus a handful of Eagles. Indications are that AMC's future lies in continuing as an assembly operation for its French partner, with the firm's former automotive design and engineering resources eventually limited to 4wd vehicles.

AMC Specifications

1966

Marlin (wb 112.0)

		Wght	Price	Prod
6659-7	fstbk cpe	3,050	2,601	4,547

Ambassador 880 (wb 116.0)*

6685-2	sdn 4d	3,006	2,455	—
6686-2	sdn 2d	2,970	2,404	—
6688-2	wgn 4d	3,160	2,759	—

Ambassador 990 (wb 116.0)*

6685-5	sdn 4d	3,034	2,574	—
6687-5	conv cpe	3,462	2,968	—
6688-5	wgn 4d	3,180	2,880	—
6689-5	htp cpe	3,056	2,600	—

DPL (wb 116.0)*

6689-7	htp cpe	3,090	2,756	—

1966 Engines	bore×stroke	bhp	availability
L6, 232	3.75×3.50	145	S-Marlin
L6, 232	2.75×3.50	155	S-Ambassador
V8, 287	3.75×3.25	198	O-all
V8, 327	4.00×3.25	250/270	O-all

*Total 1966 calendar year 279,225; includes Rambler American and Classic models and early 1967 production.

1967

Marlin (wb 118.0)

		Wght	Price	Prod
6759-7	fstbk cpe	3,342	2,963	2,545

Ambassador 880 (wb 118.0)*

		Wght	Price	Prod
6785-2	sdn 4d	3,279	2,657	—
6786-2	sdn 4d	3,310	2,519	—
6788-2	wgn 4d	3,486	2,962	—

Ambassador 990 (wb 118.0)*

6785-5	sdn 4d	3,324	2,776	—
6788-5	wgn 4d	3,545	3,083	—
6789-5	htp cpe	3,376	2,803	—

Ambassador DPL (wb 118.0)*

6787-7	conv cpe	3,434	3,143	—
6789-7	htp cpe	3,394	2,958	—

1967 Engines	bore×stroke	bhp	availability
L6, 232	3.75×3.50	145	S-Marlin
L6, 232	3.75×3.50	155	S-Ambassador; O-Marlin
V8, 290	3.75×3.28	200	S-Amb. conv; O-others
V8, 343	4.08×3.28	235	O-all
V8, 343	4.08×3.28	280	O-all

*Total 1967 calendar year 229,058; includes Rambler American and Rebel models and early 1968 production.

1968

Rebel 550 (wb 114.0)*

		Wght	Price	Prod
6815	sdn 4d	3,062	2,443	—
6817	conv 2d	3,195	2,736	377
6818	wgn 4d	3,301	2,729	—
6819	htp cpe	3,117	2,454	—

Rebel 770 (wb 114.0)*

6815-5	sdn 4d	3,074	2,542	—
6818-5	wgn 4d	3,306	2,854	—

		Wght	Price	Prod
6819-5	htp cpe	3,116	2,556	—

Rebel SST (wb 114.0)*

		Wght	Price	Prod
6817-7	conv cpe	3,427	2,999	823
6819-7	htp cpe	3,348	2,775	—

AMX (wb 97.0)*

		Wght	Price	Prod
6839-7	fstbk cpe 2S	3,097	3,245	6,725

Javelin (wb 109.0)—56,462 built

		Wght	Price	Prod
6879-5	fstbk cpe	2,826	2,482	—
6879-7	SST fstbk cpe	2,836	2,587	—

Ambassador (wb 118.0)*

		Wght	Price	Prod
6885-2	sdn 4d	3,193	2,820	—
6889-2	htp cpe	3,258	2,892	—

Ambassador DPL (wb 118.0)*

		Wght	Price	Prod
6885-5	sdn 4d	3,265	2,920	—
6888-5	wgn 4d	3,475	3,207	—
6889-5	htp cpe	3,321	2,947	—

Ambassador SST (wb 118.0)*

		Wght	Price	Prod
6885-7	sdn 4d	3,496	3,151	—
6889-7	htp cpe	3,530	3,172	—

*Total 1968 calendar year 268,439; includes Rambler American and early 1969 production.

1968 Engines	bore×stroke	bhp	availability
L6, 232	3.75×3.50	145	S-Javelin, Rebel exc SST
L6, 232	3.75×3.50	155	S-Amb exc SST
V8, 290	3.75×3.28	200	S-Rebel SST, Amb SST; O-all
V8, 290	3.75×3.28	225	S-AMX; O-Javelin
V8, 343	4.08×3.28	235	O-Rebel, Ambassador
V8, 343	4.08×3.28	280	O-AMX Javelin, Rebel, Amb
V8, 390	4.17×3.57	315	O-all

1969

Rebel (wb 114.0)*

		Wght	Price	Prod
6915	sdn 4d	3,062	2,484	—
6918	wgn 4d	3,301	2,817	—
6919	htp cpe	3,117	2,496	—

Rebel SST (wb 114.0)*

		Wght	Price	Prod
6915-7	sdn 4d	3,074	2,584	—
6918-7	wgn 4d	3,306	2,947	—
6919-7	htp cpe	3,140	2,598	—

AMX (wb 97.0)*

		Wght	Price	Prod
6939-7	fstbk cpe 2S	3,097	3,297	8,293

Javelin (wb 109.0)—40,675 built

		Wght	Price	Prod
6979-5	fstbk cpe	2,826	2,512	—
6979-7	SST fstbk cpe	2,836	2,633	—

Ambassador (wb 122.0)*

		Wght	Price	Prod
6985-2	sdn 4d	3,276	2,914	—

Ambassador DPL (wb 122.0)*

		Wght	Price	Prod
6985-5	sdn 4d	3,358	3,165	—
6988-5	wgn 4d	3,561	3,504	—
6989-5	htp cpe	3,403	3,182	—

Ambassador SST (wb 122.0)*

		Wght	Price	Prod
6985-7	sdn 4d	3,508	3,605	—
6988-7	wgn 4d	3,732	3,998	—
6989-7	htp cpe	3,566	3,622	—

*Total 1969 calendar year 242,898; includes Rambler American and early 1970 production.

1969 Engines	bore×stroke	bhp	availability
L6, 232	3.75×3.50	145	S-Javelin, Rebel
L6, 232	3.75×3.50	155	S-Amb, Amb DPL; O-Rebel
V8, 290	3.75×3.28	200	S-Amb SST; O-Amb, Reb, Jav
V8, 290	3.75×3.28	225	S-AMX; O-Javelin
V8, 343	4.08×3.28	235	O-Rebel, Ambassador
V8, 343	4.08×3.28	280	O-AMX, Jav, Rebel, Amb
V8, 390	4.17×3.57	315	O-AMX, Jav SST, Amb SST

1970*

Hornet (wb 108.0)

		Wght	Price	Prod
7005-0	sdn 4d	2,748	2,072	—
7006-0	sdn 2d	2,677	1,994	—

Hornet SST (wb 108.0)

		Wght	Price	Prod
7005-7	sdn 4d	2,765	2,221	—
7006-7	sdn 2d	2,705	2,144	—

Rebel (wb 114.0)

		Wght	Price	Prod
7015-0	sdn 4d	3,129	2,636	—
7018-0	wgn 4d	3,356	2,766	—
7019-0	htp cpe	3,148	2,660	—

Rebel SST (wb 114.0)

		Wght	Price	Prod
7015-7	sdn 4d	3,155	2,684	—
7018-0	wgn 4d	3,375	3,072	—
7019-7	htp cpe	3,206	2,718	—

Rebel Machine (wb 114.0)

		Wght	Price	Prod
7019-0	htp cpe	3,650	3,475	2,326

AMX (wb 97.0)-—4,116 built

		Wght	Price	Prod
7039-7	fstbk cpe 2S	3,126	3,395	—

Gremlin (wb 96.0)

		Wght	Price	Prod
7046-0	sdn 2d	2,497	1,879	—
7046-5	sdn 2d	2,557	1,959	—

Javelin (wb 109.0)—28,210 built

		Wght	Price	Prod
7079-5	fstbk cpe	2,845	2,720	—
7079-7	SST fstbk cpe	2,863	2,848	—
7079-7	SST/Trans-Am fstbk cpe	3,340	3,995	—

Ambassador (wb 122.0)

		Wght	Price	Prod
7085-2	sdn 4d	3,328	3,020	—

Ambassador DPL (wb 122.0)

		Wght	Price	Prod
7085-5	sdn 4d	3,523	3,588	—
7088-5	wgn 4d	3,817	3,946	—
7089-5	htp cpe	3,555	3,605	—

Ambassador SST (wb 122.0)

		Wght	Price	Prod
7085-7	sdn 4d	3,557	3,722	—
7088-5	wgn 4d	3,852	4,122	—
7089-5	htp cpe	3,606	3,739	—

*Total 1970 calendar year 276,110; includes early 1971 production.

1970 Engines	bore×stroke	bhp	availability
L6, 199	3.75×3.00	128	S-Hornet, Gremlin
L6, 232	3.75×3.50	145	S-Hornet SST, Rebel, Javelin; O-Hornet, Gremlin
L6, 232	3.75×3.50	155	S-Amb; O-Hornet, Rebel
V8, 304	3.75×3.44	210	S-DPL, SST; O-all exc AMX
V8, 360	4.08×3.44	245	O-Rebel, Amb, Jav
V8, 360	4.08×3.44	290	S-AMX; O-Reb, Amb, Jav
V8, 390	4.17×3.57	325	O-AMX, Jav, Reb SST, Amb SST
V8, 390	4.17×3.57	340	S-Rebel Machine; O-all

1971

Gremlin (wb 96.0)

		Wght	Price	Prod
7146-0	sdn 2d 2P	2,503	1,899	53,480
7146-5	sdn 2d 4P	2,552	1,999	

Hornet (wb 108.0)—74,685 built

		Wght	Price	
7105-0	sdn 4d	2,731	2,234	L6: 23,000*
7106-0	sdn 2d	2,654	2,174	V8: 500*
7105-7	SST sdn 4d	2,732	2,334	L6: 40,000*
7106-7	SST sdn 2d	2,691	2,274	V8: 9,500*
7108-7	Sportabout wgn 5d	2,827	2,594	
7106-1	SC/360 sdn 2d	3,057	2,663	784

Javelin (wb 110.0)—29,130 built

		Wght	Price	Prod
7179-5	htp cpe L6	2,887	2,879	3,500*
7179-7	SST htp cpe 6cyl	2,890	2,999	1,000*
7179-5	htp cpe V8	3,144	2,980	4,000*
7179-7	SST htp cpe V8	3,147	3,100	17,000*
7979-8	AMX htp cpe V8	3,244	3,432	2,054

Matador (wb 118.0)—45,789 built (approx. 30,000 L6)

		Wght	Price	
7155-7	sdn 4d L6	3,165	2,770	—
7119-7	htp cpe L6	3,201	2,799	—
7118-7	wgn 4d L6	3,437	3,163	6,800
7115-7	sdn 4d V8	3,324	3,100	
7119-7	htp cpe V8	3,360	3,129	—
7118-7	wgn 4d V8	3,596	3,493	4,200

Ambassador (wb 122.0)—41,674 built

		Wght	Price	Prod
7185-2	DPL sdn 4d L6	3,315	3,616	650*
7185-2	DPL sdn 4d V8	3,488	3,717	6,000*
7185-5	SST sdn 4d V8	3,520	3,852	7,500*
7189-5	SST htp cpe V8	3,561	3,870	
7188-5	SST wgn 4d V8	3,815	4,253	8,000*
7185-7	Brougham sdn 4d V8	3,541	3,983	10,000*
7189-7	Brougham htp cpe V8	3,580	3,999	
7188-7	Brougham wgn 4d V8	3,862	4,430	10,000*

1971 Engines	bore×stroke	bhp	availability
L6, 232.0	3.75×3.50	135	S-Grem,Hrnt,Jav,Mat
L6, 258.0	3.75×3.90	150	S-Amb; O-Grem,Hrnt, Jav,Mat
V8, 304.0	3.75×3.44	210	S-Jav,Mat,Amb; O-Hrnt
V8, 360.0	4.08×3.44	245	S-Hrnt SC; O-Jav,Mat,Amb
V8, 360.0	4.08×3.44	285	O-Hrnt SC,Jav,Mat,Amb
V8, 401.0	4.17×3.68	330	O-Ambassador

1972

Gremlin (wb 96.0)—61,717 built

		Wght	Price	Prod
46-5	sdn 2d L6	2,494	1,999	53,000*
46-5	sdn 2d V8	2,746	2,153	8,500*

Hornet SST (wb 108.0)—71,056 built

		Wght	Price	
05-7	sdn 4d L6	2,691	2,265	35,000*
06-7	sdn 2d L6	2,627	2,199	
08-7	Sportabout wgn 5d L6	2,769	2,587	30,000*
05-7	sdn 4d V8	2,925	2,403	2,000*
06-7	sdn 2d V8	2,861	2,337	
08-7	Sportabout wgn 5d V8	2,998	2,725	5,000*

Javelin (wb 110.0)

		Wght	Price	
79-7	SST htp cpe L6	2,876	2,807	23,455
79-7	SST htp cpe V8	3,118	2,901	
79-8	AMX htp cpe V8	3,149	3,109	2,729

Matador (wb 118.0)—54,813 built

		Wght	Price	
15-7	sdn 4d L6	3,171	2,784	11,000*
19-7	htp cpe L6	3,210	2,818	
18-7	wgn 4d L6	3,480	3,140	3,000*
15-7	sdn 4d V8	3,355	2,883	34,000*
19-7	htp cpe V8	3,394	2,917	
18-7	wgn 4d V8	3,653	3,239	7,500*

Ambassador (wb 122.0)—44,364 built

		Wght	Price	
85-5	SST sdn 4d	3,537	3,885	18,000*
89-5	SST htp cpe	3,579	3,902	
88-5	SST wgn 4d	3,833	4,270	5,500*
85-7	Brougham sdn 4d	3,551	4,002	15,000*
89-5	Brougham htp cpe	3,581	4,018	
88-5	Brougham wgn 4d	3,857	4,437	5,500*

1972 Engines	bore×stroke	bhp	availability
L6, 232.0	3.75×3.50	100	S-Grem,Hrnt,Jav,Mat exc wgn
L6, 258.0	3.75×3.90	110	S-Mat wgn,Grem,Hrnt; O-Jav,Mat
V8, 304.0	3.75×3.44	150	S-all base V8 models
V8, 360.0	4.08×3.44	175	O-all exc Gremlin
V8, 360.0	4.08×3.44	195	O-Jav,Mat,Amb
V8, 401.0	4.17×3.68	225	O-Jav,Mat,Amb

1973

Gremlin (wb 96.0)

		Wght	Price	Prod
46-5	sdn 2d L6	2,642	2,098	
46-5	sdn 2d V8	2,867	2,252	

Hornet (wb 108.0)

		Wght	Price	
05-7	sdn 4d L6	2,854	2,343	
06-7	sdn 2d L6	2,777	2,298	
03-7	htchbk cpe L6	2,818	2,449	
08-7	Sportabout wgn 5d L6	2,921	2,675	
05-7	sdn 4d V8	3,067	2,481	
06-7	sdn 2d V8	2,990	2,436	
03-7	htchbk cpe V8	3,031	2,587	
08-7	Sportabout wgn 5d V8	3,134	2,813	

Javelin (wb 110.0)

		Wght	Price	
79-7	htp cpe L6	2,868	2,889	22,556
79-7	htp cpe V8	3,104	2,983	
79-8	AMX htp cpe V8	3,170	3,191	4,980

Matador (wb 118.0)

		Wght	Price	
15-7	sdn 4d L6	3,289	2,853	
19-7	htp cpe L6	3,314	2,887	
18-7	wgn 4d L6	3,627	3,179	
15-7	sdn 4d V8	3,502	2,952	
19-7	htp cpe V8	3,527	2,986	
18-7	wgn 4d V8	3,815	3,278	

Ambassador Brougham (wb 122.0)

		Wght	Price	
85-7	sdn 4d	3,763	4,461	
89-7	htp cpe	3,774	4,477	
88-7	wgn 4d	4,054	4,861	

1973 Engines	bore×stroke	bhp	availability
L6, 232.0	3.75×3.50	100	S-Grem,Hrnt,Jav,Mat exc wgn
L6, 258.0	3.75×3.90	110	S-Mat wgn; O-Grem,Hrnt, Jav,Mat
V8, 304.0	3.75×3.44	150	S-all base V8 models
V8, 360.0	4.08×3.44	175	O-all exc Gremlin
V8, 360.0	4.08×3.44	195	O-Jav,Mat,Amb
V8, 360.0	4.08×3.44	220	O-Jav,Mat,Amb
V8, 401.0	4.17×3.68	255	O-Jav,Mat,Amb

1974

Gremlin (wb 96.0)

		Wght	Price	Prod
46-5	sdn 2d L6	2,649	2,481	119,642
46-5	sdn 2d V8	2,888	2,635	12,263

Hornet (wb 108.0)

		Wght	Price	
05-7	sdn 4d L6	2,833	2,824	70,052
06-7	sdn 2d L6	2,767	2,774	
03-7	htchbk cpe L6	2,791	2,849	
08-7	Sportabout wgn 5d L6	2,900	3,049	57,414

		Wght	Price	Prod
05-7	sdn 4d V8	3,077	2,962	
06-7	sdn 2d V8	3,011	2,912	7,697
03-7	htchbk cpe V8	3,035	2,987	
08-7	Sportabout wgn 5d V8	3,144	3,187	10,295

Javelin (wb 110.0)

		Wght	Price	Prod
79-7	htp cpe L6	2,869	2,999	5,036
79-7	htp cpe V8	3,116	3,093	19,520
79-8	AMX htp cpe V8	3,184	3,299	4,980

Matador (wb 118.0)—99,922 built

		Wght	Price	Prod
15-7	sdn 4d L6	3,425	3,052	25,826
16-7	cpe L6	3,437	3,096	
18-7	wgn 4d L6	3,739	3,378	2,975
15-7	sdn 4d V8	3,632	3,151	35,000*
16-7	cpe V8	3,634	3,195	
18-7	wgn 4d V8	3,925	3,477	6,734
16-9	Brougham cpe L6	3,456	3,249	28,000*
16-9	Brougham cpe V8	3,663	3,348	
16-8	"X" htp cpe V8	3,672	3,699	1,500*

Ambassador Brougham (wb 122.0)

		Wght	Price	Prod
85-7	sdn 4d	3,851	4,559	17,901
88-7	wgn 4d	4,125	4,960	7,076

1974 Engines	bore×stroke	bhp	availability
L6, 232.0	3.75×3.50	100	S-Grem,Hrnt,Jav,Mat wgn
L6, 258.0	3.75×3.90	110	S-Mat wgn; O-Grem,Hrnt, Jav,Mat
V8, 304.0	3.75×3.44	150	S-all base V8 models
V8, 360.0	4.08×3.44	175	O-all exc Gremlin
V8, 360.0	4.08×3.44	195	O-Jav,Mat,Amb
V8, 401.0	4.17×3.68	255	O-Jav,Mat,Amb

1975

Gremlin (wb 96.0)

		Wght	Price	Prod
46-5	sdn 2d L6	2,694	2,798	42,630
46-5	sdn 2d V8	2,952	2,952	3,218

Hornet (wb 108.0)

		Wght	Price	Prod
05-7	sdn 4d L6	2,881	3,124	
06-7	sdn 2d L6	2,815	3,074	36,305
03-7	htchbk cpe L6	2,839	3,174	
08-7	Sportabout wgn 5d L6	2,948	3,374	3,016
05-7	sdn 4d V8	3,127	3,262	
06-7	sdn 2d V8	3,061	3,212	20,369
03-7	htchbk cpe V8	3,085	3,312	
08-7	Sportabout wgn 5d V8	3,194	3,512	4,223

Pacer (wb 100.0)

		Wght	Price	Prod
66-7	htchbk sdn 3d	2,995	3,299	72,158

Matador (wb 118.0)

		Wght	Price	Prod
85-7	sdn 4d L6	3,586	3,452	9,390
16-7	cpe L6	3,562	3,446	
88-7	wgn 4d L6	3,878	3,844	1,575
85-7	sdn 4d V8	3,746	3,551	40,500
16-7	cpe V8	3,734	3,545	
88-7	wgn 4d V8	4,038	3,943	8,117

1975 Engines	bore×stroke	bhp	availability
L6, 232.0	3.75×3.50	100	S-Grem,Hrnt,Pcr
L6, 258.0	3.75×3.90	110	S-Mat; O-Grem,Hrnt,Pcr
V8, 304.0	3.75×3.44	150	S-Grem,Hrnt,Mat
V8, 360.0	4.08×3.44	175	O-Matador

1976

Gremlin (wb 96.0)

		Wght	Price	Prod
46-3	sdn 2d L6	2,771	2,889	
46-5	Cus sdn 2d L6	2,774	2,998	
46-3	sdn 2d V8	3,020	3,051	
46-5	Cus sdn 2d V8	3,023	3,160	

Pacer (wb 100.0)

		Wght	Price	Prod
66-7	htchbk sdn 3d	3,114	3,499	

Hornet (wb 108.0)

		Wght	Price	Prod
05-7	sdn 4d L6	2,971	3,199	
06-7	sdn 2d L6	2,909	3,199	
03-7	htchbk cpe L6	2,920	3,199	
08-7	Sportabout wgn 5d L6	3,040	3,549	
05-7	sdn 4d V8	3,220	3,344	
06-7	sdn 2d V8	3,158	3,344	
03-7	htchbk cpe V8	3,169	3,344	
08-7	Sportabout wgn 5d V8	3,289	3,694	

Matador (wb 118.0)

		Wght	Price	Prod
85-7	sdn 4d L6	3,589	3,627	
16-7	cpe L6	3,562	3,621	
85-7	sdn 4d V8	3,838	3,731	
16-7	cpe V8	3,811	3,725	
88-7	wgn 4d V8	4,015	4,373	

1976 Engines	bore×stroke	bhp	availability
L6, 232.0	3.75×3.50	90	S-all exc Mat
L6, 258.0	3.75×3.90	95	S-Mat; O-others
V8, 304.0	3.75×3.44	120	S-all exc Pcr
V8, 360.0	4.08×3.44	140/180	O-Mat sdn/wgn

1977

Gremlin (wb 96.0)

		Wght	Price	Prod
46-4	sdn 2d L4	2,654	3,248	
46-5	sdn 2d L6	2,811	2,995	
36-7	Custom sdn 2d L6	2,824	3,248	

Pacer (wb 100.0)

		Wght	Price	Prod
66-7	htchbk sdn 3d	3,156	3,649	
68-7	wgn 3d	3,202	3,799	

Hornet (wb 108.0)

		Wght	Price	Prod
05-7	sdn 4d L6	3,035	2,449	
06-7	sdn 2d L6	2,971	3,399	
03-7	htchbk cpe L6	3,012	3,419	
08-7	wgn 5d L6	3,100	3,699	
05-7	sdn 4d V8	3,268	3,613	
06-7	sdn 2d V8	3,204	3,563	
03-7	htchbk cpe V8	3,245	3,662	
08-7	wgn 5d V8	3,333	3,863	

Matador (wb 118.0)

		Wght	Price	Prod
85-7	sdn 4d L6	3,713	4,549	
16-7	cpe L6	3,704	4,499	
85-7	sdn 4d V8	3,876	4,669	
16-7	cpe V8	3,872	4,619	
88-7	wgn 4d V8	4,104	4,899	

1977 Engines	bore×stroke	bhp	availability
L4, 121.0	3.41×3.22	80	S-Gremlin
L6, 232.0	3.75×3.50	88	S-all exc Matador
L6, 258.0	3.75×3.90	98	S-Matador
L6, 258.0	3.75×3.90	114	O-all exc Matador
V8, 304.0	3.75×3.44	121	S-Hornet
V8, 304.0	3.75×3.44	126	S-Matador
V8, 360.0	4.08×3.44	129	O-Matador

1978

Gremlin (wb 96.0)

		Wght	Price	Prod
46-4	sdn 2d L4	2,656	3,789	
46-5	sdn 2d L6	2,834	3,539	
46-7	Custom sdn 2d L6	2,822	3,789	

Concord (wb 108.0)

		Wght	Price	Prod
05-7	sdn 4d L6	3,099	3,849	
06-7	sdn 2d L6	3,029	3,749	
03-7	htchbk cpe L6	3,051	3,849	
08-7	wgn 5d L6	3,133	4,049	

		Wght	Price	Prod
05-7	sdn 4d V8	3,332	4,099	
06-7	sdn 2d V8	3,262	3,999	
03-7	htchbk cpe V8	3,284	4,099	
08-7	wgn 5d V8	3,366	4,299	

Pacer (wb 100.0)

		Wght	Price	Prod
66-7	htchbk sdn 3d L6	3,197	4,048	
68-7	wgn 3d L6	3,245	4,193	
66-7	htchbk sdn 3d V8	3,430	4,298	
68-7	wgn 3d V8	3,478	4,443	

AMX (wb 108.0)

		Wght	Price	Prod
03-9	htchbk cpe L6	3,159	4,649	
03-9	htchbk cpe V8	3,381	4,899	

Matador (wb 118.0)

		Wght	Price	Prod
85-7	sdn 4d L6	3,718	4,849	
16-7	cpe L6	3,709	4,799	
85-7	sdn 4d V8	3,921	5,039	
16-7	cpe V8	3,916	4,989	
88-7	wgn 4d V8	4,146	5,299	

1978 Engines	bore×stroke	bhp	availability
L4, 121.0	3.41×3.22	80	S-Gremlin
L6, 232.00	3.75×3.50	90	S-all exc Matador,AMX
L6, 258.0	3.75×3.90	120	S-Mat,AMX; O-others
V8, 304.0	3.75×3.44	130	S-all exc Gremlin
V8, 360.0	4.08×3.44	140	O-Matador

1979

Spirit (wb 96.0)

		Wght	Price	Prod
43-7	htchbk cpe L4	2,545	3,953	
46-7	sdn 2d L4	2,489	3,853	
43-7	DL htchbk cpe L4	2,635	4,190	
46-7	DL sdn 2d L4	2,579	4,090	
43-7	Limited htchbk cpe L4	2,732	5,190	
46-7	Limited sdn 2d L4	2,676	5,090	
43-7	htchbk cpe L6	2,762	4,133	
46-7	sdn 2d L6	2,706	4,033	
43-7	DL htchbk cpe L6	2,852	4,370	
46-7	DL sdn 2d L6	2,798	4,270	
43-7	Limited htchbk cpe L6	2,949	5,370	
46-7	Limited sdn 2d L6	2,893	5,270	

Concord (wb 108.0)

		Wght	Price	Prod
05-7	sdn 4d L6	2,939	4,489	
06-7	sdn 2d L6	2,873	4,389	
03-7	htchbk cpe L6	2,888	4,324	
08-7	wgn 5d L6	2,977	4,689	
05-7	DL sdn 4d L6	3,040	4,788	
06-7	DL sdn 2d L6	2,982	4,688	
03-7	DL htchbk cpe L6	3,003	4,623	
08-7	DL wgn 5d L6	3,072	4,988	
05-7	Limited sdn 4d L6	3,146	5,788	
06-7	Limited sdn 2d L6	3,090	5,688	
08-7	Limited wgn 5d L6	3,177	5,988	
05-7	sdn 4d V8	3,146	4,889	
06-7	sdn 2d V8	3,080	4,789	
03-7	htchbk cpe V8	3,095	4,724	
08-7	wgn 5d V8	3,184	5,089	
05-7	DL sdn 4d V8	3,247	5,188	
06-7	DL sdn 2d V8	3,189	5,088	
03-7	DL htchbk cpe V8	3,210	5,023	
08-7	DL wgn 5d V8	3,279	5,388	
05-7	Limited sdn 4d V8	3,353	6,188	
06-7	Limited sdn 2d V8	3,297	6,088	
08-7	Limited wgn 5d V8	3,384	6,888	

Pacer (wb 100.0)

		Wght	Price	Prod
66-7	DL htchbk sdn 3d L6	3,133	5,039	
68-7	DL wgn 3d L6	3,170	5,189	
66-7	Limited htchbk sdn 3d L6	3,218	6,039	
68-7	Limited wgn 3d L6	3,255	6,189	
66-7	DL htchbk sdn 3d V8	3,360	5,439	
68-7	DL wgn 3d V8	3,397	5,589	
66-7	Limited htchbk sdn 3d V8	3,445	6,439	
68-7	Limited wgn 3d V8	3,482	6,589	

AMX (wb 96.0)

		Wght	Price	Prod
43-9	htchbk cpe L6	2,899	6,090	
43-9	htchbk cpe V8	3,092	6,465	

1979 Engines	bore×stroke	bhp	availability
L4, 121.0	3.41×3.22	80	S-Spirit; O-Con exc wgn
L6, 232.0	3.75×3.50	90	S-Con; O-Spirit
L6, 258.0	3.75×3.90	100	S-Pacer
L6, 258.0	3.75×3.90	110	S-Sprt,AMX; O-Con
V8, 304.0	3.75×3.44	125	S-all V8 models

1980

Spirit (wb 96.0)

		Wght	Price	Prod
43-0	htchbk cpe L4	2,556	4,605	
46-0	sdn 2d L4	2,512	4,505	
43-5	DL htchbk cpe L4	2,656	5,004	
46-5	DL sdn 2d L4	2,611	4,904	
43-7	Limited htchbk cpe L4	2,675	5,451	
46-7	Limited sdn 2d L4	2,630	5,351	
43-0	htchbk cpe L6	2,758	4,734	
46-0	sdn 2d L6	2,714	4,634	
43-5	DL htchbk cpe L6	2,858	5,133	
46-5	DL sdn 2d L6	2,813	5,033	
43-7	Limited htchbk cpe L6	2,877	5,580	
46-7	Limited sdn 2d L6	2,832	5,480	

Concord (wb 108.0)

		Wght	Price	Prod
05-0	sdn 4d L4	2,712	5,219	
06-0	sdn 2d L4	2,646	5,094	
08-0	wgn 5d L4	2,741	5,419	
05-5	DL sdn 4d L4	2,834	5,618	
06-5	DL sdn 2d L4	2,764	5,493	
08-5	DL wgn 5d L4	2,855	5,818	
05-7	Limited sdn 4d L4	2,859	6,065	
06-7	Limited sdn 2d L4	2,789	5,940	
08-7	Limited wgn 5d L4	2,886	6,265	
05-0	sdn 4d L6	2,910	5,348	
06-0	sdn 2d L6	2,844	5,223	
08-0	wgn 5d L6	2,939	5,548	
05-5	DL sdn 4d L6	3,032	5,747	
06-5	DL sdn 2d L6	2,962	5,622	
08-5	DL wgn 5d L6	3,053	5,947	
05-7	Limited sdn 4d L6	3,057	6,194	
06-7	Limited sdn 2d L6	2,987	6,069	
08-7	Limited wgn 5d L6	3,084	6,394	

Pacer (wb 100.0)

		Wght	Price	Prod
66-5	DL htchbk 2d L6	3,147	5,407	
68-5	DL wgn 2d L6	3,195	5,558	
66-7	Limited htchbk 2d L6	3,172	6,031	
68-7	Limited wgn 2d L6	3,220	6,182	

AMX (wb 96.0)

		Wght	Price	Prod
43-9	htchbk cpe L4	2,901	5,653	

Eagle (wb 109.3)

		Wght	Price	Prod
35-5	sdn 4d L6	3,450	7,418	
36-5	sdn 2d L6	3,382	7,168	
38-5	wgn 5d L6	3,470	7,718	
35-7	Limited sdn 4d L6	3,465	7,815	
36-7	Limited sdn 2d L6	3,397	7,565	
38-7	Limited wgn 5d L6	3,491	8,115	

1980 Engines	bore×stroke	bhp	availability
L4, 151.0	4.00×3.00	90	S-all 4-cyl. models
L6, 258.0	3.75×3.90	110	S-all 6-cyl. models

Auburn

Auburn Automobile Company
Auburn, Indiana

The Auburns best remembered by enthusiasts today are those built in the late 1920s and in the '30s, but the marque was established much earlier than that. In 1903, two Indiana carriage builders, Frank and Morris Eckhart, launched a chain-drive, single-cylinder runabout, which they sold for $800. Two-, four-, and six-cylinder cars followed successively in the years through 1912. A notable 1919 entry was the Beauty Six, which had a streamlined body, disc wheels, step plates instead of running-boards, and windshield vent wings, all very advanced for the time. But good though they were, these early Auburns were never in great demand, and the Eckharts lacked an effective sales organization. After WWI, a deep recession cut into automobile sales generally, and Auburn produced fewer than 4000 cars annually in 1919-22.

The company's low-key image changed abruptly in 1924 with the arrival of Errett Lobban Cord, a 30-year-old industrialist variously described as a "boy wonder" and a "profane, bespectacled capitalist." His claim to fame was salesmanship. He had started as a salesman for Moon five years earlier, quickly working his way up to become general manager, then director, of the Chicago company, amassing around $100,000 in the process. His reputation preceeded him to Auburn, where he was asked to step in as general manager. He promptly disposed of 750 leftovers, which netted the company enough cash to pay off its debts, and was made a vice-president. By 1926, he had become both president and chief stockholder.

Under Cord's guidance, Auburn prospered in the 1920s. It gained a modest competition image, greatly increased its export operations, upgraded its dealer network, and passed the 20,000 mark in annual production by 1929. Auburns of the late '20s and early '30s were fast, good-looking and reliable, yet incredibly low-priced. Though its eight-cylinder models were more vivid performers than its Sixes, all Auburns were appreciated for their style.

After 1930, Cord dropped the Six to concentrate on the Eights and, ultimately, a Twelve. That year's final six-cylinder 685 series consisted of only three models, cabriolet, sedan, and sport sedan. The engine came from Lycoming, a Pennsylvania company Cord had purchased in 1929, and was a sturdy 185-cubic-inch unit that produced 70 horsepower at 3400 rpm. Despite its modest price, the 685 was by no means dull. It rode a 120-inch wheelbase and was smooth and clean-looking. Nevertheless, Auburn sales dropped by almost 50 percent in 1930, and the continuing Depression convinced management that a six was not profitable enough to continue.

Auburn's eight-cylinder cars came in two series for 1930. The lower-priced 895 rode a 125-inch wheelbase and was an unquestionable bargain. Its engine shared the 685's bore and stroke, but had two extra cylinders. Further up the price ladder was the Custom Eight 125. Though most models in this line tipped the scales at around 3900 pounds, they were capable of close to 90 mph, astonishing for the day. In 1929, this engine in a 3000-pound speedster body had powered Auburn's first 100-mph automobile.

Auburn was one of the first car companies to record increased sales *after* the 1929 stock market crash. Production zoomed to a record 32,301 units in 1931, the result of a dealer expansion program, plus an all-eight-cylinder line of fleet, luxurious, bargain-priced cars. The '31 offerings reflected Cord's cagey sales strategy. Auburn now lopped off its slower selling small-six and big-eight models and bored out its smaller eight-cylinder powerplant. Larger, more rakish bodies were placed on a longer 127-inch wheelbase, and two series were offered, Standard and Custom, the latter with a standard freewheeling transmission. Speedsters, coupes, cabriolets, broughams, phaeton sedans, and sedans were all available, as well as a seven-passenger sedan built on a special 136-inch wheelbase chassis. As *Business Week* magazine commented at the time: "It was more car for the money than the public had ever seen."

1930 Custom Eight 125 cabriolet

1931 Custom Eight four-door sedan

1931 Eight four-door sedan

1932 Custom Eight cabriolet

1932 Custom Eight four-door sedan

1933 Eight five-passenger brougham

Although the 1931 Eight was a remarkable buy, the 1932 Twelve was even more incredible. It was the least expensive V12 automobile yet offered: $975 for the Standard coupe, $1275 for the top-of-the-line Custom Speedster. The 391-cid Lycoming engine was built to the design of Auburn chief engineer George Kublin, and packed a healthy 160 bhp at 3500 rpm. The double-braced frame spanned a 133-inch wheelbase. Custom Twelves featured a Columbia dual-ratio rear axle with 4.55:1 and 3.04:1 gearing that could be switched at speeds under 40 mph, effectively providing six forward speeds. The Eights continued as before, and the usual body styles were available through the line, plus the long-wheelbase eight-cylinder sedans. The beautiful V12 boattail speedsters, so rare today, were magnificent expressions of Auburn styling that year.

Despite a peerlesss model line, Auburn sales plunged in 1932 and production for the year was only 7939 units. Output dropped to 4636 the next year, and in 1934 it fell again, to 4703. This mystified E.L. Cord, though with hindsight the reason is clear: a V12 at any price simply didn't interest buyers in the depths of the Depression. Nor, for that matter, did Auburn's Eight, which had exhausted what market it had enjoyed in 1931. Both cars had a reputation for size and performance that perhaps made people equate them with more expensive makes. By this time, Cord him-

1932 Custom Eight phaeton sedan

1933 Custom Twelve four-door sedan

1934 Eight cabriolet

self was spread too thin building his far-flung business empire. He'd already bought Duesenberg in 1926 and had launched a front-wheel-drive car bearing his name three years later. He then acquired the Lycoming and Ansted engine companies, several midwestern industrial corporations, and Checker Cab, as well as shipbuilding and aviation interests. Perhaps in order to avoid a scandal over the management of his enterprises, Cord went to England in 1934—and dropped out of sight. His conglomerate's fortunes were eventually handed over to Duesenberg president Harold T. Ames.

The lineup for 1933-34 comprised Eights and Twelves as in 1932, and 1934 brought a revival of the Six. Designated the Series 652, it was powered by 210-cid Lycoming engine rated at 85 bhp at 3500 rpm. Priced as low as $695, it was offered in Standard or Custom trim on a 119-inch wheelbase. But it didn't sell. Controversial styling, which included such radical streamlining features as a shovel nose, is often tagged with the blame, but 1934 was not a good sales year for any make.

When Ames arrived, he brought with him Gordon Miller

Buehrig and August Duesenberg. Buehrig was given a modest $50,000 budget and told to do what he could to upgrade Auburn styling for 1935. Duesenberg was handed the eight-cylinder engine assignment, in conjunction with Schwitzer-Cummins and Lycoming. The result was a line of very pretty cars crowned by the legendary 851 Speedster, Auburn's final glory. Buehrig didn't have enough money for a complete redesign, so he worked with leftover '34 Twelves. To create the new Speedster, he restyled the previous body from the cowl forward with a new radiator, a sleek hood, beautifully curved pontoon fenders, and external exhausts. To save on engine tooling costs, Duesenberg created what was basically an extension of the 1934 six, with the same bore and stroke dimensions and two more cylinders. The end product developed 150 bhp with the aid of a Schwitzer-Cummins supercharger. Speedster models, which came only with the blower, could hit 100 mph right off the showroom floor and were among the most breathtakingly beautiful automobiles of all time, yet their base price was just $2245. Again, Auburn offered tremendous value for the money.

1935 phaeton sedan with Cummins diesel engine

1936 Supercharged Eight Dual Ratio four-door sedan

The 1936 models were mainly reruns, with the Sixes now designated 653/654 and the Eights tagged 852. Despite a still brilliant line of cabriolets, broughams, phaetons, sedans, and the 852 Speedster, Auburn could only watch production plummet. Speedster output for both years totaled only about 600, for example. In 1936, Cord returned from England to salvage his crumbling empire, but he found the Securities and Exchange Commission and the IRS waiting at the dock, ready to launch major investigations of his doings. A promised 1937 Auburn never materialized.

Cord managed to keep most of his fortune, and in his later years was involved in western land speculation. He is not remembered with reverence in Auburn circles, but it is doubtful that the marque would have evolved into what it did without him. Under Cord and Harold Ames, as well, Auburn wrote some of the world's greatest motoring history in the 1930s.

Auburn Specifications

1930

605 Six (wb 120.0)

		Wght	Price	Prod
685A	sdn 4d	3,300	1,095	
685B	spt sdn 2W	3,300	995	3,984
685F	cab, 2-4P	3,125	1,095	

895 Eight (wb 125.0)

		Wght	Price	Prod
895A	sdn 4d	3,590	1,295	
895B	spt sdn 2W	3,590	1,195	5,738
895F	cab 2-4P	3,410	1,295	
895H	phtn sdn 5P	3,600	1,395	

125 Custom Eight (wb 130.0)

		Wght	Price	Prod
125A	sdn 4d	3,995	1,595	
125B	spt sdn 2W	3,995	1,495	4,658
125F	cab 2-4P	3,800	1,595	
125H	phtn sdn 5P	3,990	1,695	

1930 Engines	bore×stroke	bhp	availability
L6, 185.0	2.88×4.75	70	685
L8, 247.0	2.88×4.75	100	895
L8, 298.6	3.25×4.50	125	125

1931—36,148 built

8-98 Eight (wb 127.0; 7P-136.0)

	Wght	Price	Prod
b'ham 2d 5P	3,580	945	—
spdstr 2P	3,320	945	—
sdn 4d	3,700	995	—
cpe 2P	3,460	995	—
cab 2-4P	3,540	1,045	—
phtn sdn 5P	3,650	1,145	—
sdn 7P	3,990	1,195	—

8-98A Custom Eight (wb 127.0; 7P-136.0)

	Wght	Price	Prod
b'ham 2d 5P	3,630	1,145	—
sdn 4d	3,750	1,195	—
cpe 2P	3,510	1,195	—
cab 2-4P	3,490	1,245	—
phtn sdn 5P	3,700	1,345	—
spdstr 2P	3,370	1,395	—
sdn 7P	4,040	1,395	—

1931 Engine	bore×stroke	bhp	availability
L8, 268.6	3.00×4.75	98	8-98, 8-98A

1932

8-100 Eight (wb 127.0; 7P-136.0)

	Wght	Price	Prod
cpe 2P	3,485	675	—
b'ham 2d 5P	3,605	725	—
sdn 4d	3,725	775	—
cab 2-4P	3,495	795	—
phtn sdn 5P	3,675	845	—
spdstr 2P	3,345	845	—
sdn 7P	4,015	875	—

8-100A Custom Eight Dual Ratio (wb 127.0, 7P-136.0)

	Wght	Price	Prod
cpe 2P	3,575	805	—
b'ham 2d 5P	3,695	855	—
sdn 4d	3,815	905	—
cab 2-4P	3,585	925	—
phtn sdn 5P	3,765	975	—
spdstr 2P	3,435	975	—
sdn 7P	4,105	1,005	—

12-160 Twelve (wb 133.0)

	Wght	Price	Prod
cpe 2P	4,275	975	—
b'ham 2d 5P	4,395	1,025	—
sdn 4d	4,515	1,075	—
cab 2-4P	4,285	1,095	—
phtn sdn 5P	4,465	1,145	—
spdstr 2P	4,135	1,145	—

12-160A Custom Twelve Dual Ratio (wb 133.0)

	Wght	Price	Prod
cpe 2P	4,375	1,105	—
b'ham 2d 5P	4,495	1,155	—
sdn 4d	4,615	1,205	—
cab 2-4P	4,385	1,225	—
phtn sdn 5P	4,565	1,275	—
spdstr 2P	4,235	1,275	—

1932 Engines	bore×stroke	bhp	availability
L8, 268.6	3.00×4.75	100	all Eights
L12, 391.6	3.13×4.25	160	all Twelves

*Total 1932 registrations: 11,646

1933

8-101 Eight (wb 127.0, 7P-136.0)

	Wght	Price	Prod
cpe 2P	3,485	745	—
b'ham 2d 5P	3,605	795	—
sdn 4d	3,725	845	—
cab 2-4P	3,495	895	—

	Wght	Price	Prod
phtn sdn 5P	3,675	945	—
spdstr 2P	3,345	945	—
sdn 7P	4,015	945	—

8-101A Custom Eight Dual Ratio (wb 127.0, 7P-136.0) 4,459 built*

	Wght	Price	Prod
cpe 2P	3,575	895	—
b'ham 2d 5P	3,695	945	—
sdn 4d	3,815	995	—
cab 2-4P	3,585	1,045	—
phtn sdn 5P	3,765	1,095	—
spdstr 2P	3,435	1,095	—
sdn 7P	4,105	1,095	—

8-105 Salon Eight Dual Ratio (wb 127.0)

	Wght	Price	Prod
b'ham 2d 5P	3,800	1,045	
sdn 4d	3,920	1,095	
cab 2-4P	3,640	1,145	2,002
phtn sdn 5P	3,835	1,195	
spdstr 2P	3,510	1,195	

12-161 Twelve (wb 133.0)

	Wght	Price	Prod
cpe 2P	4,275	1,145	—
b'ham 2d 5P	4,395	1,195	—
sdn 4d	4,515	1,245	—
cab 2-4P	4,285	1,295	—
phtn sdn 5P	4,465	1,345	—
spdstr 2P	4,135	1,345	—

12-161A Custom Twelve Dual Ratio (wb 133.0) 1,261 built*

	Wght	Price	Prod
cpe 2P	4,35	1,295	—
b'ham 2d 5P	4,495	1,345	—
sdn 4d	4,615	1,395	—
cab 2-4P	4,385	1,445	—
phtn sdn 5P	4,565	1,495	—
spdstr 2P	4,235	1,495	—

12-165 Salon Twelve Dual Ratio (wb 133.0)

	Wght	Price	Prod
b'ham 2d 5P	4,715	1,595	
sdn 4d	4,870	1,645	
cab 2-4P	4,570	1,695	305
phtn sdn 5P	4,710	1,745	
spdstr 2P	4,440	1,745	

*includes 8-101; **includes 12-161

1933 Engines	bore×stroke	bhp	availability
L8, 268.6	3.00×4.75	100	all Eights
V12, 391.6	3.13×4.25	160	all Twelves

1934

652X Six (wb 119.0)

	Wght	Price	Prod*
b'ham 2d 5P	3,215	695	—
sdn 4d	3,263	745	—
cab 2-4P	3,105	795	—

652Y Custom Six Dual Ratio (wb 119.0)

	Wght	Price	Prod
b'ham 2d 5P	3,305	795	—
sdn 4d	3,353	845	—
cab 2-4P	3,195	895	—
phtn sdn 5P	3,375	945	—

850X Eight (wb 126.0)

	Wght	Price	Prod
b'ham 2d 5P	3,628	945	—
sdn 4d	3,668	995	—
cab 2-4P	3,603	1,045	—

850Y Custom Eight Dual Ratio (wb 126.0)

	Wght	Price	Prod
b'ham 2d 5P	3,688	1,075	—
sdn 4d	3,755	1,125	—
cab 2-4P	3,653	1,175	—
phtn sdn 5P	3,773	1,225	—

1250 Salon Twelve Dual Ratio (wb 133.0)

	Wght	Price	Prod
b'ham 2d 5P	4,715	1,395	—
sdn 4d	4,870	1,445	—
cab 2-4P	4,570	1,495	—
phtn sdn 5P	4,710	1,545	—

1934 Engines	bore×stroke	bhp	availability
L6, 210.0	3.06.×4.75	85	all Sixes
L8, 280.0	3.06×4.75	100	850X
L8, 280.0	3.06×4.75	115	850Y
V12, 391.6	3.13×4.25	160	1250

*Total 1934 registrations 5,536; 652X, 652Y combined

1935/36

653/654 Six (wb 120.0)

	Wght	Price	Prod*
b'ham 2d 5P	3,214	745	—
sdn 4d	3,279	795	—
cpe 2P	3,105	835	—
cab 2-4P	3,182	945	—
phtn sdn 5P	3,248	995	—

653 Custom Six Dual Ratio (from February 1935) (wb 120.0)

	Wght	Price	Prod
b'ham 2d 4P	3,321	852	—
cpe 2P	3,201	942	—
sdn 4d	3,388	952	—
cab 2-4P	3,282	1,052	—
phtn sdn 5P	3,248	1,102	—

653 Salon Six Dual Ratio (wb 120.0)

	Wght	Price	Prod
b'ham 2d 4P	3,471	932	—
sdn 4d	3,533	982	—
cpe 2P	3,371	990	—
cab 2-4P	3,432	1,100	—
phtn sdn 5P	3,498	1,182	—

851/852 Eight (wb 127.0)

	Wght	Price	Prod
b'ham 2d 5P	3,475	995	—
cpe 2P	3,395	1,085	—
sdn 4d	3,580	1,095	—
cab 2-4P	3,415	1,225	—
phtn sdn 5P	3,565	1,275	—
sdn 7P	3,870	1,195	—

851/852 Custom Eight Dual Ratio (wb 127.0)

	Wght	Price	Prod
b'ham 2d 5P	3,574	1,088	—
cpe 2P	3,493	1,173	—
sdn 4d	3,679	1,188	—
cab 2-4P	3,511	1,313	—
phtn sdn 5P	3,664	1,368	—
sdn 7P	3,969	1,288	—

851/852 Salon Eight Dual Ratio (wb 127.0)

	Wght	Price	Prod
b'ham 2d 5P	3,724	1,168	—
cpe 2P	3,643	1,221	—
sdn 4d	3,835	1,268	—
cab 2-4P	3,641	1,361	—
phtn sdn 5P	3,814	1,448	—
sdn 7P	4,125	1,368	—

851/852 Supercharged Eight Dual Ratio (wb 127.0)

	Wght	Price	Prod
b'ham 2d 5P	3,655	1,445	—
sdn 4d	3,729	1,545	—
cpe 2P	3,565	1,545	—
cab 2-4P	3,633	1,675	—
phtn sdn 5P	3,714	1,725	—
spdstr 2P	3,706	2,245	—

1935/6 Engines	bore×stroke	bhp	availability
L6, 210.0	3.06×4.75	85	all Sixes
L8, 280.0	3.06×4.75	115	Eights exc Sprchd
L8, 280.0	3.06×4.75	150	Supercharged

*Total 1935-37 registrations: 7,160

Avanti II
Avanti Motor Corp.
South Bend, Indiana

Studebaker fled to Canada in 1963. Leo Newman and the late Nathan Altman had been partners in one of the oldest Studebaker dealerships in the country. Two years later, Newman and Altman resurrected the Avanti, Studebaker's greatest car of the '60s.

The Studebaker Avanti, designed by a team of stylists working under Raymond Loewy, had been a failure in the marketplace. But it was loved by hardcore Studebaker enthusiasts—the only Studebaker in two generations to have inspired such interest. Before it was phased out by Studebaker, the Avanti had captured virtually every major U.S. Auto Club speed record, including a 170.78-mph flying-mile at Bonneville. Newman and Altman decided the Avanti was too good to lose. So, they bought the name, the production rights, and the tooling for it, along with a portion of Studebaker's abandoned factory in South Bend. Production of a revised version called the Avanti II commenced in late 1965. The goal was an output of 300 cars a year. That figure was never achieved, but production has been adequate and consistent ever since.

Unlike its predecessor, the Avanti II has been a commercial success. The car's fiberglass body panels insured there would be no expensive sheetmetal dies to maintain. Construction could be done by hand on a miniature assembly line so each car could be built carefully and tailored to each customer's personal specifications. Altman, a born salesman, reveled in the Avanti II business. Visitors to the factory would frequently find him with telephone in hand, talking long-distance to an affluent customer about individualizing his car.

The Avanti II is still in production today, though its base price at this writing has soared to about $36,000. In the 1960s, it was a far better buy: prices began at $6550. And in those days, even the most dedicated devotee of high living would have been hard put to push the price of a tailor-made Avanti II past $10,000, though Newman and Altman tried their best to help. The option list included a Hurst four-speed shifter, power steering, air conditioning, electric window lifts, tinted windshield and rear window, AM/FM radio, Eppe fog or driving lights, limited-slip differential, Magnum 500 chromed wheels, and a variety of Firestone and Michelin bias-ply and radial tires. The basic Avanti II came with vinyl trim, but textured "Raphael vinyl" could be ordered for $200 extra. Genuine leather seats and door panel trim cost $300, and full leather trim went for $500. Paint color could be ordered to suit any preference.

Although early Avanti IIs used the same modified Studebaker convertible frame as the original Avanti, they were not powered by Studebaker V8s. The supply had dried up when Studebaker left South Bend. Instead, the factory switched to the Chevrolet 327 cubic-inch V8 in Corvette tune. Displacement was later enlarged to 350 cid. Buyers could choose either a fully synchronized Borg-Warner four-speed manual transmission or Avanti's "power-shift" automatic, designed to permit manual selection of first and second gears. All these mechanical changes were hidden from view under a body that was almost identical with that of the original

1966 Avanti II sport coupe

Avanti. The main visual clues for identifying the new model were its more level stance (Altman's customers disliked the original's noticeable front-end rake), the addition of a Roman numeral II to the Avanti script, and reduced-radius wheel openings.

The Corvette engine provided excellent performance for the aerodynamic four-place grand tourer. A typical 0-60 mph acceleration time for an Avanti II with automatic was under nine seconds; with a 3.54:1 rear axle ratio, the car could achieve 125 miles per hour. The Chevy V8 was lighter than the old Studebaker engine, and this improved front/rear weight distribution from the 59/41 of the original car to 57/43 for the Avanti II. The new car still understeered, but final oversteer could be induced by a judicious poke at the throttle. The front-disc/rear-drum brakes resisted fade, and provided nearly 1 G deceleration from 80 mph in a panic stop. Obviously Newman and Altman cared about safety as much as straight-line performance.

The Avanti II sold to a somewhat different clientele than Studebaker's version. In the 1960s, its $6500 base price was Cadillac Eldorado money. The original Avanti had sold for $4445, which was Chrysler territory. Newman and Altman realized this difference meant a change in market appeal. Accordingly, their promotion was aimed at the customer interested more in "personal-luxury" than performance.

On the open road, the Avanti II was in its element. Road testers gave it points for safety, quietness, structural rigidity, and a ride that was firm but comfortable. "In this day of great concern over automotive safety," wrote John R. Bond in 1966, "the Avanti II should make new friends, for obviously there was more thought given to safety in its conception than in most American cars. Good brakes, sensible interior design and decent handling impart security to the driver . . . It's a better car than it was three years ago."

Most of what changes were evident in the Avanti II of the '70s were made only to meet the growing number of federal safety and emissions standards. One of the most obvious was an ugly, rubber-tipped "cow catcher" grafted onto the original bumpers to pass the 5-mph barrier crash test, although Avanti Motor Corporation was exempted from the 2½-mph side-impact regulation. For 1973 the company switched from Chevrolet's 350 small-block to the division's detoxed 400-cubic-inch V8. Net horsepower ratings took effect the following year, and this unit came in at a relatively anemic 180 bhp. The 350 returned as the standard powerplant for 1976, and would remain so into the early '80s.

With Nate Altman's death in 1976, Avanti seemed to lose direction, at times appearing half-hearted about its product and its own future. Build quality suffered a noticeable decline even as prices, partly due to inflationary pressures, were scampering upward (they broke the $10,000 barrier in 1976). Federal rules dictated minor changes to interior fittings, mainly switchgear, which were made with an afterthought carelessness suggesting lack of really thorough engineering and design work. On the

1968 Avanti II sport coupe

plus side, the company reduced the number of outlandish special-order paint jobs and far-out interior trims in an attempt to make its cars somewhat more standardized and thus hold down inventory costs. But little if any money and effort were put toward updating the original Avanti concept as Altman had done. Both car and company were surviving but hardly thriving.

Over the years, several entrepreneurs had inquired about purchasing Avanti Motor Corporation. All were put off by a strong reluctance even to discuss the matter on the part of the Altman family and the outsiders who together comprised the 13-member board of directors. All but one, that is: Stephen Blake, a young and very successful construction magnate from Washington D.C. An Avanti II owner, Blake loved the car and wanted to see its maker move ahead. Ironically, Nate Altman died only days after agreeing to serious negotiations with him, but it would take fully seven more years before Blake could conclude the deal, officially taking over as owner, president, and CEO of Avanti in October 1982.

The management and product housecleaning swept in by Blake's new broom is beyond the scope of this book, but briefly, it seems likely to insure Avanti's future. For example, Blake has completely revamped that portion of the old Studebaker plant where the cars are built, calling in industry consultants Arthur Anderson, Inc. to advise him on space planning, assembly sequencing, and other production matters. Also, he threw out the firm's existing "dealers," most of whom were merely owners who occasionally sold a car, and has drawn up proper businesslike agreements with prominent luxury car outlets in cities like Houston, Los Angeles, Miami, and Chicago. Although he is adamant about keeping the distinctive Avanti style, Blake has set up a wholesale product improvement program, already underway at this writing. This involves most every aspect of the car, from more logical switchgear and better-quality carpeting to a new-for-'84 convertible and a completely redesigned chassis with all-independent suspension, the latter slated for 1985. Blake has also tightened up labor practices and quality standards for his firm's small workforce, which rejected an organizing bid by the United Auto Workers union.

All of this costs money, of course, and the current Avanti (Blake has dropped the "II") sells for around $36,000 at this writing. But to its host of admirers, this is little enough to pay for an exclusive sports coupe built almost entirely—and well—by hand, boasting an interesting heritage and a timeless appeal. Avanti is moving forward once more.

Avanti II Specifications

1965

(wb 109.0)			Wght	Price	Prod
spt cpe			3,217	6,550	21

1965 Engine	bore×stroke	bhp	availability
V8, 327.0	4.00×3.25	300	S-all

1966

(wb 109.0)			Wght	Price	Prod
spt cpe			3,181	7,200	98

1966 Engine	bore×stroke	bhp	availability
V8, 327.0	4.00×3.25	300	S-all

1967

(wb 109.0)			Wght	Price	Prod
spt cpe			3,217	7,200	60

1967 Engine	bore×stroke	bhp	availability
V8, 327.0	4.00×3.25	300	S-all

1968

(wb 109.0)			Wght	Price	Prod
spt cpe			3,217	6,645	89

1968 Engine	bore×stroke	bhp	availability
V8, 327.0	400×3.25	300	S-all

1969

(wb 109.0)			Wght	Price	Prod
spt cpe			3,217	7,145	103

1969 Engine	bore×stroke	bhp	availability
V8, 327.0	4.00×3.25	300	S-all
V8, 350.0	4.00×3.48	300	O-all

1970

(wb 109.0)			Wght	Price	Prod
spt cpe			3,342	7,500	111

1970 Engine	bore×stroke	bhp	availability
V8, 350.0	4.00×3.48	300	S-all

1971

(wb 109.0)			Wght	Price	Prod
spt cpe			3,217	7,645	107

1971 Engine	bore×stroke	bhp	availability
V8, 350.0	4.00×3.48	270	S-all

1972

(wb 109.0)			Wght	Price	Prod
spt cpe			3,217	8,145	127

1972 Engine	bore×stroke	bhp	availability
V8,350.0	4.00×3.48	270	S-all

1973

(wb 109.0)			Wght	Price	Prod
spt cpe			3,250	8,145	106

1973 Engine	bore×stroke	bhp	availability
V8, 400.0	4.13×3.75	245	S-all

1974

(wb 109.0)			Wght	Price	Prod
spt cpe			3,250	8,645	123

1974 Engine	bore×stroke	bhp	availability
V8, 400.0	4.13×3.75	180	S-all

1975

(wb 109.0)			Wght	Price	Prod
spt cpe			3,250	9,945	125

1975 Engine	bore×stroke	bhp	availability
V8, 400.0	4.13×3.75	180	S-all

1976

(wb 109.0)			Wght	Price	Prod
spt cpe			3,500	12,195	156

1976 Engine	bore×stroke	bhp	availability
V8, 350.0	4.00×3.48	210	S-all

1977

(wb 109.0)			Wght	Price	Prod
spt cpe			3,500	13,195	146

1977 Engine	bore×stroke	bhp	availability
V8, 350.0	4.00×3.48	180	S-all

1978

(wb 109.0)			Wght	Price	Prod
spt cpe			3,500	15,980	165

1978 Engine	bore×stroke	bhp	availability
V8, 350.0	4.00×3.48	180	S-all

1979

(wb 109.0)			Wght	Price	Prod
spt cpe			3,500	17,670	142

1979 Engine	bore×stroke	bhp	availability
V8, 350.0	4.00×3.48	180	S-all

1980

(wb 109.0)			Wght	Price	Prod
spt cpe			3,500	18,995	168

1980 Engine	bore×stroke	bhp	availability
V8, 350.0	4.00×3.48	190	S-all

Buick

**Buick Motor Division, General Motors Corporation
Flint, Michigan**

David Dunbar Buick was a canny Scottish industrialist who saw an opportunity to profit from the horseless carriage phenomenon. The first car to bear his name appeared in 1903, powered by a flat-twin engine and using chain drive. One of its significant features was overhead valves—very rare then, but a Buick feature ever since. The company prospered, and became one of the firms brought together by William C. Durant to create General Motors in 1908. Six-cylinder powerplants arrived in 1914, and were the only type offered in 1925-30. By then, Buick buyers comprised mostly upper-class and professional people who had moved up from a Chevrolet, Oakland, or Oldsmobile, and this remains the make's primary market to this day. Though the Depression reduced the size of this segment considerably, the division recovered later in the '30s, rising to fourth in industry production by 1938.

The decisions to move up the price scale and adopt eight-cylinder engines were made before the Wall Street crash, so Buick's sales problems in the early 1930s were the result of bad timing. There was certainly little to fault about the 1931 models. They were powered by five-main-bearing straight eights developed by chief engineer F.A. Bower, smooth and reliable, and among the most advanced engines of their day. There were three in all. The bottom-line Series 50 used a 77-horsepower 220.7-cid unit; displacement for the Series 60 was 272.6 cid, good for 90 bhp; the upper-echelon Series 80 and 90 packed a 104-bhp 344.8-cid engine. That year's very lengthy model roster included sedans, coupes, phaetons, convertibles, roadsters, and a limousine in the Series 90. The low-priced Series 50, including the second-series line introduced in early 1931, were built on the 114-inch wheelbase formerly applied to Marquette, Buick's short-lived junior make (see entry), while the Series 60, 80 and 90 were built on wheelbases of 118, 124, and 132 inches, respectively.

In various forms, the Buick straight eight would serve the division for the next 22 years. The company proved its new engine's mettle right away. At the 1931 Indianapolis 500, a Buick-powered racer driven by Phil Shafer qualified at 105.1 mph and averaged 86.4 mph. Even in showroom form, the '31s were quick: 10-60 mph took about 25 seconds, quite speedy for the day, and a top end of 90 mph was possible.

For 1932, the big news was "Silent Second Synchro-Mesh" transmission, plus more horsepower on all three engines. Power and wheelbase lengths went up again for 1933, but sales did not. In October of that year, Harlow H. Curtice was appointed Buick president, and the division's fortunes changed almost immediately under his leadership. His goal was "more speed for less money," and his first move toward that end was an all-new 117-inch-wheelbase Series 40 for 1934. The result was a sales upturn, aided by more modern, streamlined styling that was a complete contrast to the boxy "Roaring '20s"

1930 Series 60 seven-passenger sedan

1932 Series 90 seven-passenger limousine

1933 Series 60 five-passenger victoria coupe

1934 Series 60 convertible coupe

look of yore. All models also featured GM's new "Knee-Action" independent front suspension. Though it skipped flashy soft-top bodies in favor of the more popular coupes and sedans, the Series 40 was a masterful blend of an inexpensive, Chevrolet-size platform and imposing Buick styling, and it helped boost division output that year. Buick

43

Buick

1935 Series 60 five-passenger club sedan

1936 Series 80 Roadmaster four-door sedan

was back over the 100,000-unit mark in calendar 1935, and production would reach record levels just four years later.

Also in 1934, Curtice launched a $64 million factory modernization program, though it was not fully completed until 1940. Ploughing back receipts into the Flint facilities left little money for product improvements, however, so the 1935 offerings weren't changed much. The lineup continued to consist of the Series 40, 50, 60, and 90, with straight eights of 233, 235, 278, and 344 cubic inches, respectively. A belated addition was a convertible coupe for the Series 40.

The 1936 models saw more extensive changes as Buick adopted GM's all-steel "Turret Top" construction, plus more powerful engines with aluminum pistons. Revised styling was accompanied by four new model designations still remembered today: Special (Series 40), Century (60), Roadmaster (80) and Limited (90). For 1940, these would be joined by the Series 50 Super, another name that would continue through the 1950s. The new styling was a big factor in the division's resurgence, and was the work of Harley J. Earl, founder and head of GM's Art & Colour Studio, the first formal styling department at a major automaker. Earl liked streamlining, and the '36 Buick had it. The overall shape was more rounded than ever, with windshields swept back at a greater angle, trunks integrated with the body (instead of being separate, detachable fixtures), and massive, vertical-bar grilles. The public loved this package, and responded by buying over 200,000 Buicks that year. Calendar 1936 production was close to 180,000 units, as the division's fortunes returned to their pre-Depression height.

Equally important in this success was a new 320-cid eight with 120 bhp, standard for all models except the Series 40 Special, which retained its 233-cid, 93-bhp powerplant. Predictably, the bigger engine delivered its best performance in the lighter Century models, which had genuine 100-mph cruising capability and 10-60 mph acceleration in the 18-19-second range. Besides its speed and sleek good looks, the Century was attractively priced: as little as $1035 for the sport coupe and $1135 for the rakish convertible. This series quickly gained a reputation as a factory-built hot rod for anyone with $1000 or so in hand who wanted to be faster off the line than almost anything else at that price. The Century would continue to be Buick's bomb well into the '50s.

After the design and production triumphs of the '36s, there was little need for drastic change on the 1937 models. But Harley Earl wasn't quite satisfied, so a facelift was ordained. The basic Turret Top body acquired enlongated fenders with blunt trailing edges, plus horizontal grille bars and complementing side hood vents. Buick was arguably GM's best-looking entry that year, and a styling leader for the rest of the industry. On the mechanical side, the big eight in the upper three series returned unchanged, but a stroke increase boosted the Special's displacement to 248 cid and rated horsepower to an even 100. Factory figures indicated a Special could now scale 10-60 mph in 19.2 seconds, fine performance for the class and only a second slower than the hot Century. Several new features appeared across the board: hypoid rear axle, improved generator, running board-mounted radio antenna, standard windshield defroster, and front and rear anti-sway bars. Buick claimed an industry first this year with introduction of a steering wheel horn ring.

It was with the 1936 models that the top-line Limited became rather uncommon cars, so it's puzzling that they've generally been overlooked by today's enthusiasts. All body types in this series were of the "trunkback" style, with a faired-in luggage compartment and dual spare tires nestled in long, pontoon fenders. A formal sedan of elegant proportions was issued for 1936-37, complete with a glass division window between front and rear compartments and the expected luxury trim. The series included six- and eight-passenger sedans and a limousine in 1936-39, and Limited chassis were supplied in quantity to body builders such as Eureka, Miller, Sayers & Scoville, and Flexible for hearse, ambulance, and flower car applications.

A new grille with fewer and thicker horizontal bars was Buick's main styling distinction for 1938, but under the skin were extensive alterations that made a good car even better. All-coil suspension—another Buick first—made for a much improved ride, aided by shock absorbers four times the size of those used on most other cars of the period. Domed, high-compression pistons boosted horsepower on both engines, which were now dubbed "Dynaflash." A new item for the Special was a five-speed semi-automatic transmission, which compiled a poor service record and was abandoned after only one year. Buick would not attempt another clutchless drive until Dynaflow automatic appeared about a decade later.

Buick closed out the 1930s with a lower, mildly face-lifted lineup for 1939, marked by waterfall-type grille styling, "streamboards" (optional closed-in running boards), and a sunroof option on some models. Sidemount spares were still available, though they weren't ordered as often as in the past. The Special, which had grown to a 122-inch wheelbase for 1937-38, now rode a 120-inch-wheelbase chassis. Body style choices were as extensive as ever and prices as moderate, ranging from the $894 Special business coupe to the $2453 Limited limousine. The natty Century convertible sport phaeton sold at $1713, the sport coupe at $1175. Rumble seat convertibles disappeared this year, but Buick scored a safety innovation with flashing turn signal lights, installed at the rear only, where they were part of the trunk emblem. Also new were column-mounted gearshift and refillable shock absorbers. Though the grille was questionable aesthetically, the '39s retained the individuality and generally clean design of the '38s. Buick styling and engineering had improved steadily through the decade, rewarding the division with steadily improved sales.

During the 1940s, Buick was GM's number-two producer after Chevrolet, and usually fourth in the industry behind the "Big Three"—Chevy, Ford, and Plymouth. The division normally turned out upwards of 300,000 cars a year. After the war, as GM endured an extended strike, Buick took awhile to regain momentum, but by 1949 it was producing nearly 400,000 cars. In 1950, it would top half a million.

"Valve in Head—Ahead in Value" was Buick's slogan, and the cars reflected that characteristic throughout the '40s. They were big, but only slightly ostentatious. For those who felt status was everything, there was always Cadillac. Buick's buyers were, for the most part, professional people, a loyal group that returned to the cars from Flint time and time again. The prewar line was one of the widest in Buick's history, one that wouldn't be matched in scope until well into the 1950s.

For 1940, the Buick lineup was divided into four series, bearing names as well as numbers. The Series 40 Special ranged from simple sedans to spectacular open styles. The Series 50 Super comprised a smaller number of models, including a wood-bodied estate wagon.

1940 Series 80 Limited Streamlined formal sedan

1941 Series 70 Roadmaster convertible phaeton

1941 Series 60 Century four-door sedan

1941 Series 90 Limited eight-passenger sedan

1941 Series 60 Century business coupe

1941 Series 70 Roadmaster four-door sedan

Buick

Harley Earl's Y-Job show car

1942 Series 70 Roadmaster convertible coupe

Specials and Supers rode a 121-inch wheelbase, and were powered by the 248 cubic-inch Buick five-main-bearing straight eight, a smooth and respected powerplant.

The larger cars were the Series 60 Century, Series 70 Roadmaster, and the Series 80 and 90 Limiteds, all powered by a 320.2-cid engine, also with five main bearings. The long sedans and limousines used a 140-inch wheelbase.

A number of interesting special bodies were offered for 1940, some of them for the last time. The crop of convertible sedans had started to thin out by the start of the decade, and the last in the Century line appeared that year. The Super and Roadmaster versions continued for one more season. In the Limited series, Buick built just 14 Streamlined Sedans, with fastback styling reminiscent of the Lincoln-Zephyr. More popular was the Limited convertible sedan or phaeton, which had conventional "trunkback" styling and sold for $1952. Buick sold just seven streamlined phaetons and 250 trunkbacks. Similar body alternatives were offered for the formal sedans.

Custom bodies occasionally appeared in 1940, but not as regular catalog offerings. Rakish town cars from Brewster, one of which rode the Series 90 chassis, were not identified as Buicks at all. But the Series 90 Brewster Buick was the first to earn coveted "Classic" status from the Classic Car Club of America. Buffalo's Brunn Company also designed custom models, including a fairly conventional town car body on the Roadmaster chassis—strictly a one-off.

Buick had a banner year in 1941. Model year production totaled 374,000 units. Leading the line was a beautiful series of opulent customs by Brunn on the Limited

chassis. These included a phaeton, town car, landau brougham, and full landau. Most flamboyant was the Brunn convertible coupe, offered to dealers for $3500. At that price, only the prototype was sold. The car was significant because of its "sweep-spear" side motif, which prefigured a postwar production styling trademark.

The Roadmaster lineup continued unchanged in 1941, while the Century series was trimmed of its convertible, convertible sedan, and club coupe. The station wagon shifted from the Super to the Special series, but nevertheless sold for about $200 more than its 1940 counterpart. Specials were split into two sub-series: the 40, which rode a 118-inch wheelbase, and the 40A on a 121-inch span.

The 1941 Special/Super 248-cid engine featured a new piston design that provided better compression of the fuel/air mixture before combustion and a corresponding increase in horsepower. Available for the 40A Special touring sedan and sedanet was Compound Carburetion, two carburetors with a progessive linkage, which further boosted horsepower to 125. Compound Carburetion was standard on other models, resulting in 165 bhp for the Century, Roadmaster, and Limited. The 1941 chassis design was a carryover for all but the Limited, which used a new X-member frame. No Buick was yet available with automatic transmission.

Styling was evolutionary, marked mainly by a bolder, heavier grille and revised ports along the sides of the hood. One new idea was the fastback, offered as the 40A Special and Century touring sedan, business coupe, and sedanet. It did away with anachronisms of the "trunkback" age. Apparently it appealed to the public: over 100,000 Special fastback touring sedans were sold.

World War II came at the wrong time for Buick. Car production ended after February 2, 1942. The new models had been completely restyled along the lines of Harley Earl's Y-Job show car, and were much sleeker than any that had gone before. A wide, low, vertical-bar grille arrived, and would be continued on postwar models through 1954. Fastback, or "torpedo," styling was more popular than ever. The Century put in its last appearance until 1954, and was available in only two styles, both fastbacks. The streamlined models continued to dominate Special sales, and also appeared as sedanets in the Super and Roadmaster Series.

Most '42 Buicks featured Harley Earl's new "Airfoil" front fenders, which swept back through almost the entire length of the car to meet the leading edge of the rear fenders. Limiteds and Specials lacked the full-sweep treatment, but their fenders extended back well into the doors. Streamlining had truly arrived in Flint.

Cars built after January 1, 1942 used painted metal instead of plated parts, as per government order. On Specials and Supers, cast-iron pistons were used in place of aluminum ones. Base horsepower dropped to 110 bhp (118 with Compound Carburetion). By the time production ground to a halt, more than 92,000 of the

1942 models had been built. Production would not begin again until October 1945.

When cars started rolling off the Flint lines again, there were no exotic Brunn customs. Only standard production bodies were offered. Buick built a mere 2482 cars in the closing months of 1945. But production picked up the following year when more than 150,000 units were built. Naturally, the postwar cars were warmed-over '42s, but were available in a few new body styles: sedans and sedanets in Special, Super, and Roadmaster guise; Super and Roadmaster convertibles; and a Super estate wagon. Styling was cleaned up. Most models bore single instead of double side moldings, a simpler grille, and the first of Buick's distinctive "gunsight" hood ornaments. Wheelbase choices, now without a Limited in the field, were restricted to 121 inches for the Special, 124 for the Super, and 129 for Roadmaster. Compound Carburetion was not offered, so Specials and Supers were both rated at 110 bhp. This combination of models, wheelbases, and engines would endure through 1948 with only minor changes in horsepower.

Undoubtedly, Buick's production potential in the early postwar years was left unexploited. The Special, which would set many records in the 1950s, actually accounted for the smallest number of sales in this period. Supers were the most popular. The Special did not outstrip the Super in production until 1950, when it became Buick's biggest success story. By 1954, it would help the division surpass Plymouth.

Styling changes for the 1947-48 models were minimal, since GM planned to introduce its first all-new postwar cars for 1949. The '47 Buicks were marked by a wing-top grille that gave them a very low look. A new, more elaborate crest appeared above it. In 1948, Specials received a full-length belt molding; Supers and Roadmasters acquired chrome fender nameplates. Instrument panel gauges were gold-colored, and steering wheels were three-spoke, flexible types with semi-circular horn rings. The most important news in 1948 was Dynaflow, Buick's excellent automatic transmission. It was offered as a $244 option on the Roadmaster only. Demand for this torque-converter automatic was so high the division had to double its planned production. By 1950, Dynaflow was being fitted to 85 percent of all Buicks sold.

The long-awaited 1949 design helped model year production surge to 324,276 units, right behind the Chevy-Ford-Plymouth trio. The '49s were sleek and graceful compared to their predecessors, and re-

1946 Roadmaster sedanet

1946 Special sedanet

1947 Roadmaster convertible coupe

1949 Roadmaster Riviera hardtop coupe

1950 Special sport coupe

1950 Roadmaster four-door sedan

1950 Super Riviera hardtop coupe

1951 Super Deluxe two-door sedan

1951 Special sport coupe

LeSabre show car of 1951

viewers agreed they were worth all the attention they got. Harley Earl's Art & Colour Studio had successfully adapted aircraft fuselage lines to an automobile. Only a hint of the separate rear fender remained on the Super and Roadmaster (the Special retained 1948 fender styling). The new bodies featured the first of Buick's now-legendary portholes, an idea inspired by Ned Nickles of Earl's staff. Easily the most eye-catching model was the Roadmaster Riviera. Together with Cadillac's Coupe deVille and Oldsmobile's Holiday, it was the first mass-production hardtop in the modern sense, and ushered in a new trend that would eventually make the convertible obsolete. Roadmaster Rivieras were good-looking, luxurious cars with beautiful pillarless rooflines. They were available with either conventional straight side moldings or with sweep-spear trim. The latter quickly became another Buick trademark.

With the emphasis mainly on styling, the '49 Buicks were much the same mechanically as the earlier post-war models. The Special's horsepower remained at 110 bhp, the Super's at 115. Supers equipped with Dynaflow also got higher 6.9:1 compression heads for an output of 120 bhp. The Roadmaster had been raised to 150 bhp in 1948, and it continued in that form with Dynaflow Drive standard. Bodies remained unaltered for the most part. The woody wagon was reworked to fit the new styling. Although the result was very pleasing, the wagon sold in small numbers.

Thanks to the 1942 redesign, Buick emerged from the war in fine fettle. While nearly all manufacturers were forced to stay with their prewar designs, Flint's styling was technically only one year old in 1945 and still fairly fresh. Packard, by contrast, was left with a two-year-old design in its very handsome Clipper, and felt obliged to undertake a severe facelift by 1948. Buick was able to stretch out its '42 tooling through the 1949 Special—and come back with a brand-new model for 1950. One year makes a difference.

Three different styling periods, a 50th anniversary, and the advent of V8 engines marked Buick history in the '50s. Throughout the decade, Buicks were big, powerful, and sometimes garish cars. They reflected what could be considered as either the best contemporary thinking—or the worst depravity of those glittery years before the advent of compacts, pollution controls, and safety regulations. Buicks of the '50s were very different from the division's present-day cars. Yet both generations share a tradition of quality, high performance in their class, and product lines carefully orchestrated to fit the times and the market.

The 1949 restyling adopted by all General Motors lines resulted in the lowest, sleekest Buicks in history. But there was more to come in 1950. If '49 had been the Year of the Porthole, 1950 was the Year of the Sweep-spear. Through 1953, the lineup comprised the Special, Super, and Roadmaster series. The Special was sleekly styled and competitively priced, designed to catch third-place Plymouth in the production race. Yet it began the decade as a rather utilitarian series. Attractive,

sporty hardtops and convertibles were added later. The pioneering two-door Riviera hardtop of 1949 continued in Super and Roadmaster trim, and was extended to the Special by 1951. The Riviera name was also applied to a very well-proportioned four-door sedan in the Super and Roadmaster series riding a special extended wheelbase. There were also two woody wagons offered with wooden body parts made of mahogany and white ash. They were big, expensive haulers: the 1953 Roadmaster estate wagon cost $4031 and weighed 4315 pounds.

For all 1950-52 models and the '53 Special, Buick continued to rely on its aging but proven valve-in-head straight eight. Displacement, compression, and horsepower varied from model to model. The base Special engine of 1950 produced 115 bhp, or 120 bhp with Dynaflow automatic. Supers and the 1951-53 Specials offered up to 143 bhp. Roadmasters used a hefty 320-cid version that put out 170 bhp at 3800 rpm by 1952.

Dynaflow Drive (some called it "Dyna-slush") had been introduced as a standard Roadmaster item in late 1947. It became increasingly popular on other models at around $200 extra. Its torque converter system depended on induced rotation of a drive turbine through an oil bath by a facing crankshaft-driven turbine. Dynaflow was smooth, but none too exciting in performance. The Twin-Turbine Dynaflow of 1953 was more positive in operation. By the end of the decade, an even better Triple-Turbine setup was offered across the board as a $296 option. But Dynaflow in all its forms couldn't deliver acceleration like Hydra-Matic, and was therefore handicapped in an age of horsepower and hot rods.

Golden Anniversary year 1953 was significant. It saw the arrival of power steering, a 12-volt electrical system, and a fine new overhead-valve V8 for the Super and Roadmaster. The engine was an oversquare design of 322 cid developing up to 188 bhp thanks to an industry-topping 8.5:1 compression ratio.

That year also saw the debut of the limited-edition Skylark sports convertible, a car for flashy Hollywood types and Texas oil barons. Buick made only 1690 of them, priced at an extraordinary $5000 each. Many custom features were standard, including wraparound windshield and special bodywork.

Skylark was another of those Harley Earl styling projects for which GM had long been famous. Typical of company thinking, it was designed for the broadest possible appeal. Instead of being a two-seat sports car—which accounted for only 0.27 percent of the market in 1953—it was a luxurious, sporty "personal" four-seater like Ford's post-1957 Thunderbirds and Buick's own Riviera of the '60s. Like the similar Oldsmobile Fiesta and Cadillac Eldorado, the Skylark was a large chopped-and-sectioned convertible. Four inches were removed from windshield height, and the top was correspondingly lower. Skylark was much cleaner-looking than standard Buicks. It had no portholes and no hubcaps, but sported the Kelsey-Hayes chrome wire wheels that were coming into fashion

throughout the industry by 1953.

Skylark was back again the following year, but the '54 version was much less radical and sold for only $4483. It arrived with tack-on tailfins and huge, chrome-plated, die-cast taillight housings. Its full circular wheel cutouts approximated those of the Wildcat II show car. But

1952 Special Riviera hardtop coupe

1953 Skylark convertible coupe

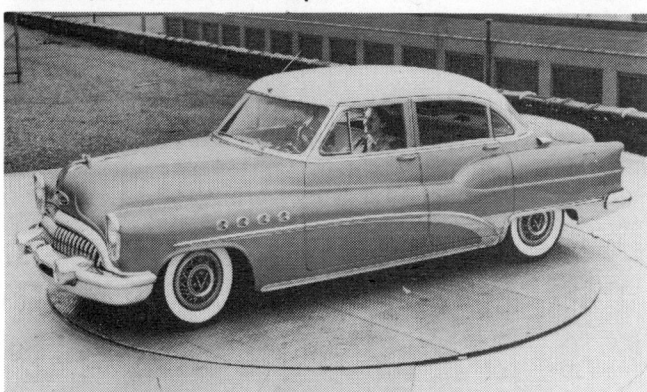

1953 Roadmaster four-door sedan

1954 Century four-door sedan

apparently, the '54 Skylark was less impressive than the '53, for only 836 were sold and the model was discontinued for 1955.

Buick's show cars of the '50s were among the wildest in the industry. Led by the XP-300 and the LeSabre of 1951, they were rolling laboratories—test vehicles for a number of unique ideas.

Both the XP-300 and the LeSabre used an experimental 215-cid aluminum V8. This was *not* a forerunner of the 215 V8 of the early '60s, but rather a very special job, exactly square with 3.25-inch bore-and-stroke dimensions. It boasted a 10:1 compression ratio and over 300 bhp. Induction was boosted by a Roots-type supercharger. All this meant a combination of methanol and gasoline had to be used for fuel.

Styling on these two showpieces was radical. On a 116-inch wheelbase, LeSabre sported the wraparound windshield and "Dagmar" bumpers that would be featured on production models a few years later. The XP-300 sat on a 115-inch-wheelbase chassis and featured a concave grille and mesh-backed headlamp nacelles that would be seen on the '54s.

Meanwhile, Buick production was pushing relentlessly toward the industry's number-three spot. The division broke an all-time record in calendar year 1950 with more than 550,000 cars. Flint built 531,000 units in 1954, and found itself trailing only Chevrolet and Ford—a position it had not held since 1930. In 1955, output hit 781,000, another record and nearly 50 percent higher than the previous best figure. This success was based largely on the Special, which had become one of the industry's best sellers.

Special sales began to take off with the arrival of a 264-cid V8 in 1954. In the industry's banner year of 1955, Specials were everywhere. Over 380,000 were made, including 155,000 Riviera two-door hardtops, the single most popular model of the day. The entire Buick line had been restyled in 1954, with a longer, squarer body style and wraparound windshield. That only helped keep sales booming.

Buicks became really fast cars in 1954, too. The Century series reappeared with a 195-bhp V8 in the smaller, lighter Special bodyshell. It immediately became the "hot" Buick.

Four-door and two-door Rivieras joined the Special and Century series in 1955, followed by Super and Roadmaster versions in 1956. The rest of the industry had to play catch-up while Buick dealers enjoyed unprecedented success.

The mild 1956 facelift left the line relatively unchanged, and the cars didn't sell as well as the year before. The division added model year designation to exterior nameplates beginning in '56. This practice was later abandoned after customers complained it made last year's model obsolete even sooner than without it. With the horsepower race in full swing, the '56s were the most powerful Buicks yet. The Special delivered 220 bhp, the rest of the line had 255. A '56 Century could leap from 0 to 60 mph in 10.5 seconds and top 110

mph—and every model in the line could do at least 100 mph.

The line was fully restyled again in 1957. Ed Ragsdale, Buick's general manager, never said how much the retooling had cost, but it must have run several hundred million. Yet, despite the most sweeping alterations since 1949, the '57s didn't sell particularly well, possibly because Buick's rivals were pressing hard. At

1955 Century convertible coupe

Centurion show car of 1956

1956 Roadmaster Riviera hardtop sedan

1956 Special four-door sedan

Chrysler, Virgil Exner's tailfinned "Forward Look" had been introduced. Highland Park was selling almost as many 1956 cars as it had sold in 1955, and Plymouth was forging its way back into third place. But the '57 Buicks were clean, well-styled automobiles. Model additions were few but interesting: the four-door hardtop Caballero station wagon in the Century and Special series, and a Series 75 Roadmaster based on the Series 70, offering every possible accessory except air conditioning as standard. Series 75s came with Dynaflow, power steering, power brakes, flexible-spoke steering wheel, dual exhausts, automatic windshield washers and wide-angle wipers, backup lights, clock, special interior with deep-pile carpeting, and a host of other features. Though 1957 was a good year for Buick, it was even better for Plymouth, which knocked Flint out of third place for the first time in three years.

In those days, the answer to sales problems was to pile on more chrome. Thus, the ugliest Buicks in history materialized for 1958. From a monstrous grille that contained 160 chrome squares within a huge shell, to hastily contrived chrome-draped tailfins, it was a ghastly looking machine(and the revived Limited series in particular). It didn't sell, but the '58 recession was probably more to blame than the awful styling. Buick production dropped to 240,000 units, and the division slipped behind Oldsmobile to fifth place. Air suspension was offered, but seldom ordered. Altogether, '58 was a very bad year.

So was 1959. But while the '58 design had been tasteless, the '59 went the other way in a peak year for Buick styling. Though dominated by the now-omnipresent tailfin, the new design was at least smooth, clean, and fairly dignified (the grille had fewer chrome squares, too). Buick now shared the corporate A-body with other GM lines, but it wasn't obvious. Gone were the traditional model names: the Special was renamed LeSabre, the Century became Invicta, the Super and Roadmaster were dubbed Electra and Electra 225. At the bottom end, LeSabre and Invicta retained the old Special/Century body styles. The hardtop wagon, which hadn't sold well, was dropped. The two Electras were priced down quite a bit from 1958, and rode slightly shorter wheelbases. Buick was called 1959's most changed car, and the change was for the better.

There were some new mechanical developments that year: a 401-cid V8 with 325 bhp was offered for the upper three models, a 364 V8 for the LeSabre. Power brakes and steering were standard on Electras, a $150 option for the other series. Air conditioning was a $430 extra. Air suspension, for the rear only, was still not popular.

Significantly, Buick dealers were selling more Opels in 1959 than ever before. The captive German import assigned to Buick in 1958 grabbed an increasing number of customers as people saw penalties in oversize, overweight automobiles. But Buick Division was already planning its own compact, the 1961 Special/Skylark, and its star would rise again.

1957 Century Caballero hardtop wagon

1957 Roadmaster convertible coupe

1958 Limited hardtop coupe

1959 Electra 225 convertible

1959 LeSabre hardtop sedan

Buick

1960 LeSabre four-door sedan

1961 Special four-door sedan

1961 LeSabre hardtop sedan

1962 Special Deluxe convertible coupe

1962 Electra 225 hardtop coupe

1963 Wildcat hardtop sedan

For Buick, the 1960s were very successful years. The division built about 250,000 cars in 1960, ranking ninth in the industry. For the 1969 model year Buick built more than 665,000 units, and enjoyed a tight hold on fifth place. The improvement was due in part to the debut of the Special and Skylark, and in part to increased production of the larger models. For example, some 56,000 Electras came off the lines in 1960; nearly 159,000 in 1969. LeSabre production was about 152,000 units in 1960, and nearly 198,000 in '69. The Wildcat, which replaced the Invicta in 1964, began at the 35,000 level but almost doubled that figure by 1969.

The 1961 Special was one of the "second-wave" GM compacts—the Buick-Oldsmobile-Pontiac cars that followed the 1960 Chevrolet Corvair. The Special's first engine was a 215-cid aluminum-block V8 that was light, smooth-running, efficient, and economical. This quiet, powerful engine would have a long life. After GM sold manufacturing rights to British Leyland, it went on in modified form to power Rover sedans in the late '60s through the 1976 3500 sedan and V8 Land-Rover of 1980.

To profit from the sporty-car market pioneered in 1960 by the Corvair Monza, Buick introduced the mid-1961 Special Deluxe Skylark. This coupe had bucket seats, deluxe trim, vinyl-covered roof, and a 185-bhp version of the aluminum V8. More than 12,000 were sold before the end of the model year. In 1962, Buick introduced a Skylark convertible and an optional Borg-Warner four-speed transmission—and watched sales increase to more than 42,000.

In the early part of the decade, the big Buicks changed dramatically. The 1960 LeSabre, Invicta, Electra, and Electra 225—sedans, station wagons, two-door and four-door hardtops, and convertibles—were heavy iron objects of dubious styling merit, basically face-lifted '59s. Their 1961 replacements had shorter wheelbases, weighed 100 to 200 pounds less, and looked much cleaner. In 1962, the Wildcat appeared as a specialty model based on the Invicta. It was a two-ton, 123-inch-wheelbase luxury hardtop priced at nearly $4000, equipped with bucket seats, vinyl roof, and distinctive exterior trim. It was well received and returned for 1963. Fewer than 3,500 Invictas were sold that year. From 1964 on, Wildcat was Buick's middle full-size series.

Production of the top-of-the-line Electra steadily increased throughout the '60s. Buick offered two Electras in '61—the basic model, and the longer, more luxurious

Electra 225 (named for its overall length). In 1962, the base model was dropped, and all Electras became "225s"; the division then concentrated on fewer offerings. Electras were powered by Buick's largest engine, the 401-cid V8. Its output was 325 bhp at 4400 rpm for 1960-63.

During these years, Buick styling was hardly exceptional. But the 1963 Riviera, a personal-luxury sports coupe, changed the division's stodgy image almost overnight. Many people felt that Bill Mitchell, chief of GM styling, had created one of the best automotive shapes of all time.

The Riviera's origins can be found in Mitchell's project to revive the LaSalle, Cadillac's low-priced cousin, which had disappeared after 1940. Numerous renderings and clay models had been completed—notably, an experimental convertible shown at the 1955 Motorama featuring a LaSalle-type grille. Designed by Buick stylist Ned Nickles, it was named LaSalle II. Although it never went into production, it encouraged GM to build a "personal-luxury" competitor to Ford's Thunderbird. Ultimately, management tapped Buick to design and build it. Cadillac didn't have the facilities, Chevrolet was enjoying record sales, and Oldsmobile and Pontiac were occupied with other things. Buick sales needed a shot in the arm, though. The name Riviera was a natural, having been associated with the make since 1949.

The Riviera borrowed some of its design features from various sources. For example, English custom coachwork inspired its razor-edged body styling. But the finished product was handsome and individual. The final clay model was approved by early 1961, and a production run of 40,000 was scheduled for the 1963 model year. Riding a 117-inch wheelbase, Riviera was about 14 inches shorter than other Buicks. The 325-bhp 401 V8 was standard in its debut year. A 425-cid powerplant with up to 360 bhp was a 1964 option. Transmission was two-speed Turbine Drive in '63; three-speed Twin-Turbine Hydra-Matic was used from 1964 on.

The Riviera's handling was well up to its performance. Standing quarter-mile time was 16 seconds at 85 mph with the standard V8; 15.5 seconds and 90-plus mph with the 360-bhp engine.

In 1964, Buick's compact line was restyled and enlarged. Wheelbases went up to 115 inches for sedans, 120 inches for station wagons. There were new engines, too: a 225-cid V6 with 155 bhp and a 300-cid V8 with 210 bhp. The plush Skylark was now considered part of the Special series, though it is listed individually in our model year production charts. People liked the luxury it offered. By 1964, Skylark was rapidly becoming Buick's most popular compact. The production ratio of Skylarks to Specials was about 9 to 10 in 1964. From 1965 on, Skylark pulled away. By 1969, Buick was building nearly five Skylarks to every one Special.

The large Buicks—LeSabre, Wildcat, and Electra—were lengthened for 1964, although there was no change in wheelbase. The LeSabre's standard engine became a 300-cid V8. Wildcats were the hot rods of the

1963 Riviera hardtop coupe

1964 Wildcat hardtop coupe

1964 Riviera hardtop coupe

1965 LeSabre Custom hardtop coupe

1965 Riviera hardtop coupe

1966 Electra 225 hardtop coupe

1966 Special Deluxe four-door sedan

1967 Riviera GS hardtop coupe

1967 Special Deluxe four-door sedan

family, since they carried the 401-cid Electra engine in the lighter, shorter LeSabre chassis. As such, the Wildcat was Buick's performance model, much like the Century had been in the '50s. Riviera, meanwhile, remained basically unchanged, though a 425-cid V8 was added to the option list.

In the first half of the decade, Buick production rose by 50 percent, the division climbing from ninth to fifth place. And instead of a limited lineup of large cars priced just below Cadillac, Buick offered full-size and intermediate models, plus the unique Riviera. Riviera sales consistently ran at 35,000 to 40,000 units a year. In 1965, Riviera's headlights were hidden behind the grille, and the taillights were integrated with the rear bumper.

The year 1965 was significant in other ways, too. Numerous trim and model variations were offered so the buyer could custom-build his Buick. There were standard, Deluxe, and Skylark versions of the compact Special, with V6 or V8 engines, priced from about $2350 to $3000; and V8 Special Sportwagons in the $3000–$3200 range. The Wildcat was offered with standard, deluxe, and Custom trim packages as a sedan, hardtop sedan, and coupe, and as a deluxe and Custom convertible. LeSabres and Electra 225s came in standard and Custom versions. The most expensive Buick was the Electra 225 Custom convertible, priced at $4440. LeSabres were fitted with the 300-cid V8; Wildcats and Electras had the big 401.

An important performance option for '65 was the Gran Sport package for Riviera and Skylark. Gran Sports were equipped with $250 worth of roadability improvements. Fitted with oversize tires, Super-Turbine 300 automatic transmission, and the Wildcat 401 engine, the Skylark Gran Sport was every inch a grand touring car. The Riviera version was, of course, even grander. Using the 425-cid engine, it could reach 125 mph on the straight. *Motor Trend* magazine pronounced it superb in every category: "It goes and handles better than before, and that's quite an improvement."

There were many changes for the 1966-67 Riviera. Although the crisp, razor-edged body was now much more massive, it rode a wheelbase only two inches longer than that of the 1965 model. The second-generation model's smooth sheetmetal, clean hidden-headlight grille, and large windows melded to create an impressive effect. Yet it sold for only about $4400—an amount that seems unbelievably low today.

Riviera was Buick's main news in '66 because the rest of the line was mostly a carryover. Modest facelifts of grilles, side trim, and taillights were the only alterations again in '67. Riviera got a new grille with a horizontal crossbar and redesigned parking lights. Specials and Skylarks, which continued with the 225 V6 or the 300 V8, were distinguished by different grilles.

For 1967, Buick introduced one of its largest engines ever: the 430-cid V8 standard on Wildcat, Electra, and Riviera. It had no more horsepower than previous engines, but it ran more smoothly and quietly. Also new

1968 LeSabre convertible

1968 Electra 225 hardtop coupe

1968 Skylark Custom hardtop sedan

1969 Riviera hardtop coupe

was a 400-cid cast-iron V8 for the Special/Skylark chassis. This powerplant appeared in a sporty series with bucket seats dubbed GS400, offered as a convertible, hardtop, or pillared coupe. An identical hardtop with the 340 engine appeared as the GS340. Sales were excellent. Model year production came to over 560,000

units, and the division ranked fifth in the industry.

In 1968, Skylark dominated sales among the "small" Buicks, although by then it had grown from compact to intermediate size. A record number were built for the model year. The junior editions used three different wheelbases: 112 inches for Special and Skylark two-

1969 Sportwagon four-door station wagon

1969 GS400 hardtop coupe

1969 Wildcat Custom hardtop coupe

1969 Electra 225 hardtop coupe

doors, 116 inches for four-doors and Special Deluxe station wagons, and 121 inches for Sportwagons. Again, a group of Gran Sport models was fielded. They were the GS350 hardtop, and the GS400 hardtop and convertible. The V6 gave way to a 250-cid Chevy six, but compression was lowered to meet emissions requirements. There was a new 350-cid V8 with 280 bhp for the GS350. It also powered LeSabres, which rode the wheelbase length they'd had in 1960. The 430 was still reserved for Wildcat, Electra, and Riviera.

Buick's restyling for its 1968 big cars included new divided grilles, altered rear bumpers, and concealed windshield wipers. Skylarks and Specials were given a down-sloped side contour line and new grilles. The Riviera got a much heavier divided grille and was not quite as clean-looking as it had been in 1966-67. The senior cars featured bodyside moldings somewhat reminiscent of the old sweep-spear of the '50s. Many Buicks kept with tradition in another way stylized "ventiports," a design trademark dating from the '40s.

No engine changes were made for the record-breaking 1969 model year when Buick produced more than 665,000 cars—its highest output for any year in the '60s. The Electra 225, Wildcat, and LeSabre were given new bodies with ventless side glass and busier grilles. Gran Sports and Sportwagons, meanwhile, were all but separate models now. GS350 and GS400 hardtops and convertibles, plus Sportwagons with two or three bench seats, were offered as in 1968. LeSabres remained structurally unchanged, but the Wildcat was switched back from the Electra chassis to the LeSabre's, and handling was improved.

With this hot-selling lineup, Buick stood pat for 1970. Skylark, Sportwagon, Gran Sports, Wildcat, Electra 225, and the inevitable Riviera were continued. A new model designation was the Estate Wagon, actually a pair of upper-class haulers designed to do battle with the likes of the Chrysler Town & Country. The full-size line received new grilles, bumpers, and lights. Intermediates were restyled with a longer hood, shorter deck, and different grilles for each series. The '70 Riviera had a thin-line vertical-bar grille extending below the bumper. The big hardtop also reverted to exposed headlamps and adopted a longer hood and wider rear window than in 1969. Altered bumpers completed the package.

Mechanically, the big news in 1970 was an enormous 455 V8, the largest ever, which gulped premium gas at the rate of 12 mpg and was offered with compression ratios of at least 10:1. The last mammoth V8 Buick would build, the 455 was available in three versions with up to 370 bhp. In one of these guises it was standard on the GS and LeSabre 455, Riviera, Electra 225, Wildcat, and both Estate wagons.

Buick was staunchly committed to big cars throughout most of the '70s. As the decade wore on, energy economics, backed by government mandates, inexorably led the division to progressively smaller models in an expanding lineup, but full-size cars remained the make's bread and butter through 1975, accounting for over 40 percent

1970 Estate Wagon four-door station wagon

1970 Riviera hardtop coupe

1970 GS455 hardtop coupe

1970 Wildcat Custom convertible

of total sales that year.

GM completely redesigned its B- and C-body cars for 1971, so Buick's biggies emerged larger and heavier—as big as American cars would ever get, in fact. Styling was more smoothly rounded, marked by curved "fuselage" bodysides, massive hoods, and broad expanses of glass. The Wildcat name disappeared on the midrange series in favor of Centurion, another name first seen on a mid-'50s Buick show car. This line shared the B-body platform with the popular LeSabre, while the upmarket Electra stayed with the long-wheelbase C-body, also used for the Olds Ninety-Eight and Cadillac DeVille. The big Buicks continued in this form through 1976, with mostly minor year-to-year changes to meet safety and emissions requirements. They were thirsty cars all, and in their final season, the year before their downsized successors appeared, the 455-cid Electra was good for only 8.7 mpg in Environmental Protection Agency city fuel economy ratings.

The personal-luxury Riviera was also beefed up for 1971, growing longer between wheel centers and gaining needless pounds in the process. There was swoopy new styling courtesy of Bill Mitchell, marked by a dramatic "boattail" rear deck that proved so controversial it had to be toned down the very next year. By 1974 it was gone altogether. The one remaining reminder of sport, the GS option, vanished the year after that, but Buick tried to keep enthusiasts interested with a substitute Rallye package consisting of reinforced front stabilizer bar, heavy-duty springs, specially calibrated shocks, and a rear stabilizer bar. It was claimed to deliver even better ride and handling

characteristics than the GS, and it probably should have been standard to handle the size and weight of these mammoths. The oddball styling was partly responsible for sagging sales in this period, which by 1975 were less than half of what they'd been five years earlier.

Buick reentered the compact field for the first time in 10 years with the Apollo, launched at mid-model year 1973. Essentially a badge-engineered version of the X-body Chevrolet Nova introduced for 1968, it was offered in the same three body styles, and even had Chevy's straight six initially as standard power. It was a definite asset during the big-car sales slump brought on by the Arab oil embargo late that year, but intermediates would prove increasingly more important in the post-energy crisis period. The last of the "split-wheelbase" generation of Skylarks appeared for 1972. They were still solid, good-looking middleweights, though engines had been emasculated by then due to power-sapping emissions controls, and the interesting Gran Sport versions existed in name only. The next year saw a brand-new intermediate line reviving the respected Century label. These cars were built on GM's newly designed A-body platform, with so-called "Colonnade" styling that completely did away with pillarless coupes and sedans as well as convertibles, GM's reaction to a proposed federal rule on rollover crash protection that, ironically, never materialized. The Century sold well in this form through 1977, and provided an important "safety net" for Buick sales at times when inflation and rising fuel prices sent would-be big-car buyers scurrying for thriftier alternatives. Confusing buyers for

1971 Gran Sport Stage I hardtop coupe

1972 Centurion hardtop coupe

1971 Electra Limited hardtop sedan

1972 Skylark Custom hardtop coupe

1972 Riviera hardtop coupe

1974 LeSabre hardtop coupe

1973 Apollo two-door sedan

1974 Riviera coupe

1973 LeSabre Custom hardtop sedan

1975 Century Special Colonnade hardtop coupe

1973 Century Colonnade hardtop coupe

1975 Riviera coupe

1975 was the return of the Skylark name at the top of the compact line, where it eventually supplanted Apollo. In common with all X-body variants that year, Buick's version gained heavily revised outer panels that gave it something of a European sports sedan flair.

A brand new entry for '75 was the Skyhawk, the smallest Buick in living memory. A near twin to the Vega-based Chevrolet Monza, this 97-inch-wheelbase subcompact coupe took a bit more than eight percent of total division sales in the first six months of that year, and typified some new thinking in Flint. "To be in tune with today's market," said one official, "we want to emphasize that Buick means small, exciting cars as well as traditional prestige models." Though it was not light for its size, the Skyhawk had a

decent performance/economy balance thanks to Buick's new 90-degree V6 engine, the only one available. With the short-lived Borg-Warner five-speed manual gearbox introduced for '76, this car was rated by the government at nearly 30 mpg in highway driving.

Model year 1977 brought the first of GM's downsized cars. The advent of corporate average fuel economy (CAFE) standards, effective with the 1978 model year, prompted the firm to move to smaller, lighter, more economical models in every size and price category, and the company's largest models were the logical starting point for this program. The new order was dramatically apparent at Buick, which shrunk the LeSabre and Electra down to almost Century size, losing several hundred pounds in the process.

This made it possible to fit smaller engines, yet interior dimensions were within inches of what they'd been on the old behemoths. The Riviera was temporarily made a high-spec version of the B-body LeSabre, though it would return to the corporate E-body platform two years later. The big Buicks were treated to a mid-life facelift for 1980, with subtly restyled sheetmetal intended to reduce wind resistance as an aid to economy. There was also more extensive use of lightweight materials, which netted an average 150-pound weight saving, about half that achieved on the '77s. It's odd how perspective changes: when these first downsized models first appeared, they seemed quite small next to other big cars of the day; now they look just as large as their outsized predecessors did a decade ago.

Intermediates were next on the corporate slenderizing schedule, and a smaller Century bowed for 1978 along with a companion personal-luxury coupe called Regal, a name previously reserved for the top-line mid-size series. Regal sold well from the start, but the Century didn't. Clumsy sloped-roof "aeroback" styling on the two- and four-door sedans was out of phase with buyer tastes, though there was nothing wrong with the handsome new A-body wagon. Buick corrected its mistake for 1980 with a more formal-looking notchback four-door bearing a faint resemblance to the first-generation Cadillac Seville, and sales took off. A gesture to performance was optional turbocharging for the Buick V6, available initially in special Century and Regal Sport Coupe models and still in production at this writing, albeit with many interim refinements.

Riviera was downsized a second time for 1979. Styling was crisper and tighter than before, and at long last the model fell into line with its Toronado and Eldorado cousins by adopting front-wheel drive. A turbo V6 was available here, too, though most buyers opted for the standard powerplants. The blown Riv was a fine performer, though, able to leap 0-60 mph in under 12 seconds while averaging close to 20 mpg in more restrained driving, this despite a still-bulky 3800-pound curb weight. The 1980 followup was basically a rerun, but introduced to Buick a long-time Cadillac feature. This was "Twilight Sentinel," the automatic headlamp on/off device that also incorporated a delay timer for keeping the lights on for up to three minutes after switching off the ignition, thus illuminating a path from car to house.

Though it promised much, the little Skyhawk had never been a big seller, and Buick retired it after 1980. One interesting 1979-80 variation was the Road Hawk, an option package aimed at the younger buyer more interested in the sports car look than genuine performance. It comprised fore and aft spoilers, special paint and tape treatment, identifying decals, mag-style wheels, and larger tires, but there was little action to back up the brag.

One of the most important cars ever to bear the Buick tri-shield was unveiled in the spring of 1979 as an early-1980 entry. This was the front-drive replacement for the long-running rear-drive Skylark, sharing GM's technically advanced new X-body platform with siblings Chevrolet Citation, Pontiac Phoenix, and Oldsmobile Omega. The division had learned its styling lesson, so this new smaller

1976 Century Custom Colonnade hardtop coupe

1976 Electra Limited hardtop sedan

1977 Skyhawk hatchback coupe

1977 Electra 225 four-door sedan

1978 Regal Sport Coupe

compact was offered only in traditional notchback form. Design highlights included rack-and-pinion steering, all-coil suspension, and transversely mounted engines. With the optional Chevy-built 60-degree V6, the Skylark performed well, and there were tastefully done Sport Coupe and Sport Sedan models with upgraded suspension components, full instrumentation, and sportier trim for more serious-minded drivers. Mainly on the strength of the Buick name, the Skylark became the second best-selling X-car variant after the higher-volume, lower-priced Citation. Unfortunately, GM's execution left much to be desired,

and the X-cars quickly compiled a worrisome record of safety recalls and driveability quirks.

Despite the occasional flawed product and market miscalculation, Buick continued to move correctly with changing buyer demands in the '70s, reaping the benefit of good sales while some other makes faltered. The division has traditionally been able to anticipate market trends well in advance, and to respond with cars that, if not always on the leading edge of design, are at least very much in tune with the times. Strong sales year after year is proof positive that Buick not only knows its market, but how to satisfy it.

1978 LeSabre Custom four-door sedan

1978 Riviera coupe

1979 Electra Park Avenue four-door sedan

1980 Skyhawk "Road Hawk" hatchback coupe

1980 Skylark Sport Coupe

1980 Regal Somerset coupe

1980 LeSabre Limited coupe

1980 Riviera S Type coupe

Buick Specifications

1930

Series 40 (wb 118.0)

		Wght	Price	Prod
30-40	sdn 2d	3,600	1,270	6,144
30-44	spt rdstr 2P	3,420	1,310	3,639
30-45	phtn 4P	3,410	1,310	1,100
30-46	bus cpe	3,540	1,260	5,716
30-46S	special cpe 4P	3,600	1,300	10,748
30-47	sdn 4d	3,700	1,330	47,496
—	chassis	—	—	3,288

Series 50 (wb 124.0)

		Wght	Price	Prod
30-57	sdn 4d	4,235	1,540	23,139
30-58	cpe 4P	4,120	1,510	5,275

Series 60 (wb 132.0)

		Wght	Price	Prod
30-60	sdn 7P	4,415	1,910	6,650
30-60L	limo 7P	4,475	2,070	836
30-61	special sdn 4d	4,330	1,760	12,557
30-64	rdstr 2P	4,015	1,585	2,009
30-64C	special cpe 4P	4,225	1,695	5,381
30-68	cpe 5P	4,220	1,740	10,216
30-69	phtn 7P	4,110	1,595	1,618
—	chassis	—	—	924

1930 Engines	bore×stroke	bhp	availability
L6, 257.5	3.44×4.63	81	S-40
L6, 331.3	3.75×5.00	99	S-50, 60

1931

Series 50 (wb 114.0)

		Wght	Price	Prod
8-50	sdn 2d	3,065	1,035	
8-54	spt rdstr 2-4P	2,840	1,055	
8-55	phtn 5P	2,840	1,055	combined
8-56	bus cpe	2,980	1,025	below
8-56S	spt cpe 2-4P	3,060	1,055	
8-57	sdn 4d	3,170	1,095	

Series 50 (wb 114.0; intro. 1/31)

		Wght	Price	Prod
8-50	sdn 2d	3,145	1,035	3,677
8-54	spt rdstr 2-4P	2,935	1,055	977
8-55	phtn 5P	2,970	1,055	388
8-56	bus cpe	3,055	1,025	2,782
8-56C	conv cpe 4P	3,095	1,095	1,540
8-56S	spt cpe 2-4P	3,135	1,055	5,757
8-57	sdn 4d	3,265	1,095	33,358
—	chassis	—	—	2,008

Series 60 (wb 118.0)

		Wght	Price	Prod
8-64	spt rdstr 2-4P	3,465	1,335	1,078
8-65	phtn 5P	3,525	1,335	495
8-66	bus cpe	3,615	1,285	2,732
8-66S	spt cpe 2-4P	3,695	1,325	6,501
8-67	sdn 4d	3,795	1,355	30,775
—	chassis	—	—	1,692

Series 80 (wb 124.0)

		Wght	Price	Prod
8-86	cpe 4P	4,120	1,535	3,579
8-87	sdn 4d	4,255	1,565	14,769

Series 90 (wb 132.0)

		Wght	Price	Prod
8-90	sdn 7P	4,435	1,935	4,202
8-90L	limo 7P	4,505	2,035	620
8-91	brgm 4d 5P	4,340	1,785	7,858
8-94	spt rdstr 4P	4,010	1,610	843
8-95	phtn 7P	4,125	1,620	450
8-96	cpe 5P	4,260	1,765	7,715

		Wght	Price	Prod
8-96C	conv cpe	4,195	1,785	1,070
8-96S	spt cpe 2-4P	4,250	1,720	2,993
—	chassis	—	—	290

1931 Engines	bore×stroke	bhp	availability
L8, 220.7	2.88×4.25	77	S-50
L8, 272.6	3.06×4.63	90	S-60
L8, 344.8	3.13×5.00	104	S-80, 90

1932

Series 50 (wb 114.0)

		Wght	Price	Prod
32-55	spt phtn 5P	3,270	1,155	116
32-56	bus cpe	3,275	935	1,726
32-56C	conv cpe-rdstr 4P	3,335	1,080	643
32-56S	special cpe 4P	3,395	1,040	1,914
32-57	sdn 4d	3,450	995	10,803
32-57S	special sdn 4d	3,510	1,080	9,941
32-58	victoria cpe 5P	3,420	1,060	2,196
32-58C	conv phtn 5P	3,425	1,080	400
—	chassis	—	—	664

Series 60 (wb 118.0)

		Wght	Price	Prod
32-65	spt phtn 5P	3,795	1,390	103
32-66	bus cpe	3,795	1,250	636
32-66C	cpe-rdstr 4P	3,795	1,310	452
32-66S	special cpe 4P	3,860	1,270	1,684
32-67	sdn 4d	3,980	1,310	9,060
32-68	victoria cpe 5P	3,875	1,290	1,514
32-68C	conv phtn 5p	3,880	1,310	384
—	chassis	—	—	408

Series 80 (wb 126.0)

		Wght	Price	Prod
32-86	victoria cpe 5P	4,335	1,540	1,800
32-87	sdn 4d	4,450	1,570	4,092

Series 90 (wb 134.0)

		Wght	Price	Prod
32-90	sdn 7P	4,657	1,955	1,387
32-90L	limo 7P	4,740	2,055	190
32-91	club sdn 5P	4,620	1,820	2,238
32-95	spt phtn 7P	4,400	1,675	146
32-96	victoria cpe 5P	4,460	1,785	1,460
32-96C	cpe rdstr 4P	4,390	1,805	289
32-96S	Country Club cpe 4P	4,470	1,740	586
32-97	sdn 4d	4,565	1,805	1,485
32-98	conv phtn 5P	4,480	1,830	269
—	chassis	—	—	216

1932 Engines	bore×stroke	bhp	availability
L8, 230.4	2.94×4.25	82	S-50
L8, 272.6	3.06×4.63	95	S-60
L8, 344.8	3.13×5.00	113	S-80, 90

1933

Series 50 (wb 119.0)

		Wght	Price	Prod
33-56	bus cpe	3,520	995	1,321
33-56C	conv cpe 4p	3,525	1,115	350
33-56S	spt cpe 2-4P	3,585	1,030	1,653
33-57	sdn 4d	3,705	1,045	19,259
33-58	victoria cpe 5P	3,605	1,065	4,123
—	chassis	—	—	870

Series 60 (wb 127.0)

		Wght	Price	Prod
33-66C	conv cpe 2-4P	3,940	1,365	152
33-66S	spt cpe 2-4P	3,975	1,270	1,000
33-67	sdn 4d	4,115	1,310	7,450
33-68	victoria cpe 5P	4,005	1,310	2,887

		Wght	Price	Prod
33-68C	conv phtn 5P	4,110	1,585	183
—	chassis	—	—	399

Series 80 (wb 130.0)

		Wght	Price	Prod
33-86	victoria cpe 5P	4,420	1,540	758
33-86C	conv cpe 2-4P	4,325	1,575	90
33-86S	spt cpe 2-4P	4,355	1,495	401
33-87	sdn 4d	4,505	1,570	1,545
33-88C	conv phtn 5P	4,525	1,845	124
—	chassis	—	—	90

Series 90 (wb 138.0)

		Wght	Price	Prod
33-90	sdn 7P	4,705	1,955	902
33-90L	limo 7P	4,780	2,055	338
33-91	club sdn 5P	4,595	1,820	1,639
33-96	victoria cpe 5P	4,520	1,785	557
33-97	sdn 4d	4,595	1,805	641
—	chassis	—	—	192

1933 Engines	bore×stroke	bhp	availability
L8, 230.4	2.94×4.25	86	S-50
L8, 272.6	3.06×4.63	97	S-60
L8, 344.8	3.13×5.00	113	S-80, 90

1934

Series 40 (wb 117.0)

		Wght	Price	Prod
34-41	club sdn T/B 5P	3,175	925	11,495
34-46	cpe 5P	2,995	795	1,808
34-46S	spt cpe 2-4P	3,085	855	1,279
34-47	sdn 4d	3,155	895	7,805
34-48	tng sdn 2d T/B	3,120	865	4,779
—	chassis	—	—	1,727

Series 50 (wb 119.0)

		Wght	Price	Prod
34-56	bus cpe 2P	3,682	1,110	1,082
34-56C	conv cpe 2-4P	3,692	1,230	589
34-56S	spt cpe 2-4P	3,712	1,145	1,192
34-57	sdn 4d	3,852	1,190	12,805
34-58	victoria cpe 5P	3,767	1,160	4,405

		Wght	Price	Prod
—	chassis	—	—	1,777

Series 60 (wb 128.0)

		Wght	Price	Prod
34-61	club sdn 5P	4,318	1,465	5,629
34-66C	conv cpe 2-4P	4,133	1,495	263
34-66S	spt cpe 2-4P	4,193	1,375	825
34-67	sdn 4d	4,303	1,425	5,365
34-68	victoria T/B cpe 5P	4,213	1,395	1,966
34-68C	conv phtn 5P	4,353	1,675	587
—	chassis	—	—	717

Series 90 (wb 136.0)

		Wght	Price	Prod
34-90	sdn 7P	4,806	2,055	1,234
34-90L	limo 7P	4,876	2,175	428
34-91	club sdn 5P	4,696	1,965	1,507
34-96C	conv cpe 4P	4,511	1,945	83
34-96C	spt cpe 2-4P	4,546	1,875	137
34-97	sdn 4d	4,691	1,945	654
34-98	victoria cpe 5P	4,571	1,895	348
34-98C	conv phtn 5P	4,691	2,145	138
—	chassis	—	—	405

1934 Engines	bore×stroke	bhp	availability
L8, 233.0	3.09×3.88	93	S-40
L8, 235.3	2.97×4.25	88	S-50
L8, 278.1	3.09×4.63	100	S-60
L8, 344.8	3.13×5.00	110	3-90

1935

Series 40 (wb 117.0)

		Wght	Price	Prod
35-41	sdn T/B 4d	3,210	925	19,173
35-46	bus cpe	3,020	795	2,858
35-46C	conv cpe 2-4P	3,140	925	1,000
35-46S	spt cpe 2-4P	3,090	855	1,200
35-47	sdn 4d	3,180	895	6,641
35-48	sdn 2d T/B	3,160	865	5,027
—	chassis	—	—	2,621

Series 50 (wb 119.0)

		Wght	Price	Prod
35-56	bus cpe	3,652	1,110	257
35-56C	conv cpe 2-4P	3,662	1,230	187
35-56S	spt cpe 2-4P	3,682	1,145	279
35-57	sdn 4d	3,822	1,190	3,998
35-58	victoria cpe 5P	3,737	1,160	1,618
—	chassis	—	—	197

Series 60 (wb 128.0)

		Wght	Price	Prod
35-61	club sdn 5P	4,288	1,465	2,854
35-66C	conv cpe 2-4P	4,103	1,495	111
35-66S	spt cpe 2-4P	4,163	1,375	261
35-67	sdn 4d	4,273	1,425	1,792
35-68	victoria cpe 5P	4,183	1,395	603
35-68C	conv phtn 6W 5P	4,323	1,675	308
—	chassis	—	—	309

Series 90 (wb 136.0)

		Wght	Price	Prod
35-90	sdn 7P	4,776	2,055	651
35-90L	limo 7P	4,846	2,175	296
35-91	club sdn 5P	4,666	1,965	580
35-96C	conv cpe 2-4P	4,481	1,945	11
35-96S	spt cpe 2-4P	4,516	1,875	42
35-97	sdn 4d	4,661	1,945	119
35-98	victoria cpe 5P	4,541	1,895	32
35-98C	conv phtn 6W 5P	4,661	2,145	43
—	chassis	—	—	181

1935 Engines	bore×stroke	bhp	availability
L8, 233.0	3.09×3.88	93	S-40
L8, 235.3	2.97×4.25	88	S-50
L8, 278.1	3.09×4.63	100	S-60
L8, 344.8	3.13×5.00	116	S-90

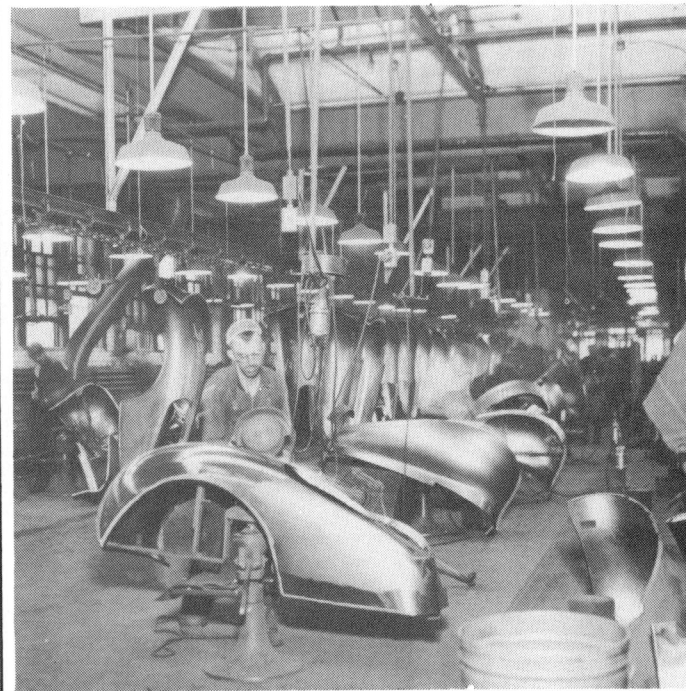

Buick's Flint, Michigan factory in 1937

1936

Series 40 Special (wb 118.0)

		Wght	Price	Prod
36-41	sdn 4d T/B	3,660	885	78,803
36-46	bus cpe	3,150	765	10,928
36-46C	conv cpe 2-4P	3,590	905	1,650
36-46S	spt cpe 3P	3,180	820	1,103
36-46S	spt cpe 2-4P R/S	3,180	820	1,494
36-48	victoria cpe T/B 5P	3,305	835	22,323
—	chassis	—	—	5,413

Series 60 Century (wb 122.0)

		Wght	Price	Prod
36-61	sdn 4d T/B	3,780	1,090	18,203
36-66C	conv cpe 2-4P	3,595	1,135	766
36-66S	spt cpe 3P T/B	3,195	1,035	1,079
36-66S	spt cpe 2-4P R/S	3,195	1,035	1,018
36-68	victoria cpe T/B 5P	3,730	1,055	3,799
—	chassis			1,115

Series 80 Roadmaster (wb 131.0)

		Wght	Price	Prod
36-80C	conv phtn T/B 6P	4,100	1,565	1,230
36-81	sdn 4d T/B 6P	4,100	1,255	15,328
—	chassis			534

Series 90 Limited (wb 138.0)

		Wght	Price	Prod
36-90	sdn T/B 8P		1,845	1,709
36-90L	limo T/B 8P		1,945	947
36-91	sdn T/B 6P		1,695	1,726
36-91F	form sdn T/B 4d	1,635	1,895	75
—	chassis			352

1936 Engines

	bore×stroke	bhp	availability
L8, 233.0	3.09×3.88	93	S-40
L8, 320.2	3.44×4.31	120	S-60, 80, 90

1937

40 Special (wb 122.0)

		Wght	Price	Prod
37-40C	conv phtn 5P	3,630	1,302	1,945
37-41	sdn 4d T/B	3,490	1,021	85,195
37-44	sdn 2d	3,490	959	9,342
37-46	bus cpe	3,380	913	13,773
37-46C	conv cpe 4P	3,480	1,056	2,399
37-46S	spt cpe 4P	3,445	975	5,284
37-47	sdn 4d	3,510	995	22,517
37-48	tng sdn T/B 2d	3,480	985	16,034
—	chassis	—	—	6,860

60 Century (wb 126.0)

		Wght	Price	Prod
37-60C	conv phtn 5P	3,840	1,524	425
37-61	tng sdn T/B 4d	3,720	1,233	21,140
37-64	sdn 2d	3,720	1,172	1,118
37-66C	conv cpe 4P	3,715	1,269	843
37-66S	spt cpe 4P	3,660	1,187	2,873
37-67	sdn 4d	3,750	1,297	4,771
37-68	tng sdn T/B 2d	3,750	1,197	2,897
—	chassis			1,026

80 Roadmaster (wb 131.0)

		Wght	Price	Prod
37-80C	conv phtn T/B 6P	4,214	1,856	1,155
37-81	sdn T/B 4d	4,159	1,518	14,981
37-81F	formal sdn 6P	4,229	1,641	489
—	chassis	—	—	606

90 Limited (wb 138.0)

		Wght	Price	Prod
37-90	sdn T/B 8P	4,549	2,240	1,710
37-90L	limo T/B 8P	4,599	2,342	965
37-91	sdn T/B 4d	4,469	2,066	1,242
37-91F	form sdn T/B 4d	4,409	2,240	158
—	chassis			598

1937 Engines

	bore×stroke	bhp	availability
L8, 248.0	3.09×4.13	100	S-40
L8, 320.2	3.44×4.31	130	S-60, 80, 90

1938

40 Special (wb 122.0)

		Wght	Price	Prod
38-40C	conv phtn 5P	3,705	1,406	946
38-41	tng sdn 4d T/B	3,560	1,047	82,191
38-44	spt sdn 2d 5P	3,515	981	5,951
38-46	bus cpe	3,385	945	11,368
38-46C	conv cpe 4P	3,575	1,103	2,625
38-46S	spt cpe T/B 4P	3,425	1,001	5,574
38-47	spt sdn 4d	3,535	1,022	11,341
38-48	tng sdn T/B 2d	3,520	1,006	14,213
—	chassis	—	—	7,092

Series 60 Century (wb 126.0)

		Wght	Price	Prod
38-60C	conv phtn 5P	3,950	1,713	219
38-61	tng sdn T/B 4d	3,780	1,297	12,673
38-66C	conv cpe 4P	3,815	1,359	694
38-66S	spt cpe T/B 4P	3,690	1,226	2,030
38-67	spt sdn 4d	3,785	1,272	1,516
38-68	tng sdn T/B 2d	3,760	1,256	1,393
—	chassis	—	—	762

Series 80 Roadmaster (wb 133.0)

		Wght	Price	Prod
37-80C	conv phtn 6P	4,235	1,983	411
37-81	tng sdn T/B 4d	4,245	1,645	4,704
37-81F	form sdn 6P	4,305	1,758	296
37-87	spt sdn 6P	4,245	1,645	466
—	chassis	—	—	223

Series 90 Limited (wb 140.0)

		Wght	Price	Prod
37-90	tng sdn T/B 8P	4,585	2,350	706
37-90L	limo T/B 8P	4,665	2,453	577
37-91	tng sdn T/B 4d	4,580	2,176	441
—	chassis	—	—	277

1938 Engines

	bore×stroke	bhp	availability
L8, 248.0	3.09×4.13	107	S-40
L8, 320.2	3.44×4.31	141	S-60, 80, 90

1939

Series 40 Special (wb 120.0)

		Wght	Price	Prod
41	tng sdn T/B 4d	3,482	966	111,493
41C	spt phtn T/B 5P	3,642	1,406	830
46	bus cpe	3,322	894	14,609
46C	conv cpe T/B 4P	3,452	1,077	4,809
46S	spt cpe T/B 4P	3,372	950	10,276
48	tng sdn T/B 2d	3,417	955	27,290
—	chassis	—	—	6,281

Series 60 Century (wb 126.0)

		Wght	Price	Prod
61	tng sdn T/B 4d	3,782	1,246	18,783
61C	spt phtn T/B 5P	3,917	1,713	269
61C	conv cpe T/B 4P	3,712	1,343	850
66S	spt cpe T/B 4P	3,637	1,175	3,470
—	chassis	—	—	518

Series 80 Roadmaster (wb 133.0)

		Wght	Price	Prod
80C	spt phtn 4d 6P	4,237	1,983	3
81	tng sdn T/B 4d	4,247	1,543	5,619
81C	spt phtn T/B 4d	4,392	1,983	364
81F	form sdn T/B 6P	4,312	1,758	340
87	spt sdn 6P	4,262	1,543	20
—	chassis	—	—	143

Series 90 Limited (wb 140.0)

		Wght	Price	Prod
90	tng sdn T/B 8P	4,608	2,350	686
90L	limo T/B 8P	4,653	2,453	543
91	tng sdn T/B 4d	4,568	2,074	382
—	chassis	—	—	176

1939 Engines

	bore×stroke	bhp	availability
L8, 248.0	3.09×4.13	107	S-40
L8, 320.2	3.44×4.31	141	S-60, 80, 90

Buick

1940

Series 40 Special (wb 121.0)

		Wght	Price	Prod
41	sdn 4d	3,660	996	68,816
41C	spt phtn	3,755	1,355	597
41T	taxi	3,700	1,000	48
46	bus cpe	3,505	895	12,382
46C	conv cpe	3,665	1,077	3,763
46S	spt cpe	3,540	950	8,401
48	sdn 2d	3,605	955	20,768

Series 50 Super (wb 121.0)

		Wght	Price	Prod
51	sdn 4d	3,790	1,109	97,226
51C	spt phtn	3,895	1,549	534
56C	conv cpe	3,785	1,211	4,804
56S	spt cpe	3,735	1,058	26,462
59	wgn 4d	3,870	1,242	501

Series 60 Century (wb 126.0)

		Wght	Price	Prod
61	sdn 4d	3,935	1,210	8,708
61C	spt phtn	4,050	1,620	203
66	bus cpe	3,800	1,128	44
66C	conv cpe	3,915	1,343	550
66S	spt cpe	3,765	1,175	96

Series 70 Roadmaster (wb 126.0)

		Wght	Price	Prod
71	sdn 4d	4,045	1,359	13,733
71C	opt phtn	4,195	1,768	238
76C	conv cpe	4,055	1,431	612
76S	spt cpe	3,990	1,277	3,972

Series 80 Limited (wb 133.0)

		Wght	Price	Prod
80C	Streamlined spt phtn	4,540	1,952	7
81	sdn 4d	4,440	1,553	3,898
81C	T/B spt phtn	4,540	1,952	250
81F	T/B form sdn	4,455	1,727	270
87	Streamlined spt sdn 4d	4,380	1,553	14
87F	Streamlined form sdn	4,455	1,727	7

Series 90 Limited (wb 140.0)

		Wght	Price	Prod
90	sdn 4d, 8P, A/S	4,645	2,096	828
90L	limo 8P, A/S	4,705	2,199	634
91	sdn 4d	4,590	1,942	418

1940 Engines	bore×stroke	bhp	availability
L8, 248.0	3.09×4.13	107	S-40, 50
L8, 320.2	3.44×4.31	141	S-60, 80, 90

1941

Series 40 Special (wb 121.0)

		Wght	Price	Prod
41	sdn 4d	3,730	1,052	92,528
41SE	sdn 4d	3,790	1,134	13,402
46	bus cpe	3,630	935	9,201
46S	sedanet	3,700	1,006	88,148
46SSE	sedanet	3,690	1,063	9,614
49	wgn 4d	3,980	1,463	850

Series 40A Special (wb 118.0)

		Wght	Price	Prod
44	bus cpe	3,530	915	3,261
44C	conv cpe	3,780	1,138	4,309
44S	spt cpe	3,590	980	5,290
47	sdn 4d	3,670	1,021	14,139

Series 50 Super (wb 121.0)

		Wght	Price	Prod
51	sdn 4d	3,770	1,185	58,638
51C	conv phtn	4,014	1,555	508
56	bus cpe	3,620	1,031	2,452
56C	conv cpe	3,810	1,267	12,391
56S	spt cpe	3,670	1,113	19,876

Series 60 Century (wb 126.0)

		Wght	Price	Prod
61	sdn 4d	4,025	1,288	15,136
66	bus cpe	3,870	1,195	222
66S	sedanet	3,920	1,241	5,547

Series 70 Roadmaster (wb 128.0)

		Wght	Price	Prod
71	sdn 4d	4,010	1,364	10,553
71C	conv phtn	4,469	1,775	326
76C	conv cpe	4,045	1,457	1,869
76S	spt cpe	3,920	1,282	2,834

Series 90 Limited (wb 139.0)

		Wght	Price	Prod
90	sdn 4d, 8P, A/S	4,680	2,360	906
90L	limo 8P, A/S	4,760	2,465	669
91	sdn 4d	4,575	2,155	1,231
91F	form sdn, A/S	4,665	2,310	296

1941 Engines	bore×stroke	bhp	availability
L8, 248.0	3.09×4.13	115	S-40A, 40 exc SE
L8, 248.0	3.09×4.13	125	S-50, 41SE, 46SSE
L8, 320.2	3.44×4.31	165	S-60, 70, 90

1942

Series 40A Special (wb 118.0)

		Wght	Price	Prod
44	util cpe	3,510	990	461
44C	conv cpe	3,790	1,260	1,788
47	sdn 4d	3,650	1,080	1,652
48	bus sedanet	3,555	1,010	559
48S	fam sedanet	3,610	1,045	5,990

Series 40B Special (wb 121.0)

		Wght	Price	Prod
41	sdn 4d	3,760	1,120	17,397
41SE	sdn 4d	3,785	1,200	2,288
46	bus sedanet	3,650	1,020	1,408
46S	fam sedanet	3,705	1,075	11,856
46SSE	fam sedanet	3,725	1,130	1,809
49	wgn 4d	3,925	1,450	327

Series 50 Super (wb 124.0)

		Wght	Price	Prod
51	sdn 4d	3,890	1,280	16,265
56C	conv cpe	4,025	1,450	2,489
56S	sedanet	3,800	1,230	14,629

Series 60 Century (wb 126.0)

		Wght	Price	Prod
61	sdn 4d	4,065	1,350	3,319
66S	sedanet	3,985	1,300	1,232

Series 70 Roadmaster (wb 129.0)

		Wght	Price	Prod
71	sdn 4d	4,150	1,465	5,418
76C	conv cpe	4,300	1,675	511
76S	sedanet	4,075	1,395	2,475

Series 90 Limited (wb 139.0)

		Wght	Price	Prod
90	sdn 4d, 8P, A/S	4,710	2,445	150
90L	limo 8P, A/S	4,765	2,545	250
91	sdn 4d	4,665	2,245	215
91F	form sdn	4,695	2,395	85

1942 Engines	bore×stroke	bhp	availability
L8, 248.0	3.09×4.13	110	S-40A, 40B exc SE
L8, 248.0	3.09×4.13	118	S-50, 46SSE, 41SE
L8, 320.2	3.44×4.31	165	S-60, 70, 90

1946

Series 40 Special (121.0)

		Wght	Price	Prod
41	sdn 4d	3,720	1,580	1,650
46S	sedanet	3,670	1,522	1,350

Series 50 Super (wb 124.0)

		Wght	Price	Prod
51	sdn 4d	3,935	1,822	77,724
56C	conv cpe	4,050	2,046	5,987

		Wght	Price	Prod
56S	sedanet	3,795	1,741	34,425
59	wgn 4d	4,170	2,594	748

Series 70 Roadmaster (wb 129.0)		Wght	Price	Prod
71	sdn 4d	4,165	2,110	20,864
76C	conv cpe	4,345	2,347	2,587
76S	sedanet	4,095	2,014	8,292

1946 Engines	bore×stroke	bhp	availability
L8, 248.0	3.09×4.13	110	S-40, 50
L8, 320.2	3.44×4.31	144	S-70

1947

Series 40 Special (wb 121.0)		Wght	Price	Prod
41	sdn 4d	3,720	1,623	18,431
46S	sedanet	3,760	1,611	14,603

Series 50 Super (wb 124.0)		Wght	Price	Prod
51	sdn 4d	3,910	1,929	83,576
56C	conv cpe	4,050	2,333	28,297
56S	sedanet	3,795	1,843	46,917
59	wgn 4d	4,170	2,940	2,036

Series 70 Roadmaster (wb 129.0)		Wght	Price	Prod
71	sdn 4d	4,190	2,232	47,152
76C	conv cpe	4,345	2,651	12,074
76S	sedanet	4,095	2,131	19,212
79	wgn 4d	4,445	3,249	529

1947 Engines	bore×stroke	bhp	availability
L8, 248.0	3.09×4.13	110	S-40, 50
L8, 320.2	3.44×4.31	144	S-70

1948

Series 40 Special (wb 121.0)		Wght	Price	Prod
41	sdn 4d	3,705	1,809	14,051
46S	sedanet	3,635	1,735	11,176

Series 50 Super (wb 124.0)		Wght	Price	Prod
51	sdn 4d	3,855	2,087	53,447
56C	conv cpe	4,020	2,518	19,017
56S	sedanet	3,770	1,987	33,819
59	wgn 4d	4,170	3,127	2,018

Series 70 Roadmaster (wb 129.0)		Wght	Price	Prod
71	sedan 4d	4,160	2,418	47,569
76C	conv cpe	4,315	2,837	11,503
76S	sedanet	4,065	2,297	20,649
79	wgn 4d	4,460	3,433	350

1948 Engines	bore×stroke	bhp	availability
L8, 248.0	3.09×4.13	110	S-40
L8, 248.0	3.09×4.13	115	S-50
L8, 320.2	3.44×4.31	144	S-70

1949

Series 40 Special (wb 121.0)		Wght	Price	Prod
41	sdn 4d	3,695	1,861	5,940
46S	sedanet	3,625	1,787	4,687

Series 50 Super (wb 121.0)		Wght	Price	Prod
51	sedan 4d	3,835	2,157	136,423

Series 40 Special (wb 121.0)		Wght	Price	Prod
56C	conv cpe	3,985	2,583	22,110
56S	sedanet	3,735	2,059	66,250
59	wgn 4d	4,100	3,178	1,847

Series 70 Roadmaster (wb 126.0)		Wght	Price	Prod
71	sdn 4d	4,205	2,735	55,242
76C	conv cpe	4,370	3,150	8,244
76R	Riviera htp cpe	4,420	3,203	4,343
76S	sedanet	4,115	2,618	18,537
79	wgn 4d	4,490	3,734	653

1949 Engines	bore×stroke	bhp	availability
L8, 248.0	3.09×4.13	110	S-40
L8, 348.0	3.09×4.13	115/120	S-50
L8, 320.2	3.44×4.31	150	S-70

1950

Series 40 Special (wb 121.5)		Wght	Price	Prod
41	sdn 4d	3,710	1,941	1,141
41D	DeLuxe sdn	3,735	1,983	141,396
43	J/B sdn 4d	3,715	1,809	58,700
43D	DeLuxe J/B sdn, 4d	3,720	1,952	14,335
46	J/B cpe	3,615	1,803	2,500
46D	DeLuxe J/B cpe	3,665	1,899	76,902
46S	J/B sedanet	3,655	1,856	42,935

Series 50 Super (wb 121.5)		Wght	Price	Prod
51	sdn 4d	3,745	2,139	55,672
56C	conv cpe	3,965	2,476	12,259
56R	Riviera htp cpe	3,790	2,139	56,030
56S	J/B sedanet	3,645	2,041	10,697
59	wgn 4d	4,115	2,844	2,480

Series 50 Super (wb 125.5)		Wght	Price	Prod
52	sdn 4d	3,870	2,212	114,745

Series 70 Roadmaster (wb 125.3; 72-130.3)		Wght	Price	Prod
71	sdn 4d	4,135	2,633	6,738
72	Riviera sdn 4d	4,220	2,738	54,212
75R	Riviera htp cpe	4,135	2,633	2,300
76R	Riv DeLuxe htp cpe	4,245	2,854	8,432
76C	conv cpe	4,345	2,981	2,964
76S	J/B sedanet	4,025	2,528	2,968
79	wgn 4d	4,470	3,407	420

1950 Engines	bore×stroke	bhp	availability
L8, 248.0	3.09×4.13	115/120	S-40
L8, 263.3	3.19×4.13	124/128	S-50
L8, 320.2	3.44×4.31	152	S-70

1951

Series 40 Special (wb 121.5)		Wght	Price	Prod
41	sdn 4d	3,605	2,139	999
41D	DeLuxe sdn 4d	3,680	2,185	87,848
45R	Riviera sdn 2d	3,645	2,225	16,491
46C	conv cpe	3,830	2,561	2,099
46S	spt cpe	3,600	2,046	2,700
48D	DeLuxe sdn 2d	3,615	2,127	54,311

Series 50 Super (wb 121.5; 52-125.5)		Wght	Price	Prod
51	sdn 4d	3,755	2,356	10,000
52	Riviera sdn 4d	3,845	2,437	92,886
56C	conv cpe	3,965	2,728	8,116
56R	Riviera sdn 2d	3,765	2,356	54,512
56S	DeLuxe sdn 2d	3,685	2,248	1,500
59	wgn 4d	4,100	3,133	2,212

Series 70 Roadmaster (wb 126.3; 72R-130.3)		Wght	Price	Prod
72R	Riviera sdn 4d	4,240	3,044	48,758
76C	conv cpe	4,355	3,283	2,911
76MR	Riviera htp cpe	4,185	3,051	809

		Wght	Price	Prod
76R	Riv htp cpe, hydraulic controls	4,235	3,143	12,901
79R	wgn 4d	4,470	3,780	679

1951 Engines	bore×stroke	bhp	availability
L8, 263.3	3.19×4.13	120/128	S-40
L8, 263.3	3.19×4.13	124/128	S-50
L8, 320.2	3.44×4.31	152	S-70

1952

Series 40 Special (wb 121.5)

		Wght	Price	Prod
41	sdn 4d	3,650	2,209	137
41D	DeLuxe sdn 4d	3,665	2,255	63,346
45R	Riviera htp cpe	3,665	2,295	21,180
46C	conv cpe	3,850	2,634	600
46S	spt cpe	3,605	2,115	2,206
48D	sdn 2d	3,620	2,197	32,684

Series 50 Super (wb 121.5; 52-125.5)

		Wght	Price	Prod
52	sdn 4d	3,825	2,563	71,387
56C	conv cpe	3,970	2,869	6,904
56R	Riviera htp cpe	3,775	2,478	55,400
59	wgn 4d	4,105	3,296	1,641

Series 70 Roadmaster (wb 126.3;72R-130.3)

		Wght	Price	Prod
72R	sdn 4d	4,285	3,200	32,069
76C	conv cpe	4,395	3,453	2,402
76R	Riviera htp cpe	4,235	3,306	11,387
79R	wgn 4d	4,505	3,977	359

1952 Engines	bore×stroke	bhp	availability
L8, 263.3	3.19×4.13	120/128	S-40
L8, 263.3	3.19×4.13	124/128	S-50
L8, 320.2	3.44×4.31	170	S-70

1953

Series 40 Special (wb 121.5)

		Wght	Price	Prod
41D	DeLuxe sdn 4d	3,710	2,255	100,312
45R	Riviera htp cpe	3,705	2,295	58,780
46C	conv cpe	3,815	2,553	4,282
48D	DeLuxe sdn	3,675	2,197	53,796

Series 50 Super (wb 121.5; 52-125.5)

		Wght	Price	Prod
52	Riviera sdn 4d	3,905	2,696	90,685
56C	conv cpe	4,035	3,002	6,701
56R	Riviera htp cpe	3,845	2,611	91,298
59	wgn 4d	4,150	3,430	1,830

Series 70 Roadmaster (wb 121.5; 72R-125.5)

		Wght	Price	Prod
72R	Riviera sdn 4d	4,100	3,254	50,523
76C	conv cpe	4,250	3,506	3,318
76R	Riviera htp cpe	4,125	3,358	22,927
76X	Skylark conv cpe	4,315	5,000	1,690
79R	wgn 4d	4,315	4,031	670

1953 Engines	bore×stroke	bhp	availability
L8, 263.3	3.19×4.13	125/130·	S-40
V8, 322.0	4.00×3.20	164/170	S-50
V8, 322.0	4.00×3.20	188	S-70

1954

Series 40 Special (wb 122.0)

		Wght	Price	Prod
41D	DeLuxe sdn 4d	3,735	2,265	70,356
46C	conv cpe	3,810	2,563	6,135
46R	Riviera htp cpe	3,740	2,305	71,186
48D	DeLuxe sdn 2d	3,690	2,207	41,557
49	DeLuxe wgn 4d	3,905	3,163	1,650

Series 50 Super (wb 127.0)

		Wght	Price	Prod
52	Riviera sdn 4d	4,105	2,711	41,756
56C	conv cpe	4,145	2,964	3,343

		Wght	Price	Prod
56R	Riviera htp cpe	4,035	2,626	73,531

Series 60 Century (wb 122.0)

		Wght	Price	Prod
61	sdn 4d	3,805	2,520	31,919
66C	conv cpe	3,950	2,963	2,790
66R	Riviera htp cpe	3,795	2,534	45,710
69	wgn 4d	3,975	3,470	1,563

Series 70 Roadmaster (wb 127.0)

		Wght	Price	Prod
72R	Riviera sdn 4d	4,250	3,269	26,862
76C	conv cpe	4,355	3,521	20,404
76R	Riviera htp cpe	4,215	3,373	3,305

Series 100 Skylark (wb 122.0)

		Wght	Price	Prod
100M	conv cpe	4,260	4,483	836

1954 Engines	bore×stroke	bhp	availability
V8, 264.0	3.63×3.20	143/150	S-40
V8, 322.0	4.00×3.20	177/182	S-50
V8, 322.0	4.00×3.20	195/200	S-60
V8, 322.0	4.00×3.20	200	S-70, 100

1955

Series 40 Special (wb 122.0)

		Wght	Price	Prod
41	sdn 4d	3,745	2,291	84,182
43	Riviera htp sdn	3,820	2,409	66,409
46C	conv cpe	3,825	2,590	10,009
46R	Riviera htp cpe	3,720	2,332	155,818
48	sdn 2d	3,715	2,233	61,879
49	wgn 4d	3,940	2,974	2,952

Series 50 Super (wb 127.0)

		Wght	Price	Prod
52	sdn 4d	4,140	2,876	43,280
56C	conv cpe	4,280	3,225	3,527
56R	Riviera htp cpe	4,075	2,831	85,656

Series 60 Century (wb 122.0)

		Wght	Price	Prod
61	sdn 4d	3,825	2,548	13,269
63	Riviera htp sdn	3,900	2,733	55,088
66C	conv cpe	3,950	2,991	5,588
66R	Riviera htp cpe	3,805	2,601	80,338
68	sdn 2d	3,795	2,490	270
69	wgn 4d	3,995	3,175	4,243

Series 70 Roadmaster (wb 127.0)

		Wght	Price	Prod
72	sdn 4d	4,300	3,349	31,717
76C	conv cpe	4,415	3,552	4,739
76R	Riviera htp cpe	4,270	3,453	28,071

1955 Engines	bore×stroke	bhp	availability
V8, 264.0	3.63×3.20	188	S-40
V8, 322.0	4.00×3.20	236	S-50, 60, 70

1956

Series 40 Special (wb 122.0)

		Wght	Price	Prod
41	sdn 4d	3,790	2,416	66,977
43	Riviera htp sdn	3,860	2,528	91,025
46C	conv cpe	3,880	2,740	9,712
46R	Riviera htp cpe	3,775	2,457	113,861
48	sdn 2d	3,750	2,357	38,672
49	wgn 4d	3,945	2,775	13,770

Series 50 Super (wb 127.0)

		Wght	Price	Prod
52	sdn 4d	4,200	3,250	14,940
53	Riviera htp sdn	4,265	3,340	34,029
56C	conv cpe	4,340	3,544	2,889
56R	Riviera htp cpe	4,140	3,204	29,540

Series 60 Century (wb 122.0)

		Wght	Price	Prod
61	sdn 4d	3,930	exp	1
63	Riviera htp sdn	4,000	3,025	20,891

Series 70 Roadmaster (wb 127.0)		Wght	Price	Prod
63D	Riviera DeLuxe htp sdn	4,000	3,041	35,082
66C	conv cpe	4,045	3,306	4,721
66R	Riviera htp cpe	3,890	2,963	33,334
69	wgn 4d	4,080	3,256	8,160

Series 70 Roadmaster (wb 127.0)				
72	sdn 4d	4,280	3,503	11,804
73	Riviera htp sdn	4,355	3,692	24,779
76C	conv cpe	4,395	3,704	4,354
76R	Riviera htp cpe	4,235	3,591	12,490

1956 Engines	bore×stroke	bhp	availability
V8, 322.0	4.00×3.20	220	S-40
V8, 322.0	4.00×3.20	255	S-50, 60, 70

1957

Series 40 Special (wb 122.0)		Wght	Price	Prod
41	sdn 4d	4,012	2,660	59,739
43	Riviera htp sdn	4,041	2,780	50,563
46C	conv cpe	4,082	2,987	8,505
46R	Riviera htp cpe	3,956	2,704	64,425
48	sdn 2d	2,596	2,596	23,180
49	wgn 4d	4,292	3,047	7,013
49D	Caballero wgn 4d	4,309	3,167	6,817

Series 50 Super (wb 127.5)				
53	Riviera htp sdn	4,356	3,681	41,665
56C	conv cpe	4,414	3,981	2,065
56R	Riviera htp cpe	4,271	3,536	26,529

Series 60 Century (wb 122.0)				
61	sdn 4d	4,137	3,234	8,075
63	Riviera htp sdn	4,163	3,354	26,589
66C	conv cpe	4,234	3,598	4,085
66R	Riviera htp cpe	4,081	3,270	17,029
68	sdn 2d	4,080	exp	2
69	Caballero wgn 4d	4,423	3,706	10,186

Series 70 Roadmaster (wb 127.5)				
73	Riviera htp sdn	4,469	4,053	11,401
73A	Riviera htp sdn, 1-piece backlight	4,455	4,066	10,526
76C	conv cpe	4,500	4,066	4,363
76R	Riviera htp sdn	4,374	3,944	3,826
76A	Riviera htp sdn, 1-piece backlight	4,370	3,944	2,812

Series 75 Roadmaster (wb 127.5)				
75	Riviera htp sdn	4,539	4,483	12,250
75R	Riviera htp cpe	4,427	4,373	2,404

1957 Engines	bore×stroke	bhp	availability
V8, 364.0	4.13×3.40	250	S-40
V8, 364.0	4.13×3.40	300	S-50, 60, 70, 75

1958

Series 40 Special (wb 122.0)		Wght	Price	Prod
41	sdn 4d	4,115	2,700	48,238
43	Riviera htp sdn	4,180	2,820	31,921
46C	conv cpe	4,165	3,041	5,502
46R	Riviera htp cpe	4,058	2,744	34,903
48	sdn 2d	4,063	2,636	11,566
49	wgn 4d	4,396	3,154	3,663
49D	Caballero htp wgn 4d	4,408	3,261	3,420

Series 50 Super (wb 127.5)				
53	Riviera htp sdn	4,500	3,789	28,460
56R	Riviera htp cpe	4,392	3,644	13,928

Series 60 Century (wb 122.0)				
61	sdn 4d	4,241	3,316	7,241

		Wght	Price	Prod
63	Riviera htp sdn	4,267	3,436	15,171
66C	conv cpe	4,302	3,680	2,588
66R	Riviera htp cpe	4,182	3,368	8,100
68	sdn 2d	4,189	exp	2
69	Caballero htp wgn 4d	4,498	3,831	4,456

Series 75 Roadmaster (wb 127.5)				
75	Riviera htp sdn	4,668	4,667	10,505
75C	conv cpe	4,676	4,680	1,181
75R	Riviera htp cpe	4,568	4,557	2,368

Series 700 Limited (wb 127.5)				
750	Riviera htp sdn	4,710	5,112	5,571
755	Riviera htp cpe	4,691	5,002	1,026
756	conv cpe	4,603	5,125	839

1958 Engines	bore×stroke	bhp	availability
V8, 364.0	4.13×3.40	250	S-40
V8, 364.0	4.13×3.40	300	S-50, 60, 75, 700

1959

4400 LeSabre (wb 123.0)		Wght	Price	Prod
4411	sdn 2d	4,159	2,740	13,492
4419	sdn 4d	4,229	2,804	51,379
4435	wgn 4d	4,565	3,320	8,286
4437	htp cpe	4,188	2,849	35,189
4439	htp sdn	4,266	2,925	46,069
4467	conv cpe	4,216	3,129	10,489

4600 Invicta (wb 123.0)				
4619	sdn 4d	4,331	3,357	10,566
4635	wgn 4d	4,660	3,841	5,231
4637	htp cpe	4,274	3,447	11,451
4639	htp sdn	4,373	3,515	20,156
4667	conv cpe	4,317	3,620	5,447

4700 Electra (wb 126.3)				
4719	sdn 4d	4,557	3,856	12,357
4737	htp cpe	4,465	3,818	11,216
4739	htp sdn	4,573	3,963	20,612

4800 Electra 225 (wb 126.3)				
4829	Riviera htp sdn	4,632	4,300	6,324
4839	htp sdn	4,641	4,300	10,491
4867	conv cpe	4,562	4,192	5,493

1959 Engines	bore×stroke	bhp	availability
V8, 364.0	4.13×3.40	250	S-LeSabre
V8, 401.0	4.19×3.64	325	S-others

1960

4400 LeSabre (wb 123.0)		Wght	Price	Prod
4411	sdn 2d	4,139	2,756	14,388
4419	sdn 4d	4,219	2,870	54,033
4435	wgn 4d, 2S	4,568	3,386	5,331
4437	htp cpe	4,163	2,915	26,521
4439	htp sdn	4,269	2,991	35,999
4445	wgn 4d, 3S	4,574	3,493	2,222
4467	conv cpe	4,233	3,145	13,588

4600 Invicta (wb 123.0)				
4619	sdn 4d	4,324	3,357	10,839
4635	wgn 4d, 2S	4,644	3,841	3,471
4637	htp cpe	4,255	3,447	8,960
4639	htp sdn	4,365	3,515	15,300
4645	wgn 4d, 3S	4,679	3,948	1,605
4667	conv cpe	4,347	3,620	5,236

4700 Electra (wb 126.3)				
4719	sdn 4d	4,544	3,856	13,794

		Wght	Price	Prod
4737	htp cpe	4,453	3,818	7,416
4739	htp sdn	4,554	3,963	14,488

4800 Electra 225 (wb 126.3)

		Wght	Price	Prod
4829	Riviera htp sdn	4,653	4,300	8,029
4839	htp sdn	4,650	4,300	5,841
4867	conv cpe	4,571	4,192	6,746

1960 Engines	bore×stroke	bhp	availability
V8, 364.0	4.13×3.40	235/250	S-LeSabre
V8, 401.0	4.19×3.64	325	S-others

1961

4000 Special (wb 112.0)

		Wght	Price	Prod
4019	sdn 4d	2,610	2,384	18,339
4027	spt cpe	2,579	2,330	4,232
4035	wgn 4d	2,775	2,681	6,101
4045	wgn 4d, 3S	2,844	2,762	798
4119	Deluxe sdn 4d	2,632	2,519	32,986
4135	Deluxe wgn 4d	2,794	2,816	11,729
4317	Skylark spt cpe	2,687	2,621	12,683

4400 LeSabre (wb 123.0)

		Wght	Price	Prod
4411	sdn 2d	4,033	2,993	5,959
4435	wgn 4d	4,450	3,623	5,628
4437	htp cpe	4,054	3,152	14,474
4439	htp sdn	4,129	3,228	37,790
4445	wgn 4d, 3S	4,483	3,730	2,423
4467	conv cpe	4,186	3,382	11,951
4469	sdn 4d	4,102	3,107	35,005

4600 Invicta (wb 123.0)

		Wght	Price	Prod
4637	htp cpe	4,090	3,447	6,382
4639	htp sdn	4,179	3,515	18,398
4667	conv cpe	4,206	3,620	3,953

4700 Electra (wb 126.0)

		Wght	Price	Prod
4719	sdn 4d	4,298	3,825	13,818
4737	htp cpe	4,260	3,818	4,250
4739	htp sdn	4,333	3,932	8,978

4800 Electra 225 (wb 126.0)

		Wght	Price	Prod
4829	Riviera htp sdn	4,417	4,350	13,719
4867	conv cpe	4,441	4,192	7,158

1961 Engines	bore×stroke	bhp	availability
V8, 215.0	3.50×2.80	155	S-Special (Slylark 185 bhp)
V8, 364.0	4.13×3.40	235/250	S-LeSabre
V8, 401.0	4.19×3.64	325	S-others

1962

Special (wb 112.1)

		Wght	Price	Prod
4019	sdn 4d	2,666	2,358	23,249
4027	cpe	2,638	2,304	19,135
4035	wgn 4d	2,876	2,655	7,382
4045	wgn 4d, 3S	2,896	2,736	2,814
4067	conv cpe	2,858	2,587	7,918
4119	Del sdn 4d	2,648	2,593	31,660
4135	Del wgn 4d	2,845	2,890	10,380
4167	Del conv cpe	2,820	2,879	8,332
4347	Skylark htp cpe	2,707	2,787	34,060
4367	Skylark conv cpe	2,871	3,012	8,913

LeSabre (wb 123.0)

		Wght	Price	Prod
4411	sdn 2d	4,041	3,091	7,418
4439	stp sdn	4,156	3,369	37,518
4447	htp cpe	4,054	3,293	25,479
4469	sdn 4d	4,104	3,227	56,783

Invicta (wb 123.0)

		Wght	Price	Prod
4435	wgn 4d	4,471	3,836	9,131

		Wght	Price	Prod
4639	htp sdn	4,159	3,667	16,443
4645	wgn 4d, 3S	4,505	3,917	4,617
4647	spt cpe	4,077	3,733	10,335
4647	Wildcat spt cpe	4,150	3,927	2,000
4667	conv cpe	4,217	3,617	13,471

Electra 225 (wb 126.0)

		Wght	Price	Prod
4819	sdn 4d	4,304	4,051	13,523
4829	Riviera htp sdn 6W	4,390	4,448	15,395
4839	htp sdn	4,309	4,186	16,734
4847	htp cpe	4,235	4,062	8,992
4867	conv cpe	4,396	4,366	7,894

1962 Engines	bore×stroke	bhp	availability
V6, 198.0	3.63×3.20	135	S-Special
V8, 215.0	3.50×2.80	155	S-Special Deluxe
V8, 215.0	3.50×2.80	185	S-Skylark
V8, 401.0	4.19×3.64	265/280	S-LeSabre, Invicta
V8, 401.0	4.19×3.64	325	S-Electra

1963

Special (wb 112.1)

		Wght	Price	Prod
4019	sdn 4d	2,696	2,363	21,733
4027	cpe	2,661	2,309	21,886
4035	wgn 4d	2,866	2,659	5,867
4045	wgn 4d, 3S	2,903	2,740	2,415
4067	conv cpe	2,768	2,591	8,082
4119	Del sdn 4d	2,720	2,521	37,695
4135	Del wgn 4d	2,854	2,818	8,771
4347	Skylark spt cpe	2,757	2,857	32,109
4367	Skylark conv cpe	2,810	3,011	10,212

LeSabre (wb 123.0)

		Wght	Price	Prod
4411	sdn 2d	3,905	2,869	8,328
4435	wgn 4d	4,320	3,526	5,566
4439	htp sdn	4,007	3,146	50,420
4445	wgn 4d, 3S	4,340	3,606	3,922
4447	htp cpe	3,924	3,070	27,997
4467	conv cpe	4,052	3,339	9,975
4469	sdn 4d	3,970	3,004	64,995

Wildcat (wb 123.0)

		Wght	Price	Prod
4639	htp sdn	4,222	3,871	17,519
4647	htp cpe	4,123	3,849	12,185
4667	conv cpe	4,228	3,961	6,021

Invicta (wb 123.0)

		Wght	Price	Prod
4635	wgn 4d	4,397	3,969	3,495

Electra 225 (wb 126.0)

		Wght	Price	Prod
4819	sdn 4d	4,241	4,051	14,268
4829	pillarless sdn	4,284	4,254	11,468
4839	htp sdn	4,272	4,186	19,714
4847	htp cpe	4,153	4,062	6,848
4867	conv cpe	4,297	4,365	6,347

Riviera (wb 117.0)

		Wght	Price	Prod
4747	htp cpe	3,988	4,333	40,000

1963 Engines	bore×stroke	bhp	availability
V6, 198.0	3.63×3.20	135	S-Special, Special Deluxe
V8, 215.0	3.50×2.80	155	O-Special Deluxe, Skylark
V8, 215.0	3.50×2.80	200	S-Skylark, O-all Specials
V8, 401.0	4.19×3.64	265/280	S-LeSabre
V8, 401.0	4.19×3.64	325	S-Invicta, Wildcat, Electra, Riviera

1964

Special (wb 115.0; wgns-120.0)

		Wght	Price	Prod
4027	cpe	2,991	2,343	15,030

		Wght	Price	Prod
4035	wgn	3,266	2,689	6,270
4067	conv cpe	3,108	2,605	6,308
4069	sdn 4d	3,008	2,397	17,983
4127	Del cpe	3,006	2,457	11,962
4135	Del wgn 4d	3,285	2,787	9,467
4169	Del sdn 4d	3,026	2,490	31,742
4337	Skyl spt cpe	3,057	2,680	42,356
4367	Skyl conv cpe	3,175	2,834	10,225
4369	Skyl sdn 4d	3,070	2,669	19,635
4255	Skyl Spt Wgn	3,557	2,989	2,709
4355	Skyl Spt Wgn	3,595	3,161	3,913
4265	Skyl Spt Wgn 4d 3S	3,689	3,124	2,586
4365	Skyl Spt Wgn	3,727	3,286	4,446

LeSabre (wb 123.0)

		Wght	Price	Prod
4439	htp sdn	3,730	3,122	37,052
4447	htp cpe	3,629	3,061	24,177
4467	conv cpe	3,787	3,314	6,685
4469	sdn 4d	3,693	2,980	56,729
4635	wgn 4d	4,352	3,554	6,517
4645	wgn 4d, 3S	4,362	3,635	4,003

Wildcat (wb 123.0)

		Wght	Price	Prod
4639	htp sdn	4,058	3,327	33,358
4647	htp cpe	4,003	3,267	22,893
4667	conv cpe	4,076	3,455	7,850
4669	sdn	4,021	3,164	20,144

Electra 225 (wb 126.0)

		Wght	Price	Prod
4819	sdn 4d	4,212	4,059	15,968
4829	pillarless sdn	4,238	4,261	11,663
4839	htp sdn	4,229	4,194	24,935
4847	htp cpe	4,149	4,070	9,045
4867	conv cpe	4,280	4,374	7,181

Riviera (wb 117.0)

		Wght	Price	Prod
4747	htp cpe	3,951	4,385	37,658

1964 Engines	bore×stroke	bhp	availability
V6, 225.0	3.75×3.40	155	S-Special
V8, 300.0	3.75×3.40	210/250	S-LeSabre 4400, Special
V8, 401.0	4.19×3.64	325	S-LeS 4600, Wildcat, Elec
V8, 425.0	4.31×3.64	340(O−360)	S-Riv; O-LeS 4600, Wldct, Elec

1965

Special (wb 115.0)

		Wght	Price	Prod
43327	cpe	2,977	2,343	12,945
43335	wgn 4d	3,258	2,688	2,868
43367	conv cpe	3,087	2,605	3,357
43369	sdn 4d	3,010	2,397	13,828
43427	cpe V8	3,080	2,414	5,309
43435	wgn 4d	3,365	2,759	3,676
43467	conv cpe	3,197	2,676	3,365
43469	sdn 4d	3,117	2,468	8,121
43535	Del wgn 4d	3,242	2,787	1,677
43569	Del sdn 4d	3,016	2,669	11,033
43635	Del wgn 4d	3,369	2,858	9,123
43669	Del sdn 4d	3,143	2,561	26,299

Skylark (wb 115.0; wgns-120.0)

		Wght	Price	Prod
44255	wgn 4d	3,642	2,989	4,226
44265	wgn 4d, 3S	3,750	3,123	4,669
44327	cpe	3,035	2,537	4,195
44337	htp cpe	3,057	2,680	4,549
44367	conv cpe	3,149	2,834	1,181
44369	sdn 4d	3,086	2,669	3,385
44427	GS cpe	3,146	2,608	11,877
44437	GS htp cpe	3,198	2,751	47,034
44455	Cus wgn 4d	3,690	3,160	8,300
44465	Cus wgn 3S	3,802	3,285	11,166
44467	GS conv cpe	3,294	2,905	10,456
44469	sdn 4d	3,194	2,740	22,335

LeSabre (wb 123.0)

		Wght	Price	Prod
45237	htp cpe	3,753	3,030	15,786
45239	htp sdn	3,809	3,090	18,384
45269	sdn 4d	3,788	2,948	37,788
45437	Cus htp cpe	3,724	3,100	21,049
45439	Cus htp sdn	3,811	3,166	23,394
45467	Cus conv cpe	3,812	3,325	6,543
45469	Cus sdn 4d	3,777	3,024	22,052

Wildcat (wb 126.0)

		Wght	Price	Prod
46237	htp cpe	3,988	3,286	6,031
46239	htp sdn	4,089	3,346	7,499
46269	sdn 4d	4,058	3,182	10,184
46437	Del htp cpe	4,014	3,340	11,617
46439	Del htp sdn	4,075	3,407	13,903
46467	Del conv cpe	4,069	3,502	4,616
46469	Del sdn 4d	4,046	3,285	9,765
46637	Cus htp cpe	4,047	3,566	15,896
46639	Cus htp sdn	4,160	3,626	14,878
46667	Cus conv cpe	4,087	3,727	4,398

Electra 225 (wb 126.0)

		Wght	Price	Prod
48237	htp cpe	4,208	4,082	6,302
48239	htp sdn	4,284	4,206	12,842
48269	sdn 4d	4,261	4,071	12,459
48437	Cus htp cpe	4,228	4,265	9,570
48439	Cus htp sdn	4,344	4,389	29,932
48467	Cus conv cpe	4,325	4,440	8,505
48469	Cus sdn 4d	4,272	4,254	7,197

Riviera (wb 117.0)

		Wght	Price	Prod
49447	htp cpe	4,036	4,408	34,586

1965 Engines	bore×stroke	bhp	availability
V6, 225.0	3.75×3.40	155	S-Special, Skylark
V8, 300.0	3.75×3.40	210/250	S-Special, Skylark, LeSabre
V8, 401.0	4.19×3.64	325	S-Wildcat, Electra, Riviera
V8, 425.0	4.31×3.64	340/360	O-Wildcat, Electra Riviera

1966

Special (wb 115.0; wgns-120.0)

		Wght	Price	Prod
43307	cpe	3,009	2,348	9,322
43335	wgn 4d	3,296	2,695	1,451
43367	conv cpe	3,092	2,604	1,357
43369	sdn 4d	3,046	2,401	8,797
43407	cpe	3,091	2,418	5,719
43435	wgn 4d	3,399	2,764	3,038
43467	conv cpe	3,223	2,671	2,036
43469	sdn 4d	3,148	2,471	9,355
43507	Del cpe	3,009	2,432	2,359
43517	Del htp cpe	3,038	2,504	2,507
43535	Del wgn 4d	3,290	2,783	824
43569	Del sdn 4d	3,045	2,485	5,573
43607	Del cpe	3,112	2,502	4,908
43617	Del htp cpe	3,130	2,574	10,350
43635	Del wgn 4d	3,427	2,853	7,592
43669	Del sdn 4d	3,156	2,555	27,909

Skylark (wb 115.0; wgns - 120.0)

		Wght	Price	Prod
44255	wgn 4d	3,713	3,025	2,469
44265	wgn 4d, 3S	3,811	3,173	2,667
44307	cpe V6	3,034	2,624	1,454
44317	htp cpe	3,069	2,687	2,552
44339	htp sdn	3,172	2,846	1,422
44367	conv cpe	3,158	2,837	608
44407	cpe	3,145	2,694	6,427
44417	htp cpe	3,152	2,757	33,326
44439	htp sdn	3,285	2,916	18,873
44455	Cus wgn 4d	3,720	3,155	6,964
44465	Cus wgn 4d, 3S	3,844	3,293	9,510
44467	conv cpe	3,259	2,904	6,129
44607	GS cpe	3,479	2,956	1,835

		Wght	Price	Prod
44617	GS htp cpe	3,428	3,019	9,934
44667	GS conv cpe	3,532	3,167	2,047

LeSabre (wb 123.0)

		Wght	Price	Prod
45237	htp cpe	3,751	3,022	13,843
45239	htp sdn	3,828	3,081	17,740
45269	sdn 4d	3,796	2,942	39,146
45437	Cus htp cpe	3,746	3,109	18,830
45439	Cus htp sdn	3,824	3,174	21,914
45467	Cus conv cpe	3,833	3,326	4,994
45469	Cus sdn 4d	3,788	3,035	25,932

Wildcat (wb 126.0)

		Wght	Price	Prod
46437	htp cpe	4,003	3,326	9,774
46439	htp sdn	4,108	3,391	15,081
46467	conv cpe	4,065	3,480	2,690
46469	sdn 4d	4,070	3,233	14,389
46637	Cus htp cpe	4,018	3,547	10,800
46639	Cus htp sdn	4,176	3,606	13,060
46667	Cus conv cpe	4,079	3,701	2,790

Electra 225 (wb 126.0)

		Wght	Price	Prod
48237	htp cpe	4,176	4,032	4,882
48239	htp sdn	4,271	4,153	10,792
48269	sdn 4d	4,255	4,022	11,740
48437	Cus htp cpe	4,230	4,211	10,119
48439	Cus htp sdn	4,323	4,332	34,149
48467	Cus conv cpe	4,298	4,378	7,175
48469	Cus sdn 4d	4,292	4,201	9,368

Riviera (wb 119.0)

		Wght	Price	Prod
49487	htp cpe	4,180	4,424	45,348

1966 Engines	bore×stroke	bhp	availability
V6, 225.0	3.75×3.40	160	S-Special, Skylark
V8, 300.0	3.75×3.40	210	O-Special, Skylark
V8, 340.0	3.75×3.85	220	S-4440 wagon, LeSabre
V8, 401.0	4.19×3.64	325	S-Skylark GS, Wildcat, Electra
V8, 401.0	4.19×3.64	340	S-Riviera; O-Wildcat, Electra

1967

Special (wb 115.0; wgns-120.0)

		Wght	Price	Prod
43307	cpe	3,071	2,411	6,989
43335	wgn 4d	3,343	2,742	908
43369	sdn 4d	3,077	2,462	4,711
43407	cpe	3,173	2,481	8,937
43435	wgn 4d	3,425	2,812	1,688
43469	sdn 4d	3,196	2,532	5,793
43517	Del htp cpe	3,127	2,566	2,357
43569	Del sdn 4d	3,142	2,545	3,650
43617	Del htp cpe	3,202	2,636	14,408
43635	Del wgn 4d	3,317	2,901	6,851
43669	Del sdn 4d	3,205	2,615	26,057

Skylark (wb 115.0; wgns-120.0)

		Wght	Price	Prod
34017	GS340 htp cpe	3,283	2,845	3,692
44307	cpe V6	3,137	2,665	894
44407	cpe V8	3,229	2,735	3,165
44417	htp cpe	3,199	2,798	41,084
44439	htp sdn	3,373	2,950	13,721
44455	wgn 4d	3,772	3,202	8,554
44465	wgn 4d, 3S	3,876	3,340	10,529
44467	conv cpe	3,335	2,945	6,319
44469	sdn 4d	3,324	2,767	9,213
44607	GS400 cpe	3,439	2,956	1,014
44617	GS400 htp cpe	3,500	3,019	10,659
44667	GS400 conv cpe	3,505	3,167	2,140

LeSabre (wb 123.0)

		Wght	Price	Prod
45239	htp sdn	3,878	3,142	17,464
45269	sdn 4d	3,847	3,002	36,220

		Wght	Price	Prod
45287	htp cpe	3,819	3,084	13,760
45439	Cus htp sdn	3,873	3,236	32,526
45467	Cus conv cpe	3,890	3,388	4,624
45469	Cus sdn 4d	3,855	3,096	27,930
45487	Cus htp cpe	3,853	3,172	22,666

Wildcat (wb 126.0)

		Wght	Price	Prod
46439	htp sdn	4,069	3,437	15,110
46467	conv cpe	4,064	3,536	2,276
46469	sdn 4d	4,008	3,277	14,579
46487	htp cpe	4,021	3,382	10,585
46639	Cus htp sdn	4,119	3,652	13,547
46667	Cus conv cpe	4,046	3,757	2,913
46687	Cus htp cpe	4,055	3,603	11,871

Electra 225 (wb 126.0)

		Wght	Price	Prod
48239	htp sdn	4,293	4,184	12,491
48257	htp cpe	4,197	4,075	6,845
48269	sdn 4d	4,246	4,054	10,787
48439	Cus htp sdn	4,336	4,363	40,978
48457	Cus htp cpe	4,242	4,254	12,156
48467	Cus conv cpe	4,304	4,421	6,941
48469	Cus sdn 4d	4,312	4,270	10,106

Riviera (wb 119.0)

		Wght	Price	Prod
49487	htp cpe	4,189	4,469	42,799

1967 Engines	bore×stroke	bhp	availability
V6, 225.0	3.75×3.40	160	S-Special, Skylark
V6, 300.0	3.75×3.40	210	O-Special, Skylark
V8, 340.0	3.75×3.85	220/260	S-4400 wgn, LeS; O-Skyl
V8, 401.0	4.19×3.64	340	S-GS400
V8, 430.0	4.19×3.90	360	S-Wildcat, Electra, Riviera

1968

Special Deluxe (wb 116.0; 2d-112.0)

		Wght	Price	Prod
43327	cpe	3,185	2,513	21,988
43369	sdn 4d	3,277	2,564	16,571
43435	wgn 4d	3,670	3,001	10,916

Skylark (wb 116.0; 2d-112.0)

		Wght	Price	Prod
43537	htp cpe	3,240	2,688	32,795
43569	sdn 4d	3,278	2,666	27,387
44437	Cus htp cpe	3,344	2,956	44,143
44439	Cus htp sdn	3,481	3,108	12,984
44467	Cus conv cpe	3,394	3,098	8,188
44469	Cus sdn 4d	3,377	2,924	8,066

Sportwagon (wb 121.0)

		Wght	Price	Prod
44455	wgn 4d	3,975	3,341	10,530
44465	wgn 4d, 3S	4,118	3,499	12,378

Gran Sport (wb 112.0)

		Wght	Price	Prod
43437	GS350 htp cpe	3,375	2,926	8,317
44637	GS400 htp cpe	3,514	3,127	10,743
44667	GS400 conv cpe	3,547	3,271	2,454

LeSabre (wb 123.0)

		Wght	Price	Prod
45239	htp sdn	3,980	3,281	18,058
45269	sdn 4d	3,946	3,141	37,433
45287	htp cpe	3,923	3,223	14,992
45439	Cus htp sdn	4,007	3,375	40,370
45467	Cus conv cpe	3,966	3,504	5,257
45469	Cus sdn 4d	3,950	3,235	34,112
45487	Cus htp cpe	3,932	3,311	29,596

Wildcat (wb 126.0)

		Wght	Price	Prod
46439	htp sdn	4,133	3,576	15,153
46469	sdn 4d	4,076	3,416	15,201
46487	htp cpe	4,065	3,521	10,708
46639	Cus htp sdn	4,162	3,791	14,059

		Wght	Price	Prod
46667	Cus conv cpe	4,118	3,873	3,572
46687	Cus htp cpe	4,082	3,742	11,276

Electra 225 (wb (126.0))

		Wght	Price	Prod
48239	htp sdn	4,270	4,330	15,376
48257	htp cpe	4,180	4,221	10,705
48269	sdn 4d	4,253	4,200	12,723
48439	Cus htp sdn	4,314	4,509	50,846
48457	Cus htp cpe	4,223	4,400	16,826
48467	Cus conv cpe	4,285	4,541	7,976
48469	Cus sdn 4d	4,304	4,415	10,910

Riviera (wb 119.0)

		Wght	Price	Prod
49487	htp cpe	4,222	4,615	49,284

1968 Engines	bore×stroke	bhp	availability
L6, 250.0	3.88×3.53	155	S-Special Del, Skylark
V8, 350.0	3.80×3.85	230	S-Swgn, Sky Cus, LeS; O-Spec, Sky
V8, 350.0	3.80×3.85	280	S-GS350; O-Sp Del, Sky, LeS, Swgn
V8, 401.0	4.19×3.64	340	S-GS400, Sportwagon 400
V8, 430.0	4.19×3.90	360	S-Wildcat, Electra, Riviera

1969

Special Deluxe (wb 116.0; 2d-112.0)

		Wght	Price	Prod
43327	cpe	3,216	2,562	15,268
43369	sdn 4d	3,182	2,613	11,113
43435	wgn 4d	3,736	3,092	2,590
43436	luxury wgn 4d	3,783	3,124	6,677

Skylark (wb 116.0; 2d-112.0)

		Wght	Price	Prod
43537	htp cpe	3,240	2,736	38,658
43569	sdn 4d	3,270	2,715	22,349
44437	Cus htp cpe	3,341	3,009	35,639
44439	Cus htp sdn	3,477	3,151	9,609
44467	Cus conv cpe	3,398	3,152	6,552
44469	Cus sdn 4d	3,397	2,978	6,423

Sportwagon (wb 121.0)

		Wght	Price	Prod
44456	wgn 4d	4,106	3,465	9,157
44466	wgn 4d, 3S	4,321	3,621	11,513

Gran Sport (wb 112.0)

		Wght	Price	Prod
43437	GS350 htp cpe	3,406	2,980	4,933
44637	GS400 htp cpe	3,549	3,181	6,356
44667	GS400 conv cpe	3,594	3,325	1,776

LeSabre (wb 123.2)

		Wght	Price	Prod
45237	htp cpe	3,936	3,298	16,201
45239	htp sdn	3,983	3,356	17,235
45269	sdn 4d	3,966	3,216	36,664
45437	Cus htp cpe	4,018	3,386	38,887
45439	Cus htp sdn	4,073	3,450	48,123
45467	Cus conv cpe	3,958	3,579	3,620
45469	Cus sdn 4d	3,941	3,310	37,136

Wildcat (wb 123.2)

		Wght	Price	Prod
46437	htp cpe	3,926	3,596	12,416
46439	htp sdn	4,304	3,651	13,805
46469	sdn 4d	4,102	3,491	13,126
46637	Cus htp cpe	4,134	3,817	12,136
46639	Cus htp sdn	4,220	3,866	13,596
46667	Cus conv cpe	4,152	3,948	2,374

Electra 225 (wb 126.2)

		Wght	Price	Prod
48239	htp sdn	4,294	4,432	15,983
48257	htp cpe	4,203	4,323	13,128
48269	sdn 4d	4,238	4,302	14,521
48439	Cus htp sdn	4,328	4,611	65,240
48457	Cus htp cpe	4,222	4,502	27,018
48467	Cus conv cpe	4,309	4,643	8,294
48469	Cus sdn 4d	4,281	4,517	14,434

Riviera (wb 119.0)

		Wght	Price	Prod
49487	htp cpe	4,199	4,701	52,872

1969 Engines	bore×stroke	bhp	availability
L6, 250.0	3.88×3.53	155	S-SD cpe & sdn, Skylark
V8, 350.0	3.80×3.85	230	S-SD wgn, Sky Cus, LeS
V8, 350.0	3.80×3.85	280	S-GS350; O-LeS, SW, SD, Sky
V8, V8, 401.0	4.19×3.64	340	S-GS400; O-Sportwagon
V8, 430.0	4.19×3.90	360	S-Riviera, Electra, Wildcat

1970

Skylark (wb 116.0; 2d-112.0)

		Wght	Price	Prod
43327	cpe	3,250	2,685	18,620
43369	sdn 4d	3,311	2,736	13,420
43537	350 htp cpe	3,277	2,859	70,918
43569	350 sdn 4d	3,320	2,838	30,281
44437	Cus htp cpe	3,435	3,132	36,367
44439	Cus htp sdn	3,565	3,220	12,411
44467	Cus conv cpe	3,499	3,275	4,954
44469	Cus sdn 4d	3,499	3,101	7,113

Sportwagon (wb 116.0)

		Wght	Price	Prod
43435	wgn 4d	3,775	3,210	2,239
43436	luxury wgn 4d	3,898	3,242	10,002

Gran Sport (wb 112.0)

		Wght	Price	Prod
43437	htp cpe	3,434	3,098	9,948
44637	455 htp cpe	3,562	3,283	8,732
44667	455 conv cpe	3,619	3,469	1,416

LeSabre (wb 124.0)

		Wght	Price	Prod
45237	htp cpe	3,866	3,419	14,163
45239	htp sdn	4,018	3,477	14,817
45269	sdn 4d	3,970	3,337	35,404
45437	Cus htp cpe	3,921	3,507	35,641
45439	Cus htp sdn	3,988	3,571	43,863
45467	Cus conv cpe	3,947	3,700	2,487
45469	Cus sdn 4d	3,950	3,431	36,682
46437	Cus 455 htp cpe	4,066	3,675	5,469
46439	Cus 455 htp sdn	4,143	3,739	6,541
46469	Cus 455 sdn 4d	4,107	3,599	5,555

Estate Wagon (wb 124.0)

		Wght	Price	Prod
46036	wgn 4d	4,691	3,923	11,427
46046	wgn 4d, 3S	4,779	4,068	16,879

Wildcat Custom (wb 124.0)

		Wght	Price	Prod
46637	htp cpe	4,099	3,949	9,447
46639	htp sdn	4,187	3,997	12,924
46667	conv cpe	4,214	4,079	1,244

Electra 225 (wb 127.0)

		Wght	Price	Prod
48239	htp sdn	4,296	4,592	14,338
48257	htp cpe	4,214	4,482	12,013
48269	sdn 4d	4,274	4,461	12,580
48439	Cus htp sdn	4,385	4,771	65,114
48457	Cus stp cpe	4,297	4,661	26,002
48467	Cus conv cpe	4,341	4,802	6,045
48469	Cus sdn 4d	4,283	4,677	14,109

Riviera (wb 119.0)

		Wght	Price	Prod
49487	htp cpe	4,216	4,854	37,336

1970 Engines	bore×stroke	bhp	availability
L6, 250.0	3.88×3.53	155	S-Skylark, Skylark 350
V8, 350.0	3.80×3.85	260	S-LeS, Sky Cus, SW; O-Sky
V8, 350.0	3.80×3.85	285	O-LeS, Sky, Sportwagon
V8, 350.0	3.80×3.85	315	S-GS; O-LeS, Sky, Swgn
V8, 455.0	4.31×3.90	350/360	S-GS455
V8, 455.0	4.31×3.90	370	S-Wldct, Est Wgn, LeS 455, Elec, Riv

Buick

1971

Skylark (wb 116.0; 2d 112.0)

		Wght	Price	Prod
43327	cpe	3,254	2,847	14,500
43337	htp cpe	3,272	2,918	61,201
43369	sdn 4d	3,326	2,897	34,037
44437	Custom htp cpe	3,391	2,317	29,536
44439	Custom htp sdn	3,547	3,397	10,814
44467	Custom conv cpe	3,431	3,462	3,993
44469	Custom sdn 4d	3,455	3,288	8,299

Sportwagon (wb 116.0)

		Wght	Price	Prod
43436	wgn 4d	3,928	3,515	12,525

Gran Sport (wb 112.0)

		Wght	Price	Prod
43437	htp cpe	3,461	3,285	8,268
43467	conv cpe	3,497	3,476	902

LeSabre (wb 124.0)

		Wght	Price	Prod
45239	htp sdn 4d	4,109	4,119	14,234
45257	htp cpe	4,049	4,061	13,385
46269	sdn 4d	4,078	3,992	26,348
45439	Custom htp sdn	4,147	4,213	41,098
45457	Custom htp cpe	4,095	4,149	20,041
45467	Custom conv cpe	4,086	4,342	1,856
45469	Custom sdn 4d	4,107	4,085	26,970

Estate Wagon (wb 127.0)

		Wght	Price	Prod
46035	wgn 4d 2S	4,906	4,640	8,699
46045	wgn 4d 3S	4,965	4,786	15,335

Centurion (wb 124.0)

		Wght	Price	Prod
46639	htp sdn	4,307	4,564	15,345
46647	htp cpe	4,195	4,678	11,892
46667	conv cpe	4,227	4,678	2,161

Electra 225 (wb 127.0)

		Wght	Price	Prod
48237	htp cpe	4,345	4,801	8,662
48239	htp sdn	4,381	4,915	17,589
48437	Custom htp cpe	4,359	4,980	26,831
48439	Custom htp sdn	4,421	5,093	72,954

Riviera (wb 122.0)

		Wght	Price	Prod
49487	htp cpe	4,325	5,253	33,810

1971 Engines

	bore×stroke	bhp	availability
L6, 250.0	3.88×3.53	145	S-Skylark
V8, 350.0	3.80×3.85	230	S-SW,GS,LeS,O-Sky
V8, 350.0	3.80×3.85	260	O-LeS
V8, 455.0	4.31×3.90	315	S-Cent,Elec,EWgn; Riv,O-Sky,LeS
V8, 455.0	4.31×3.90	330	O-Cent,Riv
V8, 455.0	4.31×3.90	345	O-Sky,LeS

1972

Skylark (wb 116.0; 2d 112.0)

		Wght	Price	Prod
4D69	sdn 4d	3,475	2,973	42,206
4D69	350 sdn 4d	3,600	3,104	
4D27	cpe	3,420	2,925	14,552
4D37	htp cpe	3,426	2,993	84,868
4D37	350 htp cpe	3,600	3,124	
4G37	GS htp cpe	3,471	3,225	7,723
4G67	GS conv cpe	3,525	3,406	852
4H69	Custom sdn 4d	3,516	3,228	9,924
4H39	Custom htp sdn	3,609	3,331	12,925
4H37	Custom htp cpe	3,477	3,255	34,271
4H67	Custom conv cpe	3,534	3,393	3,608
4F36	Sportwagon 4d 2S	3,987	3,444	14,417

LeSabre (wb 124.0)

			Wght	Price	Prod
4L69	sdn 4d		4,201	3,958	29,505
4L39	htp sdn		4,211	4,079	15,160
4L57	htp cpe		4,166	4,024	14,011
4N69	Custom sdn 4d		4,221	4,047	35,295
4N39	Custom htp sdn		4,226	4,168	50,804
4N57	Custom htp cpe		4,181	4,107	36,510
4N67	Custom conv cpe		4,235	4,291	2,037

Estate Wagon (wb 127.0)

		Wght	Price	Prod
4R45	wgn 4d 3S	5,060	4,728	18,793
4R35	wgn 4d 2S	4,975	4,589	10,175

Centurion (wb 124.0)

		Wght	Price	Prod
4P39	htp sdn	4,406	4,508	19,852
4P47	htp cpe	4,336	4,579	14,187
4P67	conv cpe	4,396	4,616	2,396

Electra 225 (wb 127.0)

		Wght	Price	Prod
4U39	htp sdn	4,515	4,890	19,433
4U37	htp cpe	4,445	4,782	9,961
4V39	Custom sdn 4d	4,530	5,060	104,754
4V37	Custom htp cpe	4,455	4,952	37,974

Riviera (wb 122.0)

		Wght	Price	Prod
1Y87	htp cpe	4,343	5,149	33,728

1972 Engines

	bore×stroke	bhp	availability
V8, 350.0	3.88×3.53	150	S-Skylark,LeSabre
V8, 350.0	3.88×3.53	190	S-GS,O-Sky,LeS
V8, 455.0	4.31×3.90	225	S-Cent,Elec,EWgn; O-Sky,GS,LeS
V8, 455.0	4.31×3.90	250	S-Riviera

1973

Apollo (wb 111.0)

		Wght	Price	Prod
B69	sdn 4d	3,239	2,628	8,450
B27	sdn 2d	3,195	2,605	14,475
B17	htchbk sdn 3d	3,297	2,754	9,868

Century (wb 116.0; 2d 112.0)

		Wght	Price	Prod
D29	Colonnade sdn 4d	3,780	3,057	38,202
D37	Colonnade cpe	3,713	3,057	56,154
F35/45	wgn 4d 2S/3S	4,156*	3,486*	7,760*
H29	Luxus Colonnade sdn 4d	3,797	3,326	22,438
H57	Luxus Colonnade cpe	3,718	3,331	71,712
K35/45	Luxus wgn 4d 2S/3S	4,190*	3,652*	10,645*
J57	Regal Colonnade cpe	3,743	3,470	91,557

LeSabre (wb 124.0)

		Wght	Price	Prod
L69	sdn 4d	4,234	3,998	29,649
L39	htp sdn	4,259	4,125	13,413
L57	htp cpe	4,210	4,067	14,061
N69	Custom sdn 4d	4,264	4,091	42,854
N39	Custom htp sdn	4,284	4,217	55,879
N57	Custom htp cpe	4,225	4,154	41,425

Centurion (wb 124.0)

		Wght	Price	Prod
P39	htp sdn	4,329	4,390	22,354
P57	htp cpe	4,260	3,336	16,883
P67	conv cpe	4,316	4,534	5,739

Estate Wagon (wb 127.0)

		Wght	Price	Prod
R35	wgn 4d 2S	4,952	4,645	12,282
R45	wgn 4d 3S	5,021	4,790	23,513

Electra 225 (wb 127.0)

		Wght	Price	Prod
T39	htp sdn	4,581	4,928	17,189
T37	htp cpe	4,488	4,815	9,224
V39	Custom htp sdn	4,603	5,105	107,031
V37	Custom htp cpe	4,505	4,993	44,328

Riviera (wb 122.0)

			Wght	Price	Prod
Y87	htp cpe		4,486	5,221	34,080

1973 Engines	bore×stroke	bhp	availability
L6, 250.0	3.87×3.50	100	S-Apollo
V8, 350.0	3.88×3.53	150	S-AP,Cnty,LeS
V8, 350.0	3.88×3.53	175	S-Cnty; O-Ap,LeS
V8, 455.0	4.31×3.90	225	S-EWgn,Elec; O-Cnty,LeS
V8, 455.0	4.31×3.90	250	S-Riv; O-LeS,EWgn,Elec
V8, 455.0	4.31×3.90	270	O-Riviera

*figures for 2S wgns shown; for 3S wgns add approx. 40 lbs and $125. Production combined.

1974

Apollo (wb 111.0)

		Wght	Price	Prod
B69	sdn 4d	3,362	3,060	16,779
B27	sdn 2d	3,322	3,037	28,286
B17	htchbk sdn 3d	3,428	3,160	11,644

Century (wb 116.0; 2d 112.0)

		Wght	Price	Prod
D29	350 Colonnade sdn 4d	3,890	3,836	22,856
D37	350 Colonnade cpe	3,845	3,790	33,166
D37	Grand Sport Colonnade cpe	3,937	3,904	
F35/45	wgn 4d 2S/3S	4,272*	4,205*	4,860*
H29	Luxus Colonnade sdn 4d	3,910	4,109	11,159
H57	Luxus Colonnade cpe	3,835	4,089	44,930
K35/45	Luxus wgn 4d 2S/3S	4,312*	4,371*	6,791*
J29	Regal Colonnade htp sdn	3,930	4,221	9,333
J57	Regal Colonnade htp cpe	3,900	4,201	57,512

LeSabre (wb 124.0)

		Wght	Price	Prod
N69	sdn 4d	4,337	4,355	18,572
N39	htp sdn	4,387	4,482	11,879
N57	htp cpe	4,297	4,424	12,522
P69	Luxus sdn 4d	4,352	4,466	16,039
P39	Luxus htp sdn	4,397	4,629	23,910
P57	Luxus htp cpe	4,307	4,575	27,243
P67	Luxus conv cpe	4,372	4,696	3,627

Estate Wagon (wb 127.0)

		Wght	Price	Prod
R35	wgn 4d 2S	5,082	5,019	4,581
R45	wgn 4d 3S	5,182	5,163	9,831

Electra 225 (wb 127.0)

		Wght	Price	Prod
T39	htp sdn	4,682	5,373	5,750
T37	htp cpe	4,607	5,260	3,339
V39	Custom htp sdn	4,702	5,550	29,089
V37	Custom htp cpe	4,627	5,438	15,099
X39	Limited htp sdn	4,732	5,921	30,051
X37	Limited htp cpe	4,682	5,886	16,086

Riviera (wb 122.0)

		Wght	Price	Prod
Y87	htp cpe	4,572	5,678	20,129

1974 Engines	bore×stroke	bhp	availability
L6, 250.0	3.87×3.50	100	S-Apollo
V8, 350.0	3.88×3.53	150	S-Ap,Cnty,LeS
V8, 350.0	3.88×3.53	175	O-Ap,Cnty,LeS
V8, 455.0	4.31×3.90	175	O-Cnty,EWgn
V8, 455.0	4.31×3.90	210	S-EWgn,Elec,Riv; O-Cnty
V8, 455.0	4.31×3.90	245	O-EWgn,Elec,Riv,Cnty

*figures for 2S wgns shown; for 3S wgns add approx. 30 lbs and $125. Production combined.

1975

Skyhawk (wb 97.0)

		Wght	Price	Prod
S07	htchbk cpe 3d	2,891	4,173	29,448
T07	S htchbk cpe 3d	2,851	3,860	

Apollo/Skylark (wb 111.0)*

		Wght	Price	Prod
B69	Apollo sdn 4d L6	3,438	3,436	21,138
W27	Skylark "S" cpe V6	3,405	3,234	27,689
B27	Skylark cpe V6	3,438	3,463	
B17	Skylark htchbk sdn 3d V6	3,512	3,586	6,814
C69	Apollo S/R sdn 4d L6	3,478	4,092	2,241
C27	Skylark S/R cpe V6	3,404	4,136	3,746
C17	Skylark S/R htchbk V6	3,514	4,253	1,505

Century (wb 116.0; 2d 112.0)*

		Wght	Price	Prod
D37	Colonnade cpe	3,762	3,894	39,556
E37	Special Colonnade cpe V6	3,613	3,815	
D29	Colonnade sdn 4d	3,818	3,944	22,075
F35	wgn 4d 2S V8	4,320	4,636	4,416
F45	wgn 4d 3S V8	4,370	4,751	
H29	Custom Colonnade sdn 4d	3,851	4,211	9,995
H57	Custom Colonnade cpe	3,759	4,154	32,966
K35	Custom wgn 4d 2S	4,350	4,802	7,078
K45	Custom wgn 4d 3S	4,400	4,917	

Regal (wb 116.0; 2d 112.0)*

		Wght	Price	Prod
J29	Colonnade sdn 4d V6	3,888	4,311	10,726
J57	Colonnade cpe V6	3,821	4,257	56,646

LeSabre (wb 123.5)

		Wght	Price	Prod
N69	sdn 4d	4,355	4,771	14,088
N39	htp sdn	4,411	4,898	9,119
N57	htp cpe	4,294	4,840	8,647
P69	Custom sdn 4d	4,388	4,934	17,026
P39	Custom htp sdn	4,439	5,061	30,005
P57	Custom htp cpe	4,316	5,007	25,016
P67	Custom conv cpe	4,392	5,133	5,300

Estate Wagon (wb 127.0)

		Wght	Price	Prod
R35	wgn 4d 2S	5,055	5,447	4,128
R45	wgn 4d 3S	5,135	5,591	9,612

Electra 225 (wb 127.0)

		Wght	Price	Prod
V39	Custom htp sdn	4,706	6,201	27,357
V37	Custom htp cpe	4,582	6,041	16,145
X39	Limited htp sdn	4,762	6,516	33,778
X37	Limited htep cpe	4,633	6,352	17,750

Riviera (wb 122.0)

		Wght	Price	Prod
Z87	htp cpe	4,539	6,420	17,306

1975 Engines	bore×stroke	bhp	availability
V6, 231.0	3.80×3.40	110	S-Skh,Skl,Cnty,Rgl
L6, 250.0	3.87×3.50	105	S-Apollo
V8, 260.0	3.50×3.39	110	S-Apollo,Skylark
V8, 350.0	3.88×3.53	145	S-Cnty exe wgns
V8, 350.0	3.88×3.53	165	S-Cnty wgns,Les; O-Cnty, Rgl
V8, 400.0	4.12×3.75	185	S-LeSabre (Cal.)
V8, 455.0	4.31×3.90	205	S-EWgn,Elec,Riv; O-LeS

*Six & V8 weights averaged. Prices for sixes shown; for V8s add approx. $80 to L6 or $20-30 to V6 models.

1976

Skyhawk (wb 97.0)

		Wght	Price	Prod
S07	htchbk cpe 3d	2,889	4,216	15,768
T07	S htchbk cpe 3d	2,857	3,903	

Skylark (wb 111.0)*

		Wght	Price	Prod
W27	S cpe	3,416	3,435	51,260
B27	cpe	3,426	3,549	
B69	sdn 4d	3,384	3,609	48,157
B17	htchbk cpe 3d	3,494	3,687	6,703
C69	S/R sdn 4d	3,406	4,324	3,243
C27	S/R cpe	3,410	4,281	3,880
C17	S/R htchbk cpe 3d	3,430	4,398	1,248

Buick

Century (wb 116.0; 2d 112.0)

D37	Colonnade cpe	3,748	4,070	⎤ 59,448
E37	Special Colonnade cpe V6	3,508	3,935	⎦
D29	Colonnade sdn 4d	3,567	4,105	33,632
H29	Custom Colonnade sdn 4d	3,817	4,424	19,728
H57	Custom Colonnade cpe	3,705	4,346	34,036
K35	Custom wgn 4d 2S V8	4,363	4,987	⎤ 16,625
K45	Custom wgn 4d 3S V8	4,413	5,099	⎦

Regal (wb 116.0; 2d 112.0)

J29	Colonnade sdn 4d V8	4,104	4,825	17,118
J57	Colonnade cpe V6	3,866	4,465	124,498

LeSabre (wb 124.0)

N69	sdn 4d V6	4,170	4,747	4,315
N39	htp sdn V6	4,059	4,871	2,312
N57	htp cpe V6	4,129	4,815	3,861
P69	Custom sdn 4d V8	4,328	5,046	34,841
P39	Custom htp sdn V8	4,386	5,166	46,109
P57	Custom htp cpe V8	4,275	5,144	45,669

Estate Wagon (wb 127.0)

R35	wgn 4d 2S	5,013	5,591	5,990
R45	wgn 4d 3S	5,139	5,731	14,384

Electra 225 (wb 127.0)

V39	htp sdn	4,641	6,527	26,655
V37	htp cpe	4,502	6,367	18,442
X39	Limited htp sdn	4,709	6,852	51,067
X37	Limited htp cpe	4,521	6,689	28,395

Riviera (wb 122.0)

Z87	htp cpe	4,531	6,798	20,082

1976 Engines	bore×stroke	bhp	availability
V6, 231.0	3.80×3.40	110	S-Skh,Skl,Cnty,Rgl,LeS
V8, 260.0	3.50×3.39	110	S-Skylark
V8, 350.0	3.88×3.53	145	S-Rgl,Cnty exc wgn; O-Skl
V8, 350.0	3.88×3.53	165	S-Cnty wgn,LeS Cus; O-Skl,Cnty,Rgl
V8, 455.0	4.31×3.90	205	S-EWgn,Elec,Riv; O-LeS Cus

1977

Skyhawk (wb 97.0)

		Wght	Price	Prod
S07	htchbk cpe 3d	2,817	4,294	⎤ 12,345
T07	S htchbk cpe 3d	2,805	3,981	⎦

Skylark (wb 111.0)*

W27	S cpe	3,286	3,642	⎤ 49,858
B27	cpe	3,286	3,765	⎦
B69	sdn 4d	3,324	3,825	48,121
B17	htchbk cpe 3d	3,408	3,942	5,316
C69	S/R sdn 4d	3,324	4,587	4,000
C27	S/R cpe	3,330	4,527	5,023
C17	S/R htchbk cpe	3,358	4,695	1,154

Century (wb 116.0; 2d 112.0)*

D37	cpe	3,582	4,304	⎤ 52,864
E37	Special cpe	3,590	4,170	⎦
D29	sdn 4d	3,754	4,364	29,065
H29	Custom sdn 4d	3,750	4,688	13,645
H57	Custom htp cpe	3,610	4,628	20,834
K35	Custom wgn 4d 2S V8	4,260	5,219	⎤ 19,282
K45	Custom wgn 4d 3S V8	4,310	5,271	⎦

Regal (wb 116.0; 2d 112.0)*

J29	sdn 4d V8	3,928	5,244	17,946
J57	cpe V6	3,612	4,713	174,560

LeSabre (wb 115.9)*

N69	sdn 4d	3,560	5,093	19,827
N37	cpe	3,522	5,033	8,455
P69	Custom sdn 4d	3,572	5,382	103,855
P37	Custom htp cpe	3,530	5,322	⎤ 58,589
F37	Custom htp cpe V8	3,634	5,819	⎦

Estate Wagon (115.9)

R35	wgn 4d 2S	4,015	5,903	⎤ 25,075
R45	wgn 4d 3S	4,141	6,078	⎦

Electra 225 (wb 119.0)

V69	sdn	3,814	6,866	25,633
V37	cpe	3,761	6,673	15,762
X69	Limited htp sdn	3,839	7,226	82,361
X37	Limited htp cpe	3,785	7,033	37,871

Riviera (wb 116.0)

Z37	htp cpe	3,784	7,385	26,138

1977 Engines	bore×stroke	bhp	availability
V6, 231.0	3.80×3.40	105	S-Skh,Skl,Cnty,Regl,LeS
V8, 301.0	4.00×3.00	135	S-Skl,LeS
V8, 305.0	3.74×3.48	145	O-Skl,Cnty wgn
V8, 350.0	3.88×3.53	140	S-Cnty exc wgn,Rgl; O-Skl
V8, 350.0	3.88×3.53	155	S-Cnty wagon,Elec,Riv; O-Skl,Cnty,Rgl
V8, 350.0	3.88×3.53	170	S-EWgn; O-Les,Elec,Riv
V8, 403.0	4.35×3.38	185	O-Cnty,LeS,E,Elec,Riv

*Six & V8 weights averaged. Prices for sixes shown; for V8s add $150

1978

Skyhawk (wb 97.0)

		Wght	Price	Prod
S07	htchbk cpe 3d	2,707	4,414	⎤ 24,589
T07	S htchbk cpe 3d	2,678	4,146	⎦

Skylark (wb 111.0)*

W27	S cpe	3,285	3,911	⎤ 42,087
B27	cpe	3,287	4,035	⎦
B69	sdn 4d	3,318	4,120	40,951
B17	htchbk cpe 3d	3,397	4,217	2,642
C69	Custom sdn 4d	3,303	4,367	14,523
C27	Custom cpe	3,270	4,282	12,740
C17	Custom htchbk cpe 3d	3,369	4,464	1,277

Century (wb 108.1)*

E09	Special sdn 4d	3,087	4,520	12,533
E87	Special sdn 2d	3,096	4,413	10,818
E37	Special wgn 4d 2S	3,231	5,021	9,586
H09	Custom sdn 4d	3,111	4,768	18,361
H87	Custom sdn 2d	3,084	4,658	12,434
H35	Custom wgn 4d 2S	3,265	5,233	20,014
G87	Sport Coupe sdn 2d	3,124	5,051	NA
L09	Limited sdn 4d	3,148	5,127	NA
L87	Limited sdn 2d	3,171	4,017	NA

Regal (wb 108.1)*

J47	cpe	3,065	4,885	236,652
M47	Limited cpe	3,114	5,268	NA
K47	Sport Coupe turbo V6	3,153	5,958	NA

LeSabre (wb 115.9)*

N69	sdn 4d	3,522	5,536	23,354
N37	cpe	3,531	5,451	8,265
P69	Custom sdn 4d	3,534	6,045	86,638
P37	Custom cpe	3,496	5,727	53,675
F37	Sport Coupe turbo V6	3,559	6,346	NA

Estate Wagon (wb 115.9)

R35	wgn 4d 2S V8	4,063	6,394	25,964

Electra 225 (wb 119.0)

V69	sdn 4d	3,730	7,431	14,590
V37	cpe	3,682	7,252	8,259
X69	Limited sdn 4d	3,757	7,817	65,335
X37	Limited cpe	3,710	7,638	33,365
U69	Park Avenue sdn 4d	3,777	8,208	NA
U37	Park Avenue cpe	3,730	7,952	NA

Riviera (wb 116.0)

			Wght	Price	Prod
Z37	cpe		3,701	9,224	20,535

1978 Engines

Engines	bore×stroke	bhp	availability
V6, 196.0	3.50×3.40	90	S-Cnty exc wgn, Rgl exc S/C
V6, 231.0	3.80×3.40	105	S-Skh, Skl, Cnty wgn, LeS; O-Rgl exc S/C
V6T, 231.0	3.80×3.40	150	S-Rgl & LeS S/Cs; O-Rgl
V6T, 231.0	3.80×3.40	165	O-Rgl & LeS S/Cs
V8, 301.0	4.00×3.00	165	S-LeS exc wgn
V8, 305.0	3.74×3.48	145	S-Skl, Cnty wgn, Rgl exc S/C, O-Cnty
V8, 305.0	3.74×3.48	160	O-Cnty, Rgl exc S/C
V8, 350.0	3.88×3.53	155	S-EWgn, Elec, Riv O-LeS
V8, 350.0	3.88×3.53	170	O-Skl, Cnty
V8, 403.0	4.35×3.38	185	O-LeS, Elec, Riv

*Six & V8 weights averaged. Prices for sixes shown; for V8s add $175.

1979

Skyhawk (wb 97.0)

		Wght	Price	Prod
S07	htchbk cpe 3d	2,740	4,778	⎤ 23,139
T07	S htchbk cpe 3d	2,724	4,560	⎦

Skylark (wb 111.0)

		Wght	Price	Prod
W27	S cpe	3,164	4,082	⎤ 10,201
B27	cpe	3,174	4,208	⎦
B69	sdn 4d	3,218	4,308	10,849
B17	htchbk cpe 3d	3,254	4,357	608
C69	Custom sdn 4d	3,226	4,562	3,822
C27	Custom cpe	3,182	4,462	3,526

Century (wb 108.1)

		Wght	Price	Prod
E09	Special sdn 4d	3,105	5,021	7,363
E87	Special sdn 2d	3,090	4,921	4,805
E35	Special wgn 4d 2S	3,222	5,492	10,413
H09	Custom sdn 4d	3,123	5,290	9,681
H87	Custom sdn 2d	3,103	5,165	2,474
H37	Custom wgn 4d 2S	3,258	5,806	21,100
G87	Sport Coupe sdn 2d	3,099	5,473	NA
L09	Limited sdn 4d	3,156	5,658	NA

Regal (wb 108.1)

		Wght	Price	Prod
J47	cpe	3,081	5,407	273,365
M47	Limited cpe	3,123	5,814	NA
K47	Sport Coupe turbo V6	3,190	6,497	NA

LeSabre (wb 115.9)

		Wght	Price	Prod
N69	sdn 4d	3,523	6,110	25,431
N37	cpe	3,492	6,010	7,542
P69	Limited sdn 4d	3,567	6,620	75,939
P37	Limited cpe	3,518	6,495	41,872
F37	Sport Coupe turbo V6	3,545	6,953	NA

Estate Wagon (wb 115.9)

		Wght	Price	Prod
R35	wgn 4d 2S V8	4,021	7,169	21,312

Electra 225 (wb 119.0)

		Wght	Price	Prod
V69	sdn 4d	3,831	8,878	11,055
V37	cpe	3,767	8,703	5,358
X69	Limited sdn 4d	3,853	9,278	76,340
X37	Limited cpe	3,789	9,103	28,878
U69	Park Avenue sdn 4d	3,860	9,959	NA
U37	Park Avenue cpe	3,794	9,784	NA

Riviera (wb 114.0)

		Wght	Price	Prod
Z57	cpe V8	3,759	10,684	⎤ 52,181
Y57	S-Type cpe	3,774	10,960	⎦

1979 Engines

Engines	bore×stroke	bhp	availability
V6, 196.0	3.50.×3.40	105	S-Cnty exc wgn, Rgl exc S/C
V6, 231.0	3.80×3.40	115	S-Skh, Skl, Cnty wgn, LeS; O-Cnty, Rgl
V6T, 231.0	3.80×3.40	175	S-Riv S; O-Cnty/Rgl/LeS Spt
V8, 301.0	4.00×3.00	140	S-Cnty, Rgl, LeS
V8, 301.0	4.00×3.00	150	O-Cnty, Rgl
V8, 305.0	3.74×3.48	130	S-Skl
V8, 305.0	3.74×3.48	155	S-EWgn, Elec, Riv; O-Cnty, Rgl, LeS, Riv S
V8, 350.0	3.88×3.53	170	O-Skl, Cnty, EW, Elec, Riv S
V8, 403.0	4.35×3.38	185	O-EWgn, Elec

1980

Skyhawk (wb 97.0)

		Wght	Price	Prod
S07	htchbk cpe 3d	2,754	5,211	⎤ 8,322
T07	S htchbk cpe 3d	2,754	4,993	⎦

Skylark (wb 111.0)*

		Wght	Price	Prod
B69	sdn 4d	2,458	5,488	80,940
B37	sdn 2d	2,430	5,342	55,114
C69	Limited sdn 4d	2,498	5,912	86,948
C37	Limited sdn 2d	2,458	5,765	42,652
D69	Sport Sedan 4d	2,490	6,102	—
D37	Sport Coupe 2d L4/V6	2,450	5,955	—

Century (wb 108.1)**

		Wght	Price	Prod
H69	sdn 4d	3,158	5,858	129,740
L69	Limited sdn 4d	3,202	6,344	—
H87	sdn 2d	3,138	5,758	1,074
G87	Sport Coupe sdn 2d	3,202	6,275	—
H35	Estate wgn 4d 2S	3,311	6,432	11,122
E35	wgn 4d 2S	3,300	6,134	6,493

Regal (wb 108.1)**

		Wght	Price	Prod
J47	cpe 2d	3,179	6,506	⎤
M47	Limited cpe 2d	3,282	6,925	⎬ 214,735
K47	Sport Coupe turbo V6 2d	3,194	7,203	⎦

LeSabre (wb 115.9)**

		Wght	Price	Prod
N69	sdn 4d	3,433	6,940	23,873
N37	cpe 2d	3,380	6,845	8,342
P69	Limited sdn 4d	3,439	7,242	37,676
P37	Limited cpe 2d	3,391	7,100	20,561
F37	Sport Coupe turbo V6	3,430	8,003	—
R35	wgn 4d 2S V8	3,898	7,844	⎤ 9,318
R35	wgn 4d 3S V8	3,928	8,037	⎦

Electra 225 (wb 119.0; wgns 115.9)**

		Wght	Price	Prod
X69	Limited sdn 4d	3,670	9,580	54,422
W69	Park Avenue sdn 4d	3,670	10,676	—
X37	Limited cpe 2d	3,664	9,425	14,058
W37	Park Avenue cpe 2d	3,692	10,537	—
V35	Estate wgn 4d 2S V8	4,105	10,806	—
V35	Estate wgn 4d 3S V8	4,135	10,999	—

Riviera (wb 114.0)

		Wght	Price	Prod
Z57	cpe V8	3,633	11,640	⎤ 48,621
Y57	S-Type cpe	3,734	12,151	⎦

1980 Engines

Engines	bore×stroke	bhp	availability
L4, 151.0	4.00×3.00	90	S-Skyhawk
V6, 173.0	3.50×3.00	115	S-Skylark
V6, 231.0	3.80×3.40	110	S-Skl, Cnty, Rgl, LeS
V6T, 231.0	3.80×3.40	170	S-Rgl S/C, LeS S/C; O-Cnty
V6T, 231.0	3.80×3.40	175	S-Cnty S/C
V6T, 231.0	3.80×3.40	185	S-Riv"S"; O-Riv
V6, 252.0	3.97×3.40	125	S-Elec; O-LeS
V8, 265.0	3.75×3.00	120	S-Cnty, Rgl
V8, 301.0	4.00×3.00	140	S-LeS, Elec wgn, EWgn, O-Cnty, Rgl
V8, 305.0	3.74×3.48	155	O-Cnty, Rgl
V8, 350.0	3.88×3.53	155	O-LeS, Elec, EWgn
V8, 350.0	3.88×3.53	160	S-Elec, Riv; O-LeS, Riv S, EWgn
V8D, 350.0	3.88×3.53	105	O-EWgn, Elec

*L4 & V6 weights averaged. Prices are for L4s; V6s add $225
**V6 & V8 weights averaged. Prices are for V6s; V8s add $105

Cadillac

Cadillac Motor Car Division, General Motors Corp. Detroit, Michigan

Cadillac was founded in late 1902 by Henry Martyn Leland, a brilliant engineer with prior experience at Ford and Oldsmobile. The first cars were single-cylinder models. The four-cylinder Cadillac 30 was introduced in 1909, and remained in production until 1915. During this period, Leland's emphasis on parts standardization came to the notice of the young auto industry. In England, three Cadillacs were disassembled, their components mixed up, and three complete cars reassembled from the pieces. This won Cadillac its first Dewar Trophy, and was the source of its slogan, "Standard of the World."

In 1909, Cadillac became part of the fledgling General Motors Corporation. In those days, it was an upper middle-priced car, not directly competitive with Packard and Pierce-Arrow, but always a high-quality item. The company's pioneer V8 engine of 1915 set new standards for smoothness, compactness, power, and reliability. Sales increased through the late Teens and '20s.

Regardless of its cars, Cadillac would have perished in the Depression had it been an independent. Including LaSalle (see entry), calendar year production reached an unprecedented 41,000 units in 1928, only to plunge after the 1929 stock market crash. Like other prestige producers, GM's finest found itself with superb cars that few wanted—or wanted to be seen in. Though many more people remained solvent in the Depression than is commonly thought, most preferred to drive around in Fords rather than flaunt any wealth they had preserved. Tellingly, events forced arch rival Packard to adopt valiant survival measures that would ultimately prove fatal. Protected by GM's vast size and enormous financial strength, Cadillac could continue to build ultra-luxurious cars selling only in small quantities without being affected much by the ailing national economy. But Packard, as an independent, had to change course or die. That firm would weather the storm with its middle-priced One-Twenty and One-Ten series, but in so doing it squandered its blue-chip image and thus began losing its traditional status-conscious clientele. So, even before World War II, Cadillac had overhauled Packard in the high-dollar market.

Perils of the Depression aside, Cadillac entered 1930 in splendid fashion. The new line leader that year was the magnificent Sixteen, powered by an overhead-valve, 452 cubic-inch engine producing 165 horsepower and 320 pounds-feet of torque. One of the greats in an era of great cars, it was theoretically available in 33 different models, sub-models or trim variations, ranging from the $5350 two-passenger roadster to the $8750 town cabriolet. Typically, the V16 could return about eight miles to a 15-cent gallon of gas, and 150 miles to a quart of oil, plus a 70-mph cruise and 90-mph top speed. But brute performance was not its forte. Rather, it was designed to please the luxury-car buyer of the age, offering smooth, effortless power that required a minimum of gearshifting. Cadillac described its performance as "a continuous flow. . .constantly at full-volume efficiency. . .flexible. . .instantly responsive."

The Sixteen was on the market only nine months when the division introduced another multi-cylinder giant, a 370-cid V12. This engine, basically the V16 with four fewer

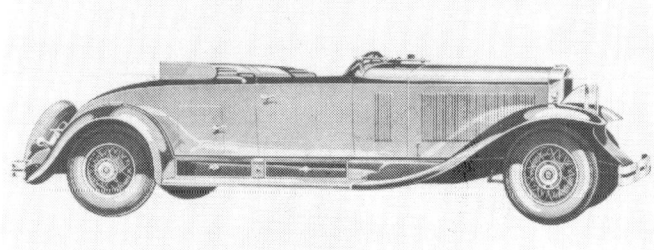

1930 Eight Fleetwood roadster

1931 Eight five-passenger phaeton

1932 Twelve Fleetwood Town Cabriolet

1932 Eight Fisher all-weather phaeton

1933 Eight Fleetwood seven-passenger sedan

1936 Series 75 Fleetwood Imperial sedan

1934 Eight Series 20 convertible coupe

1937 Series 70 Fleetwood convertible sedan

cylinders, developed 135 bhp and 285 lbs/ft torque. Bodies for the Twelve were not as large as on the Sixteens, the latter riding an enormous 148-inch wheelbase compared to the V12's 140-inch-wheelbase chassis, shared with the eight-cylinder models. Predictably, the Twelve was not as fast as the Sixteen, but its engine was free-revving and had a reputation for smooth, even power delivery. And it was considerably cheaper, available in 11 body style choices ranging from $3795 to $4985. A V12 roadster

could see about 85 mph maximum with standard rear axle ratio, and most models could cruise all day at 70 mph.

Despite their refined performance and majestic proportions, the multi-cylinder Cadillacs failed to sell strongly. The divison built 3250 Sixteens and 5725 Twelves for model years 1930-31, which would be the peak. Production was only fair for 1932, and annual output from 1933 on was never more than 300 and 1000 units, respectively. Both engines were dropped in 1938, but Cadillac had one

1935 Eight Series 10 coupe

1937 Series 65 five-passenger touring sedan

1936 Series 60 convertible coupe

1938 Series 60 Special four-door sedan

more try with an L-head V16. At 431 cid and 185 bhp, it was smaller and lighter yet more powerful than the earlier ohv powerplants, but only 508 cars were so equipped through 1940, its final year.

There were two reasons why these grand Cadillacs fared as they did. As noted, staggeringly expensive cars with more than eight cylinders seemed socially inappropriate to many people in the early '30s and, after an initial sales burst, these models were shunned by most customers in favor of the cheaper, less ostentatious, but by no means inferior, Cadillac Eights. Later the big engines were simply outmoded by advancing technology. The introduction of precision-insert connecting-rod bearings helped eliminate knock and high-speed wear in engines with fewer than 12 cylinders, so there was little reason for Cadillac buyers to choose a Twelve or Sixteen over an Eight.

Fortunately for Cadillac, its V8 line sold consistently and fairly well throughout the decade. Model year production hung around 10,000 units in 1930-31, then fell precipitously (to 2000-3000) in 1932-33, after which it recovered rapidly. With introduction of the low-priced Series 60 for 1936, the total again surged past 10,000 units, reaching over 13,000 by 1939. This creditable sales performance was due to the reliable cast-iron L-head engine, plus competitive prices and a wide range of body styles.

Cadillac's early-'30s V8 was based on a 341-cid unit introduced in 1928. Sized at 353 cid for 1930-35, it was rated at 90 to 130 bhp. A completely redesigned 346-cid L-head with 135 bhp replaced it for 1936. The Series 60 had a 322-cid engine that year, then adopted the 346. This respected powerplant would remain in production until Cadillac launched its new short-stroke ohv V8 for 1949. Though it had its limits, it was capable of excellent performance and reasonable economy. It could propel the lighter 1938-39 cars to nearly 100 mph and deliver 0-60 mph acceleration of 15-16 seconds—no mean feat for 4500-pound luxury liners in the years before the war.

Unlike its prestige rivals, Cadillac designed and built most of its bodies in-house, via Fisher and Fleetwood, and few chassis were sent to independent body builders. This enabled designer Harley Earl to maintain a consistent Cadillac look throughout the car instead of in just the radiator and hood. The marque's best styling undoubtedly came in 1930-31, distinguished by opulent, thick-collared vertical radiators announcing a beautifully rounded hood,

plus clean, flowing lines and a bewildering array of body styles. The 1930 Fisher line spanned seven models priced from $3300 to $4000. Fleetwood Custom offerings numbered no fewer than 14, with prices from $3450 to $5145. Perhaps the most elegant of all were several Madame X styles, identified by their slender, chrome-edged door and windshield moldings.

Square-rigged styling began to dissolve with the more rounded 1932 design, but the big switch from classic to streamlined forms came the following year. While the 1933 models retained the basic '32 body, Earl enhanced its appearance with such devices as skirted fenders, vee'd radiators, and less vertically angled windshields. A noteworthy innovation that year was front door vent wing windows, called "No-Draft Ventilation." These cars are prized by many today as the epitome of late Classic-era design.

Styling for 1934 was fully revised, previewed by an exotic show car seen at the 1933 Chicago's World's Fair. Earl now moved away completely from upright forms and into the realm of pontoon fenders, sloped radiators, bullet-style headlights, and rakish rear decks. He also conjured up novel two-piece front and rear bumpers likely inspired by the biplane configuration, but they were as unpopular as they were clumsy and were abandoned after only one season. The 1935-36 models were relatively dumpy by comparison, with roundness prevailing over squareness throughout; even the door windows were potato-shaped.

Everything changed again for 1938, when young William L. Mitchell, an Earl protegé, drew up the Sixty Special as an addition to the Series 60. Successfully introduced two years earlier, this line also included three regular models priced about $600 less than their least-expensive predecessors. Mitchell's new sedan was very square yet crisply elegant, distinguished by chrome-edged side windows and flat-backed pontoon fenders, and was quite compact for a Cadillac. Today, the Sixty Special is considered one of the most beautiful cars of all time.

Cadillac promoted its wide variety of Eights for 1939 and scored a gain of 10,000 units over the previous year's output. Though there was only a mild facelift and the 346 engine was unchanged, the division now blanketed the luxury market. The new 126-inch-wheelbase Series 61 offered four models priced from $1610 to $2170, while the Sixty Special returned as a distinct series on its own 127-inch wheelbase and priced from $2090. The Series

1938 Series 75 Fleetwood convertible coupe

1939 Series 60 Special four-door sedan

1939 Series 75 Fleetwood two-passenger coupe

1940 Series 75 Fleetwood two-passenger coupe

1940 Series 72 Fleetwood five-passenger formal sedan

1940 Sixteen (Series 90) five-passenger town sedan

1940 Series 60 Special four-door sedan

1940 Series 62 convertible sedan

75 comprised the usual plethora of Fleetwood bodies on a long 141-inch chassis; prices ranged from $2995 to $5115.

The 1930s were years of great technological progress at Cadillac. The division had introduced clashless Syncro-Mesh transmission in 1929, and followed up for 1932 with "Triple-Silent" Syncro-Mesh, a reference to helical-cut gears for all three forward speeds. "No-Draft Ventilation" and vacuum-assisted brakes appeared for 1933; independent front suspension bowed for 1934; all-steel "Turret Top" construction made news for 1935; hydraulic brakes were offered on all models except Sixteens for 1936; the first of what would become Cadillac's traditional eggcrate grilles was seen for 1937; and column gearshift and optional turn signals were featured for 1938.

Some of Cadillac's most important engineering developments, as well as many of its most beautiful automobiles, made their debut in the '40s. The decade began with the last of the opulent V16s and no fewer than four variations of Bill Mitchell's brilliant 60 Special. Like Buick, Cadillac offered facelifted models in 1940 and '41, then brought out a completely restyled line for 1942. This put the division in a good position to resume civilian car production after World War II.

Most 1940 Cadillacs were relatively plain-looking—almost Chevrolet-like at the front end, with simple bar-type grilles. One exception was the V16 Series 90, which had an eggcrate grille that would inspire postwar styling. The V16 shared its 141-inch wheelbase (the longest for Cadillac up to that time) with the V8 Series

Cadillac

1941 Series 60 Special four-door sedan

1940 Series 75 Fleetwood convertible coupe

75. The V12 models had been discontinued earlier. Except for their engines, the Series 90 and 75 offered an identical lineup of two coupes, a convertible, a touring sedan with and without divider window, a trunkback convertible sedan, formal sedans for five or seven passengers, and a variety of seven-passenger sedans. The big difference was price. A basic Series 75 five-passenger sedan sold for $2995, while the same car in V16 guise cost $5140. The price spread was not really justified by the powerplant, for the Cadillac 346 cubic-inch V8 was one of the smoothest engines anywhere. V16 sales were therefore low, and 1940 proved the last year for this exotic engine.

One step down from the 90 and 75 was the Series 72, mounted on a 138-inch wheelbase. The 72 would also be making its last appearance that year. It offered slightly fewer models priced between $2670 and $3695. The 72 was an impressive and well-designed automobile, but its market was limited due to competition from the more luxurious 75. Even counting 75s, Cadillac produced only a little over 2500 long-wheelbase models. In later years, when the 75 was mainly a limousine line, production often neared 5000 units per year.

The crisp 60 Special, with its thin door and window pillars and squared-off roofline, was the first direct evidence of young Bill Mitchell's talent. Later, in 1958, Mitchell would relieve the legendary Harley Earl as GM

chief of styling; his rise to prominence is due directly to the success of this, his first production design.

The 60 Special came in many varieties for 1940. Both the town sedan and Imperial (division-window sedan) could be ordered with a sunroof; the town car was available with either painted metal or leather-covered rear roof. Only 15 town cars were built, however. The bulk of 60 Special production was the basic sedan, which accounted for 4472 units.

Least expensive of the 1940 Cadillacs was the 62, which came as a coupe, convertible, and convertible sedan or touring sedan, ranging in price from $1685 up to $2195. Mounted on a 129-inch wheelbase, the 62 accounted for the bulk of Cadillac sales, and was chiefly responsible for the division's success in 1940, as in later years. It was cleanly styled, lushly upholstered, and offered a broad variety of body styles designed to appeal to every buyer.

All Cadillacs except the Series 90 shared the 346-cid, 90-degree L-head V8 first seen in 1936. Using a unit block and cast-iron crankcase, it featured three main bearings with counterweights and dual downdraft carburetors. The 346 was heavy, but reliable and exceptionally smooth-running. It developed 135 horsepower for the 62 and 60 Special, and was tuned for 140 bhp on the 72 and 75.

The Cadillac V16 was also an L-head, but built on a narrow 135-degree angle. With 431 cid it delivered 185 bhp. Like the V8, it was made of cast iron and had dual carburetors. But it featured nine main bearings, and separate manifolding for each cylinder block. Each bank of cylinders also had its own water pump and distributor. It was a big, impressive engine, typical of motoring's classic age—but its best days were long past. Cadillac had not produced more than 300 V16s a year since 1931. After 1940, the V16 became dispensible.

A significant and attractive model change occurred for 1941. Cadillac's companion make, LaSalle, was replaced by the relatively low-priced Series 61. This was a marketing decision based on the success of Packard's contemporary One Ten/One Twenty and the Lincoln-Zephyr—but the 61 was every inch a Cadillac, and only moderately underpriced compared to the 62. Packard continued to build medium-priced models long after World War II, while Cadillac (and Lincoln) kept its cars

1941 Series 62 convertible sedan

1941 Series 62 convertible coupe

axle ratios were offered: the 3.77 and 4.27 were standard, while the 3.36 was for Hydra-Matic on the short-wheelbase models. Higher compression and more horsepower meant that most '41 Cadillacs could achieve a genuine 100 mph. Their 0–60 mph acceleration times averaged around 14 seconds—impressive performance 40 years ago.

The formula of V8s only and a broad price span helped Cadillac reach all-time record production for calendar 1941—66,130 units. This was only 6700 units short of Packard, which was selling a much higher proportion of lower-priced models. Much of the increase, of course, was due to the new 61. But the 62 line was also up dramatically—and Cadillac had added a Series 63 four-door that accounted for another 5000 sales. The outstanding 60 Special scored a healthy 4100 units, even though it was offered only as a sedan or division-window town car.

strictly in the luxury bracket. As a result, Packard's reputation as fine-car builder diminished in the '40s, and disappeared entirely in the '50s.

The 1941 models wore a fresh face—a complex egg-crate grille with the central section most prominent. This remained a Cadillac styling tradition into the 1970s. Taillights were also made more prominent, and one of them concealed the gas filler cap—another long-running feature. All '41s used the 346 V8, rated at 150 bhp. The departure of the V16 and Series 72 allowed the division to reduce the number of chassis, and only three wheelbases were used. The 75 rode a 136-inch wheelbase, the 67 a 138, and all other models a 126. Three

The 1942 lineup was similar in specification but had a brand-new look. Long pontoon fenders appeared, running back into the front doors. Matching rear fenders were blended into the rear doors on four-door models. Fastback styling, which had appeared on the 1941 Series 61, was now extended to the 62. Before production was curtailed by the war, Cadillac built 16,511 cars. In February 1942, the firm converted to war work and made tanks, aircraft engines, and munitions until V-J Day.

1942 Series 63 four-door sedan

1946 Series 62 four-door sedan

1942 Series 60 Special four-door sedan

1947 Series 62 convertible

Resuming civilian operations took several months after the war ended. The division managed to build only 1000 Series 61 sedans before the end of that year. In all, just 31,944 of the 1946 models were made. These were only slightly changed in appearance from the 1942 versions, but model offerings were greatly reduced. The 63 and 67 series were eliminated, along with the division-window 60 Special. What remained were the fastback 61s, fastback or notchback 62s, 60 Special, and the 75. Hydra-Matic transmission had become optional in 1941. It remained optional through 1949 on all models.

For one more year, Cadillac continued to rely on its prewar styling, so the '47s were quite similar to the '46s. The main visual differences were round instead of rectangular parking lights, and script instead of block-letter fender nameplates. The 60 Special lacked the previous model's three vertical chrome louvers behind the rear side window; the 1947 Series 75 omitted the stainless-steel-trimmed running boards formerly used. Prices were $150 to $200 higher than in '46, mainly due to postwar inflation. Production had now regained its prewar stride, and nearly 60,000 units were built for the calendar year. In model year totals, the 62 carried most of the volume, with just under 40,000 units.

Then came 1948—the year of the tailfin. Cadillac designers Bill Mitchell, Harley Earl, Frank Hershey, and Art Ross had been inspired before the war by the then-secret P-38 Lockheed Lightning pursuit fighter. During the war, a skeleton crew played with ideas for postwar styling that would incorporate the plane's features—pontoon front fenders, pointed noses, cockpit-like curved windshields, and tailfins.

Besides Cadillac's tailfin, the P-38 influence would be seen at other GM divisions. Oldsmobile, for example, adopted an engine-scoop motif for the headlamp bezels of its "Futuramic" 1949 models. But the fin had the most lasting impact on Cadillac styling. Said Bill Mitchell: "From a design standpoint the fins gave definition to the rear of the car for the first time. They made the back end as interesting as the front, and established a longstanding Cadillac styling hallmark."

On the 1948 Cadillac, the tailfin was the finishing touch on a magnificent overall design package. At the front, the traditional grille shape was retained, made more aggressive by a larger eggcrate pattern and a more shapely hood. The lines of the roof and fenders were clean, curvaceous, and beautiful from every angle. Attention was given to the interior as well: the 1948 dashboard was dominated by a huge, ornate drum-type housing for the speedometer, minor gauges, and controls. This lasted only a year, because it was complicated and costly to produce. For 1949, it was replaced by a simplified dash duplicating the grille shape, a design followed closely for the next eight years.

Cadillac stayed with the '47 model and body style lineup for 1948, but there was a new addition the next year: the Coupe deVille. A $3497 entry in the 62 series, it joined Oldsmobile's Holiday and Buick's Riviera as

1948 Series 62 convertible

1948 Series 62 club coupe (sedanet)

1948 Fleetwood Series 60 Special four-door sedan (prototype)

1948 Fleetwood Series 75 seven-passenger imperial sedan

the first production hardtops. Cadillac sold 2150 of them in 1949—a higher percentage of production than either Holiday or Riviera. The idea was to combine the airiness of a convertible with the snugness of a closed car—and it succeeded admirably. It started a trend that, by the late '50s, would dominate industry body styles. (There was also one 60 Special Coupe deVille built on the 133-inch wheelbase strictly as an experimental model.)

Following Cadillac's styling revolution of 1948, the

exciting overhead-valve V8 of 1949 was the second punch in a potent one-two combination delivered directly to Packard, Lincoln, and Chrysler Imperial. Designed by Ed Cole, Jack Gordon, and Harry Barr, it was the product of ten years' concentrated research and experimentation. The goals had been to reduce weight and increase compression to take advantage of the higher-octane fuels promised after the war. This dictated the valve arrangement, a stroke shorter than the bore, wedge-shaped combustion chambers, and "slipper" pistons. The latter, developed by Byron Ellis, traveled low between the crankshaft counterweights, allowing for short connecting rods and low reciprocating weight.

The new V8 displaced 331 cid and developed 160 bhp. Although this was a mere 10 percent numerical increase over the old L-head engine, there were other factors in the ohv's favor. Though built of cast iron, it weighed nearly 200 pounds less than its predecessor. Compression ratio was just 7.5:1, yet it was capable of being pushed to as high as 12:1 should the fuel become available. It produced more torque and delivered 14 percent better fuel economy. It was durable and reliable. And it could be bored and stroked to much larger displacements. The relatively light 62 model with this powerplant could clock 0–60 mph times of around 13 seconds and easily top 100 mph.

Driven by Sam and Miles Collier, a 1950 Cadillac finished 10th overall at Le Mans—a performance unmatched by any other luxury make. Its speed down the Mulsanne Straight was around 120 mph; average speed was 81.5 mph. Briggs Cunningham also raced a Cadillac at Le Mans that year—a streamlined special. He was even faster than the Colliers, but lost top gear and slid in some corners, resulting in an 11th-place finish.

Another enthusiastic Cadillac booster was Edward Gaylord of Chicago, amateur racer, later co-designer of the Gaylord automobile. "I owned one of the 1950 61s with stickshift and 3.77 rear axle ratio," Gaylord said, "along with a new Jaguar XK-120. The Cadillac was the faster car up to about 90 mph. My Cadillac set what was then a stock-car record at the original quarter-mile drag races in Santa Ana, California . . . The only competition I had in acceleration was from the small 135-horsepower Olds 88 coupe, but the Cadillac engine was substantially more efficient both in performance and economy."

The best styling in the industry and the new V8 put Cadillac firmly atop the luxury-car field. So well did the V8 meet its needs that Cadillac retained the 331-cid size through 1955. But the V8 gained over 100 horsepower in the 1949-55 period—ultimately reaching 270 bhp in the '55 Eldorado.

The good styling didn't last. The most unfortunate aspect to '50s Cadillacs was the gradual decline from smooth design to chrome-laden glitter. The trend peaked in 1958-59; a return to more conservative architecture began in the 1960s. But the Earl/Mitch-

1948 Series 61 four-door sedan

1949 Series 61 club coupe (sedanet)

1949 Series 62 Coupe deVille hardtop coupe

1950 Series 61 four-door sedan

1950 Fleetwood Series 60 Special four-door sedan

Cadillac

1951 Series 62 Coupe deVille hardtop coupe

1952 Series 62 convertible

1951 Series 62 convertible

1952 Series 62 four-door sedan

1951 Fleetwood Series 60 Special four-door sedan

1953 Series 62 convertible

ell/Hershey/Ross styling of 1948 was so good that not much facelifting was needed to keep it fresh. As Mitchell said, "a traditional look is always preserved. If a grille is changed, the tail end is left alone; if a fin is changed, the grille is not monkeyed with."

Through 1953, styling changes were fairly minor: a new grille and a one-piece windshield in 1950, small auxiliary grilles under the headlamps in 1951, a winged badge in that spot for 1952, "Dagmar" bumpers and a one-piece rear window in 1953.

The model lineup didn't change much either. The 62 series, accounting for most sales, comprised a four-door sedan, coupe, Coupe deVille (hardtop) and convertible; the 60 Special was a sedan with its own 130-inch wheelbase (down from 133 in 1949); the 75 limousine and sedan rode a wheelbase of 146.8 inches. The latter were updated for the first time in 1950; during 1948-49 the smaller Cadillacs had new styling, but the

75 retained prewar lines. Low production precluded early amortization of the prewar dies.

The Cadillac 61, on a short 122-inch wheelbase, was available in 1950-51 in sedan or sedanet (coupe) form. Manual shift was standard and the 61 was priced $575 less than the 62. But by 1952, the division no longer needed a price leader—sales of the "standard" model 62 were more than adequate. The 61 was accordingly dropped, never to appear again.

A feature at General Motors in 1953 was the ultra-expensive, Motorama-inspired limited edition: Buick's Skylark, Oldsmobile's Fiesta, and Cadillac's Eldorado. Only 532 of the latter were built, largely because each one sold for a towering $7750. Like Buick's Skylark, the Eldorado featured a custom interior and special cut-down panoramic windshield. A metal lid covered the top when lowered. It was indeed a striking car, and it prefigured many styling features of the near future.

Model year 1954 saw a major restyle—longer, lower, and wider cars with more power. Wheelbases were lengthened throughout the line, even on the Series 75. Power output on the V8 was up to 230 bhp. Cadillac reduced the price of an Eldorado to $4738 and made more of them—2150 units. Sales doubled for 1956, when the Eldorado line doubled to include the Seville coupe and Biarritz convertible, each priced at $6556. From 1955 onwards, Eldorados were distinctively styled with sharply pointed fins above round taillights. The rest of the line continued to use the small taillight-and-fin design that had become a Cadillac tradition.

Division sales had topped 100,000 cars for the first time in 1950, and continued to improve through the middle years of the decade. In 1955, Cadillac sold 140,777 units, the highest ever. Even this was only a temporary plateau. Production would break 200,000 in the '60s, and 223,000 by 1969. Despite momentary challenges—a revitalized Imperial in 1957, a crisp new Lincoln Continental in 1961—Cadillac was never really threatened as the standard of the luxury-car world. Neither Lincoln nor Imperial ever built more than 40,000

1953 Fleetwood Series 60 Special four-door sedan

1954 Series 62 convertible

1953 Series 62 Eldorado convertible

1955 Series 62 Eldorado convertible

1954 Fleetwood Series 75 eight-passenger sedan

1955 Series 62 Coupe deVille hardtop coupe

1954 Fleetwood Series 60 Special four-door sedan

1956 Series 62 Sedan deVille hardtop sedan

1956 Series 62 Eldorado Seville hardtop coupe

1956 Series 62 four-door sedan

1957 Series 62 Eldorado Biarritz convertible

1957 Fleetwood Series 60 Special hardtop sedan

1957 Series 62 Eldorado Seville hardtop coupe

1957 Eldorado Brougham hardtop sedan

1957 Fleetwood Series 75 nine-passenger limousine

1958 Fleetwood Series 60 Special hardtop sedan

cars in one year; at Cadillac, that would be considered a good quarterly output.

The line was restyled again for 1957, this time inspired by the Eldorado Brougham and Park Avenue show cars. The production 1957 Eldorado Brougham sold for a princely $13,074. One of Cadillac's most interesting cars, it had descended from the Orleans, Park Avenue, and Brougham showmobiles of 1953-55. It was a pillarless sedan with center-opening doors and a brushed stainless-steel roof—the latter one of Harley Earl's favorite touches. The Brougham also featured quad headlights—a first for the industry, shared with Nash and Lincoln that year.

Mechanically, the Brougham's most unique feature was its air suspension, designed by engineers Lester Milliken and Fred Cowin. Based on systems used for commercial vehicles since 1952, it employed an air "spring" at each wheel. The spring consisted of a dome air chamber, rubber diaphragm, and pistons. The domes were fed by a central air compressor, and were continually adjusted for load and road conditions by valves and solenoids. These devices kept the

Brougham level and smoothed its ride. The system differed from those offered optionally by other GM divisions because it was an open arrangement: it took in air from the outside.

But the cost and complexity of air suspension proved too high in relation to its benefits. The air domes leaked, and dealer replacements were frequent. In many Broughams the system was simply rooted out in favor of conventional coil springs. Four years later, air suspension was dropped.

The Brougham itself, after two years of production totaling 704 units, was completely restyled and final assembly farmed out to Pininfarina in Italy. Only 99 were built in 1959, 101 in 1960.

Styling for 1958 was typical of GM that year, and among the most garish ever seen. The cars were big, heavy, laden with brightwork, and far less memorable than, say, the 1953 Eldorado or the Eldorado Brougham. Sales were poor, due probably to the nationwide recession rather than the styling, which was, after all, in vogue. Production, at 121,778 units, was lower than it had been since 1954. The DeVille became a 62 sub-series, pillar sedans were temporarily

eliminated, and the 62 line was expanded by a special four-door with an extended deck.

Cadillac's durable V8, which had been bored out to 365 cid for 1956, was developing 310 bhp by 1958. All models that year were available with cruise control, high-pressure cooling system, two-speaker radio with automatic signal-seeking, and automatic parking brake release. There was even a special show Eldorado with a "thinking" convertible top that raised itself and the side windows when a sensor spotted raindrops.

The restyling for 1959 resulted in tailfins of near-ridiculous proportions, but there were some suspension improvements, a new 390-cid engine, and better power steering. The lineup included convertibles, hardtop two-doors, and four- and six-window hardtop sedans. This was the last year for the old 75 chassis, which was updated in 1960. Prices were generally higher than before, with 62s at around $5000 and Eldorados going for $7400 and up. But Cadillac built 138,000 cars for calender 1959, a fair improvement on its 1958 showing.

The line was facelifted for 1960, with a more restrained look than the chrome-laden '59. The grille was

1958 Series 62 Eldorado Seville hardtop coupe

Cadillac's futuristic Cyclone "dream car" from 1959

1959 Eldorado Brougham hardtop sedan (by Pininfarina)

1959 Series 62 hardtop coupe

1959 Series 62 six-window hardtop sedan

1959 Eldorado Biarritz convertible

1960 Fleetwood Series 60 Special hardtop sedan

1960 Eldorado Brougham hardtop sedan (by Pininfarina)

1961 Fleetwood Series 60 Special hardtop sedan

1961 Series 62 hardtop coupe

1962 six-window Sedan deVille hardtop sedan

1963 four-window Sedan deVille hardtop sedan

cleaner and the tailfins were reduced in height. A carry-over feature was a choice of rooflines on hardtop sedans in the 62 and DeVille series. Prices throughout the line were not changed from the year before. Nor were there any changes in mechanical specifications. The standard horsepower rating was still 325; the Eldorado offered 345. Cadillac had dropped to 10th place in production in 1958, but stayed 10th again in 1960. It would continue to hold 10th place—an impressive position for a luxury make—until 1965. Model year 1960 was the last for the limited-edition Eldorado Brougham. Management was already working on a successor that would sell in higher numbers and would, therefore, be more profitable.

In 1961, styling began showing the influence of William Mitchell, who favored a more chiseled look than Harley Earl and was not terribly enamored of chrome. The '61s were cleaner than any Cadillac had been in years. The grille was reduced in size to a modest grid between the headlights. The wraparound windshield was abandoned (except for the Series 75), yet Mitchell contrived to improve visibility. The model range also thinned: the Eldorado Seville was dropped

along with the Brougham. The sole remaining Eldorado was the Biarritz convertible, but the '61 edition used the standard 325-bhp engine.

At General Motors, the early '60s was a period of little styling change: the corporation had found what it wanted and was holding on to it. Predictably, Cadillac changed little for '62. Tailfins were lowered, and cornering lights were added to the front fender. Detail trim changes included a slightly flashier grille and a thin bright metal molding low on the bodysides. The roofline was squared off on some models; backup, turn, and stop lights were combined in panels that showed white in the daylight. New models were the 62 Town Sedan and the DeVille Park Avenue, a pair of short-deck four-door hardtops. The engine remained unchanged, but a new dual braking system appeared with separate front and rear hydraulic lines. Cadillac produced about 160,000 cars, some 23,000 more than the previous year.

The long-running V8 was revised for 1963 for the first time in 14 years. Displacement, bore, and stroke were unchanged, as were valves, rocker arms, cylinder heads, and connecting rods. But everything else was

different. The new block was stiffer, but 50 pounds lighter, than its predecessor. There was a lighter, stronger crankshaft. Accessory mounting points were relocated for improved accessibility. The reworked engine added little to Cadillac's already top-class performance, but it was smoother and quieter by far. And performance was already of a high order. The 1963 models would reach 115–120 mph, do 0 to 60 mph in 10 seconds and 0 to 80 mph in 16 seconds, and return about 14 miles per gallon. Most impressive was their near-silence at high speed—many testers held them superior to Rolls-Royce in this respect.

The 1963 model was, generally, a departure from recent styling traditions. The fins were still there, but lower than ever; a bulkier full-width grille contained parking lights built into grille extensions under the headlamps. New body panels and side moldings created a more slab-sided look than past models. The rear

end was more massive, with elongated vertical taillight and backup light housings.

Prices rose only slightly in 1963, and Cadillac remained an excellent buy for the money. Standard equipment included Hydra-Matic, power steering, power brakes, heater, remote-control outside mirror, and backup lights. A six-way power seat became standard on Eldorado; power windows were standard on all models except 62 sedans and coupes. Even power vent windows were offered. The specifications included self-adjusting brakes, cornering lights, and turn signal indicators atop the front fenders. Remarkably, the 62 still cost as little as $5026. Even the Eldorado Biarritz was only $6608. Production topped 164,000 in calendar 1963.

Revisions were minor for '64. New, lower tailfins—the last true Cadillac fins—created an unbroken beltline, accentuating length. There was a body-color horizontal

1964 Fleetwood Eldorado Biarritz convertible

1965 Calais hardtop coupe

1964 Series 62 hardtop coupe

1965 Fleetwood Eldorado convertible

1964 Fleetwood Series 75 nine-passenger limousine

1965 Sedan deVille hardtop sedan

grille divider bar, and new taillamp housings with the usual assortment of red and white lights. Cadillac's new Comfort-Control heating/air-conditioning system maintained a set temperature regardless of outside conditions. It has been on the Cadillac options sheet ever since. Sales were around 165,000, slightly higher than 1963 and still good for 10th place in the industry.

Cadillac had a resounding year in 1965, producing close to 200,000 cars. But it was a banner year for the rest of the industry too, and even this output was only good for 11th place. The Series 62, which had been around since 1940, was finally put to rest; its place was taken by the Calais. DeVille, Eldorado, 60 Special, and 75 were continued. The last three comprised the Fleetwood series. Each bore Fleetwood nameplates, a wreath-and-crest medallion, broad bright rocker panel and rear quarter moldings, and rectangular pattern rear appliqués. A new Fleetwood Brougham offered a vinyl roof with "Brougham" script on the rear roof pillars.

The major styling change for 1965 was a longer, lower silhouette and the disappearance of tailfins. The 60 Special regained its customary 133-inch wheelbase, after using the standard 129.5-inch-wheelbase chassis from 1959. Rear styling consisted of a straight bumper and vertical lamp clusters. There was a new flush-top contour on the rear quarter panels, and curved-glass side windows. Horsepower was now up to 340 bhp, giving Cadillac the highest power-to-weight ratio in the industry. On all models except the 75 there was dual driving range Turbo Hydra-Matic and a perimeter-type frame. All Cadillacs featured a sonically balanced exhaust system. Prices were still remarkably stable. They'd risen only a few dollars since 1961.

In 1966, Cadillac had its first 200,000-car year. For the January–December period, 205,001 were assembled. The 1966 was a mild facelift of the '65 design, with new front bumper, new grille, and integrated vertical taillight housings. The perimeter frame was now adopted for the 75, which was fully restyled for the first time since 1959. Variable-ratio power steering, which provided maximum assist at low speed and minimum at cruising speed, was introduced for all models. Another new option was carbon-cloth seat heating pads. The Fleetwood Brougham moved up one step by adopting the 133-inch 60 Special wheelbase; it was more luxuriously trimmed, and priced about $320 higher.

Management changes occurred rapidly in 1965-66. Chief engineer Fred Arnold retired in 1965, after a long and rich career, succeeded by Carleton A. Rasmussen. The following year saw general manager Harold G. Warner retire in favor of Kenneth N. Scott. Scott was replaced six months later by Calvin J. Werner, who remained general manager until 1969. In July of that year, he was relieved by George R. Elges.

The new front-wheel-drive Eldorado of 1967 was the most significant single Cadillac model of the '60s. Based on the Oldsmobile Toronado, which had appeared the year before, it was a new concept in the luxury field. Front drive gave it outstanding roadability; Bill Mitchell gave it magnificent styling. In market orientation, it was the long-awaited replacement for the 1957-60 Eldorado Brougham. Six years of careful planning and research were behind it.

The Eldorado project began with a 1959 styling exercise code-named XP-727, which underwent several re-thinks during 1960-62. By early 1962, it was decided that front-wheel drive would be used, and prototypes developed with that consideration in mind. For awhile, Cadillac considered calling the new car LaSalle, but ultimately picked Eldorado, a more current name with greater public recognition. Clay model XP-825, with razor-edged lines and a formal roofline, was the direct predecessor of the production front-drive Eldorado.

Compared with the Toronado, the new Eldorado's 1967 introduction was, in typical Cadillac fashion, very low-key. Cadillac preferred it that way, and it used the extra lead time to make some improvements on the

1966 Fleetwood Seventy-Five limousine

1966 Coupe deVille hardtop coupe

1966 Fleetwood Brougham four-door sedan

Toronado package. The Eldorado rode better than the Toronado, yet it handled at least as well. Its front suspension consisted of torsion bars, A-arms, and telescopic shocks; rear suspension was by semi-elliptic leaf springs with four shock absorbers—two horizontal, two vertical. The chassis featured self-leveling control and radially vented caliper front disc brakes.

On its own relatively compact 120-inch wheelbase, the Eldorado sold for $6277. Cadillac, orchestrating its debut with traditional precision, targeted the car for ten percent of total production, or about 20,000 units. The actual 1967 model year figure was 17,930. Sales held at over 23,000 in 1968, 1969, and 1970. The Eldorado quickly became established as a technological tour de force—the ultimate Cadillac. And, unlike the Eldorado Brougham before it, it made money from the day it appeared.

The remainder of the 1967 line was broken down into the usual Calais, DeVille, and Fleetwood series. Front ends were revised and given a forward-rake grille and fenders. Line-wide features were mylar printed circuits for the instrument panel, automatic level control (standard on all Fleetwoods), cruise control, and tilt steering wheel. Bolstered by the new Eldorado, Cadillac built 213,161 cars for the calendar year.

In 1968, the focus was on the engine again: an all-new 472-cid V8 with 375 bhp. Designed around government emission control requirements, the 472 was extensively proven, running the equivalent of 500,000 miles in laboratory testing. Other mechanical features for '68 were hidden windshield wipers and several new safety devices, most mandated by the government.

Major styling changes for the 1968 Eldorado were a new grille, longer hood, side marker lights, and larger taillights. Other models were also given a longer hood, along with a revised grille and a trunklid designed to in-

1967 Fleetwood Eldorado hardtop coupe

1968 DeVille convertible

1967 Fleetwood Brougham four-door sedan

1968 Hardtop Sedan deVille hardtop sedan

1967 Coupe deVille hardtop coupe

1968 Fleetwood Eldorado hardtop coupe

crease cargo capacity. The new engine was not as economical as the old one, but it was capable of propelling a Coupe deVille from 0 to 100 mph in 27.8 seconds.

In 1969, Cadillac broke back into the top ten producers with a record 266,798 units for the calendar year. It passed both Chrysler and American Motors, moving into ninth place. The Eldorado's front end was revised, its headlights no longer hidden as in 1967-68. The other models were completely restyled, with a new body and squarer roofline. Headlamps were now horizontal instead of vertical. Parking lights wrapped around at the front, the grille was new, and the hood was longer. A somewhat unpopular change was the elimination of front vent windows. Prices ranged from just over $5400 for the Calais to well over $10,000 for the 75 limousine.

Eldorado had a new engine for 1970, and a badge reading "8.2 litres" (500 cubic inches) to prove it. The largest production-car engine in the world, it developed 400 bhp and 550 pounds-feet of torque. Other models retained the 472 V8 with 375 bhp. New mechanical features included integral steering knuckle, bias-ply fiberglass-belted tires, a radio antenna imbedded in the windshield, and more safety features. All Cadillacs now came equipped with energy-absorbing steering column, pushbutton seatbelt buckles, shoulder harnesses, head restraints, hazard flashers, folding front seatback latches, backup lights, side marker lights, and reflectors. Cadillac offered an anti-theft ignition key warning buzzer, and anti-theft steering column/transmission lock with starter switch.

Stylewise, the major changes for 1970 were a new grille with bright vertical accents over a cross-hatch pattern, new horizontal chrome trim on parking lights, winged crests instead of Vs on hoods of the DeVille

Eldorado Biarritz Town Coupe show car, 1968

1969 Fleetwood Eldorado hardtop coupe

1969 Fleetwood Brougham four-door sedan

1969 Coupe deVille hardtop coupe

1970 Coupe deVille hardtop coupe

1970 Hardtop Sedan deVille hardtop sedan

and Calais, and new taillamps. The Eldorado grille was narrower and separate from the headlamps, while its taillamps were more slender than in 1969.

Cadillac's performance was disappointing in 1970. Calendar year output dropped over 100,000 units, putting the division back in 11th place behind Chrysler and AMC. Still, Cadillac had out-produced Lincoln 3-1 and Imperial 15-1 in a year that had been generally quiet for the industry as a whole. As before, Cadillac reigned supreme as America's number-one luxury car.

In the first half of the 1970s, Cadillac stayed with its successful basic model lineup: the lower-priced Calais (in decreasing numbers), the top-selling DeVille, and the long-wheelbase Sixty Special sedan in the full-size line, plus the front-drive Eldorado and the stretched-chassis Seventy-Five limousines. A forecast of the future was the 1975 debut of the compact Seville, the smallest Cadillac in 50 years, followed quickly by a decisively downsized big-car range for 1977.

Along with its E-body Buick Riviera and Oldsmobile Toronado stablemates, the Eldorado became much heavier and bulkier for 1971. It would continue as such through 1978, with few changes apart from government mandated safety and emissions equipment that, along with inflation, escalated prices each year. Though they accounted for upwards of 40,000 sales annually, these outsized personal-luxury cruisers were hardly the svelte, good-handling cars their predecessors had been. A new entry was the first-ever front-drive Eldo convertible, a body style not shared with its corporate cousins.

Cadillac's big cars continued to dominate division sales in the early part of the decade, helped by GM's smoother but larger new C-body platform of 1971. Calais remained the "economy" offering, the latter-day equivalent of the old Series 61, though it wasn't that much cheaper than the better-equipped DeVille. Perhaps because of this, production declined, dropping to below 10,000 units by 1974. Typically, only two models were listed, hardtops with two or four doors; the former became a fixed-pillar coupe from 1974 on. Likewise, the money-spinning DeVille was reduced to just two models for '71, the convertible being judged superfluous with the return of the Eldorado ragtop. Considering the history of the name, a pillared Coupe deVille was really a contradiction in terms and, possibly for that reason, proved less popular than the still-pillarless Sedan deVille. Styling for this full-size generation was more massive and rounded than the 1967-70 design. The premium Fleetwoods remained low-volume specialty items that were too costly even to facelift each year, and the limos and Sixty Special were stylistically the least changed big Caddys in these years. The latter remained a four-door sedan riding a special 133-inch wheelbase, but the name was progressively deemphasized, and disappeared entirely with the new downsized C-body for '77.

The main reason Cadillac's big-car appearance changed relatively little through '76 is that engineering and design talent was heavily engaged with the more pressing concerns of the day, mainly fuel economy, emissions, and occupant crash protection. It was very difficult to recon-

cile the first goal with the others, so Cadillac's engineering emphasis fell on the emissions side with both of its V8s. For example, exhaust-gas recirculation was added for 1973 to reduce oxides of nitrogen (NO_x) emissions, while the air injection reactor pump and engine pulleys were altered to lessen mechanical noise.

Along with the rest of the industry, Cadillac sales slipped in the wake of the 1973-74 oil embargo, but recovered quickly in 1975. That was the year the division broke with

1971 Sedan DeVille hardtop

1971 Fleetwood Eldorado convertible

1972 Fleetwood 60 Special Brougham four-door sedan

1972 Fleetwood Eldorado coupe

its own tradition in the form of a brand-new car that has since become one of its most important products. It was christened Seville, a name used by Cadillac (and DeSoto) in the '50s, but it was a complete departure from its thirsty, tailfinned predecessor. Cadillac had considered calling it the "Leland" in honor of the marque's founder, but decided most buyers were too young to make the connection. "LaSalle" was also in the running, but a revival of the division's junior make from the '30s was ultimately rejected because of the name's "loser" image. But the Seville was no loser. It was carefully designed for the one area of the luxury market that Cadillac had left unexplored: the quality intermediate, exemplified by Mercedes-Benz.

The Seville bowed to mixed reviews. It was clean and trim overall and compared favorably with its German rivals for interior space. But the styling struck some as unimaginative and dull, and it was an open secret that this "baby Cadillac" was actually a heavily reengineered version of GM's workaday X-body compact, a serious deficit in the prestige stakes. On the road, however, there was little to criticize. The standard powerplant, a 350-cid V8 with a new electronic fuel injection system exclusive to this model, delivered brisk, turbine-like performance. Typical 0-60 mph acceleration was in the 10-11-second range; top speed was over 110 mph. The Seville weighed 1000 pounds less and was 27 inches shorter overall than a '75 DeVille, but the reduced size and weight didn't affect ride, which was as cloudlike as buyers expected. Yet this was the best handling Cadillac in living memory, much closer to M-B and BMW than those manufacturers might have liked to admit. To be sure, it wouldn't glide over washboard surfaces with the disdain of a 450SEL—but then it didn't cost nearly as much, either.

1976 Calais hardtop sedan

1976 Fleetwood 60 Special Brougham four-door sedan

Buyers responded enthusiastically to the Seville. Sales totalled 43,000 for the first full model year, 1976, a healthy 15 percent of division output. Other Cadillacs were mostly unchanged that season, but a reviving economy meant brisk sales across the board, and the division broke the 300,000-unit mark for the first time in history. Things were even better in 1977-78 despite cancellation of the Eldo convertible and the Calais series, about 335,000 and 350,000, respectively. Volume was down in 1979-80, but Cadillac maintained its traditional 2-3 percent of total industry production, a share it had held for many years.

Perhaps only Cadillac among high-priced makes could so drastically change its cars while setting new sales records. Its 1977 models were fresh from the ground up, 8-12 inches shorter and nearly 1000 pounds lighter on the average than the '76s. Also, they had cleaner, more efficient engines, including a newly reworked, fuel-injected version of the 425, standard throughout the line except for Seville. The story was much the same for 1979, when the Eldorado was downsized by shaving off 225 pounds, 20 inches in overall length, and 12 inches in wheelbase. An unusual touch for an upmarket domestic was independent rear suspension, more compact than the previous beam axle, which made it possible to reduce wheelbase with little sacrifice in passenger room. Optional features for all Cadillacs that year included dual electric remote-control door mirrors, automatic retractable radio antenna, a choice of 8-track or cassette stereo tape players, integrated 40-channel CB radio, and "Tripmaster" on-board travel computer. First offered on the 1978 DeVille, the Trip master provided digital readouts for average mpg and speed, miles to destination and estimated arrival time, plus engine rpm, coolant temperature, and electrical system voltage.

For 1980, attention focused on a completely overhauled second-generation Seville. Its most daring and controversial aspect was a sloped "trunkback" rear end, conceived by designer Wayne Cady and a sort of valedictory for departing GM styling chief Bill Mitchell. It was reminiscent of certain razor-edge Rolls-Royce coachwork built by Hooper and Vanden Plas in the '50s, and although not everyone approved, it made this the most distinctive Cadillac since the first tailfinned models of 1948. In addition, the Seville acquired the Eldorado's front-drive mechanicals and all-independent suspension with automatic self-levelling, thus setting a new standard for engineering sophistication among U.S. cars.

Another significant 1980 Seville standard was its engine, a diesel V8 based on Oldsmobile's 350-cid gasoline unit and built in Lansing for use by other GM car divisions. Cadillac had first offered it as a 1978 option for all models except the Eldorado, which acquired it the following year. It was smooth and quiet for a diesel, and gave Cadillac a direct reply to Mercedes' compression-ignition models. More importantly, it helped the division contribute toward GM's compliance with the corporate average fuel economy (CAFE) law that took effect with the '78 model year. As time went on, however, it became clear that many people bought diesel Mercedes not for their economy or longevity,

but for the snob appeal of their three-pointed star. And unhappily for Cadillac's reputation, reliability problems surfaced early with the Olds diesel, forcing GM's finest to back away from compression ignition in later years. A further blow to the division's quality image came with 1981's problematic "V-8-6-4" variable-displacement gasoline power-plant, a costly stopgap prompted by CAFE. Further downsizing would prove far more effective in Cadillac's efforts to boost mph, and it culminated with the 1985 model year introduction of a new-generation DeVille and Fleetwood, with front drive and advanced electronics, plus more passenger room and smaller external size than even the Seville.

1976 Fleetwood Eldorado convertible

1977 Fleetwood Brougham D'Elegance four-door sedan

1979 Fleetwood Brougham D'Elegance four-door sedan

1979 Eldorado Biarritz coupe

1977 Fleetwood Eldorado coupe

1980 Coupe deVille

1977 Seville four-door sedan

1980 Eldorado coupe

1978 Fleetwood Eldorado coupe

1980 Seville four-door sedan

Cadillac Specifications

1930

353 Eight (wb 140.0)—11,005 built

		Wght	Price	Prod
Fisher:				
	cpe 2P	4,940	3,295	—
	conv cpe 2P	4,845	3,595	—
	cpe 5P	4,930	3,595	—
	town sdn 5P	5,025	3,495	—
	sdn 5P	5,055	3,695	—
	sdn 7P	5,155	3,795	—
	Imperial sdn 7P	5,195	3,995	—
Fleetwood:				
	rdstr 2P	4,610	3,450	—
	sdn 5P	5,135	4,195	—
	sdn cab 5P	5,185	4,245	—
	Imperial sdn 5P	5,205	4,395	—
	Imperial cab 5P	5,225	4,445	—
	sdn 7P	5,265	4,295	—
	Imperial sdn 7P	5,305	4,595	—
	sdnt 5P	5,055	4,500	—
	sdnt 4P	5,055	4,595	—
	phtn A/W 4P	4,075	4,700	—
	Town cab	5,215	4,995	—
	Town cab "Fleetmont"	5,135	5,145	—
	Town cab "Fleetcrest"	5,135	5,145	—
	Limo b'ham	5,305	5,145	—

370 Twelve (wb 140.0; 7P-143.0)—5,725 built (1930-31)

		Wght	Price	Prod
Fisher:				
	rdstr 2P	4,910	3,945	—
	phtn 5P	4,950	4,055	—
	A/W phtn 5P	5,290	4,895	—
	cpe 2P	5,035	3,795	—
	conv cpe 2P	5,005	4,045	—
	cpe 5P	5,055	3,895	—
	sdn 5P	5,215	3,895	—
	Town sdn 5P	5,230	3,945	—
	sdn 7P	5,345	4,195	—
	Imperial sdn 7P	5,420	4,345	—
	touring 7P	5,005	4,295	—
Fleetwood:				
	sdn 5P	5,350	4,995	—
	Imperial sdn 5P	5,420	5,200	—
	sdn cab 5P	5,400	5,095	—
	Imperial cab 5P	5,440	5,300	—
	sdn 7P	5,480	5,075	—
	Imperial sdn 7P	5,520	5,275	—
	Town cab 5P	5,430	5,750	—
	Town cab 5P CQ	5,350	5,800	—
	limo b'ham 7P	5,520	5,800	—

Sixteen (wb 148.0)—3,250 built (1930-31)

		Wght	Price	Prod
4100	*Madam X:*			
4108C	Imperial landau cab 5P	5,925	NA	4
4130	Imperial sdn 5P	5,905	7,300	17
4130S	sdn 5P	5,835	6,950	49
4155	Imperial cab 5P	5,925	7,350	10
4155S	sdn cabriolet 5P	5,885	7,121	7
4155C	Imperial landau cab 5P	5,925	NA	5
4155SC	landau sdn cab 5P	5,885	NA	2
4161	Imperial club sdn 5P	5,725	NA	1
4161S	club sdn 5P	5,655	6,950	43
4175	Imperial sdn 7P	6,005	7,525	110
4175S	sdn 7P	5,965	7,225	47
4200 series:				
4200	stationary sdn cab 7P	NA	NA	1
4206	stationary cpe cab 2P	NA	NA	1
4207	stationary cpe cab 2P	NA	NA	3

		Wght	Price	Prod
4208	Imperial cab 5P	5,885	NA	7
4212	transformable Town cab 5P	6,005	8,750	6
4212C	transformable Town cab CQ 5P	6,005	NA	1
4220	4212C w/leather roof	6,006	8,750	9
4220B	4212C w/painted roof	6,005	NA	1
4225	4212C SQ	6,005	8,750	6
4225C	4212C CQ	6,005	NA	1
4235	conv cpe 2P	5,655	6,900	94
4257A	touring 5P	NA	NA	1
4257H	touring 7P	NA	NA	1
4260	phtn 5P	NA	6,500	85
4260A	phtn 5P	NA	NA	1
4262	Imperial cab 7P	NA	NA	1
4264	transformable Town b'ham 5P	6,005	9,200	4
4264B	transformable Town b'ham 5P	6,005	9,700	6
4275	Imperial sdn 7P	6,005	6,525	1
4275C	Imperial Lnd sdn 7P	6,005	7,525	2
4276	cpe 2P	5,750	6,850	70
4280	A/W phtn 4P	5,675	7,350	8
4285	A/W spt cab 5P	NA	NA	2
4291	transformable limo b'ham 7P	6,005	8,750	14
4300 series:				
4302	rdstr 2P	5,310	5,350	105
4312	transformable Town cab 5P	NA	7,000	24
4,320	transformable Town cab 7P Q/W	NA	7,150	25
4325	transformable Town cab 7P SQ	NA	7,150	35
4325C	transformable CQ	NA	NA	3
4330	Imperial sdn 5P	5,905	6,300	50
4330S	sdn 5P	5,835	5,950	394
4335	conv cpe 2P	5,655	5,900	100
4355	Imperial cab 5P	5,925	6,350	52
4355S	sdn cap 5P	5,885	6,125	81
4355C	Imperial landau cab 5P	NA	NA	1
4361	Imperial club sdn 5P	NA	NA	2
4361S	club sdn 5P	5,725	5,950	258
4375	Imperial sdn 7P	6,005	6,525	438
4375S	sdn 7P	5,965	6,225	501
4375C	Imperial landau sdn 7P	NA	NA	2
4376	cpe 2P	5,750	5,800	98
4380	A/W phtn 4P	NA	6,650	250
4381	cpe 5P	5,740	5,950	98
4391	transformable limo b'ham 7P	6,005	7,150	30
Misc. Fisher:				
30-152	town sdn 5P	NA	NA	3
30-158	cpe 2P	NA	NA	3
30-158	sdn 5P	NA	NA	5
30-168	conv cpe 2P	NA	NA	17
30-172	cpe 5P	NA	NA	2
2901LX	sdn 7P	NA	NA	1
2951LX	snd 7P	NA	NA	1
30-X	sdn test car 7P	NA	NA	1
LX 2905	Town sdn 5P	NA	NA	1
LX 2913	cpe 5P	NA	NA	1
Misc. Fleetwood:				
3289B	transformable Town cab 7P	NA	NA	1
3981	sdnt cab 4P	NA	6,450	1
3991	transformable limo b'ham 7P	NA	NA	1
4412	transformable Town cab 5P	NA	NA	1
4476	cpe 2P	5,750	5,800	11
2950X	special sdn 7P	NA	NA	1
	Misc. chassis and unknown	—	—	37

1930 Engines	bore×stroke	bhp	availability
V8, 353.0	3.63×4.94	95	S-Eight
V12, 368.0	3.13×4.00	135	S-Twelve
V16, 452.6	3.00×4.00	165	S-Sixteen

Editor's note: Cadillac Sixteens obviously appeared in a very broad number of body styles. This analysis, the clearest ever published, appears in *Sixteen*

Cylinder Motorcars by Roy S. Schneider, Heritage House, 430 W. Longden Avenue, Arcadia, California 91006, with production figures researched from company records by Carl L. Steig.

1931

355 Eight (wb 134.0)—10,709 built	Wght	Price	Prod
rdstr 2P	4,355	2,845	—
phtn 5P	4,395	2,945	—
cpe 2P	4,480	2,695	—
conv cpe 2P	4,450	2,945	—
cpe 5P	4,500	2,795	—
sdn 4d 5P	4,660	2,795	—
Town sdn 5P	4,675	2,845	—
A/W phtn 5P	4,685	3,795	—
sdn 4d 7P	4,760	2,945	—
Imperial sdn 7P	4,835	3,095	—
touring 7P	4,450	3,195	—

370A Twelve (wb 140.0; 7P-143.0) (see 1930)

Sixteen (wb 148.0) (see 1930)

1931 Engines	bore×stroke	bhp	availability
V8, 353.0	3.63×4.94	95	S-Eight
V12, 368.0	3.13×4.00	135	S-Twelve
V16, 452.6	3.00×4.00	165	S-Sixteen

1932

355B Eight (wb 134.0)—2,693 built*	Wght	Price	Prod
rdstr 2P	4,635	2,895	—
cpe 2P	4,705	2,795	—
conv cpe 2P	4,675	2,945	—
sdn 5P	4,885	2,895	—

355B Eight (wb 140.0)

Fisher:			
phtn 5P	4,700	2,995	—
Special phtn 5P	4,750	3,095	—
spt phtn 5P	4,800	3,245	—
A/W phtn 5P	5,070	3,495	—
cpe 5P	4,715	2,995	—
special sdn 5P	4,965	3,045	—
Town sdn 5P	4,980	3,095	—
sdn 7P	5,110	3,145	—
Imperial sdn 7P	5,150	3,295	—
Fleetwood:			
sdn 5P	4,965	3,395	—
Town cpe 5P	4,915	3,395	—
sdn 7P	5,110	3,545	—
limo 7P	5,150	3,745	—
Town cab 5P	4,990	4,095	—
Town cab 7P	5,100	4,245	—
limo b'ham 7P	5,100	4,245	—

370B Twelve (wb 134.0)—1,709 built*			
rdstr 2P	4,870	3,595	—
cpe 2P	5,085	3,495	—
conv cpe 2P	5,060	3,645	—
sdn 5P	5,175	3,595	—

370B Twelve (wb 140.0)

Fisher:			
phtn 5P	5,240	3,695	—
Special phtn 5P	5,290	3,795	—
spt phtn 5P	5,340	3,945	—
A/W phtn 5P	5,385	4,195	—
cpe 5P	5,220	3,695	—
Special sdn 5P	5,345	3,745	—
Town sdn 5P	5,370	3,795	—
sdn 7P	5,460	3,845	—
Imperial sdn 7P	5,500	3,995	—

	Wght	Price	Prod
Fleetwood:			
Town cpe 5P	5,225	4,095	—
sdn 5P	5,345	4,095	—
sdn 7P	5,460	4,245	—
limo 7P	5,500	4,445	—
Town cab 5P	5,380	4,795	—
Town cab 7P	5,580	4,945	—
limo b'ham 7P	5,580	4,945	—

452B Sixteen (wb 143.0)—296 built**			
rdstr 2P	5,065	4,595	—
cpe 2P	5,530	4,495	—
conv cpe 2P	5,505	4,645	—
sdn 5P	5,625	4,595	—

452B Sixteen (wb 149.0)

Fisher:			
phtn 5P	5,400	4,695	—
Special phtn 5P	5,450	4,795	—
spt phtn 5P	5,500	4,945	—
A/W phtn 5P	5,525	5,195	—
Fleetwood:			
Town cpe 5P	5,605	5,095	—
sdn 5P	5,735	5,095	—
sdn 7P	5,865	5,245	—
limo 7P	5,935	5,445	—
Town cab 5P	5,775	5,795	—
Town cab 7P	5,935	5,945	—
limo b'ham 7P	5,935	5,945	—

*incl. 140.0-in wb; **incl. 149.0-in wb.

1932 Engines	bore×stroke	bhp	availability
V8, 353.0	3.63×4.94	115	S-Eights
V12, 368.0	3.13×4.00	135	S-Twelves
V16, 452.6	3.00×4.00	165	S-Sixteens

Note: weights listed for five wire wheels, all models.

1933

355C Eight (wb 134.0)—2,906 built*	Wght	Price	Prod
rdstr 2P	4,695	2,795	—
cpe 2P	4,855	2,695	—
conv cpe 2P	4,825	2,845	—

355 C Eight (wb 140.0)

Fisher:			
phtn 5P	4,865	2,895	—
A/W phtn 5P	5,110	3,395	—
cpe 5P	4,850	2,895	—
sdn 5P	5,000	2,895	—
Town sdn 5P	5,060	2,995	—
sdn 7P	5,105	3,045	—
Imperial sdn 7P	5,140	3,195	—
Fleetwood:			
sdn 5P	5,000	3,295	—
sdn 7P	5,105	3,445	—
limo 7P	5,140	3,645	—
Town cab 5P	5,010	3,395	—
Town cab 7P	5,200	4,145	—
limo b'ham 7P	5,225	4,145	—

370C Twelve (wb 134.0)—952 built*			
rdstr 2P	5,030	3,495	—
cpe 2P	5,165	3,395	—
conv cpe 2P	5,125	3,545	—

370C Twelve (wb 140.0)

Fisher:			
phtn 5P	5,200	3,595	—

		Wght	Price	Prod
	A/W phtn 5P	5,405	4,095	—
	cpe 5P	5,200	3,595	—
	sdn 5P	5,335	3,595	—
	Town sdn 5P	5,385	3,695	—
	sdn 7P	5,440	3,745	—
	Imperial sdn 7P	5,500	3,895	—
	Fleetwood:			
	sdn 5P	5,335	3,995	—
	sdn 7P	5,440	4,145	—
	limo 7P	5,500	4,345	—
	Town cab 5P	5,375	4,695	—
	Town cab 7P	5,575	4,845	—
	limo b'ham 7P	5,575	4,845	—

452C Sixteen (wb 149.0)—125 built

		Wght	Price	Prod
	Fleetwood:			
	A/W phtn 5P	6,110	8,000	—
	conv cpe 5P	5,910	7,500	—
	Town cpe 5P	6,000	6,250	—
	Imperial cab 5P	6,100	5,540	—
	sdn 5P	6,070	6,250	—
	sdn 7P	6,200	6,400	—
	limo 7P	6,270	6,600	—
	Town cab 5P	6,110	6,850	—
	Town cab 7P	6,270	6,850	—
	limo b'ham 7P	6,300	6,850	—

*incl. 140-in. wb.

1933 Engines	bore×stroke	bhp	availability
V8, 353.0	3.38×4.94	115	S-Eights
V12, 368.0	3.13×4.00	135	S-Twelves
V16, 452.0	3.00×4.00	165	S-Sixteens

1934

355D Eight Series 10 (wb 128.0)—2,015 built

		Wght	Price	Prod
702	Town sdn 5P	4,735	2,695	—
709	snd 5P	4,715	2,645	—
718	conv cpe 2P	4,515	2,645	—
721	conv sdn 5P	4,750	2,845	—
722	Town cpe 5P	4,630	2,695	—
728	cpe 2P	4,550	2,545	—

355D Eight Series 20 (wb 136.0)—2,729 built

652	Town sdn 5P	4,815	2,895	—
659	sdn 5P	4,825	2,845	—
662	sdn 7P	4,945	2,995	—
663	Imperial sdn 7P	4,970	3,145	—
668	conv cpe 2P	4,625	2,845	—
671	conv sdn 5P	4,860	3,045	—
678	cpe 2P	4,660	2,745	—

355D Eight Series 30 (wb 146.0)—336 built

		Wght	Price	Prod
Fleetwood (straight windshield):				
6030FL	Imperial cab 5P	5,500	3,895	—
6030S	sdn 5P	5,465	3,495	—
6033S	Town sdn 5P	5,415	3,545	—
6075	limo 7P	5,580	3,845	—
6075FL	Imperial cab 7P	5,580	4,045	—
6075S	sdn 7P	5,545	3,645	—
Fleetwood (mod. V windshield):				
5612	Town cab 5P	5,540	5,695	—
5630FL	Special Imperial cab 5P	5,500	4,345	—
5630S	Special sdn 5P	5,465	3,945	—
5625	Town cab 7P	5,650	5,795	—
5633S	Special Town sdn 5P	5,415	3,995	—
5635	conv cpe 4P	5,115	4,245	—
5675	Special limo 7P	5,580	4,295	—

		Wght	Price	Prod
5675FL	Imperial cab 7P	5,580	4,495	—
5675S	Special sdn 7P	5,545	4,095	—
5676	cpe 4P	5,150	4,095	—
5680	Imperial conv sdn 5P	5,465	4,495	—
5691	limo b'ham 7P	5,580	5,695	—

370D Twelve Series 40 (wb 146.0)—683 built

		Wght	Price	Prod
Fleetwood (straight windshield):				
6130FL	Imperial cab 5P	5,765	4,595	—
6130S	sdn 5P	5,735	4,195	—
6133S	Town sdn 5P	5,700	4,245	—
6175	limo 7P	5,790	4,545	—
6175FL	Imperial cab 7P	5,790	4,745	—
6175S	sdn 7P	5,760	4,345	—
Fleetwood (V windshield):				
5712	Town cab 5P	5,990	6,395	—
5725	Town cab 7P	6,040	6,495	—
5730FL	Special Imperial cab 5P	5,765	5,045	—
5730S	Special sdn 5P	5,735	4,645	—
5733S	Special Town sdn 5P	5,700	4,695	—
5735	conv cpe 4P	5,485	4,945	—
5775	Special limo 7P	5,790	4,995	—
5775FL	Special Imperial cab 7P	5,790	5,195	—
5775S	Special sdn 7P	5,760	4,795	—
5770	cpe 4P	5,520	4,795	—
5780	Imperial conv sdn 5P	5,800	5,195	—
5791	limo b'ham 7P	6,030	6,395	—

452D Sixteen Series 60 (wb 154.0)—60 built

		Wght	Price	Prod
Fleetwood (straight windshield):				
6275	limo 7P	6,210	7,300	9
6275S	sdn 7P	6,190	7,100	5
Fleetwood (V windshield):				
5825	Town cab 7P	6,390	9,250	4
5830	Imperial sdn 5P	NA	NA	1
5833	Imperial Town sdn 5P	NA	NA	1
5833	Town sdn 5P	6,085	7,350	2
5835	conv cpe 2P	5,900	7,900	2
5875	limo 7P	6,210	7,950	9
5875S	Special sdn 7P	6,190	7,750	5
5875FL	Special Imperial sdn 7P	NA	8,150	2
5876	stationary cpe 2P	5,840	7,750	5
5880	conv sdn 5P	6,100	8,150	5
5880S	Imperial conv sdn 5P	NA	7,950	1
5885	conv cpe 5P	NA	8,150	1
5899	Aero cpe 5P	NA	8,150	3
Chassis (1) and unknown (4)		—	—	5

1934 Engines	bore×stroke	bhp	availability
V8, 353.0	3.38×4.94	130	S-Eights
V12, 368.0	3.13×4.00	150	S-Twelves
V16, 452.0	3.00×4.00	185	S-Sixteens

1935

355D Eight Series 10 (wb 128.0)—1,130 built

		Wght	Price	Prod
702	Town sdn 5P	4,735	2,495	—
709	sdn 5P	4,715	2,445	—
718	conv cpe 2-4P	4,515	2,445	—
721	conv sdn 5P	4,750	2,755	—
722	Town cpe 5P	4,630	2,495	—
728	cpe 2-4P	4,550	2,345	—

355D Eight Series 20 (wb 136.0)—1,859 built

652	Town sdn 5P	4,815	2,695	—
659	sdn 5P	4,825	2,645	—
662	sdn 7P	4,945	2,995	—
663	Imperial sdn 7P	4,970	2,945	—
668	conv cpe 2-4P	3,625	2,645	—

		Wght	Price	Prod
671	conv sdn 5P	4,860	2,955	—
678	cpe 2-4P	4,660	2,545	—

355D Eight Series 30 (wb 146.0)—220 built

Fleetwood (straight windshield):

6030FL	Imperial cab	5,500	3,695	—
6030S	sdn 5P	5,465	2,295	—
6033S	Town sdn 5P	5,415	3,345	—
6075	limo 7P	5,580	3,645	—
6075FL	Imperial cab 7P	5,580	3,845	—
6075S	sdn 7P	5,545	3,445	—

Fleetwood (V windshield):

5612	Town cab 5P	5,540	5,495	—
5625	Town cab 7P	5,650	5,595	—
5630FL	Special Imperial cab 5P	5,500	4,145	—
5630S	Special sdn 5P	5,465	3,745	—
5633S	Special cab sdn 5P	5,415	3,795	—
5635	conv cpe 4P	5,115	4,045	—
5675FL	Special Imperial cab 7P	5,580	4,295	—
5675S	Special sdn 7P	5,545	3,895	—
5675	Special limo 7P	5,580	4,095	—
5676	cpe 4P	5,150	3,895	—
5680	Imperial conv sdn 5P	5,465	4,295	—
5691	limo b'ham 7P	5,580	5,495	—

370D Twelve Series 40 (wb 146.0)—377 built

Fleetwood (straight windshield):

6130FL	Imperical cab 5P	5,765	4,395	—
6130S	sdn 5P	5,735	3,995	—
6133S	Town sdn 5P	5,700	4,045	—
6175	limo 7P	5,790	4,345	—
6175FL	Imperial cab 7P	5,790	4,545	—
6175S	sdn 7P	5,760	4,145	—

Fleetwood (V windshield):

5712	Town cab 5P	5,990	6,195	—
5725	Town cab 7P	6,040	6,295	—
5730FL	Special Imperial cab 5P	5,765	4,845	—
5730S	Special sdn 5P	5,735	4,445	—
5733S	Special Town sdn 5P	5,700	4,495	—
5735	conv cpe 4P	5,485	4,745	—
5775	Special limo 7P	5,790	4,795	—
5775FL	Special Imperial cab 7P	5,790	4,995	—
5775S	Special sdn 7P	5,760	4,595	—
5776	cpe 4P	5,520	4,595	—
5780	Imperial conv sdn 5P	5,800	4,995	—
5791	limo b'ham 7P	6,030	6,195	—

452D Sixteen Series 60 (wb 154.0)—50 built

Fleetwood (straight windshield):

6233S	Town sdn 5P	6,085	6,800	2
6275	limo 7P	6,210	7,100	7
6275S	sdn 7P	6,190	6,900	2
6275B	Imperial sdn 7P	NA	NA	2
6275H3	limo (extra headroom) 7P	NA	NA	1

Fleetwood (V windshield):

5825	Town cab 7P	6,390	9,050	2
5830S	Special sdn 5P	NA	7,400	1
5833	Imperial Town sdn 5P	NA	8,000	2
5833S	Town sdn 5P	6,085	7,450	4
5875	limo 7P	6,210	7,750	14
5875S	sdn 7P	6,190	7,550	2
5875FL	Imperial cab 7P	NA	7,950	1
5876	stationary cpe 2P	5,840	7,550	2
5880	conv sdn 5P	6,100	7,950	4
5885	conv cpe 5P	NA	8,150	2
5891B	limo b'ham 7P	NA	NA	1
Chassis		—	—	1

1935 Engines	bore×stroke	bhp	availability
V8, 353.0	3.38×4.94	130	S-Eights

	bore×stroke	bhp	availability
V12, 368.0	3.13×4.00	150	S-Twelves
V16, 452.0	3.00×4.00	185	S-Sixteens

1936

Series 60 (wb 121.0)—6,700 built

		Wght	Price	Prod
6019	Touring sdn 5P	4,010	1,695	—
6067	conv cpe 2-4P	3,985	1,725	—
6077	cpe 2P	3,830	1,645	—

Series 70 (wb 131.0)—2,000 built

7019	Touring sdn 5P	4,670	2,445	—
7029	conv sdn 5P	4,710	2,745	—
7057	cpe 2P	4,620	2,595	—
7067	conv cpe 2-4P	4,690	2,695	—

Series 75 Fleetwood (wb 138.0)—3,227 built

7503	sdn 7P	4,885	2,795	—
7509	sdn 5P	4,805	2,645	—
7513	Imperial sdn 7P	5,045	2,995	—
7519	Touring sdn 5P	4,805	2,645	—
7523	Touring sdn 7P	4,885	2,795	—
7529	conv sdn 5P	5,040	3,395	—
7519F	formal sdn 5P	4,805	3,395	—
7533	Imperial Touring sdn 5P	5,045	2,995	—
7539	Town sdn 5P	4,840	3,145	—
7543	town car 7P	5,115	4,445	—

Series 80 Fleetwood (wb 131.0)—250 built

8019	Touring sdn 5P	4,945	3,145	—
8029	conv sdn 5P	4,990	3,445	—
8057	cpe 2P	4,690	3,295	—
8067	conv cpe 2-4P	4,800	3,395	—

Series 85 Fleetwood (wb 138.0)—651 built

8503	sdn 7P	5,195	3,495	—
8509	sdn 5P	5,115	3,345	—
8513	Imperial sdn 7P	5,230	3,695	—
8519	Touring sdn 5P	5,115	3,345	—
8519F	formal sdn 5P	5,115	4,095	—
8523	Touring sdn 7P	5,195	3,495	—
8529	conv sdn 5P	5,230	4,095	—
8533	Imperial Touring sdn 7P	5,230	3,695	—
8539	Town sdn 5P	5,065	3,845	—
8543	town car 7P	5,300	5,145	—

Series 90 Fleetwood (wb 154.0)—52 built

5825	Town cab	6,390	8,850	1
5825C	Town cab 7P CQ	6,450	NA	1
5830S	Special sdn 5P	NA	7,600	1
5830FL	Special Imperial cab	NA	8,000	3
5833S	Town sdn 5P	6,085	7,250	3
5835	conv cpe 2P	NA	7,900	2
5875	limo 7P	6,190	7,550	24
5875S	sdn 7P	6,190	7,350	2
5875FL	Imperial cab 7P	6,210	7,850	1
5876	stationary cpe 2P	NA	7,750	1
5880	conv sdn 5P	6,100	7,850	6
5899	Aero cpe 5P	NA	8,150	4
—	Chassis	—	—	3

1936 Engines	bore×stroke	bhp	availability
V8, 322.0	3.38×4.50	125	S-60
V8, 346.0	3.50×4.50	135	S-70,75
V12, 368.0	3.13×2.00	150	S-80,85
V16, 452.0	3.00×4.00	185	S-90

1937

Series 60 (wb 124.0)—7,000 built*

		Wght	Price	Prod
—	club cpe 2P	NA	1,710	—
6019	Touring sdn 5P	3,845	1,760	—

		Wght	Price	Prod
6027	cpe 2P	3,710	1,655	—
6049	conv sdn 5P	3,885	2,120	—
6067	conv cpe 2P	3,745	1,790	—

Series 65 (wb 131.0)

		Wght	Price	Prod
6519	Touring sdn 5P	4,385	2,190	2,401

Series 70 Fleetwood (wb 131.0)—1,001 built

7019	Touring sdn 5P	4,420	2,695	—
7029	conv sdn 5P	4,460	3,060	—
7057	spt cpe 2P	4,285	2,905	—
7067	conv cpe 2P	4,325	3,005	—

Series 75 Fleetwood (wb 138.0)—3,227 built**

7509F	formal sdn 5P	4,745	3,785	—
7519	Touring sdn 5P	4,745	2,915	—
7523	Touring sdn 7P	4,825	3,070	—
7523S	Touring spt sdn 7P	4,825	2,710	—
7523SL	Touring bus sdn 8P	4,825	2,845	—
7529	conv sdn 5P	4,980	3,730	—
7533	Imperial Touring sdn 7P	4,985	3,270	—
7533S	Touring Spl Imperial sdn 7P	4,985	2,910	—
7533SL	Imperial Touring bus sdn 8P	4,985	3,050	—
7539	Town sdn 5P	4,780	3,425	—
7543	town car 7P	5,055	4,866	—

Series 85 Fleetwood (wb 138.0)—474 built

8509F	formal sdn 5P	5,050	4,500	—
8519	Touring sdn 5P	5,050	3,635	—
8523	Touring sdn 7P	5,130	3,790	—
8529	conv sdn 5P	5,165	4,450	—
8533	Imperial Touring sdn 7P	5,165	3,990	—
8539	Town sdn 5P	5,000	4,145	—
8543	town car 7P	5,230	5,575	—

Series 90 (wb 154.0)—49 built

5825	Town cab	6,390	9,230	2
5833S	Town sdn 5P	6,085	7,595	2
5875	limo 7P	6,190	7,900	24
5875S	sdn 7P	6,190	7,645	1
5875SF	sdn 7P SQ	6,200	NA	1
5875FL	Imperial cab 7P	6,210	8,155	2
5875H4	limo 7P (+4 in. headroom)	NA	NA	1
5876	stationary cpe 2P	5,840	7,745	4
5880	conv sdn 5P	6,100	8,205	5
5885	conv cpe 5P	NA	8,150	2
5891	limo b'ham	NA	9,150	1
5899	Aero cpe 5P	NA	8,150	1
—	Chassis (2) & unknown (1)	—	—	3

1937 Engines	bore×stroke	bhp	availability	
V8, 346.0	3.50×4.50	135	S-60,65,70,75	
V12, 368.0	3.13×4.00	150	S-85	
V16, 452.0	3.00×4.00	185	S-90	

*Includes commercials on 160-in. wb
**Includes commercials on 155-in. wb

1938

Series 60 (wb 124.0)

		Wght	Price	Prod
6119	sdn 4d	3,940	1,730	1,295
6119	sdn 4d CKD	—	—	12
6127	cpe 2P	3,855	1,695	438
6149	conv sdn 5P	3,980	2,215	60
6167	conv cpe 2P	3,845	1,815	145
—	comm chassis (wb 159.0)	—	—	101

Series 60 (wb 127.0)

6019S	sdn 4d	4,170	2,090	3,587
6019S	sdn 4d CKD	—	—	108
—	chassis	—	—	8

Series 65 (wb 132.0)

6519	sdn 4d	4,540	2,290	1,178
6519F	Imperial div sdn 5P	4,580	2,360	110
6549	conv sdn 5P	4,580	2,605	110
—	chassis	—	—	3

Series 75 (wb 141.3)

7519	sdn 5P	4,865	3,080	475
7519F	Imperial div sdn 5P	4,925	3,155	34
7523	sdn 7P	4,945	3,210	380
7523L	bus sdn 7P	4,945	3,105	25
7529	conv sdn 5P	NA	NA	58
7533	Imperial sdn 7P	5,105	3,360	479
7533	Imperial sdn 7P CKD	—	—	84
7533F	formal sdn 7P	5,105	3,995	40
7533L	Imperial bus sdn 7P	5,105	3,260	25
7539	Town sdn 5P	4,900	3,635	56
7553	town car 7P	5,175	5,115	17
7557	cpe 2P	4,675	3,280	52
7557B	cpe 5P	4,775	3,380	42
—	chassis (incl. 8 CKD)	—	—	24
—	comm chassis (wb 161.0)	—	—	11

Series 90 (wb 141.3)

9019	sdn 5P	5,105	5,140	43
9019F	Imperial sdn 5P	5,165	5,215	5
9023	sdn 7P	5,185	5,270	65
9029	conv sdn 5P	5,350	6,000	13
9033	Imperial sdn 7P	5,345	5,420	95
9033F	formal sdn 7P	5,345	6,055	17
9039	Town sdn 5P	5,140	5,695	20
9053	town car 7P	5,415	7,175	11
9057	cpe 2P	4,915	5,340	11
9057B	cpe 5P	5,015	5,440	8
9059	formal sdn 5P	5,105	6,055	8
9067	conv cpe 2P	4,905	5,440	10
9006	Presidential limo (wb 161.0)	—	—	2
—	chassis	—	—	3

1938 Engines	bore×stroke	bhp	availability	
V8, 346.0	3.50×4.50	135	S-60,65,70	
V8, 346.0	3.50×4.50	140	S-75	
V16, 431.0	3.25×3.25	185	S-90	

1939

Series 61 (wb 126.0)

		Wght	Price	Prod
6119	sdn 4d	3,770	1,680	3,955
6119	sdn 4d CKD	—	—	196
6119A	sunroof sdn 4d	NA	NA	43
6119F	Imperial sdn 5P	NA	NA	30
6127	cpe 2-4P	3,685	1,610	1,023
6129	conv sdn 5P	3,810	2,170	140
6167	conv cpe 2-4P	3,765	1,770	350
—	comm chassis (wb 156.0)	—	—	237

Series 60 Special (wb 127.0)

6019S	sdn 4d	4,110	2,090	5,135
6019S	sdn 4d CKD	—	—	84
6019SA	sunroof sdn 4d	NA	NA	225
6019SAF	Imperial sunroof sdn 4d	NA	NA	55
—	chassis	—	—	7

Series 75 (wb 141.3)

7519	sdn 5P	4,785	2,995	543
7519F	Imperial div sdn 5P	4,845	3,155	53
7523	sdn 7P	4,865	3,210	412
7523L	bus sdn 7P	4,865	3,105	33
7529	conv sdn 5P	5,030	3,945	36
7533	Imperial sdn 7P	5,025	3,360	638
7533	Imperial sdn 7P CKD	—	—	60
7533F	formal sdn 7P	5,025	3,995	44
7533L	Imperial bus sdn 7P	5,025	3,260	2

		Wght	Price	Prod
7539	Town sdn 5P	4,820	3,635	51
7553	town car 7P	5,095	5,115	13
7557	cpe 2P	4,595	3,280	36
7557B	cpe 5P	4,695	3,380	23
7559	formal sdn 5P	4,785	3,995	53
7567	conv cpe 2P	4,675	3,380	27
—	chassis	—	—	13
—	comm chassis (wb 161.0)	—	—	28

Series 90 (wb 141.3)

		Wght	Price	Prod
9019	sdn 5P	5,190	5,140	13
9019F	Imperial sdn 5P	5,265	5,215	2
9023	sdn 7P	5,215	5,270	18
9029	conv sdn 5P	5,220	6,000	4
9033	Imperial sdn 7P	5,260	5,345	60
9033F	formal sdn 7P	5,260	6,055	8
9039	Town sdn 5P	5,230	5,695	2
9053	town car 7P	5,330	7,175	5
9057	cpe 2P	4,830	5,340	6
9057B	cpe 5P	4,930	5,440	5
9059	formal sdn 5P	5,190	6,055	4
9067	conv cpe 2P	4,970	5,440	7
—	chassis	—	—	2

1939 Engines	bore×stroke	bhp	availability
V8, 346.0	3.50×4.50	135	S-60,61
V8, 346.0	3.50×4.50	140	S-75
V16, 431.0	3.25×3.25	185	S-90

1940

Series 62 (wb 129.0)

		Wght	Price	Prod
6219	sdn 4d	4,065	1,745	4,302
6227	cpe 2–4P	3,975	1,685	1,322
6229	conv sdn	4,265	2,195	75
6267	conv cpe	4,080	1,795	200
62	chassis	—	—	1

Series 60 Special (wb 127.0)

		Wght	Price	Prod
6019F	division sdn	4,110	2,230	110
6019S	sdn 4d	4,070	2,090	4,472
6053LB	town car-leather back	4,365	3,820	6
6053MB	town car-metal back	4,365	3,465	9

Series 72 (wb 138.0)

		Wght	Price	Prod
7219	sdn 4d	4,670	2,670	455
7219F	division sdn	4,710	2,740	100
7223	sdn 4d, 7P	4,700	2,785	305
7223L	livery sdn 7P	4,700	2,690	25
7233	imperial sdn 7P	4,740	2,915	292
7233F	formal sdn 7P	4,780	3,695	20
7233L	livery imp sdn 7P	4,740	2,825	36
7259	formal sdn	4,670	3,695	18
72	comm chassis (wb 165.0)	—	—	275

Series 75 (wb 141.3)

		Wght	Price	Prod
7519	sdn 4d	4,900	2,995	155
7419F	division sdn	4,940	3,155	25
7523	sdn 4d, 7P	4,930	3,210	166
7529	conv sdn 7P, T/B	5,110	3,945	45
7533	imperial sdn 7P	4,970	3,360	338
7533F	formal sdn 7P	4,970	3,995	42
7539	town sdn	4,935	3,635	14
7553	town car 7P	5,195	5,115	14
7557	cpe 2–4P	4,785	3,280	15
7557B	cpe	4,810	3,380	12
7559	formal sdn, T/B	4,900	3,995	48
7567	conv cpe	4,915	3,380	30
75	chassis	—	—	3

		Wght	Price	Prod
75	comm chassis (wb 161.0)	—	—	52

Series 90 Sixteen (wb 141.3)

		Wght	Price	Prod
9019	sdn 4d	5,190	5,140	4
9023	sdn 4d, 7P	5,215	5,270	4
9029	conv sdn, T/B	5,265	6,000	2
9033	imperial sdn 7P	5,260	5,420	20
9033F	formal sdn 7P, T/B	5,260	6,055	20
9039	town sdn, T/B	5,220	5,695	1
9053	town car 7P, T/B	5,330	7,175	2
9057	cpe 2–4P	4,830	5,340	2
9057B	cpe	4,930	5,440	1
9059	formal sdn, T/B	5,190	6,055	2
9067	conv cpe 2–4P	4,970	5,440	2
90	chassis	—	—	1

1940 Engines	bore×stroke	bhp	availability
V8, 346.0	3.50×4.50	135	S-62, 60S
V8, 346.0	3.50×4.50	140	S-72, 75
V16, 431.0	3.25×3.25	185	S-Sixteen

1941

Series 61 (wb 126.0)

		Wght	Price	Prod
6109	sdn 4d	4,065	1,445	10,925
6109D	del sdn 4d	4,085	1,535	3,495
6127	cpe	3,985	1,345	11,812
6127D	del cpe	4,005	1,435	3,015
61	chassis	—	—	3

Series 62 (wb 126.0)

		Wght	Price	Prod
6219	sdn 4d	4,030	1,495	8,012
6219D	del sdn 4d	4,050	1,585	7,850
6227	cpe 2–4P	3,950	1,420	1,985
6227D	del cpe 2–4P	3,970	1,510	1,900
6229D	conv sdn	4,230	1,965	400
6267D	conv cpe	4,055	1,645	3,100
62	chassis	—	—	4
62	comm chassis (wb 163.0)	—	—	1,475

Series 63 (wb 126.0)

		Wght	Price	Prod
6319	sdn 4d	4,140	1,695	5,050

Series 60 Special (wb 126.0)

		Wght	Price	Prod
6019	sdn 4d	4,230	2,195	3,878
6019F	division sdn	4,290	2,345	220
6053LB	town car	4,485	—	1
60	chassis	—	—	1

Series 67 (wb 138.0)

		Wght	Price	Prod
6719	sdn 4d	4,555	2,595	315
6719F	division sdn	4,615	2,745	95
6723	sdn 4d, 7P	4,630	2,735	280
6733	imperial sdn 7P	4,705	2,890	210

Series 75 (wb 136.0)

		Wght	Price	Prod
7519	sdn 4d	4,750	2,995	422
7519F	division sdn	4,810	3,150	132
7523	sdn 4d, 7P	4,800	3,140	405
7523L	business sdn 9P	4,750	2,895	54
7533	imperial sdn 7P	4,860	3,295	757
7533F	formal sdn 7P	4,915	4,045	98
7533L	business imperial sdn 7P	4,810	3,050	6
7559	formal sdn	4,900	3,920	75
75	chassis	—	—	5
75	comm chassis (wb 163.0)	—	—	150

1941 Engine	bore×stroke	bhp	availability
V8, 346.0	3.50×4.50	150	S-all

Cadillac

1942

Series 61 (wb 126.0)

		Wght	Price	Prod
6107	club cpe	4,035	1,450	2,482
6109	sdn 4d	4,115	1,530	3,218

Series 62 (wb 129.0)

6207	club cpe	4,105	1,545	515
6207D	club cpe	4,125	1,630	530
6267D	conv cpe	4,365	1,880	308
6269	sdn 4d	4,185	1,630	1,780
6269D	sdn 4d	4,205	1,705	1,827

Series 63 (wb 126.0)

6319	sdn 4d	4,115	1,745	1,750

Series 60 Special (wb 133.0)

6069	sdn 4d	4,310	2,265	1,684
6069F	division sdn	4,365	2,415	190
60	chassis	—	—	1

Series 67 (wb 138.0)

6719	sdn 4d	4,605	2,700	200
6719F	division sdn	4,665	2,845	50
6723	sdn 7P	4,680	2,845	260
6733	imperial sdn 7P	4,755	2,995	190

Series 75 (wb 136.0)

7519	sdn 4d	4,750	3,080	205
7519F	division sdn	4,810	3,230	65
7523	sdn 4d, 7P	4,800	3,230	225
7523L	business sdn 9P	4,750	2,935	29
7533	imperial sdn 7P	4,860	3,375	430
7533F	formal sdn 7P	4,915	4,215	80
7533L	business imperial sdn 9P	4,860	3,080	6
7559	formal sdn	4,900	4,060	60
75	chassis	—	—	1
75	comm chassis (wb 163.0)	—	—	425

1942 Engine	bore×stroke	bhp	availability	
V8, 346.0	3.50×4.50	150	S-all	

1946

Series 61 (wb 126.0)

		Wght	Price	Prod
6107	club cpe	4,145	2,052	800
6109	sdn 4d	4,225	2,176	2,200
61	chassis	—	—	1

Series 62 (wb 129.0)

6207	club cpe	4,215	2,284	2,323
6267D	conv cpe	4,475	2,556	1,342
6269	sdn 4d	4,295	2,359	14,900
62	chassis	—	—	1

Series 60 Special (wb 133.0)

6069	sdn 4d	4,420	3,095	5,700

Series 75 (wb 136.0)

7519	sdn 4d	4,860	4,298	150
7523	sdn 4d, 7P	4,905	4,475	225
7523L	business sdn 9P	4,920	4,153	22
7533	imperial sdn 7P	4,925	4,669	221
7533L	business imperial sdn 9P	4,925	4,346	17
75	comm chassis (wb 163.0)	—	—	1,292

1946 Engine	bore×stroke	bhp	availability	
V8, 346.0	3.50×4.50	150	S-all	

1947

Series 61 (wb 126.0)

		Wght	Price	Prod
6107	club cpe	4,080	2,200	3,395

		Wght	Price	Prod
6109	sdn 4d	4,165	2,324	5,160

Series 62 (wb 129.0)

6207	club cpe	4,145	2,446	7,245
6267	conv cpe	4,455	2,902	6,755
6269	sdn 4d	4,235	2,523	25,834
62	chassis	—	—	1

Series 60 Special (wb 133.0)

6069	sdn 4d	4,370	3,195	8,500

Series 75 (wb 136.0)

7519	sdn 4d	4,875	4,471	300
7523	sdn 4d, 7P	4,895	4,686	890
7523L	business sdn 9P	4,790	4,368	135
7533	imperial sdn 7P	4,930	4,887	1,005
7533L	business imperial sdn 9P	4,800	4,560	80
75	chassis	—	—	3
75	comm & bus chassis (wb 163.0)	—	—	2,623

1947 Engine	bore×stroke	bhp	availability	
V8, 346.0	3.50×4.50	150	S-all	

1948

Series 61 (wb 126.0)

		Wght	Price	Prod
6107	club cpe	4,068	2,728	3,521
6169	sdn 4d	4,150	2,833	5,081
61	chassis	—	—	1

Series 62 (wb 126.0)

6207	club cpe	4,125	2,912	4,764
6267	conv cpe	4,449	3,442	5,450
6259	sdn 4d	4,179	2,996	23,997
62	chassis	—	—	2

Series 60 Special (wb 133.0)

6069	sdn 4d	4,356	3,820	6,561

Series 75 (wb 136.0)

7519	sdn 4d	4,875	4,779	225
7523	sdn 4d, 7P	4,878	4,999	499
7523L	business sdn 9P	4,780	4,679	90
7533	imperial sdn 7P	4,959	5,199	382
7533L	bus imperial sdn 9P	—	—	64
75	chassis	—	—	2
75	comm chassis (wb 163.0)	—	—	2,067

1948 Engine	bore×stroke	bhp	availability	
V8, 346.0	3.50×4.50	150	S-all	

1949

Series 61 (wb 126.0)

		Wght	Price	Prod
6107	club cpe	3,838	2,788	6,409
6169	sdn 4d	3,915	2,893	15,738
61	chassis	—	—	1

Series 62 (wb 126.0)

6207	club cpe	3,862	2,966	7,515
6237	Coupe de Ville htp cpe	4,033	3,497	2,150
6267	conv cpe	4,218	3,442	8,000
6269	sdn 4d	3,956	3,050	37,977
62	chassis	—	—	1

Series 60 Special (wb 133.0)

6037	Coupe de Ville htp cpe	4,200	exp	1
6069	sdn 4d	4,129	3,828	11,399

Series 75 (wb 136.0)

7519	sdn 4d	4,579	4,750	220
7523	sdn 4d, 7P	4,626	4,970	595
7523L	business sdn 9P	4,522	4,650	35
7533	imperial sdn 7P	4,648	5,170	626
7533L	business imperial sdn 9P	4,573	4,839	25
75	chassis	—	—	1
86	comm chassis (wb 163.0)	—	—	1,861

1949 Engine	bore×stroke	bhp	availability	
V8, 331.0	3.81×3.63	160	S-all	

1950

Series 61 (wb 122.0)

		Wght	Price	Prod
6137	club cpe	3,829	2,761	11,839
6169	sdn 4d	3,822	2,866	14,931
61	chassis	—	—	2

Series 62 (wb 126.0)

6219	sdn 4d	4,012	3,234	41,890
6237	club cpe	3,993	3,150	6,434
6237D	Coupe de Ville htp cpe	4,074	3,523	4,507
6267	conv cpe	4,316	3,654	6,986
62	chassis	—	—	1

Series 60 Special (wb 130.0)

6019	sdn 4d	4,136	3,797	13,755

Series 75 (wb 146.8)

7523	sdn 4d, 7P	4,555	4,770	716
7523L	business sdn 9P	4,235	exp	1
7533	imperial sdn 7P	4,586	4,959	743
86	comm chassis (wb 157.0)	—	—	2,052

1950 Engine	bore×stroke	bhp	availability	
V8, 331.0	3.81×3.63	160	S-all	

1951

Series 61 (wb 122.0)

		Wght	Price	Prod
6137	club cpe	3,829	2,810	2,400
6169	sdn 4d	3,827	2,917	2,300

Series 62 (wb 126.0)

6219	sdn 4d	4,062	3,528	55,352
6237	cpe	4,081	3,436	10,132
6237D	Coupe De Ville htp cpe	4,156	3,843	10,241
6267	conv cpe	4,377	3,987	6,117
62-126	chassis	—	—	2

Series 60 Special (wb 130.0)

6019	sdn 4d	4,234	4,142	18,631

Series 75 (wb 146.8)

7523	sdn 4d, 8P	4,621	5,200	1,090
7523L	business sdn 9P	4,300	exp	30
7533	imperial sdn 8P	4,652	5,405	1,085
86	comm chassis (wb 157.0)	—	—	2,960

1951 Engine	bore×stroke	bhp	availability	
V8, 331.0	3.81×3.63	160	S-all	

1952

Series 62 (wb 126.0)

		Wght	Price	Prod
6219	sdn 4d	4,140	3,684	42,625
6237	cpe	4,173	3,587	10,065
6237D	Coupe de Ville htp cpe	4,203	4,013	11,165
6267	conv cpe	4,416	4,163	6,400

Series 60 Special (wb 130.0)

6019	sdn 4d	4,255	4,323	16,110

Series 75 (wb 146.8)

7523	sdn 4d, 8P	4,698	5,428	1,400
7533	imperial sdn 8P	4,733	5,643	800
8680S	comm chassis (wb 157.0)	—	—	1,694

1952 Engine	bore×stroke	bhp	availability	
V8, 331.0	3.81×3.63	190	S-all	

1953

Series 62 (wb 126.0)

		Wght	Price	Prod
6219	sdn 4d	4,225	3,666	47,640
6237	cpe	4,320	3,571	14,353
6237D	Coupe de Ville htp cpe	4,320	3,995	14,550
6267	conv cpe	4,500	4,144	8,367
6267S	Eldorado conv cpe	4,800	7,750	532
62	chassis	—	—	4

Series 60 Special (wb 130.0)

6019	sdn 4d	4,415	4,305	20,000

Series 75 (wb 146.8)

7523	sdn 4d, 8P	4,830	5,408	1,435
7533	imperial sdn 8P	4,850	5,621	765
8680S	comm chassis (wb 157.0)	—	—	2,005

1953 Engine	bore×stroke	bhp	availability	
V8, 331.0	3.81×3.63	210	S-all	

1954

Series 62 (wb 129.0)

		Wght	Price	Prod
6219	sdn 4d	4,370	3,933	34,252
6219S	DeVille htp sdn	—	proto	1
6237	htp cpe	4,365	3,838	17,460
6237D	Coupe de Ville htp cpe	4,405	4,261	17,170
6267	conv cpe	4,610	4,404	6,310
6267S	Eldorado conv cpe	4,815	4,738	2,150
62	chassis	—	—	1

Series 60 Special (wb 133.0)

6019	sdn 4d	4,500	4,863	16,200

Series 75 (wb 149.8)

7523	sdn 4d, 8P	5,055	5,875	889
7533	imperial sdn 8P	5,105	6,090	611
8680S	comm chassis (wb 158.0)	—	—	1,635

1954 Engine	bore×stroke	bhp	availability	
V8, 331.0	3.81×3.63	230	S-all	

1955

Series 62 (wb 129.0)

		Wght	Price	Prod
6219	sdn 4d	4,370	3,977	45,300
6237	htp cpe	4,358	3,882	27,879
6237D	Coupe de Ville htp cpe	4,424	4,305	33,300
6267	conv cpe	4,627	4,448	8,150
6267S	Eldorado conv cpe	4,809	6,286	3,950
62	chassis	—	—	7

Series 60 Special (wb 133.0)

		Wght	Price	Prod
6019	sdn 4d	4,540	4,728	18,300

Series 75 (wb 149.8)

		Wght	Price	Prod
7523	sdn 4d, 8P	5,020	6,187	1,075
7533	limo 8P	5,113	6,402	841
8680S	comm chassis (wb 158.0)	—	—	1,975

1955 Engines	bore×stroke	bhp	availability
V8, 331.0	3.81×3.63	250	S-62, 60S, 75
V8, 331.0	3.81×3.63	270	S-Eldorado

1956

Series 62 (wb 129.0)

		Wght	Price	Prod
6219	sdn 4d	4,430	4,296	26,666
6237	htp cpe	4,420	4,201	26,649
6237D	Coupe de Ville htp cpe	4,445	4,624	24,086
6237S	Eldorado Seville htp cpe	4,665	6,556	3,900
6239D	Sedan de Ville htp cpe	4,550	4,753	41,732
6267	conv cpe	4,645	4,766	8,300
6267S	Eldorado Biarritz conv cpe	4,880	6,556	2,150
62	chassis	—	—	19

Series 60 Special (wb 133.0)

		Wght	Price	Prod
6019	sdn 4d	4,610	5,047	17,000

Series 75 (wb 149.8)

		Wght	Price	Prod
7523	sdn 4d, 8P	5,050	6,613	1,095
7533	limo 8P	5,130	6,828	955
8680S	comm chassis (wb 158.0)	—	—	2,025

1956 Engines	bore×stroke	bhp	availability
V8, 365.0	4.00×3.63	285	S-62, 60S, 75
V8, 365.0	4.00×3.63	305	S-Eldorado

1957

Series 62 (wb 129.5)

		Wght	Price	Prod
6237	htp cpe	4,565	4,677	25,120
6237D	Coupe de Ville htp cpe	4,620	5,116	23,813
6237S	Eldorado Seville htp cpe	4,810	7,286	2,100
6239	htp sdn	4,595	4,781	32,342
6239D	Sedan de Ville htp sdn	4,655	5,256	23,808
6239S	Eldorado Seville htp sdn	4,810	7,286	4
6267	conv cpe	4,730	5,293	9,000
6267S	Eldorado Biarritz conv cpe	4,930	7,286	1,800
62	chassis & export sdn	—	—	385

Series 60 Special (wb 133.0)

		Wght	Price	Prod
6039	htp sdn	4,735	5,614	24,000

Series 70 Eldorado Brougham (wb 129.0)

		Wght	Price	Prod
7059	htp sdn	5,315	13,074	400

Series 75 (wb 149.8)

		Wght	Price	Prod
7523	sdn 4d, 8P	5,340	7,440	1,010
7533	limo 8P	5,390	7,678	890
8680S	comm chassis (wb 156.0)	—	—	2,169

1957 Engines	bore×stroke	bhp	availability
V8, 365.0	4.00×3.63	300	S-62, 60S, 70
V8, 365.0	4.00×3.63	325	S-Eldorado

1958

Series 62 (wb 129.5)

		Wght	Price	Prod
6237	htp cpe	4,630	4,784	18,736
6237D	Coupe de Ville htp cpe	4,705	5,251	18,414
6237S	Eldorado Seville htp cpe	4,910	7,500	855
6239	htp sdn	4,675	4,891	13,335
6239E	htp sdn (ext. deck)	4,770	5,079	20,952
6239	Sedan de Ville htp sdn	4,855	5,497	23,989
6267	conv cpe	4,856	5,454	7,825
6267S	Eldorado Biarritz conv cpe	5,070	7,500	815
62	chassis & exp sdn	—	—	206

Series 60 Special (wb 133.0)

		Wght	Price	Prod
6039	htp sdn	4,930	6,232	12,900

Series 70 Eldorado Brougham (wb 126.0)

		Wght	Price	Prod
7059	htp sdn	5,315	13,074	304

Series 75 (wb 149.8)

		Wght	Price	Prod
7523	sdn 4d, 9P	5,360	8,460	802
7533	limo 9P	5,425	8,675	730
8680S	comm chassis (wb 156.0)	—	—	1,915

1958 Engine	bore×stroke	bhp	availability
V8, 365.0	4.00×3.63	310	S-all

1959

Series 62 (wb 130.0)

		Wght	Price	Prod
6229	htp sdn 6W	4,770	5,080	23,461
6237	htp cpe	4,690	4,892	21,947
6239	htp sdn 9W	4,835	5,080	14,138
6267	conv cpe	4,855	5,455	11,130
62	export sdn	—	—	60

De Ville (wb 130.0)

		Wght	Price	Prod
6329	htp sdn 6W	4,850	5,498	19,158
6337	htp cpe	4,720	5,252	21,924
6339	htp sdn 4W	4,825	5,498	12,308

Eldorado (wb 130.0)

		Wght	Price	Prod
6437	Seville htp cpe	—	7,401	975
6467	Biarritz conv cpe	—	7,401	1,320
6929	Brougham htp sdn	—	13,075	99

Series 60 Special (wb 130.0)

		Wght	Price	Prod
6039	htp sdn	4,890	6,233	12,250

Series 75 (wb 149.8)

		Wght	Price	Prod
6723	sdn 4d, 9P	5,490	9,533	710
6733	limo 9P	5,570	9,748	690
6890	comm chassis (wb 156.0)	—	—	2,102

1959 Engines	bore×stroke	bhp	availability
V8, 390.0	4.00×3.88	325	S-62, DeVille, 60S, 75
V8, 390.0	4.00×3.88	345	S-Eldorado

1960

Series 62 (wb 130.0)

		Wght	Price	Prod
6229	htp sdn 6W	4,805	5,080	26,824
6237	htp cpe	4,670	4,892	19,978
6239	htp sdn 4W	4,775	5,080	9,984
6267	conv cpe	4,850	5,455	14,000
62	chassis & export sdn	—	—	38

DeVille (wb 130.0)

		Wght	Price	Prod
6329	htp sdn 6W	4,835	5,498	22,579
6337	htp cpe	4,705	5,252	21,585
6339	htp sdn 4W	4,815	5,498	9,225

Eldorado (wb 130.0)

		Wght	Price	Prod
6437	Seville htp cpe	—	7,401	1,075

		Wght	Price	Prod
6467	Biarritz conv cpe	—	7,401	1,285
6929	Brougham htp sdn	—	13,075	101

Series 60 Special (wb 130.0)

6039	htp sdn	4,880	6,233	11,800

Series 75 (wb 149.8)

6723	sdn 4d, 9P	5,475	9,533	718
6733	limo 9P	5,560	9,748	832
6890	comm chassis (wb 156.0)	—	—	2,160

1960 Engines	bore×stroke	bhp	availability	
V8, 390.0	4.00×3.88	325	S-62, DeVille, 60S, 75	
V8, 390.0	4.00×3.88	345	S-Eldorado	

1961

Series 62 (wb 129.5)

		Wght	Price	Prod
6229	htp sdn 6W	4,680	5,080	26,216
6237	htp cpe	4,560	4,892	16,005
6239	htp sdn 4W	4,660	5,080	4,700
6267	conv	4,720	5,455	15,500
62	chassis	—	—	5

DeVille (wb 129.5)

6239	htp sdn 6W	4,710	5,498	26,415
6337	htp cpe	4,595	5,252	20,156
6339	htp sdn 4W	4,715	5,498	4,847
6399	Town Sedan htp 6W	—	5,498	3,756

Eldorado (wb 129.5)

6367	Biarritz conv cpe	—	6,477	1,450

Series 60 Special (wb 129.5)

6039	htp sdn	4,770	6,233	15,500

Series 75 (wb 149.8)

6723	sdn 4d, 9P	5,390	9,533	600
6733	limo 9P	5,420	9,748	926
6890	comm chassis (wb 156.0)	—	—	2,204

1961 Engine	bore×stroke	bhp	availability	
V8, 390.0	4.00×3.88	325	S-all	

1962

Series 62 (wb 129.5)

		Wght	Price	Prod
6229	htp sdn 6W	4,640	5,213	16,730
6239	htp sdn 4W	4,645	5,213	17,314
6247	htp cpe	4,530	5,025	16,833
6267	conv cpe	4,630	5,588	16,800
6289	Town Sedan htp sdn	4,590	5,213	2,600

DeVille (wb 129.5)

6329	htp sdn 6W	4,660	5,631	16,230
6339	htp sdn 4W	4,675	5,631	27,378
6347	htp cpe	4,595	5,385	25,675
6389	Park Avenue htp sdn	4,655	5,631	2,600

Eldorado (wb 129.5)

6367	Biarritz conv cpe	4,620	6,610	1,450

Series 60 Special (wb 129.5)

6039	htp sdn 6W	4,710	6,366	13,350

Series 75 (wb 149.8)

6723	sdn 4d, 9P	5,325	9,722	696
6733	limo 9P	5,390	9,937	904
6890	comm chassis (wb 156.0)	—	—	2,280

1962 Engine	bore×stroke	bhp	availability	
V8, 390.0	4.00×3.88	325	S-all	

1963

Series 62 (wb 129.5)

		Wght	Price	Prod
6229	htp sdn 6W	4,610	5,214	12,929
6239	htp sdn 4W	4,595	5,214	16,980
6257	htp cpe	4,505	5,026	17,786
6267	conv cpe	4,545	5,590	17,600
62	chassis	—	—	3

DeVille (wb 129.5)

6329	htp sdn 6W	4,650	5,633	15,146
6339	htp sdn 4W	4,605	5,633	30,579
6357	htp cpe	4,520	5,386	31,749
6389	Park Avenue htp sdn	4,590	5,633	1,575

Eldorado (wb 129.5)

6367	Biarritz conv cpe	4,640	6,608	1,825

Series 60 Special (wb 129.5)

6039	htp sdn	4,690	6,366	14,000

Series 75 (wb 149.8)

6723	sdn 4d, 9P	5,240	9,724	680
6733	limo 9P	5,300	9,939	795
6890	comm chassis (wb 156.0)	—	—	2,527

1963 Engine	bore×stroke	bhp	availability	
V8, 390.0	4.00×3.88	325	S-all	

1964

Series 62 (wb 129.5)

		Wght	Price	Prod
6229	htp sdn 6W	4,575	5,236	9,243
6239	htp sdn 4W	4,550	5,236	13,670
6257	htp cpe	4,475	5,048	12,166
6267	conv cpe	4,545	5,612	17,900

DeVille (wb 129.5)

6329	htp sdn 6W	4,600	5,655	14,627
6339	htp cpe 4W	4,575	5,655	39,674
6357	htp cpe	4,495	5,408	38,195

Eldorado (wb 129.5)

6367	Biarritz conv cpe	4,605	6,630	1,870

Series 60 Special (wb 129.5)

6039	htp sdn	4,680	6,388	14,550

Series 75 (wb 149.8)

6723	sdn 4d, 9P	5,215	9,746	617
6733	limo 9P	5,300	9,960	808
6890	comm chassis (wb 156.0)	—	—	2,639

1964 Engine	bore×stroke	bhp	availability	
V8, 429.0	4.13×4.00	340	S-all	

1965

Calais (wb 129.5)

		Wght	Price	Prod
68239	htp sdn	4,500	5,247	13,975
68257	htp cpe	4,435	5,059	12,515
68269	sdn 4d	4,490	5,247	7,721

DeVille (wb 129.5)

68339	htp sdn	4,560	5,666	45,535
68357	htp cpe	4,480	5,419	43,345
68367	conv cpe	4,690	5,639	19,200
68369	sdn 4d	4,555	5,666	15,000

Eldorado (wb 129.5)

68467	conv cpe	4,660	6,738	2,125

Sixty Special (wb 133.0)

68069	sdn 4d	4,670	6,479	18,100

Cadillac

Seventy-Five (wb 149.8)		Wght	Price	Prod
69723	sdn 4d, 9P	5,190	9,746	455
69733	limo 9P	5,260	9,960	795
69890	comm chassis (wb 156.0)	—	—	2,669

1965 Engine	bore×stroke	bhp	availability	
V8, 429.0	4.13×4.00	340	S-all	

1966

Calais (wb 129.5)		Wght	Price	Prod
68239	htp sdn	4,465	5,171	13,025
68257	htp cpe	4,390	4,986	11,080
68269	sdn 4d	4,460	5,171	4,575

DeVille (wb 129.5)		Wght	Price	Prod
68339	htp sdn	4,515	5,581	60,550
68357	htp cpe	4,460	5,339	50,580
68367	conv cpe	4,445	5,555	19,200
68369	sdn 4d	4,535	5,581	11,860

Eldorado (wb 129.5)		Wght	Price	Prod
68467	conv cpe	4,500	6,631	2,250

Sixty Special (wb 133.0)		Wght	Price	Prod
68069	sdn 4d	4,615	6,378	5,455
68169	Fleetwood Brougham sdn 4d	4,665	6,695	13,630

Seventy-Five (wb 149.8)		Wght	Price	Prod
69723	sdn 4d, 9P	5,320	10,312	980
69733	limo 9P	5,435	10,521	1,037
69890	comm chassis (wb 156.0)	—	—	2,463

1966 Engine	bore×stroke	bhp	availability	
V8, 429.0	4.13×4.00	340	S-all	

1967

Calais (wb 129.5)		Wght	Price	Prod
68247	htp cpe	4,447	5,040	9,085
68249	htp sdn	4,495	5,215	9,880
68269	sdn 4d	4,499	5,215	2,865

DeVille (wb 129.5)		Wght	Price	Prod
68347	htp cpe	4,486	5,392	52,905
68349	htp sdn	4,532	5,625	59,902
68367	conv cpe	4,479	5,608	18,202
68369	sdn 4d	4,534	5,625	8,800

Eldorado (wb 120.0)		Wght	Price	Prod
69347	htp cpe	4,500	6,277	17,930

Sixty Special (wb 133.0)		Wght	Price	Prod
68069	sdn 4d	4,678	6,423	3,550
68169	Fleetwood Brougham sdn 4d	4,715	6,739	12,750

Seventy-Five (wb 149.8)		Wght	Price	Prod
69723	sdn 4d, 9P	5,344	10,360	835
69733	limo 9P	5,436	10,571	965
68490	comm chassis (wb 156.0)	—	—	2,333

1967 Engine	bore×stroke	bhp	availability	
V8, 429.0	4.13×4.00	340	S-all	

1968

Calais (wb 129.5)		Wght	Price	Prod
68247	htp cpe	4,570	5,315	8,165
68249	htp sdn	4,640	5,491	10,025

DeVille (wb 129.5)		Wght	Price	Prod
68347	htp cpe	4,595	5,552	63,935
68349	htp sdn	4,675	5,785	72,662

Series 61 (wb 126.0)		Wght	Price	Prod
68367	conv cpe	4,600	5,736	18,025
68369	sdn 4d	4,680	5,785	9,850

Eldorado (wb 120.0)		Wght	Price	Prod
69347	htp cpe	4,580	6,605	24,528

Sixty Special (wb 133.0)		Wght	Price	Prod
68069	sdn 4d	4,795	6,583	3,300
68169	Fleetwood Brougham sdn 4d	4,805	6,899	15,300

Seventy-Five (wb 149.8)		Wght	Price	Prod
69723	sdn 4d, 9P	5,300	10,629	805
69733	limo 9P	5,385	10,768	995
69890	comm chassis (wb 156.0)	—	—	2,413

1968 Engine	bore×stroke	bhp	availability	
V8, 472.0	4.30×4.06	375	S-all	

1969

Calais (wb 129.5)		Wght	Price	Prod
68247	htp cpe	4,555	5,484	5,600
68349	htp sdn	4,630	5,660	6,825

DeVille (wb 129.5)		Wght	Price	Prod
68347	htp cpe	4,595	5,721	65,755
68349	htp sdn	4,660	5,954	72,958
68367	conv cpe	4,590	5,905	16,445
68369	sdn 4d	4,640	5,954	7,890

Eldorado (wb 120.0)		Wght	Price	Prod
69347	htp cpe	4,550	6,711	23,333

Sixty Special (wb 133.0)		Wght	Price	Prod
68069	sdn 4d	4,765	6,779	2,545
68169	Fleetwood Brougham sdn 4d	4,770	7,110	17,300

Seventy-Five (wb 149.8)		Wght	Price	Prod
69723	sdn 4d, 9P	5,430	10,841	880
69733	limo 9P	5,555	10,979	1,156
69890	comm chassis (wb 156.0)	—	—	2,550

1969 Engine	bore×stroke	bhp	availability	
V8, 472.0	4.30×4.06	375	S-all	

1970

Calais (wb 129.5)		Wght	Price	Prod
68247	htp cpe	4,620	5,637	4,724
68249	htp sdn	4,680	5,813	5,187

DeVille (wb 129.5)		Wght	Price	Prod
68347	htp cpe	4,650	5,884	76,043
68349	htp sdn	4,725	6,118	83,274
68367	conv cpe	4,660	6,068	15,172
68369	sdn 4d	4,690	6,118	7,230

Eldorado (wb 120.0)		Wght	Price	Prod
69347	htp cpe	4,630	6,903	28,842

Sixty Special (wb 133.0)		Wght	Price	Prod
68089	sdn 4d	4,830	6,953	1,738
68189	Fleetwood Brougham sdn 4d	4,835	7,284	16,913

Seventy-Five (wb 149.8)		Wght	Price	Prod
69723	sdn 4d, 9P	5,530	11,039	876
69733	limo 9P	5,630	11,178	1,240
69890	comm chassis (wb 156.0)	—	—	2,506

1970 Engines	bore×stroke	bhp	availability
V8, 472.0	4.30×4.06	375	S-all exc Eldorado
V8, 500.0	4.30×4.30	400	S-Eldorado

1971

Calais (wb 130.0)		Wght	Price	Prod
68247	htp cpe	4,635	5,899	3,360
68249	htp sdn	4,710	6,075	3,569

DeVille (wb 130.0)				
68347	htp cpe	4,685	6,264	66,081
68349	htp sdn	4,730	6,498	69,345

Eldorado (wb 120.0)				
69346	htp cpe	4,675	7,383	20,568
69367	conv	4,730	7,751	6,800

Sixty Special Brougham (wb 133.0)				
68169	Fleetwood sdn 4d	4,815	7,763	15,200

Seventy-Five (wb 151.5)				
69723	sdn 4d	5,510	11,869	752
69733	limo 9P	5,570	12,008	848
69890	comm chassis (wb 157.5)	—	—	2,014

1971 Engines	bore×stroke	bhp	availability	
V8, 472.0	4.30×4.06	345	S-all exc Eldorado	
V8, 500.0	4.30×4.30	365	S-Eldorado	

1972

Calais (wb 130.0)		Wght	Price	Prod
68247	htp cpe	4,642	5,771	3,900
68249	htp sdn	4,698	5,938	3,875

DeVille (wb 130.0)				
68347	htp cpe	4,682	6,168	95,280
68349	htp sdn	4,762	6,390	99,531

Eldorado (wb 126.3)				
69347	htp cpe	4,682	7,230	32,099
69367	conv	4,772	7,546	7,975

Sixty Special Brougham (wb 133.0)				
68169	Fleetwood sdn 4d	4,858	7,637	20,750

Seventy-Five (wb 151.5)				
69723	sdn 4d	5,515	11,748	955
69733	limo 9P	5,637	11,880	960
69890	comm chassis (wb 157.5)	—	—	2,462

1972 Engines	bore×stroke	bhp	availability	
V8, 472.0	4.30×4.06	220	S-all exc Eldorado	
V8, 500.0	4.30×4.30	235	S-Eldorado	

1973

Calais (wb 130.0)		Wght	Price	Prod
68247	htp cpe	4,900	5,866	4,275
68249	htp sdn	4,953	6,038	3,798

DeVille (wb 130.0)				
68347	htp cpe	4,925	6,268	112,849
68349	htp sdn	4,985	6,500	103,394

Eldorado (wb 126.3)				
69347	htp cpe	4,880	7,360	42,136
69367	conv	4,966	7,681	9,315

Sixty Special Brougham (wb 133.0)				
68169	Fleetwood sdn 4d	5,102	7,765	24,800

Seventy-Five (wb 151.5)				
69723	sdn 4d	5,620	11,948	1,043
69733	limo 9P	5,742	12,080	1,017
69890	comm chassis (wb 157.5)	—	—	2,212

1973 Engines	bore×stroke	bhp	availability	
V8, 472.0	4.30×4.06	220	S-all exc Eldorado	
V8, 500.0	4.30×4.30	235	S-Eldorado	

1974

Calais (wb 130.0)		Wght	Price	Prod
68247	cpe	4,900	7,371	4,559
68249	sdn 4d	4,979	7,545	2,324

DeVille (wb 130.0)				
68347	cpe	4,924	7,867	112,201
68349	sdn 4d	5,032	8,100	60,419

Eldorado (wb 126.3)				
69347	htp cpe	4,960	9,110	32,812
69367	conv	5,019	9,437	7,600

Sixty Special Brougham (wb 133.0)				
68169	Fleetwood sdn 4d	5,143	9,537	18,250

Seventy-Five (wb 151.5)				
69723	sdn 4d	5,719	13,120	895
69733	limo 9P	5,883	13,254	1,005
69890	comm chassis (wb 157.5)	—	—	2,265

1974 Engines	bore×stroke	bhp	availability	
V8, 472.0	4.30×4.06	205	S-all exc Eldorado	
V8, 500.0	4.30×4.30	210	S-Eldorado	

1975

Seville (wb 114.3)		Wght	Price	Prod
S69	sdn 4d	4,232	12,479	16,355

Calais (wb 130.0)				
68247	cpe	5,003	8,184	5,800
68249	sdn 4d	5,087	8,377	2,500

DeVille (wb 130.0)				
68347	cpe	5,049	8,600	110,218
68349	sdn 4d	5,146	8,801	63,352

Eldorado (wb 126.3)				
69347	cpe	5,108	9,935	35,802
69367	conv	5,167	10,354	8,950

Sixty Special Brougham (wb 133.0)				
68169	Fleetwood sdn 4d	5,242	10,414	18,755

Seventy-Five (wb 151.5)				
69723	sdn 4d	5,720	14,218	876
69733	limo 9P	5,862	14,557	795
69890	comm chassis (wb 157.5)	—	—	1,329

1975 Engines	bore×stroke	bhp	availability	
V8, 350.0	4.06×3.39	180	S-Seville	
V8, 500.0	4.30×4.30	190	S-all exc Seville	

1976

Seville (wb 114.3)		Wght	Price	Prod
S69	sdn 4d	4,232	12,479	43,772

Calais (wb 130.0)				
68247	cpe	4,989	8,629	4,500
68249	sdn 4d	5,083	8,825	1,700

DeVille (wb 130.0)				
68347	cpe	5,025	9,067	114,482
68349	sdn 4d	5,127	9,265	67,677

Eldorado (wb 126.3)				
69347	cpe	5,085	10,586	35,184
69367	conv	5,153	11,049	14,000

Sixty Special Brougham (wb 133.0)				
68169	Fleetwood sdn 4d	5,213	10,935	24,500

Seventy-Five (wb 151.5)				
69723	sdn 4d	5,746	14,889	981
69733	limo 9P	5,889	15,239	834
69890	comm chassis (wb 157.5)	—	—	1,509

1976 Engines	bore×stroke	bhp	availability
V8, 350.0	4.06×3.39	180	S-Seville
V8, 500.0	4.30×4.30	190	S-all exc Seville
V8, 500.0	4.30×4.30	215	O-all exc Seville

1977

Seville (wb 114.3)		Wght	Price	Prod
S69	sdn 4d	4,192	13,359	45,060

DeVille (wb 121.50)				
68347	cpe	4,186	9,810	138,750
68349	sdn 4d	4,222	10,020	95,421

Eldorado (wb 126.3)				
69347	cpe	4,955	11,187	47,344

Fleetwood Brougham (wb 121.5)				
68169	sdn 4d	4,340	11,546	28,000

Fleetwood limousine (wb 144.5)				
69723	sdn 4d	4,738	18,349	1,582
69773	formal sdn 4d	4,806	19,014	1,032
69890	comm chassis (wb 157.5)	—	—	1,299

1977 Engines	bore×stroke	bhp	availability
V8, 350.0	4.06×3.39	180	S-Seville
V8, 425.0	4.08×4.06	180	S-all exc Seville
V8, 425.0	4.08×4.06	195	O-Brgm,DeVille,Eldo

1978

Seville (wb 114.3)		Wght	Price	Prod
S69	sdn 4d	4,179	14,710	56,985

1977 Seville four-door sedan

DeVille (wb 121.5)				
68347	cpe	4,163	10,584	117,750
68349	sdn 4d	4,236	10,924	88,951

Eldorado (wb 126.3)				
69347	cpe	4,906	12,401	46,816

Fleetwood Brougham (wb 121.5)				
68169	sdn 4d	4,314	12,842	36,800

Fleetwood limousine (wb 144.5)				
69723	sdn 4d	4,772	20,007	848
69773	formal sdn 4d	4,858	10,742	682
69890	comm chassis (wb 157.5)	—	—	852

1978 Engines	bore×stroke	bhp	availability
V8, 350.0	4.06×3.39	170	S-Seville
V8, 350.0 Dsl	4.06×3.39	120	0-Seville
V8, 425.0	4.08×4.06	180	S-all exc Seville
V8, 425.0	4.08×4.06	195	S-Brgm,DeVille,Eldo

1979

Seville (wb 114.3)		Wght	Price	Prod
S69	sdn 4d	4,179	14,710	53,487

Eldorado (wb 113.9)				
L57	cpe	3,792	14,668	67,436

DeVille (wb 121.5)				
D47	cpe	4,143	11,728	121,890
D69	sdn 4d	4,212	12,093	93,211

Fleetwood Brougham (wb 121.5)				
B69	sdn 4d	4,250	14,102	42,200

Fleetwood limousine (wb 144.5)				
F23	sdn 4d	4,782	21,869	2,025
F33	formal sdn 4d	4,866	22,640	2,025
—	comm chassis (wb 157.5)	—	—	864

1979 Engines	bore×stroke	bhp	availability
V8, 350.0	4.06×3.39	170	S-Seville,Eldo
V8, 350.0 Dsl	4.06×3.39	125	O-all
V8, 425.0	4.08×4.06	180	S-all exc Seville
V8, 425.0	4.08×4.06	195	O-Brgm,DeVille

1980

Eldorado (wb 113.9)		Wght	Price	Prod
L57	cpe	3,806	16,141	52,685

DeVille (wb 121.5)				
D47	cpe	4,048	12,899	55,490
D69	sdn 4d	4,084	13,282	49,188

Fleetwood Brougham (wb 121.5)				
B47	cpe	4,025	15,307	2,300
B69	sdn 4d	4,092	15,564	29,659

Fleetwood limousine (wb 144.5)				
F23	sdn 4d	4,629	23,509	1,612
F33	formal sdn 4d	4,718	24,343	—
—	comm chassis (wb 157.5)	—	—	750

Seville (wb 114.3)				
S69	sdn 4d	3,911	20,477	38,344

1980 Engines	bore×stroke	bhp	availability
V8, 350.0 Dsl	4.06×3.39	105	S-Seville O-Flt/Brgm,Eldo
V8, 350.0	4.06×3.39	160	O-Seville,Eldo
V8, 368.0	3.80×4.06	150	O-Seville; S-DeV,Fltwd
V8, 368.0	3.80×4.06	145	S-Eldo

Checker
Checker Motors Corp.
Kalamazoo, Michigan

Checker, the Kalamazoo builder of taxicabs and airport limousines, began marketing passenger cars in 1960. The company's practical four-door, the Superba, had the same upright, tank-like styling that had become familiar to anyone who'd ever seen a taxi. Checker president Morris Markin was steadfast: there'd be no change to this utilitarian, but unattractive, design from year to year as long as there were customers who wanted a car with a taxi's reliability and durability. The Superba's design dated back to the A8 taxicab of 1956.

The engine used in Checkers of this era was of Continental Motor Company design, roughly the same as that used in Kaisers of the late-1940s and 1950s. It displaced 226 cubic inches, but was offered with either side or overhead valves. The side-valve version had a 7.3:1 compression ratio, and produced 80 horsepower at 3100 rpm. The ohv engine had an 8.0:1 compression ratio and an output of 122 bhp at 4000 rpm. Either engine could be ordered in 1960 for the same price.

The 1960 Checker Superba was available as a four-door sedan and a four-door station wagon, in standard or Special form. The Special came with upgraded interior trim. True to its taxicab heritage, the Superba sedan had a pair of jump seats in the rear compartment and could carry up to eight adults. The wagon's rear seat could be folded up or down by means of an electronic servo controlled from the dashboard. This gimmick, and its different bodywork, made the Checker wagon about $350 more expensive than the sedan.

For 1961, the Superba Special was renamed

1965 Marathon four-door sedan

1970 Marathon DeLuxe four-door sedan

Marathon. The sedan's 15-inch wheels were replaced by 14-inchers for a slightly lower ride height. The overhead-valve engine became standard on station wagons. Prices did not change. Air conditioning cost $411 extra; power steering was a $64 option. Like Checker cabs, the Superba and Marathon had a full bank of gauges, a spartan but well-padded interior, wide doors, and a spacious rear compartment.

The same four offerings were continued for 1962. The only change was a return to 15-inch wheels for the sedans. In 1963, output on the overhead-valve engine was increased to 141 bhp at 4000 rpm. Prices rose in 1964—about $100 across the board. Optimistically, Checker decided to introduce a $7500 Town Custom limousine on a 129-inch wheelbase in '62. In addition to a glassed-off driver's compartment, the limousine offered a full range of power options. Production was limited, probably because demand for this most expensive of taxis was low.

The Superba name was dropped in 1964, which was also the last year for the old 226-cid engine. Checker than switched to Chevrolet engines for 1965: a 230-cid six, a 283 V8, and a 327 V8. The Town Custom limousine was still offered, but only on special order. The optional 283 V8 cost $110 extra, automatic transmission was priced at $248, and overdrive cost $108.

The 1966 Checker added a deluxe sedan, and a lower-priced limousine at $4541, temporarily reestablishing its four-model lineup. These two models were dropped the following year. The deluxe sedan was revived for 1968, and the deluxe limousine reappeared for 1969.

Checkers became faster cars during these years as their Chevy V8s became increasingly more potent. The big 350 was producing 300 bhp when Checker introduced it as an option in 1969; emission controls cut output to 250 bhp in its 1970 form, however. Prices for the optional engines were usually low: In 1968, these were $108 for the 307 and $195 for the 327.

Sales were moderate for Checker in the '60s, although adequate to sustain the level of production the firm desired—6000 to 7000 units a year. Checker's best year of the decade was 1962, when 8173 cars were built. Most of these, of course, were sold as commercial taxis.

Morris Markin, Checker's founder, never waivered from his goal to build a tough taxicab. If he could also sell a few of them as passenger cars, so much the better. But the fickle public, he insisted, would never control Checker styling or engineering. (It isn't widely known, but Nathan Altman once made overtures to Checker as a possible builder of his Avanti II. Markin, however, said the Avanti was too ugly to sell.)

Markin died in 1970, and his son David then took over the company. A flurry of interest surrounded the marque

in the mid-'70s when Edward N. Cole, having retired as president of GM in 1974, joined Checker to launch a powerful development program. But Cole was killed in a plane crash before his efforts came to fruition and with him perished what appeared to be the firm's last best hope for survival. Taxicabs had always been Checker's main business; passenger cars were strictly secondary. The problem was that the major manufacturers were placing increased emphasis on fleet sales, particularly when hard times hit the industry in the late '70s and made the fleet market an important outlet for excess production.

Checker's economic difficulties were evident in its reduced passenger-car offerings through the '70s. The decade began with a four-car lineup on two wheelbases. In 1972, the long-wheelbase limousine was dropped, and in 1975 the remaining long-wheelbase sedan also disappeared. For 1976 the line was down to only the basic

Marathon sedan, available with either six or V8. Passenger-car sales continued to hover around 300-400 per year—but it was taxicabs, not private cars, that would determine Checker's future.

The Markin management seemed unwilling to alter what was, by the late '60s, an extremely dated design. With the addition of "federal" bumpers in 1974—big, girder-style lumps of steel—a car that had once simply looked old was now also distinctly ugly. Markin Sr. hadn't seemed to mind, but neither, apparently, did Markin Jr. A handsome new-generation Checker prototype was designed for the company by Ghia in 1970, but not adopted, though it's possible that financial difficulties were more responsible for this than management's stubbornness.

In the end, it may not have made any difference. Checker's taxi business continued to decline, and the Kalamazoo company ceased car production in mid-1982.

1966 Marathon four-door sedan

1967 Marathon four-door sedan

1969 Marathon wagon

Checker Specifications

1960—6,980 built, inc taxis

Superba (wb 120.0)

	Wght	Price	Prod
sdn 4d	3,410	2,542	—
Special sdn 4d	3,410	2,650	—
wgn 4d	3,780	2,896	—
Special wgn 4d	3,780	3,004	—

1960 Engines	bore×stroke	bhp	availability
L6, 226.0	3.31×4.38	80	S-all
L6, 226.0	3.31×4.38	122	O-all

1961—5,683 built, inc taxis

Superba (wb 120.0)

	Wght	Price	Prod
sdn 4d	3,320	2,542	—
wgn 4d	3,570	2,896	—

Marathon (wb 120.0)

	Wght	Price	Prod
sdn 4d	3,345	2,650	—
wgn 4d	3,615	3,004	—

1961 Engines	bore×stroke	bhp	availability
L6, 226.0	3.31×4.38	80	S-all
L6, 226.0	3.31×4.38	122	S-wgn; O-sdn

1962—8,173 built, inc taxis

Superba (wb 120.0)

	Wght	Price	Prod
sdn 4d	3,320	2,642	—
wgn 4d	3,570	2,991	—

Marathon (wb 120.0)

	Wght	Price	Prod
sdn 4d	3,345	2,793	—
wgn 4d	3,615	3,140	—

Town Custom (wb 129.0)

	Wght	Price	Prod
limo 8P	5,000	7,500	—

1962 Engines	bore×stroke	bhp	availability
L6, 226.0	3.31×4.38	80	S-all
L6, 226.0	3.31×4.38	122	O-all

1963—7,050 built, inc taxis

Superba (wb 120.0)

	Wght	Price	Prod
sdn 4d	3,485	2,642	—
wgn 4d	3,625	2,991	—

Marathon (wb 120.0)

	Wght	Price	Prod
sdn 4d	3,485	2,773	—
wgn 4d	3,625	3,140	—

Town Custom (wb 129.0)

	Wght	Price	Prod
limo 8P	5,000	7,500	—

1963 Engines	bore×stroke	bhp	availability
L6, 226.0	3.31×4.38	80	S-all
L6, 226.0	3.31×4.38	141	O-all

1964—6,310 built, inc taxis

Marathon (wb 120.0)

	Wght	Price	Prod
sdn 4d	3,625	2,814	—
wgn 4d	3,720	3,160	—

Town Custom (wb 129.0)

	Wght	Price	Prod
limo 8P	5,000	8,000	—

1964 Engines	bore×stroke	bhp	availability
L6, 226.0	3.31×4.38	80	S-all
L6, 226.0	3.31×4.38	141	O-all

1965—6,136 built, inc taxis

Marathon (wb 120.0)

	Wght	Price	Prod
sdn 4d	3,360	2,793	—
wgn 4d	3,450	3,140	—

Town Custom (wb 129.0)

	Wght	Price	Prod
limo 8P	4,800	8,000	—

1965 Engines	bore×stroke	bhp	availability
L6, 230.0	3.88×3.25	140	S-all
V8, 283.0	3.88×3.00	195	O-all
V8, 327.0	4.00×3.25	250	O-all

1966—1,056 built; 5,761 inc taxis

Marathon (wb 120.0)

		Wght	Price	Prod
A12	sdn 4d	3,400	2,874	—
A12E	Deluxe sdn 4d	3,800	3,567	—
A12E	limo 8P	3,800	4,541	—
A12W	wgn 4d	3,500	3,500	—

1966 Engines	bore×stroke	bhp	availability
L6, 230.0	3.88×3.25	140	S-all
V8, 327.0	4.00×3.25	250	O-all

1967—935 built; 5,822 inc taxis

Marathon (wb 120.0)

		Wght	Price	Prod
A12	sdn 4d	3,400	2,874	—
A12W	wgn 4d	3,500	3,075	—

1967 Engines	bore×stroke	bhp	availability
L6, 230.0	3.88×3.25	140	S-all
V8, 327.0	4.00×3.25	250	O-all

1968—992 built; 5,477 inc taxis

Marathon (wb 120.0)

		Wght	Price	Prod
A12	sdn 4d	3,390	3,221	—
A12E	Deluxe sdn 4d	3,590	3,913	—
A12W	wgn 4d	3,480	3,491	—

1968 Engines	bore×stroke	bhp	availability
L6, 230.0	3.88×3.25	140	S-all
V8, 307.0	3.88×3.25	200	O-all
V8, 327.0	4.00×3.25	275	O-all

1969—760 built; 5,417 inc taxis

Marathon (wb 120.0)

		Wght	Price	Prod
A12	sdn 4d	3,390	3,290	—
A12W	wgn 4d	3,480	3,560	—

DeLuxe (wb 129.0)

		Wght	Price	Prod
A12E	sdn 4d	3,590	3,984	—
A12E	limo 8P	3,802	4,969	—

1969 Engines	bore×stroke	bhp	availability
L6, 230.0	3.88×3.25	155	S-all
V8, 327.0	4.00×3.25	235	O-all
V8, 350.0	4.00×3.48	300	O-all

1970—397 built

Marathon (wb 120.0)

		Wght	Price	Prod
A12	sdn 4d	3,268	3,671	—
A12W	wgn 4d	3,470	3,941	—

Marathon DeLuxe (wb 129.0)

		Wght	Price	Prod
A12E	sdn 4d	3,378	4,364	—
A12E	limo 8P	3,578	5,338	—

1970 Engines	bore×stroke	bhp	availability
L6, 230.0	3.88×3.25	155	S-all
V8, 350.0	4.00×3.48	250	O-all

Checker

1971

Marathon (wb 120.0)		Wght*	Price*	Prod*
A12	sdn 4d	3,400	3,843	500
A12W	wgn 4d	3,600	4,113	

Marathon DeLuxe (wb 129.0)				
A12E	sdn 4d	3,700	4,536	100
A12E	limo 8P	3,975	5,510	

1971 Engines	bore×stroke	bhp	availability
L6, 250.0	3.88×3.53	145	S-all
V8, 350.0	4.00×3.48	245	O-all

*L6 weight/price given; V8 adds 100 lbs & $110. Production estimated.

1972

Marathon (wb 120.0)		Wght*	Price*	Prod*
A12	sdn 4d	3,400	3,654	750
A12W	wgn 4d	3,600	3,910	

Marathon DeLuxe (wb 129.0)				
A12E	sdn 4d	3,700	4,312	100

1972 Engines	bore×stroke	bhp	availability
L6, 250.0	3.88×3.53	145	S-all
V8, 350.0	4.00×3.48	245	O-all

*L6 weight/price given; V8 adds 100 lbs & $250. Production estimated.

1973

Marathon (wb 120.0)		Wght*	Price*	Prod*
A12	sdn 4d	3,622	3,955	800
A12W	wgn 4d	3,825	4,211	

Marathon DeLuxe (wb 129.0)				
A12E	sdn 4d 8P L6	3,822	4,612	100
A12E	sdn 4d 8P V8	3,923	4,727	

1973 Engines	bore×stroke	bhp	availability
L6, 250.0	3.88×3.53	145	S-all
V8, 350.0	4.00×3.48	245	O-Marathon

*L6 weight/price given; V8 adds 100 lbs & $115. Production estimated.

1974

Marathon (wb 120.0)		Wght*	Price*	Prod*
A12	sdn 4d	3,720	4,453	900
A12W	wgn 4d	3,925	4,710	

Marathon DeLuxe (wb 129.0)				
A12E	sdn 4d 8P	3,920	5,394	50

1974 Engines	bore×stroke	bhp	availability
L6, 250.0	3.88×3.53	100	S-all
V8, 350.0	4.00×3.48	145	O-all

*L6 weight/price given; V8 adds 100 lbs & $150. Production estimated.

1975

Marathon (wb 120.0)		Wght	Price	Prod*
A12	sdn 4d L6	3,774	5,394	450
A12	sdn 4d V8	3,839	5,539	
A12	DeLuxe sdn 4d V8	4,137	6,216	

1975 Engines	bore×stroke	bhp	availability
L6, 250.0	3.88×3.53	100	S-sixes
V8, 350.0	4.00×3.48	145	S-V8s

*Production estimated.

1969 Marathon four-door sedan

1976

Marathon (wb 120.0)		Wght	Price	Prod*
A12	sdn 4d L6	3,774	5,749	400
A12	sdn 4d V8	3,839	5,894	

1976 Engines	bore×stroke	bhp	availability
L6, 250.0	3.88×3.53	105	S-sixes
V8, 350.0	4.00×3.48	145	S-V8s

*Production estimated.

1977

Marathon (wb 120.0)		Wght	Price	Prod*
A12	sdn 4d L6	3,765	6,156	300
A12	sdn 4d V8	3,830	6,301	

1977 Engines	bore×stroke	bhp	availability
L6, 250.0	3.88×3.53	110	S-sixes
V8, 305.0	3.74×3.48	145	S-V8s
V8, 305.0	4.00×3.48	170	O-V8s

*Production estimated.

1978

Marathon (wb 120.0)		Wght	Price	Prod*
A12	sdn 4d L6	3,765	6,814	300
A12	sdn 4d V8	3,830	6,959	

1978 Engines	bore×stroke	bhp	availability
L6, 250.0	3.88×3.53	110	S-sixes
V8, 305.0	3.74×3.53	145	S-V8s
V8, 350.0	4.00×3.48	170	O-V8s

*Production estimated.

1979

Marathon (wb 120.0)		Wght	Price	Prod*
A12	sdn 4d L6	3,765	7,314	200
A12	sdn 4d V8	3,830	7,515	

1979 Engines	bore×stroke	bhp	availability
L6, 250.0	3.88×3.53	110	S-sixes
V8, 305.0	3.74×3.48	145	S-V8s
V8, 350.0	4.00×3.48	160	O-V8s

Production estimated.

1980

Marathon (wb 120.0)		Wght	Price	Prod*
A12	sdn 4d L6	3,765	7,800	250
A12	sdn 4d V8	3,830	8,000	

1980 Engines	bore×stroke	bhp	availability
L6, 250.0	3.88×3.53	110	S-sixes
V8, 305.0	3.74×3.48	145	S-V8s
V8, 350.0	4.00×3.48	160	O-V8s

*Production estimated

Chevrolet

Chevrolet Motor Division, General Motors Corp.
Detroit, Michigan

General Motors' largest volume division first passed Ford in production in 1927, the year Dearborn stopped building its venerable Model T and retooled in preparation for the Model A. Chevrolet's strength that year—and throughout the '30s—was its Stovebolt Six, also called the Cast Iron Wonder. The nicknames stemmed from the engine's ¼ × 20 slotted-head bolts and cast-iron pistons—not esoteric maybe, but wonderfully effective and as reliable as Old Faithful.

The Chevy six was developed by engineer Ormond E. Hunt, who took his cue from an earlier design by Henry M. Crane that had evolved into the 1926 Pontiac engine. The Chevy powerplant used the same stroke as the Pontiac but a larger bore, and by 1930 was producing an even 50 horsepower. With certain improvements over time, this solid, overhead-valve engine remained the division's standard powerplant for nearly three decades. For the 1933 Eagle and 1934 Master series it was given a new combustion chamber, a four-inch stroke, and the name Blue Flame Six. Then, for 1937, it was fully redesigned. Bore and stroke became nearly square, there were now four (instead of three) main bearings, and it was shorter and

1930 Universal coach

1932 Confederate Deluxe Special sedan

1930 Universal sport roadster

1933 Eagle two-door Town Sedan

1931 Independence sport roadster

1934 Master five-passenger coach

1935 Master DeLuxe five-passenger coach

1936 Master DeLuxe five-passenger coach

lighter than its predecessor. It was behind one of these engines in 1940 that young Juan Manuel Fangio won the car-breaking 5900-mile road race from Buenos Aires, Argentina to Lima, Peru and back with an average speed of 53.6 mph. Fangio continued to race his Chevy after World War II, but eventually switched to Grand Prix cars and became a legendary five-time world champion.

Throughout its history, Chevrolet has usually made the right decisions at precisely the right time. After he'd introduced the Stovebolt Six, division general manager William "Big Bill" Knudsen assigned styling to company design director Harley Earl. The result was a line of elegant-looking little cars for 1929-31 that resembled a Cadillac. For 1930 and 1931, a single series consisting of roadsters for two or four passengers, a phaeton, three coupes, and two sedans was offered at $495 to $685.

Each year's Chevys were identified by a special name: Universal for 1930, Independence for '31, Confederate for '32, Eagle (deluxe) and Mercury (standard) in 1933. Styling developed along the lines of the more expensive GM cars. The '33s, with their skirted fenders and graceful lines, were perhaps the most attractive Chevrolets of the entire decade. Body styles proliferated, and included such exotics as a $640 landau phaeton in 1932. The 1933 Eagles had many features designed to win buyers from Ford: a Fisher body with "No-Draft Ventilation," airplane-type instruments, Cadillac-style hood doors, a cowl vent, synchromesh transmission, selective free-wheeling, safety plate glass, adjustable driver's seat, and even an octane selector. Many of these features were also carried on the standard Mercury line. These were good years for the division despite the prevailing Depression. Chevy production outpaced Ford's each year in 1931-34. Output bottomed out at 300,000 units in 1932, rose to 480,000 in 1933, and was back to the 1931 level the following year.

Along with new streamlined body styling, 1934 brought a vital decision: "Knee-Action" independent front suspension on the Master series. This was Bill Knudsen's last act before leaving in October, 1933. According to writer Karl Ludvigsen, suspension engineer Maurice Olley tried to discourage Knudsen from using Knee-Action on the high-volume Chevy, saying there weren't enough centerless grinding machines in America to produce the necessary coil springs. Knudsen replied that this was just what the machine tool industry needed to get back on its feet, but nevertheless, he restricted the new feature to only the one

series. Not every buyer liked the suspension, and Masters with solid front axles were also offered in 1935-40. Standards continued to use the solid axle, and Knee-Action didn't spread throughout the line until 1941.

The 1935s were the last Chevys with any styling relationship to the classic era, and a wide model lineup was offered. Standards kept a 107-inch wheelbase, while Masters used a 113-inch span topped by very rakish bodies with V-shaped windshields and streamlined fenders. The raked-back radiator had its cap concealed under the hood, an innovation at the time. This dual-range marketing approach worked in the showrooms. Ford built more cars than Chevy in 1935, but it was the last time Dearborn would do so until 1959.

Continued modernization occurred in 1936 as Chevrolets adopted the rounded styling of the streamlined school. They had die-cast waterfall grilles, steel-spoked wheels (wires remained optional), smooth fenders and body lines, and all-steel "Turret Top" bodies. A big plus in the continuing battle with Ford was hydraulic brakes, which Ford failed to adopt until 1939, mainly due to the stubbornness of Henry Ford. The year also saw Chevy's two series become more alike as both used the 80-bhp Stovebolt Six, and the dated phaeton was dropped. The Master series had mostly the same styles, but substituted a sport coupe for a cabriolet. The Master wasn't offered as a cabriolet until 1937, and even then it came with a beam front axle rather than the Knee-Action suspension.

With the new 85-bhp engine for 1937, Chevrolet was particularly well equipped for the sales battle. Styling became rather dull, as it did for several other GM cars that year. Grilles were skinny and uninteresting, bodies high and bulky. Chevys looked pretty clumsy in the closing years of the decade, particularly compared to the increasingly streamlined Fords. Still, Chevrolet continued to outproduce Ford.

Competitiveness was evident in the 1940 line. The cars were thoroughly facelifted with what Chevrolet called Royal Clipper styling. Though not a drastic change from the past, it was sufficiently fresh to make the cars much newer-looking than the '39s. A new Special DeLuxe series was created for the top of the line, and included a convertible that was not available the previous year. The soft-top was quite successful: nearly 12,000 copies were sold.

Special and Master DeLuxe lines came standard with

1937 Master DeLuxe five-passenger coach

Knee-Action, the independent front suspension developed in 1934 by Maurice Olley. Chevrolet had reintroduced a cheaper model with a solid front axle in 1935, and this remained available through 1940, when it was called the Master 85. Both Master series were available as business coupes and two- and four-door sedans; the Master 85 included a woody wagon. The top-line Special DeLuxe also came in wagon form. These wagons, of course, were far different from today's all-steel wagons. Wooden construction made them heavy, ungainly, and hard to maintain. Later, Chevrolet and Plymouth would lead the trend to all-steel station wagons.

In model year production, 1941 was also a million-car year for Chevrolet. The division fielded the body/chassis combination that would carry it through 1948: 116-inch wheelbase, Knee-Action on all models, 90-bhp six, and attractive new styling by Harley Earl's Art & Colour Studio. The Master 85 series was dropped. The Master DeLuxe and Special DeLuxe retained the 1940 body styles. The Fleetline four-door sedan was a special addition, and 34,000 were sold that year. It was distinguished by a new, more formal-looking roofline with closed-in rear quarters, a takeoff on styling ideas first seen on the Cadillac 60 Special. The engine's 90 bhp

was obtained by means of a 6.5:1 compression head, new pistons, and reduced combustion chambers. Valves, rocker arms, and water pump were also reworked.

Further refinements to the '41 styling were made for '42: fenders were extended back into the front doors as on the more expensive GM cars; and a smart, clean grille replaced the somewhat busy '41 rendition. The model line stayed mostly the same, but new names were added: Stylemaster for the lower-priced Master DeLuxe coupes and sedans; Fleetmaster for the Special DeLuxe. An offshoot of the upper series was the Fleetline, comprising a new torpedo-style two-door Aerosedan and a conventionally styled four-door Sportmaster sedan. Both were distinguished by triple bands of brightwork on front and rear fenders.

Civilian car production stopped in February 1942. Chevrolet's model year total up to then was 254,885 units, of which only 45,472 were produced in calendar year 1942. In the Special DeLuxe series, only a handful of convertibles, wagons, and business coupes were built. Because they are so rare, 1942 Chevys are highly sought-after by collectors today.

Production at GM was hampered after the war by strikes and material shortages. If you count Chevy's tiny output in 1945 as a calendar year, it was outpaced by Ford by about three to one. But after that, Chevy was on top again, even though its 1946-48 cars were only slightly modified versions of the '42 design.

The differences were slight, but they were there. The '46s had fewer grille bars and a hood emblem with upright instead of horizontal wings. Parking lights were rectangular, fitted horizontally into the lower corners of the grille instead of vertically as before. The model line-up went unchanged, although the old Master series was simply called Stylemaster. This line comprised two- and four-door sedans, sport coupe, and business coupe.

1938 Master DeLuxe five-passenger coach

Fleetmaster sedans, coupes, convertible and wagon, and the Fleetline Aerosedan and Sportmaster were all continued.

It was during this period that Chevrolet experimented with and rejected a new rear-engine small car code-named Cadet. The design team was led by Maurice Olley. Several different configurations were considered. After spending a few million dollars on development, management concluded there was no market for it. Ford had reached the same conclusion at about the same time. Neither of the two giants fielded a small car until 1960, when the Corvair and Falcon were introduced.

Styling for each of the next two model years was basically a rerun of 1946. There was no change in the line-up of four Stylemasters, five Fleetmasters, and two Fleetlines, except for increased prices. But there were detail appearance changes. For 1947, the horizontal grille bars were wider, the nameplate went from the bottom to the top of the grille, the hood medallion was now horizontal, and side hood and beltline moldings were eliminated. For 1948, the grille acquired a central vertical bar rising to the base of the top horizontal molding with a small "Chevrolet" emblem near its top. The 1947-48 Fleetlines had horizontal chrome moldings on front and rear fenders; Sportmaster sedans had pivoting wind wings in the rear doors.

Although there was little visible change at Chevy during this period, the division that had written the industry's greatest success story was never known for standing pat, or for making wrong decisions. Management was changing, and new ideas were being discussed for the future: sports cars, hardtop convertibles, and all-steel station wagons.

In June 1946, Nick Dreystadt, former Cadillac general manager, replaced M. E. Coyle as general manager of

1940 Master DeLuxe four-door Sport Sedan

1946 Stylemaster four-door Sport Sedan

1941 Master DeLuxe two-door Town Sedan

1947 Fleetmaster four-door Sport Sedan

1942 Special DeLuxe Fleetmaster five-passenger coupe

1948 Fleetline two-door Aerosedan

Chevrolet. Dreystadt encouraged development of new models, and with a forceful engineering program brought new life to a make that had a rather stodgy image by then. But Dreystadt unexpectedly died two years later, and his successor, W. E. Armstrong, resigned early because of illness. Thomas H. Keating then stepped up. He followed Dreystadt's policies and spoke bullishly about Chevrolet's future. Soon after Keating took over, Edward N. Cole joined the team as Chevy's chief engineer.

The first order of business after the war was to change Chevy's look completely. GM had scheduled its first corporate postwar redesign for the 1949 model year, and Chevy's version was among the most attractive. Although wheelbase was actually an inch shorter, the '49 was cleanly styled from nose to tail and looked much more streamlined than the 1948 model. Its two-piece windshield was curved and two inches lower; fenders swept back smoothly through the cowl and doors, while the rear fenders rolled forward. Suspension revisions and a lower center of gravity made the '49 one of the best-handling Chevrolets ever—probably superior to that year's Plymouth and Ford. The '49s were also beautifully put together. The precise fit of body panels, the way the shifter snicked cleanly through the gears, and the car's positive response to controls testified that engineers and production people had gone to extremes to make them "right."

For the first time in years, the model line was overhauled for '49. The less expensive Series 1500GJ comprised the Special Styleline and the fastback Special Fleetline sedans. The more luxurious Series 2100GK included the Deluxe Styleline models—two- and four-door sedans, a coupe, convertible, and two station wagons. One of the wagons was trimmed with wood, one was all-steel, both carried eight passengers. This series also offered a pair of fastback sedans named DeLuxe Fleetline, a two-door and a four-door. Initially, the fastbacks sold well, but as time went on they fell out of favor, and disappeared at the end of 1952.

In the 1950s, Chevrolet evolved from staid family car to hot performance machine. The division moved from dull sedans to fast, sporty cars. Chevy also dropped from number-one in the industry to number-two—but only briefly.

Most of Chevrolet's decisions between 1950 and '59 were the right ones. It was right to build the Bel Air, first as a single hardtop and later as a separate series. It was highly successful, dominating production by 1957. It was right to build the 265 and 283 cubic-inch V8s, the engines that changed Chevrolet's performance reputation almost overnight. And it was right to market the Impala, because it added strength to the top of the line. Chevrolet would no longer be just one of the "low-priced three": now, it was an alternative for those who previously would have bought Pontiacs, Dodges, or Mercurys.

The 1950-52 period saw the last of the traditional low-cost, low-suds Chevys; 1953-54 saw a transition; 1955 a

revolution. In the early years, the Special accounted for about 15–20 percent of total production. The costlier DeLuxe accounted for the rest, and offered a wide variety of models. Specials came in two- or four-door sedans, coupes, and business coupes known as Stylelines, and two- and four-door fastback sedans called Fleetlines. The DeLuxe lineup had no business coupe,

1949 Styleline DeLuxe four-door Sport Sedan

1950 Styleline DeLuxe four-door Sport Sedan

1951 Styleline DeLuxe Bel Air hardtop coupe

1951 Styleline DeLuxe four-door sedan

but offered wagon, hardtop, convertible, and the Fleetline fastbacks.

Fleetlines did well enough in the seller's market of 1946-50, but the fastback fad had faded by the early '50s. Accordingly, Chevrolet phased them out. The last was a two-door in the '52 Deluxe series, and relatively few were made. As rapidly as the fastbacks disappeared, Bel Air hardtops took their place. Chevrolet was a year ahead of Ford and Plymouth in introducing a pillarless coupe, and sales were brisk. All 1950-52 Chevys were powered by the hoary old "stovebolt six." By this time, the 216.5-cid mill had been coaxed up to 92 bhp at 3400 rpm, or 105 bhp at 3600 when teamed with optional Powerglide two-speed automatic. Prices in those years were competitive and styling was consistent, varying only in minor details like grille, taillights, and side moldings.

In 1953, all GM cars got a major facelift, but Chevy and Pontiac looked newest. Chevy renamed the Special the One-Fifty and the Deluxe became the Two-Ten; the Bel Air was made a series in its own right with a full range of body styles. The big news that year was the Corvette, America's first postwar sports car (see separate chapter). The Blue Flame Six was revised again, with much higher compression giving up to 115 bhp. It was continued through the '50s and beyond, grinding out as much as 145 bhp. It was sound and reliable, but not very exciting. Ed Cole's V8 took care of that.

Without question, the 265-cid V8 that appeared for 1955 was one of the industry's milestone engines. Though designed to be efficient and cheap to build, it was really one of those "blue sky" projects of the type that comes along only once or twice in an engineer's career. Said Cole, "I had worked on V8 engines all my professional life. I had lived and breathed engines. [Motor engineer Harry F.] Barr and I were always say-

1952 Styleline DeLuxe four-door sedan

1952 Styleline DeLuxe two-door sedan

1953 Bel Air four-door sedan

1953 Bel Air convertible

1954 Bel Air four-door sedan

1954's Nomad show car — forerunner of Nomad wagons

1955 Bel Air Nomad two-door station wagon

1956 Bel Air hardtop sedan

1955 Two-Ten hardtop coupe

1956 Bel Air Nomad two-door station wagon

1958 styling preview—Biscayne show car, 1955

1957 Bel Air convertible

ing how we would do it if we could ever design a new engine. You just know you want five main bearings—there's no decision to make. We knew that a certain bore-stroke relationship was the most compact. We knew we'd like a displacement of 265 cubic inches . . . And we never changed any of this. We released our engine for tooling direct from the drawing boards—that's how crazy and confident we were.''

Cole and Barr had reason to be enthusiastic. The 265 weighed even less than the six. It had low reciprocating mass, which allowed high rpm; die-cast heads with integral, interchangeable valve guides; aluminum slipper pistons; and a crankshaft of forged pressed-steel instead of alloy iron. It performed beautifully, putting out 162 bhp at 4400 rpm, or 180 bhp at 4600 with Power-pak (a four-barrel carburetor and dual exhausts). It became the basis of all the great Chevy engines of the immediate future: the 225-bhp '56 Corvette and the bored-out fuel-injected 283 of 1957, the first mass-production engine with one horsepower per cubic inch. Chevrolet developed a new 348-cid V8 as a big-car option for 1958, and it was a good one. But the 283 remained the

best-known, best-loved engine of the period, earning Chevy a reputation for performance it had never enjoyed with the sixes.

Powerglide automatic, a torque converter using the Dynaflow principle, was an increasingly popular option in those years at a price under $200. Smooth in operation, it was well-suited to all but the high-powered models. These were available with a manual or stick-overdrive, three-speed Turboglide automatic from 1957 on, and an all-synchromesh four-speed manual starting in 1959.

Styling was as much a part of the mid-1950s picture as engineering. Harley Earl's Chevy design team—Clare MacKichan, Chuck Stebbins, Bob Veryzer, Carl Renner, and others—worked under Earl's guideline: "Go all the way, then back off." Though the '55 didn't reach production looking the way it had in fanciful renderings, it wasn't far off. The beltline dip and wraparound windshield had been inspired by the Cadillac Eldorado, Oldsmobile Fiesta, and Buick Skylark limited editions of 1953; the eggcrate grille had been inspired by Ferrari and was one of Earl's favorite touches. The

1957 Two-Ten four-door sedan

1957 One-Fifty two-door utility sedan

1957 Bel Air Nomad two-door station wagon

1958 Impala hardtop coupe

1958 Bel Air hardtop sedan

1958 Biscayne four-door sedan

grille was unpopular with the public though, so the '56 version was broader, brighter, and more conventional.

Carl Renner was the man responsible for a unique hardtop wagon called the Bel Air Nomad. Actually, it was too impractical as a wagon, too bulky as a hardtop. But it was the ideal stylistic blend of both. If it didn't sell well, it was more because two-door wagons were generally less popular than four-doors rather than lack of appeal. The Nomad was relatively expensive, but there had never been such a beautiful wagon. Had anybody else built it, the Nomad would probably be quite rare today. Volume, however, was relatively high: 8386 were built for 1955; 7886 for '56, 6103 for 1957.

A mild facelift came about for '56, another in '57. Both Ford and Plymouth were completely restyled in 1957, so Chevrolet suffered by comparison. Yet record market penetration of close to 28 percent was achieved in 1956, and the '57 facelift was a good one. The engines previously described had the go to match the looks. A '57 Bel Air four-door hardtop with the 270-bhp engine would streak from 0 to 60 mph in 9.9 seconds, do the quarter-mile in 17.5 seconds, and run up to well over 110 mph. The lighter One-Fifty with the injected V8 was even faster.

Properly equipped, the 1955-57 Chevy was, and is, a formidable competitor on the race track. Before the Automobile Manufacturers Association recommended the industry withhdraw from organized racing in 1957, Chevy did quite well on NASCAR and other circuits. At the 1957 Daytona Speed Weeks, it added more achievements. In Class 4 (213 to 259 cubic inches) Chevrolets won the first three places in the two-way flying-mile; in Class 5 (259 to 305 cubic inches) they took 33 out of 37 places, with the best car averaging 131.076 mpg. Chevy also won the Pure Oil Manufacturers Trophy in '57 with 574 points, against only 309 for runner-up Ford.

The effects of the racing ban didn't take long. For 1958, Chevy back-pedaled on performance with a line of softer, more luxurious cars. Most reviewers were unhappy. Said Tom McCahill of *Mechanix Illustrated,* "When an ad man can't write about his product's success at Pikes Peak, Daytona Beach or Darlington, or how fast it gets away from a traffic light, what's he got left? All he can do is tell about the hand-woven Indian

rugs on the floor, the Da Vinci sculptured door handles, or the 'ten miles per gallon' it averaged under the featherfoot of a professional economy jockey.''

McCahill was right. The '58 Chevys were longer, lower, wider, heavier . . . and slower. The division was reaching for a new market sector—the solid, substantial Pontiac-types it had never gone after before—with such cars as the Impala. People who bought Impalas, then as now, didn't care about performance or handling. They wanted size and comfort. The Impala delivered.

Despite a rough year for the U.S. economy in '58, Chevy managed to build over 1.1 million cars: 60,000 were Impalas. That was a decent showing for a new series consisting of only a hardtop and convertible. The One-Fifty was renamed Delray; Biscayne replaced the Two-Ten title. Bel Air was still top of the line, with Impala as a sub-series for '58 only. "Station Wagon" became a separate series with no fewer than five models: the two-door Yeoman; four-door Yeoman, Brookwood, and Nomad; and the nine-passenger Brookwood. The '58 Nomad wasn't the same car it had been in 1955-57. It was now just a conventional wagon, and it remained so through 1961, its last year.

Chevrolet probably deserves credit for bucking the tailfin trend in 1958, but the stylists made up for it the following year with an overdecorated bat-wing tail. The result was a rear deck, as Tom McCahill said, "big enough to land a Piper Cub." It could have been worse. Carl Renner said one 1959 proposal called for an upright, Edsel-like grille and was one of the ugliest things

he'd ever seen. As it turned out, the front end of the '59 was relatively mild, but the rear was a thing from another world. This was the year Ford beat Chevy in calendar year production, so Chevrolet's rear end was a lot more subdued for 1960.

Delray disappeared in 1959, leaving the Biscayne, Bel Air, Impala, and Station Wagon in the lineup. All rode a 119-inch wheelbase, the longest in postwar history. The growth between 1957 and 1959 was amazing. Wheelbases were up by four inches, length by nearly eleven inches, width by seven inches, and weight increased by 300 pounds. The '59s were the first of the overstuffed generation that would live on for the next 15 years. Only recently has GM been weaning the public from these enormous vehicles. At the time, of course, they made a degree of sense. In order to compete, the low-priced three—Ford, Chevy and Plymouth—needed larger and larger dimensions, cars the size of Cadillacs and Lincolns that would sell at half the price. Chevy led; Ford and Plymouth followed suit.

During the 1960s, Chevrolet expanded into at least five new market areas: compacts with the Corvair and Chevy II, intermediates with the Chevelle, super stockers with the Malibu and Impala SS, luxury full-size models with the Caprice, and "ponycars" with the Camaro. (The Corvette and Corvair are different enough to be treated separately.) Each new product of the decade was carefully designed to fill a basic need. Nearly every one succeeded.

Moving into so many new markets would seem to imply increased production. The division did set some

1959 Biscayne two-door sedan

1960 Impala convertible

1959 Impala four-door sedan

1961 Impala two-door sedan

1962 Impala convertible

1962 Chevy II 300 two-door sedan

1963 Impala convertible

1963 Chevy II 100 two-door sedan

1964 Impala hardtop coupe

records during the decade. But it was only producing some 500,000 more cars at the end of the '60s than it had been at the beginning, despite introducing four new lines in different size categories. Actually, the market had been subdivided. The departure of the independent automakers and the rise of compacts, sporty compacts, and intermediates in the '60s generated more competition than there had been in the '50s. In many cases, Chevy was competing against itself or other GM divisions.

Chevrolet offered a wide range of cars by the end of the decade, built on just four wheelbases: 108 inches for the Corvair and Camaro, 110 for the Chevy II and Nova, 115 for the Chevelle, and 119 for the big Chevrolets. The only exception was the 1968-72 Chevelle. Like other GM compacts of those years, it used a 112-inch wheelbase for two-door models and a 116-inch wheelbase for the four-doors.

The big Chevrolet progressed from overstyled outrageousness to clean, crisp elegance. The '60 model was a facelift of the horrendously finned '59 edition. The fins were cropped and completely disappeared for '61. By 1963, there was a new sculptured body without a trace of the outlandish '50s. Without a change in wheelbase, the large Chevrolet grew bulkier in the last years of the decade, but was deftly styled nonetheless. Another complete restyle in 1965 brought flowing lines and a slight upward sweep to the rear quarter panels. This shape continued until 1969, when a new look was fashioned with elliptical wheel openings, emphasized by subtle bulges. The prettiest full-size Chevy of the period might be the 1962. It had straight, correct lines and interesting roof styling with "bow" sculpturing like a raised convertible top.

Biscayne was still the price leader, but buyer interest fell during the decade. The Bel Air had become the mid-priced big Chevrolet in 1959 but its sales also decreased in the '60s. The top-line Impala had rapidly become the most popular single model in the United States. Its best sales year of the decade was 1964, when 889,600 units were built.

One Impala worthy of particular attention is the performance-bred Super Sport of 1962-67. Like Corvair and Camaro, the Impala SS is already a collector's item. The concept was simple: take the big, 119-inch standard-wheelbase chassis, add sporty styling touches, and offer options designed to enhance performance and handling. The Impala SS was available as either a two-door hardtop or convertible. A six-cylinder engine was offered, but only 3600 were equipped with one in 1965. The exterior featured special SS emblems and deleted the regular Impala's rocker panel brightwork. Vinyl bucket seats and a central gearshift console were standard. Tachometer and sport steering wheel were optional. Big-displacement V8s were offered, like the famous 409 that developed 425 bhp. Equipped with exciting handling options like stiffer springs and shocks, sintered metallic brake linings, four-speed gearbox, and ultra-quick power steering, the Impala SS was the

Prototype for 1964 Chevelle Malibu four-door sedan

1965½ Caprice hardtop sedan

1965 Impala hardtop coupe

1966 Caprice hardtop sedan

highest-performance big Chevy in history.

But it didn't last. Government regulations, a decline in demand for race-bred automobiles, and the increased popularity of smaller sporty cars all combined to do in the Impala SS after 1967. Production fell rapidly during the five model years. Meanwhile, Chevrolet had found a far more lucrative market by dolling up the Impala with the best grades of upholstery and trim, and calling it Caprice. This top-of-the-line Chevy arrived in 1965 and captured some 180,000 buyers in 1966.

Next in Chevrolet's size hierarchy of the '60s was the intermediate Chevelle, introduced in 1964 to compete against Ford's Fairlane. The Chevelle was conventional: front engine, rear drive, coil springs in front, leaf springs in the rear. It provided almost as much interior room as the Impala, but had a more sensibly sized ex-

terior. In effect, it was a revival of the ideally proportioned, middle-wheelbase "classic" Chevrolet of 1955-57. Sales went nowhere but up, from 328,400 units in its first year to nearly 440,000 by 1969. The addition of numerous performance options and its own SS variations only enhanced Chevelle's appeal.

Third down the size scale was the 110-inch-wheelbase Chevy II. It had been rushed into production for 1962 as a stopgap against Ford's Falcon, which was handily trimming Corvair in the compact market. While Corvair appealed mainly to car enthusiasts, Falcon pleased the much broader range of average buyers. Chevy IIs were available with a 153-cid four-cylinder engine with 90 bhp, or a 194-cid 120-bhp six. (Falcons had only six-cylinder powerplants.)

Chevrolet hoped to outflank and outproduce Ford in this segment. But through 1966, Chevy IIs outnumbered Falcons only once, in 1963. Between 1963 and '64, sales dropped nearly 50 percent, due partly to competition from the Chevelle. A spate of Super Sport models didn't help. By the middle of the decade, Chevy II seemed destined for oblivion.

Then in 1968, Chevy gave its compact an all-new body with a 111-inch wheelbase for two-door coupes and four-door sedans. The new cars were known by the name of the previous top-line series, Nova. Backed by a strong ad campaign and competitive prices, the Chevy II Nova made a comeback. The division concentrated on just the two body styles, which sold as fast as they could be built. Sales were up to 201,000 units in 1968, the best year since '63. The Chevy II title was dropped, and the basic design continued as the Nova through 1979, when it was replaced by the front-wheel-drive Citation.

The Camaro is one of the more interesting Chevrolets of the '60s, and potentially the most collectible (aside from Corvettes). Introduced for 1967, it was an immediate hit. Production topped 220,000 cars the first year, followed by 235,100 for 1968, and 243,100 for 1969.

The Camaro was born out of a need to replace the ailing Corvair. Despite the beautiful styling and impressive performance of the all-new 1965 models, Corvair was no threat to Ford's incredibly successful Mustang in the burgeoning "ponycar" market. Furthermore, the Corvair was expensive to build; it was entirely different in concept and technology from mainstream Chevrolet models. Six months after the '65s arrived, division managers decided Corvair would be allowed to fade away. Its replacement would be a conventional front-engine sporty car—the ultimate solution to the Mustang.

The Camaro's design became the responsibility of William L. Mitchell, GM's vice-president of styling, and head of the corporation's Styling Staff. There was no better team of designers in the industry during this period. The look that resulted—flat nose, chiseled profile, chopped-off rear deck, and low roofline—was exactly right. The Camaro appealed to those who wanted a four-seater with handling to match its straight-line performance.

1967 Impala hardtop coupe

1967 Camaro hardtop coupe

1967 Chevy II Nova SS hardtop coupe

1968 Impala convertible

1968 Camaro convertible

1968 Chevy II Nova coupe

1968 Chevelle SS 396 hardtop coupe

1969 Chevelle SS 396 hardtop coupe

The Camaro was more than a new Chevrolet: it was a new concept. Mustang had pointed the way, and GM has never been reticent about borrowing a good idea. Some 81 factory options and 41 dealer-installed accessories were offered so the buyer could tailor the car to taste and budget. Prices started at $2466 f.o.b. for the 140-bhp six-cylinder coupe and $2704 for the convertible. The 155-bhp, 250-cid six cost $26 extra; the 210-bhp 327 V8 was an additional $106. Next on the list was a 350-cid V8 with 295 bhp, exclusive to Camaro in '67. (Later, it became the most popular Corvette powerplant.) To get it, the buyer had to order the Super Sports package.

The SS option cost $211 and included a tight suspension (stiff springs and shocks), D70-14 Firestone Wide Oval tires, modified hood with extra sound insulation,

SS emblems, and special hood striping. Early in the model year, the L-35 Chevrolet 396-cid V8 and Turbo Hydra-Matic became available at a cost of nearly $400. Scores of other options tempted buyers: custom carpeting, bucket seats, fold-down back seat, a special interior group, full instrumentation, and console-mounted shifters for the Turbo Hydra-Matic, heavy-duty three speed manual or four-speed manual. For $105, the Rally Sport package added a hidden-headlight grille, special taillights and emblems, aluminum rocker panel moldings, black-painted rocker bottoms, and miscellaneous trim. There were five different wheels and wheel covers, three types of steering wheels, plus headrests, shoulder belts, tinted glass, radios, heater, air conditioning, clock, cruise control, and a vinyl-covered roof for hardtops. Mechanical options included

sintered metallic brake linings, ventilated front disc brakes, vacuum brake booster, power steering, fast-ratio manual steering, stiff suspension, Positraction, and a dozen different axle ratios. Without too much trouble, a Camaro's price could be boosted to $5000.

The Camaro wasn't significantly changed in 1968 or '69, although interim facelifts were proposed. The ultimate restyling was scheduled for 1970. The '68 model received a new horizontal grille texture, ventless side glass, and restyled taillights. For 1969 there were slimmer body contours, lower front and rear wheel openings, a V-shaped grille, and a new rear styling.

A successful competition Chevrolet of these years

was the Z/28 Camaro, which won 18 of 25 Sports Car Club of America Trans-Am races and was Trans-Am sedan class champion in 1968 and 1969. Vincent W. Piggins, veteran competition engineer, had convinced management a car should be built expressly for SCCA sedan racing. Piggins combined the 327 V8 block with the 283 crankshaft to get a bore and stroke of 4×3 inches for a displacement of 302.4 cubic inches. Officially, this engine delivered 290 bhp at 5800 rpm (actually it was more like 350) and 290 pounds-feet of torque at 4200 rpm. This engine was combined with heavy-duty suspension, front disc brakes, metallic-lined rear drums, 11-inch clutch, close-ratio four-speed

1969 Impala Custom hardtop coupe

1970 Monte Carlo hardtop coupe

1969 Nova coupe

1970 Nova coupe

1969 Camaro 2-28 hardtop coupe

1970 Chevelle SS 396 hardtop coupe

1970 Caprice hardtop coupe

1970 Camaro sport coupe

1971 Caprice Classic hardtop coupe

1971 Monte Carlo hardtop coupe

1971 Chevelle Malibu hardtop coupe

1971 Vega 2300 two-door sedan

1972 Monte Carlo hardtop coupe

transmission with a 2.20:1 first gear, quick steering, and wide Corvette wheels. The hood was reworked to increase airflow to the carburetor.

The Z/28 name came from the package's option number (not from Zora Arkus-Duntov, the famed Corvette engineer). It was a whale of an automobile for about $3300. Few Z/28s were intended for the general public, of course; the object was to win the Trans-Am championship. But production quickly climbed, from 602 in 1967 to 7199 in 1968 and 19,014 in 1969. The Z/28s are the ultimate performance Camaros. A decade or two from now, they will be one of the ultimate collector's Chevys.

In 1970, Chevrolet entered the personal-luxury field with the Monte Carlo and fielded an all-new Camaro. A 65-day strike prevented the division from outproducing Ford for the calendar year, but the 12-month total of near 1.5 million cars was respectable nonetheless.

The cleanly styled Monte Carlo hardtop sat on the 116-inch wheelbase used for the Chevelle four-doors. Fitted with the 350-cid V8 as standard, it was available with a variety of luxury and performance options to suit every buyer. Numerous engine choices were offered, up to the huge 454-cid V8. At a base price of nearly $3000, the Monte Carlo sold well: over 130,000 copies in its first year, against a mere 40,000 of Ford's Thunderbird. Of course, the T-Bird was considerably more costly, but the Monte Carlo must be judged a success.

Shorn of its Chevy II designation, the Nova was facelifted for 1970, receiving a fine-mesh grille and large front, side, and rear lights. The intermediate Chevelle was vastly altered, and now bore a family resemblance to the full-size models. It had a divided grille, sculptured sides, and was offered as both a hardtop and a fixed-pillar coupe. The big-car sales emphasis was still on the luxurious Impala and Caprice; Biscayne and Bel Air were reduced to one four-door sedan each, offered with either six or V8.

The brilliant new 1970 Camaro was introduced in the spring of that year; the 1969 model was sold through the previous December. The new Camaro brought dramatic European-inspired GT styling to the ponycar field. Over 143,000 examples were sold that year. Its styling was so good that it was still around with surprisingly few changes ten years later.

The 1970s were years of new product experiments at Chevrolet. Some of them were good and are still with us. Others were minor blunders the division would rather forget. Yet is is very hard for the most successful nameplate on earth to make a really serious mistake. What could be a disaster of major proportions for a smaller company end up as mere hiccoughs on the graph of Chevrolet history. The Vega, for example, is viewed now as a pretty bad car, yet it remained in the lineup for eight model years and sold respectably in every one.

The Vega seemed like a good idea when it bowed for 1971. Mounted on Chevy's shortest wheelbase at that time, it was powered by a newly designed all-aluminum

1972 Camaro Rally Sport coupe

1972 Chevelle Malibu hardtop coupe

1972 Caprice Classic hardtop sedan

1973 Chevelle Laguna Colonnade hardtop coupe

1973 Chevelle Malibu Colonnade hardtop coupe

1974 Caprice Classic convertible

1974 Monte Carlo Landau coupe

four that was pretty stingy with gas, and it was offered in practical body styles like a hatchback coupe and a neat little "Kammback" wagon. Chevrolet spent vast sums designing, launching and promoting this latterday import fighter, and on a special factory to build it. But the Vega missed its target from the beginning. Instead of economical utility, it soon became seen as a small sporty car of low versatility. The bodies were notorious rusters, and persistent oil leak and cylinder head warping troubles in the linerless engine were not cured until 1976. By that time the smaller Chevette was ready, and the Vega was being crowded out of contention by a number of domestic and foreign rivals. Though the name was dropped after 1977,

the car itself (minus the problematic engine) lived on through 1979 as part of the Monza line.

An exception to most of the above was the exciting, short-lived Cosworth-Vega of 1975-76, a good performer that has already gained a degree of status with car collectors. The engine was its main attraction, a destroked Vega powerplant with a special 16-valve aluminum head designed by Cosworth Engineering in England. Bendix electronic fuel injection fed the cyclinders, actuated by a glovebox-mounted "computer." Available only as a hatchback coupe, the "CosVeg" was initially offered only with black paint, set off by special gold bodyside striping and cast-aluminum wheels. Wide radial tires, full instrumenta-

1974 Chevelle Laguna S-3 Colonnade coupe

1974 Nova Custom four-door sedan

1974 Camaro Type LT sport coupe

1974 Vega Estate Wagon

1975 Monte Carlo Landau coupe

1975 Chevelle Malibu Classic Colonnade coupe

1975 Monza 2+2 hatchback coupe

1976 Chevette Rally three-door sedan

tion in an engine-turned dash panel, anti-roll bars at both ends, special-ratio four-speed transmission, quick steering, and discreet badges completed the package. Unfortunately, the engine yielded only 21 extra horsepower after all emission standards were accounted for, so this was not the BMW-beater Chevy had hoped. The 1976 version was available in any Vega color and an optional five-speed gearbox was offered, but many Cosworths were still unsold at year's end. Today, this model is sought after as one of Chevy's rarer and more interesting cars of the '70s.

A more successful Vega offshoot was the Monza, introduced for 1975. Intially sharing the same basic chassis and drivetrain, this was a handsome 2 + 2 coupe with lift-up rear door and a fastback greenhouse reminiscent of certain Ferrari roofs. A major 1976 improvement was a redesigned overhead-cam engine, with hydraulic valve lifters giving quieter performance and greater valvetrain durability. The Monza finished a close second in the 1976 EPA fuel economy tests, behind Ford's lighter Mustang II, with city/highway ratings of 22/35 mpg. Enthusiasts could opt for several interesting Regular Production options such as RPO Z01, a performance and handling package. After 1977, the Monza name was applied to the remnants of the Vega range.

continued on page 145

▲1930 American Austin coupe ▼1930 Cord L-29 cabriolet

▲1930 Nash Twin-Ignition Six roadster   ▼1930 Ruxton four-door sedan

▲1931 Cadillac Series 90 V16 phaeton   ▼1930 Packard Speedster Eight boattail roadster

▲ 1933 Chrysler Imperial Custom phaeton   ▼ 1931 Ford Model A cabriolet (body by Buehrig)

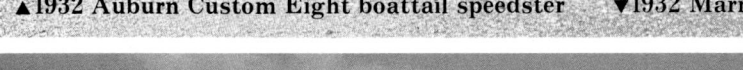

▲1932 Auburn Custom Eight boattail speedster ▼1932 Marmon Sixteen convertible by LeBaron

▲ 1936 Cord 810 Westchester sedan   ▼ 1937 Ford DeLuxe convertible sedan

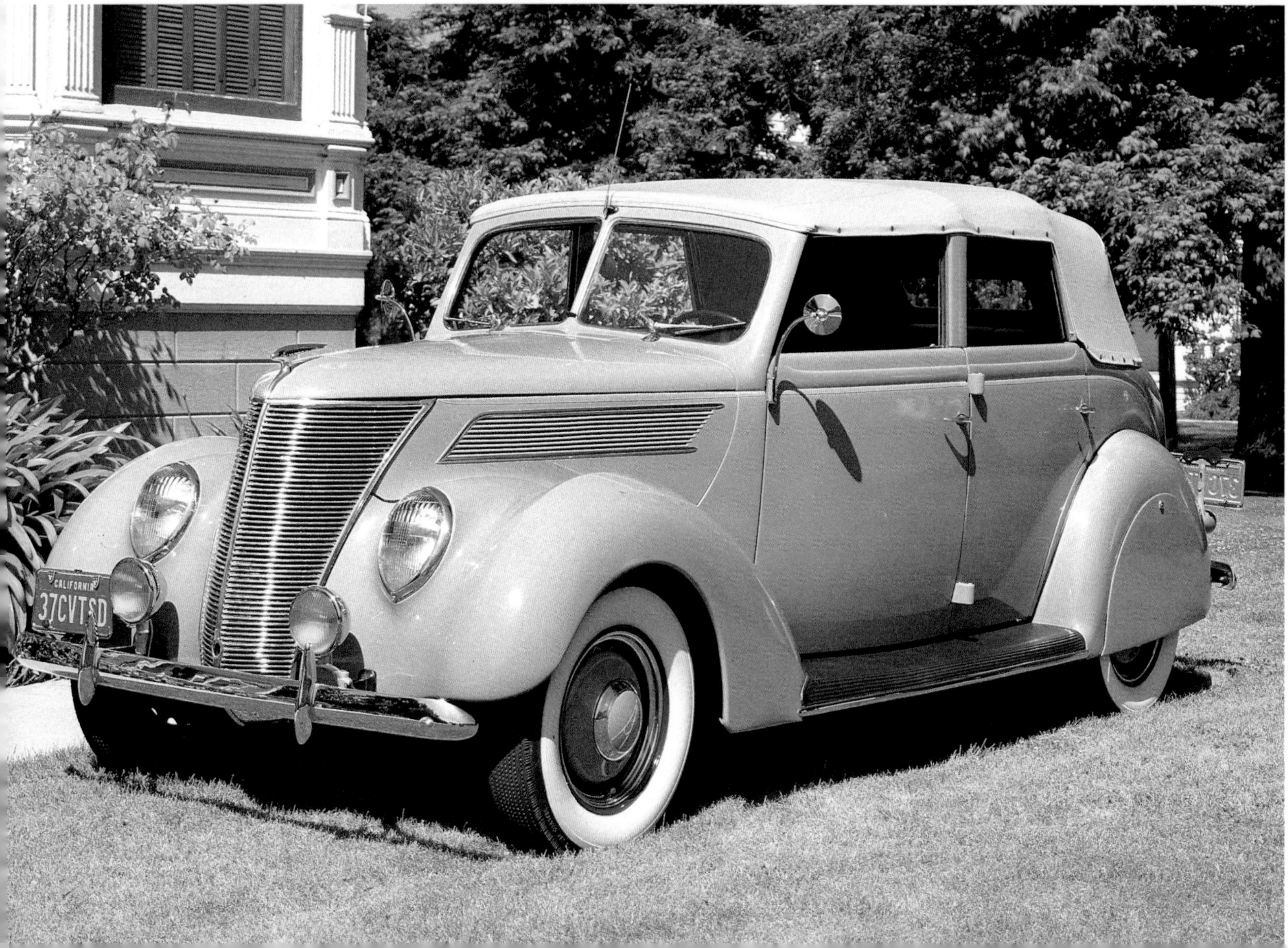

▲1938 Buick Special four-door touring sedan ▼1938 Cadillac Series 90 V16 formal sedan

▲1939 Ford DeLuxe coupe   ▼1939 Graham Custom Supercharger four-door sedan

▲1938 Hudson Terraplane Super Six brougham ▼1939 Crosley Series 1A convertible coupe

▲1939 American Bantam DeLuxe roadster   ▼1940 Ford DeLuxe convertible coupe

▲1940 Mercury Town Sedan   ▼1940 Chrysler Royal coupe

▲1941 Lincoln Continental club coupe　　▼1941 Graham Custom Hollywood sedan

▲1940 Packard Super Eight 160 convertible   ▼1948 Dodge Custom four-door sedan

▲1948 Nash Ambassador Custom cabriolet    ▼1948 Cadillac Sixty Special sedan

▲1948 Tucker "Torpedo" four-door sedan ▼1946 Lincoln Continental cabriolet

▲1949 Oldsmobile Futuramic 98 four-door sedan   ▼1949 Buick Roadmaster Riviera hardtop coupe

continued from page 128

Further up the size scale, the division reaped steady success with the 111-inch-wheelbase Nova, the long-running compact that had evolved from the original Chevy II and last redesigned for 1968. Chevrolet engineered a lot of value into the Nova, which carried on in this form through 1974. The next year it was extensively reworked, with a new roofline and more glass, plus steering and front suspension borrowed from the Camaro. Nova captured 15 percent of total Chevrolet sales that year to become the best-selling American compact. The engine lineup was simplified for 1976, and the "performance" option was now a 305-cid V8, replacing the older 262 and 350 engines with two-barrel carburetors. It was not a revived 307, though, but a debored version of the 350. The standard six through 1979 remained the workhorse 250-cid inline unit, after which both engine and the car were scrubbed in favor of a new generation of V6s and the first of Chevy's front-drive X-body models, the Citation.

Unveiled in April 1979, the Citation was a runaway success its first year, though the arrival of another fuel crisis helped. Buyers could choose from three body styles, two-door and four-door hatchback sedans (the later looking quite similar to the Lancia Beta, several of which were studied by GM during the X-body's development) and a two-door "slantback" coupe unique among the four versions of this corporate design. The new X-body afforded excellent space utilization at moderate weight, which averaged only about 2500 pounds. Pontiac's well-proven 2.5-liter Iron Duke four was standard and Chevy's new 60-degree 2.8-liter (173-cid) V6 was optional, both mounted transversely to enhance the space-saving front-drive mechanicals. A four-speed manual transmission was standard, three-speed automatic optional. To make a Citation sporty you ordered the X-11 package, with handling suspension and other mods, plus brash exterior identification. Though it had no more power than other models at first, the X-11 was a capable all-rounder when equipped with the V6. Unfortunately, like most new designs, the Citation had a hefty helping of engineering "bugs" and quality control problems, and would be recalled many times. But the car's practicality, performance and overall liveability made it a hot number, and Chevy's main problem was keeping up with demand.

The bigger Chevrolets saw relatively little change during the early '70s. In the full-size arena, the marketing emphasis gradually centered on the Impala and Caprice series, the familiar, less expensive Biscayne and Bel Air lines being dropped for 1973 and 1976, respectively. Then came the revolution: the first-wave of GM's corporate-wide downsizing program, which saw the 1977 Impala/Caprice trimmed by 5½ inches in wheelbase and 600-800 pounds in gas-wasting bulk. It seemed like a huge gamble then, and Ford cranked up its promotion machine to tell people its still-enormous full-size cars had kept their size. But Chevrolet, as usual, knew exactly what it was doing. The following year, the intermediate Chevelle/Malibu and the companion personal-luxury Monte Carlo got a similar re-

furbishing. It was all to the good, for the new models were not only lighter but more agile, far easier on gas, more fun to drive and, to some, better looking.

The Monte Carlo, introduced for 1970 as Chevy's "personal car" reply to the Thunderbird from Ford and similar models from other GM divisions, rapidly won a loyal following. It split into S and Landau sub-models for 1973, the first year for "Colonnade" styling on GM intermediates. The only Monte Carlo with any claim to performance was the SS454 of 1970-71. This was actually an option package, RPO Z20, consisting of a 360-bhp version of the big-block Mark IV V8, plus square-tip dual exhausts and a chassis fortified with automatic level control rear shocks, stiffer front shocks, and power front disc brakes. Discreet badges and black rocker panel accents were the only clues to what was under the hood. Acceleration was vivid, with 0-60 mph taking only about 7.5 seconds. A handful of non-standard options found their way onto SS Montes too, including the 450-bhp LS-6 engine and the M-series four-speed manual gearbox (Turbo Hydra-matic was standard). But most Monte Carlos of the '70s were equipped with much milder engines, and offered luxury and smoothness, plus the longest hood ever bolted onto a Chevrolet.

The popular Camaro had its ups and downs in the '70s as the golden age of ponycars receded further into history. But a determined effort by enthusiasts within GM saved the striking second-generation design from a premature end after the Arab oil embargo, and it enjoyed a remarkable sales resurgence on into the 1980s, when an even more exciting third generation took its place. The 1971-72 models were little changed from the inaugural "1970½"

1976 Monza Towne Coupe

1976 Chevelle Malibu Classic coupe

1977½ Camaro Z28 sport coupe

1977 Vega GT hatchback coupe

1978 Caprice Classic four-door sedan

1978 Monte Carlo Landau coupe

1978 Monza Estate wagon

1978 Camaro Z28 sport coupe

1978 Malibu Classic Landau coupe

edition, with most of the modifications prompted by federal regulations. The 1973s had to meet stricter bumper standards, but stylists handled this beautifully by moving the front and rear bumpers farther away from the body and reinforcing them with braces and an inner support bar. The macho SS was replaced that year by the less pretentious LT (Luxury Touring), carrying a 165-bhp V8, variable-ratio power steering, and appearance touches like hidden wipers, black painted rockers and accents, Rally wheels, and woodgrain dash trim. Prices started to gallop with the '74s, which received a really serious front-end facelift to accommodate that year's new bumper impact standards. A wraparound rear window marked the 1975s, which began the Camaro's sales revival after a four-year dry spell. Capitalizing on renewed buyer interest in ponycars,

Chevy reinstated the Rally Sport package as a mid-season option: matte-black hood and front fender tops, special paint and the further option of color-matched Z 28 wheels. The '74 facelift kept going for 1976-77, and Camaro reached, then exceeded, its old sales record of the 1960s. The big news for 1977 was the return of the racy Z 28, which had been absent for two years. The emphasis now, however, was on grand touring road manners instead of raw acceleration. Engineer Jack Turner took a straightforward approach to the chassis: tighter springs at each corner, a thicker front roll bar, more flexible rear bar, larger wheels and tires. And there were bold exterior graphics and bright colors well suited to the smooth lines. Midyear introduction kept production low for '77, but sales took off the next year. Low numbers plus status at the "first of the last" per-

formance models among the second-generation cars makes the "1977½" Z-car a potential collector's item.

If Chevrolet couldn't meet the needs of American motorists, probably nobody else could. The division spent the 1970s revolutionizing its model lineup, reordering its priorities to cope with the vast changes taking place in customer buying habits. A good example of these ardent efforts was the Chevette, the smallest car ever to carry the Chevrolet badge. Announced for 1976, it tipped the scales at under 2000 pounds and was 17 inches shorter than a Vega. Its basic engineering was derived from the newly designed 1974 German Opel Kadett, the first of GM's "world car" T-body models (England's Vauxhall Chevette and Japan's Isuzu Gemini were other variants). The Chevette was unique for a U.S. car in being built entirely to metric measurements. Its principal aim was economy, which it delivered: 35 mpg was not uncommon in highway driving, although Chevrolet had wanted 40 mpg. The Chevette was offered initially as a two-door hatchback sedan, and a four-door arrived for 1978 on a slightly longer wheelbase. Built to sell at a low price, the Chevette was always offered with a lengthy list of options. Like so many Chevrolets before it, it was exactly right for its time, well built, and engaging to drive as well. It was a far better entry than Vega in the increasingly competitive subcompact market, and proved once again that Chevrolet Division makes very few mistakes. Chevy weathered the 1970s better than most of its competitors, even within General Motors, and by the 1980s its lineup was fully up to date.

1979 Camaro Berlinetta sport coupe

1979 Nova two-door sedan

1979 Monte Carlo coupe

1980 Malibu Classic coupe

1980 Camaro Z28 sport coupe

1980 Monte Carlo coupe with turbo option

1980 Caprice Classic coupe

Chevrolet Specifications

1930

AD Universal (wb 107.0)		Wght	Price	Prod
	rdstr 2P	2,195	495	5,684
	spt rdstr 2-4P	2,250	515	27,651
	phtn 5P	2,265	495	1,713
	cpe 2	2,415	565	100,373
	spt cpe 2-4P	2,525	615	45,311
	coach 5P	2,515	565	255,027
	club sdn 5P	2,575	625	24,888
	sdn 5P	2,615	675	135,193
	Special sdn 5P	2,625	685	35,929
	cpe 2P R/S	2,540	n.a.	9,211

1930 Engine	bore×stroke	bhp	availability
L6, 194.0	3.13×3.75	50	S-all

1931

AE Independence (wb 109.0)		Wght	Price	Prod
	rdstr 2P	2,275	475	2,939
	spt rdstr 2P	2,330	495	24,050
	Deluxe phtn 5P	2,370	510	852
	cpe 2P 3W	2,490	535	57,741
	spt cpe 2-4P	2,565	575	66,029
	cpe 2P 5W	2,490	545	28,379
	coach 5P	2,585	545	228,316
	sdn 5P	2,685	635	52,465
	Special sdn 5P	2,725	650	109,775
	cpe 5P	2,610	595	20,297
	cab 2-4P	2,520	615	23,077
	conv sdn 5P	2,610	650	5,634

1931 Engine	bore×stroke	bhp	availability
L6, 194.0	3.13×3.75	50	S-all

1932

BA Confederate (wb 109.0)		Wght	Price	Prod
	rdstr 2P	2,410	445	1,118
	cpe 2P 3W	2,580	490	8,874
	coach 5P	2,665	495	132,109
	sdn 5P	2,750	590	27,718
	spt cpe 2-4P	2,645	535	26,623
	Deluxe spt cpe 2-4P	2,695	550	
	cpe 2P 5W	2,580	490	34,796
	Deluxe cpe 2P 5W	2,630	505	
	cpe 5P	2,700	575	7,566
	Deluxe cpe 5P	2,700	590	
	landau phtn 5P	2,700	625	1,602
	Deluxe landau phtn 5P	2,750	640	
	Deluxe phtn 5P	2,520	495	419
	Deluxe spt rdstr 2-4P	2,530	500	8,552
	Deluxe cpe 2P	2,630	510	2,226
	Deluxe coach 5P	2,715	515	9,346
	Deluxe Special sdn 5P	2,850	630	52,446

1932 Engine	bore×stroke	bhp	availability
L6, 194.0	3.13×3.75	60	S-all

1933

CA Eagle (wb 110.0)		Wght	Price*	Prod
	spt rdstr 2P	2,675	485	2,876
	phtn 5P	2,715	515	543
	cpe 2P	2,715	495	60,402
	spt cpe 2-4P	2,780	535	26,691
	coach 5P	2,820	515	162,629
	Town sdn 2d 5P	NA	545	30,657
	sdn 5P	2,880	565	162,361
	cab 2-4P	2,715	565	4,276

*all models $15 extra with 6-wire wheel equipment

CC Mercury (wb 107.0)		Wght	Price	Prod
	cpe 2p	2,335	445	8,909
	cpe 2-4P	2,395	475	1,903
	coach 5P	2,425	455	25,033

1933 Engines	bore×stroke	bhp	availability
L6, 181.0	3.31×3.50	60	S-Mercury series
L6, 206.8	3.31×4.00	65	S-Eagle series

1934

DA Master (wb 112.0)		Wght	Price*	Prod
	spt rdstr 2-4P	2,815	540	1,974
	cpe 2P	2,935	560	53,018
	spt cpe 2-4P	2,995	600	18,365
	cab 2-4P	2,990	665	3,276
	coach 5P	2,995	580	163,948
	sdn 5P	3,080	640	124,754
	Town sdn 2d 5P	3,020	615	10,131
	spt sdn 4d 5P	3,155	675	37,646

DC Standard (wb 107.0)		Wght	Price	Prod
	spt rdstr 2-4P	2,380	465	1,038
	phtn 5P	2,400	495	234
	cpe 2P	2,470	485	16,765
	sdn 2d	2,580	495	69,082
	sdn 4d	2,655	540	11,840

*all DA/DC models exc DC sdn 4d $30 extra with 6-wire wheel equipment

1934 Engines	bore×stroke	bhp	availability
L6, 181.0	3.31×3.50	60	S-Standard
L6, 206.8	3.31×4.00	80	S-Master

1935

EC Standard (wb 107.0)		Wght	Price	Prod
	spt rdstr 2-4P	2,430	465	1,176
	phtn 5P	2,495	485	217
	cpe 2P	2,540	475	32,193
	coach 5P	2,645	485	126,138
	sdn 5P	2,700	550	42,049

ED/EA Master DeLuxe (wb 113.0)*		Wght	Price	Prod
	cpe 2P 5W	2,910	560	40,201
	spt cpe 2-4P 3W	2,940	600	11,904
	coach 5P	3,010	580	102,996
	sdn 5P	3,055	640	57,771
	Town sdn 2d 5P	3,055	615	66,231
	spt sdn 4d 5P	3,130	675	67,339

*ED had no Knee-Action. For EA Knee-Action, add 60 lbs & $20

1935 Engines	bore×stroke	bhp	availability
L6, 181.0	3.31×3.50	74	S-Standard
L6, 206.8	3.31×4.00	80	S-Master DeLuxe

1936

FC Standard (wb 109.0)		Wght	Price	Prod
	cpe 2P	2,645	495	59,356
	cab 2-4P	2,745	595	3,629
	coach 5P	2,750	510	76,646
	sdn 5P	2,775	575	11,142
	Town sdn 2d 5P	2,775	535	220,884
	spt sdn 4d 5P	2,805	600	46,760

FD/FA Master DeLuxe (wb 113.0)*

		Wght	bhp	Prod
cpe 2P 5W		2,895	560	49,319
spt cpe 2-4P		2,940	590	10,985
coach 5P		2,985	580	40,814
sdn 5P		3,060	640	14,536
Town sdn 2d 5P		3,030	605	244,134
spt sdn 4d 5P		3,080	665	140,073

*FD had no Knee-Action. For FA Knee-Action, add 50 lbs & $20

1936 Engine	bore×stroke	bhp	availability
L6, 206.8	3.31×4.00	79	S-all

1937

GB Master (wb 112.3)

	Wght	Price	Prod
bus cpe 2P	2,770	619	54,683
cab 2-4P	2,790	725	1,724
coach 5P	2,800	637	15,349
Town sdn 2d 5P T/B	2,830	655	178,645
sdn 4d 5P	2,845	698	2,755
spt sdn 4d 5P T/B	2,885	716	43,240

GA Master DeLuxe (wb 112.3)

	Wght	Price	Prod
cpe 2P	2,840	685	56,166
spt cpe 2-4P	2,870	724	8,935
coach 5P	2,910	703	7,260
Town sdn 2d 5P T/B	2,935	721	300,332
sdn 4d 5P	2,935	770	2,221
spt sdn 4d 5P T/B	2,960	788	144,110

1937 Engine	bore×stroke	bhp	availability
L6, 216.5	3.50×3.75	85	S-all

1938

HB Master (wb 112.3)

	Wght	Price	Prod
cpe 2P	2,770	648	39,793
cab 2-4P	2,790	755	2,787
coach 5P	2,795	668	3,326
Town sdn 2d T/B	2,825	689	95,050
sdn 4d	2,840	730	522
spt sdn 4d T/B	2,845	750	20,952

HA Master DeLuxe (wb 112.3)

	Wght	Price	Prod
cpe 2P	2,840	714	36,108
spt cpe 4P	2,855	750	2,790
coach 5P	2,900	730	1,038
Town sdn 2d T/B	2,915	750	186,233
sdn 4d	2,915	796	236
spt sdn 4d T/B	2,940	817	76,323

1938 Engine	bore×stroke	bhp	availability
L6, 216.5	3.50×3.75	85	S-all

1939

JB Master 85 (wb 112.3)

	Wght	Price	Prod
cpe 2P	2,780	628	41,770
coach 5P	2,795	648	1,404
Town sdn 2d T/B	2,820	669	124,059
sdn 4d	2,805	689	336
spt sdn 4d T/B	2,845	710	22,623
wgn 4d	3,010	848	430*

*229 with folding end gates, 201 with rear door

JA Master DeLuxe (wb 112.3)

	Wght	Price	Prod
bus cpe 2P	2,845	684	33,809
spt cpe 4P	2,845	715	20,908
coach 5P	2,865	699	180
Town sdn 2d T/B	2,875	720	220,181
sdn 4d	2,875	745	68

		Wght	Price	Prod
spt sdn 4d T/B		2,910	766	110,521
wgn 4d		3,060	883	989

1939 Engine	bore×stroke	bhp	availability
L6, 216.5	3.50×3.75	85	S-all

1940

KB Master 85 (wb 113.0)

	Wght	Price	Prod
bus cpe	2,865	659	25,734
Town Sedan 2d, T/B	2,915	699	66,431
Sport Sedan 4d, T/B	2,930	740	11,468
wgn 4d, 8P	3,106	903	411

KH Master DeLuxe (wb 113.0)

	Wght	Price	Prod
bus cpe	2,920	684	28,090
Sport Coupe	2,925	715	17,234
Town Sedan 2d, T/B	2,965	725	143,125
Sport Sedan 4d, T/B	2,990	766	40,924

KA Special DeLuxe

	Wght	Price	Prod
bus cpe	2,930	720	25,537
Sport Coupe	2,945	750	46,628
conv cpe	3,160	898	11,820
Town Sedan 2d, T/B	2,980	761	205,910
Sport Sedan 4d, T/B	3,010	802	138,811
wgn 4d, 8P	3,158	934	2,493

1940 Engine	bore×stroke	bhp	availability
L6, 216.5	3.50×3.75	85	S-all

1941

AG Master DeLuxe (wb 116.0)

	Wght	Price	Prod
bus cpe	3,020	712	48,763
cpe	3,025	743	79,124
Town Sedan 2d	3,050	754	219,438
Sport Sedan 4d	3,090	795	59,538

AH Special DeLuxe (wb 116.0)

	Wght	Price	Prod
bus cpe	3,040	769	17,602
cpe	3,050	800	155,889
conv cpe	3,285	949	15,296
Town Sedan 2d	3,095	810	228,458
Sport Sedan 4d	3,127	851	148,661
wgn 4d, 8P	3,410	995	2,045
Fleetline sdn 4d	3,130	877	34,162

1941 Engine	bore×stroke	bhp	availability
L6, 216.5	3.50×3.75	90	S-all

1942

BG Stylemaster (wb 116.0)

	Wght	Price	Prod
cpe 2P	3,055	760	8,089
cpe 5P	3,060	790	17,442
Town Sedan 2d	3,090	800	41,872
Sport Sedan 4d	3,110	840	14,093

BH Fleetmaster (wb 116.0)

	Wght	Price	Prod
cpe 2P	3,070	815	1,716
cpe 5p	3,085	845	22,187
conv cpe	3,385	1,080	1,182

		Wght	Price	Prod
	Town Sedan 2d	3,120	855	39,421
	Sport Sedan 4d	3,145	895	31,441
	wgn 4d, 8P	3,425	1,095	1,057

BH Fleetline (wb 116.0)

		Wght	Price	Prod
	Aerosedan 2d	3,105	880	61,885
	Sportmaster sdn 4d	3,165	920	14,530

1942 Engine	bore×stroke	bhp	availability
L6, 216.5	3.50×3.75	90	S-all

1946

DJ Stylemaster (wb 116.0)

		Wght	Price	Prod
	Sport Sedan 4d	3,175	1,205	75,349
	Town Sedan 2d	3,170	1,152	61,104
	spt cpe	3,130	1,137	19,243
	bus cpe	3,105	1,098	14,267

DK Fleetmaster (wb 116.0)

		Wght	Price	Prod
	Sport Sedan 4d	3,225	1,280	73,746
	Town Sedan 2d	3,190	1,225	56,538
	spt cpe	3,145	1,212	27,036
	conv cpe	3,445	1,476	4,508
	wgn 4d, 8P	3,465	1,712	804

DK Fleetline (wb 116.0)

		Wght	Price	Prod
	Sportmaster sdn 4d	3,240	1,309	7,501
	Aerosedan 2d	3,165	1,249	57,932

1946 Engine	bore×stroke	bhp	availability
L6, 216.5	3.50×3.75	90	S-all

1947

EJ Stylemaster (wb 116.0)

		Wght	Price	Prod
	Sport Sedan 4d	3,130	1,276	42,571
	Town Sedan 2d	3,075	1,219	88,534
	spt cpe	3,060	1,202	34,513
	bus cpe	3,050	1,160	27,403

EK Fleetmaster (wb 116.0)

		Wght	Price	Prod
	Sport Sedan 4d	3,185	1,345	91,440
	Town Sedan 2d	3,125	1,286	80,128
	spt cpe	3,090	1,281	59,661
	conv cpe	3,390	1,628	28,443
	wgn 4d, 8P	3,465	1,893	4,912

EK Fleetline (wb 116.0)

		Wght	Price	Prod
	Sportmaster sdn 4d	3,150	1,371	54,531
	Aerosedan 2d	3,125	1,313	159,407

1947 Engine	bore×stroke	bhp	availability
L6, 216.5	3.50×3.75	90	S-all

1948

FJ Stylemaster (wb 116.0)

		Wght	Price	Prod
1502	Town Sedan 2d	3,095	1,313	70,228
1503	Sport Sedan 4d	3,115	1,371	48,456
1504	bus cpe	3,045	1,244	18,396
1524	spt cpe	3,020	1,323	34,513

FK Fleetmaster (wb 116.0)

		Wght	Price	Prod
2102	Town Sedan 2d	3,110	1,381	66,208
2103	Sport Sedan 4d	3,150	1,439	93,142
2109	wgn 4d, 8P	3,430	2,013	10,171
2124	spt cpe	3,050	1,402	58,786

		Wght	Price	Prod
2134	conv cpe	3,340	1,750	20,471

FK Fleetline (wb 116.0)

		Wght	Price	Prod
2113	Sportmaster sdn 4d	3,150	1,492	64,217
2144	Aerosedan 2d	3,100	1,434	211,861

1948 Engine	bore×stroke	bhp	availability
L6, 216.5	3.50×3.75	90	S-all

1949

GJ Styleline Special (wb 115.0)

		Wght	Price	Prod
1502	Town Sedan 2d	3,070	1,413	69,398
1503	Sport Sedan 4d	3,090	1,460	46,334
1504	bus cpe	3,015	1,339	20,337
1524	spt cpe	3,030	1,418	9,310

GJ Fleetline Special (wb 115.0)

		Wght	Price	Prod
1552	sdn 2d	3,060	1,413	58,514
1553	sdn 4d	3,095	1,460	36,317

GK Styleline DeLuxe (wb 115.0)

		Wght	Price	Prod
2102	Town Sedan 2d	3,100	1,492	147,347
2103	Sport Sedan 4d	3,125	1,539	191,357
2109	wgn 4d, wood body	3,485	2,267	3,342
2119	wgn 4d, steel body	3,465	2,267	6,006
2124	spt cpe	3,065	1,508	78,785
2134	conv cpe	3,375	1,857	32,392

GK Fleetline DeLuxe (wb 115.0)

		Wght	Price	Prod
2152	sdn 2d	3,100	1,492	180,251
2153	sdn 4d	3,135	1,539	130,323

1949 Engine	bore×stroke	bhp	availability
L6, 216.5	3.50×3.75	90	S-all

1950

HJ Styleline Special (wb 115.0)

		Wght	Price	Prod
1502	Town Sedan 2d	3,085	1,403	89,897
1503	Sport Sedan 4d	3,120	1,450	55,644
1504	bus cpe	3,025	1,329	20,984
1524	spt cpe	3,050	1,408	28,328

HJ Fleetline Special (wb 115.0)

		Wght	Price	Prod
1552	sdn 2d	3,080	1,403	43,682
1553	sdn 4d	3,115	1,450	23,277

HK Styleline DeLuxe (wb 115.0)

		Wght	Price	Prod
2102	Town Sedan 2d	3,100	1,482	248,567
2103	Sport Sedan 4d	3,150	1,529	316,412
2119	wgn 4d, steel body	3,460	1,994	166,995
2124	spt cpe	3,090	1,498	81,536
2134	conv cpe	3,380	1,847	32,810
2154	Bel Air htp cpe	3,225	1,741	76,662

HK DeLuxe Fleetline (wb 115.0)

		Wght	Price	Prod
2152	sdn 2d	3,115	1,482	189,509
2153	sdn 4d	3,145	1,529	124,287

1950 Engine	bore×stroke	bhp	availability
L6, 216.5	3.50×3.75	92	S-all
L6, 235.5	3.56×3.94	105	S-Powerglide

1951

JJ Special Styleline (wb 115.0)

		Wght	Price	Prod
1502	sdn 2d	3,095	1,540	75,566
1503	sdn 4d	3,130	1,595	63,718

		Wght	Price	Prod
1504	bus cpe	3,040	1,460	17,020
1524	spt cpe	3,060	1,545	18,981

JJ Special Fleetline (wb 115.0)

1552	sdn 2d	3,090	1,540	6,441
1553	sdn 4d	3,130	1,594	3,364

JK DeLuxe Styleline (wb 115.0)

2102	sdn 2d	3,110	1,629	262,933
2103	sdn 4d	3,140	1,680	380,270
2119	wgn 4d	3,470	2,191	23,586
2124	spt cpe	3,115	1,647	64,976
2134	conv cpe	3,380	2,030	20,172
2154	Bel Air htp cpe	3,225	1,914	103,356

JK DeLuxe Fleetline (wb 115.0)

2152	sdn 2d	3,125	1,629	131,910
2153	sdn 4d	3,155	1,680	57,693

1951 Engine	bore×stroke	bhp	availability
L6, 216.5	3.50×3.75	92	S-all
L6, 235.5	3.56×3.94	105	S-Powerglide

1952

KJ Special Styleline (wb 115.0)

		Wght	Price	Prod
1502	sdn 2d	3,085	1,614	54,781
1503	sdn 4d	3,115	1,670	35,460
1504	bus cpe	3,045	1,530	10,359
1524	spt cpe	3,050	1,620	8,906

KK DeLuxe Styleline (wb 115.0)

2102	sdn 2d	3,110	1,707	215,417
2103	sdn 4d	3,145	1,761	319,736
2119	wgn 4d	3,475	2,297	12,756
2124	spt cpe	3,100	1,726	36,954
2134	conv cpe	3,380	2,128	11,975
2154	Bel Air htp cpe	3,215	2,006	74,634

KK DeLuxe Fleetline (wb 115.0)

2152	sdn 2d	3,110	1,707	37,164

1952 Engines	bore×stroke	bhp	availability
L6, 216.5	3.50×3.75	92	S-manual shift
L6, 235.5	3.56×3.94	105	S-Powerglide

1953

150 Special (wb 115.0)

		Wght	Price	Prod
1502	sdn 2d	3,180	1,613	79,416
1503	sdn 4d	3,215	1,670	54,207
1504	bus cpe	3,140	1,524	13,555
1509	Handyman wgn 4d	3,420	2,010	22,408
1524	club cpe	3,140	1,620	6,993

210 DeLuxe (wb 115.0)

2102	sdn 2d	3,215	1,707	247,455
2103	sdn 4d	3,250	1,761	332,497
2109	Handyman wgn 4d	3,450	2,123	18,258
2119	Townsman wgn 4d, 8P	3,495	2,273	7,988
2124	club cpe	3,190	1,726	23,961
2134	conv cpe	3,435	2,093	5,617
2154	htp cpe	3,295	1,967	14,045

240 Bel Air (wb 115.0)

2402	sdn 2d	3,230	1,820	144,401
2403	sdn 4d	3,275	1,874	247,284
2434	conv cpe	3,470	2,175	24,047
2454	htp cpe	3,310	2,051	99,028

1953 Engines	bore×stroke	bhp	availability
L6, 235.5	3.56×3.94	105	S-manual shift
L6, 235.5	3.56×3.94	115	S-Powerglide

1954

150 Special (wb 115.0)

		Wght	Price	Prod
1502	sdn 2d	3,165	1,680	64,855
1503	sdn 4d	3,210	1,623	32,430
1509	Handyman wgn 4d	3,455	2,020	21,404
1512	Utility sdn 2d, 3P	3,145	1,539	10,770

210 DeLuxe (wb (115.0)

2102	sdn 2d	3,185	1,717	195,498
2103	sdn 4d	3,230	1,771	235,146
2109	Handyman wgn 4d	3,470	2,133	27,175
2124	Delray cpe	3,185	1,782	66,403

240 Bel Air (wb 115.0)

2402	sdn 2d	3,220	1,830	143,573
2403	sdn 4d	3,255	1,884	248,750
2419	Townsman wgn 4d, 8P	3,540	2,283	8,156
2434	conv cpe	3,445	2,185	19,383
2454	Sport Coupe htp cpe	3,300	2,061	66,378

1954 Engines	bore×stroke	bhp	availability
L6, 235.5	3.56×3.94	115	S-manual
L6, 235.5	3.56×3.94	125	S-Powerglide

1955

150 (wb 115.0)

		Wght	Price	Prod
1502	sdn 2d	3,145	1,685	66,416
1503	sdn 4d	3,150	1,728	29,898
1512	Util sdn	3,070	1,593	11,196
1529	Handyman wgn 4d	3,275	2,030	17,936

210 (wb 115.0)

2102	sdn 2d	3,130	1,775	249,105
2103	sdn 4d	3,165	1,819	317,724
2109	Townsman wgn 4d	3,355	2,127	82,303
2124	Delray cpe	3,130	1,835	115,584
2129	Handyman wgn 2d	3,315	2,079	28,918
2154	htp cpe	—	—	11,675

Bel Air (wb 115.0)

2402	sdn 2d	3,140	1,888	168,313
2403	sdn 4d	3,185	1,932	345,372
2409	Beauville wgn 4d	3,370	2,262	24,313
2429	Nomad wgn 2d	3,285	—	8,386
2434	conv cpe	3,300	2,206	41,292
2454	Sport Coupe htp cpe	3,180	2,067	185,562

1955 Engines	bore×stroke	bhp	availability
L6, 235.5	3.56×3.94	123/136	S-manual/Powerglide
V8, 265.0	3.75×3.00	162/170	O-manual/Powerglide
V8, 265.0	3.75×3.00	180	O-all

1956

150 (wb 115.0)

		Wght	Price	Prod
1502	sdn 2d	3,154	1,826	82,384
1503	sdn 4d	3,196	1,869	51,544
1512	Util sdn	3,117	1,734	9,879
1529	Handyman wgn 2d	3,299	2,171	13,487

210 (wb 115.0)

2102	sdn 2d	3,167	1,912	205,545
2103	sdn 4d	3,202	1,955	283,125
2109	Townsman wgn 4d	3,371	2,263	113,656
2113	Sport htp sdn	3,252	2,117	20,021
2119	Beauville wgn 4d, 9P	3,490	2,348	17,988
2124	Delray cpe	3,172	1,971	56,382
2129	Handyman wgn 2d	3,334	2,215	22,038
2154	Sport htp cpe	3,194	2,063	18,616

Bel Air (wb 115.0)		Wght	Price	Prod
2402	sdn 2d	3,187	2,025	104,849
2403	sdn 4d	3,221	2,068	269,798
2413	Sport htp sdn	3,270	2,230	103,602
2419	Beauville wgn 4d, 9P	3,506	2,482	13,279
2429	Nomad wgn 2d	3,352	2,608	7,886
2434	conv cpe	3,330	2,344	41,268
2454	Sport htp cpe	3,222	2,176	128,382

1956 Engines	bore×stroke	bhp	availability
L6, 235.5	3.56×3.94	140	S-all
V8, 265.0	3.75×3.00	162/170	O-manual/Powerglide
V8, 265.0	3.75×3.00	205/225	O-all

1957

150 (wb 115.0)		Wght	Price	Prod
1502	sdn 2d	3,211	1,996	70,774
1503	sdn 4d	3,236	2,048	52,266
1512	Util sdn 2d	3,163	1,885	8,300
1529	Handyman wgn 2d	3,406	2,307	14,740

210 (wb 115.0)				
2102	sdn 2d	3,225	2,122	160,090
2103	sdn 4d	3,270	2,174	260,401
2109	Townsman wgn 4d	3,461	2,456	127,803
2113	Sport htp sdn	3,320	2,270	16,178
2119	Beauville wgn 4d	3,561	2,563	21,083
2124	Delray cpe	3,220	2,162	25,644
2129	Handyman wgn 2d	3,406	2,402	17,528
2154	Sport htp cpe	3,260	2,204	22,631

Bel Air (wb 115.0)				
2402	sdn 2d	3,232	2,238	62,757
2403	sdn 4d	3,276	2,290	254,331
2409	Townsman wgn 4d	3,460	2,580	27,375
2413	Sport htp sdn	3,340	2,364	137,672
2429	Nomad wgn 2d	3,465	2,757	6,103
2434	conv cpe	3,409	2,511	47,562
2454	Sport htp cpe	3,278	2,299	166,426

1957 Engines	bore×stroke	bhp	availability
L6, 235.5	3.56×3.94	140	S-all
V8, 265.0	3.75×3.00	162	O-all w/manual shift
V8, 283.0	3.88×3.00	185	S-all w/automatic
V8, 283.0	3.88×3.00	245/250	O-all
V8, 283.0	3.88×3.00	270/283	O-manual shift

1958

Delray (wb 117.5)—178,000* built		Wght	Price	Prod
1121	Util sdn 2d, L6	3,351	2,013	—
1141	sdn 2d, L6	3,396	2,101	—
1149	sdn 4d, L6	3,439	2,155	—
1221	Util sdn 2d, V8	3,156	2,120	—
1241	sdn 2d, V8	3,399	2,208	—
1249	sdn 4d, V8	3,442	2,262	—

Biscayne (wb 117.5)—100,000* built exc 1541				
1541	sdn 2d, L6	3,404	2,236	76,229
1549	sdn 4d, L6	3,447	2,290	—
1641	sdn 2d, V8	3,407	2,343	—
1649	sdn 4d, V8	3,450	2,397	—

Bel Air (wb 117.5)—592,000* built				
1731	Sport htp cpe, L6	3,455	2,447	—
1739	Sport htp sdn, L6	3,511	2,511	—
1741	sdn 2d, L6	3,424	2,386	—

		Wght	Price	Prod
1747	Impala htp cpe, L6	3,458	2,586	—
1749	sdn 4d, L6	3,467	2,440	—
1767	Impala conv cpe, L6	3,522	2,734	—
1831	Sport htp cpe, V8	3,458	2,554	—
1839	Sport htp sdn, V8	3,514	2,618	—
1841	sdn 2d, V8	3,427	2,493	—
1847	Impala htp cpe, V8	3,459	2,693	—
1849	sdn 4d, V8	3,470	2,547	—
1867	Impala conv cpe, V8	3,523	2,841	—

Station Wagon (wb 117.5)—187,063 built				
1191	Yeoman 2d, L6	3,693	2,413	—
1193	Yeoman 4d, L6	3,740	2,467	—
1291	Yeoman 2d, V8	3,696	2,520	—
1292	Yeoman 4d, V8	3,743	2,574	—
1593	Brookwood 4d, 6P, L6	3,748	2,571	—
1594	Brookwood 4d, 9P, L6	3,837	2,678	—
1693	Brookwood 4d, 6P, V8	3,751	2,678	—
1694	Brookwood 4d, 9P, V8	3,839	2,785	—
1793	Nomad 4d, L6	3,768	2,728	—
1893	Nomad 4d, V8	3,771	2,835	—

*To nearest 100. Impalas approximately 60,000.

1958 Engines	bore×stroke	bhp	availability
L6, 235.5	3.56×3.94	145	S-six
V8, 283.0	3.88×3.00	185	S-V8
V8, 348.0	4.13×3.25	250	O-all
V8, 348.0	4.13×3.25	280	O-all

1959

Biscayne (wb 119.0)—311,800* built		Wght	Price	Prod
1111	sdn 2d, L6	3,535	2,247	—
1119	sdn 4d, L6	3,605	2,301	—
1121	Util sdn 2d, L6	3,480	2,160	—
1211	sdn 2d, V8	3,530	2,365	—
1219	sdn 4d, V8	3,600	2,419	—
1221	Util sdn 2d, V8	3,490	2,278	—

Bel Air (wb 119.0)—447,100* built				
1511	sdn 2d, L6	3,515	2,386	—
1519	sdn 4d, L6	3,600	2,440	—
1539	Sport htp sdn, L6	3,660	2,556	—
1611	sdn 2d, V8	3,510	2,504	—
1619	sdn 4d, V8	3,615	2,558	—
1639	Sport htp sdn, V8	3,630	2,674	—

Impala (wb 119.0)—407,200* built exc 1867				
1719	sdn 4d, L6	3,625	2,592	—
1737	Sport htp cpe, L6	3,570	2,599	—
1739	Sport htp sdn, L6	3,665	2,664	—
1767	conv cpe, L6	3,660	2,849	—
1819	sdn 4d, V8	3,620	2,710	—
1837	Sport htp cpe, V8	3,580	2,717	—
1839	Sport htp sdn, V8	3,670	2,782	—
1867	conv cpe, V8	3,650	2,967	65,800

Station Wagon (wb 119.0)—195,583 built exc 1215				
1115	Brookwood 2d, L6	3,870	2,571	—
1135	Brookwood 4d, L6	3,955	2,638	—
1215	Brookwood, 2d, V8	3,860	2,689	18,800
1235	Brookwood, 4d, V8	3,955	2,756	—
1535	Parkwood 4d, V8	3,965	2,749	—
1545	Kingswood, 4d, 9P, L6	4,020	2,852	—
1635	Parkwood 4d, V8	3,970	2,867	—
1645	Kingswood 4d, 9P, V8	4,015	2,970	—
1735	Nomad 4d, L6	3,980	2,891	—
1835	Nomad 4d, V8	3,975	3,009	—

*To nearest 100.

1959 Engines	bore×stroke	bhp	availability
L6, 235.5	3.56×3.94	135	S-six
V8, 283.0	3.88×3.00	185	S-V8
V8, 348.0	4.13×3.25	250–315	O-all

1960

Biscayne (wb 119.0)—287,700* built		Wght	Price	Prod
1111	sdn 2d, L6	3,485	2,262	—
1119	sdn 4d, L6	3,555	2,316	—
1121	Util sdn 2d, L6	3,455	2,175	—
1211	sdn 2d, V8	3,500	2,369	—
1219	sdn 4d, V8	3,570	2,423	—
1221	Util sdn 2d, V8	3,470	2,282	—

Biscayne Fleetmaster (wb 119.0)—prod included with Biscayne				
1311	sdn 2d, L6	3,480	2,230	—
1319	sdn 4d, L6	3,545	2,284	—
1411	sdn 2d, V8	3,495	2,337	—
1419	sdn 4d, V8	3,560	2,391	—

Bel Air (wb 119.0)—381,500* built				
1511	sdn 2d, L6	3,490	2,384	—
1519	sdn 4d, L6	3,565	2,438	—
1537	Sport htp cpe, L6	3,515	2,489	—
1539	Sport htp sdn, L6	3,605	2,554	—
1611	sdn 2d, V8	3,505	2,491	—
1619	sdn 4d, V8	3,500	2,545	—
1637	Sport htp cpe, L6	3,530	2,596	—
1639	Sport htp sdn, V8	3,620	2,661	—

Impala (wb 119.0)—411,000* built exc 1867				
1719	sdn 4d, L6	3,575	2,590	—
1737	Sport htp cpe, L6	3,530	2,597	—
1739	Sport htp sdn, L6	3,625	2,662	—
1767	conv cpe, L6	3,625	2,847	—
1819	sdn 4d, V8	3,580	2,697	—
1837	Sport htp cpe, V8	3,540	2,704	—
1839	Sport htp sdn, V8	3,625	2,769	—
1867	conv cpe, V8	3,635	2,954	100,000*

Station Wagon (wb 119.0)—212,700* built				
1115	Brookwood 2d, L6	3,845	2,586	—
1135	Brookwood 4d, L6	3,935	2,653	—
1215	Brookwood 2d, V8	3,855	2,693	—
1235	Brookwood 4d, V8	3,935	2,760	—
1535	Parkwood 4d, L6	3,945	2,747	—
1545	Kingswood, 4d, 9P, L6	3,990	2,850	—
1635	Parkwood 4d, V8	3,950	2,854	—
1645	Kingswood 4d, 9P, V8	4,000	2,957	—
1735	Nomad 4d, L6	3,955	2,889	—
1835	Nomad 4d, V8	3,960	2,996	—

*To nearest 100; model 1645 dropped.

1960 Engines	bore×stroke	bhp	availability
L6, 235.5	3.56×3.94	135	S-six
V8, 283.0	3.88×3.00	170	S-V8
V8, 348.0	4.13×3.25	250–335	O-all

1961

Biscayne (wb 119.0)—201,000* built		Wght	Price	Prod
1111	sdn 2d, L6	3,415	2,262	—
1121	Util sdn 2d, L6	3,390	2,175	—
1169	sdn 4d, L6	3,500	2,316	—
1211	sdn 2d, V8	3,425	2,369	—
1221	Util sdn 2d, V8	3,395	2,282	—
1269	sdn 4d, V8	3,505	2,423	—

Biscayne Fleetmaster (wb 119.0)				
1311	sdn 2d, L6	3,410	2,230	**
1369	sdn 4d, L6	3,495	2,284	**

		Wght	Price	Prod
1411	sdn 2d, V8	3,415	2,337	3,000
1469	sdn 4d, V8	3,500	2,391	

Bel Air (wb 119.0)—330,000* built				
1511	sdn 2d, L6	3,430	2,384	—
1537	Sport htp cpe, L6	3,475	2,489	—
1539	Sport htp sdn, L6	3,550	2,554	—
1569	sdn 4d, L6	3,515	2,438	—
1611	sdn 2d, V8	3,435	2,491	—
1637	Sport htp cpe, V8	3,480	2,596	—
1639	Sport htp sdn, V8	3,555	2,661	—
1669	sdn 4d, V8	3,520	2,545	—

Impala (wb 119.0)—426,400* built exc 1867				
1711	sdn 2d, L6	3,445	2,536	—
1737	Sport htp cpe, L6	3,485	2,597	—
1739	Sport htp sdn, L6	3,575	2,662	—
1767	conv cpe, L6	3,605	2,847	—
1769	sdn 4d, L6	3,530	2,590	—
1811	sdn 2d, V8	3,440	2,643	—
1837	Sport htp cpe, V8	3,480	2,704	—
1839	Sport htp sdn, V8	3,570	2,769	—
1867	conv cpe, V8	3,600	2,954	64,600
1869	sdn 4d, V8	3,525	2,697	—

Station Wagon (wb 119.0)***				
1135	Brookwood 4d, L6	3,850	2,653	—
1145	Brookwood 4d, 9P, L6	3,900	2,756	—
1235	Brookwood 4d, V8	3,845	2,760	—
1245	Brookwood 4d, 9P, V8	3,895	2,864	—
1535	Parkwood 4d, L6	3,865	2,747	—
1545	Parkwood 4d, 9P, L6	3,910	2,850	—
1635	Parkwood 4d, V8	3,860	2,854	—
1645	Parkwood 4d, 9P, V8	3,905	2,957	—
1735	Nomad 4d, L6	3,885	2,889	—
1745	Nomad 4d, 9P, L6	3,935	2,992	—
1835	Nomad 4d, V8	3,880	2,996	—
1845	Nomad 4d, 9P, V8	3,930	3,099	—

*To nearest 100.
**Included with Biscayne.
***Included with models above.

1961 Engines	bore×stroke	bhp	availability
L6, 235.5	3.56×3.94	135	S-six
V8, 283.0	3.88×3.00	170	S-V8
V8, 348.0	4.13×3.25	250–335	O-all
V8, 409.0	4.31×3.50	360	O-all

1962

Chevy II 100 (wb 110.0)		Wght	Price	Prod
0111	sdn 2d, L4	2,410	2,003	11,500*
0135	wgn 4d, L4	2,665	2,399	
0169	sdn 4d, L4	2,445	2,041	
0211	sdn 2d, L6	2,500	2,063	35,500*
0235	wgn 4d, L6	2,755	2,399	
0269	sdn 4d, L6	2,535	2,101	

Chevy II 300 (wb 110.0)				
0311	sdn 2d, L4	2,425	2,084	—
0345	wgn 4d, 9P, L4	2,765	2,517	—
0369	sdn 4d, L4	2,460	2,122	—
0411	sdn 2d, L6	2,515	2,144	92,800*
0445	wgn 4d, 9P, L6	2,855	2,577	
0469	sdn 4d, L6	2,550	2,182	

Chevy II Nova 400, L6 (wb 110.0)				
0435	wgn 4d	2,775	2,497	—
0437	Sport htp cpe	2,550	2,254	59,586
0441	sdn 2d	2,540	2,198	44,390
0449	sdn 4d	2,575	2,336	139,004
0467	conv cpe	2,745	2,475	23,741

Biscayne (wb 119.0)—160,000** built

		Wght	Price	Prod
1111	sdn 2d, L6	3,405	2,324	—
1135	wgn 4d, L6	3,845	2,725	—
1169	sdn 4d, L6	3,480	2,378	—
1211	sdn 2d, V8	3,400	2,431	—
1235	wgn 4d, V8	3,840	2,832	—
1269	sdn 4d, V8	3,475	2,485	—

Bel Air (wb 119.0)—365,000** built

1511	sdn 2d, L6	3,410	2,456	—
1535	wgn 4d, L6	3,845	2,819	—
1537	Sport htp cpe, L6	3,445	2,561	—
1545	wgn 4d, 9P, L6	3,895	2,922	—
1569	sdn 4d, L6	3,480	2,510	—
1611	sdn 2d, V8	3,405	2,563	—
1635	wgn 4d, V8	3,840	2,926	—
1637	Sport htp cpe, V8	3,440	2,668	—
1645	wgn 4d, 9P, V8	3,890	3,029	—
1669	sdn 4d, V8	3,475	2,617	—

Impala (wb 119.0)—704,900** built (includes SS models)

1735	wgn 4d, L6	3,870	2,961	—
1739	Sport htp sdn, L6	3,540	2,734	—
1745	wgn 4d, 9P, L6	3,925	3,064	—
1747	Sport htp cpe, L6	3,455	2,669	—
1767	conv cpe, L6	3,565	2,919	—
1769	sdn 4d, L6	3,510	2,662	—
1835	wgn 4d, V8	3,865	3,068	—
1839	Sport htp sdn, V8	3,535	2,841	—
1845	wgn 4d, 9P, V8	3,920	3,171	—
1847	Sport htp cpe, V8	3,450	2,776	—
1867	conv cpe, V8	3,560	3,026	—
1869	sdn 4d, V8	3,505	2,769	—

*To nearest 100.
**Does not include wagons.

1962 Engines

1962 Engines	bore×stroke	bhp	availability
L4, 153.0	3.88×3.25	90	S-Chevy II 100, 300
L6, 194.0	3.56×3.25	120	S-Chevy II all
L6, 235.5	3.56×3.94	135	S-Chevrolet
V8, 283.0	3.88×3.00	170	S-Chevrolet
V8, 327.0	4.00×3.25	250/300	O-V8-all Chev
V8, 409.0	4.31×3.50	380/409	O-V8-all Chev

1963

Chevy II 100 (wb 110.0)—50,400* built

		Wght	Price	Prod
0111	sdn 2d, L4	2,430	2,003	—
0135	wgn 4d, L4	2,725	2,338	—
0169	sdn 4d, L4	2,455	2,040	—
0211	sdn 2d, L6	2,520	2,062	—
0235	wgn 4d, L6	2,810	2,397	—
0269	sdn 4d, L6	2,545	2,099	

Chevy II 300 (wb 110.0)—78,800* built

0311	sdn 2d, L4	2,440	2,084	—
0345	wgn 4d, 9P, L4	2,810	2,516	—
0369	sdn 4d, L4	2,470	2,121	—
0411	sdn 2d, L6	2,530	2,143	
0445	wgn 4d, 9P, L6	2,900	2,575	—
0469	sdn 4d, L6	2,560	2,180	

Chevy II Nova 400, L6 (wb 110.0)

0435	wgn 4d	2,835	2,494	—
0437	Sport htp cpe	2,590	2,267	87,415
0449	sdn 4d	2,590	2,235	58,862
0467	conv cpe	2,760	2,472	24,823

Biscayne (wb 119.0)—186,500* built

1111	sdn 2d, L6	3,205	2,322	—
1135	wgn 4d, L6	3,685	2,723	—

(Biscayne continued)

		Wght	Price	Prod
1169	sdn 4d, L6	3,280	2,376	—
1211	sdn 2d, V8	3,340	2,429	—
1235	wgn 4d, V8	3,810	2,830	—
1269	sdn 4d, V8	3,415	2,483	—

Bel Air (wb 119.0)—354,100* built

1511	sdn 2d, L6	3,215	2,454	—
1535	wgn 4d, L6	3,685	2,818	—
1545	wgn 4d, 9P, L6	3,720	2,921	—
1569	sdn 4d, L6	3,280	2,508	—
1611	sdn 2d, V8	3,345	2,561	—
1635	wgn 4d, V8	3,810	2,925	—
1645	wgn 4d, 9P, V8	3,850	3,028	—
1669	sdn 4d, V8	3,415	2,615	—

Impala (wb 119.)—832,600* built (includes SS models)

1735	wgn 4d, L6	3,705	2,960	—
1739	Sport htp sdn, L6	3,350	2,732	—
1745	wgn 4d, 9P, L6	3,745	3,063	—
1747	Sport htp cpe, L6	3,265	2,667	—
1767	conv cpe, L6	3,400	2,917	—
1769	sdn 4d, L6	3,310	2,661	—
1835	wgn 4d, V8	3,835	3,067	—
1839	Sport htp sdn, V8	3,475	2,839	—
1845	wgn 4d, 9P, V8	3,870	3,170	—
1847	Sport htp cpe, V8	3,390	2,774	—
1867	conv cpe, V8	3,525	3,024	—
1869	sdn 4d, V8	3,435	2,768	—

*To nearest 100; does not include wagons. Total wagons 187,600; Chevy II wagons 75,274.

1963 Engines

1963 Engines	bore×stroke	bhp	availability
L4, 153.0	3.88×3.25	90	S-Chevy II
L6, 194.0	3.56×3.25	120	S-Chevy II
L6, 230.0	3.87×3.25	140	S-Chevrolet
V8, 283.0	3.88×3.00	170	S-Chevrolet
V8, 327.0	4.00×3.25	250/300	O-Chevrolet
V8, 409.0	4.31×3.50	340–425	O-Chevrolet

1964

Chevy II 100 (wb 110.0)—53,100 built*

		Wght	Price	Prod
0110	sdn 2d, L4	2,455	2,011	—
0169	sdn, L4	2,495	2,048	—
0211	sdn 2d, L6	2,540	2,070	—
0235	wgn 4d, L6	2,840	2,406	—
0269	sdn 4d, L6	2,580	2,108	—

Chevy II Nova 400, L6 (wb 110.0)—102,900* built (includes SS)

0411	sdn 2d	2,560	2,206	—
0435	wgn 4d	2,860	2,503	—
0437	Sport htp cpe	2,660	2,271	—
0469	sdn 4d	2,595	2,243	—

Chevy II Nova SS, L6 (wb 110.0)

0447	Sport htp cpe	2,675	2,433	

Chevelle 300 (wb 115.0)—68,300* built

5311	sdn 2d, L6	2,825	2,231	—
5315	wgn 2d, L6	3,050	2,528	—
5335	wgn 4d, L6	3,130	2,566	—
5369	sdn 4d, L6	2,850	2,268	—
5411	sdn 2d, V8	2,995	2,339	—
5415	wgn 2d, V8	3,170	2,636	—
5435	wgn 4d, V8	2,250	2,674	—
5469	sdn 4d, V8	2,980	2,376	—

Chevelle Malibu (wb 115.0) 149,000* built

5535	wgn 4d, L6	3,140	2,647	—
5537	Sport htp cpe, L6	2,850	2,376	—
5545	wgn 4d, 9P, L6	3,240	2,744	—

		Wght	Price	Prod
5567	conv cpe, L6	2,995	2,587	—
5569	sdn 4d, L6	2,870	2,349	—
5635	wgn 4d, V8	3,265	2,755	—
5637	Sport htp cpe, V8	2,975	2,484	—
5645	wgn 4d, 9P, V8	3,365	2,852	—
5667	conv cpe, V8	3,120	2,695	—
5669	sdn 4d, V8	2,996	2,457	—

Chevelle Malibu SS (wb 115.0) —78,800 built

		Wght	Price	Prod
5737	Sport htp cpe, L6	2,875	2,538	—
5767	conv cpe, L6	3,020	2,749	—
5837	Sport htp cpe, V8	3,000	2,646	—
5867	conv cpe, V8	3,145	2,857	—

Biscayne (wb 119.0)—173,900* built

		Wght	Price	Prod
1111	sdn 2d, L6	3,230	2,363	—
1135	wgn 4d, L6	3,700	2,763	—
1169	sdn 4d, L6	3,300	2,417	—
1211	sdn 2d, V8	3,365	2,471	—
1235	wgn 4d, V8	3,820	2,871	—
1269	sdn 4d, V8	3,430	2,524	—

Bel Air (wb 119.0)—318,100* built

		Wght	Price	Prod
1511	sdn 2d, L6	3,235	2,465	—
1535	wgn 4d, L6	3,745	2,828	—
1545	wgn 4d, 9P, L6	3,705	2,931	—
1569	sdn 4d, L6	3,305	2,519	—
1611	sdn 2d, V8	3,370	2,573	—
1635	wgn 4d, V8	3,825	2,935	—
1645	wgn 4d, 9P, V8	3,865	3,039	—
1669	sdn 4d, V8	3,440	2,626	—

Impala (wb 119.0)—889,600* built (includes SS)

		Wght	Price	Prod
1735	wgn 4d, L6	3,725	2,970	—
1739	Sport htp sdn, L6	3,370	2,742	—
1745	wgn 4d, 9P, L6	3,770	3,073	—
1767	conv cpe, L6	3,400	2,927	—
1769	sdn 4d, L6	3,340	2,671	—
1835	wgn 4d, V8	3,850	3,077	—
1839	Sport htp sdn, V8	3,490	2,850	—
1845	wgn 4d, 9P, V8	3,895	3,181	—
1847	Sport htp cpe, V8	3,415	2,786	—
1867	conv cpe, V8	3,525	3,035	—
1869	sdn 4d, V8	3,460	2,779	—

Impala SS (wb 119.0)

		Wght	Price	Prod
1347	htp cpe, L6	3,325	2,839	—
1367	conv cpe, L6	3,435	3,088	—
1447	Sport htp cpe, V8	3,450	2,947	—
1467	conv cpe, V8	3,555	3,196	—

*To nearest 100; does not include wagons. Wagon production: Chevy II 35,700; Chevelle 44,000; others 192,800.

1964 Engines	bore×stroke	bhp	availability
L4, 153.0	3.88×3.25	90	S-Chevy II 100
L6, 194.0	3.56×3.25	120	S-Chevy II 100/400, Chevelle
L6, 230.0	3.87×3.25	140	S-Chevrolet; O-others
L6, 230.0	3.87×3.25	155	O-all
V8, 283.0	3.88×3.00	195	S-V8 Chvlle, Chvrlet; O-Chevy II
V8, 283.0	3.88×3.00	220	O-Chevelle
V8, 327.0	4.00×3.25	250/300	O-Chevrolet, Chevelle
V8, 409.0	4.31×3.50	340–425	O-Chevrolet

1965

Chevy II 100 (wb 110.0)

		Wght	Price	Prod
11111	sdn 2d, L4	2,505	2,011	} 1,300*
11169	sdn 4d, L4	2,520	2,048	

		Wght	Price	Prod
11311	sdn 2d, L6	2,605	2,077	}
11335	wgn 4d, L6	2,875	2,413	—39,200*
11369	sdn 4d, L6	2,620	2,115	}

Chevy II Nova 400, L6 (wb 110.0)—51,700* built

		Wght	Price	Prod
11535	wgn 4d	2,880	2,510	—
11537	htp cpe	2,645	2,270	—
11569	sdn 4d	2,645	2,243	—

Chevy II Nova SS, L6 (wb 110.0)

		Wght	Price	Prod
11737	htp cpe	2,690	2,433	9,100

Chevelle 300 (wb 115.0)—31,600* built

		Wght	Price	Prod
13111	sdn 2d, L6	2,870	2,156	—
13115	wgn 2d, L6	3,140	2,453	—
13169	sdn 4d, L6	2,900.	2,193	—
13211	sdn 2d, V8	3,010	2,262	—
13215	wgn 2d, V8	3,275	2,561	—
13269	sdn 4d, V8	3,035	2,301	—
13311	Del sdn 2d, L6	2,870	2,231	—
13335	Del wgn 4d, L6	3,185	2,567	—
13369	Del sdn 4d, L6	2,910	2,269	—
13411	Del sdn 2d, V8	3,010	2,339	—
13435	Del wgn 4d, V8	3,320	2,674	—
13469	Del sdn 4d, V8	3,050	2,377	—

Chevelle Malibu (wb 115.0) 152,200* built

		Wght	Price	Prod
13535	wgn 4d, L6	3,225	2,647	—
13537	htp cpe, L6	2,930	2,377	—
13567	conv cpe, L6	3,025	2,588	—
13569	sdn 4d, L6	2,945	2,250	—
13635	wgn 4d, V8	3,355	2,755	—
13637	htp cpe, V8	3,065	2,485	—
13667	conv cpe, V8	3,160	2,696	—
13669	sdn 4d, V8	3,080	2,458	—

Chevelle Malibu SS (wb 115.0)—101,577 built (201 SS 396)

		Wght	Price	Prod
13737	htp cpe, L6	2,980	2,539	—
13767	conv cpe, L6	3,075	2,750	—
13837	htp cpe, V8	3,115	2,647	—
13867	conv cpe, V8	3,210	2,858	—

Biscayne (wb 119.0)

		Wght	Price	Prod
15311	sdn 2d, L6	3,305	2,363	}
15335	wgn 4d, L6	3,765	2,764	—107,700*
15369	sdn 4d, L6	3,365	2,417	}
15411	sdn 2d, V8	3,455	2,470	}
15435	wgn 4d, V8	3,900	2,871	—37,600*
15469	sdn 4d, V8	3,515	2,524	}

Bel Air (wb 119.0)

		Wght	Price	Prod
15111	sdn 2d, L6	3,310	2,465	}
15535	wgn 4d, L6	3,765	2,828	—107,800*
15545	wgn 4d, 9P, L6	3,810	2,931	
15569	sdn 4d, L6	3,380	2,519	}
15611	sdn 2d, V8	3,460	2,573	}
15635	wgn 4d, V8	3,905	2,936	
15645	wgn 4d, 9P, V8	3,950	3,039	—163,000*
15669	sdn 4d, V8	3,530	2,626	}

Impala (wb 119.0)—803,400* built (includes Caprice pkg)

		Wght	Price	Prod
16335	wgn 4d, L6	3,825	2,970	—
16337	htp cpe, L6	3,385	2,678	—
16339	htp sdn, L6	3,490	2,742	—
16345	wgn 4d, 9P, L6	3,865	3,073	—
16367	conv cpe, L6	3,470	2,943	—
16369	sdn 4d, L6	3,460	2,672	—
16435	wgn 4d, V8	3,960	3,078	—
16437	htp cpe, V8	3,525	2,785	—
16439	htp sdn, V8	3,630	2,850	—
16445	wgn 4d, 9P, V8	4,005	3,181	—

		Wght	Price	Prod
16467	conv cpe, V8	3,605	3,051	—
16469	sdn 4d, V8	3,595	2,779	—

Impala SS (wb 119.0)—243,100* built

		Wght	Price	Prod
16537	htp cpe, L6	3,435	2,839	—
16567	conv cpe, L6	3,505	3,104	—
16637	htp cpe, V8	3,570	2,947	—
16667	conv cpe, V8	3,655	3,212	—

*To nearest 100; does not include wagons. Wagon production: Chevy II 21,500; Chevelle 37,600; others 184,400. Convertible production: Malibu 19,765; Impala SS 27,842.

1965 Engines	bore×stroke	bhp	availability
L4, 153.0	3.88×3.25	90	S-Chevy II 100
L6, 194.0	3.56×3.25	120	S-Chevy II, Chevelle
L6, 230.0	3.87×3.25	140	S-Chevrolet; O-others
V8, 283.0	3.88×3.00	195	S-Chevrolet, Chevelle; O-Chevy II
V8, 283.0	3.88×3.00	220	O-all
V8, 327.0	4.00×3.25	250/300	O-all
V8, 327.0	4.00×3.25	350	O-Chevelle
V8, 396.0	4.09×3.75	325/425	O-Chevrolet, Chevelle
V8, 409.0	4.31×3.50	340/400	O-Chevrolet

1966

Chevy II 100 (wb 110.0)

		Wght	Price	Prod
11111	sdn 2d, L4	2,520	2,028	
11169	sdn 4d, L4	2,535	2,065	
11311	sdn 2d, L6	2,620	2,090	44,500*
11335	wgn 4d, L6	2,855	2,430	
11369	sdn 4d, L6	2,635	2,127	
11411	sdn 2d, V8	2,775	2,197	
11435	wgn 4d, V8	2,990	2,536	2,500*
11469	sdn 4d, V8	2,790	2,234	

Chevy II Nova (wb 110.0)

		Wght	Price	Prod
11535	wgn 4d, L6	2,885	2,518	
11537	htp cpe, L6	2,675	2,271	54,300*
11569	sdn 4d, L6	2,640	2,245	
11635	wgn 4d, V8	3,010	2,623	
11637	htp cpe, V8	2,830	2,377	19,600*
11669	sdn 4d, V8	2,800	2,351	

Chevy II Nova SS (wb 110.0)

		Wght	Price	Prod
11737	htp cpe, L6	2,740	2,430	6,700*
11837	htp cpe, V8	2,870	2,535	16,300*

Chevelle 300 (wb 115.0)

		Wght	Price	Prod
13111	sdn 2d, L6	2,895	2,156	23,300*
13169	sdn 4d, L6	2,935	2,202	
13211	sdn 2d, V8	3,040	2,271	5,300*
13269	sdn 4d, V8	3,080	2,308	
13311	Del sdn 2d, L6	2,910	2,239	
13335	Del wgn 4d, L6	3,210	2,575	
13369	Del sdn 4d, L6	2,945	2,276	
13411	Del sdn 2d, V8	3,060	2,345	37,600*
13435	Del wgn 4d, V8	3,350	2,681	
13469	Del sdn 4d, V8	3,095	2,382	

Chevelle Malibu (wb 115.0)—241,600* built

		Wght	Price	Prod
13517	htp cpe, L6	2,935	2,378	—
13535	wgn 4d, L6	3,235	2,651	—
13539	htp sdn, L6	3,035	2,458	—
13567	conv cpe, L6	3,030	2,588	—
13569	sdn 4d, L6	2,960	2,352	—
13617	htp cpe, V8	3,075	2,484	—
13635	wgn 4d, V8	3,375	2,766	—
13639	htp sdn, V8	3,180	2,564	—
13667	conv cpe, V8	3,175	2,693	—
13669	sdn 4d, V8	3,110	2,456	—

Chevelle Malibu SS, V8 (wb 115.0)-72,300* built

		Wght	Price	Prod
13817	htp cpe	3,375	2,776	—
13867	conv cpe, V8	3,470	2,984	—

Biscayne (wb 119.0)

		Wght	Price	Prod
15311	sdn 2d, L6	3,310	2,379	
15335	wgn 4d, L6	3,770	2,772	83,200*
15369	sdn 4d, L6	3,375	2,431	
15411	sdn 2d, V8	3,445	2,484	
15435	wgn 4d, V8	3,895	2,877	39,200*
15469	sdn 4d, V8	3,519	2,537	

Bel Air (wb 119.0)

		Wght	Price	Prod
15111	sdn 2d, L6	3,315	2,479	
15535	wgn 4d, 2S, L6	3,770	2,835	72,100*
15545	wgn 4d, 3S, L6	3,815	2,948	
15569	sdn 4d, L6	3,390	2,531	
15611	sdn 2d, V8	3,445	2,584	
15635	wgn 4d, 2S, V8	3,895	2,940	164,500*
15645	wgn 4d, 9P, V8	3,940	3,053	
15669	sdn 4d, V8	3,525	2,636	

Impala (wb 119.0)

		Wght	Price	Prod
16335	wgn 4d, 2S, L6	3,805	2,971	
16337	htp cpe, L6	3,430	2,684	
10039	htp sdn, L6	3,525	2,747	
16345	wgn 4d, 3S, L6	3,860	3,083	33,100*
16367	conv cpe, L6	3,484	2,935	
16369	sdn 4d, L6	3,435	2,678	
16435	wgn 4d, 2S, V8	3,990	3,076	
16437	htp cpe, V8	3,555	2,789	
16439	htp sdn, V8	3,650	2,852	
16445	wgn 4d, 3S, V8	4,005	3,189	621,800*
16467	conv cpe, V8	3,610	3,041	
16469	sdn 4d, V8	3,565	2,783	

Impala SS (wb 119.0)—119,300* built

		Wght	Price	Prod
16737	htp cpe, L6	3,460	2,842	—
16767	conv cpe, L6	3,505	3,093	—
16837	htp cpe, V8	3,585	2,947	—
16867	conv cpe, V8	3,630	3,199	—

Caprice, V8 (wb 119.0)—181,000* built

		Wght	Price	Prod
16635	wgn 4d, 2S	3,970	3,234	—
16639	htp sdn	3,675	3,063	—
16645	wgn 4d, 3S	4,020	3,347	—
16647	htp cpe	3,600	3,000	—

*To nearest 100; does not include wagons. Wagon production: Chevy II 21,400; Chevelle 31,900; others 185,500. Impala SS convertible cpe 15,872.

1966 Engines	bore×stroke	bhp	availability
L4, 153.0	3.88×3.25	90	S-Chevy II 100
L6, 194.0	3.56×3.25	120	S-Chevy II, Chevelle
L6, 230.0	3.87×3.25	140	S-Chevrolet; O-others
V8, 283.0	3.88×3.00	195	S-Chevelle, Chevrolet; O-Chevy II
V8, 327.0	4.00×3.25	250/300	O-all
V8, 327.0	4.00×3.25	350	O-Chevelle, Chevy II
V8, 396.0	4.09×3.76	325	S-Chvlle 396; O-Chvrlet, Chvlle
V8, 409.0	4.31×3.50	340/400	O-Chevrolet

1967

Chevy II 100 (wb 110.0)

		Wght	Price	Prod
11111	sdn 2d, L4	2,555	2,090	
11169	sdn 4d, L4	2,560	2,120	
11311	sdn 2d, L6	2,640	2,152	34,200*
11335	wgn 4d, L6	2,865	2,478	
11369	sdn 4d, L6	2,650	2,182	
11411	sdn 2d, V8	2,770	2,258	
11435	wgn 4d, V8	2,985	2,583	1,700*
11469	sdn 4d, V8	2,780	2,287	

Chevy II Nova (wb 110.0)		Wght	Price	Prod
11535	wgn 4d, L6	2,890	2,566	
11537	htp cpe, L6	2,660	2,330	34,400*
11569	sdn 4d, L6	2,660	2,298	
11635	wgn 4d, V8	3,015	2,671	
11637	htp cpe, V8	2,790	2,435	13,200*
11669	sdn 4d, V8	2,790	2,403	

Chevy II Nova SS (wb 110.0)				
11737	htp cpe, L6	2,690	2,487	1,900*
11837	htp cpe, V8	2,820	2,590	8,200*

Camaro (wb 108.1) (includes 602 Z-28s)				
12337	htp cpe, L6	2,770	2,466	
12367	conv cpe, L6	3,025	2,704	58,808
12437	htp cpe, V8	2,920	2,572	
12467	conv cpe, V8	3,180	2,809	162,109

Chevelle 300 (wb 115.0)				
13111	sdn 2d, L6	2,935	2,221	
13169	sdn 4d, L6	2,955	2,250	19,900*
13211	sdn 2d, V8	3,070	2,326	
13269	sdn 4d, V8	3,090	2,356	4,800*
13311	Del sdn 2d, L6	2,955	2,295	
13335	Del wgn 4d, L6	3,230	2,619	19,300*
13369	Del sdn 4d, L6	2,980	2,324	
13411	Del sdn 2d, V8	3,090	2,400	
13435	Del wgn 4d, V8	3,360	2,725	7,000*
13469	Del sdn 4d, V8	3,110	2,430	

Chevelle Malibu (wb 115.0)				
13517	htp cpe, L6	2,980	2,434	
13535	wgn 4d, L6	3,260	2,695	
13539	htp sdn, L6	3,065	2,506	40,600*
13567	conv cpe, L6	3,050	2,637	
13569	sdn 4d, L6	3,000	2,400	
13617	htp cpe, V8	3,115	2,540	
13635	wgn 4d, V8	3,390	2,801	
13639	htp sdn, V8	3,200	2,611	187,200*
13667	conv cpe, V8	3,185	2,743	
13669	sdn 4d, V8	3,130	2,506	

Chevelle Concours (wb 115.0)				
13735	wgn 4d, L6	3,270	2,827	5,900
13835	wgn 4d, V8	3,405	2,933	21,400

Chevelle Super Sports (wb 115.0)—63,000* built				
13817	htp cpe	3,415	2,825	—
13867	conv cpe, V8	3,485	3,033	—

Biscayne (wb 119.0)				
15311	sdn 2d, L6	3,335	2,442	
15335	wgn 4d, L6	3,765	2,817	54,200*
15369	sdn 4d, L6	3,395	2,484	
15411	sdn 2d, V8	3,465	2,547	
15435	wgn 4d, V8	3,885	2,923	38,600*
15469	sdn 4d, V8	3,525	2,589	

Bel Air (wb 119.0)				
15111	sdn 2d, L6	3,340	2,542	
15535	wgn 4d, 2S, L6	3,770	2,881	
15545	wgn 4d, 3S, L6	3,825	2,993	41,500*
15569	sdn 4d, L6	3,410	2,584	
15611	sdn 2d, V8	3,470	2,647	
15635	wgn 4d, 2S, V8	3,890	2,986	
15645	wgn 4d, 9P, V8	3,940	3,098	138,200*
15669	sdn 4d, V8	3,535	2,689	

Impala (wb 119.0)		Wght	Price	Prod
16335	wgn 4d, 2S, L6	3,805	3,016	
16339	htp sdn, L6	3,540	2,793	
16345	wgn 4d, 3S, L6	3,868	3,129	18,800*
16367	conv cpe, L6	3,515	2,991	
16369	sdn 4d, L6	3,455	2,723	
16387	htp cpe, L6	3,475	2,740	
16435	wgn 4d, 2S, V8	3,920	3,122	
16439	htp sdn, V8	3,660	2,899	
16445	wgn 4d, 3S, V8	3,990	3,234	556,800*
16467	conv cpe, V8	3,625	3,097	
16469	sdn 4d, V8	3,575	2,828	
16487	htp cpe, V8	3,590	2,845	

Impala SS (wb 119.0)				
16767	conv cpe, L6	3,535	3,149	
16787	htp cpe, L6	3,500	2,898	400*
16867	conv cpe, V8	3,650	3,254	
16887	htp cpe, V8	3,615	3,003	73,600*

Caprice, V8 (wb 119.0)—124,500* built				
16635	wgn 4d, 2S	3,935	3,301	—
16639	htp sdn	3,710	3,130	—
16645	wgn 4d, 3S	3,990	3,413	—
16647	htp cpe	3,605	3,078	—

*To nearest 100; does not include wagons. Wagon production: Chevy II 12,900; Chevelle 27,300; others 155,100. Convertible production: Camaro 25,141; Impala SS 9,545.

1967 Engines	bore×stroke	bhp	availability
L4, 153.0	3.88×3.25	90	S-Chevy II 100 sdns
L6, 194.0	3.56×3.25	120	S-Chevy II
L6, 230.0	3.88×3.25	140	S-Camaro, Chevelle
L6, 250.0	3.88×3.53	155	S-Chevrolet exc Caprice; O-others
V8, 283.0	3.88×3.00	195	S-all exc Camaro
V8, 327.0	4.00×3.25	210	O-Camaro
V8, 327.0	4.00×3.25	275	O-all
V8, 327.0	4.00×3.25	325	O-Chevelle
V8, 350.0	4.00×3.48	295	O-Camaro
V8, 396.0	4.09×3.76	325	S-Chevelle 396; O-Chevrolet
V8, 396.0	4.09×3.76	350	O-Chevelle 396
V8, 427.0	4.25×3.76	385	O-Chevrolet

1968

Chevy II Nova (wb 111.0)—201,000* built		Wght	Price	Prod
11127	cpe L4	2,760	2,222	—
11169	sdn 4d, L4	2,790	2,252	—
11327	cpe L6	2,860	2,284	—
11369	sdn 4d, L6	2,890	2,314	—
11427	cpe, V8	2,995	2,390	—
11469	sdn 4d, V8	3,025	2,419	—

Camaro (wb 108.1) (includes 7,199 Z-28s)				
12337	htp cpe, L6	2,810	2,588	
12367	conv cpe, L6	3,110	2,802	50,937
12437	htp cpe, V8	2,955	2,694	
12467	conv cpe, V8	3,245	2,908	184,178

Chevelle 300 (wb 112.0; 4d-116.0)				
13127	cpe, L6	3,020	2,341	
13135	Nomad wgn 4d, L6	3,370	2,625	2,900*
13227	cpe, V8	3,155	2,447	
13235	Nomad wgn 4d, V8	3,500	2,731	9,700*
13327	Del cpe, L6	3,035	2,415	
13335	Cus Nomad wgn 4d, L6	3,415	2,736	
13337	Del htp cpe, L6	3,050	2,479	25,500*
13369	Del sdn 4d, L6	3,105	2,445	
13427	Del cpe, V8	3,170	2,521	
13435	Cus Nomad wgn 4d, V8	3,545	2,841	
13437	Del htp cpe, V8	3,185	2,584	17,700*
13469	Del sdn 4d, V8	3,240	2,550	

Chevelle Malibu (wb 112.0; 4d-116.0)		Wght	Price	Prod
13535	wgn 4d, L6	3,440	2,846	
13537	htp cpe, L6	3,070	2,558	
13539	htp sdn, L6	3,185	2,629	33,100*
13567	conv cpe, L6	3,135	2,757	
13569	sdn 4d, L6	3,125	2,524	
13635	wgn 4d, V8	3,575	2,951	
13637	htp cpe, V8	3,204	2,663	
13639	htp sdn, V8	3,315	2,735	233,200*
13667	conv cpe, V8	3,260	2,863	
13669	sdn 4d, V8	3,255	2,629	

Chevelle Concours (wb 116.0)				
13835	wgn 4d, V8	3,580	3,083	

Chevelle SS 396 (wb 112.0)				
13837	htp cpe	3,550	2,899	60,499
13867	conv cpe	3,570	3,102	2,286

Biscayne (wb 119.0)				
15311	sdn 2d, L6	3,400	2,581	
15335	wgn 4d, L6	3,790	2,957	44,500*
15369	sdn 4d, L6	3,465	2,623	
15411	sdn 2d, V8	3,520	2,686	
15435	wgn 4d, V8	3,900	3,062	37,600*
15469	sdn 4d, V8	3,585	2,728	

Bel Air (wb 119.0)				
15511	sdn 2d, L6	3,405	2,681	
15535	wgn 4d, 2S, L6	3,800	3,020	
15545	wgn 4d, 3S, L6	3,845	3,133	28,800*
15569	sdn 4d, L6	3,470	2,723	
15611	sdn 2d, V8	3,525	2,786	
15635	wgn 4d, 2S, V8	3,910	3,125	
15645	wgn 4d, 3S, V8	3,955	3,238	123,400*
15669	sdn 4d, V8	3,590	2,828	

Impala (wb 119.0)				
16339	hpt sdn, L6	3,605	2,917	
16369	sdn 4d, L6	3,520	2,846	11,400*
16387	htp cpe, L6	3,250	2,863	
16435	wgn 4d, 2S, V8	3,940	3,245	
16439	htp sdn, V8	3,715	3,022	
16445	wgn 4d, 3S, V8	3,905	3,358	
16447	Cus htp cpe, V8	3,645	3,021	699,500*
16467	conv cpe, V8	3,680	3,197	
16469	sdn 4d, V8	3,630	2,951	
16487	htp cpe, V8	3,630	2,968	

Caprice (wb 119.0)—115,500* built				
16635	wgn 4d, 2S	3,950	3,458	—
16639	htp sdn	3,755	3,271	—
16645	wgn 4d, 3S	4,005	3,570	—
16647	htp cpe	3,660	3,219	—

*To nearest 100; does not include wagons. Wagon production: Chevelle 45,500; others 175,600. Chevy II Nova SS cpe 5,571; Camaro convertible cpe 20,440.

1968 Engines	bore×stroke	bhp	availability
L4, 153.0	3.88×3.25	90	S-Chevy II
L6, 230.0	3.88×3.25	140	S-Chevy II, Camaro, Chevelle
L6, 250.0	3.88×3.53	155	S-Chevrolet; O-Camaro, Chevelle
V8, 307.0	3.88×3.25	200	S-Chevy II, Chevelle, Chevrolet
V8, 327.0	4.00×3.25	210	S-Camaro
V8, 327.0	4.00×3.25	250	O-Chevrolet
V8, 327.0	4.00×3.25	275	O-all
V8, 327.0	4.00×3.25	325	O-Chevelle
V8, 350.0	4.00×3.48	295	O-Chevy II, Camaro
V8, 396.0	4.09×3.76	325	S-Chevelle 396; O-Camaro, Chevr
V8, 396.0	4.09×3.76	350	O-Chevrolet
V8, 427.0	4.25×3.76	385	O-Chevrolet

1969

Chevy II Nova (wb 111.0)		Wght	Price	Prod
11127	cpe, L4	2,785	2,237	
11169	sdn 4d, L4	2,810	2,267	6,100*
11327	cpe L6	2,895	2,315	
11369	sdn 4d, L6	2,920	2,345	10,200*
11427	cpe, V8	3,035	2,405	
11469	sdn 4d, V8	3,065	2,434	89,900*

Camaro (wb 108.1) (includes 19,014 Z-28s)				
12337	htp cpe, L6	3,040	2,638	
12367	conv cpe, L6	3,160	2,852	65,008**
12437	htp cpe, V8	3,050	2,726	
12467	conv cpe, V8	3,295	2,940	178,087**

Note: wagon designation "CT" refers to conventional tailgate, opening from top. Most wagons had dual-action tailgates, opening from top or from side, from 1969 onward.

Chevelle Nomad (wb 116.0)				
13135	wgn 4d, CT, L6	3,390	2,668	—
13136	wgn 4d, L6	3,475	2,710	—
13235	wgn 4d, CT, V8	3,515	2,758	—
13236	wgn 4d, V8	3,600	2,800	—

Chevelle 300 Del (wb 112.0; 4d-116.0)				
13327	cpe, L6	3,035	2,458	
13337	htp cpe, L6	3,075	2,521	11,000*
13369	sdn 4d, L6	3,100	2,488	
13427	cpe, V8	3,165	2,548	
13437	htp cpe, V8	3,205	2,611	31,000*
13469	sdn 4d, V8	3,230	2,577	

Chevelle Greenbrier (wb 116.0)				
13335	wgn 4d, CT, L6	3,445	2,779	
13336	wgn 4d, L6	3,530	2,821	7,400*
13435	wgn 4d, CT, V8	3,585	2,869	
13436	wgn 4d, 2S, V8	3,665	2,911	38,500*
13446	wgn 4d, 3S, V8	3,740	3,020	

Chevelle Malibu (wb 112.0; 4d-116.0)				
13537	htp cpe, L6	3,095	2,601	
13539	htp sdn, L6	3,205	2,672	
13567	conv cpe, L6	3,175	2,800	23,500*
13569	sdn 4d, L6	3,130	2,567	
13637	htp cpe, V8	3,230	2,690	
13639	htp sdn, V8	3,340	2,762	
13667	conv cpe, V8	3,300	2,889	343,600*
13669	sdn 4d, V8	3,265	2,657	

Chevelle Concours (wb 116.0)				
13536	wgn 4d, L6	3,545	2,931	—
13636	wgn 4d, 2S, V8	3,685	3,021	—
13646	wgn 4d, 3S, V8	3,755	3,141	—
13836	del wgn 4d, 2S, V8	3,680	3,153	—
13846	del wgn 4d, 3S, V8	3,730	3,266	—

Biscayne (wb 119.0)				
15311	sdn 2d, L6	3,530	2,645	
15336	wgn 4d, L6	4,045	3,064	27,400*
15369	sdn 4d, L6	3,590	2,687	
15411	sdn 2d, V8	3,670	2,751	
15436	wgn 4d, V8	4,170	3,169	41,300*
15469	sdn 4d, V8	3,725	2,793	

Bel Air (wb 119.0)				
15511	sdn 2d, L6	3,540	2,745	
15536	wgn 4d, 2S, L6	4,045	3,127	
15546	wgn 4d, 3S, L6	4,100	3,240	17,000*
15569	sdn 4d, L6	3,590	2,787	

		Wght	Price	Prod
15611	sdn 2d, V8	3,675	2,851	
15636	wgn 4d, 2S, V8	4,175	3,232	139,700*
15646	wgn 4d, 3S, V8	4,230	3,345	
15669	sdn 4d, V8	3,725	2,893	

Impala (wb 119.0)

16337	htp cpe, L6	3,650	2,927	
16339	htp sdn, L6	3,735	2,981	8,700*
16369	sdn 4d, L6	3,640	2,911	
16436	wgn 4d, 2S, V8	3,725	3,352	
16437	htp cpe, V8	3,775	3,033	
16439	htp sdn, V8	3,855	3,056	
16446	wgn 4d, 3S, V8	4,285	3,465	768,300*
16447	Cus htp cpe, V8	3,800	3,085	
16467	conv cpe, V8	3,835	3,261	
16469	sdn 4d, V8	3,760	3,016	

Caprice, V8 (wb 119.0)—166,900* built

16636	wgn 4d, 2S	4,245	3,565	—
16639	htp sdn	3,895	3,346	—
16646	wgn 4d, 3S	4,300	3,678	—
16647	htp cpe	3,815	3,294	—

*To nearest 100; does not include wagons.
**Includes 1970 extension of 1969 model. Wagon production: Chevelle 45,900; others 59,300. Chevy II Nova SS cpe 17,564; Camaro convertible cpe 17,573.

1969 Engines	bore×stroke	bhp	availability
L4, 153.0	3.88×3.25	90	S-Chevy II
L6, 230.0	3.88×3.25	140	S-Chevelle, Chevy II
L6, 250.0	3.88×3.53	155	S-Chvr; O-Chvl, Chev II, Cam
V8, 307.0	3.88×3.25	200	S-Chevy II, Chevelle
V8, 327.0	4.00×3.25	210	S-Camaro
V8, 327.0	4.00×3.25	235	S-Chevrolet
V8, 350.0	4.00×3.48	255	O-all
V8, 350.0	4.00×3.48	300	O-Chevr, Chevl, II SS, Cam SS
V8, 396.0	4.09×3.76	265	S-Chevelle 396; O-Chevrolet
V8, 396.0	4.09×3.76	325	O-Chevelle 396, Camaro SS
V8, 396.0	4.09×3.76	350	O-Chevelle
V8, 427.0	4.25×3.76	335/390	O-Chevrolet

Note: Station wagon engines—for wb 116 read Chevelle; for wb 119 read Chevrolet.

1970

Nova (wb 111.0)—254,242* built

		Wght	Price	Prod
11127	htp cpe, L4	2,820	2,335	—
11169	sdn 4d, L4	2,843	2,365	—
11327	cpe, L6	2,919	2,414	—
11369	sdn 4d, L6	2,942	2,443	—
11427	cpe, V8	3,048	2,503	—
11469	sdn 4d, V8	3,071	2,533	—

Camaro (wb 108.1) (includes 8,733 Z-28s)

12387	spt cpe, L6	3,076	2,749	12,566
12487	spt cpe, V8	3,190	2,839	112,323

Chevelle (wb 112.0; 4d-116.0)—354,855 built (including Malibu)

13337	htp cpe, L6	3,142	2,620	—
13369	sdn 4d, L6	3,196	2,585	—
13437	htp cpe, V8	3,260	2,710	—
13469	sdn 4d, V8	3,312	2,679	—

Chevelle Malibu (wb 112.0; 4d-116.0)

13537	htp cpe, L6	3,197	2,719	—
13539	htp sdn, L6	3,302	2,790	—

		Wght	Price	Prod
13567	conv cpe, L6	3,243	2,919	—
13569	sdn 4d, L6	3,221	2,685	—
13637	htp cpe, V8	3,307	2,809	—
13639	htp sdn, V8	3,409	2,881	—
13667	conv cpe, V8	3,352	3,009	—
13669	sdn 4d, V8	3,330	2,775	—

Station Wagon (wb 116.0)

13136	Nomad 4d, 2S, L6	3,615	2,835	—
13236	Nomad 4d, 2S, V8	3,718	2,925	—
13336	Greenbrier 4d, 2S, L6	3,644	2,946	—
13436	Greenbrier 4d, 2S, V8	3,748	3,100	—
13446	Greenbrier 4d, 3S, V8	3,794	3,213	—
13536	Concours 4d, 2S, L6	3,687	3,056	—
13636	Concours 4d, 2S, V8	3,794	3,210	—
13646	Concours 4d, 3S, V8	3,836	3,323	—
13836	Concours del wgn 4d, 2S, V8	3,821	3,342	—
13846	Concours del wgn 4d, 3S, V8	3,880	3,455	—

Biscayne (wb 119.0)

15369	sdn 4d, L6	3,600	2,787	—
15469	sdn 4d, V8	3,759	2,898	

Bel Air (wb 119.0)

15569	sdn 4d, L6	3,604	2,887	—
15669	sdn 4d, V8	3,763	2,998	—

Impala (wb 119.0)—495,909 built exc 16467

16337	htp cpe, L6	3,641	3,038	—
16369	sdn 4d, L6	3,655	3,021	—
16437	htp cpe, V8	3,788	3,149	—
16439	htp sdn, V8	3,871	3,203	—
16447	Cus htp cpe, V8	3,801	3,266	—
16467	conv cpe, V8	3,843	3,377	9,562
16469	sdn 4d, V8	3,802	3,132	—

Caprice (wb 119.0)

16639	htp sdn	3,905	3,527	—
16647	htp cpe	3,821	3,474	—

Monte Carlo (wb 116.0)

13857	htp cpe	3,460	3,123	130,657

Station Wagon (wb 119.0)

15436	Brookwood 4d, 2S	4,204	3,294	—
15636	Townsman 4d, 2S	4,208	3,357	—
15646	Townsman 4d, 3S	4,263	3,469	—
16436	Kingswood 4d, 2S	4,269	3,477	—
16446	Kingswood 4d, 3S	4,329	3,589	—
16636	Kingswood del 4d, 2S	4,295	3,753	—
16646	Kingswood del 4d, 3S	4,361	3,886	—

*Includes 19,558 SS coupes.

1970 Engines	bore×stroke	bhp	availability
L4, 153.0	3.88×3.25	90	S-Nova
L6, 230.0	3.88×3.25	140	S-Camaro; O-Nova
L6, 250.0	3.88×3.53	155	S-Chevrolet exc Caprice & Impala cpe, Chevelle; O-Nova, Camaro
V8, 307.0	3.88×3.25	200	S-Nova, Camaro; O-Chevelle
V8, 350.0	4.00×3.48	250	S-Chevr, MC; O-others
V8, 350.0	4.00×3.48	300	O-Chevr, MC, Chevl, Cam, Nova SS
V8, 396.0	4.09×3.76	325	O-Camaro
V8, 396.0	4.09×3.76	350	O-Chevelle
V8, 400.0	4.12×3.75	265	O-Chevrolet, Monte Carlo
V8, 400.0	4.12×3.75	330	O-Monte Carlo, Chevelle
V8, 454.0	4.25×4.00	345	O-Chevrolet
V8, 454.0	4.25×4.00	360	O-Monte Carlo
V8, 454.0	4.25×4.00	390	O-Chevrolet

Note: Station wagon engines—for wb 116 read Chevelle; for wb 119 read Chevrolet.

Chevrolet

1971

Vega (wb 97.0)

		Wght	Price	Prod
14111	sdn 2d	2,146	2,090	58,804
14177	htchbk cpe 3d	2,190	2,196	168,308
14115	Kammback wgn 3d	2,230	2,328	42,793

Nova (wb 111.0)

11327	cpe 2d L6	2,952	2,376	65,891
11369	sdn 4d L6	2,976	2,405	29,037
11427	cpe 2d V8	3,084	2,471	77,344
11469	sdn 4d V8	3,108	2,501	22,606

Camaro (wb 108.1; incl. 4,862 Z/28s)

12387	spt cpe L6	3,094	2,921	11,178
12487	spt cpe V8	3,218	3,016	103,452

Chevelle (wb 112.0; 4d-116.0)

11337	htp cpe L6	3,166	2,712	6,660
11369	sdn 4d L6	3,210	2,677	6,621
13437	htp cpe V8	3,296	2,807	17,117
13469	sdn 4d V8	3,338	2,773	9,042
13537	Malibu htp cpe L6	3,212	2,885	6,220
13569	Malibu sdn 4d L6	3,250	2,851	4,241
13637	Malibu htp cpe V8	3,342	2,980	180,117
13639	Malibu htp sdn V8	3,450	3,052	20,775
13667	Malibu conv V8	3,390	3,260	5,089
13669	Malibu sdn 4d V8	3,380	2,947	37,385

Chevelle Wagon (wb 116.0)

13136	Nomad 4d 2S L6	3,632	2,997	2,801
13236	Nomad 4d 2S V8	3,746	3,097	6,528
13436	Greenbrier 4d 2S V8	3,820	3,228	6,128
13446	Greenbrier 4d 3S V8	3,882	3,340	2,129
13636	Concours 4d 2S V8	3,864	3,337	12,716
13646	Concours 4d 3S V8	3,908	3,450	4,276
13836	Concours Estate 4d 2S V8	3,892	3,514	4,502
13846	Concours Estate 4d 3S V8	3,944	3,626	3,219

Biscayne (wb 121.5)

15369	sdn 4d L6	3,732	3,096	5,846
15469	sdn 4d V8	3,888	3,448	16,463

Bel Air (wb 121.5)

15569	sdn 4d L6	3,732	3,233	3,452
15669	sdn 4d V8	3,888	3,585	38,534

Impala (wb 121.5)

16357	htp cpe L6	3,742	3,408	939
16369	sdn 4d L6	3,760	3,391	1,606
16439	htp sdn V8	3,978	3,813	140,300
16447	Custom htp cpe V8	3,912	3,826	139,437
16457	htp cpe V8	3,896	3,759	52,952
16467	conv V8	3,960	4,021	4,576
16469	sdn 4d V8	3,914	3,742	135,334

Caprice (wb 121.5)

16639	htp sdn 4d	4,040	4,134	64,093
16647	htp cpe	3,964	4,081	46,404

Monte Carlo (wb 116.0)

13857	htp cpe	3,488	3,416	128,600

Chevrolet Wagon (wb 125.0)

15435	Brookwood 4d 2S	4,542	3,929	5,314
15635	Townsman 4d 2S	4,544	4,020	12,951
15645	Townsman 4d 3S	4,598	4,135	6,870
16435	Kingswood 4d 2S	4,588	4,112	26,638
16445	Kingswood 4d 3S	4,648	4,227	32,311
16635	Kingswood Estate 4d 2S	4,678	4,384	11,913
16645	Kingswood Estate 4d 3S	4,738	4,498	19,010

1971 Engines

1971 Engines	bore×stroke	bhp	availability
L4, 140.0	3.50×3.63	90	S-Vega
L4, 140.0	3.50×3.63	110	O-Vega
L6, 250.0	3.88×3.53	145	S-Nova,Chevl,Cam,Chevr
V8, 307.0	3.88×3.25	200	S-Nova,Chevl,Cam
V8, 350.0	4.00×3.48	245	S-MC,Chevr exc K/Est & Cap O-Nova,Chevl,Cam
V8, 350.0	4.00×3.48	270	O-Chevl,Cam,MC,Chevr
V8, 350.0	4.00×3.48	330	O-Camaro
V8, 400.0	4.12×3.75	255	S-Chevr K/Est & Cap; O-Chevr
V8, 402.0**	4.13×3.76	300	O-Chevl,Cam,MC,Chevr
V8, 454.0	4.25×4.00	365	O-Chevl,MC,Chevr
V8, 454.0	4.25×4.00	425	O-Chevl,MC

*"Chevr" for 1971-80 means full-size Chevrolets. In above context, this includes Biscayne, Bel Air, Impala, Caprice and full-size (125-in. wb) station wagons. **Commonly known as "396", actual displacement 402 cid.

1972

Vega (wb 97.0)

		Wght	Price	Prod
1V11	sdn 2d	2,158	2,060	55,839
1V15	wgn 3d	2,333	2,285	71,957
1V77	htchbk cpe 3d	2,294	2,160	262,682

Nova (wb 111.0)

1X27	cpe 2d L6	2,949	2,351	96,740
1X27	cpe 2d V8	3,083	2,441	163,475
1X69	sdn 4d L6	2,982	2,379	43,029
1X69	sdn 4d V8	3,116	2,469	46,489

Camaro (wb 108.1; includes 2,575 Z/28s)

1Q87	spt cpe L6	3,121	2,730	4,824
1Q87	spt cpe V8	3,248	2,820	63,832

Chevelle (wb 112.0; 4d-116.0)

1C37	htp cpe L6	3,172	2,669	6,993
1C37	htp cpe V8	3,300	2,759	22,714
1C69	sdn 4d L6	3,204	2,636	6,764
1C69	sdn 4d V8	3,332	2,726	12,881
1D37	Malibu htp cpe L6	3,194	2,833	4,790
1D37	Malibu htp cpe V8	3,327	2,923	207,598
1D39	Malibu htp sdn V8	3,438	2,991	24,192
1D67	Malibu conv V8	3,379	3,187	4,853
1D69	Malibu sdn 4d L6	3,240	2,801	3,562
1D69	Malibu sdn 4d V8	3,371	2,891	45,013

Chevelle Wagon (wb 116.0)

1B36	Nomad 4d 2S L6	3,605	2,926	2,956
1B36	Nomad 4d 2S V8	3,732	3,016	7,768
1C36	Greenbrier 4d 2S V8	3,814	3,140	6,975
1C46	Greenbrier 4d 3S V8	3,870	3,247	2,370
1D36	Concours 4d 2S V8	3,857	3,244	17,968
1D46	Concours 4d 3S V8	3,909	3,351	6,560
1H36	Concours Estate 4d 2S V8	3,887	3,431	5,331
1H46	Concours Estate 4d 3S V8	3,943	3,538	4,407

Chevrolet (wb 122.0)

1K69	Biscayne sdn 4d L6	3.857	3,074	1,504
1K59	Biscayne sdn 4d V8	4,045	3,408	19,034
1L69	Bel Air sdn 4d L6	3,854	3,204	868
1L69	Bel Air sdn 4d V8	4,042	3,538	41,020
1M39	Impala htp sdn V8	4,150	3,771	170,304
1M47	Impala Custom htp cpe V8	4,053	3,787	183,493
1M57	Impala htp cpe L6	3,864	3,385	289
1M57	Impala htp cpe V8	4,049	3,720	52,403
1M67	Impala conv V8	4,125	3,979	6,456
1M69	Impala sdn 4d L6	3,928	3,369	1,235
1M69	Impala sdn 4d V8	4,113	3,708	183,361
1N39	Caprice htp sdn V8	4,203	4,076	78,768
1N47	Caprice htp cpe V8	4,102	4,026	65,513
1N69	Caprice sdn 4d	4,166	4,009	34,174

Chevrolet Station Wagon (wb 125.0)

		Wght	Price	Prod
1K35	Brookwood 4d 2S	4,686	3,882	8,150
1L35	Townsman 4d 2S	4,687	3,969	16,482
1L45	Townsman 4d 3S	4,769	4,078	8,667
1M35	Kingswood 4d 2S	4,734	4,056	43,152
1M45	Kingswood 4d 3S	4,817	4,165	40,248
1N35	Kingswood Estate 4d 2S	4,798	4,314	20,281
1N45	Kingswood Estate 4d 3S	4,883	4,423	34,723

Monte Carlo (wb 116.0)

		Wght	Price	Prod
1H57	htp cpe V8	3,506	3,362	180,819

1972 Engines	bore×stroke	bhp	availability
L4, 140.0	3.50×3.63	80	S-Vega
L4, 140.0	3.50×3.63	90	O-Vega
L6, 250.0	3.88×3.53	110	S-Nova,Chevl,Cam,Chevr exc Cap & K/Est
V8, 307.0	3.88×3.25	130	S-Nova,Chevl, & Cam exc Cal
V8, 350.0	4.00×3.48	165	S-Chevl & Cam in Cal. O-Nova, Chevl, Chevr
V8, 350.0	4.00×3.48	175	O-Chevl, MC
V8, 350.0	4.00×3.48	200	O-Cam, Chevr
V8, 350.0	4.00×3.48	255	O-Chevr
V8, 350.0	4.00×3.48	275	O-Camaro
V8, 400.0	4.12×3.75	170	S-Chevr Cap & K/Est; O-Chevr
V8, 402.0	4.13×3.76	210	O-Chevr
V8, 402.0	4.13×3.76	240	O-Chevl,Cam, MC
V8, 454.0	4.25×4.00	270	O-Chevl, MC, Chevr

1973

Vega (wb 97.0)

		Wght	Price	Prod
V11	sdn 2d	2,219	2,087	58,425
V15	wgn 3d	2,317	2,323	102,751
V77	htchbk cpe 3d	2,313	2,192	266,124

Nova (wb 111.0)

X17	htchbk cpe 3d L6	3,145	2,528	11,005
X17	htchbk cpe 3d V8	3,274	2,618	33,949
X27	cpe L6	3,033	2,377	54,140
X27	cpe V8	3,162	2,467	81,679
X69	sdn 4d L6	3,065	2,407	27,440
X69	sdn 4d V8	3,194	2,497	32,843
Y17	Custom htchbk cpe 3d L6	3,152	2,701	3,172
Y17	Custom htchbk cpe 3d V8	3,281	2,792	42,886
Y27	Custom cpe L6	3,073	2,551	6,336
Y27	Custom cpe V8	3,202	2,741	52,042
Y69	Custom sdn 4d L6	3,105	2,580	4,344
Y69	Custom sdn 4d V8	3,234	2,671	19,673

Camaro (wb 108.1; incl. 11,574 Z/28s)

Q87	spt cpe L6	3,119	2,781	3,614
Q87	spt cpe V8	3,238	2,872	60,810
S87	Type LT spt cpe V8	3,349	3,268	32,327

Chevelle (wb 112.0; 4d-116.0)

C29	Deluxe Colonnade sdn 4d L6	3,435	2,719	5,253
C29	Deluxe Colonnade sdn 4d V8	3,585	2,835	15,502
C37	Deluxe Colonnade cpe L6	3,423	2,743	6,332
C37	Deluxe Colonnade cpe V8	3,580	2,860	15,045
D29	Malibu Colonnade sdn 4d L6	3,477	2,871	2,536
D29	Malibu Colonnade sdn 4d V8	3,627	2,987	58,143
D37	Malibu Colonnade cpe L6	3,430	2,894	3,157
D37	Malibu Colonnade cpe V8	3,580	3,010	165,627
E29	Laguna Colonnade sdn 4d V8	3,627	3,179	13,095
E37	Laguna Colonnade cpe V8	3,678	3,203	42,941

Chevelle Wagon (wb 116.0)

C35	Deluxe 5d 2S L6	3,849	3,106	1,870
C35	Deluxe 5d 3S V8	4,054	3,331	1,316
C37	Deluxe 5d 2S V8	4,006	3,198	7,754

		Wght	Price	Prod
D37	Malibu 5d 3S V8	4,075	3,423	5,961
D35	Malibu 5d 2S V8	4,027	3,290	18,592
G35	Malibu Estate 5d 3S V8	4,080	3,608	4,099
G35	Malibu Estate 5d 2S V8	4,032	3,475	5,527
E35	Laguna 5d 3S V8	4,158	3,616	2,200
E35	Laguna 5d 2S V8	4,110	3,483	4,419
H35	Laguna Estate 5d 3S V8	4,189	3,795	3,709
H35	Laguna Estate 5d 2S V8	4,141	3,662	3,661

Chevrolet (wb 121.5)

K69	Bel Air sdn 4d L6	3,895	3,247	1,394
K69	Bel Air sdn 4d V8	4,087	3,595	40,438
L39	Impala htp sdn V8	4,162	3,822	139,143
L47	Impala Custom cpe V8	4,110	3,836	176,824
L57	Impala cpe V8	4,096	3,769	42,979
L69	Impala sdn 4d	4,138	3,752	190,536
N39	Caprice Classic htp sdn V8	4,208	4,134	70,155
N47	Caprice Classic htp cpe V8	4,103	4,082	77,134
N67	Caprice Classic conv cpe V8	4,191	4,345	7,339
N69	Caprice Classic sdn 4d V8	4,176	4,064	58,126

Chevrolet Station Wagon (wb 125.0)

K47	Bel Air 4d 3S	4,770	4,136	6,321
K35	Bel Air 4d 2S	4,717	4,022	14,549
L35	Impala 4d 2S	4,742	4,119	46,940
L45	Impala 4d 3S	4,807	4,233	43,664
N35	Caprice Estate 4d 2S	4,779	4,382	22,969
N45	Caprice Estate 4d 3S	4,858	4,496	39,535

Monte Carlo (wb 116.0)

H57	spt cpe	3,713	3,415	4,960
H57	S spt cpe	3,720	3,562	177,963
H57	Landau spt cpe	3,722	3,806	107,770

1973 Engines	bore×stroke	bhp	availability
L6, 140.0	3.50×3.63	72	S-Vega
L4, 140.0	3.50×3.63	85	O-Vega
L6, 250.0	3.88×3.53	100	S-Nova,Chevl,Cam exc Lt,Chevr
V8, 307.0	3.88×3.25	115	S-Nova,Chevl exc Lag,Cam exc Lt
V8, 350.0	4.00×3.48	145	S-Lag,CamLT,MC, Chevr exc Cap O-Nova,Chevl, exc Lag, Cam exc Lt, Chevr exc Cap.
V8, 350.0	4.00×3.48	175	O-Nova, Chevl,Cam,MC
V8, 400.0	4.12×3.75	150	S-Cam; O-Chevr
V8, 454.0	4.25×4.00	215	O-Caprice
V8, 454.0	4.25×4.00	245	O-Chevl,Cam,MC,Cap

1974

Vega (wb 97.0)

		Wght	Price	Prod
V11	sdn 2d	2,369	2,505	58,724
V11	LX sdn 2d	—	2,833	5,996
V15	wgn 3d 2S	2,514	2,748	88,248
V15	Estate wgn 3d 2S	—	2,976	27,089
V77	hatchback cpe 3d	—	—	276,028

Nova (wb 111.0)

X17	htchbk cpe 3d L6	3,260	2,935	13,722
X17	htchbk cpe 3d V8	3,398	3,034	20,627
X27	cpe L6	3,150	2,811	87,399
X27	cpe V8	3,288	2,919	72,558
X69	sdn 4d L6	3,192	2,841	42,105
X69	sdn 4d V8	3,330	2,949	32,017
Y17	Custom htchbk cpe 3d L6	3,299	3,108	9,631
Y17	Custom htchbk cpe 3d V8	3,437	3,217	36,653
Y27	Custom cpe L6	3,206	2,985	11,115
Y27	Custom cpe V8	3,344	3,093	39,912
Y69	Custom sdn 4d L6	3,233	3,014	7,458
Y69	Custom sdn 4d V8	3,371	3,123	17,340

Chevrolet

Camaro (wb 108.1; incl 13,802 Z/28s)

Q87	spt cpe L6	3,309	3,162	22,210
Q87	spt cpe V8	3,450	3,366	79,835
S87	Type LT spt cpe V8	3,566	3,713	48,963

Chevelle (wb 112.0; 4d-116.0)

C29	Malibu sdn Colonnade 4d L6	3,638	3,049	11,399
C29	Malibu sdn Colonnade 4d V8	3,788	3,340	26,841
C37	Malibu Colonnade cpe L6	3,573	3,054	15,790
C37	Malibu Colonnade cpe V8	3,723	3,345	37,583
D29	Malibu Classic Colonnade sdn 4d L6	3,695	3,304	4,457
D29	Malibu Classic Colonnade sdn 4d V8	3,845	3,595	51,468
D37	Malibu Classic Colonnade cpe L6	3,609	3,307	4,132
D37	Malibu Classic Colonnade cpe V8	3,759	3,598	116,962
D37	Malibu Classic Colonnade Landau cpe L6	—	3,518	351
D37	Malibu Classic Colonnade Landau cpe V8	—	3,800	27,490
E37	Laguna S3 Colonnade cpe V8	3,951	3,723	15,792

Chevelle Wagon (wb 116.0) (all V8)

C35	Malibu 5d 3S	4,223	3,834	2,500
C37	Malibu 5d 2S	4,191	3,701	12,408
D35	Malibu Classic 5d 3S	4,315	4,251	4,909
D35	Malibu Classic 5d 2S	4,283	4,118	13,986
G35	Malibu Classic Estate 5d 3S	4,338	4,424	4,742
G35	Malibu Classic Estate 5d 2S	4,306	4,291	5,480

Chevrolet (wb 121.5)

K69	Bel Air sdn 4d	4,148	3,960	24,778
L39	Impala spt sdn 4d	4,256	4,215	76,492
L47	Impala Custom cpe	4,169	4,229	98,062
L57	Impala spt cpe	4,167	4,162	50,036
L69	Impala sdn 4d	4,205	4,135	133,164
N39	Caprice Classic spt sdn 4d	4,344	4,534	48,387
N47	Caprice Classic Custom cpe	4,245	4,483	59,484
N67	Caprice Classic conv cpe	4,308	4,745	4,670
N69	Caprice Classic sdn 4d	4,294	4,465	43,367

Chevrolet Wagon (wb 125.0)

K35	Bel Air 4d 2S	4,829	4,464	6,437
K45	Bel Air 4d 3S	4,884	4,578	2,913
L35	Impala 4d 2S	4,891	4,561	23,455
L45	Impala 4d 3S	4,936	4,675	23,259
N35	Caprice Estate 4d 2S	4,960	4,800	12,280
N45	Caprice Estate 4d 3S	5,004	4,914	23,063

Monte Carlo (wb 116.0)

H57	S spt cpe	3,926	3,885	184,873
H57	Landau spt cpe	3,928	4,129	127,344

1974 Engines	bore×stroke	bhp	availability
L4, 140.0	3.50×3.63	75	S-Vega
L4, 140.0	3.50×3.63	85	O-Vega
L6, 250.0	3.88×3.53	100	S-Nova,Chevl,Cam
V8, 350.0	4.00×3.48	145	S-Nova,Chevl,Cam,MC, Chevr exc Cap
V8, 350.0	4.00×3.48	160	O-as above
V8, 350.0	4.00×3.48	185	O-Nova, Camaro
V8, 400.0	4.12×3.75	150	S-Caprice exc wgns
V8, 400.0	4.12×3.75	180	S-wgns; O-Chevl, MC
V8, 454.0	4.25×4.00	235	O-Chevl,MC,Cap

1975

Vega (wb 97.0)

		Wght	Price	Prod
V11	sdn 2d	2,415	2,786	33,878
V11	LX sdn 2d	—	3,119	1,255
V15	wgn 3d 2S	2,531	3,016	47,474
V15	Estate wgn 3d 2S	—	3,244	8,659
V77	htchbk cpe 3d	2,478	2,899	112,912
V77	Cosworth htchbk cpe 3d	—	5,916	2,061

Monza (wb 97.0)

M27	Towne cpe	2,675	3,570	69,238
R07	S htchbk cpe 3d	—	3,648	9,795
R07	2+2 htchbk cpe 3d	2,753	3,953	57,170

Nova (wb 111.0)

X17	htchbk cpe 3d L6	3,391	3,347	7,952
X17	htchbk cpe 3d V8	3,493	3,422	8,421
X27	cpe L6	3,276	3,205	48,103
X27	S cpe L6	—	3.099	16,655
X27	cpe V8	3,378	3,280	33,921
X27	S cpe V8	—	3,174	5,070
X69	sdn 4d L6	3,306	3,209	43,760
X69	sdn 4d V8	3,408	3,284	22,587
Y17	Custom htchbk cpe 3d L6	3,421	3,541	3,812
Y17	Custom htchbk cpe 3d V8	3,523	3,616	11,438
Y27	Custom cpe L6	3,335	3,402	7,214
Y27	LN Cpe L6	—	3,782	1,138
Y27	Custom cpe V8	3,437	3,477	19,074
Y27	LN cpe V8	—	3,857	11,395
Y69	Custom sdn 4d L6	3,367	3,415	8,959
Y69	LN sdn 4d L6	—	3,795	1,286
Y69	Custom sdn 4d V8	3,469	3,490	13,221
Y69	LN sdn 4d V8	—	3,870	8,976

Camaro (wb 108.1)

Q87	spt cpe L6	3,421	3,540	29,749
Q87	spt cpe V8	3,532	3,685	76,178
S87	Type LT spt cpe V8	3,616	4,057	39,843

Chevelle (wb 112.0; 4d-116.0)

C29	Malibu sdn 4d L6	3,713	3,402	12,873
C29	Malibu sdn 4d V8	3,833	3,652	24,989
C37	Malibu cpe L6	3,642	3,407	13,292
C37	Malibu cpe V8	3,762	3,657	23,708
D29	Malibu Classic sdn 4d L6	3,778	3,695	1
D29	Malibu Classic sdn 4d V8	3,898	3,945	51,070
D37	Malibu Classic cpe L6	3,681	3,698	4,330
D37	Malibu Classic cpe V8	3,801	3,948	76,607
D37	Malibu Classic Landau cpe L6	—	3,930	378
D37	Malibu Classic Landau cpe V8	—	4,180	22,691
E37	Lagunna S3 cpe V8	3,908	4,113	—

Chevelle Malibu Wagon (wb 116.0)

C35	5d 3S	4,237	4,463	2,377
C35	5d 2S	4,207	4,318	11,600
D36	Classic 5d 3S	4,305	4,701	6,394
D36	Classic 5d 2S	4,275	4,556	15,974
G35	Classic Estate 5d 3S	4,331	4,893	4,600
G35	Classic Estate 5d 2S	4,301	4,748	4,637

Chevrolet (wb 121.5)

K69	Bel Air sdn 4d	4,179	4,345	15,871
L39	Impala spt sdn 4d	4,265	4,631	47,125
L47	Impala Custom cpe	4,190	4,626	49,455
L47	Impala Landau cpe	—	4,901	2,465
L57	Impala spt cpe	4,207	4,575	21,333
L69	Impala sdn 4d	4,218	4,548	91,330
N39	Caprice Classic spt sdn 4d	4,360	4,891	40,482
N47	Caprice Classic cpe	4,275	4,837	36,041
N47	Caprice Classic Landau cpe	—	5,075	3,752
N67	Caprice Classic conv cpe	4,343	5,113	8,349
N69	Caprice Classic sdn 4d	4,311	4,819	33,715

Chevrolet Wagon (wb 125.0)

K35	Bel Air 4d 2S	4,856	4,878	4,032
K45	Bel Air 4d 3S	4,913	4,998	2,386

		Wght	Price	Prod
L35	Impala 4d 2S	4,910	5,001	17,998
L45	Impala 4d 3S	4,959	5,121	19,445
N35	Caprice Estate 4d 2S	4,978	5,231	9,047
N45	Caprice Estate 4d 3S	5,036	5,351	18,858

Monte Carlo (wb 116.0)

		Wght	Price	Prod
H57	S spt cpe	3,927	4,249	148,529
H57	Landau spt cpe	3,930	4,519	110,380

1975 Engines	bore×stroke	bhp	availability
L4, 122.0	3.50×3.16	111	S-Cosworth Vega
L4, 140.0	3.50×3.63	78	S-Vega, Monza exc 2+2
L4, 140.0	3.50×3.63	87	S-Monza 2+2; O-Vega
L6, 250.0	3.88×3.53	105	S-Nova, Chevl, Cam
V8, 262.0	3.67×3.10	110	O-Nova, Monza
V8, 350.0	4.00×3.48	125	O-Monza
V8, 350.0	4.00×3.48	145	S-Nova, Chevl, Cam, MC, Chevr exc wgns
V8, 350.0	4.00×3.48	155	O-Nova, Chevl, Cam, MC, Chev
V8, 400.0	4.12×3.75	175	S-Chevr wgns; O-Chevl, MC, Chevr
V8, 454.0	4.25×4.00	235	O-Chevl, MC, Chevr

1976

Chevette (wb 94.3)

		Wght	Price	Prod
B08	htchbk sdn 3d	1,927	3,098	178,007
J08	Scooter htchbk sdn 3d	1,870	2,899	9,810

Vega (wb 97.0)

		Wght	Price	Prod
V11	sdn 2d	2,443	2,984	27,619
V15	wgn 3d 2S	2,578	3,227	46,114
V15	Estate wgn 3d 2S	—	3,450	7,935
V77	htchbk cpe 3d	2,534	3,099	77,409
V77	Cosworth htchbk cpe 3d	—	6,066	1,447

Monza (wb 97.0)

		Wght	Price	Prod
M27	Towne cpe	2,625	3,359	46,735
RO7	2+2 htchbk cpe 3d	2,668	3,727	34,170

Nova (wb 111.0)

		Wght	Price	Prod
X17	htchbk cpe 3d L6	3,391	3,417	10,853
X17	htchbk cpe 3d V8	3,475	3,579	7,866
X27	cpe L6	3,188	3,248	87,438
X27	cpe V8	3,272	3,413	44,421
X69	sdn 4d L6	3,221	3,283	86,600
X69	sdn 4d V8	3,305	3,448	37,167
Y17	Concours htchbk cpe 3d L6	3,401	3,972	2,088
Y17	Concours htchbk cpe 3d V8	3,485	4,134	5,486
Y27	Concours cpe L6	3,324	3,795	6,568
Y27	Concours cpe V8	3,408	3,960	15,730
Y69	Concours sdn 4d L6	3,367	3,830	10,151
Y69	Concours sdn 4d V8	3,451	3,995	20,360

Camaro (wb 108.1)

		Wght	Price	Prod
Q87	spt cpe L6	3,421	3,762	38,047
Q87	spt cpe V8	3,511	3,927	92,491
S87	Type LT spt cpe V8	3,576	4,320	52,421

Chevelle (wb 112.0; 4d-116.0)

		Wght	Price	Prod
C29	Malibu sdn 4d L6	3,729	3,671	13,116
C29	Malibu sdn 4d V8	3,834	4,201	25,353
C37	Malibu cpe L6	3,650	3,636	12,616
C37	Malibu cpe V8	3,755	4,166	17,976
D29	Malibu Classic sdn 4d L6	3,827	4,196	4,253
D29	Malibu Classic sdn 4d V8	3,932	4,490	73,307
D37	Malibu Classic cpe L6	3,688	3,926	5,791
D37	Malibu Classic cpe V8	3,793	4,455	76,843

		Wght	Price	Prod
D37	Malibu Classic Landau cpe L6	—	4,124	672
D37	Malibu Classic Landau cpe V8	—	4,640	29,495
E37	Laguna S3 cpe V8	3,978	4,621	9,100

Chevelle Malibu Wagon (wb 116.0)

		Wght	Price	Prod
C35	5d 3S	4,268	4,686	2,984
C35	5d 2S	4,238	4,543	13,581
D35	Classic 5d 3S	4,330	4,919	11,617
D35	Classic 5d 2S	4,300	4,776	24,635
G35	Malibu Classic Estate 5d 3S	4,356	5,114	6,386
G35	Malibu Classic Estate 5d 2S	4,326	4,971	5,518

Chevrolet (wb 121.5)

		Wght	Price	Prod
L39	Impala spt sdn 4d	4,245	4,798	39,849
L47	Impala Custom cpe	4,175	4,763	43,219
L47	Impala Landau cpe	—	5.058	10,841
L69	Impala S spt sdn 4d	—	4,507	18,265
L69	Impala sdn 4d	4,222	4,706	86,057
N39	Caprice Classic spt sdn 4d	4,314	5,078	55,308
N47	Caprice Classic cpe	4,244	5,043	28,161
N47	Caprice Classic Landau cpe	—	5,284	21,926
N69	Caprice Classic sdn 4d	4,285	5,013	47,411

Chevrolet Wagon (wb 125.0)

		Wght	Price	Prod
L35	Impala 4d 2S	4,912	5,166	19,657
L45	Impala 4d 3S	4,972	5,283	21,329
N35	Caprice Estate 4d 2S	4,948	5,429	10,029
N45	Caprice Estate 4d 3S	5,007	5,546	21,804

Monte Carlo (wb 116.0)

		Wght	Price	Prod
H57	S spt cpe	3,907	4,673	191,370
H57	Landau spt cpe	—	4,966	161,902

1976 Engines	bore×stroke	bhp	availability
L4, 85.0	3.23×2.61	52	S-Chevt
L4, 97.6	3.23×2.98	60	O-Chevt
L4, 122.0	3.50×3.15	111	S-Cosworth Vega
L4, 140.0	3.50×3.63	70	S-Vega, Monza
L4, 140.0	3.50×3.63	84	O-Vega, Monza
L6, 250.0	3.88×3.53	105	S-Nova, Chevl, Cam
V8, 262.0	3.67×3.10	110	O-Monza
V8, 305.0	3.74×3.48	140	S-Nova, Chevl, Cam, MC; O-Monza
V8, 305.0	3.74×3.48	145	S-Chevl wgn, Chevr; O-MC
V8, 350.0	4.00×3.48	165	O-Nova, Chevl, Cam, MC, Chevr
V8, 400.0	4.12×3.75	175	S-Chevr wgn; O-Chevl, MC, Chevr
V8, 454.0	4.25×4.00	225	O-Chevr

1977

Chevette (wb 94.3)

		Wght	Price	Prod
B08	htchbk sdn 3d	1,958	3,225	120,278
J08	Scooter htchbk sdn 3d	1,898	2,999	13,191

Vega (wb 97.0)

		Wght	Price	Prod
V11	sdn 2d	2,459	3,249	12,365
V15	wgn 3d 2S	2,571	3,522	25,181
V15	Estate wgn 3d 2S	—	3,745	3,461
V77	htchbk cpe 3d	2,522	3,359	37,395

Monza (wb 97.0)

		Wght	Price	Prod
M27	Town cpe	2,580	3,560	34,133
RO7	2+2 htchbk cpe 3d	2,671	3,840	39,215

Nova (wb 111.0)

		Wght	Price	Prod
X17	htchbk cpe 3d L6	3,217	3,646	} 18,048
X17	htchbk cpe 3d V8	3,335	3,766	
X27	cpe L6	3,139	3,482	} 132,833
X27	cpe V8	3,257	3,602	

1977 Monza 2+2 hatchback coupe

		Wght	Price	Prod
X69	sdn 4d L6	3,174	3,532	141,028
X69	sdn 4d V8	3,292	3,652	
Y17	Concours htchbk cpe 3d L6	3,378	4,154	5,481
Y17	Concours htchbk cpe 3d V8	3,486	4,274	
Y27	Concours cpe L6	3,283	3,991	28,602
Y27	Concours cpe V8	3,391	4,111	
Y69	Concours sdn 4d L6	3,329	4,066	39,272
Y69	Concours sdn 4d V8	3,437	4,186	

Camaro (wb 108.1)

		Wght	Price	Prod
Q87	spt cpe	3,369	4,113	131,717
S87	Type LT spt cpe	3,422	4,478	72,787
Q87	Z/28 spt cpe V8	—	—	14,349

Chevelle Malibu (wb 112.0; 4d-116.0)

		Wght	Price	Prod
C29	sdn 4d L6	3,628	3,935	39,064
C29	sdn 4d V8	3,727	4,055	
C37	cpe L6	3,551	3,885	28,793
C37	cpe V8	3,650	4,005	
D29	Classic sdn 4d L6	3,725	4,475	76,776
D29	Classic sdn 4d V8	3,824	4,595	
D37	Classic cpe L6	3,599	4,125	73,739
D37	Classic cpe V8	3,698	4,245	
D37	Classic Landau cpe L6	—	4,353	37,215
D37	Classic Landau cpe V8	—	4,473	

Chevelle Malibu Wagon (wb 116.0)

		Wght	Price	Prod
C35	5d 3S	4,169	4,877	4,014
C35	5d 2S	4,139	4,734	18,023
D35	Classic 5d 3S	4,263	5,208	19,053
D35	Classic 5d 2S	4,233	5,065	31,539

Chevrolet (wb 116.0)

		Wght	Price	Prod
L35	Impala wgn 4d 3S V8	4,072	5,406	28,255
L35	Impala wgn 4d 2S V8	4,042	5,289	37,108
L47	Impala Custom cpe L6	3,533	4,876	55,347
L47	Impala Custom cpe V8	3,628	4,996	
L47	Impala Landau cpe	—	—	2,745
L69	Impala sdn 4d L6	3,564	4,901	196,824
L69	Impala sdn 4d V8	3,659	5,021	
N35	Caprice Classic wgn 4d 3S V8	4,118	5,734	33,639
N35	Caprice Classic wgn 4d 2S V8	4,088	5,617	22,930
N47	Caprice Classic cpe L6	3,571	5,187	62,366
N47	Caprice Classic cpe V8	3,666	5,307	
N69	Caprice Classic sdn 4d L6	3,606	5,237	212,840
N69	Caprice Classic sdn 4d V8	3,701	5,357	
N69	Caprice Landau cpe	—	—	9,607

Monte Carlo (wb 116.0)

		Wght	Price	Prod
H57	S spt cpe	3,852	4,968	224,327
H57	Landau spt cpe	—	5,298	186,711

1977 Engines

1977 Engines	bore×stroke	bhp	availability
L4, 85.0	3.23×2.61	57	S-Chevt
L4, 97.6	3.23×2.98	63	O-Chevt
L4, 140.0	3.50×3.15	84	S-Vega, Monza
L6, 250.0	3.88×3.53	110	S-Nova,Chevl,Cam,Chevr
V8, 305.0	3.74×3.48	145	S-Nova,Chevl exc Clsc wgn, Cam, MC,Chevr; O-Monza
V8, 350.0	4.00×3.48	170	S-Chevl Clsc wgn; O-Nova, Chevl,Cam,MC,Chevr

1978

Chevette (wb 94.3; 5d-97.3)

		Wght	Price	Prod
B08	htchbk sdn 3d	1,965	3,644	118,375
B68	hthcbk sdn 5d	2,035	3,764	167,769
J08	Scooter htchbk sdn 3d	1,932	3,149	12,829

Monza (wb 97.0)

		Wght	Price	Prod
M07	2+2 htchbk cpe 3d	2,732	3,779	36,227
M15	wgn 3d	2,723	3,868	24,255
M15	Estate wgn 3d	—	4,102	2,478
M27	cpe	2,688	3,622	37,878
M77	S htchbk cpe 3d	2,643	3,697	2,326
R07	2+2 htchbk cpe 3d	2,777	4,247	28,845
R27	spt cpe	2,730	4,100	6,823

Nova (wb 111.0)

		Wght	Price	Prod
X17	htchbk cpe 3d L6	3,258	3,866	12,665
X17	htchbk cpe 3d V8	3,403	4,051	
X27	cpe L6	3,132	3,702	101,858
X27	cpe V8	3,277	3,887	
X69	sdn 4d L6	3,173	3,777	123,158
X69	sdn 4d V8	3,318	3,962	
Y27	Custom cpe L6	3,261	3,960	23,953
Y27	Custom cpe V8	3,396	4,145	
Y69	Custom sdn 4d L6	3,298	4,035	26,475
Y69	Custom sdn 4d V8	3,443	4,220	

Camaro (wb 108.1)

		Wght	Price	Prod
Q87	spt cpe	3,300	4,414	134,491
Q87	Rally sport cpe	—	4,784	11,902
S87	Type LT spt cpe	3,352	4,814	65,635
S87	Type LT Rally sport cpe	—	5,065	5,696
Q87	Z/28 spt cpe V8	—	5,604	54,907

Malibu (wb 108.1)

		Wght	Price	Prod
T19	sdn 4d V6	3,006	4,276	44,426
T19	sdn 4d V8	3,143	4,469	
T27	cpe V6	3,001	4,204	27,089
T27	cpe V8	3,138	4,394	
T35	wgn 4d 2S V6	3,169	4,516	30,850
T35	wgn 4d 2S V8	3,550	4,706	
W19	Classic sdn 4d V6	3,039	4,561	102,967
W19	Classic sdn 4d V8	3,175	4,751	
W27	Classic spt cpe V6	3,031	4,461	60,992
W27	Classic spt cpe V8	3,167	4,651	
W27	Classic Landau cpe V6	—	4,684	29,160
W27	Classic Landau cpe V8	—	4,874	
W35	Classic wgn 4d 2S V6	3,196	4,714	63,152
W35	Classic wgn 4d 2S V8	3,377	4,904	

Chevrolet (wb 116.0)

		Wght	Price	Prod
L35	Impala wgn 4d 3S V8	4,071	5,904	28,518
L35	Impala wgn 4d 2S V8	4,037	5,777	40,423
L47	Impala cpe L6	3,511	5,208	33,990
L47	Impala cpe V8	3,619	5,393	
L47	Impala Landau cpe L6	—	5,598	4,652
L47	Impala Landau cpe V8	—	5,783	
L69	Impala sdn 4d L6	3,530	5,283	183,161
L69	Impala sdn 4d V8	3,638	5,468	
N35	Caprice Classic wgn 4d 3S V8	4,109	6,151	32,952
N35	Caprice Clasic wgn 4d 2S V8	4,079	6,012	24,792

1978 Impala coupe

		Wght	Price	Prod
N47	Caprice Classic cpe L6	3,548	5,526	37,301
N47	Caprice Classic cpe V8	3,656	5,711	
N47	Caprice Landau cpe L6	—	5,830	22,771
N47	Caprice Landau cpe V8	—	6,015	
N69	Caprice Classic sdn 4d L6	3,578	5,628	203,837
N69	Caprice Classic snd 4d V8	3,686	5,811	

Monte Carlo (wb 108.1)

		Wght	Price	Prod
Z37	spt cpe V6	3,040	4,785	216,730
Z37	spt cpe V8	3,175	4,935	
Z37	Landau spt cpe V6	—	5,678	141,461
Z37	Landau spt cpe V8	—	5,828	

1978 Engines	bore×stroke	bhp	availability
L4, 97.6	3.23×2.98	63	S-Chevt
L4, 97.6	3.23×2.98	68	O-Chevt
L4, 151.0	4.00×3.00	85	S-Monza
V6, 196.0	3.50×3.40	90	O-Monza
V6, 200.0	3.50×3.48	95	S-Malibu
V6, 231.0	3.80×3.40	105	S-MC; O-Malibu, Monza
L6, 250.0	3.88×3.53	110	S-Nova,Cam exc Z/28 Chevr
V8, 305.0	3.74×3.48	145	S-Nova,Mal,Cam exc Z/28, MC, Chevr; O-Monza
V8, 350.0	4.00×3.48	170	O-Nova, Mal wgns, Cam, Chevr
V8, 350.0	4.00×3.48	185	S-Camaro Z/28

1979

Chevette (wb 94.3; 5d-97.3)

		Wght	Price	Prod
B08	htchbk sdn 3d	1,978	3,948	136,145
B68	htchbk sdn 5d	2,057	4,072	208,865
J08	Scooter htchbk sdn 3d	1,929	3,437	24,099

Monza (wb 97.0)

		Wght	Price	Prod
M07	2+2 htchbk cpe 3d	2,630	4,161	56,871
M15	wgn 3d	2,631	4,167	15,190
M27	cpe	2,577	3,850	61,110
R07	2+2 htchbk cpe 3d	2,676	4,624	30,662

Nova (wb 111.0)

		Wght	Price	Prod
X17	htchbk cpe 3d L6	3,264	4,118	4,819
X17	htchbk cpe 3d V8	3,394	4,353	
X27	cpe L6	3,135	3,955	36,800
X27	cpe V8	3,265	4,190	
X69	sdn 4d L6	3,179	4,055	40,883
X69	sdn 4d V8	3,309	4,290	

		Wght	Price	Prod
Y27	Custom cpe L6	3,194	4,164	7,529
Y27	Custom cpe V8	3,324	4,399	
Y69	Custom sdn 4d L6	3,228	4,264	7,690
Y69	Custom sdn 4d V8	3,358	4,499	

Camaro (wb 108.0)

		Wght	Price	Prod
Q87	spt cpe	3,305	5,163	111,357
Q87	Rally sport cpe	—	5,572	19,101
S87	Berlinetta cpe	3,358	5,906	67,236
Q87	Z/28 spt cpe V8	—	6,748	84,877

Malibu (wb 108.1)

		Wght	Price	Prod
T19	sdn 4d V6	2,988	4,915	59,674
T19	sdn 4d V8	3,116	5,180	
T27	cpe V6	2,983	4,812	41,848
T27	cpe V8	3,111	5,077	
T35	wgn 2d 2S V6	3,155	5,078	50,344
T35	wgn 2d 2S V8	3,297	5,343	
W19	Classic sdn 4d V6	3,024	5,215	104,222
W19	Classic sdn 4d V8	3,152	5,480	
W27	Classic cpe V6	3,017	5,087	60,751
W27	Classic cpe V8	3,145	5,352	
W27	Classic Landau cpe V6	—	5,335	25,213
W27	Classic Landau cpe V8	—	5,600	
W35	Classic wgn 4d V6	3,183	5,300	70,095
W35	Classic wgn 4d V8	3,325	5,565	

Chevrolet (wb 116.0)

		Wght	Price	Prod
L35	Impala wgn 4d 3S V8	4,045	6,636	28,710
L35	Impala wgn 4d 2S V8	4,013	6,497	39,644
L47	Impala cpe V6	3,495	5,828	26,589
L47	Impala cpe V8	3,606	6,138	
L47	Impala Landau cpe L6	—	6,314	3,247
L47	Impala Landau cpe V8	—	6,624	
L69	Impala sdn 4d L6	3,513	5,928	172,717
L69	Impala sdn 4d V8	3,624	6,238	
N35	Caprice Classic wgn 4d 3S V8	4,088	6,960	32,693
N35	Caprice Classic wgn 4d 2S V8	4,056	6,800	23,568
N37	Caprice Classic cpe L6	3,538	6,198	36,629
N37	Caprice Classic cpe V8	3,649	6,508	
N47	Caprice Classic Landau cpe L6	—	6,617	21,824
N47	Caprice Classic Landau cpe V8	—	6,927	
N69	Caprice Classic sdn 4d L6	3,564	6,323	203,017
N69	Caprice Classic sdn 4d V8	3,675	6,633	

Monte Carlo (wb 108.1)

		Wght	Price	Prod
Z37	spt cpe V6	3,039	5,333	225,073
Z37	spt cpe V8	3,169	5,598	

		Wght	Price	Prod
Z37	Landau spt cpe V6	—	6,183	91,850
Z37	Landau spt cpe V8	—	6,448	

1979 Engines	bore×stroke	bhp	availability
L4, 97.6	3.23×2.98	70	S-Chevt
L4, 97.6	3.23×2.98	74	O-Chevt
L4, 151.0	4.00×3.00	90	S-Monza 4s
V6, 196.0	3.50×3.40	105	S-Monza 6s
V6, 200.0	3.50×3.48	94	S-Malibu, MC
V6, 231.0	3.80×3.40	115	O-Mal, Monza, MC
L6, 250.0	3.88×3.53	115	S-Nova,CAm exc Z/28, Chevr exc wgns
V8, 267.0	3.50×3.48	125	S-Malibu, MC
V8, 305.0	3.74×3.48	130	S-Nova, Cam exc Z/28, Chevr O-Monza
V8, 305.0	3.74×3.48	160	O-Monte Carlo Chev
V8, 350.0	4.00×3.48	170	O-Nova, Mal, Cam exc Z/28
V8, 350.0	4.00×3.48	175	S-Camaro Z/28

1980

Chevette (wb 94.3; 5d-97.3)

		Wght	Price	Prod
B08	htchbk sdn 3d	1,989	4,601	148,686
B68	htchbk sdn 5d	2,048	4,736	261,477
J08	Scooter htchbk	1,935	4,057	40,998

Monza (wb 97.0)

		Wght	Price	Prod
M07	2+2 htchbk cpe 3d	2,672	4,746	53,415
M27	cpe	2,617	4,433	95,469
R07	Sport 2+2 htchbk cpe 3d	2,729	5,186	20,534

Citation (wb 104.9)*

		Wght	Price	Prod
H11	cpe L4	2,391	4,800	42,909
H11	cpe V6	2,428	4,925	
X08	htchbk sdn 3d L4	2,417	5,422	210,258
X08	htchbk sdn 3d V6	2,454	5,547	
X11	club cpe L4	2,397	5,214	100,340
X11	club cpe V6	2,434	5,339	
X68	htchbk sdn 5d L4	2,437	5,552	458,033
X68	htchbk 5d V6	2,474	5,677	

Camaro (wb 108.1)

		Wght	Price	Prod
P87	spt cpe	3,218	5,843	68,174
P87/Z85	RS cpe	—	6,086	12,015
S87	Berlinetta cpe	3,253	6,606	26,679
P87	Z/28 spt cpe V8	—	7,363	45,137

Malibu (wb 108.1)

		Wght	Price	Prod
T19	sdn 4d V6	3,001	5,617	67,696
T19	sdn 4d V8	3,122	5,697	

		Wght	Price	Prod
T27	spt cpe V6	2,996	5,502	28,425
T27	spt cpe V8	3,117	5,582	
T35	wgn 4d 2S V6	3,141	5,778	30,794
T35	wgn 4d 2S V8	3,261	5,858	
W19	Classic sdn 4d V6	3,031	5,951	77,938
W19	Classic sdn 4d V8	3,152	6,031	
W27	Classic spt cpe V6	3,027	5,816	28,425
W27	Classic spt cpe V8	3,148	5,896	
W27/Z03	Classic Landau cpe V6	—	6,009	9,342
W27/Z03	Classic Landau cpe V8	—	6,149	
W35	Classic wgn 4d 2S V6	3,167	6,035	35,730
W35	Classic wgn 4d 2S V8	3,307	6,115	

Full-size Chevrolet (wb 116.0)

		Wght	Price	Prod
L35	Impala wgn 4d 3S V8	3,924	7,186	6,767
L35	Impala wgn 4d 2S V8	3,892	7,041	11,203
L47	Impala spt cpe V6	3,344	6,535	10,756
L47	Impala spt cpe V8	3,452	6,615	
L69	Impala sdn 4d V6	3,360	6,650	70,801
L69	Impala sdn 4d V8	3,468	6,730	
N35	Caprice Clsc wgn 4d 3S V8	3,962	7,536	13,431
N35	Caprice Clsc wgn 4d 2S V8	3,930	7,369	9,873
N47	Caprice Clsc cpe V6	3,376	6,946	13,919
N47	Caprice Clsc cpe V8	3,484	7,026	
N47/Z03	Cap Clsc Lndu cpe V6	—	7,400	8,857
N47/Z03	Cap Clsc Lndu cpe V8	—	7,480	
N69	Caprice Classic sdn 4d V6/V8	—	—	91,208

Monte Carlo (wb 108.1)

		Wght	Price	Prod
Z37	spt cpe V6	3,104	6,524	116,580
Z37	spt cpe V8	3,219	6,604	
Z37/Z03	Landau cpe V6	—	6,772	32,262
Z37/Z03	Landau cpe V8	—	6,852	

1980 Engines	bore×stroke	bhp	availability
L4, 97.6	3.23×2.98	70	S-Chevt
L4, 97.6	3.23×2.98	74	O-Chevt
L4, 151.0	4.00×3.00	86	S-Monza
L4, 151.0	4.00×3.00	90	S-Citation
V6, 173.0	3.50×3.00	115	S-Citation
V6, 229.0	3.74×3.48	115	S-Mal,Cam,MC,Chevr exc wgn
V6, 231.0	3.80×3.40	110	O-Cam, Monza, MC, Chevr exc wgn
V6T, 231.0	3.80×3.40	170	O-MC
V8, 267.0	3.50×3.48	120	S-Mal,Cam,MC,Chevr
V8, 305.0	3.74×3.48	155	O-Mal,Cam,MC,Chevr
V8, 350.0	4.00×3.48	190	S-Camaro Z/28; O-other Cam
V8D, 350.0	4.00×3.48	105	O-Chevr wgn

1980 Citation club coupe

1980 Monza Sport 2+2 hatchback coupe with Spyder option

Chevrolet Corvair
Chevrolet Motor Division, General Motors Corp. Detroit, Michigan

Chevrolet's work on a small rear-engine car began after World War II, with a stillborn prototype called the Cadet. But postwar buyers were so hungry for cars, even warmed-over prewar models, that the division saw no need to build Cadets. By the late 1950's, however, the situation had changed radically. Import makes, led by Volkswagen and Renault, were biting into the domestic market. The growing number of economy-car sales was becoming too large to ignore.

The first modern compact, Studebaker's 1959 Lark, was so successful that it temporarily halted Studebaker's slide into oblivion. The Lark soon had rivals. In Detroit, Ford had laid plans for the Falcon, Chrysler was ready with the Valiant, and both were introduced as 1960 models. In 1958-59, General Motors had stemmed the tide with its so-called "captive imports," the British Vauxhall and the German Opel. For 1960, GM pinned its small-car sales hopes on the Corvair.

Largely the work of Edward N. Cole, long-time GM engineer (and future GM president), the Corvair was a technician's car, by far the most radical of the Big Three's new compacts. Its powerplant was a flat six that developed 80 or 95 horsepower. Relatively complicated, it had two cylinder heads, six separate cylinder barrels, and a divided crankcase. Flat sixes were not common in automobiles; Corvair's powerplant might have been inspired by Cole's interest in airplanes. Unfortunately, the production engine weighed 388 pounds, some 100 pounds more than the target weight. This miscalculation would have a negative effect on the car's handling.

The suspension of the 108-inch-wheelbase chassis was basic—perhaps too basic. Up front were wishbones and coil springs; in back were semi-trailing swing axles. There was no anti-sway bar, although GM had known this was one of several ways to achieve acceptable handling with swing axles in a car with a rear-end weight bias. Management's decision to reduce cost while maximizing ease of service and efficiency of assembly prevented the use of more sophisticated suspension components until 1962, when a regular production option including stiffer springs, shorter rear axle limit straps, and a front sway bar was made available. A major suspension improvement was made in 1964, when a transverse compensating spring was adopted.

It should be pointed out, however, that the 1960-63 Corvair's rather basic four-wheel independent suspension did not create a "dangerous, ill-handling car," as lawsuits claimed. The car did oversteer, to be sure. But the oversteer was not excessive when the tires were inflated to the recommended pressures: 15 psi front, 26

1958 clay for 1960 Corvair

1960 prototype for production 1962 convertible

1961 700 Lakewood four-door station wagon

1962 700 four-door station wagon

psi rear. The point was argued for years, and was settled only by a congressional investigation, which found in the Corvair's favor.

The Corvair's 10-year production run can be divided into two segments: the first generation of 1960-64, and the second generation of 1965-69.

Corvairs were initially offered in three series. The 500 was the most basic package. The 700 was slightly better trimmed. Most interesting was the 900 Monza with its deluxe interior and bucket seats. When Chevy offered an optional four-speed gearbox in 1961, Monza sales caught fire. A new market had been uncovered almost by accident: the sporty, fun-to-drive, bucket-seat compact. This was fortunate, because the 500 and 700 series Corvairs were not competitive in price with the Falcon and were being outsold by it.

The most highly prized first-generation Corvair is the turbocharged Monza Spyder of 1962-64. Its 150-bhp engine, multi-gauge instrument panel, many handling and performance options, and choice of coupe and convertible models made it highly desirable. Unfortunately, it wasn't cheap: the price was about $2800 plus options. Production was limited to about 40,000 units over three years.

For 1961, the flat six was bored out to 145 cid and optional horsepower went up to 98. In 1964, the engine was stroked for a displacement of 164 cubic inches and 95 to 110 hp in nonsupercharged form.

Another interesting first-generation Corvair was the Lakewood station wagon, which appeared in 1961. The

1963 900 Monza Spyder convertible

1966 Corsa convertible

Lakewood offered a surprising amount of cargo space—58 cubic feet behind the front seat, and 10 more cubic feet under the hood. This was more than other compact wagons, and even more than some larger models. The wagon didn't sell well, however, and production barely topped 25,000 units in 1961. For 1962, the Lakewood name was dropped, but the wagon was offered in both the 700 and Monza series. The Monza wagon was plush, equipped with bucket seats and deluxe trim. Only about 6000 of the 1962 models were built before this body style was dropped entirely to make room on the assembly line for the hot Chevy II.

The sleek 1965 Corvairs were a design revolution. Good-looking even from normally unflattering angles, they were a tribute to the fine edge honed on GM cars by then styling chief William L. Mitchell and his designers. The new Corvair looked almost like the work of an Italian coachbuilder. (In fact, Pininfarina built a specially bodied 1964 Corvair with similar lines.) It was nicely shaped and not overdone, with just the right amount of trim. The car was new under the skin also. The turbocharged engine produced 180 bhp at 400 rpm, making it the most powerful stock powerplant. But probably the best all-around Corvair engine was the new 140-bhp version. New cylinder heads, redesigned manifolds, and four progressively linked carburetors gave it its extra power.

The 1960 Corvair had been the first mass-produced American car to offer a swing-axle rear suspension. The 1965 Corvair was the first to offer fully independent suspension (aside from the Corvette). There was only one difference between the two: Corvette's suspension design used a transverse leaf spring while Corvair's had a coil spring at each wheel. The rest of the two systems were the same: upper and lower control arms were used at each rear wheel. The uppers were actually the axle half-shafts; the lowers were unequal length, nonparallel bars. These four arms controlled all lateral wheel motion. Small rubber-mounted rods extended from each arm to the main rear cross-member to absorb shocks from movement at the trailing-arm pivot points.

No longer was there any question of tricky handling on hard corners. The Corvair's cornering was now nearly neutral, tending toward mild understeer at high speeds. The rear wheels, remaining at a constant angle with the ground, took most of the car's weight and enabled it to be pushed around corners at great speeds. Attention was also given to the front suspension, which was tuned to complement the new rear-end design and to provide roll stiffness.

Of all second-generation Corvairs, the 1965-66 Corsa was the most desirable. It came as a sport coupe with a base price of $2519 and as a convertible at $2665, complete with a full set of instruments, special exterior trim (including an aluminum rear panel for instant identification), deluxe interior, and the 140-bhp engine. The turbocharged six was a $158 option. With it, the Corsa was definitely in the high-performance category. A typical 0–60 mph acceleration time was less than 11 sec-

1967 Monza hardtop sedan

1969 Monza hardtop coupe

onds, and the car could do the standing-start quarter-mile in 18 seconds at 80 mph. The Corsa could hit 115 mph when given enough straightaway, yet deliver more than 20 miles per gallon at moderate highway speeds.

Unfortunately, the Corsa didn't sell particularly well against Ford's Mustang, which could better the Chevy's performance. Even more critical was a decline in Monza sales. This most popular Corvair rallied slightly in 1965, but the following year production plunged to about one-third the '65 level. By that time, Ralph Nader's book *Unsafe at Any Speed* was having an effect on Corvair sales. But according to Karl Ludvigsen in his history of Corvair, the car's fate had already been sealed by a GM directive in April 1965: "No more development work," was the order.

When the Camaro was added to the sporty-car lists for 1967, the Corvair line was trimmed to just two series: the 500 sedan and coupe; and the Monza sedan, coupe, and convertible. It would be the last year for the hardtop sedans, which are collector's items today.

The 1968-69 Corvairs were the rarest of the breed, available in just three models—500 hardtop, Monza coupe, and Monza convertible. These cars are readily identifiable by their front side marker lights—clear lenses in 1968, amber ones in 1969. Monza convertibles were the scarcest of all.

It was obvious by 1968 that the Corvair was becoming an orphan. Some Chevrolet dealers wouldn't handle them, and others refused to service them. Cole's vision had faded, and Corvair died an undeserved death.

Chevrolet Corvair Specifications

1960

500 (wb 108.0)

		Wght	Price	Prod
0527	cpe	2,270	1,984	14,628
0569	sdn 4d	2,305	2,038	47,683

700 (wb 108.0)

| 0727 | cpe | 2,290 | 2,049 | 36,562 |
| 0769 | sdn 4d | 2,315 | 2,103 | 139,208 |

900 Monza (wb 108.0)

| 0927 | cpe | 2,280 | 2,238 | 11,926 |

1960 Engines	bore×stroke	bhp	availability	
flat 6, 140.0	3.38×2.60	80	S-all	
flat 6, 140.0	3.38×2.60	95	O-all	

1961

500 (wb 108.0)

		Wght	Price	Prod
0527	cpe	2,320	1,920	16,857

		Wght	Price	Prod
0535	Lakewood wgn 4d	2,530	2,266	5,591
0569	sdn 4d	2,355	1,974	18,752

700 (wb 108.0)

0727	cpe	2,350	1,985	24,786
0735	Lakewood wgn 4d	2,555	2,331	20,451
0769	sdn 4d	2,380	2,039	51,948

900 Monza (wb 108.0)

| 0927 | cpe | 2,395 | 2,201 | 109,945 |
| 0969 | sdn 4d | 2,420 | 2,201 | 33,745 |

1961 Engines	bore×stroke	bhp	availability	
flat 6, 145.0	3.44×2.60	80	S-all	
flat 6, 145.0	3.44×2.60	98	O-all	

1962

500 (wb 108.0)

		Wght	Price	Prod
0527	cpe	2,350	1,992	16,245

700 (wb 108.0)

0727	cpe	2,390	2,057	18,474
0735	wgn 4d	2,590	2,407	3,716
0769	sdn 4d	2,410	2,111	35,368

Chevrolet Corvair

900 Monza (wb 108.0)		Wght	Price	Prod
0927	cpe	2,440	2,273	144,844
0927	Spyder cpe	2,465	2,636	6,894
0935	wgn 4d	2,590	2,569	2,362
0967	conv cpe	2,625	2,483	13,995
0967	Spyder conv cpe	2,650	2,846	2,574
0969	sdn 4d	2,455	2,273	48,059

1962 Engines	bore×stroke	bhp	availability
flat 6, 145.0	3.44×2.60	80	S-all exc Spyder
flat 6, 145.0	3.44×2.60	98	O-all exc Spyder
flat 6, 145.0	3.44×2.60	150	S-Monza Spyder

1963

500 (wb 108.0)		Wght	Price	Prod
0527	cpe	2,330	1,992	16,680

700 (wb 108.0)				
0727	cpe	2,355	2,056	12,378
0769	sdn 4d	2,385	2,110	20,684

900 Monza (wb 108.0)				
0927	cpe	2,415	2,272	117,917
0927	Spyder cpe	2,440	2,589	11,627
0967	conv cpe	2,525	2,481	36,693
0967	Spyder conv cpe	2,550	2,798	7,472
0969	sdn 4d	2,450	2,326	31,120

1963 Engines	bore×stroke	bhp	availability
flat 6, 145.0	3.44×2.60	80	S-all exc Spyder
flat 6, 145.0	3.44×2.60	98	O-all exc Spyder
flat 6, 145.0	3.44×2.60	150	S-Monza Spyder

1964

500 (wb 108.0)		Wght	Price	Prod
0527	cpe	2,365	2,000	22,968

600 Monza Spyder (wb 108.0)				
0627	cpe	2,470	2,599	6,480
0667	conv cpe	2,580	2,811	4,761

700 (wb 108.0)				
0769	sdn 4d	2,415	2,119	16,295

900 Monza (wb 108.0)				
0927	cpe	2,445	2,281	88,440
0967	conv cpe	2,555	2,492	31,045
0969	sdn 4d	2,470	2,335	21,926

1964 Engines	bore×stroke	bhp	availability
flat 6, 164.0	3.44×2.94	95	S-all exc 600
flat 6, 164.0	3.44×2.94	110	O-all exc 600
flat 6, 164.0	3.44×2.94	150	S-600

1965

500 (wb 108.0)		Wght	Price	Prod
10137	htp cpe	2,385	2,066	36,747
10139	htp sdn	2,405	2,142	17,560

Monza (wb 108.0)				
10537	htp cpe	2,440	2,347	88,954
10539	htp sdn	2,465	2,422	37,157
10567	conv cpe	2,675	2,493	26,466

Corsa (wb 108.0)				
10737	htp cpe	2,475	2,519	20,291
10767	conv cpe	2,710	2,665	8,353

1965 Engines	bore×stroke	bhp	availability
flat 6, 164.0	3.44×2.94	95	S-all exc Corsa
flat 6, 164.0	3.44×2.94	110	O-all exc Corsa
flat 6, 164.0	3.44×2.94	140	S-Corsa; O-others
flat 6, 164.0	3.44×2.94	180	O-Corsa

1966

500 (wb 108.0)		Wght	Price	Prod
10137	htp cpe	2,400	2,083	24,045
10139	htp sdn	2,445	2,157	8,779

Monza (wb 108.0)				
10537	htp cpe	2,445	2,350	37,605
10539	htp sdn	2,495	2,424	12,497
10567	conv cpe	2,675	2,493	10,345

Corsa (wb 108.0)				
10737	htp cpe	2,485	2,519	7,330
10767	conv cpe	2,720	2,662	3,142

1966 Engines	bore×stroke	bhp	availability
flat 6, 164.0	3.44×2.94	95	S-all exc Corsa
flat 6, 164.0	3.44×2.94	110	O-all exc Corsa
flat 6, 164.0	3.44×2.94	140	S-Corsa; O-others
flat 6, 164.0	3.44×2.94	180	O-Corsa

1967

500 (wb 108.0)		Wght	Price	Prod
10137	htp cpe	2,435	2,128	9,257
10139	htp sdn	2,470	2,194	2,959

Monza (wb 108.0)				
10537	htp cpe	2,465	2,398	9,771
10539	htp sdn	2,515	2,464	3,157
10567	conv cpe	2,695	2,540	2,109

1967 Engines	bore×stroke	bhp	availability
flat 6, 164.0	3.44×2.94	95	S-all
flat 6, 164.0	3.44×2.94	110/140	O-all

1968

500 (wb 108.0)		Wght	Price	Prod
10137	htp cpe	2,470	2,243	7,206

Monza (wb 108.0)				
10537	htp cpe	2,500	2,507	6,807
10567	conv cpe	2,725	2,626	1,386

1968 Engines	bore×stroke	bhp	availability
flat 6, 164.0	3.44×2.94	95	S-all
flat 6, 164.0	3.44×2.94	110	O-all

1969

500 (wb 108.0)		Wght	Price	Prod
10137	htp cpe	2,515	2,528	2,762

Monza (wb 108.0)				
10537	htp cpe	2,545	2,522	2,717
10567	conv cpe	2,770	2,641	521

1969 Engines	bore×stroke	bhp	availability
flat 6, 164.0	3.44×2.94	95	S-all
flat 6, 164.0	3.44×2.94	110	O-all

Chevrolet Corvette

Chevrolet Motor Division, General Motors Corp. Detroit, Michigan

Chevrolet's Corvette was America's first and only successful fiberglass sports car. It debuted in 1953, the product of a 30-month cooperative development program between Harley Earl's Art & Colour Studio and the Chevrolet Division Engineering Staff. A simple managerial decision to have a sports car in the Chevy lineup was all it took to get the Corvette project in motion. The decision was a brave one, since sales of imported sports cars in the middle-'50s amounted to less than one percent of the market.

The first-generation 1953-55 Corvette was marked by rounded, rather bulbous styling derived from a variety of Motorama show cars and studio sketches. With ex-

tended pod-type taillights, a busy front end, and the then-mandatory wraparound windshield, it was hardly a timeless design. Indeed, the Corvette almost expired after 1955 due to disappointing sales, which some blamed on its rather awkward combination of features. Dyed-in-the-wool driving enthusiasts found it hard to accept the Corvette's two-speed Powerglide automatic transmission, even though its modified Chevrolet six developed a commendable 150 horsepower. "Boulevardier" types, on the other hand, disliked the plastic side curtains, and would have preferred proper rolldown windows like those of regular passenger cars. A V8 finally arrived in 1955: the 265 cubic-inch Chevrolet

Corvette Motorama show car of 1953

Corvair fastback show car of 1954

1953 Corvette convertible roadster

1955 Corvette convertible roadster

Motorama hardtop showcar, 1954

1956 Corvette with optional hardtop

1956 Corvette convertible roadster

1957 Corvette with optional hardtop

Racing show car from '57—Corvette SR-2

Sebring SS racer with Duntov at the wheel

1958 Corvette with optional hardtop

small-block created by Ed Cole, John Gordon, and others. This powerplant delivered vastly improved performance, and almost all Corvettes that year were V8-equipped. Still, total 1955 model year production failed to surpass 700 units.

Late in 1954, a decision was made to give the Corvette a reprieve, and a fully redesigned model was readied for 1956. It was a considerable improvement on the stubby look of the earlier cars. Harley Earl had developed a beautifully sculptured body featuring a curving, concave section just aft of the front wheel openings, and a "toothy" grille. Engine changes—the six was dropped completely after 1955—eventually put Corvette in the serious performance class. Earl's styling lasted a full seven years before it was replaced by Bill Mitchell's Sting Ray design in 1963. In the process, Corvette became America's favorite sports car. The '56-'62 series was aggressive-looking, which nicely matched its performance. Manual as well as Powerglide transmissions were available from 1956 on, and eventually a close-ratio four-speed joined the list.

For 1957, the 265-cid V8 was bored out to 283 cid, and fuel injection versions of this were offered. "Fuelie" Corvettes developed a phenomenal 250 to 283 bhp that year. Though they were thunderingly fast in a straight line, they were only moderately successful in road racing competition. There were three carbureted and two injected V8s offered through the end of the '50s, and handling options improved roadability of the later models. Though GM had begun deemphasizing racing with the rest of the industry in 1957, numerous private drivers continued to campaign Corvettes. By dint of their numbers, Chevy's sports car began piling up wins in road racing as well as on the dragstrips by the end of the decade.

For 1960, Corvette was substantially the same as it had been in 1958-59—flashy and fast. But there was an increase in the use of aluminum: in the clutch housing, the radiator, and the cylinder heads of fuel-injected engines. The 1960 model also featured anti-sway bars front and rear, which greatly improved ride and handling. It was the first use of a rear sway bar on an American car.

Also that year, Corvette achieved international recognition in the 24-hour race at Le Mans in France. Three cars entered by Briggs Cunningham in the GT class all performed exceptionally well: one hit 151 miles per hour on the long Mulsanne Straight. A Corvette finished eighth overall in that race, the toughest of all international endurance contests.

The 1960-61 period was the last for the 283 V8. During those two years, six variations were offered. They ranged from a single four-barrel-carburetor engine to a fuel-injected version with 315 bhp. A wide assortment of rear axle ratios and three transmission choices (three-speed and four-speed manual plus automatic) were available. It was now possible to tailor a Corvette to very specific requirements, from boulevard touring to all-out competition.

1958 Corvette with optional hardtop

1959 Corvette convertible roadster

XP-700 show car of 1958

Mitchell's Sting Ray racer in "street" trim

Sting Ray racer in '61— officially a "Corvette"

Styling for 1961-62 was a mild facelift of the 1960 model, but it was highly effective. The cars retained the basic 1958-60 front end and midsection, but were completely restyled at the rear. By that time, Mitchell had relieved Harley Earl as GM styling chief, and the new rear-end treatment was his idea. A "ducktail" shape, it was derived from Mitchell's Stingray racer and the experimental XP-700.

Engine and gearbox options for 1961 were unchanged from 1960. More than 85 percent of Corvette buyers ordered manual transmission, and more than half of them requested the four-speed. The 315-bhp engine was most impressive when coupled to stump-pulling rear axle ratios. With the 4.11:1 gearset, for example, the car could accelerate from 0 to 60 mph in 5.5 seconds, and cover the standing quarter-mile in 14.2 seconds at 99 mph. Despite this short gearing, top speed could approach 130 mph.

For 1962, Mitchell further refined the Corvette's styling. De-emphasizing the concave bodyside "cove," he eliminated its chrome outline. He also replaced the "speed streaks" inside it with a vertical grid. The grille

was blacked out, and a decorative strip of anodized aluminum was added to the rocker panels. Also in '62, stiffer springs were brought back as an option. Dr. Richard Thompson won the Sports Car Club of America (SCCA) A-production championship that year with a Corvette so equipped.

After Semon E. "Bunkie" Knudsen became Chevrolet's general manager in 1962, Corvette was slated for increased production. The car had turned the profit corner in 1958, and the division was seeing an adequate return on its investment. Production continued to rise in the years that followed.

In 1962, a new 327-cid V8, created by enlarging the 283, was introduced. The fuel-injection system was also modified. A 3.08:1 final drive ratio was adopted for quieter cruising with the two lowest-horsepower engines.

The 327 remained the basic Corvette powerplant through 1968. With its improved torque, the 327 Corvette with 3.70:1 rear axle could run the quarter-mile in 15 seconds at more than 100 mph. And, with its new optional sintered metallic brake linings, Corvette could

173

1961 Corvette convertible roadster

1963 Corvette Sting Ray "split-window" coupe

1962 Corvette convertible roadster

1963 Corvette Sting Ray roadster with hardtop

'63 Sting Ray roadsters with and without tops

stop as well as it could go. In SCCA racing, it was now the undisputed champion in both A- and B-production classes, and it competed in good form at Sebring.

The 1963 Sting Ray was a revolution, a complete revision of Chevrolet's sports car, which had been mostly unchanged up to that point. The only items carried over from 1962 were the engines. In addition to the Sting Ray roadster, there was a beautiful new fastback grand touring coupe. More than 10,000 copies of each were sold, and both were unquestionably landmark designs.

Prototypes for what became the 1963 Corvette began appearing in late 1959. The first of these cars was the experimental XP-720. Based on the Mitchell-designed Stingray racer, this coupe featured a smooth fastback fuselage set off by a distinctive split rear window. That window was Mitchell's idea, but it stayed in production only one year, 1963. To his disgust, but for better visibility, it was replaced on the 1964 coupes by a one-piece window.

The XP-720 package was practical as well as attractive. Early alterations from the Stingray racer included hidden headlights, achieved through the use of pivot-

ing sections that lay flush with the creased front end. There was an attractive dip in the beltline at the upper trailing edges of the doors. The coupe's doors were cut into the roof. A new "dual cockpit" dashboard was a fresh approach that worked remarkably well.

After the XP-720 was firmed up, a roadster version was developed. A four-passenger Corvette was considered too, but the idea was dropped because it seemed out of character with the car's concept. Final prototypes were intensively evaluated. Wind tunnel tests were made to determine aerodynamics. Body engineers added as well as subtracted weight. As a result, the 1963 model had almost twice as much steel support in its central body structure as the 1962 Corvette and less fiberglass in its body.

The 1963 Sting Ray had a shorter wheelbase than the 1962 model, and its rear track was two inches narrower. Frontal area was reduced by one square foot. Interior space, however, was at least as good in every dimension. And, thanks to the added steel reinforcement, the cockpit was stronger and safer than before.

Compared to the '62 model, the '63 was a superior

car. There were no engine changes from the previous year, but the chassis was extensively reworked, primarily at the rear. Its most significant feature was the fully independent rear suspension, a three-link type with double-jointed open driveshafts at either side, control arms, and trailing radius rods. A single transverse leaf spring was mounted to the frame with rubber-cushioned struts. In accord with the wishes of leading Corvette engineer Zora Arkus-Duntov, the differential was bolted to the rear cross-member. The frame itself was a well-reinforced box. Weight distribution was 48/52, compared to the previous 53/47. As a result of all this, the '63's ride and handling were significantly better. A new recirculating-ball steering gear, combined with a dual-arm, three-link ball-joint front suspension made the steering quicker. The front brake drums were wider, and all brakes were self-adjusting. There was an alternator instead of a generator, positive crankcase ventilation, a smaller flywheel, and a new aluminum clutch

housing. Competition options included stiff suspension, metallic brake linings, cast-aluminum knock-off wheels, and a 36.5-gallon long-distance fuel tank.

Styling actually became cleaner during the five years of the Sting Ray's life. In 1964, the fake hood louvers were deleted, and the coupe's rear quarter vents were made functional. In 1965, the sculptured hood panel was smoothed out, and the front fender slots were opened up. By 1967, the car had reached its styling peak, and the only changes were an oblong back-up light, bolt-on instead of knock-off aluminum wheels, revised front fender louvers, and an optional vinyl covering for the roadster's removable hardtop.

Mechanically, important advancements were made through the mid-1960s. The new fuel-injected small-block engine of 1964 developed 1.15 bhp per cubic inch. For 1965, Corvettes were equipped with disc brakes on all four wheels, and the new Mark IV engine that developed 425 bhp made its debut.

1964 Corvette Sting Ray coupe

Mako Shark II show car from 1965

1965 Corvette Sting Ray coupe

1966 Corvette Sting Ray coupe

1966 Corvette Sting Ray roadster

The first Mark IV displaced 396 cid, but this was increased to 427 in 1966. To handle its bruce force, Chevrolet used a stiffer suspension, extra-heavy-duty clutch, and a larger radiator and fan. With the 4.11:1 rear axle ratio, a 1966 Mark IV could go from 0 to 60 in less than five seconds, with a top-end maximum of more than 140 mph. Fuel injection was dropped after 1965 for the smaller-displacement engines. This was mainly due to its high production costs and low sales.

Chevrolet had considered building a mid-engine Corvette for 1968, but that was ruled out due to the high cost of making the transaxle that would be needed. Instead, there was a complete restyling, chiefly the work of the division's design studio under David Holls. The 1968 model was an aggressive, swoopy-looking car with an air dam at the front and a spoiler at the rear. Its aerodynamic properties, however, were not especially good. A roadster and a notchback hardtop were offered. Pop-up hidden headlights and concealed windshield wipers were featured. The 1968 model retained

the 1967 engine lineup. From 1967 on, buyers could specify the potent L88, a competition engine that produced up to a staggering 560 bhp. It had aluminum heads, and came with an extra-heavy-duty clutch. It was joined in 1969 by the ZL-1 racing engine, with a dry sump and aluminum block. The ZL-1 weighed 100 pounds less than the L88, but it cost $3000!

The Sting Ray name disappeared in 1968, only to return—as one word—for 1969. These cars were improved in detail. The exterior door handles were cleaner than before, black-painted grille bars replaced the chrome, and the back-up lights were integrated with the inner taillights. Handling was improved by wider wheels, and the frame was stiffened. The interior was revised to create more room for passengers and their belongings. The 327 engine was stroked to 350 cid and was offered in 300- and 350-bhp tune. Four 427 engines were also available, with an array of axle ratios from 4.56:1 to 2.75:1.

The 1968 package, however, was not received with

1966 Corvette Sting Ray coupe

1966 Corvette Sting Ray coupe

1967 Corvette Sting Ray coupe

1968 Corvette coupe

1968 Corvette convertible roadster

1968 Corvette convertible roadster

1969 Corvette Stingray coupe

1970 Corvette Stingray convertible roadster

unamimous praise, and debate surrounds it to this day. *Road & Track* magazine summed up the case for the opposition, saying that the car was "highly reminiscent of certain older Ferraris, laid around a chassis that seemed fairly modern in 1962 but is now quite dated by the march of progress ... We feel that the general direction of the change is away from sports car and toward image-and-gadget car."

The new body was seven inches longer than its 1967 predecessor, most of that in extra front overhang. The car's wheelbase was unchanged at 98 inches, but its interior was more cramped, and there was less luggage space. About 150 pounds had been added to what *Road & Track* called the "already gross avoirdupois." It was a great machine, the magazine said, "for those who like their cars big, flashy, and full of blinking lights and trap doors ... The connoisseur who values finesse, efficiency, and the latest chassis design will have to look, unfortunately, to Europe."

Although the 1963-67 Sting Ray is considered *the* classic Corvette of the '60s, the 1968-70 models were more successful with the public. The production peak was set in 1969, with 38,762 units—a record that would stand until 1976. They were longer, heavier, and clumsier than their predecessors, but they were still very fast and appealing. They remained America's only true sports cars. "Corvettes are for driving, by drivers," *Car Life* magazine said. "The Corvette driver will be tired of smiling long before he's tired of the car."

1971 Corvette Stingray coupe

1972 Corvette Stingray coupe

1973 Corvette Stingray coupe

1972 Corvette Stingray coupe

1974 Corvette Stingray coupe

Chevrolet Corvette

The 1970s might have seen dramatic changes in the Corvette. Had Bill Mitchell had his way, the 1977-78 model would have been patterned after his Aerovette, a strikingly streamlined mid-engine prototype originally created as part of GM's aborted Wankel engine project. This design was modified for production and nearly made the 1980 program. But Mitchell's retirement in 1977 plus the fifth generation's continuing strong sales precluded any radical alterations until model year 1984. Meantime, the Corvette continued on into the early '80s with its basic 1968 engineering (and the chassis it inherited from the Sting Ray) with mostly detail year-to-year updates.

For 1970, a new 454-cid enlargement of the big-block Mark IV V8 designed to meet tightening emissions standards arrived to replace the previously optional 427. An even more powerful (465-bhp gross) version was planned but never actually offered, because it couldn't be made sufficiently "clean." For the same reason, the solid-lifter LT-1 small-block engine also bit the dust after 1970. The effects of government mandates on the 'Vette's power ratings (bearing in mind that horsepower was quoted in SAE net

1979 Corvette coupe

measure after 1971) are obvious from the accompanying charts.

With all this, a change in the Corvette's character was inevitable. By 1975 the car had become more balanced, less outlandish, and arguably more pleasant—a high-speed *boulevardier* instead of a rumbling straightline screamer. Even so, physical changes were relatively minor through 1977. The most noticeable were a revised nose for 1073, with the mandated "5-mph bumper" nicely integrated with the original styling via a body-color polyure-

1977 Corvette Stingray coupe

1978 Corvette Pace Car Replica coupe

1980 Corvette coupe

1980 Corvette coupe

thane cover. A similarly reworked tail followed for 1974. Meanwhile, comfort and convenience features proliferated and standard equipment became more comprehensive with each passing year. Prices predictably pushed upward.

Though somewhat emasculated compared to the Corvettes that had gone before, "America's only true sports car" was more popular than ever in the '70s. Production ran to nearly 40,000 units annually for 1974-75. The next two years saw two successive sales records despite the loss of the convertible, dropped after 1975 because of threatened government rollover standards. Production broke the 50,000-unit barrier for 1979, another first. Such high demand was surprising for a heavy, obsolete car in an age of rapid inflation, soaring fuel prices and occasional gas shortages— but then, there was nothing else remotely like the Corvette.

GM vetoed an Aerovette-like mid-engine layout for the next-generation Corvette in early 1977, and started work on a new front-engine/rear-drive design. Pending its arrival—and a drop in sales—the fifth generation was spruced up with a revised roofline for 1978, the Corvette's 25th anniversary year. A large wraparound backlight was grafted on to give the car a completely different, fastback profile, and the Stingray surname disappeared. By this time, the sole surviving powerplant was Chevy's workhorse 350-cid small-block, which would be continued with varying (and comparatively anemic) horsepower ratings on into the '80s.

Chevrolet Corvette Specifications

1953

290 (wb 102.0)		Wght	Price	Prod
2934	conv rdstr	2,705	3,513	315

1953 Engine	bore×stroke	bhp	availability
L6, 235.5	3.56×3.94	150	S-all

1954

290 (wb 102.0)		Wght	Price	Prod
2934	conv rdstr	2,705	3,523	3,640

1954 Engine	bore×stroke	bhp	availability
L6, 235.5	3.56×3.94	150	S-all

1955

290 (wb 102.0)		Wght	Price	Prod
2934	conv rdstr	2,650	2,799	674

1955 Engines	bore×stroke	bhp	availability
L6, 235.5	3.56×3.94	150	S-all
V8, 265.0	3.75×3.00	162	O-all

1956

290 (wb 102.0)		Wght	Price	Prod
2934	conv rdstr	2,764	3,149	3,467

1956 Engine	bore×stroke	bhp	availability
V8, 265.0	3.75×3.00	225	S-all

1957

290 (wb 102.0)		Wght	Price	Prod
2934	conv rdstr	2,730	3,465	6,339

1957 Engines	bore×stroke	bhp	availability
V8, 283.0	3.88×3.00	220	S-all
V8, 283.0	3.88×3.00	245/270	O-all
V8, 283.0	3.88×3.00	250/283	O-all (FI)

1958

(wb 102.0)		Wght	Price	Prod
867	conv rdstr	2,793	3,631	9,168

1958 Engines	bore×stroke	bhp	availability
V8, 283.0	3.88×3.00	230	S-all
V8, 283.0	3.88×3.00	245/270	O-all
V8, 283.0	3.88×3.00	250/290	O-all (FI)

1959

(wb 102.0)		Wght	Price	Prod
867	conv rdstr	2,840	3,875	9,670

Chevrolet Corvette

1959 Engines	bore×stroke	bhp	availability
V8, 283.0	3.88×3.00	230	S-all
V8, 283.0	3.88×3.00	245/270	O-all
V8, 283.0	3.88×3.00	250/290	O-all (FI)

1960

(wb 102.0)		Wght	Price	Prod
0867	conv rdstr	2,840	3,872	10,261

1960 Engines	bore×stroke	bhp	availability
V8, 283.0	3.88×3.00	230	S-all
V8, 283.0	3.88×3.00	245/270	O-all
V8, 283.0	3.88×3.00	275/315	O-all (FI)

1961

(wb 102.0)		Wght	Price	Prod
0867	conv rdstr	2,905	3,934	10,939

1961 Engines	bore×stroke	bhp	availability
V8, 283.0	3.88×3.00	230	S-all
V8, 283.0	3.88×3.00	245/270	O-all
V8, 283.0	3.88×3.00	275/315	O-all (FI)

1962

(wb 102.0)		Wght	Price	Prod
0867	conv rdstr	2,925	4,038	14,531

1962 Engines	bore×stroke	bhp	availability
V8, 327.0	4.00×3.25	250	S-all
V8, 327.0	4.00×3.25	300/340	O-all
V8, 327.0	4.00×3.25	360	O-all (FI)

1963

Sting Ray (wb 98.0)		Wght	Price	Prod
0837	cpe	2,859	4,252	10,594
0867	conv rdstr	2,881	4,037	10,919

1963 Engines	bore×stroke	bhp	availability
V8, 327.0	4.00×3.25	250	S-all
V8, 327.0	4.00×3.25	300/340	O-all
V8, 327.0	4.00×3.25	360	O-all (FI)

1964

Sting Ray (wb 98.0)		Wght	Price	Prod
0837	cpe	2,960	4,252	8,304
0867	conv rdstr	2,945	4,037	13,925

1964 Engines	bore×stroke	bhp	availability
V8, 327.0	4.00×3.25	250	S-all
V8, 327.0	4.00×3.25	300	O-all
V8, 327.0	4.00×3.25	395	O-all (FI)

1965

Sting Ray (wb 98.0)		Wght	Price	Prod
19437	cpe	2,975	4,321	8,186
19467	conv rdstr	2,985	4,106	15,376

1965 Engines	bore×stroke	bhp	availability
V8, 327.0	4.00×3.25	250	S-all
V8, 327.0	4.00×3.25	300/350	O-all
V8, 327.0	4.00×3.25	395	O-all (FI)
V8, 396.0	4.09×3.75	425	O-all

1966

Sting Ray (wb 98.0)		Wght	Price	Prod
19437	cpe	2,985	4,295	9,958
19467	conv rdstr	3,005	4,084	17,762

1966 Engines	bore×stroke	bhp	availability
V8, 327.0	4.00×3.25	300	S-all
V8, 327.0	4.00×3.25	350	O-all
V8, 427.0	4.25×3.76	390/425	O-all

1967

Sting Ray (wb 98.0)		Wght	Price	Prod
19437	cpe	3,000	4,353	8,504
19467	conv rdstr	3,020	4,141	14,436

1967 Engines	bore×stroke	bhp	availability
V8, 327.0	4.00×3.25	300	S-all
V8, 327.0	4.00×3.25	350	O-all
V8, 427.0	4.25×3.76	390–435	O-all

1968

(wb 98.0)		Wght	Price	Prod
19437	cpe	3,055	4,663	9,936
19467	conv rdstr	3,065	4,320	18,630

1968 Engines	bore×stroke	bhp	availability
V8, 327.0	4.00×3.25	350	S-all
V8, 427.0	4.25×3.76	400–435	O-all

1969

Stingray (wb 98.0)		Wght	Price	Prod
19437	cpe	3,140	4,781	22,154
19467	conv rdstr	3,145	4,438	16,608

1969 Engines	bore×stroke	bhp	availability
V8, 350.0	4.00×3.48	300	S-all
V8, 350.0	4.00×3.48	350	O-all
V8, 427.0	4.25×3.76	390–435	O-all

1970

Stingray (wb 98.0)		Wght	Price	Prod
19437	cpe	3,184	5,192	10,668
19467	conv rdstr	3,196	4,849	6,648

1970 Engines	bore×stroke	bhp	availability
V8, 350.0	4.00×3.48	300	S-all
V8, 350.0	4.00×3.48	350/370	O-all
V8, 427.0	4.25×3.76	390/460	O-all

Note: 1967-70 racing engines not listed; see text.

1971

Stingray (wb 98.0)		Wght	Price	Prod
19437	cpe	3,202	5,533	14,680
19467	conv rdstr	3,216	5,296	7,121

1971 Engines	bore×stroke	bhp	availability
V8, 350.0	4.00×3.48	270	S-all
V8, 350.0	4.00×3.48	330	O-all
V8, 454.0	4.25×4.00	365/425	O-all

1972

Stingray (wb 98.0)		Wght	Price	Prod
1Z37	cpe	3,215	5,472	20,486
1Z67	conv rdstr	3,216	5,246	6,508

1972 Engines	bore×stroke	bhp	availability
V8, 350.0	4.00×3.48	200	S-all
V8, 350.0	4.00×3.48	255	O-all
V8, 454.0	4.25×4.00	270	O-all

1973—30,465 built

Stingray (wb 98.0)		Wght	Price	Prod
Z37	cpe	3,326	5,635	24,372*
Z67	conv rdstr	3,333	5,399	} 6,093*
Z67	above, two tops	3,387	5,676	

1973 Engines	bore×stroke	bhp	availability
V8, 350.0	4.00×3.48	190	S-all
V8, 350.0	4.00×3.48	250	O-all
V8, 454.0	4.25×4.00	275	O-all

*estimates; proportioned from total

1974

Stingray (wb 98.0)		Wght	Price	Prod
Z37	cpe	3,309	6,082	32,028
Z67	conv rdstr	3,315	5,846	5,474

1974 Engines	bore×stroke	bhp	availability
V8, 350.0	4.00×3.48	195	S-all
V8, 350.0	4.00×3.48	250	O-all
V8, 454.0	4.25×4.00	270	O-all

1975

Stingray (wb 98.0)		Wght	Price	Prod
Z37	cpe	3,433	6,797	33,836
Z67	conv rdstr	3,446	6,537	4,629

1975 Engines	bore×stroke	bhp	availability
V8, 350.0	4.00×3.48	165	S-all
V8, 350.0	4.00×3.48	205	O-all

1976

Stingray (wb 98.0)		Wght	Price	Prod
Z37	cpe	3,445	7,605	46,558

1976 Engines	bore×stroke	bhp	availability
V8, 350.0	4.00×3.48	180	S-all
V8, 350.0	4.00×3.48	210	O-all

1977

Stingray (wb 98.0)		Wght	Price	Prod
Z37	cpe	3,448	8,648	49,213

1977 Engines	bore×stroke	bhp	availability
V8, 350.0	4.00×3.48	180	S-all
V8, 350.0	4.00×3.48	210	O-all

1978

(wb 98.0)		Wght	Price	Prod
Z87	cpe	3,401	9,645	41,467*
Z87/Z78	Pace Car Replica cpe	3,450	13,653	6,200

*includes 2,500 Silver Anniversary editions

1978 Engines	bore×stroke	bhp	availability
V8, 350.0	4.00×3.48	185	S-all
V8, 350.0	4.00×3.48	220	O-all

1979

(wb 98.0)		Wght	Price	Prod
Z87	cpe	3,372	12,313	53,807

1979 Engines	bore×stroke	bhp	availability
V8, 350.0	4.00×3.48	195	S-all
V8, 350.0	4.00×3.48	225	O-all

1980

(wb 98.0)		Wght	Price	Prod
Z87	cpe	3,206	13,965	40,614

1980 Engines	bore×stroke	bhp	availability
V8, 350.0	4.00×3.48	190	S-all
V8, 350.0	4.00×3.48	230	O-all
V8, 305.0	3.74×3.48	180	O-all

1980 coupe

Chrysler

Chrysler Division, Chrysler Corporation
Detroit, Michigan

One of the best descriptions of Walter Percy Chrysler was provided by the late Ray Dietrich, the great coachbuilder who headed styling at Chrysler Corporation in the 1930s. Said he of the company founder: "Like Edsel Ford, Mr. Chrysler was a gentleman. There was dynamite in his step, his walk, his smile, and his piercing blue eyes. Like Edsel, he would never doubt what you were saying, but he was always trying to get more out of you. In later life he told me that if the damn engineers would leave him alone he'd be able to enjoy himself a lot more. Every time he'd ask for something they'd say he couldn't get it."

But that was in later life. When Walter P. built his first Chrysler in 1924, he had instrumental assistance from three very talented engineers: Fred Zeder, Carl Breer, and Owen Skelton. This trio continued to dominate the design of Chrysler products throughout the '30s. Chrysler built some spectacular automobiles early in the decade, and its 1934 Airflow was an innovation if hardly a success.

Chrysler's very first car, the 1924 Six, had been the foundation of the company's early sales success. It was powered by a high-compression 202-cid L-head unit with seven main bearings and developed 68 horsepower—0.3 bhp per cubic inch, which was almost astounding for the early '20s. The car also featured four-wheel hydraulic brakes, full-pressure lubrication, attractive styling, and a competitive price of around $1500. It couldn't miss—and it didn't. By 1927, production had soared from 32,000 to some 182,000 units.

Sixes continued to be Chrysler's mainstay through 1930. There were four different engines offered that year ranging in size from 195.6 to 309.3 cid. The smallest was the four-main-bearing unit used on the cheap CJ series. The others were all derived from the original powerplant. Model offerings totalled no fewer than 28, and spanned a price spread from the least costly CJ at $845 the most imposing Imperial at $3075.

The Imperial, conceived more as a prestige leader than a high money-earner, reached its pinnacle in 1931. It featured Chrysler's first eight, a smooth, low-revving 385-cid L-head with nine main bearings. This engine was capable of propelling the nearly 5000 pounds of this car to 96 mph and from 0 to 60 mph in 20 seconds. But what was most distinctive—and distinguished—about the 1931 Imperials was their styling: long and low, with gracefully curved fenders and a rakish grille strongly resembling Duesenberg's. They provided glorious motoring at a surprisingly low price, but the Depression kept 1931 sales down. Coachwork was available from Locke, Derham, Murphy, Waterhouse, and LeBaron. In design, these cars were flawless—the most beautiful Chryslers ever built.

On a more plebian level, Chrysler also introduced an eight-cylinder engine on its 1931 CD series, priced about half as much as the Imperials. The year also saw the debut of "Floating Power" (rubber engine mounts) on all models, which had automatic spark control, free-wheeling

1930 Model 77 Royal coupe

1930 Imperial seven-passenger sedan

1930-31 Model CJ6 roadster

1931 Imperial Custom convertible coupe

transmission, and rustproofed bodies as well. Interiors were lavish, especially on Imperials and Chrysler Eights, which featured a comprehensive set of instruments in a polished walnut panel. Walnut was also used for interior moldings. Welded steel bodies were another innovation. To prove their strength, Chrysler got a five-ton elephant to stand on a sedan at Coney Island; happily, the body held. Another feature of early-'30s Chryslers was an optional four-speed manual transmission, though it was more than they really needed. Basically, it was a three-speed unit with an extra-low first gear. Since hardly anyone used "emergency low," this gearbox was dropped after 1933. The 1931 models were continued in 1932-33 with few changes.

Engineering has always been Chrysler's strong suit, so it isn't surprising that the 1934 Airflow was a product of engineers. What *was* curious was that canny business-man Walter Chrysler approved this advanced concept without much regard for whether the public would go for it. And that amounted to Chrysler's (the man's and the company's) first serious mistake.

As the story goes, engineer Carl Breer got the idea for a streamlined automobile when he saw a squadron of Army Air Corps planes flying overhead in 1927. Back at the factory, Breer got together with Zeder and Skelton to consider an automobile employing aircraft-type design principles. Wind tunnel tests suggested its shape: tear-drop altered to allow for a hood and windshield. A forward-mounted engine (directly over the front axle) afforded considerable interior space, and a strong beam-and-truss body provided rigidity without sacrificing room. The Airflow's seats were 50 inches wide, which was pretty impressive for the time, and it had more head, hip, shoulder, and legroom than even big Walter Chrysler himself needed. Exterior styling, by Oliver Clark, followed the dictates of the engineers.

To protect itself with a traditional-style model, Chrysler produced a line of square-rigged Model CA sixes. Everything else was an Airflow, and all were eight-cylinder cars. The Custom Imperial was the best-looking of the bunch because its long wheelbase allowed the rounded body to be stretched out more. From an aesthetic point of view, the basic styling needed every inch of stretch it could get.

But the Airflows did have fine performance. In 1934, an Imperial coupe ran 95.7 mph for the flying-mile and 90 mph for 500 miles at the Bonneville Salt Flats, capturing 72 national speed records in the process. They were not flimsy, either: in Pennsylvania, one was purposely driven off a 110-foot cliff; it landed wheels down and was driven away. The Airflow's main problem was its strange new shape—and its initial scarcity in Chrysler showrooms.

Because of the considerable retooling necessary to convert to Airflow production, Chrysler delayed the cars' debut until January 1934; the Custom Imperials didn't arrive until June. Lack of cars blunted public interest and created rumors that the Airflow was a problem child, a lemon. Sales were underwhelming. In a year that saw most companies increase production by up to 60 percent from rock-bottom 1933, Chrysler's volume was up only 20 percent, and the division continued to lag behind its competitors

1932 Imperial eight-passenger sedan

1932 Six roadster (second series)

1932 Imperial convertible sedan

for several years. In calendar 1936, Chrysler dropped out of the top ten contenders in the production race.

Detroit's lead times are long and it takes several years to alter a plan once it's in motion. Chrysler had banked heavily on the Airflow's success to inspire the design and sales of its cheaper makes. In addition to the Airflow for 1935-36 the division offered the more conventional Airstream Sixes and Eights. Though they were not pure Airflow in design, their bodies had pontoon fenders, raked-backed radiators, and teardrop headlamp pods. Overall, there was a strong family resemblance between the two lines, yet the Airstreams weren't so far out as to turn off customers completely, and they literally carried the division in those years.

The bulk of Chrysler's 1937 models, and all the '38s were of a transitional styling period sometimes called the "age of the potato." Eight-cylinder engines were five-main bearing side-valve units (the nine-main-bearing engine had disappeared after 1934). Chrysler moved back up into 10th place in production for calendar 1937, but the 1938 recession pushed output down to the 40,000 level for that year and again, Chrysler finished 11th. In 1939, when it built 68,000 cars, the division dropped to 12th place.

1934 Airflow Eight four-door sedan

1935 Airstream Eight DeLuxe seven-passenger sedan

1932 Imperial Airflow Eight four-door sedan

1936 Airflow Imperial four-door sedan

1936 Airstream coupe

1937 Royal coupe

1938 Imperial five-passenger touring sedan

1939 New Yorker four-door sedan

The 1937-38 models wore barrel grilles, round fenders, and pod-type headlamps. Dashboards were ornate and varied; instruments were grouped in front of the driver for 1937, and in a central dash panel for 1938. The Royal Six, Imperial, and Custom Imperial Eights soldiered on in both years. A new model for 1938 was the New York Special, a hybrid car on the Royal's 119-inch wheelbase and power-ed by the Imperial's 229-cid eight. Distinguished by its color-keyed interior, it came only as a four-door sedan. A business coupe was planned but not produced.

The Chrysler line was fully redesigned for 1939 by Ray Dietrich. Headlamps were moved stylishly into the fenders, the barrel-shaped front end was deemphasized by a lower grille composed of vertical bars, and all fenders were

elongated. Maintaining its reputation for sound engineering, Chrysler introduced "Superfinish," a process of mirror-finishing engine and chassis components to produce a minimum of friction. Several once-familiar model names appeared for the first time: Windsor (a six-cylinder Royal sub-series), New Yorker, and Saratoga. The C-22 Royal/Royal Windsor were powered by the 95/102-bhp six from 1938, and all models rode a 119-inch wheelbase except for a long sedan and a limousine. The New Yorker and Saratoga joined the Imperial in series C-23 on a 125-inch chassis, with the Custom Imperial above in series C-24 on a 144-inch wheelbase. All the eight-cylinder cars now used the same 323.5-cid engine, rated at 135 bhp this year. Dating from 1934, it would remain in production until the breakthrough hemi-head V8 arrived for 1951.

Walter Chrysler died in August 1940, but not before he had turned over the presidency of his firm to his chosen successor, K.T. Keller, in 1935. Engineers continued to run Chrysler in the latter half of the decade. Though its cars were more conservative in the aftermath of the Airflow debacle, they were soundly built, reasonably well styled for the period, and good value.

The early '40s were good years for Chrysler Division. From dangerously low production in recession year 1938, the make rose steadily from 11th to eighth place in the industry between 1939 and '41. Its success was due partly to the 1940 line, which spanned a price scale ranging from $895 for the Royal coupe to $2445 for the Crown Imperial eight-passenger limousine.

Styling was not radical: notchbacked, smooth at the front and rear, individual fenders. The design work had been directed by Raymond H. Dietrich, the famed coachbuilder. Yet engineering prevailed over styling, and was supported wholeheartedly by Keller, an arch-conservative. The design that resulted, as one wag put it, "wouldn't knock your eyes out but wouldn't knock your hat off either." (Chrysler's radical Airflow had sold poorly in the 1930s, so the division had gone to quieter-looking cars in the '40s.)

The line was set up in six- and eight-cylinder ranks. Six-cylinder Royals and Windsors rode a 122.5-inch wheelbase, with a 139.5-inch wheelbase for the eight-passenger sedans and limousines. The eight-cylinder Traveler, New Yorker, and Saratoga rode a 128.5-inch wheelbase (the last two included formal sedans as well). A 145.5-inch wheelbase carried the Crown Imperial sedans and limousine. All of the upper models used a 323.5 cubic-inch eight that developed 135–143 bhp at 3400 rpm.

Adding a little class to the 1940 line were two striking show cars from the house of LeBaron—the Newport and Thunderbolt. Six of each were built. The Newport, designed by Ralph Roberts of LeBaron, was a dual-cowl phaeton built on the Imperial chassis. It had a rakish envelope body and smooth fenders. The Thunderbolt, designed by Alex Tremulis of Briggs, had a similar envelope body, but was a retractable hardtop with single bench seat mounted on the New Yorker chassis. Designed to wow the public at auto shows, these two

dream cars would later inspire postwar styling.

After the war, Chrysler would continue to use separate fenders, even for the total redesign of 1949. More customs, one-offs mainly, were turned out by the Derham Body Company. These included town cars and a dual-cowl phaeton. Chrysler itself built a custom formal sedan, and A. J. Miller of Ohio built a long-wheelbase limousine/hearse.

The most interesting new model of 1941 was Dave Wallace's unique Town & Country station wagon, the first of that body style for Chrysler. Unlike other woodies of the day, the Town & Country had a clean, rounded shape and "clamshell" type rear doors that opened from the center. Built on the Windsor chassis, Town & Country was available with six- or nine-passenger seating. It sold for a remarkably low price, and a to-

1940 Royal coupe

Thunderbolt show car by Le Baron

Newport phaeton show car by Le Baron

1942 New Yorker four-door sedan

Prototype 1946 Town & Country hardtop coupe

1946 Town & Country four-door sedan

1946 Royal club coupe

1946 Windsor convertible coupe

tal of 999 were built, mostly the nine-passenger variety.

Styling changes for the rest of the '41 line were minor, including simpler grilles and more ornate taillamps. The Traveler was eliminated. The Saratoga series was expanded from two models to include club and business coupes, two- and four-door sedans, and a town sedan. Chrysler also issued a wide variety of upholstery in '41. There was Highlander Plaid, a striking combination of Scots plaid and leatherette trim; Saran trim, a woven plastic and leatherette designed for certain open models; and Navajo, a pattern resembling the blankets of the Southwest Indians. One new mechanical feature was optional Vacamatic transmission, a self-shifter that operated between the two lower and two higher gears. Manual shifting was still required from the low to high ranges.

A significant front facelift marked the 1942 models. A smooth appearance was achieved by wrapping the grille's chrome bands right around to the front fenders. The hoodline looked slooker than before, and opened from the front instead of the side. The running boards were hidden from view, concealed under flares at the bottoms of the doors. Highlander Plaid was optional; another special upholstery called Thunderbird also borrowed Indian motifs. The Town & Country wagon was moved to the Windsor series. The six-cylinder engine was bored out to yield 120 bhp at 3800 rpm. The eight, which remained at 323.5 cid, was rated at 140 bhp for other models.

Like other cars, Chryslers built after January 1, 1942 used painted trim instead of chrome. In early February, production ended altogether. In those two months, the firm built only 5292 cars. During the war, Chrysler built anti-aircraft guns, Wright Cyclone airplane engines, land mine detectors, radar units, marine engines, and Sea Mule harbor tugs. But tanks were its most famous wartime product.

When they could during the war, small teams of designers and engineers would work on postwar car ideas, most of which never reached production. Planned but not implemented were smoother versions of the 1940-42 styles, with fully wrapped bumpers and grilles, thinner A- and B-pillars, and skirted rear fenders. Ultimately, Chrysler produced warmed-over versions of its 1942 cars from 1946 through the first part of 1949. Even the full redesign of mid-1949 was conservative compared to rival makes.

For 1946, fender brightwork was reduced. The grille was given prominent vertical bars, which made it one of the most highly chromed in the industry. The four wheelbases were continued with the same body style offerings as before. The six- and eight-passenger Crown Imperial sedans were dropped, leaving only the limousine. The '46 Town & Country was no longer a wagon, but a three-car line consisting of six-cylinder and eight-cylinder sedans and convertibles. Originally, Chrysler had promised an array of non-wagon woodies, including two-door broughams, roadsters, and a hardtop, but only a handful were built.

1947 Crown Imperial eight-passenger limousine

1947 Windsor Traveler four-door sedan

Prototype Town & Country hardtop coupe for 1949

1949 Saratoga club coupe

There were seven hardtops in all, made by grafting an elongated coupe top onto a Town & Country convertible. The eight-cylinder Town & Country sedan was eliminated after a run of one hundred 1946 models. Prewar engines were carried over, but were detuned slightly.

Prices increased dramatically between 1942 and 1946, mainly as a result of wartime and postwar infla-

tion. A Chrysler Royal could be bought for a little more than $1000 in 1942; by '46, its minimum price had risen to nearly $1500. Prices would continue to rise through the rest of the decade, to the point where a Crown Imperial sold for nearly double its 1940 figure. Even so, Chrysler was back among the top ten in model year production in both 1947 and '48.

For 1947, there were only detail alterations to fender trim, hubcaps, colors, carburetion, wheels, and instruments. Between August and November, Goodyear low-pressure Super Cushion tires were adopted. One new model in the Windsor series was the Traveler, a luxury utility car with special paint and interior, and an attractive wooden luggage rack. Unlike the comparable DeSoto Suburban, the Traveler did not have fold-down triple seats or wooden floorboards in the rear, having a separate trunk compartment instead. The eight-cylinder series went unchanged, except for a new eight-passenger sedan in the Crown Imperial series.

Chrysler's extravagant "jukebox" dashboard was one of the flashiest in the immediate postwar period. Making use of solid or mottled plastics, it was a symmetrical affair with gauges at the left, a glovebox at the right, and a huge radio speaker and a bank of control knobs in the middle. The knobs were made of clear lucite; chrome plating was everywhere. The radio had a tone selector providing adjustment from "Mello" to "Speech," with its dial changing from blue to red in the process. The steering wheel was 18 inches in diameter, and had three spokes with an enormous chrome horn ring. Over on the far left, the umbrella-handle hand-brake was a long reach, but it was highly effective. It operated on the driveshaft rather than the rear brake drums—a heavy-handed approach, but it worked.

The 1948 line was a continuation of the '47 model run. The six-cylinder Town & Country sedan was discontinued at mid-year, but the eight-cylinder convertible carried on. Eventually, 8569 would be built from 1946, including a handful reserialed for the first part of 1949.

Chrysler wasn't ready on time with its redesigned Silver Anniversary models for 1949, so from December to March the old models were offered again—without the Town & Country. Prices weren't changed, and none of the old-style "first series" cars were actually built that year.

Many ideas had been considered for a streamlined '49 design with integral, skirted fenders. None of them came to pass. Keller insisted on bolt-upright styling with vast interior space, and he got it—with some loss of sales appeal. The '49 Chrysler was ornate, with a massive chrome-laden grille, prominent brightwork on the sides, and curious vertical taillights ending in a little hump. (Only the Crown Imperial was spared those gaudy devices.) There was a new Imperial sedan and a convertible Town & Country. Along with the new styling came a host of gimmick names for certain desirable features: Safety-Level Ride, Hydra-Lizer shock absorbers, Safety-Rim wheels, Full-Flow oil filter, and Cycle-bonded brake linings.

1950 Crown Imperial limousine by Derham

1951 Windsor club coupe

1952 Saratoga eight-passenger sedan

An assortment of customs were built on Chrysler chassis in the late '40s, mainly by Derham of Pennsylvania. It offered a town limousine and a dual-cowl phaeton in the 1946-48 period, and tried the same padded-top treatment on the '49 New Yorker. But the wildest of all was a New Yorker promotion car with a mid-section designed to look like a giant Zippo lighter.

As the 1950s began, Chrysler was a high-volume line comprising no fewer than seven different series and 22 models. When the decade ended, it had become an upper medium-price make with just 15 models in four basic series. The lineup shrank when Imperial became a separate make in 1955 and the Windsor sixes were dropped after 1954. But over the years, styling and engineering improved. The dowdy 1950 cars powered by plodding L-head engines would give way to performance machines with exciting styling by 1955. Eventually, Chrysler would have some of the best-looking tail-

fins of the age.

Those tailfins, which arrived in grafted-on form in 1956, were nicely integrated into the all-new '57 styling. They were the work of Virgil M. Exner, who joined Chrysler after leaving Studebaker in 1949. Exner's tastes ran to classic cars—meaning bold, upright radiator grilles, open-wheel designs, and rakish lines. On arriving at Chrysler he found the engineering-oriented boxes of K. T. Keller, who was then preparing for retirement. Unfortunately, people didn't want practical compact cars in the early '50s—at least, not the people who bought Chryslers. The division was having sales troubles, and before Exner was able to get any completely new designs into production, Chrysler sank from 180,000 units to barely 100,000.

For 1950, the boxy cars that had emerged as Chrysler's first new postwar design were largely carryovers. Several models were on their way out. The six-cylinder Royals, which sold for less than $2200, were dropped after that year. The exotic wood-decorated Town & Country series was down to one model—the Newport, a hardtop powered by the straight eight and equipped with four-wheel disc brakes. By then, it had outlived its purpose, to glamorize an unglamorous lineup by offering something vividly different, so the T & C hardtop was dropped for '51. After that, the Town & Country name was reserved for station wagons only. The Saratoga, also a peripheral seller, was dropped after 1952.

For a short time, there were standard and luxury versions of the Windsor and New Yorker. But by the time the "Hundred Million Dollar Look" arrived in 1955, the line was down to just two series sans Imperial, which had become a separate make in its own right.

It's easy to summarize the 1950-54 Chryslers because they were all so much alike. All except the Crown Imperial and the long-wheelbase Windsor sedan were built on 125.5- or 131.5-inch wheelbases. All were styled pretty much the same way.

The '50 models wore broad, chrome, eggcrate smiles; the 1951-52 models had a more conservative three-bar grille. There were no significant differences between the '51s and '52s, (the firm didn't even keep separate production figures for those two years). The only way to tell them apart is by the taillights: the '52s had built-in backup lamps.

While it lasted, the Saratoga was the quickest Chrysler and a notable stock-car contender. It used a Hemi V8 in the shorter Windsor chassis. New Yorkers came in roughly the same form as Windsor DeLuxe models, but on the longer wheelbase. Imperials were built as sedans, club coupes, hardtops, convertibles, and long-wheelbase cars in those years. For 1950, there was a special Imperial sedan with custom interior.

Perhaps it was the plain styling of this period that gave rise to Chrysler's reputation for engineering. It was certainly the company's great strength in the early '50s. A change in powerplants was part of that emphasis. The Chrysler six had been a dominant seller for some years, so its disappearance after 1954 came as a

surprise to many. But in reality it was part of a broad-based plan, partly instigated by Keller's successor, Lester Lum "Tex" Colbert.

Colbert set several early goals, among which were the decentralization of divisional management, the total redesign of all passenger cars as soon as possible, and an ambitious program of plant expansion and financing. Giving the divisions freer rein meant that people closer to the sales level could take more control in mapping policy. At Chrysler Division, the only market sector available was the top one. DeSoto had staked out the lower ground.

When the hemi-head V8 arrived in 1951, the six was gradually de-emphasized. It had taken close to 100,000 sales in 1950, but dropped to 84,000 by 1953 and to 45,000 in 1954.

The 331-cid hemi-head V8 was first offered on the '51 Saratoga-New Yorker-Imperial. Though not really a new idea at the time, the Hemi offered exceptionally good volumetric efficiency for truly outstanding performance. Also, it had a lower compression ratio and could therefore use lower-octane fuel than non-Hemis. Yet it was capable of producing as much power as a conventional engine with more displacement.

The Hemi's output was more than ample: one early demonstration version achieved 352 bhp on the dynamometer after minor modifications to the camshaft, carburetors, and exhaust. Drag racers would later get as much as 1000 horsepower from it. On the other hand, it was complex and costly, requiring double the number of rocker shafts, pushrods, and rockers. The heads were heavy and expensive to manufacture. As result, the Hemi was replaced for '59 by more conventional 383- and 413-cid wedge-head V8s. But while it was around, it wrote a great story.

A stock Saratoga Hemi would run from 0 to 60 mph in as little as 10 seconds and achieve close to 110 mph flat out. Bill Sterling won the Mexican Road Race stock-car class in a Saratoga and was third overall—behind two Ferraris—in 1951. Chryslers placed high in NASCAR racing, though they were eclipsed in 1952-54 by the remarkable Hudson Hornets. Briggs Cunningham began running his outstanding Chrysler-powered sports cars in European road races. In 1953, he drove his C-5R to third place at Le Mans, averaging 104.14 mph against 105.85 mph for the winning Jaguar C-Type.

Chrysler engineers had built four special Hemi engines for the 1953 Indianapolis 500, all of which developed over 400 horsepower using Hillborn fuel injection. But a displacement limit prevented them from reaching their full potential. Then came the Chrysler 300 in 1955, delivering 300 bhp from its stock Hemi. The 300 dominated NASCAR events in 1955-56, and probably would have done so for several more years had the Auto Manufacturers Association not agreed to de-emphasize racing in 1957.

The 300 was part of Virgil Exner's all-new 1955 line, which rallied Chrysler from a 100,000-unit year in 1954 to 150,000, and finally brought styling up to par with

performance. Based on a long line of Ghia-bodied Exner show cars, the '55s were clean and aggressive-looking. Their 1956 successors were generally even better—something rare for a facelift during the '50s. The modestly grilled, gracefully finned Forward Look cars of 1957 were probably Exner's design pinnacle, and that year's 300C was a breathtaking machine—big and powerful, yet safe and controllable. It was available as a convertible for the first time.

For 1955-56, there was a second two-door hardtop in the Windsor and New Yorker lines called Nassau and St. Regis, respectively. They were more conservatively two-toned and offered slightly better interiors. There were six- and nine-passenger Town & Country station wagons from 1958 on. A hastily conceived item in '56, the new four-door hardtop sedan was especially pretty in its 1957 form.

Exner-styled C-200 show car by Ghia from 1952

1953 Custom Imperial four-door sedan

1953 New Yorker Deluxe Newport hardtop coupe

Chrysler

Bubble-top Le Comte show car, 1954

Chrysler's Falcon show car from 1955

1955 Windsor four-door sedan

1956 300B hardtop coupe

1955 New Yorker Deluxe convertible

Exner's Dart show car by Ghia, 1956

1955 300 hardtop coupe

1957 Chrysler 300C convertible

The Saratoga returned for '57, and over 37,000 were sold that year. It again offered a performance premium—a 295-bhp version of the Hemi. PowerFlite two-speed automatic transmission had come along in 1953, joined by the three-speed TorqueFlite in mid-'56, one of the finest automatics ever built. In 1956, Chrysler automatics adopted the famous (or infamous) pushbutton controls, mounted in a handy pod to the left of the steering wheel.

While the 1957 styling was superb, Chrysler's rush to set the pace had a negative effect on overall quality. Workmanship was also hampered by a series of strikes.

No discussion of Chrysler in the '50s is complete without a mention of Torsion-Aire ride, offered from 1957 on. Torsion bars were not a new idea—Packard had introduced an excellent four-wheel system in 1955—but Torsion-Aire went a long way toward proving big American cars could handle decently. Instead of sending road shocks up into the car like coil or leaf springs did, torsion bars absorbed force by winding up

against their anchor points. The resultant twisting motion eliminated most of the upward force caused by road irregularities. Unlike Packard, Chrysler put torsion bars on the front wheels only. It's likely they were used mainly to provide more engine compartment space rather than to improve suspension geometry. Nevertheless, torsion bars must be regarded as a major step toward better handling. They were still used on Chrysler products into the '80s, an indication of how well they worked.

1957 Windsor hardtop sedan

1957 New Yorker hardtop coupe

1958 300D hardtop coupe

1959 New Yorker hardtop sedan

Partly as a result of buyer dissatisfaction with quality control, and partly because of a recession, 1958 was a terrible year for the division. There was no major styling change to enhance the line's allure. Higher hopes were pinned on Exner's restyle for '59. The result was less graceful, but the new soaring tailfins seemed to solve the sales problem anyway. The "lion-hearted" 1959 Chrysler scored close to 70,000 sales for the model year.

A Windsor convertible was added in 1958, but otherwise the '59 line stayed the same: Windsors rode the 122-inch wheelbase that had appeared the year before; other models kept the 126-inch wheelbase that had been used since 1955. The new wedge-head V8 wasn't as powerful as the Hemi, but it was much simpler to build, and would survive for a long time.

That year's 300E has been unduly criticized as a performance weakling compared to its Hemi-powered predecessors, but road tests do not bear this out. It was just as quick as the 300D before it. With 10.1:1 compression, TorqueFlite, and a 3.31:1 rear axle ratio, the E could accelerate from rest to 60 mph in less than 8.5 seconds; in 17.5 seconds, it would be doing 90. But production in 1959 was a record low for the 300 series.

During the '60s, Chrysler advertising had a strident, almost belligerent tone, as the company repeatedly declared there would never be a small Chrysler. (Of course there would be, when the time was right and the government would allow little else.) As rival manufacturers were rushing compacts into production, Chrysler cried out it would do no such thing. Let Dodge and Plymouth divisions handle the compacts; Chryslers would always be the large, brawny, luxurious cars they'd traditionally been. And so they remained through the end of the decade.

The 1960-61 Chryslers were Exner's last outlandishly plumed creations. In the vernacular of the stylist, they were clean—uncluttered by excess chrome—and fitted with lots of glass and aggressive, inverted trapezoid grilles. Detail improvements for 1960 included four-way hazard flashers and optional swivel seats that pivoted outward through an automatic latch release when a door was opened.

The Saratoga had its last year in 1960. The Windsor lasted through 1961, replaced by the attractive Newport that became Chrysler's volume car into the '70s. Newports were competitively priced at just under $3000 through 1964, a point emphasized in division advertising. Sales soared, exceeding 125,000 units by 1965. The larger-engine models comprised six varieties of the luxury New Yorker, which sold at a rate of about 20,000 units a year. It was priced just under Imperial, and was competitive with the larger Buicks.

The most exciting of all Chryslers in 1960 was the sixth edition of the "letter series" line, the 300F. It combined racy styling with a road-hugging suspension and an optional Pont-a-Mousson four-speed gearbox. A set of ram-induction manifolds boosted output of its 413-cid V8 to 375 bhp. The 300F would do the standing

Turbo-Flite gas turbine experimental, 1961

1962 300 hardtop coupe

1961 New Yorker hardtop sedan

1962 New Yorker hardtop sedan

quarter-mile in 16 seconds at 85 mph. It rode hard, but cornered better than any other car of its size. A half dozen different axle ratios could be ordered. (Using the 3.03 ratio, special tuning, and some streamlining, Andy Granatelli came close to 190 mph for the flying-mile.) Offered as a hardtop or convertible, the 300F wasn't cheap, but it offered a lot of performance for the money.

The 1960 models were significant in that they were the first Chryslers with unit body construction instead of the traditional body on frame attached with flexible mountings. Since unit bodies were held together more by welds than by nuts and bolts, they were not as prone to looseness or rattles, though they were more susceptible to rust.

The 1961 line was mostly a repeat of 1960, except for the advent of the Newport and the demise of the Saratoga. The Newport was equipped with a smaller engine, and that year's 300G did not use the F's optional four-speed French gearbox. The letter series also returned to 15-inch wheels for the first time since 1956. Two engines were offered with 375 and 400 bhp, both with ram-induction.

Management changes during 1961 had an immediate effect on Chrysler products. At the end of July, corporate president Lester Lum "Tex" Colbert retired under fire and turned over the presidency to his chosen successor, William Newberg. But Newberg quit after two months when he was found to have financial interests in several of Chrysler's suppliers. Lynn A. Townsend, former administrative vice-president, ultimately replaced Colbert. In 1967, Townsend became board chairman. Chrysler's president from January 1967 to January 1970 was Virgil Boyd.

This shakeup brought with it a new styling head. Exner departed after shaping the 1962-64 models. His replacement was Elwood Engle, the former Ford designer generally credited for the elegant 1961 Lincoln Continental. As a result, the mid-1960s were years of change for Chrysler styling. For 1962, the division fielded what Exner called the "plucked chicken": a repeat of the conservative '61 but without the fins. The 1963-64 models had what Chrysler called "the crisp, clean custom look." They were chiseled, chunky cars, the last designed by Exner before he departed. For 1965, Engle unveiled his smooth, concave-sided styling with fenders edged in bright metal, one of his trademarks. This shape continued through 1968, when Engle came up with more rounded, less bulky "fuselage" styling for '69.

For 1962, the Windsor name was dropped, replaced in the three-tier model lineup by the "non-letter" 300s. These were sporty-looking cars having fashionable features such as a center console and front bucket seats. Offered as hardtops or convertibles, they were quite popular.

The New Yorker rode a 126-inch wheelbase in '62; all other Chryslers had a wheelbase of 122 inches. For 1963-64, the shorter wheelbase was adopted across the board, making New Yorker the same general size as the less expensive models. This did not hamper New Yorker sales, which were strong in both years. Two special models in this period were the 300 Pace Setter, two-door hardtop and convertible; and the New Yorker Salon, a four-door hardtop sedan. The Pace Setter commemorated Chrysler's selection as pace car for the 1963 Indianapolis 500, and was identified by crossed

checkered-flag emblems and special trim. The Salon came with such standard luxury accessories as air conditioning; AM/FM radio; auto-pilot; power brakes, steering, seats, and windows; TorqueFlite automatic transmission; color-keyed wheel covers; and vinyl-covered roof. Chrysler stayed with the same basic line-up in 1964.

The 1963-64 300J and 300K (they skipped the letter "I" to avoid confusion with the number "1") were big, burly cars in the letter series tradition, the J only in

hardtop form. Some 400 of the 300Js were built (an all-time low), but 300K production (with the convertible now reinstated) was increased considerably. The 1965 300L was the last of the true letter series cars. The 1963-65 letter series 300s weren't quite the potent machines their predecessors had been, but they did have tight suspensions and were the most roadable Chryslers in the lineup. The series was discontinued after 1965 because of low volume; Chrysler had successfully attracted a sporty-car clientele with its "non-letter" 300.

1964 Newport Town & Country hardtop wagon

1964 300K convertible

1966 Newport hardtop sedan

1967 300 hardtop coupe

1967 Newport Custom hardtop coupe

1968 Newport convertible

1968 300 hardtop coupe

1969 Town & Country Station wagon

Chrysler

All models did well in 1965 and 1966. The division built over 125,000 Newports, nearly 30,000 300s, and almost 50,000 New Yorkers in '65. Sales were even better in '66. Production of 300s nearly doubled, and Newport climbed by 42,000 units.

The Engle Chryslers of 1965-69 were shorter than their predecessors, but just as big inside. Wheelbase on all models except wagons was 124 inches, up two inches from 1964. During the late 1960s, the lineup grew. The Newport was joined in '67 by a Newport Cus-

Concept 70X show car, 1969

1969 Newport Custom hardtop sedan

1970 Town & Country station wagon

1970 New Yorker hardtop coupe

tom, priced about $200 higher. Promoted as "a giant step in luxury, a tiny step in price," the Custom comprised two-door and four-door hardtops and a four-door sedan. Deluxe interiors were done in jacquard or textured vinyl upholstery and featured pull-down center armrests. The dash of a fully equipped Newport Custom had eight toggle switches, three thumbwheels, 16 pushbuttons, three sliding levers, and 12 other controls that, as Chrysler brochures proclaimed, "put you in charge of almost every option in the book." It was the ultimate in gadgetry. Vinyl-covered lift handles were used on the trunk.

Chrysler wagons went through many changes during the late '60s. The luxurious New Yorker Town & Country was dropped after 1965 (very few units were sold that year). During 1966-68, wagons carried the Newport name. All-vinyl upholstery was used instead of the cloth-and-vinyl in Newport sedans. Standard features included power steering, power brakes, and automatic transmission. Wagons also had a three-in-one front seat that looked like a conventional bench. Each half could be adjusted individually, and there was a reclining seatback on the passenger's side. For 1969, the Town & Country returned as a separate series in its own right.

Mid-year specials were the focus of the 1968 spring selling season. Sportsgrain simulated wood paneling (like that of the wagons) was offered as a $126 option for Newport hardtops and convertibles. Newport Special two-door and four-door hardtops were available with turquoise color schemes, later extended to the 300 series.

After record calendar year production in 1968, the fuselage-styled 1969s did almost as well. The '69s were handsome, with a combination bumper/grille, clean lines, and smooth contours. If not the most beautiful Chryslers of the decade, they were close rivals to the good-looking '62s and '65s. Wheelbase remained at 124 inches. Length kept growing, to almost 225 inches overall with width of nearly 80 inches—about as big as an American passenger car would get.

Mid-year 1970 saw the first Cordobas: hardtop coupes and hardtop sedans in the Newport line, painted gold with special vinyl roof and bodyside moldings, gold wheels and grille, and "Aztec Eagle" upholstery. Newports were now offered with the 440-cid V8. A special Newport 440 hardtop was listed, complete with TorqueFlite, vinyl roof, and special accessories.

Another flashy product that year was the 300-H, formally known as the 300-Hurst because of the floor-mounted shifter used for its automatic gearbox. Performance options were standard, including special road wheels and H70×15 white-letter tires, the 440 engine, and heavy-duty suspension. All this was set off by a gold-and-white paint job, customized hood, rear deck spoiler, special grille paint, pinstriping, and a custom interior.

Vast changes were evident in corporate administration by 1969-70. Quality control had become an end in

itself for the first time in history, as engineers struggled to correct the firm's reputation for poor body durability. The old centralized structure had been decentralized under Colbert. Townsend recentralized it, but retained some divisional identity between Chrysler-Plymouth and Dodge. Still, the Chrysler marque would face tough sledding in the 1970s, partly because of its decision not to produce a smaller car until the very last minute.

Model year 1971 was the last for what Chrysler called "fuselage styling," though the 1972-73 models continued to be based on the 1969 shell. Styling remained clean-limbed overall, even if easy-change items like grilles, taillights and side decoration became a bit more tacky with time. A new engine more adaptable to emissions tuning than the old 383 was introduced for 1972, and the smaller 360 was dropped for the Newport Royal. Electronic ignition was now *de rigueur,* but New Yorkers retained the big-block with only added emission controls.

The one-millionth Chrysler came down the Jefferson Avenue lines on June 26, 1973. It was a Newport sedan and thus a base-series model with the departure of the low-priced Royal. All the '73s used new sheetmetal, and the bumper-framed grille gave way to a more conventional front end with bulkier bumpers, in line with federal impact regulations.

Chrysler was still plugging the big car, but sales sank mightily in the wake of the energy crisis. Still riding a 124-inch wheelbase, the 1974 models arrived on a completely new platform, about five inches shorter overall and bearing a crisp new look. Chryslers and Imperials both wore pseudo-classic square grilles of the sort they'd studiously avoided when this design fad took hold in the early '70s, and engine options and horsepower were down. The lineup consisted of Newport, New Yorker, and the Town and Country wagons as well as the Imperial, which was being marketed again as a Chrysler, though it was still registered as a separate make (and is so treated for purposes of this book).

Few people at Chrysler had foreseen the energy crisis, which only accelerated the buyer resistance to big cars that had been building because of galloping sticker prices. Sales of the record-priced 1975s dropped to 1970 levels, and a two-month backlog of unsold cars quickly piled up. Chrysler Corporation chairman Lynn Townsend refused to slash prices. Instead, he slashed production. By early November 1974, Chrysler sales were down 34 percent, not as bad as GM's 43 percent but really more serious, because Chrysler's fixed costs were spread over a much smaller volume. The result was employee layoffs and an unsold inventory of 300,000 units by early 1975. Finally Chrysler did something it and the rest of the industry had never done before: instituted a cash rebate to buyers. Other Detroit producers had little choice but to join in. What rebates amounted to was throwing money away in an attempt to lose less on the balance sheets, but it was a necessary, if drastic, step: that big inventory was costing Chrysler $300,000 a week.

These sharp sales reversals prompted a complete rethink that must have seemed quite alien for a make that

had solemnly promised never to build a "small" car. But the new philosophy that emerged only echoed the 1958 suggestions of outgoing company president K. T. Keller, who had wanted Chrysler to "get back to design for function, with more stress on utility." The most visible product of the new order was the Cordoba. Though it broke new ground for the marque, this personal-luxury coupe wasn't really new. In fact, it was a twin in most respects to a revamped Dodge Charger that arrived for '75, with styling that seemed to be a cross between a Jaguar XJ6 and

1971 Newport hardtop coupe

1972 Town & Country wagon

1973 New Yorker Brougham four-door sedan

1974 New Yorker hardtop sedan

Chrysler

a Chevrolet Monte Carlo, though that was a very good cross. The Cordoba's 115-inch wheelbase was the shortest seen on any Chrysler since the war, and was only 2.5 inches longer than on the first car to bear the badge way back in 1924. Trumpeted as "the new small Chrysler," it was marketed as something of a road car, which it really wasn't, standard steel-belted radial tires and front and rear sway bars notwithstanding. Reflecting the Cordoba's true

character, power seats, windows and door locks were optional, and interiors were beautifully upholstered in crushed velour or brocade cloth and vinyl, with "fine Corinthian" leather available at extra cost.

The rest of the line was basically unchanged for 1975-76—except for price. The accent was now less on performance and much more on luxury, with a modicum of "efficiency" thrown in. The most opulent offering was the New

1975 Cordoba coupe

1976 Newport Custom hardtop coupe

1977 LeBaron Medallion coupe

1977 Cordoba coupe

1978 New Yorker Brougham hardtop sedan

1979 New Yorker Fifth Avenue Edition four-door sedan

1980 LeBaron Medallion four-door sedan

1980 Cordoba Crown hardtop coupe

Yorker Brougham, which took over for the Imperial as the division's luxury leader after 1975. It boasted standard leather, velour or brocade upholstery, plus shag carpeting, imitation walnut trim, and filigree moldings. Economy, such as it was, was boosted with numerically lower final drive ratios and an optional "Fuel Pacer" system, which consisted of an intake manifold pressure sensor connected to a warning light that glowed during heavy-footed moments.

Chrysler fielded a yet smaller model for 1977, this time the shortest in its history: the compact, 3500-pound Le-Baron. Cleanly styled in the boxy Mercedes idiom, it was initially available in two trim levels as either a coupe or four-door sedan. Despite its origins in the workaday Dodge Aspen/Plymouth Volare compacts, it sold extremely well, providing timely sales assistance in a market gone wild for smaller cars. Elsewhere, the Newport/Town & Country/New Yorker trio were mildly updated, and Cordoba soldiered on in two versions. The next year, LeBaron got more emphasis as the line was expanded with lower-priced S versions and a brace of Town & Country wagons, along with the buyer's option of slant six or V8. The full-size T&Cs

vanished entirely for '78, and the other two series were cut to just two models apiece. The 440 V8 was still available as a big-car option, but relatively few were ordered. The bread-and-butter engine was now the old 318, an artifact from the mid-'60s.

For 1979, both the 440 and 400 V8s were scrubbed, and a solitary downsized sedan was issued in both Newport and New Yorker guise. This new R-body four-door was considerably smaller and lighter (3500-4000 pounds) than the old mastadons, but it managed to look big and heavy, which may explain why its sales were underwhelming. Much the same lineup returned for 1980, while Chrysler-watchers did double-takes over the developing business crisis in Highland Park. But help was on the way in the person of Lee A. Iacocca, who took the helm of his one-time rival that year.

Since then, the Chrysler story—at least so far—has been one of innovation and a solid improvement in quality, and its mid-'80s models are among the more sensible and pleasant American cars. At this writing, the firm has just bounced back from the very brink of disaster, and its future once again seems bright.

Chrysler Specifications

1930

Model CJ6 (wb 109.0)

	Wght	Price	Prod*
rdstr 2-4P	2,390	805	1,616
touring 5P	2,455	835	279
bus cpe 2P	2,560	795	2,267
Royal cpe 2-4P	2,590	835	3,593
Royal sdn 4d 5P	2,695	845	20,748
conv cpe	—	—	705
chassis	—	—	31

Model 66 (wb 112.8)

rdstr 2-4P	2,625	1,025	1,213
phtn 5P	2,695	1,025	26
bus cpe 2P	2,750	995	2,014
Royal cpe 2-4P	2,850	1,075	3,257
brougham 5P	2,850	995	2,343
Royal sdn 5P	2,930	1,095	3,753

Model 70 (wb 116.5)

rdstr 2-4P	3,205	1,345	1,431
phtn 5P	3,235	1,295	279
bus cpe 2P	3,410	1,345	766
Royal cpe 2-4P	3,490	1,395	3,135
brougham 5P	3,490	1,345	1,204
Royal sdn 5P	3,590	1,445	11,213
conv cpe 2-4P	3,450	1,545	705

Model 77 (wb 124.0)

rdstr 2-4P	3,370	1,665	1,729
phtn 5P	3,495	1,795	173
bus cpe 2P	3,560	1,395	230
Royal cpe 2-4P	3,615	1,495	2,954

	Wght	Price	Prod
Crown cpe 4P	3,580	1,575	883
conv cpe 2-4P	3,580	1,825	418
Royal sdn 5P	3,750	1,495	7,211
Town sdn 5P	3,720	1,445	436
Crown sdn 5P	3,760	1,595	2,654

Imperial (wb 136.0)

rdstr 2-4P	3,955	2,995	—
spt phtn 4P	4,225	3,955	—
phtn 7P	3,925	3,195	15**
cpe 2P	4,025	3,095	—
conv cpe 2-4P	4,120	3,095	50**
sdn 5P	4,335	3,075	300**
Town sdn 5P	4,310	3,075	100**
sdn 7P	4,460	3,195	150**
sdn limo 7P	4,510	3,575	—

*Some figures include later years; see 1931, 1932.
**Estimates based on one-third of 1929-30 model year production.

1930 Engines	bore×stroke	bhp	availability
L6, 195.6	3.13×4.25	62	S-CJ6
L6, 195.6	3.13×4.25	65	S-66s built 1929
L6, 218.6	3.13×4.75	75	S-70s built 1929
L6, 218.6	3.13×4.75	68	S-66s built 1930
L6, 268.4	3.38×5.00	93	S-70s built 1930, 77
L6, 309.3	3.63×5.00	100	S-Imperial

1931

Model CJ6 (wb 109.0)

Production was carried over from 1930, with 1931 model output commencing July 1, 1930. Production figures combined with 1930 CJ6 models. Body styles and weights identical; prices $20-50 below 1930 prices.

Chrysler

Model 66 (wb 112.8)

Production was carried over from 1930 commencing July 1, 1930. Production figures combined with 1930 Model 66. Body styles and weights identical; prices $5 above 1930 prices.

Model 70 (wb 116.5)

Production was carried over from 1930 commencing July 1, 1930. Production figures combined with 1930 Model 70. Body styles and weights identical. Open car prices unchanged; closed car prices lowered $100 except for Royal sedan, which was lowered $150.

CM6 New Six (wb 116.0)	Wght	Price	Prod
rdstr 2-4P	2,565	885	2,281
cpe 2-4P	2,700	885	5,327
sdn 4d	2,815	895	28,620
phtn 5P	2,740	915	196
bus cpe 2P	2,730	865	802
conv cpe 2-4P	2,750	935	1,492
chassis	—	—	99

CD8 New Eight (wb 124.0)*	Wght	Price	Prod
rdstr 2-4P	3,100	1,495	1,462
spts rdstr 2-4P	3,225	1,595	
Royal Standard cpe	3,235	1,495	3,000
Royal Sport cpe	3,235	1,535	
conv cpe 2-4P	3,195	1,665	700
Royal Standard sdn	3,365	1,525	9,000
Royal Special sdn	3,365	1,565	
phtn 5P	3,490	1,970	85
chassis	—	—	108

*First series commenced July 1930. Second series commenced January 1931; discontinued April 1931 and replaced by DeLuxe Eight.

DeLuxe Eight (wb 124.0)	Wght	Price	Prod
rdstr 2-4P	3,330	1,545	511
phtn 5P	3,545	1,970	113
cpe 2-4P	3,525	1,525	1,506
conv cpe 2-4P	3,445	1,585	501
cpe 5P	3,575	1,565	500
sdn 5P	3,640	1,565	5,843
chassis	—	—	126

CG Imperial (wb 145.0)	Wght	Price	Prod
Custom rdstr 2-4P	4,530	3,220	100
Custom spt phtn 5P	4,645	3,575	85
Custom cpe 2-4P	4,605	3,150	135
Custom conv cpe	4,570	3,320	10
sdn 5P	4,705	2,745	909
close-coupled sdn 5P	4,685	2,845	1,195
sdn 7P	4,825	2,945	403
sdn limo 8P	4,915	3,145	271
conv sdn	4,825	3,995	25
chassis	—	—	95

1931 Engines	bore×stroke	bhp	availability
L6, 195.6	3.13×4.25	62	S-CJ6
L6, 217.8	3.25×4.38	78	S-CM6
L6, 218.6	3.13×4.75	68	S-66
L6, 268.4	3.38×5.00	93	S-70
L8, 240.3	3.00×4.25	82	S-CD8s built 1930
L8, 260.8	3.13×4.25	90	S-CD8s built 1931
L8, 282.1	3.25×4.25	95	S-DeLuxe Eight
L8, 384.8	3.50×5.00	125	S-CG

1932

Model 70 (wb 116.5)

Listed by Chrysler for 1932, although production ceased in May 1931. Engine numbers from #V-29414. Production combined with 1931 and 1930 (see entries).

Model CM6 (wb 116.0)

Production continued from 1931 commencing July 1, ending in December. Engine numbers from #CM-30829. Production combined with 1931 (see entry).

Model CD DeLuxe Eight (wb 124.0)

Production continued from 1931 commencing July 1, ending in November. Engine numbers from #CD-21141. Production combined with 1931 (see entry).

CG Imperial (wb 145.0)

Production continued from 1931 commencing July 1, ending in December. Engine numbers from #CG-3752.

CI6 "Second Series" Six (wb 116.0)	Wght	Price	Prod
rdstr 2-4P	2,830	885	474
phtn 5P	2,905	915	59
bus cpe 2P	2,915	865	354
cpe 2-4P	3,040	885	2,913
conv cpe 2-4P	2,970	935	1,000
sdn 5P	3,135	895	13,772
conv sdn 5P	3,160	1,125	322
chassis	—	—	70

CP8 Eight (wb 125.0)	Wght	Price	Prod
cpe 2-4P	3,735	1,435	718
conv cpe 2-4P	3,705	1,495	396
cpe 5P	3,810	1,475	502
sdn 5P	3,885	1,475	3,198
conv sdn 5P	4,090	1,695	251
chassis	—	—	48

CH Imperial (wb 135.0)	Wght	Price	Prod
cpe 2-4P	4,480	1,925	239
sdn 5P	4,645	1,945	1,002
conv sdn 5P	4,890	2,195	152
chassis	—	—	9

CL Imperial (wb 146.0)	Wght	Price	Prod
conv cpe	4,930	3,295	28
phtn 5P	5,065	3,395	14
close-coupled sdn 5P	5,150	2,895	57
conv sdn 5P	5,125	3,595	49
sdn 8P	5,295	2,995	35
sdn limo 7P	5,330	3,295	32
chassis	—	—	5

1932 Engines	bore×stroke	bhp	availability
L6, 217.8	3.25×4.38	78	S-CM6
L6, 224.0	3.25×4.50	82	S-CI6
L6, 268.4	3.38×5.00	93	S-70
L8, 282.1	3.25×4.25	95	S-CD
L8, 298.6	3.25×4.50	100	S-CP8
L8, 384.8	3.50×5.00	125	S-CG,CH,CL

1933

CO Six (wb 117.0)	Wght	Price	Prod
bus cpe 2P	2,968	745	587
cpe 2-4P	3,018	775	1,454
conv cpe 2-4P	3,013	795	677
brougham 5P	3,078	745	1,207
sdn 5P	3,143	785	13,264
sdn 7P (special interior)	3,200	845	51
conv sdn 5P	3,212	945	205
sdn 7P	—	—	151
chassis	—	—	267

CT Royal Eight (wb 120.0)	Wght	Price	Prod
bus cpe 2P	3,303	895	226
cpe 2-4P	3,343	915	1,033
conv cpe 2-4P	3,363	945	539
sdn 5P	3,483	925	7,993

	Wght	Price	Prod
conv sdn 5P	3,617	1,085	257
sdn 7P	3,658	1,125	246
chassis	—	—	95

CQ Imperial Eight (wb 126.0)

	Wght	Price	Prod
cpe 2-4P	3,734	1,275	364
conv cpe 2-4P	—	1,325	243
cpe 5P	3,754	1,295	267
sdn 5P	3,864	1,295	2,584
conv sdn 5P	4,144	1,495	364
chassis	—	—	16

CL Imperial Custom (wb 146.0)

	Wght	Price	Prod
rdstr 2-4P	4,910	3,295	9
phtn 5P	4,890	3,395	36
close-coupled sdn 5P	5,045	2,895	43
sdn 7P	5,240	2,995	21
limo sdn 7P	5,245	3,295	22
conv sdn	—	—	11
stationary cpe	—	—	3
chassis	—	—	6

1933 Engines	bore×stroke	bhp	availability
L6, 224.0	3.25×4.50	83/89	S-CO
L8, 273.8	3.25×4.13	90/98	S-CT
L8, 298.7	3.25×4.50	108/100	S-CQ
L8, 384.8	3.50×5.00	135/125	S-CL

1934

CA Six (wb 118.0)

	Wght	Price	Prod
bus cpe 2P	2,868	740	1,650
cpe 2-4P	2,903	815	1,875
conv cpe 2-4P	—	850	700
brougham 5P	3,019	760	1,575
sdn 5P	3,123	820	17,617
chassis	—	—	385

CB Custom Six (wb 121.0)

	Wght	Price	Prod
close-coupled sdn 5P	—	900	980
conv sdn 5P	—	970	450
chassis	—	—	20

CU Airflow Eight (wb 123.0)

	Wght	Price	Prod
cpe 5P	—	1,345	732
brougham 5P	3,741	1,345	306
sdn 6P	3,760	1,345	7,226
Town sdn 6P	—	1,345	125

CV Airflow Imperial Eight (wb 128.0)

	Wght	Price	Prod
cpe 5P	3,929	1,625	212
sdn 6P	3,974	1,625	1,997
Town sdn 6P	3,969	1,625	67
chassis	—	—	1

CX Airflow Imperial Eight (wb 137.5)

	Wght	Price	Prod
sdn 5P	4,154	2,245	25
Town sdn 5P	4,160	2,245	1
sdn limo 8P	4,299	2,345	78
Town sdn limo	4,304	2,345	2

CW Airflow Imp Custom Eight (wb 146.0)

	Wght	Price	Prod
sdn 8P	5,780	5,000	17
Town sdn 8P	5,815	5,000	28
limo sdn 8P	5,900	5,145	20
Town limo sdn 8P	5,935	5,145	2

1934 Engines	bore×stroke	bhp	availability
L6, 241.5	3.38×4.50	93	S-CA,CB
L6, 241.5	3.38×4.50	100	O-CA,CB
L8, 298.7	3.25×4.50	122	S-CU
L8, 323.5	3.25×4.88	130	S-CV,CX
L8, 384.8	3.50×5.00	150	S-CW

1935

C6 Airstream Six (wb 118.0)

	Wght	Price	Prod
bus cpe 2P	2,863	745	1,975
cpe 2-4P	2,953	810	861
touring brougham 5P	2,988	820	1,901
fstbk sdn 4d 5P	3,013	830	6,055
touring sdn 5P	3,048	860	12,790
fstbk sdn 2d 5P	2,990	820	400
chassis	—	—	476

CZ Airstream Eight (wb 121.0; lwb-133.0)

	Wght	Price	Prod
bus cpe 2P	3,103	910	} 100
Deluxe bus cpe 2P	3,138	930	
cpe 2-4P	3,138	935	} 550
Deluxe cpe 2-4P	3,233	955	
touring brougham 2d	3,203	960	} 500
Deluxe touring brougham 2d	3,293	980	
sdn 4d	3,213	975	} 2,958
Deluxe sdn 4d	3,333	985	
touring sdn 4d	3,263	995	} 4,394
Deluxe touring sdn 4d	3,338	1,015	
Deluxe conv cpe 2-4P	3,298	1,015	101
Deluxe Traveler sdn 5P	3,513	1,235	245
Deluxe lwb sdn 7P	3,538	1,235	212
chassis	—	—	237

C1 Airflow 8 (wb 123.0)

	Wght	Price	Prod
bus cpe 2P	3,823	1,245	72
cpe 6P	3,883	1,245	307
sdn 6P	3,828	1,245	4,617

C2 Imperial Airflow 8 (wb 128.0)

	Wght	Price	Prod
cpe 6P	4,003	1,475	200
sdn 4d 6P	3,998	1,475	2,398

C3 Custom Imperial Airflow 8 (wb 137.5)

	Wght	Price	Prod
sdn 4d 6P	4,208	2,245	69
Town sdn 4d 6P	4,308	2,245	1
sdn limo 8P	4,378	2,345	53
Town sdn limo 8P	4,478	2,345	2

CW Custom Imperial Airflow 8 (wb 146.5)

	Wght	Price	Prod
sdn 8P	4,785	5,000	15
sdn limo 8P	5,990	5,145	15
Town sdn limo 8P	5,090	5,145	2

1935 Engines	bore×stroke	bhp	availability
L6, 241.5	3.38×4.50	93	S-C6
L6, 241.5	3.38×4.50	100	O-C6
L8, 273.8	3.25×4.13	105	S-CZ
L8, 273.8	3.25×4.13	110	O-CZ
L8, 323.5	3.25×4.88	115	S-C1
L8, 323.5	3.25×4.88	120	O-C1
L8, 323.5	3.25×4.88	130	S-C2,C3
L8, 323.5	3.25×4.88	138	O-C2,C3
L8, 384.8	3.50×5.00	150	S-CW

1936

C7 Airstream (wb 118.0)

	Wght	Price	Prod
bus cpe 2P	2,963	760	3,703
cpe 2-4P	3,037	825	759
conv cpe 2-4P	3,053	925	650
touring brougham 5P	3,082	825	3,177
conv sdn 5P	3,282	1,125	497
touring sdn 4d	3,137	874	34,099
chassis	—	—	586

C8 Airstream Deluxe (wb 121.0; lwb-133.0)

	Wght	Price	Prod
bus cpe 2P	3,155	925	520
cpe 2-4P	3,220	995	325
conv cpe 2-4P	3,350	1,075	240
touring brougham 5P	3,330	995	268

	Wght	Price	Prod
conv sdn 5P	3,495	1,265	362
touring sdn 4d	3,345	1,045	6,547
Traveler sdn 5P	3,500	1,255	350
lwb sdn 7P	3,550	1,245	619
lwb sdn limo 7P	3,595	1,865	67
lwb Town sdn 7P	3,550	4,995	8
chassis	—	—	196

C9 Airflow Eight (wb 123.0)

	Wght	Price	Prod
cpe 6P	3,997	1,395	110
sdn 4d 6P	4,102	1,345	1,590

C10 Airflow Imperial (wb 128.0)

	Wght	Price	Prod
cpe 6P	4,105	1,475	240
sdn 4d 6P	4,175	1,475	4,259
chassis	—	—	1

C11 Airflow Custom Imperial (wb 137.0; lwb-146.5)

	Wght	Price	Prod
sdn 4d 5P	5,900	2,475	38
sdn limo 7P	6,000	2,575	37
lwb sdn 4d 8P	6,200*	5,000*	
lwb limo 8P	6,250*	5,000*	10

1936 Engines	bore×stroke	bhp	availability
L0, 241.5	3.38×4.50	93	S-C7
L6, 241.5	3.38×4.50	100	O-C7
L8, 273.8	3.25×4.13	105	S-C8
L8, 273.8	3.25×4.13	110	O-C8
L8, 323.5	3.25×4.88	115	S-C9
L8, 323.5	3.25×4.88	130	S-C10,C11

1937

C16 Royal (wb 116.0; lwb-133.0)

	Wght	Price	Prod
bus cpe 2P	3,049	810	9,830
cpe 2-4P	3,099	860	1,050
conv cpe 2-4P	3,274	1,020	767
brougham 5P F/B	3,114	870	750
touring brougham 5P	3,094	880	7,835
fstbk sdn 4d 5P	3,124	910	1,200
touring sdn 4d 5P	3,134	920	62,408
conv sdn 5P	3,484	1,355	642
lwb sdn 7P	3,544	1,145	856
lwb sdn limo 7P	3,550	1,245	138
chassis	—	—	524

C14 Imperial (wb 121.0)

	Wght	Price	Prod
bus cpe 2P	3,374	1,030	1,075
cpe 2-4P	3,449	1,070	225
conv cpe 2-4P	3,609	1,170	351
touring brougham 5P	3,544	1,070	430
touring sdn 5P	3,564	1,100	11,796
conv sdn 5P	3,824	1,500	325
chassis	—	—	118

C17 Airflow (wb 128.0)

	Wght	Price	Prod
cpe 6P	4,225	1,610	230
sdn 4d 6P	4,300	1,610	4,370

C15 Custom Imperial (wb 140.0)

	Wght	Price	Prod
sdn 4d	4,500	2,060	187
sdn 7P	4,522	2,060	721
sdn limo 7P	4,644	2,160	276
chassis	—	—	16

1937 Engines	bore×stroke	bhp	availability
L6, 228.0	3.38×4.25	93	S-C16
L6, 228.0	3.38×4.25	100	O-C16
L8, 273.8	3.25×4.13	110	S-C14
L8, 273.8	3.25×4.13	115	O-C14
L8, 323.5	3.25×4.88	130	S-C17,C15

		Wght	Price	Prod
L8, 323.5	3.25×4.88	138	O-C17,C15	

1938

C18 Royal (wb 119.0; lwb-136.0)

	Wght	Price	Prod
bus cpe 2P	3,090	918	4,840
cpe 2-4P	3,135	963	363
conv cpe 2-4P	3,250	1,085	480
fstbk brougham 5P	3,160	963	88
touring brougham 5P	3,165	975	3,802
fstbk sdn 5P	3,170	998	112
touring sdn 5P	3,180	1,010	31,991
conv sdn 5P	3,450	1,425	177
chassis	—	—	564
lwb sdn T/B 7P	3450	1235	722
limo T/B 7P (lwb)	3545	1325	161

C19 Imperial (wb 125.0)

	Wght	Price	Prod
bus cpe 2P	3,450	1,123	766
New York Special bus cpe 2P	3,475	1,255	
touring sdn 5P	3,565	1,198	8,554
New York Spl touring sdn 5P	3,600	1,378	
cpe 2-4P	3,515	1,160	80
conv cpe 2-4P	3,630	1,275	189
touring brougham 5P	3,560	1,165	245
conv sdn 5P	3,950	1,595	113
chassis	—	—	55

C20 Custom Imperial (wb 144.0)

	Wght	Price	Prod
sdn 5P	4,495	2,295	252
sdn 7P	4,510	2,295	122
sdn limo 7P	4,635	2,395	145
chassis	—	—	11

1938 Engines	bore×stroke	bhp	availability
L6, 241.5	3.38×4.50	95	S-C18
L6, 241.5	3.38×4.50	102	O-C18
L8, 298.7	3.25×4.50	110	S-C19
L8, 298.7	3.25×4.50	122	O-C19
L8, 323.5	3.25×4.88	130	S-C20
L8, 323.5	3.25×4.88	138	O-C20

1939

C-22 Royal (wb 119.0; lwb-136.0)

	Wght	Price	Prod
cpe 2P	3,120	918	4,780
Windsor cpe 2P	3,130	983	
Victoria cpe 4P	3,160	970	239
Windsor Victoria cpe 4P	3,165	1,065	
brougham 5P	3,200	975	4,838
sdn 4d	3,265	1,010	45,955
Windsor sdn 4d	3,275	1,075	
Windsor club cpe 5P	3,245	1,185	2,983
lwb sdn 7P	3,520	1,235	621
lwb sdn limo 7P	3,625	1,325	191
chassis	—	—	394

C-23 Imperial/New Yorker/Saratoga (wb 125.0)

	Wght	Price	Prod
Imperial bus cpe 2P	3,520	1,123	492
Imperial Victoria cpe 4P	3,555	1,160	35
Imperial brougham 5P	3,610	1,165	185
Imperial sdn 4d	3,640	1,198	
New Yorker sdn 4d	3,695	1,298	10,536
Saratoga sdn 4d	3,720	1,443	

	Wght	Price	Prod
New Yorker Victoria cpe 4P	3,665	1,395	99
New Yorker bus cpe 2P	3,540	1,223	⎤
New Yorker club cpe 5P	3,550	1,260	⎦ 606
Saratoga club cpe 5P	3,665	1,495	134
chassis	—	—	48

C-24 Custom Imperial (wb 144.0)

		Wght	Price	Prod
sdn 5P		4,590	2,595	88
sdn 7P		4,620	2,595	95
sdn limo 7P		4,665	2,695	117
chassis		—	—	7

1939 Engines	bore×stroke	bhp	availability
L6, 241.5	3.38×4.50	95	S-C22
L6, 241.5	3.38×4.50	102	O-C22
L8, 323.5	3.25×4.88	130	S-C23
L8, 323.5	3.25×4.88	132	S-C24
L8, 323.5	3.25×4.88	138	O-C24

1940

Series C-25 (wb 122.5; 8P-139.5)

	Wght	Price	Prod
Royal sdn 4d	3,175	995	23,274
Windsor sdn 4d	3,210	1,025	28,477
Royal sdn 2d	3,150	960	⎤
Windsor sdn 2d	3,175	995	⎦ 9,851
Royal bus cpe	3,075	895	⎤
Windsor bus cpe	3,095	935	⎦ 5,117
Royal cpe	3,110	960	⎤
Windsor cpe	3,135	995	⎦ 4,315
Windsor Highlander cpe	3,135	1,020	
Windsor conv cpe	3,360	1,160	⎤ 2,275
Windsor Highlander conv cpe	3,360	1,185	⎦
Royal sdn 4d, 8P	3,550	1,235	⎤ 439
Windsor sdn 4d, 8P	3,575	1,275	⎦
Royal limo	3,640	1,310	⎤ 98
Windsor limo	3,660	1,350	⎦
chassis	—	—	152

Series C-26 (wb 128.5)

	Wght	Price	Prod
Traveler sdn 4d	3,590	1,180	⎤
New Yorker sdn 4d	3,635	1,260	⎥ 14,603
Saratoga sdn 4d	3,790	1,375	⎦
Traveler cpe	3,525	1,150	⎤
New Yorker cpe	3,570	1,230	⎥ 1,117
New Yorker Highlander cpe	3,570	1,255	⎦
Traveler bus cpe	3,475	1,095	⎤ 731
New Yorker bus cpe	3,490	1,175	⎦
Traveler sdn 2d	3,555	1,150	⎤ 275
New Yorker sdn 2d	3,610	1,230	⎦
New Yorker conv cpe	3,775	1,375	⎤ 845
New Yorker Highlndr conv cpe	3,775	1,400	⎦

Series C-27 Crown Imperial (wb 145.5)

		Wght	Price	Prod
sdn 4d		4,340	2,245	355
sdn 4d, 8P		4,330	2,345	284
limo, 8P		4,365	2,445	210
chassis		—	—	1

1940 engines	bore×stroke	bhp	availability
L6, 241.5	3.38×4.50	108	S-Royal, Windsor
L6, 241.5	3.38×4.50	112	O-Royal, Windsor
L8, 323.5	3.25×4.88	135	S-Traveler, NY, Saratoga
L8, 323.5	3.25×4.88	143	O-Traveler, NY, Saratoga
L8, 323.5	3.25×4.88	132	S-Crown Imperial
L8, 323.5	3.25×4.88	143	O-Crown Imperial

1941

Series C-28S Royal (wb 121.5; 8P-139.5)

	Wght	Price	Prod
sdn 4d	3,300	1,091	51,378
club cpe	3,260	1,085	10,830
luxury brougham 2d	3,270	1,066	8,006
bus cpe	3,170	995	6,846
town sdn 4d	3,320	1,136	1,277
sdn 4d, 8P	3,650	1,345	297
limo 8P	3,695	1,415	31
chassis	—	—	3

C-28W Windsor (wb 121.5; 8P-139.5)

	Wght	Price	Prod
sdn 4d	3,300	1,165	36,396
club cpe	3,260	1,142	8,513
conv cpe	3,470	1,315	4,432
luxury brougham 2d	3,270	1,128	2,898
town sdn 4d	3,315	1,198	2,704
bus cpe	3,170	1,045	1,921
Town & Country wgn 4d, 9P	3,595	1,492	797
Town & Country wgn 4d, 6P	3,540	1,412	200
sdn 4d, 8P	3,575	1,410	116
limo, 8P	3,660	1,487	54

C-30K/30N (wb 127.5)

	Wght	Price	Prod
Saratoga sdn 4d	3,755	1,320	⎤ 15,868
New Yorker sdn 4d	3,775	1,389	⎦
Saratoga club cpe	3,685	1,299	⎤ 2,845
New Yorker club cpe	3,690	1,369	⎦
Saratoga town sdn 4d	3,750	1,350	⎤ 2,326
New Yorker town sdn 4d	3,785	1,399	⎦
Saratoga bus cpe	3,600	1,245	⎤ 771
New Yorker bus cpe	3,635	1,325	⎦
Saratoga luxury brougham 2d	3,715	1,293	⎤ 293
New Yorker luxury brougham 2d	3,745	1,369	⎦
New Yorker conv cpe	3,945	1,548	1,295
Town & Country wgn 4d	exp	proto	1
chassis	—	—	9

C-33 Crown Imperial (wb 145.5)

	Wght	Price	Prod
sdn 4d	4,435	2,595	179
sdn 4d, 8P	4,495	2,696	205
limo 8P	4,560	2,795	316
special town sdn 4d*	3,900	1,760	894
chassis	—	—	1

*C-30 body and chassis, C-33 engine and nameplates.

1941 Engines	bore×stroke	bhp	availability
L6, 241.5	3.38×4.50	108/112	S-Royal, Windsor
L6, 241.5	3.38×4.50	115	O-Royal, Windsor
L8, 323.5	3.25×4.88	137	S-Saratoga, NY
L8, 323.5	3.25×4.88	140	O-Saratoga, NY
L8, 323.5	3.25×4.88	143	S-Crown Imperial

1942

Series C-34S Royal (wb 121.5; 8P-139.5)

	Wght	Price	Prod
bus cpe	3,331	1,075	479
club cpe	3,406	1,168	779
brougham 2d	3,431	1,154	709
sdn 4d	3,476	1,177	7,424
town sdn 4d	3,481	1,222	73
sdn 4d, 8P	3,854	1,535	79
limo 8P	3,895	1,605	21

C-34W Windsor (wb 121.5; 8P-139.5)

	Wght	Price	Prod
bus cpe	3,351	1,140	250
club cpe	3,426	1,228	1,713
conv cpe	3,661	1,420	574
brougham 2d	3,441	1,220	317

	Wght	Price	Prod
sdn 4d	3,496	1,255	10,054
town sdn, 4d	3,506	1,295	479
Town & Country wgn 4d, 6P	3,614	1,595	150
Town & Country wgn 4d, 9P	3,699	1,685	849
sdn 4d, 8P	3,879	1,605	29
limo 8P	3,900	1,685	12

C-36K Saratoga (wb 127.5)

	Wght	Price	Prod
bus cpe	3,703	1,325	80
club cpe	3,788	1,380	193
brougham 2d	3,798	1,365	36
sdn 4d	3,833	1,405	1,239
town sdn 4d	3,843	1,450	46
chassis	—	—	2

C-36N New Yorker (wb 127.5)

	Wght	Price	Prod
bus cpe	3,728	1,385	158
club cpe	3,783	1,450	1,234
conv cpe	4,033	1,640	401
brougham 2d	3,798	1,440	62
Town & Country wgn 4d, 9P	—	proto	1
sdn 4d	3,873	1,475	7,045
town sdn 4d	3,893	1,520	1,648

C-33 Crown Imperial (wb 145.5)

	Wght	Price	Prod
sdn 4d	4,565	2,815	81
sdn 4d, 8P	4,620	2,915	152
limo 8P	4,685	3,065	215
chassis	—	—	2

1942 Engines	bore×stroke	bhp	availability
L6, 250.6	3.44×4.50	120	S-Royal, Windsor
L8, 323.5	3.25×4.88	140	S-others

1946

Series C-38S Royal (wb 121.5; 8P-139.5)*	Wght	Price	Prod
sdn 4d	3,523	1,561	—
sdn 2d	3,458	1,526	—
club cpe	3,443	1,551	—
bus cpe	3,373	1,431	—
sdn 4d, 8P	3,997	1,943	—
limo 8P	4,022	2,063	—
chassis	—	—	—

C-38W Windsor (wb 121.5; 8P-139.5)*

	Wght	Price	Prod
sdn 4d	3,528	1,611	—
sdn 2d	3,468	1,591	—
club cpe	3,448	1,601	—
bus cpe	3,383	1,481	—
conv cpe	3,693	1,861	—
sdn 4d, 8P	3,977	1,993	—
limo 8P	4,052	2,113	—
Traveler sdn 4d	3,610	1,746	—

C-39K Saratoga (wb 127.5)*

	Wght	Price	Prod
sdn 4d	3,972	1,863	—
sdn 2d	3,932	1,838	—
club cpe	3,892	1,848	—
bus cpe	3,817	1,753	—

C-39N New Yorker (wb 127.5)*

	Wght	Price	Prod
sdn 4d	3,973	1,963	—
sdn 2d	3,932	1,938	—
club cpe	3,897	1,948	—
bus cpe	3,837	1,853	—
conv cpe	4,132	2,193	—
chassis	—	—	—

C-38/39 Town & Country (wb 121.5; L8-127.5)*

	Wght	Price	Prod
sdn 4d, L6	3,917	2,366	4,124
brougham 2d, L6	—	proto	1

	Wght	Price	Prod
conv cpe, L6	—	proto	1
sdn 4d, L8	4,300	2,718	100
conv cpe, L8	4,332	2,743	1,935
htp cpe, L8	—	proto	7

C-40 Crown Imperial (wb 145.5)*

	Wght	Price	Prod
limo 8P	4,814	3,875	—

1946 Engines	bore×stroke	bhp	availability
L6, 250.6	3.44×4.50	114	S-Royal, Windsor, T&C six
L8, 323.5	3.25×4.88	135	S-others

1947

Series C-38S Royal (wb 121.5; 8P-139.5)*	Wght	Price	Prod
sdn 4d	3,523	1,661	—
sdn 2d	3,458	1,626	—
club cpe	3,443	1,651	—
bus cpe	3,373	1,561	—
sdn 4d, 8P	3,997	2,043	—
limo 8P	4,022	2,163	—

C-38W Windsor (wb 121.5; 8P-139.5)*

	Wght	Price	Prod
sdn 4d	3,528	1,711	—
Traveler sdn 4d	3,610	1,846	—
sdn 2d	3,468	1,691	—
club cpe	3,448	1,701	—
bus cpe	3,383	1,611	—
conv cpe	3,693	2,075	—
sdn 4d, 8P	3,977	2,093	—
limo 8P	4,052	2,213	—

C-39K Saratoga (wb 127.5)*

	Wght	Price	Prod
sdn 4d	3,972	1,973	—
sdn 2d	3,900	1,948	—
club cpe	3,930	1,958	—
bus cpe	3,817	1,873	—

C-39N New Yorker (wb 127.5)*

	Wght	Price	Prod
sdn 4d	3,987	2,073	—
sdn 2d	3,932	2,048	—
club cpe	3,940	2,058	—
bus cpe	3,837	1,973	—
conv cpe	4,132	2,447	—

C-38/39 Town & Country (wb 121.5; L8-127.5)

	Wght	Price	Prod
sdn 4d, L6	3,955	2,713	2,651
conv cpe, L8	4,332	2,998	3,136

C-40 Crown Imperial (wb 145.5)*

	Wght	Price	Prod
sdn 4d, 8P	4,865	4,205	—
limo 8P	4,875	4,305	—

1947 Engines	bore×stroke	bhp	availability
L6, 250.6	3.44×4.50	114	S-Royal, Windsor, T&C six
L8, 323.5	3.25×4.88	135	S-others

1948–1949 First Series

Series C-38S Royal (wb 121.5; 8P-139.5)*	Wght	Price	Prod
sdn 4d	3,523	1,955	—
sdn 2d	3,485	1,908	—
club cpe	3,475	1,934	—
bus cpe	3,395	1,819	—
sdn 4d, 8P	3,925	2,380	—
limo 8P	4,022	2,506	—

C-38W Windsor (wb 121.5; 8P-139.5)*

	Wght	Price	Prod
sdn 4d	3,528	2,021	—
Traveler sdn 4d	3,610	2,163	—
sdn 2d	3,510	1,989	—

	Wght	Price	Prod
club cpe	3,475	2,000	—
bus cpe	3,395	1,884	—
conv cpe	3,693	2,414	—
sdn 4d, 8P	3,935	2,434	—
limo 8P	4,035	2,561	—

C-39K Saratoga (wb 127.5)*

	Wght	Price	Prod
sdn 4d	3,972	2,291	—
sdn 2d	3,900	2,254	—
club cpe	3,930	2,265	—
bus cpe	3,817	2,165	—

C-39N New Yorker (wb 127.5)*

	Wght	Price	Prod
sdn 4d	3,987	2,411	—
sdn 2d	3,932	2,374	—
club cpe	3,940	2,385	—
bus cpe	3,837	2,285	—
conv cpe	4,132	2,815	—

C-38/39 Town & Country (wb 121.5; L8-127.5)

	Wght	Price	Prod
sdn 4d, L6	3,955	2,860	1,175
conv cpe, L8	4,332	3,395	3,309

C-40 Crown Imperial (wb 145.5)*

	Wght	Price	Prod
sdn 4d, 8P	4,865	4,662	—
limo 8P	4,875	4,767	—

1948 Engines	bore×stroke	bhp	availability
L6, 250.6	3.44×4.50	114	S-Royal, Windsor, T&C six
L8, 323.5	3.25×4.88	135	S-others

Note: First Series 1949 models sold December 1948 through March 1949 identical in weight and price to 1948 models and comprised about 15% of total production.

*Factory combined production figures for 1946 through 1949 first series and breakdowns are not available from Chrysler archives. However, since the Town & Country figures have been obtained (by historian Donald Narus), it is very likely that breakdowns exist for other models.

Combined 1946–1949 First Series Production:

C-38S Royal (wb 121.5; 8P-139.5)

	Prod
sdn 4d	24,279
sdn 2d	1,117
club cpe	4,318
bus cpe	1,221
sdn 4d, 8P	626
limo 8P	169
chassis	1

C-38W Windsor (wb 121.5; 8P-139.5)

	Prod
sdn 4d	161,139
Traveler sdn 4d	4,182
sdn 2d	4,034
club cpe	26,482
bus cpe	1,980
conv cpe	11,200
sdn 4d, 8P	4,390
limo 8P	1,496

C-39K Saratoga (wb 127.5)

	Prod
sdn 4d	4,611
sdn 2d	155
club cpe	765
bus cpe	74

C-39N New Yorker (wb 127.5)

	Prod
sdn 4d	52,036
sdn 2d	545
club cpe	10,735
bus cpe	701

	Prod
conv cpe	3,000
chassis	2

C-38/39 Town & Country (wb 121.5; L8-127.5)

	Prod
sdn 4d, L6	3,950
brougham 2d, L6 (proto)	1
conv cpe, L6 (proto)	1
sdn 4d, L8	100
conv cpe, L8	8,380
htp cpe, L8 (proto)	7

C-40 Crown Imperial (wb 145.5)

	Prod
sdn 4d, 8P	750
limo 8P	650

1949 Second Series

C-45-1 Royal (wb 125.5; 8P-139.5)

	Wght	Price	Prod
sdn 4d	3,550	2,134	13,192
club cpe	3,495	2,114	4,849
wgn 4d, 9P	4,060	3,121	850
sdn 4d, 8P	4,200	2,823	185

C-45-2 Windsor (wb 125.5; 8P-139.5)

	Wght	Price	Prod
sdn 4d	3,681	2,329	55,879
club cpe	3,631	2,308	17,732
conv cpe	3,845	2,741	3,234
sdn 4d, 8P	4,290	3,017	373
limo 8P	4,430	3,144	73

C-46-1 Saratoga (wb 131.5)

	Wght	Price	Prod
sdn 4d	4,103	3,610	1,810
club cpe	4,037	2,585	465

C-46-2 New Yorker (wb 131.5)

	Wght	Price	Prod
sdn 4d	4,113	2,726	18,799
club cpe	4,048	2,700	4,524
conv cpe	4,277	3,206	1,137
chassis	—	—	1

C-46-2 Town & Country (wb 131.5)

	Wght	Price	Prod
conv cpe	4,630	3,970	1,000

C-46-2 Imperial (wb 131.5)

	Wght	Price	Prod
sdn 4d	4,300	4,665	50

C-47 Crown Imperial (wb 145.5)

	Wght	Price	Prod
sdn 4d, 8P	5,250	5,229	40
limo 8P	5,295	5,334	45

1949 Engines	bore×stroke	bhp	availability
L6, 250.6	3.44×4.50	116	S-Royal, Windsor
L8, 323.5	3.25×4.88	135	S-others

1950

C-48-1 Royal (wb 125.5; 8P-139.5)

	Wght	Price	Prod
sdn 4d	3,610	2,134	17,713
club cpe	3,540	2,114	5,900
Town & Country wgn 4d, wood	4,055	3,163	599
Town & Country wgn 4d, steel	3,964	2,735	100
sdn 4d, 8P	4,190	2,855	375

C-48-2 Windsor (wb 125.5; 8P-139.5)

	Wght	Price	Prod
sdn 4d	3,765	2,329	78,199
Traveler sdn 4d	3,830	2,560	900
club cpe	3,670	2,308	20,050
Newport htp cpe	3,875	2,637	9,925
conv cpe	3,905	2,741	2,201
sdn 4d, 8P	4,295	3,050	763
limo 8P	4,400	3,176	174
chassis	—	—	1

C-49-1 Saratoga (wb 131.5)	Wght	Price	Prod
sdn 4d	4,170	2,642	1,000
club cpe	4,110	2,616	300

C-49-2 New Yorker (wb 131.5)			
sdn 4d	4,190	2,758	22,633
club cpe	4,110	2,732	3,000
Newport htp cpe	4,370	3,133	2,800
conv cpe	4,360	3,232	899
wgn 4d, wood	—	proto	1
chassis	—	—	2

C-49-2 Town & Country (wb 131.5)			
Newport htp cpe	4,670	4,003	700

C-49-2 Imperial (wb 131.5)			
sdn 4d	4,245	3,055	9,500
Deluxe sdn 4d	4,250	3,176	1,150

C-50 Crown Imperial (wb 145.5)			
sdn 4d, 8P	5,235	5,229	209
limo 8P	5,305	5,334	205
chassis	—	—	1

1950 Engines	bore×stroke	bhp	availability
L6, 250.6	3.44×4.50	116	S-Royal, Windsor
L8, 323.5	3.25×4.88	135	S-others

1951

C-51W Windsor (wb 125.5; 8P-139.5)	Wght	Price	Prod
sdn 4d	3,527	2,390	10,151*
club cpe	3,570	2,368	4,243*
Town & Country wgn 4d	3,965	3,063	1,239*
sdn 4d, 8P	4,145	3,197	399*
ambulance (sp. order)	—	—	153
Deluxe sdn 4d	3,775	2,608	47,573*
Deluxe Traveler sdn 4d	3,890	2,867	850
Deluxe club cpe	3,700	2,585	8,365
Deluxe Newport htp cpe	3,855	2,953	6,426*
Deluxe conv cpe	3,945	3,071	2,646*
Deluxe sdn 4d, 8P	4,295	3,416	720
Deluxe limo 8P	4,415	3,557	152

C-55 Saratoga (wb 125.5; 8P-139.5)			
sdn 4d	4,018	3,016	22,375*
club cpe	3,948	2,989	5,355*
Newport htp cpe	—	proto	1
Town & Country wgn 4d	4,310	3,681	818*
sdn 4d, 8P	4,465	3,912	115*
ambulance (sp. order)	—	—	1

C-52 New Yorker (wb 131.5)			
sdn 4d	4,260	3,378	25,461*
club cpe	4,145	3,348	3,533
Newport htp cpe	4,330	3,798	3,654*
conv cpe	4,460	3,916	1,386*
Town & Country wgn 4d (4 C51s)	4,455	4,026	251
chassis	—	—	1

C-54 Imperial (wb 131.5)			
sdn 4d	4,350	3,674	13,678*
club cpe	4,230	3,661	2,226*
Newport htp cpe	4,380	4,042	749*
conv cpe	4,570	4,402	650

C-53 Crown Imperial (wb 145.5)			
sdn 4d, 8P	5,360	6,573	227*
limo 8P	5,450	6,690	213*
chassis	—	—	2

1951 Engines	bore×stroke	bhp	availability
L6, 250.6	3.44×4.50	116	S-Windsor
V8, 331.1	3.81×3.63	180	S-others

1952

C-51W Windsor (wb 125.5; 8P-139.5)	Wght	Price	Prod
sdn 4d	3,640	2,498	5,961*
club cpe	3,550	2,475	2,492*
Town & Country wgn 4d	4,015	3,200	728*
sdn 4d, 8P	4,145	3,342	234*
Deluxe sdn 4d	3,775	2,727	27,940*
Deluxe Newport htp cpe	3,855	3,087	3,774*
Deluxe conv cpe	3,990	3,210	1,554*

C-55 Saratoga (wb 125.5; 8P-139.5)			
sdn 4d	4,010	3,215	13,141*
club cpe	3,935	3,187	3,145*
Town & Country wgn 4d, 8P	4,345	3,925	481*
sdn 4d, 8P	4,510	4,172	68*

C-52 New Yorker (wb 131.5)			
sdn 4d	4,205	3,530	14,954*
Newport htp cpe	4,325	3,969	2,146*
conv cpe	4,450	4,093	814*

C-54 Imperial (wb 131.5)			
sdn 4d	4,315	3,839	8,033*
club cpe	4,220	3,826	1,307*
Newport htp cpe	4,365	4,224	440*

C-53 Crown Imperial (wb 145.5)			
sdn 4d, 8P	5,395	6,872	133*
limo 8P	5,430	6,994	125*

1952 Engines	bore×stroke	bhp	availability
L6, 264.5	3.44×4.75	119	S-Windsor
V8, 331.1	3.81×3.63	180	S-others

*As with other corporate makes, Chrysler combined model year production for 1951–52. However, production figures are known for several 1951-only body styles, making production estimates of remaining body styles (spanning both years) more accurate. In the above cases (*), estimates are based on the known percentages of the two-year run: 63% in 1951 and 37% in 1952.

1953

C-60-1 Windsor (wb 125.5; 8P-139.5)	Wght	Price	Prod
sdn 4d	3,660	2,462	18,879
club cpe	3,600	2,442	11,646
Town & Country wgn 4d	3,960	3,259	1,242
sdn 4d, 8P	4,170	3,403	425

C-60-2 Windsor Deluxe (wb 125.5)			
sdn 4d	3,775	2,691	45,385
Newport htp cpe	3,775	2,995	5,642
conv cpe	4,005	3,217	1,250

C-56-1 New Yorker (wb 125.5; 8P-139.5)			
sdn 4d	4,005	3,150	37,540
club cpe	3,925	3,121	7,749
Newport htp cpe	4,020	3,487	2,525
Town & Country wgn 4d	4,265	3,898	1,399
sdn 4d, 8P	4,510	4,334	100

C-56-2 New Yorker Deluxe (wb 125.5)			
sdn 4d	4,025	3,293	20,585
club cpe	3,925	3,264	1,934
Newport htp cpe	4,025	3,653	3,715
conv cpe	4,295	3,945	950
chassis	—	—	21

C-58 Custom Imperial (wb 133.5; htp cpe-131.5)			
sdn 4d	4,305	4,225	7,793
town limo 6P	4,525	4,762	243
Newport htp cpe	4,290	4,525	823

C-59 Crown Imperial (wb 145.5)			
sdn 4d, 8P	5,235	6,872	48

	Wght	Price	Prod
limo 8P	5,275	6,994	111
chassis	—	—	1

1953 Engines	bore×stroke	bhp	availability
L6, 264.5	3.44×4.75	119	S-Windsor
V8, 331.1	3.81×3.63	180	S-others

1954

C-62 Windsor Del (wb 125.5; 8P-139.5)

	Wght	Price	Prod
sdn 4d	3,655	2,562	33,563
club cpe	3,565	2,541	5,659
Newport htp cpe	3,685	2,831	3,655
conv cpe	3,915	3,046	500
Town & Country wgn 4d	3,955	3,321	650
sdn 4d, 8P	4,185	3,492	500

C-63-1 New Yorker (wb 125.5; 8P-139.5)

	Wght	Price	Prod
sdn 4d	3,970	3,229	15,788
club cpe	3,910	3,202	2,079
Newport htp cpe	4,005	3,503	1,312
Town & Country wgn 4d	4,245	4,024	1,100
sdn 4d, 8P	4,450	4,368	140

C-63-2 New Yorker Deluxe (wb 125.5)

	Wght	Price	Prod
sdn 4d	4,065	3,433	26,907
club cpe	4,005	3,406	1,861
Newport htp cpe	4,095	3,707	4,814
conv cpe	4,265	3,938	724
chassis	—	—	17

C-64 Custom Imperial (wb 133.5)

	Wght	Price	Prod
sdn 4d	4,355	4,260	4,324
town limo 6P	4,465	4,797	83
special town limo 6P	4,475	—	2
Newport htp cpe	4,345	4,560	1,249
conv cpe	—	proto	1
chassis	—	—	2

C-66 Crown Imperial (wb 145.5)

	Wght	Price	Prod
sdn 4d, 8P	5,220	6,922	23
limo 8P	5,295	7,044	77

1954 Engines	bore×stroke	bhp	availability
L6, 264.5	3.44×4.75	119	S-Windsor Deluxe
V8, 331.1	3.81×3.63	195	S-NY
V8, 331.1	3.81×3.63	235	S-others

1955

C-67 Windsor Deluxe (wb 126.0)

	Wght	Price	Prod
sdn 4d	3,925	2,660	63,896
Nassau htp cpe	3,930	2,703	18,474
Newport htp cpe	3,925	2,818	13,126
conv cpe	4,075	3,090	1,395
Town & Country wgn 4d	4,295	3,332	1,983

C-68 New Yorker Deluxe (wb 126.0)

	Wght	Price	Prod
sdn 4d	4,160	3,494	33,342
Newport htp cpe	4,140	3,652	5,777
St. Regis htp cpe	4,125	3,690	11,076
conv cpe	4,285	3,924	946
Town & Country wgn 4d	4,430	4,209	1,036
chassis	—	—	1

C-68 300 (wb 126.0)

	Wght	Price	Prod
htp cpe	4,005	4,110	1,725

1955 Engines	bore×stroke	bhp	availability
V8, 301.0	3.63×3.63	188	S-Windsor Deluxe
V8, 331.1	3.81×3.63	250	S-NY Deluxe
V8, 331.1	3.81×3.63	300	S-300

1956

C-71 Windsor (wb 126.0)

	Wght	Price	Prod
sdn 4d	3,900	2,870	53,119
Newport htp sdn	3,990	3,128	7,050
Nassau htp cpe	3,910	2,905	11,400
Newport htp cpe	3,920	3,041	10,800
conv cpe	4,100	3,336	1,011
Town & Country wgn 4d	4,290	3,598	2,700

C-72 New Yorker (wb 126.0)

	Wght	Price	Prod
sdn 4d	4,110	3,779	24,749
Newport htp sdn	4,220	4,102	3,599
Newport htp cpe	4,175	3,951	4,115
St. Regis htp cpe	4,175	3,995	6,686
conv cpe	4,360	4,243	921
Town & Country wgn 4d	4,460	4,523	1,070

C-72 300B (wb 126.0)

	Wght	Price	Prod
htp cpe	4,145	4,419	1,102

1956 Engines	bore×stroke	bhp	availability
V8, 331.1	3.81×3.63	225	S-Windsor
V8, 331.1	3.81×3.63	250	O-Windsor
V8, 354.0	3.94×3.63	280	S-NY
V8, 354.0	3.94×3.63	340	S-300B
V8, 354.0	3.94×3.63	355	O-300B

1957

C-75-1 Windsor (wb 126.0)

	Wght	Price	Prod
sdn 4d	3,995	3,088	17,639
htp sdn	4,030	3,217	14,354
htp cpe	3,925	3,153	14,027
Town & Country wgn 4d	4,210	3,575	2,035

C-75-2 Saratoga (wb 126.0)

	Wght	Price	Prod
sdn 4d	4,165	3,718	14,977
htp sdn	4,195	3,832	11,586
htp cpe	4,075	3,754	10,633

C-76 New Yorker (wb 126.0)

	Wght	Price	Prod
sdn 4d	4,315	4,173	12,369
htp sdn	4,330	4,259	10,948
htp cpe	4,220	4,202	8,863
conv cpe	4,365	4,638	1,049
Town & Country wgn 4d	4,490	4,746	1,391

C-76 300C (wb 126.0)

	Wght	Price	Prod
htp cpe	4,235	4,929	1,918
conv cpe	4,390	5,359	484

1957 Engines	bore×stroke	bhp	availability
V8, 354.0	3.94×3.63	285	S-Windsor
V8, 354.0	3.94×3.63	295	S-Saratoga
V8, 392.0	4.00×3.90	325	S-NY
V8, 392.0	4.00×3.90	375	S-300C
V8, 392.0	4.00×3.90	390	O-300C

1958

LC-1-L Windsor (wb 122.0)

	Wght	Price	Prod
sdn 4d	3,895	3,129	12,861
htp sdn	3,915	3,279	6,254
htp cpe	3,860	3,214	6,205
Town & Country wgn 4d, 9P	4,245	3,803	862
Town & Country wgn 4d, 6P	4,155	3,616	791
conv cpe	—	—	2

LC-2-M Saratoga (wb 126.0)

	Wght	Price	Prod
sdn 4d	4,120	3,818	8,698
htp sdn	4,145	3,955	5,322

		Wght	Price	Prod
	htp cpe	4,045	3,878	4,466

LC-3-H New Yorker (wb 126.0)

		Wght	Price	Prod
	sdn 4d	4,195	4,295	7,110
	htp sdn	4,240	4,404	5,227
	htp cpe	4,205	4,347	3,205
	conv cpe	4,350	4,761	666
	Town & Country wgn 4d, 9P	4,445	5,083	775
	Town & Country wgn 4d, 6P	4,435	4,868	428

LC-3-S 300D (wb 126.0)

		Wght	Price	Prod
	htp cpe	4,305	5,173	618
	conv cpe	4,475	5,603	191

1958 Engines

	bore×stroke	bhp	availability
V8, 354.0	3.94×3.63	290	S-Windsor
V8, 354.0	3.94×3.63	310	S-Saratoga
V8, 392.0	4.00×3.90	345	S-NY
V8, 392.0	4.00×3.90	380	S-300D
V8, 392.0	4.00×3.90	390	O-300D

1959

MC-1-L Windsor (wb 122.0)

		Wght	Price	Prod
512	htp cpe	3,830	3,289	6,775
513	sdn 4d	3,800	3,204	19,910
514	htp sdn	3,735	3,353	6,084
515	conv cpe	3,950	3,620	961
576	Town & Country wgn 4d, 6P	4,045	3,691	751
577	Town & Country wgn 4d, 9P	4,070	3,878	992

MC-2-M Saratoga (wb 126.0)

532	htp cpe	3,970	4,026	3,753
533	sdn 4d	4,010	3,966	8,783
534	htp sdn	4,035	4,104	4,943

MC-3-H New Yorker (wb 126.0)

552	htp cpe	4,080	4,476	2,434
553	sdn 4d	4,120	4,424	7,792
554	htp sdn	4,165	4,533	4,805
555	conv cpe	4,270	4,890	286
578	Town & Country wgn 6P	4,295	4,997	444
579	Town & Country wgn 9P	4,360	5,212	564
—	chassis	—	—	3

MC-3-H 300E (wb 126.0)

592	htp cpe	4,290	5,319	550
595	conv cpe	4,350	5,749	140

1959 Engines

	bore×stroke	bhp	availability
V8, 383.0	4.03×3.75	305	S-Windsor
V8, 383.0	4.03×3.75	325	S-Saratoga
V8, 413.0	4.18×3.75	350	S-NY
V8, 413.0	4.18×3.75	380	S-300E

1960

PC-1-L Windsor (wb 122.0)

		Wght	Price	Prod
23	htp cpe	3,855	3,279	6,496
27	conv cpe	3,855	3,623	1,467
41	sdn 4d	3,815	3,194	25,152
43	htp sdn	3,850	3,343	5,897
46	Town & Country wgn 4d, 6P	4,235	3,733	1,120
46	Town & Country wgn 4d, 9P	4,390	3,814	1,026

PC-2-M Saratoga (wb 126.0)

23	htp cpe	4,030	3,989	2,963
41	sdn 4d	4,010	3,929	8,463
43	htp sdn	4,035	4,067	4,099

PC-3-H New Yorker (wb 126.0)

23	htp cpe	4,175	4,461	2,835

		Wght	Price	Prod
27	conv cpe	4,185	4,875	556
41	sdn 4d	4,145	4,409	9,079
43	htp sdn	4,175	4,518	5,625
46	Town & Country wgn 6P	4,515	5,022	624
46	Town & Country wgn 9P	4,535	5,131	671

PC-3-H 300F (wb 126.0)

23	htp cpe	4,270	5,411	964
27	conv cpe	4,310	5,841	248

1960 Engines

	bore×stroke	bhp	availability
V8, 383.0	4.03×3.75	305	S-Windsor
V8, 383.0	4.03×3.75	325	S-Saratoga
V8, 413.0	4.18×3.75	350	S-NY
V8, 413.0	4.18×3.75	375	S-300F
V8, 413.0	4.18×3.75	400	O-300F

1961

RC-1-L Newport (wb 122.0)

		Wght	Price	Prod
812	htp cpe	3,690	3,025	9,405
813	sdn 4d	3,710	2,964	34,370
814	htp sdn	3,730	3,104	7,789
815	conv cpe	3,760	3,442	2,135
858	Town & Country wgn 4d, 6P	4,070	3,541	1,832
859	Town & Country wgn 4d, 9P	4,155	3,622	1,571

RC-2-M Windsor (wb 122.0)

822	htp cpe	3,710	3,303	2,941
823	sdn 4d	3,730	3,218	10,239
824	htp sdn	3,765	3,367	4,156

RC-3-H New Yorker (wb 126.0)

832	htp cpe	4,065	4,175	2,541
833	sdn 4d	4,055	4,123	9,984
834	htp sdn	4,100	4,261	5,862
835	conv cpe	4,070	4,592	576
878	Town & Country wgn 4d, 6P	4,425	4,764	676
879	Town & Country wgn 4d, 9P	4,455	4,871	760

RC-4-P 300G (wb 126.0)

842	htp cpe	4,260	5,411	1,280
845	conv cpe	4,315	5,841	337

1961 Engines

	bore×stroke	bhp	availability
V8, 361.0	4.12×3.38	265	S-Newport
V8, 383.0	4.25×3.38	305	S-Windsor
V8, 413.0	4.18×3.75	350	S-NY
V8, 413.0	4.18×3.75	375	S-300G
V8, 413.0	4.18×3.75	400	O-300G

1962

SC1-L Newport (wb 122.0)

		Wght	Price	Prod
812	htp cpe	3,650	3,027	11,910
813	sdn 4d	3,690	2,964	54,813
814	htp sdn	3,715	3,106	8,712
815	conv cpe	3,740	3,399	2,051
858	Town & Country wgn 4d, 6P	4,060	3,478	3,271
859	Town & Country wgn 4d, 9P	4,090	3,586	2,363

SC2-M 300 (wb 122.0)

822	htp cpe	3,750	3,323	11,341
823	sdn 4d	—	—	1,801
824	htp sdn	3,760	3,400	10,030
825	conv cpe	3,815	3,883	1,848

SC3-H New Yorker (wb 126.0)

833	sdn 4d	3,925	4,125	12,056
834	htp sdn	4,005	4,263	6,646
878	Town & Country wgn 4d, 6P	4,225	4,766	728

		Wght	Price	Prod
879	Town & Country wgn 4d, 9P	4,455	4,873	793

SC2-M 300H (wb 122.0)

842	htp cpe	4,010	5,090	435
845	conv cpe	4,080	5,461	123

1962 Engines	bore×stroke	bhp	availability
V8, 361.0	4.12×3.38	265	S-Newport
V8, 383.0	4.25×3.38	305	S-300
V8, 413.0	4.18×3.75	340	S-NY
V8, 413.0	4.18×3.75	380	S-300H
V8, 413.0	4.18×3.75	405	O-300H

1963

TC1-L Newport (wb 122.0)

		Wght	Price	Prod
812	htp cpe	3,760	3,027	9,809
813	sdn 4d	3,770	2,964	49,067
814	htp sdn	3,800	3,106	8,437
815	conv cpe	3,825	3,399	2,093
858	Town & Country wgn 4d, 6P	4,200	3,478	3,618
859	Town & Country wgn 4d, 9P	4,215	3,586	2,948

TC2-M 300 (wb 122.0)

802	Pace Setter htp cpe	3,790	3,769	306
822	htp cpe	3,790	3,430	9,423
805	Pace Setter conv cpe	3,840	4,129	1,861
825	conv cpe	3,845	3,790	1,535
823	sdn 4d	3,790	—	1,625
824	htp sdn	3,815	3,400	9,915

TC3-H New Yorker (wb 122.0)

833	sdn 4d	3,910	4,981	14,884
834	htp sdn	3,950	4,118	10,229
884	Salon htp sdn	4,290	5,860	593
878	Town & Country wgn 4d, 6P	4,350	4,708	950
879	Town & Country wgn 4d, 9P	4,370	4,815	1,244

TC2-M 300J (wb 122.0)

842	htp cpe	4,000	5,184	400

1963 Engines	bore×stroke	bhp	availability
V8, 361.0	4.12×3.38	265	S-Newport
V8, 383.0	4.25×3.38	305	S-300
V8, 413.0	4.19×3.75	340	S-NY
V8, 413.0	4.19×3.75	360	S-300J; O-300
V8, 413.0	4.19×3.75	390	S-300J

1964

VC1-L Newport (wb 122.0)

		Wght	Price	Prod
812	htp cpe	3,760	2,962	10,579
813	sdn 4d	3,805	2,901	55,957
814	htp sdn	3,795	3,042	9,710
815	conv cpe	3,810	3,334	2,176
858	Town & Country wgn 4d, 6P	4,175	3,414	3,720
859	Town & Country wgn 4d, 9P	4,200	3,521	3,041

VC2-M 300 (wb 122.0)*

822	htp cpe	3,850	3,443	18,379
824	htp sdn	3,865	3,521	11,460
823	sdn 4d	—	—	2,078
825	conv cpe	4,120	3,803	1,401

VC3-H New Yorker (wb 122.0)

832	htp cpe	—	—	300
833	sdn 4d	4,015	3,994	15,443
834	htp sdn	4,035	4,131	10,887
878	Town & Country wgn 4d, 6P	4,385	4,721	1,190

		Wght	Price	Prod
879	Town & Country wgn 4d, 9P	4,395	4,828	1,603
884	Salon htp sdn	4,280	5,860	1,621

VC2-M 300K (wb 122.0)*

842	htp cpe	3,965	4,056	3,022
845	conv cpe	3,995	4,522	625

*Silver 300 models: 300—2,152; 300K series—255.

1964 Engines	bore×stroke	bhp	availability
V8, 361.0	4.12×3.38	265	S-Newport
V8, 383.0	4.25×3.38	305	S-300
V8, 413.0	4.19×3.75	340	S-NY; O-300
V8, 413.0	4.19×3.75	360	S-300K; O-300
V8, 413.0	4.19×3.75	390	O-300K

1965

AC1-L Newport (wb 124.0; wgns-121.0)

		Wght	Price	Prod
C12	htp cpe	4,035	3,070	23,655
C13	sdn 4d, 4W	4,045	3,009	61,054
C14	htp sdn	4,050	3,149	17,062
C15	conv cpe	4,025	3,442	3,192
C18	town sdn 4d, 6W	4,000	3,146	12,411
C56	Town & Country wgn 4d, 6P	4,360	3,521	4,683
C57	Town & Country wgn 4d, 9P	4,455	3,629	3,738

AC2-M 300 (wb 124.0)

C22	htp cpe	4,085	3,551	11,621
C24	htp sdn 4W	4,150	3,628	12,452
C25	conv cpe	4,140	3,911	1,418
C28	htp town sdn 6W	—	—	2,187

AC3-H New Yorker (wb 124.0; wgns-121.0)

C32	htp cpe	4,270	4,161	9,357
C34	htp sdn	4,295	4,238	21,110
C38	town sdn 4d, 6W	4,265	4,104	16,239
C76	Town & Country wgn 4d, 6P	4,650	4,827	1,368
C77	Town & Country wgn 4d, 9P	4,745	4,935	1,697

AC2-P 300L (wb 124.0)

C42	htp cpe	4,245	4,153	2,405
C45	conv cpe	4,170	4,618	440

1965 Engines	bore×stroke	bhp	availability
V8, 383.0	4.25×3.38	270	S-Newport; O-300
V8, 383.0	4.25×3.38	315	S-300; O-Newport
V8, 413.0	4.19×3.75	340	S-NY
V8, 413.0	4.19×3.75	360	S-300L; O-300, NY

1966

BC1-L Newport (wb 124.0; wgns-121.0)

		Wght	Price	Prod
23	htp cpe	3,920	3,112	37,622
27	conv cpe	4,020	3,476	3,085
41	sdn 4d, 4W	3,875	3,052	74,964
42	sdn 4d, 6W	3,910	3,183	9,432
43	htp sdn	4,010	3,190	24,966
45	wgn 4d, 6P	4,370	4,086	9,035
46	wgn 4d, 9P	4,550	4,192	8,567

BC2-M 300 (wb 124.0)

23	htp cpe	3,940	3,583	24,103
27	conv cpe	4,015	3,936	2,500
41	sdn 4d	3,895	3,523	2,353
43	htp sdn	4,000	3,659	20,642

BC3-H New Yorker (wb 124.0)

23	htp cpe	4,095	4,157	7,955
42	sdn 4d	4,100	4,101	13,025

			Wght	Price	Prod
43	htp sdn		4,140	4,233	26,599

1966 Engines	bore×stroke	bhp	availability
V8, 383.0	4.25×3.38	270	S-Newport
V8, 383.0	4.25×3.38	325	S-300; O-Newport
V8, 440.0	4.32×3.75	350	S-NY

1967

CC1-E Newport (wb 124.0; wgns-122.0)		Wght	Price	Prod
23	htp cpe	3,920	3,219	26,583
27	conv cpe	3,970	3,583	2,891
41	sdn 4d	3,955	3,159	48,945
43	htp sdn	3,980	3,296	14,247
45	wgn 4d, 6P	4,495	4,264	7,183
46	wgn 4d, 9P	4,550	4,369	7,520

CC1-L Newport Custom (wb 124.0)		Wght	Price	Prod
23	htp cpe	3,935	3,407	14,193
41	sdn 4d	3,975	3,347	23,101
43	htp sdn	3,995	3,485	12,728

CC2-M 300 (wb 124.0)		Wght	Price	Prod
23	htp cpe	4,070	3,936	11,556
27	conv cpe	4,105	4,289	1,594
43	htp sdn	4,135	4,012	8,744

CC3-H New Yorker (wb 124.0)		Wght	Price	Prod
23	htp cpe	4,170	4,264	6,885
41	sdn 4d	4,185	4,208	10,907
43	htp sdn	4,240	4,339	21,665

1967 Engines	bore×stroke	bhp	availability
V8, 383.0	4.25×3.38	270	S-Newport
V8, 383.0	4.25×3.38	325	O-Newport
V8, 440.0	4.32×3.75	350	S-300, NY; O-wgns
V8, 440.0	4.32×3.75	375	O-all exc wgns

1968

DC1-E Newport (wb 124.0; wgns-122.0)		Wght	Price	Prod
CE23	htp cpe*	3,840	3,366	36,768
CE27	conv cpe*	3,910	3,704	2,847
CE41	sdn 4d	3,850	3,306	61,436
CE43	htp sdn	3,865	3,444	20,191
CE45	Town & Country wgn 4d, 6P	4,340	4,418	9,908
CE46	Town & Country wgn 4d, 9P	4,410	4,523	12,223

DC1-L Newport Custom (wb 124.0)		Wght	Price	Prod
CL23	htp cpe	3,890	3,552	10,341
CL41	sdn 4d	3,855	3,493	16,915
CL43	htp sdn	3,860	3,631	11,640

DC2-M 300 (wb 124.0)		Wght	Price	Prod
CM23	htp cpe	3,985	4,010	16,953
CM27	conv cpe	4,050	4,337	2,161
CM43	htp sdn	4,015	4,086	15,507

DC3-H New Yorker (wb 124.0)		Wght	Price	Prod
CH23	htp cpe	4,060	4,424	8,060
CH41	sdn 4d	4,055	4,367	13,092
CH43	htp sdn	4,090	4,500	26,991

*Sportsgrain models: htp cpe 965; conv cpe 175.

1968 Engines	bore×stroke	bhp	availability
V8, 383.0	4.25×3.38	290	S-Newport, T&C
V8, 383.0	4.25×3.38	330	O-Newport, T&C
V8, 440.0	4.32×3.75	350	S-300, NY; O-T&C
V8, 440.0	4.32×3.75	375	O-all exc T&C

1969

EC-E Newport (wb 124.0)*		Wght	Price	Prod
CE23	htp cpe	3,891	3,485	33,639
CE27	conv cpe	4,026	3,823	2,169
CE41	sdn 4d	3,941	3,414	55,083
CE43	htp sdn	4,156	3,549	20,608

EC-L Newport Custom (wb 124.0)		Wght	Price	Prod
CL23	htp cpe	3,891	3,652	10,995
CL41	sdn 4d	3,951	3,580	18,401
CL43	htp sdn	3,971	3,730	15,981

EC-P Town & Country (wb 122.0)		Wght	Price	Prod
CP45	wgn 4d, 6P	4,435	4,583	10,108
CP46	wgn 4d, 9P	4,485	4,669	14,408

EC-M 300 (wb 124.0)		Wght	Price	Prod
CM23	htp cpe	3,965	4,104	16,075
CM27	conv cpe	4,095	4,450	1,933
CM43	htp sdn	4,045	4,183	14,464

EC-H New Yorker (wb 124.0)		Wght	Price	Prod
CH23	htp cpe	4,070	4,539	7,539
CH41	sdn 4d	4,135	4,487	12,253
CH43	htp sdn	4,165	4,615	27,157

*Sportsgrain models 195.

1969 Engines	bore×stroke	bhp	availability
V8, 383.0	4.25×3.38	290	S-Newport, T&C
V8, 383.0	4.25×3.38	330	O-Newport, T&C
V8, 440.0	4.32×3.75	350	S-300, NY; O-T&C
V8, 440.0	4.32×3.75	375	O-all exc T&C

1970

FC-E Newport (wb 124.0)		Wght	Price	Prod
CE23	htp cpe*	4,030	3,589	21,664
CE27	conv cpe	4,085	3,925	1,124
CE41	sdn 4d	4,080	3,514	39,285
CE43	htp sdn*	4,110	3,652	16,940

FC-L Newport Custom (wb 124.0)		Wght	Price	Prod
CL23	htp cpe	4,035	3,781	6,639
CL41	sdn 4d	4,091	3,710	13,767
CL43	htp sdn	4,125	3,861	10,873

FC-P Town & Country (wb 122.0)		Wght	Price	Prod
CP45	wgn 4d, 6P	4,490	4,738	5,686
CP46	wgn 4d, 9P	4,555	4,824	9,583

FC-M 300 (wb 124.0)		Wght	Price	Prod
CM23	htp cpe*	4,135	4,234	10,084
CM27	conv cpe	4,175	4,580	1,077
CM43	htp sdn	4,220	4,313	9,846

FC-H New Yorker (wb 124.0)		Wght	Price	Prod
CH23	htp cpe	4,235	4,681	4,917
CH41	sdn 4d	4,310	4,630	9,389
CH43	htp sdn	4,335	4,761	19,903

*CE23 includes 1,868 Cordoba htp cpes; CE43 includes 1,873 Cordoba htp sdns; CM23 includes 400 300-H "Hurst" htp cpes.

1970 Engines	bore×stroke	bhp	availability
V8, 383.0	4.25×3.38	290	S-Newport, T&C
V8, 383.0	4.25×3.38	330	O-Newport auto, T&C
V8, 440.0	4.32×3.75	350	S-NY, 300; O-T&C
V8, 440.0	4.32×3.75	375	O-all exc T&C

1971

CE Newport (wb 124.0)		Wght	Price	Prod
23	Royal htp cpe	4,121	4,153	8,500
23	htp cpe	4,121	4,265	13,549
41	Royal sdn 4d	4,171	4,078	19,662
41	sdn 4d	4,171	4,190	24,834
43	Royal htp sdn	4,191	4,216	5,188
43	htp sdn	4,191	4,265	10,800

CP Town & Country (wb 122.0)				
45	wgn 4d 2S	4,525	4,951	5,697
46	wgn 4d 3S	4,580	5,037	10,993

CL Newport Custom (wb 124.0)				
23	htp cpe	4,126	4,391	5,527
41	sdn 4d	4,181	4,319	11,254
43	htp sdn	4,211	4,471	10,207

CS 300 (wb 124.0)				
23	htp cpe	4,246	4,608	7,256
43	htp sdn	4,321	4,687	6,683

CH New Yorker (wb 124.0)				
23	htp cpe	4,250	4,961	4,485
41	sdn 4d	4,335	4,910	9,850
43	htp sdn	4,355	5,041	20,633

1971 Engines	bore×stroke	bhp	availability
V8, 360.0	4.00×3.58	255	S-CE, Royal
V8, 383.0	4.25×3.38	275	S-CL,CP; O-CE Royal
V8, 383.0	4.25×3.38	300	O-CL,CP,CE Royal
V8, 440.0	4.32×3.75	335	O-CE,CL,CP;S-CS,CH
V8, 440.0	4.32×3.75	370	O-CE,CL,CP,CS,CH

1972

CL Newport Royal (wb 124.0)		Wght	Price	Prod
23	htp cpe	4,035	4,124	22,622
41	sdn 4d	4,095	4,051	47,437
43	htp sdn	4,100	4,186	15,185

CM Newport Custom (wb 124.0)				
23	htp cpe	4,130	4,357	10,326
41	sdn 4d	4,185	4,435	19,278
43	htp sdn	4,195	4,435	15,457

CP Town & Country (wb 122.0)				
45	wgn 4d 2S	4,610	5,055	6,473
46	wgn 4d 3S	4,665	5,139	14,116

CH New Yorker (wb 124.0)				
23	htp cpe	4,270	4,915	5,567
41	sdn 4d	4,335	4,865	7,296
43	htp sdn	4,365	4,993	10,013

CS New Yorker Brougham (wb 124.0)				
23	htp cpe	4,270	5,271	4,635
41	sdn 4d	4,335	5,222	5,971
43	htp sdn	4,365	5,350	20,328

1972 Engines	bore×stroke	bhp	availability
V8, 360.0	4.00×3.58	175	S-CL
V8, 400.0	4.34×3.38	190	S-CM,CP; O-CL
V8, 440.0	4.32×3.75	225	S-CH,CS;O-CL,CM,CP

1973

CL Newport (wb 124.0)		Wght	Price	Prod
23	htp cpe	4,160	4,254	27,456
41	sdn 4d	4,200	4,181	54,147
43	htp sdn	4,210	4,316	20,175

CM Newport Custom (wb 124.0)				
23	htp cpe	4,145	4,484	12,293
41	sdn 4d	4,200	4,419	20,092
43	htp sdn	4,225	4,567	20,050

CP Town & Country (wb 122.0)				
45	wgn 4d 2S	4,670	5,241	5,353
46	wgn 4d 3S	4,725	5,266	14,687

CH New Yorker (wb 124.0)				
41	sdn 4d	4,355	4,997	7,991
43	htp sdn	4,375	5,125	7,619

CS New Yorker Brougham (wb 124.0)				
23	htp cpe	4,335	5,413	9,190
41	sdn 4d	4,425	5,364	8,541
43	htp sdn	4,440	5,492	26,635

1973 Engines	bore×stroke	bhp	availability
V8, 400.0	4.34×3.38	185	S-CL,CM
V8, 440.0	4.32×3.75	215	S-CP,CH,CS; O-CL,CM

1974

CL Newport (wb 124.0)		Wght	Price	Prod
23	htp cpe	4,380	4,752	13,784
41	sdn 4d	4,430	4,677	26,944
43	htp sdn	4,440	4,816	8,968

CM Newport Custom (wb 124.0)				
23	htp cpe	4,430	5,105	7,206
41	sdn 4d	4,480	5,038	10,569
43	htp sdn	4,500	5,190	9,892

CP Town & Country (wb 124.0)				
45	wgn 4d 2S	4,915	5,767	2,236
46	wgn 4d 3S	4,970	5,896	5,958

CH New Yorker (wb 124.0)				
41	sdn 4d	4,560	5,554	3,072
43	htp sdn	4,595	5,686	3,066

CS New Yorker Brougham (wb 124.0)				
23	htp cpe	4,540	5,982	7,980
41	sdn 4d	4,640	5,931	4,533
43	htp sdn	4,655	6,063	13,165

1974 Engines	bore×stroke	bhp	availability
V8, 400.0	4.34×3.38	185	S-CL,CM
V8, 400.0	4.34×3.38	205	O-CL,CM
V8, 440.0	4.32×3.75	230	S-CP,CH,CS; O-CL,CM
V8, 440.0	4.32×3.75	275	O-CH,CS

1975

SS Cordoba (wb 115.0)		Wght	Price	Prod
22	cpe	3,975	5,072	150,105

CL Newport (wb 124.0)				
23	htp cpe	4,395	4,937	10,485
41	sdn 4d	4,440	4,854	24,339
43	htp sdn	4,475	5,008	6,846

CM Newport Custom (wb 124.0)				
23	htp cpe	4,450	5,329	5,831
41	sdn 4d	4,500	5,254	9,623
43	htp sdn	4,520	5,423	11,626

CP Town & Country (wb 124.0)				
45	wgn 4d 2S	5,015	6,099	1,891
46	wgn 4d 3S	5,050	6,244	4,764

CS New Yorker Brougham (wb 124.0)				
23	htp cpe	4,650	6,334	7,567

Chrysler

		Wght	Price	Prod
41	sdn 4d	4,630	6,277	5,698
43	htp sdn	4,690	6,424	12,774

1975 Engines	bore×stroke	bhp	availability
V8, 318.0	3.91×3.31	150	O-SS
V8, 360.0	4.00×3.58	180	S-SS; O-CL,CM
V8, 360.0	4.00×3.58	190	O-CL,CM
V8, 400.0	4.34×3.38	165	O-SS
V8, 400.0	4.34×3.38	175	S-CL,CM; O-CS
V8, 400.0	4.34×3.38	190	O-SS
V8, 400.0	4.34×3.38	195	O-CL,CM,CS
V8, 400.0	4.34×3.38	235	O-SS
V8, 440.0	4.32×3.75	215	S-CP,CS; O-others
V8, 440.0	4.32×3.75	260	O-CP

1976

SS Cordoba (wb 115.0)		Wght	Price	Prod
22	cpe	4,130	5,392	120,462

CL Newport (wb 124.0)		Wght	Price	Prod
23	htp cpe	4,455	5,076	6,109
41	sdn 4d	4,490	4,993	10,370
43	htp sdn	4,525	5,147	5,908

CM Newport Custom (wb 124.0)		Wght	Price	Prod
23	htp cpe	4,530	5,479	6,448
41	sdn 4d	4,565	5,407	11,587
43	htp sdn	4,585	5,576	9,893

CP Town & Country (wb 124.0)		Wght	Price	Prod
45	wgn 5d 2S	5,045	6,084	1,770
46	wgn 5d 3S	5,075	6,244	3,769

CS New Yorker Brougham (wb 124.0)		Wght	Price	Prod
23	htp cpe	4,865	6,641	11,510
43	htp sdn	4,950	6,737	28,327

1976 Engines	bore×stroke	bhp	availability
V8, 318.0	3.91×3.31	150	O-SS
V8, 360.0	4.00×3.58	170/175	O-SS,CL,CM
V8, 400.0	4.34×3.38	175	S-SS,CL,CM; O-CS
V8, 400.0	4.34×3.38	210	O-all
V8, 400.0	4.34×3.38	240	O-SS
V8, 440.0	4.32×3.75	205	S-CP,CS; O-others

1977

FH LeBaron (wb 112.7)—54,851 built (incl. FP)		Wght	Price	Prod
22	cpe	3,510	5,066	—
41	sdn 4d	3,560	5,224	—

FP LeBaron Medallion (wb 112.7)				
22	cpe	3,615	5,436	—
41	sdn 4d	3,675	5,594	—

Cordoba (wb 115.0)				
SP22	cpe	NA	5,368	183,146
SS22	cpe	4,045	5,418	

CL Newport (wb 124.0)				
23	htp cpe	4,400	5,374	16,227
41	sdn 4d	4,455	5,280	39,424
43	htp sdn	4,485	5,433	20,738

CP Town & Country (wb 124.0)				
45	wgn 5d 2S	5,025	6,461	2,488
46	wgn 5d 3S	5,060	6,647	6,081

CS New Yorker Brougham (wb 124.0)				
23	htp cpe	4,685	7,090	19,732
43	htp sdn	4,770	7,215	56,010

1977 Engines	bore×stroke	bhp	availability
V8, 318.0	3.91×3.31	135	O-Cordoba
V8, 318.0	3.91×3.31	145	S-LeB; O-Crdba
V8, 360.0	4.00×3.58	155	O-Crdba,Nwpt
V8, 360.0	4.00×3.58	170	O-Crdba
V8, 400.0	4.34×3.38	190	S-Crdba,Nwpt; O-T&C,NY
V8, 440.0	4.32×3.75	195	S-T&C,NY; O-others

1978

LeBaron (wb 112.7)		Wght	Price	Prod
FM22	"S" cpe L6	3,335	4,894	NA
FM22	"S" cpe V8	3,415	5,080	NA
FM41	"S" sdn 4d L6	3,400	5,060	NA
FM41	"S" sdn 4d V8	3,485	5,246	NA
FH22	cpe L6	3,420	5,144	16,273
FH22	cpe V8	3,505	5,330	
FH41	sdn 4d L6	3,465	5,310	22,732
FH41	sdn 4d V8	3,550	5,496	

1978 LeBaron Medallion coupe

1977 Cordoba coupe

1978 LeBaron Town & Country wagon

		Wght	Price	Prod
FP22	Medallion cpe L6	3,495	5,526	37,138
FP22	Medallion cpe V8	3,580	5,712	
FP41	Medallion sdn 4d L6	3,550	5,692	44,291
FP41	Medallion sdn 4d V8	3,635	5,878	
FH45	Town & Country wgn 5d 2S L6	3,600	5,724	25,256
FH45	Town & Country wgn 5d 2S V8	3,685	5,910	

Cordoba (wb 114.9)

		Wght	Price	Prod
SS22	cpe	4,020	5,811	124,825
SS22	S cpe	NA	5,611	

Newport (wb 123.9)

		Wght	Price	Prod
CL23	htp cpe	4,395	5,804	8,877
CL43	htp sdn	4,460	5,888	30,078

New Yorker Brougham (wb 123.9)

		Wght	Price	Prod
CS23	htp cpe	4,620	7,702	11,469
CS43	htp sdn	4,670	7,831	33,090

1978 Engines	bore×stroke	bhp	availability
L6, 225.0	3.40×3.12	90	O-LeBaron
L6, 225.0	3.40×3.12	110	S-LeBaron
V8, 318.0	3.91×3.31	140	S-LeB; O-Crdba
V8, 318.0	3.91×3.31	155	O-LeB; Crdba
V8, 360.0	4.00×3.58	155	S-Crdba S; O-others
V8, 360.0	4.00×3.58	170	O-all
V8, 400.0	4.34×3.38	190	S-Crdba,Nwpt,NY; O-Crdba S
V8, 440.0	4.32×3.75	185/195	O-Nwpt,NY

1979

LeBaron (wb 112.7)

		Wght	Price	Prod
FM22	cpe L6	3,270	5,381	10,987
FM22	cpe V8	3,365	5,692	
FM41	sdn 4d L6	3,330	5,479	14,297
FM41	sdn 4d V8	3,425	5,790	
FH22	Salon cpe L6	3,285	5,623	17,637
FH22	Salon cpe V8	3,385	5,934	
FH41	Salon sdn 4d L6	3,350	5,851	18,843
FH41	Salon sdn 4d V8	3,450	6,162	

		Wght	Price	Prod
FP22	Medallion cpe L6	3,345	6,017	21,762
FP22	Medallion cpe V8	3,440	6,328	
FP41	Medallion sdn 4d L6	3,425	6,425	25,041
FP41	Medallion sdn 4d V8	3,520	6,556	
FH45	Town & Country wgn 4d 2S L6	3,585	6,331	19,932
FH45	Town & Country wgn 4d 2S V8	3,675	6,642	

Cordoba (wb 114.9)

		Wght	Price	Prod
SS22	cpe	3,680	6,337	88,015
SP22	"300" cpe	3,880	8,034	

Newport (wb 118.5)

		Wght	Price	Prod
TH42	sdn 4d L6	3,530	6,405	78,296
TH42	sdn 4d V8	3,605	6,720	

New Yorker (wb 118.5)

		Wght	Price	Prod
TP42	sdn 4d	3,800	10,026	54,640

1979 Engines	bore×stroke	bhp	availability
L6, 225.0	3.40×3.12	100	S-LeBaron
L6, 225.0	3.40×3.12	110	S-Nwpt; O-LeB
V8, 318.0	3.91×3.31	135	S-LeB,Crdba,Nwpt; O-NY
V8, 360.0	4.00×3.58	150	S-NY; O-others
V8, 360.0	4.00×3.58	195	S-"300"; O-others

1980

LeBaron (wb 112.7)

		Wght	Price	Prod
FL41	Special sdn 4d L6	3,260	5,995	—
FM22	cpe L6	3,220	6,362	8,181
FM22	cpe V8	3,300	6,457	
FM41	sdn 4d L6	3,300	6,518	8,470
FM41	sdn 4d V8	3,385	6,613	
FM45	wgn 4d 2S L6	3,455	6,723	1,887
FM45	wgn 4d 2S V8	3,535	6,818	
FH22	Salon cpe L6	3,230	6,643	18,538
FH22	Salon cpe V8	3,310	6,738	
FH41	Salon sdn 4d L6	3,325	6,764	10,762
FH41	Salon sdn 4d V8	3,405	6,859	
FP22	Medallion cpe L6	3,285	7,185	10,448
FP22	Medallion cpe V8	3,360	7,280	
FP41	Medallion sdn 4d L6	3,400	7,329	13,079
FP41	Medallion sdn 4d V8	3,485	7,424	
FH45	Town & Country wgn 5d 2S L6	3,525	7,324	11,100
FH45	Town & Country wgn 5d 2S V8	3,610	7,419	

Cordoba (wb 112.7)

		Wght	Price	Prod
SH22	cpe L6	3,270	6,978	31,238
SH22	cpe V8	3,355	7,073	
SP22	Crown cpe L6	3,320	7,428	
SP22	Crown cpe V8	3,400	7,523	
SS22	LS cpe L6	3,270	6,745	22,233
SP22	LS cpe V8	3,365	6,840	
SP22	"300" cpe V8	NA	NA	

Newport (wb 118.5)

		Wght	Price	Prod
TH42	sdn 4d L6	3,545	7,247	15,061
TH42	sdn 4d V8	3,630	7,343	

New Yorker (wb 118.5)

		Wght	Price	Prod
TP42	sdn 4d	3,810	10,872	13,513

1980 Engines	bore×stroke	bhp	availability
L6, 225.0	3.40×3.12	90	S-all sixes
V8, 318.0	3.91×3.31	120	S-all V8s exc "300"
V8, 360.0	4.00×3.58	130	O-Nwpt,NY
V8, 360.0	4.00×3.58	185	S-Crdba "300"

Note: Chrysler production includes export models, usually a small fraction of the total, which makes figures in this book somewhat higher than those quoted elsewhere.

Clipper

Packard-Clipper Division, Studebaker-Packard Corp. Detroit, Michigan

Marketing wizard James J. Nance became president of Packard in 1952. Immediately, he started to divorce the medium-priced 200 models from Packard's luxury lines, declaring that continued emphasis on cheaper models after World War II had been "bleeding the Packard name white." Accordingly, the 200 became the Packard Clipper in 1953. For 1956, Nance registered Clipper as a separate make. There were also separate Packard and Clipper dealer signs, and even the factory was renamed Packard-Clipper Division of Studebaker-Packard Corporation. The Packard name appeared nowhere on Clippers except for a tiny script on the decklid. Early production models didn't even have that.

Nance's aim was to distinguish the Clipper still further from the "senior" Packard. Plans for 1957 called for Clipper to use the larger Studebaker bodyshell while Packard would continue with one of its own. That never materialized, however, because lenders failed to commit sufficient funds for the corporation to finance its all-new 1957 line. Nance resigned in August 1956.

Studebaker-Packard received temporary reprieve by way of a management agreement with Curtiss-Wright Corporation, which needed S-P mainly as a tax loss. Under C-W management, the Packard name was saved for 1957's deluxe line of Studebaker-based cars. But these were called Packard Clippers, so Clipper disappeared as a distinct make after only a year.

The 1956 Clipper line comprised five models in DeLuxe, Super, and Custom series with a choice of two body styles. All shared a 122-inch wheelbase and an overhead-valve Packard V8. Clippers also featured Packard's innovative Torsion-Level suspension, although a conventional suspension was available on the bottom-line DeLuxe. Options included overdrive transmission ($110), Ultramatic transmission ($199), power steering, power brakes, and air conditioning.

Clippers were luxuriously trimmed and nicely styled, though their sales volume wasn't sufficient to help the

1956 Super hardtop coupe

1956 Custom four-door sedan

1956 Deluxe four-door sedan

company. The DeLuxe sedan was the best seller. The handsome Custom Constellation hardtop was rarest, accounting for fewer than 1500 units.

Making Clipper a separate make was a good idea, but it came too late. Had the firm begun this marketing approach in the huge seller's market of 1946, the story might have had a happier ending.

Clipper Specifications

1956

5640 Deluxe-Super (wb 122.0)

		Wght	Price	Prod
5622	Deluxe sdn 4d	3,745	2,731	5,715
5642	Super sdn 4d	3,800	2,866	5,173
5647	Super htp cpe	3,825	2,916	3,999

5660 Custom (wb 122.0)

5662	sdn 4d	3,860	3,069	2,129
5667	Constellation htp cpe	3,860	3,164	1,466

1956 Engines	bore×stroke	bhp	availability
V8, 352.0	4.00×3.50	240	S-Deluxe, Super
V8, 352.0	4.00×3.50	275	S-Custom

Continental

Continental Division, Ford Motor Co.
Dearborn, Michigan

The Continental "Marks" of 1956-60 and 1968-on were, and are, not officially Lincolns. The first of these were products of a separate division at Ford, created with the goal of establishing the firm's dominance in the uppermost reaches of the market—even higher than Cadillac. Only one model was offered for 1956 and 1957: the flawlessly styled, beautifully crafted Mark II. It was priced at $10,000, and worth every penny. Yet Ford lost about $1000 on every Mark II it sold, because this was primarily an "image" car—more of an ego trip than a calculated profit-maker. An attempt was made to put Continental into the black with a lower-priced 1958-60 model based on the standard Lincoln, but it never sold particularly well. The separate division was gone by 1961, and the Continental name was applied to a new line of four-door hardtops and convertibles designed by Elwood Engle.

Ever since the demise of the original Lincoln Continental in 1948, Ford had been pressured by its dealers and customers to build a successor. In 1953, with profits looking up, the effort was begun. William Clay Ford, younger brother of Henry Ford II, was put in charge of a Special Products Division to come up with a design. He called in five outside consultants to submit their ideas

for comparison. Management reviewed 13 different proposals using front, side, rear, and ¾-front views, and unanimously selected the design from Special Products. Harley F. Copp, chief engineer of the Special Products Division, designed a unique chassis that dipped low between front and rear axles to permit high seating without a high roofline. The starkly simple cockpit and dash were inspired by aircraft and locomotive designs. The engines were Lincoln V8s specially selected from the assembly line and individually balanced. These were connected to Multi-Drive three-speed automatic transmissions and 3.07:1 rear axles. The sleek and timeless coupe measured 218.5 inches overall. It was greeted with wonderment on both sides of the Atlantic, and has been considered one of the all-time great design achievements ever since its debut. It was in a class by itself.

But the euphoria didn't last. Though the Continental Division was hoping to add a beautiful four-door berline and perhaps a convertible to the line for 1958, word from the sales department deflated those hopes. The Mark II had not had much impact on luxury-car production; General Motors was still the leader. A moneyed few were indeed buying Mark IIs, but the car was not

Mark II clay model

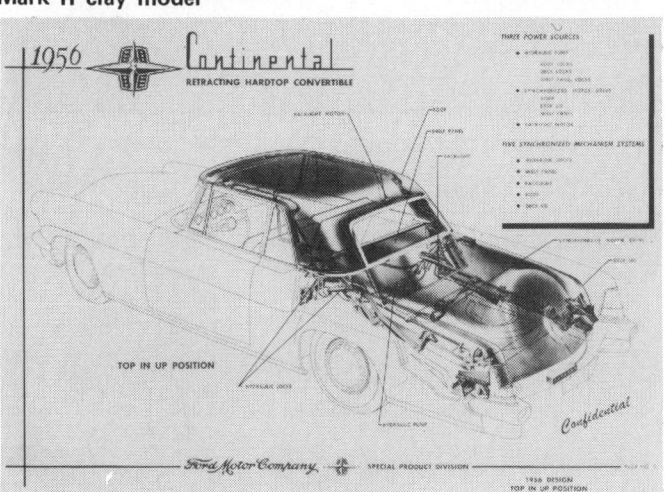

Proposed Mark II retractable hardtop

Chanelled Lincoln test mule for Mark II chassis

1956 Mark II hardtop coupe

1957 Mark II convertible (prototype)

1957 Mark II hardtop coupe

1958 Mark III Landau hardtop sedan

1958 Mark III convertible

convincing those with slightly less cash to buy Lincolns.

One Ford executive said years later that the Mark II program was, on balance, a big mistake. "For obvious reasons we don't like to talk about it... What we had going for us in the Mark II was literally a revival of the Duesenberg concept. What we ended up with was something much less—and even that didn't last long...it was a project that for a time broke Bill Ford's heart, and I guess you could say that in many ways it broke ours too."

In line with an upper management decision, the $10,000 price of 1956-57 was cut to about $6000 for 1958's "new" Continental. A Mercury cost analyst was brought in and the car was dubbed "Mark III." This Lincoln-based giant had a 131-inch wheelbase, elongated fenders, large chrome appliqués, huge tailfins and canted quad head-

lamps—but more important, it had been "built to a price." Shortcuts were made everywhere on the four models offered—and sales improved.

For 1959, "Continental" disappeared as a separate marque and again became a Lincoln model as it had been before the Mark II. Continental Division was absorbed by Lincoln-Mercury, which also acquired fast-faltering Edsel Division, thus ending Ford's dream of a GM-like hierarchy. The 1968 Mark III was given that numeral to emphasize the model's "official" status as lineal successor to the 1956-57 Mark II. Even so, its genealogy is a bit hazy: to some people it is a Lincoln Continental, for others strictly a Continental. Ford Motor Company itself generally includes the Mark III and its successors under the "Lincoln" badge, so we do too (see entry).

Continental Specifications

1956

Mark II (wb 126.0)

		Wght	Price	Prod
60A	htp cpe	4,825	9,695	1,325

1956 Engine	bore×stroke	bhp	availability
V8, 368.0	4.00×3.66	285	S-all

1957

Mark II (wb 126.0)

		Wght	Price	Prod
60A	htp cpe	4,800	9,966	444

1957 Engine	bore×stroke	bhp	availability
V8, 368.0	4.00×3.66	300	S-all

1958

Mark III (wb 131.0)

		Wght	Price	Prod
54A	sdn 4d	4,800	6,072	1,283
65A	htp cpe	4,865	5,825	2,328
68A	conv cpe	5,040	6,283	3,048
75A	Landau htp sdn	4,965	6,072	5,891

1958 Engine	bore×stroke	bhp	availability
V8, 430.0	4.30×3.70	375	S-all

Cord

Cord Corporation
Auburn and Indianapolis, Indiana

One can only hope to avoid criticism, a wise man once wrote, by saying nothing, doing nothing, and being nothing. Errett Lobban Cord handily avoided all those pitfalls, and he was criticized a lot. Born in 1894, the industry's golden boy (or unwelcome intruder, depending on whose opinion you hear) came literally from nowhere. A roustabout Los Angeles used-car salesman in 1920, Cord had become president and chief stockholder of Auburn by 1926. By the early '30s he had acquired both Duesenberg and Checker, as well as Auburn and a host of other industrial enterprises. His method of gaining control was all too clear: he dumped large quantities of common stock until its value was so low he could buy controlling interest for a song. When Cord left for England in 1934, he left to avoid an SEC investigation, not for a holiday. When he returned three years later it was to close the doors on three Classic marques. Few enthusiasts have forgiven him for that.

But during his wheeling-dealing decade of success, E.L.Cord was responsible for some of the most magnificent cars ever to put tire to road. Take 1929, for example. In that one year, he was the impressario behind three significant Classics: the Auburn speedster, the Model J Duesenberg, and the front-wheel-drive Cord L-29. The L-29 proved to be rather less than its backers had hoped, but eventually it led to the Cord 810 and 812, which are among the most memorable cars of the '30s.

The spirit of uninhibited optimism in the '20s saw many auto manufacturers expand with new models and even new makes. Ford bought Lincoln and turned it into a rival for Cadillac and Packard. Chrysler bought Dodge, then launched Plymouth and DeSoto. General Motors' various divisions introduced the Pontiac, Viking, Marquette, and LaSalle. Nash built the Ajax, Hudson the Essex, and Willys the Whippet. Even in the esoteric market inhabited by E.L. Cord's cars, there seemed to be a price gap between the eight-cylinder Auburn and the mighty Duesenberg. Cord's gap-filler was a rakish new model bearing his own name and the unorthodox feature of front-wheel drive.

The L-29 was designed by race-car builder Harry Miller and Detroit engineer Cornelius Van Ranst, both avid proponents of the "horse-pulls-cart" principle. Their engine was based on Auburn's 198.6-cid straight eight, with 115 bhp at 3300 rpm, but it was not a carbon copy of it. For the Cord's front-drive chassis it had to be turned around 180 degrees so that the clutch, flywheel, and chain drive faced forward. The cylinder head was altered so that a water outlet would be up front, and the crankcase was changed to accept a rear engine mount so the powerplant would bolt up to the L-29 frame. According to Cord authority Robert Fabris, more than 70 parts in the L-29 engine were not interchangeable with their Auburn counterparts.

The L-29's three-speed sliding-pinion transimission was mounted between the clutch and differential, following the

1930 L-29 town car by LeBaron

1930 L-29 four-door sedan

1930 L-29 phaeton sedan

1930 L-29 cabriolet

1931 L-29 cabriolet

Cord

1931 L-29 cabriolet

practice of a 1927 Miller Indianapolis racer. The brakes were also Miller-designed: inboard-mounted Lockheed hydraulics. Front suspension was by quarter-elliptic leaf springs, by semi-elliptics at the rear, and Houdaille-Hershey shock absorbers were used all around. The driveshaft to each front wheel employed Cardan constant-velocity joints.

This layout was not without its disadvantages. Owing to the distance between the front wheels and the cowl, the L-29's wheelbase was a tremendous 137.5 inches. The un-

usual gearbox/differential arrangement and long straight-eight engine put more than half the car's weight over its rear wheels, where it did nothing for traction, and L-29s were notoriously twitchy over any kind of loose surface. The universal joints weren't up to the pounding of both steering and driving, and wore out with merciless frequency. Miller and Van Ranst could have licked these problems given more time, but Cord was adamant the car debut before 1930.

1931 L-29 four-door sedan

1932 L-29 five-passenger brougham

1932 L-29 phaeton sedan

1936 Model 810 Beverly four-door sedan (prototype)

216

1937 Model 810 cabriolet

The L-29's styling was sensational. All that length up front allowed body engineer John Oswald to create a flowing hood and fenders that looked about 20 feet long. Auburn chief designer Al Leamy applied a Duesenberg-type radiator grille, which added to the impressive appearance. For 1930, the L-29 was priced from $3095 to $3294 and was offered as a convertible cabriolet, sedan, phaeton, and brougham. The same lineup continued in 1931-32, but prices were cut $800 across the board to spark sales.

Sales didn't spark. Aside from the dearth of traction and the U-joint wear problem, front-wheel drive was difficult to sell to buyers in the conservative $3000 market. Furthermore, against the powerful Packards, Lincolns, and Cadillacs of the day, the L-29 was a pig: 0-60 mph acceleration took over 30 seconds, and top speed was barely 75 mph. One writer optimistically described this performance as "pleasant tepidity," which is excusable only because it is easy to be overwhelmed by the car's styling. At the time, Cord couldn't give away the L-29. A used-car price guide published in 1935 quoted a cash value of $145 for a convertible that had sold for $3295 just five years earlier.

Historically, the L-29 is certified Classic by the Classic Car Club of America. Technically, it is a sort of primitive forefather of the Olds Toronado. In its time, however, it was a dismal failure. When production ended in early 1932, the count barely exceeded 4400 units, and the Cord name went into limbo for the next three years.

But it returned in 1936 on one of the most beautiful cars of all time: the 810. Like the L-29 it had front-wheel drive, but there was one key difference in the layout. The L-29 mounted its long straight eight behind the transmission, and both sat far behind the front axle. The 810 engine, on the other hand, was located just aft of the axle, and the differential/clutch assembly extended forward to the transmission, which was located ahead of the axle line. The key to all this was the engine, a V8 approximately half as long as the straight eight. The overall result was much more even weight distribution than in the L-29.

The 810 suspension consisted of independent front trailing arms with a single transverse leaf spring and constant-velocity U-joints. Its transmission was a four-speed unit with electric pre-selector. You selected the next gear by means of a lever located on an extension of the steering column; then, when you were ready, you stabbed the clutch to make the shift. The 288.6-cid engine was made by Lycoming and had nearly square bore/stroke dimensions. It produced 125 bhp at 3500 rpm or, with the Schwitzer-Cummins centrifugal supercharger also offered, 170 bhp at 4200 rpm. A higher-boost blower was fitted almost immediately, which brought output up to 190. An unblown Cord would do 90 mph and 0-60 mph in 20 seconds. The blown version would do nearly 110 mph and in 13 seconds, performance that made it one of the fastest prewar American production cars.

All this good engineering seems almost superfluous

1937 Model 812 Custom Berline

1937 Model 812 Supercharged Beverly sedan

1936 Model 810 cabriolet

compared to the body design, developed by Gordon Buehrig, Dale Cosper, Dick Roberson, and Paul Laurenzen. Initially, the shape was proposed for a junior Duesenberg that never made it, but whatever its origins, the 810 was unforgettable. Its smoothly formed "coffin-nose" hood, wraparound radiator louvers, exposed exhaust pipes, and clean side elevation were faultless design elements. Its turned-metal dash with functional needle gauges was one of the most beautiful ever to grace an automobile. The 810 also bristled with innovations. Concealed headlights were a production first, and dual taillights with a separate license plate light, full wheel covers, a roof-mounted radio speaker, and a hidden gasoline cap were equally futuristic.

The 125-inch wheelbase Cord 810 came in four models: Westchester and Beverly sedans (the main difference between them was their upholstery patterns), the Sportsman two-passenger coupe, and a four-passenger phaeton-sedan (convertible victoria). For 1937 the model designation was 812, and two long sedans on a 132-inch wheel base were added, the Custom Beverly and Custom Berline. Cord also built a handful of hardtop coupes and speedsters. With prices in the $3000s, the cars were expensive— but worth every penny.

E.L.Cord's empire collapsed in 1937 and with it, the Cord automobile. Only 1174 model 810s and 1146 model 812s were built. While the L-29 was ignored by collectors for years, the 810 and 812 began appreciating in value almost immediately after production ceased. As with the mighty Duesenberg J/SJ, peerless styling was the principal factor in several postwar revival attempts. So far, none has managed even the original's modest success.

Cord Specifications

1930—1,700 registered

L29 (wb 137.5)		Wght	Price	Prod
	cabriolet 2-4P	4,300	3,295	—
	sdn 4d 5P	4,530	3,095	—
	phaeton sdn 5P	4,500	3,295	—
	brougham 5P	4,500	3,095	—

1930 Engine	bore×stroke	bhp	availability
L8, 298.6	3.25×4.50	125	S-all

1931—1,433 built

L29 (wb 137.5)		Wght	Price	Prod
	cabriolet 2-4P	4,300	2,495	—
	sdn 4d 5P	4,530	2,395	—
	phaeton sdn 5P	4,500	2,595	—
	brougham 5P	4,500	2,395	—

1931 Engine	bore×stroke	bhp	availability
L8, 298.6	3.25×4.50	125	all

1932—335 registered

L29 (wb 137.5)		Wght	Price	Prod
	cabriolet 2-4P	4,300	2,495	—
	sdn 4d 5P	4,560	2,395	—
	phaeton sdn 5P	4,500	2,595	—
	brougham 5P	4,560	2,395	—

1932 Engine	bore×stroke	bhp	availability
L8, 298.6	3.25×4.50	125	all

1936—1,174 registered

810 (wb 125.0)		Wght	Price	Prod
	Westchester sdn 4d	3,715	1,995	—
	Beverly sdn 4d	3,740	2,095	—
	cabriolet	3,815	2,145	—
	phaeton	3,864	2,195	—

1936 Engine	bore×stroke	bhp	availability
V8, 288.6	3.50×3.75	115	S-all

1937—1,146 registered

812 (wb 125.0; Custom-132.0)		Wght	Price	Prod
	Westchester sdn 4d	3,715	2,445	—
	Beverly sdn 4d	3,800	2,545	—
	cabriolet	3,815	2,595	—
	phaeton	3,864	2,645	—
	Custom Beverly sdn 4d	3,900	2,960	—
	Custom Berline	4,120	3,060	—

812 Supercharged (wb 125.0; Custom-132.0)		Wght	Price	Prod
	Westchester sdn 4d	3,765	2,860	—
	Beverly sdn 4d	3,850	2,960	—
	cabriolet	3,865	3,010	—
	phaeton	3,914	3,060	—
	Custom Beverly sdn 4d	3,950	3,375	—
	Custom Berline	4,170	3,575	—

1937 Engines	bore×stroke	bhp	availability
V8, 288.6	3.50×3.75	115	S-812
V8, 288.6	3.50×3.75	190	S-Schgd 812

Crosley

Crosley Motors Inc.
Richmond-Marion, Indiana and Cincinnati, Ohio

The Midwestern businessman who'd brought us radios and refrigerators in the '20s and '30s decided to get into the car business in 1939. Powel Crosley, Jr. offered a very small economy vehicle on an 80-inch wheelbase and carrying the lowest price in the land. In its first year, Crosley sold 2017 of them. To buy one, you visited your local hardware store or appliance shop—a novel if shortsighted marketing scheme. About 5000 Crosleys had been produced by 1942, when the war brought passenger-car production to a halt.

1939 Series 1A convertible coupe

1946 CC Four pickup

1948½ CC Four two-door sedan

The 1940 Crosley line consisted of five models priced as low as $299 It included a standard and DeLuxe sedan with convertible top; station wagon; convertible; a "covered wagon" with full canvas top; plus several commercial bodies. Styling was basic, dominated by low, freestanding fenders and a prominent hood bulging out ahead of small horizontal grilles built into the front apron. Headlamps were attached to either side of the hood. Interiors were barren—just a central speedometer flanked by fuel and water gauges.

For its 1940-42 models, Crosley chose an air-cooled Waukeshaw two-cylinder engine with two main bearings. Performance wasn't quite as bad as the specifications suggest, since Crosleys were geared low at 5.14:1 and 5.57:1. Mechanical brakes, six-gallon fuel tank, disc wheels, and tiny 4.25×12-inch tires completed the economy package.

This design changed little for 1941. The same models were carried over, and the mechanical specifications were identical with the 1940 version. Prices were raised, however. The cars were now sold by separate automobile dealers besides Crosley's appliance outlets. The lineup was repeated for 1942.

During the war, Crosley developed the overhead-cam four-cylinder Cobra engine for a U.S. Navy project, using brazed copper and sheet steel for the block. This engine was selected to power the postwar civilian cars. This five-main-bearing engine had been fairly successful during the war in a variety of machines from truck refrigerators to Mooney Mite airplanes. It was less useful in its automotive application. The copper-steel block was subject to electrolysis, which caused holes to develop in cylinders and resulted in early rebuilds. Crosley soon rectified the fault by offering a cast-iron block that retained the original cylinder dimensions. Significantly, used-car price guides of the day gave a higher trade-in value for cars with the cast-iron engine, including 1946-48 models that had been retrofitted with the new unit.

The 1946 Crosley first appeared as a two-door four-seat sedan. Production began in June 1946. Later that year, a two-door convertible was added. A wagon and utility model followed by 1948. Commercial bodies were also offered, and in this period the future looked bright. After building almost 5000 cars in model year 1946, Crosley went on to produce 19,000 1947 models, and close to 29,000 of the 1948s. But this marked the end of prosperity. New designs from the Big Three, innovative new cars from the independents, and Crosley's growing reputation for engine problems combined to lower production drastically in model year 1949.

The sales slide was ironic in that the Crosley had become a much better car by 1949 than it had ever been before. New styling was introduced: a smooth hood,

1946-47 CC Four convertible and Powel Crosley

1949-50 CD Four two-door sedan and wagon

integral front fenders with sealed-beam headlights, remote-control door handles, and turn indicators on sedans and convertibles. In addition to the 80-inch wheelbase for sedan, delivery, convertible, and station wagon models, Crosley fielded an 85-inch wheelbase for its new Hotshot roadster.

The 1950 line comprised wagon, convertible, and sedan body styles in standard and Super trim, and a choice of two roadsters: the spartan, doorless Hotshot, and the slightly better-trimmed Super Sports (with conventional doors).

With its low prices Crosley was in a class by itself—but its engineering was also unique. For example, the 1949-50 model featured disc brakes. Along with Chrysler's 1950 Town & Country Newport, it was the first disc-braked car in series production. Unfortunately, Crosley's design proved troublesome, due to insufficient pre-production development. The brakes quickly deteriorated when exposed to road salt and grime,

causing tremendous service woes. Since Crosley had only recently recovered from a rash of service difficulties with its unlamented sheetmetal engines, the disc brake problem was the last thing dealers wanted to hear about. Conventional drum brakes were reinstituted for 1951.

Though the Crosley roadster failed to sell, they were tremendous class competitors in racing. Right off the showroom floor, the little roadsters could do up to 90 mph. Their handling, thanks to semi-elliptic-and-coil-spring front suspension with quarter-elliptics at the rear, was outstanding. The Hotshot's greatest accomplishment was winning the Index of Performance at Sebring in 1951 after a fine showing in the 12-hour endurance race. Buyers were not impressed, however, and Crosley ended car production in mid-1952. The company merged with General Tire and Rubber, which quickly disposed of the automotive business. In all, the venture had cost Powel Crosley about $3 million.

1951 CD Four Hotshot roadster

Courtesy Henry Ford Museum

Crosley Specifications

1939

Series 1A (wb 80.0)		Wght	Price	Prod
	conv cpe, 2P	925	325	—
	conv sdn, 4P	925	350	—

1939 Engine	bore×stroke	bhp	availability
L2, 35.3	3.00×2.50	12	S-all

1940

Series 2A (wb 80.0)—422 built	Wght	Price	Prod
sdn 2d	975	349	—
Deluxe sdn 2d	975	359	—
conv cpe	950	299	—
covered wgn 2d	1,125	399	—
wgn 2d	1,160	450	—

1940 Engine	bore×stroke	bhp	availability
L2, 35.3	3.00×2.50	12	S-all

1941

Series CB41 (wb 80.0)—2,289 built	Wght	Price	Prod
sdn 2d	975	390	—
Deluxe sdn 2d	975	400	—
conv cpe	950	339	—
covered wgn 2d	1,125	441	—
wgn 2d	1,160	496	—

1941 Engine	bore×stroke	bhp	availability
L2, 35.3	3.00×2.50	12	S-all

1942

Series CB42 (wb 80.0)—1,029 built	Wght	Price	Prod
sdn 2d	975	468	—
Deluxe sdn 2d	1,050	516	—
conv cpe	975	413	—
wgn 2d	1,105	582	—

1942 Engine	bore×stroke	bhp	availability
L2, 35.3	3.00×2.50	7.5	S-all

1946

CC Four (wb 80.0)	Wght	Price	Prod
sdn 2d	1,145	905	4,987
conv cpe	1,150	proto	12

1946 Engine	bore×stroke	bhp	availability
L4, 44.0	2.50×2.25	26.5	S-all; O-cast-iron block

1947

CC Four (wb 80.0)	Wght	Price	Prod
sdn 2d	1,155	888	14,090
conv cpe	1,150	949	4,005
wgn 2d	1,305	929	1,249

1947 Engine	bore×stroke	bhp	availability
L4, 44.0	2.50×2.25	26.5	S-all; O-cast-iron block

1948

CC Four (wb 80.0)	Wght	Price	Prod
sdn 2d	1,280	869	2,750
Sport Utility sdn 2d	1,160	799	
conv cpe	1,210	899	2,845
wgn 2d	1,305	929	23,489

1948 Engine	bore×stroke	bhp	availability
L4, 44.0	2.50×2.25	26.5	S-all; O-cast-iron block

1949

CD Four (wb 80.0; rdstr-85.0)	Wght	Price	Prod
DeLuxe sdn 2d	1,363	866	2,231
conv cpe	1,320	866	645
wgn 4d	1,403	894	3,803
Hotshot rdstr	1,175	849	752

1949 Engine	bore×stroke	bhp	availability
L4, 44.0	2.50×2.25	26.5	S-all; O-cast-iron block

1950

CD Four (wb 80.0; rdstr-85.0)	Wght	Price	Prod
sdn 2d	1,363	882	1,367
Super sdn 2d	1,363	951	
conv cpe	1,320	882	478
Super conv cpe	1,320	954	
wgn 2d	1,403	916	4,205
Super wgn 2d	1,403	984	
Hotshot rdstr	1,175	872	742
Super Sports rdstr	1,175	925	

1950 Engine	bore×stroke	bhp	availability
L4, 44.0	2.50×2.25	26.5	S-all

1951

CD Four (wb 80.0; rdstr-85.0)	Wght	Price	Prod
bus cpe	1,355	943	1,077
Super sdn 2d	1,370	1,033	
wgn 2d	1,002	1,420	9,500
Super wgn 2d	1,077	1,450	
Super conv cpe	1,035	1,310	391
Hotshot rdstr	1,180	952	646
Super Sports rdstr	1,180	1,029	

1951 Engine	bore×stroke	bhp	availability
L4, 44.0	2.50×2.25	26.5	S-all

1952

CD Four (wb 80.0; rdstr-85.0)	Wght	Price	Prod
Standard bus cpe	1,355	943	216
Super sdn 2d	1,400	1,033	
Standard wgn 2d	1,430	1,002	1,355
Super wgn 2d	1,480	1,077	
Super conv cpe	1,400	1,035	146
Hotshot rdstr	1,240	952	358
Super Sports rdstr	1,240	1,029	

1952 Engine	bore×stroke	bhp	availability
L4, 44.0	2.50×2.25	25.5	S-all

DeSoto
DeSoto Division, Chrysler Corp.
Detroit, Michigan

In the '20s, when it seemed as if prosperity would go on forever, auto manufacturers looked upon expansion as the natural way of life. From GM and Chrysler, new makes proliferated. General Motors brought forth the Marquette, Viking, and Pontiac; Chrysler purchased Dodge, then created Plymouth and DeSoto.

DeSoto's design evolution in the 1930s paralleled Chrysler's with one notable exception: while Chrysler fielded conventionally styled companion models for 1934, DeSoto relied exclusively on the radical Airflow. The result was a sales disaster. By the middle of the decade, it was even money whether DeSoto would survive or wither away.

The 1930-33 Desotos reflected general Chrysler Corporation design trends. The 1930-31s were formal, bolt-upright styles; the 1932-33s were modified somewhat with barrel-like grilles. Both six- and eight-cylinder engines were offered for 1930-32, all orthodox side-valve units. The five-main-bearing eight was smoother and quieter than the six, but neither was a powerhouse. The eights appealed to only about one in three customers, and DeSoto would offer nothing but sixes from 1932 until the hemi-head "Firedome" V8 appeared for 1952.

DeSoto's sixes were cast-iron, four-main-bearing engines, smaller versions of their Chrysler counterparts. Eight prices averaged around $1000 early in the decade, and sixes ran around $800-850. For 1933, with sales at an all-time low, DeSoto cut prices: as little as $665 for the standard sedan or coupe, $875 for the top-line Custom convertible sedan.

Early Desotos were not revised for each model year. The first to be designated that way was the "All New Six" or SC series, introduced in January 1932 and bearing chunky but attractive lines. Model offerings comprised a standard sedan, a seven-passenger sedan, and a Custom sedan, convertible, and phaeton. The 1933 season brought more coupes and a new brougham (two-door sedan).

All the pros and cons of the 1934 Chrysler Airflow also held for the DeSoto version, which was powered by the make's largest and most powerful six to date. The engine, at least, was a survivor, and continued in production for 1935-36. It was destroked for 1937, but rated power stayed the same. Enlarged again for 1941 and 1951, it remained the division's mainstay until the last of its kind was offered for 1954. Vice-free and reliable, it would run forever in exchange for an occasional quart of oil. And it could return good gas mileage, up to 22 mpg.

DeSoto's Airflow initially came in one series and four

1931 Model SA Six roadster

1933 Standard two-door brougham sedan

1933 Custom coupe

1933 Standard four-door sedan

1933 Custom coupe

1936 Custom Airstream four-door touring sedan

body styles. A hasty retreat for 1935 saw the much more conventional and saleable Airstream styling on seven companion models, marked by a Plymouth-like raked grille, slab sides, and a rounded deck. Sedans were offered with and without outside spare tire, "without" meaning that a faired-in trunk housed the spare. There was also a $35 two-tone paint option. Though 1935 sales were up 116 percent, DeSoto dropped to 13th place in the production race, largely because of Packard's highly successful One Twenty series.

The division rode out the rest of the decade with increas-ingly larger and duller cars. The Airflows disappeared after 1936. Long sedans and limousines began coming off the lines, and grew to a 136-inch wheelbase by 1938. Styling, by Dietrich, was very conservative in this period, though it did match contemporary tastes. The 1938 recession cut output, and DeSoto finished 12th in volume. The recovery year of 1939 was good, but rivals were doing much better.

The DeSoto line had settled into a consistent pattern by 1938: Deluxes and Customs priced at around $900 and $1000, respectively, powered by the same engines and

1934 Airflow coupe

1936 Airflow III four-door sedan

1936 Airflow coupe

1937 Six convertible coupe

1939 Custom four-door touring sedan

sharing the same conventional chassis. Long sedans and limousines were available in each series. Significantly, there weren't any open cars by 1939, though a sliding sunroof was offered, and styling was still heavily influenced by Chrysler's junior makes: a 1939 DeSoto looked like a Plymouth that had taken pep pills. Dumpy appear-

ance would remain one of the make's big sales handicaps until well after World War II.

Production soared with introduction of the '41s: good-looking cars with lower hoods and bolder front ends. Grilles featured the prominent vertical "teeth" that would be a DeSoto hallmark through 1955. Al-

1940 Custom coupe

1941 Custom four-door sedan

1941 Studio rendering for postwar DeSoto styling

1942 Sky-View taxicab

1942 Custom convertible coupe

1946 Custom Suburban eight-passenger sedan

1948 Custom club coupe

1949 Custom four-door sedan

though the division had produced only about 65,000 of the 1940 models, model year production reached nearly 100,000 on the strength of the new '41 line.

The standard-size cars lost an inch in wheelbase, but were 5.5 inches longer overall than the '40 models, as well as wider and lower. For the first time, DeSoto offered Fluid Drive, which greatly simplified gear changing. A new model was the Custom Town Sedan, a formal adaptation of the standard sedan with blind rear roof quarters. This very pretty car sold for about $50 more than the standard Custom four-door. DeSoto wooed the buyer with many optional extras, including an underseat heater, pushbutton radio, and streamlined fender skirts.

One of the more interesting model years was 1942, when the division adopted "Airfoil" hidden headlamps. They remained "out of sight, except at night." While not a first, they were the only hidden lamps in the industry that year, and imparted a clean look to the front end. Designers placed the entire grille on the lower half of the car's face. A sculpted lady was introduced as a hood mascot, and stayed into 1949.

Although the 1942 model line was identical with 1941's, there was a "squarer" L-head six. Somewhat detuned, it would power all DeSotos for the the rest of the decade. Stroked slightly, it would continue in production as the Powermaster Six through 1954—the last year for six-cylinder models.

There wasn't much time in 1942 for specials before civilian production ceased, but DeSoto did manage a plush Fifth Avenue version of the Custom Town Sedan. Distinguished on the exterior only by a nameplate, it sported a luxurious leather and Bedford cloth interior, and sold for about $75 more than the standard Town Sedan. Because production was so low, 1942 DeSotos are rare indeed. Fewer than 25,000 were built altogether, with fewer than 1000 of some styles.

When the division opened its doors again after World War II, the model lineup was cut, though the drivetrain and chassis combinations used for '42 were retained. The long-wheelbase DeLuxe was discontinued, and a convertible was substituted for the business coupe in the Custom series. Only three models rode the long wheelbase: a seven-passenger sedan, a limousine, and the intriguing DeSoto Suburban.

Designed to provide the ultimate in stylish cargo hauling for hotels, airports, and well-heeled individuals, the Suburban featured a fold-down rear seat without trunk partition, providing a huge cargo hold. A metal-and-wood roof rack and beautifully fitted wooden interior panels completed the package. Not surprisingly, it was the most expensive model in the 1946 lineup, listing at nearly $100 more than the limousine.

The 1947 and '48 models were largely 1946 carry-overs. Serial numbers are the only guide to model years. The '46 facelift had been mild: fenders flowed

1950 Custom wood-trimmed four-door station wagon

1952 Firedome four-door sedan

1951 Custom Sportsman hardtop coupe

1953 Firedome eight-passenger sedan

into the front doors, the grille was heavier and wider, medallions and parking lights were shuffled, and the rear fenders were deepened. Horsepower was listed at 109 for 1946-48, down 6 bhp from 1942. This was not a result of mechanical alterations, just a new rating method.

DeSoto built 11,600 taxicabs in 1946-48, making this the fifth most popular model in its line. Suburban production was also quite satisfactory: 7500 of the luxurious carryalls were built in the three-year period.

For 1949, the line was completely restyled, as was the rest of Chrysler Corporation. Standard models used a longer wheelbase, and DeSoto took on the boxy, upright styling typical of Chrysler products that year, which were conservative compared to their Ford and GM competition. The 236-cid six was continued with slightly more horsepower. Fluid Drive with "Tip-Toe hydraulic shift" became standard for Customs and a $121 option on DeLuxes. The front end sported a vertical-bar grille similar to that of the 1942-48 design. The lady mascot was replaced by a bust of Hernando DeSoto. Like all proper hood ornaments of those years, Hernando glowed brightly in the dark.

The 1949s appeared in March after a brief run of old-style models to fill the gap, and featured some interesting new utility vehicles. DeSoto's DeLuxe series included a new woody wagon priced at $2959. More significant was the all-steel Carry-All, similar to the

Suburban but on the standard wheelbase. The Carry-All's rear seat folded down to provide a long cargo bed.

In the Custom line, the long-wheelbase Suburban was continued on a chassis shared with an eight-passenger sedan. As before, the Suburban provided great cargo space and a rooftop luggage rack. It was also fitted with jump seats, giving it true nine-passenger capacity.

Of these three utility models, the Carry-All pointed the way of the future by handily selling 2690 copies. Woody wagon production was only 680; Suburban output, a mere 129. The woody continued only through 1950. Emphasis was then placed on the Carry-All.

Generally, 1949 had been a spectacular year for DeSoto. For the 1949 model year, it built three times as many Customs as DeLuxes, an indication of buyer preference for more luxurious, higher-priced cars. The division built its first V8 in 1952. But production declined to barely more than a trickle by the end of the '50s. Nevertheless, DeSoto had several good years during the decade. By the start of 1959, there was little indication the make would be phased out within 24 months.

In early 1950s, DeSoto still had six-cylinder cars with engines with up to 250.6 cid. They were still L-heads, providing up to 116 bhp for two series. The DeLuxe was utilitarian, while the Custom offered hardtops, convertibles, and long-wheelbase sedans. The 1950 model was boxy-looking, wearing more chrome up front than per-

haps any other Chrysler product. Stylist Virgil Exner brought in a somewhat sleeker style for '51.

For 1952, DeSoto introduced its version of the hemispherical-head V8, the 276.1-cid Firedome. Based on the larger Chrysler Hemi, it developed 160 bhp at 4400 rpm, and put DeSoto firmly in the horsepower race. Immediately, Firedome Eights accounted for nearly 50,000 sales. The six-cylinder Custom and DeLuxe series were combined in 1953 as the Powermaster Six, but sales didn't fare as well as the eight-cylinder models. By the end of 1953, Firedomes were outselling Powermasters by a margin of two to one. Both series included Sportsman hardtops.

Model year 1954 marked the debut of PowerFlite two-speed automatic transmission. Through that year, DeSotos came with three-speed manual transmission standard. Fluid Drive was the major gearbox option at $130, followed by overdrive at $96. That year also marked the end of the Powermaster and the long-wheelbase sedans. Two brilliantly engineered, good-looking 1955 series, the Firedome and the new top-of-the-line Fireflite, came with a 291-cid V8. With its

attractive two-tone color schemes, "gullwing" dash, and highly chromed front end, the '55 was just in time to save the division temporarily. Sales had been very poor in 1954—a nightmare period for all of Chrysler Corporation.

No '55 Chrysler product was really sedate in appearance, but DeSotos were possibly the most glittery of all. They appealed to buyers and sold well, putting the division over the 100,000 mark. The Firedome series offered a cheap Special hardtop at $110 less than the Sportsman; the Coronado sedan led the Fireflite series at a $100 premium over the $2800 standard sedan. The Coronado is a minor collector's item today. It is significant because it brought us one of the first three-tone paint jobs—turquoise, black, and white.

Horsepower went up to 230 and 255 bhp for 1956. The teeth were yanked out of the grille, replaced with a wire mesh. Unreadable gold-on-white instruments appeared, and DeSotos grew tailfins as did other Chrysler lines. Generally, this facelift produced questionable results. A highlight, however was the new limited-edition Adventurer, a gold-bedecked two-door hardtop super-

1954 Firedome convertible

Adventurer I show car by Ghia, 1954

1955 Fireflite four-door sedan

1955 Fireflite convertible

1955 Fireflite Sportsman hardtop coupe

1956 Adventurer hardtop coupe

car. Equipped with a 341-cid, 320-bhp V8, it was part of the wild performance assortment that also included the Chrysler 300B, Plymouth Fury, and Dodge D-500.

One other introduction for '56 was DeSoto's first four-door hardtop. The Firedome version was called Seville, and appeared just as Cadillac was adopting that name for its two-door Eldorado hardtop. No legal entanglements developed.

DeSoto fared extremely well in 1956, while other Chrysler divisions suffered extensive production cut-backs. And 1957 proved to be another successful year. A low-cost Firesweep series on the 122-inch Dodge wheelbase joined the two upper lines in a last effort to extend DeSoto's market territory. It helped; customers could buy a Firesweep for only $2777 (the cheapest Firedome was $2958), and there was a full line of

1957 Fireflite Sportsman hardtop sedan

1957 Fireflite Shopper six-passenger station wagon

1957 Adventurer hardtop coupe

1957 Firesweep four-door sedan

1957 Fireflite Sportsman hardtop coupe

1957 Firedome four-door sedan

sedans, hardtops, and wagons to choose from.

In 1957, DeSoto came as near as it ever did to passing Chrysler in production, ending up less than 8000 units behind. The '57s were big, heavy, powerful cars. The two upper series used a V8 with up to 290 bhp. The Firesweep engine was more conservative, producing about 260 bhp. An Adventurer soft-top now made its debut, offering 345 bhp.

Of all the Exner finned fantasies that arrived that year, DeSoto was the cleanest. Smooth rear panels, attractive taillights, simple but pleasant side moldings, and a front bumper unique to the division all helped give the '57 DeSotos first-rate styling. Yet, as good as they looked, the division would not be able to survive on looks alone. From a production level of 118,000 units in calendar year 1957, DeSoto fell to 50,000 the following year—the division's lowest output since 1938. The recession, a reputation for poor quality, and unwise marketing decisions all contributed to the downward spiral.

The 1958 models were basically the same as the '57s, except for a mild facelift. The grille became busier, and all models came with four lights. (As of 1957, some states still had not legalized "quadrilights," so DeSoto front fenders had been designed to accept either one or two headlamps.) Wagons and Sportsman hardtops proliferated along with four-door sedans; no fewer than four convertibles were offered. The Adventurer ragtop was the most expensive DeSoto in history, though Chrysler's corresponding 300D convertible cost $1300 more.

As ever, DeSotos were extremely quick. Fast-shifting TorqueFlite automatic transmission and torsion-bar suspension made them among the most roadworthy cars as well. A DeSoto Firedome with Turboflash V8 and the optional 305-bhp setup could accelerate from 0 to 60 in 7.7 seconds, to 80 mph in 13.5 seconds, and could reach 115 mph with little strain.

DeSoto said its towering tailfins of 1957-61 "added stability at speed," but this was advertising propaganda. Although they did little from an aerodynamic standpoint under 80 mph, they did make the cars look dramatically different from the opposition. The tailfins reached their height in 1959, the year that marked the beginning of the end.

DeSoto had joined the corporate switch to wedge-head engines in '58. For 1959, Firesweeps used the 361-cid unit, and other models got the more potent 383. Maximum horsepower—standard on the Adventurer—was 350 bhp at 5000 rpm. The wedge-heads gave away little to the Hemis in acceleration. As before, there was a wide choice of hardtops, wagons, sedans, and convertibles. The Adventurer became a regular series, and sales improved slightly. But it was hardly the kind of volume that had sustained DeSoto earlier in the decade.

DeSoto show cars in the '50s vied with those of the Chrysler label. They were built mainly by Ghia of Italy to Exner's designs. Adventurer I was the first, part of Exner's early series that began with the 1951 Chrysler

1958 Fireflite convertible

1959 Firedome Sportsman hardtop sedan

Cella I show car of 1959

K-310. Built in 1954, the Adventurer I rode a shortened 111-inch wheelbase, and accommodated four passengers. Its off-white coupe body was fitted with outside exhausts, wire wheels, and full instrumentation. It came closer to production than any other Exner special. "Had it been mass-produced," Exner said, "it would have been the first four-passenger sports car made in this country. It was better than a two-plus-two, and of course it had the DeSoto Hemi. It was my favorite car."

1959 Fireflite Sportsman hardtop coupe

1960 Adventurer hardtop coupe

1961 hardtop sedan

1961 hardtop coupe

Adventurer II followed in 1955. This standard-wheelbase, four-passenger coupe was designed more by Ghia's craftsmen than Exner. It was painted deep red, was fitted with wire wheels, and had no bumper. Adventurer II lacked the sleek integrated styling of its predecessor, and was not seriously considered for production.

DeSoto was discontinued in 1961 after 33 years of production. Its demise was hastened by a change in Chrysler's marketing approach. In the past there had been three types of dealers: Chrysler-Plymouth, DeSoto-Plymouth, and Dodge-Plymouth. The advent of Imperial as a separate make in 1955 prompted Chrysler Division to concentrate on the lower end of its market, while larger and more luxurious Dodge models in-

creased that division's spread upward. Both Chrysler and Dodge ate into DeSoto's territory. Rumors of DeSoto's imminent demise were heard as early as 1959, and they naturally affected sales.

The statistics were ominous. Although 1959 calendar year production had increased slightly from 1958, the volume for both years was less than half that of 1957, when DeSoto built nearly 120,000 cars. The division was in the same kind of trouble as many other middle-priced cars, including Oldsmobile, Buick, and Mercury. But those rivals had higher volume and could stand to lose more money. Furthermore, all of them had smaller models ready for introduction in 1961. Although DeSoto's 1962 plans included downsized standard models, there was no program for a compact.

Initially, rumors of DeSoto's termination were strongly denied, and in 1959 a celebration was held to mark the division's two-millionth car. Press releases noted there were almost a million DeSotos still registered. The division announced $25 million would be invested in the engineering and styling of future cars, $7 million of which would be earmarked for the 1960 models. Officials said commitments had been made for 1961, and work on the 1962-63 line was in the development stage. It was also pointed out that Chrysler had regularly made a profit on DeSoto.

In 1960, however, Chrysler merged DeSoto and Plymouth into one division, with Valiant as an ostensibly separate make. Valiant did very well and Plymouth did fairly well, but DeSoto fared poorly. During the first two months of 1960, sales totaled 4746, or 0.51 percent of the industry total. This was down considerably from the first two months of 1959, when the figures were 6134 units and 0.72 percent. By the end of 1960, plans for the restyled 1962 models had been shelved, and the '61 DeSotos, announced in October, were taken off the market. Some DeSoto-Plymouth dealers became Chrysler-Plymouth agencies, much to the chagrin of existing Chrysler-Plymouth dealers nearby.

For 1960, the DeSoto line was reduced to two series, each with three body styles: sedan, hardtop sedan, and hardtop coupe. The Adventurer took the place of the Fireflite, though its price was a few hundred dollars less than the '59 Fireflite. The Fireflite was moved down into the $3000 area formerly occupied by the Firesweep, which was eliminated along with the mid-line Firedome. Station wagons and convertibles were also dropped. The most popular DeSoto was the Fireflite sedan, production of which failed to exceed 10,000.

All models rode the 122-inch wheelbase shared with Chrysler, and adopted the company's "unibody" construction, new that year. Adventurers used the Chrysler 383-cid V8 with the same compression, but 305 bhp at 4600 rpm. Automatic transmission, either PowerFlite or TorqueFlite, was optional on the Fireflite. Styling featured a blunt, trapezoidal grille similar to Chrysler's, composed of small horizontal bars and carried over a huge, curved bumper with rubber-capped bumper guards. Fins were as high as they'd ever been, and

glass area was huge. Performance was mediocre. The Adventurer's specification duplicated the Chrysler Windsor's; the Fireflite's V8 was borrowed from Dodge. In a drag race, an Adventurer could stay with a Windsor, but would lose to a Saratoga or the lighter 383 Dodge Phoenix.

The '61 DeSoto's brief appearance resulted in very low production figures. No series names were used; the cars were simply "DeSotos." The four-door pillared sedan was eliminated. Publicity concentrated on the design's individuality. Odd might be a more apt description. The front displayed a curious double grille flanked by diagonally stacked headlights. A lattice-like lower grille was topped by a large, blunt oval bearing the name DeSoto in stylized letters against a fine mesh. Production tapered off by Christmas 1960, after which the few existing orders were filled mostly with Chrysler Windsors. It was a sad finale for a marque that had brought considerable prestige and profits to Chrysler for more than three decades.

De Soto Specifications

1930

Model K Six (wb 109.0)—29,860 built**

	Wght	Price	Prod*
rdstr 2-4P	2,350	845	—
touring (phaeton) 5P	2,445	845	—
bus cpe 2P	2,465	845	—
DeLuxe cpe 2-4P	2,525	885	—
sdn 2d 5P	2,580	845	—
sdn 4d 5P	2,645	885	—
DeLuxe sdn 4d 5P	2,655	955	—

Model CF Eight (wb 114.0)—19,525 built (est.)**

rdstr 2-4P	2,720	985	1,457*
phaeton 5P	2,800	1,035	179*
bus cpe 2P	2,835	965	1,015*
DeLuxe cpe 2-4P	2,875	1,025	2,735*
conv cpe 2-4P	2,845	1,075	524*
sdn 4d 5P	2,965	995	9,653*
DeLuxe sdn 4d 5P	2,975	1,065	4,139*
chassis	—	—	373*

Model CK Finer Six (wb 109.0)—7,443 built (est.)**

rdstr 2-4P	2,385	810	⎤
DeLuxe rdstr 2-4P	2,520	835	⎦ 1,086*
touring (phaeton) 5P	2,475	830	209*
bus cpe 2P	2,515	830	858*
DeLuxe cpe 2-4P	2,585	860	1,521*
conv cpe 2-4P	2,540	945	184*
sdn 4d	2,705	875	8,248*
chassis	—	—	94*

*combined 1930-31 individual model exact production
**Available Model K figures include 1929 production. 1930 model production began August 15. Engine number span for 1930: K83241 to K11310. If no engine numbers were skipped, total 1930 Model K production was 29,860. Available Model CF and CK figures include 1931 production. 1930 Model CF production began January 1. 1930 Model CK production began April 29. Sources of serial number spans suggest that of 20,075 Model CFs built, approximately 19,575 were 1930s and 550 1931s. Same sources indicate 7,443 CKs were 1930s and 4,757 1931s.

1930 Engines	bore×stroke	bhp	availability
L6, 174.9	3.00×4.13	57	S-K
L8, 207.7	2.88×4.00	70	S-CF
L6, 189.8	3.13×4.13	60	S-CK

1931

Model CF Eight (wb 114.0)—550 built (est.)

Production was carried over from 1930, with 1931 model output commencing July 1. Production figures combined with 1930 CF Eight. Body styles, weights and prices identical.

Model CK Finer Six (wb 109.0)—4,757 built (est.)

Production was carried over from 1930, with 1931 model output commencing July 1. Production figures combined with 1930 CK Finer Six. Body styles, weights and prices identical.

Model SA Six (wb 109.0)

	Wght	Price	Prod*
rdstr 2-4P	2,465	795	1,949
touring (phaeton) 5P	2,580	795	100
bus cpe 2P	2,585	740	1,309
cpe 2-4P	2,635	775	2,663
conv cpe 2-4P	2,630	825	638
sdn 2d 5P	2,680	695	2,349
sdn 4d 5P	2,695	775	17,866
DeLuxe sdn 4d 5P	2,834	825	1,450
chassis	—	—	32

Model CF Eight Second Series (wb 114.0)

rdstr 2-4P	2,785	995	73
touring (phaeton) 5P	2,800	1,035	22
bus cpe 2P	2,915	965	102
DeLuxe cpe 2-4P	2,970	995	486
conv cpe 2-4P	2,970	1,075	48
sdn 4d 5P	2,025	995	⎤ 3,490
DeLuxe sdn 4d 5P	3,115	1,065	⎦
chassis	—	—	3

1930-31 Eight roadster

*Model SA and CF 2nd Series production continued into 1932; production figures are for 1931-32 combined. Approximately one-third of total SA models were 1931s, the rest 1932s. Second Series Model CF production began January 1, 1931.

1931 Engines	bore×stroke	bhp	availability
L8, 207.7	2.88×4.00	70	S-CF
L6, 189.8	3.13×4.13	60	S-CF
L6, 205.3	3.25×4.13	67	S-SK
L8, 220.7	2.88×4.25	77	S-CF Second Series

1932

Model SA Six (wb 109.0)

Production was carried over from 1931, with 1932 model output commencing July 23. Production figures combined with 1931 SA Six. Body styles, weights and prices identical.

Model SC New Six (wb 112.4)	Wght	Price	Prod
Standard rdstr 2P	2,725	675	894
Custom rdstr 2-4P	2,748	775	
phaeton 5P	NA	775	30
Standard cpe 2P	2,778	695	1,691
Standard cpe 2-4P	2,848	735	2,897
Custom cpe 2-4P	2,908	700	
sdn 2d (brougham)	2,883	695	3,730
Standard sdn 4d	2,978	775	8,924
Custom sdn 4d	3,018	835	4,791
Custom conv sdn 5P	3,175	975	275
sdn 7P	3,175	925	221
chassis	—	—	83

1932 Engines	bore×stroke	bhp	availability
L6, 205.3	3.25×4.13	67	S-SA
L8, 220.7	2.88×4.25	77	S-CF 2nd Series
L6, 211.5	3.25×4.25	75	S-SC

Model CF Eight Second Series (wb 114.0)

Production was carried over from 1931, with 1932 model output commencing July 23. Production figures combined with 1931 CF Second Series. Body styles, weights and prices identical.

1933

Model SD (wb 114.4)	Wght	Price	Prod
bus cpe 2P	2,930	665	800
Standard cpe 2-4P	2,940	705	2,705
Custom cpe 2-4P	2,995	750	
Standard sdn 2d	2,995	665	2,436
Special sdn 2d	3,000	725	
Custom conv cpe 2-4P	2,990	775	412
Standard sdn 4d	3,060	735	7,890
Custom sdn 4d	3,150	795	8,133
Custom conv sdn 5P	NA	875	132
sdn 7P (export only)	NA	NA	104
chassis	—	—	124

1933 Engine	bore×stroke	bhp	availability
L6, 217.8	3.25×4.38	82	S-all

1934

Model SE Airflow (wb 115.5)	Wght	Price	Prod
cpe 5P	3,323	995	1,584
brougham 6P	3,323	995	522
sdn 4d	3,378	995	11,713
Town sdn 6P	3,343	995	119
chassis	—	—	2

1934 Engine	bore×stroke	bhp	availability
L6, 241.5	3.38×4.50	100	S-all

1935

Model SS Airstream Six (wb 116.0)	Wght	Price	Prod
bus cpe 2P	2,840	695	1,760
cpe 2-4P	2,925	760	900
conv cpe 2-4P	3,035	835	226
sdn 2d	2,915	745	1,350
touring sdn 2d	2,960	775	2,035
sdn 4d	2,990	795	5,714
touring sdn 4d	3,035	825	8,018

Model SG Airflow Six (wb 115.5)	Wght	Price	Prod
bus cpe 3P	3,390	1,015	70
cpe 5P	3,390	1,015	418
sdn 4d	3,390	1,015	6,269
Town sdn 6P	3,400	1,015	40

1935 Engine	bore×stroke	bhp	availability
L6, 241.5	3.38×4.50	100	S-all

1936

S1 DeLuxe Airstream (wb 118.0)	Wght	Price	Prod
bus cpe 2P	2,941	695	2,592
touring brougham 5P	3,051	770	2,207
touring sdn 5P	3,111	810	13,093
chassis	—	—	99

S1 Custom Airstream (wb 118; lwb-130.0)	Wght	Price	Prod
bus cpe 2P	—	745	940
cpe 2-4P	—	795	641
conv cpe 2-4P	3,031	895	350
touring brougham 5P	3,031	825	1,120
touring sdn 4d	3,126	865	13,801
conv sdn 5P	—	1,095	215
Traveler sdn 4d*	—	1,075	23
lwb sdn 7P	—	1,075	208
limo 7P (lwb)	—	NA	10

S2 Airflow II (wb 115.5)	Wght	Price	Prod
cpe 5P	NA	1,095	250
sdn 4d	NA	1,095	4,750

1936 Engine	bore×stroke	bhp	availability
L6, 241.5	3.38×4.50	100	S-all

1937

S3 Six (wb 116.0; lwb-133.0)	Wght	Price	Prod
bus cpe 3P	3,038	770	11,050
cpe 3-5P	3,088	820	1,030
conv cpe 3-5P	3,225	975	992

1934 Airflow five-passenger coupe

	Wght	Price	Prod
brghm F/B 6P	3,123	830	1,200
touring 6P	3,148	840	11,660
sdn F/B 4d	3,123	870	2,265
touring sdn 4d	3,148	880	51,889
conv sdn 5P	3,441	1,300	426
lwb sdn 7P	3,451	1,120	695
limo sdn 7P (lwb)	3,475	1,220	71
chassis	—	—	497

1937 Engine	bore×stroke	bhp	availability
L6, 228.1	3.38×4.25	93	S-all

1938

S5 Six (wb 119.0; lwb-136.0)	Wght	Price	Prod
bus cpe 3P	3,039	870	5,160
conv cpe 3-5P	3,229	1,045	431
touring brougham 6P	3,119	930	5,367
sdn F/B 4d 6P	3,134	958	498
touring sdn 4d 6P	3,139	970	23,681
conv sdn 5P	3,394	1,375	88
lwb sdn 7P	3,439	1,195	513
sdn limo 7P (lwb)	3,524	1,285	81
Custom Traveler sdn 4d (lwb)	NA	NA	2,550
cpe 2-4P	NA	NA	38
fstbk brougham	NA	NA	11
chassis	—	—	413

1938 Engines	bore×stroke	bhp	availability
L6, 228.1	3.38×4.25	93	S-all
L6, 228.1	3.38×4.25	100	O-all

1939

S6 DeLuxe (wb 119.0; lwb-136.0)	Wght	Price	Prod
bus cpe 2P	3,064	870	5,176
cpe A/S 2-4P	3,089	925	2,124
touring sdn 2d 5P	3,129	930	7,472
touring sdn 4d 5P	3,174	970	31,513
lwb touring sdn 7P	3,454	1,195	425
sdn limo 7P	3,549	1,285	84
chassis	—	—	154

S6 Custom (wb 119.0; lwb-136.0)			
cpe 2P	3,069	923	498
cpe A/S 2-4P	3,094	978	287
club cpe 4P	3,164	1,145	264
touring sdn 2d 5P	3,134	983	424
touring sdn 4d 5P	3,179	1,023	5,993
lwb touring sdn 7P	3,459	1,248	30
sdn limo 7P	3,554	1,338	5

1939 Engines	bore×stroke	bhp	availability
L6, 228.1	3.38×4.25	93	S-all
L6, 228.1	3.38×4.25	100	O-all

1940

S-7S DeLuxe (wb 122.5; 7P-139.5)	Wght	Price	Prod
bus cpe	3,001	845	3,650
cpe, A/S	3,026	905	2,098
sdn 2d	3,066	905	7,072
sdn 4d	3,086	945	18,666
sdn 4d, 7P	3,490	1,175	142

S-7C Custom (wb 122.5; 7P-139.5)			
bus cpe	3,024	885	1,898
cpe, A/S	3,044	945	2,234
conv cpe	3,329	1,095	1,085
sdn 2d	3,084	945	3,109
sdn 4d	3,104	985	25,221

	Wght	Price	Prod
sdn 4d, 7P	3,490	1,215	206
limo 7P	3,550	1,290	34
chassis	—	—	52

1940 Engines	bore×stroke	bhp	availability
L6, 228.1	3.38×4.25	100	S-all
L6, 228.1	3.38×4.25	105	O-all

1941

S-8S DeLuxe (wb 121.5; 7P-139.5)	Wght	Price	Prod
bus cpe	3,134	945	4,449
club cpe	3,219	1,025	5,603
sdn 2d	3,224	1,008	9,228
sdn 4d	3,254	1,035	26,417
sdn 4d, 7P	3,629	1,270	101

S-8C Custom (wb 121.5; 7P-139.5)			
bus cpe	3,144	982	2,033
club cpe	3,239	1,080	6,726
conv cpe	3,494	1,240	2,937
brougham 2d	3,264	1,060	4,609
sdn 4d	3,269	1,085	30,876
town sdn	3,329	1,133	4,362
sdn 4d, 7P	3,649	1,310	120
limo 7P	3,700	1,390	35
chassis	—	—	1

1941 Engine	bore×stroke	bhp	availability
L6, 228.1	3.38×4.25	105	S-all

1942

S-10S DeLuxe (wb 121.5; 7P-139.5)	Wght	Price	Prod
bus cpe	3,190	1,010	469
club cpe	3,270	1,092	1,968
conv cpe	3,500	1,250	79
sdn 2d	3,270	1,075	1,781
sdn 4d	3,315	1,103	6,463
town sdn	3,335	1,147	291
sdn 4d, 7P	3,705	1,455	49

S-10C Custom (wb 121.5; 7P-139.5)			
bus cpe	3,205	1,046	120
club cpe	3,270	1,142	2,236
conv cpe	3,510	1,317	489
sdn 2d	3,305	1,142	913
sdn 4d	3,330	1,152	7,974
town sdn	3,365	1,196	1,084
sdn 4d, 7P	3,725	1,504	79
limo 7P	3,820	1,580	20

1942 Engine	bore×stroke	bhp	availability
L6, 236.6	3.44×4.25	115	S-all

1946

S-11S DeLuxe (wb 121.5)*	Wght	Price	Prod
bus cpe	3,302	1,331	—
club cpe	3,392	1,451	—
sdn 2d	3,397	1,426	—
sdn 4d	3,427	1,461	—

S-11C Custom (wb 121.5; 7–8P-139.5)*			
club cpe	3,378	1,501	—
conv cpe	3,618	1,761	—
sdn 2d	3,423	1,491	—
sdn 4d	3,433	1,511	—
sdn 4d, 7P	3,837	1,893	—

DeSoto

	Wght	Price	Prod
limo 8P	3,937	2,013	—
Suburban sdn 4d, 8P	4,012	2,093	—

1946 Engine	bore×stroke	bhp	availability
L6, 236.6	3.44×4.25	109	S-all

1947

S-11S DeLuxe (wb 121.5)*

	Wght	Price	Prod
bus cpe	3,323	1,451	—
club cpe	3,413	1,541	—
sdn 2d	3,418	1,516	—
sdn 4d	3,448	1,551	—

S-11C Custom (wb 121.5; 7–8P-139.5)*

	Wght	Price	Prod
club cpe	3,398	1,591	—
conv cpe	3,618	1,965	—
sdn 2d	3,443	1,581	—
sdn 4d	3,453	1,601	—
sdn 4d, 7P	3,837	1,983	—
limo 7P	3,995	2,013	—
Suburban sdn 4d, 8P	4,012	2,283	—

1947 Engine	bore×stroke	bhp	availability
L6, 236.6	3.44×4.25	109	S-all

1948

S-11S DeLuxe (wb 121.5)*

	Wght	Price	Prod
bus cpe	3,285	1,699	—
club cpe	3,385	1,815	—
sdn 2d	3,375	1,788	—
sdn 4d	3,435	1,825	—

S-11C Custom (wb 121.5; 7–9P-139.5)*

	Wght	Price	Prod
club cpe	3,389	1,874	—
conv cpe	3,599	2,296	—
sdn 2d	3,399	1,860	—
sdn 4d	3,439	1,892	—
sdn 4d, 7P	3,819	2,315	—
limo 7P	3,995	2,442	—
Suburban sdn 4d, 9P	3,974	2,631	—

1948 Engine	bore×stroke	bhp	availability
L6, 236.6	3.44×4.25	109	S-all

1949 First Series

S-11S DeLuxe (wb 121.5)*

	Wght	Price	Prod
bus cpe	3,285	1,699	—
club cpe	3,385	1,815	—
sdn 2d	3,375	1,788	—
sdn 4d	3,435	1,825	—

S-11C Custom (wb 121.5; 7–9P-139.5)*

	Wght	Price	Prod
club cpe	3,389	1,874	—
conv cpe	3,599	2,296	—
sdn 2d	3,399	1,860	—
sdn 4d	3,439	1,892	—
sdn 4d, 7P	3,819	2,315	—
limo 7P	3,995	2,442	—
Suburban 4d, 9P	3,974	2,631	—

1949(1) Engine	bore×stroke	bhp	availability
L6, 236.6	3.44×4.25	109	S-all

*Factory combined production figures for 1946 through 1949 First Series.

Combined 1946–1949 First Series Production:

S-11S DeLuxe (wb 121.5)

	Prod
bus cpe	1,950
club cpe	8,580
sdn 2d	12,751
sdn 4d	32,213

S-11C Custom (wb 121.5; 7–9P-139.5)

	Prod
club cpe	38,720
conv cpe	8,100
sdn 2d	1,600
sdn 4d	126,226
sdn 4d, 7P	3,530
limo 7P	120
Suburban 4d, 8–9P	7,500
chassis	105

1949 Second Series

S-13-1 DeLuxe (wb 125.5)

	Wght	Price	Prod
club cpe	3,455	1,976	6,807
sdn 4d	3,520	1,986	13,148
Carry-All sdn 4d, 6P	3,565	2,191	2,690
wgn 4d, 9P	3,915	2,959	680

S-13-2 Custom (wb 125.5; 8–9P-139.5)

	Wght	Price	Prod
club cpe	3,585	2,156	18,431
conv cpe	3,785	2,578	3,385
sdn 4d	3,645	2,174	48,589
sdn 4d, 8P	4,200	2,863	342
Suburban 4d, 9P	4,410	3,179	129

1949(2) Engine	bore×stroke	bhp	availability
L6, 236.6	3.44×4.25	112	S-all

1950

S-14-1 DeLuxe (wb 125.5; 8P-139.5)

	Wght	Price	Prod
club cpe	3,450	1,976	10,704
sdn 4d	3,525	1,986	18,489
Carry-All sdn 4d, 5P	3,600	2,191	3,900
sdn 4d, 8P	3,995	2,676	235
chassis	—	—	1

S-14-2 Custom (wb 125.5; 8–9P-139.5)

	Wght	Price	Prod
club cpe	3,575	2,156	18,302
Sportsman htp cpe	3,735	2,489	4,600
conv cpe	3,815	2,578	2,900
sdn 4d	3,640	2,174	72,664
wgn 4d (wood)	4,035	3,093	600
wgn 4d (steel)	3,900	2,717	100
sdn 4d, 8P	4,115	2,863	734
Suburban 4d, 9P	4,400	3,179	623
chassis	—	—	2

1950 Engine	bore×stroke	bhp	availability
L6, 236.6	3.44×4.25	112	S-all

1951

S-15-1 DeLuxe (wb 125.5; 8P-139.5)*

	Wght	Price	Prod
club cpe	3,475	2,215	—
sdn 4d	3,570	2,227	—
Carry-All sdn 4d	3,685	2,457	—
sdn 4d, 8P	4,045	3,001	—

S-15-2 Custom (wb 125.5; 8–9P-139.5)*	Wght	Price	Prod
club cpe	3,585	2,418	—
Sportsman htp cpe	3,760	2,761	—
conv cpe	2,862	2,840	—
sdn 4d	3,685	2,438	—
wgn 4d	3,960	3,047	—
sdn 4d, 8P	4,122	2,211	—
Suburban 4d, 9P	4,395	3,566	—

1951 Engine	bore×stroke	bhp	availability
L6, 250.6	3.44×4.50	116	S-all

1952

S-15-1 DeLuxe (wb 125.5; 8P-139.5)*	Wght	Price	Prod
club cpe	3,435	2,319	—
sdn 4d	3,540	2,333	—
Carry-All sdn 4d	3,650	2,572	—-
sdn 4d, 8P	4,035	3,142	—

S-15-2 Custom (wb 125.5; 8–9P-139.5)*	Wght	Price	Prod
club cpe	3,565	2,531	—
Sportsman htp cpe	3,720	2,890	—
conv cpe	3,865	2,996	—
sdn 4d	3,660	2,552	—
wgn 4d	4,020	3,189	—
sdn 4d, 8P	4,155	3,362	—
Suburban 4d, 9P	4,370	3,734	—

S-17 Firedome (wb 125.5; 8P-139.5)	Wght	Price	Prod
club cpe	3,675	2,718	5,699
Sportsman htp cpe	3,850	3,078	3,000
conv cpe	3,950	3,183	850
sdn 4d	3,760	2,740	35,651
wgn 4d	4,080	3,377	550
sdn 4d, 8P	4,325	3,547	50

1952 Engines	bore×stroke	bhp	availability
L6, 250.6	3.44×4.50	116	S-Deluxe, Custom
V8, 276.1	3.63×3.34	160	S-Firedome

*Factory combined 1951–1952 Deluxe and Custom production figures.

1951–1952 Deluxe and Custom Production:

S-15-1 DeLuxe (wb 125.5; 8P-139.5)	Prod
club cpe	6,100
sdn 4d	13,506
Carry-All sdn 4d	1,700
sdn 4d, 8P	343

S-15-2 Custom (wb 125.5; 8–9P-139.5)	Prod
club cpe	19,000
Sportsman htp cpe	8,750
conv cpe	3,950
sdn 4d	88,491
wgn 4d	1,440
sdn 4d, 8P	769
Suburban 4d, 9P	600

1953

S-18 Powermaster (wb 125.5; 8P-139.5)	Wght	Price	Prod
club cpe	3,480	2,334	8,063
Sportsman htp cpe	3,585	2,604	1,470
sdn 4d	3,535	2,356	33,644
wgn 4d	3,845	3,078	500
sdn 4d, 8P	4,080	3,251	225

S-16 Firedome (wb 125.5; 8P-139.5)	Wght	Price	Prod
club cpe	3,655	2,622	14,591
Sportsman htp cpe	3,740	2,893	4,700
conv cpe	3,990	3,114	1,700
sdn 4d	3,720	2,643	64,211
wgn 4d	3,995	3,351	1,100
sdn 4d, 8P	4,270	3,529	200

1953 Engines	bore×stroke	bhp	availability
L6, 250.6	3.44×4.50	116	S-Powermaster
V8, 276.1	3.63×3.34	160	S-Firedome

1954

S-20 Powermaster (wb 125.5; 8P-139.5)	Wght	Price	Prod
club cpe	3,505	2,364	3,499
Sportsman htp cpe (discont'd.)	3,590	2,635	250
sdn 4d	3,570	2,386	14,967
wgn 4d	3,855	3,108	225
sdn 4d, 8P	4,100	2,381	263

S-19 Firedome (wb 125.5; 8P-139.5)	Wght	Price	Prod
club cpe	3,735	2,652	5,762
Sportsman htp cpe	3,815	2,923	4,382
conv cpe	4,015	3,144	1,025
sdn 4d	3,790	2,673	45,095
wgn 4d	4,045	3,381	946
sdn 4d, 8P	4,305	3,559	165
chassis	—	—	1

1954 Engines	bore×stroke	bhp	availability
L6, 250.6	3.44×4.50	116	S-Powermaster
V8, 276.1	3.63×3.34	170	S-Firedome

1955

S-22 Firedome (wb 126.0)	Wght	Price	Prod
Special htp cpe	3,801	2,541	28,944
Sportsman htp cpe	3,805	2,654	
conv cpe	4,010	2,824	625
sdn 4d	3,870	2,498	46,388
wgn 4d	4,185	3,170	1,083

S-21 Fireflite (wb 126.0)	Wght	Price	Prod
Sportsman htp cpe	3,890	2,939	10,313
conv cpe	4,115	3,151	775
sdn 4d (inc. Coronado)	3,940	2,727	26,637

1955 Engines	bore×stroke	bhp	availability
V8, 291.0	3.72×3.34	185	S-Firedome
V8, 291.0	3.72×3.34	200	S-Fireflite

1956

S-23 Firedome (wb 126.0)	Wght	Price	Prod
Seville htp cpe	3,800	3,734	19,136
Seville htp sdn	3,920	2,833	4,030
Sportsman htp cpe	3,835	2,854	4,589
Sportsman htp sdn	3,945	2,953	1,645
conv cpe	4,080	3,081	646
sdn 4d	3,780	2,678	44,909
wgn 4d	4,095	3,371	2,950

S-24 Fireflite (wb 126.0)	Wght	Price	Prod
Sportsman htp cpe	3,905	3,346	8,475
Sportsman htp sdn	3,970	3,431	3,350
conv cpe	4,075	3,544	1,385*
Pacesetter conv cpe	4,070	3,615	100*

		Wght	Price	Prod
	sdn 4d	3,860	3,119	18,207
	Adventurer htp cpe	3,870	3,728	996

*Estimated; total conv cpes 1,485.

1956 Engines	bore×stroke	bhp	availability
V8, 330.4	3.72×3.80	230	S-Firedome
V8, 330.4	3.72×3.80	255	S-Fireflite exc Adventurer
V8, 341.4	3.78×3.80	320	S-Adventurer

1957

S-27 Firesweep (wb 122.0)		Wght	Price	Prod
	Sportsman htp cpe	3,645	2,836	13,333
	Sportsman htp sdn	3,720	2,912	7,168
	sdn 4d	3,675	2,777	17,300
	Shopper wgn 4d, 6P	3,965	3,169	2,270
	Explorer wgn 4d, 9P	3,970	3,310	1,198

S-25 Firedome (wb 126.0)				
	Sportsman htp cpe	3,910	3,085	12,179
	Sportsman htp sdn	3,960	3,142	9,050
	conv cpe	4,065	3,361	1,297
	sdn 4d	3,955	2,958	23,330

S-26 Fireflite (wb 126.0)				
	Sportsman htp cpe	4,000	3,614	7,217
	Sportsman htp sdn	4,125	3,671	6,726
	conv cpe	4,085	3,890	1,151
	sdn 4d	4,025	3,487	11,565
	Shopper wgn 4d, 6P	4,290	3,982	837
	Explorer wgn 4d, 9P	4,250	4,124	934

S-26A Adventurer (wb 126.0)				
	htp cpe	4,040	3,997	1,650
	conv cpe	4,235	4,272	300

1957 Engines	bore×stroke	bhp	availability
V8, 325.0	3.69×3.80	245	S-Firesweep
V8, 325.0	3.69×3.80	260	O-Firesweep
V8, 341.0	3.78×3.80	270	S-Firedome
V8, 341.0	3.78×3.80	290	S-Fireflite
V8, 345.0	3.80×3.80	345	S-Adventurer

1958

LS1-L Firesweep (wb 122.0)		Wght	Price	Prod
23	Sportsman htp cpe	3,660	2,890	5,635
27	conv cpe	3,850	3,219	700
41	sdn 4d	3,660	2,819	7,646
43	Sportsman htp sdn	3,720	2,953	3,003
45A	Shopper wgn 4d, 6P	3,955	3,266	1,305
45B	Explorer wgn 4d, 9P	3,980	3,408	1,125

LS2-M Firedome (wb 126.0)				
23	Sportsman htp cpe	3,825	3,178	4,325
27	conv cpe	4,065	3,489	519
41	sdn 4d	3,855	3,085	9,505
43	Sportsman htp sdn	3,920	3,235	3,130

LS3-H Fireflite (wb 126.0)				
23	Sportsman htp cpe	3,920	3,675	3,284
27	conv cpe	4,105	3,972	474
41	sdn 4d	3,990	3,583	4,192
43	Sportsman htp sdn	3,980	3,731	3,243
45A	Shopper wgn 4d, 6P	4,225	4,030	318
45B	Explorer wgn 4d, 9P	4,295	4,172	609

LS3-S Adventurer (wb 126.0)				
23	htp cpe	4,000	4,071	350
27	conv cpe	4,180	4,369	82

1958 Engines	bore×stroke	bhp	availability
V8, 350.0	4.06×3.38	280	S-Firesweep
V8, 350.0	4.06×3.38	295	O-Firesweep
V8, 361.0	4.13×3.38	295	S-Firedome
V8, 361.0	4.13×3.38	305	S-Fireflite; O-Firedome
V8, 361.0	4.13×3.38	345	S-Adventurer
V8, 361.0	4.13×3.38	355	O-Adventurer

1959

MS1-L Firesweep (wb 122.0)		Wght	Price	Prod
23	Sportsman htp cpe	3,625	2,967	5,481
27	conv cpe	3,840	3,315	596
41	sdn 4d	3,670	2,904	9,649
43	Sportsman htp sdn	3,700	3,038	2,875
45A	Shopper wgn 4d, 6P	3,950	3,366	1,054
45B	Explorer wgn 4d, 9P	3,980	3,508	1,179

MS2-M Firedome (wb 126.0)				
23	Sportsman htp cpe	3,795	3,341	2,862*
27	conv cpe	4,015	3,653	299*
41	sdn 4d	3,840	3,234	9,171*
43	Sportsman htp sdn	3,895	3,398	2,744*

MS3-H Fireflite (wb 126.0)				
23	Sportsman htp cpe	3,910	3,831	1,393
27	conv cpe	4,105	4,152	186
41	sdn 4d	3,920	3,763	4,480
43	Sportsman htp sdn	3,950	3,888	2,364
45A	Shopper wgn 4d, 6P	4,170	4,216	271
45B	Explorer wgn 4d, 9P	4,205	4,358	433

MS3-S Adventurer (wb 126.0)				
23	htp cpe	3,980	4,427	590
27	conv cpe	4,120	4,749	97

*Includes Seville htp cpe, conv cpe, sdn 4d, and htp sdn, trim variation introduced in Spring 1959 to mark DeSoto's 30th anniversary.

1959 Engines	bore×stroke	bhp	availability
V8, 361.0	4.13×3.38	295	S-Firesweep
V8, 383.0	4.25×3.38	305	S-Firedome
V8, 383.0	4.25×3.38	325	S-Fireflite
V8, 383.0	4.25×3.38	350	S-Adventurer; O-others

1960

PS1-L Fireflite (wb 122.0)		Wght	Price	Prod
23	htp cpe	3,885	3,102	3,494
41	sdn 4d	3,865	3,017	9,032
43	htp sdn	3,865	3,167	1,958

PS3-M Adventurer (wb 122.0)				
23	htp cpe	3,945	3,663	3,092
41	sdn 4d	3,895	3,579	5,746
43	htp sdn	3,940	3,727	2,759

1960 Engines	bore×stroke	bhp	availability
V8, 361.0	4.13×3.38	295	S-Fireflite
V8, 383.0	4.25×3.38	305	S-Adventurer

1961

(wb 122.0)				
612	htp cpe	3,760	3,102	911
614	htp sdn	3,820	3,167	2,123

1961 Engine	bore×stroke	bhp	availability
V8, 361.0	4.13×3.38	265	S-all

Dodge

**Dodge Division, Chrysler Corp.
Detroit and Hamtramck, Michigan**

Chrysler bought the 14-year-old Dodge Brothers Corporation in 1928, and managed to produce 125,000 Dodge cars the following year before the Depression altered the economic climate. Yet, while other manufacturers were bottoming out in 1933 and 1934, the new division of Chrysler was producing an average of 100,000 units a year, running fourth in the industry behind Chevrolet, Ford, and Plymouth.

In its early years, Dodge had never made any pretense at sportiness. The Dodge brothers were traditional industrialists who believed in practicality and dollar-for-dollar value. Even in the 1940s, there was little about the marque that suggested the high-performance cars to come. Dodge was simply a solid, reliable, low-to-middle-priced car, the next step up from a Plymouth.

Dodge's market position shifted around in the early '30s; with prices sometimes above DeSoto's, sometimes below. By 1933, the Chrysler regime had decreed that Dodge should occupy the attractive territory just above Plymouth and below DeSoto. Because of the Depression, it took the

firm eight years to rebuild its new acquisition, but Dodge output began surging, and hit over 200,000 a year by 1935. Two years later, a prewar record was reached with 299,841 units. By then, Dodge was firmly established as the number-four producer, after Chevy, Ford, and Plymouth.

The early-'30s models retained Dodge Brothers styling barely long enough for Chrysler to alter it. Engines were also altered, and the company experimented with a wide range of L-head sixes and eights, the latter built through 1933 in three displacements. The Eights offered a slight performance advantage over the Six, but smoothness and low-end torque were their big attractions. They were also more graceful than the lower-priced cars because of their longer wheelbases. They were not really built for performance, being intended to compete with the likes of Pontiac, but they were available in several sporty body styles.

Dodge had the most conservative styling of any Chrysler Corporation make in the '30s and, fortunately for the division, was never saddled with a version of the Airflow. Lines were four-square and upright through 1934, the only con-

1930 DD New Six four-door sedan

1933 DP Six coupe

1932 DK Eight two/four-passenger coupe

1934 New Standard Six four-door sedan

1936 Beauty Winner Six two-door touring sedan

1937 Series D5 two-door trunkback sedan

cession to the streamlining craze being a rakish grille on the 1933-34s. The famous ram hood ornament, a manifestation of the Chrysler takeover, was first used on the '32s. A waterfall grille and rounder, skirted fenders crept into the formula for 1935 as part of Chrysler's company-wide "Airstream" look. By 1939, Dodges had acquired extended pontoon-style fenders, elongated rear decks, and a sharp-edge frontal motif under the direction of body designer Ray Dietrich. Meanwhile, the firm's costlier cars had backed away from the radical Airflow look, so that by the end of the decade, Dodge was right in line with both DeSoto and Chrysler.

The Dodge six, the engine foundation on which Walter Chrysler built, saw many forms in the '30s. Displacement ranged from 190 to 242 cubic inches, horsepower from 60 to 78. Numerous six-cylinder body styles were fielded encompassing all the popular open types of the period, and a convertible sedan was fielded throughout most of the decade, absent only in 1935 and finally dropped after 1938

due to low demand. A long-wheelbse chassis appeared for 1936 under seven-passenger sedans and limousines, and had been stretched to 134 inches by 1939.

Chrysler would give its cars almost any name if it meant better sales, so the Dodge line included such prosaic titles as the "New Standard" of 1934, the "New Value" for 1935, the "Beauty Winner" of 1936, and 1939's "Luxury Liner" (the last later becoming something of a slang expression). Sales picked up as the Depression eased, and proved far better than those of the Airflow-plagued Chrysler and DeSoto divisions. Dodge also made a strong effort to win custom body business by selling chassis to hearse, ambulance, and station wagon builders.

One of Dodge's more innovative years was 1937. Though the cars were not vastly altered from the "Air Styled" '36s they did introduce non-snag door handles, recessed dash knobs, flush-mounted dash gauges, ultra-low driveshaft tunnels, one-piece steel roof construction, and built-in defroster vents. And the 1937 Series D5 marked a first

1938 Series D8 four-door trunkback sedan

1939 Luxury Liner DeLuxe four-door fastback sedan

by employing fully insulated rubber body mounts.

The totally redesigned 1939s arrived simultaneously with a futuristic world's fair and Dodge's Silver Anniversary. In apparent celebration of the twin events, Dodge reinstated a dual model lineup for the first time since 1934. Dubbed Special and Deluxe, the two series differed mainly in interior trim. The economic doldrums were over at last.

Dodge had built eight-cylinder engines in the early '30s, and would do so again in the '50s. But in the '40s, all models were powered by sixes. This was a cast-iron flathead unit with design roots going back to 1933. Since then, it had been enlarged to 217.8 cubic inches. For 1942, it was stroked for 230.2 cid, and its Stromberg carburetor was replaced by a Carter. In this form, it developed 105 bhp at 3600 rpm, and would be continued through 1949 and beyond.

Dodge retained the same body from 1940 through its "first series" 1949 models. The standard wheelbase was 119.5 inches. The car's 1940-41 styling was typical of Chrysler in that era: freestanding fenders; built-in headlamps; prominent, peaked radiator grille; high superstructure; limited glass area.

The 1940 line was grouped into Special and DeLuxe series. The Special comprised three body styles: a two-seat coupe, and two- and four-door sedans. The De-Luxe offered these plus a convertible, a larger coupe, and a seven-passenger sedan and limousine. DeLuxe prices ranged up to $1170 for the limousine. The running board was declining in popularity, so it was a $10 option for all models. Of about 195,000 cars built for 1940, 120,000 were DeLuxes, although only 1000 of these were on the long wheelbase. A feature that year was optional two-tone paint, with fenders, hood, and deck done in a contrasting shade. Predictably, it gave the car a taxicab look and was not popular.

In 1941, a clean facelift using a bold, horizontal grille greatly improved Dodge appearance. The DeLuxe name now designated the inexpensive three-model line. The new top-of-the-line series was labeled Custom. The 2-4 passenger coupe was replaced by a Town Sedan (with blind rear roof quarters); the two-door sedan was called the Brougham. Fluid Drive became an option, and the engine was boosted to 91 bhp through changes in compression. Parking lights were moved inboard to the grille. Turn indicators were housed in large chrome pods atop the fenders.

As it was for most manufacturers, 1941 was a banner year for Dodge. Model year production was one of the highest in the division's history: some 106,000 DeLuxes and 131,000 Customs were built. The new Town Sedan was a modest success. Long-wheelbase models continued to sell in small quantities. The division held seventh place in the industry, then crept ahead of sixth-place Oldsmobile in 1942.

When the federal government ordered car production halted in February 1942, Dodge had built only about 68,000 of its new models. They were good-looking cars—not quite as radical as the hidden-headlamp De-Sotos, but nicely done throughout. Grilles were now full-width, heavier and wider than before, featuring a prominent eggcrate central section. Optional fender skirts carried bright moldings to blend with rear fender trim. Performance was improved by means of an enlarged engine that provided 105 bhp. A club coupe was added to the DeLuxe line. Production wasn't low enough to make the '42 Dodge as rare as some other makes that year. Of the standard wheelbase models, the convertible coupe—1185 units—is the scarcest.

After the war, Dodge got off to an especially slow start, and only 420 of the '46s were built before December 31, 1945. Wartime studies had produced a variety of interesting postwar styling proposals for the 1940-42 body. Among them were smooth grilles, wraparound bumpers, thin door pillars, and integral fenders. But body tooling was far from amortized in 1942, and Dodge's decision to produce a mildly facelifted version of its prewar designs for 1946-48 was typical of the postwar industry. Between January and December 1946, Dodge turned out these cars rapidly, finishing the year fourth behind the low-priced three.

Facelifting for the 1946-48 Dodges (which were physically identical except for serial numbers) was carried out by stylists A. B. Grisinger, John Chika, and Herb Weissinger—a trio later to win fame at Kaiser-Frazer. Allowed bolt-on alterations only, they opted for a new grille with very wide horizontal and vertical bars forming a pattern of rectangles. Parking lights were square, located at either side of the grille with the Dodge nameplate mounted above it. Mechanical changes included relocation of the starter from a foot pedal to a button on the dash, and front brakes equipped with double wheel cylinders. The transmission was also revised. An in-line fuel filter and full-flow oil filter became standard.

One part that is easy to change, despite carryover bodies, is the dashboard. This underwent continuous alteration at Dodge in the '40s. The 1940 edition was a relatively plain affair, flat and square, with instruments grouped under a big three-spoke steering wheel. In '41, the steering wheel came with two pairs of horizontal spokes and the dash was symmetrical: speedometer and large clock flanked a central radio-speaker panel,

with minor gauges positioned in a row to the left of the speedometer. In 1942, the dash got a woodgrain finish, and the steering wheel went back to three spokes. This pattern was retained for the 1946-48 models, with the addition of more brightwork. Dashboard symmetry was standard fare in the '40s—often at the expense of visibility. Dodge paid attention to practicality, however, by retaining needle gauges that were clear and readable.

After 1946, Fluid Drive was made standard for all models. This was an important selling point in an age when people were tiring of manual shift. Inaugurated in 1938, Fluid Drive was a complicated solution to a simple problem. Combining a conventional clutch with torque converter and electrical shifting circuits, it provided what one writer called a "full range of potential transmission trouble." But it did replace the conventional flywheel with a fluid-coupling torque converter. The converter performed the usual flywheel functions— storing energy, smoothing power impulses, and carrying the ring gear that meshed with the starter pinion. Lacking a clutch plate contact, a clutch was mounted in tandem. The fluid coupling itself was a drum, filled with low-viscosity mineral oil. As the engine ran, a set of vanes attached to the inner casing rotated, throwing oil outward onto a facing runner that had another set of vanes. The oil turned the runner, allowing a smooth flow of power and avoiding any metal-to-metal contact.

There were two gear positions: Low for first and second; High for third and fourth. Low was used mainly for fast starts or towing situations. For normal driving, you simply shifted into High and pressed on the accelerator. At 14 mph when the accelerator was released, a "thump" announced the car had switched from third to fourth gear. Stops and starts were accomplished without any clutching or gear shifting at all. Fluid Drive eliminated 95 percent of gear shifting. The clutch was there, but it was used only to change between Low and High, or to back up.

Dodge's restyled 1949 models were not ready at new-car announcement time, so leftover '48s were sold as '49s until April. The "second series" 1949, powered by a 100-bhp version of the old six, was entirely redesigned.

continued on page 257

1940 DeLuxe four-door sedan

1941 Custom convertible coupe

1940 Special two-door sedan

1942 DeLuxe club coupe

1941 Custom four-door sedan

1946 Deluxe three-passenger coupe

▲1950 Oldsmobile Futuramic 88 convertible   ▼1950 Ford Custom Crestliner Tudor sedan

▲1950 Oldsmobile Futuramic 88 two-door sedan ▼1951 Ford Custom convertible

▲1952 Chevrolet Styleline Deluxe convertible   ▼1953 Buick Super convertible

▲1953 Kaiser Manhattan four-door sedan   ▼1953 Packard Caribbean convertible

▲1953 Ford Crestline Sunliner convertible   ▼1953 Hudson Hornet club coupe

▲1953 Nash-Healey roadster ▼1954 Kaiser-Darrin DKF-161 roadster

▲1955 Ford Fairlane Crown Victoria club coupe   ▼1955 Lincoln Capri hardtop coupe

▲1955 Oldsmobile Super 88 Holiday hardtop sedan    ▼1956 Packard Caribbean convertible

▲1956 Cadillac Series 62 Coupe deVille hardtop ▼1956 Buick Special Riviera hardtop coupe

▲1956 Ford Fairlane Victoria hardtop coupe

▼1957 Lincoln Premiere Landau hardtop sedan

▲1957 Ford Thunderbird convertible with hardtop ▼1957 Pontiac Star Chief convertible

▲1957 Cadillac Series 62 Sedan de Ville hardtop   ▼1957 Chrysler New Yorker hardtop sedan

▲1957 Continental Mark II hardtop coupe   ▼1957 Oldsmobile Golden Rocket 88 two-door sedan

▲1958 Pontiac Bonneville hardtop coupe   ▼1958 Chevrolet Impala convertible

▲1958 Edsel Pacer convertible   ▼1958 Plymouth Belvedere Sport Sedan hardtop

▲1959 Ford Thunderbird hardtop coupe   ▼1959 Oldsmobile Ninety-Eight convertible

1949 Coronet four-door sedan

1949 Wayfarer roadster

A-227 front-wheel-drive prototype, 1949-50

1950 Coronet four-door sedan

1950 Wayfarer Sportabout roadster

continued from page 240

First came the inexpensive Wayfarer series on a 115-inch wheelbase. It comprised a sedan, coupe, and a novel roadster with side curtains, in a price range of $1611 to $1738. The Meadowbrook and Coronet—the volume cars of the line—rode a 123.5-inch wheelbase. They were more luxuriously trimmed and available in a wider variety of body styles. The Coronet Town Sedan was a luxury trim option, about $85 more expensive than the standard model. It featured beautiful and luxurious Bedford cord upholstery. The Meadowbrook was a single four-door sedan, trimmed more simply and offered at about $75 less than the comparable Coronet.

The new squared-off body styling remained quite conservative. A bold eggcrate grille bore some resemblance to the 1946-48 design, but was more massive. Bolt-on rear fenders were capped by taillights visible from three sides. The slab-sided body was embellished by stainless-steel moldings. Collectors today agree that the Wayfarer roadster is the most desirable '49 Dodge, and many of these have been restored. By contrast, the 1949 woody wagon was not successful: only 800 unit sales were recorded for the model year. After 600 were sold in 1950, it was phased out. Dodge produced nearly 257,000 cars in 1949—a new record.

Dodge's image was transformed in the '50s. The cars began the decade as stodgy six-bangers, but soon became V8 track stars. Styling kept pace with performance. The division had its ups and downs in sales, however, as it deserted one kind of buyer for another.

The three-box '49 bodyshell got a major facelift for 1950 and a new Diplomat hardtop was added. Gyro-Matic drive, an improvement on standard Fluid Drive that eliminated gear changing, also appeared. All models were powered by the sturdy flathead six, which would serve Dodge through the decade. Two basic model lines were fielded. The D33 Wayfarer, including a winsome sport convertible, was priced just above the more expensive Plymouths. The D34 series comprised Meadowbrook and Coronet sedans and Coronet wagons, coupes, convertibles, and hardtops. Through 1952, Coronet would also be offered as a long-wheelbase sedan, Dodge's heaviest car, for taxi and limousine purposes.

Styling in the early '50s was pretty dull. But Dodge represented a step up in prestige for Plymouth owners in those years, and the cars did well. The division built over 340,000 in 1950, and 290,000 in 1951 to nail down seventh place in the industry. Dodge held onto seventh in 1952 by building only 206,000 cars, but dropped back to eighth for 1954 as production reached only 154,000 units.

Without a switch in wheelbases, styling became smoother and sleeker for 1951-52. A lower grille opening, clean flanks, and faired-in taillights gave a new look. The model lineup remained exactly as it had been in 1950. Wayfarers set the price pace; Coronets supplied the widest variety of body styles; and the Meadow-

brook filled the gap between them with a lone four-door sedan. Appearance changed only slightly for '52—the grille bar immediately above the bumper was painted.

For 1953, a major revamping was accompanied by the Red Ram V8 for the first Dodge performance cars of the decade. Originally, the Red Ram produced 140 bhp, though it was capable of much more than that. It was essentially a scaled-down version of the 331-cid Chrysler Hemi introduced in 1951. Chrysler had long been experimenting with hemispherical combustion chambers, and was now cashing in on what it had learned. The Hemi's advantages included smoother manifolding and porting, larger valves set farther apart, improved thermal efficiency, plenty of room for water passages, a more central spark plug location, and low heat rejection into coolant. Its main disadvantage was cost: engine for engine, Red Rams were more expensive to build than Chevy 265s, for example.

The 1953 Dodge was among the first production Chrysler automobiles styled by Virgil Exner, who had come from Studebaker a few years earlier. Surprisingly light, they handled well, and were known for economy

as well as performance. A Dodge V8 scored 23.4 miles per gallon in the '53 Mobilgas Economy Run; the same year, other V8s broke 196 AAA stock-car records at Bonneville, and Danny Eames drove one to a record 102.62 mph at El Mirage dry lake in California. Dodge's V8 was a small-displacement, high-efficiency power-plant—unique in its hemi-head construction, reliable, and strong.

Only detail changes were made for '54. However, a new, luxurious Royal series appeared, joined at mid-year by the Royal 500 convertible, named for the Indianapolis race. Dodge had paced the Indiana classic that year, and a round of pace-car replicas seemed like a good idea. Included in the 500 package (at only $2632) were Kelsey-Hayes chrome wire wheels, a "continental" spare tire, special ornamentation, and a 150-bhp Red Ram V8. Dealers could even specify a four-barrel Offenhauser manifold that must have made the 500 a screamer, though Chrysler never quoted the actual horsepower.

Of the Royal convertibles sold in 1954, only 701 were 500s, but the package was far more successful than that

1952 Wayfarer two-door sedan

1952 Coronet four-door sedan

April 1950 proposal for 1953 Dodge restyle

1953 Coronet 500 convertible

1953 Coronet four-door sedan

Firearrow show car of 1954 by Ghia

figure suggests. The division had established itself as the "performance team" at Chrysler, and had begun to roll up victories. Lincoln is famous for its dominance in the Mexican Road Race of those years. What is not widely known is that Dodge overwhelmed the race's Medium Stock class, taking the 1-2-3-4-6-9 positions in the 1954 marathon.

Competition successes helped boost sales. In a generally poor year for Chrysler products, the Dodge sold well in '54. The division came back with another major restyling that was mainly the work of Exner staff member Murray Baldwin. Set on a new 120-inch wheelbase, the '55 Coronets, Royals, and Custom Royals offered engine options of up to 193 bhp. They were much larger, but nicely styled and well-built.

In 1956, all Chrysler products grew tailfins and Dodge was no exception. PowerFlite automatic transmission, which had arrived with gear lever control in '54, now had pushbuttons. Facelifted styling and new

interiors were enhanced by a new engine, the optional D-500 V8, which developed a hefty 260 bhp at 4400 rpm. Dodge also unveiled a four-door Lancer hardtop in all three series. In a declining year for the industry, the division built only 240,000 cars but still managed to hold onto eighth place. The following year, with torsion-bar suspension and all-new styling, Dodge climbed to seventh place, building nearly 290,000 units.

Exner's Forward Look was new from the ground up for 1957, yet it hadn't progressed to extremes. That year's Dodge was smoothly styled and aggressive-looking, with a massive bumper/grille, lots of glass, and still more power. An array of Hemi engines, ranging from the mild 325 to the top 354-cid D-500 with 340 bhp, offered performance enthusiasts much to choose from. Even the old six got a horsepower boost.

Dodge did not follow Chrysler, DeSoto, and Plymouth with a limited-edition "supercar" for '57. Instead, it offered the D-500 option across the board, even on the

1954 Royal V8 convertible

1956 Custom Royal Lancer hardtop sedan

1955 Royal V8 four-door sedan

"La Femme" show car based on 1956 Custom Royal Lancer

1955 Royal Lancer V8 hardtop coupe

1957 Royal Lancer hardtop coupe

plain Coronet two-door sedan. All D-500s were equipped with stiff shocks, stiff springs, and torsion bars for what *Motor Trend* magazine called "close liaison with the road." The soft ride of conventional Chrysler cars was replaced by firm suspension settings that put D-500s at the top of the class in handling. And with the 245-bhp engine, the car ran 0 to 60 in 9.4 seconds in the magazine's tests. The D-500 model continued in 1958-59, but its expensive Hemi engine was replaced with a wedge-head V8. Offered with optional fuel injection for 1958, the 361-cid wedge would produce 333 bhp at 4800 rpm—the highest power offered by Dodge that year.

Riding a 122-inch wheelbase in 1957, Dodge continued with the same body and chassis for 1958-59. The '58s got a mild but attractive facelift with four headlamps and a less massive frontispiece. The model lineup was generally unchanged, but the Regal Lancer hardtop made its debut in February.

Fuel injection was a short-lived venture, marked by little success. Few buyers opted for it. More popular were the conventional V8s ranging up to 320 bhp. The old flathead six was still around, but was relegated to the Coronet series only and was not a wise buy. According to one tester: "It could be pretty much of a white elephant when you go to sell it." Dodge itself was somewhat of a white elephant in 1958, a disastrous year. Production plunged to 138,000 for the model year, barely enough to beat out Cadillac. Management remained calm—it was, after all, an abnormally poor year—and rebounded with a restyled 1959 line composed of the same basic models. The division built about 156,000 cars for its traditional eighth-place finish.

Fins went wild on most 1959 Chrysler Corporation cars, but remained fairly modest at Dodge. The front end was given a new look, the interior revised, and several interesting options premiered. Dodge and its companion divisions now had the popular swivel seat, a

1957 Custom Royal Lancer hardtop sedan

1957 Custom Royal convertible

1958 Regal Lancer hardtop coupe

1958 Custom Royal Lancer hardtop coupe

1959 Custom Sierra nine-passenger station wagon

1960 Matador hardtop sedan

semi-bucket affair that pivoted outward as the door opened. The twin four-barrel 383 V8 produced 1959's top horsepower—345 at 5000 rpm. Also available were 325 and 361 wedges, and the flathead six was marketed for the last time. Incidentally, the D-500 engines weren't cheap. The 383 with four-barrel cost $304 extra; the Super version with twin four-barrel cost $446. Both were thirsty, but it was the age of 30-cent gasoline. People were willing to spend extra money on the engines and gas to get the added performance.

Exner's Dodge show cars are worth mention. There was a Firearrow series beginning in 1953 with a mock-up roadster that was made road-ready the following year. In late 1954 came a Firearrow sport coupe and convertible. The latter inspired the limited-production Dual-Ghia of 1956. The Firearrow coupe was aerodynamically stable and achieved 143.44 mph on the banked oval at Chrysler's Proving Grounds.

Another show car was 1955's La Femme, a Custom Royal Lancer two-door hardtop painted pink and upholstered in white. Many custom accoutrements were featured, including a folding umbrella and fitted handbag stored in the backs of the front seats. La Femme was back again for the 1956 show route, and was all the rage. For awhile, it was considered for volume production, but no more than a handful were ultimately produced.

By 1970, Dodge was one of the leading names in high performance. In product orientation, the division had pushed upward into the market vacated by DeSoto, and downward into the compact and "ponycar" fields. As a result, volume increased rapidly. From 1964 through 1969, Dodge built an average of over half a million cars a year. In the industry's peak year of 1968, the division built a record 627,533 cars. But the competition was increasing output too, so Dodge's standing in the production race varied. In its best years, the division ranked fifth or sixth; in the worst 1961-63 period, it was eighth or ninth. The relatively poor showing in the early 1960s was temporary; Dodge quickly reoriented its product line and recovered rapidly. As Robert McCurry assumed the post of division president in the mid-1960s, Dodge achieved new status as a builder of hot cars.

Only one series on a fairly long wheelbase had been offered in 1959. For 1960, Dodge recognized the growing interest in smaller cars and added the new Dart line of sixes and V8s with a 118-inch wheelbase for sedans and hardtop and a 122-inch wheelbase for wagons. Darts were available in three series: Seneca, Pioneer, and Phoenix. The "senior" Matador and Polara rode the 122-inch wheelbase and were offered with V8s only.

Dart's six-cylinder engine was the larger of two excellent Chrysler Corporation slant sixes. Displacing 225 cid, it continued in various Dodge models on through the '70s. The Dart 318 V8 was another solid, reliable unit. Matadors used the Chrysler 361-cid V8; Polaras got the 383 V8, the latter offered optionally on Matador and Phoenix.

1960 Dart Phoenix hardtop coupe

1961 Dart Phoenix convertible

Unit body/chassis construction was new for 1960, accompanied by a complete restyling. The Dart and the large Dodges got "chrome-y" front ends, large blunt grilles, and reworked tailfins. On the big cars the fins ended ahead of the taillights; the Dart's ran all the way back. Despite the heavy-handed appearance, most models were relatively light and offered good performance with reasonable economy. The year brought an industry-wide recovery from the 1958-59 recession, and volume was up by over 200,000 units.

For 1961, Dodge was ready with its twin to the compact Valiant. Called Lancer, it used a modestly reworked version of the Valiant body/chassis. Lancers had a horizontal-bar grille, instead of Valiant's square one, and slightly better trim. There were two series, 170 and 770, each with sedans and wagons. The 770 also had a hardtop. Power came from a 170-cid slant six with 101 bhp. The Dart's 225-cid was optional.

The Dart was facelifted for 1961, with a full-width concave grille incorporating quad headlights, and reverse-slant tailfins. The six and V8 Seneca, Pioneer, and Phoenix models continued. The senior line was pared down to the Polara series only, though a convertible was added in the V8 Phoenix series. Darts and Polaras retained 1960's lineup of V8s. The top powerplant was the 383-cid D-500 with 330 bhp. Twin four-barrel carburetors and ram-induction were responsible for this outstanding output, and made the Polara extraordinarily fast, fully capable of 120 mph. Oversized Chrysler brakes and torsion-bar front suspension combined to make the D-500 as roadable as it was quick. Since the ram-induction engine was available on Darts

1961 Polara hardtop sedan

1962 Lancer GT hardtop coupe

1962 Custom 880 hardtop sedan

1963 Custom 880 hardtop sedan

as well as Polaras, Dodge also had an extremely rapid "intermediate." The D-500 Dart Phoenix had almost one horsepower for every 10 pounds of weight.

Sales dropped by over 25 percent in 1961, as a result of increased competition in the compact-car market, and an overall downtrend in the industry. Lancer did not sell well, but it was a temporary entry anyway. As development work progressed on its successor, Lancer returned for '62 with a busier grille as the only significant change.

Dart and Polara were treated to a brand-new body on a 116-inch wheelbase for 1962. Inspired by Virgil Exner, these cars were as much as 400 pounds lighter and six inches shorter than the '61s. If Americans like compacts, Exner reasoned, they'd also prefer downsized versions of standard-size models. Unfortunately, the designer was about 15 years ahead of his time: the '62s did not sell well. Most manufacturers enjoyed increased sales that year, but Dodge dropped. What

saved the division was a separate line of Chrysler-based large cars introduced at mid-year on a 122-inch wheelbase, the 880 and Custom 880. The year's performance news was marked by release of two 413-cid wedge engines, offering 410 and 420 bhp.

While Plymouth struggled on for another year with its shortened '62 design, Dodge increased standard wheelbase to 119 inches for 1963 and emphasized performance. The 413-cid wedge with 360 bhp was available for 880s. The performance version was punched out to 426 cid as the Ramcharger. With aluminum pistons and high-lift cam, it developed 415 or 425 bhp. Ramchargers were available in the light 330, 440, and Polara cars that won the 1962 National Hot Rod Association Championship for Dodge. The 330 reigned supreme on literally every dragstrip. They were also strong contenders at Daytona.

Also new for 1963 was the compact replacement for the Lancer. Dodge added five inches to the Valiant

1962 Polara 500 convertible

1964 Custom 880 convertible

1964 Polara hardtop coupe

1964 Dart GT hardtop coupe

1965 Dart GT convertible

1965 Monaco hardtop coupe

1965 Coronet 500 hardtop coupe

1965 Coronet 500 hardtop coupe

wheelbase for all models except wagons to create an all-new Dart. Hardtops, sedans, wagons, and convertibles were offered. Sales rebounded, and Dodge moved ahead of Rambler into seventh place.

The 1964 lineup was substantially the same as 1963's, distinguished by facelifts. Darts could be ordered with the 273-cid Valiant V8. The GT hardtop and convertible were snazzy, and priced remarkably low. The big Dodges came with the usual assortment of sixes and V8s. This year's Ramcharger was powered by the fabled Hemi, making its return to the performance wars. Dodge's Hemi-powered intermediates (and their Plymouth counterparts) dominated the NASCAR ovals that season, sweeping the Daytona 500, for example, 1-2-3. The 880 continued to satisfy big-car customers. Dodge climbed back into sixth place for the first time since 1960.

Dart received only a minor facelift for 1965. The division renamed its midrange line Coronet, which featured new styling and a 117-inch wheelbase for all models but the wagons, which rode a 116-inch wheelbase. A special 115-inch wheelbase Coronet Hemi-Charger was also offered, a two-door sedan weighing just 3165 pounds. The Hemi-Charger was perhaps one of the greatest performance bargains of the decade. It sold at a base price of $3165, which included heavy-duty springs and shocks, anti-roll bar, four-speed transmission, and strong "police" brakes. It could accelerate to 60 mph in seven seconds, and hit a top speed of 120 mph. In racing tune, developing up to 430 bhp, it ruled the tracks in 1965.

The '65 line also included the glamorous Coronet 500 hardtop and convertible with bucket seats and center console, plus a completely new 121-inch wheelbase line of Polaras, Custom 880s, and the sports/luxury Monaco hardtop. Aside from the wagons, the Monaco was the most expensive of the senior Dodges.

For 1966, the offerings continued to be six and V8 Darts; six and V8 Coronets in standard, Deluxe, 440, and 500 guise; V8 Polaras and Monacos; and a hardtop Monaco 500. The Custom 880 was dropped in favor of a full-line Monaco series. A bright new addition was the fastback Charger on the 117-inch wheelbase. Although it shared some sheetmetal with the Coronet, the Charger had a look all its own: hidden headlamps, folddown split-back rear seat, a sporty interior. Standard power was the 318 V8, but the 361, 383, and 426 Hemi V8s were available as options. So were manual transmission, "Rallye" suspension, and long list of luxury equipment. A 383 Charger with TorqueFlite automatic could run 0–60 mph in about nine seconds and hit 110 mph.

Dodge restyled most of its models for 1967. Dart hardtops, sedans, and convertibles continued on the 111-inch wheelbase, but the wagons were dropped. The new body styling was good-looking and clean-lined. Monaco and Polara adopted the Chrysler Newport's styling and sleeker roofline for a much lower profile than their predecessors. The Charger retained its 1966

Dodge

look, while the Coronet had a minor facelift and two new additions, the R/T (Road/Track) hardtop and convertible. Standard R/T equipment included the 440-cid 375-bhp engine, heavy-duty suspension, wide tires, and oversize brakes. The 426 Hemi V8 was again listed as an option for the Coronet R/T and the Charger.

The approach for 1968 was to facelift the Dart, Polara, and Monaco, and to completely restyle the Coronet and Charger. These were the best-looking Dodge intermediates of the decade, with a long, low, bullet-shaped fuselage; larger windows; a plain grille; and strong but light bumpers. The Charger featured hidden headlamps and a "flying buttress" roofline.

Several new variations appeared in the compact and intermediate lines. The Dart GTS comprised plush, grand touring hardtops and convertibles available with a new lightweight 340-cid V8. The Coronet Super Bee was a light, fast two-door coupe, equipped with a special 335-bhp version of the 383 engine. R/T equipment was made available for the Charger as well as the Coronet and resulted in a fine road car.

The Super Bee, Dart GTS, Coronet and Charger R/Ts

1966 Charger fastback hardtop coupe

1967 Dart GT hardtop coupe

1966 Coronet 500 hardtop coupe

1967 Coronet 500 hardtop coupe

1966 Dart GT convertible

1967 Monaco hardtop sedan

1966 Monaco 500 hardtop coupe

1968 Dart GTS hardtop coupe

composed what Dodge called its "Scat Pack," each denoted by bumble-bee stripes. These were among the most roadable machines in America during 1968. The R/T's ultimate engines, a 375-bhp Magnum 440 or a 425-bhp Hemi, made it a winning entry on the nation's dragstrips once again.

Like other Chrysler models that shared the same bodyshell, Polara and Monaco received all-new "fuselage" styling for 1969, but retained their 122-inch wheelbase. The Dart, Coronet, and Charger were facelifted. Chargers were given a split grille; Coronet R/Ts and 500s sported full-width taillamps. The usual wide range of engines was offered. A new variation was the

Dart Swinger two-door hardtop, which came with special identifying trim, a bright aluminum grille, and a choice of 318- or 340-cid V8s.

The pride of the '69 fleet was the exotic Charger Daytona, built especially for the Daytona 500. It featured a wind-cheating bullet nose with hidden headlights, a front spoiler, an aerodynamic full-fastback roof, and a towering rear-deck stabilizer. Compared with the previous Charger 500 racing car, the Daytona was about 20 percent more aerodynamic, which gave it an advantage of 500 yards per lap. Dodge built only 505 Charger Daytonas—just enough to qualify the model as a production car for NASCAR racing. The list price was

1968 Monaco 500 hardtop coupe

1968 Coronet R/T hardtop coupe

1968 Coronet 440 hardtop coupe

1968 Charger hardtop coupe

1969 Charger hardtop coupe

1969 Charger Daytona hardtop coupe

1969 Polara 500 hardtop coupe

1969 Dart Swinger hardtop coupe

about $8000. A Daytona won the Talledega 500 in September 1969, but arch-rival Ford failed to show up. In 1970, the Daytonas and Plymouth's similar Superbird won 38 of 48 major NASCAR races.

For 1970, Dodge fielded its answer to the Mustang and Camaro ponycars, fittingly named Challenger. Like its Ford and GM rivals, Challenger was offered with both six-cylinder and V8 engines. There were three models: hardtop coupe, convertible, and the Special Edition. The latter was a coupe with a padded vinyl roof and smaller ''formal'' rear window. Priced attractively in the $3000-3500 range and offering a broad list of options, the Challenger sold extremely well. Six-cylinder

models outpaced the V8s. Hardtops were the most popular; only about 10,000 Special Edition coupes found buyers.

Though specifications and dimensions of the 1970 line largely duplicated those of 1969, some significant styling changes occurred. Darts and Coronets received a new split grille. The Dart was particularly well-executed, with a longer hood and new rear styling. The Charger, closely resembling its 1969 predecessor, had a full-width grille surrounded by a massive loop bumper and was offered in six-cylinder form for the first time. The exotic Daytona had proved its point on the race tracks and was dropped.

1969 Coronet 500 hardtop coupe

1969 Coronet R/T hardtop coupe

1969 Charger 500 hardtop coupe

1970 Polara Custom hardtop coupe

1970 Dart Swinger 340 hardtop coupe

1970 Charger hardtop coupe

1970 Coronet 500 hardtop coupe

1970 Challenger R/T convertible

The senior-series Polara and Monaco were restyled following the general '70 theme. Loop-type bumpers surrounded grille and taillights; side marker lights were set into the bumper ends. Ignition/steering column locks, fiberglass-belted tires, dual-action wagon tailgates, and a long list of federally mandated safety equipment completed the 1970 equipment package. With some 400,000 sales, the year proved encouraging.

Dodge's path through the '70s was strewn with the same obstacles that made life difficult for all U.S. automakers in those years—mainly an increasing number of ever-stricter government regulations and a dramatically altered business climate stemming from the Arab oil embargo of 1973-74. However, the division began the decade ill-prepared for what lay ahead, its model line heavy with full-size behemoths motivated by thirsty big-block V8s and wallowing on overly soft suspensions. To be sure, the compact Dart still sold like hotcakes even if the Challenger ponycar didn't, but Dodge was handicapped by too many dinosaurs that hung around too long—along with the indifferent workmanship that hampered sales and contributed greatly to Chrysler Corporation's near-demise by 1980-81. Yet by that time, the division had been through its trial by fire and was building nothing remotely like its early-'70s models, save the 118.5-inch-wheelbase St. Regis sedan and the Mirada personal-luxury coupe, both remnants of what used to be the "intermediate" field.

It didn't take much corporate cogitating to dispose of the poor Challenger. Dodge had been the last major nameplate to field a ponycar, and though it tried hard, the clumsy, poorly built Challenger never posed a serious sales challenge to the Camaro/Firebird or even the Mustang II (if you call that one a ponycar). Discretion being the better part of valor, Dodge discreetly put this overweight latecomer to rest after 1974, when only about 16,000 were sold.

The first energy crisis seemed to make the brontosaurus-like Polara/Monaco full-size cars equally good bets for the automotive tar pits, but Dodge tried hard to save them by instituting cash rebates and various discount offers beginning in 1974. The Polara name vanished after 1977, when the Monaco name transferred to the intermediate line, replacing Coronet. But the big Dodge still hung on grimly as the Royal Monaco through 1978, still with the basic design introduced for '74 and selling in decent numbers largely on the strength of police orders. By 1979, the nine-model mid-size group had been reduced to just a pair of heavily facelifted coupes called Charger and Magnum, plus the similarly reworked St. Regis sedan, a twin to Chrysler's Newport/New Yorker.

The ultra-reliable Dart had made Dodge a leader in the compact class for many years, but its successor was a big disappointment. Introduced for 1976, the Aspen was little more than a slightly larger, slightly heavier Dart with a bit more passenger space and a wider range of luxury options. In other words, it was much like the Granada was to Maverick at Ford. Unfortunately, it earned the dubious distinction (along with the near-identical Plymouth Volare) of being the most recalled car in history, due mainly to

1971 Charger R/T hardtop coupe

1971 Coronet Brougham four-door sedan

1971 Polara hardtop sedan

1971 Challenger hardtop coupe

1972 Charger hardtop coupe

poor quality control and widespread body rust-through in particular. The other side of Aspen was its better performance, at least with the extra-cost 360 V8s initially available, and nicer furnishings compared to later Darts. Also, Aspen marked the return of a compact Dodge wagon, something Dart had lacked since its 1967 redesign, and there were pseudo-muscle R/T coupes and, later, a "finish it yourself" kit-car racer for the performance crowd.

Despite its problems, the Aspen was an important car for Dodge, and underlined one of the few things Detroit began doing well in the mid- to late '70s: putting big-car comfort in smaller packages. Dodge called it the "family car of the future," which was hyperbole exceeding the bounds of even P. T. Barnum, but it was a necessary step on the way to the genuine article. By contrast, the Dart's appeal was mainly as basic transportation, though the 1974-75 Special Edition models were a belated attempt to broaden it. An unusual Aspen (and Volare) design feature was the front suspension, which retained torsion bars per Chrysler tradition but mounted crosswise instead of longitudinally. Some critics sneered that this was merely a convoluted gimmick with no real advantage for ride or quietness, and some said it actually hampered handling. Nevertheless, the transverse arrangement did allow the

1972 Dart Swinger hardtop coupe

1973 Charger SE hardtop coupe

1973 Polara Custom hardtop sedan

1973 Monaco hardtop coupe

1973 Challenger hardtop coupe with Rallye option

1974 Monaco Brougham hardtop sedan

1974 Dart Sport fastback coupe

1974 Challenger hardtop coupe

suspension to be better isolated from the body, which made for smoother going than in the Dart. Both Aspen powerplants were hoary old affairs, but they had seen years of refinement, and the thrifty slant six (which could yield up to 25 mpg on the highway with manual shift and a gentle right foot) remained about as bulletproof as Detroit engines ever get.

Aspen may have not realized its full potential, but it was nothing compared to what was happening further up the line. The mid-size Coronet/Monaco became more like the equivalent Plymouth Satellite/Fury with each passing year (both were built nose-to-tail at Chrysler's Lynch Road facil-

ity in Detroit), and it was hardly a bargain at prices averaging $100 higher. It was also thirsty, and styling wasn't the best. As for the Charger, it simply got lost in all the name shuffling, and was progressively watered down. By 1974, not even the Dukes of Hazzard would have recognized it.

Better things were in store for the Diplomat, launched for 1977 as Dodge's counterpart to the Chrysler LeBaron and, like it, essentially a stretched-wheelbase version of the Aspen/Volare platform. It sold well from the start, and its more sensible design made the old-style intermediates more or less superfluous. Thus, the Coronet-turned-Monaco was deep-sixed after 1978 and the Cordoba-based Mag-

1975 Charger SE coupe

1976 Charger SE coupe

1975 Coronet Brougham hardtop coupe

1976 Charger Sport coupe

1975 Royal Monaco Brougham hardtop coupe

1976 Aspen Special Edition coupe

1975 Dart Special Edition hardtop coupe

1977 Diplomat Medallion four-door sedan

269

1976 Coronet Custom four-door sedan

1977 Monaco Brougham coupe

1978 Diplomat station wagon

1978 Monaco Brougham four-door sedan

1978 Aspen R/T coupe

1978 Magnum XE coupe

1978 Omni five-door sedan

1978 Charger SE coupe

1979 Magnum XE coupe

1979 Diplomat Medallion coupe

1979 Aspen R/T coupe

1979 St. Regis four-door sedan

1979 Omni 024 hatchback coupe

1980 Diplomat Medallion coupe

1980 Aspen SE coupe

1980 Mirada hardtop coupe

num coupe vanished a year later. For 1980, the smooth-looking Mirada arrived as the division's entry in the personal-luxury class. Mounted on the Diplomat platform, it was one of the few true hardtop coupes left in Detroit, and it was strikingly styled, especially the front end that vaguely recalled the "coffin-nose" of the Cord 810/812. The Mirada got a lot of good copy in the "buff" magazines, mainly because of its looks. And, considering how much things had changed since the end of the muscle-car era, it was decently quick—if you ordered the optional 185-horsepower (SAE net) 360 V8, the hairiest Dodge engine that season. Unhappily, this would be another model that arrived just a shade too late to be of any real sales value.

Capping Dodge's enforced product overhaul in the '70s was the Omni, a sensible, front-drive subcompact introduced for 1978 and cut very much from the same pattern Volkswagen had established with its trend-setting Rabbit. In its first couple of years, the Omni was even powered by a special version of VW's overhead-cam four (mounted transversely) but it was slightly larger and not as much

fun to drive. Even so, it offered the same boxy, hatchback body styling and a similar high level of practicality. Along with its Plymouth Horizon twin, it would prove to be one of the few bright spots in Chrysler's mostly gloomy sales outlook at the time. For 1979, a slicker coupe version of the Omni bowed on a slightly shorter wheelbase. Curiously named 024, it gained an immediate following, and even managed a few conquest sales among import buyers seeking a sporty and nimble 2 + 2 that was easy on the pocketbook. A further development was the de Tomaso, a one-year-only 1980 package option. It was marked by loud yellow or red paint, set off by black-finished rocker panels, a rear spoiler, and vertical louvers over the rear side windows. You also got beefed-up springs and shocks and wider Aramid-belted tires on cast-aluminum wheels. After Lee Iacocca took over as Chrysler's savior, he would again team up with his old friend Carroll Shelby to make make the 024 more of a genuine high-performance machine. Under the name Shelby Charger, it continues to win friends for Dodge Division at this writing.

Dodge Specifications

1930

DA Six (wb 112.0)—15,000 built (est.)*	Wght	Price	Prod
rdstr 2-4P	2,687	995	—
phtn 5P	2,730	1,025	—
bus cpe 2P	2,750	945	—
DeLuxe cpe 2-4P	2,812	1,025	—
victoria 4P	2,846	1,025	—
brougham 5P	2,834	995	—
sdn 2d 5P	2,876	925	—
sdn 4d 5P	2,894	995	—
DeLuxe sdn 4d 5P	2,898	1,065	—

DB Six Senior (wb 120.0)—7,000 built (est.)*	Wght	Price	Prod
rdstr 2-4P	3,303	1,615	—
cpe 2-4P	3,426	1,595	—
brougham 5P	3,419	1,545	—
sdn 4d	3,513	1,595	—
landau sdn 4d	3,525	1,645	—

DC Eight (wb 114.0)—19,993 built**	Wght	Price	Prod
rdstr 2P	2,802	1,095	598
phtn 5P	2,690	1,225	234
cpe 2-4P	2,981	1,125	2,999
conv cpe 2-4P	2,938	1,195	728
sdn 4d	3,043	1,145	20,315
bus cpe	NA	NA	123
chassis	—	—	253

DD New Six (wb 109.0)—29,651 built***	Wght	Price	Prod
rdstr 2-4P	2,462	855	772
phtn 5P	2,521	875	542
bus cpe 2P	2,534	835	3,877
cpe 2-4P	2,603	855	3,363
conv cpe 2-4P	2,605	935	620
sdn 4d	2,668	865	33,432
chassis	—	—	899

*Available 1930 figures combined with 1929 production.
**Total based on serial number spans. Individual model totals for 1930-32 combined. Approximately 80 percent of the individual model totals were 1930 models.
***Total based on serial number spans. Individual model totals for 1930-32 combined. Approximately 70 percent of the individual model totals were 1930 models.

1930 Engines	bore×stroke	bhp	availability
L6, 208.0	3.38×3.88	63	S-DA
L6, 241.5	3.38×4.50	78	S-DB
L6, 189.8	3.13×4.13	61	S-DD
L8, 220.7	2.88×4.25	75	S-DC

1931

DC Eight (wb 114.0)—4,268 built

Production was carried over from 1930, with 1931 model output commencing July 15. Production figures combined with 1930 DC; total 1931 production based on serial number spans. Body styles and weights identical. Prices $100 less except phaeton, which was $145 less than 1930.

DD New Six (wb 109.0)—12,854 built

Production was carried over from 1930, with 1931 model output commencing July 15. Production figures combined with 1930 DD; total 1931 production based on serial number spans. Body styles and weights identical. Prices $100 less than 1930.

DG Eight (wb 118.5)—9,520 built*	Wght	Price	Prod
rdstr 2-4P	2,936	1,095	64
cpe 2-4P	3,094	1,095	2,181
conv cpe	3,240	1,170	500
sdn 4d	3,175	1,135	8,937
chassis	—	—	20

DH Six (wb 114.0)—20,558 built**	Wght	Price	Prod
rdstr 2-4P	2,638	825	160
bus cpe 2P	2,661	815	3,178
cpe 2-4P	2,745	835	4,187
sdn 4d	2,820	845	33,090
chassis	—	—	47

*Total based on serial number spans. Individual model totals for 1931-32 combined (see also additional models under 1932). Approximately 80 percent of the individual model totals were 1931 models.
**Total based on serial number spans. Individual model totals for 1931-32 combined (see also additional models under 1932). Approximately 50 percent of the individual model totals were 1931 models.

1931 Engines	bore×stroke	bhp	availability
L8, 220.7	2.88×4.25	75	S-DC
L6, 189.8	3.13×4.13	61	S-DD
L8, 240.3	3.00×4.25	84	S-DG
L6, 211.5	3.25×4.25	68	S-DH

1932

DG Eight (wb 118.5)—2,344 built*	Wght	Price	Prod
rdstr 2-4P	2,976	1,095	**
phtn 5P	NA	1,155	43**
bus cpe 2P	3,003	1,095	119**
cpe 2-4P	3,094	1,095	**
conv cpe 5P	3,240	1,145	**
sdn 4d	3,175	1,135	**
chassis	—	—	**

*Total production based on serial number spans for 1932.
**Production combined with 1931 except for phaeton (43) and business coupe (119), which were new models for 1932.

DH Six (wb 114.0)—20,268 built*	Wght	Price	Prod
rdstr 2-4P	2,638	850	**
phtn 5P	2,655	865	164
bus cpe 2P	2,661	815	**
cpe 2-4P	2,745	835	**
sdn 4d	2,820	845	**
chassis	—	—	**

*Total production based on serial number spans for 1932.
**Production combined with 1931 except for phaeton (164), which was a new model for 1932.

DC Eight (wb 114.0)—631 built

Leftover 1930-31 models sold as 1932s commencing July 1, 1931. Total volume based on serial number spans. Body styles, weights and prices as for 1931.

DD New Six (wb 109.0)—1,000 built (est.)

Leftover 1930-31 models sold as 1932s commencing July 1 1931. Total volume estimated. Body styles, weights and prices as for 1931.

DL Six (wb 114.3)—21,042 built	Wght	Price	Prod
bus cpe 2P	2,928	795	1,963
cpe 2-4P	2,995	835	1,815
conv cpe 2-4P	2,988	895	224
sdn 4d	3,094	945	16,901
conv sdn	NA	NA	12
cpe 5P	NA	NA	1
chassis	—	—	126

DK Eight (wb 122.0)—6,187 built	Wght	Price	Prod
cpe 2-4P	3,417	1,115	821
cpe 5P	3,504	1,145	651

	Wght	Price	Prod
conv cpe 2-4P	3,438	1,220	126
sdn 4d	3,527	1,145	4,422
conv sdn 5P	3,706	1,395	88
bus cpe 2P	NA	NA	57
chassis	—	—	22

1932 Engines	bore×stroke	bhp	availability
L8, 220.7	2.88×4.25	75	S-DC
L6, 189.8	3.13×4.13	61	S-DD
L8, 240.3	3.00×4.25	84	S-DG
L6, 211.5	3.25×4.25	74	S-DH
L6, 217.8	3.25×4.38	79	S-DL
L8, 282.1	3.25×4.25	90	S-DK

1933

DP Six (wb 111.3; lwb-115.0)	Wght	Price	Prod
bus cpe 2P	2,452	595	11,236
lwb bus cpe 2P	2,501	595	
cpe 2-4P	2,506	640	8,875
lwb cpe 2-4P	2,551	640	
conv cpe 2-4P	2,511	695	1,563
conv cpe 2-4P	2,556	695	
sdn 2d	2,591	630	8,523
lwb sdn 2d	2,636	630	
sdn 4d	2,632	670	69,074
lwb sdn 4d	2,661	675	
salon brougham 5P	2,651	660	4,200
lwb salon brougham 5P	2,678	660	
chassis	—	—	980

DO Eight (wb 122.0)	Wght	Price	Prod
cpe 2-4P	3,451	1,115	212
cpe 5P	3,540	1,145	159
conv cpe 2-4P	3,465	1,185	56
sdn 4d	3,580	1,145	1,173
conv sdn 5P	3,961	1,395	39
chassis	—	—	13

1933 Engines	bore×stroke	bhp	availability
L6, 201.3	3.13×4.38	75	S-DP
L8, 282.1	3.25×4.25	92	S-DO

1934

DR DeLuxe Six (wb 117.0)	Wght	Price	Prod
bus cpe 2P	2,695	665	8,723
cpe 2-4P	2,745	715	5,323
conv cpe 2-4P	2,845	765	1,239
sdn 2d	2,855	715	7,308
sdn 4d	2,940	765	53,479
sdn 4d 7P	NA	NA	710
chassis	—	—	1,475

DS DeLuxe Six (wb 121.0)	Wght	Price	Prod
Special brougham 4d 5P	2,905	845	1,397
Special conv sdn 5P	2,915	875	350
chassis	—	—	3

DRXX New Standard Six (wb 117.0)	Wght	Price	Prod
bus cpe 2P	2,695	645	2,284
cpe 2-4P	2,745	690	105
sdn 2d	2,855	695	3,133
sdn 4d	2,940	745	9,481
chassis	—	—	1

1934 Engines	bore×stroke	bhp	availability
L6, 217.8	3.25×4.38	87	S-all

1935

DU New Value Six (wb 116.0; lwb-128.0)	Wght	Price	Prod
cpe 2P	2,731	645	17,800
cpe 2-4P	2,801	710	4,499
conv cpe 2-4P	2,883	770	950
fstbk sdn 2d	2,821	690	7,891
sdn T/B 2d	2,868	715	18,069
fstbk sdn 4d	2,861	735	33,118
sdn T/B 4d	2,868	760	74,203
Caravan sdn 4d 5P (lwb)	3,221	995	193
lwb sdn 4d 7P	3,118	995	1,018
chassis	—	—	1,258

1935 Engine	bore×stroke	bhp	availability
L6, 217.8	3.25×4.38	87	S-all

1936

D2 Beauty Winner Six (wb 116.0; lwb-128.0)	Wght	Price	Prod
cpe 2P	2,773	640	32,952
cpe 2-4P	2,823	695	4,317
conv cpe 2-4P	2,887	795	1,525
fstbk sdn 2d	2,903	695	2,453
sdn T/B 2d	2,893	720	37,468
fstbk sdn 4d	2,923	735	5,996
sdn T/B 4d	2,958	760	174,334
conv sdn 5P	3,018	995	750
lwb sdn 4d 7P	3,238	975	1,942
chassis	—	—	1,910

1936 Engine	bore×stroke	bhp	availability
L6, 217.8	3.25×4.38	87	S-all

1937

D5 (wb 115.0; lwb-132.0)	Wght	Price	Prod
bus cpe 2P	2,902	715	41,702
cpe 2-4P	2,967	770	3,500
conv cpe 2-4P	3,057	910	1,345
fstbk sdn 2d	2,992	780	5,302
sdn T/B 2d	2,997	790	44,750
fstbk sdn 4d	2,982	820	7,555
sdn T/B 4d	2,997	830	185,483
conv sdn 5P	3,262	1,230	473
lwb sdn 7P	3,367	1,075	2,207
limo 7P (lwb)	NA	1,175	216
chassis	—	—	2,514

1937 Engine	bore×stroke	bhp	availability
L6, 217.8	3.25×4.38	87	S-all

1938

D8 (wb 115.0; lwb-132.0)	Wght	Price	Prod
bus cpe 2P	2,877	808	15,552
cpe 2-4P	2,952	858	950
conv cpe 2-4P	3,122	960	701
fstbk sdn 2d	2,977	858	999
sdn T/B 2d	2,957	870	17,282
fstbk sdn 4d	2,977	898	714
sdn T/B 4d	2,967	910	73,417
conv sdn T/B 5P	3,308	1,275	132
lwb sdn 7P	3,332	1,095	1,953
limo 7P (lwb)	NA	1,185	153

Dodge

	Wght	Price	Prod
wgn 4d	NA	NA	375
chassis	—	—	2,301

1938 Engine	bore×stroke	bhp	availability
L6, 217.8	3.25×4.38	87	S-all

1939

D11 Luxury Liner Special (wb 117.0)

	Wght	Price	Prod
bus cpe 2P	2,905	756	12,300
sdn 2d	2,955	815	26,700
sdn 4d	2,995	855	32,000

D11 Luxury Liner DeLuxe (wb 117.0)

	Wght	Price	Prod
bus cpe 2P	2,940	803	630
fstbk sdn 2d	3,010	865	270
sdn T/B 2d	2,990	895	1,585
fstbk sdn 4d	3,045	905	270
sdn T/B 4d	3,035	915	5,545
Town cpe 5P	3,075	1,055	300*

1939 Engine	bore×stroke	bhp	availability
L6, 217.8	3.25×4.38	87	S-all

*Estimated from total of 1000 built by Hayes for Dodge, Chrysler and Plymouth.
Note: Many sources also list a 2-4 passenger rumble-seat coupe (2,985 lbs/$860), and a 134-inch wheelbase 7-passenger sedan (3,440 lbs/$1,095) and limousine (3,545 lbs/$1,185). However, Dodge gives no production figures for these models, and their production in 1939 is in doubt.

1940

D-17 Special (wb 119.5)

	Wght	Price	Prod
bus cpe	2,867	755	12,001
sdn 2d	2,942	815	27,700
sdn 4d	2,997	855	26,803

D-14 DeLuxe (wb 119.5; 7P-139.5)

	Wght	Price	Prod
bus cpe	2,905	803	12,750
cpe, A/S	2,973	855	8,028
conv cpe	3,190	1,030	2,100
sdn 2d	2,990	860	19,838
sdn 4d	3,028	905	84,976
sdn 4d, 7P	3,460	1,095	932
limo 7P	3,500	1,170	79
chassis	—	—	298

1940 Engine	bore×stroke	bhp	availability
L6, 217.8	3.25×4.38	87	S-all

1941

D-19 DeLuxe (wb 119.5)

	Wght	Price	Prod
bus cpe	3,034	862	22,318
sdn 2d	3,109	915	34,566
sdn 4d	3,149	954	49,579

D-19 Custom (wb 119.5; 7P-137.5)

	Wght	Price	Prod
club cpe	3,154	995	18,024
conv cpe	3,384	1,162	3,554
brougham 2d	3,169	962	20,146
sdn 4d	3,194	999	72,067
town sdn	3,234	1,062	16,074
sdn 4d, 7P	3,579	1,195	604
limo 7P	3,669	1,262	50
chassis	—	—	20

1941 Engine	bore×stroke	bhp	availability
L6, 217.8	3.25×4.38	91	S-all

1942

D-22 DeLuxe (wb 119.5)

	Wght	Price	Prod
bus cpe	3,056	895	5,257
club cpe	3,131	995	3,314
sdn 2d	3,131	958	9,767
sdn 4d	3,171	998	13,343

D-22 Custom (wb 119.5; 7P-137.5)

	Wght	Price	Prod
club cpe	3,171	1,045	4,659
conv cpe	3,476	1,245	1,185
brougham 2d	3,171	1,008	4,685
sdn 4d	3,206	1,048	22,055
town sdn	3,256	1,105	4,047
sdn 4d, 7P	3,693	1,395	201
limo 7P	3,768	1,475	9

1942 Engine	bore×stroke	bhp	availability
L6, 230.2	3.25×4.63	105	S-all

1946

D-24S DeLuxe (wb 119.5)*

	Wght	Price	Prod
bus cpe	3,146	1,229	—
sdn 2d	3,206	1,299	—
sdn 4d	3,256	1,339	—

D-24C Custom (wb 119.5; 7P-137.5)*

	Wght	Price	Prod
club cpe	3,241	1,384	—
conv cpe	3,461	1,649	—
sdn 4d	3,281	1,389	—
town sdn	3,331	1,444	—
sdn 4d, 7P	3,757	1,743	—

1946 Engine	bore×stroke	bhp	availability
L6, 230.2	3.25×4.63	102	S-all

1947

D-24S DeLuxe (wb 119.5)*

	Wght	Price	Prod
bus cpe	3,147	1,347	—
sdn 2d	3,236	1,417	—
sdn 4d	3,256	1,457	—

D-24C Custom (wb 119.5; 7P-137.5)*

	Wght	Price	Prod
club cpe	3,241	1,502	—
conv cpe	3,461	1,871	—
sdn 4d	3,281	1,507	—
town sdn	3,331	1,577	—
sdn 4d, 7P	3,757	1,861	—

1947 Engine	bore×stroke	bhp	availability
L6, 230.2	3.25×4.63	102	S-all

1948

D-24S DeLuxe (wb 119.5)*

	Wght	Price	Prod
bus cpe	3,146	1,587	—
sdn 2d	3,236	1,676	—
sdn 4d	3,256	1,718	—

D-24C Custom (wb 119.5; 7P-137.5)*

	Wght	Price	Prod
club cpe	3,241	1,774	—
conv cpe	3,461	2,189	—
sdn 4d	3,281	1,788	—
town sdn	3,331	1,872	—
sdn 4d, 7P	3,757	2,179	—

1948 Engine	bore×stroke	bhp	availability
L6, 230.2	3.25×4.63	102	S-all

1949 First Series

D-24S DeLuxe (wb 119.5)*

	Wght	Price	Prod
bus cpe	3,146	1,587	—
sdn 2d	3,236	1,676	—
sdn 4d	3,256	1,718	—

D-24C Custom (wb 119.5; 7P-137.5)*

	Wght	Price	Prod
club cpe	3,241	1,774	—
conv cpe	3,461	2,189	—
sdn 4d	3,281	1,788	—
town sdn	3,331	1,872	—
sdn 4d, 7P	3,757	2,179	—

1949(1) Engine	bore×stroke	bhp	availability
L6, 230.2	3.25×4.63	102	S-all

*Factory combined production figures for 1946 through 1949 First Series.

Combined 1946–1949 First Series Production:

D-24S DeLuxe (wb 119.5)

	Prod
bus cpe	27,600
sdn 2d	81,399
sdn 4d	61,987

D-24C Custom (wb 119.5; 7P-137.5)

	Prod
club cpe	103,800
conv cpe	9,500
sdn 4d	333,911
town sdn	27,800
sdn 4d, 7P	3,698
limo 7P (proto)	2
chassis	302

1949 Second Series

D-29 Wayfarer (wb 115.0)

	Wght	Price	Prod
cpe	3,065	1,611	9,342
sdn 2d	3,180	1,738	49,058
rdstr	3,145	1,727	5,420

D-30 (wb 123.5; 8P-137.5)

	Wght	Price	Prod
Meadowbrook sdn 4d	3,355	1,848	144,390
Coronet sdn 4d	3,380	1,927	
Coronet club cpe	3,325	1,914	45,435
Coronet conv cpe	3,570	2,329	2,411
Coronet wgn 4d, 9P	3,830	2,865	800
chassis	—	—	1

1949(2) Engine	bore×stroke	bhp	availability
L6, 230.2	3.25×4.53	103	S-all

1950

D-33 Wayfarer (wb 115.0)

	Wght	Price	Prod
bus cpe	3,095	1,611	7,500
sdn 2d	3,200	1,738	65,000
Sportabout rdstr	3,155	1,727	2,903

D-34 (wb 123.5; 8P-137.5)

	Wght	Price	Prod
Meadowbrook sdn 4d	3,395	1,848	221,791
Coronet sdn 4d	3,405	1,927	
Coronet club cpe	3,340	1,914	38,502
Coronet conv cpe	3,590	2,329	1,800
Coronet Diplomat htp cpe	3,515	2,233	3,600
Coronet wgn 4d (wood)	3,850	2,865	600
Coronet Sierra wgn 4d (steel)	3,726	2,485	100
chassis	—	—	1

1950 Engine	bore×stroke	bhp	availability
L6, 230.2	3.25×4.63	103	S-all

1951

D-41 Wayfarer (wb 115.0)

	Wght	Price	Prod
bus cpe	3,125	1,795	*
sdn 2d	3,210	1,936	*
Sportabout rdstr	3,175	1,924	1,002

D-42 (wb 123.5; 8P-137.5)*

	Wght	Price	Prod
Meadowbrook sdn 4d	3,415	2,059	—
Coronet sdn 4d	3,415	2,148	—
Coronet club cpe	3,320	2,132	—
Coronet Diplomat htp cpe	3,515	2,478	—
Coronet conv cpe	3,575	2,568	—
Coronet Sierra wgn 4d	3,750	2,768	—
Coronet sdn 4d, 8P	3,935	2,916	—

1951 Engine	bore×stroke	bhp	availability
L6, 230.2	3.25×4.63	103	S-all

1952

D-41 Wayfarer (wb 115.0)*

	Wght	Price	Prod
bus cpe	3,053	1,886	—
sdn 2d	3,140	2,034	—

D-42 (wb 123.5; 8P-137.5)*

	Wght	Price	Prod
Meadowbrook sdn 4d	3,355	2,164	—
Coronet sdn 4d	3,385	2,256	—
Coronet club cpe	3,290	2,240	—
Coronet conv cpe	3,520	2,698	—
Coronet Diplomat htp cpe	3,475	2,602	—
Coronet Sierra wgn 4d	3,735	2,908	—
Coronet sdn 4d, 8P	3,935	3,064	—

1952 Engine	bore×stroke	bhp	availability
L6, 230.2	3.25×4.63	103	S-all

*Factory combined 1951–1952 production.

Combined 1951–1952 production:

D-41 Wayfarer (wb 115.0)

	Prod
bus cpe	6,702
sdn 2d	70,700
Sportabout rdstr (1951 only)	1,002

D-42 (wb 123.5; 8P-137.5)

	Prod
Meadowbrook-Coronet sdn 4d	329,202
Coronet club cpe	56,103
Coronet conv cpe	5,550
Coronet Diplomat htp cpe	21,600
Coronet Sierra wgn 4d	4,000
Coronet sdn 4d, 8P	1,150

1953

D-46 (wb 119.0)

	Wght	Price	Prod
Meadowbrook Special cpe	3,100	1,958	36,766
Meadowbrook cpe	3,085	1,958	
Coronet cpe	3,155	2,084	
Meadowbrook Special sdn 4d	3,195	2,000	84,158
Meadowbrook sdn 4d	3,175	2,000	
Coronet sdn 4d	3,220	2,111	

D-47 Meadowbrook Suburban (wb 114.0)

	Wght	Price	Prod
wgn 2d	3,190	2,176	15,751

D-44 Coronet Eight (wb 119.0)

	Wght	Price	Prod
club cpe	3,325	2,198	32,439
sdn 4d	3,385	2,220	124,059

D-48 Coronet Eight (wb 114.0)	Wght	Price	Prod
conv cpe	3,438	2,494	4,100
Diplomat htp cpe	3,310	2,361	17,334
Sierra wgn 2d	3,425	2,503	5,400
chassis	—	—	1

1953 Engines	bore×stroke	bhp	availability
L6, 230.2	3.25×4.63	103	S-D-46, D-47
V8, 241.3	3.44×3.25	140	S-D-44, D-48

1954

D51-1 Meadowbrook L6 (wb 119.0)	Wght	Price	Prod
club cpe	3,120	1,983	3,501
sdn 4d	3,195	2,025	7,894

D50-1 Meadowbrook V8 (wb 119.0)	Wght	Price	Prod
club cpe	3,335	2,154	750
sdn 4d	3,390	2,176	3,299

D51-2 Coronet L6 (wb 119.0)	Wght	Price	Prod
club cpe	3,165	2,109	4,501
sdn 4d	3,235	2,136	14,900

D52 Coronet L6 (wb 119.0; 2d-114.0)	Wght	Price	Prod
Suburban wgn 2d	3,185	2,229	6,389
Sierra wgn 4d, 6P	3,430	2,719	312
Sierra wgn 4d, 8P	3,435	2,790	

D50-2 Coronet V8 (wb 119.0)	Wght	Price	Prod
club cpe	3,345	2,223	7,998
sdn 4d	3,405	2,245	36,063

D53-2 Coronet V8 (wb 114.0; 4d-119.0)	Wght	Price	Prod
Sport htp cpe	3,310	2,380	100
conv cpe	3,505	2,514	50
Suburban wgn 2d	3,400	2,517	3,100
Sierra wgn 4d, 6P	3,605	2,960	988
Sierra wgn 4d, 8P	3,660	3,031	

D50-3 Royal V8 (wb 119.0)	Wght	Price	Prod
club cpe	3,365	2,349	8,900
sdn 4d	3,425	2,373	50,050

D53-3 Royal V8 (wb 114.0)	Wght	Price	Prod
Sport htp cpe	3,355	2,503	3,852
conv cpe (prod inc 701 model 500)	3,575	2,632	2,000
chassis	—	—	1

1954 Engines	bore×stroke	bhp	availability
L6, 230.2	3.25×4.63	110	S-all 6s
V8, 241.3	3.44×3.25	140	S-Meadowbrook V8
V8, 241.3	3.44×3.25	150	S-others (Offenhauser manifold available)

1955

D56-1 Coronet L6 (wb 120.0)	Wght	Price	Prod
sdn 2d	3,235	2,013	13,277
sdn 4d	3,295	2,093	15,976
Suburban wgn 2d	3,410	2,349	3,248
Suburban wgn 4d, 6P	3,480	2,463	1,311
Suburban wgn 4d, 8P	3,595	2,565	

D55-1 Coronet V8 (wb 120.0)	Wght	Price	Prod
sdn 2d	3,360	2,116	10,827
club sdn 2d	3,235	2,124	
sdn 4d	3,395	2,196	30,098
Lancer htp cpe	3,375	2,281	26,727
Suburban wgn 2d	3,550	2,452	4,867
Suburban wgn 4d, 6P	3,590	2,566	4,641
Suburban wgn 4d, 8P	3,695	2,668	

D55-2 Royal V8 (wb 120.0)	Wght	Price	Prod
sdn 4d	3,425	2,310	45,323
Lancer htp cpe	3,425	2,395	25,831
Sierra wgn 4d, 6P	3,655	2,659	5,506
Sierra wgn 4d, 8P	3,730	2,761	

D55-3 Custom Royal V8 (wb 120.0)	Wght	Price	Prod
sdn 4d	3,485	2,473	55,503
Lancer sdn 4d	3,505	2,516	
Lancer htp cpe	3,480	2,543	30,499
Lancer conv cpe	3,610	2,748	3,302

1955 Engines	bore×stroke	bhp	availability
L6, 230.2	3.25×4.63	123	S-all 6s
V8, 270.1	3.63×3.25	175	S-all V8s exc Custom Royal
V8, 270.1	3.63×3.25	183	S-Custom Royal
V8, 270.1	3.63×3.25	193	O-Custom Royal

1956

D62 Coronet L6 (wb 120.0)— 142,613 built (includes D63-1)	Wght	Price	Prod
sdn 2d	3,250	2,194	—
sdn 4d	3,295	2,267	—
Suburban wgn 2d	3,455	2,491	—

D63-1 Coronet V8 (wb 120.0)	Wght	Price	Prod
club sdn 2d	3,380	2,302	—
sdn 4d	3,435	2,375	—
Lancer htp sdn	3,560	2,552	—
Lancer htp cpe	3,430	2,438	—
conv cpe	3,600	2,678	—
Sierra wgn 4d, 6P	3,600	2,716	—
Sierra wgn 4d, 8P	3,715	2,822	—
Suburban wgn 2d	3,605	2,599	—

D63-2 Royal V8 (wb 120.0)—48,780 built	Wght	Price	Prod
sdn 4d	3,475	2,513	—
Lancer htp sdn	3,625	2,697	—
Lancer htp cpe	3,505	2,583	—
Sierra wgn 4d, 6P	3,710	2,869	—
Sierra wgn 4d, 8P	3,800	2,974	—
Suburban wgn 2d	3,620	2,729	—

D63-3 Custom Royal V8 (wb 120.0)—49,293 built	Wght	Price	Prod
sdn 4d	3,520	2,623	—
Lancer htp sdn	3,675	2,807	—
Lancer htp cpe	3,505	2,693	—
conv cpe	3,630	2,913	—

1956 Engines	bore×stroke	bhp	availability
L6, 230.2	3.25×4.63	131	S-all 6s
V8, 270.0	3.63×3.25	189	S-Coronet V8
V8, 315.0	3.63×3.80	218	S-Royal, Custom Royal
V8, 315.0	3.63×3.80	260	O-all

1957

D72 Coronet L6 (wb 122.0)—160,979 built (includes D66 and D501)	Wght	Price	Prod
club sdn 2d	3,400	2,370	—
sdn 4d	3,470	2,451	—

D66 Coronet V8 (wb 122.0)	Wght	Price	Prod
club sdn 2d	3,530	2,478	—
sdn 4d	3,620	2,559	—
Lancer htp sdn	3,665	2,665	—
Lancer htp cpe	3,570	2,580	—
conv cpe	3,815	2,842	—

D501 Coronet D-500 V8 (wb 122.0)	Wght	Price	Prod
club sdn 2d	3,885	3,314	—
conv cpe	3,975	3,670	—

D67-1 Royal V8 (wb 122.0)—40,999 built			
sdn 4d	3,620	2,712	—
Lancer htp sdn	3,690	2,818	—
Lancer htp cpe	3,585	2,769	—

D67-2 Custom Royal V8 (wb 122.0)—55,149 built			
sdn 4d	3,690	2,881	—
Lancer htp sdn	3,750	2,991	—
Lancer htp cpe	3,670	2,920	—
conv cpe	3,810	3,146	—

D70 Station Wagon V8 (wb 122.0)–30,481 built (includes D71)			
Sierra wgn 4d, 6P	3,930	2,946	—
Sierra wgn 4d, 9P	4,015	3,073	—
Suburban wgn 2d	3,830	2,861	—

D71 Custom Station Wgn V8 (wb 122.0)			
Sierra wgn 4d, 6P	3,960	3,087	—
Sierra wgn 4d, 9P	4,030	3,215	—

1957 Engines	bore×stroke	bhp	availability
L6, 230.2	3.25×4.63	138	S-D72
V8, 325.0	3.69×3.80	245	S-all exc D72, D67-2, D501
V8, 325.0	3.69×3.80	260	S-D67-2
V8, 325.0	3.69×3.80	285/310	O-all (D-500)
V8, 354.0	3.94×3.63	340	O-all (D-500)

1958

LD-1 Coronet L6 (wb 122.0)—77,388 built (includes LD-2 Coronet)	Wght	Price	Prod
club sdn 2d	3,360	2,449	—
sdn 4d	3,410	2,530	—
Lancer htp cpe	3,400	2,572	—

LD-2 Coronet V8 (wb 122.0)			
club sdn 2d	3,505	2,556	—
sdn 4d	3,555	2,637	—
Lancer htp sdn	3,605	2,764	—
Lancer htp cpe	3,540	2,679	—
conv cpe	3,725	2,942	—

LD-2 Royal V8 (wb 122.0)—15,165 built			
sdn 4d	3,570	2,797	—
Lancer htp sdn 4d	3,640	2,915	—
Lancer htp cpe	3,565	2,854	—

LD-3 Custom Royal V8 (wb 122.0)			
sdn 4d	3,640	3,030	
Lancer htp sdn	3,670	3,142	
Lancer htp cpe	3,610	3,071	23,949
conv cpe	3,785	3,298	
Regal Lancer htp cpe	3,650	3,245	1,163

LD-3 Station Wagon V8 (wb 122.0)—20,196 built			
Sierra wgn 4d, 6P	3,930	3,035	—
Sierra wgn 4d, 9P	3,990	3,176	—
Suburban wgn 2d	3,875	2,970	—
Custom Sierra wgn 4d, 6P	3,955	3,212	—
Custom Sierra wgn 4d, 9P	4,035	3,354	—

1958 Engines	bore×stroke	bhp	availability
L6, 230.2	3.25×4.63	138	S-Coronet 6
V8, 325.0	3.69×3.80	252	S-Coronet V8
V8, 325.0	3.69×3.80	265	S-Royal V8
V8, 350.0	4.06×3.38	285	S-Cus Royal, wgns
V8, 361.0	4.12×3.38	305/333	O-all (D-500)

1959

MD1-L Coronet L6 (wb 122.0)—96,782 built (includes MD2-L)		Wght	Price	Prod
21	club sdn 2d	3,375	2,516	—
23	Lancer htp cpe	3,395	2,644	—
41	sdn 4d	3,425	2,587	—

MD2-L Coronet V8 (wb 122.0)				
21	club sdn 2d	3,565	2,636	—
23	Lancer htp cpe	3,590	2,764	—
27	conv cpe	3,775	3,089	—
41	sdn 4d	3,615	2,707	—
43	Lancer htp sdn	3,620	2,842	—

MD3-M Royal V8 (wb 122.0)—14,807 built				
23	Lancer htp cpe	3,625	2,990	—
41	sdn 4d	3,640	2,934	—
43	Lancer htp sdn	3,690	3,069	—

MD3-H Custom Royal V8 (wb 122.0)—21,206 built				
23	Lancer htp cpe	3,675	3,201	—
27	conv cpe	3,820	3,422	—
41	sdn 4d	3,660	3,145	—
43	Lancer htp sdn	3,745	3,270	—

MD3-L Sierra V8 (wb 122.0)–23,590 built (includes Customs)				
45A	wgn 4d, 6P	3,940	3,103	—
45B	Sierra wgn 4d, 9P	4,015	3,224	—

MD3-H Custom V8 (wb 122.0)				
45A	wgn 4d, 6P	3,980	3,318	—
45B	wgn 4d, 9P	4,020	3,439	—

1959 Engines	bore×stroke	bhp	availability
L6, 230.2	3.25×4.63	138	S-Coronet 6
V8, 326.0	3.95×3.31	255	S-Coronet V8
V8, 361.0	4.12×3.38	305	S-all exc Coronet
V8, 383.0	4.25×3.38	320/345	O-all (D-500, Super D-500)

1960

PD3 Dart L6 (wb 118.0; wgns-122.0)		Wght	Price	Prod
L21	Seneca sdn 2d	3,385	2,278	
L41	Seneca sdn 4d	3,420	2,330	93,167
L45	Seneca wgn 4d	3,805	2,695	
M21	Pioneer sdn 2d	3,375	2,410	
M23	Pioneer htp cpe	3,410	2,488	
M41	Pioneer sdn 4d	3,430	2,459	36,434
M45A	Pioneer wgn 4d, 6P	3,820	2,787	
M45B	Pioneer wgn 4d, 9P	3,875	2,892	
H23	Phoenix htp cpe	3,410	2,618	
H27	Phoenix conv cpe	3,460	2,868	
H41	Phoenix sdn 4d	3,420	2,595	6,567
H43	Phoenix htp sdn	3,460	2,677	

PD4 Dart V8 (wb 118.0; wgns-122.0)				
L21	Seneca sdn 2d	3,530	2,397	
L41	Seneca sdn 4d	3,600	2,449	45,737
L45	Seneca wgn 4d	3,975	2,815	
M21	Pioneer sdn 2d	3,540	2,530	
M23	Pioneer htp cpe	3,610	2,607	
M41	Pioneer sdn 4d	3,610	2,578	74,655
M45A	Pioneer wgn 4d, 6P	4,000	2,906	
M45B	Pioneer wgn 4d, 9P	4,065	3,011	
H23	Phoenix htp cpe	3,605	2,737	
H27	Phoenix conv cpe	3,690	2,988	
H41	Phoenix sdn 4d	3,610	2,715	66,608
H43	Phoenix htp sdn	3,655	2,796	

PD1-L Matador (wb 122.0)—27,908 built				
23	htp cpe	3,705	2,996	—
41	sdn 4d	3,725	2,930	—
43	htp sdn	3,820	3,075	—

		Wght	Price	Prod
45A	wgn 4d, 6P	4,045	3,239	—
45B	wgn 4d, 9P	4,120	3,354	—

PD2-H Polara (wb 122.0)—16,728 built

23	htp cpe	3,740	3,196	—
27	conv cpe	3,765	3,416	—
41	sdn 4d	3,735	3,141	—
43	htp sdn	3,815	3,275	—
45A	wgn 4d, 6P	4,085	3,506	—
45B	wgn 4d, 9P	4,220	3,621	—

1960 Engines	bore×stroke	bhp	availability
L6, 225.0	3.40×4.13	145	S-Dart 6
V8, 318.0	3.91×3.31	230	S-Seneca, Pioneer V8
V8, 318.0	3.91×3.31	255	S-Phoenix V8
V8, 361.0	4.12×3.38	295	S-Matador; O-Pioneer, Phoenix
V8, 383.0	4.25×3.38	325	S-Polara; O-Matador, Phoenix
V8, 383.0	4.25×3.38	330	O-Polara, Matador, Phoenix

1961

RW1-L Lancer 170 (wb 106.5)—25,508 built

		Wght	Price	Prod
711	sdn 2d	2,585	1,979	—
713	sdn 4d	2,595	2,041	—
756	wgn 4d	2,760	2,354	—

RW1-H Lancer 770 (wb 106.5)—49,268 built

723	htp cpe	2,595	2,164	—
731	spt cpe	2,643	2,075	—
733	sdn 4d	2,605	2,137	—
776	wgn 4d	2,775	2,449	—

RD3 Dart L6 (wb 118.0; wgns-122.0)

L411	Seneca sdn 2d	3,290	2,278	
L413	Seneca sdn 4d	3,335	2,330	60,527
L456	Seneca wgn 4d	3,740	2,695	
M421	Pioneer sdn 2d	3,290	2,410	
M422	Pioneer htp cpe	3,335	2,488	
M423	Pioneer sdn 4d	3,335	2,459	18,214
M466	Pioneer wgn 4d, 6P	3,740	2,787	
M467	Pioneer wgn 4d, 9P	3,825	2,892	
H432	Phoenix htp cpe	3,325	2,618	
H433	Phoenix sdn 4d	3,350	2,595	4,273
H434	Phoenix htp sdn	3,385	2,677	

RD4 Dart V8 (wb 118.0; wgns-122.0)

L511	Seneca sdn 2d	3,470	2,397	
L513	Seneca sdn 4d	3,515	2,449	27,174
L556	Seneca wgn 4d	3,920	2,815	
M521	Pioneer sdn 2d	3,460	2,530	
M522	Pioneer htp cpe	3,500	2,607	
M523	Pioneer sdn 4d	3,510	2,578	39,054
M566	Pioneer wgn 4d, 6P	3,940	2,906	
M567	Pioneer wgn 4d, 9P	4,005	3,011	
H532	Phoenix htp cpe	3,520	2,737	
H533	Phoenix sdn 4d	3,535	2,715	
H534	Phoenix htp sdn	3,555	2,796	34,319
H535	Phoenix conv cpe	3,580	2,988	

RD1-L Polara (wb 122.0)—14,032 built

542	htp cpe	3,690	3,032	—
543	sdn 4d	3,700	2,966	—
544	htp sdn	3,740	3,110	—
545	conv cpe	3,765	3,252	—
578	wgn 4d, 6P	4,115	3,294	—
579	wgn 4d, 9P	4,125	3,409	—

1961 Engines	bore×stroke	bhp	availability
L6, 170.0	3.40×3.13	101	S-Lancer
L6, 225.0	3.40×4.13	145	S-Dart 6; O-Lancer
V8, 318.0	3.91×3.31	230	S-Dart V8

	bore×stroke	bhp	availability
V8, 318.0	3.91×3.31	260	O-Dart V8
V8, 361.0	4.12×3.38	265	S-Polara
V8, 361.0	4.12×3.38	305	O-Dart V8 (D-500)
V8, 383.0	4.25×3.38	325	O-Polara (D-500)
V8, 383.0	4.25×3.38	330	O-Polara, Dart V8 (ram ind)

1962

SL1-L Lancer 170 (wb 106.5)—19,780 built

		Wght	Price	Prod
711	sdn 2d	2,495	1,951	—
713	sdn 4d	2,525	2,011	—
756	wgn 4d	2,685	2,306	—

SL1-H Lancer 770 (wb 106.5)—30,888 built

731	sdn 2d	2,520	2,052	—
733	sdn 4d	2,540	2,114	—
776	wgn 4d	2,705	2,408	—

SL1-P Lancer GT (wb 106.5)

742	htp cpe	2,560	2,257	13,683

SD1 Dart L6 (wb 116.0)

L401	Fleet Special sdn 2d	2,965	2,158	
L403	Fleet Special sdn 4d	2,995	2,214	
L411	sdn 2d	2,970	2,241	43,927
L413	sdn 4d	3,000	2,297	
L456	wgn 4d	3,270	2,644	
M421	330 sdn 2d	2,965	2,375	
M422	330 htp cpe	2,985	2,463	
M423	330 sdn 4d	3,000	2,432	11,606
M466	330 wgn 4d	3,275	2,739	
H432	440 htp cpe	3,025	2,606	
H433	440 sdn 4d	3,045	2,584	3,942

SD2 Dart V8 (wb 116.0)

L501	Fleet Special sdn 2d	3,130	2,316	
L503	Fleet Special sdn 4d	3,165	2,372	
L511	sdn 2d	3,135	2,348	17,981
L513	sdn 4d	3,170	2,404	
L556	wgn 4d	3,435	2,751	
M521	330 sdn 2d	3,135	2,482	
M522	330 htp cpe	3,155	2,570	
M523	330 sdn 4d	3,170	2,540	26,544
M566	330 wgn 4d, 6P	3,435	2,848	
M567	330 wgn 4d, 9P	3,500	2,949	
H532	440 htp cpe	3,185	2,713	
H533	440 sdn 4d	3,205	2,691	
H534	440 htp sdn	3,260	2,763	
H535	440 conv cpe	3,285	2,945	42,360
H576	440 wgn 4d, 6P	3,460	2,989	
H577	440 wgn 4d, 9P	3,530	3,092	

SD2-P Polara 500 (wb 116.0)—12,268 built

542	htp cpe	3,315	3,019	—
544	htp sdn	3,360	2,960	—
545	conv cpe	3,430	3,268	—

SD3-L Custom 880 (wb 122.0)—17,505 built

612	htp cpe	3,615	3,030	—
613	sdn 4d	3,655	2,964	—
614	htp sdn	3,680	3,109	—
615	conv cpe	3,705	3,251	—
658	wgn 4d, 6P	4,025	3,292	—
659	wgn 4d, 9P	4,055	3,407	—

1962 Engines	bore×stroke	bhp	availability
L6, 170.0	3.40×3.13	101	S-Lancer
L6, 225.0	3.40×4.13	145	S-Dart 6; O-Lancer
V8, 318.0	3.91×3.31	230	S-Dart V8
V8, 318.0	3.91×3.31	260	O-Dart V8
V8, 361.0	4.12×3.38	265	S-Custom 880
V8, 361.0	4.12×3.38	305	S-Polara 500; O-Dart V8

1963

TL1-L Dart 170 (wb 111.0; wgns-106.0)—58,536 built

		Wght	Price	Prod
711	sdn 2d	2,605	1,983	—
713	sdn 4d	2,625	2,041	—
756	wgn 4d	2,710	2,309	—

TL1-H Dart 270 (wb 111.0; wgns 106.0)—61,159 built

731	sdn 2d	2,610	2,079	—
733	sdn 4d	2,635	2,135	—
735	conv cpe	2,740	2,385	—
776	wgn 4d	2,735	2,433	—

TL1-P Dart GT (wb 111.0)—34,227 built

742	htp cpe	2,690	2,289	—
745	conv cpe	2,765	2,512	—

TD1-L 330 L6 (wb 119.0; wgns-116.0)—51,761 built

401	Fleet Special sdn 2d	3,040	2,205	—
403	Fleet Special sdn 4d	3,065	2,261	—
411	sdn 2d	3,050	2,245	—
413	sdn 4d	3,070	2,301	—
456	wgn 4d, 2S	3,320	2,648	—
457	wgn 4d, 3S	3,380	2,749	—

TD1-M 440 L6 (wb 119.0; wgns-116.0)—13,146 built

421	sdn 2d	3,050	2,381	—
422	htp cpe	3,050	2,470	—
423	sdn 4d	3,075	2,438	—

TD1-H Polara L6 (wb 119.0)—68,262 built

432	htp cpe	3,105	2,624	—
433	sdn 4d	3,105	2,602	—

TD2-L 330 V8 (wb 119.0; wgns 116.0)—33,602 built

601	Fleet Special sdn 2d	3,310	2,313	—
603	Fleet Special sdn 4d	3,335	2,369	—
611	sdn 2d	3,220	2,352	—
613	sdn 4d	3,245	2,408	—
656	wgn 4d, 2S	3,490	2,756	—
657	wgn 4d, 3S	3,550	2,857	—

TD2-M 440 V8 (wb 119.0; wgns 116.0)—49,591 built

621	sdn 2d	3,215	2,489	—
622	htp cpe	3,245	2,577	—
623	sdn 4d	3,250	2,546	—
666	wgn 4d, 2S	3,495	2,854	—
667	wgn 4d, 3S	3,555	2,956	—

TD2-H Polara V8 (wb 119.0)—40,323 built

632	htp cpe	3,255	2,732	—
633	sdn 4d	3,275	2,709	—
634	htp sdn	3,330	2,781	—
635	conv cpe	3,340	2,963	—

TD2-P Polara 500 V8 (wb 119.0)—7,256 built

642	htp cpe	3,375	2,965	—
645	conv cpe	3,455	3,196	—

TA3 880 V8 (wb 122.0)

E503	sdn 4d	3,800	2,815	
E556	wgn 4d, 6P	4,145	3,142	9,831
E557	wgn 4d, 9P	4,175	3,257	
L512	Custom htp cpe	3,825	3,030	
L513	Custom sdn 4d	3,815	2,964	
L514	Custom htp sdn	3,840	3,109	
L515	Custom conv cpe	3,845	3,251	18,435
L558	Custom htp wgn 4d, 2S	4,160	3,292	
L559	Custom htp wgn 4d, 3S	4,186	3,407	

1963 Engines

	bore×stroke	bhp	availability
L6, 170.0	3.40×3.13	101	S-Dart
L6, 225.0	3.40×4.13	145	S-330/440/Polara 6; O-Dart

	bore×stroke	bhp	availability
V8, 318.0	3.91×3.31	230	S-330, 440, Polara V8
V8, 361.0	4.13×3.38	265	S-880, Custom 880
V8, 383.0	4.25×3.38	305	S-Polara 500; O-others exc Dart
V8, 383.0	4.25×3.38	230	O-all exc Dart
V8, 413.0	4.19×3.75	360	O-880, Custom 880
V8, 426.0	4.25×3.75	415/425	O-all exc Dart (ram ind)

1964

VL1-L Dart 170 (wb 111.0; wgns-106.0)

		Wght	Price	Prod
711	sdn 2d	2,615	1,988	L6: 74,625
713	sdn 4d	2,640	2,053	V8: 2,509
756	wgn 4d, 2S	2,740	2,315	

VL1-H Dart 270 (wb 111.0; wgns-106.0)

731	sdn 2d	2,625	2,094	L6: 58,972
733	sdn 4d	2,645	2,160	V8: 7,097
735	conv cpe	2,735	2,389	
776	wgn 4d, 2S	2,745	2,414	

VL1-P Dart GT (wb 111.0)

742	htp cpe	2,670	2,318	L6: 37,660
745	conv cpe	2,770	2,536	V8: 12,170

VD1-L 330 L6 (wb 119.0; wgns-116.0)—57,957 built

411	sdn 2d	3,115	2,264	—
413	sdn 4d	3,145	2,317	—
456	wgn 4d, 2S	3,400	2,654	—
457	wgn 4d, 3S	3,475	2,755	—

VD1-M 440 L6 (wb 119.0)—15,147 built

421	sdn 2d	3,110	2,401	—
422	htp cpe	3,120	2,483	—
423	sdn 4d	3,145	2,454	—

VD1-H Polara L6 (wb 119.0)—3,810 built

432	htp cpe	3,135	2,637	—
433	sdn 4d	3,170	2,615	—

VD2-L 330 V8 (wb 119.0; wgns-116.0)—46,438 built

611	sdn 2d	3,285	2,372	—
613	sdn 4d	3,325	2,424	—
656	wgn 4d, 2S	3,570	2,762	—
657	wgn 4d, 3S	3,620	2,863	—

VD2-M 440 V8 (wb 119.0; wgns-116.0)—68,861 built

621	sdn 2d	3,280	2,508	—
622	htp cpe	3,295	2,590	—
623	sdn 4d	3,330	2,562	—
666	wgn 4d, 2S	3,585	2,861	—
667	wgn 4d, 3S	3,640	2,962	—

VD2-H Polara V8 (wb 119.0)—66,988 built

632	htp cpe	3,320	2,745	—
633	sdn 4d	3,365	2,722	—
634	htp sdn	3,395	2,794	—
645	conv cpe	3,435	2,994	—

VD2-P Polara 500 V8 (wb 119.0)—discont'd—17,787 built

642	htp cpe	3,340	2,978	—
645	conv cpe	3,550	3,227	—

VA3 880 V8 (wb 122.0)

E513	sdn 4d	3,795	2,826	
E556	wgn 4d, 6P	4,165	3,155	10,526
E557	wgn 4d, 9P	4,185	3,270	
L522	Custom htp cpe	3,765	3,043	
L523	Custom sdn 4d	3,825	2,977	
L524	Custom htp sdn	3,860	3,122	
L525	Custom conv cpe	3,850	3,264	21,234
L568	Custom htp wgn 4d, 2S	4,155	3,305	
L569	Custom htp wgn 4d, 3S	4,185	3,420	

Dodge

1964 Engines	bore×stroke	bhp	availability
L6, 170.0	3.40×3.13	101	S-Dart
L6, 225.0	3.40×4.13	145	S-330/440/Polara 6;O-Dart
V8, 273.5	3.63×3.31	180	O-Dart
V8, 318.0	3.91×3.31	230	S-330, 440, Polara V8
V8, 361.0	4.13×3.38	265	S-880, Custom 880
V8, 383.0	4.25×3.38	305/330	O-all exc Dart
V8, 426.0	4.25×3.75	365	O-all exc Dart
V8, 426.0	4.25×3.75	415/425	O-all exc Dart (ram ind)

1965

AL1-L Dart 170 (wb 111.0; wgns-106.0)—86,013 built

		Wght	Price	Prod
L11	sdn 2d	2,645	2,074	—
L13	sdn 4d	2,660	2,139	—
L56	wgn 4d	2,770	2,407	—

AL1-H Dart 270 (wb 111.0; wgns 106.0)—78,245 built

L31	sdn 2d	2,650	2,180	—
L32	htp cpe	2,675	2,274	—
L33	sdn 4d	2,670	2,247	—
L35	conv cpe	2,765	2,481	—
L76	wgn 4d	2,770	2,506	—

AL1-P Dart GT (wb 111.0)—45,118 built

L42	htp cpe	2,715	2,404	—
L45	conv cpe	2,795	2,628	—

AW1-L Coronet L6 (wb 117.0; wgns-116.0)*

W11	Deluxe sdn 2d	3,090	2,257	—
W13	Deluxe sdn 4d	3,140	2,296	—
W21	sdn 2d	3,070	2,217	—
W23	sdn 4d	3,095	2,256	—
W56	Deluxe wgn 4d	3,390	2,592	—

AW2-H Coronet 440 L6 (wb 117.0; wgns-116.0)*

W32	htp cpe	3,100	2,403	—
W33	sdn 4d	3,125	2,377	—
W35	conv cpe	3,230	2,622	—
W76	wgn 4d	3,395	2,674	—

AW2-L Coronet V8 (wb 117.0; wgns-116.0)*

W01	Hemi-Charger sdn 2d	3,165	—	—
W11	Deluxe sdn 2d	3,160	2,353	—
W13	Deluxe sdn 4d	3,210	2,392	—
W21	sdn 2d	3,145	2,313	—
W23	sdn 4d	3,195	2,352	—
W56	Deluxe wgn 4d	3,470	2,688	—

AW2-H Coronet 440 V8 (wb 117.0; wgns-116.0)*

W32	htp cpe	3,180	2,499	—
W33	sdn 4d	3,230	2,473	—
W35	conv cpe	3,295	2,718	—
W76	wgn 4d, 6P	3,490	2,770	—
W77	wgn 4d, 9P	3,560	2,868	—

AW2-P Coronet 500 V8 (wb 117.0)—32,745 built

W42	htp cpe	3,255	2,674	—
W45	conv cpe	3,340	2,894	—

AW2-L Polara V8 (wb 121.0)—12,705 built

D12	htp cpe	3,850	2,837	—
D13	sdn 4d	3,905	2,806	—
D14	htp sdn	3,965	2,913	—
D15	conv cpe	3,940	3,131	—
D23	sdn 4d (318)	3,847	2,730	—
D56	wgn 4d, 6P	4,220	3,153	—
D57	wgn 4d, 9P	4,255	3,259	—

AD2-H Custom 880 V8 (wb 121.0)—44,496 built

D32	htp cpe	3,945	3,085	—
D34	htp sdn	4,155	3,150	—

		Wght	Price	Prod
D35	conv cpe	3,965	3,335	—
D38	sdn 4d	3,915	3,010	—
D76	wgn 4d, 6P	4,270	3,422	—
D77	wgn 4d, 9P	4,355	3,527	—

AD2-P Monaco V8 (wb 121.0)

D42	htp cpe	4,000	3,355	13,096

*Combined L6 and V8 production: Coronet 71,880; Coronet 440 104,767.

1965 Engines	bore×stroke	bhp	availability
L6, 170.0	3.40×3.13	101	S-Dart
L6, 225.0	3.40×4.13	145	S-Coronet/440 6; O-Dart
V8, 273.5	3.63×3.31	180	S-Coronet/440/500 V8s; O-Dart
V8, 273.5	3.63×3.31	235	O-Coronet/440/500 V8s, Dart
V8, 318.0	3.91×3.31	230	O-Coronet/440/500 V8s
V8, 361.0	4.12×3.38	265	O-Coronet/440/500 V8s
V8, 383.0	4.25×3.38	315	S-Monaco; O-Coronets
V8, 383.0	4.25×3.38	270	S-Polara, Custom 880
V8, 383.0	4.25×3.38	330	O-Coronet, 440, 500 V8s
V8, 413.0	4.19×3.75	340	O-Polara, Custom 880, Monaco
V8, 426.0	4.25×3.75	365	S-Hemi-Charger; O-others
V8, 426.0	4.25×3.75	425	S-Hemi-Charger 425

1966

BLL Dart (wb 111.0; wgns-106.0)—75,990 built

		Wght	Price	Prod
1-21	sdn 2d, L6	2,670	2,094	—
2-21	sdn 2d, V8	2,860	2,222	—
1-41	sdn 4d, L6	2,695	2,158	—
2-41	sdn 4d, V8	2,895	2,286	—
1-45	wgn 4d, L6	2,780	2,436	—
2-45	wgn 4d, V8	2,990	2,564	—

BLH Dart 270 (wb 111.0; wgns 106.0)—69,996 built

1-23	htp cpe, L6	2,720	2,307	—
2-23	htp cpe, V8	2,890	2,435	—
1-27	conv cpe, L6	2,805	2,570	—
2-27	conv cpe, V8	2,995	2,698	—
1-41	sdn 4d, L6	2,680	2,280	—
2-41	sdn 4d, V8	2,895	2,408	—
1-45	wgn 4d, L6	2,795	2,533	—
2-45	wgn 4d, V8	3,020	2,661	—

BLP Dart GT (wb 111.0)—30,041 built

1-23	htp cpe, L6	2,735	2,417	—
2-23	htp cpe, V8	2,915	2,545	—
1-27	conv cpe, L6	2,830	2,700	—
2-27	conv cpe, V8	2,995	2,828	—

BWL Coronet (wb 117.0)—66,161 built

1-21	sdn 2d, L6	3,055	2,264	—
2-21	sdn 2d, V8	3,215	2,358	—
1-41	sdn 4d, L6	3,077	2,306	—
2-41	sdn 4d, V8	3,245	2,396	—
1-21	Deluxe sdn 2d, L6	3,050	2,303	—
2-21	Deluxe sdn 2d, V8	3,215	2,391	—
1-41	Deluxe sdn 4d, L6	3,075	2,341	—
2-41	Deluxe sdn 4d, V8	3,240	2,435	—
1-45	Deluxe wgn 2d, L6	3,480	2,631	—
2-45	Deluxe wgn 2d, V8	3,595	2,725	—

BWH Coronet 440 (wb 117.0)—128,998 built

1-23	htp cpe, L6	3,075	2,457	—
2-23	htp cpe, V8	3,235	2,551	—
1-27	conv cpe, L6	3,185	2,672	—
2-27	conv cpe, V8	3,310	2,766	—
1-41	sdn 4d, L6	3,095	2,432	—
2-41	sdn 4d, V8	3,220	2,526	—
1-45	wgn 4d, L6	3,515	2,722	—
2-45	wgn 4d, 2S, V8	3,585	2,816	—

		Wght	Price	Prod
2-46	wgn 4d, 3S, V8	3,680	2,926	—

BWP Coronet 500 (wb 117.0)—55,683 built

		Wght	Price	Prod
1-23	htp cpe, L6	3,115	2,611	—
2-23	htp cpe, V8	3,275	2,705	—
1-27	conv cpe, L6	3,180	2,827	—
2-27	conv cpe, V8	3,345	2,921	—
1-41	sdn 4d, L6	3,120	2,586	—
2-41	sdn 4d, V8	3,280	2,680	—

BX2-P Charger (wb 117.0)

		Wght	Price	Prod
29	htp cpe 4P	3,499	3,122	37,344

BD2-L Polara (wb 121.0)—107,832 built

		Wght	Price	Prod
23	htp cpe	3,820	2,874	—
27	conv cpe	3,885	3,161	—
41	sdn 4d	3,860	2,838	—
41	sdn 4d (318)	3,765	2,763	—
43	htp sdn	3,880	2,948	—
45	wgn 4d, 2S	4,265	3,183	—
46	wgn 4d, 3S	4,295	3,286	—

BD2-H Monaco (wb 121.0)—49,773 built

		Wght	Price	Prod
23	htp cpe	3,855	3,107	—
41	sdn 4d	3,890	3,033	—
43	htp sdn	4,835	3,170	—
45	wgn 4d, 2S	4,270	3,436	—
46	wgn 4d, 3S	4,315	3,539	—

BD2-P Monaco 500 (wb 121.0)

		Wght	Price	Prod
23	htp cpe	3,895	3,604	10,840

1966 Engines	bore×stroke	bhp	availability
L6, 170.0	3.40×3.13	101	S-Dart 6s
L6, 225.0	3.40×4.13	145	S-Coronet 6; O-Dart 6
V8, 273.5	3.63×3.31	180	S-Coronet V8, Dart V8
V8, 273.5	3.63×3.31	235	O-Dart V8
V8, 318.0	3.91×3.31	230	S-Chrgr; O-Cor V8, Pol 318 sdn 4d
V8, 361.0	4.13×3.38	265	O-Charger, Coronet V8
V8, 383.0	4.25×3.38	270	S-Pol, Pol 500, Mon; O-Mon 500
V8, 383.0	4.25×3.38	325	S-Monaco 500; O-all exc Dart
V8, 426.0	4.25×3.75	425	O-Charger (max perf cam avail)
V8, 440.0	4.32×3.75	350	O-Pol, Pol 500, Mon, Mon 500

1967

CLL Dart (wb 111.0)—53,043 built

		Wght	Price	Prod
1-21	sdn 2d, L6	2,710	2,187	—
2-21	sdn 2d, V8	2,895	2,315	—
1-41	sdn 4d, L6	2,725	2,224	—
2-41	sdn 4d, V8	2,910	2,352	—

CLH Dart 270 (wb 111.0)—63,227 built

		Wght	Price	Prod
1-23	htp cpe, L6	2,725	2,388	—
2-23	htp cpe, V8	2,910	2,516	—
1-41	sdn 4d, L6	2,735	2,362	—
2-41	sdn 4d, V8	2,915	2,490	—

CLP Dart GT (wb 111.0)—38,225 built

		Wght	Price	Prod
1-23	htp cpe, L6	2,750	2,499	—
2-23	htp cpe, V8	2,930	2,627	—
1-27	conv cpe, L6	2,850	2,732	—
2-27	conv cpe, V8	3,030	2,860	—

CWE Coronet (wb 117.0)—4,933 built

		Wght	Price	Prod
1-45	wgn 4d, L6	3,485	2,622	—
2-45	wgn 4d, V8	3,650	2,716	—

CWL Coronet Deluxe (wb 117.0)—29,022 built

		Wght	Price	Prod
1-21	sdn 2d, L6	3,045	2,359	—
2-21	sdn 2d, V8	3,210	2,453	—

		Wght	Price	Prod
1-41	sdn 4d, L6	3,070	2,397	—
2-41	sdn 4d, V8	3,235	2,491	—
1-45	wgn 2d, L6	3,495	2,693	—
2-45	wgn 2d, V8	3,625	2,787	—

CWH Coronet 440 (wb 117.0)—106,368 built

		Wght	Price	Prod
1-23	htp cpe, L6	3,065	2,500	—
2-23	htp cpe, V8	3,235	2,594	—
1-27	conv cpe, L6	3,140	2,740	—
2-27	conv cpe, V8	3,305	2,834	—
1-41	sdn 4d, L6	3,060	2,475	—
2-41	sdn 4d, V8	3,225	2,569	—
1-45	wgn 4d, L6	3,495	2,771	—
2-45	wgn 4d, 2S, V8	3,605	2,865	—
2-46	wgn 4d, 3S, V8	3,705	2,975	—

CWP Coronet 500 (wb 117.0)—39,260 built (includes R/T)

		Wght	Price	Prod
1-23	htp cpe, L6	3,115	2,679	—
2-23	htp cpe, V8	3,280	2,773	—
1-27	conv cpe, L6	3,190	2,919	—
2-27	conv cpe, V8	3,355	3,013	—
1-41	sdn 4d, L6	3,075	2,654	—
2-41	sdn 4d, V8	3,235	2,748	—

CW2-P Coronet R/T (wb 117.0)

		Wght	Price	Prod
23	htp cpe, V8	3,565	3,199	—
27	conv cpe, V8	3,640	3,438	—

CW2-P Charger (wb 117.0)

		Wght	Price	Prod
29	htp cpe 4P, V8	3,480	3,128	15,788

CD2-L Polara (wb 122.0)—69,798 built

		Wght	Price	Prod
23	htp cpe	3,870	2,953	—
27	conv cpe	3,930	3,241	—
41	sdn 4d	3,885	2,915	—
41	sdn 4d (318)	3,765	2,843	—
43	htp sdn	3,920	3,028	—
45	wgn 4d, 2S	4,440	3,265	—
46	wgn 4d, 3S	4,450	3,368	—

CD2-M Polara 500 (wb 122.0)—5,606 built

		Wght	Price	Prod
23	htp cpe	3,880	3,155	—
27	conv cpe	3,940	3,443	—

CD2-H Monaco (wb 122.0)—35,225 built

		Wght	Price	Prod
23	htp cpe	3,885	3,213	—
41	sdn 4d	3,895	3,138	—
43	htp sdn	3,945	3,275	—
45	wgn 4d, 2S	4,425	3,543	—
46	wgn 4d, 3S	4,475	3,646	—

CD2-P Monaco 500 (wb 122.0)

		Wght	Price	Prod
23	htp cpe	3,970	3,712	5,237

1967 Engines	bore×stroke	bhp	availability
L6, 170.0	3.40×3.13	115	S-Dart 6
L6, 225.0	3.40×4.13	145	S-Coronet 6; O-Dart 6
V8, 273.5	3.63×3.31	180	S-Dart V8, Coronet V8
V8, 273.5	3.63×3.31	235	O-Dart V8
V8, 318.0	3.91×3.31	230	S-Chrgr, Polara 318; O-Cor V8
V8, 383.0	4.25×3.38	270	S-Polara, Monaco; O-Cor, Mon 500
V8, 383.0	4.25×3.38	325	S-Mon 500; O-Cor, Chrgr, Pol, Mon
V8, 426.0	4.25×3.75	425	O-Coronet R/T, Charger
V8, 440.0	4.32×3.75	350	O-Polara, Monaco
V8, 440.0	4.32×3.75	375	S-Cor R/T; O-Chrgr, Pol, Mon

1968

DLL Dart (wb 111.0)—60,250 built

		Wght	Price	Prod
1-21	sdn 2d, L6	2,705	2,323	—
2-21	sdn 2d, V8	2,875	2,451	—

		Wght	Price	Prod
1-41	sdn 4d, L6	2,725	2,360	—
2-41	sdn 4d, V8	2,900	2,488	—

DLH Dart 270 (wb 111.0)—76,497 built

		Wght	Price	Prod
1-23	htp cpe, L6	2,725	2,525	—
2-23	htp cpe, V8	2,885	2,653	—
1-41	sdn 4d, L6	2,710	2,499	—
2-41	sdn 4d, V8	2,900	2,627	—

DLP Dart GT (wb 111.0)—26,280 built

		Wght	Price	Prod
1-23	htp cpe, L6	2,715	2,637	—
2-23	htp cpe, V8	2,895	2,675	—
1-27	conv cpe, L6	2,790	2,831	—
2-27	conv cpe, V8	2,970	2,959	—

DL2-S Dart GTS (wb 110.0)—8,745 built

		Wght	Price	Prod
23	htp cpe, V8	3,065	3,189	—
27	conv cpe, V8	3,150	3,383	—

DWL Coronet Deluxe (wb 117.0)—46,299 built

		Wght	Price	Prod
1-21	cpe, L6	3,015	2,487	—
2-21	cpe, V8	3,200	2,581	—
1-41	sdn 4d, L6	3,035	2,525	—
2-41	sdn 4d, V8	3,220	2,610	—
1-45	wgn 4d, L6	3,455	2,816	—
2-45	wgn 4d, V8	3,590	2,910	—

DWH Coronet 440 (wb 117.0)—116,348 built (includes Super Bee)

		Wght	Price	Prod
1-21	cpe, L6	3,015	2,565	—
2-21	cpe, V8	3,200	2,671	—
1-23	htp cpe, L6	3,040	2,627	—
2-23	htp cpe, V8	3,225	2,733	—
1-41	sdn 4d, L6	3,035	2,603	—
2-41	sdn 4d, V8	3,320	2,709	—
1-45	wgn 4d, L6	3,450	2,924	—
2-45	wgn 4d, 2S, V8	3,585	3,030	—
2-46	wgn 4d, 3S, V8	3,680	3,140	—

DWH Coronet Super Bee (wb 117.0)

		Wght	Price	Prod
M-21	cpe, V8	3,395	3,027	—

DW2-P Coronet 500 (wb 117.0)—40,139 built

		Wght	Price	Prod
23	htp cpe, V8	3,260	2,879	—
27	conv cpe, V8	3,360	3,036	—
41	sdn 4d, V8	3,240	2,912	—
45	wgn 4d, 2S, V8	3,610	3,212	—
46	wgn 4d, 3S, V8	3,700	3,322	—

DW2-S Coronet R/T (wb 117.0)—10,849 built

		Wght	Price	Prod
23	htp cpe, V8	3,530	3,379	—
27	conv cpe, V8	3,630	3,613	—

DX1-S Charger (wb 117.0)—96,108 built

		Wght	Price	Prod
1P-29	htp cpe 4P, L6	3,100	2,934	—
2P-29	htp cpe 4P, V8	3,305	3,040	—
2X-29	R/T htp cpe, 4P, V8	3,575	3,506	—

DD2-L Polara (wb 122.0)—99,055 built

		Wght	Price	Prod
23	htp cpe	3,700	3,027	—
27	conv cpe	3,755	3,288	—
41	sdn 4d	3,735	3,005	—
43	htp sdn	3,755	3,100	—
45	wgn 4d, 2S	4,155	3,388	—
46	wgn 4d, 3S	4,210	3,454	—

DD2-M Polara 500 (wb 122.0)—4,983 built

		Wght	Price	Prod
23	htp cpe	3,740	3,226	—
27	conv cpe	3,780	3,487	—

DD2-H Monaco (wb 122.0)—37,412 built

		Wght	Price	Prod
23	htp cpe	3,845	3,369	—
41	sdn 4d	3,885	3,294	—
43	htp sdn	3,910	3,432	—
45	wgn 4d, 2S	4,295	3,702	—
46	wgn 4d, 3S	4,360	3,835	—

DD2-P Monaco 500 (wb 122.0)

		Wght	Price	Prod
23	htp cpe	3,885	3,869	4,568

1968 Engines	bore×stroke	bhp	availability
L6, 170.0	3.40×3.13	115	S-Dart 6
L6, 225.0	3.40×4.13	145	S-Coronet 6; O-Dart 6
V8, 273.5	3.63×3.31	190	S-Dart V8, Coronet V8
V8, 318.0	3.91×3.31	230	S-Chrgr, Pol; O-Dart V8, Cor V8
V8, 340.0	4.04×3.31	275	S-Dart GTS
V8, 383.0	4.25×3.38	300	O-Dart GTS
V8, 383.0	4.25×3.38	290	S-Mon; O-Cor V8, Chrgr, Pol
V8, 383.0	4.25×3.38	330	O-Cor V8, Chrgr, Pol, Mon
V8, 383.0	4.25×3.38	335	S-Coronet Super Bee
V8, 426.0	4.25×3.75	425	O-Cor R/T, Chrgr R/T; S-Chrgr Dayt
V8, 440.0	4.32×3.75	350	O-Polara & Monaco wgns
V8, 440.0	4.32×3.75	375	S-Cor R/T, Chrgr R/T; O-Pol, Mon

1969

LL Dart (wb 111.0)—106,329 built (includes Swinger 340)

		Wght	Price	Prod
23	Swinger htp cpe	2,795	2,400	—
41	sdn 4d	2,810	2,413	—

LM Dart Swinger 340 (wb 111.0)

		Wght	Price	Prod
23	htp cpe	3,097	2,836	—

LH Dart Custom (wb 110.0)—63,740 built

		Wght	Price	Prod
23	htp cpe	2,795	2,577	—
41	sdn 4d	2,810	2,550	—

LP Dart GT (wb 111.0)—20,914 built

		Wght	Price	Prod
23	htp cpe	2,800	2,672	—
27	conv cpe	2,905	2,865	—

LS Dart GTS V8 (wb 110.0)—6,702 built

		Wght	Price	Prod
23	htp cpe	3,105	3,226	—
27	conv cpe	3,210	3,419	—

WL Coronet Deluxe (wb 117.0)—23,988 built

		Wght	Price	Prod
21	cpe	3,067	2,554	—
41	sdn 4d	3,097	2,589	—
45	wgn 4d	3,552	2,922	—

WH Coronet 440 (wb 117.0)—105,882 built

		Wght	Price	Prod
21	cpe	3,067	2,630	—
23	htp cpe	3,097	2,692	—
41	sdn 4d	3,102	2,670	—
45	wgn 4d, 2S	3,557	3,033	—
46	wgn 4d, 3S, V8 only	3,676	3,246	—

WM Coronet Super Bee V8 (wb 117.0)—27,846 built

		Wght	Price	Prod
21	cpe	3,440	3,076	—
23	htp cpe	3,470	3,138	—

WP Coronet 500 V8 (wb 117.0)—32,050 built

		Wght	Price	Prod
23	htp cpe	3,171	2,929	—
27	conv cpe	3,306	3,069	—
41	sdn 4d	3,206	2,963	—
45	wgn 4d, 2S	3,611	3,280	—
46	wgn 4d, 3S	3,676	3,392	—

WS Coronet R/T (wb 117.0)—7,238 built

		Wght	Price	Prod
23	htp cpe	3,601	3,442	—
27	conv cpe	3,721	3,660	—

XP/XS Charger (wb 117.0)

		Wght	Price	Prod
XP29	htp cpe, L6	3,103	3,020	69,142
XP29	htp cpe, V8	3,256	3,126	

		Wght	Price	Prod
XS29	R/T htp cpe, V8	3,646	3,592	20,057
—	Daytona htp cpe, V8	—	4,000	505

XX Charger 500 V8 (wb 117.0)*

		Wght	Price	Prod
XX29	htp cpe	3,671	3,860	—

DL Polara (wb 122.0)—83,122 built

		Wght	Price	Prod
23	htp cpe	3,646	3,117	—
27	conv cpe	3,791	3,377	—
41	sdn 4d	3,701	3,095	—
43	htp sdn	3,731	3,188	—
45	wgn 4d, 2S	4,161	3,522	—
46	wgn 4d, 3S	4,211	3,629	—

DM Polara 500 (wb 122.0)—5,564 built

		Wght	Price	Prod
23	htp cpe	3,681	3,314	—
27	conv cpe	3,801	3,576	—

DH Monaco (wb 122.0)—38,566 built

		Wght	Price	Prod
23	htp cpe	3,811	3,528	—
41	sdn 4d	3,846	3,452	—
43	htp sdn	3,891	3,591	—
45	wgn 4d, 2S	4,306	3,917	—
46	wgn 4d, 3S	4,361	4,046	—

*Production included with XP 29 models

1969 Engines	bore×stroke	bhp	availability
L6, 170.0	3.40×3.13	115	S-Dart
L6, 225.0	3.40×4.13	145	S-Coronet Del/440; O-Dart
V8, 273.5	3.63×3.31	190	S-Dart V8
V8, 318.0	3.91×3.31	230	S-Cor Del/440/500, Chrgr, Pol; O-Dart
V8, 340.0	4.04×3.31	275	S-GTS, Swinger 340
V8, 383.0	4.25×3.38	290	S-Monaco; O-Polara, Chrgr, Coronet
V8, 383.0	4.25×3.38	330	O-GTS, Cor V8, Mon, Pol, Chrgr
V8, 383.0	4.25×3.38	335	S-Coronet Super Bee
V8, 426.0	4.25×3.75	425	O-Coronet R/T, Charger R/T
V8, 440.0	4.32×3.75	350	O-Monaco & Polara wgns
V8, 440.0	4.32×3.75	375	O-Monaco & Polara exc wagons

1970

LL Dart (wb 111.0)

		Wght	Price	Prod
23	Swinger htp cpe	2,903	2,261	119,883
41	sdn 4d	2,900	2,308	35,499

LH Dart Custom (wb 111.0)

		Wght	Price	Prod
23	htp cpe	2,898	2,463	17,208
41	sdn 4d	2,905	2,467	23,779

LM Dart Swinger 340 (wb 111.0)

		Wght	Price	Prod
23	htp cpe	3,130	2,631	13,785

JH Challenger (wb 110.0)

		Wght	Price	Prod
23	htp cpe	3,028	2,851	53,337
27	conv cpe	3,103	3,120	3,173
29	S.E. htp cpe	3,053	3,083	6,584

JS Challenger R/T (wb 110.0)

		Wght	Price	Prod
23	htp cpe (inc T/A)	3,405	3,226	14,889
27	conv cpe	3,470	3,535	1,070
29	S.E. htp cpe	3,440	3,498	3,979

WL Coronet Deluxe (wb 117.0)

		Wght	Price	Prod
21	cpe	3,150	2,669	2,978
41	sdn 4d	3,188	2,704	7,894
45	wgn 4d	3,675	3,048	3,694

WH Coronet 440 (wb 117.0)

		Wght	Price	Prod
21	cpe	3,170	2,743	1,236
23	htp cpe	3,185	2,805	24,341
41	sdn 4d	3,190	2,783	33,258
45	wgn 4d	3,673	3,156	3,964
46	wgn 4d	3,775	3,368	3,772

WM Coronet Super Bee (wb 117.0)

		Wght	Price	Prod
21	cpe	3,500	3,012	3,966
23	htp cpe	3,535	3,074	11,540

WP Coronet 500 (wb 117.0)

		Wght	Price	Prod
23	htp cpe	3,235	3,048	8,247
27	conv cpe	3,345	3,188	924
41	sdn 4d	3,255	3,082	2,890
45	wgn 4d, 2S	3,715	3,404	1,657
46	wgn 4d, 3S	3,785	3,514	1,779

WS Coronet R/T (wb 117.0)

		Wght	Price	Prod
23	htp cpe	3,545	3,569	2,319
27	conv cpe	3,610	3,785	296

XH/XP Charger (wb 117.0)

		Wght	Price	Prod
XH29	htp cpe	3,293	3,001	39,431
XP29	500 htp cpe	3,293	3,139	

XS/XX Charger R/T (wb 117.0)

		Wght	Price	Prod
XS29	htp cpe	3,610	3,711	10,337
XX29	Daytona htp cpe	3,710	3,993	

DE Polara (wb 122.0)*

		Wght	Price	Prod
41	sdn 4d, L6	3,775	2,960	—
45	wgn 4d, 2S, V8	4,180	3,513	—
46	wgn 4d, 3S, V8	4,235	3,621	—

DL Polara "Deluxe" V8 (wb 122.0)

		Wght	Price	Prod
23	htp cpe	3,770	3,224	*
27	conv cpe	3,830	3,527	842
41	sdn 4d	3,805	3,222	*
43	htp sdn	3,850	3,316	*
45	wgn 4d, 2S	4,180	3,670	*
46	wgn 4d, 3S	4,235	3,778	*

DM Polara Custom V8 (wb 122.0)*

		Wght	Price	Prod
23	htp cpe	4,005	3,458	—
41	sdn 4d	3,975	3,426	—
43	htp sdn	3,925	3,528	—

DH Monaco (wb 122.0)

		Wght	Price	Prod
23	htp cpe	3,950	3,679	3,522
41	sdn 4d	4,010	3,604	4,721
43	htp sdn	4,045	3,743	10,974
45	wgn 4d, 2S	4,420	4,110	2,211
46	wgn 4d, 3S	4,475	4,242	3,264

*Dodge combined production figures for most Polara models. Available figures are:

23	htp cpe (DL, DM)	15,243
27	conv cpe (DL)	842
41	sdn 4d (DE, DL, DM)	18,740
43	htp sdn (DL, DM)	19,223
45	wgn 4d, 2S (DE, DL)	3,074
46	wgn 4d, 3s (DE, DL)	3,546

1970 Engines	bore×stroke	bhp	availability
L6, 198.0	3.40×3.64	125	S-Dart
L6, 225.0	3.40×4.13	145	S-Chal/Cor/Chrgr/Polara 6s; O-Dart
V8, 318.0	3.91×3.31	230	S-Dart exc Swngr 340, Chal, Cor, Chrgr, Pol
V8, 340.0	4.04×3.31	275	S-Swngr 340; O-Chal
V8, 383.0	4.25×3.38	290	S-Mon, Pol Cus; O-Chal/Cor/Chrgr/ Polara V8s
V8, 383.0	4.25×3.38	330	O-Chal, Cor, Pol, Pol Cus, Monaco
V8, 383.0	4.25×3.38	335	S-Super Bee, Chal R/T; O-Chal, Chrgr R/T
V8, 426.0	4.25×3.75	425	O-Chal, Super Bee, Cor/Chrgr R/Ts
V8, 440.0	4.32×3.75	350	O-Monaco, Polara, Polara Custom
V8, 440.0	4.32×3.75	375	S-Chrgr/Coronet/Challenger R/Ts
V8, 440.0	4.32×3.75	390	O-Chrgr/Cor/Chal R/Ts, Super Bee

Dodge

1971

Dart (wb 111.0; fstbk cpes-108.0)		Wght	Price	Prod
LL29	Demon fstbk cpe	2,845	2,343	69,861
LL23	Swinger Special htp cpe	2,900	2,402	13,485
LL41	sdn 4d	2,900	2,450	32,711
LH23	Swinger htp cpe	2,900	2,561	102,480
LH41	Custom sdn 4d	2,900	2,609	21,785
LM29	Demon fstbk 340 cpe V8	3,165	2,721	10,098

Challenger (wb 110.0)				
JL23	cpe	3,050	2,727	23,088
JH23	htp cpe	3,092	2,848	
JH27	conv cpe	3,180	3,105	2,165
JS23	R/T htp cpe V8	3,495	3,273	4,630

Coronet (wb 118.0)				
WL41	sdn 4d	3,302	2,777	11,794
WL45	wgn 4d 2S	3,778	3,101	5,470
WH41	Custom sdn 4d	3,308	2,951	37,817
WH45	Custom wgn 4d 2S	3,812	3,196	5,365
WH46	Custom wgn 4d 3S V8	3,890	3,454	5,717
WP41	Brougham sdn 4d V8	3,475	3,232	4,700
WP45	Crestwood wgn 4d 2S V8	3,845	3,601	2,884
WP46	Crestwood wgn 4d 3S V8	3,900	3,682	3,981

Charger (wb 115.0)				
WL21	cpe	3,270	2,707	46,183
WH23	htp cpe	3,138	2,975	
WP23	500 htp cpe V8	3,350	3,223	11,948
WM23	Super Bee htp cpe V8	3,640	3,271	5,054
WP29	SE htp cpe V8	3,375	3,422	15,811
WS23	R/T htp cpe V8	3,685	3,777	3,118

Polara (wb 122.0)				
DE41	sdn 4d	3,788	3,298	16,444
DE23	htp cpe	3,755	3,319	11,500
DE43	htp sdn V8	3,875	3,497	2,487
DL41	Custom sdn 4d V8	3,835	3,593	13,850
DL43	Custom htp sdn V8	3,875	3,681	17,458
DL23	Custom htp cpe V8	3,805	3,614	9,682
DL45	Custom wgn 4d 2S V8	4,280	3,992	9,682
DL46	Custom wgn 4d 3S V8	4,335	4,098	
DM43	Brougham htp sdn V8	4,035	3,884	2,570
DM23	Brougham htp cpe V8	3,965	3,818	2,024

Monaco (wb 122.0)				
DH41	sdn 4d	4,050	4,223	16,900
DH43	htp sdn	4,080	4,362	
DH23	htp cpe	4,000	4,298	3,195
DH45	wgn 4d 2S	4,525	4,689	5,449
DH46	wgn 4d 3S	4,585	4,821	

1971 Engines	bore×stroke	bhp	availability
L6, 198.0	3.40×3.64	125	S-Dart,Chal JL
L6, 225.0	3.40×4.13	145	S-Chal JH,Cor,Chrgr,Pol; O-Dart,Chal JL
V8, 318.0	3.91×3.31	230	S-Chal,Cor,Chrgr,Pol; O-Dart
V8, 340.0	4.04×3.31	275	S-Demon 340; O-Chal
V8, 360.0	4.00×3.58	275	O-Polara
V8, 383.0	4.25×3.38	275	S-Chal RT,Chrgr SuperBee, Pol B'ham, Mon; O-Chal, Cor, Chrgr, Pol
V8, 383.0	4.25×3.38	300	O-Chal,Cor,Chrgr,Pol,Mon
V8, 426.0	4.25×3.75	335	O-Polara, Monaco
V8, 426.0	4.25×3.75	425	S-Charger, Challenger
V8, 440.0	4.32×3.75	335	O-Polara, Monaco
V8, 440.0	4.32×3.75	370	S-Charger RT; O-Charger
V8, 440.0	4.32×3.75	385	O-Challenger, Charger

1972

Dart (wb 111.0; fstbk cpes 108.0)		Wght	Price	Prod
LL29	Demon fstbk cpe	2,800	2,316	39,880
LL23	Swinger Special htp cpe	2,845	2,373	19,210
LL41	sdn 4d	2,855	2,420	26,019
LH23	Swinger htp cpe	2,835	2,528	119,618
LH41	Custom sdn 4d	2,855	2,574	49,941
LM29	Demon 340 fstbk cpe V8	3,125	2,759	8,750

Challenger (wb 110.0)				
JH23	cpe	3,098	2,790	18,535
JS23	Rallye htp cpe V8	3,225	3,082	8,123

Coronet (wb 118.0)				
WL41	sdn 4d	3,362	2,721	11,293
WL45	wgn 4d 2S V8	3,795	3,209	5,452
WH45	Custom wgn 4d 2S V8	3,800	3,382	
WH46	Custom wgn 4d 3S V8	3,840	3,460	
WH41	Custom sdn 4d	3,370	2,998	43,132
WP45	Crestwood wgn 4d 2S V8	3,810	3,604	6,471
WP46	Crestwood wgn 4d 3S V8	3,850	3,683	

Charger (wb 115.0)				
WL21	cpe	3,278	2,652	7,803
WH23	htp cpe	3,292	2,913	45,361
WP29	SE htp cpe V8	3,390	3,249	22,430

Polara (wb 122.0)				
DL41	sdn 4d	3,835	3,618	25,187
DL43	htp sdn	3,875	3,709	8,212
DL23	htp cpe	3,800	3,641	7,000
DM41	Custom sdn 4d	3,845	3,808	19,739
DM43	Custom htp sdn	3,890	3,898	22,505
DM23	Custom htp cpe	3,815	3,830	15,039
DM45	Custom wgn 4d 2S	4,320	4,262	3,497
DM46	Custom wgn 4d 3S	4,370	4,371	7,660

Monaco (wb 122.0)				
DP41	sdn 4d	3,980	4,095	6,474
DP43	htp sdn	4,030	4,216	15,039
DP23	htp cpe	3,960	4,153	7,786
DP45	wgn 4d 2S	4,445	4,627	2,569
DP46	wgn 4d 3S	4,490	4,756	5,145

1972 Engines	bore×stroke	bhp	availability
L6, 198.0	3.40×3.64	100	S-Dart
L6, 225.0	3.40×4.13	100	O-Dart
L6, 225.0	3.40×4.13	110	S-Chal,Cor,Chrgr; O-Dart
V8, 318.0	3.91×3.31	150	S-Chal,Cor,Chrgr,Pol; O-Dart
V8, 340.0	4.04×3.31	240	S-Demon 340; O-Dart, Chal,Chrgr
V8, 360.0	4.00×3.58	175	S-Mon; O-Pol
V8, 400.0	4.34×3.38	190	O-Chrgr,Pol,Mon
V8, 400.0	4.34×3.38	250	O-Pol,Mon
V8, 400.0	4.34×3.38	255	O-Charger
V8, 440.0	4.32×3.75	230	O-Monaco
V8, 440.0	4.32×3.75	235	O-Polara
V8, 440.0	4.32×3.75	280	O-Monaco
V8, 440.0	4.32×3.75	285	O-Pol,Mon

1973

Dart (wb 111.0; fstbk cpes-108.0)		Wght	Price	Prod
LL29	Sport fstbk cpe	2,850	2,424	68,113
LL23	Swinger Special htp cpe	2,895	2,462	17,480
LL41	sdn 4d	2,910	2,504	21,539
LH23	Swinger htp cpe	2,890	2,617	107,619
LH41	Custom sdn 4d	2,910	2,658	62,626
LM29	340 fstbk cpe V8	3,205	2,853	11,315

Challenger (wb 110.0)				
JH23	htp cpe V8	3,155	3,011	32,596

Coronet (wb 118.0)

WL41	sdn 4d	3,472	2,867	14,395
WL45	wgn 4d 2S V8	3,955	3,314	4,874
WH41	Custom sdn 4d	3,962	3,017	46,491
WH45	Custom wgn 4d 2S V8	3,955	3,442	
WH46	Custom wgn 4d 3S V8	4,000	3,560	13,018
WP45	Crestwood wgn 4d 2S V8	3,970	3,671	
WP46	Crestwood wgn 4d 3S V8	4,005	3,791	8,755

Charger (wb 115.0)

WL21	cpe	3,428	2,810	11,995
WH23	htp cpe	3,465	3,060	45,415
WP29	SE htp cpe V8	3,540	3,375	61,908

Polara (wb 122.0)

DL41	sdn 4d	3,865	3,729	15,015
DL23	htp cpe	3,835	3,752	6,432
DL45	wgn 4d 2S	4,420	4,186	3,327
DM41	Custom sdn 4d	3,870	3,911	23,939
DM43	Custom htp sdn	3,905	4,001	29,341
DM23	Custom htp cpe	3,835	3,928	17,406
DM45	Custom wgn 4d 2S	4,440	4,370	3,702
DM46	Custom wgn 4d 3S	4,485	4,494	8,839

Monaco (wb 122.0)

DP41	sdn 4d	4,020	4,218	6,316
DP43	htp sdn	4,060	4,339	9,031
DP23	htp cpe	3,985	4,276	6,133
DP45	wgn 4d 2S	4,470	4,730	2,337
DP46	wgn 4d 3S	4,515	4,859	5,579

1973 Engines	bore×stroke	bhp	availability
L6, 198.0	3.40×3.64	95	S-Dart
L6, 225.0	3.40×4.13	105	S-Cor,Chrgr; O-Dart
V8, 318.0	3.91×3.31	150	S-Chal,Cor,Chrgr, Pol exc wgns; O-Dart
V8, 340.0	4.04×3.31	240	S-Dart Sport 340; O-Chal,Cor,Chrgr
V8, 360.0	4.00×3.58	170	S-Pol wgns, Mon; O-Pol
V8, 400.0	4.34×3.38	175	O-Coronet, Charger
V8, 400.0	4.34×3.38	185	S-Mon wgns; O-Pol, Mon
V8, 400.0	4.34×3.38	220	O-Polara, Monaco
V8, 400.0	4.34×3.38	260	O-Coronet, Charger
V8, 440.0	4.32×3.75	220	O-Polara, Monaco
V8, 440.0	4.32×3.75	280	O-Coronet, Charger

1974

Dart (wb 111.0; fstbk cpes-108.0)

		Wght	Price	Prod
LL29	Sport fstbk cpe	2,990	2,878	59,567
LL23	Swinger Special htp cpe	3,035	2,918	16,155
LH23	Swinger htp cpe	3,030	3,077	89,242
LL41	sdn 4d	3,055	2,961	
LH41	Custom sdn 4d	3,055	3,119	78,216
LM29	360 fstbk cpe V8	3,330	3,320	3,951
LP41	Special Edition sdn 4d	3,641	3,837	
LP23	Special Edition htp cpe	3,599	3,794	12,385

Challenger (wb 110.0)

JH23	htp cpe V8	3,225	3,143	16,437

Coronet (wb 118.0)

WL41	sdn 4d	3,548	3,271	8,752
WL45	wgn 4d 2S V8	4,085	3,699	2,968
WH41	Custom sdn 4d	3,538	3,374	36,021
WH45	Custom wgn 4d 2S V8	4,090	3,882	2,975
WH46	Custom wgn 4d 3S V8	4,130	4,196	4,950
WP45	Crestwood wgn 4d 2S V8	4,100	4,117	1,916
Wp46	Crestwood wgn 4d 3S V8	4,135	4,433	3,146

Charger (wb 115.0)

WL21	cpe	3,510	3,212	8,876

		Wght	Price	Prod
WH23	htp cpe	3,528	3,412	29,101
WP29	SE htp cpe V8	3,625	3,742	36,399

Monaco (wb 122.0; wgns-124.0)

DM41	sdn 4d	4,170	4,259	9,101
DM23	htp cpe	4,150	4,283	3,347
DM45	wgn 4d 2S	4,760	4,706	1,583
DH41	Custom sdn 4d	4,175	4,446	12,655
DH43	Custom htp sdn	4,205	4,539	10,585
DH23	Custom htp cpe	4,155	4,464	6,649
DH45	Custom wgn 4d 2S	4,770	4,839	1,253
DH46	Custom wgn 4d 3S	4,815	4,956	3,272
DP41	Brougham sdn 4d	4,410	4,891	3,954
DP43	Brougham htp sdn	4,445	4,999	5,649
DP23	Brougham htp cpe	4,370	4,951	4,863
DP45	Brougham wgn 4d 2S	4,860	5,360	1,042
DP46	Brougham wgn 4d 3S	4,905	5,477	2,718

1974 Engines	bore×stroke	bhp	availability
L6, 198.0	3.40×3.64	95	S-Dart exc SE
L6, 225.0	3.40×4.13	105	S-Dart SE, Cor; O-Dart
V8, 318.0	3.91×3.31	150	S-Chal,Cor,Chrgr; O-Dart
V8, 360.0	4.00×3.58	180	S-Mon exc B'ham/wgns; O-Chrgr
V8, 360.0	4.00×3.58	200	O-Cor,Chrgr,Mon exc B'ham,wgn
V8, 360.0	4.00×3.58	245	S-Dart 360; O-Chal,Chrgr
V8, 400.0	4.34×3.38	185	S-Mon B'ham,wgns; O-Cor,Chrgr
V8, 400.0	4.34×3.38	205	O-Coronet, Charger
V8, 400.0	4.34×3.38	240	O-Monaco exc wagons
V8, 400.0	4.34×3.38	250	O-Coronet, Charger
V8, 440.0	4.32×3.75	230	O-Monaco exc wagons
V8, 440.0	4.32×3.75	250	O-Monaco wagons
V8, 440.0	4.32×3.75	275	O-Coronet, Charger

1975

Dart (wb 111.0; fstbk cpes-108.0)

		Wght	Price	Prod
LL29	Sport fstbk cpe	2,980	3,297	50,312
LM29	360 fstbk cpe V8	3,335	4,014	1,043
LL23	Swinger Special htp cpe	3,045	3,341	9,304
LL41	sdn 4d	3,060	3,269	24,193
LH23	Swinger htp cpe	3,035	3,518	45,495
LH41	Custom sdn 4d	3,060	3,444	60,818
LP23	Special Edition htp cpe	3,260	4,232	5,680
LP41	Speical Edition sdn 4d	3,280	4,159	13,194

Coronet (wb 117.5; htps-115.0)

WL41	sdn 4d	3,652	3,641	8,138
WL21	htp cpe	3,620	3,591	6,058
WL45	wgn 4d 2S V8	4,185	4,358	2,852
WH41	Custom sdn 4d	3,692	3,754	26,219
WH23	Custom htp cpe	3,702	3,777	18,513
WH45	Custom wgn 4d 2S V8	4,240	4,560	2,623
WH46	Custom wgn 4d 3S V8	4,290	4,674	5,052
WP23	Brougham htp cpe V8	3,800	4,154	10,292
WP45	Crestwood wgn 4d 2S V8	4,230	4,826	1,784
WP46	Crestwood wgn 4d 3S V8	4,290	4,918	2,967

Charger (wb 115.0)

XS22	SE htp cpe	3,950	4,903	30,812

Monaco (wb 121.5; wgns-124.0)

DM41	sdn 4d	4,280	4,605	7,097
DM23	htp cpe	4,225	4,631	2,116
DH41	Royal sdn 4d	4,285	4,848	10,126
DH43	Royal htp sdn	4,310	4,951	8,117
DH23	Royal htp cpe	4,240	4,868	4,001
DP41	Royal Brougham sdn 4d	4,455	5,262	5,126

		Wght	Price	Prod
DP43	Royal Brougham htp sdn	4,485	5,382	5,964
DP29	Royal Brougham htp cpe	4,370	5,460	
DM45	wgn 4d 2S	4,885	5,109	1,547
DH45	Royal wgn 4d 2S	4,905	5,292	1,279
DH46	Royal wgn 4d 3S	4,945	5,415	2,666
DP45	Royal Brougham wgn 4d 2S	4,980	5,779	1,165
DP46	Royal Brougham wgn 4d 3S	5,025	5,905	2,909

1975 Engines	bore×stroke	bhp	availability
L6, 225.0	3.40×4.13	95	S-Dart, Coronet
V8, 318.0	3.91×3.31	135	O-Charger
V8, 318.0	3.91×3.31	145	O-Dart
V8, 318.0	3.91×3.31	150	S-Cor;O-Chrgr, Monaco
V8, 360.0	4.00×3.58	180	S-Chrgr,Mon exc B'ham wgns; O-Cor, Ryl Monaco B'ham
V8, 360.0	4.00×3.58	190	O-Chrgr,Ryl Monaco B'ham
V8, 360.0	4.00×3.58	230	S-Dart 360
V8, 400.0	4.34×3.38	165/190/235	O-Coronet, Charger
V8, 400.0	4.34×3.38	175	S-Ryl Mon B'ham; O-Mon
V8, 400.0	4.34×3.38	185	O-Charger
V8, 400.0	4.34×3.38	195	O-Monaco
V8, 440.0	4.32×3.75	195	O-Monaco exc Ryl B'ham
V8, 440.0	4.32×3.75	215	O-all Monaco

1976

Dart (wb 111.0; fstbk cpes-108.0)

		Wght	Price	Prod
LL29	Sport fstbk cpe	2,990	3,258	18,873
LL23	Swinger Special htp cpe	3,050	3,337	3,916
LL41	sdn 4d	3,070	3,295	34,864
LH23	Swinger htp cpe	3,035	3,510	10,885

Aspen (wb 112.7; cpes-108.7)

		Wght	Price	Prod
NL41	sdn 4d	3,252	3,371	17,573
NL29	cpe	3,222	3,336	27,730
NL45	wgn 5d 2S	3,605	3,658	37,642
NH41	Custom sdn 4d	3,240	3,553	32,163
NH29	Custom cpe	3,232	3,518	23,782
NP41	SE sdn 4d	3,470	4,440	24,378
NP29	SE cpe	3,432	4,413	21,564
NP45	SE wgn 5d 2S	3,630	3,988	34,617

Coronet (wb 117.5; htps-115.0)

		Wght	Price	Prod
WL41	sdn 4d	3,742	3,770	15,658
WL45	wgn 4d 2S V8	4,285	4,634	2,632
WL46	wgn 4d 3S V8	4,350	4,776	3,336
WH41	Brougham sdn 4d	3,760	4,059	15,215
WH45	Crestwood wgn 4d 2S V8	4,285	5,023	1,725
WH46	Crestwood wgn 4d 3S V8	4,360	5,165	2,597

Charger (wb 115.0)

		Wght	Price	Prod
WL23	htp cpe	3,712	3,736	9,906
WH23	cpe	3,718	4,025	13,826
XS22	SE htp cpe V8	3,945	4,763	42,168

Monaco (wb 121.5; wgns-124.0)

		Wght	Price	Prod
DM41	sdn 4d	4,160	4,388	6,221
DM45	wgn 4d 2S	4,910	4,948	1,116
DH41	Royal sdn 4d	4,325	4,763	11,320
DH23	Royal htp cpe	4,280	4,778	2,915
DH45	Royal wgn 4d 2S	4,915	5,241	923
DH46	Royal wgn 4d 3S	4,950	5,364	1,429
DP41	Royal Brougham sdn 4d	4,520	5,211	5,111
DP29	Royal Brougham htp cpe	4,430	5,382	4,076
DP46	Royal Brougham wgn 4d 3S	4,995	5,869	2,480

1976 Engines	bore×stroke	bhp	availability
L6, 225.0	3.40×4.13	100	S-all sixes
V8, 318.0	3.91×3.31	150	S-Asp,Cor exc wgns,Chrgr, Mon exc Wgns/Ryl; O-Dart

	bore×stroke	bhp	availability
V8, 360.0	4.00×3.58	170	S-Cor wgns, Ryl Mon; O-Asp,Cor,Chrgr,Ryl Mon B'ham
V8, 360.0	4.00×3.58	175	O-Coronet, Charger
V8, 360.0	4.00×3.58	220	O-Dart, Coronet
V8, 400.0	4.34×3.38	175	S-Mon wgns/Ryl B'hams; O-Cor Chrgr, Monaco
V8, 400.0	4.34×3.38	185/240	O-Coronet, Charger
V8, 400.0	4.34×3.38	210	O-Monaco
V8, 400.0	4.34×3.38	255	O-Coronet
V8, 440.0	4.32×3.75	205	O-Monaco

1977

Aspen (wb 112.7; cpes-108.7)

		Wght	Price	Prod
NL41	sdn 4d	3,290	3,631	32,662
NL29	cpe	3,235	3,582	33,102
NL45	wgn 5d 2S	3,492	3,953	67,294
NH41	Custom sdn 4d	3,295	3,813	45,697
NH29	Custom cpe	3,240	3,764	29,946
BP41	SE sdn 4d	3,492	4,366	25,949
NP29	SE cpe	3,428	4,317	19,985
NH45	SE wgn 5d 2S	3,518	4,283	58,011

Charger (wb 115.0)

		Wght	Price	Prod
XS22	SE htp cpe V8	3,895	5,098	42,542

Monaco (wb 117.4; htps-115.0)

		Wght	Price	Prod
WL41	sdn 4d	3,772	3,988	20,633
WL23	htp cpe	3,630	3,911	14,054
WS23	Special htp cpe	NA	3,995	NA
WL45	wgn 4d 2S V8	4,335	4,724	3,896
WL46	wgn 4d 3S V8	4,395	4,867	4,594
WH41	Brougham sdn 4d	3,782	4,217	17,224
WH23	Brougham htp cpe	3,752	4,146	14,430
WH45	Crestwood wgn 4d 2S V8	4,330	5,224	1,948
WH46	Crestwood wgn 4d 3S V8	4,405	5,367	3,301

Diplomat (wb 112.0)

		Wght	Price	Prod
GH41	sdn 4d	3,560	5,101	9,647
GH22	cpe	3,510	4,943	14,023
GP41	Medallion sdn 4d	3,675	5,471	4,667
GP22	Medallion cpe	3,615	5,313	9,215

Royal Monaco (wb 121.5; wgns-124.0)

		Wght	Price	Prod
DM41	sdn 4d	4,125	4,716	12,646
DM23	htp cpe	4,050	4,731	3,360

1977 Royal Monaco Brougham four-door sedan

		Wght	Price	Prod
DM45	wgn 4d 2S	4,905	5,353	2,010
DH41	Brougham sdn 4d	4,270	4,996	21,440
DH23	Brougham htp cpe	4,205	5,011	8,309
DH45	Brougham wgn 4d 2S	4,900	5,607	1,418
DH46	Brougham wgn 4d 3S	4,935	5,730	4,251

1977 Engines	bore×stroke	bhp	availability
L6, 225.0	3.40×4.13	100	S-Aspen exc wgns
L6, 225.0	3.40×4.13	110	S-Asp wgns, Mon; O-Aspen
V8, 318.0	3.91×3.31	145	S-Asp,Dip,Mon exc wgns, Chrgr, Ryl Mon
V8, 318.0	3.91×3.31	135	O-Mon,Chrgr
V8, 360.0	4.00×3.58	155	S-Mon wgns,Ryl Mon B'ham;O-Asp,Mon,Chrgr,Ryl Mon
V8, 360.0	4.00×3.58	170	O-Monaco, Charger
V8, 400.0	4.34×3.38	190	S-Ryl Mon wgns; O-Mon, Chrgr, Ryl Mon
V8, 440.0	4.32×3.75	195	O-Ryl Mon

1978

Omni (wb 99.2)

		Wght	Price	Prod
ZL44	htchbk sdn 5d	2,145	3,976	81,611

Aspen (wb 112.7; cpe-108.7)

NL41	sdn 4d	3,235	3,911	60,191
NL29	cpe	3,195	3,783	75,599
NL45	wgn 5d 2S	3,448	4,253	61,917

Charger/Magnum (wb 114.9)

XP22	Charger SE htp cpe V8	3,895	5,368	2,800
XS22	Magnum XE htp cpe V8	3,895	5,509	55,431

Monaco (wb 117.4; cpes-114.9)

WL41	sdn 4d	3,760	4,344	20,292
SL23	htp cpe	3,738	4,254	10,291
WL45	wgn 4d 2S V8	4,310	5,103	2,376
WL46	wgn 4d 3S V8	4,375	5,246	2,944
WH41	Brougham sdn 4d	3,775	4,568	8,665
WH23	Brougham htp cpe	3,742	4,507	6,842
WH45	Crestwood wgn 4d 2S V8	4,305	5,549	1,329
WH46	Crestwood wgn 4d 3S V8	4,380	5,692	2,112

Diplomat (wb 112.7)

GM41	S sdn 4d	3,438	4,937	NA
GM22	S cpe	3,358	4,771	NA
GH41	sdn 4d	3,508	5,187	21,094
GH22	cpe	3,462	5,021	19,000
GH45	wgn 5d 2S	3,598	5,538	11,226
GP41	Medallion sdn 4d	3,592	5,569	11,628
GP22	Medallion cpe	3,538	5,403	12,372

1978 Engines	bore×stroke	bhp	availability
L4, 104.7	3.13×3.40	70	S-Omni
L4, 104.7	3.13×3.40	75	O-Omni
L6, 225.0	3.40×4.13	90	O-Asp exc wgns, Dip
L6, 225.0	3.40×4.13	100	S-Aspen exc wgns, Chrgr
L6, 225.0	3.40×4.13	110	S-Asp wgns; O-Asp,Dip,Mon
V8, 318.0	3.91×3.31	140	S-Asp,Dip,Mag,Mon exc wgns
V8, 318.0	3.91×3.31	150	S-Charger
V8, 318.0	3.91×3.31	155	O-Asp,Dip,Mag,Mon
V8, 360.0	4.00×3.58	155	S-Mon wgns; O-Asp,Dip, Mag,Mon
V8, 360.0	4.00×3.58	165	O-Aspen
V8, 360.0	4.00×3.58	170	O-Dip,Mag,Mon,Chrgr
V8, 360.0	4.00×3.58	175	O-Aspen,Chrgr
V8, 400.0	4.34×3.38	190	O-Magnum, Monaco
V8, 400.0	4.34×3.38	175/185/240	O-Charger
V8, 440.0	4.32×3.75	195	O-Monaco

1979

Omni (wb 99.2; 024-96.7)

		Wght	Price	Prod
ZL44	htchbk sdn 5d	2,135	4,469	84,093
ZL24	024 htchbk cpe 3d	2,195	4,864	57,384

Aspen (wb 112.7; cpe-108.7)

NL41	sdn 4d	3,175	4,516	62,568
NL29	cpe	3,110	4,399	42,833
NL45	wgn 5d 2S	3,380	4,838	38,183

Magnum (wb 114.9)

XS22	XE htp cpe V8	3,675	6,039	30,354

Diplomat (wb 112.7)

GM41	sdn 4d	3,378	5,336	10,675
GM22	cpe	3,318	5,234	8,733
GH41	Salon sdn 4d	3,400	5,714	5,479
GH22	Salon cpe	3,335	5,482	6,849
GH45	Salon wgn 5d 2S	3,588	6,127	9,511
GP41	Medallion sdn 4d	3,472	6,198	5,995
GP22	Medallion cpe	3,392	5,966	6,637

St. Regis (wb 118.5)

EH42	sdn 4d	3,602	6,532	34,972

1979 Engines	bore×stroke	bhp	availability
L4, 104.7	3.13×3.40	70	S-Omni
L6, 225.0	3.40×4.13	100	S-Aspen, Diplomat
L6, 225.0	3.40×4.13	110	S-St. Regis; O-Asp, Dip
V8, 318.0	3.91×3.31	135	S-Asp,Dip,St. Regis, Mag
V8, 360.0	4.00×3.58	150	O-Dip,St.Regis,Magnum
V8, 360.0	4.00×3.58	195	O-Asp,Dip,St.Regis, Magnum

1980

Omni (wb 99.2; 2dr 96.7)

		Wght	Price	Prod
ZL44	htchbk sdn 5d	2,095	5,681	76,505
ZL24	024 htchbk cpe 3d	2,135	5,526	61,650

Aspen (wb 112.7; cpe-108.7)

NE41	Special sdn 4d L6	3,210	5,151	19,225
NE29	Special cpe L6	3,155	5,151	13,166
NL41	sdn 4d L6/V8	3,242	5,162	26,239
NL29	cpe L6/V8	3,185	5,045	11,895
NL45	wgn 5d 2S L6/V8	3,410	5,434	14,944

Diplomat (wb 112.7; cpes 108.7)

GL22	Special spt cpe L6	3,130	5,995	NA
GM41	sdn 4d	3,342	6,202	7,941
GM22	spt cpe	3,260	6,048	5,884
GM45	wgn 4d 2S	3,495	6,346	2,093
GH41	Salon sdn 4d	3,205	6,501	5,479
GH22	Salon cpe	3,270	6,372	6,849
GH45	Salon wgn 5d 2S	3,525	7,041	2,664
GP41	Medallion sdn 4d	3,442	7,078	2,159
GP22	Medallion cpe	3,322	6,931	2,131

Mirada (wb 112.7)

XS22	S htp cpe	3,328	6,645	32,746
XH22	htp cpe	3,230	6,850	

St. Regis (wb 118.5)

EH42	sdn 4d	3,608	7,129	17,068

1980 Engines	bore×stroke	bhp	availability
L4, 104.7	3.13×3.40	65	S-Omni
L6, 225.0	3.40×4.13	90	S-Asp,Dip,St.Regis,Mirada
V8, 318.0	3.91×3.31	120	S-Asp exc Spcls, Dip,St.Regis,Mirada
V8, 360.0	4.00×3.58	130/185	O-St.Regis,Mirada

Note: The Mitsubishi-built Dodge Colt (1971-80) and Dodge Challenger (1978-80) are imports and thus not included in the above tabulations.

Duesenberg

Duesenberg Motor Company
Indianapolis, Indiana

The story of what many still consider the finest automobiles ever built in America begins with Frederick Samuel Duesenberg. Born in Lippe, Germany in 1876, he emigrated to America as a child and adopted Iowa as his home state. In his 20s, Fred built bicycles, racing bikes famed for their precision. In Des Moines, with his brother August, he designed the Mason, named for the brothers' backer, in 1906. It was succeeded by the Maytag, which expired after 1911, though that company is still famous today for its washing machines. By 1912 the Duesenbergs were starting to put together impressive racing engines. In 1917, they moved to Elizabeth, New Jersey, where they set up a factory to build them, as well as powerplants for aircraft, tractors, boats, and other vehicles.

Duesenberg racing engines grew in prestige after World War I. A special 16-cylinder unit powered a Land Speed Record car to 158 mph at Daytona in 1919 and the only time an American car won the French Grand Prix was when a Duesenberg did it in 1921. In the '20s, Duesenbergs won the Indianapolis 500 three times.

With their considerable experience in building complete racing cars, the Duesenberg brothers moved to Indianapolis and set up a factory for their first production car.

Designated the Model A, it appeared in late 1921 and sold for $6500. Genuinely derived from competition experience, it had a potent 259.6-cid overhead-valve straight eight, and was good for 85 mph. A first among American cars was its four-wheel hydraulic brake system, something Fred had developed for his race cars as early as 1914. The Model A was a brilliant design and fastidiously built, but the brothers were never good businessmen. Less than 500 cars were sold through 1926, when the company was purchased by Errett Lobban Cord. The following year, a dozen makeshift derivatives of the Model A, called Model X, were fielded, but this was only a stopgap measure: E.L. Cord wanted something far more esoteric.

The result was the Model J, introduced to universal applause in December 1928, the product of Fred Duesenberg's engineering genius and E. L. Cord's money. To an appreciative public, Cord proclaimed the birth of "the world's finest motor car." By almost any measurement, it was.

In any discussion of Duesenbergs, the subject of engines and horsepower inevitably comes up. The Model J was advertised with 265 horsepower at 4250 rpm from its 420-cid Lycoming-built straight eight. This was a mind-boggling

1930 Model J cabriolet by Letourneur & Marchand

1932 Model SJ dual-cowl phaeton by Murphy

1931 Model J convertible sedan by Murphy

1932 Model J Beverly sedan by Murphy

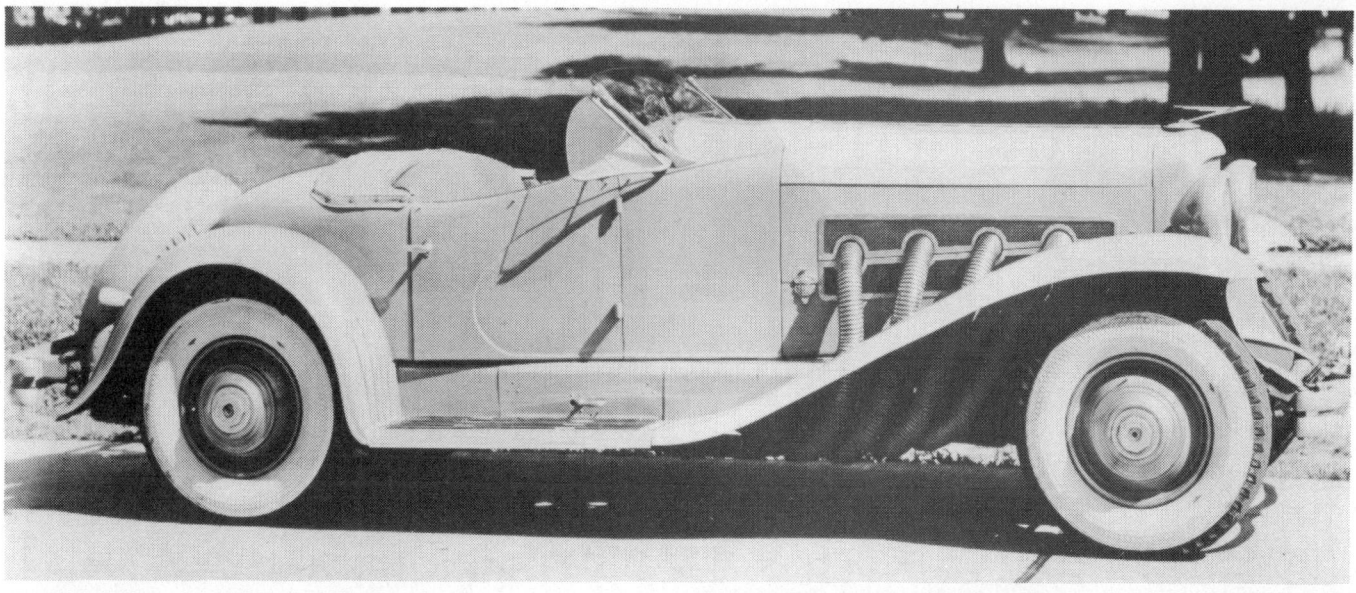

1932 Model SSJ roadster by LeGrande

1934 Model SJN "Twenty Grand" sedan by Rollston

1933 Model J roadster by Fernandez and Darrin

figure for the day, easily more then twice the output of the industry's previous horsepower leader, Chrysler. Doubters have since argued that the J's actual power rating was closer to 200 bhp, but there is evidence the factory wasn't exaggerating. The stock Lycoming eight had a compression ratio of only 5.2:1, yet one modified engine with an 8:1 compression ratio allegedly delivered 390 bhp. Former *Road & Track* publisher John R. Bond has a famous Lycoming chart showing a *reject* Model J engine delivering 208 bhp at 3500 rpm, and he projected 245-250 bhp at the 4250 rpm rev limit. So, the odds are that the production unit developed at least 250 bhp.

But forget horsepower and consider some of the mighty J's other details. Its cylinder head contained 32 valves—16 to a side or four to a cylinder. These were actuated by twin overhead camshafts driven by chains the size of ankle bracelets. The engine itself was enameled in bright green and its fittings were finished in nickel, chrome, or stainless steel. The standard 142.5-inch-wheelbase chassis used 8.5-inch-deep, quarter-inch-thick frame rails and oversize hydraulic brakes (vacuum assisted after 1930). Aluminum alloy was used extensively in engine, dash, steering col-

umn, differential/pinion/flywheel housings, crankcase, camshaft, timing chain covers water pump, intake manifold, brake shoes, and gas tank. Despite their size, most Duesies didn't weight much over 5200 pounds, so they could do a staggering 89 mph in second gear and 112-116 mph in high.

The Model J cockpit was opulent but thoroughly functional. The most comprehensive instrumentation yet seen in an automobile consisted of brake pressure gauge, ammeter, oil pressure gauge, tachometer, split-second stopwatch, 150-mph speedometer, gas gauge, altimeter/barometer, and water temperature gauge. Warning lights reminded the driver to add chassis oil (the chassis lubricated itself every 75 miles), change engine oil, or replenish battery water. But all this was only typical of Fred Duesenberg's dedication to excellence—his insistence that his car be superior in all respects.

Down through the years, there's been much confusion about Duesenberg prices. The bare chassis listed for $8500 in 1929-30, $9500 in 1931. Though bodies were announced as low as $2500, the lowest-price Murphy coupe body actually seems to have retailed for $3500 minimum. The

1934 Model SJ town car by Murphy

1935 Model SJ roadster for Prince Mdivani

1935 Model J long-wheelbase Sport Berline by Rollston

majority of Model Js sold for less than $17,000 complete. A few sold for up to $20,000 and a handful for up to $25,000. Even so, given equivalent dollar values, most of these prices would be well above the most expensive production cars available today, and were roughly 20 times the price of the contemporary Model A Ford.

Duesenberg bodies were as regal as their drivetrains. They were, after all, designed not as sports cars but *grand luxe* carriages, so only the finest woods, fabrics, and leathers money could buy were used throughout. Vanity cases, radios, bars, and rear instrument panels were all commonplace features. One town car was upholstered in silk, trimmed in ebony, and had ivory and silver fittings. Another car reportedly had solid gold hardware and inlaid mosaic wood in the rear compartment (its owner covered the floor with an oriental prayer rug worth more than the car itself). Despite its astonishing performance, the J remained primarily an ultra-luxurious automobile capable of running at any speed in eerie silence, as customers demanded.

Who were those demanding customers? Since only 470 J chassis and 480 engines were built between 1929 and

1936, it's safe to say the clientele was quite exclusive. Duesie advertising pinpointed those buyers. Typically, the ad contained not one word of hype or any specifications—not even a picture of the car. Instead, it might illustrate a yachtsman, commanding his boat against what looked like a 40-knot gale, or a smoking-jacketed tycoon relaxing in a library that would do justice to a university. In all the ads, there would be but a single line of type: "He Drives a Duesenberg." The factory was not at all chauvanistic, however. One ad showed an elegantly attired woman, conferring with a hat-in-hand gardener; in the background are gardens that would put Versailles to shame. "She Drives a Duesenberg," read the headline.

Between 1932 and 1935, Duesenberg ran off 36 supercharged models designated SJ, with the chassis priced at $11,750. The centrifugal supercharger delivered five psi of boost at 4000 rpm, and the engine used tubular-steel connecting rods instead of the aluminum-alloy variety. The first SJs developed 320 horsepower, but August Duesenberg, in a search for more power, half-heartedly tried a set of manifolds with a "rams horn" configuration. He was amazed to see output jump to 400 bhp.

1935 Model SJ convertible coupe by Bowman & Schwartz

1935 Model SJ convertible coupe by Bowman & Schwartz

The SJ's performance is well documented. A stock example could reach 104 mph in second gear and had a top speed of 140 mph. Famed driver Ab Jenkins took a lightweight roadster with no mechanical modifications to the Bonneville Salt Flats in Utah in late 1934, and ran for 24 hours at an *average* of 135 mph. For one hour he averaged 152 mph, and toward the end he clocked one lap at 160 mph. All things considered, the SJ was simply incredible.

Yet there was more to a Duesenberg than mere power and luxury. Despite their size, these cars had balance, precision, finesse, and the heaviness so often displayed by their high-priced domestic and imported contemporaries was absent. A Duesenberg was not "trucky"; it did not steer like a tank; the clutch did not demand the leg muscles of a Purdue football player; the vacuum-servo brakes were more than adequate. The car did understeer, but its exquisitely accurate steering allowed this to be corrected easily. With the exhaust cut-out open, an SJ throbbed with a din even extroverts couldn't long endure, but with it closed, the car was little louder than a healthy Cadillac Sixteen.

The only Duesenbergs that could genuinely be called sports cars were two specials, unofficially titled SSJ. They were built by E. L. Cord's Union City Body Company, usually known as La Grande, and had "short" 125-inch wheelbases. The first was bought right off the showroom floor by Gary Cooper; the second was purchased by Clark Gable, who evidently couldn't bear the thought of being outclassed by his friend. There is no definite information on how these cars performed, and though both survive today, their current owners are understandably reluctant about giving demonstration drives. But with a chassis 17 inches shorter than standard and relatively lean bodies, the SSJs must have been devastating flat-out. They were also among the most beautiful Duesenbergs ever built.

Another low-production offshoot was the JN appearing in 1935. Only 10 were built, all with Rollston coachwork. In contrast to the SSJ, the JN used a longer wheelbase of 153.5 inches plus smaller-diameter wheels (17 instead of 19 inches) and skirted fenders. But its main characteristic was a very low body drawn down below the frame rails. Of the ten built, two received the supercharged engine and the logical designation SJN. But again, there is a lot of confusion. Some SJs were relieved of their superchargers, while a few blowers were added to unsupercharged Js. (A longtime legend among the uninformed was that any car with outside exhaust pipes had a supercharger, like the classic Auburns, Cords, and Mercedes. Like Auburn, far more Duesies with that beautiful external plumbing were unblown than blown.)

As a company, Duesenberg was never meant to make money, only "the world's finest motor car," so it wasn't seriously damaged by the business slowdown of the Depression. Instead, it continued to plod along, building its magnificent cars on a cost-no-object basis, the prestige line in E. L. Cord's car company. Ultimately, Duesenberg was killed by the 1937 collapse of Cord's business empire.

The last Duesenberg was ordered by German artist Rudolf Bauer early that year. Its chassis was assembled by the Chicago dealership after the Indianapolis factory closed its doors. Because of the approaching war, the last chassis was never shipped to its owner, but Bauer eventually made his way to America and had a four-door convertible sedan body completed for it in 1940. The last Duesenberg's overall cost: $21,000.

Sadly, Fred Duesenberg would not survive his company. Ironically, he was the victim of an auto accident in 1932, behind the wheel of an SJ. His brother August carried on for a time, but failed in an attempt to revive the marque in 1947. Several subsequent revival schemes would prove equally fruitless. These included a short-lived 1966 venture headed by Fred's son "Fritz," an abortive 1980 Cadillac-based creation cooked up by two of the brothers' nephews, plus various replicas (a very good one is being built in very small numbers at this writing). If these efforts were largely unsuccessful, perhaps it was because they lacked the heart and soul of Fred himself. Wrote pioneering automotive journalist Ken Purdy: "...he died content...Fred Duesenberg had done what is given few men to do; he had chosen a good course and held unswervingly to it...With his mind and his two good hands, he had created something new and good and, it its way, immortal. And the creator is, when all is said and done, the most fortunate of men."

Edsel
Edsel Division, Ford Motor Co.
Dearborn, Michigan

A comedy of errors, or a good idea at the wrong time? The Edsel was both—proof that even giant multinational corporations sometimes make mistakes. "Its aim was right," said a prominent auto historian, "but the target moved."

The Edsel was developed in 1955, when sales of lower-medium-price cars were booming. Pontiac, Buick, and Dodge were producing nearly two million vehicles combined. By the time Edsel appeared in late 1957, the market had bottomed out. New-car sales were in a slump generally, and the market share for medium-price cars had dropped from 25 percent to about 18 percent. Edsel Division started with a goal of selling 100,000 of the first-year 1958 models. It produced a little over 50,000 cars by the end of calendar 1957. From there it was all downhill. In calendar 1958, only 26,563 Edsels were built. Output was less than 30,000 units in

1959, and the line disappeared for good by the end of November that year.

The car was never intended to bear the name of Henry Ford's son, but it wasn't for lack of trying. Ford had recruited poetess Marianne Moore to name the new car and she came up with some stunners: "Mongoose Civique," "Turcotinga," and "Utopian Turtletop." Ranger, Pacer, Corsair, and Citation were the top finishers of the 6000 names considered by the ad agency. Ernest Breech, Ford Motor Company's chairman of the board, didn't like any of them, though they were adopted as series designations for 1958. When told that Henry Ford II was against calling the car Edsel, Breech replied, "I'll take care of Henry." And he did.

Ranger and Pacer came on a 116- or 118-inch wheelbase shared with the '58 Ford. Corsair and Citation rode Mercury's 124-inch wheelbase. Bodyshells were simi-

1958 Citation hardtop sedan

1959 Corsair hardtop sedan

1960 Ranger four-door sedan

1960 Ranger convertible

larly shared and Edsel offered a wide choice of body styles. Prices were about $500 downstream of comparable Mercurys. Along with its unique "horse-collar" grille and narrow horizontal taillights (which one cynic called the ingrown toenail), Edsel featured numerous gadgets. The "Teletouch" automatic transmission was controlled by pushbuttons recessed in the steering wheel hub; the speedometer was a rotating drum; and almost everything except the rearview mirror could be power-assisted.

Two V8s were offered. A 361 cubic-inch engine was fitted to the two lower series and station wagons; the 410-cid unit was installed in the Corsair/Citation. Edsels were quite rapid, especially when equipped with the big engine.

For 1959, with sales dropping to basement level, the lineup was radically cut. Only Rangers, Corsairs, and station wagons were offered on a single wheelbase.

The Corsair line disappeared for 1960.

The 1960 Edsel's standard engine was a 292-cid V8, but at no extra cost, a buyer could order Ford's 223-cid inline six. For $58 more, the customer could have the "Super Express" V8, which developed 300 horsepower. Cars so equipped were capable of 0–60 mph times of less than 10 seconds.

For 1960, the upright central grille was replaced by a horizontal motif, divided in the center, which looked suspiciously like the '59 Pontiac. Heavy chrome accents were used on the fenders and sides of the body, which was a mildly restyled version of the all-new 1960 Ford design. Two-speed or three-speed automatic transmission, power steering, and air conditioning were options. The Ranger convertible, equipped with air conditioning and other options, could run up to $3800. Extremely low production makes the 1960 model the rarest of Edsel's three model years.

Edsel Specifications

1958

Ranger (wb 118.0; wgns-116.0)

		Wght	Price	Prod
21	sdn 2d	3,729	2,519	4,615
22	sdn 4d	3,805	2,592	6,576
23	htp cpe	3,724	2,593	5,546
24	htp sdn	3,796	2,678	3,077
26	Roundup wgn 2d	3,761	2,876	963
27	Villager wgn 4d, 6P	3,827	2,933	2,294
28	Villager wgn 4d, 9P	3,900	2,990	978

Pacer (wb 118.0; wgns-116.0)

		Wght	Price	Prod
42	sdn 4d	3,826	2,375	6,083
43	htp cpe	3,773	2,805	6,139
44	htp sdn	3,857	2,863	4,959
45	conv cpe	3,909	3,028	1,876
47	Bermuda wgn 4d, 6P	3,853	3,190	1,456
48	Bermuda wgn 4d, 9P	3,919	3,247	779

Corsair (wb 124.0)

		Wght	Price	Prod
63	htp cpe	4,134	3,346	3,312
64	htp sdn	4,235	3,425	5,880

Citation (wb 124.0)

		Wght	Price	Prod
83	htp cpe	4,136	3,535	2,535
84	htp sdn	4,230	3,615	5,112
85	conv cpe	4,311	3,801	930

1958 Engines

	bore×stroke	bhp	availability
V8, 361.0	4.05×3.50	303	S-Ranger, Pacer
V8, 410.0	4.20×3.70	345	S-Corsair, Citation

1959

Ranger (wb 120.0)

		Wght	Price	Prod
57F	htp sdn	3,682	2,756	2,352
58D	sdn 4d	3,774	2,684	12,814
63F	htp cpe	3,591	2,691	5,474
64C	sdn 2d	3,547	2,629	7,778

Corsair (wb 120.0)

		Wght	Price	Prod
57B	htp sdn	3,709	2,885	1,694
58B	sdn 4d	3,696	2,812	3,301
63B	htp cpe	3,778	2,819	2,315
76E	conv cpe	3,790	3,072	1,343

Station Wagon (wb 120.0)

		Wght	Price	Prod
71E	Villager wgn 4d, 9P	3,930	3,055	2,133
71F	Villager wgn 4d, 6P	3,842	2,971	5,687

1959 Engines

	bore×stroke	bhp	availability
L6, 223.0	3.62×3.60	145	O-Ranger, Station Wagon
V8, 292.0	3.75×3.30	200	S-Ranger, Station Wagon
V8, 332.0	4.00×3.30	225	S-Corsair; O-others
V8, 361.0	4.05×3.50	303	O-all

1960

Ranger (wb 120.0)

		Wght	Price	Prod
57A	htp sdn	3,718	2,770	135
58A	sdn 4d	3,700	2,697	1,288
63A	htp cpe	3,641	2,705	295
64A	sdn 2d	3,601	2,643	777
76B	conv cpe	3,836	3,000	76

Station Wagon (wb 120.0)

		Wght	Price	Prod
71E	Villager wgn 4d, 9P	4,046	3,072	59
71F	Villager wgn 4d, 6P	4,029	2,989	216

1960 Engines

	bore×stroke	bhp	availability
L6, 223.0	3.62×3.50	145	O-all
V8, 292.0	3.75×3.30	185	S-all
V8, 352.0	4.00×3.50	300	O-all

Essex
Hudson Motor Car Company
Detroit, Michigan

Introduced in 1922, the Hudson-built Essex was a sales winner in its first two years on the market. It not only had a lively four-cylinder engine, but was the first mass-produced car to offer closed body types in the popular price field. Then Essex adopted a less reliable six in 1924, and its image and popularity suffered accordingly. Though this unit was enlarged and improved in 1930 and 1931, the make failed to win back its early reputation for ruggedness and durability, and the fortunes of Hudson Motor Company fell with it. However, there was an important development that put the brakes on the slide.

Roy D. Chapin Sr., one of Hudson's founders, was still active in the company in 1930-32, even though he was working for the Hoover Administration at that time. When Hoover left office, Chapin immediately returned to Hudson and prepared to make some long-needed changes in the price-leading Essex lineup. For 1932 he ordered the six bored and stroked to 193 cubic inches, which yielded 70 horsepower. Initially, the revised engine powered the 113-inch wheelbase Pacemaker and Challenger. But at mid-year, Chapin dumped it into a new 106-inch-wheelbase series dubbed Terraplane: "In the air, it's aeroplaning; on the water, it's hydroplaning; on the ground, hot diggety dog, that's Terraplaning!"

The 1932-33 Essex Terraplane turned Hudson's fortunes around. It was fast—up to 80 mph; it was economical—up to 25 mpg; and it was cheap—as little as $425. Adding to its appeal was the 1933 appearance of an extra-cost eight-cylinder engine evolved from the original six. Essex Terraplanes set numerous speed marks, including over 100 stock car records. The public responded enthusiastically, and in 1934, the Essex name was dropped in favor of Terraplane, which became a marque in its own right.

1931 Challenger Six Special four-door sedan

1932 Pacemaker four-door Town Sedan

1932 Pacemaker convertible coupe

1930 Challenger Six Sun Sedan

1930 Challenger Six phaeton

1933 Terraplane Eight convertible coupe (with Roy D. Chapin)

Essex Specifications

1930—68,593 built

Challenger Six (wb 113.0)	Wght	Price	Prod
rdstr 2-4P	2,550	695	—
phtn 5P	2,620	695	—
cpe 2P	2,660	650	—
cpe 2-4P	2,700	685	—
coach 5P	2,730	650	—
Standard sdn 4d	2,805	715	—
Touring sdn 4d	2,850	775	—
brougham 4d	2,850	795	—
Sun sdn 4d	2,760	695	—

1930 Engine	bore×stroke	bhp	availability
L6, 160.0	2.75×4.50	58	S-all

1931—47,418 built

Challenger Six (wb 113.0; 7P 119.0)	Wght	Price	Prod
rdstr 2-4P	2,400	725	—
cpe 2P	2,595	595	—
cpe 2-4P	2,645	645	—
Special cpe 2-4P	2,800	725	—
coach 5P	2,690	595	—
Standard sdn 4d	2,750	695	—
Touring sdn 4d	2,815	775	—
Town sdn 4d	2,815	735	—
Special sdn 4d	2,950	855	—
sdn 7P	2,945	895	—

1932—18,700 built

Pacemaker (wb 113.0)	Wght	Price	Prod
phtn 5P	—	765	—
bus cpe 2P	2,775	695	—
cpe 2-4P	2,840	745	—
Special cpe 2-4P	2,895	795	—
conv cpe 2-4P	2,760	845	—
coach 5P	2,860	705	—
Standard sdn 4d	2,980	775	—
Town sdn 4d	2,950	745	—
Special sdn 4d	3,010	845	—

Standard (wb 113.0)	Wght	Price	Prod
bus cpe	—	660	NA
cpe 4P	2,750	710	NA
coach 5P	2,785	665	NA
Standard sdn 4d	2,870	735	NA

Terraplane (wb 106.0)—14,125 built	Wght	Price	Prod
rdstr 2P	2,010	425	—
phtn 5P	2,170	495	—
bus cpe 2P	2,135	470	—
cpe 2-4P	2,190	510	—
coach 5P	2,205	475	—
Standard sdn 4d	2,250	550	—
Sport rdstr 2-4P	2,110	525	—
Special bus cpe 2P	2,135	510	—
Special cpe 2-4P	2,190	550	—
Special conv cpe 2-4P	2,145	610	—
Special coach 5P	2,205	515	—
Special sdn 4d	2,250	590	—

1932 Engine	bore×stroke	bhp	availability
L6, 193.0	2.94×4.75	70	S-all

1933

Terraplane Six (wb 106.0)	Wght	Price	Prod*
rdstr 2P	2,135	425	—

1930 Challenger Six coupe

	Wght	Price	Prod
phtn 5P	2,260	515	—
cpe 2P	2,220	485	—
cpe 2-4P	2,260	535	—
coach 5P	2,275	505	—
sdn 4d	2,345	555	—
Special rdstr 2-4P	2,220	505	—
Special cpe 2-4P	2,310	555	—
Special conv cpe 2-4P	2,275	575	—
Special coach 5P	2,335	525	—
Special sdn 5P	2,415	575	—

Terraplane Special Six (wb 113.0)	Wght	Price	Prod
Spt rdstr 2-4P	2,290	505	—
phtn 5P	—	535	—
bus cpe 2P	2,320	505	—
cpe 2-4P	2,330	555	—
conv cpe 2-4P	—	575	—
coach 5P	2,270	525	—
sdn 4d	2,420	575	—

Terraplane DeLuxe Six (wb 113.0)	Wght	Price	Prod
cpe 2P	2,395	585	—
cpe 2-4P	2,405	635	—
conv cpe 2-4P	2,395	655	—
coach 5P	2,450	605	—
sdn 4d	2,500	655	—

Terraplane Eight (wb 113.0)	Wght	Price	Prod
rdstr 2P	2,410	565	—
rdstr 2-4P	2,455	625	—
cpe 2P	2,485	615	—
cpe 2-4P	2,545	655	—
conv cpe 2-4P	2,495	695	—
coach 5P	2,565	615	—
sdn 4d	2,640	675	—

Terraplane DeLuxe Eight (wb 113.0)	Wght	Price	Prod
cpe 2P	2,540	685	—
cpe 2-4P	2,600	725	—
conv cpe 2-4P	2,550	765	—
coach 5P	2,625	685	—
sdn 4d	2,700	745	—

*Production not available.

1933 Engines	bore×stroke	bhp	availability
L6, 193.0	2.94×4.75	70	S-all Sixes
L8, 243.9	2.94×4.50	94	S-all Eights

Note:
Essex production figures shown above are based on serial number spans listed in industry sources and may be presumed reliable, though it is always possible that some numbers were skipped. For comparison, Essex *calendar* year production, as reported by Don Butler in *The History of Hudson,* was as follows:

1930	76,158	1932	34,007
1931	40,338	1933	38,150

See "Terraplane" for 1934-37 models and "Hudson" for 1938-39 Terraplane models.

Excalibur

SS Automobiles, Inc., and
Excalibur Automobile Corporation
Milwaukee, Wisconsin

America's most successful builder of cars fashioned in the image of the great classics is Excalibur, the Milwaukee concern founded by the two sons of industrial designer Brooks Stevens. Fastidiously assembled, the Excalibur is a superb road machine. It's also exclusive.

The Excalibur Series I, introduced in 1964, remained in its original form until it was replaced by the Series II in 1970. Its styling echoed the classic 1928 Mercedes-Benz SSK, and even the firm's sales literature was patterned after that of the prewar Mercedes. Careful engineering and clever design distinguished the Excalibur from a motley group of VW-powered replicas that followed it.

In 1964, Stevens was finishing four years as design consultant to the ill-fated Studebaker Corporation. The old-line automaker had ceased car production at its South Bend, Indiana plant in late 1963, but continued some operations at its Hamilton, Ontario factory. Stevens hoped production would go on. But he was unimpressed by the firm's mundane cars at the 1964 Chicago Auto Show, and was determined to build a more exciting Studebaker "special" for the New York show in April. So, he ordered up a Lark Daytona convertible chassis with power disc brakes and a 290-horsepower, supercharged 289-cubic-inch Avanti V8. Company managers tentatively approved his plan to build "a modern classic" for their company's New York display. The prototype Excalibur was created in just six weeks by Stevens' two sons, David and William. No sooner had it left for New York than Studebaker officials changed their minds. A "contemporary classic," they said would conflict with the "common-sense" image they were trying to establish.

More than time and money was at stake, and the Stevenses refused to scrap the project. Through hurried phone calls to the show's management, they arranged to display the Excalibur on a separate stand. The car was a hit, and in August 1964 the sons founded SS Automobiles to manufacture it—with their dad's blessing and assistance. Some 100 copies had been sold by the beginning of 1966.

Studebaker's demise ended the supply of 289 V8s after 1965, so the Stevens brothers went shopping for a new engine. The 327-cid Corvette unit was duly provided by their friends Ed Cole and Semon E. "Bunkie" Knudsen at General Motors. After 1966, Excaliburs were also offered with a Paxton-supercharged V8 rated at 400 bhp, and high-performance Corvette engines. With the standard 3.31:1 rear axle ratio, the car was claimed to have a 0-60 mph time of less than five seconds and a top speed in the area of 160 mph.

The 109-inch wheelbase Studebaker Daytona convertible chassis was hardly modern, but it offered some advantages. Unlike concurrent torque-box frames, it was quite narrow, as its frame rails were not spread as far apart as on other chassis that had to accommodate more modern, wider body sills. Thus, it was perfectly suited for the Excalibur's narrower, vintage-style body. As a convertible chassis it was firmly X-braced. But it needed considerable re-engineering to insure safe handling in a high-powered car that weighed at least 500 pounds less than a Corvette.

David Stevens was largely responsible for the engineering. The classic-style cowl forced him to lower the Studebaker steering column and control pedals. It was also necessary to alter the suspension geometry drastically by decreasing spring rates and changing caster and camber. This modified Studebaker chassis was retained for all Series I models. Like the Excaliburs that followed them, these cars were fast on both curves and straights.

Brooks Stevens was responsible for the styling, which was a surprisingly accurate rendition of the fabulous SSK. He considered outside exhaust pipes mandatory, but no one in the United States could supply them. Ultimately, he bought the flexible tubing from the same German firm that had supplied it for the Mercedes back in the 1920s. Bodies on the first few cars were made of hammered aluminum; but the firm soon switched to fiberglass, mainly for reasons of cost and practicality. The radiator was made of sheet brass on the prototype; production radiators were cast aluminum. The Mercedes three-pointed star suggested the hood ornament, an Excalibur sword in a circle, which resembled, but was not too close to, the symbol jealously protected by the German firm. French-built free-standing headlamps closely resembled the original SSK units. White-on-black instruments from the Studebaker Hawk were placed in an SSK-like engine-turned dash panel. The seats used were modified Studebaker buckets, covered in expanded vinyl (leather upholstery would be

1965-69 Series I SSK roadster

1967-69 Series I phaeton

1970-74 Series II phaeton

1975-79 Series III roadster

1975-79 Series III phaeton

1980-84 Series IV phaeton

used later). The initial price was almost unbelievably low: $7250 for a hand-built car having one of the most competently engineered chassis in the business.

For 1966, the firm changed its name to Excalibur Automobile Corporation and added a more elaborate roadster. Unlike the aggressive-looking SSK, this model had full fenders and running boards. A four-passenger phaeton was offered beginning that same year. Prices began going up, but so did materials quality and standard equipment. By 1969 the list included air conditioning, heater and defroster, variable-ratio power steering, tilt steering wheel, power front disc brakes, Positraction rear axle, chrome-plated wire wheels, luggage rack, AM-FM stereo, leather seats, Turbo Hydra-Matic transmission, twin side mounted spare tires, all weather hardtop, air horns, driving lights, steel-belted radial tires, and automatically controlled self-leveling rear shock absorbers.

For 1970, the Series II was introduced on a longer wheelbase and powered by a larger Corvette V8. The same body styles were offered, but the old Lark frame was replaced by a new box-section chassis designed by David Stevens around Corvette suspension components. GM's

four-speed "Muncie" manual gearbox was standard, and the Turbo Hydra-Matic became optional. Independent suspension and four-wheel disc brakes combined with Goodyear Polyglas tires mounted on specially designed wire wheels to offer a fine balance between ride and handling. The factory claimed a Series II would leap from 0 to 60 mph in six seconds flat and reach 150 mph.

Prices and production began taking off with the Series III, announced in 1975 (the firm does not adhere strictly to a model year cycle). Basically, this was the Series II design modified to meet federal safety and emissions regulations, but not so much as to compromise the styling or roadability that were, by this time, traditional for the marque. Besides "shock mounted solid aluminum alloy [bumpers that] meet government standards for absorbing impact," the Series III boasted fuller clamshell-style fenders and standard high-back bucket seats covered in leather and—like most of the rest of the car—made by Excalibur itself. The major mechanical alteration was adoption of Chevy's big-block Mark IV V8, an engine more amenable to emissions tuning than the previous unit.

By any standard, this was still a tiny producer, but the

Excalibur

1980-84 Series IV roadster

Stevens brothers would not be rushed. Nor did they want to dilute their market with too much of a good thing. As it had since 1969, the more practical four-seat phaeton continued to outsell the two-passenger roadster, but total production was still miniscule even for a specialty maker. A mere 1141 Series III cars were built through 1979, compared with 342 for the Series II and 359 for the Series I.

Excalibur had come a long way since David and William C. "Steve" Stevens had built their first cars (the latter even worked on the assembly line until 1968). Striking evidence of the firm's progress appeared in January 1981 in the elegant new Series IV. More a luxury tourer than a lightweight big-inch sports machine, it was the most radically changed Excalibur in history—and the best yet. Wheelbase was extended to near limousine length, and the new model boasted more standard accoutrements than any

of its predecessors. Styling remained firmly in the classic tradition, but was smoother, sleeker, and evolutionary in much the same way that the late-'30s Mercedes 500/540K was related to the SS/SSK. The phaeton acquired a new lift-off hardtop plus a fully powered soft top, and the roadster gained a functional rumble seat. Another round of engineering improvements was made in line with federal requirements, and running gear was switched to GM's well-known 5.0-liter (305-cid) V8 and four-speed overdrive automatic transmission.

Appropriately, the Series IV marked the 30th anniversary of the Excalibur marque (Brooks Stevens designed and built the first car to bear the name around Henry J components in 1951). It remains in production at this writing, a glorious tribute to the Stevens family's dedication to excellence and a timeless automotive idea.

1980-84 Series IV phaeton

Excalibur Specifications

1965

Series I (wb 109.0)*			Wght	Price	Prod
	SSK rdstr		2,100	7,250	56

1965 Engine	bore×stroke	bhp	availability
V8, 289.0	3.56×3.62	290	S-all

1966

Series I (wb 109.0)*			Wght	Price	Prod
	SSK rdstr		2,100	7,250	87
	rdstr		2,500	8,000	
	phtn		2,500	7,950	3

1966 Engine	bore×stroke	bhp	availability
V8, 327.0	4.00×3.25	300	S-all

1967

Series I (wb 109.0)*			Wght	Price	Prod
	SSK rdstr		2,100	8,000	38
	rdstr		2,500	8,500	
	phtn		2,600	8,250	33

1967 Engines	bore×stroke	bhp	availability
V8, 327.0	4.00×3.25	300	S-all
V8, 327.0	4.00×3.25	400	O-all

1968

Series I (wb 109.0)*			Wght	Price	Prod
	SSK rdstr		2,300	8,650	37
	rdstr		2,500	8,650	
	phtn		2,600	9,850	20

1968 Engines	bore×stroke	bhp	availability
V8, 327.0	4.00×3.25	300	S-all
V8, 327.0	4.00×3.25	435	O-all

1969

Series I (wb 109.0)*			Wght	Price	Prod
	SSK rdstr		2,400	9,000	47
	rdstr		2,550	9,000	
	phtn		2,650	10,000	44

1969 Engines	bore×stroke	bhp	availability
V8, 327.0	4.00×3.25	300	S-all
V8, 327.0	4.00×3.25	435	O-all

*Production 1965-69; SSK 168; rdstr 59; phtn 89.

1970

Series II (wb 111.0)			Wght	Price	Prod
	SSK rdstr		2,750	12,000	11
	SS rdstr		2,900	12,500	
	SS phtn		3,000	12,900	26

1970 Engine	bore×stroke	bhp	availability
V8, 350.0	4.00×3.48	300	S-all

1971

Excalibur records show no 1971 model production.

1972

Series II (wb 111.0)			Wght	Price	Prod
	SS rdstr		2,900	12,500	13
	SS phtn		3,000	13,500	52

1972 Engine	bore×stroke	bhp	availability	Wght	Price	Prod
V8, 350.0	4.00×3.48	300	S-all			

1973

Series II (wb 111.0)			Wght	Price	Prod
	SS rdstr		2,900	13,500	22
	SS phtn		3,000	16,000	100

1973 Engine	bore×stroke	bhp	availability
V8, 350.0	4.00×3.48	300	S-all

1974

Series II (wb 111.0)			Wght	Price	Prod
	SS rdstr		2,900	17,000	26
	SS phtn		3,000	17,000	92

1974 Engine	bore×stroke	bhp	availability
V8, 350.0	4.00×3.48	300	S-all

1975

Series III (wb 112.0)			Wght	Price	Prod
	SS rdstr		4,350	18,900	8
	SS phtn		4,350	18,900	82

1975 Engine	bore×stroke	bhp	availability
V8, 454.0	4.25×4.00	215	S-all

1976

Series IV (wb 112.0)			Wght	Price	Prod
	SS rdstr		4,350	21,500	11
	SS phtn		4,350	21,500	173

1976 Engine	bore×stroke	bhp	availability
V8, 454.0	4.25×4.00	215	S-all

1977

Series IV (wb 112.0)			Wght	Price	Prod
	SS rdstr		4,350	23,600	15
	SS phtn		4,350	23,600	222

1977 Engine	bore×stroke	bhp	availability
V8, 454.0	4.25×4.00	215	S-all

1978

Series III (wb 112.0)			Wght	Price	Prod
	SS rdstr		4,350	25,600	15
	SS phtn		4,350	25,600	248

1978 Engine	bore×stroke	bhp	availability
V8, 454.0	4.25×4.00	215	S-all

1979

Series III (wb 112.0)			Wght	Price	Prod
	SS rdstr		4,350	28,600	27
	SS phtn		4,350	28,600	340

1979 Engine	bore×stroke	bhp	availability
V8, 350.0	4.00×3.48	180	S-all

1980

Series IV (wb 125.0)			Wght	Price	Prod
	SS rdstr		4,300	NA	0
	SS phtn		4,300	37,700	93

1980 Engine	bore×stroke	bhp	availability
V8, 305.0	3.74×3.48	155	S-all

Ford

Ford Division, Ford Motor Company
Dearborn, Michigan

Ford entered 1930 by giving its still-popular Model A more in the way of major changes than it had the previous year. Though basic styling remained the same, there were lower and wider fenders, a higher hoodline, and stainless steel instead of nickel plate on the radiator shell and headlight shells and rims. Ford also switched to balloon tires and decreased wheel diameter from 21 to 19 inches. Running changes made during the year comprised a numerically higher steering ratio to reduce effort at the wheel and standardization of vacuum-operated windshield wipers. In June a completely new DeLuxe two-door phaeton was added to the line. Sportier than the four-door, it had a side-mount spare, chrome-trimmed trunk rack, all-leather upholstery, and a lower steering wheel and windshield frame. Another new body style, bowing in the autumn of 1930, was the Victoria coupe. It had no exterior sunvisor, but did boast a slanted windshield, a feature that prefigured many cars of the next few years. There was little change to the Model A for 1931 aside from a painted section on the top front of the radiator shell, which made identification easy.

It took Model A assembly about a year to hit full stride. Once it did, Ford pulled ahead of Chevrolet in both the 1929 and 1930 production contests. Its output of 1,155,162 units in calendar 1930 would be its best for the entire decade. But Ford fell behind again in 1932, caused in part by the changeover to a new engine for the majority of that year's models: the first low-priced V8 offered in the U.S.

Henry Ford had wanted to replace the faithful old Model T with an eight-cylinder car for a long time. A new V8 had been scheduled for release along with the Model A in 1928, but sales pressures and the peculiar conditions Henry imposed on his engineers delayed it considerably. So, the Model A was introduced without the V8 as an interim measure. Production ended officially in the autumn of 1931, though sales continued through April 1932. Then, a revised four-cylinder car, the Model B, was announced. Both this and the new V8 Model 18 shared a 106.5-inch wheelbase and the same body styles. The big difference, of course, was under the hood. The V8 was a tremendous bargain: the roadster, coupe, and phaeton all listed for less than $500. Still, some buyers preferred the four-cylinder cars, which would be continued through 1933.

The cast-iron flathead V8 initially developed 65 bhp at 3400 rpm from its 221 cubic inches. With a relatively sensational top speed of 78 mph, the peppy new Ford caused a storm of public interest. Even before it was introduced it garnered over 50,000 orders, and millions flocked to dealers to see it in March 1932.

Henry kept a close watch over the new engine's design and development, and was constantly telling his engineers what to do. The need to get the car on the market as soon as possible left insufficient time for durability testing, so engine troubles surfaced early: some used a lot of oil, cylinder heads developed cracks, engine mounts worked

1930 Model A phaeton

1931 Modle A DeLuxe roadster

1931 Model A convertible sedan

1932 Model 18 V-8 DeLuxe roadster

1933 Model 40 V-8 station wagon

1934 DeLuxe three-window coupe

1933 Model 40 V-8 DeLuxe roadster

1935 DeLuxe three-window coupe

1934 DeLuxe roadster

1935 DeLuxe phaeton

loose, and ignition problems cropped up. Ford supplied replacement pistons by the thousands to ease the crisis, but the engine difficulties hurt sales, and Chevrolet continued to lead by a comfortable margin in 1933-34.

There was a completely new look for 1933. The hood was now extended back to the windshield, doors were hinged at the rear on closed body styles, and fenders were skirted and dipped low in front. Wheelbase grew to 112 inches and wheel diameter shrank to 17 inches. On the mechanical side, engine durability was improved and the frame completely redesigned. Henry's son Edsel had always played an important part in Ford styling, and his tasteful '33 was universally applauded. Production rose by 100,000 units which, if not better than Chevrolet's total, was at least a decent gain. The speedy Ford V8 was the favorite of many buyers—including the notorious John Dillinger. He once wrote Henry to tell him just how much he liked the product, an unbiased plug from Public Enemy Number One.

Minor styling alterations marked the 1934 models, and

the 112-inch wheelbase was locked up for the remainder of the decade. The V8 got a new carburetor and manifold that increased output to 85 bhp; most of its early problems had been eliminated by this time. The standard two-passenger coupe still sold for little more than $500, while the Deluxe four-door sedan ("Fordor" in company parlance) cost only $615 and featured standard safety glass all around.

Beginning with the Model A, Ford began offering a wood-bodied station wagon constructed of birch or maple as a regular production model. Initially, the bodies were made by the Mingel Company of Kentucky, and assembly was carried out by Murray and Briggs in Detroit. In 1935, Ford started building the wagons itself in a plant at Iron Mountain, Michigan, an ideal location because of the nearby hardwood forests that minimized transportation costs.

Ford styling took on a more rounded look for 1935 and, for the first time, an integral trunk could be ordered on the sedan. Another round of engine improvements brought a new camshaft and a better crankcase ventilation system.

Also, the frame and rear axle were beefed up. The simple suspension still consisted of single transverse leaf springs front and rear, an archaic arrangement that would not be abandoned for another 13 years. This and the use of mechanical brakes were two areas in which Ford was distinctly behind the times, but old Henry refused to believe any of his ideas were outdated. However, he did give up on traditional wire wheels in favor of all-steel wheels after 1935.

Model year 1936 again saw only minor styling changes, but they were good ones. The hood became longer and more pointed, and the grille was given a sharper V-shape. Industry design practices dictated hiding some components previously visible, so horns now sat behind "catwalk" grilles that followed the pattern of the main grille. Though the spare tire could be mounted either inside or outside on sedans, external spares were still the rule rather than the exception.

An additional flathead V8 debuted for 1937. This was a smaller unit originally conceived for the European market to take advantage of tax laws based on displacement (in Britain, on bore but not stroke). The V8/60, as it came to be called, therefore had a much reduced bore compared to the familiar V8/85. The latter got a relocated water pump this year, which made a vast improvement to the cooling system. It also benefited from larger insert bearings and new cast alloy steel pistons. Car prices had been on the rise, but while the smaller V8 made for cheaper Fords, it didn't sell nearly as well as expected. Mediocre performance was a big factor. Also for 1937, Ford adopted all-steel construction for closed bodies, discarding the fabric roof insert of yore. Evidence of streamlining was ample in the handsome new styling. Headlamps were now incorporated into the front fenders, the grille was stretched and sloped backwards at the top, and fine horizontal bars decorated the front end and hood sides. The result was one of the best-looking cars of the decade; even President Franklin Roosevelt bought a convertible sedan to use at his Warm Springs, Georgia retreat. In a year of questionable styling throughout

1936 DeLuxe trunkback convertible sedan

1937 DeLuxe five-window coupe

1936 DeLuxe three-window coupe

1938 DeLuxe Fordor sedan

1937 DeLuxe Fordor sedan

1939 DeLuxe five-window coupe

the industry, Ford was a standout—proof that streamlining did not necessarily mean an end to distinctive, timelessly styled automobiles.

For 1938, Ford instituted a two-tier model line. The previous year's Deluxe body was retained for this year's Standard series, while the costlier models were given an entirely new look. The romantic roadster was gone, and the phaeton was making its last stand. Both these body styles had long since lost whatever favor they once had, but Ford was far behind its competition in realizing this (Plymouth's last roadster and phaeton appeared in 1932, Chevrolet's for 1935). The rumble-seat models were also in their last year. The 60-bhp V8 was available in just three body styles: coupe, four-door sedan, and two-door sedan. Styling was a warmed-over version of 1937. The grille/hood section became more bulbous, and the Standards were saddled with a fulsome swept-back grille.

Deluxe models were again fully restyled for 1939, distinguished by a vertical stainless-steel grille and clean front fenders with flush headlamps. Prices were reduced $5 across the board, and the convertible sedan put in its last appearance. Mechanical changes included column-mounted, instead of floor-mounted, gearshift and hydraulic, instead of mechanical, brakes. Henry had finally given in on the last point, three years after Chevrolet and 11 years after Plymouth.

After the war, Henry would pass the reins of his company over at last—but not to his son. Edsel had died in 1943, at age 49. Henry had continued to manage his increasingly troubled firm until his family insisted on a change in 1945. Control then passed to grandson Henry Ford II. "HFII" retired in 1980 after 33 years at the helm, years marked by great success. Unlike his grandfather, he consistently sought and encouraged talented managers. However, he just as consistently encouraged their retirement when they reached a certain level of power. Though the family no longer owns a majority of common stock, Ford is still very much a family operation.

Styling of the first Ford of the '40s was good—so good that this car has become one of the most desirable single models made by any manufacturer. The hood was crisply pointed, meeting a handsome grille composed mainly of delicate horizontal bars, flowing smoothly back to a rakishly angled windshield. The headlamps, sealed-beams for the first time, were faired into neat fender nacelles. The fenders themselves were beautifully curved to complement the body contours, and were often skirted at the rear for the ultimate streamlined appearance.

On a 112-inch wheelbase, Ford mounted two different engines: 60- and 85-bhp L-head V8s. The V8/60, never very popular, was a price leader. The larger V8/85 came in a wider range of models and two trim stages—standard and DeLuxe.

When Mercury arrived in 1939, many dealers were disappointed, since they felt a six-cylinder Ford would have been a better seller. Edsel Ford promised them one, but then had to reckon with his father. Henry ap-

proved a six in one of those strange about-faces for which he was noted. Edsel went to work, and brought out an L-head six in 1941, the Ford Special. This car replaced the unpopular V8/60. Its well-built flathead displaced 226 cubic inches, 90 more than the small V8, for a horsepower increase of 50 percent. In 1941, it actually delivered more horsepower than the V8/85. A vast array of six and V8 Specials, DeLuxes, and Super DeLuxes was offered. Styling, if not entirely new in the middle, was altered at each end. There were wider and more integral front fenders, a busy grille composed of vertical bars, a chromed-up hood, and larger rear fenders.

None of these changes did much for Ford production. It remained about the same in '41 as it was in 1940: less than two-thirds of Chevrolet's output. Ford had surpassed Chevrolet just once in the '30s. Chevy would reign supreme throughout the '40s, except for model years 1946 and '49.

A more cohesive, lower grille was introduced for

1940 DeLuxe Fordor sedan

1940 DeLuxe coupe

Wartime prototype for postwar Ford

1942. Ford built only 43,000 cars from January 1 through February 2, when civilian production ended. The low-priced Specials were restricted to six cylinders only that year, but otherwise the model lineup was unchanged. Prices were increased about $100 throughout, making the convertible coupe the first Ford (aside from wagons) to sell for over $1000 since the Model A town cars of about 10 years earlier.

The elder Henry had been a renowned pacifist before Pearl Harbor. After the Japanese attack, he grasped the altered situation, and quickly converted to war production. Ford built a variety of military vehicles including Jeeps (with Willys-Overland and American Bantam) during the conflict. Ford also built the mile-long Willow Run plant near Detroit, which produced a variety of bombers through 1945. Young Henry II moved into car production fast after Japan surrendered. For model year 1946, the company was once again the industry leader. Chevrolet, however, was back in full swing by 1947, and led production totals that year.

The 1946 Ford used prewar dies and the old 114-inch wheelbase, but important mechanical changes were made and body offerings were revised. The six remained at 90 bhp, but the V8 was boosted to 100 bhp, the result of a bore increase that gave 239 cid. The Special series of low-priced sixes was eliminated, leaving the DeLuxe and Super DeLuxe with six- and eight-cylinder engines. There was no six-cylinder convertible, but there were two convertible V8s, the standard model and a novel variation called the Sportsman.

Developed from design sketches made by Gregorie during the war, the Sportsman featured white ash and mahogany trim over its doors, rear body panels, and deck like the Chrysler Town & Country. This was an attractive way to add something new to an old-fashioned design, and helped increase floor traffic at

1942 Super DeLuxe four-door station wagon

1946 Super DeLuxe Fordor sedan

1946 Super DeLuxe Sportsman convertible

1948 DeLuxe Fordor sedan

1948 Super DeLuxe convertible

1948 Super DeLuxe Fordor sedan

Ford dealerships. The Sportsman was quite expensive, however, some $500 more than the regular convertible. As such it did not sell in high numbers.

Little outward change marked the 1947-48 models. Alterations involved a shuffle of nameplates and lower-mounted round parking lights in 1947. No styling changes were made for '48. The six was now rated at 95 instead of 90 bhp. Responding to postwar inflation, prices were on the rise, increasing about $100 model for model in 1947 and again in '48.

In the booming postwar seller's market, no styling or engineering changes were really needed. Ford output exceeded 429,000 units in 1947, but was only 236,000 in '48. That drop did not indicate trouble in Dearborn, only an early end to 1948 model production. Ford management had realized that a new car was needed. Work on the all-new postwar design began in early 1946, and the '49s were introduced earlier than usual, in June 1948.

Styling for the '49s was a competitive operation, as Ford solicited ideas from freelance designers as well as from its own design department. One of the competitors was George Walker, who employed a young stylist named Dick Caleal. The Walker team developed a package incorporating integral fenders. However, as the deadline approached, Caleal ran into trouble with the front and rear styling. According to Robert Bourke, then chief designer for the Loewy Studios at Studebaker, Caleal approached Bourke and his assistant Bob Koto for help. The Loewy people agreed to lend their friend Caleal whatever expertise they could on their own time. Late-night sessions at the Caleal home in Mishawaka, Indiana found the three men concocting a smooth-looking clay model with a bullet or spinner-type grille reminiscent of the later '50 Studebaker. According to Bourke, the quarter-scale clay was submitted to Walker, who put it under his arm and took it to Dearborn. It was accepted almost without alteration. The only significant change was in the taillights: horizontal lenses were used instead of the vertical tail-lights the team had planned. The design, of course, had none of the Studebaker's radical lines. But it brought Ford a calendar year production level the likes of which the company hadn't seen since 1937. In 1955, Walker became design director at Ford, mainly on the strength of this contribution.

The 1949s used the 100-bhp V8, which made for a sprightly performer able to run circles around rival Chevys and Plymouths. If a '49 Ford couldn't actually achieve 100 mph, the modifications necessary to make it do so weren't that involved. Multiple carburetors, headers, dual exhausts, and other speed equipment were all available at local auto accessory stores.

The low-selling Sportsman was eliminated for 1949, but a wider range of body types was offered. Again prices increased. Overdrive was optional on all models at $97. Ford would not have its own automatic transmission until 1951, though it had tried hard to get one earlier. Studebaker had developed an excellent auto-

Clay proposal for 1949 station wagon

1949 Custom V8 station wagon

1949 Custom V8 Tudor sedan

matic for 1950, in association with Warner Gear. Ford tried to buy the rights to use it on its own cars, but Studebaker refused—much to its regret later.

The '49 Fords were without doubt worthy automobiles. They were the first tangible evidence of a new hand at the controls—Henry II, ably assisted by a team of youthful executives.

The 1950-53 Ford continued to offer sixes and the famous flathead V8 so popular with hot rodders. By 1953, this engine was pumping out 110 bhp at 3800 rpm. Ford replaced the flathead six with an overhead-valve unit in 1952. From 1951 on, all these engines were accompanied by an optional two-speed Ford-O-Matic shiftless transmission.

Through these early years of the decade Ford Motor Company experienced a revival, moving ahead of Chrysler into the number-two spot. The reason? Interesting cars that sold well.

A special confection for 1950-51 was the V8 Crestliner. This limited-edition two-door was distinguished by a vivid contrasting color sweep on its sides and a

1950 Custom Crestliner two-door sedan

1951 Custom Tudor sedan

1952 Crestline Sunliner convertible

1953 Customline Fordor sedan

1954 Crestline Skyliner hardtop coupe

1954 Crestline Country Squire station wagon

padded vinyl top. Only 26,304 were sold before the series was canceled in 1952, but the wildly colored cars remain collector's items to this day. The rest of the line was divided between DeLuxes and Customs, sixes and V8s, sedans and coupes, Custom wagons, and the Custom V8 convertible. Styling was rather high and wide compared to arch-rival Chevrolet, but was better than Plymouth's. Ford built over a million cars in model year 1950, its highest total since 1930.

For '51, the hardtop Victoria with the same styling as the rest of the line appeared in the Custom V8 series. This neat alteration of the two-door coupe sold much better than the Crestliner. A new bodyshell came in 1952, with a look that would be mostly untouched for the next several years. The cars were lower and wider on a longer 115-inch wheelbase. Mainline and Customline now replaced the Deluxe and Custom designations. The Crestline became a top-of-the-line V8 series comprising the Victoria hardtop, Sunliner convertible, and the posh Country Squire station wagon. The latter

was the first all-steel Ford wagon, with wood decal trim.

Though 1953 was Ford's Golden Anniversary year, no significant changes were made to celebrate the event—except for an increase in prices. Ford Division built 1.2 million cars that year—an output shattered in 1955 with nearly 1.5 million cars. Ford was closing in on Chevy, but was straining its dealers to do so. A Ford could be bought at "less than cost" in 1953-54 when the "Ford Blitz" reached its peak. Chevrolet was not seriously damaged by the onslaught, but the independents were. Unable to discount as much, Studebaker, American Motors, and Kaiser-Willys dealers were hit hard. The Ford Blitz is generally considered one of the most important factors in the decline of the independents in the mid-'50s.

Ford made headlines in 1954 when it introduced its new overhead-valve, "Y-block" V8 with 130 bhp. This was easily the hottest engine in the low-price field. Together with ball-joint front suspension, also new that year, the Y-block greatly narrowed the engineering gap

between expensive and inexpensive cars. Though it displaced 239 cubic inches (exactly the same as its flathead predecessor), it was entirely different in bore and stroke with oversquare dimensions. The Y-block had a 7.2:1 compression ratio in standard trim, but could be upped to 12:1 if required.

In styling, 1954 was mainly the same story as '53 except for one noteworthy addition: the Crestline Skyliner hardtop, with a novel front roof section made of transparent plastic. The concept was developed by interior styling director L. David Ash. Its current counterpart is the moonroof, though these are made of glass and cover a smaller area.

The 1955 Ford, bearing some resemblance to the 1952-54 models, was a good design, clean if highly chromed, with a rakish look of motion. Frank Hershey was the man in charge of styling. (Hershey also gets most of the credit for the '55 Thunderbird, one of the most important Fords in history. See separate chapter.)

Ford retained its basic line for '56—Mainline, Customline, Fairlane, and Station Wagon. This year the company tried to make safety a selling point. Standard for all models were a dished steering wheel, breakaway rearview mirror, and crashproof door locks; padded dash and sunvisors cost $16 extra, and factory-installed seatbelts cost $9. The public took to safety in a modest way early in the model year. But the rush to install seatbelts overtaxed Ford's supplier, and only 20 percent of the cars were so equipped. Ford continued to stress safety for a few years, but after Ford failed to catch Chevrolet in 1956, a lot of dealers said performance was more important.

An interesting 1955-56 model was the two-door Crown Victoria, developed from the 1954 Skyliner. Some featured the transparent half-top. All had a broad, stainless-steel wrapover roof band that looked like a roll bar, but added little if any strength. The model was dropped for 1957. Altogether, Ford sold 13,344 plastic-roof cars for 1954, 1999 for '55; and only 603 for '56. Though attractive, they were expensive and the plastic roof made them hot on a summer day.

Ford met dealer demand with an all-new '57 line, offering a vast array of V8 engines from the 190-bhp "300" powerplant on up to the Thunderbird's supercharged 312 V8 with 300 bhp. Wheelbase grew slightly, and there were now two of them, 116 and 118 inches. The model lineup was rearranged accordingly. There were Customs, including a business sedan; Custom 300s; Fairlanes; Fairlane 500s, including a Sunliner convertible and a retractable hardtop convertible; and Station Wagons. All were available with six or V8 power. The new styling was particularly simple for the period. It featured a clean, full-width rectangular grille; rakish side moldings; and tiny tailfins. It was a good year for the division. Some statisticians showed Ford ahead of Chevrolet in calendar year output for the first time since 1935, but the final tabulation indicated Chevy ahead by 130 cars. In model year production, though, Ford scored a substantial victory.

1955 Fairlane Crown Victoria hardtop coupe

1956 Fairlane Victoria hardtop sedan (prototype)

1957 Fairlane 500 Skyliner retractable hardtop

1957 Fairlane 500 Victoria hardtop sedan

1957 Fairlane four-door Town sedan

1958 Fairlane 500 Skyliner retractable hardtop

Prototype for 1959 Galaxie hardtop coupe

The Skyliner retractable hardtop was a unique mid-1957 arrival based on earlier developmental engineering by Continental Division. (A Mark II retractable was considered, but not produced.) Ford sold 20,766 retractables in 1957, but production tapered off quickly. The Skyliner was complicated and expensive: in '57, it cost $350 more than a standard convertible.

Ford settled for a facelift in 1958, using a bumper/grille reminiscent of the '58 Thunderbird and quad headlights. The cheaper of the two Custom series was retained. A recession now slowed sales. Ford sold fewer cars than Chevrolet, but hadn't invested as much money that year and was still able to keep production near a million units.

In 1959, Chevrolet fielded its all-new line of radical bat-fin models that didn't strike the public's fancy. Ford passed Chevy by some 12,000 units for the 12 months. The '59 Ford used the basic '57 body with updated, though still conservative, styling. Bizarre two-toning

and radical fins were avoided in favor of a squared-off grille with floating, starlike ornaments, and simple side moldings. A new Galaxie series with a T-Bird-like roofline was added. It included sedans, hardtops, and a convertible.

For Ford Motor Company as a whole, 1959 justified the strenuous efforts of Henry Ford II and board chairman Ernest Breech. They had assumed control of a third-rate company in 1945, and had turned it into something approaching General Motors in less than 15 years.

Ford's history in the '60s closely parallels Chevrolet's. When the decade ended, the division was producing about 100,000 more cars each year than in 1960. During the period, Ford expanded into several important new markets, including economy compacts and sportier versions of regular production models. And like Chevrolet, Ford built these diverse types on relatively few wheelbases. (The two most highly specialized Fords, Mustang and Thunderbird, are discussed separately.)

Management changed rapidly. Lee A. Iacocca arrived as division general manager in 1960. In 1961, George Walker left as chief stylist, and Eugene Bordinat became Ford's chief of automotive design. Iacocca soon put an end to Robert S. McNamara's concept of building mundane people-haulers. By 1970, Ford was offering some of the world's best road cars. For much of the decade, Fords were the cars to beat on the nation's racetracks. In fact, the 1968-69 Dodge Charger racing program was an all-out effort to halt the Ford superstockers. In this period, the division also evolved from a "Chevy-follower" to a "Chevy-leader." Its compact Falcon outsold the Corvair; its 1962 Fairlane intermediate was a bit ahead of, and more popular than, the Chevy II; its Mustang changed the public's attitude toward compact cars and sent Chevrolet racing to the drawing boards to develop the Camaro.

Looking at the size of Ford's products is the best way to summarize its cars of the '60s. The smallest was the Falcon, which rode a 109.5-inch wheelbase through 1965, and longer wheelbases from 1966 on. Falcon production gradually decreased, largely because of competition from both inside and outside Ford Division, but the car was always a profit-maker. To many, it was the ultimate "throw-away" car—built to sell at a low price, and designed to be discarded within a few years. Compared with the Corvair, Falcon's conventional independent front suspension, beam-axle rear suspension, and ordinary six-cylinder engine were uninteresting. But they added up to a simple little car that rode well, stopped well, provided excellent space utilization, and delivered 20–25 miles per gallon.

Ford brought out the bucket-seated Falcon Futura coupe as an answer to the Corvair Monza in the spring of 1961. This sporty little car was restyled for '64 with a much less distinctive, squared-off shape. The ultimate collector's Falcon, however, is the Futura Sprint, introduced for 1963½. Offered as a convertible or hardtop, it

1962 Falcon Futura two-door coupe

1963 Falcon Futura Sprint hardtop coupe

1964 Falcon two-door sedan

1967 Falcon Futura Sports Coupe

1968 Falcon Futura four-door station wagon

1969 Falcon Futura Sports Coupe

was powered by the compact yet lively small-block Fairlane V8. It was one of the finest engines built, and one of the most economical. The 260 completely transformed the Falcon's performance without greatly affecting gas mileage. Sprints had special trim, bucket seats, console, and full instrumentation including a 6000-rpm tachometer. When equipped with optional four-speed transmission, they were great fun to drive.

In 1966, Falcon was restyled a third time. It received a longer wheelbase and long-hood/short-deck proportions like the Mustang's. It remained in this form through the rest of the '60s. Ford later enlarged the small-block V8 to 289 cid and it also became a Falcon option. In its last year before emission controls, the 289 "Stage 2" offered 225 bhp with four-barrel carburetors, and made Falcon Sprints very fast. For 1968, the 289 was detuned to 195 bhp, but the larger 302-cid V8 appeared as an option. Equipped with a two-barrel carburetor, the 302 ran on regular gas and developed 210 bhp. With the four barrel, it required premium fuel, but developed 230 bhp. Stringent emissions controls meant

the end of the four-barrel package by 1969.

Ford held pat in early 1970 with a Falcon identical to the '69 version. Then it brought out a new mid-year model using the intermediate Torino bodyshell. These were much larger cars, from 10 to 22 inches longer than their predecessors. Ultimately, Falcon was displaced by another new 1970 offering, the compact Maverick.

In 1962, Ford broke new ground with the "intermediate-size" Fairlane. The name (originally derived from Henry Ford's estate) had been lifted from a series in the large Ford line. In concept, the Fairlane was identical with Virgil Exner's downsized '62 Plymouths and Dodges. But unlike Chrysler, Ford retained its full-size cars—a wise move, even though Fairlane sold more than 297,000 units for 1962, and broke the 300,000-unit level in 1963.

The Fairlane was significant for reasons other than first-year sales. It was the first Ford to use the small-block V8, the basis for some of Ford's hottest performance models. Bored out to 289 cid as a 1963 option, it developed 271 bhp, almost one horsepower per cubic

1970 Falcon Futura four-door sedan

1963 Fairlane 500 four-door sedan

1967 Fairlane 500XL hardtop coupe

1968 Torino GT fastback hardtop coupe

1969 Torino Squire four-door station wagon

1969 Fairlane 500 convertible

inch. Stroked to 302 cid in 1968, it delivered 230 bhp when equipped with the special carburetion setup. Powerful and smooth, yet surprisingly economical, this engine in all three displacements was the definitive small V8. Tuned versions used in racing and sports cars like the Ford GT40 and the Shelby Cobra disproved the old saw about there being no substitute for cubic inches. The GT40 nearly took the world GT Manufacturers Trophy away from Ferrari in its first full year of competition, 1964. In 1966 and again in '67, it won the LeMans 24 Hours outright.

Initially, Fairlane rode a 115.5-inch wheelbase and offered only two-door and four-door sedan body styles. As time went on, the line got more exciting. Along with a number of station wagons, a new Fairlane 500 series was added for 1963. The best Fairlanes appeared in '66 with a completely restyled body mounted on a 116-inch wheelbase (113 inches for wagons). These were long, sleek cars with smooth lines, curved side glass, and vertical taillights. The top of the line that year was the bucket-seat 500XL series, a hardtop coupe and a con-

vertible in standard and GT trim. Although they could be ordered with the 120-bhp six, most were equipped with the 289 V8. The fastest were the GTs, powered by Ford's new 390 V8 as standard equipment. Rated at 335 horsepower, this potent powerplant had a 10.5:1 compression ratio that necessitated premium fuel. Since the 390 could be ordered on any Fairlane, racing drivers slotted it into the lighter two-door sedans that quickly earned respect for their competitive prowess. From 1964 on, Ford offered a growing assortment of handling and performance options, including stiffer suspensions and four-speed gearboxes.

For 1968, Fairlane was again restyled and the Torino introduced as the top-line series. The base Torino came with the 115-bhp six, but the GTs were far more exciting, featuring bucket seats, center console, paint striping, and more performance options than a salesman could memorize.

For 1969, Torino was largely unchanged except for two new arrivals, the fastback and hardtop Torino Cobra. The name symbolized Ford's close relationship

with Carroll Shelby's muscular sports cars. The Cobra came with the 428-cid engine from the Mach I Mustang. This powerplant had first appeared in the 1968½ Mercury Cyclone, and was known as the Cobra Jet. A $133 option was "Ram-Air," a fiberglass hood scoop with a special air cleaner assembly that ducted incoming air directly into the carburetor through a valve in the air cleaner. Four-speed gearbox, competition suspension including stiff shocks and springs, and functional hood locking pins were all standard. One magazine was ac-

tually disappointed when its Torino Cobra ran from 0 to 60 in 7.2 seconds and the quarter-mile in 15 seconds at 98.3 miles per hour! On the other hand, just about everyone admitted that of all the '69 "supercars"— Plymouth GTX, Dodge Charger R/T, Pontiac GTO, Chevelle 396, and Buick GS 400—the Torino Cobra was the tightest, the best built, and the quietest.

Torinos were potent racing machines. Ford found that the styling of the Torino's Mercury counterpart, the Cyclone, was slightly more aerodynamic, and in 1969

1969 Torino GT fastback hardtop coupe

1970 Torino Brougham hardtop coupe

1970 Torino GT fastback hardtop coupe

1961 Galaxie two-door sedan

1962 Galaxie two-door sedan

1963 Galaxie 500 hardtop coupe

Ford

only Cyclones were usually run in races more than 250 miles long. Nevertheless, both the Torino and the Cyclone could achieve about 190 mph. Lee Roy Yarborough won the 1969 Daytona 500 in a Ford.

For 1970, the Fairlane name was applied to an offshoot of the Torino line. There was all-new aerodynamic styling on a one-inch longer wheelbase. Profiles were lower and five inches longer than in '69.

Despite the Falcon and Fairlane, Ford was still a determined producer of full-size cars in the 1960s. The big models—the Custom, pre-1962 Fairlane, Galaxie, Galaxie 500, 500 XL, and LTD—all used Ford's 119-inch wheelbase (increased to 121 inches for 1969). They were heavy and not particularly exciting to drive on anything other than a superhighway. But plenty of interesting variations developed that made these 3000–4000-pound cruisers surprisingly capable, even on winding roads.

The big-car lineup for 1960 comprised Custom, Fairlane, Galaxie, and station wagon models available with

1965 Galaxie 500 LTD hardtop sedan

1968 Galaxie 500 convertible

1966 Country Squire four-door station wagon

1968 LTD hardtop sedan

1967 Galaxie 500XL hardtop coupe

1969 Country Squire four-door station wagon

1969 Galaxie 500 fastback hardtop coupe

1969 LTD hardtop sedan

1970 XL convertible

1970 Maverick two-door sedan

sixes and V8s. The all-new bodyshell had been hastily developed to keep pace with the completely redesigned '59 Chevrolet. But to everyone's surprise, the boxy Ford outsold Chevy in '59. So for 1961, Ford facelifted its one-year-old styling by clipping its modest bat-wing fins and reverting to round taillights topped by discreet blades. A full-width concave grille with a texture similar to that of the '59 Galaxie appeared in front. The bucket-seat Galaxie 500 XL Victoria hardtop coupe and Sunliner convertible bowed for 1962½. The "500" stood for the 500-mile races in which Fords were doing well. (In 1963, Ford won every 500 race.) Although the standard powertrain was a 292 V8 with Cruise-O-Matic, a large number of options could be ordered to turn a 500 XL into a real fire-breather. There were 300-bhp, 340-bhp, and 401-bhp versions of the 390, plus a Borg-Warner four-speed gearbox. In 1963, an even larger 427-cid engine was added, but was rarely ordered on "street Fords," even 500XLs.

The 1963 Galaxie was a facelifted version of the chunky '62 styling. The line was augmented at mid-year by a set of 500 and 500XL sports hardtops with ultra-thin fastback rooflines. Both were available with 427 cubic-inch engines. For 1964, the big cars had more sculptured sheetmetal and a horizontal-bar grille, as well as a new roofline for four-door hardtops.

The 1964 lineup collectively won *Motor Trend* magazine's "Car of the Year" award on the basis of its "total performance" image. Performance was just what the big Fords delivered. A pair of Galaxie 500XLs tested by the magazine that year were truly impressive. The 390 V8 powered one of them from 0 to 60 mph in 9.3 sec-

onds; the 427 made that run in 7.4 seconds. The only complaints were the car's tendency to nosedive in panic stops and a slight roughness in the power brakes.

The 1965 Fords were completely restyled with longer, sleeker lines. They were also fitted with a new, sophisticated front suspension. Making their debut were the Galaxie LTD hardtop coupe and sedan, priced at about $3300. LTDs were favorably compared in quietness at speed to Rolls-Royces—at least in Ford advertising.

Ford held onto the '65 design through 1967, along with the 119-inch wheelbase. The 1968 models had new sheetmetal below the beltline, and concealed headlights on XL and LTD models. The '69 edition had new sheetmetal everywhere, a two-inch longer wheelbase, a tunneled backlight for SportsRoof (fastback) models, and ventless door glass on hardtops and convertibles. The LTD had become a separate series in 1967, and quickly became a strong sales contender. Ford built nearly 139,000 of them for '68, and more than twice that many for '69.

Throughout the decade, Ford production kept pace with Chevrolet's, often coming close to leading. In 1965, Ford enjoyed its first two-million-car year.

The full-size 1970 Fords had new grilles with a 'poke-through' center section on LTDs and XLs, new sheetmetal, and a new rear bumper with integral, horizontal taillamps. No less than five series were offered, with the LTD Brougham at the top of the line. A brand-new entry was the Maverick, a compact semi-fastback two-door sedan on a 103-inch wheelbase. Ideal for the '70s, Maverick took off in sales and succeeded the Falcon as the economy car in the lineup.

1971 Pinto two-door fastback sedan

1971 Torino Brougham hardtop coupe

1971 Maverick four-door sedan

1971 Maverick two-door fastback sedan

Ford Motor Company was the last of the Big Three to realize that traditional full-size cars were dead by the mid-'70s. Not surprisingly, it was the first to suffer for it. In the wake of the Arab oil embargo and the first energy crisis, Chrysler pushed compacts while GM went forward with plans to downsize its entire fleet. Ford stubbornly resisted the winds of change, instead trying to promote its aging big cars on the basis of their greater passenger space and the presumed safety of "road-hugging weight." But the public wasn't buying this cynical line—or the cars. This situation in large measure reflected the personal view of chairman Henry Ford II, who decreed there would be no rush to smaller cars in Dearborn, no vast capital investment in new technology. As a result, Ford greeted 1980 a critical two to three years behind GM in the fuel efficiency and "space" races—and at a critical sales disadvantage

1972 LTD Brougham hardtop coupe

next to its domestic foes and a growing hoarde of ever-more-prosperous Japanese companies. The firm has since made drastic changes to its products, but its recovery is by no means complete at this writing.

Ford Division's 1971 lineup was top-heavy with full-size cars and the Torinos. The latter were nominally intermediates, but they were larger outside than their Chrysler and GM rivals and smaller inside than even some compacts. Ford did have a plus in the Maverick, new the previous year and now bolstered by a stretched-wheelbase notchback four-door sedan as well as the sporty Grabber version of the fastback two-door. Maverick would carry the division's entire compact sales effort for most of the decade, which it did tolerably well, but its old-fashioned engineering looked increasingly so with time and the arrival of more capable domestic and foreign competitors.

A major introduction for 1971 was the four-cylinder subcompact Pinto, the smallest Ford in living memory. A direct reply to Chevrolet's Vega, also new that year, it was smaller, less technically daring, and less accommodating, and its performance and fuel economy were nothing special compared to that of imports like the Datsun 510. Yet the Pinto must be considered a success. It usually outsold the trouble-prone Vega as well as most overseas contenders, and it was progressively dressed up and civilized with larger, more powerful engines, nicer trim, and more optional conveniences. By 1973 there was even a wood-sided Squire wagon, although Pinto remained primarily basic transportation throughout its long 10-year life. But though it served Ford well in a difficult period, this car seems destined to be remembered mainly as what one wag called "the barbeque that seats four." That's a reference

to the dangerously vulnerable fuel tank and filler neck design of the 1971-76 models, which was implicated in a rash of highly publicized (and fatal) fires following rear-end collisions. Sadly, Ford stonewalled in a number of lawsuits all the way to federal court, which severely tarnished its public image, even if Pinto sales didn't seem to suffer much. What really put Pinto out to pasture after 1980 was not bad publicity but the relative lack of change in a design that, by then, was simply old hat next to roomier, thriftier front-drive minicars from both home and abroad.

Like its subcompact sibling, the Maverick changed little during its production run, which ended with the 1977 models. That's remarkable considering the greater importance of compacts in the post-energy-crisis era. There was little here to interest the enthusiast. The Grabber may have looked jazzy, but it was pretty tame, even with the optional 302 V8. And certain requisites for a sporty car, like decent engine instruments and front disc brakes, were either late in coming or not available (the latter arrived for '76). Ford's last gesture to the youth market was the Stallion package, a 1976 trim treatment also available for Pinto and Mustang II. The Maverick kit, offered only on the two-door, comprised mainly black paint (on grille and exterior moldings), plus twin door mirrors, styled steel wheels, raised-white-letter tires, and special i.d. More popular was the Luxury Decor Option (LDO), a 1973 package continued through the end of the line. It offered upgraded interior appointments color-keyed to a special paint scheme and crowned by a matching vinyl top. It was available for either Maverick body style.

The mid-size Torino proved exceptionally popular early in the decade, only to fall from buyer favor once fuel economy became a pressing consumer concern. The 14-model 1971 lineup was basically a carryover of the previous year's heavy facelift on the 1968-69 platform. The Cobra fastback coupe remained the most exciting of this

1972 Gran Torino Sport fastback hardtop coupe

1973 Maverick four-door sedan with LDO option

1973 Pinto wagon with Squire option

1973 Gran Torino formal hardtop coupe

1973 LTD hardtop sedan

1974 LTD Brougham pillared hardtop sedan

bunch, even though its standard engine was downgraded from a 429 V8 to a 240-horsepower version of the ubiquitous 351 small-block. It was a sign of the times, and the Cobra would not return. High-power engines began disappearing at Ford (and elsewhere in Detroit) the following year, and by 1980 only a mildly tuned 351 remained, an option for the full-size line.

Except for engines, the 1972 Torino was all-new—and a big disappointment. Models were now split on two different wheelbase lengths depending on body style, and body-on-frame construction was adopted for the first time. Dimensions ballooned close to what the big Galaxies and LTDs had had a few years before. These cars were symbolic of most everything that was going wrong in Detroit at the time. They were needlessly oversized, overweight, and thirsty, with limited interior space and a soggy chassis that sent the adrenalin pumping in quick direction changes. There was wasted space everywhere, incredible for such a large car. You saw it ahead of the radiator, in the bulky dash, and in the doors (a full seven inches wide). Ford tried in vain to make these rigs passably economical, gave up and simply fitted a larger fuel tank. CONSUMER GUIDE® magazine's test of a 1976 Torino Brougham

yielded a dismal 13.5 mpg. The report aptly concluded: "The more buyers learn about the Torino, the more reasons they will find to opt for a Granada."

An altogether different and more rational proposition, the Granada was arguably Ford's best idea of the decade. It was certainly one of the most timely. Introduced during 1975, it was originally intended as a slightly larger replacement for the Maverick, built around the older compact's basic chassis and drivetrains. When the fuel crunch boosted small car sales, Ford decided to retain the Maverick while launching its erstwhile successor as a more luxurious compact half a step up the price scale. This explains why the Granada appeared on the same 109.9-inch wheelbase used by the Maverick four-door. In typical Ford fashion, it was keyed to the new needs of the market, perhaps more accurately than any Ford since the original Mustang. Its general concept blended American-style luxury with the mock-Mercedes look then favored in Detroit. Buyers wholeheartedly approved, and the Granada zoomed from nowhere to become Ford Division's top-selling model line, outdistancing the big Fords and the swollen Torinos by a wide margin. After a year or so, it had achieved all the acceptance and familiarity of a model 20 years old—which

1974 Gran Torino Brougham hardtop coupe

1975 Granada two-door sedan

1975 Maverick two-door fastback sedan

1976 LTD Landau pillared hardtop coupe

1976 Pinto two-door fastback sedan with Stallion option

1976 Granada Ghia four-door sedan

it *was* in some ways, notably its untidy cornering response and a roly-poly ride on rough roads. Nevertheless, it enabled Ford to bridge a big market gap at a crucial time, appealing to both compact-car buyers with upscale aspirations and big-car owners now energy-conscious for the first time.

The Maverick's true successor bowed for 1978 bearing a name borrowed from the Australian subsidiary: Fairmont. It was undoubtedly the firm's single most significant new product of the decade because, although no one knew it then, its basic engineering would be the foundation for most Ford Motor Company cars introduced through the mid-1980s, including a new-generation Mustang and Thunderbird (see following entries). Billed as the first FoMoCo car designed with the aid of computer analysis, the Fairmont (and its Zephyr twin at Mercury) was mainly a car of common sense, and pretty conventional at that. It was one of the last all-new U.S. models conceived around the traditional front-engine/rear-drive layout, yet it was a big improvement over the Maverick: cleanly styled, sensibly boxy for good interior space on a shorter wheelbase, lighter and thus more economical than most people expected. Engines were familiar, but there was a new all-

coil suspension system featuring modified MacPherson-strut geometry at the front, with the springs mounted on lower A-arms. Aside from better handling, this arrangement opened up more underhood space for easier servicing. A front stabilizer bar was standard, as was rack-and-pinion steering, offered at extra cost with variable-ratio power assist, a new item shared with several other Ford models that year.

The "Fox" program that produced Fairmont was one of Ford's first design projects initiated after the 1973-74 energy crisis. But it wasn't the firm's only attempt at downsizing. For 1977, the old Torino was refurbished with cleaner exterior sheetmetal and "badge engineered" to pass as a new-generation full-size car. Called LTD II, it was only a little lighter than before, and sales went nowhere. One reason was the arrival of a new "downsized" Thunderbird, another version of this basic platform and much less costly than the earlier bigger Birds. With that magical name going for it, it swamped the LTD II in sales until this unhappy design was retired

Besides a new Fairmont-based Mustang, model year 1979 saw the fruition of the "Panther" design project in a new LTD that was genuinely downsized. But this trim-

1976 Elite hardtop coupe

1978 Fairmont four-door sedan

1977 LTD II Brougham hardtop coupe

1979 LTD Landau four-door sedan

1978 Pinto two-door fastback sedan

1979 Pinto Runabout hatchback sedan with Rallye option

1979 Fairmont Futura coupe

1980 Fairmont two-door sedan with turbo option

1980 Granada Ghia four-door sedan

1980 LTD four-door sedan

mer, tauter big Ford was less successful than the new ponycar, and that was curious. In size and execution it was fully a match for its GM competition, riding a seven-inch shorter wheelbase yet offering more claimed passenger and trunk space than the outsized 1973-78 cars. Styling was boxier but much less pretentious, and visibility and fuel economy were better. So, too, were ride and handling, courtesy of a new all-coil suspension system with short-arm/long-arm front geometry and more precise four-bar link location for the live rear axle. With all this, "the new American road car" should have scored higher

sales, yet model year deliveries actually fell by some 80,000 units compared to 1978. The new LTD thus barely beat out the big Oldsmobiles for second place in full-size sales, and ran far behind Chevy's Caprice/Impala. Two factors seemed to be at work. One was GM's two-year head start. The other was a severe downturn in the national economy that begin in the spring of '79 and put a crimp in big-car sales generally. The LTD would enjoy a sales resurgence in the '80s, but not before Ford and the U.S. industry as a whole had passed through three of their bleakest years in history.

Ford Specifications

1930

Model A (wb 103.5)	Wght	Price	Prod
rdstr 2P	2,155	435	122,703
rdstr 2-4P	2,230	460	
phtn 5P	2,212	440	39,886
Standard cpe 2P	2,257	495	232,564
spt cpe 2-4P	2,283	525	72,572
cabriolet 2-4P	2,273	625	29,226
Tudor sdn 5P	2,375	495	425,124
Fordor sdn 2W 5P	2,441	600	7,838
Town sdn 5P	2,475	660	122,534
town car 5P	2,525	1,200	96
Standard sdn 3W 5P	2,462	600	53,958
DeLuxe rdstr 2-4P	2,230	520	11,629
DeLuxe phtn 5P	2,285	625	4,635
DeLuxe cpe 2P	2,265	545	29,777
victoria 5P	2,265	625	6,447

	Wght	Price	Prod
DeLuxe sdn 5P	2,488	640	13,710
wgn 4d	—	650	3,799
bus cpe 2P	—	—	110

1930 Engine	bore×stroke	bhp	availability
L4, 200.5	3.88×4.25	40	S-all

1931

Model A (wb 103.5)	Wght	Price	Prod
rdstr 2P	2,155	430	7,793
rdstr 2-4P	2,230	455	
phtn 5P	2,212	435	11,060
Standard cpe 2P	2,257	490	82,885
spt cpe 2-4P	2,283	500	21,272
cabriolet 2-4P	2,273	595	13,706
Tudor sdn 5P	2,375	490	170,645
Standard sdn 3W 5P	2,462	590	25,720
DeLuxe rdstr 2-4P	2,230	475	56,702
DeLuxe phtn 5P	2,285	580	2,875

	Wght	Price	Prod
DeLuxe cpe 2P	2,265	525	23,653
victoria 5P	2,265	580	36,830
DeLuxe Tudor sdn 5P	2,388	525	23,490
DeLuxe Fordor sdn 5P	2,488	630	4,967
DeLuxe town sdn 5P	2,475	630	65,447
conv sdn 5P	2,360	640	5,072
wgn 4d	—	625	3,018

1931 Engine	bore×stroke	bhp	availability
L4, 200.5	3.88×4.25	40	S-all

1932

Model B (wb 106.5)	Wght	Price	Prod*
rdstr 2P	2,077	410	—
rdstr 2-4P	2,119	435	—
phtn 5P	2,213	445	—
cpe 2P	2,236	440	—
spt cpe 2-4P	2,261	485	—
Tudor sdn 5P	2,353	450	—
Fordor sdn 5P	2,388	540	—
DeLuxe rdstr 2-4P	2,153	450	—
DeLuxe phtn 5P	2,243	495	—
DeLuxe cpe 2P	2,339	525	—
victoria 5P	2,319	550	—
cabriolet 2-4P	2,370	560	—
DeLuxe Tudor sdn 5P	2,373	500	—
DeLuxe Fordor sdn 5P	2,407	595	—
conv sdn 5P	2,324	600	—
wgn 4d	—	—	—

Model 18 V8 (wb 106.5)	Wght	Price	Prod
rdstr 2P	2,217	460	—
rdstr 2-4P	2,258	485	—
phtn 5P	2,344	495	—
cpe 2P	2,387	490	—
spt cpe 2-4P	2,397	535	—
Tudor sdn 5P	2,487	500	—
Fordor sdn 5P	2,524	590	—
DeLuxe rdstr 2-4P	2,283	500	—
DeLuxe phtn 5P	2,350	545	—
DeLuxe cpe 2P	2,477	575	—
victoria 5P	2,463	600	—
cabriolet 2-4P	2,390	610	—
DeLuxe Tudor sdn 5P	2,497	550	—
DeLuxe Fordor snd 5P	2,543	643	—
conv sdn 2-4P	2,455	650	—
wgn 4d	—	600	—

1932 Engines	bore×stroke	bhp	availability
L4, 200.5	3.88×4.25	50	S-Model B
V8, 221.0	3.06×3.75	65	S-Model 18

*Production of both models was combined, though V8s far exceeded Model Bs. Factory production figures by body style:

cabriolet	7,063
conv sdn	1,142
coupe	54,597
Fordor sdn	36,649
phaeton	2,705
roadster	8,996
wagon	334
Tudor sdn	90,568
victoria	8,870

1933

Model 46 (wb 106.5)	Wght	Price	Prod*
rdstr	2,021	425	—
rdstr 2-4P	2,064	450	—
phtn 5P	2,124	445	—
cpe 3W/5W 2P	2,147	440	—
cpe 3W/5W 2-4P	2,202	465	—
Tudor sdn 5P	2,418	450	—
Fordor sdn 5P	2,465	510	—
DeLuxe rdstr 2-4P	2,264	460	—
DeLuxe phtn 5P	2,154	495	—
DeLuxe cpe 3W/5W 2P	2,196	490	—
DeLuxe cpe 3W/5W/ 2-4P	2,202	515	—
victoria 5P	2,230	545	—
cabriolet 2-4P	2,181	535	—
DeLuxe Tudor sdn 5P	2,435	500	—
DeLuxe Fordor sdn 5P	2,505	560	—
wgn 4d	—	—	—

Model 40 (wb 112.0)	Wght	Price	Prod
rdstr 2P	2,337	475	—
rdstr 2-4P	2,420	500	—
phtn 5P	2,435	495	—
cpe 3W/5W 2P	2,448	490	—
cpe 3W/5W 2-4P	2,380	515	—
Tudor sdn 5P	2,536	500	—
Fordor sdn 5P	2,590	560	—
DeLuxe rdstr 2-4P	2,376	510	—
DeLuxe phtn 5P	2,444	545	—
DeLuxe cpe 3W/5W 2P	2,453	540	—
DeLuxe cpe 3W/5W 2-4P	2,450	565	—
victoria 5P	2,510	595	—
cabriolet 2-4P	2,460	585	—
DeLuxe Tudor sdn 5P	2,540	550	—
DeLuxe Fordor sdn 5P	2,599	610	—
wgn 4d	—	640	—

1933 Engines	bore×stroke	bhp	availability
L4, 200.5	3.88×4.25	50	S-Model 46
V8, 221.0	3.06×3.75	75	S-Model 40

*Production of both models plus 1934 V8 combined, though V8s far exceeded Model 46s. Factory production figures for all models by body style:

cabriolet	24,299
coupe 5W	120,735
coupe 3W	52,111
Fordor sdn	220,225
phaeton	8,365
roadster	11,187
wagon	4,562
Tudor sdn	426,389
victoria	26,552

1934

Model 40A (wb 112.0)	Wght	Price	Prod*
Standard cpe 5W 2P	2,448	505	—
Standard cpe 5W 2-4P	2,534	530	—
victoria 5P	2,670	600	—
conv cabriolet 2-4P	2,460	590	—
Tudor sdn 5P	2,536	520	—
Fordor sdn 5P	2,590	575	—
DeLuxe rdstr 2-4P	2,376	525	—
DeLuxe phtn 5P	2,444	550	—
DeLuxe cpe 2P	2,453	545	—
DeLuxe cpe 2-4P	2,450	570	—
DeLuxe Tudor sdn 5P	2,540	560	—
DeLuxe Fordor sdn 5P	2,599	615	—
wgn 4d	—	660	—

1934 Engine	bore×stroke	bhp	availability
V8, 221.0	3.06×3.75	90	S-all

*See 1933

1935

Model 48 (wb 112.0)	Wght	Price	Prod
cpe 5W 2P	2,620	495	111,542
DeLuxe cpe 5W 2P	2,643	560	

	Wght	Price	Prod
conv cabriolet 2-4P	2,687	625	17,000
Tudor sdn 5P	2,717	510	322,575
DeLuxe Tudor sdn 5P	2,735	575	
Tudor touring sdn 5P	2,772	595	87,326
Fordor sdn 5P	2,760	575	124,984
DeLuxe Fordor sdn 5P	2,767	635	
Fordor touring sdn 5P	2,787	655	105,157
DeLuxe rdstr 2-4P	2,597	550	4,896
DeLuxe phtn 5P	2,667	580	6,073
DeLuxe cpe 3W 2P	2,647	570	31,513
conv sdn 5P	2,827	750	4,234
victoria 5P	—	630	235
wgn 4d	—	670	4,536
sdn 7P	—	—	182

1935 Engine	bore×stroke	bhp	availability
V8, 221.0	3.06×3.75	90	S-all

1936

Model 68 Standard (wb 112.0)

	Wght	Price	Prod
cpe 5W 2P	2,599	510	*
cpe 5W 2-4P	2,641	535	*
Tudor sdn 5P	2,659	520	*
Tudor T/B sdn 5P	2,718	545	*
Fordor sdn 5P	2,699	580	*
Fordor T/B sdn 5P	2,771	605	*
wgn 4d	3,020	670	7,044

Model 68 DeLuxe (wb 112.0)

	Wght	Price	Prod
rdstr 2-4P	2,561	560	3,862
phtn 5P	2,641	590	5,555
cpe 3W 2P	2,621	570	*
cpe 3W 2-4P	2,656	595	*
cpe 5W 2P	2,641	555	*
cpe 5W 2-4P	2,666	580	*
cabriolet 2-4P	2,649	625	14,068
club cabriolet 2-4P	2,661	675	4,616
Tudor sdn 5P	2,691	565	*
Tudor T/B sdn 5P	2,786	590	*
Fordor sdn 5P	2,746	625	*
Fordor T/B sdn 5P	2,816	650	*
conv sdn 5P	2,791	760	5,601
conv sdn T/B 5P	2,916	780	

1936 Engines	bore×stroke	bhp	availability
V8, 221.0	3.06×3.75	90	S-all

*Production combined by body style as follows:

coupe 5W	108,472
coupe 3W	21,446
Tudor sdn	486,310
Fordor sdn	273,804

1937

Model 74 (wb 112.0)

	Wght	Price	Prod
cpe 5W 2P	2,275	529	*
Tudor sdn 5P	2,405	579	
Tudor T/B sdn 5P	2,415	604	
Fordor sdn 5P	2,435	639	
Fordor T/B sdn 5P	2,445	664	
wgn 4d s/curtains	2,691	744	
wgn 4d glass windows	2,776	764	

Model 78 Standard (wb 112.0)

	Wght	Price	Prod
cpe 5W 2P	2,496	586	*
Tudor sdn 5P	2,616	611	
Tudor T/B sdn 5P	2,648	638	
Fordor sdn 5P	2,649	671	
Fordor T/B sdn 5P	2,666	696	
wgn 4d s/curtains	2,906	754	

	Wght	Price	Prod
wgn 4d glass windows	2,991	775	

Model 78 DeLuxe (wb 112.0)

	Wght	Price	Prod
rdstr 2-4P	2,576	694	1,250
phtn 5P	2,691	749	3,723
cpe 5W 2P	2,506	659	26,783
cabriolet 2-4P	2,616	719	10,184
club cpe 5W 5P	2,616	719	16,992
club cabriolet 4P	2,636	759	8,001
Tudor sdn 5P	2,656	674	33,683
Tudor T/B sdn 5P	2,679	699	73,690
Fordor sdn 5P	2,671	734	22,885
Fordor T/B sdn 5P	2,696	759	98,687
conv sdn 5P	2,861	859	4,378
sdn 7P	—	—	521

1937 Engines	bore×stroke	bhp	availability
V8, 136.0	2.60×3.20	60	S-74
V8, 221.0	3.06×3.75	85	S-78

*Production combined by body style as follows:

coupe	90,347
Tudor sdn	308,446
Tudor T/B sdn	138,538
Fordor sdn	49,062
Fordor T/B sdn	45,531
wagons	9,304

1938

Model 82A (wb 112.0)

	Wght	Price	Prod
cpe 5W 2P	2,354	595	*
Tudor sdn 5P	2,455	640	*
Fordor sdn 5P	2,481	685	*

Model 81A (wb 112.0)

	Wght	Price	Prod
cpe 5W 2P	2,575	625	*
Tudor sdn 5P	2,674	665	*
Fordor sdn 5P	2,697	710	*
wgn 4d	2,981	825	6,944
DeLuxe phtn 5P	2,748	820	1,169
DeLuxe cpe 5W 2P	2,606	685	22,225
DeLuxe conv cpe 2-4P	2,679	770	4,702
DeLuxe club cpe 5P	2,688	745	7,171
DeLuxe Tudor sdn 5P	2,742	725	101,647
DeLuxe Fordor sdn 5P	2,773	770	92,020
DeLuxe conv sdn 5P	2,883	900	2,743
DeLuxe sdn 7P	—	—	449

1938 Engines	bore×stroke	bhp	availability
V8, 136.0	2.60×3.20	60	S-82A
V8, 221.0	3.06×3.75	85	S-81A

*Production combined by body style as follows:

coupe	34,789
Tudor sdn	106,117
Fordor sdn	30,287

1939

Model 92A (wb 112.0)

	Wght	Price	Prod
cpe 5W 2P	2,463	599	*
Tudor sdn 5P	2,608	640	*
Fordor sdn 5P	2,623	686	*

Model 91A (wb 112.0)

	Wght	Price	Prod
cpe 5W 2P	2,710	640	*
Tudor sdn 5P	2,830	681	*
Fordor sdn 5P	2,850	727	*
wgn 4d	3,080	840	3,277
DeLuxe cpe 5W 2P	2,752	702	37,326
DeLuxe conv cpe 2-4P	2,840	788	10,422
DeLuxe Tudor sdn 5P	2,867	742	144,333

	Wght	Price	Prod
DeLuxe Fordor sdn 5P	2,898	788	90,551
DeLuxe conv sdn 5P	2,935	921	3,561
DeLuxe wgn 4d	3,095	916	6,155
DeLuxe sdn 7P	—	—	192

1939 Engines	bore×stroke	bhp	availability
V8, 136.0	2.60×3.20	60	S-92A
V8, 221.0	3.06×3.75	85	S-91A

*Production combined by body style as follows:

coupe	38,197
Tudor sdn	124,866
Fordor sdn	28,151

1940—541,896 built

01A V8/85 (wb 112.0)	Wght	Price	Prod
cpe	2,763	660	—
bus cpe	2,801	681	—
Tudor sdn	2,909	701	—
Fordor sdn	2,936	747	—
wgn 4d	3,249	875	—
DeLuxe cpe	2,791	722	—
DeLuxe bus cpe	2,831	742	—
DeLuxe conv cpe	2,956	849	—
DeLuxe Tudor sdn	2,927	762	—
DeLuxe Fordor sdn	2,966	808	—
DeLuxe wgn 4d	3,262	947	—

02A V8/60 (wb 112.0)			
cpe	2,519	619	—
bus cpe	2,549	640	—
Tudor sdn	2,669	660	—
Fordor sdn	2,696	706	—

1940 Engines	bore×stroke	bhp	availability
V8, 136.0	2.60×3.20	60	S-V8/60
V8, 221.0	3.06×3.75	85	S-V8/85

1941—691,896 built

1GA Six (wb 114.0)	Wght	Price	Prod
Special cpe	2,870	684	—
Special Tudor sdn	2,975	720	—
Special Fordor sdn	3,020	761	—
Deluxe cpe	2,947	715	—
DeLuxe cpe, A/S	2,970	746	—
DeLuxe Tudor sdn	3,065	756	—
DeLuxe Fordor sdn	3,100	797	—
DeLuxe wgn 4d	3,395	946	—
Super DeLuxe cpe	2,934	761	—
Super DeLuxe cpe, A/S	2,974	792	—
Super DeLuxe sdn cpe	3,030	833	—
Super DeLuxe conv cpe	3,145	931	—
Super DeLuxe Tudor sdn	3,096	802	—
Super DeLuxe Fordor sdn	3,131	843	—
Super DeLuxe wgn 4d	3,400	998	—

11A V8 (wb 114.0)			
Special cpe	2,878	700	—
Special Tudor sdn	2,983	736	—
Special Fordor sdn	3,033	777	—
Deluxe cpe	2,953	730	—
DeLuxe cpe, A/S	2,981	761	—
DeLuxe Tudor sdn	3,095	772	—
DeLuxe Fordor sdn	3,121	813	—
DeLuxe wgn 4d	3,412	962	—
Super DeLuxe cpe	2,969	777	—
Super DeLuxe cpe, A/S	3,001	807	—
Super DeLuxe sdn cpe	3,052	849	—
Super DeLuxe conv cpe	3,187	946	—
Super DeLuxe Tudor sdn	3,110	818	—

	Wght	Price	Prod
Super DeLuxe Fordor sdn	3,146	859	—
Super DeLuxe wgn 4d	3,419	1,013	—

1941 Engines	bore×stroke	bhp	availability
L6, 226.0	3.30×4.40	90	S-Six
V8, 221.0	3.06×3.75	85	S-V8

1942—160,432 built

2GA Six (wb 114.0)	Wght	Price	Prod
70C	Special Tudor sdn	3,053	815	—
73C	Special Fordor sdn	3,093	850	—
77C	Special cpe	2,910	780	—
70A	DeLuxe Tudor sdn	3,122	840	—
72A	DeLuxe sdn cpe	3,045	865	—
73A	DeLuxe Fordor sdn	3,141	875	—
77A	DeLuxe cpe	2,958	805	—
79A	DeLuxe wgn 4d, 8P	3,405	1,035	—
70B	Super DeLuxe Tudor sdn	3,136	885	—
72B	Super DeLuxe sdn cpe	3,109	910	—
73B	Super DeLuxe Fordor sdn	3,179	920	—
76	Super DeLuxe conv cpe	3,218	1,080	—
77B	Super DeLuxe cpe	3,030	850	—
79B	Super DeLuxe wgn 4d, 8P	3,453	1,115	—

21A V8 (wb 114.0)				
70A	DeLuxe Tudor sdn	3,141	850	—
72A	DeLuxe sdn cpe	3,065	875	—
73A	DeLuxe Fordor sdn	3,161	885	—
77A	DeLuxe cpe	2,978	815	—
79A	DeLuxe wgn 4d	3,420	1,090	—
70B	Super DeLuxe Tudor sdn	3,159	895	—
72B	Super DeLuxe sdn cpe	3,120	920	—
73B	Super DeLuxe Fordor sdn	3,200	930	—
76	Super DeLuxe conv cpe	3,238	1,090	—
77B	Super DeLuxe cpe	3,050	860	—
79B	Super DeLuxe wgn 4d, 8P	3,468	1,125	—

1942 Engines	bore×stroke	bhp	availability
L6, 226.0	3.30×4.40	90	S-Six
V8, 221.0	3.06×3.75	90	S-V8

1946

6GA Six (wb 114.0)*	Wght	Price	Prod
70A	DeLuxe Tudor sdn	3,157	1,136	—
73A	DeLuxe Fordor sdn	3,187	1,198	—
77A	DeLuxe cpe	3,007	1,074	—
70B	Super DeLuxe Tudor sdn	3,157	1,211	—
72B	Super DeLuxe cpe sdn	3,107	1,257	—
73B	Super DeLuxe Fordor sdn	3,207	1,273	—
77B	Super DeLuxe cpe	3,007	1,148	—
79B	Super DeLuxe wgn 4d	3,457	1,504	—

69A V8 (wb 114.0)*				
70A	DeLuxe Tudor sdn	3,190	1,185	—
73A	DeLuxe Fordor sdn	3,220	1,248	—
77A	DeLuxe cpe	3,040	1,123	—
70B	Super DeLuxe Tudor sdn	3,190	1,260	—
71	Super DeLuxe Sprtsmn conv	3,340	1,982	1,209
72B	Super DeLuxe cpe sdn	3,140	1,307	—
73B	Super DeLuxe Fordor sdn	3,240	1,322	—
76	Super DeLuxe conv cpe	3,240	1,488	—
77B	Super DeLuxe cpe	3,040	1,197	—
79B	Super DeLuxe wgn 4d, 8P	3,490	1,533	—

*Model Year Production by Body Style (Six/V8):

DeLuxe (wb 114.0)

Tudor sdn	74,954
Fordor sdn	9,246

	Wght	Price	Prod
cpe			10,670
chassis			86

Super DeLuxe (wb 114.0)

Tudor sdn			163,370
Fordor sdn			92,056
sdn cpe			70,826
conv cpe			16,359
cpe			12,249
wgn 4d			16,960
chassis			37

1946 Engines	bore×stroke	bhp	availability
L6, 226.0	3.30×4.40	90	S-Six
V8, 239.4	3.19×3.75	100	S-V8

1947

7GA Six (wb 114.0)*	Wght	Price	Prod
DeLuxe Fordor sdn	3,213	1,270	—
DeLuxe Tudor sdn	3,183	1,212	—
Deluxe cpe	3,033	1,154	—
Super DeLuxe Fordor sdn	3,233	1,372	—
Super DeLuxe Tudor sdn	3,183	1,309	—
Super DeLuxe cpe sdn	3,133	1,330	—
Super DeLuxe cpe	3,033	1,251	—
Super DeLuxe wgn 4d, 8P	3,487	1,893	—

79A V8 (wb 114.0)*	Wght	Price	Prod
DeLuxe Fordor sdn	3,246	1,346	—
DeLuxe Tudor sdn	3,216	1,288	—
DeLuxe cpe	3,066	1,230	—
Super DeLuxe Fordor sdn	3,266	1,440	—
Super DeLuxe Tudor sdn	3,216	1,382	—
Super DeLuxe cpe sdn	3,166	1,409	—
Super DeLuxe conv cpe	3,266	1,740	22,159
Super DeLuxe Sprtsmn conv	3,366	2,282	2,250
Super DeLuxe wgn 4d, 8P	3,520	1,972	—

*Model Year Production by Body Style (Six/V8):

DeLuxe (wb 114.0)

Tudor sdn			44,523
Fordor sdn			20
cpe			10,872
chassis			23

Super DeLuxe (wb 114.0)

Tudor sdn			136,126
Fordor sdn			116,744
cpe sdn			80,830
wgn 4d, 8P			16,104
chassis			23

1947 Engines	bore×stroke	bhp	availability
L6, 226.0	3.30×4.40	90	S-Six
V8, 239.4	3.19×3.75	100	S-V8

1948

87HA Six (wb 114.0)*	Wght	Price	Prod
70A	DeLuxe Tudor sdn	3,183	1,212	—
77A	Deluxe cpe	3,033	1,154	—
70B	Super DeLuxe Tudor sdn	3,183	1,309	—
72B	Super DeLuxe cpe sdn	3,133	1,330	—
73B	Super DeLuxe Fordor sdn	3,233	1,372	—
79B	Super DeLuxe wgn 4d, 8P	3,487	1,893	—

89A V8 (wb 114.0)*	Wght	Price	Prod
70A	DeLuxe Tudor sdn	3,216	1,288	—

		Wght	Price	Prod
77A	DeLuxe cpe	3,066	1,230	—
70B	Super DeLuxe Tudor sdn	3,216	1,382	—
71B	Super DeLuxe Sprtsmn conv	3,366	2,282	28
72B	Super DeLuxe cpe sdn	3,166	1,409	—
73B	Super DeLuxe Fordor sdn	3,266	1,440	—
76B	Super DeLuxe conv cpe	3,266	1,740	12,033
79B	Super DeLuxe wgn 4d, 8P	3,520	1,972	—

*Model Year Production by Body Style (Six/V8):

DeLuxe (wb 114.0)

Tudor sdn			23,356
cpe			5,048

Super DeLuxe (wb 114.0)

Tudor sdn			82,161
Fordor sdn			71,358
cpe sdn			44,826
wgn 4d, 8P			8,912

1948 Engines	bore×stroke	bhp	availability
L6, 226.0	3.30×4.40	95	S-Six
V8, 239.4	3.19×3.75	100	S-V8

1949

Standard (wb 114.0)		Wght	Price	Prod
70A	Tudor sdn	2,965	1,425	126,770
72A	club cpe	2,945	1,415	4,170
72C	bus cpe	2,891	1,333	28,946
73A	Fordor sdn	3,010	1,472	44,563
—	chassis	—	—	1

Custom V8 (wb 114.0)				
70B	Tudor sdn	2,968	1,511	433,316
72B	club cpe	2,948	1,511	150,254
73B	Fordor sdn	3,013	1,559	248,176
76	conv cpe	3,254	1,886	51,133
79	wgn 2d, 8P	3,543	2,119	31,412
—	chassis	—	—	18

1949 Engines	bore×stroke	bhp	availability
L6, 226.0	3.30×4.40	95	S-Six
V8, 239.4	3.19×3.75	100	O-V8

1950

DeLuxe (wb 114.0)		Wght	Price	Prod
D70	Tudor sdn	3,007	1,424	275,360
D72C	bus cpe	2,949	1,333	35,120
D73	Fordor sdn	3,064	1,472	77,888

Custom (wb 114.0)				
C70	Tudor sdn	3,015	1,511	398,060
C70C	Crestliner sdn 2d	3,050	1,711	17,601
C72	club cpe	2,981	1,511	85,111
C73	Fordor sdn	3,078	1,558	247,181
C76	conv cpe	3,263	1,948	50,299
C79	Country Squire wgn 2d	3,511	2,028	22,292

1950 Engines	bore×stroke	bhp	availability
L6, 226.0	3.30×4.40	95	S-all exc C70C, C76
V8, 239.4	3.19×3.75	100	S-C70C, C76; O-others

1951

DeLuxe (wb 114.0)		Wght	Price	Prod
70	Tudor sdn	3,043	1,417	146,010

		Wght	Price	Prod
72C	bus cpe	2,979	1,324	20,343
73	Fordor sdn	3,102	1,465	54,265

Custom (wb 114.0)

		Wght	Price	Prod
60	Victoria htp cpe	3,188	1,925	110,286
70	Tudor sdn	3,043	1,505	317,869
70C	Crestliner sdn 2d	3,065	1,595	8,703
72	club cpe	3,015	1,505	53,263
73	Fordor sdn	3,102	1,553	232,691
76	conv cpe	3,268	1,949	40,934
79	Country Squire wgn 2d	3,530	2,029	29,017

1951 Engines	bore×stroke	bhp	availability		
L6, 226.0	3.30×4.40	95	S-all exc 60, 70C, 76		
V8, 239.4	3.19×3.75	100	S-60, 70C, 76; O-others		

1952

Mainline (wb 115.0)

		Wght	Price	Prod
59A	Ranch Wagon 2d	3,212	1,832	32,566
70A	sdn 2d	3,111	1,485	79,931
72C	bus cpe	3,035	1,389	10,137
73A	sdn 4d	3,190	1,530	41,227

Customline (wb 115.0)

		Wght	Price	Prod
70B	sdn 2d	3,111	1,570	175,762
72B	club cpe	3,116	1,579	26,550
73B	sdn 4d	3,190	1,615	188,303
79C	Country Sedan wgn 4d, 6P	3,617	2,060	11,927

Crestline (wb 115.0)

		Wght	Price	Prod
60B	Victoria htp cpe	3,274	1,925	77,320
76B	Sunliner conv cpe	3,339	2,027	22,534
79B	Country Squire wgn 4d, 8P	3,640	2,186	5,426

1952 Engines	bore×stroke	bhp	availability		
L6, 215.3	3.56×3.60	101	S-all exc 79C, Crestline (ohv)		
V8, 239.4	3.19×3.75	110	S-79C, Crestline; O-others		

1953

Mainline (wb 115.0)

		Wght	Price	Prod
59A	Ranch Wagon 2d	3,406	1,917	66,976
70A	sdn 2d	3,092	1,497	152,995
72C	bus cpe	3,018	1,400	16,280
73A	sdn 4d	3,138	1,542	69,463

Customline (wb 115.0)

		Wght	Price	Prod
70B	sdn 2d	3,100	1,582	305,433
72B	club cpe	3,084	1,591	43,999
73B	sdn 4d	3,154	1,628	374,487
79B	Country Sedan wgn 4d, 6P	3,539	2,076	37,743

Crestline (wb 115.0)

		Wght	Price	Prod
60B	Victoria htp cpe	3,250	1,941	128,302
76B	Sunliner conv cpe	3,334	2,043	40,861
79C	Country Squire wgn 4d, 8P	3,609	2,203	11,001
—	chassis	—	—	2

1953 Engines	bore×stroke	bhp	availability		
L6, 215.3	3.56×3.60	101	S-all exc 79B, Crestline		
V8, 239.4	3.19×3.75	110	S-79B, Crestline; O-others		

1954

Mainline (wb 115.5)

		Wght	Price	Prod
59A	Ranch Wagon 2d	3,399	2,029	44,315
70A	sdn 2d	3,147	1,651	123,329
72C	bus cpe	3,082	1,548	10,665
73A	sdn 4d	3,203	1,701	55,371

Customline (wb 115.5)

		Wght	Price	Prod
59B	Ranch Wagon 2d	3,405	2,122	36,086
70B	sdn 2d	3,160	1,744	293,375
72B	club cpe	3,141	1,753	33,951
73B	sdn 4d	3,216	1,793	262,499
79B	Country Sedan wgn 4d, 6P	3,574	2,202	48,384

Crestline (wb 115.5)

		Wght	Price	Prod
60B	Victoria htp cpe	3,245	2,055	95,464
60F	Skyliner htp cpe	3,265	2,164	13,344
73C	sdn 4d	3,220	1,898	99,677
76B	Sunliner conv cpe	3,292	2,164	36,685
79C	Country Squire wgn 4d, 8P	3,624	2,339	12,797

1954 Engines	bore×stroke	bhp	availability		
L6, 223.0	3.62×3.60	115	S-all exc 79B		
V8, 239.4	3.50×3.10	130	S-79B; O-others (ohv)		

1955

Mainline (wb 115.5)

		Wght	Price	Prod
70A	sdn 2d	3,119	1,707	76,698
70D	bus cpe	3,081	1,606	8,809
73A	sdn 4d	3,161	1,753	41,794

Customline (wb 115.5)

		Wght	Price	Prod
70B	sdn 2d	3,139	1,801	236,575
73B	sdn 4d	3,181	1,845	235,417

Fairlane (wb 115.5)

		Wght	Price	Prod
60B	Victoria htp cpe	3,251	2,095	113,372
64A	Crown Victoria htp cpe	3,313	2,202	33,165
64B	Crown Vic htp cpe, glass top	3,321	2,272	1,999
70C	club sdn 2d	3,155	1,914	173,311
73C	Town Sedan	3,201	1,960	254,437
76B	Sunliner conv cpe	3,315	2,224	49,966

Station Wagon (wb 115.5)

		Wght	Price	Prod
59A	Ranch 2d, 6P	3,376	2,043	40,493
59B	Custom Ranch 2d, 6P	3,394	2,109	43,671
79B	Country Sedan 4d, 8P	3,536	2,287	53,209
79C	Country Squire 4d, 8P	3,538	2,392	19,011
79D	Country Sedan 4d, 6P	3,460	2,156	53,075

1955 Engines	bore×stroke	bhp	availability		
L6, 223.0	3.62×3.60	120	S-all		
V8, 272.0	3.62×3.30	162	O-all		
V8, 272.0	3.62×3.30	182	O-all		

1956

Mainline (wb 115.5)

		Wght	Price	Prod
70A	sdn 2d	3,143	1,850	106,974
70D	bus sdn 2d	3,088	1,748	8,020
73A	sdn 4d	3,183	1,895	49,448

Customline (wb 115.5)

		Wght	Price	Prod
64D	Victoria htp cpe	3,202	1,985	33,130
70B	sdn 2d	3,163	1,939	164,828
73B	sdn 4d	3,203	1,985	170,695

Fairlane (wb 115.5)

		Wght	Price	Prod
57A	Victoria htp sdn	3,369	2,249	32,111
64A	Crown Victoria htp cpe	3,289	2,337	9,209
64B	Crown Vic htp cpe, glass top	3,299	2,407	603
64C	Victoria htp cpe	3,274	2,194	177,735
70C	club sdn 2d	3,179	2,047	142,629

		Wght	Price	Prod
73C	Town Sedan	3,219	2,093	224,872
76B	Sunliner conv cpe	3,384	2,359	58,147

Station Wagon (wb 115.5)

		Wght	Price	Prod
59A	Ranch 2d, 6P	3,402	2,185	48,348
59B	Custom Ranch 2d, 6P	3,417	2,249	42,317
59C	Parklane 2d	3,432	2,428	15,186
79B	Country Sedan 4d, 8P	3,555	2,428	85,374
79C	Country Squire 4d, 8P	3,566	2,533	23,221

1956 Engines	bore×stroke	bhp	availability	
L6, 223.0	3.62×3.60	137	S-all	
V8, 272.0	3.62×3.30	173	O-Mainline, Customline	
V8, 292.0	3.75×3.30	200	O-Fairlane wgn, (202 bhp w/auto)	
V8, 312.0	3.80×3.44	215	O-all (225 bhp w/auto)	

1957

Custom (wb 116.0)

		Wght	Price	Prod
70A	sdn 2d	3,211	1,991	116,963
70D	bus sdn 2d	3,202	1,879	6,888
73A	sdn 4d	3,254	2,042	68,924

Custom 300 (wb 116.0)

		Wght	Price	Prod
70B	sdn 2d	3,224	2,105	160,360
73B	sdn 4d	3,269	2,157	194,877

Fairlane (wb 118.0)

		Wght	Price	Prod
57B	Victoria htp sdn	3,411	2,357	12,695
58A	Town Sedan 4d	3,376	2,286	52,060
63B	Victoria htp cpe	3,366	2,293	44,127
64A	club sdn 2d	3,331	2,235	39,843

Fairlane 500 (wb 118.0)

		Wght	Price	Prod
51A	Skyliner retrac conv cpe	3,916	2,942	20,766
57A	Victoria htp sdn	3,426	2,404	68,550
58B	Town Sedan 4d	3,384	2,286	193,162
63A	Victoria htp cpe	3,381	2,339	183,202
64B	club sdn 2d	3,346	2,281	93,756
76B	Sunliner conv cpe	3,536	2,505	77,726

Station Wagon (wb 116.0)

		Wght	Price	Prod
59A	Ranch 2d, 6P	3,455	2,301	60,486
59B	Del Rio 2d, 6P	3,462	2,397	46,105
79C	Country Sedan 4d, 9P	3,614	2,556	49,638
79D	Country Sedan 4d, 6P	3,525	2,451	137,251
79E	Country Squire 4d, 9P	3,628	2,684	27,690

1957 Engines	bore×stroke	bhp	availability	
L6, 223.0	3.62×3.60	144	S-all exc 51A	
V8, 272.0	3.62×3.30	190	S-51A; O-others	
V8, 292.0	3.75×3.30	212	O-Fairlane, Fairlane 500, wgns	
V8, 312.0	3.80×3.44	245	O-all	

1958

Custom (wb 116.0)

		Wght	Price	Prod
70A	sdn 2d	3,250	2,055	36,272
70D	bus sdn	3,227	1,967	4,062
73A	sdn 4d	3,278	2,109	27,811

Custom 300 (wb 116.0)

		Wght	Price	Prod
70B	sdn 2d	3,300	2,305	137,169
73B	sdn 4d	3,328	2,159	135,557

Fairlane (wb 118.0)

		Wght	Price	Prod
57B	Victoria htp sdn	3,450	2,419	5,868
58A	Town Sedan 4d	3,427	2,275	57,490
63B	Victoria htp cpe	3,373	2,354	16,416
64A	club sdn 2d	3,375	2,221	38,366

Fairlane 500 (wb 118.0)

		Wght	Price	Prod
51A	Skyliner retrac conv cpe	4,069	3,163	14,713
57A	Victoria htp sdn	3,488	2,499	36,509
58B	sdn 4d	3,452	2,428	105,698
63A	Victoria htp cpe	3,390	2,435	80,439
64B	club sdn 2d	3,380	2,374	34,041
76B	Sunliner conv	3,556	2,650	35,029

Station Wagon (wb 116.0)

		Wght	Price	Prod
59A	Ranch 2d, 6P	3,552	2,397	34,578
59B	Del Rio 2d, 6P	3,734	2,503	12,687
79A	Ranch 4d, 6P	3,608	2,451	32,854
79C	Country Sedan 4d, 9P	3,682	2,664	20,702
79D	Country Sedan 4d, 6P	3,614	2,557	68,772
79E	Country Squire 4d, 9P	3,718	2,794	15,020

1958 Engines	bore×stroke	bhp	availability	
L6, 223.0	3.62×3.60	145	S-all exc 51A	
V8, 292.0	3.75×3.30	205	S-51A; O-others	
V8, 332.0	4.00×3.30	240	O-wgns (265 bhp w/auto)	
V8, 332.0	4.00×3.30	265	O-all	
V8, 352.0	4.00×3.50	300	O-all	

1959

Custom 300 (wb 118.0)

		Wght	Price	Prod
58E	sdn 4d	3,436	2,273	249,553
64F	sdn 2d	3,360	2,219	228,576
64G	bus sdn	3,334	2,132	4,084

Fairlane (wb 118.0)

		Wght	Price	Prod
58A	Town Sedan 4d	3,466	2,411	64,663
64A	club sdn 2d	3,382	2,357	35,126

Fairlane 500 (wb 118.0)

		Wght	Price	Prod
57A	Victoria htp sdn	3,502	2,602	9,308
58B	sdn 4d	3,468	2,530	35,670
63A	Victoria htp cpe	3,416	2,537	23,892
64B	club sdn 2d	3,388	2,476	10,141

Galaxie (wb 118.0)

		Wght	Price	Prod
51A	Skyliner retrac htp cpe	4,064	3,346	12,915
54A	sdn 4d	3,456	2,582	183,108
64H	club sdn 2d	3,388	2,528	52,848
65A	Victoria htp cpe	3,428	2,589	121,869
75A	Victoria htp sdn	3,544	2,654	47,728
76B	Sunliner conv cpe	3,578	2,839	45,868

Station Wagon (wb 118.0)

		Wght	Price	Prod
59C	Ranch 2d, 6P	3,640	2,567	45,588
59D	Del Rio 2d, 6P	3,664	2,678	8,663
71E	Country Sedan 4d, 9P	3,818	2,829	28,811
71F	Country Sedan 4d, 6P	3,768	2,745	94,601
71G	Country Squire 4d, 9P	3,808	2,958	24,336
71H	Ranch 4d, 6P	3,736	2,634	67,339

1959 Engines	bore×stroke	bhp	availability	
L6, 223.0	3.62×3.60	145	S-all exc 51A	
V8, 292.0	3.75×3.30	200	S-51A; O-others	
V8, 332.0	4.00×3.30	225	O-all	
V8, 352.0	4.00×3.50	300	O-all	

1960

Falcon (wb 109.5)

		Wght	Price	Prod
58A	sdn 4d	2,288	1,974	167,896
59A	wgn 2d	2,540	2,225	27,552
64A	sdn 2d	2,259	1,912	193,470
71A	wgn 4d	2,575	2,287	46,758

Custom 300 (wb 119.0)		Wght	Price	Prod
58F	sdn 4d	3,576	2,284	572
64H	sdn 2d	3,465	2,230	302

Fairlane (wb 119.0)		Wght	Price	Prod
58E	sdn 4d	3,656	2,311	109,801
64F	sdn 2d	3,582	2,257	93,256
64G	bus sdn	3,555	2,170	1,733

Fairlane 500 (wb 119.0)		Wght	Price	Prod
58A	Town Sedan 4d	3,663	2,388	153,234
64A	club sdn 2d	3,586	2,334	91,041

Galaxie (wb 119.0)		Wght	Price	Prod
54A	Town Sedan 4d	3,684	2,603	104,784
62A	club sdn 2d	3,603	2,549	31,866
63A	Starliner htp cpe	3,617	2,610	68,461
75A	Victoria htp sdn	3,692	2,675	39,215
76B	Sunliner conv cpe	3,791	2,860	44,762

Station Wagon (wb 119.0)		Wght	Price	Prod
59C	Ranch 2d, 6P	3,881	2,586	27,136
71E	Country Sedan 4d, 9P	4,058	2,837	19,277
71F	Country Sedan 4d, 6P	4,012	2,752	59,302
71G	Country Squire 4d, 9P	4,072	2,967	22,237
71H	Ranch 4d, 6P	3,998	2,656	43,872

1960 Engines	bore×stroke	bhp	availability
L6, 144.3	3.50×2.50	90	S-Falcon only
L6, 223.0	3.62×3.60	145	S-all exc Falcon
V8, 292.0	3.75×3.30	185	O-all exc Falcon
V8, 352.0	4.00×3.50	235	O-all exc Falcon
V8, 352.0	4.00×3.50	300	O-all exc Falcon

1961

Falcon (wb 109.5)		Wght	Price	Prod
58A	sdn 4d	2,289	1,976	159,761
59A	wgn 2d	2,525	2,227	32,045
62A	Futura cpe	2,322	2,162	44,470
64A	sdn 2d (inc 50 Economy sdns)	2,254	1,914	150,032
71A	wgn 4d	2,558	2,270	87,933

Custom 300 (wb 119.0)		Wght	Price	Prod
58F	sdn 4d	3,516	—	303
64H	sdn 2d	3,405	—	49

Fairlane (wb 119.0)		Wght	Price	Prod
58E	sdn 4d	3,634	2,317	96,602
64F	sdn 2d	3,536	2,263	66,875

Fairlane 500 (wb 119.0)		Wght	Price	Prod
58A	sdn 4d	3,642	2,432	98,917
64A	sdn 2d	3,551	2,378	42,468

Galaxie (wb 119.0)		Wght	Price	Prod
54A	sdn 4d	3,619	2,592	141,823
62A	sdn 2d	3,537	2,538	27,780
63A	Starliner htp cpe	3,566	2,599	29,669
65A	Victoria htp cpe	3,594	2,599	75,437
75A	Victoria htp sdn	3,637	2,664	30,342
76B	Sunliner conv cpe	3,743	2,849	44,614

Station Wagon (wb 119.0)		Wght	Price	Prod
59C	Ranch 2d, 6P	3,865	2,588	12,042
71E	Country Sedan 4d, 9P	4,011	2,858	16,356
71F	Country Sedan 4d, 6P	3,983	2,754	46,311
71G	Country Squire 4d, 9P	4,015	3,013	14,657
71H	Ranch 4d, 6P	3,960	2,658	30,292
71J	Country Squire 4d, 6P	3,969	2,943	16,961

1961 Engines	bore×stroke	bhp	availability
L6, 144.3	3.50×2.50	85	S-Falcon
L6, 170.0	3.50×2.94	101	O-Falcon
L6, 223.0	3.62×3.30	135	S-all exc Falcon
V8, 292.0	3.75×3.30	175	S-all exc Falcon
V8, 352.0	4.00×3.50	220	O-all exc Falcon
V8, 390.0	4.05×3.78	300	O-all exc Falcon

1962

Falcon (wb 109.5)		Wght	Price	Prod
58A	sdn 4d	2,279	2,047	126,041
58B	Deluxe sdn 4d	2,285	2,133	
59A	wgn 2d	2,539	2,298	20,025
59B	Deluxe wgn 2d	2,545	2,384	
62C	Futura cpe	2,343	2,273	17,011
64A	sdn 2d	2,243	1,985	143,650
64B	Deluxe sdn 2d	2,249	2,071	
71A	wgn 4d	2,575	2,341	66,819
71B	Deluxe wgn 4d	2,581	2,427	
71C	Squire wgn 4d	2,591	2,603	22,583

Fairlane (wb 115.5)		Wght	Price	Prod
54A	sdn 4d	2,848	2,216	45,342
62A	sdn 2d	2,815	2,154	34,264
54B	500 sdn 4d	2,865	2,304	129,258
62B	500 sdn 2d	2,832	2,242	68,624
62C	500 spt cpe	2,928	2,403	19,628

Galaxie (wb 119.0)		Wght	Price	Prod
54B	sdn 4d	3,636	2,507	115,594
62B	sdn 2d	3,554	2,453	54,930

Galaxie 500 (wb 119.0)		Wght	Price	Prod
54A	sdn 4d	3,650	2,667	174,195
62A	sdn 2d	3,568	2,613	27,824
65A	Victoria htp cpe	3,568	2,674	87,562
65B	XL Victoria htp cpe	3,672	2,268	28,412
75A	Victoria htp sdn	3,640	2,739	30,778
76A	Sunliner conv cpe	3,730	2,924	42,646
76B	XL Sunliner conv cpe	3,831	3,518	13,183

Station Wagon (wb 119.0)		Wght	Price	Prod
71A	Country Squire 4d, 9P	4,022	3,088	15,666
71B	Country Sedan 4d, 6P	3,992	2,829	47,635
71C	Country Sedan 4d, 9P	4,010	2,933	16,562
71D	Ranch 4d, 6P	3,968	2,733	33,674
71E	Country Squire 4d, 6P	4,006	3,018	16,114

1962 Engines	bore×stroke	bhp	availability
L6, 144.3	3.50×2.50	85	S-Falcon
L6, 170.0	3.50×2.94	101	O-Falcon
L6, 223.0	3.62×3.60	138	S-all exc Falcon
V8, 221.0	3.50×2.87	145	O-Fairlane
V8, 260.0	3.80×2.87	164	O-Fairlane
V8, 292.0	3.75×3.30	170	S-76B; O-all exc Falc, Fair
V8, 352.0	4.00×3.50	220	O-all exc Falcon, Fairlane
V8, 390.0	4.05×3.78	300/340	O-all exc Falcon, Fairlane
V8, 390.0	4.05×3.78	375/401	O-all exc Falcon, Fairlane

1963

Series 0 Falcon (wb 109.5)		Wght	Price	Prod
54A	sdn 4d	2,337	2,047	62,365
62A	sdn 2d	2,300	1,985	70,630

Series 10 Falcon Futura (wb 109.5)		Wght	Price	Prod
54B	sdn 4d	2,345	2,161	31,736
62B	sdn 2d	2,308	2,116	27,018

		Wght	Price	Prod
63B	htp cpe	2,438	2,198	28,496
63C	Sprint htp cpe	2,438	2,320	10,479
76A	conv cpe	2,645	2,470	31,192
76B	Sprint conv cpe	2,645	2,600	4,602

Series 20 Falcon Wagon (wb 109.5)

59A	wgn 2d	2,580	2,298	7,322
59B	Deluxe wgn 2d	2,586	2,384	4,269
71A	wgn 4d	2,617	2,341	18,484
71B	Deluxe wgn 4d	2,623	2,427	23,477
71C	Squire wgn 4d	2,639	2,603	8,269

Series 30 Fairlane (wb 115.5)

54A	sdn 4d	2,930	2,216	44,454
62A	sdn 2d	2,890	2,154	28,984
71B	Cus Ranch Wagon 4d	3,298	2,613	29,612
71D	Ranch Wagon 4d	3,281	2,525	24,006
71E	Squire Wagon 4d	3,295	2,781	7,983

Series 40 Fairlane 500 (wb 115.5)

54B	sdn 4d	2,945	2,304	104,175
62B	sdn 2d	2,905	2,242	34,764
65A	htp cpe	2,923	2,324	41,641
65B	htp cpe, bkt sts	2,929	2,504	28,268

Series 50 300 (wb 119.0)

54E	sdn 4d	3,627	2,378	44,142
62E	sdn 2d	3,547	2,324	26,010

Series 50 Galaxie (wb 119.0)

54B	sdn 4d	3,647	2,507	82,419
62B	sdn 2d	3,567	2,453	30,335

Series 60 Galaxie 500 (wb 119.0)

54A	sdn 4d	3,667	2,667	205,722
62A	sdn 2d	3,587	2,613	21,137
63B	XL htp cpe, fstbk	3,772	2,674	134,370
65A	htp cpe	3,599	2,674	49,733
75A	htp sdn	3,679	2,739	39,154
76A	Sunliner conv cpe	3,757	2,924	29,713

Series 70 Station Wagon (wb 119.0)

71A	Country Squire 4d, 9P	4,003	3,088	19,567
71B	Country Sedan 4d, 6P	3,977	2,829	64,954
71C	Country Sedan 4d, 9P	3,989	2,933	22,250
71E	Country Squire 4d, 6P	3,991	3,018	20,359

1963 Engines	bore×stroke	bhp	availability
L6, 144.3	3.50×2.50	85	S-Falcon
L6, 170.0	3.50×2.94	101	O-Falcon
L6, 200.0	3.68×3.13	116	S-Fairlane
L6, 223.0	3.62×3.60	138	S-all exc Falcon, Fairlane
V8, 221.0	3.50×2.87	145	O-Fairlane
V8, 260.0	3.80×2.87	164	S-Falcon Sprint; O-others
V8, 289.0	4.00×2.87	271	O-Fairlane
V8, 352.0	4.00×3.50	220	O-all exc Falcon, Fairlane
V8, 390.0	4.05×3.78	300/330	O-all exc Falcon, Fairlane
V8, 406.0	4.13×3.78	385/405	O-all exc Falcon, Fairlane
V8, 427.0	4.23×3.78	410/425	O-all exc Falcon, Fairlaine

1964

Series 0 Falcon (wb 109.5)

		Wght	Price	Prod
01	sdn 4d	2,365	1,996	36,441
01	Deluxe sdn 2d	2,380	2,096	28,411
02	sdn 4d	2,400	2,058	27,722
02	Deluxe sdn 4d	2,420	2,158	26,532

Series 10 Falcon Futura (wb 109.5)

11	htp cpe, bkt seats	2,545	2,325	8,607
12	conv cpe, bkt seats	2,735	2,597	2,980
13	Sprint htp cpe	2,813	2,436	13,830

		Wght	Price	Prod
14	Sprint conv cpe	3,008	2,671	4,278
15	conv cpe	2,710	2,481	13,220
16	sdn 4d	2,410	2,176	38,032
17	htp cpe	2,515	2,209	32,608
19	sdn 2d	2,375	2,127	16,833

Series 20 Falcon Wagon (wb 109.5)

21	wgn 2d	2,660	2,326	6,034
22	wgn 4d	2,695	2,360	17,779
24	Deluxe wgn 4d	2,715	2,446	20,697
26	Squire wgn 4d	2,720	2,622	6,766

Series 30 Fairlane (wb 115.5)

31	sdn 2d	2,855	2,194	20,421
32	sdn 4d	2,895	2,235	36,693
38	Ranch wgn 4d	3,290	2,531	20,980

Series 40 Fairlane 500 (wb 115.5)

41	sdn 2d	2,863	2,276	23,447
42	sdn 4d	2,910	2,317	86,919
43	htp cpe	2,925	2,341	42,733
47	htp cpe, bkt sts	2,945	2,502	21,431
48	Ranch Cus wgn 4d	3,310	2,612	24,962

Series 50 Custom (wb 119.0)

51	500 sdn 2d	3,559	2,464	20,619
52	500 sdn 4d	3,659	2,518	68,828
53	sdn 2d	3,529	2,361	41,359
54	sdn 4d	3,619	2,415	57,964

Series 60 Galaxie 500 (wb 119.0)

60	XL htp sdn	3,722	3,298	14,661
61	sdn 2d	3,574	2,624	13,041
62	sdn 4d	3,674	2,678	198,805
64	htp sdn	3,689	2,750	49,242
66	htp cpe	3,584	2,685	206,998
—	Sunliner conv cpe	3,759	2,947	37,311
68	XL htp cpe	3,622	3,233	58,306
69	XL conv cpe	3,687	3,495	15,169

Series 70 Station Wagon (wb 119.0)

72	Country Sedan 4d, 6P	3,973	2,840	68,578
74	Country Sedan 4d, 9P	3,983	2,944	25,661
76	Country Squire 4d, 6P	3,988	3,029	23,570
78	Country Squire 4d, 9P	3,998	3,099	23,120

1964 Engines	bore×stroke	bhp	availability
L6, 144.3	3.50×2.50	85	S-Flcn exc conv, Sprnt, Del wgns
L6, 170.0	3.50×2.94	101	S-Flcn conv, Sprnt, Del wgn; O-other Flcn
L6, 200.0	3.68×3.13	116	S-Fairlane; O-Falcon
L6, 223.0	3.62×3.60	138	S-all exc Fairlane, Falcon
V8, 260.0	3.80×2.87	116	S-Flcn Sprnt, Fairlane; O-Flcn
V8, 289.0	4.00×2.87	195/271	S-60, 68, 69; O-all exc Flcn
V8, 352.0	4.00×3.50	250	O-all exc Falcon, Fairlane
V8, 390.0	4.05×3.78	300/330	O-all exc Falcon, Fairlane
V8, 427.0	4.23×3.78	425	O-all exc Falcon, Fairlane

1965

Series 0 Falcon (wb 109.5)

		Wght	Price	Prod
01	sdn 4d	2,366	2,020	35,858
01	Deluxe sdn 2d	2,381	2,120	13,824
02	sdn 4d	2,406	2,082	30,186
02	Deluxe sdn 4d	2,426	2,182	13,850

Series 10 Falcon Futura (wb 109.5)

13	Sprint htp cpe	2,749	2,337	2,806
14	Sprint conv cpe	2,971	2,671	300
15	conv cpe	2,673	2,481	6,215
16	sdn 4d	2,413	2,192	33,985

		Wght	Price	Prod
17	htp cpe	2,491	2,226	25,754
19	sdn 2d	2,373	2,144	11,670

Series 20 Falcon Wagon (wb 109.5)

21	wgn 2d	2,611	2,333	4,891
22	wgn 4d	2,651	2,367	14,911
24	Deluxe wgn 4d (Futura)	2,667	2,506	12,548
26	Squire wgn 4d	2,669	2,665	6,703

Series 30 Fairlane (wb 115.5)

31	sdn 2d	2,902	2,230	13,685
32	sdn 4d	2,954	2,271	25,378
38	wgn 4d	3,279	2,567	13,911

Series 40 Fairlane 500 (wb 115.5)

41	sdn 2d	2,901	2,312	16,092
42	sdn 4d	2,959	2,353	77,836
43	htp cpe	2,973	2,377	41,405
47	htp cpe, bkt sts	2,984	2,538	15,141
48	wgn 4d	3,316	2,648	20,506

Series 50 Custom (wb 119.0)

51	sdn 2d	3,336	2,464	49,034
52	sdn 4d	3,408	2,518	96,393
53	500 sdn 2d	3,306	2,361	19,603
54	500 sdn 4d	3,378	2,415	71,727

Series 60 Galaxie 500 (wb 119.0)

60	LTD htp sdn	3,578	3,313	68,038
62	sdn 4d	3,440	2,678	181,183
64	htp sdn	3,480	2,765	49,982
65	conv cpe	3,592	2,950	31,930
66	htp cpe	3,380	2,685	157,284
67	LTD htp cpe	3,486	3,233	37,691
68	XL htp cpe	3,497	3,233	28,141
69	XL conv cpe	3,665	3,498	9,849

Series 70 Station Wagon (wb 119.0)

71	Ranch 4d, 6P	3,869	2,763	30,817
72	Country Sedan 4d, 6P	3,879	2,855	59,693
74	Country Sedan 4d, 9P	3,893	2,959	32,344
76	Country Squire 4d, 6P	3,925	3,104	24,308
78	Country Squire 4d, 9P	3,937	3,174	30,502

1965 Engines	bore×stroke	bhp	availability
L6, 170.0	3.50×2.94	101	S-Flcn exc Futura, Squire until 9/25/64
L6, 200.0	3.68×3.13	120	S-Futura/Squire, Fairlane; O-Flcn
L6, 240.0	4.00×3.18	150	S-all exc Flcn, Fairlane, LTD, XL
V8, 289.0	4.00×2.87	200–271	S-LTD, XL;O-others
V8, 352.0	4.00×3.50	250	O-all exc Falcon, Fairlane
V8, 390.0	4.05×3.78	300/330	O-all exc Falcon, Fairlane
V8, 427.0	4.23×3.78	425	O-all exc Falcon, Fairlane

1966

Series 0 Falcon (wb 110.5; wgn-113.0)		Wght	Price	Prod
01	club cpe	2,519	2,060	41,432
02	sdn 4d	2,559	2,114	34,685
06	wgn 4d	3,037	2,442	16,653

Series 10 Falcon Futura (wb 110.9; wgn-113.0)

11	club cpe	2,527	2,183	21,997
12	sdn 4d	2,567	2,237	34,039
13	spt cpe	2,597	2,328	20,289
16	wgn 4d	3,045	2,553	13,574

Series 30 Fairlane (wb 116; wgn 113.0)

31	club cpe	2,832	2,240	13,498
32	sdn 4d	2,877	2,280	26,170
38	wgn 4d	3,267	2,589	12,379

Series 40 Fairlane 500 (wb 116; wgn-113.0)		Wght	Price	Prod
40	XL GT htp cpe, V8	3,493	2,843	33,015
41	club cpe	2,839	3,317	14,118
42	sdn 4d	2,884	2,357	68,635
43	htp cpe	2,941	2,378	75,947
44	XL GT conv cpe	3,070	3,068	4,327
45	conv cpe	3,169	2,603	9,299
46	XL conv cpe	3,184	2,768	4,560
47	XL htp cpe	2,969	2,533	23,942
48	Deluxe wgn 4d	3,277	2,665	19,826
49	Squire wgn 4d	3,285	2,796	11,558

Series 50 Custom (wb 119.0)

51	500 sdn 2d	3,397	2,481	28,789
52	500 sdn 4d	3,466	2,533	109,449
53	sdn 2d	3,355	2,380	32,292
54	sdn 4d	3,455	2,432	72,245

Series 60 Galaxie 500 (wb 119.0)

60	LTD htp sdn	3,649	3,278	69,400
61	7 Litre htp cpe	3,914	3,621	8,705
62	sdn 4d	3,478	2,677	171,886
63	7 Litre conv cpe, V8	4,059	3,872	2,368
64	htp sdn	3,548	2,762	54,884
65	conv cpe	3,655	2,934	27,454
66	htp cpe	3,459	2,685	198,532
67	LTD htp cpe	3,601	3,201	31,696
68	XL htp cpe	3,616	3,231	25,715
69	XL conv cpe	3,761	3,480	6,360

Series 70 Station Wagon (wb 119.0)

71	Ranch 4d	3,941	2,793	33,306
72	Country Sedan 4d, 6P	3,956	2,882	55,616
74	Country Sedan 4d, 9P	3,997	2,999	36,633
76	Country Squire 4d, 6P	4,026	3,182	27,645
78	Country Squire 4d, 9P	4,040	3,265	41,953

1966 Engines	bore×stroke	bhp	availability
L6, 170.0	3.50×2.94	105	S-Falcon
L6, 200.0	3.68×3.13	120	S-Flcn Futura/wgn, Fair exc GT, GTA; O-Flcn
L6, 240.0	4.00×3.18	150	S-all exc Flcn, Fair; O-Flcn wgns
V8, 289.0	4.00×2.87	200/225	S-XL, LTD; O-Flcn, Fair exc GT, GTA; 50, 60, 70 exc 7L
V8, 352.0	4.00×3.50	250	O-all exc 7L, Fairlane, Falcon
V8, 390.0	4.05×3.78	265	O-all exc 7L, Fair GT/GTA, Flcn
V8, 390.0	4.05×3.78	315	O-all exc 7L, Fairlane, Falcon
V8, 390.0	4.05×3.78	335	S-Fair GT/GTA; O-other Fair
V8, 427.0	4.23×3.78	410/425	O-all exc 7L, 70, Fairlane, Flcn
V8, 428.0	4.13×3.98	345	S-7L; O-others exc Fairlane, Flcn

1967

Falcon (wb 110.9; wgn-113.0)		Wght	Price	Prod
10	sdn 2d	2,520	2,118	16,082
11	sdn 4d	2,551	2,167	13,554
12	wgn 4d	3,030	2,497	5,553

Falcon Futura (wb 110.9; wgns-113.0)

20	club cpe	2,528	2,280	6,287
21	sdn 4d	2,559	2,322	11,254
22	spt cpe	3,062	2,437	7,053
23	Squire wgn 4d	2,556	2,609	4,552

Fairlane (wb 116.0; wgns-113.0)

30	sdn 2d	2,832	2,297	10,628
31	sdn 4d	2,867	2,339	19,740
32	Ranch wgn 4d	3,283	2,643	10,881
33	500 club cpe	2,840	2,377	8,473
34	500 sdn 4d	2,887	2,417	51,522

		Wght	Price	Prod
35	500 htp cpe	2,927	2,439	70,135
36	500 conv cpe	3,244	2,664	5,428
37	Deluxe wgn 4d	3,291	2,718	15,902
38	Country Squire wgn 4d	3,302	2,902	8,348
Fairlane 500XL (wb 116.0)				
40	htp cpe	2,955	2,724	14,871
41	conv cpe	3,272	2,950	1,943
42	GT htp cpe	3,301	2,839	18,670
43	GT conv cpe	3,607	3,064	2,117
Series 50 Custom (wb 119.0)				
50	sdn 2d	3,430	2,441	18,107
51	sdn 4d	3,488	2,496	41,417
52	500 sdn 2d	3,482	2,553	18,146
53	500 sdn 4d	3,490	2,595	83,260
Galaxie 500 (wb 119.0)				
54	sdn 4d	3,500	2,732	130,063
55	htp cpe	3,503	2,755	197,388
56	htp sdn	3,571	2,808	57,087
57	conv cpe	3,682	3,003	19,068
58	XL htp sdn	3,594	3,243	18,174
59	XL conv cpe	3,794	3,103	6,101
LTD (wb 119.0)				
62	htp cpe	3,626	3,362	46,036
64	sdn 4d	3,795	3,298	12,491
66	htp sdn	3,676	3,363	51,978
Station Wagon (wb 119.0)				
70	Ranch 4d, 6P	3,930	2,836	23,932
71	Country Sedan 4d, 6P	3,943	2,935	50,818
72	Country Sedan 4d, 9P	4,023	3,061	34,377
73	Country Squire 4d, 6P	3,990	3,234	25,600
74	Country Squire 4d, 9P	4,030	3,359	44,024

1967 Engines	bore×stroke	bhp	availability
L6, 170.0	3.50×2.94	105	S-Falcon exc Futura, wagons
L6, 200.0	3.68×3.13	120	S-Flcn Futura/wgns, Fair exc GTs
L6, 240.0	4.00×3.18	150	S-all exc Falcon, Fairlane
V8, 289.0	4.00×2.87	200	S-Fair GT, 500XL, LTD; O-others
V8, 289.0	4.00×2.87	225	O-Falcon
V8, 390.0	4.05×3.78	270	O-Fairlane
V8, 390.0	4.05×3.78	315	O-Cus, Gal, LTD, Station Wgn
V8, 390.0	4.05×3.78	320	O-Fairlane
V8, 427.0	4.23×3.78	410/425	O-all exc Falcon
V8, 428.0	4.13×3.98	345	O-all exc Falcon, Fairlane

1968

Falcon (wb 110.9; wgn-113.0)		Wght	Price	Prod
10	sdn 2d	2,680	2,252	29,166
11	sdn 4d	2,714	2,301	36,443
12	wgn 4d	3,123	2,617	15,576
Falcon Futura (wb 110.9; wgn-113.0)				
20	sdn 2d	2,685	2,415	10,633
21	sdn 4d	2,719	2,456	18,733
22	spt cpe	2,713	2,541	10,077
23	wgn 4d	3,123	2,728	10,761
Fairlane (wb 116.0; wgn-113.0)				
30	htp cpe	3,028	2,456	44,683
31	sdn 4d	2,986	2,464	18,146
32	wgn 4d	3,333	2,770	14,800
33	500 htp cpe	3,066	2,591	33,282
34	500 sdn 4d	3,024	2,543	42,930
35	500 fstbk htp cpe	3,080	2,566	32,452
36	500 conv cpe	3,226	2,822	3,761
37	500 wgn 4d	3,377	2,880	10,190

Torino (wb 116.0; wgn-113.0)		Wght	Price	Prod
38	Squire wgn 4d	3,425	3,032	14,773
40	htp cpe	3,098	2,710	35,964
41	sdn 4d	3,062	2,688	17,962
42	GT fstbk htp cpe	3,208	2,747	74,135
43	GT conv cpe	3,352	3,001	5,310
44	GT htp cpe	3,194	2,772	23,939
Custom (wb 119.0)				
50	sdn 2d	3,471	2,584	18,485
51	sdn 4d	3,498	2,642	45,980
52	500 sdn 2d	3,460	2,699	8,983
53	500 sdn 4d	3,511	2,741	49,398
Galaxie 500 (wb 119.0)				
54	sdn 4d	3,516	2,864	117,877
55	fstbk htp cpe	3,534	2,881	69,760
56	htp sdn	3,562	2,936	55,461
57	conv cpe	3,679	3,108	11,832
58	htp cpe	3,540	2,916	84,332
60	XL fstbk htp cpe	3,588	2,985	50,048
61	XL conv cpe	3,745	3,214	6,066
LTD (wb 119.0)				
62	htp cpe	3,679	3,153	54,163
64	sdn 4d	3,596	3,135	22,834
66	htp sdn	3,642	3,206	61,755
Station Wagon (wb 119.0)				
70	Ranch 4d, 6P	3,925	3,000	18,237
71	Ranch 500 4d, 6P	3,935	3,063	18,181
72	Ranch 500 4d, 9P	3,981	3,176	13,421
73	Country Sedan 4d, 6P	3,944	3,184	39,335
74	Country Sedan 4d, 9P	4,001	3,295	29,374
75	Country Squire 4d, 6P	4,013	3,539	33,994
76	Country Squire 4d, 9P	4,059	3,619	57,776

1968 Engines	bore×stroke	bhp	availability
L6, 170.0	3.50×2.94	100	S-base Falcon cpes, sdns
L6, 200.0	3.68×3.13	115	S-Fair, Tor, Flcn Fut wgn; O-Flcn
L6, 240.0	4.00×3.18	150	S-all exc Futura, Tor GT, LTD
V8, 289.0	4.00×2.87	195	O-Falcon
V8, 302.0	4.00×3.00	210	S-LTD, Tor GT; O-all
V8, 302.0	4.00×3.00	230	O-Falcon, Fairlane, Torino
V8, 390.0	4.05×3.78	265	O-all exc Falcon
V8, 390.0	4.05×3.78	315	O-all exc Falcon, Fairlane
V8, 390.0	4.05×3.78	335	O-Fairlane
V8, 427.0	4.23×3.78	390	O-Fairlane/Torino htps
V8, 428.0	4.13×3.98	340	O-all exc Falcon, Fairlane

1969

Falcon (wb 110.9; wgn-113.0)		Wght	Price	Prod
10	sdn 2d	2,700	2,283	29,262
11	sdn 4d	2,735	2,333	22,719
12	wgn 4d	3,100	2,660	11,568
Falcon Futura (wb 110.9; wgn-113.0)				
20	sdn 2d	2,715	2,461	6,482
21	sdn 4d	2,748	2,498	11,850
22	spt cpe	2,738	2,598	5,931
23	wgn 4d	3,120	2,771	7,203
Fairlane (wb 116.0; wgn-113.0)				
30	htp cpe	3,079	2,499	85,630
31	sdn 4d	3,065	2,488	27,296
32	wgn 4d	3,441	2,841	10,882
33	500 htp cpe	3,090	2,626	28,179
34	500 sdn 4d	3,082	2,568	40,888
35	500 fstbk htp cpe	3,137	2,601	29,849
36	500 conv cpe	3,278	2,851	2,264
37	500 wgn 4d	3,469	2,951	12,869

Torino (wb 116.0; wgn-113.0)		Wght	Price	Prod
38	Squire wgn 4d	3,503	3,107	14,472
40	htp cpe	3,143	2,754	20,789
41	sdn 4d	3,128	2,733	11,971
42	GT fstbk htp cpe	3,220	2,840	61,319
43	GT conv cpe	3,356	3,090	2,552
44	GT htp cpe	3,173	2,865	17,951

Custom (wb 121.0)				
50	sdn 2d	3,605	2,649	15,439
51	sdn 4d	3,628	2,691	45,653
52	500 sdn 2d	3,590	2,748	7,585
53	500 sdn 4d	3,640	2,790	45,761
70	Ranch wgn 4d	4,089	3,091	17,489
71	500 wgn 4d, 6P	4,102	3,155	16,432
72	500 wgn 4d, 9P	4,152	3,268	11,563

Galaxie 500 (wb 121.0)				
54	sdn 4d	3,690	2,914	104,606
55	fstbk htp cpe	3,700	2,930	63,921
56	htp sdn	3,725	2,983	64,031
57	conv cpe	3,860	3,159	6,910
58	htp cpe	3,655	2,982	71,920
73	Country Sedan wgn 4d, 6P	4,087	3,274	36,387
74	Country Sedan wgn 4d, 9P	4,112	3,390	27,517

XL (wb 121.0)				
60	fstbk htp cpe	3,805	3,069	54,557
61	conv cpe	3,955	3,297	7,402

LTD (wb 119.0)				
62	htp cpe	3,745	3,251	111,565
64	sdn 4d	3,745	3,209	63,709
66	htp sdn	3,840	3,278	113,168
75	Country Squire wgn 4d, 6P	4,202	3,661	46,445
76	Country Squire wgn 4d, 9P	4,227	3,738	82,790

1969 Engines	bore×stroke	bhp	availability
L6, 170.0	3.50×2.94	100	S-Falcon exc Futura
L6, 200.0	3.68×3.13	115	S-Futura
L6, 240.0	4.00×3.18	150	S-all exc Flcn, Fair, Tor GT, LTD
L6, 250.0	3.68×3.91	155	S-Fairlane, Tor exc GT, Cobra
V8, 302.0	4.00×3.00	220	S-LTD, Tor GT; O-others
V8, 351.0	4.00×3.50	250	O-Fairlane, Tor exc Cobra
V8, 351.0	4.00×3.50	290	O-Fairlane, Tor exc Cobra
V8, 390.0	4.05×3.78	265	O-full-size
V8, 390.0	4.05×3.78	320	O-Fairlane, Tor exc Cobra
V8, 428.0	4.13×3.98	335*	S-Tor Cobra; O-Fairlane
V8, 429.0	4.36×3.59	320/360	O-full-size

*Available in standard and Ram Air versions.

1970

Maverick (wb 103.0)		Wght	Price	Prod
91	sdn 2d	2,411	1,995	578,914

Falcon (wb 110.9, wgn-113.0)				
10	sdn 2d	2,708	2,390	4,373
11	sdn 4d	2,753	2,438	5,301
12	wgn 4d	3,155	2,767	1,624

Falcon Futura (wb 110.9; wgn-113.0)				
20	sdn 2d	2,727	2,542	1,129
21	sdn 4d	2,764	2,579	2,262
23	wgn 4d	3,191	2,878	1,005

"1970½" Falcon (wb 117.0)				
26	sdn 2d	3,100	2,460	26,071
27	sdn 4d	3,116	2,500	30,443
40	wgn 4d	3,483	2,801	10,539

Fairlane 500 (wb 117.0; wgn-114.0)		Wght	Price	Prod
28	sdn 4d	3,166	2,627	25,780
29	htp cpe	3,178	2,660	70,636
41	wgn 4d	3,558	2,957	13,613

Torino (wb 117.0; wgn-114.0)				
30	htp cpe	3,223	2,722	49,826
31	sdn 4d	3,208	2,689	30,117
32	htp sdn	3,239	2,795	14,312
33	Brougham htp cpe	3,293	3,006	16,911
34	fstbk htp cpe	3,261	2,899	12,490
35	GT htp cpe	3,366	3,105	56,819
36	Brougham htp sdn	3,309	3,078	14,543
37	GT conv cpe	3,490	3,212	3,939
38	Cobra fstbk htp cpe	3,774	3,270	7,675
42	wgn 4d	3,603	3,164	10,613
43	Squire wgn 4d	3,673	3,379	13,166

Custom (wb 121.0)				
51	sdn 4d	3,545	2,850	42,849
52	500 htp cpe	3,510	2,918	2,677
53	500 sdn 4d	3,585	2,872	41,261
70	Ranch wgn 4d	4,079	3,305	15,086
71	500 wgn 4d, 6P	4,049	3,368	15,304
72	500 wgn 4d, 9P	4,137	3,481	9,943

Galaxie 500 (wb 121.0)				
54	sdn 4d	3,601	3,026	101,784
55	fstbk htp cpe	3,610	3,043	50,825
56	htp sdn	3,672	3,096	53,817
58	htp cpe	3,611	3,094	57,059
73	Country Sedan wgn 4d, 6P	4,089	3,488	32,209
74	Country Sedan wgn 4d, 9P	4,112	3,600	22,645

XL (wb 121.0)				
60	fstbk htp cpe	3,750	3,293	27,251
61	conv cpe	3,983	3,501	6,348

LTD (wb 121.0)				
62	htp cpe	3,727	3,356	96,324
62	Brougham htp cpe	3,855	3,537	
64	sdn 4d	3,701	3,307	78,306
64	Brougham sdn	3,829	3,502	
66	htp sdn	3,771	3,385	90,390
66	Brougham htp sdn	4,029	3,579	
75	Country Squire wgn 4d, 6P	4,139	3,832	39,837
76	Country Squire wgn 4d, 9P	4,185	3,909	69,077

1970 Engines	bore×stroke	bhp	availability
L6, 170.0	3.50×2.94	105	S-Maverick
L6, 200.0	3.68×3.13	120	S-Falcon; O-Maverick
L6, 240.0	4.00×3.18	150	S-full-size exc XL, LTD
L6, 250.0	3.68×3.91	155	S-Tor exc GT, Brghm, Squire, Cobra
V8, 302.0	4.00×3.00	220	S-Tor GT/Brghm/Squire, Cobra; O-others
V8, 351.0	4.00×3.50	250	S-XL, LTD, big wgns; O-all exc Flcn, Cobra
V8, 351.0	4.00×3.50	300	O-Torino exc Cobra
V8, 390.0	4.05×3.78	265	O-all full-size
V8, 429.0	4.36×3.59	320	O-all full-size
V8, 429.0	4.36×3.59	360	S-Tor Cobra; O-Ford, Torino
V8, 429.0	4.36×3.59	370*	O-Torino exc wgns
V8, 429.0	4.36×3.59	375	O-Torino, Cobra

*Available in standard and Ram Air versions.

1970½ Engines	bore×stroke	bhp	availability
L6, 250.0	3.68×3.91	155	S-Falcon
V8, 302.0	4.00×3.00	220	O-Falcon
V8, 351.0	4.00×3.50	250/300	O-Falcon
V8, 429.0	4.36×3.59	360	O-Falcon
V8, 429.0	4.36×3.59	370	O-Falcon (w/o Ram Air)

1971

Pinto (wb 94.2)

		Wght	Price	Prod
10	fstbk sdn 2d	1,949	1,919	288,606
11	Runabout htchbk sdn 3d	1,993	2,062	63,796

Maverick (wb 103.0; 4d-109.9)

		Wght	Price	Prod
91	fstbk sdn 2d	2,546	2,175	159,726
92	sdn 4d	2,641	2,234	73,208
93	Grabber fstbk sdn 2d	2,601	2,354	38,963

Torino (wb 117.0; wgns-114.0)

		Wght	Price	Prod
25	formal htp cpe	3,168	2,706	37,518
27	sdn 4d	3,163	2,672	29,501
40	wgn 5d	3,514	3,023	21,570
30	500 formal htp cpe	3,170	2,887	89,966
31	500 sdn 4d	3,160	2,855	35,650
32	500 htp sdn	3,196	2,959	12,724
34	500 fstbk htp cpe	3,179	2,943	11,150
42	500 wgn 5d	3,514	3,170	23,270
33	Brougham formal htp cpe V8	3,209	3,175	8,593
36	Brougham formal htp sdn V8	3,256	3,248	4,408
43	Squire wgn 5d V8	3,583	3,560	15,805
35	GT fstbk htp cpe V8	3,287	3,150	31,641
37	GT conv V8	3,428	3,408	1,613
38	Cobra fstbk htp cpe	3,525	3,295	3,054

Ford (wb 121.0)

		Wght	Price	Prod
51	Custom sdn 4d	3,700	3,288	41,062
70	Custom Ranch Wagon 4d V8	4,222	3,890	16,696
53	Custom 500 sdn 4d	3,705	3,426	33,765
72	Custom 500 Ranch Wagon 5d 2S V8	4,231	3,982	25,957
72	Custom 500 Ranch Wagon 5d 3S V8	4,281	4,097	
54	Galaxie 500 sdn 4d	3,782	3,594	98,130
56	Galaxie 500 htp sdn	3,838	3,665	46,595
58	Galaxie 500 htp cpe	3,783	3,628	117,139
74	G500 Ctry Sdn wgn 5d 2S V8	4,246	4,074	60,487
74	G500 Ctry Sdn wgn 5d 3S V8	4,296	4,188	
61	LTD conv V8	4,053	4,094	5,750
62	LTD htp cpe V8	3,919	3,923	103,896
63	LTD sdn 4d V8	3,981	3,931	92,260
64	LTD htp sdn V8	3,976	3,969	48,166
76	Country Squire wgn 5d 2S V8	4,306	4,380	130,644
76	Country Squire wgn 5d 3S V8	4,356	4,496	
66	LTD Brougham sdn 4d V8	4,111	4,094	26,186
67	LTD Brougham htp sdn V8	4,016	4,140	27,820
68	LTD Brougham htp cpe V8	3,945	4,097	43,303

1971 Engines

	bore×stroke	bhp	availability
L4, 98.6	3.19×3.06	75	S-Pinto
L4, 122.0	3.58×3.03	100	0-Pinto
L6, 170.0	3.50×2.94	100	S-Maverick
L6, 200.00	3.68×3.13	115	0-Maverick
L6, 240.0	4.00×3.18	140	S-Ford
L6, 250.0	3.68×3.91	145	S-Tor exc Cobra; O-Mav
V8, 302.0	4.00×3.00	210	S-Mav, Ford Cus, Tor exc Cobra
V8, 351.0	4.00×3.50	240	S-Tor Cobra, Ford exc Cus
V8, 351.0	4.00×3.50	285	O-Torino
V8, 400.0	4.00×4.00	260	O-Ford
V8, 429.0	4.36×3.59	320/360	O-Ford
V8, 429.0	4.36×3.59	370	O-Torino

1972

Pinto (wb 94.2)

		Wght	Price	Prod
10	fstbk sdn 2d	2,061	1,960	181,002
11	Runabout htchbk sdn 3d	2,099	2,078	197,290
12	wgn 3d	2,283	2,265	101,483

Maverick (wb 103.0; 4d-109.9)

		Wght	Price	Prod
91	fstbk sdn 2d	2,654	2,140	145,931
92	sdn 4d	2,751	2,195	73,686
93	Grabber fstbk sdn 2d	2,708	2,309	35,347

Torino (wb 118.0; 2d-114.0)

		Wght	Price	Prod
25	formal htp cpe	3,374	2,673	33,530
27	sdn 4d	3,442	2,641	33,486
40	wgn 5d	3,840	2,955	22,204
30	Gran Torino Formal htp cpe	3,410	2,878	132,284
31	Gran Torino sdn 4d	3,484	2,856	102,300
42	Gran Torino wgn 5d	3,874	3,096	45,212
35	GT Sport fstbk htp cpe V8	3,470	3,094	60,794
38	Gran Torino form htp cpe V8	3,466	3,094	31,239
43	Squire wgn 5d V8	3,938	3,486	35,595

Ford (wb 121.0)

		Wght	Price	Prod
51	Custom sdn 4d	3,742	3,246	33,014
70	Custom Ranch wgn 5d V8	4,304	3,852	13,064
53	Custom 500 sdn 4d	3,808	3,377	24,870
72	C 500 Ranch Wagon 5d 2S V8	4,314	3,941	16,834
72	C 500 Ranch Wagon 5d 3S V8	4,364	4,051	
54	Galaxie 500 sdn 4d	3,848	3,537	104,167
56	Galaxie 500 htp sdn	3,910	3,604	28,939
58	Galaxie 500 htp cpe	3,852	3,572	80,855
74	G500 Ctry Sdn wgn 5d 2S V8	4,349	4,028	55,238
74	G500 Ctry Sdn wgn 5d 3S V8	4,399	4,136	
62	LTD htp cpe V8	3,999	3,882	101,048
63	LTD sdn 4d V8	4,065	3,890	104,167
64	LTD htp sdn V8	4,060	3,925	33,742
61	LTD conv V8	4,165	4,057	4,234
76	LTD Ctry Squire wgn 5d 2S V8	4,393	4,318	121,419
76	LTD Ctry Squire wgn 5d 3S V8	4,443	4,430	
66	LTD Brougham sdn 4d V8	4,095	4,031	36,909
67	LTD Brougham htp sdn V8	4,090	4,074	23,364
68	LTD B'ham formal htp cpe V8	4,031	4,034	50,409

1972 Engines

	bore×stroke	bhp	availability
L4, 98.6	3.19×3.06	54	S-Pinto exc wgn
L4, 122.0	3.58×3.03	86	S-Pinto wgn; O-Pinto
L6, 170.0	3.50×2.94	82	S-Maverick
L6, 200.0	3.68×3.13	91	O-Maverick
L6, 240.0	4.00×3.18	103	S-Ford
L6, 250.0	3.68×3.91	95	S-Torino
L6, 250.0	3.68×3.91	98	O-Maverick
V8, 302.0	4.00×3.00	140	S-Torino, Ford Cus V8
V8, 302.0	4.00×3.00	143	S-Maverick
V8, 351.0	4.00×3.50	153	S-Ford wgn; O-Ford
V8, 351.0	4.00×3.50	161	O-Torino
V8, 351.0	4.00×3.50	248	O-Torino
V8, 400.0	4.00×4.00	168	O-Torino
V8, 400.0	4.00×4.00	172	O-Ford
V8, 429.0	4.36×3.59	205	O-Torino
V8, 429.0	4.36×3.59	208	O-Ford

1973

Pinto (wb 94.2)

		Wght	Price	Prod
10	fstbk sdn2d	2,115	2,021	116,146
11	Runabout htchbk sdn 3d	2,145	2,144	150,603
12	wgn 3d	2,386	2,343	217,763

Maverick (wb 103.0; 4d-109.9)

		Wght	Price	Prod
91	fstbk sdn 2d	2,730	2,248	148,943
92	sdn 4d	2,844	2,305	110,382
93	Grabber fstbk sdn 2d	2,770	2,427	32,350

Torino (wb 118.0; 2d-114.0)

		Wght	Price	Prod
25	htp cpe	3,548	2,732	28,005
27	sdn 4d	3,620	2,701	37,524
40	wgn 5d V8	4,063	3,198	23,982
30	Gran Torino htp cpe	3,591	2,921	138,962
30	Gran Torino B'ham htp cpe	3,598	3,071	
31	Gran Torino sdn 4d	3,675	2,890	98,404
31	Gran Torino B'ham sdn 4d	3,690	3,051	

		Wght	Price	Prod
42	Gran Torino wgn 5d V8	4,097	3,344	60,738
43	Gran Torino Squire wgn 5d V8	4,129	3,559	40,023
35	Gran Torino Sport fstbk htp cpe V8	3,664	3,154	51,853
38	Gran Torino formal htp cpe V8	3,650	3,154	17,090

Ford (wb 121.0)

		Wght	Price	Prod
53	Custom 500 sdn 4d	4,059	3,606	42,549
72	C 500 Ranch Wagon 5d 2S	4,529	4,050	22,432
72	C 500 Ranch Wagon 5d 3S	4,579	4,164	
54	Galaxie 500 sdn 4d	4,086	3,771	85,654
56	Galaxie 500 htp sdn	4,102	3,833	25,802
58	Galaxie 500 htp cpe	4,034	3,778	70,808
74	G500 Country Sdn Wgn 5d 2S	4,555	4,146	51,290
74	G500 Country Sdn wgn 5d 3S	4,605	4,260	
62	LTD htp cpe	4,059	3,950	120,864
63	LTD sdn 4d	4,107	3,958	122,851
64	LTD htp sdn	4,123	4,001	28,606
76	LTD Coutnry Squire wgn 5d 2S	4,579	4,401	142,933
76	LTD Country Squire wgn 5d 3S	4,629	4,515	
66	LTD Brougham sdn 4d	4,130	4,113	49,553
67	LTD Brougham htp sdn	4,148	4,157	22,268
68	LTD Brougham htp cpe	4,077	4,107	68,901

1973 Engines	bore×stroke	bhp	availability
L4, 98.6	3.19×3.06	54	S-Pinto exc wgn
L4, 122.0	3.58×3.03	83	S-Pinto wgn; O-Pinto
L6, 200.0	3.68×3.13	84	S-Maverick
L6, 250.0	3.68×3.91	88	O-Maverick
L6, 250.0	3.68×3.91	92	O-Torino
V8, 302.0	4.00×3.00	137/138	Torino 35 & wgns; O-other Torino
V8, 351.0	4.00×3.50	158/159	S-Ford; O-Torino
V8, 400.0	4.00×4.00	168	O-Torino, Ford
V8, 429.0	4.36×3.59	201	O-Torino, Ford
V8, 460.0	4.36×3.85	202	O-Ford

1974

Pinto (wb 94.2)		Wght	Price	Prod
10	fstbk sdn 2d	2,372	2,527	132,061
11	Runabout htchbk sdn 3d	2,406	2,676	174,754
12	wgn 3d	2,576	2,771	237,394

Maverick (wb 103.0; 4d-109.9)

		Wght	Price	Prod
91	fstbk sdn 2d	2,739	2,790	139,818
92	sdn 4d	2,932	2,824	137,728
93	Grabber fstbk sdn 2d	2,868	2,923	23,502

Torino (wb 118.0; 2d-114.0)

		Wght	Price	Prod
25	htp cpe	3,709	3,236	22,738
27	sdn 4d	3,793	3,239	31,161
40	wgn 5d	4,175	3,818	15,393
30	Gran Torino htp cpe	3,742	3,411	76,290
31	Gran Torino sdn 4d	3,847	3,454	72,728
42	Gran Torino wgn 5d	4,209	4,017	29,866
32	Gran Torino Brougham htp cpe	3,794	3,975	26,402
33	Gran Torino Brougham sdn 4d	3,887	3,966	11,464
43	Gran Torino Squire wgn 5d	4,250	4,300	22,837
38	Gran Torino Sport htp cpe	3,771	3,824	23,142
21	Gran Torino Elite htp cpe	NA	4,437	96,604

Ford (wb 121.0)

		Wght	Price	Prod
53	Custom 500 sdn 4d	4,180	3,982	28,941
72	C 500 Ranch Wagon 5d 2S	4,654	4,488	12,104
72	C 500 Ranch Wagon 5d 3S	4,687	4,608	
54	Galaxie 500 sdn 4d	4,196	4,164	49,661
56	Galaxie 500 htp sdn	4,212	4,237	11,526
58	Galaxie 500 htp cpe 5d	4,157	4,211	34,214
74	G500 Country Sdn wgn 5d 2S	4,690	4,584	22,400
74	G500 Country Sdn wgn 5d 3S	4,722	4,704	
62	LTD htp cpe	4,215	4,389	73,296

		Wght	Price	Prod
63	LTD sdn 4d	4,262	4,370	72,251
64	LTD htp sdn	4,277	4,438	12,375
76	LTD Cntry Squire wgn 5d 2S*	4,752	4,898	64,047
76	LTD Cntry Squire wgn 5d 3S*	4,785	5,018	
66	LTD Brougham sdn 4d	4,292	4,647	30,203
67	LTD Brougham htp sdn	4,310	4,717	11,371
68	LTD Brough htp cpe	4,247	4,669	39,084

*Prices with optional woodgrain bodyside trim. Non-woodgrain version $136 less.

1974 Engines	bore×stroke	bhp	availability
L4, 122.0	3.58×3.03	80	S-Pinto
L4, 140.0	3.78×3.13	82	O-Pinto
L6, 200.0	3.68×3.13	84	S-Maverick
L6, 250.0	3.68×3.91	91	O-Maverick, Torino
V8, 302.0	4.00×3.00	140	S-Maverick, Torino
V8, 351.0	4.00×3.50	162	S-Ford exc 76; O-Tor
V8, 400.0	4.00×4.00	170	S-Ford 76; O-Tor, Ford
V8, 460.0	4.36×3.85	220	O-Torino, Ford

1975

Pinto (wb 94.4; wgns-94.7)		Wght	Price	Prod
10	fstbk sdn 2d	2,495	2,769	64,081
11	Runabout htchbk sdn 3d	2,528	2,984	68,919
12	wgn 3d	2,692	3,153	90,763

Maverick (wb 103.0; 4d 109.9)

		Wght	Price	Prod
91	fstbk sdn 2d	2,896	3,025	90,695
92	sdn 4d	3,018	3,061	63,404
93	Grabber fstbk sdn 2d	2,903	3,282	8,473

Granada (wb 109.9)

		Wght	Price	Prod
81	sdn 4d	3,279	3,756	118,168
82	sdn 2d	3,230	3,698	100,810
83	Ghia sdn 4d	3,392	4,283	43,652
84	Ghia sdn 2d	3,342	4,225	40,028

Torino (wb 118.0; 2d-114.0)

		Wght	Price	Prod
25	htp cpe	3,981	3,954	13,394
27	sdn 4d	4,053	3,957	22,928
40	wgn 4d	4,406	4,336	13,291
30	Gran Torino htp cpe	3,992	4,314	35,324
31	Gran Torino sdn 4d	4,084	4,338	53,161
42	Gran Torino wgn 5d	4,450	4,673	23,951
43	Gran Torino Squire wgn 5d	4,490	4,952	
32	Gran Torino Brougham htp cpe	4,081	4,805	4,849
33	Gran Torino Brougham sdn 4d	4,157	4,837	5,929
38	Gran Torino Sport htp cpe	4,038	4,790	5,126
21	Elite htp cpe	4,154	4,767	123,372

Ford (wb 121.0)

		Wght	Price	Prod
53	Custom 500 sdn 4d	4,377	4,477	31,043
72	Custom 500 Ranch Wagon 5d	4,787	5,067	6,930
62	LTD htp cpe	4,359	4,753	47,432
63	LTD sdn 4d	4,408	4,712	82,382
74	LTD wgn 5d 2S	4,803	5,158	22,936
74	LTD wgn 5d 3S	4,836	5,283	
66	LTD Brougham sdn 4d	4,419	5,099	32,327
68	LTD Brougham sdn 2d	4,391	5,133	24,005
76	LTD Country Squire wgn 5d 2S	4,845	5,440	41,550
76	LTD Country Squire wgn 5d 3S	4,878	5,565	
64	LTD Landau sdn 4d	4,446	5,453	32,506
65	LTD Landau sdn 2d	4,419	5,484	26,919

1975 Engines	bore×stroke	bhp	availability
L4, 140.0	3.78×3.13	83	S-Pinto
V6, 170.0	3.66×2.70	97	O-Pinto #11,12
L6, 200.0	3.68×3.13	65	S-Mav, Granada exc Ghia
L6, 250.0	3.68×3.91	72	S-Granada Ghia; O-Mav, Grnda
V8, 302.0	4.00×3.00	122	S-Maverick, Granada

	bore×stroke	bhp	availability
V8, 351.0	4.00×3.50	143	O-Granada
V8, 351.0	4.00×3.50	148-150	S-Torino
V8, 400.0	4.00×4.00	144	S-Ford 74,76; O-Torino, other Ford
V8, 460.0	4.36×3.85	216	O-Torino, Ford

1976

Pinto (wb 94.4; wgns-94.7)

		Wght	Price	Prod
10	Pony MPG fstbk sdn 2d L4	2,450	2,895	
10	MPG fstbk sdn 2d L4	2,452	3,025	92,264
10	sdn 2d V6	2,590	3,472	
11	MPG htchbk sdn 3d L4	2,482	3,200	
11	Squire MPG htchbk sdn 3d L4	2,518	3,505	
11	Runabout htchbk sdn 3d V6	2,620	3,647	92,540
11	Squire htchbk sdn 3d V6	2,656	3,952	
12	MPG wgn 3d L4	2,635	3,365	
12	Squire MPG wgn 3d L4	2,672	3,671	
12	wgn 3d V6	2,773	3,865	105,328
12	Squire wgn 3d V6	2,810	4,171	

Maverick (wb 109.9; 2d-103.0)

91	fstbk sdn 2d	2,846	3,117	60,611
92	sdn 4d	2,950	3,109	79,070

Granada (wb 109.9)

81	sdn 4d	3,222	3,798	187,923
82	sdn 2d	3,172	3,707	161,618
83	Ghia sdn 4d	3,392	4,355	52,457
84	Ghia sdn 2d	3,334	4,265	46,786

Torino (wb 118.0; 2d-114.0)

25	htp cpe	3,976	4,172	34,518
27	sdn 4d	4,061	4,206	17,394
30	Gran Torino htp cpe	3,999	4,461	23,939
31	Gran Torino sdn 4d	4,081	4,495	40,568
32	Gran Torino Brougham htp cpe	4,063	4,883	3,183
33	Gran Torino Brougham sdn 4d	4,144	4,915	4,473
40	wgn 5d	4,409	4,521	17,281
42	Gran Torino wgn 5d	4,428	4,769	30,596
43	Gran Torino Squire wgn 5d	4,454	5,083	21,144

Elite (wb 114.0)

21	htp cpe	4,169	4,879	146,475

Ford (wb 121.0)

52	Custom 500 sdn 2d	—	—	7,037
53	Custom 500 sdn 4d	4,298	4,493	23,447
72	Custom 500 Ranch Wagon 5d	4,737	4,918	4,633
62	LTD sdn 2d	4,257	4,780	62,844
63	LTD sdn 4d	4,303	4,752	108,168
74	LTD wgn 5d 2S	4,752	5,207	
74	LTD wgn 5d 3S	4,780	5,333	30,237
66	LTD Brougham sdn 4d	4,332	5,245	32,917
68	LTD Brougham sdn 2d	4,299	5,299	20,863
76	LTD Country Squire wgn 5d 2S	4,809	5,523	
76	LTD Country Squire wgn 5d 3S	4,837	5,649	47,379
64	LTD Landau sdn 4d	4,394	5,560	35,663
65	LTD Landau sdn 2d	4,346	5,613	29,673

1976 Engines

	bore×stroke	bhp	availability
L4, 140.0	3.78×3.13	92	S-Pinto
V6, 170.0	3.66×2.70	103	O-Pinto
L6, 200.0	3.68×3.13	81	S-Mav, Gran exc Ghia
L6, 250.0	3.68×3.91	90	S-Gran Ghia; O-Mav, Gran
V8, 302.0	4.00×3.00	134/138	S-Granada, Maverick
V8, 351.0	4.00×3.50	152/154	S-Tor, Elite, Ford exc wgns; O-Granada
V8, 400.0	4.00×4.00	180	S-Ford wgns; O-Tor, Ford, Elite
V8, 460.0	4.36×3.85	202	O-Torino, Elite, Ford

1977

Pinto (wb 94.4; wgns-94.7)

		Wght	Price	Prod
10	Pony sdn 2d L4	2,313	3,099	
10	sdn 2d	2,376	3,237	48,863*
11	Runabout htchbk sdn 3d	2,412	3,353	74,237*
12	wgn 3d	2,576	3,548	
12	Squire wgn 3d	2,614	3,891	79,449*

Maverick (wb 109.9; 2d-103.0)

91	fstbk sdn 2d	2,864	3,322	40,086
92	sdn 4d	2,970	3,395	58,420

Granada (wb 109.9)

81	sdn 4d	3,222	4,118	163,071
82	sdn 2d	3,172	4,022	157,612
83	Ghia sdn 4d	3,276	4,548	35,730
84	Ghia sdn 2d	3,222	4,452	34,166

LTD II (wb 118.0; 2d-114.0)

25	S htp cpe	3,789	4,528	9,531
27	S sdn 4d	3,894	4,579	18,775
30	htp cpe	3,789	4,785	57,449
31	sdn 4d	3,904	4,870	56,704
32	Brougham htp cpe	3,898	5,121	20,979
33	Brougham sdn 4d	3,930	5,206	18,851
40	S wgn 5d 2S	4,393	4,806	
40	S wgn 5d 3S	4,410	4,906	0,636
42	wgn 5d 2S	4,404	5,064	
42	wgn 5d 3S	4,421	5,164	23,237
43	Squire wgn 5d 3S	4,430	5,335	
43	Squire wgn 5d 3S	4,447	5,435	17,162

LTD (wb 121.0)

52	Custom 500 sdn 2d	—	—	4,139
53	Custom 500 sdn 4d	—	—	5,582
62	LTD sdn 2d	4,190	5,128	73,637
63	LTD sdn 4d	4,240	5,152	160,255
64	LTD Landau sdn 4d	4,319	5,742	65,030
65	LTD Landau sdn 2d	4,270	5,717	44,396
	Custom 500 Ranch Wagon 5d	—	—	1,406
74	LTD wgn 5d 2S	4,635	5,415	
74	LTD wgn 5d 3S	4,679	5,541	
74	Country Squire wgn 5d 2S	4,674	5,866	90,711
74	Country Squire wgn 5d 3S	4,718	5,992	

1977 Engines

	bore×stroke	bhp	availability
L4, 140.0	3.78×3.13	89	S-Pinto
V6, 170.0	3.66×2.70	93	O-Pinto, exc. Pony
L6, 200.0	3.68×3.13	96	S-Maverick, Granada
L6, 250.0	3.68×3.91	98	O-Maverick, Granada
V8, 302.0	4.00×3.00	122	O-Granada
V8, 302.0	4.00×3.00	130	S-LTD II exc wgns
V8, 302.0	4.00×3.00	137	O-Maverick
V8, 351.0	4.00×3.50	135	O-Granada
V8, 351.0	4.00×3.50	149	S-LTD II wgns; O-LTD II
V8, 351.0	4.00×3.50	161	S-LTD exc wgns; O-LTD II wgns
V8, 400.0	4.00×4.00	173	S-LTD wgns; O-LTD II, LTD
V8, 460.0	4.36×3.85	197	O-LTD

*incl. some units produced as 1978 models but sold as 1977 models.

1978

Pinto (wb 94.4; wgns-94.7)

		Wght	Price	Prod
10	Pony sdn 2d L4	2,321	3,139	
10	sdn 2d	2,400	3,629	62,317
11	Runabout htchbk sdn 3d	2,444	3,744	74,313
12	wgn 3d	2,579	4,028	
12	Squire wgn 3d	2,614	4,343	52,269

Fairmont (wb 105.5)

91	sdn 2d	2,590	3,624	78,776
92	sdn 4d	2,632	3,710	136,849

		Wght	Price	Prod
93	Futura cpe	2,626	4,103	116,966
94	wgn 5d	2,740	4,063	⎤ 128,390
94	Squire wgn 5d	2,748	4,428	⎦

Granada (wb 109.9)

		Wght	Price	Prod
81	sdn 2d	3,132	4,300	⎤
81	Ghia sdn 2d	3,192	4,685	⎥ 110,481
81	ESS sdn 2d	3,190	4,872	⎦
82	sdn 4d	3,167	4,390	⎤
82	Ghia sdn 4d	3,275	4,776	⎥ 139,305
82	ESS sdn 4d	3,225	4,962	⎦

LTD II (wb 118.0; 2d-114.0)

		Wght	Price	Prod
25	S htp cpe	3,746	4,850	9,004
27	S sdn 4d	3,836	4,935	21,122
30	htp cpe	3,773	5,112	⎤ 76,285
30	Brougham htp cpe	3,791	5,448	⎦
31	sdn 4d	3,872	5,222	⎤ 64,133
31	Brougham sdn 4d	3,901	5,558	⎦

LTD (wb 121.0)

		Wght	Price	Prod
62	LTD htp cpe	3,972	5,398	57,466
63	LTD sdn 4d	4,032	5,483	112,392
64	LTD Landau htp cpe	4,029	5,970	27,305
65	LTD Landau sdn 4d	4,081	6,055	39,836
74	LTD wgn 5d 2S	4,532	5,885	⎤
74	LTD wgn 5d 3S	4,567	6,028	⎥ 71,285
74	Country Squire wgn 5d 2S	4,576	6,304	⎥
74	Country Squire wgn 5d 3S	4,601	6,447	⎦

Note: Fiesta not included (import).

1978 Engines	bore×stroke	bhp	availability
L4, 140.0	3.78×3.13	88	S-Pinto, Fairmont
V6, 170.0	3.66×2.70	90	O-Pinto, exc Pony
L6, 200.0	3.68×3.13	85	S-Fairmont
L6, 250.0	3.68×3.91	97	S-Granada
V8, 302.0	4.00×3.00	134	S-LTD II, Ford exc wgns
V8, 302.0	4.00×3.00	139	S-Granada; O-Fairmont
V8, 351.0	4.00×3.50	144/145	S-Ford wgns; O-LTD II, LTD
V8, 351.0	4.00×3.50	152	O-LTD II
V8, 400.0	4.00×4.00	166	O-LTD II, LTD
V8, 460.0	4.36×3.85	202	O-LTD

1979

Pinto (wb 94.4; wgns-94.7)

		Wght	Price	Prod
10	Pony fstbk sdn 2d L4	2,329	3,434	⎤ 75,789
10	fstbk sdn 2d	2,396	3,939	⎦
11	Runabout htchbk sdn 3d	2,442	4,055	69,383
12	Pony wgn 3d L4	NA	3,899	⎤
12	wgn 3d	2,571	4,338	⎥ 53,846
12	Squire wgn 3d	2,607	4,654	⎦

Fairmont (wb 105.5)

		Wght	Price	Prod
91	sdn 2d	2,524	4,102	54,798
92	sdn 4d	2,578	4,220	133,813
93	Futura cpe	2,580	4,463	106,065
94	wgn 5d	2,708	4,497	⎤ 100,691
94	Squire wgn 5d	NA	4,856	⎦

Granada (wb 109.9)

		Wght	Price	Prod
81	sdn 2d	3,088	4,678	⎤
81	Ghia sdn 2d	3,124	5,051	⎥ 76,850
81	ESS sdn 2d	3,140	5,211	⎦
82	sdn 4d	3,134	4,782	⎤
82	Ghia sdn 4d	3,168	5,157	⎥ 105,526
82	ESS sdn 4d	3,210	5,317	⎦

LTD II (wb 118.0; 2d-114.0)

		Wght	Price	Prod
25	S htp cpe	3,781	5,561	834
27	S sdn 4d	3,844	5,661	9,649
30	htp cpe	3,797	5,799	⎤ 18,300
30	Brougham htp cpe	3,815	6,135	⎥
31	sdn 4d	3,860	5,924	⎤ 19,781
31	Brougham sdn 4d	3,889	6,259	⎦

LTD (wb 114.3)

		Wght	Price	Prod
62	LTD sdn 2d	3,421	6,184	54,005
63	LTD sdn 4d	3,463	6,284	117,730
64	LTD Landau sdn 2d	3,472	6,686	42,314
65	LTD Landau sdn 4d	3,527	6,811	74,599
74	LTD wgn 5d 2S	3,678	6,550	⎤ 37,955
74	LTD wgn 5d 3S	—	6,699	⎦
76	Country Squire wgn 5d 2S	3,719	7,006	⎤ 29,932
76	Country Squire wgn 5d 3S	—	7,155	⎦

1979 Engines	bore×stroke	bhp	availability
L4, 140.0	3.78×3.13	88	S-Pinto, Fairmont
V6, 170.0	3.66×2.70	102	O-Pinto exc Pony
L6, 200.0	3.68×3.13	85	O-Fairmont
L6, 250.0	3.68×3.91	97	S-Granada
V8, 302.0	4.00×3.00	129	S-LTD
V8, 302.0	4.00×3.00	133	S-LTD II
V8, 302.0	4.00×3.00	137	O-Granada
V8, 302.0	4.00×3.00	140	O-Fairmont
V8, 351.0	4.00×3.50	142	O-LTD
V8, 351.0	4.00×3.50	151	O-LTD II, LTD

1980

Pinto (wb 94.4; wgns-94.7)

		Wght	Price	Prod
10	Pony fstbk sdn 2d	2,377	4,117	⎤ 84,053
10	fstbk sdn 2d	2,385	4,605	⎦
11	Runabout htchbk sdn 3d	2,426	4,717	61,842
12	Pony wgn 2d	2,545	4,627	⎤
12	wgn 3d	2,553	5,004	⎥ 39,159
12	Squire wgn 3d	2,590	5,320	⎦

Fairmont (wb 105.5)

		Wght	Price	Prod
91	sdn 2d	2,576	4,894	45,074
92	sdn 4d	2,610	5,011	⎤ 143,118
92	Futura sdn 4d	—	5,390	⎦
93	Futura cpe	2,623	5,325	51,878
94	wgn 5d	2,735	5,215	77,035

Granada (wb 109.9)

		Wght	Price	Prod
81	sdn 2d	3,135	5,541	⎤
81	Ghia sdn 2d	3,168	5,942	⎥ 60,872
81	ESS sdn 2d	3,199	6,031	⎦
82	sdn 4d	3,168	5,664	⎤
82	Ghia sdn 4d	3,209	6,065	⎥ 29,557
82	ESS sdn 4d	3,240	6,154	⎦

LTD (wb 118.0, 2d 114.0)

		Wght	Price	Prod
	S sdn 2d	—	—	553
61	S sdn 4d	3,464	6,875	19,283
62	sdn 2d	3,447	7,003	15,333
63	sdn 4d	3,475	7,117	51,630
64	Crown Victoria sdn 2d	3,482	7,628	7,725
65	Crown Victoria sdn 4d	3,524	7,763	21,962
72	S wgn 5d 2S	3,707	7,198	⎤ 3,490
72	S wgn 5d 3S	3,748	7,344	⎦
74	wgn 5d 2S	3,717	7,463	⎤ 11,718
74	wgn 5d 2S	3,758	7,609	⎦
76	Crown Victoria wgn 5d 2S	3,743	7,891	⎤ 9,868
76	Crown Victoria wgn 5d 3S	3,704	8,042	⎦

1980 Engines	bore×stroke	bhp	availability
L4, 140.0	3.78×3.13	88	S-Pinto, Fairmont
L6, 200.0	3.68×3.13	91	O-Fairmont
L6, 250.0	3.68×3.91	90	S-Granada
V8, 255.0	3.68×3.00	119	O-Fairmont, Granada
V8, 302.0	4.00×3.00	130	S-LTD
V8, 302.0	4.00×3.00	134	O-Granada
V8, 351.0	4.00×3.50	140	O-LTD

Ford Mustang
**Ford Division, Ford Motor Co.
Dearborn, Michigan**

The greatest single automotive success of the 1960s raised Ford volume by well over half a million cars, and set an all-time record for first-year sales of any new model. Between its April 1964 introductory date and January 1965, a total of 680,989 Mustangs were sold. Truck drivers drove through showroom windows staring at them, housewives entered contests to win them, and dealers auctioned them off because buyer demand exceeded supply by 15 to 1. America loved the Mustang.

This remarkable accomplishment can be credited to Lee A. Iacocca, the engineer turned salesman, who worked his way from an obsure sales position to vice-president and general manager of Ford Division in five years. Later, Iacocca became president of Ford Motor Company and would go on to become chairman of the board at Chrysler Corporation.

Iacocca's idea was a new "personal car." In his early days as sales manager, people had pleaded with the firm to bring back the two-seat Thunderbird. Iacocca dreamed, doodled, and scribbled down thoughts in the little black book by which he governed his career. By

Mid-engine Mustang I experimental model

1965 2+2 fastback coupe

Mustang II show car of 1963

1965 hardtop coupe

1964½ convertible

1966 GT 2+2 fastback coupe

1961 he had a plan. His young-person's car would be inexpensive to build, but peppy and sporty-looking. It would sell for less than $2500. Projected volume was 100,000 units a year.

The first Mustang prototype was a low, mid-engine fiberglass two-seater on a 90-inch wheelbase, powered by a Ford Cardinal (soon to become the German Ford Taunus 12M) two-liter V4 with 90 horsepower. This Mustang I was pretty but impractical. When Iacocca looked at the people who gathered around it at a show, he said: "That's sure not the car we want to build, because it can't be a volume car. It's too far out." More prototypes followed, culminating in the four-seat, conventionally laid out, 108-inch-wheelbase production Mustang of 1964½. From a marketing standpoint, it

couldn't have been better.

For the 1965 through '68 model years, Mustang came in three basic forms: a hardtop, a convertible, and a semi-fastback coupe. Convertible sales started at the 100,000-unit annual level but had dropped to less than 15,000 a year by 1969. The crisp notchback hardtop was the sales leader. The coupe, known as the "2+2," was introduced with the rest of the Ford line in autumn 1964. It soon overtook the convertible in sales, and averaged about 50,000 units a year through 1970.

The standard Mustang engines during the first six months of production were the 170 cubic-inch Falcon and the 260-cid small-block V8. By fall, these had been replaced by Ford's 200-cid six and the bored-out 289 V8. In the last years of the '60s, before government reg-

1966 hardtop coupe

1967 hardtop coupe

1967 GT 2+2 fastback coupe

GT/SC package on 1968 hardtop coupe

1967 convertible

1968 GT 2+2 fastback coupe

ulations put an end to Ford's "Total Performance" program, the company offered increasingly hairy engine options. For 1967, there was a 390 V8 with 320 bhp; for 1968, the most powerful engine was a 427 of 390 bhp; for 1969, a 335-bhp 428 was available. The 1970 Boss series included a 429 V8 with 375 bhp.

Part of Mustang's appeal lay in its myriad options, which enabled a customer to personalize the car. Careful use of the order form could result in anything from a cute economy car to a thunderingly fast drag racer or a deceptively nimble sporty car. Transmission choices comprised automatics, four-speeds, three-speeds, and stick-overdrive units. Handling packages, power steering, disc brakes, air conditioning, tachometer, and a clock were available. A Mustang could be ordered with bench seats instead of the standard buckets, though few people did so. For $170, the GT package offered a pleasant assortment of goodies, including front disc brakes, a full-gauge instrument panel, and special badges. A variety of interiors was available, along with accent stripes and special moldings for the exterior.

Mustang's shape was inspired, the work of Joe Oros, L. David Ash, and Gayle L. Halderman of the Ford Division styling studio. The long-hood/short-deck style was to fascinate many buyers in the '60s and early '70s. For the next several years, it was the only formula for what soon became known, in honor of Iacocca's brainchild, as the "ponycar." Styling was so good that it was

hardly changed at all during the first few years. The '66s were mostly unaltered; the '67s had a deeper grille and sculptured side panels that ended in twin simulated air scoops; the '68s had a new grille with an inner bright ring around the Mustang emblem. The 2+2 adopted full-fastback styling for '67. Only in 1969 was the package changed more extensively. The '69 version was lower, longer, and wider than earlier models, with ventless side glass and an eggcrate grille. A "SportsRoof" fastback with simulated air scoops and rear deck spoiler joined the line, along with the six or V8 Grandé hardtop coupe priced at $2866 to $2971, and the Mach I fastback at $3139. The Mach I had a 351 V8.

The 1970 Boss Mustang was even more unique than the '69—flashily painted, well-suspended, and fitted with the hottest engines ever. A competition shifter with Hurst linkage was new. Up the price scale was the Boss 429, powered by Ford's Cobra-Jet NASCAR engine with cast-magnesium rocker arm covers and semi-hemispherical combustion chambers.

Available Mach I engines for 1970 ranged from a 351 V8 to a 428-cid four-barrel unit with Ram Air. Mach I styling features included a special grille with driving lamps, a dull-finish black center hood section, functional hood scoop, quick-fill gas cap, and black honeycomb rear panel appliqué. The luxury Grandé was still offered with either six or V8 power. Like all Mustangs that year, it inherited the '69 Mach I's high-back front

1969 Mach I fastback coupe

1969 convertible

1969 Grande hardtop coupe

1970 Boss 302 fastback coupe

bucket seats. A landau-style black or white vinyl roof, racing-type mirrors, special identification, and bright wheelwell moldings completed the package.

There were still basic Mustangs in 1970, available with the standard six or 302 V8 in hardtop, convertible, and SportsRoof fastback styles. Like other models, they featured new front-end styling and reverted to single headlights. Recessed taillamps appeared at the rear. Convertibles became much scarcer now; buyer preference for air conditioning and closed coupes had transformed the market, keeping ragtop production low.

In late 1970, Ford abandoned most of its Trans-Am, USAC, NASCAR, and international competition efforts, and also began to change the Mustang's character. After what Ford Division had called the "Sizzlin' '70s," later Mustangs would seem relatively tame.

An all-new third-generation design bowed for 1971. Largely the product of Semon E. "Bunkie" Knudsen, who served briefly as Ford Motor Company president in the late '60s, the new model was intended to answer a frequent criticism of early ponycars, namely insufficient passenger room. The result was the most changed Mustang yet: larger, heavier, and thirstier—as "fat" as Mustang would ever get. Though it grew only an inch in wheelbase, the '71 was eight inches longer overall, six inches wider, and close to 600 pounds heavier than the original '65 Mustang. Styling was also more massive, with busier sheetmetal, Shelby-like grilles, and a sweeping, full-fastback roofline on the "SportsRoof" 2 + 2 inspired by Ford's GT 40-series international endurance racers. Reflecting a greater emphasis on luxury and convenience, the performance-oriented Mach 1 with 429 Cobra Jet engine could now be ordered with air conditioning and automatic transmission, plus power steering, tilt wheel, and other niceties. Yet almost any '71 could be blindingly quick. With automatic and 3.25:1 final drive, the 429 CJ Mach 1 could do 0-60 mph in 6.5 seconds and the standing-start quarter-mile in 14.5 seconds.

The "fat" Mustang lumbered onto the market just as ponycar demand was starting to wane and fuel prices and insurance costs were starting to rise. Predictably, its sales fell far short of expectations. Model year 1971 production was down to under 150,000, with other Ford products like the compact Maverick accounting for some of the loss. The 1972s were little changed, but there were fewer engine options, performance and horsepower were both down, and the previous year's interesting Boss 351 model vanished. Ford promoted new colors and fabrics, the prettiest of which was the Sprint decor option. This was marked by white paint with broad, blue, Shelby-style racing stripes edged in red. Complementary colors were used inside, and mag wheels, raised-white-letter tires, and competition suspension were all available. Mustang remained its hefty self for one final year, 1973. By this time, Ford was well along on a much smaller successor—and more willing to admit its error: "We started out with a secretary car," said design vice-president Eugene Bordinat, "and all of a sudden we had a behemoth." Most of the changes for '73 were made in line with federal regulations: 5-mph

bumpers (an optional color-keyed cover helped them from looking like afterthoughts), rubber-covered control knobs, flame-retardant upholstery, an EGR system to hold down emissions.

The smaller, lighter Mustang II, introduced for 1974, marked a major turning point for the original ponycar. Its appearance couldn't have been better timed, coinciding neatly with the onset of the first national fuel shortage. Sales boomed. With a production run of nearly 400,000 units in its first year, Mustang II came within 10 percent of the original's first-year record.

Lee Iacocca, by now Ford president, had specified a wheelbase of 96-100 inches for the Mustang II, plus a scaled-down version of the familiar long-hood/short-deck styling, the target being sporty import coupes like the Toyota Celica and Ford's own German-built Capri. Compared to the 1971-73 Mustang, the II was 20 inches shorter, four inches narrower, an inch lower, and 400-500 pounds lighter. Like the Pinto (which borrowed some of its engineering from 1974 on), it employed unit construction and a conventional front suspension with coil springs and unequal-length upper and lower arms. However, the Mustang's lower arm was attached to a rubber-mounted subframe instead of being bolted directly to the body structure. The subframe, which carried the rear of the engine/transmission assembly, added to production costs, but it was deemed necessary to provide more precise steering and a smoother, quieter ride than Pinto. At the rear, the Mustang II's leaf springs were longer than Pinto's, and its shock absorbers were staggered to give better balance and handling. Notchback and fastback coupe body styles returned (the latter now a hatchback), but not the convertible. And for the first time in history, a new Mustang was planned without a V8, the initial engine offerings limited to a 2.3-liter inline four and a 2.8-liter V6. The four was the first American engine built to metric (instead of English) measurements; it had originally been created for Ford's larger European cars. The V6 standard on the Mach 1 hatchback was also based on a Ford Europe design, but had greater displacement and separate, instead of siamesed, exhaust ports. The Mustang II's four-speed gearbox was derived from the English Ford unit used in the Pinto, and was strengthened when teamed with the V6 to handle its extra power and torque. A typical V6/four-speed car could do 0-60 mph in 13-14 seconds and had a top speed of 100 mph.

The Mustang II didn't change significantly during its five-year production run. Ghia notchbacks in both four-cylinder and V6 form as well as the Mach 1 were available throughout, and the II continued a Mustang tradition in its lengthy option list. Air conditioning, power steering and brakes, a raft of sound equipment, fancier trim, a vinyl top for notchbacks, sunroof, and forged-aluminum wheels were among the items available. For 1975 a moonroof ($454) and a luxury package were added as options for the already posh Ghia.

Mustang II sales never came near their 1974 level in subsequent years, but they were a lot better than 1971-73. The total fell by over half for '75, then held steady. Ford

1971 Mach 1 SportsRoof fastback hardtop coupe

1973 Mach 1 SportsRoof fastback hardtop coupe

1972 convertible

1974 II Mach 1 hatchback coupe

1972 hardtop coupe

1975 II Ghia coupe

made a gesture toward performance buyers for '75 by reviving a V8 option, the workhorse 302-cid unit, which initially delivered 122 bhp. This was followed by the Cobra II, basically a trim option for hatchbacks only, arriving at mid-'76. It included sports steering wheel, dual remote-control door mirrors, brushed-aluminum dash and door panel appliques, black grille, styled steel wheels, radial tires, flip-out rear side windows with add-on louvers, front air dam, rear spoiler, and simulated hood scoop. Available at first only in white with blue stripes, the Cobra II could be ordered in other colors from 1977 on. It was flashy, but a far cry from the great Shelby Mustang it tried to ape. Ford again tried "paint-on performance" with the King Cobra package for 1978. It had many of the aforementioned items, plus a gaudy snake decal on the hood and tape stripes from stem to stern, but you also got the 302

V8, power steering, handling suspension, and Goodrich 70-series radial tires, all for about $1300. A 17-second quarter-mile time didn't make this a really hot car, but it was decent for its day.

The new-generation Mustang that appeared in 1979 was in many ways the best car ever to wear the galloping pony. From the rear it looked vaguely like a BMW—clean, taut and tight—and its surface execution, downswept nose, ample glass area, and lack of superfluous ornamentation combined the best of contemporary American and European design. At long last, Ford had returned to the sort of restrained, efficient and elegant ponycar it had built in the first place. Though many styling ideas were proposed, the one chosen for production originated with a team headed by Jack Telnack, executive director of Ford North American Light Truck and Car Design (this group

1975 II Mach 1 hatchback coupe

1978 II Mach 1 hatchback coupe with King Cobra option

1976 II Mach 1 Cobra II hatchback coupe

1979 Indy Pace Car Replica hatchback coupe

1977 II hatchback coupe

1980 Cobra hatchback coupe

also styled the European front-drive Fiesta minicar). Body construction made extensive use of lightweight materials—mainly plastics, low-alloy steel, and aluminum—so the '79 weighed roughly 200 pounds less than a comparable Mustang II. It was equally impressive inside: rear legroom was up five inches, overall interior volume up 14-16 cubic feet, shoulder room up 3.5/5 inches (front/rear), cargo volume up by two cubic feet.

The '79 Mustang ran on a new suspension borrowed from the Fairmont/Zephyr compacts. It employed modified MacPherson-strut geometry in front, four-bar-link rear axle location, anti-sway bars at both ends, and coil springs all around. A handling package with higher spring rates, different shock valving, and stiffer bushings was available with mandatory 14-inch tires. There was also a premium setup featuring Michelin TRX tires, specially sized forged-

aluminum wheels, and appropriately tuned chassis pieces for maximum roadability. The 1978 engine lineup was carried over, and expanded with a turbocharged version of the standard four, which produced 0-60 mph times of 10 seconds or so and fuel economy in the low to mid-20s.

Mustang paced the 1979 Indianapolis 500, and a Pace Car Replica was accordingly issued as a mid-year commemorative. For 1980, this model's special styling features were applied to a revised Cobra package: front and rear spoilers, integral fog lamps, slatted grille, non-functional hood scoop. Also standard on Cobra was the TRX suspension package, and a new 255-cid V8 was optional across the board. Substituting for the 302, the 255 was the latest in a long line of Ford small-blocks going back to the original Fairlane 221 V8 of 1962, and was intended to boost fuel economy while still providing a modicum of go.

Ford Mustang

During the latter part of the 1979 model year, Ford brought back its 200-cid six because V6 supplies from the firm's German subsidiary in Cologne weren't adequate. This engine was even older than the V8.

Ford deserves a lot of credit for sticking with the ponycar concept it originated. After a rocky start in the early '70s, Mustang was transformed in to an adequate sporty compact well tuned to market needs, and became really exciting again with the 1979 design. The latter was proof positive that Americans could build nimble, handsome, efficient cars that are as much fun on a winding road as on a straightaway. By the end of the decade, the Mustang was once more the kind of car it had been in the beginning.

Ford Mustang Specifications

1965

(wb 108.0)		Wght	Price	Prod
07	htp cpe	2,583	2,372	501,965
08	conv cpe	2,789	2,614	101,945
09	fstbk cpe	2,633	2,589	77,079

1965 Engines	bore×stroke	bhp	availability
L6, 170.0	3.50×2.94	101	S-all through 9/24/64
L6, 200.0	3.68×3.13	120	S-all after 9/25/64
V8, 260.0	3.80×2.87	164	O-all through 9/25/64
V8, 289.0	4.00×2.87	200	O-all after 9/25/64
V8, 289.0	4.00×2.87	225/271	O-all

1966

(wb 108.0)		Wght	Price	Prod
01	htp cpe	2,488	2,416	499,751
02	fstbk cpe	2,519	2,607	35,698
03	conv cpe	2,650	2,653	72,119

1966 Engines	bore×stroke	bhp	availability
L6, 200.0	3.68×3.13	120	S-all
V8, 289.0	4.00×2.87	200	O-all
V8, 289.0	4.00×2.87	225/271	O-all

1967

(wb 108.0)		Wght	Price	Prod
01	htp cpe	2,568	2,461	356,271
02	fstbk cpe	2,605	2,592	71,042
03	conv cpe	2,738	2,698	44,808

1967 Engines	bore×stroke	bhp	availability
L6, 200.0	3.68×3.13	120	S-all
V8, 289.0	4.00×2.87	200	O-all
V8, 289.0	4.00×2.87	225/271	O-all
V8, 390.0	4.05×3.78	320	O-all

1968

(wb 108.0)		Wght	Price	Prod
01	htp cpe	2,635	2,602	249,447
02	fstbk cpe	2,659	2,712	42,581
03	conv cpe	2,745	2,814	25,376

1968 Engines	bore×stroke	bhp	availability
L6, 200.0	3.68×3.13	115	S-all
V8, 289.0	4.00×2.87	195	O-all
V8, 302.0	4.00×3.00	230	O-all
V8, 390.0	4.05×3.78	325	O-all
V8, 427.0	4.23×3.78	390	O-all

1969

(wb 108.0)		Wght	Price	Prod
01	htp cpe	2,798	2,635	128,458
02	fstbk cpe	2,822	2,635	60,046
02	Boss 302 fstbk cpe, V8	3,210	3,588	1,934
03	conv cpe	2,908	2,849	14,746
04	Grande htp cpe	2,873	2,866	22,182
05	Mach I fstbk cpe	3,175	3,139	72,458

1969 Engines	bore×stroke	bhp	availability
L6, 200.0	3.68×3.13	115	S-all exc Mach I, Boss 302
L6, 250.0	3.68×3.91	155	O-all exc Mach I, Boss 302
V8, 302.0	4.00×3.00	220	O-all exc Mach I, Boss 302
V8, 351.0	4.00×3.50	250	S-Mach I; O-others exc Boss 302
V8, 351.0	4.00×3.50	290	O-all
V8, 390.0	4.05×3.78	320	O-all
V8, 428.0	4.13×3.98	335	O-Mach I (Ram Air avail)

1970

(wb 108.0)		Wght	Price	Prod
01	htp cpe	2,822	2,721	82,569
02	fstbk cpe	2,846	2,771	39,316
02	Boss 302 fstbk cpe, V8	3,227	3,720	6,319
03	conv cpe	2,932	3,025	7,673
04	Grande htp cpe	2,907	2,926	13,581
05	Mach I cpe	3,240	3,271	40,970

1970 Engines	bore×stroke	bhp	availability
L6, 200.0	3.68×3.13	115	S-all exc Mach I, Boss 302
L6, 250.0	3.68×3.91	155	O-all exc Mach I, Boss 302
V8, 302.0	4.00×3.00	220	O-all exc Mach I, Boss 302
V8, 351.0	4.00×3.50	250	S-Mach I; O-others exc Boss 302
V8, 351.0	4.00×3.50	300	O-all
V8, 428.0	4.13×3.98	335	O-Mach I (Ram Air avail)
V8, 429.0	4.36×3.59	375	O-Mach 1, Boss

1971

(wb 109.0)		Wght	Price	Prod
01	htp cpe	2,982	2,911	65,696
02	fstbk cpe	2,950	2,973	
02	Boss 351 fstbk cpe V8	3,281	4,124	23,956
03	conv	3,102	3,227	6,121
04	Grandé htp cpe	3,006	3,117	17,406
05	Mach 1 fstbk cpe V8	3,220	3,268	36,499

1971 Engines	bore×stroke	bhp	availability
L6, 250.0	3.68×3.91	145	S-all exc Mach 1, Boss 351
V8, 302.0	4.00×3.00	210	O-all exc Mach 1, Boss 351
V8, 351.0	4.00×3.50	240	O-all exc Boss 351
V8, 351.0	4.00×3.50	285	O-all exc Boss 351
V8, 351.0	4.00×3.50	330	S-Boss 351; O-others
V8, 429.0	4.36×3.59	370	O-all

1972

(wb 109.0)		Wght	Price	Prod
01	htp cpe	2,983	2,729	57,350
02	fstbk cpe	2,952	2,786	15,622
03	conv	3,099	3,015	6,401
04	Grandé htp cpe	3,008	2,915	18,045
05	Mach 1 fstbk cpe V8	3,046	3,053	27,675

1972 Engines	bore×stroke	bhp	availability
L6, 250.0	3.68×3.91	99	S-all exc Mach I
V8, 302.0	4.00×3.00	141	S-Mach 1; O-others
V8, 351.0	4.00×3.50	177/266 /275	O-all

1973

(wb 109.0)		Wght	Price	Prod
01	htp cpe	3,040	2,760	51,480
02	fstbk cpe	3,053	2,820	10,820
03	conv	3,171	3,102	11,853
04	Grandé htp cpe	3,059	2,946	25,674
05	Mach 1 fstbk cpe V8	3,115	3,088	35,440

1973 Engines	bore×stroke	bhp	availability
L6, 250.0	3.68×3.91	95	S-all exc Mach 1
V8, 302.0	4.00×3.00	136	S-Mach 1; O-others
V8, 351.0	4.00×3.50	154/156	O-all

1974

II (wb 96.2)		Wght	Price	Prod
02	cpe 2d	2,654	3,134	177,671
03	htchbk cpe 3d	2,734	3,328	74,799
04	Ghia cpe 2d	2,820	3,480	89,477
05	Mach 1 htchbk cpe 3d V6	2,778	3,674	44,046

1974 Engines	bore×stroke	bhp	availability
L4, 140.0	3.78×3.13	88	S-all exc Mach 1
V6, 170.0	3.66×2.70	105	S-Mach 1; O-others

1975

II (wb 96.2)		Wght	Price	Prod
02	cpe 2d	2,718	3,529	85,155
03	htchbk cpe 3d	2,754	3,818	30,038
04	Ghia cpe 2d	2,762	3,938	52,320
05	Mach 1 htchbk cpe 3d V6	2,879	4,188	21,062

1975 Engines	bore×stroke	bhp	availability
L4, 140.0	3.78×3.13	83	S-all exc Mach 1
V6, 170.0	3.66×2.70	97	S-Mach 1; O-others

	bore×stroke	bhp	availability
V8, 302.0	4.00×3.00	122	O-all

1976

II (wb 96.2)		Wght	Price	Prod
02	cpe 2d	2,717	3,525	78,508
03	htchbk cpe 3d	2,745	3,781	62,312
04	Ghia cpe 2d	2,768	3,859	37,515
05	Mach 1 htchbk cpe V6 3d	2,822	4,209	9,232

1976 Engines	bore×stroke	bhp	availability
L4, 140.0	3.78×3.13	92	S-all exc Mach 1
V6, 170.0	3.66×2.70	103	S-Mach 1; O-others
V8, 302.0	4.00×3.00	134	O-all

1977

II (wb 96.2)		Wght	Price	Prod
02	cpe 2d	2,688	3,702	67,783
03	htchbk cpe 3d	2,734	3,901	49,161
04	Ghia cpe 2d	2,728	4,119	29,510
05	Mach 1 htchbk cpe V6 3d	2,785	4,332	6,719

1977 Engines	bore×stroke	bhp	availability
L4, 140.0	3.78×3.13	89	S-all exc Mach 1
V6, 170.0	3.66×2.70	93	S-Mach 1; 0-others
V8, 302.0	4.00×3.00	139	O-all

1978

II (wb 96.2)		Wght	Price	Prod
02	cpe 2d	2,656	3,731	81,304
03	htchbk cpe 3d	2,702	3,975	68,408
04	Ghia cpe 2d	2,694	4,149	34,730
05	Mach 1 htchbk cpe V6 3d	2,733	4,430	7,968

1978 Engines	bore×stroke	bhp	availability
L4, 140.0	3.78×3.13	88	S-all exc Mach 1
V6, 170.0	3.66×2.70	90	S-Mach 1; O-others
V8, 302.0	4.00×3.00	139	O-all

1979

(wb 104.4)		Wght	Price	Prod
02	cpe 2d	2,471	4,494	156,666
03	htchbk cpe 3d	2,491	4,828	120,535
04	Ghia cpe 2d	2,579	5,064	56,351
05	Ghia htchbk cpe 3d	2,588	5,216	36,384

1979 Engines	bore×stroke	bhp	availability
L4, 140.0	3.78×3.13	88	S-all
L4T, 140.0	3.78×3.13	140	O-all
V6, 170.0	3.66×2.70	109	O-all
L6, 200.0	3.68×3.13	91	O-all (late)
V8, 302.0	4.00×3.00	140	O-all

1980

(wb 104.4)		Wght	Price	Prod
02	cpe 2d	2,514	5,338	128,893
03	htchbk cpe 3d	2,548	5,616	98,497
04	Ghia cpe 2d	2,582	5,823	23,647
05	Ghia htchbk cpe 3d	2,606	5.935	20,285

1980 Engines	bore×stroke	bhp	availability
L4, 140.0	3.78×3.13	88	S-all
L4T, 140.0	3.78×3.13	140	O-all
L6, 200.0	3.68×3.13	91	O-all
V8, 255.0	2.68×3.00	118	O-all

Ford Thunderbird

**Ford Division, Ford Motor Co.
Dearborn, Michigan**

The two-seat Thunderbird was a spectacular-looking newcomer in 1955, and still turns heads today. Initially, it was Ford's answer to the Chevrolet Corvette. Styling came from Ford Division designers working under Frank Hershey, and not directly from the George Walker consultant team as is often quoted. Also, it's not likely the project started with division general manager Lewis Crusoe admiring foreign sports cars at the 1951 Paris Automobile Show. Hershey and others say a two-seater was already in the works at Ford Styling well before that. Early market surveys had indicated a demand for a two-seater. But later, an even greater market was pinpointed for a four-seat model. As a result, the two-seaters planned for 1958 and beyond were dropped. T-Bird was enlarged and began stressing luxury over sportiness. It proved an intelligent move from a sales standpoint: the 1958 and later Thunderbirds handily outsold the Corvettes, and were always well ahead in sales of the 1955-57 two-seaters.

The 1955 Thunderbird was priced just below $3000 without options. Unlike the first Corvettes, manual and stick-overdrive transmissions were available as well as automatic. Power came from the 292-cid "Y-block" V8, and a detachable hardtop was offered as an option. For 1956, engine output was 202 bhp. Due to complaints about limited trunk space, Ford placed the spare tire outside, "continental" style, for the '56 edition. A popular no-cost option on '56–'57 hardtops was the famous T-Bird portholes, derived from vintage coachwork by Ford stylist Bill Boyer. Porthole hardtops outsold non-porthole versions heavily in 1956, and virtually all '57 Thunderbirds had them.

For 1957, the two-seater got what would be the only major restyle for its three-year design cycle. Modest tailfins were added, trailing back from midway on the body, and the front end featured a combination bumper/grille. Though basic stickshift models still came with the 292 V8, other versions had larger engines—all the way to a supercharged 312-cid unit with 300 bhp. With a base price still under $3500, the '57 T-Bird was an attractive buy. Because it remained in production through the end of the year, more '57s were built than either of the first two models.

The four-seater followed in 1958. It was a dramatic

1955 two-seat convertible with hardtop (pre-production)

1956 two-seat convertible with hardtop

1955 two-seat convertible (pre-production)

1956 two-seat convertible

1957 two-seat convertible with hardtop

1957 two-seat convertible

design with unibody construction, all-coil suspension, and rakish lowness. Crisp new styling popularized the square-cut "formal" hardtop roofline. The 113-inch wheelbase was compact, yet provided ample interior room for four. Both hardtop and convertible models were offered, though a rumored retractable hardtop model like the Ford Skyliner was canceled in the design stage.

With two models and room for four, the '58 Thunderbird was a solid success. Almost twice as many found buyers as any of the previous two-seaters. The

'59s changed only in detail: a horizontal instead of honeycomb pattern for grille, air scoop, and taillight panels; projectile-like door moldings; reworked Thunderbird script; a bird emblem for the hardtop's rear roof pillar instead of the '58's round emblem. Owing to production over a full model year, the '59 bested the '58 in sales.

The 1960 version was the last "squarebird" in the three-year styling cycle. It was substantially the same as its predecessor, but had a new grille with a main horizontal bar bisecting three vertical bars ahead of a grid

1958 hardtop coupe

1960 hardtop coupe

1959 convertible

1960 hardtop coupe

1961 hardtop coupe

1962 convertible

1963 Sports Roadster

1964 Landau hardtop coupe

1965 convertible

insert, new triple taillight clusters, and small trim changes. A 352-cid V8 was standard. The Lincoln Continental 430 V8 was optional. Hardtops outsold convertibles by nearly an eight to one ratio, indicating T-Bird customers wanted luxury first and sportiness second.

The 1961 model was entirely new, though a 113-inch wheelbase was retained. This styling and engineering would be continued through the 1963 model year. The bullet-shaped '61s had severely pointed front profiles, modest tailfins, and the traditional Ford circular taillights. Only one engine was now offered: the 390 V8 (created by stroking the old 352 a quarter-inch). In 1962, the 390 was offered with a powerpack option. With minor horsepower alterations, these two would be the basic Thunderbird powerplants through 1968, to be accompanied by big-block options in 1966-68.

Thunderbird engineering in the early and middle '60s was conservative but sound. Ford had considered front-wheel-drive for 1961, but felt it was too unorthodox for this market. Instead, engineers stressed quality control, solid construction, high ride standards, and minimum noise at speed. Extensive use of rubber bushings for the independent front suspension and leaf-spring rear suspension made the 1961-63 Thunderbirds among the best-riding cars of the day.

Styling for 1962 and 1963 was generally the same as for '61, but two new models were added. These were the Sports Roadster and the Landau.

The Sports Roadster was the only production four-seat car to become a two-seater. (There are many examples of the opposite, of course, including the 1958 Thunderbird.) The decision to build it was made by Lee A. Iacocca, Ford Division general manager, because dealers were beseiged with requests for another two-seater. Iacocca concluded there was no significant market for anything like the 1955-57 Thunderbird, but a semi-sports model wouldn't hurt.

The designer most responsible for the Sports Roadster was Bud Kaufman. He developed a fiberglass tonneau cover to hide the area behind the front seat. When fitted, the cover formed twin headrests for the front seats. Kaufman overcame fitting problems so the car's soft top could be raised and lowered with the cover in place. Kelsey-Hayes wire wheels were fitted to all Sports Roadsters. The stock rear fender skirts were left off because they wouldn't clear the pseudo knock-off hubcaps.

Limited demand made the Sports Roadster rare. The problem was price. It sold for about $650 more than the standard Thunderbird convertible. In 1964, dealers offered the tonneau cover and wire wheels as accessories. These are even scarcer today.

The Landau was more popular, because it cost only $77 more than the standard hardtop. It sported a vinyl-covered roof with a fake landau ("S") bar on each rear pillar. This distinctive touch made the Landau a hit. By 1966, it was outselling the unadorned hardtop, and composed the bulk of T-Bird production by 1969.

The 1963 model run also included 2000 examples of a

1966 Landau hardtop coupe

1967 hardtop coupe

1968 hardtop coupe

1968 Landau four-door sedan

1969 Landau four-door sedan

1969 Landau hardtop coupe

Limited Edition Landau, introduced in the spring of that year. It was identified by a special numbered plaque on the console, all-white background in the rear roof quarter, all-white interiors, and spinner wheel covers.

Thunderbird received completely new sheetmetal in 1964, along with a lot of bodyside sculpture. The third-generation four-seater, still on the original-length wheelbase, would be continued without major change through 1966. These were years of increasing emphasis on quiet, refined luxury. During this period, convertible sales declined noticeably. The last convertibles were run off for 1966, and accounted for only 7.5 percent of production.

Among features introduced on the '64-'66 cars were a cockpit-style passenger compartment and Silent-Flo ventilation (1964); front disc brakes (1965); full-width taillight housings including backup lights and sequential turn signals; and a "Town" (formal) roofline for the Landau and hardtop (1966). A popular accessory, which had first appeared in 1961, was the "Swing-Away" steering wheel. It shifted about 10 inches in-

board so the driver could be seated more easily.

Throughout the '60s, the pros and cons of offering a Thunderbird sedan were steadily debated by Ford officials. By 1965, Iacocca was satisfied that the sporting image was being handled by other Fords: he had launched the Mustang, and had an attractive array of Falcons and Fairlanes. Market surveys indicated that Thunderbird, now firmly entrenched as a personal-luxury car, no longer needed an image of sportiness. Accordingly, the car was completely restyled for 1967. In place of the convertible came a four-door Landau on a 117-inch wheelbase. The hardtop and two-door Landau were continued on a two-inch shorter wheelbase. The front featured a deeply recessed honeycomb grille with concealed headlamps. The front bumper was wrapped underneath. On two-door models, rear quarter windows retracted horizontally into the roof pillars.

This series was continued through 1970, despite the fact that the plain hardtop was a slow seller, as were other models in the line. Sales moved slowly but consistently downward in the last three years of the de-

Ford Thunderbird

1970 Landau four-door sedan

cade. The four-door Landau was not very practical; its rear doors seemed to detract from the formal roofline. It dropped in sales from almost 25,000 cars in 1967 to slightly more than 8400 for 1970.

Styling changes to distinguish the 1968 and 1969 Thunderbirds were minor. For 1968, an eggcrate grille pattern replaced the '67 honeycomb, and bodysill moldings were narrowed. For 1969, the grille texture was changed to horizontal louvers with three vertical dividers, and divided taillamps replaced the full-width cluster. The Landau coupe's rear quarter windows were eliminated. The '70 was restyled on the same wheelbase; it received a longer hood and a more prominent, snout-like grille. Windshield wipers and radio antenna were concealed, and two-door models had a "faster" roofline.

1971 Landau coupe

1972 Landau hardtop coupe

Although Thunderbird had no performance image to uphold by now, the Ford slogan was "Total Performance." Big-block V8s were offered, but they did not sell well. The 1966-67 option was Ford's 428. For 1968-70, the 429 became standard. The 390 engine, which had powered Thunderbirds for eight years, was no longer offered although it was used in some Fairlanes, Torinos, Mustangs, and full-size Fords.

The sixth-generation Thunderbird made its final appearance for 1971. The customary three-model lineup returned, but two-door Landaus were now available without dummy S-bars on the rear roof quarters (a Bird emblem substituted). Four-door Landaus continued to carry the bars, and any vinyl-roof mdoel could now be ordered with the electric sliding sunroof that had returned as an option for '69. Styling changes were limited to wheel covers, grille insert, and minor trim. In all, the 1970-71 was among the best Thunderbirds of the '70s. One reviewer called it "almost a limousine . . . for something under $7000."

Thunderbird was completely redesigned for 1972, becoming larger and heavier than any generation before—or since. The slow-selling sedans were dropped, and the brace of hardtop coupes now shared basic structure with the new Continental Mark IV. Besides list prices starting $2500 below the Lincoln's, a big selling point for this bigger Bird was a new suspension, with coil springs all-round and four-bar link location for the live rear axle. Not surprisingly, the greater size and weight conspired with more restrictive emissions tuning to hurt both performance and economy. The typical '72 needed 12 seconds for the 0-60 mph sprint and returned a dismal 11-12 miles per gallon of increasingly more expensive gas. Yet buyers apparently didn't care. Perhaps because of its closer similarity with the prestigious Mark, the new model posted a healthy 60-percent sales gain, followed by a near all-time Thunderbird record for 1973. This basic package would be continued for five model years, the longest of any Thunderbird generation. While the Arab oil embargo of 1973-74 put a big dent in big-car sales generally, the personal-luxury Ford maintained a solid lead in this period over its nearest rivals, the Buick Rivera and Oldsmobile Toronado.

Federal bumper standards took effect for 1973. Like other cars that year, the Bird had to withstand a 5-mph frontal impact (and a 2.5-mph rear shunt the next year) without damage to safety-related components. Heavier bumpers met the standard, but they only added to the weight problem and the Bird was now over two tons at the curb. Styling was similar to 1972 except for the front end, where headlights were set into square holes and a gaudy eggcrate replaced horizontal bars in the grille. A stand-up hood ornament appeared, and the dummy landau irons gave way to optional "opera" windows, curious little oblong panes in the rear roof quarters. As before, the 429 V8 was standard and the 460 optional.

The 1974 model had to be the least pleasant to of all Birds to live with. The infamous, short-lived seatbelt interlock system mandated by the feds forced you to buckle in a bag of groceries placed on the front seat before the car could be started, and the heftier rear bumpers added

to overall length with no gain in interior space. With weight up and emissions standards stricter, the whopping 460 V8 became standard equipment this year, along with vinyl roof, opera windows, solid-state ignition, AM radio, air conditioning, power windows, and tinted glass. There were eight variations of metalflake paint available, and a glass moonroof appeared as an optional alternative to the steel sunroof.

Aside from details, such as segmented taillights for 1974, the last three years of the seventh generation saw few styling changes. Emissions tuning continued to strangle the 460 V8, and horsepower for 1975-76 declined to ridiculously low levels for such a large engine, despite a switch to the catalytic converter. Ford went all-out to promote the '75 as "the best luxury car buy", trumpeting "new softness, new ease, with ample room for six . . . rich, lavish fabrics . . . 24-oz. cut-pile carpeting . . . woodtone appliques." More practical options included four-wheel disc brakes (an option since '72), Sure-Track anti-lock braking device, and

a fuel monitor warning light. The latter was really needed, because these Birds were among the thirstiest products ever to come from Dearborn.

Ford had long since become a master at keeping interest alive in an aging model via special editions, and the mid-'70s Thunderbird was no exception. An optional gold-tint moonroof was announced at mid-1974, along with the Burgundy and White-and-Gold Luxury Groups, color-keyed to a fare-the-well inside and out. There were Copper and Silver Luxury Groups for '75, with either velour or leather upholstery, joined by the Jade LG in April 1975. These had a padded vinyl half-roof with opera windows, the latter being deleted when a moonroof was specified. For 1976, the similarly done Creme-and-Gold, Bordeaux, and Lipstick LGs were issued.

Thunderbird marked a first in its history for 1977 by being smaller than it had been the year before. This new "downsized" model was nothing more than a derivative of the existing intermediate platform, and was suggested

1973 hardtop coupe

1974 hardtop coupe

1976 hardtop coupe with Creme-and-Gold Luxury Group option

1979 Heritage coupe

1975 hardtop coupe

1978 coupe with Sport Decor Group option

1977 coupe

1980 coupe

by the Gran Torino Elite, introduced in 1974 as a test to see if the public would accept a Monte Carlo-size Thunderbird. Though the Elite sold tolerably well, it was nothing compared to what this "new" Bird would achieve.

Compared to the 1972-76 models, the '77 was lighter and more economical, reflecting big reductions in almost every dimension: nearly 10 inches shorter overall and seven inches in wheelbase, three inches narrower, 1800 pounds lighter. There were big reductions in price, too: nearly $3000 less for the base model. It was an expedient move in the face of CAFE (corporate average fuel economy) standards and other obvious needs of the times, but it was the low price and the Thunderbird name that sent sales soaring. Better fuel efficiency was merely incidental. Not surprisingly, Thunderbird enjoyed 300,000-unit years in 1977-78—better than three times the previous model year record set in distant 1960. And it easily outsold its LTD II sibling despite far fewer model choices (see "Ford").

Though the '77 was smaller and less unique than previous Birds, it had many of the same overtones and brash touches. Prices soon started climbing to where they had been. Ford announced a new top-line variant called Town Landau in January 1977, listing at nearly $8000 base and carrying a long list of standard luxury features plus a brushed-aluminum "tiara" roof band. The standard engine for all models was the trusty 302 V8 except for California, where only the 351 was available. The big-blocks of old were all but gone now.

There was little change for 1978-79. The collector's Thunderbird for 1978 was the Diamond Jubilee model, issued to commemorate the company's 75th anniversary and tagged at close to $10,000. It was finished in Diamond Blue Metallic or Ember Metallic, and came with the owner's initials on the door and a 22-carat gold nameplate on the dash. This package proved so popular that Ford retained it for 1979 as the Heritage, offered with either special maroon or light blue paint.

Thunderbird was downsized again and in much the same manner for 1980. Instead of an intermediate, the foundation this time was a compact, the practical "Fox" platform developed for the Ford Fairmont/Mercury Zephyr. But the size reductions for this ninth generation were just as dramatic as they'd been for the eighth: 16 inches in overall length, 4.5 inches in width, 5.5 inches between wheel centers. And compared to the '76 models, this new Bird looked positively tiny: two feet shorter, eight inches narrower, a foot less wheelbase, and a full half-ton lighter. Yet it was no less comfortable or luxurious than its immediate predecessors. And, thanks to a skilled design team headed by Toshie Saito, it was one of the most distinctive Birds in a long time. In the interest of reduced weight and better interior space utilization, construction reverted from body-on-frame to unitized for the first time since 1966. The interior was a pleasing blend of opulence and convenience, centered around what Ford called a "Master Control" seating position (new seats and instrument panel). Driver comfort got close attention, and a split front bench, buckets, and purpose-designed Recaro bucket seats were all available. The 302 V8 shifted to the options column, and its debored 255-cid relative moved in as standard. At mid-model year, Ford made its 200-cid six available as a credit option, a first in Thunderbird history.

Other important developments for 1980 included Ford's new four-speed overdrive automatic transmission, providing the traditional economy benefit of OD without the hassle of shifting; rack-and-pinion steering for precision unknown in previous Birds; and the all-coil suspension system proven in the Fairmont/Zephyr. Another bonus was greatly reduced service intervals. Over 50,000 miles, a 1980 required 29 scheduled maintenance procedures costing about $160, compared to 76 and about $700 for a '73. A mid-year offering expected in the Thunderbird's 25th year was the special Silver Anniversary edition, again featuring a tiara roof appliqué, plus standard 302 V8, the overdrive automatic, and gray-and-silver upholstery with complementing paintwork.

Ford's biggest problem with the Thunderbird in the 1970s was maintaining the individuality that had made the car so popular in the '50s and '60s. The corrective measures applied for 1977 and 1980 were successful from the sales standpoint, but it would be left to the aerodynamic 1983-84 model to reestablish the Bird as a unique product within the Ford lineup. Even then, it would have to share the limelight with a Mercury derivative. Nevertheless, the Thunderbird is once again much more interesting and likeable compared to the rolling pleasure palaces of the early '70s—and enthusiasts can be grateful for that.

Ford Thunderbird Specifications

1955

(wb 102.0)			Wght	Price	Prod
40A	conv 2S		2,980	2,944	16,155

1955 Engines	bore×stroke	bhp	availability
V8, 292.0	3.75×3.30	193	S-stickshift
V8, 292.0	3.75×3.30	198	S-automatic

1956

(wb 102.0)			Wght	Price	Prod
40A	conv 2S		3,038	3,151	15,631

1956 Engines	bore×stroke	bhp	availability
V8, 292.0	3.75×3.30	202	S-3-speed trans
V8, 312.0	3.80×3.44	215	S-overdrive
V8, 312.0	3.80×3.44	225	S-automatic

1957

(wb 102.0)			Wght	Price	Prod
40	conv 2S		3,145	3,408	21,380

1957 Engines	bore×stroke	bhp	availability
V8, 292.0	3.75×3.30	212	S-3-speed trans
V8, 312.0	3.80×3.44	245	S-overdrive, automatic
V8, 312.0	3.80×3.44	270/285	O-all (3-speed briefly)
V8, 312.0	3.80×3.44	300	O-auto; few od/3sp (superchgd)

1958

(wb 113.0)			Wght	Price	Prod
63A	htp cpe		3,876	3,631	35,758
76A	conv cpe		3,944	3,929	2,134

1958 Engines	bore×stroke	bhp	availability
V8, 352.0	4.00×3.50	300	S-all
V8, 430.0	4.30×3.70	350	O-prod questionable

1959

(wb 113.0)			Wght	Price	Prod
63A	htp cpe		3,813	3,696	57,195
76A	conv cpe		3,903	3,979	10,261

Ford Thunderbird

1959 Engines	bore×stroke	bhp	availability
V8, 352.0	4.00×3.50	300	S-all
V8, 430.0	4.30×3.70	350	O-all

1960

(wb 113.0)		Wght	Price	Prod
63A	htp cpe	3,799	3,755	78,447
63B	htp cpe, gold top	3,799	3,900*	2,536
76A	conv cpe	3,897	4,222	11,860

1960 Engines	bore×stroke	bhp	availability
V8, 352.0	4.00×3.50	300	S-all
V8, 430.0	4.30×3.70	350	O-all

*Estimated.

1961

(wb 113.0)		Wght	Price	Prod
63A	htp cpe	0,050	1,172	62,535
76A	conv cpe	4,130	4,639	10,516

1961 Engine	bore×stroke	bhp	availability
V8, 390.0	4.05×3.78	300	S-all

1962

(wb 113.0)		Wght	Price	Prod
63A	htp cpe	4,132	4,321	69,554*
63B	Landau htp cpe	4,144	4,398	
76A	conv cpe	4,370	4,788	7,030*
76B	Sports Roadster conv cpe	4,471	5,439	1,427*

*Some sources list total of 68,127 hardtops/Landaus and 9,884 convertibles.

1962 Engines	bore×stroke	bhp	availability
V8, 390.0	4.05×3.78	300	S-all
V8, 390.0	4.05×3.78	340	O-all

1963

Series 80 (wb 113.0)		Wght	Price	Prod
63A	htp cpe	4,195	4,445	42,806*
63B	Landau htp cpe	4,203	4,548	14,139*
76A	conv cpe	4,322	4,912	5,913*
76B	Sports Roadster conv cpe	4,396	5,563	455*

*Some sources list total of 59,000 hardtops/Landaus and 5,457 convertibles. Model 63B includes 2,000 Limited Edition Landaus with special trim; model 76B includes 37 units with 340-bhp engine.

1963 Engines	bore×stroke	bhp	availability
V8, 390.0	4.05×3.78	300	S-all
V8, 390.0	4.05×3.78	340	O-all

1964

Series 80 (wb 113.2)		Wght	Price	Prod
83	htp cpe	4,431	4,486	60,552
85	conv cpe	4,586	4,953	9,198
87	Landau htp cpe	4,441	4,589	22,715

1964 Engine	bore×stroke	bhp	availability
V8, 390.0	4.05×3.78	300	S-all

1965

Series 80 (wb 113.2)		Wght	Price	Prod
83	htp cpe	4,470	4,486	42,652
85	conv cpe	4,588	4,953	6,846
87	Landau htp cpe	4,478	4,589	20,974
87	Limited Ed Special Landau	4,500	4,639	4,500

1965 Engine	bore×stroke	bhp	availability
V8, 390.0	4.00×3.78	300	S-all

1966

Series 80 (wb 113.2)		Wght	Price	Prod
81	Town Hardtop cpe	4,359	4,483	15,633
83	htp cpe	4,386	4,426	13,389
85	conv cpe	4,496	4,879	5,049
87	Landau htp cpe	4,367	4,584	35,105

1966 Engines	bore×stroke	bhp	availability
V8, 390.0	4.00×3.78	315	S-all
V8, 428.0	4.13×3.98	345	O-all

1967

Series 80 (wb 114.7; 4d-117.2)		Wght	Price	Prod
81	htp cpe	4,248	4,603	15,567
82	Landau htp cpe	4,256	4,704	37,422
84	Landau sdn 4d	4,348	4,825	24,967

1967 Engines	bore×stroke	bhp	availability
V8, 390.0	4.00×3.78	315	S-all
V8, 428.0	4.13×3.98	345	O-all

1968

Series 80 (wb 114.7; 4d-117.2)		Wght	Price	Prod
83	htp cpe	4,366	4,716	9,977
84	Landau htp cpe	4,372	4,845	33,029
87	Landau sdn 4d	4,458	4,924	21,925

1968 Engines	bore×stroke	bhp	availability
V8, 390.0	4.00×3.78	315	S-all
V8, 429.0	4.36×3.59	360	O-all

1969

Series 80 (wb 114.7; 4d-117.2)		Wght	Price	Prod
83	htp cpe	4,348	4,824	5,913
84	Landau htp cpe	4,360	4,964	27,664
87	Landau sdn 4d	4,460	5,043	15,695

1969 Engine	bore×stroke	bhp	availability
V8, 429.0	4.36×3.59	360	S-all

1970

Series 80 (wb 114.7; 4d-117.2)		Wght	Price	Prod
83	htp cpe	4,354	4,961	5,116
84	Landau htp cpe	4,630	5,104	36,847
87	Landau sdn 4d	4,464	5,182	8,401

1970 Engine	bore×stroke	bhp	availability
V8, 429.0	4.36×3.59	360	S-all

1971

Series 80 (wb 115.0, 4d 118.0)		Wght	Price	Prod
83	htp cpe	4,389	5,295	9,146
84	Landau htp cpe	4,360	5,438	6,553
87	Landau sdn 4d	4,496	5,516	20,356

1971 Engine	bore×stroke	bhp	availability
V8, 429.0	4.36×3.59	360	S-all

1972

Series 80 (wb 120.4)		Wght	Price	Prod
87	htp cpe	4,373	5,293	57,814

1972 Engines	bore×stroke	bhp	availability
V8, 429.0	4.36×3.59	212	S-all
V8, 460.0	4.36×3.85	224	O-all

1973

Series 80 (wb 120.4)		Wght	Price	Prod
87	htp cpe	4,505	6,437	87,269

1973 Engines	bore×stroke	bhp	availability
V8, 429.0	4.36×3.59	208	S-all
V8, 460.0	4.36×3.85	219	O-all

1974

Series 80 (wb 120.4)		Wght	Price	Prod
87	htp cpe	4,825	7,330	58,443

1974 Engine	bore×stroke	bhp	availability
V8, 460.0	4.36×3.85	220	S-all

1975

Series 80 (wb 120.4)		Wght	Price	Prod
87	htp cpe	4,893	7,701	42,685

1975 Engine	bore×stroke	bhp	availability
V8, 460.0	4.36×3.85	194	S-all

1976

Series 80 (wb 120.4)		Wght	Price	Prod
87	htp cpe	4,808	7,790	52,935*

1976 Engine	bore×stroke	bhp	availability
V8, 460.0	4.36×3.85	202	S-all

*includes 30 commemorative editions.

1977

(wb 114.0)		Wght	Price	Prod
87	htp cpe	3,907	5,063	318,140
87	Town Landau cpe	4,104	7,990	

1977 Engines	bore×stroke	bhp	availability
V8, 302.0	4.00×3.00	130	S-all
V8, 351.0	4.00×3.50	135	S-in Calif.; O-all
V8, 400.0	4.00×4.00	173	O-all

1979 Heritage coupe

1978

(wb 114.0)		Wght	Price	Prod
87	htp cpe	3,907	5,498	333,757
87	Town Landau cpe	4,104	8,533	
87	Diamond Jubilee cpe	4,200	9,800	18,994

1978 Engines	bore×stroke	bhp	availability
V8, 302.0	4.00×3.00	134	S-all
V8, 351.0	4.00×3.50	152	O-all
V8, 400.0	4.00×4.00	166	O-all

1979—284,141 built

(wb 114.0)		Wght	Price	Prod
87	cpe	3,893	6,328	—
87	Town Landau cpe	4,284	9,239	—
87	Heritage cpe	4,178	11,060	—

1979 Engines	bore×stroke	bhp	availability
V8, 302.0	4.00×3.00	133	S-all
V8, 351.0	4.00×3.50	135/151	O-all

1980—156,803 built

(wb 108.4)		Wght	Price	Prod
87	cpe	3,118	6,816	—
87	Town Landau cpe	3,357	10,424	—
87	Silver Anniversary cpe	3,225	12,172	—

1980 Engines	bore×stroke	bhp	availability
V8, 255.0	3.68×3.00	115	S-all
V8, 302.0	4.00×3.00	131	S-Sil.Ann.; O-others

1980 coupe with Exterior Luxury Group option

Franklin

**Franklin Automobile Company
Syracuse, New York**

Franklin has a special distinction in being the only U.S. luxury make to achieve any real success with air-cooled engines. Since its founding in 1902, the firm had been known for high quality and innovation, with an emphasis on lightweight construction. In the 1920s and '30s, when cast iron was the standard stuff of engine blocks, pistons, and cylinder heads, Franklin used high-grade aluminum. And the company's commitment to air cooling got a boost when Charles A. Lindbergh made his historic transatlantic flight in 1927. His "Spirit of St. Louis" had an air-cooled engine, and Franklin advertising pointed out that these cars had something similar. The company even used the "Airman" name on some of its later models in honor of the Lone Eagle.

Like most manufacturers, Franklin greeted 1930 with an overly optimistic attitude towards the future. The firm had just had a banner sales year in 1929, and interest in aviation and air-cooled engines was at its peak. The 140-series models for 1930 reflected this optimism with new styling and a brand-new engine. The restyled radiator shell (which Franklin always called a "hood front," believing that a conventional-looking front end was essential for sales) had shutters that governed the amount of air entering the engine compartment. The shutter opening was auto-matically controlled by a thermostat connected to the number-one cylinder. The engine was supercharged and had six individually cast cylinders and overhead valves as before, but differed in having its incoming air directed to the sides of the cylinders from left to right. It thus became known as the "side-blast engine" among owners.

Franklin had always been a luxury make, and its chassis were the basis for many custom bodies by Derham, Dietrich, Locke, and Brunn. One of the more unusual 1930 styles was the Pirate, a four-door convertible designed by Dietrich and available as either a five-passenger phaeton or a seven-passenger touring. Its most striking feature was flared doors and runningboards completely covered by the lower body. Also new that year was the Pursuit dual-cowl phaeton, which had no external door handles in the interest of cleaner appearance. Upholstery in the driver's compartment wrapped up and over the outer edge of the doors, a feature that recalled aircraft cockpits of the period. Dietrich also built a popular four-door four-passenger speedster, which had a shortened body ending midway over the rear wheels. Most speedsters were closed cars with a permanent canvas tops, but a full-convertible option was available at extra cost.

As you might guess, aviators and aviatrix of the era consistently chose Franklins: Lindbergh, Amelia Earhart, and Frank Hawks were among them. But, though Franklin had its sporty models, it never sold on that basis. Most of these cars were purchased by professionals—doctors, attorneys, and business executives—and were painted in conservative colors and usually fitted with blackwall tires. The firm had pioneered closed cars by offering sedans before 1920, and these were the models favored in the '30s. So, Franklins may be described as conservative, elegant, and expensive. Their owners were loyal, and many were repeat customers.

Franklin reported that its share of what it called the "fine car business" gained 100 percent in the first quarter of 1930 compared to the same period in 1928. But in fact, there was no "fine car business" by then. The Depression had a death grip on the prestige market, and by the end of 1930, total sales had fallen to less than half of the 1929 record. In an attempt to maintain previous production levels, Franklin introduced the Transcontinent Six in May 1930. Though it was the lowest-priced sedan the company had ever offered, its $2395 asking price was still four times as much as for a new Model A Ford. In those days, remember, that sum amounted to a very nice annual salary.

The 1931 lineup was similar to 1930's, but prices were cut in an attempt to spark sales. Above the Transcontinent was a new series, the DeLuxe Six, strikingly handsome with more rakish clamshell fenders and flowing body lines designed by Ray Dietrich. Advertising continued to push the similarities with aircraft engineering, and phrases such as "riding like Gliding" dominated promotional material. But this enthusiasm was countered by the gloom of the

1930 Six coupe

1930 Six four-door sedan

1930 Six Pirate four-door touring

1932 Twelve club brougham

1931 DeLuxe Six victoria brougham

1933 Olympic four-door sedan

1931 DeLuxe Six Custom convertible speedster

1934 Airman four-door sedan

Depression, and sales for the model year were well below the previous total.

Franklin hatched a startling idea for 1932: a supercharged air-cooled V12. At 398 cubic inches and 150 bhp, it was initially planned for the new 132-inch-wheelbase Airman series. The engine had been ready for 1931, but financial problems held up introduction. Franklin had failed to meet payment on certain notes, and the banks sent in managers to protect their investment. Company president Edwin McEwan, meanwhile, had decided some changes were needed for the new Twelve, which accordingly bowed as an entirely new and larger car. It resembled previous Franklins in engine only. Instead of the traditional full-elliptic springs and tubular front axle, it had semi-elliptics and an I-beam front axle. Instead of bodies built by the Walker Company of Massachusetts, Franklin's long-time supplier, Twelve coachwork was hand-built at the company's own Syracuse factory. LeBaron was responsible for the

styling, distinguished by a sharply vee'd "hood cover" extending back to a rakishly angled windshield. By the standards of 1932, it was exotic and magnificent to look at: its size alone was overwhelming. But sales were hardly that, and Franklin's outlook was now quite desperate.

The lowest-priced Franklin line ever debuted for 1933. Dubbed Olympic, it was the product of a collaboration with Reo (see entry), another firm facing imminent demise. The basic recipe consisted of the Franklin six in the Reo Flying Cloud platform, with Franklin handling final assembly. Reo shipped 30 Flying Cloud bodies a day from its Lansing, Michigan factory to Syracuse, where they would roll out as new Olympics the following day. The tooling cost for this venture was a paltry $2500, so the Olympic's retail price was very attractive. But though it was a very good car, it arrived too late to save Franklin. The marque's last years were 1933-34, when a full line of Olympics, Airman Sixes, and Twelves was ostensibly offered.

Franklin Specifications

1930—5,744 built

145 Six (wb 125.0)

	Wght	Price	Prod
cpe 3-5P	3,880	2,610	—
conv cpe 3-5P	3,790	2,710	—
victoria brougham 4-6P	3,790	2,695	—
sdn 4d	3,930	2,585	—

147 Six (wb 132.0)

rdstr 2-4P	3,950	2,885	—
Pirate phtn 5P	4,120	2,885	—
Pirate touring 7P	4,050	2,885	—
Salon spdstr sdn 5P	4,130	2,715	—
sdn 7P	4,230	2,875	—
Pursuit phtn	4,120	2,885	—

141 Transcontinent Six (wb 125.0)*

cpe 305P	3,850	2,445	—
conv cpe 3-5P	3,775	2,495	—
victoria brougham 4P	3,845	2,495	—
sdn 4d	3,930	2,395	—

*Production combined with 1931 Series 151.

1930 Engine	bore×stroke	bhp	availability
L6, 274.0	3.50×4.75	95	S-all

1931—2,851 built

151 Transcontinent Six (wb 125.0)*

	Wght	Price	Prod
cpe 3-5P	3,850	1,845	—
conv cpe 3-5P	3,775	1,895	—
victoria brougham 4P	3,845	1,895	—
sdn 4d	3,930	1,795	—

153 DeLuxe Six (wb 132.0)

Cus conv spdstr 4P	4,110	2,695	—
conv cpe 3-5P	4,185	2,465	—
victoria brougham 5P	4,200	2,495	—
sdn 4d	4,220	2,395	—

*incl. 1930 Series 141.

1931 Engine	bore×stroke	bhp	availability
L6, 274.0	3.50×4.75	100	S-all

1932

16 S'Chgd Airman Six (wb 132.0)—1,700 blt*

	Wght	Price	Prod
cpe 3-5P	4,210	2,345	—
conv cpe 3-5P	4,285	2,390	—
victoria brougham 4P	4,390	2,445	—
sdn 4d	4,420	2,345	—

1930 Six Pirate seven-passenger touring

17 Supercharged Twelve (wb 144.0)—200 built*

sdn 4d	5,600	3,885	—
club brougham	5,515	3,885	—
sdn 7P	5,900	3,985	—
limo 7P	5,890	4,185	—

1932 Engines	bore×stroke	bhp	availability
L6, 274.0	3.50×4.75	100	S-16
V12, 398.0	3.25×4.00	150	S-17

*estimated.

1933

18 Olympic (wb 118.0)—889 built

	Wght	Price	Prod
cpe 3-5P	3,500	1,385	—
conv cpe 3-5P	3,425	1,500	—
sdn 4d	3,625	1,385	—

16-B Supercharged Airman Six (wb 132.0)—171 built

sdn 4d	4,420	1,935	—
Oxf sdn 4d	4,420	1,995	—
club sdn 5P	4,425	1,985	—
sdn 7P	4,500	2,135	—

17-A Supercharged Twelve (wb 144.0)—98 built*

sdn 4d	5,630	2,885	—
club brougham 5P	5,515	2,885	—
sdn 7P	5,900	2,985	—
limo 7P	5,890	3,185	—

*Incl. 1934 Series 17-B.

18-B Olympic (wb 118.0)—329 built

	Wght	Price	Prod
cpe 3-5P	3,500	1,435	—
conv cpe 3-5P	3,425	1,550	—
sdn 4d	3,625	1,435	—

1933 Engines	bore×stroke	bhp	availability
L6, 274.0	3.50×4.75	100	S-18,18-B, 16-B
V12, 398.0	3.25×4.00	150	S-17-B

1934

18-C Olympic (wb 118.0)—109 built

	Wght	Price	Prod
cpe 3-5P	3,500	1,435	—
conv cpe 3-5P	3,425	1,550	—
sdn 4d	3,625	1,435	—

19A S'Chgd Airman (wb 132.0)—186 built

cpe 3-5P	4,270	2,185	—
sdn 4d	4,500	2,185	—
club sdn 5P	4,610	2,285	—
sdn 7P	4,710	2,385	—

19-B S-Chgd Airman (wb 132.0)—111 built

cpe 3-5P	4,270	2,185	—
sdn 4d	4,500	2,185	—
club sdn 5P	4,610	2,285	—
sdn 7P	4,710	2,385	—

17-B S'Chgd Twelve (wb 144.0)—98 built*

sdn 4d	5,630	2,885	—
club brougham 5P	5,515	2,885	—
sdn 7P	5,900	2,985	—
limo 7P	5,890	3,185	—

1934 Engines	bore×stroke	bhp	availability
L6, 274.0	3.50×4.75	100	S-18-C,19,19-B
V12, 398.0	3.25×4.00	150	S-17-B

*incl. 1933 Series 17-A.

Frazer
Graham-Paige Motors/Kaiser-Frazer Corp.
Willow Run, Michigan

Joseph Washington Frazer, a descendant of the Virginia Washingtons, was a high-born aristocrat who loved motorcars. Shunning the high society in which he would have blended nicely, he enrolled in a technical college, and learned salesmanship with Packard, Pierce-Arrow, and General Motors. He was one of many talented men who helped Walter Percy Chrysler build a great corporation in the 1920s. He even named the Plymouth in 1928. During the '30s, Frazer breathed new life into Willys-Overland. In the '40s, he and his associates acquired old-line Graham-Paige Motors with the idea of producing a postwar car. The Frazer was the result.

Early in 1945, Frazer was looking for a moneyed partner. Friends introduced him to Henry J. Kaiser, the West Coast sand-and-gravel tycoon and wartime builder of Liberty ships. Kaiser-Frazer Corporation was founded in July 1945.

Initially, Frazers were to be produced by Graham-Paige and Kaisers by Kaiser-Frazer under a joint tenancy agreement at Willow Run, the huge factory 17 miles outside Detroit that once had produced bombers. In early 1947, however, Graham-Paige was unable to sustain plant investment and sold its automotive interests to Kaiser-Frazer. J. W. Frazer was company president from 1945 to early 1949; Henry J. Kaiser was chairman of the board.

During the closing years of the war, Frazer had asked inventor William Stout and custom-car designer Howard Darrin to come up with ideas for the new postwar model. Stout's creation, called Project-Y, was derived from his novel rear-engined Scarab. It was too unorthodox and complicated for G-P to build. Darrin, however, designed a smooth-looking sedan body with flow-through fenders, a high and blunt hood, and acres of space inside. Although the end result was not all Darrin's work, it led directly to the production Frazer.

Built initially as a four-door sedan only, the Frazer of-

1947 Standard four-door sedan

1948 Manhattan four-door sedan

Joseph W. Frazer (left) and Henry J. Kaiser (right) with their cars in 1946

355

Clay models (original smaller) for 1947 Frazer

1949-50 Manhattan convertible sedan

1949-50 Manhattan four-door sedan

fered tremendous interior space. At 64 inches, its front seat was one of the widest in the industry. Well over 80 percent of its total width was available for passenger room. Frazer's six-cylinder powerplant was derived from the Continental "Red Seal" industrial engine, incorporating improvements for its automotive application. Most of the engines were built by Kaiser-Frazer; a few were assembled by Continental. Frazer had no automatic transmission until 1951. Up to then, a three-speed manual transmission was offered, with Borg-Warner overdrive an $80 option. The box-section chassis was equipped with a conventional suspension—coils and wishbones in front, a beam axle and semi-elliptic leaf springs at the rear.

Production began in June 1946, with a ratio of one Frazer to every two Kaisers. The base sedan was joined by the elegantly upholstered (and usually two-toned) Manhattan, priced about $400 higher.

In a market laden with prewar designs, the all-new Frazer was a refreshing standout. It was extremely clean, with no side trim to speak of and only a modest horizontal grille. It demonstrated Darrin's styling ideals

in its lack of sheetmetal sculpture or decorative chrome. The long wheelbase provided a smooth ride, and the six-cylinder engine delivered excellent fuel economy. Some people thought these were shortcomings, however, and would have preferred eight cylinders and more chrome. Frazer ultimately offered optional hood ornaments and more glittery interiors, but was not able to provide an eight-cylinder engine, though several were considered.

The 1948 models were changed only in detail, such as redesigned nameplates. Prices increased. Despite the relatively tall prices, Frazer continued to do well in what was a seller's market. A total 48,071 cars were sold for 1948.

Kaiser-Frazer surprised the industry with its volume during those years. Observers had expressed a lack of confidence in the managerial combination. Henry Kaiser was a shipbuilder, they said, and didn't know an automobile from a motorboat. And Frazer had never built cars before; he'd only sold them. Yet, despite postwar material shortages, K-F succeeded. It formed a crack team of expeditors who foraged the country for everything from sheetmetal steel to copper wire. They usually got what they wanted—at a price. Thus, Kaiser-Frazer had the highest output of any independent in 1947-48, and a volume sufficient for ninth place in the industry production race.

The situation changed in 1949. Joseph Frazer realized this would be a facelift year for the company, and that its cars would be opposed by all-new designs from the Big Three and Nash. He recommended cutting back on production, but Henry Kaiser wanted even more output. The two were at loggerheads, so Frazer stepped down as president, taking the meaningless position of board vice-chairman. Kaiser's son Edgar assumed the presidency, tooled up for 200,000 cars—and sold only 58,000. The firm's downhill slide had begun.

The facelifted 1949 Frazers were well-built, good-looking cars. They adopted an egg-crate grille with prominent rectangular parking lamps and large, vertical, two-lens taillamps. A novel four-door convertible was added to the Manhattan series. It was a makeshift

1951 Vagabond four-door utility sedan

1951 Manhattan hardtop sedan

Proposed 1952 Manhattan based on '51 Kaiser

job at best. Engineers John Widman and Ralph Isbrandt, directed to do or die, sheared the top off a sedan, put little glass panes where the door pillars were, and purchased beefed-up X-member frames for an inordinate price. Priced at over $3000, they simply weren't salable in large quantities.

Frazer's 1949 sales were generally disappointing. About 5000 leftovers were reserialed for the brief 1950 model run, which ended in the spring of that year.

Model year 1951 was cleanup time for Frazer. At that point, Kaiser had a brand-new body, but the Frazer was merely a restyled 1949-50 Kaiser. The restyling made the Frazers look radically different, however, and 50,000 orders were placed. Yet far fewer than that were delivered, and the marque came to an end as soon as

all the old Kaiser bodies were used up.

For the abbreviated 1951 model year, the Frazer took on a new look. Leftover Kaiser utility sedans, with rear hatches and folding rear seat, were converted into Frazer Vagabonds; former Kaiser Virginian four-door hardtops became Manhattan sedans; pillared sedans were assigned to the standard Frazer series, but were trimmed similarly to the previous year's Manhattans. Altogether, 10,214 of the '51s were sold.

Kaiser-Frazer's styling department had created numerous renderings for future Frazers, based on the new 1951 Kaiser styling. However, with Joe Frazer out of the corporate picture, the Kaisers decided to discontinue the Frazer and concentrate on their new small car, the Henry J.

Frazer Specifications

1947

Standard (wb 123.5)		Wght	Price	Prod
F47	sdn 4d	3,340	2,295	36,120

Manhattan (wb 123.5)				
F47C	sdn 4d	3,375	2,712	32,655

1947 Engines	bore×stroke	bhp	availability
L6, 226.2	3.31×4.38	100	S-all
L6, 226.2	3.31×4.38	112	O-Manhattan

1948

F485 Standard (wb 123.5)		Wght	Price	Prod
4851	sdn 4d	3,340	2,483	29,480

F486 Manhattan (wb 123.5)				
4861	sdn 4d	3,375	2,746	18,591

1948 Engines	bore×stroke	bhp	availability
L6, 226.2	3.31×4.38	100	S-all
L6, 226.2	3.31×4.38	112	O-Manhattan

1949-50

F495/505 Standard (wb 123.5)		Wght	Price	Prod
4951/5051	sdn 4d	3,386	2,395	14,700*

F496/506 Manhattan (wb 123.5)				
4961/5051	sdn 4d	3,391	2,595	9,950*
4962/5052	conv sdn	3,726	3,295	70*

*Estimated: actual total 24,923. Years were combined by factory; estimated breakdown 85% 1949, 15% 1950.

1949-50 Engine	bore×stroke	bhp	availability
L6, 226.2	3.31×4.38	112	S-all

1951

F515 Standard (wb 123.5)		Wght	Price	Prod
5151	sdn 4d	3,456	2,359	6,900*
5155	Vagabond util sdn 4d	3,556	2,399	3,000*

F516 Manhattan (wb 123.5)				
5161	htp sdn	3,771	3,075	152
5162	conv sdn	3,941	3,075	131

*Estimated from actual total of 9,931.

1951 Engines	bore×stroke	bhp	availability
L6, 226.2	3.31×4.38	115	S-all

Graham

Graham-Paige Motors Corp.
Detroit, Michigan

The three Graham brothers—Joseph, Robert, and Ray—purchased the declining Paige Motor Company in 1927 to build their own car, in addition to a line of farm equipment. The car was called Graham-Paige through 1930 and simply Graham afterward, though Paige remained part of the company name. Production reached nearly 80,000 vehicles in 1929. Then came the Depression and company fortunes plunged. Graham-Paige lost money in every year of the '30s except 1933. Its attempt to rebound in 1938, dubbed "Spirit of Motion," was too radical for the public and was unsuccessful in the market.

The 1930 lineup comprised L-head sixes, straight eights, and several body styles arrayed in five series. The largest Eight included a beautiful town car by LeBaron on its basic 137-inch-wheelbase chassis. Special Sixes and Eights and Custom Eights all featured Graham-Paige's famous four-speed transmission. These offerings were continued through early 1932, along with a mid-1931 price leader called the "Prosperity Six." But Graham-Paige failed to prosper. Sales in 1930 were 33,560, only half the previous year's total, and slid to 20,428 in 1931.

Graham dug in for 1932, offering a conventional six-cylinder car and the new Blue Streak Eight. The latter featured magnificent styling by Amos Northup, who had also created the 1931 Reo Royale, with novel skirted fenders that would become a near-universal design element a few years later. Powered by a 245.4-cid eight, it had lots of special engineering: "banjo" frame, outboard springs, aluminum cylinder head. In good times it would have sold well, but 1932 was hardly a good year for anyone in the U.S. industry.

For 1934, Graham fielded another fine car, the Supercharged Custom Eight. Its blower ran at 23,000 rpm, and boosted rated output to 135 bhp. This was the first moderately priced supercharged car in America, and over the next six years, Graham would build more supercharged models than any company before or since. Production rose to 15,745 for model year 1934.

The line was reworked for 1935. Styling was now quite ugly, but sales nevertheless improved and would remain high for two more years. The Eights were dropped for 1936, but Graham-Paige now offered America's first supercharged six, which would be the company's basic engine through 1941. This year's Supercharger and Cavalier series shared their Hayes-built bodies with the Reo Flying Cloud, a result of merger talks between the two automakers during 1935. A marriage was never consummated, though Graham used Reo bodies through 1937, which resulted in some very ordinary-looking cars. The smaller 1936-37 Crusader was based on the 1935 design. Graham sold the tooling for it to Nissan of Japan in 1937 as a way to bolster sagging finances.

There was nothing ordinary about the "Spirit of Motion"

1930 Special Eight convertible sedan

1931 Prosperity Six four-door sedan

1932 Blue Streak Eight DeLuxe convertible coupe

design for 1938, dominated by a sharply undercut front end that soon earned the nickname "sharknose." It was Northup's last styling effort before his death. Again, Graham was far ahead in styling, and again the public did not respond: production dropped to less than 5000 units. For 1939, a "sharknose" two-door sedan and club coupe joined the existing four-door sedan, but Grahams remained poor sellers, and the "sharknose" was cancelled after 1940.

Company president Joseph Graham had put a half-

million dollars of his own money into the firm to keep it going. He realized a new model was needed, and quickly. In 1939 he was approached by Norman De Vaux, who'd once built his own cars and later was general manager of Hupmobile. Hupp was in similarly dire financial straits in '39, but De Vaux had an idea. He'd bought the tooling for the discontinued 1936-37 Cord Beverly sedan and wanted to build a Hupp version of it with rear-wheel drive instead of front drive. Graham said he'd agree to share the project's cost by building the bodies, provided his company could produce its own version with a Graham-Paige engine. The resulting Graham Hollywood had its own special "face" to distinguish it from Hupmobile's car, called the Skylark. But getting the line ready for production took many months, and the sleek new Hollywood sedans didn't roll out of the factory until May 1940.

The 1940 Graham line began with a slightly facelifted "Spirit of Motion" in two series, DeLuxe and Custom, available with or without supercharger. The blower was Graham's own centrifugal type, and was the only such unit available on a popularly priced car. Three body styles were offered: a combination coupe, and sedans with two or four doors. The powerplant, designed by Continental, developed 93 horsepower at 3800 rpm in standard form, or 120 bhp at 4000 rpm with supercharger. A high numerical axle ratio of 4.27:1 gave excellent acceleration. But production was a mere 1000 units.

The Hollywood was first billed as a convertible and sedan, priced at $1380 and $1250. In fact, only one or two convertible prototypes were built. The sedan used the supercharged 120-bhp six and a 115-inch wheelbase, 10 inches shorter than the Cord's. To fit the tall Graham engine into the Beverly's body, engineers had to offset the carburetor and air cleaner that gave clearance for the Hollywood's low hoodline. The front end featured a pleasing two-grille combination with freestanding headlamps and delicately curved front fenders.

The big problem in using the old Cord dies was their complexity: it took seven separate pieces of metal to make a top, for example. Joseph Graham had hoped to simplify such matters, but assembly operations were hampered. Perhaps production wouldn't have been high in any case, because the public had lost confidence in Graham by 1940. The "Spirit of Motion" models sold in such small quantities that they were dropped from the 1941 line. After July 1940, only the Hollywood was listed.

For 1941, Graham increased horsepower and sold the Hollywood for $968; the supercharger cost an additional $97. The low prices didn't help, and in November the factory closed for good.

Graham-Paige's departure from the car business a year before U.S. entry into World War II proved to be beneficial. The company received $20 million worth of defense contracts and prospered through the war. Joseph W. Frazer bought the firm in 1944, and built the

1932 Blue Streak Eight DeLuxe four-door sedan

1934 Standard Eight convertible coupe

1935 Special Eight convertible coupe

1936 Supercharger four-door touring sedan

1937 Supercharger four-door touring sedan

1937 Cavalier coupe

1940 Supercharger Custom four-door sedan

1939 Special two-door sedan

1940 Hollywood Custom Super convertible coupe (prototype)

Frazer as a G-P product in 1946-47 at Kaiser's Willow Run factory rather than G-P's old Detroit plant. In early 1947, Graham-Paige sold its automotive interests to Kaiser-Frazer, and in 1952 quit the farm product field as well. The firm then became a closed investment corporation, dropping the word 'Motors' from its title. Later, Graham-Paige operated Madison Square Garden and owned several professional New York athletic teams. All these non-automotive endeavors proved far more profitable than car making had ever been.

1940 Hollywood Custom Super four-door sedan

Graham Specifications

Note: all production figures approximate, based on assigned serial number spans.

1930

Standard Six (wb 115.0)—18,000 built

	Wght	Price	Prod
rdstr 2-4P	2,865	995	—
phtn 5P	2,910	1,015	—
cpe 2P	2,940	845	—
cpe 2-4P	2,995	895	—
cabriolet 2-4P	2,950	1,065	—
sdn 2d	3,015	895	—
Universal sdn 3W 5P	3,160	895	—
DeLuxe sdn 3W 5P	3,175	995	—
Town sdn 2W 5P	3,145	845	—
DeLuxe cpe 2P	2,940	895	—
DeLuxe cpe 2-4P	2,995	945	—
DeLuxe Town sdn 5P	3,145	945	—

Special Six (wb 115.0)—2,600 built

	Wght	Price	Prod
cpe 2P	3,230	1,195	—
cpe 2-4P	3,355	1,225	—
sdn 4d	3,390	1,225	—

Standard Eight (wb 122.0; 7P-134.0)—925 built

	Wght	Price	Prod
cpe 2-4P	3,735	1,445	—
sdn 4d	3,795	1,445	—
conv sdn 5P	3,725	1,985	—
sdn 7P	4,040	1,745	—

Special Eight (wb 122.0; 7P-134.0)—2,025 built

	Wght	Price	Prod
cpe 2-4P	3,805	1,595	—
sdn 4d	3,875	1,595	—
conv sdn 5P	3,785	2,085	—
sdn 7P	4,120	1,845	—

Custom Eight (wb 127.0; lwb-137.0)—575 built

	Wght	Price	Prod
rdstr 2-4P	4,009	2,225	
phtn 5P	3,975	2,295	
cpe 2-4P	4,105	2,225	250
cabriolet 2-4P	4,075	2,245	
sdn 4d	4,300	2,025	
lwb phtn 7P	4,200	2,295	
lwb sdn 4d	4,405	2,445	
Town sdn 4d (1wb)	4,465	2,455	
lwb sdn 7P	4,340	2,525	325
limo 7P (1wb)	4,590	2,595	
LeBaron limo sdn 7P (1wb)	4,535	3,940	
LeBaron town car 7P (1wb)	4,545	4,255	
LeBaron limo 7P (1wb)	4,545	4,505	

1930 Engines

	bore×stroke	bhp	availability
L6, 207.0	3.13×4.50	66	S-Standard 6
L6, 224.0	3.25×4.50	76	S-Special 6
L8, 298.6	3.25×4.50	100	S-Standard 8, Sp 8
L8, 322.0	3.38×4.50	120	S-Custom 8

1931

Standard Six (wb 115.0)—9,000 built

	Wght	Price	Prod
rdstr 2-4P	2,865	995	—
phtn 5P	2,910	1,015	—
bus cpe 2P	2,940	845	—
cpe 2-4P	2,995	895	—
spt cpe 2-4P	2,995	1,045	—
sdn 2d	3,015	895	—
Town sdn 5P	3,145	845	—
Univ sdn 5P	3,160	895	—
DeLuxe sdn 5P	3,175	995	—
DeLuxe Town sdn 5P	3,145	945	—

Special Six (wb 115.0)—1,400 built

	Wght	Price	Prod
bus cpe 2P	3,230	1,195	—
cpe 2-4P	3,355	1,225	—
sdn 5P	3,390	1,225	—

621 Six (wb 121.0)

	Wght	Price	Prod
rdstr 2-4P	3,835	1,795	NA
phtn 5P	3,805	1,865	NA
victoria cpe 4P	3,905	1,595	NA
cpe 2-4P	3,935	1,795	NA
sdn 5P	4,130	1,595	NA

Standard Eight (wb 122.0; lwb-134.0)

	Wght	Price	Prod
cpe 2-4P	3,735	1,445	NA
sdn 5P	3,795	1,445	NA
conv sdn 5P	3,725	1,985	NA
lwb sdn 7P	4,040	1,745	NA
lwb sdn5P	3,980	1,695	NA
limo 7P (1wb)	4,090	1,945	NA

Special Eight (wb 122.0; lwb-134.0)—2,025 built

		Wght	Price	Prod
822	cpe 2-4P	3,805	1,595	
822	sdn 5P	3,875	1,635	1,125
822	conv sdn 5P	3,785	1,635	
	lwb sdn 7P	4,120	1,845	
	lwb sdn 5P	4,060	1,795	900
	limo 7P (1wb)	4,110	2,045	

Custom Eight (wb 127.0; 1wb-137.0)

	Wght	Price	Prod
rdstr 2-4P	4,005	2,225	NA
phtn 5P	3,975	2,295	NA
victoria cpe 4P	4,075	2,025	NA
cabriolet 2-4P	4,075	2,245	NA
sdn 5P	4,300	2,025	NA
lwb phtn 7P	4,270	2,595	NA
lwb sdn 5P	4,470	2,455	NA
LeBaron limo 7P (1wb)	4,620	4,505	NA

1931 Engines

	bore×stroke	bhp	availability
L6, 207.0	3.13×4.50	66	S-Standard 6
L6, 224.0	3.25×4.50	76	S-Special 6
L6, 228.0	3.50×5.00	97	S-Standard 621
L8, 298.6	3.25×4.50	100	S-Standard 8, Special 8
L8, 322.0	3.38×4.50	120	S-Custom 8

1931 Second Series (Production began Jan. 1, '31)

Standard Six (wb 115.0)—11,600 built

	Wght	Price	Prod
rdstr 2-4P	2,930	895	—
sdn 5P	3,265	955	—
bus cpe 2P	3,120	845	—
cpe 2-4P	3,170	895	—
Town sdn 5P	3,220	895	—

Special Six (wb 115.0)—2,000 built

	Wght	Price	Prod
bus cpe 2P	3,175	925	—
cpe 2-4P	3,235	975	—
sdn 4d	3,330	1,035	—
Town sdn 5P	3,270	975	—

820 Special Eight (wb 120.0)—2,800 built

	Wght	Price	Prod
bus cpe 2P	3,445	1,155	—
cpe 2-4P	3,500	1,195	—
spt sdn 5P	3,565	1,195	—
sdn 5P	3,560	1,245	—

834 Custom Eight (wb 134.0)—200 built

	Wght	Price	Prod
sdn 4d	4,100	1,845	—
sdn 7P	4,190	1,895	—
limo 7P	4,245	2,095	—

Graham

1934 Custom Eight coupe

Prosperity Six (wb 113.0)—1,000 built

cpe 2P	3,015	785	—
cpe 2-4P	3,070	825	—
sdn 5P	3,100	825	—
Town sdn 5P	3,100	795	—

1931(2) Engines	bore×stroke	bhp	availability
L6, 207.0	3.13×4.50	70	S-Prosperity Six
L6, 224.0	3.25×4.50	76	S-Std 6, Sp 6
L8, 245.4	3.13×4.50	85	S-820
L8, 298.6	3.25×4.50	100	S-834

1932

Prosperity Six (wb 113.0)—700 built

	Wght	Price	Prod
cpe 2P	3,015	785	—
cpe 2-4P	3,070	825	—
sdn 5P	3,100	825	—
Town sdn 5P	3,100	795	—

Standard Six (wb 115.0)

rdstr 2-4P	2,930	945	NA
bus cpe 2P	3,120	934	NA
cpe 2-4P	3,170	985	NA
sdn 5P	3,265	995	NA
Town sdn 5P	3,220	975	NA

Special Six (wb 115.0)

rdstr 2-4P	2,995	985	NA
bus cpe 2P	3,175	985	NA
cpe 2-4P	3,235	1,025	NA
sdn 4d	3,330	1,035	NA
Town sdn 5P	3,270	1,015	NA

820 Special Eight (wb 120.0)

bus cpe 2P	3,445	1,185	NA
cpe 2-4P	3,500	1,225	NA
spt sdn 5P	3,565	1,235	NA
sdn 5P	3,560	1,285	NA

822 Special Eight (wb 122.0)

sdn 5P	3,875	1,635	NA
conv sdn 5P	3,785	1,635	NA

834 New Custom Eight (wb 134.0)

sdn 4d	4,100	1,895	NA
sdn 7P	4,190	1,945	NA
limo 7P	4,245	2,145	NA

57 Blue Streak Eight (wb 123.0)—9,714 built

cpe 2P	3,600	1,095	—
cpe 2-4P	3,675	1,145	—
sdn 5P	3,665	1,145	—
DeLuxe cpe 2P	3,620	1,170	—
DeLuxe cpe 2-4P	3,685	1,220	—
DeLuxe conv cpe	3,730	1,270	—
DeLuxe sdn 5P	3,690	1,220	—

Six (wb 113.0)—700 built

sdn 5P	3,205	795	—
Town sdn 5P	3,190	765	—

1932 Engines	bore×stroke	bhp	availability
L6, 207.0	3.13×4.50	70	S-Prosp Six, Six
L6, 224.0	3.25×4.50	76	S-Standard 6, Special 6
L8, 245.4	3.13×4.50	85	S-820
L8, 245.4	3.13×4.50	90	S-57
L8, 298.6	3.25×4.50	100	S-822, 834

1933

Six(a) (wb 118.0)

	Wght	Price	Prod
bus cpe 2P	3,480	825	NA
cpe 2-4P	3,545	875	NA
conv cab 2-4P	3,590	895	NA
sdn 5P	3,570	875	NA

Six(b) (wb 113.0)

sdn 5P	3,205	710	NA
Town sdn 5P	3,190	680	NA

57A Eight (wb 123.0)

cpe 2P	3,600	925	NA
cpe 2-4P	3,675	975	NA
sdn 5P	3,665	975	NA
DeLuxe cpe 2P	3,620	1,000	NA
DeLuxe cpe 2-4P	3,685	1,050	NA
DeLuxe conv cpe 2-4P	3,730	1,070	NA
DeLuxe sdn 5P	3,690	1,050	NA

65 Standard Six (wb 113.0)—4,000 built

bus cpe 2P	3,230	745	—
cpe 2-4P	3,295	795	—
conv cpe 2-4P	3,255	835	—
sdn 5P	3,265	795	—

64 Standard Eight (wb 119.0)—2,000 built

bus cpe 2P	3,455	845	—
cpe 2-4P	3,510	895	—
conv cpe 2-4P	3,470	935	—
sdn 5P	3,500	895	—

57A Custom Eight (wb 123.0)—1,000 built

cpe 2P	3,625	1,045	—
cpe 2-4P	3,680	1,095	—
sdn 5P	3,695	1,095	—

1933 Engines	bore×stroke	bhp	availability
L6, 207.0	3.13×4.50	70	S-Six(b)
L6, 224.0	3.25×4.50	80	S-Six(a)
L6, 224.0	3.25×4.50	85	S-Std Six
L8, 245.4	3.13×4.50	90	S-57A Eight
L8, 245.4	3.13×4.50	95	S-64, 57A Custom Eight

1934

65 Standard Six (wb 113.0)—6,000 built

	Wght	Price	Prod
cpe 2P	3,205	745	—
cpe 2-4P	3,275	795	—
conv cpe 2-4P	3,230	835	—

	Wght	Price	Prod
sdn 5P	3,240	795	—

64 Standard Eight (wb 119.0)—3,000 built

	Wght	Price	Prod
cpe 2P	3,415	845	—
cpe 2-4P	3,485	895	—
conv cpe 2-4P	3,430	935	—
sdn 5P	3,460	895	—

57A Custom Eight (wb 123.0)—4,000 built

	Wght	Price	Prod
cpe 2P	3,600	1,045	—
cpe 2-4P	3,640	1,095	—
sdn 5P	3,670	1,095	—

68 Six (wb 116.0)—8,550 built

	Wght	Price	Prod
Standard bus cpe 2P	3,135	695	
Standard cpe 2-4P	3,190	765	
Standard sdn 5P	3,165	775	
Standard sdn T/B 5P	3,260	810	
DeLuxe bus cpe 2P	3,165	805	5,320
DeLuxe cpe 2-4P	3,210	855	
DeLuxe conv cpe 2-4P	3,195	845	
DeLuxe sdn 5P	3,215	855	
DeLuxe sdn T/B 5P	3,300	890	

later production (from April 1934)

	Wght	Price	Prod
Standard bus cpe 2P	3,100	745	
Standard cpe 2-4P	3,165	795	
Standard conv cpe 2-4P	3,165	845	3,230
Standard sdn 5P	3,120	795	
Standard sdn T/B 5P	3,210	830	

67 Eight (wb 123.0)—915 built

	Wght	Price	Prod
Special bus cpe 2P	3,365	875	—
Special cpe 2-4P	3,450	925	—
Special sdn 5P	3,490	925	—
Special sdn T/B 5P	3,500	960	—
Standard bus cpe 2P	3,415	965	—
Standard cpe 2-4P	3,475	1,015	—
Standard conv cpe 2-4P	3,445	995	—
Standard sdn 5P	3,470	1,015	—
Standard sdn T/B 5P	3,555	1,050	—

69 Custom Eight (wb 123.0)—89 built

	Wght	Price	Prod
bus cpe 2P	3,505	1,245	—
cpe 2-4P	3,590	1,295	—
conv cpe 2-4P	3,535	1,295	—
sdn 5P	3,600	1,295	—
sdn T/B 5P	3,660	1,330	—

71 Custom Eight (wb 138.0)

	Wght	Price	Prod
sdn 7P	—	1,695	NA
sdn T/B 7P	—	1,730	NA

1934 Engines	bore×stroke	bhp	availability
L6, 224.0	3.25×4.50	85	S-65, 68
L8, 245.4	3.13×4.50	95	S-57A, 64, 67
L8, 265.4	3.25×4.50	135	S-69, 71

1935

68 Standard Six (wb 116.0)—4,000 built

	Wght	Price	Prod
bus cpe 3P	3,105	695	—
cpe 3-5P	3,165	765	—
conv cpe 3-5P	3,155	845	—
sdn 6P	3,135	775	—
sdn T/B 6P	3,225	810	—

67 Special Eight (wb 123.0)

	Wght	Price	Prod
cpe 3P	3,365	875	NA
cpe 3-5P	3,450	925	NA
conv cpe 3-5P	3,445	995	NA
sdn 6P	3,385	925	NA
sdn T/B 6P	3,480	960	NA

69 Special Eight (wb 123.0)—2,419 built

	Wght	Price	Prod
bus cpe 3P	3,445	1,045	—
cpe 3-5P	3,505	1,095	—
conv cpe 3-5P	3,490	1,165	—
sdn 6P	3,475	1,095	—
sdn T/B 6P	3,560	1,130	—

69 Supercharged Custom Eight (wb 123.0)—1,862 built

	Wght	Price	Prod
cpe 3P	3,505	1,245	—
cpe 3-5P	3,590	1,295	—
conv cpe 3-5P	3,535	1,295	—
sdn 6P	3,560	1,295	—
sdn T/B 6P	3,640	1,330	—

74 Six (wb 111.0)—11,470 built

	Wght	Price	Prod
touring sdn 2d	2,620	595	—
touring sdn 4d	2,655	635	—
DeLuxe touring sdn 2d	2,645	645	—
DeLuxe touring sdn 4d	2,680	685	—

73 Special Six (wb 116.0)—4,903 built

	Wght	Price	Prod
cpe 2P	3,130	795	—
cpe 2-4P	3,215	845	—
conv cpe 2-4P	3,190	915	—
touring sdn 4d	3,265	845	—

72 Eight (wb 123.0)—1,020 built

	Wght	Price	Prod
cpe 2P	3,385	925	—
cpe 2-4P	3,445	975	—
conv cpe 2-4P	3,425	1,045	—
touring sdn 4d	3,530	975	—

75 Supercharged Eight (wb 123.0)—1,252 built

	Wght	Price	Prod
cpe 2P	3,480	1,095	—
cpe 2-4P	3,585	1,145	—
conv cpe 2-4P	3,545	1,215	—
touring sdn 4d	3,640	1,145	—

1935 Engines	bore×stroke	bhp	availability
L6, 169.6	3.00×4.00	70	S-74
L6, 224.0	3.25×4.50	85	S-68, 73
L8, 245.4	3.13×4.50	95	S-67, 72
L8, 265.4	3.25×4.50	135	S-69/Sp 8
L8, 265.4	3.25×4.50	140+	S-69/S'chgd, 75

1936

80/80A Crusader (wb 111.0)—3,220 built

	Wght	Price	Prod
touring sdn 2d	2,665	640	—
touring sdn 2d T/B	2,690	655	—
touring sdn 4d	2,700	680	—
touring sdn 4d T/B	2,735	695	—

90 Cavalier (wb 115.0)—2,755 built

	Wght	Price	Prod
bus cpe 3P	2,815	725	—
cpe 3-5P	2,880	710	—
conv cpe 3-5P	2,960	775	—
touring sdn 2d	2,930	720	—
touring sdn 2d T/B	2,930	825	—
touring sdn 4d	3,015	750	—
touring sdn 4d T/B	3,015	825	—

90A Cavalier (wb 115.0)—7,750 built

	Wght	Price	Prod
bus cpe 3P	2,730	750	—
cpe 3-5P	2,795	735	—
conv cpe 3-5P	2,875	800	—
touring sdn 2d	2,785	745	—
touring sdn 2d T/B	2,785	850	—
touring sdn 4d	2,870	775	—
touring sdn 4d T/B	2,870	850	—

110 Supercharger (wb 115.0)—5,500 built

	Wght	Price	Prod
bus cpe 2P	2,930	865	—

	Wght	Price	Prod
cpe 2-4P	2,995	875	—
conv cpe 3-5P	3,075	910	—
touring sdn 2d	3,060	850	—
touring sdn 2d T/B	3,060	880	—
touring sdn 4d	3,080	895	—
touring sdn 4d T/B	3,080	925	—
Custom touring sdn 4d T/B	3,200	1,170	—

1936 Engines	bore×stroke	bhp	availability
L6, 169.6	3.00×4.00	70	S-80, 80A
L6, 199.1	3.25×4.00	80	S-90A
L6, 217.8	3.25×4.38	85	S-90
L6, 217.8	3.25×4.38	112	S-110

1937

85 Crusader (wb 111.0)—4,218 built

	Wght	Price	Prod
touring sdn 2d	2,660	690	—
touring sdn 2d T/B	2,675	720	—
touring sdn 4d	2,695	770	—
touring sdn 4d T/B	2,715	795	—

95 Cavalier (wb 116.0)—8,250 built

	Wght	Price	Prod
bus cpe 3P	2,815	850	
cpe 3-5P	2,880	900	—
conv cpe 3-5P	2,960	945	—
touring sdn 2d	2,930	875	—
touring sdn 2d T/B	2,930	905	—
touring sdn 4d	2,960	905	—
touring sdn 4d T/B	2,945	935	—

116 Supercharger (wb 116.0)—5,551 built

	Wght	Price	Prod
bus cpe 3P	2,975	1,015	—
cpe 3-5P	3,040	1,045	—
conv cpe 3-5P	3,120	1,080	—
touring sdn 2d	3,105	1,020	—
touring sdn 2d T/B	3,105	1,050	—
touring sdn 4d	3,125	1,050	—
touring sdn 4d T/B	3,125	1,080	—

120 Custom Supercharger (wb 116.0; lwb-120.0)—200 built

	Wght	Price	Prod
bus cpe 3P	3,020	1,105	—
cpe 3-5P	3,055	1,135	—
conv cpe 3-5P	3,135	1,170	—
lwb touring sdn 4d	3,200	1,160	—
lwb touring sdn 4d T/B	3,200	1,190	—

1937 Engines	bore×stroke	bhp	availability
L6, 169.6	3.00×4.00	70	S-85
L6, 199.1	3.25×4.00	85	S-95
L6, 199.1	3.25×4.00	106	S-116
L6, 217.8	3.25×4.38	116	S-120

1938

96 Six (wb 120.0)—2,610 built

	Wght	Price	Prod
Standard sdn 4d T/B	3,250	1,025	—
Special sdn 4d T/B	3,275	1,075	—

97 Supercharger (wb 120.0)—2,410 built

	Wght	Price	Prod
sdn 4d T/B	3,345	1,198	—
Custom sdn 4d T/B	3,350	1,320	—

1938 Engines	bore×stroke	bhp	availability
L6, 217.8	3.25×4.38	90	S-96
L6, 217.8	3.25×4.38	116	S-97

1939

96 Special (wb 120.0)—2,913 built

	Wght	Price	Prod
Combination cpe 5P	3,185	940	—
sdn 2d T/B	3,230	940	—
sdn 4d T/B	3,240	965	—
Custom Combination cpe 5P	3,200	1,070	—
Custom sdn 2d T/B	3,245	1,070	—
Custom sdn 4d T/B	3,255	1,095	—

97 Supercharger (wb 120.0)—2,479 built

	Wght	Price	Prod
Combination cpe 5P	3,260	1,070	—
sdn 2d T/B	3,285	1,070	—
sdn 4d T/B	3,295	1,095	—
Custom Combination cpe 5P	3,290	1,200	—
Custom sdn 2d T/B	3,315	1,200	—
Custom sdn 4d T/B	3,325	1,225	—

1939 Engines	bore×stroke	bhp	availability
L6, 217.8	3.25×4.38	90	S-96
L6, 217.8	3.25×4.38	116	S-97; O-96 Custom

Note:
Production figures shown are based on published serial number spans and may be deemed reasonably accurate, though some numbers may have been skipped. For comparison, Graham *calendar* year production figures were as follows:

1930	33,560	1935	15,965
1931	28,428	1936	16,439
1932	12,967	1937	13,987
1933	10,970	1938	4,139
1934	11,430	1939	3,876

1940

107 Supercharger (wb 120.0)—est. 1,000 built (includes Standard)

	Wght	Price	Prod
Deluxe cpe	3,245	1,160	—
Deluxe sdn 2d	3,250	1,135	—
Deluxe sdn 4d	3,250	1,160	—
Custom cpe	3,370	1,295	—
Custom sdn 2d	3,365	1,265	—
Custom sdn 4d	3,370	1,295	—

108 Standard (wb 120.0)

	Wght	Price	Prod
Deluxe cpe	3,190	1,020	—
Deluxe sdn 2d	3,195	995	—
Deluxe sdn 4d	3,195	1,015	—
Custom cpe	3,315	1,160	—
Custom sdn 2d	3,315	1,135	—
Custom sdn 4d	3,320	1,160	—

Hollywood Custom Super (wb. 115.0)

	Wght	Price	Prod
sdn 4d	2,965	1,250	*
conv cpe (prototype)	3,075	—	1–2

1940 Engines	bore×stroke	bhp	availability
L6, 217.8	3.25×4.38	93	S-unsupercharged
L6, 217.8	3.25×4.38	120	S-supercharged

1941

109 Custom Hollywood Schgd (wb 115.0)

	Wght	Price	Prod
sdn 4d	2,965	1,065	*

113 Custom Hollywood (wb 115.0)

	Wght	Price	Prod
sdn 4d	2,915	968	*

1941 Engines	bore×stroke	bhp	availability
L6, 217.8	3.25×4.38	95	S-unsupercharged
L6, 217.8	3.25×4.38	124	S-supercharged

*Total 1940–41 Hollywood production 1,859.

Henry J
Kaiser-Frazer Corp.
Willow Run, Michigan

Kaiser-Frazer was at the crossroads in 1949. The company had degenerated from healthy, record-high production in 1948 to just a skeleton the following year—from ninth place in the industry to fourteenth. Henry Kaiser, deciding to press on, borrowed $44 million from the Reconstruction Finance Corporation to maintain inventories, and tooled up for new models. This caused the abrupt departure of cofounder Joseph W. Frazer. Kaiser promised his lenders that part of the loan would go toward a new small car that all Americans could afford to buy: the Henry J.

Designer Howard "Dutch" Darrin had suggested a short-wheelbase compact related to his beautiful 1951 Kaiser, which was already locked up during Henry J

planning. But Mr. Kaiser wanted something all-new. He settled on a prototype built by American Metal Products, a Detroit supplier of frames and springs for car seats. Darrin reluctantly tried to improve the styling of this ungainly little two-door sedan, applying his trademark "dip" in the beltline and little tailfins.

Henry Js were powered by Willys L-head fours and sixes of 134 and 161 cubic inches, respectively. Incredible economy was promised for the four, while the six-cylinder car turned out to be a hot rod, giving 0 to 60 times of around 14 seconds thanks to its light body. Though built on a 100-inch wheelbase, the Henry J could handle four passengers and a considerable amount of luggage. The basic four-cylinder model cost

K-F 1948 proposal for Henry J based on '51 Kaiser

1952 Corsair DeLuxe (six) two-door sedan

1951 Standard (four) two-door sedan

1952 Corsair (four) two-door sedan

1951 DeLuxe (six) two-door sedan

1952 Vagabond DeLuxe (six) two-door sedan

1953 Corsair (four) two-door sedan

1954 Corsair DeLuxe (six) two-door sedan

about $200 less than a Chevrolet.

K-F began its 1951 model year early, in March 1950. For a while, the Henry J was in demand: nearly 82,000 of the '51s were sold. Unfortunately, that saturated the market and sales were down sharply by the end of 1952.

The 1952-54 models received a mild facelift—a restyled full-width grille, repositioned taillights, and new interiors. An interim model, marketed in an effort to use up unwanted '51s, was the 1952 Vagabond. This was merely the previous year's model fitted with a "continental" outside spare tire, identifying script, and a black-plastic-and-chrome hood ornament.

By 1954 when the last Henry Js (reserialed 1953s) were sold, it was evident the project had failed. Many felt the original approach was wrong. The austere, stripped 1951 models lacked gloveboxes, trunklids, and other features normally held essential—they were just too plain for most buyers. "I would have brought it out dressed up," said J. W. Frazer, "and undressed it later." Advance plans for hardtops, wagons, four-door sedans, and convertibles died with the last Henry J. Total production came to about 30,000 units.

Henry J Specifications

1951

K513 Standard (wb 100.0)		Wght	Price	Prod
5134	sdn 2d	2,293	1,363	38,500*
K514 DeLuxe (wb 100.0)				
5144	sdn 2d	2,341	1,499	43,400*

1951 Engines	bore×stroke	bhp	availability
L4, 134.2	3.13×4.38	68	S-K513
L6, 161.0	3.13×3.50	80	S-K514

1952

K523 Vagabond (wb 100.0)		Wght	Price	Prod
5234	sdn 2d	2,365	1,407	3,000*
K524 Vagabond DeLuxe (wb 100.0)				
5244	sdn 2d	2,385	1,552	4,000*
K523 Corsair (wb 100.0)				
5234	sdn 2d	2,370	1,517	7,600*
K524 Corsair DeLuxe (wb 100.0)				
5244	sdn 2d	2,405	1,664	8,900*

1952 Engines	bore×stroke	bhp	availability
L4, 134.2	3.13×4.38	68	S-K523
L6, 161.0	3.13×3.50	80	S-K524

1953

K533 Corsair (wb 100.0)		Wght	Price	Prod
5334	sdn 2d	2,395	1,399	8,500*
K534 Corsair DeLuxe (wb 100.0)				
5344	sdn 2d	2,445	1,561	8,100*

1953 Engines	bore×stroke	bhp	availability
L4, 134.2	3.13×4.38	68	S-K533
L6, 161.0	3.13×3.50	80	S-K534

1954

K543 Corsair (wb 100.0)		Wght	Price	Prod
5434	sdn 2d	2,405	1,404	800*
K544 Corsair DeLuxe (wb 100.0)				
5444	sdn 2d	2,455	1,566	300*

1954 Engines	bore×stroke	bhp	availability
L4, 134.2	3.13×4.38	68	S-K543
L6, 161.0	3.13×3.50	80	S-K544

*Estimates based on highest serial numbers found. Total model year production:

1951 all	81,942
1952 Vagabond	7,017
1952 Corsair	23,568
1953 all	16,672
1954 all	1,123

Hudson

Hudson Motor Car Co.
Detroit, Michigan (1930-54)

American Motors Corp.
Kenosha, Wisconsin (1955-57)

Founded in 1908, Hudson produced some of America's finest, fleetest automobiles throughout its history, and was usually among the industry production leaders. The low-priced four-cylinder Essex, introduced in 1919, had boosted the company to third place behind Ford and Chevrolet by 1925, and the firm ranked third, fourth, or fifth overall through 1930. Then Hudson began to flounder. From 300,000 units in 1929, production declined to barely 40,000 by 1933 as the firm reeled under the effects of the Depression. Had it not been for the success of the speedy, inexpensive Essex Terraplane (see Essex), the company might not have survived to see 1940.

Hudson had forged its reputation during the '20s largely on its Super and Special Sixes, big, smooth-looking,

solidly built cars that offered a lot of performance for the money. In 1930, however, Hudson introduced the Great Eight, powered by an engine that was actually smaller than its previous sixes and delivering only 80 horsepower to propel a heavy chassis. Though this powerplant had an integrally cast block and crankcase and the first counterweighted crankshaft ever designed for a straight eight, its splash lubrication system was outmoded. Yet the company stayed with this mill for several more years.

Sadly for Hudson, 1930 saw the closure of the Biddle and Smart coachworks, its long-time supplier of magnificent open bodies. The company turned to Murray and Briggs for phaeton and speedster designs in the early '30s, and a few eight-cylinder chassis were clothed in dashing

1930 Great Eight brougham

1933 Super Six Pacemaker four-door sedan

1931 Greater Eight Family Sedan

1933 Pacemaker Eight Major brougham by Briggs

1932 Greater Eight Major club sedan

1933 Super Six Pacemaker coupe

LeBaron coachwork. Through 1933, the last year for classic four-square styling at Hudson, there were numerous body styles listed on wheelbases from 119 to 133 inches: roadsters, victorias, convertibles, sedans, town sedans, coupes, and broughams. It was an attractive line that would have done justice to many more expensive makes.

Hudson did not field six-cylinder models in 1930-32, selling them instead under the Essex label. It was a mistake. Not only did Hudson sixes have a flawless reputaion, but the general economy would have been conducive to sales. To fill the void, the company launched a new Hudson Super Six in 1933, essentially the 193-cid Terraplane engine in the 113-inch-wheelbase Hudson chassis. But the firm hit bottom this year and sales of all models were few. For 1934, Hudson combined its sixes in its new Terraplane junior line.

Along with just about everybody else, Hudson embraced

streamlining in the mid-'30s as the old classic look, with its roots in Greek architecture, gradually gave way to the new style. The 1934-35s were transitional designs, still basically boxy but less so than before. Styling was all-new for 1936 and could be compared to the Chrysler and DeSoto Airstreams of a year earlier—not quite Airflow-radical, but much more modern. These Hudsons had skirted fenders, and their rear wheel openings were often covered. They also had tall, rounded, Plymouth-like die-cast grilles and all-steel bodies with rather dowdy appearance.

This move toward the popular "potato shape" came a bit late for Hudson, as its decreased market share during 1935-36 suggests. While 85,000 units had earned it fifth place in production during 1934, its annual volume of more than 100,000 units in 1935-37 was only good for eighth place. There is also evidence the company was cutting prices past the point of profitability, and it continued to lose money despite increased volume. It made less than $1

1934 Eight DeLuxe coupe

1937 DeLuxe Eight convertible coupe

1935 Custom Eight touring brougham

1938 Model 112 Six DeLuxe four-door sedan

1936 DeLuxe Eight convertible coupe

1938 Custom Eight Country Club four-door sedan

million profit in 1934 and 1937; with the 1938 recession, it lost close to $5 million. The decline continued through 1940, when defense work helped the company recover.

By 1938, and in the face of that year's economic downturn, Roy D. Chapin reversed his emphasis on performance and concentrated on economy. The Terraplane became a Hudson series that year, only to vanish the next, and there was an all-new big-car entry, the 112 (named for its wheelbase). In performance, the 112 was the complete opposite of the Terraplane: 0-60 mph took 35 seconds and top speed was barely 70 mph. But it did return up to 24 miles per gallon, and prices were low.

For 1939, the 112 was reduced to a single group of Deluxe models. With the national economy looking up again, Hudson launched the 118-inch-wheelbase Pacemaker and the 122-inch-wheelbase Country Club Series, both powered by the 212.1-cid Terraplane engine. Two large, comfortable closed models were offered under the curious Big Boy badge, and a Country Club Eight series on longer wheelbases topped the lineup. This year's Hudsons were the last based on the bulky body introduced for 1936, and they were probably the best looking, thanks to some deft design work. The long-wheelbase models were especially graceful, but all models had horizontal grilles with thick bars that made for a cleaner frontal appearance than the controversial waterfall grille of 1937-38.

Hudson had completely restyled its 1939 line, so the 1940 models were merely facelifted. The look was not innovative, but pleasing and clean: a rakishly pointed nose, a divided horizontal grille, and little side ornamentation. Hudson added another page to its book of endurance runs in 1940 by traveling over 20,000 miles at an average of 70.5 miles an hour, setting a new American Automobile Association record.

The 1940 line comprised seven distinct series, three wheelbases, and three different engines. On a 113-inch wheelbase were the Traveler and DeLuxe, offered as a convertible and convertible sedan powered by Hudson's smaller L-head six. A larger six powered the 118-inch-wheelbase Super, offered in a wide variety of body styles, and the 125-inch-wheelbase "Big Boy" series, made up of a carry-all and a seven-passenger sedan. The L-head eight was available for the 118-inch-wheelbase models, including some deluxe variants. The 125-inch-wheelbase eight-cylinder models formed the Country Club series. This consisted of two six-passenger sedans and one seven-passenger sedan. Registrations in 1940 did not exceed 80,000; the company lost about $1.5 million for the calendar year.

Another facelift was performed for 1941, several new models appeared, and Hudson's unit body was revised for new wheelbases: 116 inches for Traveler and DeLuxe Sixes, 121 and 128 inches for the larger Sixes and Eights. A new Commodore series debuted, listing a wide range of models on the two longer wheelbases. All the '41s had new parking lights mounted in large chrome housings atop the front fenders. Registrations were almost the same as in 1940, but the company made a profit of nearly $4 million. Credit this to defense

1939 Country Club Eight convertible brougham

1940 Eight convertible coupe

1941 Super Six four-door sedan

1941 Commodore Eight convertible coupe

contracts, which began materializing in early 1941 and increased the company's total sales by 10 percent.

The defense bonus allowed Hudson a breather. The 1942 line, announced in August 1941, was one of the prettiest of all. Running boards were hidden, the grille was lowered and cleaned up, and optional lights were placed on the fenders. Hudson's famous white triangle logo, placed on either side of the hood, was illuminated to add a touch of distinction after dark. The cars were soundly built and richly appointed. Again, the line began with the series of small sixes—coupes, sedans, and convertible sedans. Next was the Super Six, offering the same body choices plus a station wagon. At the top of the line were the Commodore Six and

Eight. Most of them rode the 121-inch wheelbase, though one long sedan was offered as well. The war put an end to all car production by February 2, so Hudson registered only 5396 cars in calendar year 1942.

During World War II, Hudson built Helldiver airplanes, Hudson Invader engines for landing craft, sections for B-29 bombers and Aircobras, and a variety of naval munitions. The company made a small profit in the war years, and jumped back into car production quickly after V-J Day. Hudson's output of 4735 cars in 1945 was enough for fifth place in this abbreviated calendar year. The firm hadn't held that slot since 1934— and would not hold it again.

The 1946-47 cars were slightly facelifted prewar mod-

1942 Commodore Eight four-door sedan

1947 Super Six four-door sedan

1942 Super Six convertible coupe

1946 Super Six convertible

1948 Super Six Brougham convertible

1948 Super Six club coupe

els. The engines were still sixes and eights; the wheelbase still 121 inches. There were three transmission options: overdrive, priced at $101; Drive-Master, $112; and Vacumotive Drive, $47. Vacumotive automatically engaged and disengaged the clutch; Drive-Master eliminated both clutch and gear lever motion. Hudson built over 90,000 of its 1946 models, two-thirds of which were Super Sixes.

The 1947s were unchanged except in details such as a new chrome nameplate on the trunk, right-hand as well as left-hand door locks, and a small lip around the center grille emblem housing. Again, Hudson produced around 90,000 cars, though its industry ranking changed. Ninth in production for 1946, Hudson dropped to 11th in '47, despite a 10 percent gain in actual volume. Other manufacturers were growing faster as all Detroit responded to the unprecedented seller's market. Hudson sales exceeded $120 million in 1946, and the firm made a profit of over $2.3 million. For 1948, Hudson had a brand-new car with a new engine, and made more money than it had at any other time after the war, netting $13.2 million on gross sales of $274 million.

The Step-down unit-body Hudson of 1948-49 (both models were identical except for serial numbers) was one of the great postwar designs. Low and sleek, it hugged the ground and handled well, thanks to a radically low center of gravity. The design team was led by Frank Spring, a fixture at Hudson and ahead of his time. The Step-down evolved from wartime doodling—sleek, aerodynamic forms modeled in quarter-scale clay and plaster. Like all Hudsons since 1932, it had a unit body and chassis that was extremely strong and rattle-free. The nickname Step-down referred to the dropped floorpan, which was completely surrounded by frame girders. It was probably the safest automotive package of its time, and perhaps one of the safest ever.

It was also beautiful in an understated way. The sides were clean, the grille was low and horizontal, the taillights were modest. The dashboard was flat and positioned upright in front of the driver. It contained a big speedometer and clock, warning lights for battery discharge and low oil pressure, and gauges for fuel and water temperature.

As the new Hudsons were introduced in mid-1948, dealers cheered. Here was precisely the formula they needed for good sales in those heady days when there were lots of eager customers. Four models, all riding a new 124-inch wheelbase, were offered: the Super Six and Eight, and the Commodore Six and Eight.

Violating an old Detroit rule about restyling and re-engineering in the same year, Hudson also brought out a new engine for '48: the 262-cid Super Six. It developed 121 bhp at 4000 rpm, only seven horsepower less than the eight. Although it had only four main bearings instead of five like the eight-cylinder unit, the six was a smooth-running, durable engine. By 1951, it had evolved into the 308-cid Hornet powerplant, the largest modern L-head six ever built. The Hornet was king of

stock-car racing from 1952 through 1954. Even in 1948 tune, the big six packed surprising power. The car could do 0 to 40 mph in 12 seconds using Drive-Master. Manual-shift cars were even faster. Hudsons had been adequate but not outstanding performers in 1946-47; the gutsy sixes made them some of the quickest, most roadable American cars for 1948-49.

There was one problem. In creating the beautiful Step-down, Hudson committed itself to a design that would be difficult and costly to change. Unit bodies are almost impossible to rework, and Hudson lacked the financial base to add new Step-down derivatives such as a station wagon, which probably would have sold well.

1950 Pacemaker four-door sedan

1951 Commodore Six Custom Hollywood hardtop coupe

1953 Super Wasp four-door sedan

1954 Jet-Liner four-door sedan

1954 Hornet Special club coupe

1954 Super Wasp Hollywood hardtop coupe

Marshall Teague, AAA point leader, in '53

For too many years, each new Hudson would look too much like last year's model. This, combined with the natural decline of the seller's market after 1950, eventually destroyed the make in the mid-'50s. By 1952, production had dropped to well under 100,000 units. In early 1954, Hudson merged with Nash, forming American Motors. To a large extent, Hudson's problems were common to all independents after the war: they had too little money for really significant production, and too little depth for sufficient change and innovation to keep the public interested.

Roy D. Chapin, Jr., who was a Hudson sales executive in the 1950s, explained the situation this way: "If you don't have enough money to do something and do it right, and if you haven't learned to specialize in a given thing . . . sooner or later you find you just can't do everything. [Hudson was] usually reacting, rather than anticipating."

Nevertheless, the firm entered the '50s in fine fettle. It sold more than 143,000 cars in 1950, including more than 60,000 of its new Pacemaker. Generally priced under $2000, the Pacemaker used a destroked version of the flathead Super Six. Performance was as good as that of Nash's top-line Ambassador, and put it well ahead in its price class. The Super Six and Super Eight and the Commodore Six and Commodore Eight were carried over from 1948-49.

All models were available with overdrive, and Drive-Master or Supermatic Drive—two Hudson semi-automatics of repute. Drive-Master relieved the driver of the need to shift and declutch. The car was started by placing the shift lever in "High" and accelerating. The driver would ease up on the accelerator when the shift to regular drive was desired. With Supermatic, a high cruising gear was added; the shift to high occurred automatically at 22 mph when a dashboard button was engaged. In 1950, overdrive cost $95 extra; Drive-Master cost $105; Supermatic was priced at $199. None of these was a substitute for full automatic transmission, of course. When Hudson offered proprietary Hydra-Matic in '51 (at only $158 extra) Supermatic was dropped.

The Hudson Hornet, with its powerful six, was introduced in 1951 with four body styles, and was priced the same as the Commodore Eight. The Hornet powerplant produced only 145 bhp at 3800 rpm in stock form, but was capable of much more than that in the hands of precision tuners. The most famous of these, Marshall Teague, claimed he could get 112 mph from a Hornet certified as stock by AAA or NASCAR. He was helped by an enthusiastic cadré of Hudson engineers who developed "severe usage" options that were really thinly disguised racing parts. Twin H-Power, offered in 1953, consisted of twin carbs and dual manifold induction (the first dual manifold on a six) for greatly improved breathing. The "7-X" racing engine, which arrived in late 1953, used .020 overbored bylinders, special cam and head, larger valves, higher compression, Twin H-Power, and headers. Output was about 210 bhp.

1954 Italia sport coupe

1955 Hornet Custom Hollywood hardtop coupe

1955 Rambler Custom Cross Country station wagon

1956 Hornet Custom four-door sedan

The Hornet was invincible in AAA and NASCAR racing during most of 1951-54. Teague finished his 1952 AAA season with a 1000-point lead over his nearest rival after winning 12 of the 13 stock-car events. NASCAR drivers like Herb Thomas, Dick Rathmann, Al Keller, and Frank Mundy drove Hornets to 27 victories in 1952, 21 in 1953, and 17 in 1954. Usually, three out of every four Hornets that entered a race would finish. Even after 1955 when the Step-down was replaced by the Nash-bodied model, Hornets were still winning races.

But racing success wasn't enough to keep the Hudson ship afloat. Though the company kept adding and subtracting series through 1954, it was unable to add new body styles. The standard Pacemaker and the Super Eight were dropped for '51, when the Hornet and the Hollywood hardtop were added; the Wasp replaced the Super Six for '52. All the Commodores were discontinued for '53, and the line of big cars was cut. A lower-priced Hornet Special for '54 failed to spark sales. Throughout this period, Hudson could offer only two wheelbases and four basic body styles. Production dropped accordingly.

The Step-down cried for restyling in 1952, but Hudson couldn't afford it. The firm had sunk $12 million into a compact, the ill-fated Jet, in 1953. Using old Commodore Eight tooling, the Jet's 202-cid six produced 104 bhp. Twin H-power and a high-compression head were optional, and made for a speedy package. Jets were

roadable and well-built, but not very pretty. Over the objections of chief designer Spring, management had insisted on bolt-upright, slab-sided styling that failed to impress many customers. Hudson tried hard, adding a very cheap Family Club sedan and luxurious Jet-Liner models in 1954, but the car still sold poorly.

The Jet did spark a project that might have become the long-awaited and much-needed new Hudson: the Italia. This four-place *gran turismo* on the Jet chassis was designed by Spring and built by Carrozzeria Touring of Milan. Italias had wraparound windshields, doors cut into the roof, fender scoops that ducted cooling air to the brakes, flow-through ventilation, and form-fitting leather seats. They were 10 inches lower than the production '54 Hornet. Though powered by the 114-bhp Hornet engine, Italias weren't very fast, and the aluminum body was not very solid. But these were problems that might have been solved if Hudson only had money for a major commitment. The firm's conservative engineers held little hope for the wild European styling anyway. Only 25 "production" Italias, plus the prototype and a four-door derivative called X-161, were built. Roy D. Chapin, Jr., later AMC President, served as Italia sales manager. He shoved them out as fast as he could at $4800 a copy. "I got rid of them," he said, adding, "It wasn't one of my greatest accomplishments."

Late in 1953, rumors began circulating about a Hudson-Nash merger. Nash couldn't have come calling at a better time. Hudson sales were sinking: the books were

1957 Hornet Custom four-door sedan

1957 Hornet Custom Hollywood hardtop coupe

written in red ink. Between January 1, 1954 and the end of April when it closed as an independent company, Hudson had lost over $6 million on sales of only $28.7 million. Old-hat styling; the ugly, slow-selling Jet; a weak dealer network; and insufficient capital for development of new models were the reasons.

In merger talks, George Mason of Nash insisted on one big condition: the Jet had to go. Hudson President A. E. Barit fought this, but not for long. He was in a very poor position to bargain.

The merger was really a Nash takeover. Hudson's Detroit plant was soon shut down, and production was transferred to Kenosha, Wisconsin. Naturally, everybody recognized the all-new 1955 Hudson: it was a restyled Nash. It used Nash's unit-construction sedan and hardtop bodyshell, with a special eggcrate grille, distinct trim, and reworked rear end. The only link to previous Hudsons was the dashboard, which used the old 1954 instruments. Wasps were powered by the former 202 Jet engine; the big six was retained for the Hornet; the Hornet V8 used a 320 Packard mill of 208 bhp. Twin H-Power was available on the sixes, increasing Hornet and Wasp horsepower. A line of Metropolitans and Ramblers with Hudson emblems was also offered.

American Motors introduced its own 190-bhp V8 for 1956, replacing the Packard unit in mid-season for the Hornet Special. The small Wasp Six remained, as did the Hornet Six, along with the usual assortment of so-called Hudson Ramblers. "V-line Styling" was the way AMC described the horrendous chrome-plated nightmare created by Edmund E. Anderson. It was the ugliest Hudson in a generation. And the AMC V8 was far less powerful than the Packard unit. An anemic engine and terrible styling made for depressing sales. Only 10,671 non-Rambler Hudsons were peddled in '56. In the next year—Hudson's last—styling didn't improve, and only 3876 were sold, all V-8s. Rambler was listed as a separate make in 1957, but a rumor that Ramblers would diverge into very different 1958 Hudson and Nash models came to naught. There was no money for that.

AMC's decision to drop Hudson and Nash was only common sense. Said Roy Chapin, "We ran Hudson and Nash Metropolitans and Ramblers—it was a charade. They were basically the exact same automobiles, and the decision really was one that said we've got to spend our money and our effort and our concentration on the Rambler because we haven't got the dough to update the big Nashes and the big Hudsons."

Hudson Specifications

1930

Great Eight (wb 119.0; lwb-126.0)	Wght	Price	Prod
rdstr 2-4P	2,870	995	
phtn 5P	2,940	965	
cpe 2P	3,010	885	
cpe 2-4P	3,060	925	74,891
coach 5P	3,080	895	
sdn 4d	3,200	1,025	
Sun sdn 5P	3,100	1,045	
lwb phtn 7P	3,080	1,160	
lwb brougham 4d	3,210	1,195	10,516
lwb touring sdn 5P	3,270	1,145	
lwb sdn 7P	3,385	1,295	

1930 Engine	bore×stroke	bhp	availability
L8, 213.5	2.75×4.50	80	S-all

1931

Greater Eight (wb 119.0; 1wb-126.0)	Wght	Price	Prod
rdstr 2-4P	2,675	995	
phtn 5P	2,745	1,095	
cpe 2P	3,865	875	
cpe 2-4P	2,955	925	16,477
coach 5P	2,975	895	
Town sdn 5P	3,055	945	
Std sdn 4d	3,115	995	
spt cpe 2-4P	3,145	1,065	
lwb phtn 7P	3,055	1,295	
lwb touring sdn 5P	3,190	1,145	

	Wght	Price	Prod
lwb Family sdn 5-7P	3,230	1,195	
lwb brougham 5P	3,190	1,225	
lwb club sdn 5P	3,225	1,445	5,769
lwb sdn 7P	3,305	1,450	
lwb DeLuxe brougham 5P	3,480	1,375	
lwb Special sdn 5P	3,430	1,325	

1931 Engine	bore×stroke	bhp	availability
L8, 233.7	2.88×4.50	87	S-all

1932*

Greater Eight—Standard (wb 119.0)—5,933 built

	Wght	Price	Prod
cpe 2P	3,145	995	—
cpe 2-4P	3,175	1,045	—
conv cpe 2-4P	3,085	1,195	—
Special cpe 2-4P	3,215	1,195	—
coach 5P	3,190	1,025	—
Town sdn 5P	3,270	1,050	—
Std sdn 5P	3,285	1,095	—

Greater Eight—Sterling (wb 126.0)

	Wght	Price	Prod
Suburban 5P	3,350	1,275	NA
Special sdn 5P	3,415	1,295	NA

Greater Eight—Major (wb 132.0)—1,116 built

	Wght	Price	Prod
phtn 7P	3,350	1,395	—
touring sdn 5P	3,475	1,445	—
club sdn 5P	3,555	1,495	—
brougham 5P	3,560	1,495	—
sdn 7P	3,590	1,595	—

*(Cal. year prod. 57,550)

1932 Engine	bore×stroke	bhp	availability
L8, 254.0	3.00×4.50	101	S-all

1933

Super Six Pacemaker (wb 113.0)—962 built

	Wght	Price	Prod
phtn 5P	2,700	765	—
bus cpe 2P	2,780	695	—
cpe 2-4P	2,845	735	—
conv cpe 2-4P	—	845	—
coach 5P	2,900	695	—
sdn 4d	2,980	765	—

Pacemaker Eight (wb 119.0; Major-132.0)—1,890 built

	Wght	Price	Prod
Standard cpe 2-4P	3,190	995	—
Standard conv cpe 2-4P	3,145	1,145	—
Standard coach 5P	3,245	975	—
Standard sdn 4d	3,345	1,045	—
Major phtn 7P	—	1,250	—
Major sdn 4d T/B	3,485	1,250	—
Major brougham 5P	3,650	1,350	—
Major club sdn 5P	3,630	1,350	—
Major sdn 7P	3,605	1,350	—

1933 Engines	bore×stroke	bhp	availability
L6, 193.0	2.94×4.75	73	S-Six
L8, 354.1	3.00×4.50	101	S-Eight

1934

LT/LU Eight (wb 116.0)—18,679 built

	Wght	Price	Prod
Special bus cpe 2P	2,720	695	—
Special cpe 2P	2,750	725	—
Special cpe 2-4P	2,795	775	—
Special conv cpe 2-4P	2,815	835	—
Special comp. victoria 5P	2,880	785	—
Special coach 5P	2,855	745	—
Special sdn 4d	2,905	805	—
Special sdn 4d T/B	2,930	845	—
DeLuxe cpe 2P	2,805	815	—
DeLuxe cpe 2-4P	2,850	855	—
DeLuxe comp. victoria 5P	2,895	875	—
DeLuxe coach 5P	2,870	835	—
DeLuxe sdn 4d	2,930	895	—
DeLuxe sdn 4d T/B	2,955	935	—

LL/LLU Major Eight (wb 123.0)—4,158 built

	Wght	Price	Prod
Special sdn 4d touring	2,950	970	—
Special sdn 4d T/B touring	2,975	1,000	—
DeLuxe club sdn 4P	3,085	1,070	—
DeLuxe 5P brougham	3,075	1,145	—
DeLuxe club sdn 4P T/B	3,110	1,125	—

LTS Challenger Eight (wb 116.0)—4,217 built

	Wght	Price	Prod
cpe 2P	2,720	685	—
cpe 2-4P	2,765	735	—
conv cpe 2-4P	2,785	800	—
coach 5P	2,860	705	—
sdn 4d	2,910	765	—

1934 Engines	bore×stroke	bhp	availability
L8, 254.7	3.00×4.00	108	S-Eight, Challenger
L8, 254.7	3.00×4.00	113	S-Major

1935

GH Big Six (wb 116.0)—7,624 built

	Wght	Price	Prod
cpe 2P	2,600	695	—
cpe 2-4P	2,665	740	—
conv cpe 2-4P	2,640	790	—
touring brougham 5P	2,735	742	—
coach 5P	2,720	710	—
sdn 4d	2,780	770	—
Suburban sdn 5P	2,795	802	—

Eight (wb 117.0)

		Wght	Price	Prod
HT	Special cpe 2P	2,740	760	
HT	Special cpe 2-4P	2,810	810	
HT	Special conv cpe 2-4P	2,765	860	
HT	Special touring b'ham 5P	2,855	812	7,150
HT	Special coach 5P	2,840	780	
HT	Special sdn 4d	2,890	840	
HT	Suburban sdn 5P	2,905	872	
HU	DeLuxe cpe 2P	2,790	845	
HU	DeLuxe cpe 2-4P	2,855	895	
HU	DeLuxe conv cpe 2-4P	2,805	955	
HU	DeLuxe touring b'ham 5P	2,895	907	3,097
HU	DeLuxe coach 5P	2,880	875	
HU	DeLuxe sdn 4d	2,945	935	
HU	DeLuxe Suburban sdn 5P	2,960	967	

HHU Custom Eight (wb 124.0)—1,460 built

	Wght	Price	Prod
brougham 5P	3,055	1,095	—
touring brougham 5P	3,070	1,127	—
club sdn 5P	3,130	1,025	—
Suburban sdn 5P	3,145	1,057	—

Eight (wb 124.0)

	Wght	Price	Prod
HTL Special brougham 5P	2,995	930	
HTL Special touring b'ham 5P	3,010	962	
HTL club sdn 5P	2,975	880	968
HTL Special Suburban sdn 5P	2,990	912	
HUL DeLuxe brougham 5P	3,055	1,025	
HUL DeLuxe touring b'ham 5P	3,070	1,057	
HUL DeLuxe club sdn 5P	3,015	975	721
HUL DeLuxe Suburban sdn 5P	3,030	1,007	

1935 Engines	bore×stroke	bhp	availability
L6, 212.1	3.00×5.00	93	S-Big Six
L8, 254.5	3.00×4.50	113	S-all Eights

Hudson

1936

63 Custom Six (wb 120.0)—9,720 built

		Wght	Price	Prod
63	cpe 2P	2,730	710	—
63	cpe 2-4P	2,810	755	—
63	conv cpe 2-4P	2,870	810	—
63	brougham 2d 5P	2,830	730	—
63	touring 2d 5P	2,830	755	—
63	sdn 4d	2,880	785	—
63	touring sdn 4d	2,880	810	—

64/66 DeLuxe Eight (wb 120.0; lwb-127.0)*

64	cpe 2P	2,865	760	—
64	cpe 2-4P	2,965	810	—
64	conv cpe 2-4P	3,000	875	—
64	brougham 2d 5P	2,985	790	—
64	touring brougham 2d 5P	2,985	815	—
64	sdn 4d	3,045	830	—
64	touring sdn 4d	3,045	855	—
66	sdn 4d (lwb)	3,110	855	—
66	lwb touring sdn 4d	3,110	880	—

65/67 Custom Eight (wb 120.0; lwb 127.0)*

65	cpe 2P	2,915	845	—
65	cpe 2-4P	3,000	895	—
65	conv cpe 2-4P	3,015	970	—
65	brougham 2d 5P	3,034	885	—
65	touring brougham 2d 5P	3,034	910	—
65	sdn 4d	3,075	925	—
65	touring sdn 4d	3,075	950	—
67	lwb sdn 4d	3,140	950	—
67	lwb touring sdn 4d	3,140	975	—

*Total Eight production: 16,627

1936 Engines	bore×stroke	bhp	availability
L6, 212.0	3.00×5.00	93	S-63
L8, 254.5	3.00×4.50	113	S-Eights

1937

73 Custom Six (wb 122.0)—6,813 built

		Wght	Price	Prod
73	bus cpe 2P	2,760	865	—
73	cpe 3P	2,805	905	—
73	victoria cpe 3P	2,865	950	—
73	conv cpe 2P	2,870	1,005	—
73	brougham 2d 5P	2,925	930	—
73	touring brougham 2d 5P	2,925	955	—
73	sdn 4d	2,990	980	—
73	touring sdn 4d	2,990	1,005	—
73	conv brougham 4P	2,945	1,000	—

74/76 DeLuxe (wb 122.0; lwb-129.0)

74	cpe 3P	3,010	950	
74	victoria cpe 3P	3,055	1,015	
74	conv cpe 2P	3,020	1,080	
74	brougham 2d 5P	3,105	1,000	
74	touring brougham 2d 5P	3,105	1,025	5,628
74	sdn 4d	3,135	1,040	
74	touring sdn 4d	3,135	1,065	
74	conv brougham 4P	3,125	1,165	
76	sdn 4d	3,205	1,065	
76	lwb touring sdn 4d	3,205	1,090	1,097

75/77 Custom Eight (wb 122.0; lwb-129.0)

75	cpe 3P	3,055	1,050	
75	victoria cpe 3P	3,085	1,100	
75	conv cpe 2P	3,070	1,175	
75	brougham 2d 5P	3,135	1,090	
75	touring brougham 2d 5P	3,135	1,115	3,274
75	sdn 4d	3,195	1,140	
75	touring sdn 4d	3,195	1,165	
75	conv brougham 4P	3,160	1,260	
77	lwb sdn 5P	3,260	1,165	
77	lwb touring sdn 5P	3,260	1,190	3,652

1937 Engines	bore×stroke	bhp	availability
L6, 212.0	3.00×5.00	101	S-73
L6, 212.0	3.00×5.00	107	O-73
L8, 254.5	3.00×4.50	122	S-Eights
L8, 254.5	3.00×4.50	128	O-Eights

1938

80/88 Terraplane Six (wb 117.0; lwb-124.0)

		Wght	Price	Prod
80	Util cpe 3P	2,840	789	—
80	Util coach 6P	2,835	779	—
80	Util touring cabriolet 6P	2,840	799	—
80	Util wgn 4d	3,055	965	—
88	lwb sdn 6P	2,965	974	—
88	lwb touring sdn 6P	2,970	995	—

81 Terraplane DeLuxe Six (wb 117.0)

81	cpe 3P	2,725	789	—
81	victoria cpe 3-5P	2,775	835	—
81	conv cpe 3P	2,780	926	—
81	brougham 6P	2,820	822	—
81	touring brougham 6P	2,825	843	—
81	sdn 6P	2,885	864	—
81	touring sdn 6P	2,890	884	—
81	conv brougham 6P	2,860	990	—

82 Terraplane Super Six (wb 117.0)

82	cpe 3P	2,755	845	—
82	victoria cpe 3-5P	2,805	886	—
82	conv cpe 3P	2,835	971	—
82	brougham 6P	2,865	878	—
82	touring brougham 6P	2,870	899	—
82	sdn 6P	2,925	915	—
82	touring sdn 6P	2,930	935	—
82	conv brougham 6P	2,880	1,034	—

89 "112" Six (wb 112.0)

	Standard cpe 3P	2,500	694	
	Standard victoria cpe 4P	2,540	740	
	Standard conv cpe 3P	2,545	835	
	Standard brougham 6P	2,595	724	
	Standard touring brougham 6P	2,600	743	
	Standard sdn 4d	2,600	755	27,475
	Standard touring sdn 5d	2,625	775	
	Standard conv brougham 6P	2,610	886	
	Utility cpe 3P	2,660	724	
	Utility coach 6P	2,600	697	
	Utility coach T/B 6P	2,605	716	
	Deluxe cpe 3P	2,500	704	
	Deluxe victoria cpe 4P	2,540	750	
	Deluxe conv cpe 3P	2,545	840	
	Deluxe brougham 6P	2,595	734	NA
	Deluxe touring brougham 6P	2,600	753	
	Deluxe sdn 4d	2,620	765	
	Deluxe touring sdn 4d	2,625	785	
	Deluxe conv brougham 6P	2,610	891	

83 Custom Six (wb 122.0)

	cpe 3P	2,825	909	—
	victoria cpe 3-5P	2,880	955	—
	conv cpe 3P	2,895	1,041	—
	brougham 6P	2,935	948	—
	touring brougham 6P	2,940	968	—
	sdn 4d	3,005	984	—
	touring sdn 4d	3,010	1,005	—
	conv brougham 6P	2,975	1,104	—

84 Deluxe Eight (wb 122.0)

	cpe 3P	3,010	990	—
	victoria cpe 3-5P	3,060	1,031	—

		Wght	Price	Prod
	conv cpe 3P	3,060	1,121	—
	brougham 6P	3,115	1,028	—
	touring brougham 6P	3,120	1,049	—
	sdn 4d	3,155	1,060	—
	touring sdn 4d	3,160	1,080	—
	conv brougham 6P	3,140	1,185	—

85/87 Custom Eight (wb 122.0; 1wb-129.0)

		Wght	Price	Prod
85	cpe 3P	3,020	1,080	—
85	victoria cpe 3-5P	3,080	1,131	—
85	brougham 6P	3,140	1,134	—
85	touring brougham 6P	3,145	1,155	—
85	sdn 4d	3,190	1,171	—
85	touring sdn	3,195	1,191	—
87	Country Club sdn 4d (lwb)	3,270	1,199	—
87	Country Club vic sdn 4d (lwb)	3,275	1,299	—

1938 Engines	bore×stroke	bhp	availability
L6, 175.0	3.00×4.13	83	S-89
L6, 212.0	3.00×5.00	96	S-80,81,88
L6, 212.0	3.00×5.00	101	S-82,83
L6, 212.0	3.00×5.00	107	O-83
L8, 254.4	3.00×4.50	122	S-84,85,87

1939

90 "112" Deluxe Six (wb 112.0)

	Wght	Price	Prod
Traveler cpe 3P	2,544	695	—
cpe 3P	2,587	745	—
victoria cpe 4P	2,622	791	—
conv cpe 3P	2,627	886	—
touring brougham 6P	2,682	775	—
conv brougham 6P	2,732	936	—
touring sdn 4d	2,712	806	—
Utility coach 6P	2,634	725	—
Utility cpe 3P	2,714	750	—
Utility wgn 4d	2,880	931	—

91 Pacemaker Six (wb 118.0)

	Wght	Price	Prod
cpe 3P	2,717	793	—
victoria cpe 5P	2,752	844	—
touring brougham 6P	2,832	823	—
touring sdn 4d	2,867	854	—

92 Six (wb 118.0)

	Wght	Price	Prod
cpe 3P	2,757	833	—

		Wght	Price	Prod
	victoria cpe 5P	2,787	879	—
	conv cpe 3P	2,782	982	—
	touring brougham 6P	2,847	866	—
	conv brougham 6P	2,892	1,042	—
	touring sdn 4d	2,897	908	—

93 Country Club Six (wb 122.0)

	Wght	Price	Prod
cpe 3P	2,848	919	—
victoria cpe 5P	2,893	967	—
conv cpe 3P	2,898	1,052	—
touring brougham 6P	2,968	960	—
conv brougham 6P	2,983	1,115	—
touring sdn 4d	3,023	995	—

98 Big Boy Six (wb 119.0)

	Wght	Price	Prod
sdn 4d	2,909	884	—
sdn 7P	3,022	1,114	—

95/97 Country Club Eight (wb 122.0; lwb-129.0)

		Wght	Price	Prod
95	cpe 3P	3,003	1,009	—
95	victoria cpe 5P	3,053	1,051	—
95	conv cpe 3P	3,033	1,138	—
95	touring brougham 6P	3,138	1,049	—
95	conv brougham 6P	3,123	1,201	—
95	touring sdn 4d	3,193	1,079	—
97	lwb touring sdn 4d	3,268	1,174	—
97	lwb sdn 7P	3,378	1,430	—

1939 Engines	bore×stroke	bhp	availability
L6, 175.0	3.00×4.13	86	S-90, 98 sdn 4d
L6, 212.0	3.00×5.00	101	S-91, 92, 93, 98 sdn 7P
L8, 254.4	3.00×4.50	122	S-95, 97

Note:
Production figures for 1930-39 shown above were compiled via analysis of serial number spans listed by industry sources. Since serials coincided roughly with calendar year production, the figures shown may be deemed reasonably accurate, although it is possible that some figures may be actually lower due to skipping within a number span. Where published spans were obviously assigned in advance, and have no bearing on the true quantity produced, they are omitted. For compaison, Hudson *calendar year* production according to Don Butler's *History of Hudson* is as follows:

1930	36,674	1935	29,476
1931	17,487	1936	25,409
1932	7,777	1937	19,848
1933	2,401	1938	50,270
1934	27,130	1939	81,521

1940

40-T Traveler (wb 113.0)*

	Wght	Price	Prod
cpe 3P	2,800	670	—
Victoria cpe 4P	2,830	750	—
sdn 2d	2,895	735	—
sdn 4d	2,940	763	—

40-P Deluxe (wb 113.0)*

	Wght	Price	Prod
cpe 3P	2,840	745	—
Victoria cpe 4P	2,865	791	—
conv cpe	2,860	930	—
sdn 2d	2,930	775	—
sdn 4d	2,965	808	—
conv sdn	2,920	955	—

41 Super (wb 118.0)*

	Wght	Price	Prod
cpe 3P	2,950	809	—
Victoria cpe 4P	2,980	860	—
conv cpe	2,980	995	—
sdn 2d	3,020	839	—
sdn 4d	3,050	870	—
conv sdn	3,020	1,030	—

1939 Model 112 DeLuxe Six four-door touring sedan

43 Country Club (wb 125.0)*

	Wght	Price	Prod
sdn 4d	3,240	1,018	—
Special sdn 4d	3,240	1,044	—
sdn 4d, 7P	3,355	1,230	—

44 Eight (wb 118.0)*

	Wght	Price	Prod
cpe 3P	3,040	860	—
Victoria cpe 4P	3,075	942	—
conv cpe	3,065	1,087	—
sdn 2d	3,140	918	—
sdn 4d	3,185	952	—
conv sdn	3,130	1,122	—

47 Country Club Eight (wb 125.0)*

	Wght	Price	Prod
sdn 4d	3,285	1,118	—
Special sdn 4d	3,285	1,144	—
sdn 4d, 7P	3,400	1,330	—

48 Big Boy (wb 125.0)*

	Wght	Price	Prod
Carry-all sdn 4d	3,245	989	—
sdn 4d, 7P	3,140	1,095	—

*Total model year production: 87,915; Sixes: 77,295; Eights: 10,620.

1940 Engines	bore×stroke	bhp	availability
L6, 175.0	3.00×4.13	92	S-40
L6, 212.0	3.00×5.00	98	S-48
L6, 212.0	3.00×5.00	102	S-41, 43
L8, 254.0	3.00×4.50	128	S-44, 47

1941

10-T Traveler (wb 116.0)*

	Wght	Price	Prod
cpe 3P	2,765	754	—
club cpe 4P	2,835	847	—
sdn 2d	2,870	824	—
sdn 4d	2,900	852	—

10-P Deluxe (wb 116.0)*

	Wght	Price	Prod
cpe 3P	2,840	870	—
club cpe 4P	2,880	917	—
sdn 2d	2,905	891	—
sdn 4d	2,945	925	—
conv sdn	3,085	1,132	140 est

11 Super (wb 121.0)*

	Wght	Price	Prod
cpe 3P	2,925	956	—
club cpe 4P	2,995	1,011	—
sdn 2d	3,005	976	—
sdn 4d	3,040	1,007	—
conv sdn	3,145	1,230	300 est
wgn 4d	3,315	1,298	100 est

12 Commodore Six (wb 121.0)*

	Wght	Price	Prod
cpe 3P	2,970	1,028	—
club cpe 4P	3,045	1,090	—
sdn 2d	3,070	1,059	—
sdn 4d	3,135	1,087	—
conv sdn	3,160	1,297	200 est

14 Commodore Eight (wb 121.0)*

	Wght	Price	Prod
cpe 3P	3,110	1,071	—
club cpe 4P	3,195	1,133	—
sdn 2d	3,200	1,096	—
sdn 4d	3,250	1,132	—
conv sdn	3,350	1,347	200 est
wgn 4d	3,400	1,384	80 est

15-17 Commodore Eight (wb 121–128)*

	Wght	Price	Prod
cpe 3P, wb 121.0	3,185	1,162	—
club cpe 4P, wb 121.0	3,235	1,225	—
sdn 4d, wb 128.0	3,370	1,330	—
sdn 4d, 7P, wb 128.0	3,440	1,537	—

18 Big Boy (wb 128.0)*

	Wght	Price	Prod
sdn 4d, 7P	3,155	1,223	—

*Total model year production: 91,769; Sixes: 82,051; Eights: 9,718.

1941 Engines	bore×stroke	bhp	availability
L6, 175.0	3.00×4.13	92	S-10
L6, 212.0	3.00×5.00	98	S-18
L6, 212.0	3.00×5.00	102	S-11, 12
L8, 254.0	3.00×4.50	128	S-14, 15, 17

1942

20T Traveler (wb 116.0)*

	Wght	Price	Prod
cpe 3P	2,795	828	—
club cpe 4P	2,845	897	—
sdn 2d	2,895	878	—
sdn 4d	2,940	905	—

20P Deluxe (wb 116.0)*

	Wght	Price	Prod
cpe 3P	2,845	916	—
club cpe 4P	2,900	967	—
sdn 2d	2,935	940	—
sdn 4d	2,971	978	—
conv sdn	3,140	1,212	—

21 Super (wb 121.0)*

	Wght	Price	Prod
cpe 3P	2,950	1,036	—
club cpe 4P	3,010	1,090	—
sdn 2d	3,035	1,065	—
sdn 4d	3,080	1,093	—
conv sdn	3,200	1,332	—
wgn 4d	3,315	1,412	—

22 Commodore Six (wb 121.0)*

	Wght	Price	Prod
cpe 3P	2,995	1,115	—
club cpe 5P	3,090	1,175	—
sdn 2d	3,090	1,152	—
sdn 4d	3,145	1,182	—
conv sdn	3,280	1,402	—

24 Commodore Eight (wb 121.0)*

	Wght	Price	Prod
cpe 3P	3,130	1,156	—
club cpe 5P	3,205	1,215	—
sdn 2d	3,230	1,187	—
sdn 4d	3,280	1,224	—
conv sdn	3,400	1,451	—

25 Commodore Custom Eight (wb 121.0)*

	Wght	Price	Prod
club cpe 4P	3,235	1,311	—

27 Commodore Custom Eight (wb 128.0)*

	Wght	Price	Prod
sdn 4d, 6P	3,395	1,430	—

*Total model year production: 40,661; Sixes: 34,069; Eights: 6,592.

1942 Engines	bore×stroke	bhp	availability
L6, 175.0	3.00×4.13	92	S-20
L6, 212.0	3.00×5.00	102	S-21, 22
L8, 254.0	3.00×4.50	128	S-24, 25, 27

1946

51 Super Six (wb 121.0)—61,787 built

	Wght	Price	Prod
sdn 4d	3,085	1,555	—
Brougham sdn 2d	3,030	1,511	—
club cpe	3,015	1,553	—
cpe 3P	2,950	1,481	—
Brougham conv cpe	3,195	1,879	1035*

52 Commodore Six (wb 121.0)—17,685 built	Wght	Price	Prod
sdn 4d	3,150	1,699	—
club cpe	3,065	1,693	—

53 Super Eight (wb 121.0)—3,961 built			
sdn 4d	3,235	1,668	—
club cpe	3,185	1,664	—

54 Commodore Eight (wb 121.0)—8,193 built			
sdn 4d	3,305	1,774	—
club cpe	3,235	1,760	—
Brougham conv cpe	3,410	2,050	140*

*Estimated; total convertibles 1,177.

1946 Engines	bore×stroke	bhp	availability
L6, 212.0	3.00×5.00	102	S-51, 52
L8, 254.0	3.00×4.50	128	S-53, 54

1947

171 Super Six (wb 121.0)—49,276 built	Wght	Price	Prod
sdn 4d	3,110	1,749	—
Brougham sdn 2d	3,055	1,704	—
club cpe	3,040	1,744	—
cpe 3P	2,975	1,628	—
Brougham conv cpe	3,220	2,021	1,460*

172 Commodore Six (wb 121.0)—25,138 built			
sdn 4d	3,175	1,896	—
club cpe	3,090	1,887	—

173 Super Eight (wb 121.0)—5,076 built			
sdn 4d	3,260	1,862	—
club cpe	3,210	1,855	—

174 Commodore Eight (wb 121.0)—12,593 built			
sdn 4d	3,330	1,972	—
club cpe	3,260	1,955	—
Brougham conv cpe	3,435	2,196	360*

*Estimated; total convertibles 1,823.

1947 Engines	bore×stroke	bhp	availability
L6, 212.0	3.00×5.00	102	S-171, 172
L8, 254.0	3.00×4.50	128	S-173, 174

1948

481 Super Six (wb 124.0)—49,388 built	Wght	Price	Prod
sdn 4d	3,500	2,222	—
Brougham sdn 2d	3,470	2,172	—
club cpe	3,480	2,219	—
cpe 3P	3,460	2,069	—
Brougham conv cpe	3,750	2,836	88*

482 Commodore Six (wb 124.0)—27,159 built			
sdn 4d	3,540	2,399	—
club cpe	3,550	2,374	—
Brougham conv cpe	3,780	3,057	48*

483 Super Eight (wb 124.0)—5,338 built			
sdn 4d	3,525	2,343	—
club cpe	3,495	2,340	—

484 Commodore Eight (wb 124.0)—35,315 built			
sdn 4d	3,600	2,514	—
club cpe	3,570	2,490	—
Brougham conv cpe	3,800	3,138	64*

*Estimated; total convertibles 200.

1948 Engines	bore×stroke	bhp	availability
L6, 262.0	3.56×4.38	121	S-481, 482
L8, 254.0	3.00×4.50	128	S-483, 484

1949

491 Super Six (wb 124.0)—91,333 built	Wght	Price	Prod
sdn 4d	3,555	2,207	—
Brougham sdn 2d	3,515	2,156	—
club cpe	3,480	2,203	—
cpe 3P	3,485	2,053	—
Brougham conv cpe	3,750	2,799	1,870*

492 Commodore Six (wb 124.0)—32,715 built			
sdn 4d	3,625	2,383	—
club cpe	3,585	2,359	—
Brougham conv cpe	3,780	2,952	655*

493 Super Eight (wb 124.0)—6,365 built			
sdn 4d	3,565	2,296	—
Brougham sdn 2d	3,545	2,245	—
club cpe	3,550	2,292	—

494 Commodore Eight (wb 124.0)—28,687 built			
sdn 4d	3,650	2,472	—
club cpe	3,600	2,448	—
Brougham conv cpe	3,800	3,041	595*

*Estimated; total convertibles 3,119.

1949 Engines	bore×stroke	bhp	availability
L6, 262.0	3.56×4.38	121	S-491, 492
L8, 254.0	3.00×4.50	128	S-493, 494

1950

500 Pacemaker (wb 119.0)—39,455 built	Wght	Price	Prod
sdn 4d	3,510	1,933	—
Brougham sdn 2d	3,475	1,912	—
club cpe	3,460	1,933	—
cpe 3P	3,445	1,807	—
Brougham conv cpe	3,655	2,428	1,100*

50A Pacemaker Deluxe (wb 119.0)—22,297 built			
sdn 4d	3,520	1,959	—
Brougham sdn 2d	3,485	1,928	—
club cpe	3,470	1,959	—
Brougham conv cpe	3,665	2,444	630*

501 Super Six (wb 124.0)—17,246 built			
sdn 4d	3,590	2,105	—
Brougham sdn 2d	3,565	2,068	—
club cpe	3,555	2,102	—
Brougham conv cpe	3,750	2,629	465*

502 Commodore Six (wb 124.0)—24,605 built			
sdn 4d	3,655	2,282	—
club cpe	3,640	2,257	—
Brougham conv cpe	3,840	2,809	700*

503 Super Eight (wb 124.0)—1,074 built			
sdn 4d	3,605	2,189	—
Brougham sdn 2d	3,575	2,152	—
club cpe	3,560	2,186	—

504 Commodore Eight (wb 124.0)—16,731 built			
sdn 4d	3,675	2,366	—
club cpe	3,655	2,341	—
Brougham conv cpe	3,865	2,893	425*

*Estimated; total convertibles 3,322.

1950 Engines	bore×stroke	bhp	availability
L6, 232.0	3.56×3.88	112	S-500
L6, 262.0	3.56×4.38	123	S-50A, 501, 502
L8, 254.0	3.00×4.50	128	S-503, 504

1951

4A Pacemaker Custom (wb 119.0)— 34,495 built

	Wght	Price	Prod
sdn 4d	3,460	2,145	—
Brougham sdn 2d	3,430	2,102	—
club cpe	3,410	2,145	—
cpe 3P	3,380	1,965	—
Brougham conv cpe	3,600	2,642	430*

5A Super Six Custom (wb 124.0)—22,532 built

	Wght	Price	Prod
sdn 4d	3,565	2,287	—
Brougham sdn 2d	3,535	2,238	—
club cpe	3,525	2,287	—
Hollywood htp cpe	3,590	2,605	1,100*
Brougham conv cpe	3,720	2,827	280*

6A Commodore Six Custom (wb 124.0) 16,070 built

	Wght	Price	Prod
sdn 4d	3,600	2,480	—
club cpe	3,585	2,455	—
Hollywood htp cpe	3,640	2,780	820*
Brougham conv cpe	3,785	3,011	210*

7A Hornet (wb 124.0)—43,656 built

	Wght	Price	Prod
sdn 4d	3,600	2,568	—
club cpe	3,580	2,543	—
Hollywood htp cpe	3,630	2,869	2,100*
Brougham conv cpe	3,780	3,099	550*

8A Commodore Eight Custom (wb 124.0)—14,243 built

	Wght	Price	Prod
sdn 4d	3,620	2,568	—
club cpe	3,600	2,543	—
Hollywood htp cpe	3,650	2,869	670*
Brougham conv cpe	3,800	3,099	180*

*Estimated; total convertibles 1,651; total hardtops 4,689.

1951 Engines	bore×stroke	bhp	availability
L6, 232.0	3.56×3.88	112	S-Pacemaker
L6, 262.0	3.56×4.38	123	S-Super & Commodore Six
L6, 308.0	3.81×4.50	145	S-Hornet
L8, 254.0	3.00×4.50	128	S-Commodore Eight

1952

4B Pacemaker (wb 119.0)—7,486 built

	Wght	Price	Prod
sdn 4d	3,390	2,311	—
Brougham sdn 2d	3,355	2,264	—
club cpe	3,335	2,311	—
cpe 3P	3,305	2,116	—

5B Wasp (wb 119.0)—21,876 built

	Wght	Price	Prod
sdn 4d	3,485	2,466	—
Brougham sdn 2d	3,470	2,413	—
club cpe	3,435	2,466	—
Hollywood htp cpe	3,525	2,812	1,320*
Brougham conv cpe	3,635	3,048	220*

6B Commodore Six (wb 124.0)—1,592 built

	Wght	Price	Prod
sdn 4d	3,595	2,674	—
club cpe	3,550	2,647	—
Hollywood htp cpe	3,625	3,000	100*
Brougham conv cpe	3,750	3,247	20*

7B Hornet (wb 124.0)—35,921 built

	Wght	Price	Prod
sdn 4d	3,600	2,769	—
club cpe	3,550	2,742	—
Hollywood htp cpe	3,630	3,095	2,160*
Brougham conv cpe	3,750	3,342	360*

8B Commodore Eight (wb 124.0)—3,125 built

	Wght	Price	Prod
sdn 4d	3,630	2,769	—
club cpe	3,580	2,742	—
Hollywood htp cpe	3,660	3,095	190*
Brougham conv cpe	3,770	3,342	30*

*Estimated; total convertibles 636; total hardtops 3,777.

1952 Engines	bore×stroke	bhp	availability
L6, 232.0	3.56×3.88	112	S-Pacemaker
L6, 262.0	3.56×4.38	127	S-Wasp, Commodore Six
L6, 308.0	3.81×4.50	145	S-Hornet
L8, 254.0	3.00×4.50	128	S-Commodore Eight

1953

1C Jet (wb 105.0)—21,143 built (includes Super Jet)

	Wght	Price	Prod
sdn 4d	2,650	1,858	—

2C Super Jet (wb 105.0)

	Wght	Price	Prod
sdn 4d	2,700	1,954	—
sdn 2d	2,695	1,933	—

4C Wasp (wb 119.0)—17,792 built (includes Super Wasp)

	Wght	Price	Prod
sdn 4d	3,380	2,311	—
sdn 4d	3,350	2,264	—
club cpe	3,340	2,311	—

5C Super Wasp (wb 119.0)

	Wght	Price	Prod
sdn 4d	3,480	2,466	—
sdn 2d	3,460	2,413	—
club cpe	3,455	2,466	—
Hollywood htp cpe	3,525	2,812	590*
Brougham conv cpe	3,655	3,048	50*

7C Hornet (wb 124.0)—27,208 built

	Wght	Price	Prod
sdn 4d	3,570	2,769	—
club cpe	3,530	2,742	—
Hollywood htp cpe	3,610	3,095	910*
Brougham conv cpe	3,760	3,342	—

*Estimated; total hardtops 1,501.

1953 Engines	bore×stroke	bhp	availability
L6, 202.0	3.00×4.75	104	S-Jet
L6, 202.0	3.00×4.75	106/114	O-Jet
L6, 232.0	3.56×3.88	127	S-Wasp
L6, 308.0	3.81×4.50	145	S-Hornet
L6, 308.0	3.81×4.50	160	O-Hornet
L6, 308.0	3.81×4.50	170	O-Hornet (7-X)

1954

1D Jet (wb 105.0)—14,224 built (includes Super Jet and Jet-Liner)

	Wght	Price	Prod
sdn 4d	2,675	1,858	—
Utility sdn 2d	2,715	1,837	—
Family Club sdn 2d	2,635	1,621	—

2D Super Jet (wb 105.0)

	Wght	Price	Prod
sdn 4d	2,725	1,954	—
club sdn 2d	2,710	1,933	—

3D Jet-Liner (wb 105.0)

	Wght	Price	Prod
sdn 4d	2,760	2,057	—
club sdn 2d	2,740	2,046	—

4D Wasp (wb 119.0)—11,603 built

(includes Super Wasp)	Wght	Price	Prod
sdn 4d	2,256	3,440	—
club sdn 2d	2,209	3,375	—
club cpe	2,256	3,360	—

5D Super Wasp (wb 119.0)

	Wght	Price	Prod
sdn 4d	3,525	2,466	—
club sdn 2d	3,490	2,413	—
club cpe	3,475	2,466	—
Hollywood htp cpe	3,570	2,704	—
Brougham conv cpe	3,680	3,004	—

6D Hornet Special (wb 124.0)—24,833 built (includes Hornet)

	Wght	Price	Prod
sdn 4d	3,560	2,619	—
club sdn 2d	3,515	2,571	—
club cpe	3,505	2,619	—

7D Hornet (wb 124.0)

	Wght	Price	Prod
sdn 4d	3,620	2,769	—
club cpe	3,570	2,742	—
Hollywood htp cpe	3,655	2,988	—
Brougham conv cpe	3,800	3,288	—

Italia (wb 105.0)

	Wght	Price	Prod
cpe	2,710	4,800	20

1954 Engines	bore×stroke	bhp	availability
L6, 202.0	3.00×4.75	104	S-Jet
L6, 202.0	3.00×4.75	106/114	S-Italia; O-Jet
L6, 232.0	3.56×3.88	126	S-Wasp
L6, 262.0	3.56×4.38	140	S-Super Wasp
L6, 308.0	3.81×4.50	160	S-Hornet
L6, 308.0	3.81×4.50	170	O-Hornet (7-X)

1955

54 Metropolitan (wb 85.0)—3,000* built

		Wght	Price	Prod
1	conv cpe 3P	1,803	1,469	—
2	htp cpe	1,843	1,445	—

55 Rambler (wb 100.0)

		Wght	Price	Prod
12	Deluxe bus sdn	2,400	1,457	34
14-1	Super Suburban wgn 2d	2,532	1,869	1,335
16-1	Super club sdn	2,450	1,683	2,970
17-2	Custom Cntry Club htp cpe	2,518	2,098	1,601

55 Rambler (wb 108.0)

		Wght	Price	Prod
15	Deluxe sdn 4d	2,567	1,695	
15-1	Super sdn 4d	2,570	1,798	7,210
15-2	Custom sdn 4d	2,606	1,989	
18-1	Super Cross Cntry wgn 4d	2,675	1,975	12,023
18-2	Custom Cross Cntry wgn 4d	2,685	1,995	

3554 Wasp (wb 114.3)

		Wght	Price	Prod
5-1	Super sdn 4d	3,254	2,290	5,561
5-2	Custom sdn 4d	3,347	2,460	
7-2	Custom Hollywood htp cpe	3,362	2,570	1,640

3556 Hornet 6 (wb 121.3)

		Wght	Price	Prod
5-1	Super sdn 4d	3,495	2,565	5,357
5-2	Custom sdn 4d	3,562	2,760	
7-2	Custom Hollywood htp cpe	3,587	2,880	1,554

3558 Hornet V8 (wb 121.3)

		Wght	Price	Prod
5-1	Super sdn 4d	3,806	2,825	4,449
5-2	Custom sdn 4d	3,846	3,015	
7-2	Custom Hollywood htp cpe	3,878	3,145	1,770

Italia (wb 105.0)

	Wght	Price	Prod
cpe	2,710	4,800	5

*Estimated; total Nash & Hudson, 3,849.

1955 Engines	bore×stroke	bhp	availability
L4, 73.2	2.56×3.50	42	S-Metropolitan
L6, 195.6	3.13×4.25	90	S-Rambler
L6, 195.6	3.13×4.25	100	S-Rambler fleet model
L6, 202.0	3.00×4.75	110	S-Wasp
L6, 202.0	3.00×4.75	114	S-Italia
L6, 202.0	3.00×4.75	120	O-Wasp
L6, 308.0	3.81×4.50	160	S-Hornet 6
L6, 308.0	3.81×4.50	170	O-Hornet 6 (Twin-H)
V8, 320.0	2.81×3.50	208	S-Hornet V8

1956

54 Metropolitan (wb 85.0)—3,000* built

		Wght	Price	Prod
1	conv cpe 3P	1,803	1,469	—
2	htp cpe 3P	1,843	1,445	—

56 Rambler DeLuxe (wb 108.0)—5,000 built (includes Super and Custom)

		Wght	Price	Prod
15	sdn 4d	2,891	1,829	—

56 Rambler Super (wb 108.0)

		Wght	Price	Prod
15-1	sdn 4d	2,096	1,939	—
18-1	Cross Cntry wgn 4d	2,992	2,233	—

56 Rambler Custom (wb 108.0)

		Wght	Price	Prod
13-2	Cross Cntry htp wgn 4d	3,095	2,494	—
15-1	sdn 4d	2,929	2,059	—
18-2	Cross Cntry wgn 4d	3,110	2,329	—
19-2	htp sdn	2,990	2,224	—

3564 Wasp (wb 114.3)

	Wght	Price	Prod
sdn 4d	3,264	2,214	2,519

3565 Hornet Special (wb 121.3)

	Wght	Price	Prod
sdn 4d	3,467	2,405	1,528
Hollywood htp cpe	3,488	2,512	229

3566 Hornet 6 (wb 121.3)

	Wght	Price	Prod
Super sdn 4d	3,545	2,544	3,022
Custom sdn 4d	3,636	2,777	
Hollywood htp cpe	3,646	2,888	358

3568 Hornet V8 (wb 121.3)

	Wght	Price	Prod
sdn 4d	3,826	3,026	1,962
Hollywood htp cpe	3,026	3,159	1,053

*Estimated; total Nash & Hudson 7,645.

1956 Engines	bore×stroke	bhp	availability
L4, 73.2	2.56×3.50	42	S-Metropolitan
L6, 195.6	3.13×4.25	120	S-Rambler
L6, 202.0	3.00×4.75	120	S-Wasp
L6, 202.0	3.00×4.75	130	O-Wasp (Twin-H)
L6, 308.0	3.81×4.50	165	S-Hornet 6
L6, 308.0	3.81×4.50	175	O-Hornet 6 (Twin-H)
V8, 320.0	3.81×3.50	208	S-Hornet V8 (through 3/56)
V8, 250.0	3.50×3.25	190	S-Hornet Special (3/56 on)

1957—3,876 built

357-1 Hornet Super (wb 121.3)

	Wght	Price	Prod
sdn 4d	3,631	2,821	—
Hollywood htp cpe	3,655	2,911	—

357-2 Hornet Custom (wb 121.3)

	Wght	Price	Prod
sdn 4d	3,678	3,011	—
Hollywood htp cpe	3,693	3,101	—

1957 Engine	bore×stroke	bhp	availability
V8, 327.0	4.00×3.25	255	S-all

Hupmobile

Hupp Motor Car Corporation
Detroit, Michigan and Cleveland Ohio

Hupmobile's best year ever was 1928, when the company recorded over 50,000 registrations. From there it was all downhill. After 1932, the company never produced more than 9500 cars annually. Ironically, the "Aerodynamic" series introduced in 1934 was among the better designs of the period. But buyers just didn't respond. Hupmobile closed down midway through 1936, reopened to produce a handful of 1937-38 models, then struggled on without much success into 1939.

After two record sales years, Hupp watched production plunge to 22,183 for 1930. That year's line comprised the six-cylinder S series, assembled in Cleveland at the former Chandler plant, and three Detroit-built straight-eight models, the C, H, and U. The S and C were the firm's bread-and-butter cars. The H and U series had a larger eight, and included some luxurious limousines on a 137-inch wheelbase.

The next year saw more of the same, plus the new L-series Century with a smaller straight eight. Added to the U series was one of the handsomest Hupmobiles ever, a two-door victoria, and freewheeling was a sales point for all models. Hupp flew buyers to Detroit and Cleveland in a ploy to stimulate sales, but production remained low, totaling 17,456 for the 1931 model year.

Beginning in 1932, Hupp designated model year and

1930 Standard Eight Town Sedan (with Helen Kane)

1931 Century Six convertible cabriolet

1932 Eight four-door sedan

1933 Eight cabriolet roadster

1933 Series 321 Six victoria coupe

1934 Series 421-J "Aerodynamic" four-door sedan

wheelbase in its series codes. Thus, the B-216, for example, was a six-cylinder series on a 116-inch wheelbase. This was also the year Hupp acquired the services of designer Raymond Loewy, who styled the F-222 and I-226 eight-cylinder models with tire-hugging cycle-type fenders, vee'd radiator grilles, sloping windshields, and chrome wheel discs. These graceful, handsome cars won Loewy many awards, but Hupmobile production dropped gain.

Sales were the worst yet in 1933, just 7316 units. These cars were essentially '32 carryovers, a sloping grille being the only major change. A new cycle-fender six-cylinder model, the K-321, was followed by a cheaper derivative, the K-321A, with stationary hood louvers and a single windshield wiper and taillight. It didn't help.

For 1934, Hupp released the radical Loewy-designed 421-J and 427-T, a six and eight, respectively. Billed under the name "Aerodynamic", they had three-piece wrapped windshields, faired-in headlights and flush-mounted spare tires. Also available was the six-cylinder 417-W series with more orthodox looks, thanks to a good many body parts borrowed from Ford. Hupp's sales rose to 9420. The '34s were largely unchanged for 1935, but there were two new entries, the smaller 518-D series Aerodynamic six with flat windshield, and the 121-inch-wheelbase eight-cylinder Model O.

The big news in this period was the fight over company ownership. Archie Andrews, the promoter of the front-drive Ruxton, had gained control of Hupp in late 1934, and the firm was in ruins by the time he was forced out a year later. Hupp closed in early 1936, and stayed closed for over 18 months. The company came back in 1938 with the conventional 822-E six and 825-H eight—just in time for a recession. Production totaled just 1020 units.

Norman De Vaux, Hupmobile's general manager, had bought the body dies for the defunct front-drive Cord 810/812 Beverly sports sedan from Auburn. He then proposed to build a rear-drive derivation, and reportedly had 6000 orders. But Hupmobile was unable to get the reborn Cord into production beyond 35 handmade prototypes in 1939. De Vaux now approached Graham-Paige, which agreed to manufacture the bodies provided it could have its own version of the car. The deal gave Hupp a ready supplier and Graham had a new model to supplement its languishing "sharknose" design. This cooperation, said Hupp's president, J. W. Drake, "does not mean a merger of the two corporations. The Hupp-Graham contract is a most favorable one for both of us as careful checking of all production costs demonstrated that great savings could be made." Actually, it was a partnership of desperation.

Hupp's Cord-derived sedan was called the Skylark. Like Graham's Hollywood, it was identical with the Cord from the cowl back, but had a shorter hood and overall length. While the Hollywood used a double grille, the Skylark had a single, horizontal-bar design, not unlike the grille of the legendary Cord itself—except that the headlamps were freestanding, not hidden.

Each company used its own engine. In Hupp's case, this was an L-head six with four main bearings and a

1934 421-J "Aerodynamic" four-door sedan

Initial design for 1939 Skylark

1940 Skylark four-door sedan

displacement of 245 cubic inches, as opposed to Graham's 217.8 cid. The Hupp powerplant was a bit livelier than the regular Graham engine, but the supercharged Hollywood had 120 bhp and was faster.

Bad luck plagued the Hupp-Graham operation from the start. Graham took nine months to set up the assembly line, and production didn't begin until May 1940. By that time, most of the advance orders had been canceled, and sales were low for both companies. Graham grabbed the lion's share of publicity with its blown engine, and built six times as many cars as its partner. Hupp gave up in October 1940, only three weeks after 1941 model production had started. Just 319 of the '41 Skylarks had been built. Registrations were equally dismal: 211 in 1940; 103 in 1941.

Hupp recovered slightly during the war by way of defense contracts. After 1945, management elected not to return to the car business. Instead, the firm turned to making accessories for other auto companies.

Hupmobile Specifications

1930

S Standard Six (wb 111.0)

	Wght	Price	Prod
phaeton 5P	2,690	1,135	—
bus cpe 2P	2,710	995	—
cabriolet 2-4P	2,690	1,110	—
sdn 4d	2,885	1,095	—
cpe 2-4P	2,740	1,095	—
DeLuxe sdn 4d	—	1,160	

C Standard Eight (wb 121.0)

touring div. sdn 7P	3,600	1,785	—
cpe 2-4P	3,560	1,695	—
conv cabriolet 2-4P	3,500	1,770	—
victoria cpe 5P	3,535	1,715	—
sdn 4d	3,640	1,695	—
Town div. sdn 5P	—	1,805	—

H Standard Eight (wb 125.0)

touring div. sdn 7P	3,870	2,190	—
cpe 2-4P	3,915	2,080	—
conv cabriolet 2-4P	3,880	2,155	—
victoria cpe 5P	3,830	2,100	—
sdn 4d	3,995	2,080	—
Town div. sdn 4d window	3,995	2,190	—

U Standard Eight (wb 137.0)

sdn 7P	4,225	2,495	—
sdn limo 7P	4,390	2,645	—

1930 Engines	bore×stroke	bhp	availability
L6, 211.6	3.25×4.25	70	S-S
L8, 268.6	3.00×4.75	100	S-C
L8, 365.6	3.50×4.75	133	S-H,U

1931

S Century Six (wb 114.0)

	Wght	Price	Prod
rdstr 2-4P	2,855	1,075	—
phtn 5P	2,900	1,050	—
comp. cpe 2P	2,825	995	—
cpe 2-4P	2,865	995	—

1934 Series 427-T "Aerodynamic" four-door sedan

	Wght	Price	Prod
conv cabriolet 2-4P	2,855	1,050	—
sdn 4d	2,985	995	

L Century Eight (wb 118.0)

rdstr 2-4P	3,055	1,375	—
phaeton 5P	3,330	1,350	—
cpe 2P	3,100	1,295	—
cpe 2-4P	3,165	1,295	—
conv cabriolet 2-4P	3,125	1,350	—
sdn 4d	3,275	1,295	—

C Standard Eight (wb 121.0)

touring sdn 7P	3,715	1,685	—
cpe 2-4P	3,650	1,595	—
conv cabriolet 2-4P	3,610	1,595	—
victoria cpe 5P	3,695	1,615	—
cpe 4P	3,695	1,615	—
sdn 4d	3,730	1,595	—
Town sdn 4d	3,785	1,705	—

H Standard Eight (wb 125.0)

touring sdn 7P	3,975	2,005	—
cpe 2-4P	4,015	1,895	—
conv cabriolet 2-4P	3,975	1,895	—
victoria cpe 5P	4,010	1,915	—
cpe 4P	4,010	1,915	—
sdn 4d	4,095	1,895	—
Town sdn 4d	4,230	2,005	—

U Standard Eight (wb 137.0)—474 built

victoria cpe 5P	4,165	2,295	—
sdn 4d	4,360	2,295	—
sdn limo 7P	4,400	2,445	—

1931 Engines	bore×stroke	bhp	availability
L6, 211.6	3.25×4.25	70	S-S
L8, 240.2	2.88×4.63	90	S-L
L8, 268.6	3.00×4.75	100	S-C
L8, 365.6	3.50×4.75	133	S-H,U

1932 First Series

S "214" Six (wb 114.0)—2,210 built

	Wght	Price	Prod
rdstr 2-4P	2,855	875	—
phaeton 5P	2,900	850	—
cpe 2P	2,825	795	—
cpe 2-4P	2,865	795	—
conv cabriolet 2-4P	2,855	850	—
sdn 4d	2,985	795	—

L "218" Eight (wb 118.0)—1,096 built

rdstr 2-4P	3,055	1,075	—
phaeton 5P	3,330	1,050	—
cpe 2P	3,100	995	—
cpe 2-4P	3,165	995	—
conv cabriolet 2-4P	3,125	1,050	—
sdn 4d	3,275	995	—

C "221" Eight (wb 121.0)—675 built

phaeton 7P	3,715	1,305	—
cpe 2-4P	3,650	1,195	—
cpe 4P	3,695	1,215	—
victoria cpe 5P	3,695	1,215	—
sdn 4d	3,730	1,195	—
Town sdn 4d	3,825	1,195	—

H "225" Eight (wb 125.0)—446 built

phaeton 7P	3,985	1,585	—
cpe 2-4P	4,015	1,455	—
cpe 4P	4,010	1,475	—
victoria cpe 5P	4,010	1,475	—
sdn 4d	4,095	1,455	—

	Wght	Price	Prod
Town sdn 4d	4,300	1,430	—
U "237" Eight (wb 137.0)—132 built			
victoria cpe	4,165	1,795	—
sdn 7P	4,360	1,895	—
limo 7P	4,400	1,955	—

1932/1 Engines	bore×stroke	bhp	availability
L6, 211.6	3.25×4.25	70	S-S
L8, 240.2	2.88×4.63	90	S-L
L8, 268.6	3.00×4.75	100	S-C
L8, 365.6	3.50×4.75	133	S-H,U

1932 Second Series (from Jan 1)

B "216" Six (wb 116.5)—3,500 built	Wght	Price	Prod
rdstr 2-4P	2,825	795	—
phaeton 5P	2,925	795	—
cpe 2-4P	2,975	895	—
cpe 2P	2,935	895	—
conv cabriolet 2-4P	2,985	895	—
sdn 4d	3,095	895	—
F "222" Eight (wb 122.0)—3,755 built			
rdstr cab 2-4P	3,415	1,395	—
cpe 2-4P	3,505	1,295	—
victoria cpe	3,585	1,360	—
sdn 4d	3,550	1,295	—
I "226" Eight (wb 126.0)—713 built			
rdstr cab 2-4P	3,650	1,695	—
cpe 2-4P	3,740	1,595	—
victoria cpe 5P	3,820	1,660	—
sdn 4d	3,785	1,595	—

1932/2 Engines	bore×stroke	bhp	availability
L6, 228.1	3.38×4.25	75	S-B
L8, 250.7	2.94×4.63	93	S-F thru #6905
L8, 261.5	3.00×4.63	NA	S-F from #6906
L8, 279.9	3.06×4.75	103	S-I

1933

B "316" Six (wb 116.0)—1,463 built	Wght	Price	Prod
rdstr 2P	2,825	795	—
phaeton 5P	2,925	795	—
cpe 2P	2,935	895	—
cpe 2-4P	2,975	895	—
conv cab 2-4P	2,965	895	—
sdn 4d	3,095	895	—
K "321" Six (wb 121.0)—4,600 built			
cab rdstr 2-4P	3,235	1,095	—
cpe 2-4P	3,235	995	—
victoria cpe 5P	3,250	1,060	—
sdn 4d	3,290	995	—
F "332" Eight (wb 122.0)—700 built			
cab rdstr 2-4P	3,600	1,295	—
cpe 2-4P	3,545	1,195	—
victoria cpe 5P	3,605	1,260	—
sdn 4d	3,650	1,195	—
I "326" Eight (wb 126.0)—250 built			
cab rdstr 2-4P	3,810	1,545	—
cpe 2-4P	3,795	1,445	—
victoria cpe 5P	3,830	1,510	—
sdn 4d	3,845	1,445	—
KK "321-A" Six (wb 121.0)—300 built			
cpe 2-4P	3,135	895	—
victoria cpe 5P	3,150	960	—
sdn 4d	3,190	895	—

1933 Engines	bore×stroke	bhp	availability
L6, 228.1	3.38×4.25	75	S-B
L6, 228.1	3.38×4.25	90	S-K,KK
L8, 261.5	3.00×4.63	96	S-F
L8, 303.2	3.19×4.75	109	S-I

1934

KK "421-A" Six (wb 121.0)—300 built	Wght	Price	Prod
cpe 2-4P	3,160	795	—
victoria cpe 5P	3,165	860	—
sdn 4d	3,200	795	—
K "421" Six (wb 121.0)*			
rdstr cab 2-4P	3,235	895	—
cpe 2-4P	3,250	795	—
victoria cpe 5P	3,255	860	—
sdn 4d	3,290	895	—
F "422" Eight (wb 122.0)*			
rdstr cab 2-4P	3,600	1,045	—
cpe 2-4P	3,545	945	—
victoria cpe 5P	3,630	1,010	—
sdn 4d	3,665	1,045	—
I "426" Eight (wb 126.0)*			
rdstr cab 2-4P	3,810	1,145	—
cpe 2-4P	3,795	1,045	—
victoria cpe 5P	3,830	1,110	—
sdn 4d	3,845	1,145	—
W "417" Six (wb 117.0)*			
cpe 2-4P	2,940	795	—
sdn 4d	3,040	795	—
touring sdn 4d T/B	3,075	845	—
DeLuxe cpe 2-4P	2,940	845	—
DeLuxe sdn 4d	3,040	845	—
DeLuxe touring sdn 4d T/B	3,075	895	—
J "421" Six (wb 121.0)*			
cpe 3-5P	3,230	1,195	—
victoria cpe 5P	3,325	1,195	—
sdn 4d	3,325	1,095	—
T "427" Eight (wb 127.0)*			
cpe 3-5P	3,675	1,345	—
victoria cpe 5P	3,700	1,265	—
sdn 4d	3,700	1,245	—

*Production not available

1934 Engines	bore×stroke	bhp	availability
L6, 228.1	3.38×4.25	90	S-K,KK
L6, 245.3	3.50×4.25	93	S-J
L6, 224.0	3.50×3.88	80	S-W
L8, 261.5	3.00×4.63	96	S-F
L8, 303.2	3.19×4.75	109	S-I
L8, 303.2	3.19×4.75	116	S-T

1935

W "517" Six (wb 117.0)—2,586 built	Wght	Price	Prod
cpe 2P	2,900	695	—
cpe 2-4P	2,940	695	—
sdn 4d	3,040	695	—
touring sdn 5P	3,075	745	—
DeLuxe cpe 2P	2,900	745	—
DeLuxe cpe 2-4P	2,940	745	—
DeLuxe sdn 4d	3,040	745	—
DeLuxe touring sdn 4d	3,075	795	—

D "518" Six (wb 118.0)—5,900 built

		Wght	Price	Prod
	sdn 4d	2,930	795	—
	touring sdn 4d	2,945	845	—
	DeLuxe sdn 4d	2,930	835	—
	DeLuxe touring sdn 4d	2,945	885	—

J "521" Six (wb 121.0)—993 built

		Wght	Price	Prod
	cpe 3-5P	3,230	1,095	—
	victoria sdn 4d	3,325	1,095	—
	sdn 4d	3,325	1,095	—
	DeLuxe cpe 3-5P	3,230	1,170	—
	DeLuxde vic sdn 4d	3,325	1,170	—
	DeLuxe sdn 4d	3,325	1,170	—

T "527" Eight (wb 127.0)—902 built

		Wght	Price	Prod
	cpe 3-5P	3,625	1,395	—
	victoria sdn 4d	3,700	1,395	—
	sdn 4d	3,700	1,395	—
	DeLuxe cpe 3-5P	3,625	1,445	—
	DeLuxe vic sdn 4d	3,700	1,445	—
	DeLuxe sdn 4d	3,700	1,445	—

O "521" Eight (wb 121.0)—400 built

		Wght	Price	Prod
	cpe 3-5P	3,300	1,195	—
	victoria cpe 5P	3,402	1,195	—
	sdn 4d	3,432	1,195	—
	touring vic cpe 5P	3,447	1,195	—
	touring sdn 4d	3,447	1,195	—
	DeLuxe cpe 3-5P	3,330	1,245	—
	DeLuxe vic cpe 5P	3,432	1,245	—
	DeLuxe sdn 4d	3,432	1,245	—
	DeLuxe touring vic 5P	3,447	1,245	—
	DeLuxe touring sdn 4d	3,447	1,245	—

1935 Engines	bore×stroke	bhp	availability
L6, 224.0	3.50×3.88	91	S-W
L6, 245.3	3.50×4.75	101	S-D,J
L8, 303.2	3.19×4.75	120	S-T,O

1936

D "618" Six (wb 118.0)—1,873 built

		Wght	Price	Prod
	sdn 4d	2,930	795	—
	touring sdn 4d	2,945	845	—
	DeLuxe sdn 4d	2,930	835	—
	DeLuxe touring sdn 4d	2,945	885	—

O "621" Eight (wb 121.0)—298 built

		Wght	Price	Prod
	cpe 3-5P	3,330	1,195	—
	victoria 5P	3,432	1,195	—
	sdn 4d	3,432	1,195	—
	touring victoria 5P	3,447	1,195	—
	touring sdn 4d	3,447	1,195	—
	DeLuxe cpe 3-5P	3,330	1,245	—
	DeLuxe victoria 5P	3,432	1,245	—
	DeLuxe sdn 4d	3,432	1,245	—
	DeLuxe touring victoria 5P	3,447	1,245	—
	DeLuxe touring sdn 4d	3,447	1,245	—

1936 Engines	bore×stroke	bhp	availability
L6, 245.3	3.50×4.25	101	S-D
L8, 303.2	3.19×4.75	120	S-O

1937

Note: Hupp closed in early 1936 and remained closed for 18 months. Most sources state no 1937 models were produced, but industry records do quote the following model listings (production based on announced serial number spans):

G Six (wb 118.0)—199 built

		Wght	Price	Prod
	bus cpe 3P	3,010	795	—
	cpe 3-5P	3,060	840	—
	sdn 2d	2,980	815	—
	touring sdn 2d	3,030	850	—
	sdn 4d	3,000	855	—
	touring sdn 4d	3,040	890	—

N Eight (wb 121.0)—39 built

		Wght	Price	Prod
	cpe 3-5P	3,565	1,035	—
	sdn 2d	3,535	995	—
	touring sdn 2d	3,565	1,035	—
	sdn 4d	3,535	1,035	—
	touring sdn 4d	3,550	1,075	—

1937 Engines	bore×stroke	bhp	availability
L6, 245.3	3.50×4.25	101	S-G
L8, 303.2	3.19×4.75	120	S-N

1938

E "822" (wb 122.0)—1,804 built

		Wght	Price	Prod
	Standard sdn 4d T/B	3,320	1,045	—
	Regular sdn 4d T/B	3,370	1,180	—
	DeLuxe sdn 4d T/B	3,400	1,222	—
	Custom sdn 4d T/B	3,440	1,340	—

H "825" (wb 125.0)—197 built

		Wght	Price	Prod
	Regular sdn 4d T/B	3,955	1,325	—
	DeLuxe sdn 4d T/B	4,085	1,365	—
	Custom sdn 4d T/B	4,125	1,485	—

1938 Engines	bore×stroke	bhp	availability
L6, 245.3	3.50×4.25	101	S-E
L8, 303.2	3.19×4.75	120	S-H

1939

E "922" Senior Six (wb 122.0)—800 built

		Wght	Price	Prod
EQ	DeLuxe touring sdn 4d	3,400	995	—
EQD	Custom touring sdn 4d	3,440	1,095	—

H "925" Senior Eight (wb 125.0)—200 built

		Wght	Price	Prod
HQ	DeLuxe touring sdn 4d	4,085	1,145	—
HQD	Custom touring sdn 4d	4,215	1,245	—

Skylark (wb 115.0)

		Wght	Price	Prod
	Custom sdn 4d	3,000	1,145	35*

*handbuilt prototypes

Note: Production figures for 1930-39 were compiled via serial number spans listed by industry sources, although it is possible some numbers were skipped within a span. When published spans were obviously assigned in advance, with round numbers, they were not listed. Comparison production figures by *calendar year* are as follows:

1930	22,183	1935	9,346
1931	17,456	1936	1,556
1932	10,476	1937	138
1933	7,316	1938	1,020
1934	9,420	1939	1,400

1940

R-015 Skylark Custom (wb 115.0)

		Wght	Price	Prod
RQK	sdn 4d	3,000	1,145	—

1940 Engine	bore×stroke	bhp	availability
L6, 245.0	3.50×4.25	101	S-all

1941

R-115 Skylark Custom (wb 115.0)

		Wght	Price	Prod
RQK	sdn 4d	3,000	1,095	—

1941 Engine	bore×stroke	bhp	availability
L6, 245.0	3.50×4.25	101	S-all

Imperial

Chrysler - Imperial Division, Chrysler Corp.
Detroit, Michigan

Imperial became a separate and distinct make in 1955, and remained as such through 1975. Long before that, it had been Chrysler's most luxurious model. Indeed, Imperial couldn't shake its image as a Chrysler, though it had some of its most successful years in the 1950s.

The beautiful 1955-56 models, based extensively on Virgil Exner's Parade Phaeton show cars and the Chrysler K-310, are recognized by many today as the most desirable Imperials of all. Wearing a distinctive split grille up front and elegantly trimmed inside and out, these big sedans and hardtops still look very good today. The infamous "gunsight" taillights were the only

Parade Phaeton show car of 1954-56

1955 Newport hardtop coupe

1955 Newport hardtop coupe

non-functional design feature, though the treatment was certainly distinctive. The '55s were powered by a 331 cubic-inch hemi-head V8; the '56 models used a bored-out version of the same engine.

The 1956s rode a longer wheelbase, which made them the longest Imperials. (Wheelbase shrank to 129 inches in 1957.) They were given tailfins, perhaps the only Chrysler product of the day to wear them as well. Styling was nicely integrated, and almost appeared to have been a ground-up design, rather than the quick facelift it was. The only significant optional extra for 1955-56 was air conditioning, priced at $567. The cars were comprehensively equipped, with PowerFlite transmission standard. Though not in the class of Chrysler's 300, Imperials were lively performers yet surprisingly economical. Imperials steadily won luxury-class laurels in the Mobilgas Economy Runs.

Crown Imperial long-wheelbase sedans or limousines were available in 1955-56. Built in Detroit, they replaced all previous Dodge, DeSoto, and Chrysler long-wheelbase cars. Though well styled along the lines of the standard Imperial, they sold slowly.

For 1957 came Exner's all-new Forward Look. Imperial sprouted huge tailfins and a full-width, complicated-looking grille. In an effort to surpass Lincoln, then second to Cadillac in the luxury field, Imperial added two new series, the Crown and LeBaron. More elaborately trimmed than standard cars, the Crown came as a sedan, two- and four-door hardtops, and a new convertible—the first soft-top Imperial since 1953. The LeBaron series was added in January and comprised a pillar sedan and four-door Southampton hardtop. Both new series were priced considerably higher than the basic models. TorqueFlite three-speed automatic transmission (new that year) and a 392 Hemi were standard for all.

From 1957 through 1965, Crown Imperial limousines were built by Ghia of Turin, Italy. Based on potential sales, Chrysler could no longer justify the time and space necessary to build such cars in Detroit. Against a potential $3.3 million tooling bill at home, Ghia offered to tool Crown Imperials for only $15,000, provided Chrysler could ship the basic "kit" to Torino.

Each Ghia limousine began as an unfinished two-door hardtop body mounted on a rigid convertible chassis, and was shipped with all body panels intact. Ghia cut the car apart, added 20.5 inches to the wheelbase, reworked the structure above the beltline, fitted and trimmed the luxurious interior, and finished off the exterior using 150 pounds of lead filler. Construction of each car took a month, and initial delays made the Crown Imperial a very late 1957 introduction, priced at a stratospheric $15,075. Sales were not impressive: only 132 Ghia Crowns had been built by the time the line ended in 1965, but all of them were impeccably tailored.

Imperial's best year ever was 1957. Nearly 38,000 cars were built, almost edging out Lincoln. Accordingly, the 1958 Imperial was changed only slightly. Circular parking lights and a complex mesh-and-eggcrate grille were the main styling features for this facelift. The model lineup was unchanged, but prices were marginally higher. Horsepower was boosted again. The year proved to be a poor one for Chrysler products in general; Imperial produced only about 16,000 units. In model years 1959 and 1960, Imperial finally outsold Lincoln, but these were the only times it did. Frustrating dealers, people still called the cars "Chrysler Imperials"—and a "Chrysler," though prestigious, didn't have the charisma of a Cadillac.

The basic 1957 styling was more extensively facelifted for '59, with a toothy grille and added brightwork along the sides. For the first time the standard series had its own model name, Custom. The lineup was otherwise unchanged. Offered again were Torsion-Aire front suspension, TorqueFlite automatic, and "Full-Time" power steering. Along with other Chrysler products, Imperial switched to the 413-cid wedge-head V8, which provided performance comparable to that of the Hemi, but was more economical to build and maintain.

Exner's heroically finned Imperials of the early '60s were the kind of cars that cause modern stylists to grimace, but they seemed perfectly valid at the time. They sold well, though not in record numbers. Imperial remained strictly an also-ran among luxury makes. Cadillac was the overwhelming choice among luxury-car buyers, Lincoln was a distant second, and Imperial was usually an even more distant third.

Imperial rode Chrysler's largest standard wheelbase, but unlike the firm's other 1960 products retained sep-

1956 Crown Imperial limousine

1957 four-door sedan

1956 four-door sedan

1958 LeBaron four-door sedan

1957 Crown convertible

D'Elegance show car from 1958

Styling clays under development, probably for 1958

1960 Crown Imperial limousine by Ghia

1959 Crown Imperial for Queen of England's Canadian tour

1961 Crown Southampton hardtop sedan

1960 Custom Southampton hardtop sedan

1961 LeBaron Southampton hardtop sedan

arate body-and-frame construction. This allowed greater insulation between body and frame, necessary in those days to achieve the level of smoothness and silence Imperial buyers demanded. The only engine available was held over from 1959, the wedge-head V8 that required premium fuel and had 10:1 compression.

The 1960 line was a repeat of '59. Three standard series were offered: Custom, Crown, and LeBaron, each separated by about $600. Custom-built Crown Imperial limousines were still available on the longer 149.5-inch wheelbase. Styling was again a facelift, with a new grille and a "wrapover" bright metal roof panel that extended all the way to the windshield. Comfort was the big feature for 1960, with a new high-back driver's seat padded in thick foam rubber, adjustable "spot" air conditioning, six-way power seat with single rotary-knob control, Auto-Pilot cruise control, and automatic headlamp dimmer. Customs were upholstered in pretty crown-pattern nylon. Crown upholstery was nylon and vinyl, wool, or leather. Wool broadcloth was used for LeBarons.

The 1961 model was altered considerably, though it used the 1960 shell. Fins were the most blatant ever to appear on an Imperial, and were accompanied by a new gimmick: freestanding headlamps pocketed in the curve of the front fenders. This was another idea from Exner, who was influenced by classic cars. Freestanding taillights suspended from the towering fins were also used. The strange-looking headlights survived through 1963, but rear styling was gradually improved during 1962 and '63. Custom, Crown, and LeBaron models were again offered, but the four-door pillared sedans were eliminated.

Before Exner left the corporation during 1961, he had envisioned a completely new, truncated Imperial for '62 as a companion for his downsized Dodges and Plymouths of that year. This didn't reach production, which is fortunate considering the failure of the cheaper makes. The production Imperial's small changes for '62 added up to a much improved appearance. The fins were shorn down to mere nubs of what they'd been. The new, elongated bullet taillights were

1962 LeBaron Southampton hardtop sedan

1963 LeBaron Southampton hardtop sedan

1964 Crown Coupe hardtop

1965 LeBaron hardtop sedan

1966 Crown hardtop sedan

1967 Crown convertible

freestanding, but blended better with the rear fenders than the earlier "gunsight" versions. Predictably, sales were better than in '61.

Imperial received another mild facelift for 1963, which included a new grille composed of elongated rectangles, a crisp new roofline, and a restyled rear deck. Freestanding taillights were discontinued. The stylist responsible for much of this revision was Elwood Engel, who had replaced Exner in mid-1961. The lineup was unchanged, except for the Ghia Crown Imperial. Model year production totals were about the same as in '62.

Engel's styling completely replaced the old Exner silhouette for 1964. Imperial was now very reminiscent of the four-door Lincoln Continentals he had styled during his Ford days. Fenderlines were traced in brightwork, just like on the big Lincolns. A divided grille appeared, and the freestanding headlamps were replaced by integral units. The Custom had not sold well and was eliminated, along with the Southampton designation for pillarless body styles. This pared the line down to just five models. Sales were exceedingly good with over 23,000 units for the model year. This performance would not be approached until 1969.

Good sales and the big '64 redesign dictated a stand-pat lineup for the 1965 season. The only significant change was a new grille with glass-enclosed dual headlights. At the New York Automobile Show, Imperial displayed its exotic LeBaron D'Or show car, which used gold striping and embellishments, and was painted a special color, Royal Essence Laurel Gold. The usual range was again offered. Prices were about $100 to $200 higher than they'd been in 1964.

Ghia stopped building limousines in 1965, though 10 more Crown Imperials were constructed in Spain using grilles and rear decks from the '66 models. When Imperial finally went to unit body construction in 1967, Chrysler worked out a limousine program with Stageway Coaches of Fort Smith, Arkansas. Built from 1967 through 1971 at the rate of about six per year, the Stageway cars were called LeBarons rather than Crown Imperials. They were much longer than their predecessors, having an unbelievable 163-inch wheelbase, by far the longest in the American industry. Prices ranged from $12,000 to $15,000, depending on equipment.

Once more in 1966, the Engel-styled Crowns and LeBarons were offered with only detail changes. The grille was a cellular affair, each "cell" housing the familiar elongated rectangles. The rear deck was cleaned up by removing the fake spare tire cover, a throwback to the Exner years. Backup lights were inset in the rear bumper. The wedgehead V8 was bored out to 440 cubic inches and rated at 350 bhp. Model year production dropped considerably, however.

By 1967, Chrysler engineers had enough experience with unit construction to be satisfied with this approach for their most expensive product. Vast technological improvements had also occured, allowing computerized stress testing of any given shape before actual

construction. Unibody construction also cut weight by 100 pounds compared to 1966. As a result, the '67s were all-new and completely restyled. A new grille with a prominent nameplate was accompanied by sharp front fenders that housed the parking lights. Headlights were still integrated with the grille. There were vertical rear bumpers and horizontal "character lines" along the bodysides. Wheelbase contracted to 127 inches. The four-door pillar-type sedan returned without a series name. Other models were continued as before.

Volume dropped for 1968, and caused Chrysler to make a far-reaching decision: for 1969-70 and beyond, Imperial would share its sheetmetal with Chrysler. Among the casualties of this decision was the Crown convertible, which made its last appearance in 1968. The '68s were only slightly altered from the '67s. Changes included a new grille that extended around the front end to enclose the parking and cornering lights, dual moldings on the lower bodysides, and rear side marker lights (now required by the government). Narrow paint stripes were applied along the beltline on all models. The 440 V8 was still standard. Dual exhausts and twin-snorkel air cleaners were an option.

The Chrysler-like cars of 1969-70 were certainly the cleanest Imperials in history. They had long, low "fuselage styling," a full-width eggcrate grille, concealed headlamps, and sequential turn signals set into the rear bumper. Ventless side glass was a feature of air-conditioned coupes. Although the 127-inch wheelbase was retained, the new styling stretched overall length by five inches, yet curb weight was about 100 pounds less. The engine, as before, was the 350-bhp 440 V8. A hardtop coupe and sedan were offered in both Crown and LeBaron trim, plus a pillared Crown sedan priced identically with the Crown hardtop. LeBaron was no longer the $7000 semi-custom it had been in past years. Its list price was slashed by about $800. Combined sales of the two LeBarons exceeded those of the Crown for the first time. This was a genuine boost to sales, which reached 22,183 units in 1969, the third best figure in Imperial history.

An increasing resemblance to Chrysler and the steady

1968 Crown hardtop sedan

1969 LeBaron hardtop sedan

1970 LeBaron hardtop sedan

buyer shift toward more manageable cars contributed to a sales decline in the early '70s and the Imperial's ultimate demise. Chrysler Corporation had had mixed success with its luxury line since making it on a separate nameplate for 1955. The name, of course, had been around as the top Chrysler series almost from the company's beginnings, so it was well known. Yet that apparently wasn't enough, and the basic car marketed as an Imperial for '75 was continued under the Chrysler New Yorker Brougham label through 1978. Inperial would return briefly in the early '80s as a personal-luxury coupe that failed to catch on and was dropped after only two years.

Imperial retained its 127-inch wheelbase through 1973, the last year for the body/chassis platform introduced with the '60 redesign. LeBaron two- and four-door hardtops were the only models left by this time, but they were not priced slightly lower to fill the gap left by the departed Crown series. The Bendix anti-skid brake system, a $250 option exclusive to Imperial for '71, was extended to the entire Chrysler line for 1972.

Ironically, Imperial was the first of the Big Three luxury cars that suffered—or seemed to suffer—from the effects of the first energy crisis. The brand-new 1972 models had crisper lines and bold upright grillework, plus a three-inch shorter wheelbase and about 100 pounds less weight. But

1971 LeBaron hardtop sedan

1972 LeBaron hardtop coupe

1974 LeBaron hardtop sedan

1973 LeBaron hardtop sedan

1975 LeBaron hardtop sedan

these modest reductions had nothing to do with the fuel shortage, which Chrysler hadn't even dreamed of, but rather were mandated by sharing that year's redesigned New Yorker platform. They were good-looking in their way, and distinctly different from the Chryslers. But prices were rapidly moving upward, and these Imperials were none

too successful compared with their predecessors. Volume, at just over 14,000 for the model year, was the lowest since 1971, and by the following year it was down to fewer than 10,000. The last of this line left the Jefferson Avenue plant in Detroit on June 12, 1975, bearing serial number YM43-T5C-182947. It was a LeBaron four-door hardtop.

Imperial Specifications

1955

C69 (wb 130.0)

	Wght	Price	Prod
sdn 4d	4,565	4,483	7,840
Newport htp cpe	4,490	4,720	3,418
conv cpe (proto)	4,600	—	1
chassis	—	—	1

C70 Crown Imperial (wb 149.5)

	Wght	Price	Prod
sdn 4d, 8P	5,180	6,973	45
limo	5,230	7,095	127

1955 Engine	bore×stroke	bhp	availability
V8, 331.0	3.81×3.63	250	S-all

1956

C73 (wb 133.0)

	Wght	Price	Prod
sdn 4d	4,575	4,832	6,821
Southampton htp sdn	4,680	5,225	1,543
Southampton htp cpe	4,555	5,094	2,094

C70 Crown Imperial (wb 149.5)

	Wght	Price	Prod
sdn 4d, 8P	5,145	7,603	51
limo	5,205	7,737	175

1956 Engine	bore×stroke	bhp	availability
V8, 354.0	3.94×3.63	280	S-all

1957

IM1-1 (wb 129.0)

	Wght	Price	Prod
sdn 4d	4,640	4,838	5,654
Southampton htp sdn	4,780	4,838	7,527
Southampton htp cpe	4,640	4,736	4,885

IM1-2 Crown (wb 129.0)

	Wght	Price	Prod
sdn 4d	4,740	5,406	3,642
Southampton htp sdn	4,920	5,406	7,843
Southampton htp cpe	4,755	5,269	4,199
conv cpe	4,830	5,598	1,167

IM1-4 LeBaron (wb 129.0)

	Wght	Price	Prod
sdn 4d	4,765	5,743	1,729
Southampton htp sdn	4,900	5,743	911

Crown Imperial (wb 149.5)

	limo	5,960	15,075	36

1957 Engine	bore×stroke	bhp	availability	
V8, 392.0	4.00×3.90	325	S-all	

1958

LY1-L (wb 129.0)

		Wght	Price	Prod
23	Southampton htp cpe	4,640	4,839	1,801
41	sdn 4d	4,590	4,945	1,926
43	Southampton htp sdn	4,795	4,945	3,336

LY1-M Crown (wb 129.0)

23	Southampton htp cpe	4,730	5,388	1,939
27	conv cpe	4,820	5,729	675
41	sdn 4d	4,755	5,632	1,240
43	Southampton htp sdn	4,915	5,632	4,146

LY1-H LeBaron (wb 129.0)

41	sdn 4d	4,780	5,969	501
43	Southampton htp sdn	4,940	5,969	538

Crown Imperial (wb 149.5)

	limo	5,960	15,075	31

1958 Engines	bore×stroke	bhp	availability	
V8, 392.0	4.00×3.90	345	S-all exc Crown Imperial	
V8, 392.0	4.00×3.90	325	S-Crown Imperial	

1959

MY1-L (wb 129.0)

		Wght	Price	Prod
612	Southampton htp cpe	4,675	4,910	1,743
613	sdn 4d	4,735	5,016	2,071
614	Southampton htp sdn	4,745	5,016	3,984

MY1-M Crown (wb 129.0)

		Wght	Price	Prod
632	Southampton htp cpe	4,810	5,403	1,728
633	sdn 4d	4,830	5,647	1,335
634	Southampton htp sdn	4,840	5,647	4,714
		Wght	Price	Prod
635	conv cpe	4,850	5,774	555

MY1-H LeBaron (wb 129.0)

653	sdn 4d	4,865	6,103	510
654	Southampton htp sdn	4,875	6,103	622

Crown Imperial (wb 149.5)

	limo	5,960	15,075	7

1959 Engines	bore×stroke	bhp	availability	
V8, 413.0	4.18×3.75	350	S-all exc Crown Imperial	
V8, 392.0	4.00×3.90	325	S-Crown Imperial	

1960

PY1-L Custom (wb 129.0)

		Wght	Price	Prod
912	Southampton htp cpe	4,655	4,923	1,498
913	sdn 4d	4,700	5,029	2,335
914	Southampton htp sdn	4,760	5,029	3,953

PY1-M Crown (wb 129.0)

922	Southampton htp cpe	4,720	5,403	1,504
923	sdn 4d	4,770	5,647	1,594
924	Southampton htp sdn	4,765	5,647	4,510
925	conv cpe	4,820	5,774	618

PY1-H LeBaron (wb 129.0)

933	sdn 4d	4,860	6,318	692
934	Southampton htp sdn	4,835	6,318	999

Crown Imperial (wb 149.5)

	limo	5,960	16,500	16

1960 Engine	bore×stroke	bhp	availability	
V8, 413.0	4.18×3.75	350	S-all	

1961

RY1-L Custom (wb 129.0)

		Wght	Price	Prod
912	Southampton htp cpe	4,715	4,923	889
914	Southampton htp sdn	4,740	5,109	4,129

RY1-M Crown (wb 129.0)

922	Southampton htp cpe	4,790	5,403	1,007
924	Southampton htp sdn	4,855	5,647	4,769
925	conv cpe	4,865	5,774	429

RY1-H LeBaron (wb 129.0)

934	Southampton htp sdn	4,875	6,426	1,026

Crown Imperial (wb 149.5)

	limo	5,960	16,500	9

1961 Engine	bore×stroke	bhp	availability	
V8, 413.0	4.18×3.75	350	S-all	

1962

SY1-L Custom (wb 129.0)

		Wght	Price	Prod
912	Southampton htp cpe	4,540	4,920	826
914	Southampton htp sdn	4,620	5,106	3,587

SY1-M Crown (wb 129.0)

922	Southampton htp cpe	4,650	5,400	1,010
924	Southampton htp sdn	4,680	5,644	6,911
925	conv cpe	4,765	5,770	554

SY1-H LeBaron (wb 129.0)

934	Southampton htp sdn	4,725	6,422	1,449

1962 Engine	bore×stroke	bhp	availability	
V8, 413.0	4.18×3.75	340	S-all	

1963

TY1-L Custom (wb 129.0)

		Wght	Price	Prod
912	Southampton htp cpe	4,640	5,058	749
914	Southampton htp sdn	4,690	5,243	3,264

TY1-M Crown (wb 129.0)

922	Southampton htp cpe	4,720	5,412	1,067
924	Southampton htp sdn	4,740	5,656	6,960
925	conv cpe	4,795	5,782	531

TY1-H LeBaron (wb 129.0)

934	Southampton htp sdn	4,830	6,434	1,537

Crown Imperial (wb 149.5)

	limo	6,100	18,500	13

1963 Engine	bore×stroke	bhp	availability	
V8, 413.0	4.18×3.75	340	S-all	

1964

VY1-M Crown (wb 129.0)

		Wght	Price	Prod
922	htp cpe	4,950	5,739	5,233
924	htp sdn	4,970	5,581	14,181
925	conv cpe	5,185	6,003	922

VY1-H LeBaron (wb 129.0)

934	htp sdn	5,005	6,455	2,949

Crown Imperial (wb 149.5)

	limo	6,100	18,500	10

1964 Engine	bore×stroke	bhp	availability
V8, 413.0	4.18×3.75	340	S-all

1965

AY1-M Crown (wb 129.0)		Wght	Price	Prod
922	htp cpe	5,075	5,930	3,974
924	htp sdn	5,015	5,772	11,628
925	conv cpe	5,345	6,194	633

AY1-H LeBaron (wb 129.0)		Wght	Price	Prod
934	htp sdn	5,080	6,596	2,164

Crown Imperial (wb 149.5)		Wght	Price	Prod
	limo	6,100	18,500	10

1965 Engine	bore×stroke	bhp	availability
V8, 413.0	4.18×3.75	340	S-all

1966

BY3-M Crown (wb 129.0)		Wght	Price	Prod
23	htp cpe	5,000	5,887	2,373
27	conv cpe	5,315	6,164	514
43	htp sdn	4,990	5,733	8,977

BY3-H LeBaron (wb 129.0)		Wght	Price	Prod
43	htp sdn	5,090	6,540	1,878

1966 Engine	bore×stroke	bhp	availability
V8, 440.0	4.32×3.75	350	S-all

1967

CY1-M (wb 127.0)		Wght	Price	Prod
23	Crown htp cpe	4,780	6,011	3,235
27	conv cpe	4,815	6,244	577
41	sdn 4d	4,830	5,374	2,193
43	Crown htp sdn	4,860	5,836	9,415

CY1-H LeBaron (wb 127.0)		Wght	Price	Prod
43	htp sdn	4,970	6,661	2,194

LeBaron, Stageway body (wb 163.0)		Wght	Price	Prod
	limo	6,300	15,000	6

1967 Engine	bore×stroke	bhp	availability
V8, 440.0	4.32×3.75	350	S-all

1968

YM Crown (wb 127.0)		Wght	Price	Prod
23	htp cpe	4,660	5,722	2,656
27	conv cpe	4,795	6,497	474
41	sdn 4d	4,685	5,654	1,887
43	htp sdn	4,715	6,115	8,492

YH LeBaron (wb 127.0)		Wght	Price	Prod
43	htp sdn	4,815	6,940	1,852

LeBaron, Stageway body (wb 163.0)		Wght	Price	Prod
	limo	6,300	15,000	6

1968 Engines	bore×stroke	bhp	availability
V8, 440.0	4.32×3.75	350	S-all
V8, 440.0	4.32×3.75	360	O-all (dual exhaust)

1969

Crown (wb 127.0)		Wght	Price	Prod
YL23	htp cpe	4,555	5,592	224
YL43	htp sdn	4,690	5,770	823
YM41	sdn 4d	4,620	5,770	1,617

LeBaron (wb 127.0)				
YM23	htp cpe	4,610	5,898	4,592
YM43	htp sdn	4,710	6,131	14,821

LeBaron, Stageway body (wb 163.0)				
	limo	6,300	16,000	6 est

1969 Engine	bore×stroke	bhp	availability
V8, 440.0	4.32×3.75	350	S-all

1970

YL Crown (wb 127.0)		Wght	Price	Prod
23	htp cpe	4,610	5,779	254
43	htp sdn	4,735	5,956	1,333

YM LeBaron (wb 127.0)		Wght	Price	Prod
23	htp cpe	4,660	6,095	1,803
43	htp sdn	4,805	6,328	8,426

LeBaron, Stageway body (wb 163.0)		Wght	Price	Prod
	limo	6,500	16,500	6 est

1970 Engine	bore×stroke	bhp	availability
V8, 440.0	4.32×3.75	350	S-all

1971

YM LeBaron (wb 127.0)		Wght	Price	Prod
23	htp cpe	4,800	6,632	1,442
43	htp sdn	4,950	6,864	10,116

1971 Engine	bore×stroke	bhp	availability
V8, 440.0	4.32×3.75	335	S-all

1972

YM LeBaron (wb 127.0)		Wght	Price	Prod
23	htp cpe	4,790	6,550	2,332
43	htp sdn	4,955	6,778	13,472

1972 Engine	bore×stroke	bhp	availability
V8, 440.0	4.32×3.75	225	S-all

1973

YM LeBaron (wb 127.0)		Wght	Price	Prod
23	htp cpe	4,905	6,829	2,563
43	htp sdn	5,035	7,057	14,166

1973 Engine	bore×stroke	bhp	availability
V8, 440.0	4.32×3.75	215	S-all

1974

YM LeBaron (wb 124.0)		Wght	Price	Prod
23	htp cpe	4,825	7,673	3,850
43	htp sdn	4,965	7,804	10,576

1974 Engine	bore×stroke	bhp	availability
V8, 440.0	4.32×3.75	230	S-all

1975

YM LeBaron (wb 124.0)		Wght	Price	Prod
23	htp cpe	4,965	8,698	2,728
43	htp sdn	5,065	8,844	6,102

Kaiser

Kaiser-Frazer Corp.
Willow-Run, Michigan

Kaiser Motors Corp.
Toledo, Ohio

Henry J. Kaiser and Joseph W. Frazer had a disagreement long before they went into business together. In 1942, Kaiser was experimenting with $400 to $600 plastic cars and suggesting that auto companies announce their postwar plans immediately. Frazer angrily replied: "I resent a West Coast shipbuilder asking us if we have the courage to plan postwar automobiles when the President has asked us to forego all work which would take away from the war effort. Kaiser has done a great job as a shipbuilder . . . but I think his challenge to automobile men is as half-baked as some of his other statements . . . I think the public is being misled by all these pictures of plastic models with glass tops, done by artists who probably wouldn't want to sit under those tops in the summer and sweat."

After the two came together to form Kaiser-Frazer in July 1945, their relationship appeared amicable. Both sides compromised. Henry Kaiser was unable to build his cheap plastic car for the common man, but he had high hopes for a Kaiser with torsion-bar suspension and front-wheel drive.

The proposed front-drive Kaiser K-85 used a unit body/chassis based on the conventional Frazer, but its drivetrain and suspension, conceived by engineer Henry C. McCaslin, were very different. Its 85-horsepower engine, designed by Continental, drove the front wheels. Power was taken through a conventional three-speed transmission, routed to the front wheels by a helical-gear transfer case, and carried to the front-mounted differential by a universal joint. The torsion bar for each wheel was a 1.3-inch steel rod, 44.5 inches long, running the length of the car. The bars twisted to provide the springing. Unit construction was adopted, McCaslin said, because "we needed to use more of the operation in the plant. We had the welding equipment but lacked large dies and cranes. It was a compromise to get the car into production."

But the front-drive Kaiser never saw production. Huge problems developed—hard steering, gear whine, wheel shimmy. With so much weight over the front wheels, the K-85 needed power steering, which would have added $900 to its retail price. In May 1946, the decision was made to drop the project. Instead, K-F would build a conventional, rear-drive Kaiser similar to the Frazer but priced lower.

This Kaiser Special was introduced for 1947 at $1868, but the price quickly rose to over $2000. It shared the Frazer's body and 100-bhp six-cylinder engine. Kaiser used a multi-piece grille that was cheaper to produce than the Frazer's because the pieces were smaller. It was mundane inside, using conventional pin-striped upholstery. Late in the model year, a fancier model called the Kaiser Custom appeared, priced about $350 higher than the Special, $150 higher than the standard

Frazer, and about $250 less than the top-line Frazer Manhattan.

Willow Run, Ford's ex-bomber plant, was quickly converted for car production, and K-F was turning out finished vehicles by June 1946. The original plan had been to build two Kaisers for every Frazer, but in 1947 the company built about one to one to satisfy initial orders. The cars were basically unchanged for '48, but very few Customs were built. Both 1947 and 1948 were outstanding years for the young corporation. Profits were near $20 million in '47 and $10 million in '48. Combined output put K-F ninth in the industry, the best of any independent.

A facelift in 1949 gave Kaiser a broad horizontal grille

K-85 front-wheel-drive prototype, 1946

1947 Special four-door sedan

1947 Custom four-door sedan

and larger taillights. Several new models were added. Henry Kaiser had thought up the Traveler/Vagabond utility car—a conventional sedan with a double-door hatch cut into the rear section and a fold-down rear seat. The economical Traveler and the leather-upholstered Vagabond enabled the company to build a wagon-type model without the tooling expense normally required for a separate wood- or steel-bodied station wagon.

Two other new Kaisers for '49 were the Virginian four-door hardtop and the DeLuxe four-door convertible, the first postwar models to use those body styles. Both were lavishly upholstered, and offered excellent visibility because they had no steel "B" pillars. But they were as expensive as Cadillacs, and only a handful were produced. The ones that didn't sell in '49 were given new serial numbers for 1950.

A unique Kaiser-Frazer feature was a wide range of unusual colors, the work of color and fabric designer

1949-50 Deluxe convertible sedan

1949 Virginian (originally "Hard Top") sedan

1949 Deluxe Vagabond utility sedan

Carleton Spencer. He and K-F also worked with color research for home interiors with *House & Garden* magazine. The results were hues like Indian Ceramic (a vivid pink), Crystal Green, Caribbean Coral, and Arena Yellow. On Kaiser's DeLuxe sedan, the color name was written in chrome script on the front fenders. There were 150 different interior fabrics offered by the automobile industry in 1949, and K-F owned 62 of them. Of the 218 exterior colors offered that year, 37 were Kaiser-Frazer's.

Between 1948 and '49, Kaiser's dashboard changed dramatically. It had been an inexpensive unit with horizontal gauges in 1947-48. In '49, it became more ornate with a giant speedometer in front of the driver and a matching clock on the passenger's side. In Deluxe models, the dash sparkled with chrome, stainless steel, and a massive ivory steering wheel with a big semicircular chrome horn ring. The flashy interior design, colorful paint, and fashion upholstery did much to doll up what was basically an unaltered '47–'48 body.

Kaiser Customs were improved in performance with optional dual intake and exhaust manifolds that boosted horsepower to 112. This became standard on the 1949 DeLuxe, Vagabond, and Virginian. Kaiser had no automatic; its only transmission alternative was overdrive, priced at $80 extra.

Unfortunately, K-F sales plumeted in 1949. The main reason was the introduction of brand-new postwar designs by GM, Ford, and Chrysler, while K-F had a mere facelift. Joseph Frazer saw the onrush coming and warned against making too many '49s. New K-F designs were scheduled for release in early 1950, and Frazer's advice was to retrench until then. But Henry Kaiser wouldn't have it. "The Kaisers never retrench," he said. By this time, the influence of Kaiser's people was far greater than Frazer's, so Joe Frazer yielded the presidency to Kaiser's son Edgar, remaining on the board only for appearance's sake.

K-F tooled up for 200,000 units in '49, but built only some 101,000. About 20 percent of these couldn't be sold, and had to be given 1950 serial numbers. It is impossible to separate 1949 model year production from 1950's except to say that the '49s account for about 84 percent of the total.

By early 1950, the new '51 Kaiser was in production. Its debut was set for March of that year, six months ahead of normal introduction time. Sales rocketed. Close to 140,000 were sold, against about 15,000 of the 1950s. From a dismal 17th place in the industry in '49, Kaiser shot up to 12th—the highest it would ever achieve.

There was reason to be enthusiastic about the '51 Kaiser. From every angle it was unlike any other American car of the day. It offered 700 square inches more glass area than its nearest competitor, and a lower beltline than any Detroit car produced through 1956. Unique styling was complemented by an array of bright exterior colors and exciting interiors—again the work of color engineer Spencer.

Kaiser was probably the first company to really push safety. It advertised the new model's padded dash, recessed instruments, narrow windshield corner posts, outstanding visibility, and a windshield that popped out if struck with a force of more than 35 pounds per square inch. The engineering, too, was commendable. Engineers John Widman and Ralph Isbrandt shunned unit construction, but designed a very rigid separate body for a frame that weighed only 200 pounds. A low center of gravity gave Kaiser fine handling, yet curb weight was only about 3100 pounds. Many felt a V8 would have made the car unbeatable in the performance stakes. The lack of one would hurt Kaiser sales as the '50s wore on.

The facelifted '52s weren't quite ready by the end of 1951; in the interim, Kaiser offered the Virginian. About 5500 of these were built. They were nearly identical to the '51 design with similar body style offerings.

A smaller lineup and a mild facelift marked the "regular" '52 series. The most significant styling changes were "teardrop" taillights and a heavier-looking grille. Kaiser now called its top series Manhattan (the old Frazer model name) and the cheaper Special became the Deluxe. The later '52s are fairly rare: only 7500 Deluxes and 19,000 Manhattans were built in the short production run before the new-model changeover.

The 1953 Kaiser "Hardtop" Dragon sedan was the most luxurious Kaiser of all, inspired by Spencer's Dragon trim option from '51. Distinguished by gold-plated exterior trim (hood ornament, badges, script, and keyhole cover) the Dragon featured a padded top, usually made of "bambu" vinyl. This tough, oriental-style material also covered the dash and parts of the seats and door panels. Seat inserts were done in "Laguna" cloth, a fabric with an oblong pattern created by fashion designer Marie Nichols. The Dragon came standard with every possible option: tinted glass, Hydra-Matic drive, whitewalls, dual-speaker radio, and Calpoint custom carpeting on the floor and in the trunk. A gold medallion on the dash was engraved with the owner's name. The Dragon was a spectacular car, but its high price restricted sales. Only 1277 were built altogether, and the last few were almost given away.

Aside from the Dragon, changes for 1953 were slight. Kaiser offered a stripped Carolina model starting at $2313, but sold only a few copies. The company admitted the Carolina's chief purpose was to draw people into the showrooms. The two-door Travelers were eliminated, along with the club coupes. Engine output went up to 118 bhp, and power steering was offered late in the season as a $122 option.

Kaiser sales were plummeting in these years. The make had fallen again to its accustomed low standing in the production race, scoring only 32,000 units for 1952 and just 28,000 for '53. The Toledo-built '54 models were a last-ditch effort, cleverly facelifted by stylist Buzz Grisinger. The front end was much like the Buick XP-300 show car (one of Edgar Kaiser's favorite designs) with a wide, concave grille and "floating"

1951 Traveler four-door utility sedan

1951 Deluxe club coupe

1952 Manhattan four-door sedan

1953 "Hardtop" Dragon four-door sedan

1954 Special two-door sedan

headlights. Rear styling was set off by "Safety-Glo" taillights—big, rounded affairs with a lighted strip running up along the top of the fenders.

In an effort to wring more power out of its 226-cid six, Kaiser bolted a McCulloch centrifugal supercharger to Manhattan engines. Boosting power to 140 bhp, the blower went into full operation only when the accelerator was pressed to the floor. Alongside the two- and four-door Manhattans, K-F sold the unsupercharged Special in two models. The first series was a group of warmed-over 1953 Manhattans with '54 front ends—another effort to use up leftovers. The second was a genuine '54 with a wraparound rear window like the '54 Manhattan's. Neither version did well.

For 1955, Kaiser fielded Manhattans only, distinguished by a higher fin on the hood scoop and little else. Less than 300 genuine '55s were sold. About 100 were loaded on a ship bound for Argentina, where Kaiser Motors hoped to keep the model in production. It's a tribute to this design's durability that it was built there as the Kaiser Carabella through 1962.

Another memorable but unsuccessful experiment was the Kaiser Darrin sliding-door sports car of 1954, based on the 100-inch-wheelbase Henry J chassis. "Dutch" Darrin designed it in late 1952, and talked Henry Kaiser into marketing it for $3668. Only 435 were built before company operations wound down.

The fiberglass Darrin was beautifully styled, and still looks good today. In addition to the unique sliding doors, it featured a landau top with an intermediate half-up position. Full instrumentation was featured, and the car was usually fitted with a three-speed floorshift and overdrive, which gave economy of around 30 mpg. Yet, the Darrin could do the 0–60 mph sprint in about 13 seconds, and approach 100 mph flat out. The project was a big disappointment to Dutch Darrin. At the last minute, he bought about 100 leftovers from the factory, fitted some with Cadillac V8s, and sold them for $4350 each at his Los Angeles showroom. The Cadillac-powered cars were potent indeed, capable of about 140 mph at the top end.

1954 Manhattan four-door sedan

1953 prototype for Darrin sports car

1954 Darrin roadster (production model)

The Kaiser itself came to an end in America in 1955, after 10 years and a loss of $100 million. They were usually good cars, offering many innovative features, but they never seemed to make it with the public. Edgar Kaiser liked to say: "Slap a Buick nameplate on it, and it would sell like hotcakes."

Kaiser Specifications

1947

K100 Special (wb 123.5)		Wght	Price	Prod
1005	sdn 4d	3,295	2,104	65,062

K101 Custom (wb 123.5)		Wght	Price	Prod
1015	sdn 4d	3,295	2,456	5,412

1947 Engines	bore×stroke	bhp	availability
L6, 226.2	3.31×4.38	100	S-all
L6, 226.2	3.31×4.38	112	O-Custom

1948

K481 Special (wb 123.5)		Wght	Price	Prod
4815	sdn 4d	3,295	2,244	90,588

K482 Custom (wb 123.5)		Wght	Price	Prod
4825	sdn 4d	3,295	2,466	1,263

1948 Engines	bore×stroke	bhp	availability
L6, 226.2	3.31×4.38	100	S-all
L6, 226.2	3.31×4.38	112	O-Custom

1949-50

K491 Special (wb 123.5)		Wght	Price	Prod
4911	sdn 4d	3,311	1,995	29,000*
4915	Traveler util sdn 4d	3,456	2,088	22,000*

K492 Deluxe (wb 123.5)				
4921	sdn 4d	3,341	2,195	38,250*
4922	conv sdn	3,726	3,195	54*
4923	Virginian htp sdn	3,541	2,995	946*
4925	Vagabond util sdn 4d	3,501	2,288	4,500*

*1949-50 production combined by factory; approximate breakdown 84 percent 1949, 16 percent 1950. Estimates for body styles based on body numbers in extant vehicles. Actual 1949-50 production: 95,175.

1949-50 Engines	bore×stroke	bhp	availability
L6, 226.2	3.31×4.38	100	S-Special
L6, 226.2	3.31×4.38	112	S-Deluxe

1951

K511 Special (wb 118.5)		Wght	Price	Prod
5110	Traveler util sdn 2d	3,210	2,265	1,500*
5111	sdn 4d	3,126	2,212	43,500*
5113	bus cpe	3,061	1,992	1,500*
5114	sdn 2d	3,106	2,160	10,000*
5115	Traveler util sdn 4d	3,270	2,317	2,000*
5117	club cpe	3,066	2,058	1,500*

K512 Deluxe (wb 118.5)				
5120	Traveler util sdn 2d	3,285	2,380	1,000*
5121	sdn 4d	3,171	2,328	70,000*
5124	sdn 2d	3,151	2,275	11,000*
5125	Traveler util sdn 4d	3,345	2,433	1,000*
5127	club cpe	3,111	2,296	6,000*

*Estimates based on extant vehicles. Actual total model year production: 139,452.

1951 Engine	bore×stroke	bhp	availability
L6, 226.2	3.31×4.38	115	S-all

1952

K521 Virginian Special (wb 118.5)*		Wght	Price	Prod
5110	Traveler util sdn 2d	3,210	2,085	—
5111	sdn 4d	3,126	2,036	—
5113	bus cpe	3,061	1,832	—
5114	sdn 2d	3,106	1,988	—
5115	Traveler util sdn 4d	3,270	2,134	—

K522 Virginian Deluxe (wb 118.5)*				
5120	Traveler util sdn 2d	3,285	2,192	—
5121	sdn 4d	3,171	2,143	—
5124	sdn 2d	3,151	2,095	—
5125	Traveler util sdn 4d	3,345	2,241	—
5127	club cpe	3,111	2,114	—

K521 Deluxe (wb 118.5)				
5211	sdn 4d	3,195	2,537	5,000**
5214	sdn 2d	3,145	2,484	2,000**
5215	Traveler util sdn 4d	3,369	2,643	***
5217	club cpe	3,045	2,296	500**

K522 Manhattan (wb 118.5)				
5221	sdn 4d	3,220	2,654	16,500**
5224	sdn 2d	3,185	2,601	2,000**
5227	club cpe	3,185	2,622	500**

*Total Virginian production: 5,579
**Estimates based on extant vehicles. Total Deluxe/Manhattan production: 26,552.
***Actual production questionable.

1952 Engine	bore×stroke	bhp	availability
L6, 226.2	3.31×4.38	115	S-all

1953

K530 "Hardtop" Dragon (wb 118.5)		Wght	Price	Prod
5301	sdn 4d	3,320	3,924	1,277

K531 Deluxe (wb 118.5)				
5311	sdn 4d	3,200	2,513	5,800*
5314	sdn 2d	3,150	2,459	1,500*
5315	Traveler util sdn 4d	3,315	2,619	1,000*

K532 Manhattan (wb 118.5)				
5321	sdn 4d	3,265	2,650	15,450*
5324	sdn 2d	3,235	2,597	2,500*
5325	Traveler util sdn 4d	3,371	2,755	**

K538 Carolina (wb 118.5)				
5381	sdn 4d	3,185	2,373	1,400*
5384	sdn 2d	3,135	2,313	400*

1953 Engine	bore×stroke	bhp	availability
L6, 226.2	3.31×4.38	118	S-all

*Estimates based on extant vehicles. Model year production:

K531	Deluxe	7,883
K532	Manhattan	17,957
K538	Carolina	1,182

**One example found; volume production questionable.

1954

161 Darrin (wb 100.0)		Wght	Price	Prod
161	rdstr	2,175	3,668	435

K542 Manhattan (wb 118.5)				
5421	sdn 4d	3,375	2,670	3,860*
5424	sdn 2d	3,265	2,334	250*

K545 Special (wb 118.5)**				
5451	sdn 4d	3,265	2,389	3,000*
5454	sdn 2d	3,235	2,334	500*

K545 Special, late (wb 118.5)				
5451	sdn 4d	3,305	2,389	800*
5454	sdn 2d	3,265	2,334	125*

1954 Engines	bore×stroke	bhp	availability
L6, 161.0	3.13×3.50	90	S-Darrin
L6, 226.2	3.31×4.38	118	S-Special
L6, 226.2	3.31×4.38	140	S-Manhattan

*Estimates based on extant vehicles. Model year production:

K542	Manhattan	4,110
K545	Special**	3,500
K545	Special, late	929

**Converted leftover 1953 Manhattans.

1955

Manhattan (wb 118.5)		Wght	Price	Prod
51363	sdn 4d (export)	3,350	—	1,021
51367	sdn 4d	3,375	2,670	226
51467	sdn 2d	3,335	2,617	44

1955 Engine	bore×stroke	bhp	availability
L6, 226.2	3.31×4.38	140	S-all

LaSalle

**Cadillac Motor Car Division, General Motors Corp.
Detroit, Michigan**

Cadillac's romantic companion make was inspired by the desire of General Motors president Alfred Sloan to offer "a car for every price and pocketbook," the basic philosophy that would make GM the giant it is today. Sloan had detected a gap in the price spread between Buick and Cadillac in the mid-'20s, and assigned the latter to come up with a model line to fill it. The division chose the name LaSalle, honoring another French explorer like Cadillac, and introduced the junior series in 1927 on a wheelbase shorter than that of its senior cars. A big attraction was the new line's elegant body styling created by Harley Earl, the young designer Sloan had hired specifically for this project. LaSalle amply fulfilled its makers' hopes, and

launched Earl on his illustrious 30-year career as the company's dean of design. In its first year, it accounted for no less than 25 percent of total division sales, and by 1929 it was outselling Cadillac 11 to 9.

Throughout the 1930s, LaSalle provided the sales volume that helped Cadillac survive. Though the division's total production rarely exceeded Packard's, the LaSalle's share was usually substantial—and sometimes crucial. In the hard Depression year of 1933, for example, the division's model year production slid to 6700 units, but LaSalle accounted for half of that. In 1937, when Cadillac built 46,000 cars altogether, fully 32,000 were LaSalles. Yet even with all this, LaSalle sales never really satisfied GM

1930 Series 340 five-passenger coupe

1932 Series 345B convertible coupe

1931 Series 345A two-passenger coupe

1933 Series 345C four-door Town Sedan

1931 Series 345A four-door Town Sedan

1934 Series 350 coupe

1936 Series 50 four-door sedan

1937 Series 50 four-door sedan

1940 Series 52 Special coupe

1940 Series 52 Special four-door sedan

1940 Series 52 Special convertible sedan

One of two prototypes for 1941 LaSalle never produced

management, who wanted much more.

In line with general industry thinking at the time, the 1930 LaSalles were longer, heavier, and more expensive than the 1929 models, riding a nine-inch longer wheelbase and available with six luxurious Fleetwood body styles instead of the previous year's two. The Fisher-bodied models—coupes, sedans, and a convertible—spanned a $2500-3000 price span, while the Fleetwood line went up to $4000 and included a phaeton, roadster, and cabriolet. Model year production was respectable in the aftermath of the Great Crash.

Unfortunately, the Depression deepened quickly, and Cadillac was forced to adopt cost-cutting measures for 1931-33. As a result, LaSalle was given the senior line's 353-cid V8 and the 134-inch-wheelbase LaSalle chassis was standardized for the eight-cylinder Cadillacs. Though La Salle prices were reduced to about $500 under those of comparable Cadillac V8s, the senior models began to look like better buys. Their production matched LaSalle's in these years, and actually exceeded it in 1931.

A new approach was tried for 1934. Abandoning any attempt to win traditional luxury-car buyers, Cadillac gave LaSalle a look all its own and slashed prices to $1000 under those of least expensive senior V8s. An L-head straight eight from Oldsmobile with aluminum pistons was substituted, GM's new "Knee-Action" front suspension was adopted, and styling was revised with a narrow rounded grille and curious portholes on the hood sides. This basic design and pricing were continued for another two years, although stroke was increased for 1936. Model offerings consisted of coupe, convertible, and two- and four-door sedans on 119- and 120-inch wheelbases. However, this formula didn't work well enough, and sales were well below those of rival luxury-class junior editions.

For 1937, wheelbase was stretched and the Oldsmobile engine was ditched in favor of the V8 from the 1936 Cadillac Series 60. The public responded, and LaSalle production rose to set a record. Due mainly to a temporary recession, output for 1938 was down to about half that figure, much to the chagrin of GM accountants. LaSalle was floundering, yet its cars were marvelous bargains.

By 1939, dual-make lineups had long since disappeared

LaSalle II roadster, 1955 show car

LaSalle II hardtop sedan shown at 1955 Motorama

from all GM divisions—except Cadillac. In an effort to boost languishing sales, the division completely reworked the LaSalle this year, with new styling, more glass area, a shorter wheelbase, and an optional metal sunroof for sedans. Running boards were deleted from all body styles save the convertible (where they were optional). Despite all this, sales again proved disappointing, and only about 23,000 units were built for the model year.

The new styling for 1940 was one of the high points in the marque's 14-year history. Instead of Cadillac's free-standing headlamps, LaSalle's sealed-beams were integrated into the fenders. Lines were gently rounded, functional, and clean. Windows were large, and the interior spacious because of a wheelbase increase from 120 inches in 1939 to 123 for 1940. The trademark La-Salle grille had always been more narrow and delicate than Cadillac's. The 1940 rendition retained these characteristics and was flanked by "catwalk" openings (an idea of Earl's) built into the leading edges of the front fenders.

LaSalles for 1940 came in two series, the 40-50 and the plush 40-52 Special. The Special line was expanded at mid-year by a convertible and convertible sedan, the most elegant LaSalles that final season.

But the marque's exclusive price niche had disappeared by 1940. While the Cadillac nearest in price was the 62 at $1685, Buicks listed from as little as $895 up to $2199. LaSalle's original market position below Cadillac was being covered by a more popular GM make.

Cadillac Division did well in 1940. Out of about 37,000 cars, LaSalle accounted for 24,130. But the junior make ranked only slightly ahead of Lincoln, and remained far behind Packard. So, the most romantic of GM's "companion" cars was discontinued for 1941, its place taken by the new low-priced Cadillac 61.

In the long run, the decision to drop LaSalle was a correct one. Buyers could have a 1941 Cadillac for about $1300, and the magic of that name was important to dealers. Cadillac continued to price the 61 in luxury territory to prevent cheapening its image. Eventually, this would help Cadillac dominate the fine-car market.

LaSalle never really died in the minds of designers, though. To them it had always stood for distinction, refinement, and class. GM Styling had actually prepared a LaSalle design for 1941. A pretty car with the traditional narrow grille and "catwalk" fender inlets, it featured thin horizontal parking lights, spinner hubcaps, and a revival of the earlier LaSalle radiator badge—the "LaS" monogram in a circle. In 1955, Harley Earl's studio produced a four-door hardtop sedan and a two-seat roadster, both dubbed LaSalle II, for that year's Motorama. Interestingly, both these cars had grilles composed of vertical slats like that of their 1940 forebear, and the traditional LaSalle badge graced their hoods. In the early 1960s, the name was again considered for what became the Buick Riviera. And only at the last minute was LaSalle dropped in favor of Seville as the moniker for Cadillac's 1976 compact.

La Salle Specifications

1930—14,986 built

340 Fisher (wb 134.0)

	Wght	Price	Prod
cpe 2P	4,465	2,490	—
conv cpe 2P	4,435	2,590	—
cpe 5P	4,485	2,590	—
sdn 4d	4,645	2,565	—
Town sdn 4d	4,660	2,590	—
sdn 7P	4,745	2,775	—

Imp sdn 7P	4,820	2,925	—

340 Fleetwood Custom (wb 134.0)

rdstr 2P	4,340	2,450	—
phtn 5P	4,380	2,385	—
touring 7P	4,435	2,525	—
phtn A/W 5P	4,670	3,995	—
sdnt cab 5P	4,600	3,725	—
sdnt 5P	4,600	3,825	—

1930 Engine	bore×stroke	bhp	availability
V8, 340.0	3.31×4.94	90	S-all

1931

345A (wb 134.0)—10,095 built		Wght	Price	Prod
	rdstr 2-4P	4,345	2,245	—
	touring 7P	4,440	2,345	—
	cpe 2P	4,470	2,195	—
	conv cpe 2P	4,440	2,295	—
	cpe 5P	4,490	2,295	—
	sdn 4d	4,650	2,295	—
	Town sdn 4d	4,665	2,345	—
	phtn A/W 5P	4,675	3,245	—
	sdn 7P	4,750	2,475	—
	Imperial sdn 7P	4,825	2,595	—
	sdnt cab 5P	4,675	3,245	—
	sdnt 5P	4,650	3,245	—

1931 Engine	bore×stroke	bhp	availability
V8, 353.0	3.38×4.94	95	S-all

1932

345B (wb 130.0; lwb-136.0)—3,386 built		Wght	Price	Prod
	cpe 2P	4,660	2,395	—
	conv cpe 2P	4,630	2,545	—
	Town cpe 5P	4,695	2,545	—
	sdn 4d	4,840	2,495	—
	Town sdn 4d (lwb)	4,895	2,645	—
	lwb sdn 7P	5,025	2,645	—
	Imp 7P (lwb)	5,065	2,795	—

1932 Engine	bore×stroke	bhp	availability
V8, 353.0	3.38×4.94	115	S-all

1933

345C (wb 130.0; lwb-136.0)—3,482 built		Wght	Price	Prod
	cpe 2P	4,730	2,245	—
	conv cpe 2P	4,675	2,395	—
	Town cpe 5P	4,695	2,395	—
	sdn 4d	4,805	2,245	—
	Town sdn 4d (lwb)	4,915	2,495	—
	lwb sdn 7P	4,990	2,495	—
	Imperial sdn 7P	5,020	2,645	—

1933 Engine	bore×stroke	bhp	availability
V8, 353.0	3.38×4.94	115	S-all

1934

350 (wb 119.0)—7,195 built		Wght	Price	Prod
6330S	sdn 4d	3,960	1,695	—
633S	club sdn 5	3,960	1,695	—
6335	conv cpe 2-4P	3,780	1,695	—
6376	cpe 2P	3,815	1,595	—

1934 Engine	bore×stroke	bhp	availability
L8, 240.3	3.00×4.25	95	S-all

1935

Series 50 (wb 119.0)—8,651 built		Wght	Price	Prod
6330S	sdn 4d	3,960	1,545	—
633S	club sdn 5P	3,960	1,545	—
6335	conv cpe 2-4P	3,780	1,545	—
6376	cpe 2P	3,185	1,445	—
35-5011	sdn 2d T/B	3,620	1,255	—
35-5019	sdn 4d T/B	3,650	1,295	—
35-5067	conv cpe 2-4P	3,510	1,325	—
35-5077	cpe 2P	3,475	1,225	—

1935 Engines	bore×stroke	bhp	availability
L8, 240.3	3.00×4.25	95	S-6300 series
L8, 248.0	3.00×4.38	105	S-5000 series

1936

Series 50 (wb 120.0)—13,004 built		Wght	Price	Prod
5011	sdn 2d T/B	3,605	1,185	—
5019	sdn 4d T/B	3,635	1,225	—
5067	conv cpe 2-4P	3,540	1,255	—
5077	cpe 2P	3,460	1,175	—

1936 Engine	bore×stroke	bhp	availability
L8, 248.0	3.00×4.38	105	S-all

1937

Series 50 (wb 124.0)—32,000 built*		Wght	Price	Prod
5011	sdn 2d T/B	3,780	1,275	—
5019	sdn 4d T/B	3,810	1,320	—
5027	cpe 2-4P opt.seats	3,675	1,155	—
5049	conv sdn 5P	3,850	1,680	—
5067	conv cpe 2-4P	3,715	1,350	—

*includes some commercial chassis on 160.0" wheelbase and some CKD.

1937 Engine	bore×stroke	bhp	availability
V8, 322.0	3.38×4.50	125	S-all

1938

Series 50 (wb 124.0)		Wght	Price	Prod
5011	sdn 2d T/B	3,800	1,345	700
5019	sdn 4d T/B	3,830	1,385	9,993
5019A	Sunroof sdn 4d T/B	3,850	1,435	72
5027	cpe 2-4P opt. seats	3,745	1,295	2,710
5029	conv sdn 5P	3,870	1,825	265
5067	conv cpe 2-4P	3,735	1,420	855
	chassis	—	—	80

1938 Engine	bore×stroke	bhp	availability
V8, 322.0	3.38×4.50	125	S-all

1939

Series 50 (wb 120.0)		Wght	Price	Prod
5011	sdn 2d T/B	3,710	1,280	977
5011A	Sunroof sdn 2d T/B	3,780	1,320	23
5019	sdn 4d T/B	3,740	1,320	15,928
5019A	Sunroof sdn 4d T/B	3,810	1,380	404
5027	cpe 2-4P, opt. seats	3,635	1,240	2,525
5029	conv sdn 5P	3,780	1,800	185
5067	conv cpe 2-4P	3,715	1,395	1,056
	chassis	—	—	29

1939 Engine	bore×stroke	bhp	availability
V8, 322.0	3.38×4.50	125	S-all

1940

40-50 (wb 123.0)		Wght	Price	Prod
5011	sdn 2d	3,760	1,280	375
5019	sdn 4d	3,790	1,320	6,722
5027	cpe, A/S	3,700	1,240	1,527
5029	conv sdn	4,000	1,800	125
5067	conv cpe	3,805	1,395	599
50	chassis	—	—	1,032

40-52 Special (wb 123.0)		Wght	Price	Prod
5219	sdn 4d	3,900	1,440	10,250
5227	cpe	3,810	1,380	3,000
5229	conv sdn	4,110	1,895	75
5267	conv cpe	3,915	1,535	425

1940 Engine	bore×stroke	bhp	availability
V8, 322.0	3.38×4.50	130	S-all

Lincoln

Ford Motor Company, (Lincoln-Mercury Division from 1947) Dearborn, Michigan

Lincoln and Cadillac had a common founder, the stern, patrician Henry Martyn Leland, usually referred to as the "Master of Precision." Leland had sold Cadillac to William C. Durant, then established Lincoln a few years later. When his second enterprise ran into financial trouble, he sold out again, this time to Henry Ford in 1922. Since then, little had been done to alter or update the Model L chassis Leland had designed around 1920. Thus, Cadillac entered the '30s with its modern, prestigious Series 90 V16, while Lincoln had only an obsolete chassis and a comparatively weak 385-cubic-inch V8 rated at 90 horsepower. With all this, the Model L was an anachronism: beautifully built and lavishly furnished, yet unfashionably upright and quite slow compared to contemporary Cadillacs, Packards, and Chrysler Imperials. But Henry had a better idea.

It was announced for 1931 as the Model K (exactly why the designation went backwards in the alphabet remains a mystery). Boasting a modernized V8 and a massive new chassis, it was, in effect, a bridge for Lincoln between the '20s and '30s. Its engine retained the previous unit's bore-and-stroke dimensions, "fork-and-blade" rods, and three-piece block and crankcase assembly in cast iron, all Leland touches that allowed the ads to dwell lovingly on the "precision-built Lincoln." But the K chassis was really designed around an all-new V12 scheduled for 1932, being nine inches deep and having six crossmembers with cruciform bracing. Like the L, the K employed torque-tube drive and a floating rear axle. Steering was by worm and roller, hydraulic shocks by Houdaille, mechanical brakes by Bendix. The slightly peaked radiator led a hood far longer than the L's, punctuated by twin trumpet horns and bowl-shaped headlamps, and the K was longer, lower, and sleeker than its predecessor. It also offered an improved ride, greater stability, and more power, with faster acceleration and a higher top speed.

The Model KB of 1932 was Lincoln's answer to the multicylinder challenges from Cadillac, Packard, and others. Its 448-cid V12 provided still better performance than the V8, yet the KB sold for slightly less and came in a wider range of body types. A magnificent around-town car and an extremely fast tourer, it was an extraordinary machine standing far above the general level of cars in its day. Its performance was as impressive as its appearance.

Alongside the KB, Lincoln continued its V8 offerings as the Model KA on a 136-inch wheelbase. Though this chassis was dimensionally the same as the old Model L's, it was structurally the equal of the KB's. Bodies were simply furnished, but the car was high class, not a middle-priced product. Even so, Lincoln's V8 was still not as smooth as the Cadillac, Packard or Pierce-Arrow eights.

Its successor arrived for 1933 in the form of another V12. This was a new "small" 381.7-cid unit packing the same horsepower as the V8. It was installed in the short-wheelbase chassis and topped by Murray-built bodies

1930 Model L two-window berline by Judkins

1930 Model L convertible roadster

1931 Model K two-passenger coupe by Judkins

1931 Model K two-window Town Sedan

made of wood, steel, and aluminum. The KB continued as the senior line. All the '33s were identified by a new front end featuring a rakish vee'd radiator shell with a chrome grille concealing vertical shutters, and louvered instead of shuttered hoods. Fenders were skirted, the front bumper was vee'd, and the trunk rack was redesigned.

Lincoln merged the KA and KB into one series for 1934, but the two distinct wheelbases were retained. A bored-out version of the 1933 KA engine with aluminum cylinder head was fitted, and had a 6.3:1 compression ratio, unheard of at the time. This was made possible by the newly available 70-octane Ethyl gasoline, which in those days was almost as potent as aviation fuel. The '34 had a top speed of about 95 mph, and its engine could rev higher than the previous V12. The chassis was virtually unchanged, but the Murray custom bodies were eliminated and radiators were now lacquered in body color. Smaller headlamps and parking lamps and metal spare tire covers cleaned up appearance, and sedans and limousines had sloping tails, a fairly radical departure from contemporary styling norms. Like Pierce, Packard, and Stutz, Lincoln was reluctant to change the graceful "oh gee" fender sweep that so indelibly marked the classic era, and was untouched through '35.

Semi-teardrop fenders appeared for 1936, along with a simplified radiator grille, new disc wheels, and larger hubcaps. Styling for '37 emphasized absolute simplicity, possibly reflecting the influence of the Cord 810. Headlamps were now integral with the fenders, belt moldings were eliminated, and doors were extended down almost to the runningboards. The spare tire was enclosed in the trunk unless sidemount spares were specified, and a V-shaped windshield was used for the first time on the factory models. The standard interior was done in rich broadcloth with curly-maple garnish moldings, and rarer woods and fabrics were available for custom bodies. The engine gained hydraulic tappets and was moved farther forward, which improved ride. Output was still 150 bhp, but '37 and later models are thought to have had more power than previous Ks because of a different cam contour. Synchromesh transmission also arrived that year. In other respects, the chassis was much the same as before.

The prestige market that had been so strong in the '20s dried up like an Arizona creek bed in the economic drought of the '30s. Lincoln would not equal its near-9000 unit sales of 1926 until 1935; its best interim total was 5311 in 1931. After 1934, Lincoln never produced more than 2000 examples of the Model K in any one year, and by 1940 it was available only to special order, built on chassis completed during 1939. (The largest of these, the 160-inch-wheelbase "Sunshine Special," was the parade car of presidents Roosevelt and Truman.)

Like its Cadillac and Packard rivals, Lincoln was forced to develop a high-volume product for the decade of austerity. It was announced for the 1936 model year as the Lincoln Zephyr, with a radical unit body designed by John Tjaarda along aircraft construction principles. It was also a genuinely slippery shape. Tjaarda's prototype was built with the help of the Briggs Body Company, eager to win

1934 Model KB convertible roadster by LeBaron

1934 Model KB convertible coupe by Brunn

1934 Model KA convertible sedan phaeton

1934 Model KB sedan limousine by Judkins

1935 Model K convertible sedan phaeton by LeBaron

some volume business from Lincoln at last. The original design envisioned a rear-mounted engine, but Ford ultimately decided to go with the conventional front-engine/rear-drive layout. The rest of the package was unconventional, though. According to Tjaarda, the Zephyr was the first car in which aircraft-type stress analysis actually proved the structural advantage of unit construction. With a curb weight of 3300 pounds, the Zephyr was lighter than Chrysler's Airflow yet much stiffer. In crash tests, it sustained nearly twice the impact of conventionally built cars. Best of all, the little Lincoln was a lot cheaper to build than it would have been as a body-on-frame design.

The Zephyr was initially slated to be powered by a modified Ford V8 producing about 100 bhp. Company president Edsel Ford decided that would be inadequate, so he directed engineer Frank Johnson to come up with a V12 derived from the existing flathead engine. Johnson was one of the ablest engineers in the industry but, because of cost pressures, his engine was not an outstanding one. An L-head unit with four main bearings, it was a monobloc casting with an exhaust cored between the cylinders. In character, it was more a "12-cylinder Ford V8" than a purpose-built V12, including Lincoln's earlier ones. Ending up at 267 cid, it developed the planned 100 bhp, but it was hardly earthshaking. The rest of the Zephyr's drivetrain was also based on Ford V8 components.

Styling on the prodution Zephyr was similar to that of Tjaarda's early prototypes, but a raised hoodline and radiator intake were grafted on by Ford stylist E.T. "Bob" Gregorie. The Briggs Company actually built most of the car; Ford only did the final assembly, installing drivetrain, adding the hood and fenders, plus trimming and painting.

1936 Model K three-window sedan

1938 Zephyr four-door sedan

1936 Zephyr four-door sedan

1939 Model K five-passenger cabriolet by Brunn

1937 Model K touring cabriolet by Brunn

1939 Zephyr four-door sedan

Edsel Ford laughingly told Tjaarda that he might as well let Briggs build the whole thing, since the Zephyr assembly line was only 40 feet long!

The Zephyr was announced in November 1935 in two body styles. Intended to compete with the Packard One Twenty and Cadillac's LaSalle, it was far closer in concept to the spectacularly unsuccessful Chrysler Airflow. Nevertheless, it sold in numbers previously unheard of at Lincoln. And it was a decent performer. Its top end was over 87 mph, though its 4.33 rear axle ratio was chosen more for low-end acceleration than all-out speed. It would do 0-50 mph in 10.8 seconds and 30-50 mph in six seconds flat, yet consistently averaged 16-18 miles per gallon.

Initially designated Model H, the Zephyr continued with little change for 1937 as the HB, though coupe and town sedan body styles were added that year. Wheelbase was increased for 1938, and styling was extensively revised with an innovative "mouth organ" grille that beat everyone to the next styling plateau, the horizontal front end. Model offerings expanded once more with a convertible coupe and convertible sedan. The line grew to nine models for 1939 and, although none of the styles were new, there was now a Custom interior option for many of them.

Mechanical alterations made to the late-'30s Zephyr followed typical Ford practice. Because of Henry Ford's stubbornness, hydraulic brakes did not appear until 1939. A two-speed Columbia rear axle was made available at extra cost, and gave a 28-percent reduction in engine speed in its higher cruising ratio. As for the V12, it was improved in response to owner complaints about several problems that cropped up. Water passages, for example, proved inadequate, leading to overheating, bore warpage, and excessive ring wear. Inadequate crankcase ventilation created oil sludge buildup, and oil flow was poor. Despite the addition of hydraulic valve lifters for 1938 and cast-iron heads from 1942 on, this powerplant never shed its lackluster reliability image. Had World War II not come along, it might have been completely reengineered, but that never came to pass, and many owners of 1940s Lincolns discarded the V12 in favor of later L-heads or overhead-valve V8s.

For Lincoln, 1940 was the year of the Continental—one of the most stunning automotive designs of the decade, and perhaps of all time. The Continental was Edsel Ford's idea, styled by Bob Gregorie. Edsel had directed him to make it "thoroughly continental," complete with outside spare tire—hence the name.

Originally, this new Lincoln was a one-off custom for Edsel to use on his annual vacation in Palm Beach. But, everyone who saw it that winter of 1938-39 thought it was sensational. Scarcely a year later, the Lincoln-Zephyr Continental was on sale in Lincoln showrooms. A coupe and cabriolet were offered at about $2850 a copy, and brought customers into dealerships by the thousands. The marketing plan had been to attract all kinds of customers, and the Continental did just that.

The old 414-cid "K" series Lincoln was listed in early 1940, but only 133 were actually sold that model year. There were many styles to choose from, some built in quantities of one or two. Custom bodies by Willoughby, Brunn, LeBaron, and Judkins were offered. Prices started with the LeBaron sedan and ended with a Brunn cabriolet. The Ks were mounted on wheelbases ranging from 136 to 145 inches. Eight Customs (on a 138-inch wheelbase) were also built, powered by the Zephyr engine.

The Zephyr line was Lincoln's main sales hope in those days, but volume was low. In the early 1940s, sales dropped to around 20,000 units annually. Two Zephyr series were offered for 1940: the standard coupes, convertibles, and sedan, and custom-interior closed models. The latter group included a special five-passenger "town limousine" built by Briggs out of a four-door sedan. The Brunn Company also made four custom Zephyr town cars, three of which went to the Ford family. These were heavy-looking, with rooflines

Edsel Ford's original Continental, 1939

1940 Continental club coupe

1940 Continental club coupe

that didn't fit the chiseled lower body styling.

Continental became a separate model for 1941 instead of a Zephyr series, and production increased. The old Series K was dropped completely in favor of the Zephyr-engined, long-wheelbase Customs. The emphasis remained on Zephyr, though the town limousine was deleted. As in 1940, some were available with custom interiors. Prices increased slightly, but styling changes were slight on both Zephyr and Continental. Zephyrs can be identified by their fender-mounted parking lights; '41 Continentals have pushbutton exterior door knobs and directional signals combined with the parking lights.

The year 1942 was significant for both styling and engineering. Lincoln adopted a new 305-cid V12 that was more reliable than the engine it replaced. A flashy facelift prefigured immediate postwar styling. All models now had longer, higher fenders, which increased the Continental's length by more than seven inches. Height on all models was reduced slightly, but weight went up. The front end acquired a bold grille of horizontal bars, and headlamps flanked by parking lights on either side.

Production in the years just before World War II had been steady, but hardly spectacular. The Zephyr had been Lincoln's low-priced key to survival in the Depression—comparable to the Packard One Ten/One Twenty and Cadillac's LaSalle. But Zephyr never sold well enough to put Lincoln in the same volume league as its rivals. In its best prewar year, 1937, the firm built barely one-fourth the number of cars Packard did, and reached only two-thirds the Cadillac/LaSalle figure. The last prewar Lincoln rolled out of the factory on February 10, 1942, and model year production was therefore slim.

1940 Zephyr three-passenger coupe

1942 Continental convertible coupe ("cabriolet")

1941 Continental convertible coupe ("cabriolet")

1947 convertible and Continental club coupe

1941 Continental club coupe

1948 four-door sedan

During the war, Ford stylists were able to spend a little time devising postwar designs. The "bathtub" look, which would captivate manufacturers in the late '40s, evolved quickly. Dozens of scale models were built; hundreds of renderings were drawn. Lincoln concepts of these years were often grotesque: they looked, as one stylist put it, as if they'd been "carved out of a bar of soap." After V-J Day, civilian production resumed with 1942 dies. The first postwar cars were unchanged from 1946 through 1948 as presentation of an all-new Lincoln was put off until 1949.

Long-wheelbase offerings were dropped for 1946, along with several prewar styles, such as the three-passenger coupe. A sedan, club coupe, and convertible were fielded for 1946-48; closed models were available with custom interiors. Continentals came in prewar form—coupe and cabriolet. All Lincolns continued to use the 125-inch wheelbase and the V12, which then produced 125 bhp.

The grille was now composed of vertical and horizontal bars, with a Lincoln emblem in the upper segment. A winged globe was adopted for the hood ornament. The Continental's hood was low and clean. Body lines flowed back to a tapered rear deck and a protected spare tire mounting. Continentals were still good-looking cars, devoid of bright metal side moldings. The only name identification was a modest "Lincoln Continental" script at the rear edge of the hood. The metal tire cover was painted body color. For 1947, the Lincoln name appeared on hubcaps, pull-out door handles were used, interior armrests were "pocket" types, and the hood ornament received a longer "wing." No changes at all occured when the '47s became the '48s.

Lincoln considered a new Continental for 1949, but ultimately dropped the idea and concentrated on higher-volume models. Predictably, the '49 styling was of the bar-of-soap school, but was nevertheless a clean-looking design. Riding 121-inch and 125-inch wheelbases, the models were designated Lincoln and Lincoln Cosmopolitan, respectively. The base series comprised a sedan, coupe, and convertible. The costlier Cosmopolitan included these three body styles plus a town sedan. Lincoln now discarded the aged V12 and adopted an L-head V8 of 337 cid with 152 bhp at 3600 rpm. Overdrive was available for $96 extra.

For its time, the styling of the '49s was dignified. Fenders faded into the body on the base series, and were eliminated completely on the Cosmopolitan. Headlights and taillights were "frenched," and grilles were conservative. The Cosmopolitan used a curved one-piece (instead of two-piece) windshield, broad chrome gravel deflectors over the front wheelwells, and thin window frames. This basic styling would carry Lincoln through 1951. Model year volume for 1949 was a record 73,507 units.

The '50s would be a topsy-turvy decade for Lincoln. Its 1950-51 cars were posh, but bulky and slow. By 1952, they'd be transformed into the taut, powerful road machines that would reign supreme in their class at the

Clay model proposal for '49 styling

1949 Series 9EL sport Sedan

1950 Cosmopolitan Presidential convertible

Carrera Panamericana. The line was overhauled again for 1956. Lincoln changed dramatically into a very long, good-looking highway cruiser. From 1957 on, it grew fins, acquired some lamentable styling touches, and adopted the biggest engine in the business.

The 1950-51 Lincolns completed the three-year cycle for the '49 design. Easily distinguishable by their sunken headlamps (covered lights were intended first), they appear at first to be big Mercurys. As in 1949, the Cosmopolitan shared no body panels with Mercury, though the smaller Lincoln used Mercury panels from the cowl back.

The explanation lies in Ford's postwar planning. Originally, the 118-inch-wheelbase Mercury was to have been the '49 Ford, and the 121-inch-wheelbase Lincoln was to have been the '49 Mercury. What became the Cosmopolitan was, in fact, the proposed '49 Zephyr, which never materialized, of course. When Ford's policy committee, led by Ernest Breech and Harold Youngren, urged the adoption of a shorter, 114-

Lincoln

1950 Series OEL Sport Sedan

1951 Series 1EL coupe

1952 Cosmopolitan four-door sedan

inch-wheelbase Ford, the various designs were all moved down a notch and Zephyr was eliminated. The ex-Mercury Lincoln was thus a much cheaper car than the Cosmopolitan. The latter had heavy chrome moldings over the front wheelwells and a more complicated grille than the Lincoln. Both cars, however, used the same engine—a 336.7-cid L-head originally designed for Ford trucks.

From 1950 to 1954, Lincolns offered Hydra-Matic transmission (optional 1950-51) bought from arch-rival GM. While not known for performance, the Lincoln's specification was good enough for ninth place in the 1950 Mexican race. A high-geared Lincoln also won the Mobilgas economy run in '51 with a 25.5-mpg average.

The 1950 models featured a brand-new dashboard created by Tom Hibbard, then chief designer. An attractive, rolled affair with an oblong window covering the instruments, it was popular enough to remain in use as late as 1956. Longer rear fenders were adopted for '51, and upright taillights replaced the round 1949-50 units.

The 1951 grille was simplified, wheel covers were changed, and horsepower was increased. In both 1950 and 1951, special limited editions were offered with custom interiors and padded canvas tops. In the base Lincoln series the special was called Lido. Cosmopolitan offered the Capri. Not many of either were sold. For the completely restyled 1952 models, however, Capri became the name of the upper series, while the former ultra-luxurious Cosmopolitan became the lesser Lincoln.

Sales were up a little for 1952-54, but lagged miles behind Cadillac. Perhaps this was a result of dull uniformity: the same five models were offered in all three years. Cosmopolitan and Capri were both available as four-door sedans and two-door hardtops; Capri also was offered as a convertible. Styling was on the sedate side, which may have been another problem. Nevertheless, these were three of Lincoln's best years.

The most significant mechanical feature of 1952-54 was a new valve in head V8, a superior engine in many ways. The crankshaft, for example, had eight counterweights, rather than the usual six of its competitors. The intake valves were oversize, allowing better breathing, greater efficiency, and more output for every cubic inch. (In 1953, the Lincoln V8 produced 0.64 bhp per cubic inch, against 0.63 for Cadillac and 0.54 for the Chrysler Hemi.) There was also a deep-skirt crankcase, which extended below the crankshaft centerline to create an extremely stiff support for the shaft.

There was more to the story than the engine. In 1952, Lincoln introduced the first ball-joint front suspension. This very flexible, controllable system was a forerunner of suspensions used by most cars today. Recirculating-ball power steering, oversize drum brakes, an optional four-way power seat, and liberal sound deadening insulation were also incorporated. Models equipped with optional factory air conditioning offered flow-through ventilation when the compressor was turned off. Fabrics and leathers, fit and finish were of a quality that far exceeded conventional Ford products.

Despite a rather short 123-inch wheelbase, Lincolns of this period offered more room inside than preceding models did, and sometimes more than their successors would. Visibility was better than on any other contemporary car except Kaiser, and exterior trim was notably free of the era's excesses. The taillights were fluted, like those of a late-'70s Mercedes-Benz, which enabled them to shed water and dirt. Whether this was pure engineering or just a lucky styling idea, it functioned extremely well.

Lincoln's performance in Mexico was spectacular. In the second, third, and fourth Carrera Panamericana, the make had no rival in the International Standard Class. Lincolns took the top five places in 1952, the top four in 1953, and first and second in 1954. Major credit for the race preparation goes to Clay Smith, a gifted mechanic who was tragically killed in a pit accident in 1954. Smith had help from publicity-conscious Ford, which supplied him with "export" suspensions, Ford truck camshafts, mechanical valve lifters, special front wheel

spindles and hubs, and a choice of two rear axle ratios. The higher one enabled a stock Lincoln to top 130 mph. The 1952 race winner, Chuck Stevenson, actually finished the 2000-mile grind from Juarez to the Guatemala border nearly an hour ahead of the Ferrari that had won the year before.

Lincoln wasn't ready for a total redesign in 1955, and its line that year was the most conservative in the indus-

1953 Capri four-door sedan

1954 Capri hardtop coupe

1955 Capri hardtop coupe

1956 Premiere hardtop coupe

try. The wraparound windshield was being used almost everywhere else, but Lincoln didn't have it yet—and as a result, was more practical. Wheelbase remained at 123 inches, but weight increased by 50 to 100 pounds. The company finally offered its own automatic transmission, called Turbo-Drive. Instead of Cosmopolitan, the bottom line was now called Custom; the Capri remained with the same three body styles as before. Styling was crisp, clean, and elegant. Interiors were a luxurious combination of quality fabrics and top-grain leather. Sales, unfortunately, were down for '55: Lincoln was one of the few makes to do better in 1954 than '55 because it wasn't "new" enough.

Drastic change occurred in 1956. "Unmistakably Lincoln," read the ads—but buyers had to look twice to see vestiges of the '55s in the newer edition. Gone were the short wheelbase and trim styling, replaced by a 126-inch-wheelbase chassis and a body seven inches longer and three inches wider. Capri became the lower series; the ultimate Lincoln was now called Premiere. Styling fit the new, enlarged body extremely well. The grille was clean, with peaked headlights and simple ornamentation; two-toning was confined to the roof; at the rear were rakish vertical taillights capping long exhaust ports and a "grille" motif duplicating the front design. The engine was as new as the styling, a 368-cid V8 with 285 bhp at 4600 rpm—"True power," the ads said, "that works for your safety at every speed." Despite their bulk, the cars didn't weigh much more than the 1955 models. As the only company that year with a major restyle instead of a mere facelift, Lincoln did well in '56. Over 50,000 cars were built for the 12 months. This was still only about a third of Cadillac's total, but was encouraging to Lincoln, nevertheless.

Among the changes for '57 was the first entirely new body style since 1951, a four-door hardtop dubbed the Landau. Lincoln's response to a popular Detroit trend, the Landau was offered in both the Capri and Premiere lines. The Premiere convertible, priced at $5381, was still the most expensive model. Tailfins sprouted, and four-lamp front-end styling was adopted a bit in advance of most competitors. With 10:1 compression, the 368 V8 delivered up to 300 bhp. Lincoln had a good year in '57, but not a great one. It sold slightly more cars than Imperial, and pinned its hopes for '58 on yet another totally new design.

Model year 1958 proved to be a bad one considering the millions invested in new tooling. The economy bottomed out, and car sales dropped by 50 percent or more from '57 levels. Elsewhere at Ford, the Edsel was beginning its rapid slide to nowhere, Mercury sales were running 40 percent behind 1957, and Ford was trailing Chevrolet by a quarter-million units. The new Lincolns were longer, lower, and wider at a time when luxury-car buyers were thinking about more compact dimensions. Model year production accordingly dropped to about 17,000.

At the bottom of this avalanche stood the 1958 Lincoln, longer by six inches than the '57, with a 131-inch

Lincoln

1956 Premiere four-door sedan

1957 Capri four-door sedan

Futura show car (left) and 1956 Premiere hardtop coupe

1958 Premiere hardtop coupe

1957 Premiere hardtop coupe

1961 Continental hardtop sedan

wheelbase. It was easily recognized, for there wasn't much else like it: sharp tailfins, pointed front fenders carrying four headlights in slanted recesses, a heavily chromed grille, and gigantic flared bumpers. Under the hood was the largest engine used in an American passenger car for 1958—the 430-cid Continental V8 of 375 bhp. It could be argued the Lincoln formula was nevertheless right. Recession or not, most buyers in this class were still demanding cars like this. Yet, Cadillac was attracting more people with a less radical facelift, and Imperial was garnering residual sales with its finned wonders. The two rivals had recently expanded with new series and body styles, and Cadillac's comparable models were priced several hundred dollars lower than Lincoln's. It was the 1958 debacle that ushered in Elwood Engle and a three-year styling program that culminated in the all-new, razor-edged look for 1961.

In the meantime, Lincoln returned for 1959 with the only thing it had: more of the same. The Premiere convertible had been eliminated for '58, and the lineup stayed the same for another year. Continental now reverted to a Lin-

coln sub-series as that marque's separate division was melded back in with Lincoln-Mercury. This year's Mark IV was basically a facelifted Mark III, and was offered in the '58 body styles plus a new town car and limousine priced at about the old Mark II's level. A similar course was taken for 1960 with the Mark V, after which both lines were replaced by the smaller and more handsome Lincoln Continental.

Predictably, the less expensive 1958-60 "jumbo Marks" always far outsold the Mark II. Lincoln as a whole, however, was approaching a crisis in 1959-60. Imperial surpassed Lincoln in model year production for '59, and would do so again the next year. Mechanically the '59 Lincolns were simply '58s with less horsepower, and the division held prices to about previous levels in desperation. For 1960, the two-year-old bodyshell was facelifted with a revised grille and front bumper, with the massive bumper guards moved inboard of the canted headlights. Also, the rear end was reworked with taillights and backup lights set into a "rear grille" rather than in the fender trailing edges, roof and rear window were reshaped, and a full-length bodyside molding was added. Standard equipment included

Twin-Range Turbo-Drive automatic, self-adjusting power brakes, power steering, heater and defroster, whitewall tires, undercoating, clock, windshield washers, radio, remote-control outside mirror, padded instrument panel and sunvisors, backup lights, parking brake warning light, and full wheel covers. Premieres also came with power seat, power windows, and a rear compartment reading light.

Better things were in the making for 1961. In fact, the generation of sedans, convertibles, and hardtops that began that year was one of the most memorable of the decade. A classically beautiful design was combined with superb engineering to create the most satisfying Lincolns since the prewar K series.

The chiseled styling was the work of seven Ford designers, who received the annual award of the Industrial Designers Institute in June 1961. They were Eugene Bordinant, Don DeLaRossa, Elwood P. Engle, Gail L. Halderman, John Najjar, Robert M. Thomas, and George Walker. The IDI, which rarely gives prizes to automobile designers, called the '61 Lincoln an "outstanding contribution of simplicity and design elegance."

Although the new car—now called Lincoln Continental—looked unique, it shared tooling around the cowl with that year's revamped Thunderbird. This cut tooling costs for two low-production automobiles in half. However, the Continental was a big four-door car on a 123-inch wheelbase, the T-Bird was a two-door on a wheelbase 10 inches shorter.

Styling of the 1961 and later Lincolns involved a smooth-lined body surface set off with bright metal fender strips that ran uninterrupted from stem to stern, plus a modest grille composed of horizontal and vertical elements. The fenderline emphasis made all four fenders easily visible from behind the wheel, which helped maneuverability. In front view, the windows sloped inward toward the roof for the greatest angle of "tumblehome" yet seen on a large American luxury car, and marked one of the first uses of curved side glass in regular production.

The Continental convertible, offered through 1967, was the first four-door convertible sedan since Kaiser-Frazer's abortive 1951 Frazer Manhattan. Unlike the Frazer's, the Lincoln's side glass and window frames slid completely out of sight. So did its convertible top, with the help of 11 relays connecting mechanical and hydraulic linkages.

Aside from styling, the 1961 and later Lincolns were renowned for quality of construction. The man chiefly responsible for this was Harold C. MacDonald, chief engineer of Ford's Car and Truck Group. MacDonald created no startling innovations, but refined and perfected techniques that were already known. The new Lincolns had the most rigid unit body and chassis ever produced, the best sound insulation and shock damping in mass production, extremely close machining tolerances for all mechanical components, an unprecedented number of long-life service components, a completely sealed electrical system, and superior rust and corrosion protection.

1962 Continental convertible sedan

1963 Continental hardtop sedan

1964 Continental hardtop sedan

Finally, Continental received the most thorough product testing ever applied by Detroit. Each engine was tested on a dynamometer at 3500 rpm (equal to about 98 mph) for three hours. Then it was torn down for inspection and reassembled. Every automatic transmission was tested for 30 minutes before installation. Each finished car was road tested for 12 miles and had to pass nearly 200 individual categories. Then, black light was used to visualize a fluorescent dye in the cars' lubricants as a check for oil leaks. As proof of the Continental's invulnerability, Lincoln offered a two-year, 24,000-mile warranty.

Public response to the new line was immediate and satisfying. Sales of the 1961s exceeded 25,000 units, and put Lincoln ahead of Imperial for keeps. Styling changes for the second and third year were minimal, since Lincoln had declared its intention to make improvements only for function and not simply for the sake of change. The '62 had a cleaner grille than the 1961 with a narrower central crossbar. Headlamps were not sunk into the grille, and contours were removed from the front bumper. The '63 had a square-textured

Lincoln

Lehmann-Peterson limousine based on 1964 Continental

1967 Continental hardtop coupe

1965 Continental hardtop sedan

1968 Continental hardtop coupe

1967 Continental four-door sedan

1969 Continental four-door sedan

grille, a restyled back panel appliqué, and increased trunk space.

For 1964, Lincoln wheelbase was extended to 126 inches, a length retained into the 1970s. The basic styling theme, however, remained the same. A slightly convex grille with vertical bars, a wider roof, a broader rear window, and a low-contour convertible top were the only major alterations.

Convertibles had always accounted for just a small fraction of total sales, usually about 10 percent. Lincoln wanted a more popular body style, and added a two-door hardtop coupe for 1966. Prices were cut across the board, and sales moved sharply upward as a result. The model year total was more than 54,000 units. Although still only 25 percent of Cadillac's figure, this was a Lincoln record.

Also for 1966, the Continental V8 was bored and stroked to 462 cid and remained in this form as the standard (and only) Lincoln powerplant until 1968. At that point, the cars received the 460 V8 from the Continental Mark III with 365 bhp at 4600 rpm.

The 1965 Lincoln had a new horizontal grille, combination parking and turn signal lights housed in the front fenders, and ribbed taillights. For 1966, the hood was lengthened for an increase in overall length of about five inches. Rear wheel cutouts were enlarged, and a slight hop-up appeared in the rear beltline. A new grille and front bumper were applied; the latter wrapped all the way back to the front wheel cutouts. Another grille-and-taillight shuffle and a spring-loaded hood emblem distinguished the '67s. The convertible put in its last appearance that year and saw only 2276 copies.

During 1967-68, Lehmann-Peterson Company built special-order Continental limousines on a 160-inch wheelbase. Also, Lincoln delivered two custom convertibles to the U.S. Secret Service for official functions.

These incorporated a variety of classified features, and replaced two other cars that had been in service for a decade. They were equipped with a retractable platform for Secret Service riders. Their rear doors were designed in two sections to allow agents to enter the moving car from the running boards through a 15-inch-wide space. The tops were made of transparent vinyl. A rear-facing seat behind the front seat, advanced electronic communications systems, a PA speaker, a siren, and emergency flasher lights were all part of the specification.

In October 1968, Lincoln delivered a Presidential limousine to the White House. This custom had a glass enclosure over the passenger compartment with a hinged center section so the occupants could stand up during a parade. The rear bumper of this 21-foot Continental could be lowered like a tailgate and converted into a platform for Secret Service agents. The limousine had more advanced security, communications, and engineering features than any other automobile ever used by the White House.

Classic automobiles, it seems, are never quite forgotten. During the early '60s, Ford executives, engineers, stylists, and dealers longed for another Continental in the tradition of the Mark II. Their answer arrived for 1968 as the Continental Mark III.

According to Ford Motor Company, this new car was the one most closely linked to Henry Ford II. Just as his brother William Clay had influenced the early Mark II and his father Edsel had sponsored the "Mark I," HF II insured that the '68 Mark III was a reflection of his personal taste. Why was the Mark III designation used again, instead of the more logical Mark VI? The reason is that he viewed the heavyweight 1958-60 cars as unworthy of the Continental marque, and company promotion ballyhooed the new entry as a direct descendent of the Mark II.

The Mark III entered the product-planning stage in late 1965. From the beginning, the goal was clear: this was to be a personal-luxury car with a long hood and short deck in the Continental tradition. Styling was supervised by design chief Eugene Bordinat. Hermann Brunn, namesake of the great coachbuilder and a member of Bordinat's staff, was largely responsible for the interior. Brunn designed large, comfortable bucket seats and a wood-grained dashboard with easy-to-reach controls. Henry II selected the car's final shape from a number of designs submitted by company stylists in early 1966.

The Mark III was ready by April 1968. Because of its late introduction, only a few thousand were built that year, but there was no question about its rightness for the market: more than 20,000 were sold in 1969 and 1970.

The Mark III was set on a 117.2-inch wheelbase, some nine inches shorter than the Mark II's, and was the same length as the front-wheel-drive Cadillac Eldorado. Although the Eldorado was more technically advanced, the Continental seemed to have more magic in its name. In sales, it almost matched Eldorado during its four-year life-span and never trailed by more than 2000 units a year. This was a significant achievement, because Lincoln's annual production had never come close to Cadillac's.

The Mark III was powered by a 460-cid V8 with 10.5:1 compression, one of the industry's largest engines. It was a good-looking car, with the longest hood—more than six feet—in the land. The buyer had a wide choice of luxury interiors and could choose from 26 exterior colors, including four special "Moondust" metallic paints. The 1969-71 models cost more but carried few changes. Standard features on all Mark IIIs included Select-Shift Turbo-Drive automatic transmission, power brakes (discs in front, drums in the rear), concealed headlights, ventless side windows, power seats and windows, flow-through ventilation, and 150 pounds of sound-deadening insulation.

Accompanied by the new Continental Mark III, the Lincoln Continental sedan and coupe were the offerings for 1968. One of the easiest things to change for model identification are the front and rear treatments, so the '68s got a new horizontal texture at both ends. Front fenders housed three-function lights for turn signals, parking, and front side markers. The rear lights had four functions; turn signals, brake lights, taillamps, and rear side markers. Their clean design blended well with the fenderlines and allowed Lincoln to avoid clumsy, separate side marker lights.

For 1969, there was a new, squarish grille, with a raised center section extending into the hood. A Town Car interior option for the sedan provided "unique, super-puff leather-and-vinyl seats and door panels, luxury wood-tone front seat back and door trim inserts, extra plush carpeting and special napped nylon headlining." Government-required safety equipment included a dual hydraulic brake system with warning light, four-way emergency flasher, day/night rearview mirror, and energy-absorbing steering column and instrument panel. Continentals retained the 126-inch wheelbase, but overall length had grown to 224.5 inches.

Aside from hidden headlights and a more horizontal grille design, the 1970 Lincoln was similar to the '69 version. Ventless side glass, concealed wipers, wider doors, and full-width taillights were the major differences. The 460-cid engine with appropriate emission controls remained the sole powerplant.

By the end of the '60s, the Lincoln Continental had grown appreciably in size, if not in weight. Sales continued at a respectable level, for the marque had made many friends among luxury-car buyers.

1970 Continental four-door sedan

The heavier, bulkier-looking 1970 design carried on through 1974 with relatively few changes, most dictated by federal, not market, requirements. An even bigger generation arrived for '75 on a fractionally longer wheelbase and some eight inches longer overall, though curb weight was slightly lower than before. Styling remained resolutely blocky and formal throughout the decade as Ford designers sought to establish a closer familial resemblance with the Mark. Sales moved smartly upward for 1972-73, followed by a temporary decline in the wake of the Arab oil embargo. But along with other full-size models, the big Lincoln rallied beginning in 1975, and output was close to 100,000 units annually by 1979. That year brought another fuel shock, and volume dropped appreciably for 1980.

Longer, lower, and wider was a formula that had traditionally worked well for luxury makes, and it worked well for Lincoln with the Continental Mark IV, introduced for 1972. Sales nearly doubled over those recorded by the previous year's Mark III, and would average 50,000 or so units annually through the final 1976 models. Remarkably, the Mark IV offered less passenger room than the Mark III, and was predictably thirstier and less agile. Though it shared basic structure with the contemporary Ford Thunderbird, it wasn't immediately apparent. It also wasn't the first time a Lincoln had been related to a Bird, as the two had shared a common cowl structure back in 1961-63.

Lincoln enjoyed good success with the Town Car, an option package initially offered on the full-size four-door. It consisted of special leather inserts and vinyl bolsters for the seats, wood-like panels on the backs of the front seats, deeper cut-pile carpeting, and soft nylon headliner, all color-keyed in a choice of five hues. For 1971, these items were bolstered by special dash and front fender nameplates plus a set of keys and door-mounted owner initials done in 22-carat gold, which made the Golden Anniversary Continental, a commemorative marking Lincoln's 50th birthday. The gold goodies were dropped the following year, by which time the Town Car had become a sub-model. For 1973, the big two-door got the same treatment to become the Town Coupe, and Lincoln enjoyed a record season, with model year production spiraling to over 125,000 units. Though the big Continental wasn't outselling Cadillac's DeVille in the full-size market, the Mark IV had a solid lead over the bulky Eldorado in the personal-luxury class.

Lincoln marked time for model year 1974. The only noteworthy changes were heavier bumpers at the rear to match the beefier front ones adopted the previous year, plus a brace of Luxury Group interior/exterior packages for the Mark. The revamped big-car line for '75 brought the end of pure "hardtop styling" and the beginning of "opera window" rooflines, with fixed B-posts and heavily padded vinyl coverings. These models continued largely intact through 1979.

The Mark IV was restyled inside and out for 1977 to become the Mark V, distinguished by a crisper, lighter appearance. And appearances were not deceiving. Though it rode the Mark IV's wheelbase and was virtually the same

mechanically, the new model was some 500 pounds lighter at the curb. It also boasted 21 percent more trunk space—which seems a large gain only because the IV had so little to begin with. Engineers also paid belated attention to fuel economy by specifying the corporate 400-cid V8 as standard equipment. The old standby 460 continued as an option except in California, where it couldn't quite clear that state's tougher emissions hurdles.

Model year 1977 also saw Lincoln's first move into the luxury-compact class, its first response to the radically changed market left behind by the first energy crisis. Called Versailles, it was a hastily contrived reply to Cadillac's remarkably successful Seville, little more than a Ford Granada/Mercury Monarch carrying a Continental-style square grille, stand-up hood ornament and humped trunklid, plus more standard equipment. Established Lincoln buyers looked askance at its plebian origins (which the press never failed to point out), while buyers who wanted a posh smaller car balked at the $11,500 price. You can only fool some of the people some of the time, and Lincoln didn't fool many with this one. Versailles model year sales for '77 totaled a mere 15,434, a fraction of Seville's.

This basic three-car lineup held the fort for 1978-79, while Lincoln prepared to launch a fleet of downsized models for 1980. Amazingly, the big cars continued to sell strongly, defying the combined threat of further fuel shortages and a fleet of luxury intermediates from Big Three rivals. For 1978, Lincoln sold over 150,000 Continentals and Marks. The next year, with the industry starting to reel, volume rose to over 168,000. Part of this performance was due to circumstance. By 1979, anyone who wanted a truly

continued on page 433

1971 Continental four-door sedan

1972 Continental Mark IV hardtop coupe

▲1959 Plymouth Sport Fury hardtop coupe   ▼1957 Nash Metropolitan coupe

▲1960 Buick Electra 225 convertible   ▼1960 Edsel Ranger convertible

▲1960 Chevrolet Bel Air Sport Coupe hardtop   ▼1961 Studebaker Hawk coupe

▲1961 Oldsmobile Dynamic 88 Sceni-Coupe hardtop   ▼1961 Ford Thunderbird convertible

▲1962 Dodge Polara 500 hardtop coupe   ▼1962 Chevrolet Impala Sport Coupe hardtop

▲1962 Studebaker Gran Turismo Hawk hardtop coupe   ▼1963 Studebaker Avanti coupe

▲1963 Ford Thunderbird Sports Roadster convertible　　▼1963 Oldsmobile F-85 Jetfire Holiday hardtop coupe

▲1963 Mercury Meteor S-33 hardtop coupe   ▼1965 Buick Riviera hardtop coupe

▲1964 Chrysler 300 convertible ▼1964 Oldsmobile Ninety-Eight Custom hardtop coupe

▲1965 Ford Galaxie 500XL hardtop coupe ▼1965 Ford Mustang hardtop coupe

▲1965 Plymouth Sport Fury convertible   ▼1965 Pontiac Tempest LeMans GTO hardtop coupe

▲1965 Chevrolet Impala Sport Coupe hardtop   ▼1966 AMC Marlin fastback hardtop coupe

▲1966 Oldsmobile Cutlass Holiday hardtop coupe ▲1966 Buick Riviera hardtop coupe

▲1967 Chevrolet Corvette Sting Ray roadster ▼1967 Pontiac Grand Prix hardtop coupe

▲1967 Chevrolet Impala SS Sport Coupe hardtop   ▼1967 Rambler American Rogue convertible

▲1969 Dodge Coronet R/T hardtop coupe   ▼1969 AMC AMX two-seat coupe

1975 Continental Town Car four-door sedan

1977 Continental "Williamsburg" Town Car four-door sedan

1979 Versailles four-door sedan

1980 Continental Mark IV coupe

1980 Continental Town Car four-door sedan

continued from page 416

large luxury liner—a "traditional-size" car, as Lincoln called it—had no other choice. Following a spate of limited-edition trim packages issued for 1978 to mark Ford Motor Company's 75th anniversary, Lincoln came up with its own "Collector Series" option for the '79 Continental and Mark. These included the appropriate nameplates, gold grille accents, special midnight blue metallic paint, and a host of "custom" accoutrements such as a color-keyed umbrella and leather-bound owner's manual and toolkit. It was a timely offering, for an era was about to end.

It should be noted that the Mark V was quite good for what it was. The author recalls how impressed an English colleague was with a '77 model sampled in Detroit. It was certainly no *grand routier,* wallowing around turns and floating over straightline undulations. But it was utterly smooth and silent and built with care using high-quality materials.

One of Lincoln's most successful marketing ploys in this period was its Designer Series. American Motors had tried something similar earlier in the decade with Gucci Hornets and Pierre Cardin Javelins. But, as a luxury make, Lincoln was in a far better position to cash in on the snob appeal of high fashion names. First seen for 1976, these extra-cost *coturier* packages were decorated inside and out with colors and materials specified by various well-known designers. The schemes varied somewhat from year to year, but the results were invariably striking and usually pleasing. Perhaps the most consistently tasteful was the Bill Blass edition, a nautically inspired blend of navy blue paint and eggshell-white vinyl top outside, and navy velour or dark blue and cream leather uphostery inside. There were also versions by Givenchy (generally turquoise or jade), Emilio Pucci (maroon and gunmetal grey), and Cartier (champagne/grey), the last not a designer per se but, of course, the famous jeweler.

The big Continental and the Mark became much more alike—and much more sensible—for 1980. Lincoln now adopted the "Panther" platform introduced with the 1979 Ford LTD and Mercury Marquis as the basis for a substantially downsized Continental and an upmarket twin called Mark VI, thus resuming its late-'50s practice of fielding two versions of a single basic design. Compared to their immediate predecessors, these cars were up to 10 inches shorter between wheel centers and significantly lighter yet about as roomy, thanks to only marginal reductions in width, plus the taller, boxier body styling. The usual appearance "cues" were retained for each line, but the usual big-block engines weren't. Standard for both was the corporate 302-cid small-block V8 in newly developed fuel injected form; a 351 V8 was the only option. It was all for the sake of economy, and Lincoln boasted an important efficiency aid in a new four-speed overdrive automatic transmission, basically a three-speed unit with an extra, super-tall (0.67:1) ratio added. There was more competent handling courtesy of a revised suspension with four-bar link rear geometry and retuned body mounts and suspension bushings, plus standard high-pressure radial

tires, which also helped eke out a few more mpg. A four-door Mark bowed for the first time, and the various designer editions were bolstered by a new Signature Series offering much the same thing as the previous Collector option.

A major national recession beginning in the spring of 1979 sent U.S. car sales plunging. Lincoln fared worse than most, its 1980 model year tally down by as much as two-thirds compared to its previous level. The under-whelming Versailles was in its final year, and found fewer than 5000 buyers. The economy began to improve a few years later, and Lincoln sales improved with it, aided by a still smaller Lincoln Continental, a "bustleback" four-door compact derived from the Fairmont/Zephyr platform and introduced for 1982 as the Versailles' successor. The arrival of the sleeker and more roadable Mark VII for 1984 signalled a new age for Lincoln—and its most interesting and distinctive cars in two generations.

Lincoln Specifications

1930

Model L (wb 136.0)

		Wght	Price	Prod
	conv rdstr 2-4P	4,740	4,500	12
	spt phtn 4P	4,840	4,200	53
	spt phtn 4P, tonneau-cowl	4,850	4,400	90
	spt touring 7P	4,940	4,200	79
	cpe 5P	4,940	4,400	275
	Town sdn 2W 4P	5,010	4,400	169
	Town sdn 3W 4P	5,010	4,400	285
	sdn 4d 2-3W	5,180	4,500	541
	sdn 7P	5,245	4,700	458
	limo 7P	5,190	4,900	329
	chassis	—	3,500	47
	Custom bodies:			
	Locke spt rdstr	—	—	15
	Judkins cpe 2P	4,790	5,000	65
	Judkins berline 4P 2W	5,280	5,600	72
	Judkins berline 4P 3W	4,930	5,600	100
	Brunn brougham A/W 7P	5,045	7,000	68
	Brunn cab s.c. A/W 7P	4,985	7,200	44
	LeBaron conv rdstr	—	—	100
	LeBaron cab 7P	5,370	7,200	NA
	LeBaron A/W cab 7P	5,045	6,900	29
	LeBaron A/W cab 7P, semi-clpsble	5,190	7,100	20
	LeBaron cpe-sdn 4P	5,030	5,300	8
	Willoughby limo 6P	5,180	5,900	244
	Willoughby brougham A/W	5,900	—	5
	Dietrich conv cpe 4P	5,180	6,200	42
	Dietrich conv sdn 5P	5,235	6,600	40
	Derham conv cpe 4P	4,850	6,400	1
	Derham phaeton	6,000	—	21

1930 Engine	bore×stroke	bhp	availability
V8, 385.0	3.50×5.00	90	S-all

1931

201 Model K (wb 145.0)

		Wght	Price	Prod
202A	dual-cowl spt phaeton 5P	4,970	4,600	77
202B	spt phaeton 5P	4,960	4,400	60
203	spt tourer 7P	5,060	4,400	45
204A	Town sdn 5P 2W	5,130	4,600	195
204B	Town sdn 5P 3W	5,130	4,600	447
205	sdn 5P	5,300	4,700	552
206	cpe 5P	5,060	4,600	225
207A	sdn 7P	5,365	4,900	521
207B/C	limo 7P	5,310	5,100	401
208A	Brunn cab A/W	5,280	7,400	30
209	Brunn brougham A/W	5,165	7,200	04
210	Dietrich conv cpe 4P	5,300	6,400	25
211	Dietrich sdn 4d	5,355	6,800	65
212	Derham phtn 4P	4,970	6,200	11
213A	Judkins berline 4P 3W	5,050	5,800	171
214	LeBaron conv rdstr 2-4P	4,860	4,700	275
215	Willoughby limo 6P	5,300	6,100	151
216	Willoughby panel brougham 7P	5,340	7,400	15
217A	LeBaron Cab A/W 7P	5,165	7,100	
217B	LeBaron Cab A/W 7P, semi-clpsble	5,100	7,300	21
218	Judkins cpe 2P	4,910	5,200	86
219	Dietrich cpe 2P	5,050	NA	35
201	chassis, 145" wb	—	—	61
220	chassis, 150" wb	—	—	3
221	chassis, 155" wb	—	—	3
—	misc. specials	—	—	47

1931 Engine	bore×stroke	bhp	availability
V8, 385.0	3.50×5.00	120	S-all

1932

501 Model KA (wb 136.0)

		Wght	Price	Prod
502A	cpe 2P	5,335	3,200	86
502B	cpe 2-4P	5,205	3,245	
504	Town sdn 5P	5,330	3,100	147
505	sdn 4d	5,300	3,200	921
506	victoria 5P	5,345	3,200	265
507A	sdn 7P	5,435	3,300	508
507B	limo 7P	5,520	3,350	122
508	phaeton	5,270	3,000	29
510A	rdstr 2P	5,050	2,900	12
510B	rdstr 2-4P	5,180	2,945	
501	chassis	—	—	7
—	misc. & unaccounted for	—	—	127

231 Model KB (wb 145.0)

		Wght	Price	Prod
232A	Murphy dual-cowl spt phtn 4P	5,625	4,500	30
232B	Murphy spt phaeton 4P	5,250	4,300	13
233	spt touring 7P	5,720	4,300	24
234A	Town sdn 5P 2W	5,740	4,500	123
234B	Town sdn 5P 3W	5,740	4,500	200
235	sdn 4d	5,975	4,600	216
236	cpe 5P	5,600	4,400	83
237A	sdn 7P	5,975	4,700	266
237B	limo 7P	5,990	4,900	41
237C	limo 7P	5,900	4,000	135

		Wght	Price	Prod
238	Brunn cab A/W 5P	5,855	7,200	14
239	Brunn brougham A/W 7P	5,920	7,000	13
240	Dietrich spt berline 5P	5,605	6,500	8
241	Dietrich conv sdn 5P	5,720	6,400	20
242A	Dietrich cpe 2-4P	5,745	5,150	17
242B	Dietrich cpe 2P	5,710	5,000	
243A	Judkins berline 5P 2W	5,860	5,700	74
243B	Judkins berline 5P 3W	5,860	5,700	
244A	Judkins cpe 2-4P	5,610	5,350	23
244B	Judkins cpe 2P	5,595	5,100	
245	Willoughby limo 7P	5,950	5,900	64
246	Willoughby panel brougham 4P	5,855	7,100	4
247	Waterhouse conv victoria 5P	5,470	5,900	10
248	LeBaron rdstr 2-4P	5,535	4,600	112
249	Murphy spt rdstr 2P	5,605	6,800	3
231	chassis, 145″ wb	—	—	18
250	chassis, 150″ wb	—	—	1
—	misc. specials	—	—	13

1932 Engines	bore×stroke	bhp	availability
V8, 385.0	3.50×5.00	125	S-KA
V12, 448.0	3.25×4.50	150	S-KB

1933

511 Model KA (wb 136.0)		Wght	Price	Prod
512A	cpe 2-4P	4,929	3,145	44
512B	cpe 2P	4,909	3,100	
513A	conv rdstr 2-4P	4,769	3,200	85
514	Town sdn 5P	4,954	3,100	201
515	sdn 4d	4,989	3,200	320
516	victoria 5P	4,919	3,200	109
517A	sdn 7P	5,159	3,300	190
517B	limo 7P	5,184	3,350	111
518A	dual-cowl phaeton 5P	4,759	3,200	12
518B	phaeton 5P	4,749	3,000	12
519	phaeton 7P	4,759	3,200	10
520A	rdstr 2-4P	4,739	2,745	12
520B	rdstr 2P	4,719	2,700	
511	chassis	—	—	7
—	misc. specials	—	—	5

251 Model KB (wb 145.0)		Wght	Price	Prod
252A	dual-cowl phaeton 5P	5,310	4,400	9
252B	spt phaeton 4P	5,220	4,200	6
253	spt touring 7P	5,310	4,300	6
254A	Town sdn 2W	5,401	4,400	39
254B	Town sdn 3W	5,401	4,400	41
255	sdn 4d	5,491	4,500	52
256	victoria cpe 5P	5,511	4,300	18
257A	sdn 7P	5,521	4,600	110
257B	limo 7P	5,571	4,800	105
258C	Brunn cab 5P	5,685	6,900	8
258D	Brunn cab semi-clpsble 5P	5,386	6,900	
259B	Brunn brougham 7P	5,431	6,900	13
260	Brunn conv cpe 5P	5,171	5,700	15
260	Dietrich spt berline 5P	NA	NA	NA
261	Dietrich conv sdn 5P	5,410	6,100	15
263A	Judkins berline 2W 4P	5,411	5,500	36
263B	Judkins berline 3W 4P	5,411	5,500	
264D	Judkins cpe 2P	5,530	5,000	12
265B	Willoughby limo 7P	5,541	5,700	40
266B	Willoughby panel brougham 7P	5,541	7,000	2
267B	LeBaron conv rdstr 2-4P	5,191	4,500	37
2197	Dietrich cpe 2P	NA	4,900	8
251	chassis	—	—	4
—	chassis, 155″ wb	—	—	1
—	misc. specials	—	—	19

1933 Engines	bore×stroke	bhp	availability
V12, 381.7	3.00×4.50	125	S-KA
V12, 448.0	3.25×4.50	150	S-KB

1934

521 Model KA (wb 136.0)		Wght	Price	Prod
522A	cpe 2-4P	4,879	3,250	60
522B	cpe 2P	5,210	3,200	
523	conv rdstr 2-4P	5,050	3,400	75
524	Town sdn 5P	5,140	3,450	450
525	sdn 4d	5,044	3,400	425
526	victoria cpe 5P	5,029	3,400	115
527A	sdn 7P	5,203	3,500	275
527B	limo 7P	5,228	3,550	175
531	conv sdn phtn 5P	5,029	3,900	75
521	chassis	—	—	21
—	misc. specials	—	—	8

271 Model KB (wb 145.0)		Wght	Price	Prod
273	touring 7P	5,720	4,200	20
277A	sdn 7P	5,510	4,500	210
277B	limo 7P	5,570	4,700	215
278A	Brunn cab 5P semi-clpsble	5,315	6,800	13
278B	Brunn cab 5P	5,615	6,800	
279	Brunn brougham 7P	5,480	6,800	15
280	Brunn conv cpe 5P	5,045	5,600	25
281	Dietrich conv sdn 5P	5,330	5,600	25
282	Judkins sdn limo 7P	5,570	5,700	27
283A	Judkins berline 4P 2W	5,710	5,400	37
283B	Judkins berline 4P 3W	5,710	5,400	17
285	Willoughby limo 7P	5,605	5,600	77
287	LeBaron conv rdstr 2-4P	5,085	4,400	45
271	chassis	—	—	12
—	misc. specials	—	—	14

1934 Engine	bore×stroke	bhp	availability
V12, 414.0	3.13×4.50	150	S-all

1935

541 Model K (wb 136.0)		Wght	Price	Prod
542	LeBaron conv rdstr 2-4P	5,030	4,600	30
543	sdn 4d 2W	5,385	4,300	170
544	sdn 4d 3W	5,375	4,300	278
545	cpe 5P	5,230	4,200	44
546	LeBaron conv sdn phtn 5P	5,360	5,000	20
547	Brunn conv victoria 5P	5,135	5,500	15
548	LeBaron cpe 2P	5,030	4,600	23
541	chassis	—	—	1
—	misc. specials	—	—	5

301 Model K (wb 145.0)		Wght	Price	Prod
302	touring 7P	5,225	4,200	15
303A	sdn 7P	5,535	4,600	351
303B	limo 7P	5,630	4,700	282
304A	Brunn cab 5P	5,505	6,600	13
304B	Brunn cab 5P semi-clpsble	5,415	6,700	13
305	Brunn brougham 7P	5,530	6,700	10
307	LeBaron conv sdn 5P	5,325	5,500	20
308	Judkins limo 7P	5,645	5,700	18
309A	Judkins berline 2W	5,545	5,500	34
309B	Judkins berline 3W	5,555	5,500	13
310	Willoughby limo 7P	5,695	5,700	40
311	Willoughby spt sdn	5,075	6,800	5
301	chassis	—	—	8
—	misc. specials	—	—	26

1935 Engine	bore×stroke	bhp	availability
V12, 414.0	3.13×4.50	150	S-all

1936

Series H Zephyr (wb 122.0)		Wght	Price	Prod
902	sdn 4d	3,349	1,320	13,180
903	sdn 2d	3,289	1,275	1,814

Model K (wb 136.0)

324A	sdn 5P 2W	5,426	4,300	103
324B	sdn 5P 3W	5,476	4,300	297
326	cpe 5P	5,266	4,200	36
328	Brunn conv victoria 5P	5,176	5,500	10
330	LeBaron conv rdstr 2-4P	5,136	4,700	20
332	LeBaron cpe 2-4P	4,700	5,126	25
333	LeBaron conv sdn phtn 5P	5,296	5,000	30

Model K (wb 145.0)

323	touring 7P	5,276	4,200	8
327A	sdn 7P	5,591	4,600	368
327B	limo 7P	5,641	4,700	370
329A	Brunn cab 5P	5,511	6,600	10
329B	Brunn cab 5P semi-clpsble	5,491	6,700	10
331	Brunn brougham 7P	5,571	6,700	20
334	LeBaron conv sdn 5P	5,381	5,500	15
335	Judkins sdn limo 7P	5,671	5,800	26
337A	Judkins berline 5P 2W	5,561	5,500	51
337B	Judkins berline 5P 3W	5,581	5,600	13
339	Willoughby limo 7P	5,661	5,700	62
341	Willoughby spt sdn	5,561	6,800	11
321	chassis	—	—	9
—	misc. specials	—	—	30
322	chassis	—	—	6
—	misc. specials	—	—	4

1936 Engines	bore×stroke	bhp	availability	
V12, 267.3	2.75×3.75	110	S-Zephyr	
V12, 414.0	3.13×4.50	150	S-K	

1937

Series HB Zephyr (wb 122.0)

		Wght	Price	Prod
700	cpe sdn	3,289	1,245	1,500
720	cpe	3,323	1,165	5,199
730	sdn 4d	3,349	1,265	23,159
737	Town sdn	3,507	1,425	139

Model K (wb 136.0; lwb-145.0)

353	Willoughby touring 7P (lwb)	5,950	5,550	7
354A	sdn 5P 2W	5,700	4,450	48
354B	sdn 5P 3W	5,700	4,450	136
356	Willoughby cpe 5P	5,790	5,550	6
357A	lwb sdn 7P	5,905	4,750	212
357B	limo 7P (lwb)	5,905	4,850	248
358	Brunn conv vic 5P	5,660	5,550	13
359A	Brunn lwb cab 5P	NA	6,650	10
359B	Brunn lwb cab semi-clpsble 5P	5,960	6,750	7
360	LeBaron conv rdstr 2-4P	5,490	4,950	15
361	Brunn lwb brougham 7P	5,995	6,750	29
362	LeBaron cpe 2P	5,380	4,950	24
363A	LeBaron conv sdn/partition (lwb)	5,697	5,650	12
363B	LeBaron lwb conv sdn	5,880	5,450	37
365	Judkins sdn limo 7P (lwb)	5,940	5,950	27
367A	Judkins lwb berline 5P 2W	5,880	5,650	47
367B	Judkins lwb berline 5P 3W	5,890	5,750	19
369	Willoughby limo 7P (lwb)	6,115	5,850	60
371	Willoughby lwb spt sdn 5P	5,915	6,850	6
373	Willoughby panel b'ham 7P (lwb)	NA	7,050	4
375	Brunn lwb touring cab 5P	6,020	6,950	10

1937 Engines	bore×stroke	bhp	availability	
V12, 267.3	2.75×3.75	110	S-Zephyr	
V12, 414.0	3.13×4.50	150	S-K	

1938

Series 86H Zephyr (wb 125.0)

		Wght	Price	Prod
700	cpe sdn	3,409	1,355	800
720	cpe 3P	3,294	1,295	2,600
730	sdn 4d	3,444	1,375	14,520
737	Town limo	3,474	1,550	130
740	conv sdn 5P	3,724	1,790	461
760B	conv cpe 3P	3,489	1,700	600

Model K (wb 136.0; lwb-145.0)

403	Willoughby lwb touring 7P	5,557	5,900	5
404A	sdn 5P 2W	5,527	4,900	9
404B	sdn 5P 3W	5,532	4,900	49
406	Willoughby cpe 5P	5,407	5,900	4
407A	lwb sdn 7P	5,672	5,100	78
407B	limo 7P (lwb)	5,762	5,200	91
408	Brunn conv victoria 5P	5,322	5,900	8
409A	Brunn cab 5P	5,692	6,900	5
409B	Brunn cab 5P semi-clpsble (lwb)	5,716	7,000	6
410	LeBaron conv rdstr 2-4P	5,297	5,300	8
411	Brunn lwb brougham 7P	5,806	7,000	13
412	LeBaron cpe 2P	5,227	5,300	12
413A	LeBaron conv sdn/partition (lwb)	5,572	6,000	7
413B	LeBaron lwb conv sdn	5,462	5,800	15
415	Judkins sdn limo 7P (lwb)	5,742	6,300	11
417A	Judkins berline 5P 2W (lwb)	5,502	6,000	19
417B	Judkins berline 5P 3W (lwb)	5,632	6,100	11
419	Willoughby limo 7P (lwb)	5,826	6,200	46
421	Willoughby lwb spt sdn 5P	5,716	7,000	4
423	Willoughby panel brougham 7P (lwb)	NA	7,400	6
425	Brunn lwb touring cab 5P	5,662	7,200	9

1938 Engines	bore×stroke	bhp	availability	
V12, 267.3	2.75×3.75	110	S-Zephyr	
V12, 414.0	3.13×4.50	150	S-K	

1939

Series 96H Zephyr (wb 125.0)

		Wght	Price	Prod
700	cpe sdn	3,600	1,369	800
720	cpe 3P	3,520	1,358	2,500
730	sdn 4d	3,620	1,399	16,663
737	Town limo	3,670	1,747	95
740	conv sdn 5P	3,900	1,839	302
760B	conv cpe 2-4P	3,790	1,747	640

Model K (wb 136.0; lwb-145.0)

403	Willoughby lwb touring 7P	5,870	5,932	1
404A	sdn 5P 2W	5,735	4,905	2
404B	sdn 5P 3W	5,740	4,905	12
406	Willoughby cpe 5P	5,615	5,926	1
407A	lwb sdn 7P	5,880	5,109	25
407B	limo 7P (lwb)	5,970	5,211	58
408	Brunn conv vic 5P	5,530	5,926	2
409A	Brunn lwb cab 5P	6,010	6,947	1
409B	Brunn lwb cab 5P semi-clpsble	6,030	7,049	1
410	LeBaron conv rdstr 2-4P	5,050	5,313	2
411	Brunn lwb brougham 7P	6,120	7,049	2
412	LeBaron cpe 2P	5,435	5,313	4
413A	LeBaron lwb conv sdn	5,670	5,828	3
413B	LeBaron conv sdn/partition (lwb)	5,780	6,028	6
415	Judkins sdn limo 7P (lwb)	5,950	6,334	2
417A	Judkins lwb berline 5P 2W	5,770	6,028	2
417B	Judkins lwb berline 5P 3W	5,840	6,130	1
419	Willoughby limo 7P (lwb)	6,140	6,232	4
421	Willoughby lwb spt sdn 5P	6,300	7,049	1
423	Willoughby panel brougham 7P (lwb)	NA	NA	1
425	Brunn lwb touring cab 5P	5,870	7,253	2

1939 Engines	bore×stroke	bhp	availability
V12, 267.3	2.75×3.75	110	S-Zephyr
V12, 414.0	3.13×4.50	150	S-K

1940

06H Zephyr (wb 125.0)

		Wght	Price	Prod
56	Continental conv cpe	3,740	2,916	54
57	Continental club cpe	3,850	2,783	350
72A	cpe 3P	3,500	1,399	⎫
72A	cpe 3P, Custom interior	3,500	1,506	⎬ 1,256
72B	cpe, A/S	3,480	1,429	⎭
73	sdn 4d	3,660	1,439	⎫
73	sdn 4d, Custom interior	3,660	1,547	⎬ 15,764
76	conv cpe	3,760	1,818	700
77	club cpe	3,590	1,439	⎫
77	club cpe, Custom interior	3,590	1,547	⎬ 3,500
22	Custom Town Limousine	3,700	1,787	4
26	Custom Town Car	3,650	1,750	4

K Series (wb 136.0)*

		Wght	Price	Prod
404A	sdn 4d	5,735	4,905	—
406	cpe, Willoughby	5,615	5,926	—
408	conv Victoria, Brunn	5,530	5,926	—
410	rdstr, LeBaron	5,505	5,313	—
412	stationary cpe, LeBaron	5,415	5,313	—

K Series (wb 145.0)*

		Wght	Price	Prod
407A	sdn 4d, 7P	5,880	5,109	—
407B	limo	5,970	5,211	—
409	cabriolet, Brunn	6,010	6,947	—
411	brougham 7P, Brunn	6,120	7,049	—
413	conv sdn, LeBaron	5,670	5,823	—
415	sdn limo 7P, Judkins	5,950	6,334	—
417A	berline 2W, Judkins	5,770	6,028	—
417B	berline 3W, Judkins	5,840	6,130	—
419	limo, Willoughby	6,140	6,232	—
421	spt sdn, Willoughby	6,300	7,049	—
425	cabriolet 2P, Brunn	5,870	7,253	—

*Total K Series model year production: 133.

1940 Engines	bore×stroke	bhp	availability
V12, 292.0	3.88×3.75	120	S-Zephyr
V12, 414.0	3.13×4.50	150	S-K Series

1941

16H Zephyr (wb 125.0)

		Wght	Price	Prod
72A	cpe 3P	3,560	1,478	⎫
72A	cpe 3P, Custom interior	3,560	1,557	⎬ 972
73	sdn 4d	3,710	1,541	⎫
73	sdn 4d, Custom interior	3,710	1,641	⎬ 14,469
76	conv cpe	3,840	1,858	725
77	club cpe	3,640	1,541	⎫
77	club cpe, Custom interior	3,640	1,541	⎬ 178

16H Continental (wb 125.0)

		Wght	Price	Prod
56	conv cpe ("cabriolet")	3,860	2,865	400
57	club cpe	3,890	2,812	850

168H Custom (wb 138.0)

		Wght	Price	Prod
31	sdn 4d, 8P	4,250	2,704	355
32	limo	4,270	2,836	295

1941 Engine	bore×stroke	bhp	availability
V12, 292.0	2.88×3.75	120	S-all

1942

26H Zephyr (wb 125.0)

		Wght	Price	Prod
72A	cpe 3P	3,730	1,650	⎫
72A	cpe 3P, Custom interior	3,730	1,735	⎬ 1,236
73	sdn 4d	3,920	1,700	⎫
73	sdn 4d, Custom interior	3,920	1,795	⎬ 4,418
76	conv cpe	4,130	2,150	191
77	club cpe	3,810	1,700	⎫
77	club cpe, Custom interior	3,810	1,795	⎬ 253

26H Continental (wb 125.0)

		Wght	Price	Prod
56	conv cpe ("cabriolet")	4,020	3,000	136
57	club cpe	4,000	3,000	200

268H Custom (wb 138.0)

		Wght	Price	Prod
31	sdn 4d, 8P	4,380	2,950	47
32	limo	4,400	3,075	66

1942 Engine	bore×stroke	bhp	availability
V12, 305.0	2.94×3.75	130	S-all

1946

66H (wb 125.0)—16,179 built

		Wght	Price	Prod
73	sdn 4d	3,980	2,337	—
73	sdn 4d, Custom interior	3,980	2,486	—
76	conv cpe	4,210	2,883	—
77	club cpe	3,380	2,318	—
77	club cpe, Custom interior	3,380	2,467	—

66H Continental (wb 125.0)

		Wght	Price	Prod
56	conv cpe ("cabriolet")	4,090	4,474	201
57	club cpe	4,100	4,392	265

1946 Engine	bore×stroke	bhp	availability
V12, 292.0	2.88×3.75	125	S-all

1947

76H (wb 125.0)—19,891 built

		Wght	Price	Prod
73	sdn 4d	4,015	2,554	—
73	sdn 4d, Custom interior	4,015	2,722	—
76	conv cpe	4,245	3,142	—
77	club cpe	3,915	2,533	—
77	club cpe, Custom interior	3,915	2,701	—

76H Continental (wb 125.0)

		Wght	Price	Prod
56	conv cpe ("cabriolet")	4,135	4,746	738
57	club cpe	4,125	4,662	831

1947 Engine	bore×stroke	bhp	availability
V12, 292.0	2.88×3.75	125	S-all

1948

876H (wb 125.0)—6,470 built

		Wght	Price	Prod
73	sdn 4d	4,015	2,554	—
73	sdn 4d, Custom interior	4,015	2,722	—
76	conv cpe	4,245	3,142	—
77	club cpe	3,915	2,533	—
77	club cpe, Custom interior	3,915	2,701	—

876H Continental (wb 125.0)

		Wght	Price	Prod
56	conv cpe ("cabriolet")	4,135	4,746	452
57	club cpe	4,125	4,662	847

1948 Engine	bore×stroke	bhp	availability
V12, 292.0	2.88×3.75	125	S-all

1949

9EL (wb 121.0)—38,384 built

	Wght	Price	Prod
cpe	3,959	2,527	—
Sport Sedan 4d	4,009	2,575	—
conv cpe	4,224	3,116	—

Lincoln

9EH Cosmopolitan(wb 125.0)—35,123 built	Wght	Price	Prod
cpe	4,194	3,186	—
Sport Sedan 4d	4,259	3,238	—
Town sdn 4d	4,274	3,238	—
conv cpe	4,419	3,948	—

1949 Engine	bore×stroke	bhp	availability
V8, 336.7	3.50×4.38	152	S-all

1950

0EL (wb 121.0)		Wght	Price	Prod
L-72	cpe	4,090	2,529	5,748
L-72C	Lido cpe	4,145	2,721	
L-74	Sport Sedan 4d	4,115	2,576	11,741

0EH Cosmopolitan (wb 125.0)		Wght	Price	Prod
H-72	cpe	4,375	3,187	1,824
H-72C	Capri cpe	4,385	3,406	
H-74	Sport Sedan 4d	4,410	3,240	8,341
H-76	conv cpe	4,640	3,950	536

1950 Engine	bore×stroke	bhp	availability
V8, 336.7	3.50×4.38	152	S-all

1951

1EL (wb 121.0)		Wght	Price	Prod
L-72B	cpe	4,065	2,505	4,482
L-72C	Lido cpe	4,100	2,702	
L-74	Sport Sedan 4d	4,130	2,553	12,279

1EH Cosmopolitan (wb 125.0)		Wght	Price	Prod
H-72B	cpe	4,340	3,129	2,727
H-72C	Capri cpe	4,360	3,350	
H-74	Sport Sedan 4d	4,415	3,182	12,229
H-76	conv cpe	4,615	3,891	857

1951 Engine	bore×stroke	bhp	availability
V8, 336.7	3.50×4.38	154	S-all

1952

2H Cosmopolitan (wb 123.0)		Wght	Price	Prod
60C	Spt htp cpe	4,155	3,293	4,545
73A	sdn 4d	4,125	3,198	*

2H Capri (wb 123.0)		Wght	Price	Prod
60A	htp cpe	4,235	3,518	5,681
73B	sdn 4d	4,140	3,331	*
76A	conv cpe	4,350	3,665	1,191

*Combined sedan production: 15,854.

1952 Engine	bore×stroke	bhp	availability
V8, 317.5	3.80×3.50	160	S-all

1953

8H Cosmopolitan (wb 123.0)		Wght	Price	Prod
60C	Sport htp cpe	4,155	3,322	6,562
73A	sdn 4d	4,135	3,226	7,560

8H Capri (wb 123.0)		Wght	Price	Prod
60A	htp cpe	4,165	3,549	12,916
73B	sdn 4d	4,150	3,453	11,352
76A	conv cpe	4,310	3,699	2,372

1953 Engine	bore×stroke	bhp	availability
V8, 317.5	3.80×3.50	205	S-all

1954

Cosmopolitan (wb 123.0)		Wght	Price	Prod
60C	Sport htp cpe	4,155	3,625	2,994
73A	sdn 4d	4,135	3,522	4,447

Capri (wb 123.0)		Wght	Price	Prod
60A	htp cpe	4,250	3,869	14,003
73B	sdn 4d	4,245	3,711	13,598
76A	conv cpe	4,310	4,031	1,951

1954 Engine	bore×stroke	bhp	availability
V8, 317.5	3.80×3.50	205	S-all

1955

Custom (wb 123.0)		Wght	Price	Prod
60C	Sport htp cpe	4,185	3,666	1,362
73A	sdn 4d	4,235	3,563	2,187

Capri (wb 123.0)		Wght	Price	Prod
60A	htp cpe	4,305	3,910	11,462
73B	sdn 4d	4,245	3,752	10,724
76A	conv cpe	4,415	4,072	1,487

1955 Engine	bore×stroke	bhp	availability
V8, 341.0	3.94×3.50	225	S-all

1956

Capri (wb 126.0)		Wght	Price	Prod
60E	Sport htp cpe	4,305	4,119	4,355
73A	sdn 4d	4,315	4,212	4,436

Premiere (wb 126.0)		Wght	Price	Prod
60B	htp cpe	4,357	4,601	19,619
73B	sdn 4d	4,347	4,601	19,465
76B	conv cpe	4,452	4,747	2,447

1956 Engine	bore×stroke	bhp	availability
V8, 368.0	4.00×3.66	285	S-all

1957

Capri (wb 126.0)		Wght	Price	Prod
57A	Landau htp sdn	4,460	4,794	1,451
58A	sdn 4d	4,349	4,794	1,476
60A	htp cpe	4,373	4,649	2,973

Premiere (wb 126.0)		Wght	Price	Prod
57B	Landau htp sdn	4,538	5,294	11,223
58B	sdn 4d	4,527	5,294	5,139
60B	htp cpe	4,451	5,149	15,185
76B	conv cpe	4,676	5,381	3,676

1957 Engine	bore×stroke	bhp	availability
V8, 368.0	4.00×3.66	300	S-all

1958

Capri (wb 131.0)		Wght	Price	Prod
53A	sdn 4d	4,799	4,951	1,184
57A	Landau htp sdn	4,810	4,951	3,084
63A	htp cpe	4,735	4,803	2,591

1959

Capri (wb 131.0)		Wght	Price	Prod
53A	sdn 4d	4,823	5,090	1,312
57A	htp sdn	4,824	5,090	4,417
63A	htp cpe	4,741	4,902	2,200

Premiere (wb 131.0)		Wght	Price	Prod
53B	sdn 4d	4,887	5,594	1,282
57B	htp sdn	4,880	5,594	4,606
63B	htp cpe	4,798	5,347	1,963

Continental Mark IV (wb 131.0)		Wght	Price	Prod
23A	limo	5,061	10,230	49
23B	form sdn	5,190	9,208	78
54A	sdn 4d	5,061	6,845	955
65A	htp cpe	4,967	6,598	1,703
68A	conv cpe	5,076	7,056	2,195
75A	htp sdn	5,050	6,845	6,146

1959 Engine	bore×stroke	bhp	availability
V8, 430.0	4.30×3.70	350	S-all

1960

(wb 131.0)		Wght	Price	Prod
53A	sdn 4d	5,016	5,441	1,093
57A	Landau htp sdn	5,012	5,441	4,397
63A	htp cpe	4,917	5,253	1,670

Premiere (wb 131.0)		Wght	Price	Prod
53B	sdn 4d	5,064	5,945	1,010
57B	Landau htp sdn	5,060	5,945	4,200
63B	htp cpe	4,965	4,698	1,365

Continental Mark V (wb 131.0)		Wght	Price	Prod
23A	limo	5,481	10,230	34
23B	form sdn	5,272	9,208	136
54A	sdn 4d	5,143	6,845	807
65A	htp cpe	5,044	6,598	1,461
68A	conv cpe	5,180	7,056	2,044
75A	htp sdn	5,139	6,845	6,604

1960 Engine	bore×stroke	bhp	availability
V8, 430.0	4.30×3.70	315	S-all

1961

Continental (wb 123.0)		Wght	Price	Prod
53A	htp sdn	4,927	6,067	22,303
57C	htp sdn, special model	—	—	4
74A	conv sdn	5,215	6,713	2,857

1961 Engine	bore×stroke	bhp	availability
V8, 430.0	4.30×3.70	300	S-all

1962

Continental (wb 123.0)		Wght	Price	Prod
53A	htp sdn	4,966	6,074	27,849
74A	conv sdn	5,370	6,720	3,212

1962 Engine	bore×stroke	bhp	availability
V8, 430.0	4.30×3.70	300	S-all

1963

Continental (wb 123.0)		Wght	Price	Prod
53A	htp sdn	4,936	6,270	28,095
74A	conv sdn	5,340	6,916	3,138

1963 Engine	bore×stroke	bhp	availability
V8, 430.0	4.30×3.70	320	S-all

1964

Continental (wb 126.0)		Wght	Price	Prod
82	htp sdn	5,055	6,292	33,969
86	conv sdn	5,393	6,938	3,328

1964 Engine	bore×stroke	bhp	availability
V8, 430.0	4.30×3.70	320	S-all

1965

Continental (wb 126.0)		Wght	Price	Prod
82	htp sdn	5,075	6,292	36,824
86	conv sdn	5,475	6,938	3,356

1965 Engine	bore×stroke	bhp	availability
V8, 430.0	4.30×3.70	320	S-all

1966

Continental (wb 126.0)		Wght	Price	Prod
82	sdn 4d	5,085	5,750	35,809
86	conv sdn	5,480	6,383	3,180
89	htp cpe	4,985	5,485	15,766

1966 Engine	bore×stroke	bhp	availability
V8, 462.0	4.38×3.83	340	S-all

1967

Continental (wb 126.0)		Wght	Price	Prod
82	sdn 4d	5,049	5,795	33,331
86	conv sdn	5,505	6,449	2,276
89	htp cpe	4,940	5,553	11,060

1967 Engine	bore×stroke	bhp	availability
V8, 462.0	4.38×3.83	340	S-all

1968

Continental (wb 126.0)		Wght	Price	Prod
81	htp cpe	4,883	5,736	9,415
82	sdn 4d	4,978	5,970	29,719

Continental Mark III (wb 117.2)		Wght	Price	Prod
89	htp cpe	4,739	6,585	7,770

1968 Engine	bore×stroke	bhp	availability
V8, 460.0	4.36×3.75	365	S-all

1969

Continental (wb 126.0)		Wght	Price	Prod
81	htp cpe	4,910	5,830	9,032
82	sdn 4d	5,005	6,063	29,258

Continental Mark III (wb 117.2)		Wght	Price	Prod
89	htp cpe	4,762	6,758	23,088

1969 Engine	bore×stroke	bhp	availability
V8, 460.0	4.36×3.75	365	S-all

1970

Continental (wb 126.0)		Wght	Price	Prod
81	htp cpe	4,669	5,976	9,073
82	sdn 4d	4,719	6,211	28,622

Continental Mark III (wb 117.2)		Wght	Price	Prod
89	htp cpe	4,675	7,281	21,432

1970 Engine	bore×stroke	bhp	availability
V8, 460.0	4.36×3.75	365	S-all

Lincoln

1971

Continental (wb 127.0)

		Wght	Price	Prod
81	htp cpe	5,032	7,172	8,205
82	sdn 4d	5,072	7,419	27,346

Continental Mark III (wb 118.0)

89	htp cpe	5,003	8,813	27,091

1971 Engine	bore×stroke	bhp	availability	
V8,460.0	4.36×3.85	365	S-all	

1972

Continental (wb 127.0)

		Wght	Price	Prod
81	htp cpe	4,906	7,068	10,408
82	sdn 4d	4,958	7,302	35,561

Continental Mark IV (wb 120.4)

89	htp cpe	4,792	8,640	48,591

1972 Engines	bore×stroke	bhp	availability	
V8,460.0	4.36×3.85	224	S-81,82	
V8, 460.0	4.36×3.85	212	S-89	

1973

Continental (wb 127.0)

		Wght	Price	Prod
81	htp cpe	5,016	7,230	13,348
82	sdn 4d	5,049	7,474	45,288

Continental Mark IV (wb 120.4)

89	htp cpe	4,908	8,984	69,437

1973 Engines	bore×stroke	bhp	availability	
V8, 460.0	4.36×3.85	219	S-81,82	
V8, 460.0	4.36×3.85	208	S-89	

1974

Continental (wb 127.2)

		Wght	Price	Prod
81	htp cpe	5,366	8,053	7,316
82	sdn 4d	5,361	8,238	29,351

Continental Mark IV (wb 120.4)

89	htp cpe	5,362	10,194	57,316

1974 Engines	bore×stroke	bhp	availability	
V8, 460.0	4.36×3.85	215	S-81,82	
V8, 460.0	4.36×3.85	220	S-89	

1975

Continental (wb 127.2)

		Wght	Price	Prod
81	cpe	5,219	9,214	21,185
82	sdn 4d	5,229	9,656	33,513

Continental Mark IV (wb 120.4)

89	htp cpe	5,145	11,082	47,145

1975 Engines	bore×stroke	bhp	availability	
V8, 460.0	4.36×3.85	206	S-81,82	
V8, 460.0	4.36×3.85	194	S-89	

1976

Continental (wb 127.2)

		Wght	Price	Prod
81	cpe	5,035	9,142	68,646
82	sdn 4d	5,083	9,293	

Continental Mark IV (wb 120.4)

89	htp cpe	5,051	11,060	56,110

1976 Engine	bore×stroke	bhp	availability	
V8, 460.0	4.36×3.85	202	S-all	

1977

Versailles (wb 109.9)

		Wght	Price	Prod
84	sdn 4d	3,800	11,500	15,434

Continental (wb 127.2)

81	cpe	4,836	9,474	95,600
82	sdn 4d	4,880	9,636	

Continental Mark V (wb 120.4)

89	htp cpe	4,652	11,396	80,321

1977 Engines	bore×stroke	bhp	availability	
V8, 351.0	4.00×3.50	135	S-Versailles	
V8, 400.0	4.00×4.00	179	S-81,82,89	
V8, 460.0	4.36×3.85	208	O-81,82,89	

1978

Versailles (wb 109.9)

		Wght	Price	Prod
84	sdn 4d	3,759	12,529	8,931

Continental (wb 127.2)

81	cpe	4,659	10,196	88,087
82	sdn 4d	4,660	10,396	

Continental Mark V (wb 120.4)

89	htp cpe	4,567	12,318	72,602

1978 Engines	bore×stroke	bhp	availability	
V8, 302.0	4.00×3.00	133	S-Versailles	
V8, 400.0	4.00×4.00	166	S-81,82,89	
V8, 460.0	4.36×3.85	210	O-81,82,89	

1979

Versailles (wb 109.9)

		Wght	Price	Prod
84	sdn 4d	3,684	13,763	21,007

Continental (wb 127.2)

81	cpe	4,639	11,868	92,600
82	sdn 4d	4,649	12,093	

Continental Mark V (wb 120.4)

89	htp cpe	4,589	13,771	75,939

1979 Engines	bore×stroke	bhp	availability	
V8, 302.0	4.00×3.00	130	S-Versailles	
V8, 400.0	4.00×4.00	159	S-81,82,89	

1980

Versailles (wb 109.9)

		Wght	Price	Prod
84	4d	3,661	15,664	4,784

Continental (wb 117.3)

81	cpe	3,843	13,251	31,233
82	sdn 4d	3,919	13,593	

Continental Mark VI (wb 117.3)

89	sdn 2d	3,892	16,291	38,891
90	sdn 4d	3,988	16,691	
96	Signature sdn 2d	3,896	21,873	
96	Signature sdn 4d	3,993	22,243	

1980 Engines	bore×stroke	bhp	availability	
V8, 302.0	4.00×3.00	132	S-Versailles	
V8,302.0	4.00×3.00	129	S-Contl,Mk VI	
V8,351.0	4.00×3.50	140	O-Contl,Mk VI	

Marmon

Marmon Motor Car Company
Indianapolis, Indiana

Anybody who could invent an air-cooled V-4 engine with overhead valves and pressure lubrication in 1902—and make it work—had to be a genius. Howard Marmon was certainly that. In the economic downturn following World War I, sales of his cars started faltering, and in 1924 he hired George M. Williams to put the firm back on the track to profitability. Marmon became board chairman, but didn't care for Williams' humdrum straight eights and withdrew almost completely from corporate activities about 1926. He set up a branch company named Midwest Aircraft, and devoted himself to research. The Marmon Eights that followed and continued on into the '30s are, therefore, the work of others.

Williams wanted the Marmon Company to be a little General Motors offering nothing but straight eights, and new examples of that engine type were introduced almost yearly. The peak of activity was 1930: a facelifted Marmon-Roosevelt, revised Model 69 and 79 versions of the earlier straight-eight cars, and a luxurious Big Eight with 315 cid and 125 bhp. The price range now stretched from $1000 to $5000, but the expansion was too soon and too rapid and Marmon's public image became confused. The Roosevelt (named for President Teddy) failed to make an impression in the lower-price field and it undermined the high-class aura of the senior models. From 22,300 units in 1929, production sank to 12,300 in 1930, then to 5768 in 1931 and 1365 in 1932.

In 1931, however, Howard Marmon's five years of research would culminate in the introduction of a magnificent new car: the Marmon Sixteen. Packing 200 bhp from an engine of almost 500 cubic inches, this mighty classic would do 100 mph and was priced at $5200-5400. Unfortunately, Cadillac had introduced its own Sixteen a year earlier, and was already draining away what market existed for such extraordinary machines.

Marmon's V16 layout comprised pushrod-operated overhead valves actuated by a single camshaft and aluminum cylinders that were a triumph of the foundry art. Both block and crankcase were cast as one unit, the block actually being a "Y" in section. One dual-throat downdraft carburetor fed the fuel, and a single cast manifold served both banks of cylinders. Despite its size, the engine was relatively light at 930 pounds, complete with all accessories, some 370 pounds less than the Cadillac V16. The Marmon's low weight-to-power ratio—4.65 pounds per horsepower—was probably rivalled only by Duesenberg.

Lightweight construction was also used throughout the car. For example, hood, front and rear splash aprons, running board aprons, spare wheel mounts, headlight and taillight brackets, and fuel filler pipe were all made of aluminum. Because of this, few cars could approach this Marmon's sheer speed or acceleration through the gears. Its pickup was superior even to the Duesenberg's, though the Duesie would win going away at higher speeds due to its double-overhead-cam engine design and superior breathing. Marmon enhanced its image by guaranteeing each Sixteen purchaser that his or her car had exceeded 100 mph for two complete laps of the Indy race track.

The body design on Marmon's greatest car caused as much interest as its engine. Although the actual styling was not the work of Howard Marmon himself, he must be credited with hiring an industrial designer to create it at a time when that profession was in its infancy. That designer was 47-year-old Walter Dorwin Teague Sr., though he admitted that much of the work was done by his son. W.D. Teague Jr. did all the original sketches and drawings for the Sixteen's body, the full-sized renderings. and some interior concepts, including the unusual aircraft-type instrument panel. The junior Teague, a student at MIT at the time, completed these tasks in summer school and on weekends. Since his father's name carried considerable prestige, Marmon publicity gave credit to Teague Sr. Indeed, he handled the contract work with Marmon and translated the concept into its production form.

1930 Big Eight four-door sedan

1930 Big Eight coupe

Marmon

With no resemblance to any previous Marmon, the Sixteen looked sensationally new. The raked "V" radiator grille was devoid of ornament or badge; and the filler and fuel tank caps were under the hood. The doors extended almost to the running boards, and fender flanges hid shock absorbers and steering connections. The beltline ran absolutely straight around the entire body, windshield rake matched that of the radiator, and the roofline was ultra low. Unified in form, the Sixteen was described as a new concept in fine cars, in which engineering and body design were of equal importance. A limited range of standard body styles was offered, all built by LeBaron: five sedans, two coupes, and a victoria. Few custom bodies are known. Waterhouse built two tourers, but the most individual custom was a one-off victoria created by Alexis de Sakhnoffsky and built by Hayes. The Sakhnoffsky victorias sold for a towering $5700, while the standard models ranged from $5220 to $5400 (prices rose by about $500 in 1932).

Sixteen apart, Marmon produced five different eights in two series for 1931. The first began in August 1930 and comprised the 113-inch wheelbase Roosevelt, the 69 and the 136-inch wheelbase Big Eight. The last was retained for the second series issued beginning January 1931, when it was renamed and priced about $450 lower to spark sales. Another second-series 1931 eight was the Model 70 replacing both the Roosevelt and the 69. It used the former's chassis and the latter's engine but sold for around $900-1000, about the same as the Roosevelt. Despite this attempt to pare its offerings down to the most popular, Marmon's sales picture was far from encouraging in 1931. With production down to around half of what it had been in 1930, the company stood 25th in the production race, between Reo and LaSalle. The Sixteen suffered a sales handicap right from the start because of a long delay between its announcement and the start of production. Prototypes were displayed at the winter 1930-31 auto shows, but deliveries didn't begin until the following April. Many other luxury-car prospects had, of course, gone into hiding. Those people bought unobtrusive Fords or, at most, Chryslers. Marmon announced 32 custom body designs for the Sixteen in September 1931—town cars, all-weather models, limousines, sports styles, and various sedans with sunshine roofs. This move came too late, and it's doubtful any were built. For every Marmon Sixteen built, Cadillac built 10 of its comparable V16s.

1931 Sixteen convertible sedan by W.D. Teague

Along with declining sales, Marmon was hampered by contradictory internal policies in the early '30s. The engineering department was divided into two warring camps; production people had trouble getting Sixteens delivered; the sales force was harassed by the low-bucks image of the Roosevelt. Only three models were fielded for 1932. the Sixteen, the eight-cylinder Model 70, and a 315.2-cid eight-cylinder car now known by its wheelbase measurement, the 125. Compared to the 88, the 125 gave away nothing in engine specification, but its wheelbase had shrunk by up to 11 inches. Its price was shrunk, too: the sedan and coupe listed for just $1420 each, against $2275-$2220 for the previous year's comparable 88 models.

Price and model cuts in the eight-cylinder ranges created a feeling among buyers that Marmon was abandoning the fine-car field in 1932. Actually, the company was preparing to do just the opposite: the Sixteen was the only line listed for 1933. Price was cut by almost $1000 from before, the coupe and sedan selling for $4825, the seven-passenger sedan down to $4975, and the convertible sedan offered at $5075. There were no specifications changes, but sales were now down to a trickle.

Engineering brilliance, it should be noted, was not effective medicine for any car company in the depths of the Depression. The makes that survived did so on corporate strength and strong market base, neither of which Marmon had.

An attempt to revive the Sixteen came in January 1934, when Marmon's assets were taken over by the American Automotive Corporation, organized and backed by Harry Miller and Preston Tucker. But the effort failed, and the firm's

1931 Model 79 four-door sedan

1933 Sixteen seven-passenger sedan

assets were ultimately liquidated by receivers in 1937. Prior to this, Howard Marmon and chassis engineer George Freers had new designs on the board. One was a revolutionary V12 car, a cut-down version of the V16, with independent suspension, tubular "backbone" frame, aluminum body, and three-point chassis attachment. There was new styling by Teague, with slab sides, pontoon fenders, built-in headlights, and integral trunk. The prototype was financed out of Howard Marmon's personal fortune, as his company had nothing, and totaled $160,000. Howard lost the lot. There was no chance for production, and the car was stored on Marmon's North Carolina estate until his death in 1943. It has since made its way to industrial designer Brooks Stevens' automotive museum in Mequon, Wisconsin.

Marmon Specifications

1930

Big Eight (wb 136.0)

	Wght	Price	Prod
touring 7P	4,200	3,170	37
cpe 2-4P	4,100	2,850	123
sdn 4d	4,210	2,720	473
sdn 7P	4,307	2,920	270

Model 79 (wb 120.0)

	Wght	Price	Prod
spdstr phtn 5P	3,800	2,020	40
cpe 2-4P	3,805	1,995	124
sdn 4d	3,900	2,020	958

Model 69 (wb 114.0)

	Wght	Price	Prod
spdstr phtn 5P	3,025	1,610	32
cpe 2-4P	3,011	1,495	196
sdn 4d	3,100	1,520	1,605

1930 Engines	bore×stroke	bhp	availability
L8, 211.2	2.81×4.25	84	S-69
L8, 303.2	3.19×4.75	110	S-79
L8, 315.2	3.25×4.75	125	S-Big Eight

1931

Big Eight (wb 136.0)

	Wght	Price	Prod*
touring 7P	4,200	3,170	—
cpe 2-4P	4,100	2,850	—
sdn 4d	4,210	2,720	—
sdn 7P	4,307	2,920	—

Model 79 (wb 120.0)

	Wght	Price	Prod*
phtn 5P	3,800	2,020	—
cpe 2-4P	3,805	1,995	—
brougham 5P	3,884	2,070	—
sdn 4d	3,900	2,020	—

Model 69 (wb 114.0)

	Wght	Price	Prod*
phtn 5P	3,025	1,610	—
cpe 2-4P	3,011	1,495	—
brougham 4d	3,153	1,565	—
sdn 4d	3,103	1,520	—

Model 70 (wb 112.8)

	Wght	Price	Prod*
cpe 2-4P	2,694	950	—
conv cpe 2-4P	2,586	1,045	—
victoria cpe 2-4P	2,678	995	—
sdn 4d	2,823	995	—

Model 88 (wb 130.0; lwb-136.0)

	Wght	Price	Prod*
cpe 2-4P	4,290	2,275	—
sdn 4d	4,375	2,220	—
club sdn 5P	4,398	2,345	—
lwb sdn 7P	4,504	2,495	—

Sixteen (wb 145.0)

	Wght	Price	Prod*
cpe 2-4P	5,090	5,220	—
sdn,cl.coupled 4d	5,335	5,270	—
sdn 4d	5,360	5,200	—
sdn 7P	5,440	5,400	—

1931 Engines	bore×stroke	bhp	availability
L8, 211.2	2.81×4.25	84	S-69,70
L8, 303.2	3.19×4.75	110	S-79
L8, 315.2	3.25×4.75	125	S-Big Eight, 88
V16, 490.8	3.13×4.00	200	S-Sixteen

*not available

1932

Model 70 (wb 112.8)

	Wght	Price	Prod*
cpe 2-4P	2,694	950	—
sdn 4d	2,823	995	—

Model 125 (wb 125.0)

	Wght	Price	Prod*
cpe 2-4P	3,625	1,420	—
sdn 4d	3,653	1,420	—

Sixteen (wb 145.0)

	Wght	Price	Prod*
cpe 2-4P	5,090	5,700	—
sdn,cl.coupled 4d	5,335	5,800	—
sdn 4d	5,360	5,700	—
sdn 7P	5,440	5,900	—

1932 Engines	bore×stroke	bhp	availability
L8, 211.2	2.81×4.25	84	S-70
L8, 315.2	3.25×4.75	125	S-125
V16, 490.8	3.13×4.00	200	S-Sixteen

*not available

1933

Sixteen (wb 145.0)

	Wght	Price	Prod*
cpe 2-4P	5,090	4,825	—
sdn 4d	5,360	4,825	—
conv sdn 5P	5,285	5,075	—
sdn 7P	5,440	4,975	—

1933 Engine	bore×stroke	bhp	availability
V16, 490.8	3.13×4.00	200	S-all

*not available

Note: Because of its size and limited volume, Marmon did not record model year production per se. Calendar year registrations were as follows:

1930:	12,369
1931:	5,687
1932:	1,365
1933:	86

(source: *The Production Figure Book for U.S. Cars*)

Mercury

Ford Motor Company (Lincoln-Mercury Division from 1947)
Dearborn, Michigan

Mercury was conceived largely by Edsel Ford, who saw a place for it in the market some time before his father did. It was announced in late 1938 as a '39 model. In price, Mercury was in the same field as the eight-cylinder Pontiac and somewhat below Oldsmobile, precisely where Edsel Ford wanted it—and where Ford Motor Company needed it. While Mercury never approached the volume of those popular GM makes, it did average about 80,000 cars per year in the early '40s. This put it in 12th or 13th place in the industry, and brought the corporation important sales in the market sector between Lincoln-Zephyr and Ford.

The engine introduced with the original Mercury remained in production through 1948. It was an L-head V8 slightly larger than the Ford V8/85, having the same stroke but a larger bore. Until 1942, it produced 95 horsepower at 3600 rpm; from 1942 through '48, output was 100 bhp at 3800 rpm. Mercury quickly gained a reputation for performance equal to its name. Well-tuned models in stock form were quicker than the V8/85, and were usually capable of turning close to 100 mph.

Mercury's wheelbase was not much longer than the more expensive Ford's, but it was sufficient to balance the lines and make the car look larger than the Ford. The dash was similar to Ford's, using strip-type instruments. Mercury exclaimed about its column-mounted gearlever.

The car's 1940 styling was Ford-like: a crisp, pointed nose; flush-mounted headlamps; and rounded lines that tapered to a beetle back. There were five body styles priced from $946 to $1212. The convertible sedan was a new addition for 1940: the heaviest and most expensive model in the line. But the convertible sedan's popularity had declined by the early '40s, so Mercury discontinued its version the following year after a run of only about 1000 units.

Sales were brisk in 1940, and Mercury looked for still greater success with its restyled '41 line. Seven different models were offered, including a 2/4-passenger coupe, business coupe, and station wagon. Styling, again in the Ford mold, was chunky and awkward. Longer, higher, squared-off fenders were accompanied by a divider-bar grille and fender-mounted parking lights.

Mercury tried harder in 1942 with a serious facelift, 100-bhp engines, and a clutchless transmission called Liquidmatic. But the war prevented a full model run. Chrome was "in," at least before government regulations restricted its use. The '42s wore a broad, glittery two-section grille composed of massive horizontal bars. Double chrome bands were applied to front and rear fenders, and a bright beltline molding ran completely around the hood. Parking lights were shifted inboard, but prominent chrome moldings remained on the tops of the front fenders. The general effect was busier than the '41 design, which had been busier than the 1940. Distinctly more elaborate styling seemed to be developing.

At the close of the war, when Henry Ford II returned from the Navy to run the firm, Ford Motor Company moved back quickly into civilian car production. Mercury reached tenth place in 1946, producing 86,608 units. Though plans had been laid for an all-new postwar design, the company decided to stay with its prewar model for a few years. The '46 Mercury was therefore quite similar to the '42. The inboard parking lights and two-band fender moldings remained, but the grille was reshaped with a vertical-bar motif, and the hood ornament was blended into the hood. The words "Mercury Eight" were prominently displayed front and center. Mechanically, the car was unchanged. A possible disadvantage was that it still shared its engine with the lower-priced Ford.

In 1946, the business coupe was replaced by the novel Sportsman convertible, comparable to Ford's Sportsman. Designated model 71, it was a convertible coupe with woodwork—maple or yellow birch framing mahogany inserts. The paneling was structural, not merely decorative. This created a problem at the rear, where the standard production fenders could not be fitted. To solve this, the company used 1941 sedan delivery fenders, and designed the wooden structure around them. The frame was constructed of solid wood, mitred together with beautiful craftsmanship and finished with multiple coats of varnish.

The Mercury Sportsman cost over $200 more than its Ford counterpart. Ford produced quite a few, but Mercury made only 205. Ford continued the Sportsman through 1948, but it was dropped from the Mercury lineup after '46.

An important corporate realignment in 1947 was the organization of Lincoln-Mercury Division. Up to that time, Lincoln and Mercury had been intrinsic parts of Ford, but Henry Ford II decided that the two makes could be more competitive as an autonomous operation, in the style of the various General Motors divisions. Lincoln-Mercury has remained a separate division ever since.

The 1947 Mercurys were proof that raw materials that had been scarce during World War II were now in greater supply: aluminum pistons and hood ornament, chrome-plated interior hardware, and a chrome grille frame rather than a painted one. Dashboard gauges were more legible than before, having silver letters on black backgrounds. The beltline molding no longer wrapped around the hood, but stopped just ahead of the cowl. Body styles decreased to five with the deletion of the Sportsman. Prices increased by about $150 model for model. Production of the glittery '47s didn't begin until February of that year, so model year output was

1940 convertible sedan

1941 Town Sedan

1942 convertible coupe

Wartime proposal for postwar front-end styling

1947 Town Sedan

1949 restyle taking shape on 1946 clay model

about the same as the year before.

No changes at all were recorded for 1948, and the only identification for these models was their serial numbers. Mercury offered the same body styles and prices (less the two-door sedan), and sold 1948-model cars from November 1947 until mid-April 1948, when the '49s appeared. As a result, 1948 production was the lowest for any postwar year.

Mercury was fully restyled for '49 with smooth, curving lines that made it appear much longer than before—though its 118-inch wheelbase was the same as before. In fact, it shared its bodyshell with the smaller 1949 Lincoln. Initial planning had called for a new Lincoln-Zephyr in this position. Mercury was to use a 116-inch wheelbase and Ford a shorter one. But management decided a smaller Ford was unnecessary, so the Zephyr was dropped in favor of the new Mercury. Styling was

good—clean, massive, streamlined. The new grille retained a resemblance to the '48 design, but was lower and wider, and had a faired-in cavity. A single piece of bright metal decorated the flanks. Overall, it was a pleasing style that still looks good today. The 1949 models quickly became hot items among customizers, who gave them special grilles, lowered bodies, and skirted rear fenders. The tail-dragging custom Merc, with cruiser skirts, foxtail, and fog lights, became a common sight around high schools in the '50s.

The 1949 Mercury also benefited from a heftier engine: the L-head had been stroked 0.25 inch for a displacement of 255.4 cubic inches, and delivered 110 bhp at 3600 rpm. Dual downdraft Holley carburetors were standard. Mercury thus became a genuine 100-mph car for the first time. Also introduced was an automatic overdrive option priced at $97, teamed up with a 4.27:1 rear

axle ratio instead of the standard 3.90:1. Mercury remained a one-series make. There were no "deluxe" versions until 1950.

The 1949-51 Mercury was an excellent value, considering it was styled like the Lincoln but had a lower price. Its V8 was about 12 percent larger than Ford's and offered 15 more horsepower. Many felt this made up for the Mercury's extra 300-some pounds in curb weight.

Essentially, the 1950-51 line consisted of only one series, but within it was a variety of new offerings. These included the Monterey, a low-production sport coupe with special trim and a padded top of either canvas or leather. Mercury would get a true hardtop, but somewhat later than its GM and Chrysler competitors. Monterey filled the gap in the meantime.

The 1950 and '51 models were very much alike. The '51 had a semicircular crest and Mercury name above the grille, while the '50 had the name spelled out on a hood chrome strip and the crest was smaller. Parking light housings were larger on the '51, sweeping back to the front wheel wells. The '51s also used a different rear fender treatment—more upright, with rounded corners dropping straight down to the rear bumper. Mercury's V8 developed 100 bhp in 1950, 112 in 1951. And '51 was the first year for Merc-O-Matic, the two-speed automatic developed in cooperation with the Warner Gear Division of Borg-Warner. Mercury ran sixth in production in both 1949 and 1951.

Ford Motor Company was the only maker to introduce completely new styling for 1952, and Mercury received the same sort of tight, clean lines as that year's Lincoln. Wheelbase length was unchanged. The L-head V8 was retained, but power was boosted to 125

1949 eight-passenger station wagon

1951 Sport Sedan

1949 convertible

1952 Custom hardtop coupe

1950 coupe

1953 Monterey four-door sedan

bhp by means of a higher compression ratio.

For 1953, Mercury did some model shuffling, and emerged with two series. The Custom offered two- and four-door sedans and a hardtop. The Monterey became a separate series offering convertible, hardtop, wagon, and sedan. Monterey sedans were luxuriously upholstered in quality broadcloth; convertibles and hardtops used leather and vinyl. Solid colors were used for the sedan, but the hardtop came with two-tone paint standard. The dashboard was interesting, with aircraft-type toggle levers for heating and ventilation flanking a central gauge cluster. Sales fell along with those of the rest of the industry in 1952, partly because of Korean War restrictions on production. Yet the restyled line accounted for over 170,000 units, enough to put Mercury in eighth place. Business picked up in 1953 as Mercury built over 300,000 cars—though staying in eighth.

A significant engineering change was made for 1954 as Mercury joined Ford in a switch to the overhead-valve V8. Mercury's version was the same size as its previous L-head, but had squarer bore-and-stroke dimensions. With a low 3.9:1 rear axle ratio and standard transmission, the '54 was a fast car off the line. The new engine used a five-main-bearing crankshaft and came in standard form with a four-barrel carburetor. Another major mechanical change was the use of ball-joint front suspension. Styling was measurably improved by the addition of wraparound taillights and a clean grille. The model lineup stayed the same, except for the addition of one new model that is more famous today than it was then: the Monterey Sun Valley.

Ford's styling department had for some time experimented with plastic-topped cars: the Sun Valley (and the companion Ford Skyliner) was the result. In theory, it was sort of a cross between the airy convertible and the comfortable closed hardtop. In practice, it was something else. Though the plastic front half of the roof was tinted and a shade provided for really hot weather, customers complained the interior heated up like an oven. Predictably, sales weren't impressive. The '54 Sun Valley was the most attractive of this short-lived breed. It came in select color combinations of yellow or mint green to complement its dark green top. Embellished with gold-anodized fender script, it was a handsome automobile. The price, however, was forbidding. Mercury was more successful with the '54 Sun Valley than with the '55 version, which sold only 1787 copies. The glasstop was then dropped—to nobody's great surprise.

At 260,000 units, 1954 wasn't the greatest sales year ever, but there were high hopes for 1955. With all-new styling, a new V8, and the first wheelbase increase since 1941, the '55 couldn't miss, and over 329,000 were run up. It was the most appealing Mercury in years, offered in more models and series than ever before.

The line leader that season was the brand-new Montclair, offered as a four-door sedan, hardtop, convertible, and Sun Valley. Nicely styled, it used an evolutionary form of the '54 grille, and was distinguished by a

thin color panel outlined in bright metal under the side windows. Next came the Monterey sedan, hardtop, and wagon, followed by the Custom series with the same body styles plus a two-door sedan. The standard Custom and Monterey engine was a 188-bhp 292-cid V8. For Montclair, and optional on other models, was a 198-bhp version with an 8.5:1 compression ratio, offered only with Merc-O-Matic transmission.

1954 Monterey hardtop coupe

1954 Monterey Sun Valley coupe

1955 Monterey four-door sedan

TV host Ed Sullivan announced the "Big M" line for '56, an ambitious expansion into somewhat uncharted territory. Prices were on the rise, so to stay competitive Mercury offered the cut-rate Medalist for the bottom-line buyer. There was a full range of body styles: two- and four-door hardtops and two- and four-door sedans. Unfortunately, inflation took its toll. The "low-priced" Medalist was actually more expensive than the previous year's Custom. At the same time, it wasn't priced far enough below the better-trimmed 1956 Custom. Although Lincoln-Mercury dealers pushed hard with the price-leading two-door sedan, a total of only 45,812 Medalists were sold. Customs, Montereys, and Montclairs all surpassed the Medalist by at least double its production, and the series was accordingly dropped for 1957. Curiously, it reappeared in '58, interfering in a price bracket that should have been sole territory for the new Edsel.

The '56 facelift was a useful update of the '55 styling. Side moldings were connected front-to-back in a sort of lightning-bolt motif that was attractive and looked new. Four-door hardtops now arrived in force in all four series. Known as Phaetons, they sold well, out-selling the standard four-door sedan in the Montclair series. Throughout the line, Mercury used an enlarged V8 that provided 210 bhp in standard form, up to 235 bhp for Monterey and Montclair. It was a downbeat year for the auto industry, but Mercury was an exception. Some 328,000 rolled off the lines, a bit below the '55 pace. Most promising was the Montclair, which managed to sell almost as well as it had in 1955. It was positioned in a higher price bracket than Monterey, however, and the junior model continued to be emphasized as Mercury's breadwinner.

In 1957, everyone's eyes were on the Turnpike Cruiser—a "dramatic expression of dream car design" offered as the top-of-the-line series in two- and four-door hardtop and convertible form. It had, Mercury thought, just about everything. There was the "skylight dual curve windshield" and a retractable, reverse-slanted rear window. There were dual air intakes over the windshield corners that housed little protruding radio antennae. There was even the creatively named "Seat-O-Matic" device, which automatically adjusted the driver's seat to any one of 49 preset positions at the twist of a dial. The Cruiser used pushbuttons like Chrysler's to control its Merc-O-Matic transmission. The convertible was a replica of the 1957 Indy pace car. Despite all the gadgetry, the Cruiser failed miserably. It was priced too high, for one thing. And while it could be said that today's kitsch was high style in the '50s, the Cruiser was too far out even then.

For the rest of the line, 1957 brought a major redesign on a new 122-inch-wheelbase chassis. A full range of Montereys and Montclairs was offered. Station wagons were made a separate series, with no fewer than six entries. There was a Colony Park four-door nine-seater, a Voyager in the same configuration along with a two-door version, and three Commuters with the various

1957 Monterey two-door sedan

1957 Turnpike Cruiser hardtop sedan

1957 Turnpike Cruiser convertible

1958 Park Lane Phaeton hardtop coupe

seat and door combinations. It was a complex lineup, but fairly successful. The Big M had grown a bit heavy-looking by '57, with big, oblong bumpers up front. The Turnpike Cruiser with its quad headlights looked even weightier. The V8 had grown commensurately, and now offered up to 290 bhp.

Similar, slightly quieter styling was offered for 1958, but the year was a disaster. From 286,000 units in 1957, production fell to 153,000. The Turnpike Cruiser was

1959 Monterey two-door sedan

1962 Comet S-22 two-door sedan

1962 Meteor two-door sedan

1964 Comet Cyclone hardtop coupe

called Multi-Drive made its debut.

What had happened was that the bottom had dropped out of the middle-priced market. This is evident from the fact that Mercury didn't lose its eighth place position in 1958, despite building only 40 percent of its '57 volume. But significantly, an independent from Kenosha had passed Mercury in sales and was gaining fast on Pontiac, Olds, and Buick. The Rambler revolution was underway. In its wake, Mercury would never be the same.

A little more of the same old stuff had to be cleared out before Mercury joined the rush to compacts and intermediates. Accordingly, the '59s were given a longer chassis that resulted in a more conventional full-width grille and an extension of the odd concave rear fender styling of 1957-58. The Medalist and Turnpike Cruiser were blessedly forgotten as the line thinned to four: Monterey, Montclair, Park Lane, and Station Wagon. Even these survivors were severely cropped. The Montclair went down from six models to just four, and there were only four varieties of wagons. Despite retrenchment, Mercury built 150,000 cars—hardly the improvement expected. A new engine for '58 was the 383-cid V8—same displacement as Chrysler's engine but with more oversquare dimensions. It was standard equipment for Montclair and station wagons.

In the '60s, Mercury evolved through a plethora of models, sizes, body types, and wheelbases, complicated by several changes in model names from year to year. This is perhaps symbolic of the make's mixed fortunes during the decade and its struggle to make improvements. Despite the confusion, many familiar names at the start of the decade were still around toward its end. Comet and Monterey spanned the entire 10 years; Montclairs and Park Lanes were still being offered in '68. Meteor, the long-time brand for a Canadian-made Mercury derivative, was seen on two different U.S. models between 1961 and 1963.

The first American Meteor appeared as a budget-priced version of the '61 full-size Mercury Monterey. 600 and 800 series were offered, powered by the 223-cid overhead-valve Ford six. Although Meteor actually outsold Monterey in '61, it was replaced the following year by a basic Monterey as the Meteor name went on Mercury's version of the intermediate Ford Fairlane.

Everything recorded about the Fairlane also applies to the 1962-63 Meteor. The cars shared the same body (although the Mercury's styling was busier) and came with an optional small-block 221-cid V8. This was supplemented in 1963 by an optional 260-cid small-block for the Meteor Custom and S-33 luxury hardtop. But the Meteor didn't sell as well as the Fairlane, and Mercury dropped it for 1964 to put its compact-car development funds into an extensively facelifted Comet.

The Comet arrived in 1960 as a companion of the Ford Falcon, and sold over 116,000 copies. Sales rose in '61 and were strong in '62. Except for station wagons,

made an upper model in the Montclair series. The Medalist was back for a short encore, with two- and four-door sedans attempting to reach into the low-price field. Again, sales were disappointing: only 18,732. Up in the higher bracket above Montclair came the new Park Lane hardtops and convertible, ostensibly to replace the Turnpike Cruiser, with less outlandish looks and the 430-cid Lincoln V8. The same group of station wagons was offered, and a new automatic

Comet had a wheelbase five inches longer than Falcon. One of the reasons Meteor didn't sell is that Comet was comparably sized, yet priced lower. The decision to make Comet the only "small Mercury" after 1963 was a good one. Sales jumped by 55,000 units for '64 and remained high into '67.

Compared with the Falcon, Comet was better

1967 Comet Cyclone GT hardtop coupe

1969 Cyclone CJ428 fastback hardtop coupe

1970 Cyclone GT hardtop coupe

1960 Colony Park four-door station wagon

trimmed and more elaborately styled, but priced less than $100 higher. Several interesting models were offered. When it became obvious that people liked sporty compacts, Mercury introduced the $2300 bucket-seated S-22 two-door sedan in 1961. At the same time, all Comets became available with an optional 101-bhp six. For 1963, an S-22 hardtop and convertible were added. With the squarish facelift of 1964, the S-22 was renamed Caliente. By then, any Comet could be equipped with the outstanding 260-cid small-block. For all-out performance, there was a special Cyclone hardtop powered by the 210-bhp, 289-cid V8.

Comet received its first major overhaul in 1966, when it deserted the compact-car field and became an intermediate sharing that year's sleek new Fairlane bodyshell. This shift underlined a basic marketing decision: Mercury customers were assumed to be wealthier than Ford buyers, and would therefore probably be happier with a car larger than the Falcon. Comet retained this 116-inch-wheelbase platform through 1969, but experienced several lean years along the way as the name was gradually phased out. In 1967, for example, it appeared only on the very basic "Comet 202" model. The rest of the intermediate line consisted of the Capri, Caliente, Cyclone, and Station Wagon. For 1968, these were replaced by the luxurious Montego in three trim levels: the basic sedan and hardtop coupe; the MX sedan, hardtop coupe, convertible, and wagon; and the top-line MX Brougham four-door sedan and hardtop coupe. The MX was outfitted with high-quality cloth upholstery and other luxury details. The Comet name was retained for a price leader coupe, and disappeared after 1969.

The 1964-70 Cyclone and Montego intermediates were the basis for some of the most roadworthy Mercurys of the decade, including several champion race cars. After adopting the Fairlane shell in 1966, Mercury offered the Cyclone GT hardtop coupe and convertible. Powered by Ford's 335-bhp 390 V8, the Cyclone offered a variety of useful suspension options. The '67 edition was even more impressive with the optional 427-cid Ford V8, which provided 410–425 bhp. Similar street racers were available in 1968, though the 427 was detuned to 390 bhp that year.

An exciting pair of fastback hardtops, the Cyclone and Cyclone CJ, hit the streets for '69. Both had special identification, narrow racing paint stripes, and unique rear-end and taillight styling. Options included wide belted tires, turbine-style wheel covers, and racing-style outside mirrors. Both models had clean sides, no chrome, and a blacked-out grille. The CJ carried a functional hood scoop for its Ram-Air 428 Cobra-Jet engine. Although Ford was NASCAR Grand National Champion in 1968-69, the Cyclone turned in many notable performances. The best was Cale Yarborough's victory in the 1968 Daytona 500, at an average speed of 143.250 mph.

Mercury's most consistent and steady sales in the '60s came from its standard-size cars. Production levels

were usually around 100,000 units annually, except for those back-to-back record years of 1965 and '66. Of all the big Mercs, only Monterey spanned the entire decade. The upper-priced Montclair and Park Lane were dropped in 1961, revived for 1964-68, and dropped again in '69 to be replaced by the Marquis and Brougham.

The 1960 full-size line rode a 126-inch wheelbase. As before, the standard engine for Montclair and Park Lane was the Lincoln 430-cid V8. Montereys and Commuter wagons were available with a 312-cid unit, and a 383 V8 with 280 bhp was an option. Styling was a more modest rendition of '59: a short, concave, full-width grille; restyled taillights; a single bright metal side strip; and revised bumpers. The Monterey dominated sales.

For 1961, Mercury moved down into the market vacated by Edsel. Montclair and Park Lane were dropped, as were the high-priced Cruiser hardtops from the Monterey series, and the aforementioned six-cylinder Meteor was added. The 430 V8 was canceled, and a 292-cid engine was standard. Sales were not spectacular. Comet, however, had a record year with over 197,000 units sold.

Meteor was made an intermediate for '62, so the standard line now consisted of two Monterey series, plus Colony Park and Commuter wagons. There was another move up-market with the Monterey Custom series, which included a convertible. Joining the bucket-seat brigade at mid-year were the S-55 hardtop coupe and convertible. Styling was busier in '62, with tunnel-mounted taillights and a gaudy grille. The previous V8 lineup stayed intact, and a six was offered for the standard Monterey.

Once more, the Monterey and wagons made up the entire full-size line in '63. Mercury introduced "Breezeway Styling"—a reverse-slant rear window like that of the old Turnpike Cruiser, which dropped down for better ventilation. Monterey and Monterey Custom returned, and wagons were pared down to just the Colony Park. The S-55 notchback hardtop coupe and convertible were joined by a slopeback hardtop for 1963½, paralleling Ford's XL offerings.

By '64, tradition had returned. Mercury restored its old series lineup of Monterey, Montclair, Park Lane, and Commuter and Colony Park wagons. The first three included two-door and four-door hardtops, four-door sedans, and fastback "Marauder" hardtop sedans. The 390 V8 that became the standard powerplant in 1963 was joined by an optional 427-cid engine for all models except wagons. Marauders with the 425-bhp version were awesome performers.

In record year 1965, the full-size Mercury shared a restyle with Ford. The wagons rode a 119-inch wheelbase; others had 123 inches. Breezeway and conventional four-door models were found in all series, with the usual line of 390 and 427 V8s. Mercury touted "Torque Box" body construction: frames tuned for each body style to minimize noise, vibration, and harshness.

1961 Colony Park four-door station wagon

1962 Monterey two-door sedan

1964 Montclair Marauder fastback hardtop sedan

1965 Park Lane Breezeway four-door sedan

1966 Montclair fastback hardtop coupe

For 1966, a new die-cast grille was adopted. Two-door models got a new "sweep-style roof" with concave backlight—a dramatic break with the Breezeway design. Styling was revised again on the '67s. The limited-production Marquis was announced: a two-door hardtop with broad rear roof pillars and vinyl top. Another newcomer was the vinyl-topped Park Lane Brougham, a hardtop sedan that was expanded into a complete series the following year. Marquis and Brougham replaced the long-running Montclair and Park Lane for 1969.

A high-performance, low-production '69 entry was the Marauder fastback hardtop, which accounted for 14,666 sales. Its sleek, clean bodywork featured the Marquis grille, concealed headlights, quad taillights, and ventless side windows. The 1970 lineup was a repeat of '69. All models sported new grilles, side ornamentation, rear trim, and taillights.

One of the more interesting and desirable Mercurys of the decade was the 111-inch-wheelbase Cougar, premiering as a hardtop for 1967 and joined by a convertible in '69. Based on the Mustang but riding a 3-inch longer wheelbase, it was a deluxe version of Ford's highly successful "ponycar," priced about $200 higher. While Mustang came with a six-cylinder engine as standard, Cougar's base engine was a 200-bhp V8. In 1969-70 the CJ 428 packing 335 bhp was available at extra cost.

The original Cougar was a dashing car, identified by its "electric-shaver" grille and hidden headlights. Sequential turn signals were a feature from the first. The vertical grille bars were blacked out for 1968, giving the car a more conventional look. For '69, the body was widened and lengthened. A full-length contour line, ventless curved side glass, die-cast grille, and full-width taillights were also featured. The '70 model adopted a divided grille with blacked-out section for the luxury XR-7. The best of the Cougar line, the XR-7 was equipped with a rich leather interior and comprehensive instrumentation set into a simulated walnut dashboard.

GT and GTE Cougars powered by the 427 V8 were available beginning in 1968, offered with a variety of handling and performance options. Though it never ap-

1968 Marquis hardtop coupe

1968 Cougar XR7-GTE hardtop coupe

1969 Marauder X-100 hardtop coupe

1969 Cougar hardtop coupe with "Eliminator" option

1970 Marquis Brougham hardtop sedan

1970 Cougar hardtop coupe with "Eliminator" option

proached the Mustang in sales, Cougar was a boost to Mercury. It was also more solid and luxurious than Mustang, but equally roadable. Among collectors, the appeal of the 1967-68 Cougars has long been acknowledged.

Cougar put the finishing touch on a decade that witnessed a complete reversal of Mercury's image. By 1967 the make was known for performance as well as luxury. By 1970, Mercury had again become the hot car it had been in the late '40s and early '50s.

But it wouldn't last. In the '70s, the various Mercury models became less distinctive and more like equivalent Fords, while government mandates and the vagaries of petroleum power politics conspired to sacrifice performance on the twin altars of safety and fuel economy. By the end of the decade, Mercury had more or less resumed its original role as a plusher, pricier and, occasionally, larger Ford. The only differences by this time were that the parallel model lineups were spread across five or six different size classes instead of one or two, and that styling was usually more closely related to Lincoln's than Ford's.

The one area where the divisions parted company during the decade was the ponycar field. Actually, Cougar began diverging from Mustang as early as 1971, when both models were completely redesigned. It jumped two inches in wheelbase instead of one and was notably bulkier, though it had always been somewhat larger overall than than the Ford. Convertibles in both standard and more luxurious XR-7 guise were offered through the end of this generation in 1973, and have already become minor collector's items, primarily by dint of low production.

Meantime, ponycar demand fell off abruptly in the early '70s, so Mercury decided on a new course for 1974. While Mustang became a smaller, lighter, Pinto-based sporty car, Cougar grew into a kind of ersatz Thunderbird, moving up to the intermediate Montego platform. Oddly enough, Lincoln-Mercury had created the design chosen for the production Mustang II. But rather than field a badge-engineered clone of that car, the division opted to continue with the German-built Ford Capri it had been selling successfully since 1970, the same sort of "mini ponycar" but better built and more roadable. Cougar continued as Mercury's entry in the mid-size personal-luxury segment

1971 Montego MX hardtop coupe

1973 Montego MX Brougham hardtop coupe

1972 Monterey Custom hardtop coupe

1973 Marquis Brougham hardtop sedan

1972 Cougar XR-7 hardtop coupe

1973 Comet two-door fastback sedan

1974 Marquis Brougham four-door pillared hardtop

1975 Grand Marquis four-door pillared hardtop

1975 Cougar XR-7 hardtop coupe

1976 Montego MX coupe

1977 Comet two-door fastback sedan

1977 Monarch Ghia two-door sedan

through 1976, competing against the likes of Chevrolet's Monte Carlo and Pontiac's Grand Prix. The name was diluted the following year, when it replaced Montego on the entire intermediate line, the XR-7 label being reserved for a single top-shelf coupe. Things were temporarily sorted out again for 1980, only now Cougar really *was* a Thunderbird, a twin to that year's new downsized model.

In between, Ford redesigned the Mustang yet again, and this time Mercury wanted in. The result was a new American-made Capri, introduced for 1979. The direct descendent of the genuine Cougar ponycar, it was virtually identical with the new-generation Mustang (see entry) save for slightly busier styling and lack of the Ford's notchback body style. The same four engines were offered in a choice of base and Ghia models, and buyers could opt for the sporty RS package (Mercury never called it "Rally Sport," perhaps out of deference to Chevrolet), which was roughly equivalent to the Mustang Cobra.

One of the last cars with a distinctively Mercury character was the Cyclone, which bowed out after 1971. Offered that year with standard 351 and optional 429 V8s, this muscular mid-size remained as impressively fast as ever.

As before, swoopier sheetmetal set it clearly apart from its run-of-the-mill Montego linemates and Ford's corresponding Torino GT and Cobra, particularly the protruding nose and "gunsight" grille appearing with the 1970-71 facelift. Reflecting the muscle-car market's sad state of affairs at that time, the Cyclone sold poorly in its farewell season, which is of interest to collectors today. These cars, especially the desirable, limited-edition Spoiler, can only become rarer and more highly prized as the memorable high-performance era recedes further into history.

Elsewhere, new-model development at Mercury during the '70s is primarily a story of badge engineering. It began when the Comet name was revived for a slightly restyled version of the compact Ford Maverick. Announced for 1971, it soldiered on through 1974 as the division's sole representative in a size and price sector that took on urgent new importance in the wake of the 1973-74 Arab oil embargo. Help arrived for 1975 in the form of two new entries. One was the Comet's once-and-future replacement, the slightly larger, Granada-based Monarch. The other was Mercury's belated rendition of the subcompact Ford Pinto, bearing the Bobcat name and a pretentious little stand-

up grille. When Ford replaced Maverick with the more able Fairmont for 1978, Mercury got its own lookalike derivative, the Zephyr. If none of these moves was exactly original, they at least combined to leave Mercury much more competitive in a market that had been forever changed by an unprecedented combination of forces.

As with Buick and Oldsmobile, intermediate and full-size cars remained Mercury's mainstay through most of the decade, and it was here that the changes were most dramatic—and most needed. Mercury's mid-size contender wallowed along as a near duplicate of the Ford Torino/LTD II, under the Montego name for 1972-76 and, as noted, with the Cougar badge from 1977 through the last of this body-on-frame design for 1979. Like the Fords, there was little praiseworthy about them, though the Mercurys were arguably nicer looking.

In what was loosely called the "standard" class sat the big Marquis and Monterey, which began the decade weighing up to and over two tons and riding wheelbases of up to 124 inches. They didn't change much through

1978. Model names centered on Marquis exclusively after 1974, and styling became progressively more like that of the big Lincoln Continental, particularly at the front. These Mercs may have been mammoths, but they were good ones: smooth and reliable, powered by reasonably potent V8s, fairly restrained in appearance, and fully (if not always tastefully) equipped. Hardtop styling gave way to "pillared hardtops" after 1974, which was something of a sham. Marquis and Colony Park wagons were built on a slightly shorter wheelbase shared with Ford—and their fuel "economy" was as you'd expect from such ponderous haulers. Along with the Ford LTD, the Marquis underwent the "big shrink" for '79, losing 10 inches in wheelbase and up to 1200 pound in curb weight. It was the right move, even if it came about two years too late.

In retrospect, the '70s were not particularly good years for Mercury. The make had just reestablished its reputation for performance, only to lose it again a few years later. A succession of heavier, clumsier Cougars and confusingly named intermediates hardly helped. Its attempt to

1979 Bobcat two-door fastback sedan

1979 Cougar XR-7 coupe

1979 Zephyr Z-7 coupe

1979 Grand Marquis two-door sedan

1980 Cougar XR-7 coupe

1980 Capri RS Turbo hatchback coupe

move down into the compact and subcompact arenas was blunted by higher prices on cars that offered little more than the Fords they so obviously were. Meantime, its traditional big-car foundation was rocked by the new economic order of a more energy-conscious world. Yet by 1980, Mercury had begun turning the corner with cars like the exciting Capri, the practical Zephyr, and the reborn Cougar and Marquis. How it will fare in the '80s is a story yet to be finished, but at this writing we can say that Mercury's prospects seem brighter than they have for a long time.

Mercury Specifications

1939—75,000 built*

*estimated

Series 99A (wb 116.0)

		Wght	Price	Prod
	conv club cpe 5P	2,995	1,018	—
	sdn 2d 5P	2,997	916	—
	cpe sdn 2d 5P	3,000	957	—
	Town Sedan 4d 5P	3,013	957	—

1939 Engine	bore×stroke	bhp	availability
V8, 239.0	3.19×3.75	95	S-all

1940

Series 09A (wb 116.0)—81,128* built

		Wght	Price	Prod
	conv cpe	3,107	1,079	—
	sdn 2d	3,068	946	—
	cpe-sdn 2d	3,030	987	—
	Town Sedan 4d	3,103	987	—
	conv sdn	3,249	1,212	—

*Estimate (see note below 1942).

1940 Engine	bore×stroke	bhp	availability
V8, 239.4	3.19×3.75	95	S-all

1941

Series 19A (wb 118.0)—82,391* built

		Wght	Price	Prod
67	cpe, A/S	3,049	936	—
70	Tudor sdn	3,184	946	—
72	cpe-sdn 2d	3,118	977	—
73	Town Sedan 4d	3,221	987	—
76	conv cpe	3,222	1,100	—
77	cpe, 2P	3,008	910	—
79	wgn, 4d	3,468	1,141	—

*Estimate (see note below 1942).

1941 Engine	bore×stroke	bhp	availability
V8, 239.4	3.19×3.75	95	S-all

1942

Series 29A (wb 118.0)—22,816* built

		Wght	Price	Prod
70	Tudor sdn	3,228	1,030	—
72	cpe-sdn 2d	3,148	1,055	—
73	Town Sedan 4d	3,263	1,065	—
76	conv cpe	3,288	1,215	—
77	cpe, 3P	3,073	995	—
79	wgn, 4d, 8P	3,528	1,260	—

*Estimate (see below).

Note: Factory records provide only calendar year production during 1940-41. Estimates are calculated by adding 25% of previous year's calendar production to 75% of current year's production. Model year production began in October each year.

1942 Engine	bore×stroke	bhp	availability
V8, 239.0	3.19×3.75	100	S-all

1946

Series 69M (wb 118.0)

		Wght	Price	Prod
70	sdn 2d	3,240	1,448	13,108
71	Sportsman conv cpe	3,407	2,209	205
72	cpe-sdn 2d	3,190	1,495	24,163
73	Town Sedan 4d	3,270	1,509	40,280
76	conv cpe	3,340	1,711	6,044
79	wgn 4d	3,540	1,729	2,797
—	chassis	—	—	11

1946 Engine	bore×stroke	bhp	availability
V8, 239.4	3.19×3.75	100	S-all

1947

Series 79M (wb 118.0)

		Wght	Price	Prod
70	sdn 2d	3,268	1,592	34
72	cpe-sdn 2d	3,218	1,645	29,284
73	Town Sedan 4d	3,298	1,660	42,281
76	conv cpe	3,368	2,002	10,221
79	wgn 4d	3,571	2,207	3,558
—	chassis	—	—	5

1947 Engine	bore×stroke	bhp	availability
V8, 239.4	3.19×3.75	100	S-all

1948

Series 89M (wb 118.0)

		Wght	Price	Prod
72	cpe-sdn 2d	3,218	1,645	16,476
73	Town Sedan 4d	3,298	1,660	24,283
76	conv cpe	3,368	2,002	7,586
79	wgn 4d	3,571	2,207	1,889
—	chassis	—	—	34

1948 Engine	bore×stroke	bhp	availability
V8, 239.4	3.19×3.75	100	S-all

1949

Series 9CM (wb 118.0)

		Wght	Price	Prod
72	cpe	3,321	1,979	120,616
74	Sport Sedan 4d	3,386	2,031	155,882
76	conv cpe	3,591	2,410	16,765
79	wgn 2d, 8P	3,626	2,716	8,044
—	chassis	—	—	12

1949 Engine	bore×stroke	bhp	availability
V8, 255.4	3.19×4.00	110	S-all

1950

Series 0CM (wb 118.0)

		Wght	Price	Prod
M-72A	cpe (economy)	3,345	1,875	151,489
M-72B	club cpe	3,430	1,980	
M-72C	Monterey cpe, canvas top	3,480	2,146	
M-72C	Monterey cpe, vinyl top	3,480	2,157	

		Wght	Price	Prod
M-74	Sport Sedan 4d	3,470	2,032	132,082
M-76	conv cpe	3,710	2,412	8,341
M-79	wgn 2d, 8P	3,755	2,561	1,746

1950 Engine	bore × stroke	bhp	availability
V8, 255.4	3.19 × 4.00	110	S-all

1951

Series 1CM (wb 118.0)		Wght	Price	Prod
M-72B	cpe	3,485	1,947	
M-72C	Monterey cpe, canvas top	3,485	2,116	142,168
M-72C	Monterey cpe, vinyl top	3,485	2,127	
M-74	Sport Sedan 4d	3,550	2,000	157,648
M-76	conv cpe	3,760	2,380	6,759
M-79	wgn 2d, 8P	3,800	2,530	3,812

1951 Engine	bore × stroke	bhp	availability
V8, 255.4	3.19 × 4.00	112	S-all

1952

Series 2M (wb 118.0)		Wght	Price	Prod
60B	Monterey htp cpe	3,520	2,225	24,453
60E	Sport Coupe	3,435	2,100	30,599
70B	sdn 2d	3,335	1,987	25,812
73B	sdn 4d	3,390	2,040	83,475
73C	Monterey sdn 4d	3,375	2,115	
76B	Monterey conv cpe	3,635	2,370	5,261
79B	wgn 4d, 6P	3,795	2,525	2,487
79D	wgn 4d, 8P	3,795	2,570	

1952 Engine	bore × stroke	bhp	availability
V8, 255.4	3.19 × 4.00	125	S-all

1953

3M Custom (wb 118.0)		Wght	Price	Prod
60E	Sport Coupe	3,465	2,117	39,547
70B	sdn 2d	3,405	2,004	50,183
73B	sdn 4d	3,450	2,057	59,794

3M Monterey (wb 118.0)				
60B	htp cpe	3,465	2,244	76,119
73C	sdn 4d	3,425	2,133	64,038
76B	conv cpe	3,585	2,390	8,463
79B	wgn 4d, 8P	3,765	2,591	7,719

1953 Engine	bore × stroke	bhp	availability
V8, 255.4	3.19 × 4.00	125	S-all

1954

Custom (wb 118.0)		Wght	Price	Prod
60E	Sport htp cpe	3,485	2,315	15,234
70B	sdn 2d	3,435	2,194	37,146
73B	sdn 4d	3,480	2,251	32,687

Monterey (wb 118.0)				
60B	htp cpe	3,520	2,452	79,533
60F	Sun Valley htp cpe	3,535	2,582	9,761
73C	sdn 4d	3,515	2,333	65,995
76B	conv cpe	3,620	2,610	7,293
79B	wgn 4d, 8P	3,735	2,776	11,656

1954 Engine	bore × stroke	bhp	availability
V8, 256.0	3.62 × 3.10	161	S-all

1955

Custom (wb 119.0; wgn-118.0)		Wght	Price	Prod
60E	htp cpe	3,480	2,341	7,040
70B	sdn 2d	3,395	2,218	31,295
73B	sdn 4d	3,450	2,277	21,219
79B	wgn 4d	3,780	2,686	14,134

Monterey (wb 119.0; wgn-118.0)				
60B	htp cpe	3,510	2,465	69,093
73C	sdn 4d	3,500	2,400	70,392
79C	wgn 4d	3,770	2,844	11,968

Montclair (wb 119.0)				
58A	sdn 4d	3,600	2,685	20,624
64A	htp cpe	3,490	2,631	71,588
64B	Sun Valley htp cpe	3,560	2,712	1,787
76B	conv cpe	3,685	2,712	10,668

1955 Engines	bore × stroke	bhp	availability
V8, 292.0	3.75 × 3.30	188	S-Custom, Monterey
V8, 292.0	3.75 × 3.30	198	S-Montclair; O-others

1956

Medalist (wb 119.0)		Wght	Price	Prod
57D	Phaeton htp sdn	3,530	2,458	6,685
64E	Sport htp cpe	3,545	2,389	11,892
70C	sdn 2d	3,430	2,254	20,582
73D	sdn 4d	3,500	2,313	6,653

Custom (wb 119.0; wgn-118.0)				
57C	Phaeton htp sdn	3,550	2,555	12,187
64D	Sport htp cpe	3,560	2,485	20,857
70B	sdn 2d	3,505	2,351	16,343
73B	sdn 4d	3,520	2,410	15,860
76A	conv cpe	3,665	2,712	2,311
79B	wgn 4d, 8P	3,860	2,819	9,292
79D	wgn 4d, 6P	3,790	2,722	8,478

Monterey (wb 119.0;wgn-118.0)				
57B	Phaeton htp sdn	3,800	2,700	10,726
58B	Sport Sedan 4d	3,550	2,652	11,765
64C	Sport htp cpe	3,590	2,630	42,863
73C	sdn 4d	3,570	2,555	26,735
79C	wgn 4d, 8P	3,885	2,977	13,280

Montclair (wb 119.0)				
57A	Phaeton htp sdn	3,640	2,835	23,493
58A	Sport Sedan 4d	3,610	2,786	9,617
64A	Sport htp cpe	3,620	2,765	50,562
76B	conv cpe	3,725	2,900	7,762

1956 Engines	bore × stroke	bhp	availability
V8, 312.0	3.80 × 3.44	210	S-Medalist, Custom 3spd
V8, 312.0	3.80 × 3.44	225	S-Medalist, Custom auto, Mntclr
V8, 312.0	3.80 × 3.44	235	S-Montclair; Monterey auto

1957

Monterey (wb 122.0)		Wght	Price	Prod
57A	Phaeton htp sdn	3,915	2,763	22,475
58A	sdn 4d	3,890	2,645	53,839
63A	Phaeton htp cpe	3,870	2,693	42,199
64A	sdn 2d	3,875	2,576	33,982
76A	Phaeton conv cpe	4,035	3,005	5,033

Montclair (wb 122.0)				
57B	Phaeton htp sdn	3,925	3,317	21,567
58B	sdn 4d	3,905	3,188	19,836
63B	Phaeton htp cpe	3,900	3,236	30,111
76B	Phaeton conv cpe	4,010	3,430	4,248

Turnpike Cruiser (wb 122.0)		Wght	Price	Prod
65A	htp cpe	4,005	3,758	7,291
75A	htp sdn	4,015	3,849	8,305
76S	conv cpe	4,125	4,103	1,265

Station Wagon (wb 122.0)		Wght	Price	Prod
56A	Commuter 2d, 6P	4,115	2,903	4,885
56B	Voyager 2d, 6P	4,240	3,403	2,283
77A	Commuter 4d, 6P	4,195	2,973	11,990
77B	Colony Park 4d, 9P	4,165	3,677	7,386
77C	Commuter 4d, 9P	4,155	3,070	5,752
77D	Voyager 4d, 9P	4,280	3,570	3,716

1957 Engines	bore × stroke	bhp	availability
V8, 312.0	3.80 × 3.44	255	S-all exc Turnpike Cruiser
V8, 368.0	4.00 × 3.66	290	S-Turnpike Cruiser; O-others

1958

Medalist (wb 122.0)		Wght	Price	Prod
58C	sdn 4d	3,875	2,617	10,982
64B	sdn 2d	3,790	2,547	7,750

Monterey (wb 122.0)		Wght	Price	Prod
57A	Phaeton htp sdn	4,150	2,840	26,909
58A	sdn 4d	4,160	2,721	20,892
63A	Phaeton htp cpe	4,075	2,769	13,693
64A	sdn 2d	4,080	2,652	10,526
76A	conv cpe	4,225	3,081	2,292

Montclair (wb 122.0)		Wght	Price	Prod
57B	Phaeton tp sdn	4,165	3,365	3,609
58B	sdn 4d	4,155	3,236	4,801
63B	Phaeton htp cpe	4,085	3,284	5,012
65A	Turnpike Cruiser htp cpe	4,150	3,498	2,864
75A	Turnpike Cruiser htp sdn	4,230	3,577	3,543
76B	conv cpe	4,295	3,536	844

Park Lane (wb 125.0)		Wght	Price	Prod
57C	Phaeton htp sdn	4,390	3,944	5,241
63C	Phaeton htp cpe	4,280	3,867	3,158
76C	conv cpe	4,405	4,118	853

Station Wagon (wb 122.0)		Wght	Price	Prod
56A	Commuter 2d, 6P	4,400	3,035	1,912
56B	Voyager 2d, 6P	4,435	3,535	568
77A	Commuter 4d, 6P	4,485	3,105	8,601
77B	Colony Park 4d, 6-9P	4,605	3,775	4,474
77C	Commuter 4d, 9P	4,525	3,201	4,227
77D	Voyager 4d, 6-9P	4,540	3,635	2,520

1958 Engines	bore × stroke	bhp	availability
V8, 312.0	3.80 × 3.44	235	S-Medalist only
V8, 383.0	4.30 × 3.30	312	S-Monterey, Commuter
V8, 383.0	4.30 × 3.30	330	S-Montclair, Voyager, Col Park
V8, 430.0	4.30 × 3.70	360	S-Park Lane

1959

Monterey (wb 126.0)		Wght	Price	Prod
57A	htp sdn	4,013	2,918	11,355
58A	sdn 4d	3,985	2,832	43,570
63A	htp cpe	3,932	2,854	17,232
64A	sdn 2d	3,914	2,768	12,694
76A	conv cpe	4,074	3,150	4,426

Montclair (wb 126.0)		Wght	Price	Prod
57B	htp sdn	4,234	3,437	6,713
58B	sdn 4d	4,205	3,308	9,514
63B	htp cpe	4,146	3,357	7,375

Park Lane (wb 128.0)		Wght	Price	Prod
57C	htp sdn	4,386	4,031	7,206

		Wght	Price	Prod
63C	htp cpe	4,311	3,955	4,060
76C	conv cpe	4,455	4,206	1,254

Station Wagon (wb 126.0)		Wght	Price	Prod
56A	Commuter 2d, 6P	4,334	3,145	1,051
77A	Commuter 4d, 6P	4,405	3,215	15,122
77B	Colony Park 4d, 6P	4,535	3,932	5,929
77D	Voyager 4d, 6P	4,483	3,793	2,496

1959 Engines	bore × stroke	bhp	availability
V8, 312.0	3.80 × 3.44	210	S-Monterey
V8, 312.0	3.80 × 3.44	280	O-Monterey
V8, 383.0	4.30 × 3.30	280	S-Commuter
V8, 383.0	4.30 × 3.30	322	S-Montclair, Voyager, Col Park
V8, 430.0	4.30 × 3.70	345	S-Park Lane

1960

Comet (wb 114.0; wgn—109.5)		Wght	Price	Prod
54A	sdn 4d	2,432	2,053	47,416
59A	wgn 2d	2,548	2,310	5,115
62A	sdn 2d	2,399	1,998	45,374
71A	wgn 4d	2,581	2,365	18,426

Monterey (wb 126.0)		Wght	Price	Prod
57A	Cruiser htp sdn	4,011	2,845	9,536
58A	sdn 4d	3,981	2,730	49,594
63A	Cruiser htp cpe	3,931	2,781	15,790
64A	sdn 2d	3,901	2,631	21,557
76A	conv cpe	4,131	3,077	6,062

Monclair (wb 126.0)		Wght	Price	Prod
57B	Cruiser htp sdn	4,285	3,394	5,548
58B	sdn 4d	4,255	3,280	8,510
63B	Cruiser htp cpe	4,205	3,331	5,756

Park Lane (wb 126.0)		Wght	Price	Prod
57F	Cruiser htp sdn	4,380	3,858	5,788
63F	Cruiser htp cpe	4,300	3,794	2,974
76D	conv cpe	4,500	4,018	1,525

Station Wagon (wb 126.0)		Wght	Price	Prod
77A	Commuter 4d, 6-9P	4,301	3,127	14,949
77B	Colony Park 4d, 9P	4,558	3,837	7,411

1960 Engines	bore × stroke	bhp	availability
L6, 144.3	3.50 × 2.50	90	S-Comet
V8, 312.0	3.80 × 3.44	205	S-Monterey, Commuter
V8, 383.0	4.30 × 3.30	280	O-Monterey, Commuter
V8, 430.0	4.30 × 3.70	310	S-Montclair, P Lane, Col Park

1961

Comet (wb 114.0; wgn-109.5)		Wght	Price	Prod
54A	sdn 4d	2,411	2,055	85,332
59A	wgn 2d	2,548	2,312	4,199
62A	sdn 2d	2,376	2,000	71,563
62A	S-22 sdn 2d	2,441	2,284	14,004
71A	wgn 4d	2,581	2,355	22,165

Meteor (wb 120.0)		Wght	Price	Prod
58A	600 sdn 4d	3,714	2,589	18,117
64A	600 sdn 2d	3,647	2,535	
54A	800 sdn 4d	3,762	2,767	
62A	800 sdn 2d	3,680	2,713	35,005
65A	800 htp cpe	3,694	2,774	
75A	800 htp sdn	3,780	2,839	

Monterey (wb 120.0)		Wght	Price	Prod
54B	sdn 4d	3,777	2,871	22,881
65B	htp cpe	3,709	2,878	10,942
75B	htp sdn	3,795	2,943	9,252
76A	conv cpe	3,872	3,128	7,053

Station Wagon (wb 120.0)		Wght	Price	Prod
71A	Commuter 4d, 6P	4,115	2,924	8,945
71B	Colony Park 4d, 6P	4,131	3,120	7,887
71B	Colony Park 4d, 9P	4,171	3,191	
71C	Commuter 4d, 9P	4,155	2,994	6

1961 Engines	bore × stroke	bhp	availability
L6, 144.3	3.50 × 2.50	85	S-Comet
L6, 170.0	3.50 × 2.94	101	O-Comet
L6, 223.0	3.62 × 3.60	135	O-Meteor 600/800, Commuter
V8, 292.0	3.75 × 3.30	175	S-all exc Comet
V8, 352.0	4.00 × 3.50	220	O-all exc Comet
V8, 390.0	4.05 × 3.78	300	O-all exc Comet

1962

Comet (wb 114.0; wgn-109.5)		Wght	Price	Prod
54A	sdn 4d	2,457	2,139	70,227
54B	Custom sdn 4d	2,648	2,226	
59A	wgn 2d	2,626	2,396	2,121
59B	Custom wgn 2d	2,642	2,483	
62A	sdn 2d	2,420	2,084	
62B	Custom sdn 2d	2,431	2,170	73,880
62C	S-22 sdn 2d	2,458	2,368	
71A	wgn 4d	2,662	2,439	16,759
71B	Custom wgn 4d	2,679	2,526	
71C	Villager wgn 4d	2,712	2,710	2,318

Meteor (wb 116.5)		Wght	Price	Prod
54A	sdn 4d	2,956	2,340	18,708
54B	Custom sdn 4d	2,964	2,428	23,484
62A	sdn 2d	2,922	2,278	11,550
62B	Custom sdn 2d	2,930	2,366	9,410
62C	S-33 sdn 2d	2,960	2,509	5,900

Monterey (wb 120.0)		Wght	Price	Prod
54A	sdn 4d	3,772	2,726	18,975
62A	sdn 4d	3,695	2,672	5,117
65A	htp cpe	3,712	2,733	5,328
75A	htp sdn	3,781	2,798	2,691

Monterey Custom (wb 120.0)		Wght	Price	Prod
54B	sdn 4d	3,836	2,965	27,591
65B	htp cpe	3,772	2,972	10,814
65C	S-55 htp cpe	4,802	3,488	2,772
75B	htp sdn	3,851	3,037	8,932
76A	conv cpe	3,938	3,222	5,489
76B	S-55 conv cpe	3,968	3,738	1,315

Station Wagon (wb 120.0)		Wght	Price	Prod
71A	Commuter 4d, 6P	4,120	2,920	8,389
71C	Commuter 4d, 9P	4,132	2,990	
71B	Colony Park 4d, 6P	4,186	3,219	9,596
71D	Colony Park 4d, 9P	4,198	3,289	

1962 Engines	bore × stroke	bhp	availability
L6, 144.3	3.50 × 2.50	85	S-Comet
L6, 170.0	3.50 × 2.94	101	S-Meteor; O-Comet
L6, 223.0	3.62 × 3.60	138	S-Monterey, Commuter
V8, 221.0	3.50 × 2.87	145	O-Meteor
V8, 260.0	3.80 × 2.87	164	O-Meteor
V8, 292.0	3.75 × 3.30	170	S-Custom, Col Park; O-Mntry, Cmmtr
V8, 352.0	4.00 × 3.50	220	O-all except Comet, Meteor
V8, 390.0	4.05 × 3.78	330	O-all exc Comet, Meteor

1963

Comet (wb 114.0; wgn-109.5)		Wght	Price	Prod
54A	sdn 4d	2,499	2,139	24,230
54B	Custom sdn 4d	2,508	2,206	27,498
59A	wgn 2d	2,644	2,440	623
59B	Custom wgn 2d	2,659	2,527	272
62A	sdn 2d	2,462	2,084	24,351

		Wght	Price	Prod
62B	Custom sdn 2d	2,471	2,171	11,897
62C	S-22 sdn 2d	2,512	2,368	6,303
63B	Custom htp cpe	2,572	2,605	9,432
63C	S-22 htp cpe	2,613	2,635	5,807
71A	wgn 4d	2,681	2,483	4,419
71B	Custom wgn 4d	2,696	2,570	5,151
71C	Villager wgn 4d	2,736	2,754	1,529
76A	Custom conv cpe	2,784	2,557	7,354
76B	S-22 conv cpe	2,825	2,710	5,757

Meteor (wb 116.5; wgn-115.5)		Wght	Price	Prod
54A	sdn 4d	3,025	2,340	9,183
54B	Custom sdn 4d	3,031	2,428	14,498
62A	sdn 2d	2,986	2,278	3,935
62B	Custom sdn 2d	2,992	2,366	2,704
65A	Custom htp cpe	3,010	2,448	7,565
65B	S-33 htp cpe	3,030	2,628	4,865
71B	wgn 4d, 6P	3,303	2,631	2,904
71D	Cus Cruiser wgn 4d, 6–9P	3,319	2,886	1,485
71E	Custom wgn 4d, 6–9P	3,311	2,719	3,636

Monterey (120.0)		Wght	Price	Prod
54A	sdn 4d	3,944	2,887	18,177
62A	sdn 2d	3,854	2,834	4,640
65A	htp cpe	3,869	2,930	3,879
75A	htp sdn	3,959	2,995	1,692

Monterey Custom (wb 120.0)		Wght	Price	Prod
54B	sdn 4d	3,956	3,075	39,542
63B	Marauder fstbk htp cpe	3,887	3,083	7,298
63C	S-55 Marauder fstbk htp cpe	3,900	3,650	2,319
65B	htp cpe	3,881	3,083	10,693
65C	S-55 htp cpe	3,894	3,650	3,863
75B	htp sdn	3,971	3,148	8,604
75C	S-55 htp sdn	3,984	3,715	1,203
76A	conv cpe	4,043	3,333	3,783
76B	S-55 conv cpe	4,049	3,900	1,379

Station Wagon (wb 120.0)		Wght	Price	Prod
71B	Colony Park 4d, 6P	4,306	3,295	6,447
71D	Colony Park 4d, 9P	4,318	3,365	7,529

1963 Engines	bore × stroke	bhp	availability
L6, 144.3	3.50 × 2.50	85	S-Comet sdns
L6, 170.0	3.50 × 2.94	101	S-other Comet, Meteor
V8, 221.0	3.50 × 2.87	145	O-Comet, Meteor
V8, 260.0	3.80 × 2.87	164	O-Meteor/Cus, S-33, Comet
V8, 390.0	4.05 × 3.78	250	S-Monterey, Monterey Custom
V8, 390.0	4.05 × 3.78	300	S-S-55; O-other Monterey
V8, 390.0	4.05 × 3.78	330	O-Montereys, wagons
V8, 406.0	4.13 × 3.78	385	O-Monterey, Monterey Custom
V8, 406.0	4.13 × 3.78	405	O-Monterey, Monterey Custom

1964

Comet 202 (wb 114.0)		Wght	Price	Prod
01	sdn 2d	2,539	2,126	33,824
02	sdn 4d	2,580	2,182	29,147
32	wgn 4d	2,727	2,463	5,504

Comet 404 (wb 114.0)		Wght	Price	Prod
11	sdn 2d	2,551	2,213	12,512
12	sdn 4d	2,588	2,269	25,136
34	Custom wgn 4d	2,741	2,550	6,918
36	Villager wgn 4d	2,745	2,734	1,980

Comet Caliente (wb 114.0)		Wght	Price	Prod
22	sdn 4d	2,668	2,350	27,218
23	htp cpe	2,688	2,375	31,204
25	conv cpe	2,861	2,636	9,039

Comet Cyclone (wb 114.0)		Wght	Price	Prod
27	htp cpe	2,860	2,655	7,454

Mercury

Monterey (wb 120.0)		Wght	Price	Prod
41	sdn 2d	3,895	2,819	3,932
42	sdn 4d	3,985	2,892	20,234
43	htp cpe	3,910	2,884	2,926
45	conv cpe	4,027	3,226	2,592
47	Marauder fstbk htp cpe	3,916	2,884	8,760
48	Marauder fstbk htp sdn	3,914	2,957	4,143

Montclair (wb 120.0)				
52	sdn 4d	3,996	3,116	15,520
53	htp cpe	3,921	3,127	2,329
57	Marauder fstbk htp cpe	3,927	3,127	6,459
58	Marauder fstbk htp sdn	4,017	3,181	8,655

Park Lane (wb 120.0)				
62	sdn 4d	4,035	3,348	6,230
63	htp cpe	3,960	3,359	1,786
64	htp sdn	4,050	3,413	2,402
65	conv cpe	4,066	3,549	1,967
67	Marauder fstbk htp cpe	3,966	3,359	1,052
68	Marauder fstbk htp sdn	4,056	3,413	4,505

Station Wagon (wb 120.0)				
72	Commuter 4d, 6P	4,259	3,236	3,484
72	Commuter 4d, 9P	4,271	3,306	1,839
76	Colony Park 4d, 6P	4,275	3,434	4,204
76	Colony Park 4d, 9P	4,287	3,504	5,624

1964 Engines	bore × stroke	bhp	availability
L6, 170.0	3.50 × 2.94	101	S-Comet
L6, 200.0	3.68 × 3.15	116	O-Comet
V8, 260.0	3.80 × 2.87	164	O-Comet
V8, 289.0	4.00 × 2.87	210	S-Cyclone; O-other Comets
V8, 390.0	4.05 × 3.78	250	S-all exc Comet, Park Lane
V8, 390.0	4.05 × 3.78	266	O-all exc Comet, Park Lane
V8, 390.0	4.05 × 3.78	300	S-Park Lane
V8, 390.0	4.05 × 3.78	330	O-Park Lane
V8, 427.0	4.23 × 3.78	410	O-Monterey, Montclair, P Lane
V8, 427.0	4.23 × 3.78	425	O-Monterey, Montclair, P Lane

1965

Comet 202 (wb 114.0)		Wght	Price	Prod
01	sdn 2d	2,584	2,154	32,425
02	sdn 4d	2,624	2,210	23,501
32	wgn 4d	2,784	2,491	4,814

Comet 404 (wb 114.0)				
11	sdn 2d	2,594	2,241	10,900
12	sdn 4d	2,629	2,294	18,628
34	Custom wgn 4d	2,789	2,578	5,226
36	Villager wgn 4d	2,789	2,762	1,592

Comet Caliente (wb 114.0)				
22	sdn 4d	2,659	2,378	20,337
23	htp cpe	2,684	2,403	29,247
25	conv cpe	2,869	2,664	6,035

Comet Cyclone (wb 114.0)				
27	htp cpe	2,994	2,683	12,347

Monterey (wb 123.0)				
42	Breezeway sdn 4d	3,898	2,904	19,569
43	sdn 2d	3,788	2,767	5,775
44	sdn 4d	3,853	2,839	23,363
45	conv cpe	3,928	3,230	4,762
47	htp cpe	3,823	2,902	16,857
48	htp sdn	3,893	2,978	10,047

Montclair (wb 123.0)				
52	Breezeway sdn 4d	3,933	3,137	18,924
57	htp cpe	3,848	3,135	9,645
58	htp sdn	3,928	3,210	16,977

Park Lane (wb 123.0)		Wght	Price	Prod
62	Breezeway sdn 4d	3,988	3,369	8,335
65	conv cpe	4,013	3,599	3,006
67	htp cpe	3,908	3,367	6,853
68	htp sdn	3,983	3,442	14,211

Station Wagon (wb 119.0)				
72	Commuter 4d, 6P	4,178	3,235	5,453
72	Commuter 4d, 9P	4,213	3,312	2,628
76	Colony Park 4d, 6P	4,228	3,434	6,910
76	Colony Park 4d, 9P	4,263	3,511	8,384

1965 Engines	bore × stroke	bhp	availability
L6, 200.0	3.68 × 3.15	120	S-Comet
V8, 289.0	4.00 × 2.87	200	S-Cyclone; O-other Comet
V8, 289.0	4.00 × 2.87	225	O-Comet
V8, 390.0	4.05 × 3.78	250	S-Monterey, Commuter
V8, 390.0	4.05 × 3.78	266	S-Montclair, Colony Park
V8, 390.0	4.05 × 3.78	300	S-Park Lane; O-all exc Comet
V8, 390.0	4.05 × 3.78	330	O-all exc Comet
V8, 427.0	4.23 × 3.78	425	O-all exc Comet

1966

Comet 202 (wb 116.0; wgn-113.0)		Wght	Price	Prod
01	sdn 2d	2,864	2,206	35,964
02	sdn 4d	2,908	2,263	20,440
06	Voyager wgn 4d	3,282	2,553	7,595

Comet Capri (wb 116.0; wgn-113.0)				
12	sdn 4d	2,928	2,378	15,635
13	htp cpe	2,960	2,400	15,031
16	Villager wgn 4d	3,319	2,790	3,880

Comet Caliente (wb 116.0)				
22	sdn 4d	2,930	2,453	17,933
23	htp cpe	2,966	2,475	25,862
25	conv cpe	3,228	2,735	3,922

Comet Cyclone (wb 116.0)				
27	htp cpe	3,078	2,700	6,889
27	GT htp cpe	3,315	2,891	13,812
29	conv cpe	3,321	2,961	1,305
29	GT conv cpe	3,595	3,152	2,158

Monterey (wb 123.0)				
42	Breezeway sdn 4d	3,966	2,917	14,174
43	sdn 2d	3,835	2,783	2,487
44	sdn 4d	3,903	2,854	18,998
45	conv cpe	4,039	3,237	3,279
47	fstbk htp cpe	3,885	2,915	19,103
48	fstbk htp sdn	3,928	2,990	7,647

S-55 (wb 123.0)				
46	conv cpe	4,148	3,614	669
49	fstbk htp cpe	4,031	3,292	2,916

Montclair (wb 123.0)				
54	sdn 4d	3,921	3,087	11,856
57	fstbk htp cpe	3,887	3,144	11,290
58	fstbk htp sdn	3,971	3,217	15,767

Park Lane (wb 123.0)				
62	Breezeway sdn 4d	4,051	3,389	8,692
65	conv cpe	4,148	3,608	2,546
67	fstbk htp cpe	3,971	3,387	8,354
68	fstbk htp sdn	4,070	3,460	19,204

Station Wagon (wb 119.0)				
72	Commuter 4d, 6P	4,280	3,240	3,970
72	Commuter 4d, 9P	4,331	3,336	2,877
76	Colony Park 4d, 6P	4,332	3,502	7,190
76	Colony Park 4d, 9P	4,383	3,598	11,704

1966 Engines	bore × stroke	bhp	availability
L6, 200.0	3.68 × 3.15	120	S-Comet exc Cyclone
V8, 289.0	4.00 × 2.87	200	S-Cyclone; O-other Comet
V8, 390.0	4.05 × 3.78	265	S-Cyclone GT, full-size w/man
V8, 390.0	4.05 × 3.78	275	S-full-size w/auto Cyclone GT
V8, 390.0	4.05 × 3.78	335	O-Cyclone GT
V8, 410.0	4.05 × 3.98	330	S-Park Lane; O-other full-size
V8, 428.0	4.13 × 3.98	345	S-S-55; O-other full-size

1967

Comet 202 (wb 116.0)		Wght	Price	Prod
01	sdn 2d	2,868	2,284	14,251
02	sdn 4d	2,906	2,336	10,284

Comet Capri (wb 116.0)		Wght	Price	Prod
06	sdn 4d	2,940	2,436	9,292
07	htp cpe	2,970	2,459	11,671

Comet Caliente (wb 116.0)		Wght	Price	Prod
10	sdn 4d	2,952	2,535	9,153
11	htp cpe	2,982	2,558	9,966
12	conv cpe	3,250	2,818	1,539

Comet Station Wagon (wb 113.0)		Wght	Price	Prod
03	Voyager 4d	3,310	2,604	4,930
08	Villager 4d	3,332	2,841	3,140

Comet Cyclone (wb 116.0)		Wght	Price	Prod
15	htp cpe	3,075	2,737	2,682
15	GT htp cpe	3,090	3,034	3,419
16	conv cpe	3,339	2,997	431
16	GT conv cpe	3,350	3,294	378

Cougar (wb 111.0)		Wght	Price	Prod
91	htp cpe	2,988	2,851	116,260
91	GT htp cpe	3,000	3,175	7,412
93	XR7 htp cpe	3,015	3,081	27,221

Monterey (wb 123.0)		Wght	Price	Prod
44	sdn 4d	3,798	2,904	15,177
44	Breezeway sdn 4d	3,847	2,967	5,910
45	conv cpe	3,943	3,314	2,673
46	S-55 conv cpe	3,960	3,837	145
47	htp cpe	3,820	2,985	16,910
48	htp sdn	3,858	3,059	8,013
49	S-55 fstbk htp cpe	3,837	3,511	570

Montclair (wb 123.0)		Wght	Price	Prod
54	sdn 4d	3,863	3,187	5,783
54	Breezeway sdn 4d	3,881	3,250	4,151
57	htp cpe	3,848	3,244	4,118
58	htp sdn	3,943	3,316	5,870

Park Lane (wb 123.0)		Wght	Price	Prod
61	Brougham Breezeway sdn 4d	3,980	3,896	3,325
62	Brougham htp sdn	4,000	3,986	4,189
64	Breezeway sdn 4d	4,011	3,736	4,163
65	conv cpe	4,114	3,984	1,191
67	htp cpe	3,947	3,752	2,196
68	htp sdn	3,992	3,826	5,412

Marquis (wb 123.0)		Wght	Price	Prod
69	htp cpe	3,995	3,989	6,510

Station Wagon (wb 119.0)		Wght	Price	Prod
72	Commuter 4d, 6P	4,178	3,289	3,447
72	Commuter 4d, 9P	4,297	3,384	4,451
76	Colony Park 4d, 6P	4,258	3,657	5,775
76	Colony Park 4d, 9P	4,294	3,752	12,915

1967 Engines	bore × stroke	bhp	availability
L6, 200.0	3.68 × 3.15	120	S-Comet exc Cyclone
V8, 289.0	4.00 × 2.87	200	S-Cougar, Cycl; O-other Comet
V8, 289.0	4.00 × 2.87	225	O-Cougar
V8, 390.0	4.05 × 3.78	270	S-Montclair, S Wgn; O-Comet
V8, 390.0	4.05 × 3.78	320	S-Cycl/Cougar GT; O-Other Cougar
V8, 410.0	4.05 × 3.98	330	S-P Lane, Brghm, Marquis; O-Monterey, Montclair
V8, 427.0	4.23 × 3.78	410	O-Comet htps and 2d sedans
V8, 427.0	4.23 × 3.78	425	O-Comet htps and 2d sedans
V8, 428.0	4.13 × 3.98	345	S-S-55; O-other full-size

1968

Comet (wb 116.0)		Wght	Price	Prod
01	htp cpe	3,166	2,477	16,693

Montego (wb 116.0; wgn-113.0)		Wght	Price	Prod
06	sdn 4d	3,062	2,504	18,492
07	htp cpe	3,138	2,552	15,002
08	MX wgn 4d	3,460	2,876	9,328
10	MX sdn 4d *	3,088	2,657	18,413
11	MX htp cpe *	3,162	2,676	25,827
12	MX conv cpe	3,374	2,935	3,248

Cyclone (wb 116.0)		Wght	Price	Prod
15	fstbk htp cpe	3,407	2,768	6,165
15	GT fstbk htp cpe	3,430	2,936	6,105
17	htp cpe	3,361	2,768	1,034
17	GT htp cpe	3,380	2,936	334

Cougar (wb 111.0)*		Wght	Price	Prod
91	htp cpe	3,134	2,933	81,014
93	XR7 htp cpe	3,174	3,232	32,712

Monterey (wb 123.0)		Wght	Price	Prod
44	sdn 4d	3,895	3,052	30,727
45	conv cpe	3,977	3,436	1,515
47	htp cpe	3,854	3,133	15,845
48	htp sdn	3,892	3,207	8,927

Montclair (wb 123.0)		Wght	Price	Prod
54	sdn 4d	3,897	3,331	7,255
57	htp cpe	3,882	3,387	3,497
58	htp sdn	3,907	3,459	4,008

Park Lane (wb 123.0)		Wght	Price	Prod
64	sdn 4d **	4,019	3,552	6,408
65	conv cpe	4,122	3,822	1,112
67	htp cpe	3,955	3,575	2,584
68	htp sdn **	4,000	3,647	10,390

Marquis (wb 123.0)		Wght	Price	Prod
69	htp cpe	3,987	3,685	3,965

Station Wagon (wb 119.0)		Wght	Price	Prod
72	Commuter 4d, 6P	4,212	3,441	3,497
72	Commuter 4d, 9P	4,331	3,569	5,191
76	Colony Park 4d, 6P	4,259	3,460	5,674
76	Colony Park 4d, 6P	4,295	3,888	15,505

*Includes cars with Brougham trim option.
**Includes cars with GT and GTE package options.

1968 Engines	bore × stroke	bhp	availability
L6, 200.0	3.68 × 3.15	115	S-Comet, Montego
V8, 289.0	4.00 × 2.87	195	S-base Cougars; O-Comet
V8, 302.0	4.00 × 3.00	210	S-Cougar Cyclone, O-Montego
V8, 302.0	4.00 × 3.00	230	O-Cougar, Montego
V8, 390.0	4.05 × 3.78	265	S-full-size w/man; O-Montego, Cyclone
V8, 390.0	4.05 × 3.78	280	S-full-size w/auto; O-Cougar

Mercury

	bore×stroke	bhp	availability
V8, 390.0	4.05×3.78	315	S-P Lane, Brghm, Marquis; O-other full-size
V8, 390.0	4.05×3.78	325	S-Cougar GT; O-Montego exc MX wgn, Cyclone, Cougar, XR7
V8, 427.0	4.23×3.78	390	S-Cougar GTE; O-Montego htps
V8, 428.0	4.13×3.98	340	O-full-size only

1969

Comet (wb 116.0)

		Wght	Price	Prod
01	htp cpe	3,175	2,532	14,104

Montego (wb 116.0; wgn-113.0)

		Wght	Price	Prod
06	sdn 4d	3,140	2,556	21,950
07	htp cpe	3,154	2,605	17,785
08	MX wgn 4d	3,504	2,979	10,590
10	MX sdn 4d	3,174	2,718	16,148
10	MX Brougham sdn 4d	3,198	2,808	1,590
11	MX htp cpe	3,186	2,736	23,160
11	MX Brougham htp cpe	3,210	2,826	1,226

Cyclone (wb 116.0)

		Wght	Price	Prod
15	fstbk htp cpe	3,273	2,771	5,882
16	CJ fstbk htp cpe	3,634	3,224	3,261

Cougar (wb 111.0)

		Wght	Price	Prod
91	htp cpe	3,219	3,016	66,331
92	conv cpe	3,343	3,382	5,796
93	XR7 htp cpe	3,221	3,315	23,918
94	XR7 conv cpe	3,343	3,595	4,024

Monterey (wb 124.0, wgn 121.0)

		Wght	Price	Prod
44	sdn 4d	3,948	3,158	23,009
45	conv cpe	4,093	3,540	1,297
46	htp cpe	3,970	3,237	9,865
48	htp sdn	4,008	3,313	6,066
72	wgn 4d, 6–9P	4,277	3,536	5,844

Monterey Custom (wb 124.0; wgn-121.0)

		Wght	Price	Prod
54	sdn 4d	4,013	3,377	7,103
56	htp cpe	3,998	3,459	2,898
58	htp sdn	4,023	3,533	2,827
74	wgn 4d, 6–9P	4,342	3,757	1,920

Marauder (wb 121.0)

		Wght	Price	Prod
60	htp cpe	4,044	3,368	9,031
61	X-100 htp cpe	4,191	4,091	5,635

Marquis (wb 124.0; wgn-121.0)

		Wght	Price	Prod
63	sdn 4d	4,226	3,857	16,787
63	Brougham sdn 4d	4,195	4,129	14,601
65	conv cpe	4,359	4,124	2,319
66	htp cpe	4,192	3,919	9,907
66	Brougham htp cpe	4,215	4,191	8,395
68	htp sdn	4,237	3,990	14,423
68	Brougham htp sdn	4,436	4,262	14,966
76	Colony Park wgn 4d, 6–9P	4,376	3,895	25,604

1969 Engines	bore×stroke	bhp	availability
L6, 250.0	3.68×3.91	155	S-Comet, Montego
V8, 302.0	4.00×3.00	220	S-Cyclone; O-Comet, Montego
V8, 351.0	4.00×3.50	250	S-Coug; O-Montego, Comet, Cyc
V8, 351.0	4.00×3.50	290	O-Coug, Comet, Cyc, Montego
V8, 390.0	4.05×3.78	265	S-Mntry, Mrdr, SW w/man
V8, 390.0	4.05×3.78	280	S-Mntry, Mrdr, SW w/man
V8, 390.0	4.05×3.78	320	O-Coug, Montego, Cyc, Comet
V8, 428.0	4.13×3.98	335	S-CJ; O-Cougar; Montego exc Brghm, SW, conv/sdns with 4spd
V8, 428.0	4.13×3.98	335	O-Coug, Cyc, Cyc CJ (ram air)
V8, 429.0	4.36×3.59	320	S-Marquis; O-other full-size

	bore×stroke	bhp	availability
V8, 429.0	4.36×3.59	360	S- X-100; O-other full-size

1970

Montego (wb 117.0; wgn-114.0)

		Wght	Price	Prod
01	htp cpe	2,859	2,645	21,298
02	sdn 4d	3,208	2,631	13,988
06	MX sdn 4d	3,215	2,728	16,708
07	MX htp cpe	3,228	2,740	15,533
08	MX wgn 4d, 6P	3,653	3,091	5,094
10	MX Brougham sdn 4d	3,238	2,896	3,315
11	MX Brougham htp cpe	3,248	2,915	8,074
12	MX Brougham htp sdn	3,268	3,037	3,685
18	MX Brghm wgn 4d, 6P	3,668	3,304	2,682

Cyclone (wb 117.0)

		Wght	Price	Prod
15	htp cpe	3,721	3,238	1,695
16	GT htp cpe	3,462	3,226	10,170
17	Spoiler htp cpe	3,773	3,759	1,631

Cougar (wb 111.1)

		Wght	Price	Prod
91	htp cpe	3,285	3,114	49,479
92	conv cpe	3,382	3,480	2,322
93	XR7 htp cpe	3,311	3,413	18,565
94	XR7 conv cpe	3,408	3,692	1,977

Monterey (wb 124.0; wgn-121.0)

		Wght	Price	Prod
44	sdn 4d	3,926	3,248	29,432
45	conv cpe	4,071	3,668	581
46	htp cpe	3,890	3,329	9,359
48	htp sdn	3,961	3,406	5,032
72	wgn 4d, 6P	4,235	3,682	1,657
72	wgn 4d, 9P	4,327	3,774	3,507

Monterey Custom (wb 124.0)

		Wght	Price	Prod
54	sdn 4d	3,931	3,520	4,823
56	htp cpe	3,922	3,600	1,357
58	htp sdn	3,973	3,676	1,194

Marauder (wb 121.0)

		Wght	Price	Prod
60	htp cpe	3,972	3,503	3,397
61	X-100 htp cpe	4,128	4,136	2,646

Marquis (wb 124.0; wgn-121.0)

		Wght	Price	Prod
62	Brougham sdn 4d	4,166	4,367	14,920
63	sdn 4d	4,121	4,052	14,394
64	Brougham htp cpe	4,119	4,428	7,113
65	conv cpe	4,337	4,318	1,233
66	htp cpe	4,072	4,113	6,229
67	Brougham htp sdn	4,182	4,500	11,623
68	htp sdn	4,141	4,185	8,411
74	wgn 4d, 6P	4,347	3,930	959
74	wgn 4d, 9P	4,393	4,022	1,429
76	Colony Park wgn 4d, 6P	4,442	4,123	4,655
76	Colony Park wgn 4d, 9P	4,488	4,215	14,549

1970 Engines	bore×stroke	bhp	availability
L6, 250.0	3.68×3.91	155	S-Montego
V8, 302.0	4.00×3.00	220	O-Montego
V8, 302.0	4.00×3.00	290	O-Cougar Eliminator
V8, 351.0	4.00×3.50	250	S-Cyclone, Cougar; O-Montego
V8, 351.0	4.00×3.50	300	S-Cgr Elmntr; O-Coug, Montego
V8, 390.0	4.05×3.78	265	S-Monterey, Marauder, C. Park w/man
V8, 390.0	4.05×3.78	280	S-above models w/auto
V8, 428.0	4.13×3.98	335	O-Cougar
V8, 429.0	4.36×3.59	320	S-Marquis exc Colony Park
V8, 429.0	4.36×3.59	360	S-Cyc, Mrdr X-100; O-Montego exc Spoiler, Mntry, Mrdr, C Park
V8, 429.0	4.36×3.59	370	S-Spoiler; O-Cyclone, GT*
V8, 429.0	4.36×3.59	375	O-all Cyclone
V8, 429.0	4.36×3.59	375	O-all Cyclone ("Boss")

*Available in Ram-Air and non-Ram-Air versions.

1971

Comet (wb 109.9; 2d-103.0)		Wght	Price	Prod
30	sdn 4d	2,789	2,446	28,116
31	fstbk sdn 2d	2,700	2,387	54,884

Montego (wb 117.0; wgns-114.0)		Wght	Price	Prod
01	hdtp cpe	3,229	2,893	9,623
02	sdn 4d	3,228	2,888	5,718
06	MX sdn 4d	3,235	2,994	13,559
07	MX hdtp cpe	3,236	3,007	13,719
08	MX wgn 5d	3,651	3,331	3,698
10	MX Brougham sdn 4d	3,258	3,189	1,565
11	MX Brougham hdtp cpe	3,275	3,201	2,851
12	MX Brougham hdtp sdn	3,302	3,273	1,156
18	MX Villager wgn 5d	3,666	3,572	2,121

Cyclone (wb 117.0)		Wght	Price	Prod
15	fstbk hdtp cpe	3,595	3,369	444
16	GT fstbk hdtp cpe	3,492	3,680	2,287
17	Spoiler fstbk hdtp cpe	3,585	3,801	353

Cougar (wb 113.0)		Wght	Price	Prod
91	hdtp cpe	3,331	3,289	34,008
92	conv	3,461	3,681	1,723
93	XR7 hdtp cpe	3,360	3,629	25,416
94	XR7 conv	3,480	3,877	1,717

Monterey (wb 124.0; wgns-121.0)		Wght	Price	Prod
44	sdn 4d	4,029	3,858	22,744
46	hdtp cpe	3,959	3,900	9,099
48	hdtp sdn	4,024	3,968	2,483
72	wgn 5d 3S	4,451	4,410	4,160
72	wgn 5d 2S	4,401	4,283	4,160
54	Custom sdn 4d	4,144	4,030	12,411
56	Custom hdtp cpe	4,074	4,113	4,508
58	Custom hdtp sdn	4,140	4,185	1,397

Marquis (wb 124.0; wgns-121.0)		Wght	Price	Prod
63	sdn 4d	4,346	4,474	16,030
66	hdtp cpe	4,276	4,557	7,726
68	hdtp sdn	4,341	4,624	5,491
74	wgn 5d 3S	4,501	4,674	2,158
74	wgn 5d 2S	4,451	4,547	2,158
62	Brougham sdn 4d	4,346	4,880	25,790
64	Brougham hdtp cpe	4,276	4,963	14,570
67	Brougham hdtp sdn	4,341	5,033	13,781
76	Colony Park wgn 5d 3S	4,562	4,933	20,004
76	Colony Park wgn 5d 2S	4,512	4,806	20,004

1971 Engines	bore×stroke	bhp	availability
L6, 170.0	3.50×3.94	100	S-Comet
L6, 200.0	3.68×3.15	115	O-Comet
L6, 250.0	3.68×3.91	145	S-Montego; O-Comet
V8, 302.0	4.00×3.00	210	O-Montego, Comet
V8, 351.0	4.00×3.50	240	S-Cyc GT, Cgr, Mntry exc Cus & wgn
V8, 351.0	4.00×3.50	285	S-Cyc exc GT; O-Cougar
V8, 400.0	4.00×4.00	260	S-Mntry Cus Marq wgns
V8, 429.0	4.36×3.59	320/360	S-Marq wgns; O-Mintry, Marquis exc wgns
V8, 429.0	4.36×3.59	370	O-Cyclone, Cougar

1972

Comet (wb 109.9; 2d-103.0)		Wght	Price	Prod
30	sdn 4d	2,674	2,398	29,092
31	fstbk sdn 2d	2,579	2,342	53,267

Montego (wb 118.0; 2d-114.0)		Wght	Price	Prod
02	sdn 4d	3,454	2,843	8,658
03	hdtp cpe	3,390	2,848	9,963
04	MX sdn 4d	3,485	2,951	23,387
07	MX hdtp cpe	3,407	2,971	25,802

		Wght	Price	Prod
08	MX wgn 5d	3,884	3,264	6,268
10	MX Brougham sdn 4d	3,512	3,127	17,540
11	MX Brougham hdtp cpe	3,433	3,137	28,417
18	MX Villager wgn 5d	3,907	3,438	9,237
16	GT fstbk hdtp cpe	3,517	3,346	5,820

Cougar (wb 112.1)		Wght	Price	Prod
91	hdtp cpe	3,282	3,016	23,731
92	conv	3,412	3,370	1,240
93	XR7 hdtp cpe	3,298	3,323	26,802
94	XR7 conv	3,451	3,547	1,929

Monterey (wb 124.0; wgns-121.0)		Wght	Price	Prod
44	sdn 4d	4,136	3,793	19,012
46	hdtp cpe	4,086	3,832	6,731
48	hdtp sdn	4,141	3,896	1,416
72	wgn 5d 3S	4,545	4,334	4,644
72	wgn 5d 2S	4,495	4,212	4,644
54	Custom sdn 4d	4,225	3,956	16,879
56	Custom hdtp cpe	4,175	4,035	5,910
58	Custom hdtp sdn	4,230	4,103	1,583

Marquis (wb 124.0; wgns-121.0)		Wght	Price	Prod
63	sdn 4d	4,386	4,493	14,122
66	hdtp cpe	4,236	4,572	5,507
68	hdtp sdn	4,391	4,637	1,583
74	wgn 5d 3S	4,589	4,567	2,085
74	wgn 5d 2S	4,539	4,445	2,085
62	Brougham sdn 4d	4,436	4,890	38,242
64	Brougham hdtp cpe	4,386	4,969	20,064
67	Brougham hdtp sdn	4,441	5,034	12,841
76	Colony Park wgn 5d 3S	4,629	4,672	20,192
76	Colony Park wgn 5d 2S	4,579	4,550	20,192

1972 Engines	bore×stroke	bhp	availability
L6, 170.0	3.50×3.94	82	S-Comet
L6, 200.0	3.68×3.15	91	O-Comet
L6, 250.0	3.68×3.91	95	O-Montego
L6, 250.0	3.68×3.91	98	O-Comet
V8, 302.0	4.00×3.00	140	S-Montego
V8, 302.0	4.00×3.00	143	S-Comet
V8, 351.0	4.00×3.50	161	O-Montego
V8, 351.0	4.00×3.50	163	S-Mntry exc Cus wgn
V8, 351.0	4.00×3.50	164	S-Cougar
V8, 351.0	4.00×3.50	262/266	O-Cougar
V8, 400.0	4.00×4.00	168	O-Montego
V8, 400.0	4.00×4.00	172	S-Mntry Cus & Marq wgns
V8, 429.0	4.36×3.59	205	O-Montego
V8, 429.0	4.36×3.59	208	S-Marquis exc wgn

1973

Comet (wb 109.9; 2d-103.0)		Wght	Price	Prod
30	sdn 4d	2,904	2,489	28,984
31	fstbk sdn 2d	2,813	2,432	55,707

Montego (wb 118.0; 2d-114.0)		Wght	Price	Prod
02	sdn 4d	3,719	2,916	7,459
03	hdtp cpe	3,653	2,926	7,082
04	MX sdn 4d	3,772	3,009	25,300
07	MX hdtp cpe	3,683	3,041	27,812
08	MX wgn 5d	4,124	3,417	7,012
10	MX Brougham sdn 4d	3,813	3,189	24,329
11	MX Brougham hdtp cpe	3,706	3,209	40,951
18	MX Villager wgn 5d	4,167	3,606	12,396
16	GT fstbk hdtp cpe	3,662	3,413	4,464

Cougar (wb 113.0)		Wght	Price	Prod
91	hdtp cpe	3,396	3,372	21,069
92	conv	3,524	3,726	1,284
93	XR7 hdtp cpe	3,416	3,679	35,110
94	XR7 conv	3,530	3,903	3,165

Monterey (wb 124.0; wgns 121.0)

44	sdn 4d	4,225	3,961	16,622
46	hdtp cpe	4,167	4,004	6,452
72	wgn 5d 3S	4,673	4,501	⎫ 4,275
72	wgn 5d 2S	4,623	4,379	⎭
54	Custom sdn 4d	4,295	4,124	20,873
56	Custom hdtp cpe	4,239	4,207	6,962

Marquis (wb 124.0; wgns-121.0)

63	sdn 4d	4,477	4,648	15,250
66	hdtp cpe	4,411	4,727	5,973
68	hdtp sdn	4,453	4,782	2,185
74	wgn 5d 3S	4,745	4,730	⎫ 2,464
74	wgn 5d 2S	4,695	4,608	⎭
62	Brougham sdn 4d	4,547	5,072	46,624
64	Brougham hdtp cpe	4,475	5,151	22,770
67	Brougham hdtp sdn	4,565	5,206	10,613
76	Colony Park wgn 5d 3S	4,780	4,835	⎫ 23,283
76	Colony Park wgn 5d 2S	4,730	4,713	⎭

1973 Engines	bore×stroke	bhp	availability
L6, 200.0	3.68×3.15	84	S-Comet 6
L6, 250.0	3.68×3.91	88	O-Comet 6
L6, 250.0	3.68×3.91	92	O-Montego
V8, 302.0	4.00×3.00	137/138	S-Montego/Comet
V8, 351.0	4.00×3.50	159/161	S-Mntry exc Cus/wgn; O-Mntgo
V8, 351.0	4.00×3.50	168	S-Cougar
V8, 351.0	4.00×3.50	264	O-Cougar (CJ option)
V8, 400.0	4.00×4.00	168/171	S-Mntry Cus/wgn; O-Mntgo
V8, 429.0	4.36×3.59	171	S-Marquis exc wgn; O-Marquis wgn
V8, 429.0	4.36×3.59	198/200	O-Monterey,Montego
V8, 460.0	4.36×3.85	202	O-Monterey, Marquis

1974

Comet (wb 109.9; 2d-103.0)

		Wght	Price	Prod
30	sdn 4d	2,969	3,042	60,944
31	fstbk sdn 2d	2,861	3,008	64,751

Montego (wb 118.0; 2d-114.0)

02	sdn 4d	4,062	3,360	5,674
03	hdtp cpe	3,977	3,327	7,645
04	MX sdn 4d	4,092	3,478	19,446
07	MX hdtp cpe	3,990	3,443	20,957
08	MX wgn 5d	4,426	4,083	4,085
10	MX Brougham sdn 4d	4,143	3,680	13,467
11	MX Brougham hdtp cpe	4,010	3,646	20,511
18	MX Villager wgn 5d	4,463	4,307	6,234

Cougar (wb 114.0)

93	XR7 hdtp cpe	4,255	4,706	91,670

Monterey (wb 124.0; wgns-121.0)

44	sdn 4d	4,559	4,367	6,185
46	hdtp cpe	4,506	4,410	2,003
72	wgn 5d 3S	4,966	4,853	⎫ 1,669
72	wgn 5d 2S	4,916	4,731	⎭
54	Custom sdn 4d	4,561	4,480	13,113
56	Custom hdtp cpe	4,504	4,523	4,510

Marquis (wb 124.0; wgns-121.0)

63	sdn 4d	4,757	5,080	6,910
66	hdtp cpe	4,698	5,080	2,633
68	hdtp sdn	4,753	5,080	784
74	wgn 5d 3S	5,023	5,082	⎫ 1,111
74	wgn 5d 2S	4,973	4,960	⎭
62	Brougham sdn 4d	4,833	5,519	24,477
64	Brougham hdtp cpe	4,762	5,519	10,207
67	Brougham hdtp sdn	4,853	5,519	4,189
76	Colony Park wgn 5d 3S	5,056	5,188	⎫ 10,802
76	Colony Park wgn 5d 2S	5,006	5,066	⎭

1975 Bobcat Villager wagon

1974 Engines	bore×stroke	bhp	availability
L6, 200.0	3.68×3.15	84	S-Comet
L6, 250.0	3.68×3.91	91	O-Comet, Monterey
V8, 302.0	4.00×3.00	140	S-Comet, Montego
V8, 351.0	4.00×3.50	162	S-Cougar; O-Montego
V8, 400.0	4.00×4.00	170	O-Montgo, Cgr, Mntry
V8, 460.0	4.36×3.85	195	S-Marquis; O-Mntgo, Mntry
V8, 460.0	4.36×3.85	220	O-Cougar

1975

Bobcat (wb 94.5; wgn-94.8)

		Wght	Price	Prod
20	Runabout htchbk sdn 3d	2,535	3,189	20,651
22	Villager wgn 3d	2,668	3,481	13,583

Comet (wb 109.9; 2d-103.0)

30	sdn 4d	3,193	3,270	31,080
31	fstbk sdn 2d	3,070	3,236	22,768

Monarch (wb 109.9)

34	sdn 4d	3,195	3,822	34,307
35	sdn 2d	3,142	3,764	29,151
37	Ghia sdn 4d	3,281	4,349	⎫ 22,723
37	Grand sdn 4d	3,432	5,375	⎭
38	Ghia sdn 2d	3,231	4,291	17,755

Montego (wb 118.0; 2d-114.0)

02	sdn 4d	4,066	4,128	4,142
03	hdtp cpe	4,003	4,092	4,051
04	MX sdn 4d	4,111	4,328	16,033
07	MX hdtp cpe	4,030	4,304	13,666
08	MX wgn 5d	4,464	4,674	4,508
10	MX Brougham sdn 4d	4,130	4,498	8,235
11	MX Brougham hdtp cpe	4,054	4,453	8,791
18	MX Villager wgn 5d	4,522	4,909	5,754

Cougar (wb 114.0)

93	XR7 hdtp cpe	4,108	5,218	62,987

Marquis (wb 124.0; wgns-121.0)

63	sdn 4d	4,513	5,115	20,058
66	hdtp cpe	4,470	5,049	6,807
74	wgn 5d 3S	4,930	5,538	⎫ 1,904
74	wgn 5d 2S	4,880	5,411	⎭
62	Brougham sdn 4d	4,799	6,037	19,667
64	Brougham hdtp cpe	4,747	5,972	7,125
60	Grand Marquis sdn 4d	4,815	6,469	12,307
61	Grand Marquis hdtp cpe	4,762	6,403	4,945
76	Colony Park wgn 5d 2S	5,003	5,725	⎫ 11,652
76	Colony Park wgn 5d 2S	4,953	5,598	⎭

1975 Engines	bore×stroke	bhp	availability
L4, 140.0	3.78×3.13	83	S-Bobcat
V6, 170.8	3.66×2.70	97	O-Bobcat
L6, 200.0	3.68×3.15	75	S-Mnrch exc Ghia; O-Comet
L6, 250.0	3.68×3.91	72	S-Mnrch Ghia; O-Cmt, Mntry
V8, 302.0	4.00×3.00	122	S-Comet

			Wght	Price	Prod
V8, 302.0	4.00×3.00	129	S-Monarch		
V8, 351.0	4.00×3.50	148/150	S-Cougar,Montego		
V8, 351.0	4.00×3.50	154	O-Monarch		
V8, 400.0	4.00×4.00	158	S-Marq exc wgn & Bham; O-Mntgo, Cgr		
V8, 460.0	4.36×3.85	216	S-Grand Marq, wgn & Marq Brghm; O-Mntgo, Cgr, Marq		

1976

	Bobcat (wb 94.5; wgn-94.8)	Wght	Price	Prod
20	MPG Runabout htchbk sdn 3d	2,535	3,338	28,905
22	MPG Villager wgn 3d	2,668	3,643	18,731

	Comet (wb 109.9; 2d-103.0)			
30	sdn 4d	3,058	3,465	21,006
31	fstbk sdn 2d	2,952	3,398	15,068

	Monarch (wb 109.9)			
34	sdn 4d	3,195	3,864	56,351
35	sdn 2d	3,142	3,773	47,466
37	Ghia sdn 4d	3,218	4,422	27,056
37	Grand sdn 4d	3,432	5,740	
38	Ghia sdn 2d	3,231	4,331	14,950

	Montego (wb 118.0; 2d-114.0)			
02	sdn 4d	4,133	4,343	3,403
03	hdtp cpe	4,057	4,299	2,287
04	MX sdn 4d	4,133	4,498	12,666
07	MX hdtp cpe	4,085	4,465	12,367
08	MX wgn 5d	4,451	4,778	5,012
10	MX Brougham sdn 4d	4,150	4,670	5,043
11	MX Brougham hdtp cpe	4,097	4,621	3,905
18	MX Villager wgn 5d	4,478	5,065	6,412

	Cougar (wb 114.0)			
93	XR7 hdtp cpe	4,168	5,125	83,765

	Marquis (wb 124.0; wgns-121.0)			
63	sdn 4d	4,460	5,063	28,212
66	hdtp cpe	4,436	5,063	10,450
62	Brougham sdn 4d	4,693	6,035	22,411
64	Brougham hdtp cpe	4,652	5,955	10,431
60	Grand Marquis sdn 4d	4,723	6,528	17,650
61	Grand Marquis hdtp cpe	4,679	6,439	9,207
74	wgn 5d 3S	4,824	5,401	2,493
74	wgn 5d 2S	4,796	5,275	
76	Colony Park wgn 5d 3S	4,906	5,716	15,114
76	Colony Park wgn 5d 2S	4,878	5,590	

1976 Engines	bore×stroke	bhp	availability
L4, 140.0	3.78×3.13	92	S-Bobcat
V6, 170.8	3.66×2.70	100	O-Bobcat
L6, 200.0	3.68×3.15	81	S-Mnrch exc Ghia; O-Comet
L6, 250.0	3.68×3.91	90	S-Mnrch Ghia; O-Cmt, Mnrch
V8, 302.0	4.00×3.00	134	S-Monarch
V8, 302.0	4.00×3.00	138	S-Comet
V8, 351.0	4.00×3.50	154	S-Montego exc wgn
V8, 351.0	4.00×3.50	152	S-Mntgo wgn, Cgr; O-Mnrch
V8, 400.0	4.00×4.00	180	S-Marq; O-Mntgo, Cgr
V8, 460.0	4.36×3.85	202	O-Mntgo, Cgr, Marquis

1977

	Bobcat (wb 94.5; wgn-94.8)	Wght	Price	Prod
20	Runabout htchbk sdn 3d	2,369	3,438	18,405*
22	wgn 3d	2,505	3,629	13,047*
22	Villager wgn 3d	—	3,771	

	Comet (wb 109.9; 2d-103.0)			
30	sdn 4d	3,065	3,617	12,436
31	fstbk sdn 2d	2,960	3,544	9,109

	Monarch (wb 109.9)	Wght	Price	Prod
34	sdn 4d	3,250	4,154	55,952
35	sdn 2d	3,200	4,076	44,509
37	Ghia sdn 4d	3,382	4,722	16,545
38	Ghia sdn 2d	3,321	4,643	11,051

	Cougar (wb 118.0; 2d-114.0)			
90	sdn 4d	3,893	4,832	15,256
91	hdtp cpe	3,811	4,700	5,910
92	wgn 5d	4,434	5,104	4951
93	XR7 hdtp cpe	3,909	5,274	124,799
94	Brougham sdn 4d	3,946	5,230	16,946
95	Brougham hdtp cpe	3,852	4,990	8,392
96	Villager wgn 5d	4,482	5,363	8,569

	Marquis (wb 124.0; wgns-121.0)			
63	sdn 4d	4,326	5,496	36,103
66	hdtp cpe	4,293	5,496	13,242
62	Brougham sdn 4d	4,408	6,324	29,411
64	Brougham hdtp cpe	4,350	6,229	12,237
60	Grand Marquis hdtp sdn	4,572	6,975	31,231
61	Grand Marquis hdtp cpe	4,516	6,880	13,445
74	wgn 5d 3S	4,678	5,794	20,363
74	wgn 5d 2S	4,628	5,631	

1977 Engines	bore×stroke	bhp	availability
L4, 140.0	3.78×3.13	89	S-Bobcat
V6, 170.8	3.66×2.70	93	O-Bobcat
L6, 200.0	3.68×3.15	96	S-Monarch exc Ghia; O-Cmt
L6, 250.0	3.68×3.91	98	S-Mnrch Ghia; O-Mnrch, Cmt
V8, 302.0	4.00×3.00	122	S-Monarch
V8, 302.0	4.00×3.00	130	S-Cougar exc wgn
V8, 302.0	4.00×3.00	137	S-Comet
V8, 351.0	4.00×3.50	149	O-Cougar exc wgn
V8, 351.0	4.00×3.50	161	S-Cgr wgn; O-Monarch
V8, 400.0	4.00×4.00	173	S-Marq exc Grand; O-Cgr
V8, 460.0	4.36×3.85	197	S-Grand Marquis; O-Marquis

*includes some cars built as 1978 models but sold as 1977 models.

1978

	Bobcat (wb 94.5; wgn-94.8)	Wght	Price	Prod
20	Runabout htchbk sdn 3d	2,389	3,830	23,428
22	wgn 3d	2,532	4,112	8,840
22	Villager wgn 3d	—	4,244	

	Zephyr (wb 105.5)			
31	sdn 2d L4/V6	2,594	3,777	27,673
32	sdn 4d L4/V6	2,636	3,863	47,334
35	Z-7 spt cpe L4/V6	2,630	4,154	44,569
36	wgn 5d L4/V6	2,744	4,216	32,596

	Monarch (wb 109.9)			
33	sdn 2d L6/V8	3,094	4,366	38,939

1977 Marquis Brougham hardtop sedan

1980 Zephyr two-door sedan with ES option

		Wght	Price	Prod
34	sdn 4d L6/V8	3,138	4,457	52,775

Cougar (wb 118.0; 2d-114.0)

91	hdtp cpe	3,761	5,052	21,398
92	sdn 4d	3,848	5,179	25,364
93	XR7 hdtp cpe	3,865	5,720	166,508

Marquis (wb 124.0; wgns-121.0)

61	hdtp cpe	4,296	5,897	27,793
62	sdn 4d	4,328	5,949	11,176
63	Brougham hdtp cpe	4,317	6,525	10,368
64	Brougham sdn 4d	4,346	6,638	26,030
65	Grand Marquis hdtp cpe	4,342	7,290	15,624
66	Grand Marquis sdn 4d	4,414	7,399	37,753
74	wgn 5d 3S	4,606	6,292	16,883
74	wgn 5d 2S	4,578	6,106	

1978 Engines	bore×stroke	bhp	availability
L4, 140.0	3.78×3.13	88	S-Bobcat, Zephyr
V6, 170.6	3.66×2.70	90	O-Bobcat
L6, 200.0	3.68×3.13	85	S-Zephyr
L6, 250.0	3.68×3.91	97	S-Monarch
V8, 302.0	4.00×3.00	134	S-Cougar
V8, 302.0	4.00×3.00	139	S-Monarch, O-Zephyr
V8, 351.0	4.00×3.50	144/145	O-Cougar, S-Marquis
V8, 351.0	4.00×3.50	152	O-Cougar
V8, 400.0	4.00×4.00	160	O-Marquis
V8, 400.0	4.00×4.00	166	O-Cougar
V8, 460.0	4.36×3.85	202	O-Marquis

1979

Bobcat (wb 94.5; wgn-94.8)

		Wght	Price	Prod
20	Runabout htchbk sdn 3d	2,424	4,104	35,667
22	wgn 3d	2,565	4,410	9,119
22	Villager wgn 3d	—	4,523	

Capri (wb 100.4)

14	htchbk cpe 3d	2,548	4,872	92,432
16	Ghia htchbk cpe 3d	2,645	5,237	17,712

Zephyr (wb 105.5)

31	sdn 2d	2,518	4,253	15,920
32	sdn 4d	2,582	4,370	41,316
35	Z-7 spt cpe	2,553	4,504	42,923
36	wgn 5d	2,683	4,647	25,218

Monarch (wb 109.9)

33	sdn 2d	3,110	4,735	28,285
34	sdn 4d L6/V8	3,151	4,841	47,594

Cougar (wb 118.0; 2d 114.0)

91	hdtp cpe	3,792	5,379	2,831
92	sdn 4d	3,843	5,524	5,605
93	XR7 hdtp cpe	3,883	6,430	163,716

Marquis (wb 114.3)

61	hdtp cpe	3,507	6,292	10,035
62	sdn 4d	3,557	6,387	32,289
63	Brougham hdtp cpe	3,540	6,986	10,627
64	Brougham sdn 4d	3,605	7,176	24,682
65	Grand Marquis hdtp cpe	3,592	7,721	11,066
66	Grand Marquis sdn 4d	3,659	7,909	32,349
74	wgn 5d 3S	3,825	6,894	5,994
74	wgn 5d 2S	3,775	6,701	
76	Colony Park wgn 5d 3S	3,850	7,688	13,758
76	Colony Park wgn 5d 2S	3,800	7,495	

1979 Engines	bore×stroke	bhp	availability
L4, 140.0	3.78×3.13	88	S-Bobcat, Zephyr, Capri
L4T, 140.0	3.78×3.13	140	O-Capri
V6, 170.6	3.66×2.70	102	O-Bobcat
V6, 170.6	3.66×2.70	109	O-Capri
L6, 200.0	3.68×3.13	85	O-Zephyr
L6, 250.0	3.68×3.91	97	S-Monarch
V8, 302.0	4.00×3.00	129/133	S-Marquis/Cougar
V8, 302.0	4.00×3.00	137	S-Monarch
V8, 302.0	4.00×3.00	140	O-Capri, Zephyr
V8, 351.0	4.00×3.50	135	S-Cougar XR7
V8, 351.0	4.00×3.50	138	O-Marquis
V8, 351.0	4.00×3.50	151	O-Cougar

1980

Bobcat (wb 94.5; wgn-94.8)

		Wght	Price	Prod
20	Runabout htchbk sdn 3d	2,445	4,764	28,103
22	wgn 3d	2,573	5,070	5,547
22	Villager wgn 3d	—	5,183	

Capri (wb 100.4)

14	htchbk cpe 3d	2,566	5,672	72,009
16	Ghia htchbk cpe 3d	2,651	5,968	7,975

Zephyr (wb 105.5)

31	sdn 2d	2,607	5,041	10,977
32	sdn 4d	2,649	5,158	40,399
35	Z-7 spt cpe	2,646	5,335	19,486
36	wgn 5d	2,771	5,364	20,341

Monarch (wb 109.9)

33	sdn 2d L6/V8	3,126	5,628	8,772
34	sdn 4d L6/V8	3,180	5,751	21,746

Cougar (wb 108.4)

93	XR7 cpe	3,191	7,045	58,028

Marquis (wb 114.3)

61	sdn 2d	3,450	7,075	2,521
62	sdn 4d	3,488	7,185	13,018
63	Brougham sdn 2d	3,476	7,860	2,353
64	Brougham sdn 4d	3,528	8,057	8,819
65	Grand Marquis sdn 2d	3,504	8,631	3,434
66	Grand Marquis sdn 4d	3,519	8,824	15,995
74	wgn 5d 3S	3,747	7,782	2,407
74	wgn 5d 2S	3,697	7,583	
76	Colony Park wgn 5d 3S	3,793	8,676	5,781
76	Colony Park wgn 5d 2S	3,743	8,477	

1980 Engines	bore×stroke	bhp	availability
L4, 140.0	3.78×3.13	88	S-Bobcat, Zphyr, Capri
L4T, 140.0	3.78×3.13	140	O-Capri, Zephyr*
L6, 200.0	3.68×3.13	91	S-Capri, Zephyr
L6, 250.0	3.68×3.91	90	S-Monarch
V8, 255.0	3.68×3.00	115	S-Cougar
V8, 255.0	3.68×3.00	118/119	O-Capri/Zephyr, Monarch
V8, 302.0	4.00×3.00	130/131	S-Marquis/O-Cougar
V8, 302.0	4.00×3.00	134	O-Monarch
V8, 351.0	4.00×3.50	140	O-Marquis

*withdrawn for Zephyr after announcement; production doubtful

Nash

Nash-Kelvinator Corp. (1940-53); Nash Division, American Motors Corporation (1953-57)
Kenosha, Wisconsin

Crusty Charles W. Nash resigned as president of General Motors in 1916, and decided to build a car under his own name. Two years later, he bought the Thomas B. Jeffrey Company of Kenosha, Wisconsin, which manufactured the slow-selling Jeffrey and had earlier built a car called the Rambler. Now renamed Nash Motors, the firm charged up the sales charts, reaching as high as eighth place in industry production during the 1920s. Along the way, it introduced the low-cost, six-cylinder Ajax, and expanded by absorbing Mitchell and LaFayette (see entry). None of these efforts were as successful as the Nash itself, and all were gone by 1930. The firm suffered from the general economic malaise following the stock market crash, but found salvation by merging with the Kelvinator appliance company in 1937. George Mason, Kelvinator's cigar-chomping president, continued in that role with the new combine, while Charles Nash remained chairman of the board. By 1940, the firm had turned the corner and was profitable once more.

Early-'30s Nashes were sumptuous, beautifully styled automobiles with many special features. A very ordinary side-valve six powered the low-line models through 1933. More interesting were the "Twin Ignition" cars, offered in both six- and eight-cylinder form. The name referred to two sets of spark plugs and points plus dual condensers and coils, all operating from a single distributor. The Twin Ignition six had appeared in 1928; the Eight was new for 1930. Buick, which Charles Nash once headed in his GM days, traditionally espoused overhead valves, so it wasn't surprising that both these engines had them. The eight lasted far longer than the six (gaining power and displacement over time), but cost factors and public demand for greater economy led Nash to drop it. The T.I. Eights of 1935-39 were powered by a smaller-displacement unit first seen in 1932. All Nash eights in these years carried nine main bearings.

Styling on the 1930 T.I. Nashes was classically upright. The look was retained through 1934 despite a general industry shift to more rounded, streamlined shapes. Seven-passenger sedans and limousines riding long-wheelbase chassis were available in both six- and eight-cylinder T.I. series, along with tourers, coupes, cabriolets, and Ambassadors in the Eight range. The Ambassadors, luxuriously upholstered for five well-heeled passengers, were nicely proportioned.

Charles Nash believed in offering a lot for the money, and his cars bristled with innovations. Twin Ignition Eights had cowl vents, dashboard starter button, shatterproof glass, and automatic radiator vents in 1930; downdraft carburetors and Bijur automatic chassis lubrication for '31; "Syncro-Safety Shift" (with the gearlever sprouting from the dash) and optional freewheeling for 1932; combination ignition and steering wheel locks for '33; and aircraft-type instruments for 1934. Many of these features were shared with the cheaper side-valve eight offered for 1931-

1930 Twin Ignition Eight seven-passenger touring

1931 Series 870 Special four-door sedan

1932 Series 980 convertible sedan

1933 Big Six four-door Town Sedan

33 in the 870/970 Standard series. This engine fell midway between the side-valve six and Twin Ignition eight in displacement and output, and prices were arranged accordingly.

Like most companies, Nash was damaged badly by the Depression. It regularly built over 100,000 cars a year in

1934 Ambassador Eight four-door sedan

1937 Ambassador Six business coupe

1935 Advanced Six six-passenger victoria

1938 LaFayette Deluxe four-door trunkback sedan

1936 "400" Deluxe special cabriolet

1939 Ambassador Six business coupe

the late '20s, but wouldn't reach that figure in the 1930s and ranked 11th, 12th, or 13th in production. The bottom was 1933, when output totaled less than 15,000 units. Thus, 1934 was clearly a year for new approaches. A planned restyle for the larger models was postponed a year, while resources were put into the LaFayette (see entry).

Nash built its one-millionth car in 1934, and looked forward to better times. A severe cropping in the lineup left only three separate series, all with overhead-valve engines. Hydraulic brakes arrived for all 1935 models, but the Ambassador lost its smooth 322 engine and shared the 260.8-cid unit with the Advanced Eight.

The long-awaited restyle (called Aeroform design) appeared for '35, and it was a good one. The fully updated look featured sweeping fastback or curved notchback bodies and skirted fenders, and some sedans were available with swept-down decks and concealed spare tires.

Hoods were louvered, radiators vee'd, and wheels were all-steel "artillery" types. It was a good year with close to 45,000 cars. Things were even better in 1936, reaching 53,000 units with the help of the low-priced 400 series.

Nash maintained its three-tier lineup for 1937, with the new LaFayette replacing the 400 on the same chassis. The Ambassador Six rode a 121-inch wheelbase and used the 234.8-cid engine with 105 bhp; the Ambassador Eight, on a 125-inch wheelbase, continued to use the 260.8-cid Twin Ignition eight and had 105 bhp. This spread of engine types and wheelbases would continue throughout the end of the decade, with horsepower gradually increasing. Styling became more conventional as the years passed. The 1937 models bore a distinct resemblance to the Airstream Chryslers, for instance, which seemed to satisfy the public: Nash had its best year of the decade in '37, building 85,949 cars.

In 1938, however, Kenosha marched back down the hill

it had climbed so laboriously. Production sank to 32,000 units and the new Nash-Kelvinator Corporation lost $7.7 million. The cars received a severe facelift, and now resembled the dumpier GM products, though the major cause of the sales drop was the 1938 recession. Yet despite the unsuccessful appearance changes and a bad year for the economy in general, Nash still had an innovation that year: the "Weather-Eye" combination heating and ventilation system. This pioneering feature was one of the best "climatizers" ever invented, and it remained so for the next 20 years.

A total restyle was deemed necessary for 1939. Fortunately, it was a good one. The ponderous '38 look with its busy front and bustle back was eliminated. Nash and LaFayette now featured a smooth, well-integrated nose with flush-fitting headlamps. A prow-like hood blended with a center grille composed of narrow, vertically stacked bars and flanked either side by chromed catwalk grilles. The result was neat and trim, and combined all the best design elements of the art-deco era. Production, at 66,000 units, was more than double that of 1938. Although Nash-Kelvinator lost $1.6 million this year, the future looked brighter in 1939 than it had for the last 10 years.

For Nash, 1940 marked the end of an era: the last Lafayette and the last use of separate body-and-chassis construction. The line consisted of the Lafayette Six and the Nash Ambassador with six-cylinder or straight-eight power. The six was a valve-in-head design, producing 99 horsepower in the Lafayette and 105 bhp in the Ambassador. Having seven main bearings, it was an exceptionally quiet and smooth-running unit, if not exactly speedy off the line. The refined nine-main-bearing Ambassador eight was also a valve-in-head power-plant, with 115 bhp. For about $150 more than the Lafayette, the Ambassador Six offered a four-inch longer wheelbase and more horsepower. Looks were similar. Both used strong, vertical, peaked grilles and smooth, flowing lines complemented by nicely rounded fenders. Body styles in all three series were exactly the same. Nash and Lafayette combined output recorded 62,131 units for the model year.

The unit body/chassis 600 for 1941 was an important breakthrough for Nash. (The designation, incidentally, stood for 600 miles to a 20-gallon tankful.) Styling was similar to the 1940 line, but different enough to be accepted as entirely new. It was a handsome package on a 112-inch wheelbase and price was remarkable: just $805 for the fastback four-door sedan, less than the price of a Ford V8. *Time* called it "the only completely new car in 1941," and sales were high. The 600 engine

1940 Ambassador Eight four-door fastback sedan

1940 Ambassador with custom cabriolet coachwork

1941 "600" DeLuxe four-door sedan

1941 Ambassador Eight All-Purpose cabriolet

was a 172.6-cid six. Eight different models were offered with Special or Deluxe trim, all either sedans or coupes. Cabriolets (two-door convertibles) were listed in the high-priced Ambassador Six line, with the 234 engine and a 121-inch wheelbase, and the Ambassador Eight that shared this same body and chassis. Altogether, 1941 proved to be very profitable. Nash-Kelvinator closed the fiscal year with a $4.6 million profit.

Nash built only 31,780 cars for the short 1942 model year. They had distinctive styling, the result of a big facelift. Following a design trend of the day, Nash adopted a low, wraparound grille made up of three horizontal bars. This motif was repeated on the fenders. The tall '41 frontispiece was dropped in favor of a vertical nameplate and small upper grille of horizontal bars. Parking lights appeared atop the front fenders and a larger hood ornament was used. The three-model lineup—600, Ambassador Six and Eight—remained, but fewer body styles were offered.

During the war, Nash-Kelvinator manufactured $600 million worth of aircraft engines and parts, munitions, cargo trailers, and binocular cases.

Nash finished third in the first postwar production race. That was calendar year 1945, which amounted to only four months of civilian car building. But the firm resumed operations earlier than most, and actually built 6148 cars during that period—one Nash for every two Chevrolets. In 1946, the first full postwar model year, Nash produced about 94,000 cars and ranked eighth; in 1947-48, having produced 101,000 and 110,000 units, it ran 10th and 11th. These early postwar years were good ones for the company, and profits were high.

In June 1948, cigar-chomping Nash president George W. Mason succeeded the venerable Charles W. Nash as chairman of the board. Nash died that month at age 84. During the 1946 celebration of the industry's Golden Jubilee, he'd been one of a dozen industry pioneers still living to share in the honors. Among executives of independent companies, Mason was the most far-seeing. He knew the independents would eventually have to merge to survive, and hoped to put Nash together with Hudson, and ultimately with Studebaker and Packard as well.

Like most other automakers, Nash built slightly renovated versions of its 1942 models for 1946, '47, and '48. Management dropped the eight to concentrate on sixes, increasing the 600's horsepower to 82 and the Ambassador's to 112. Even though alterations were minor, styling appeared quite fresh.

The 600 series comprised three models in 1946-47: a

1942 Ambassador Eight four-door sedan

1942 "600" four-door sedan

1946 Ambassador four-door sedan

1946 Ambassador Suburban four-door sedan

two-door brougham and four-door sedans with trunk-back or fastback lines. The Ambassador Six offered those three plus the unique Sedan Suburban. Like the Chrysler Town & Country and Ford/Mercury Sportsman, it was lavishly trimmed with wood. Nash built 272 Sedan Suburbans in 1946; 595 in 1947; 130 in 1948. Because of the handwork involved, they were quite expensive, and were not fast sellers. But they played the same role as their Chrysler and Ford counterparts, attracting buyers to showrooms with the promise of something new. Suburbans were pretty cars, and ultimately became popular with collectors. Unfortunately, only about 10 to 15 are thought to exist today.

The 1946 styling was only slightly modified for '47. Nash had used inboard parking lights and a wide central grille in 1946. For '47, grilles were widened again, and new raised-center hubcaps were used. Then in 1948, the side molding below the beltline was eliminated, an inexpensive change that inadvertently made the cars appear higher and less streamlined than before.

The model line was expanded for 1948. Anticipating a significant upsurge in buyer demand, the company made the best of its prewar design, offering three styles of 600 and two of Ambassador. The price leader was the 600 DeLuxe business coupe. The usual assortment of sedans and broughams was offered in Super and Custom trim. Similarly, the Ambassador Super and Custom were listed. The Sedan Suburban was continued as a Super. The Custom included a new convertible—the first open Nash since the war. One thousand of these jaunty soft-tops were produced that year. (The company also built a limited number of trucks bearing sedan-type front ends beginning in 1947; most were exported.)

Nash officials knew they'd have to come up with an all-new car for 1949. Most of the company's independent rivals had restyled by then, and the Big Three were readying all-new designs that year. Nash's answer was the 1949-51 Airflyte. Though it looks positively awful now, it was one of the most advanced cars of its day, bristling with unusual features. Its shape was as purely aerodynamic as a postwar car ever had. Though all manufacturers had toyed with the "bathtub" look, only Nash actually put it into production. The Airflyte began during World War II. Nils Erik Wahlberg had been a Nash engineer ever since the company was formed in 1916. Ted Ulrich, who'd been a unit-body exponent since the '30s, had helped create the 1941 Nash while he was at Budd Inc., the body builders. The '41 was the first successful mass-produced unit-body car. Its success led to Wahlberg hiring Ulrich.

Actual styling of the Airflyte is claimed with some authority by Holden Koto, who, with partner Ted Pietsch, showed a small scale model very much like the eventual production version to Wahlberg in 1943. Wahlberg must have been interested because he had been experimenting with wind tunnel tests on streamlined bodies. The Airflyte's aerodynamics were superior: only 113 pounds of drag at 60 miles per hour, compared to as much as 171 pounds for the similar-looking '49 Packard.

All Airflytes had a one-piece curved windshield, "Uniscope" gauge cluster (a pod mounted atop the steering column), and fully reclining front seatbacks (pneumatic mattresses were sold as accessories). The seats, together with the Nash-Kelvinator "Weather-Eye" heating and ventilation system, made the new Nash the most habitable long-distance touring car in America.

Nash produced 135,000 cars for the 1949 model year, shooting into the industry's top 10. The Airflyte 600s and Ambassadors used the same wheelbases and powerplants that had been used the year before. Three body types were offered: a two-door sedan, a four-door

1947 Ambassador four-door sedan

1948 "600" Super four-door sedan

1949 Ambassador Super four-door sedan

sedan, and a brougham (club coupe). Prices remained competitive: under $2000 for the 600s; about $2200 to $2400 for the Ambassadors.

At the height of the seller's market, these cars did very well: better, in fact, than any big cars in Nash history. For 1950, the figure was 172,000 units—an all-time company record, though it included about 58,000 Ramblers. The Statesman (nee 600) engine at 172.6 cid also powered the Rambler. Respected since its debut as an L-head in 1928, Nash's hardy old seven-main-bearing six had one of the longest production runs in history, and was not dropped until 1956.

Riding a 100-inch wheelbase, the little Rambler was the very antithesis of the huge Airflyte. Though there had been smaller cars long before World War II, the Rambler was really the first compact to sell in high volume. It was the progenitor of an entirely new breed of American automobile. Ford and Chevrolet had experimented with (and quickly discarded) compact-car designs right after the war, but their concepts were fundamentally different from Nash's. As former AMC President George Romney said, "It's one thing for a small company—a marginal firm—to pioneer a new concept like that and really push it. But it's another thing for people who already have a big slice to begin pushing something that undercuts their basic market."

Small cars fascinated George Mason. In addition to strength-through-mergers, Mason knew that independents needed cars the Big Three didn't offer. Together with chief engineer Meade Moore, Mason kept hammering away until the Rambler was a reality. It arrived just as the sell-anything era was coming to a close, and held Nash's head above water until the company merged with Hudson to become American Motors in 1954. AMC concentrated on Ramblers after 1957.

The first-generation Rambler spanned model years 1950-52. In its first season, it was sold as a two-door station wagon and an interesting convertible, on which the window frames were permanently fixed and only the top collapsed. A Country Club hardtop was added for '51, but most sales came from the practical, attractive wagons. In those early days of all-steel wagons, Ramblers accounted for 22 percent of total U.S. sales of that body type.

Road tester Tom McCahill admired Mason and Nash tremendously. They were, he said, "busier than a mouse in a barrel of hungry cats" with their many projects. Yet another of these endeavors was the Nash-Healey sports car.

Back where production really counted, Airflyte sales had slowed. Last of that type was the '51, easily recognizable by its prominent rear fenders (1949-50 cars had rounded bustle-backs). For his 1952 redesign, Mason went to Pininfarina and the result was much nicer-looking if less aerodynamic. The new, squared-off line included the Statesman and the larger Ambassador, both with unit construction.

The story was much the same for the 1953 models, identified by small chrome spacers on the cowl air-

1951 Ambassador Super four-door sedan

1951 Rambler Greenbrier station wagon

1952 Statesman Custom four-door sedan

scoop. The Statesman engine received a boost in output to 100 bhp. Ambassadors offered a "Le Mans" power option based on the latest Nash-Healey engine: 140 bhp at 4000 rpm through dual carburetors and a high-compression aluminum head.

An attractive new "floating" grille was adopted for 1954. The lineup, however, was much the same as it had been the previous two years. One difference was the deletion of two-door sedans from the two Custom series. Dual carbs and high compression had been successful on the Ambassador, so the Statesman got these modifications in '54. Its six was raised to 110 bhp, and the setup was known (with a furtive look to Chrysler) as "Dual Powerflyte." Nash probably got away with using that name (similar to Chrysler's PowerFlite transmission) only because sales were so dismal. From the heady years of 1950-51, they'd dropped steadily: 154,000 in 1952; 121,000 in 1953; 91,000 in 1954. And a growing portion was accounted for by Rambler. The latter had been facelifted for '53 with a cleaner front end.

For 1955, the big Nash appeared with inboard headlights, an easy way to make the car look different, and a V8. Cooperation between newly formed American Motors and Studebaker-Packard put Packard's 320-cid V8 in the Ambassador Eight. It was much quicker than the six and cost $300 more. The Ambassador Six continued to use the six-cylinder engine with optional Le Mans power pack. The Statesman continued with its own L-head six. Each series came in two body styles.

After Hudson joined Nash, 1955-56 Ramblers were distributed to Hudson and Nash dealers alike with the appropriate grille badge. The model lineup grew to include the DeLuxe, Super, and Custom sedans, hardtops, and Cross Country or Suburban wagons. A completely revised model with a 108-inch wheelbase was added for '56. Initially, it was sold as a Nash, but became a separate make the following year. A boxy but practical design, the Rambler line significantly included a novel four-door hardtop (Cross Country) wagon and a hardtop sedan.

With all that, the big Nash was de-emphasized for '56.

The last Statesman, a four-door sedan, appeared that year. Ambassadors used the Packard V8 early in the season, then switched to AMC's own 190-bhp, 327-cid V8 in April.

For 1957, Nash moved the headlights back out to the fenders and fielded only two Ambassador models, Super and Custom. The latter was heroically overdecorated, and equipped with a more potent 327 V8, developing 255 bhp with the help of four-barrel carburetor, dual exhausts, and 9:1 compression ratio. The styling was pretty good by contemporary standards. Nash was among the first to offer four headlights as standard, (vertically stacked, no less), but the make was in its last year. AMC was only slowly recovering from the debts forced on it through the Hudson merger and subsequent reorganization. Romney, who became company president on Mason's death in 1954, pinned his hopes for the future solely on the Rambler.

Note: the Metropolitan, a Nash model in 1954-57, was a separate make from 1958 on. For convenience, Metropolitan is discussed under a separate heading.

1953 Ambassador Custom Country Club hardtop coupe

1954 Rambler Custom convertible

1954 Ambassador Custom Country Club hardtop coupe

1955 Ambassador Custom four-door sedan

1956 Ambassador Custom four-door sedan

1957 Ambassador Custom Country Club hardtop coupe

Nash Specifications

1930

450 Single Six (wb 114.3)—33,118 built		Wght	Price	Prod
456	rdstr 2-4P	2,550	975	—
458	touring 5P	2,650	995	—
452	cpe 2P	2,650	940	—
452R	cpe 2-4P	2,700	980	—
451	cabriolet 2-4P	2,600	1,005	—
453	sdn 2d	2,750	935	—
450	sdn 4d	2,850	1,005	—
457	Deluxe sdn 4d	2,900	1,095	—
455	landaulet	2,900	1,155	—

480 Twin Ignition Six (wb 118.0; lwb-128.3)—17,346 built				
486	rdstr 2-4P	3,250	1,365	—
488S	touring, d.c. 5P	3,540	1,595	—
488	lwb touring 7P	3,450	1,475	—
482	cpe 2P	3,400	1,345	—
482R	cpe 2-4P	3,450	1,395	—
481	cabriolet 2-4P	3,350	1,385	—
489	victoria 4P	3,400	1,410	—
483	sdn 2d	3,500	1,325	—
480	sdn 4d	3,535	1,415	—
484	lwb sdn 7P	3,750	1,745	—
485	limo 7P (lwb)	3,760	1,920	—

490 Twin Ignition Eight (wb 124.0; 1wb-133.0)—12,801 built				
498	lwb touring 7P	3,770	1,845	—
498S	lwb touring, d.c. 5P	3,840	1,975	—
492	lwb coupe 2P	3,900	1,915	—
4012R	lwb coupe 2-4P	3,945	1,975	—
401	lwb cabriolet 2-4P	3,840	1,875	—
493	sdn 2d	3,950	1,675	—
490	sdn 4d	4,000	1,795	—
492	Ambassador lwb sdn	4,050	2,095	—
497B	lwb Amb. Brougham torpedo sdn	4,050	2,095	—
494	lwb sedan 7P	4,170	2,195	—
495	limo (lwb) 7P	4,210	2,385	—
499	lwb victoria 5P	3,950	2,045	—

1930 Engines	bore×stroke	bhp	availability
L6, 201.3	3.13×4.38	60	S-Single Six
L6, 242.0	3.38×4.50	74	S-T.I. Six
L8, 298.6	3.25×4.50	100	S-T.I. Eight

1931

660 (wb 114.3)—12,241 built		Wght	Price	Prod
662	cpe 2d	2,600	795	—
662R	cpe 2-4P	2,650	825	—
663	sdn 2d	2,740	795	—
660	sdn 4d	2,800	845	—
668	touring 5P	2,640	895	—

870 (wb 116.3)—12,116 built				
872	cpe 2P	2,870	945	—
872R	cpe 2-4P	2,920	975	—
870	sdn 4d	3,000	995	—
877	Special sdn 4d	3,000	955	—
871	conv sdn 2d	2,950	1,075	—

880 (wb 121.0)—6,830 built				
882	cpe 2P	3,200	1,245	—
882R	cpe 2-4P	3,250	1,285	—
880	sdn 4d	3,360	1,295	—
887	Town sdn 4d	3,400	1,375	—
881	conv sdn 2d	3,275	1,325	—

890 (wb 133.0; lwb-124.0)—6,199 built				
892	cpe 2P	3,900	1,695	—
892R	cpe 2-4P	3,950	1,745	—
891	cabriolet 2-4P	3,850	1,695	—
890	lwb sedan 4d	4,000	1,565	—
897	Ambassador sdn 4d	4,050	1,825	—
894	sdn 7P	4,170	1,925	—
895	limo 7P	4,210	2,025	—
899	victoria 5P	3,950	1,765	—
898	touring 7P	3,880	1,595	—

1931 Engines	bore×stroke	bhp	availability
L6, 201.3	3.13×4.38	65	S-660
L8, 227.2	2.88×4.38	78	S-870
L8, 240.0	3.00×4.25	87½	S-880 (T. Ign.)
L8, 298.6	3.25×4.50	115	S-890 (T. Ign.)

1932

960 (wb 114.3)—5,787 built		Wght	Price	Prod
968	phaeton 5P	2,640	895	—
962	cpe 2P	2,600	795	—
962R	cpe 2-4P	2,650	825	—
963	sdn 2d	2,740	795	—
960	sdn 4d	2,800	845	—

970 (wb 116.3)—8,201 built				
972	cpe 2P	2,870	945	—
972R	cpe 2-4P	2,920	975	—
970	sdn 4d	3,000	995	—
977	Special sdn 4d	3,000	955	—
971	conv sdn 2d	2,950	1,075	—

980 (wb 121.0)—5,204 built				
982	cpe 2P	3,200	1,245	—
982R	cpe 2-4P	3,250	1,285	—
980	sdn 4d	3,360	1,295	—
987	Town sdn 4d	3,400	1,375	—
981	conv sdn 2d	3,275	1,325	—

990 (wb 133.0; lwb 124.0)—3,900 built				
998	touring 7P	3,880	1,595	—
992	cpe 2P	3,900	1,695	—
992R	cpe 2-4P	3,950	1,745	—
991	cabriolet 2-4P	3,840	1,695	—
999	victoria 5P	3,950	1,765	—
990	lwb sdn 4d	4,000	1,565	—
996	sdn 4d	4,100	1,825	—
997	Ambassador sdn 4d	4,050	1,825	—
994	sdn 7P	4,170	1,925	—
995	limo 7P	4,210	2,025	—

1060 Big Six (wb 116.0)—6,564 built				
1061	conv rdstr 2-4P	3,120	895	—
1062	cpe 2P	3,050	777	—

1931 Series 660 delivery sedan (conversion)

		Wght	Price	Prod
1062R	cpe 2-4P	3,100	825	—
1060	sdn 4d	3,200	840	—
1063	conv sdn 2d	3,125	935	—
1067	Town sdn 4d	3,150	825	—

1070 Standard Eight (wb 121.0)—4,069 built

1071	conv rdstr 2-4P	3,270	1,055	—
1072	cpe 2P	3,250	1,072	—
1072R	cpe 2-4P	3,300	1,015	—
1070	sdn 4d	3,400	1,015	—
1073	conv sdn 2d	3,275	1,095	—
1077	Town sdn 4d	3,400	975	—

1080 Special Eight (wb 128.0)—3,221 built

1081	conv rdstr 2-4P	3,750	1,395	—
1082	cpe 2P	3,710	1,270	—
1082R	cpe 2-4P	3,800	1,320	—
1089	victoria cpe 2d	3,840	1,395	—
1080	sdn 4d	3,870	1,320	—
1083	conv sdn 4d	4,000	1,475	—

1090 Advanced Eight (wb 133.0)—1,891 built*

1091	conv rdstr 2-4P	4,270	1,795	—
1092R	cpe 2-4P	4,300	1,695	—
1099	victoria cpe 2d	4,300	1,785	—
1090	sdn 4d	4,350	1,595	—
1093	conv sdn 4d	4,470	1,875	—

1090 Ambassador Eight (wb 142.0)*

1096	sdn 4d	4,510	1,855	—
1097	brougham 4d	4,470	1,855	—
1094	sdn 7P	4,600	1,955	—
1095	limo 7P	4,650	2,055	—

*incl. Ambassador Eight

1932 Engines	bore×stroke	bhp	availability
L6, 201.3	3.13×4.38	65	S-960
L6, 201.3	3.13×4.38	70	S-1060
L8, 227.2	2.88×4.38	78	S-970
L8, 240.0	3.00×4.25	94	S-980 (T. Ign.)
L8, 247.4	3.00×4.38	85	S-1070
L8, 260.8	3.13×4.25	100	S-1080 (T. Ign.)
L8, 298.6	3.25×4.50	115	S-990 (T. Ign.)
L8, 322.0	3.38×4.50	125	S-1090 (T. Ign.)

1933

1120 Big Six (wb 116.0)—4,600 built

		Wght	Price	Prod
1120	sdn 4d	3,125	745	—
1121	conv rdstr 2-4P	3,000	810	—
1122	cpe 2P	3,000	725	—
1122R	cpe 2-4P	3,050	745	—
1127	Town sdn 4d	3,125	695	—

1130 Standard Eight (wb 116.0)*

1130	sdn 4d	3,200	845	—
1131	conv rdstr 2-4P	3,050	900	—
1132	cpe 2P	3,050	830	—
1132R	cpe 2-4P	3,100	845	—
1137	Town sdn 4d	3,175	830	—

1170 Special Eight (wb 121.0)*

1170	sdn 4d	3,400	1,015	—
1171	conv rdstr 2-4P	3,270	1,055	—
1172	cpe 2P	3,250	965	—
1172R	cpe 2-4P	3,300	1,015	—
1173	conv sdn 2d	3,275	1,095	—
1177	Town sdn 4d	3,400	975	—

1180 Advanced Eight (wb 128.0)—780 built

1180	sdn 4d	3,870	1,320	—
1181	conv rdstr 2-4P	3,750	1,395	—

		Wght	Price	Prod
1182	cpe 2P	3,710	1,255	—
1182R	cpe 2-4P	3,800	1,275	—
1183	conv sdn 4d	4,000	1,575	—
1189	victoria 5P	3,840	1,395	—

1190 Ambassador Eight (wb 133.0; lwb 142.0)—610 built

1190	sdn 4d	4,350	1,575	—
1191	conv rdstr 2-4P	4,270	1,645	—
1192R	cpe 2-4P	4,300	1,545	—
1193	conv sdn 4d	4,470	1,875	—
1194	lwb sdn 7P	4,600	1,955	—
1195	limo 7P (lwb)	4,650	2,055	—
1196	lwb sdn 4d	4,510	1,855	—
1197	lwb brougham 4d	4,470	1,820	—
1199	victoria 5P	4,300	1,785	—

*Production not available

1933 Engines	bore×stroke	bhp	availability
L6, 217.8	3.25×4.38	75	S-1120
L8, 247.4	3.00×4.38	80	S-1130
L8, 247.4	3.00×4.38	85	S-1170
L8, 260.8	3.13×4.25	100	S-1180 (T. Ign.)
L8, 322.0	3.38×4.50	125	S-1190 (T. Ign.)

1934—23,616 built*

1220 Big Six (wb 116.0)

		Wght	Price	Prod
1220	sdn 4d	3,370	755	—
1222	cpe 2P	3,290	735	—
1222R	cpe 2-4P	3,340	755	—
1223	brougham 5P T/B	3,400	745	—
1227	Town sdn 4d	3,370	715	—
1228	brougham 5P	3,400	785	—

1280 Advanced Eight (wb 121.0)

1280	sdn 4d	3,540	995	—
1282	cpe 2P	3,460	965	—
1285R	cpe 2-4P	3,510	985	—
1283	brougham 5P T/B	3,570	995	—
1287	Town sdn 4d	3,540	965	—
1288	brougham 5P	3,370	1,025	—

1290 Ambassador Eight (wb 133.0; lwb-142.0)

1290	sdn 4d	4,330	1,475	—
1293	sdn 4d T/B	4,360	1,505	—
1294	lwb sdn 7P	4,590	1,805	—
1295	limo 7P (lwb)	4,640	1,905	—
1297	lwb brougham 5P	4,460	1,670	—

1934 Engines	bore×stroke	bhp	availability
L6, 234.0	3.38×4.38	88	S-1220 (T. Ign.)
L8, 260.8	3.13×4.25	100	S-1280 (T. Ign.)
L8, 322.0	3.38×4.50	125	S-1290 (T. Ign.)

*Calendar year registrations

1935—35,184*

3520 Advanced Six (wb 120.0)

		Wght	Price	Prod
3520	sdn 4d 6W	3,630	875	—
3525	victoria 6P	3,540	825	—

3580 Advanced Eight (wb 125.0)

3580	sdn 4d 6W	3,750	1,095	—
3585	victoria 6P	3,660	1,045	—

3580 Ambassador Eight (wb 125.0)

3588	sdn 4d 6W	3,750	1,220	—
3589	victoria 6P	3,660	1,170	—

1935 Engines	bore×stroke	bhp	availability
L6, 234.8	3.38×4.38	90	S-3520

Nash

			Wght	Price	Prod
L8, 260.8		3.13×4.25	102	S-3580 (T. Ign.)	

*Calendar year registrations

1936—43,070*

3640 "400" New Six (wb 117.0)		Wght	Price	Prod
3640	sdn 4d	2,970	765	—
3642	bus cpe 3P	2,900	675	—
3642R	cpe 3-5P	2,960	725	—
3643	touring victoria 6P T/B	2,970	745	—
3645	victoria 6P	2,950	715	—
3648	touring sdn 4d T/B	3,000	790	—

3640A "400" Deluxe (wb 117.0)		Wght	Price	Prod
3640A	sdn 4d	3,020	765	—
3641A	special cab 3-5P	3,800	800	—
3642A	bus cpe 3P	2,950	675	—
3642A-R	cpe 3-5P	3,010	725	—
3643A	touring victoria 6P T/B	3,020	745	—
3645A	victoria 5P	3,000	715	—
3648A	sdn 4d T/B	3,050	790	—

3620 Ambassador Six (wb 125.0)		Wght	Price	Prod
3620	sdn 4d T/B	3,710	885	—
3625	victoria 6P	3,710	835	—

3680 Ambassador Super Eight (wb 125.0)		Wght	Price	Prod
3680	sdn 4d T/B	3,820	995	—

1936 Engines	bore×stroke	bhp	availability
L6, 234.8	3.38×4.38	90	S-3640, 3640A
L8, 234.8	3.38×4.38	93	S-3620
L8, 260.8	3.13×4.25	102	S-3680 (T. Ign.)

*Calendar year registrations

1937

3710 Lafayette 400 (wb 117.0)—56,000 built		Wght	Price	Prod
3711	cabriolet 3-5P	3,180	885	—
3712	bus cpe 3P	3,140	740	—
3712A	All-Purpose cpe	3,160	805	—
3712R	cpe 3-5P	3,190	795	—
3713	victoria 2d 6P	3,200	800	—
3718	sdn 4d T/B	3,240	845	—

3720 Ambassador Six (wb 121.0)—15,000 built		Wght	Price	Prod
3721	cabriolet 3-5P	3,320	1,040	—
3722	bus cpe 3P	3,290	935	—
3722A	All-Purpose cpe	3,310	990	—
3722R	cpe 3-5P	3,320	975	—
3723	victoria 2d 6P	3,380	975	—
3728	sdn 4d T/B	3,400	1,025	—

3780 Ambassador Eight (wb 125.0)—6,000 built		Wght	Price	Prod
3781	cabriolet 3-5P	3,640	1,180	—
3782	bus cpe 3P	3,590	1,075	—
3782A	All-Purpose cpe	3,610	1,130	—
3782R	cpe 3-5P	3,640	1,115	—
3783	victoria 2d 6P	3,690	1,115	—
3788	sdn 4d T/B	3,720	1,165	—

1937 Engines	bore×stroke	bhp	availability
L6, 234.8	3.38×4.38	90	S-3710
L6, 234.8	3.38×4.38	105	S-3720
L8, 260.8	3.13×4.25	115	S-3780 (T. Ign.)

1938

3810 Lafayette (wb 117.0)—31,557 built		Wght	Price	Prod
3811	Deluxe cab 3-5P	3,240	940	—
3812	Deluxe All-Purpose cpe	3,230	860	—
3813	Deluxe victoria 6P	3,290	855	—

1939 LaFayette Deluxe four-door sedan

		Wght	Price	Prod
3814	Deluxe bus cpe 2P	3,160	820	—
3815	Master bus cpe 3P	3,120	770	—
3816	Master victoria 2d 6P	3,190	805	—
3817	Master sdn 4d T/B	3,200	850	—
3818	Deluxe sdn 4d T/B	3,300	900	—

3820 Ambassador Six (wb 121.0)—7,040 built		Wght	Price	Prod
3821	cabriolet 3-5P	3,340	1,099	—
3822	All-Purpose cpe	3,360	1,015	—
3823	victoria 6P	3,450	1,000	—
3825	bus cpe 3P	3,300	970	—
3828	sdn 4d T/B	3,460	1,050	—

3880 Ambassador Eight (wb 125.0)—2,945 built		Wght	Price	Prod
3881	cabriolet 3-5P	3,620	1,240	—
3882	All-Purpose cpe	3,640	1,165	—
3883	victoria 6P	3,780	1,150	—
3885	bus cpe 3P	3,580	1,120	—
3888	sdn 4d T/B	3,790	1,200	—

1938 Engines	bore×stroke	bhp	availability
L6, 234.8	3.38×4.38	95	S-3810
L6, 234.8	3.38×4.38	105	S-3820
L8, 260.8	3.13×4.25	115	S-3880 (T. Ign.)

1939

3910 Lafayette (wb 117.0)—37,302 built		Wght	Price	Prod
3910	Deluxe sdn 4d T/B	3,350	885	—
3911	Deluxe All-Purpose cab 5P	3,340	950	—
3912	Deluxe All-Purpose cpe 5P	3,260	860	—
3913	Deluxe sdn 2d	3,320	855	—
3914	Deluxe bus cpe 3P	3,270	825	—
3915	Special bus cpe 3P	3,200	770	—
3916	Special sdn 2d	3,250	810	—
3917	Special sdn 4d	3,290	840	—
3918	Deluxe sdn 4d	3,350	855	—
3919	Special sdn 4d T/B	3,285	840	—

3920 Ambassador Six (wb 121.0)—8,500 built		Wght	Price	Prod
3920	sdn 4d T/B	3,470	985	—
3921	All-Purpose cab 5P	3,430	1,050	—
3922	All-Purpose cpe 5P	3,360	960	—
3923	sdn 2d	3,420	955	—
3925	bus cpe 3P	3,370	925	—
3928	sdn 4d	3,450	985	—

3980 Ambassador Eight (wb 125.0)—17,052 built		Wght	Price	Prod
3980	sdn 4d T/B	3,820	1,235	—
3981	All-Purpose cab 5P	3,740	1,295	—
3982	All-Purpose cpe 5P	3,710	1,210	—
3983	sdn 2d	3,770	1,205	—
3985	bus cpe 3P	3,720	1,175	—
3988	sdn 4d	3,800	1,235	—

1939 Engines	bore×stroke	bhp	availability
L6, 234.8	3.38×4.38	99	S-3910

			Wght	Price	Prod
L6, 234.8	3.38×4.38	105	S-3920		
L8, 260.8	3.13×4.25	115	S-3980 (T. lgn.)		

Note on Production Figures 1930-39:

These figures have been derived from published serial number spans and may be considered reasonably accurate; however, it is always possible that some numbers within a span were skipped. Therefore, these figures represent maximum possible production according to factory statements. No individual breakdowns by body style were available.

1940—62,131 built

Lafayette (wb 117.0)

		Wght	Price	Prod
4010	T/B sdn 4d	3,280	875	—
4011	All-Purpose cabriolet	3,310	975	—
4012	All-Purpose cpe	3,190	850	—
4013	fstbk sdn 2d	3,235	845	—
4014	bus cpe	3,190	795	—
4018	fstbk sdn 4d	3,275	875	—

Ambassador Six (wb 121.0)

		Wght	Price	Prod
4020	T/B sdn 4d	3,385	985	—
4021	All-Purpose cabriolet	3,410	1,085	—
4022	All-Purpose cpe	3,295	960	—
4023	fstbk sdn 2d	3,350	955	—
4025	bus cpe	3,290	925	—
4028	fstbk sdn 4d	3,380	985	—

Ambassador Eight (wb 125.0)

		Wght	Price	Prod
4080	T/B sdn 4d	3,660	1,195	—
4081	All-Purpose cabriolet	3,640	1,295	—
4082	All-Purpose cpe	3,575	1,170	—
4083	fstbk sdn 2d	3,260	1,165	—
4085	bus cpe	3,555	1,135	—
4088	fstbk sdn 4d	3,655	1,195	—

1940 Engines

	bore×stroke	bhp	availability
L6, 234.8	3.38×4.38	99	S-Lafayette
L6, 234.8	3.38×4.38	105	S-Ambassador Six
L8, 260.8	3.13×4.25	115	S-Ambassador Eight

1941—84,007 built

600 (wb 112.0)

		Wght	Price	Prod
4140	DeLuxe T/B sdn 4d	2,655	880	—
4142	DeLuxe bus cpe	2,500	772	—
4143	DeLuxe Brougham 2d	2,575	835	—
4145	Special bus cpe	2,490	730	—
4146	Special fstbk cpe	2,630	765	—
4147	Special fstbk sdn 4d	2,615	805	—
4148	DeLuxe fstbk sdn 4d	2,630	837	—
4149	DeLuxe fstbk sdn 2d	2,640	797	—

Ambassador Six (wb 121.0)

		Wght	Price	Prod
4160	T/B sdn 4d	3,300	1,065	—
4161	All-Purpose cabriolet	3,430	1,130	—
4162	bus cpe	3,180	940	—
4163	Brougham 2d	3,235	1,009	—
4165	Special bus cpe	3,310	890	—
4167	Special fstbk sdn 4d	3,300	970	—
4168	fstbk sdn 4d	3,300	1,020	—
4169	Special sdn 2d	3,320	933	—

Ambassador Eight (wb 121.0)

		Wght	Price	Prod
4180	T/B sdn 4d	3,475	1,186	—
4181	All-Purpose cabriolet	3,580	1,250	—
4183	DeLuxe Brougham 2d	3,400	1,116	—
4187	Special fstbk sdn 4d	3,465	1,091	—
4188	DeLuxe fstbk sdn 4d	3,455	1,141	—

1941 Engines

	bore×stroke	bhp	availability
L6, 172.6	3.13×3.75	75	S-600
L6, 234.8	3.38×4.38	105	S-Ambassador Six
L8, 260.8	3.13×4.25	115	S-Ambassador Eight

1942—31,780 built

600 (wb 112.0)

		Wght	Price	Prod
4240	T/B sdn 4d	2,655	918	—
4242	bus cpe	2,540	843	—
4243	Brougham 2d	2,580	883	—
4248	fstbk sdn 4d	2,650	893	—
4249	sdn 2d	2,605	873	—

Ambassador Six (wb 121.0)

		Wght	Price	Prod
4260	T/B sdn 4d	3,335	1,069	—
4262	bus cpe	3,200	994	—
4263	Brougham 2d	3,230	1,034	—
4268	fstbk sdn 4d	3,335	1,044	—
4269	sdn 2d	3,285	1,024	—

Ambassador Eight (wb 121.0)

		Wght	Price	Prod
4280	T/B sdn 4d	3,485	1,119	—
4283	Brougham 2d	3,385	1,084	—
4288	fstbk sdn 4d	3,485	1,094	—

1942 Engines

	bore×stroke	bhp	availability
L6, 172.6	3.13×3.75	75	S-600
L6, 234.8	3.38×4.38	105	S-Ambassador Six
L8, 260.8	3.13×4.25	115	S-Ambassador Eight

1946—94,000 built

600 (wb 112.0)

		Wght	Price	Prod
4640	T/B sdn 4d	2,740	1,342	—
4643	Brougham 2d	2,685	1,293	—
4648	fstbk sdn 4d	2,780	1,298	—

Ambassador (wb 121.0)

		Wght	Price	Prod
4660	T/B sdn 4d	3,335	1,511	—
4663	Brougham 2d	3,260	1,453	—
4664	Suburban sdn 4d	3,470	1,929	272
4668	fstbk sdn 4d	3,360	1,469	—

1946 Engines

	bore×stroke	bhp	availability
L6, 172.6	3.13×3.75	82	S-600
L6, 234.8	3.38×4.38	112	S-Ambassador

1947—101,000 built

600 (wb 112.0)

		Wght	Price	Prod
4740	T/B sdn 4d	2,740	1,464	—
4743	Brougham 2d	2,685	1,415	—
4748	fstbk sdn 4d	2,780	1,420	—

Ambassador (wb 121.0)

		Wght	Price	Prod
4760	T/B sdn 4d	3,335	1,809	—
4763	Brougham 2d	3,260	1,751	—
4764	Suburban sdn 4d	4,664	2,227	595
4768	fstbk sdn 4d	3,360	1,767	—

1947 Engines

	bore×stroke	bhp	availability
L6, 172.6	3.13×3.75	82	S-600
L6, 234.8	3.38×4.38	112	S-Ambassador

1948*

600 (wb 112.0)

		Wght	Price	Prod
4840	Super T/B sdn 4d	2,786	1,587	—
4842	DeLuxe bus cpe	2,635	1,478	—
4843	Super Brougham 2d	2,731	1,538	—
4848	Super fstbk sdn 4d	2,826	1,543	—
4850	Custom T/B sdn 4d	2,786	1,776	—
4853	Custom Brougham 2d	2,731	1,727	—
4858	Custom fstbk sdn 4d	2,826	1,732	—

Nash

Ambassador (wb 121.0)		Wght	Price	Prod
4860	Super T/B sdn 4d	3,387	1,916	—
4863	Super Brougham 2d	3,312	1,858	—
4864	Super Suburban sdn 4d	3,522	2,239	130
4868	Super fstbk sdn 4d	3,412	1,874	—
4870	Custom T/B sdn 4d	3,387	2,105	—
4871	Custom cabriolet (conv)	3,465	2,345	1,000
4873	Custom Brougham 2d	3,312	2,047	—
4878	Custom fstbk sdn 4d	3,412	2,063	—

*Model year registrations: 110,000.

1948 Engines	bore × stroke	bhp	availability
L6, 172.6	3.13 × 3.75	82	S-600
L6, 234.8	3.38 × 4.38	112	S-Ambassador

1949*

600 (wb 112.0)		Wght	Price	Prod
4923	Super Special Brougham 2d	2,960	1,846	—
4928	Super Special sdn 4d	2,950	1,849	—
4929	Super Special sdn 2d	2,935	1,824	—
4943	Super Brougham 2d	2,960	1,808	—
4948	Super sdn 4d	2,950	1,811	—
4949	Super sdn 2d	2,935	1,786	—
4953	Custom Brougham 2d	2,970	1,997	—
4958	Custom sdn 4d	2,985	2,000	—
4959	Custom sdn 2d	2,985	1,975	—

Ambassador (wb 121.0)		Wght	Price	Prod
4963	Super Brougham 2d	3,390	2,191	—
4968	Super sdn 4d	3,385	2,195	—
4969	Super sdn 2d	3,365	2,170	—
4973	Custom Brougham 2d	3,415	2,359	—
4978	Custom sdn 4d	3,415	2,363	—
4979	Custom sdn 2d	3,400	2,338	—
4993	Super Special Brougham 2d	3,390	2,239	—
4998	Super Special sdn 4d	3,385	2,243	—
4999	Super Special sdn 2d	3,365	2,218	—

*Model year registrations: 135,328.

1949 Engines	bore × stroke	bhp	availability
L6, 172.6	3.13 × 3.75	82	S-600
L6, 234.8	3.38 × 4.38	112	S-Ambassador

1950*

Rambler (wb 100.0)		Wght	Price	Prod
5021	Custom Landau conv cpe	2,430	1,808	—
5024	Custom wgn 2d	2,515	1,808	—

Statesman (wb 112.0)		Wght	Price	Prod
5032	DeLuxe bus cpe	2,830	1,633	—
5043	Super club cpe	2,940	1,735	—
5048	Super sdn 4d	2,965	1,738	—
5049	Super sdn 2d	2,930	1,713	—
5053	Custom club cpe	2,965	1,894	—
5058	Custom sdn 4d	2,990	1,897	—
5059	Custom sdn 2d	2,950	1,872	—

Ambassador (wb 121.0)		Wght	Price	Prod
5063	Super club cpe	3,335	2,060	—
5068	Super sdn 4d	3,350	2,064	—
5069	Super sdn 2d	3,325	2,039	—
5073	Custom club cpe	3,385	2,219	—
5078	Custom sdn 4d	3,390	2,223	—
5079	Custom sdn 2d	3,365	2,198	—

*Model year registrations: 171,782.

1950 Engines	bore × stroke	bhp	availability
L6, 172.6	3.13 × 3.75	82	S-Rambler
L6, 184.0	3.13 × 4.00	82	S-Statesman
L6, 234.8	3.38 × 4.38	112	S-Ambassador

1951*

Rambler (wb 100.0)		Wght	Price	Prod
5114	Super Suburban wgn 2d	2,515	1,885	—
5121	Custom conv cpe	2,430	1,993	—
5124	Custom wgn 2d	2,515	1,993	—
5127	Custom Cntry Club htp cpe	2,420	1,968	—

Statesman (wb 112.0)		Wght	Price	Prod
5132	DeLuxe bus cpe	2,835	1,841	—
5143	Super club cpe	2,935	1,952	—
5148	Super sdn 4d	2,970	1,955	—
5149	Super sdn 2d	2,930	1,928	—
5153	Custom club cpe	2,950	2,122	—
5158	Custom sdn 4d	2,990	2,125	—
5159	Custom sdn 2d	2,940	2,099	—

Ambassador (wb 121.0)		Wght	Price	Prod
5163	Super club cpe	3,370	2,326	—
5168	Super sdn 4d	3,410	2,330	—
5169	Super sdn 2d	3,370	2,304	—
5173	Custom club cpe	3,395	2,496	—
5178	Custom sdn 4d	3,445	2,501	—
5179	Custom sdn 2d	3,380	2,474	—

*Model year registrations: 205,307.

1951 Engines	bore × stroke	bhp	availability
L6, 172.6	3.13 × 3.75	82	S-Rambler
L6, 184.0	3.13 × 4.00	85	S-Statesman
L6, 234.8	3.38 × 4.38	115	S-Ambassador

1952*

Rambler (wb 100.0)		Wght	Price	Prod
5214	Super Suburban wgn 2d	2,515	2,003	—
5221	Custom conv cpe	2,430	2,119	—
5224	Custom wgn 2d	2,515	2,119	—
5227	Custom Cntry Club htp cpe	2,420	2,094	—

Statesman (wb 114.3)		Wght	Price	Prod
5245	Super sdn 4d	3,045	2,178	—
5246	Super sdn 2d	3,025	2,144	—
5255	Custom sdn 4d	3,070	2,332	—
5256	Custom sdn 2d	3,050	2,310	—
5257	Custom Cntry Club htp cpe	3,095	2,433	—

Ambassador (wb 121.3)		Wght	Price	Prod
5265	Super sdn 4d	3,430	2,557	—
5266	Super sdn 2d	3,410	2,521	—
5275	Custom sdn 4d	3,480	2,716	—
5276	Custom sdn 2d	3,450	2,695	—
5277	Custom Cntry Club htp cpe	3,550	2,829	—

*Model year registrations: 154,291.

1952 Engines	bore × stroke	bhp	availability
L6, 172.6	3.13 × 3.75	82	S-Rambler
L6, 195.6	3.13 × 4.25	88	S-Statesman
L6, 252.6	3.50 × 4.38	120	S-Ambassador

1953*

Rambler (wb 100.0)		Wght	Price	Prod
5314	Super Suburban wgn 2d	2,555	2,003	—
5321	Custom conv cpe	2,590	2,150	—
5324	Custom wgn 2d	2,570	2,119	—
5327	Custom Cntry Club htp cpe	2,550	2,125	—

Statesman (wb 114.3)		Wght	Price	Prod
5345	Super sdn 4d	3,045	2,178	—
5346	Super sdn 2d	3,025	2,143	—
5355	Custom sdn 4d	3,070	2,332	—
5356	Custom sdn 2d	3,050	2,310	—
5357	Custom Cntry Club htp cpe	3,095	2,433	—

Ambassador (wb 121.3)		Wght	Price	Prod
5365	Super sdn 4d	3,430	2,557	—
5366	Super sdn 2d	3,410	2,521	—
5375	Custom sdn 4d	3,480	2,716	—
5376	Custom sdn 2d	3,450	2,695	—
5377	Custom Cntry Club htp cpe	3,550	2,829	—

*Model year registrations: 121,793.

1953 Engines	bore×stroke	bhp	availability
L6, 184.0	3.13×4.00	85	S-Rambler manual
L6, 195.6	3.13×4.25	90	S-Rambler automatic
L6, 195.6	3.13×4.25	100	S-Statesman
L6, 252.6	3.50×4.38	120	S-Ambassador
L6, 252.6	3.50×4.38	140	O-Ambassador

1954*

Rambler (wb 100.0, 4d-108.0)		Wght	Price	Prod
5406	DeLuxe sdn 2d	2,425	1,550	—
5414	Super Suburban wgn 2d	2,520	1,800	—
5415	Super sdn 4d	2,570	1,795	—
5416	Super sdn 2d	2,425	1,700	—
5417	Super Cntry Club htp cpe	2,465	1,800	—
5421	Custom conv cpe	2,555	1,980	—
5424	Custom wgn 2d	2,535	1,950	—
5425	Custom sdn 4d	2,630	1,965	—
5427	Custom Cntry Club htp cpe	2,515	1,950	—
5428	Custom Cross Cntry wgn 4d	2,715	2,050	—

Statesman (wb 114.3)				
5445	Super sdn 4d	3,045	2,158	—
5446	Super sdn 2d	3,025	2,110	—
5455	Custom sdn 4d	3,095	2,332	—
5457	Custom Cntry Club htp cpe	3,120	2,423	—

Ambassador (wb 121.3)				
5465	Super sdn 4d	3,430	2,417	—
5466	Super sdn 2d	3,410	2,365	—
5475	Custom sdn 4d	3,505	2,600	—
5477	Custom Cntry Club htp cpe	3,575	2,735	—

*Model year registrations: 91,121.

1954 Engines	bore×stroke	bhp	availability
L6, 184.0	3.13×4.00	85	S-Rambler 2dr manual
L6, 195.6	3.13×4.25	90	S-Rambler 4dr, 2dr automatic
L6, 195.6	3.13×4.25	110	S-Statesman
L6, 252.6	3.50×4.38	130	S-Ambassador
L6, 252.6	3.50×4.38	140	O-Ambassador

1955*

Rambler (wb 100.0, 4d-108.0)		Wght	Price	Prod
5512	Fleet bus sdn 2d	2,400	—	—
5514	DeLuxe Suburban wgn 2d	2,528	1,771	—
5514-1	Super Suburban wgn 2d	2,532	1,869	—
5515	DeLuxe sdn 4d	2,567	1,695	—
5515-1	Super sdn 4d	2,570	1,798	—
5515-2	Custom sdn 4d	2,606	1,989	—
5516	DeLuxe sdn 2d	2,432	1,585	—
5516-1	Super sdn 2d	2,450	1,683	—
5517-2	Custom Cntry Club htp cpe	2,518	1,995	—
5518-1	Fleet Cross Cntry wgn 4d	2,675	—	—
5518-2	Cus Cross Cntry wgn 4d	2,685	2,098	—
2504	Fleet util wgn 2d	2,500	—	—

Statesman (wb 114.5)				
5545-1	Super sdn 4d	3,134	2,215	—
5545-2	Custom sdn 4d	3,204	2,385	—
5547-2	Custom Cntry Club htp cpe	3,220	2,495	—

Ambassador Six (wb 121.3)		Wght	Price	Prod
5565-1	Super sdn 4d	3,538	2,480	—
5565-2	Custom sdn 4d	3,576	2,675	—
5567-2	Cus Cntry Club htp cpe	3,593	2,795	—

Ambassador Eight (wb 121.3)				
5585-1	Super sdn 4d	3,795	2,775	—
5585-2	Custom sdn 4d	3,827	2,965	—
5587-2	Custom Cntry Club htp cpe	3,839	3,095	—

*Model year registrations: 121,261.

1955 Engines	bore×stroke	bhp	availability
L6, 195.6	3.13×4.25	90	S-Rambler exc Fleet
L6, 195.6	3.13×4.25	100	S-Rambler Fleet, Statesman man
L6, 195.6	3.13×4.25	110	S-Statesman auto
L6, 252.6	3.50×4.38	130	S-Ambassador Six
L6, 252.6	3.50×4.38	140	O-Ambassador Six
V8, 320.0	3.81×3.50	208	S-Ambassador Eight

1956

Rambler (wb 108.0)*		Wght	Price	Prod
5613-2	Cus Cross Cntry htp wgn 4d	3,095	2,494	—
5615	DeLuxe sdn 4d	2,891	1,829	—
5615-1	Super sdn 4d	2,906	1,939	—
5615-2	Custom sdn 4d	2,929	2,059	—
5618-1	Super Cross Cntry wgn 4d	2,992	2,233	—
5618-2	Cus Cross Cntry wgn 4d	3,110	2,329	—
5619-2	Custom htp sdn	2,990	2,224	—

Statesman (wb 114.5)*				
5645-1	Super sdn 4d	3,134	2,139	—

Ambassador Special (wb 121.3)—4,145 built*				
5657-1	sdn 4d	3,397	2,355	—
5657-2	Country Club htp cpe	3,418	2,462	—
5657-3	Custom sdn 4d	3,567	2,541	—

Ambassador Six (wb 121.3)*				
5665-1	Super sdn 4d	3,555	2,425	—

Ambassador Eight (wb 121.3)*				
5685-1	Super sdn 4d	3,748	2,716	—
5685-2	Custom sdn 4d	3,846	2,939	—
5687-2	Cus Cntry Club htp cpe	3,854	3,072	—

*Estimated Rambler production 10,000; total Statesman/Ambassador 14,352.

1956 Engines	bore×stroke	bhp	availability
L6, 195.6	3.13×4.25	120	S-Rambler, Statesman
L6, 252.6	3.50×4.38	130	S-Ambassador Six
L6, 252.6	3.50×4.38	140	O-Ambassador Six
V8, 320.0	3.81×3.50	208	S-Ambassador Eight
V8, 327.0	4.00×3.25	190	S-Ambassador Special

1957*

Ambassador Super (wb 121.3)		Wght	Price	Prod
	sdn 4d	3,639	2,586	—
	Country Club htp cpe	3,655	2,670	—

Ambassador Custom (wb 121.3)				
	sdn 4d	3,701	2,763	—
	Country Club htp cpe	3,722	2,847	—

*Approximate model year production: 5,000.

1957 Engine	bore×stroke	bhp	availability
V8, 327.0	4.00×3.25	255	S-all

Nash Metropolitan

American Motors Corp., Kenosha, Wisconsin
(via Longbridge, England)
Note: Nash model 1954-57; Hudson model
1955-57; separate make 1958-62

American Motors President George W. Mason loved small cars. The Rambler was his first, the Metropolitan followed. Unfortunately, Mason died in 1954 before the "Met" had met with its greatest success. A Nash model in its early days, the Metropolitan was also badge-engineered as a Hudson during a brief period before that make was discontinued. From 1958 on, Metropolitan was considered a separate AMC nameplate.

The car's origins go back to just after World War II, when Mason and Nash engineer Meade F. Moore accepted a design by independent stylist Bill Flajole. Based on a Fiat 500 chassis/drivetrain, the prototype was named NXI (Nash Experimental International). Mason's top assistant and heir-apparent, George Romney,

displayed the NXI at a variety of private showings in 1950, carefully sizing up public reaction before moving ahead with production. Reaction was favorable, but Mason still moved slowly: it wasn't until the end of 1953 that arrangements for volume production were complete. Bodies would be built in England by the well-known Birmingham manufacturers Fisher & Ludlow, Ltd. From there, they would be shipped to Austin at Longbridge, where the 42-horsepower A-40 four-cylinder engines were installed. The Metropolitan debuted in early 1954 in hardtop and convertible styles. All had loud two-tone paint schemes resembling, as one stylist put it, Neapolitan ice cream. Sales took off and Austin shipped 13,905 cars from late 1953 through '54.

Mid-year 1956 saw a more powerful 1500cc engine

1954 Series 54 (1200) convertible

1954 Series 54 (1200) coupe

1957 Series 56 (1500) convertible

1959 Series 56 (1500) coupe

1961 Series 56 (1500) convertible

with 52 bhp. The 1500s used different paint combinations, a larger clutch, and a new oval grille bearing Nash or Hudson emblems. The fake hood scoop that had adorned the original 1200 was dropped. Compared to about 70 mph for the earlier model, the 1500 would do close to 80, though not with sports-car efficiency. It was also higher priced.

Mid-year 1959 brought more refinements, though the 1500 designation remained. Metropolitans now received opening trunklids for the first time. (Before, cargo had to be pushed into the compartment from behind the seats.) More comfortable seats, vent wings, and tubeless tires were other improvements. Prices had risen to over $1600, but Metropolitan nevertheless enjoyed its best year ever. With 20,435 built for calendar 1959, it ranked second only to Volkswagen among the "imports." On its 85-inch wheelbase, it was the smallest car sold by any domestic franchise.

Production ended in mid-1960, though leftovers accounted for 853 units sold in 1961 and another 412 in '62. Like many imports, Metropolitan was a victim of the compact onslaught from the Big Three in 1960.

Nash Metropolitan Specifications

1954

Series 54 (wb 85.0)—13,095* built		Wght	Price	Prod
541	conv cpe 3P	1,803	1,469	—
542	cpe 3P	1,843	1,445	—

*Includes 743 shipments in 1953. All production figures are calendar year shipments, including some destined for Canada.

1954 Engine	bore×stroke	bhp	availability
L4, 73.8	2.56×3.50	42	S-all

1955

Series 54 (wb 85.0)—6,096 built		Wght	Price	Prod
541	conv 3P	1,803	1,469	—
542	cpe 3P	1,843	1,445	—

1955 Engine	bore×stroke	bhp	availability
L4, 73.8	2.56×3.50	42	S-all

1956—9,068 built

Series 54 (wb 85.0)		Wght	Price	Prod
541	conv 3P	1,803	1,469	—
542	cpe 3P	1,843	1,445	—

Series 56 "1500" (wb 85.0)				
561	conv 3P	1,803	1,551	—
562	cpe 3P	1,843	1,527	—

1956 Engines	bore×stroke	bhp	availability
L4, 73.8	2.56×3.50	42	S-Series 54 (1200)
L4, 90.9	2.88×3.50	52	S-Series 56 (1500)

1957

Series 56 "1500" (wb 85.0)—15,317 built		Wght	Price	Prod
561	conv 3P	1,803	1,591	—
562	cpe 3P	1,843	1,567	—

1957 Engine	bore×stroke	bhp	availability
L4, 90.9	2.88×3.50	52	S-all

1958

Series 56 "1500" (wb 85.0)—13,128 built		Wght	Price	Prod
561	conv 3P	1,835	1,650	—
562	cpe 3P	1,875	1,626	—

1958 Engine	bore×stroke	bhp	availability
L4, 90.9	2.88×3.50	52	S-all

1959

Series 56 "1500" (wb 85.0)—22,309 built		Wght	Price	Prod
561	conv 3P	1,835	1,650	—
562	cpe 3P	1,875	1,626	—

1959 Engine	bore×stroke	bhp	availability
L4, 90.9	2.88×3.50	52	S-all

1960

Series 56 "1500" (wb 85.0)—13,103 built		Wght	Price	Prod
561	conv 3P	1,850	1,697	—
562	cpe 3P	1,890	1,673	—

1960 Engine	bore×stroke	bhp	availability
L4, 90.9	2.88×3.50	52	S-all

1961

Series 56 "1500" (wb 85.0)—853 built		Wght	Price	Prod
561	conv 3P	1,850	1,697	—
562	cpe 3P	1,890	1,673	—

1961 Engine	bore×stroke	bhp	availability
L4, 90.9	2.88×3.50	52	S-all

1962

Series 56 "1500" (wb 85.0)—412 built		Wght	Price	Prod
561	conv 3P	1,850	1,697	—
562	cpe 3P	1,890	1,673	—

1962 Engine	bore×stroke	bhp	availability
L4, 90.9	2.88×3.50	52	S-all

Oldsmobile

Oldsmobile Motor Divison, General Motors Corporation
Lansing, Michigan

There was a time when Oldsmobile and not Ford was the number-one car producer. That was in 1903-05, when Lansing rolled to success with Ransom Eli Olds' little curved dash runabout, the world's first mass-production automobile. Actually, Olds built his first experimental car in 1891 and had started production by 1897. That made Olds the second oldest automaker (after Studebaker) among all nameplates offered in the '30s. But age and tradition count for little in the automobile industry, and soon after Ransom Olds left to form the Reo company in 1904, a decline set in. General Motors bought Olds Motor Works in 1909, but even that didn't immediately help sales. It wasn't until the side-valve V8 of 1916 that Oldsmobiles really began to sell well again. Lansing's best years in the 1916-30 period were 1921 and 1929, when it finished ninth in sales.

Oldsmobile blossomed in the '30s, especially under the leadership of general manager Charles L. McCuen. It featured synchromesh transmissions from 1931, "Knee-Action" independent front suspension from 1934, a semi-automatic transmission in 1937-38, and Hydra-Matic Drive from 1939. The division's worst year in the Depression era was 1932, when it built only 17,500 cars. After that, Olds recovered rapidly, with 183,000 cars and a fifth-place finish in 1935, even more in 1936, and still more in 1937. Though the 1938 recession cut output to less than 100,000 units, the division rallied quickly with 160,000 cars in 1939 and a record-shattering 215,000 in 1940. By the end of the decade, Oldsmobile's future was secure. It would go on to surpass Dodge by capturing sixth place in industry rankings, and would do even better in the postwar years.

Olds' modern role as the "experimental division" of GM really started in the '30s. McCuen had served as chief engineer before becoming general manager in 1933. To take his place, he recruited Harold T. Youngren, a brilliant innovator. Under him were experimental engineering manager Jack Wolfram and dynamometer wizard Harold Metzel. Both Wolfram and Metzel themselves became Olds general managers in later years. Youngren left in 1945 to help develop Ford's engineering department.

Oldsmobile fielded a group of rather ordinary six-cylinder models for 1930-31. Wheelbase was about a foot shorter than that of the Viking, the division's upmarket companion make that went nowhere fast and disappeared after 1930 (see entry). For 1932, the six was bored out, a new eight-cylinder engine arrived, and a longer wheelbase was applied to both series. Unlike the Viking's V8, this new eight was a conventional side-valve inline unit. Both these Olds engines were good ones—quiet, smooth, and reliable—and both received major improvements as the decade wore on, such as aluminum pistons for 1936. A major redesign the following year brought more displacement and horsepower on both. Other changes included adoption of full-length water jacketing, stiffer piston skirts and crankshaft, stronger cams and valve lifters, and

1930 Standard Six convertible roadster

1931 DeLuxe Six two-passenger coupe

1932 Eight four-door sedan

1933 Eight convertible coupe

1933 Six five-passenger coupe

1934 Six sport coupe

1936 Six four-door touring sedan

1934 Eight four-door sedan

1937 Six two-door trunkback sedan

1935 Six station wagon (special body)

1937 Eight convertible coupe

longer valve guides. The eight continued in this form without change until 1949, when it was honorably retired in favor of the modern overhead-valve high-compression "Rocket" V8. The six continued to grow, reaching close to 260 cubic inches by the time it was phased out in 1950.

One of the reasons Olds suffered relatively less in the '30s than most companies was that it cut its losses more quickly. It also resisted constant changes to its model lineup, and only the two basic series and two wheelbases were offered from 1933 to '38. Chassis design was not altered much either, although the '34s introduced Knee-Action front suspension and the '37s received a new, lighter X-braced frame. Styling was also conservative: formal and upright for 1930-32; slightly streamlined, with an angled radiator and skirted fenders for 1933; and "potato-shaped" for 1934-35. After that, design evolutions occurred at a steady pace. Even though Olds used the same GM B-body as LaSalle and the smaller Buicks, its cars managed to retain an individual appearance. There were more massive front ends with cross-hatched or horizontal-bar grilles for 1936-37; the 1938-39s had headlamp pods partly faired into the front fender aprons, and Harley Earl's "twin catwalk" auxilliary grilles on either side of the main

grillework. Prices were accurately placed in a competitive market area below Buick and LaSalle and above Pontiac. Olds management also quickly cancelled body styles that didn't sell. The phaeton was gone after 1930, the roadster vanished after '31, and a convertible sedan was never even listed. Aside from choices in wheelbase, engine, and trim, there were styling options, such as dual outside spares in the early '30s and a choice between outside spare or "trunkback" sedans in the latter part of the decade. Convertible coupes were low-production items.

Where Oldsmobile won its reputation for innovation and experimentation was in transmissions, introducing important ideas twice during the '30s. The second of these—Hydra-Matic for 1939—later became a standard for the industry in automatic transmissions.

The first new idea in gearboxes was a semi-automatic four-speed unit introduced on the L-37 eight-cylinder cars in May 1937. Called "Automatic Safety Transmission," it operated like—but was not mechanically indentical to—Chrysler's subsequent Fluid Drive. Before moving off, the driver depressed a conventional clutch pedal and moved the gearlever to Low or High range. On the move, the transmission shifted up or down between first and second

in "Low," and first, third, and fourth in "High," with the shifts made automatically via oil pressure. It operated through two planetary units, each with one brake and one clutch band. The shift points were preset according to vehicle speed. Oldsmobile claimed up to 15 percent better gas mileage with the semi-automatic, mainly due to the higher-than-standard rear axle ratio specified. The "safety" part of the name referred to the fact that it required relatively little gear shifting, and ostensibly allowed the driver to keep his hands on the wheel. The option was offered on all 1938 models, and some 28,000 were installed altogether. But the semi-automatic's real claim to fame is that it led to Hydra-Matic the next year.

Hydra-Matic also had four speeds, but it was completely automatic, using a fluid coupling and a complicated system of clutches and brake bands. It cost only $57 extra (the semi-automatic had cost $80), but its price was probably not indicative of its true manufacturing cost. High-volume sales would largely offset its development costs, and they did. By the late '40s and early '50s, Hydra-Matic was being used by Cadillac and Pontiac as well as Oldsmobile—not to mention several independents (Nash, Hudson, and Kaiser-Frazer).

Introduced along with the new transmission for 1939 was a three-model Olds line. In addition to the Six (now Series 60) and Eight (Series 80) there was a middle-range Series 70. This employed the 80's whellbase and a tuned six-cylinder engine delivering a few extra horsepower. A few years later the 80 would become the famous 88.

The Oldsmobile line for 1940 comprised three models, each having its own wheelbase. The Series 60 and 70 used a conventional six that produced 95 horsepower at 3400 rpm. The Series 90 L-head eight developed 110 bhp at 3600 rpm. Each line offered a range of body styles in keeping with its price category. The 60 included a wagon with a Hercules all-wood body. The larger and heavier 70 offered coupes, sedans, and convertibles. Series 90 styles included Oldsmobile's most expensive model, the convertible phaeton. Styling followed standard GM practice. Headlights were flush with the fenders, freestanding fenders were used all around, and roofs were "turret tops" with closed rear quarters.

The 1941 models took a step toward streamlining. The front fenders blended into the bodysides, but the rear fenders remained separate. This design change was accompanied by a model realignment: Oldsmobile now had new wheelbases—119 and 125 inches—in six different series. The six-cylinder engine was bored out slightly, boosting output to 100 bhp. Specials used the 119-inch wheelbase; other sixes used the 125. The eight powered the Special, Dynamic Cruiser, and Custom Cruiser Eights. Body styles were identical with either engine, except for the convertible phaeton, available only with the eight. It remained almost the same as it had been the year before, but only 119 copies were produced in its last year. Oldsmobile adopted new model names for '41 that would remain familiar for years: the previous 60, 70, and 90 series designations

were altered to reflect the car's number of cylinders. For example, the Custom Cruiser Eight was called the 98; the Dynamic Cruiser Six became the 76. By 1952. names had given way to numerical disignations.

Olds built over 67,000 1942 models but slipped to seventh. A five-model lineup was offered, and the number of body styles was reduced in most series. A new Town Sedan with formal roofline was added to the 60 series. Styling was revised with "Fuselage Fend-

1938 L-38 four-door touring sedan

1939 Series 80 convertible coupe

1940 Series 90 four-door sedan

1941 Custom Cruiser 8 convertible coupe

ers"—elongated pontoon types faired into the front doors. The rear fenders were longer, and tapered beyond the drop of the trunk deck. They were still bolt-on components.

During the war, Oldsmobile manufactured 350,000 precision aircraft engine parts, 175 million pounds of gun forgings, 140,000 machine guns, and millions of rounds of artillery ammunition. On January 1, 1942, the company acquired a new name: Oldsmobile Division of

1942 Sixty 8 four-door station wagon

1942 Ninety 8 convertible coupe

1946 Special 66 convertible

1947 Dynamic Cruiser 76 club sedan

General Motors. Its previous name, Olds Motor Works, had dated from the founding of the company by Ransom Eli Olds in 1896.

Oldsmobile ran seventh in the industry during 1946-47. Production of its warmed-over prewar cars was good: output had reached nearly 200,000 units annually by 1948. The '46 lineup now consisted of four different series, and models were considerably realigned. Six-cylinder cars used the 119-inch wheelbase; the most expensive Custom Cruiser 98 series rode the long 127-inch wheelbase. All other models continued on the prewar 125-inch wheelbase. The 100-bhp six and the 110-bhp eight were retained, and would remain unaltered through 1948. Oldsmobile continued to stress its popular Hydra-Matic, and produced more automatic-equipped cars as a percentage of total volume than any other company in the industry. In styling, the 1946-47 cars were only slightly changed from the '42 models. The gaudy, complicated prewar grille was replaced by four simple bars for 1946, and a shield-type hood medallion was devised. For 1947, a V-shaped plastic hood ornament appeared, and the nameplate on the fender moldings was enlarged. Strangely, Oldsmobile did not supply parking lights on these early postwar models.

Midway through 1948 model year came a memorable new design—the "Futuramic" 98. Appearing simultaneously with a similar new style from Cadillac, Futuramic was GM's first all-new postwar body design, created by Harley Earl's Art & Colour Studio, and influenced by the wartime Lockheed P-38 fighter aircraft. (The P-38 is well-known for having inspired Cadillac's tailfins.) The beautifully shaped 98s included sedan, club sedan, and convertible styles. The sedan and club sedan were offered with standard and deluxe trim, the convertible as a deluxe only. Prices ranged from $2078 for the standard club sedan to $2624 for the convertible. The 1948 series 66, 68, 76, and 78 retained previous styling, with detail changes only. Among these were a round hood medallion, "Oldsmobile" spelled out in block letters on the hood, the omission of fender nameplates, and the addition of full-length chrome strips to the rocker panels. The public responded to the new line, particularly the Futuramics, with excitement. By the close of the model year, over 60,000 98s had been sold, over half of them four-door sedans.

Another important innovation came in 1949 with the Rocket V8 engine, designed by Gilbert Burrell. It was an automotive landmark—one of the first two high-compression valve-in-head V8s. Cadillac also introduced an ohv V8 that year, but it was developed independently of Olds. Both divisions had been encouraged to compete with each other, and Cadillac actually raised the displacement of its V8 to exceed Oldsmobile's. The Rocket displaced 303 cubic inches; Cadillac had started with 309 cid, then increased it to 331.

The Rocket V8 was a five-main-bearing engine with oversquare bore-and-stroke dimensions, and developed 135 bhp at 3600 rpm. The 88's power-to-weight

1948 Futuramic 98 Deluxe four-door sedan

1949 Futuramic 76 Deluxe four-door station wagon

1949 Futuramic 98 Deluxe convertible

1950 Futuramic 88 convertible

1951 Super 88 convertible

ratio was about 22.5:1—quite good for the era. Torque was also impressive at 240 foot-pounds. Although it had a 7.25:1 compression ratio in 1949 form, Oldsmobile had designed the Rocket for ratios as high as 12:1. Engineers had anticipated the availability of high-octane fuel after the war, though octane levels never became high enough to make such ratios practical.

The best-known application of the new V8 was in the relatively light 88 body. Management had originally planned it for the 98 only, but then elected to drop it into a short-wheelbase model as well. The result was the Rocket 88, a car that soon began writing competition history. Though Oldsmobile didn't sponsor racing, stock-car drivers soon had 88s running and winning on oval tracks all around the country. Meanwhile, the 1949 Series 76 L-head engine was bored and stroked to 257.1 cid for 105 bhp at 3400 rpm. It remained in this form through its last year, 1950.

Two new body styles that predicted future trends were released for 1949. An all-steel station wagon, offered in the 76 and 88 series, was similar to wagons from Pontiac and Plymouth—and destined for tremendous popularity in the 1950s. For the 98 series, Olds introduced the Holiday two-door "hardtop convertible." Along with Buick's Riviera and Cadillac's Coupe deVille, the Holiday was the first pillarless hardtop in volume production.

Styling for 1950-51 could be traced back to prewar renderings and clay models, which first emerged (with Cadillac) in the 1948 model year. Smooth, low, and streamlined compared to the upright styles of the past, it was extremely well received, and soon influenced the entire GM line. Oldsmobile's "Futuramic" designation adequately described this outstanding shape. Olds restyled in 1951 and again in 1954, but the basic design concept—pronounced fenders and prominent grilles—remained through 1956.

After 1950, all Oldsmobiles were powered by V8s. The Rocket 88 engine continued to impress race-goers in the early '50s, and Oldsmobile was NASCAR racing champ from 1949 through 1951. Weighing 300–500 pounds less than the 98, the Rocket 88 was an obvious competitor, and it scored early. Of nine Grand National events held in 1949, 88s won six, with "Red" Byron the national champion. In 1950, an 88 broke the class speed record at Daytona with a two-way average of 100.28 mph. That same year, it won the first Mexican Road Race, besting such formidable competitors as Alfa Romeo, Cadillac, and Lincoln. On the ovals, Olds won 10 out of 19 races in 1950; the following year, 20 out of 41. Though displaced by the Hudson Hornet in 1952-54, 88s continued to show their ability in other competitions. Paul Frére, for example, won the 1952 Francorchamps stock car race in Belgium with one, and a 1950 88 nicknamed "Roarin' Relic" was still winning the occasional modified race as late as 1959.

Such goings-on naturally helped keep sales high after the seller's market began to shrink around 1950. Olds sold about 400,000 cars that year; during 1951-53

it did less well, but never fell below eighth place in production. By 1955 Olds was running fourth, and had even passed Plymouth. Interestingly, the division managed such sales triumphs with only three basic series, and didn't even offer a station wagon between 1951 and '56.

For 1950, with the 76 still in the lineup, there was only one 88 series. Standard and DeLuxe trim versions were offered for sedans, club coupe, Holiday hardtop, wagon, convertible, and the last of Olds' special "club sedans," a four-door fastback. The 98 also came in standard or DeLuxe form in notchback and fastback sedans, Holidays, and convertibles, All three '50 convertibles—the 76, 88, and 98—were curiously placed in the "standard" category: there were no DeLuxe versions.

For 1951, the Super 88 arrived on a new 120-inch wheelbase and with revised styling. The base 88 line shrank to sedans only, the 76 vanished, and the 98 was offered as four-door sedan, Holiday hardtop, and convertible. The all-steel wagons were dropped, possibly because they were ahead of their time. Styling was a bit gaudier than before, though the grille was formed by simple bars, side decoration was minimal, and taillights were built into little upright fins on the rear fenders. The same basic appearance was continued for '52, though the 88 moved up to the 120-inch wheelbase.

Along with Cadillac's Eldorado and Buick's Skylark, Oldsmobile offered a limited-production convertible for 1953. Selling for $5717, the Fiesta featured a custom leather interior, panoramic windshield, and a special 170-bhp version of the Rocket V8. Standard features included Hydra-Matic, power brakes and steering, and hydraulic servos for windows and seat. Fiesta's spinner wheel covers were soon copied by every accessory house in the business, and appeared on hot rods and custom cars from coast to coast. Only 458 Fiestas were produced, and the model was discontinued for 1954. But it did predict a host of styling features to come.

The 1954-55 period marked another styling generation, and some of the most attractive Oldsmobiles of the decade. Each series offered the same body styles in all three years, with the addition of four-door hardtops for 1955-56. A popular feature introduced for '54 was "Autronic Eye," GM's novel automatic headlight dimmer. Wheelbase was 122 inches for both the 88s and 126 for 98. A bored-out 324-cid V8 with 3.9×3.4-inch bore and stroke appeared, tuned to deliver 170 bhp for the basic 88, and 185 bhp for Super 88 and 98. As the horsepower race continued in '56, the figures were bumped up to 230 and 240 bhp.

Olds built a record number of cars in 1955, over 50 percent more than in '54, and improved its model year standing to fourth place. Model offerings and 1954's new bodyshell were retained, though styling was drastically facelifted with a new grille and two-tone color combinations. Together with Buick, Olds introduced the four-door hardtop, destined to be one of the most popular body styles of the late '50s. All GM divisions had it by 1956, having planned for it well in advance.

1953 Fiesta convertible

1953 Series 98 convertible

1953 Starfire show car

1954 Series 88 four-door sedan

1955 Series 98 Deluxe Holiday hardtop sedan

Oldsmobile

1956 Series 88 Holiday hardtop coupe

Golden Rocket show car from 1956

1957 Golden Rocket 88 Holiday hardtop coupe

1957 Golden Rocket Super 88 convertible

F-88 rectractable-hardtop show car, 1959

The rest of the industry hurried to put hastily contrived copies into production. Four-door hardtops generally were prone to let in rain and dust as the rubber window seals began to wear, but the idea of a four-door sedan with the airiness of a hardtop attracted buyers anyway.

There was yet another redo in 1956. Most of the changes were made up front, with a large gaping grille derived from the Starfire show car. The division did exceptionally well, producing some 485,000 vehicles.

Then came the '57s—an all-new design with an expanded model lineup, including a reborn station wagon. Once again Oldsmobile was innovative: some of its wagons were also four-door hardtops. The 88s were labeled Golden Rocket, after another show car; the 98 was called Starfire. Station wagons, dubbed Fiestas, came with and without B-pillars in the 88 line; pillarless only in Super 88 form. Standard horsepower was 277, but a popular option was the famous J-2 Rocket engine with three two-barrel carburetors and 300 bhp. The J-2 could propel an 88 from 0 to 60 mph in less than eight seconds.

For a '57 GM car, Olds was rather cleanly styled. The wide-mouth grille was only mildly reshaped; a broad, stainless-steel sweep-spear dropped down from the middle of the beltline, shooting straight back to the rear fenders to delineate the two-toning area. In the face of Virgil Exner's Forward Look at Chrysler, GM styling was beginning to seem a little old-fashioned, and the age of Harley Earl was coming to an end. Nevertheless, Olds built nearly 400,000 cars and finished fifth again.

In recession year 1958, most of the industry faltered, but Olds ran fourth and held production to near the 315,000 mark. Body offerings were as for '57 except that two-door sedans were now limited to the standard 88 series only. Styling, most observers concluded, was atrocious: Ford's Alex Tremulis satirized the four rear-fender chrome strips by drawing in a clef and a few notes of music. Indeed, the '58 Fords were better-looking than GM cars, and Chrysler's products were in another league entirely. But Oldsmobile still managed to sell well—aided, no doubt, by potent engines. A 371-cid V8 had been introduced in '57, and the hottest version produced 312 bhp for '58.

Behind the scenes in Detroit and Lansing, big changes were being contemplated. For the first time, corporate cross-pollination would occur: GM divisions would share basic bodyshells. A new greenhouse design using wide wraparound windows front and rear, plus narrow pillars, was devised for all makes. Inner panels were shared between Chevrolet and Pontiac, and between Oldsmobile and Buick. Chevys rode the shortest wheelbase, while Olds and Buick shared two chassis with wheelbase of 123 and 126 inches. Pontiac was slightly shorter. Only Cadillac retained its own individual panels. Exterior styling was devised to make each division's products look different from each other, though there was more resemblance between Olds and Pontiac than Olds management would have liked. Pontiac surged past Oldsmobile in '59 model year produc-

tion, something it hadn't done since 1953.

Body sharing had other repercussions. Chevrolet, for example, had to drop its 1958 tooling after only a year. Oldsmobile's previous bodyshell had only two years behind it. Still, it was an effective move because body sharing held production costs down, and the company was able to put that much more time and money into its forthcoming compacts. Oldsmobile would follow its peers into small-car territory with the F-85 in 1961.

The 59s, however, were big, roomy cars offering high performance and low mileage. Engines ranged from the 88's 371-cid unit with 270 or 300 bhp to the new 394 V8 for the Super 88 and 98 that provided 315 bhp with 9.75:1 compression ratio and four-barrel carburetor. Performance, of course, was an Olds tradition. Compared to Buick, Olds styling was sedate in '59. The grille was a rather simple dumbbell shape with four widely spaced headlights; the tail carried modest fins. The usual vast array of colorful interiors in vinyl and jacquard was offered.

As the innovator among GM divisions, Oldsmobile also led the way with its dream cars in the '50s. After the limited-edition Fiesta came a series of two-seaters. The '53 Starfire was Corvette-like. Its grille design, taken from the Air Force's Starfire jet fighter plane, eventually found its way onto 1956 production models. Perhaps the most exotic Olds show car was the 1956 Golden Rocket, a wild-looking aerodynamic coupe made of fiberglass and equipped with a 324-bhp Rocket engine. Features included gullwing roof panels that rose when the doors were opened, swivel seats, running lights mounted in stubby fins behind the doors, and a tilt steering wheel.

During the 1960s Oldsmobile continued to experiment—with its production models. The division introduced a variety of new models from compacts to full-size cars, new engines, new powertrains—and its product decisions were rarely mistaken. In annual volume, Oldsmobile never ranked below seventh place, often placed fourth, and averaged about fifth through the decade. From a model year output of about 350,000 cars in 1960, production rose to 635,000 in 1969.

Oldsmobile joined the compact wars in 1961. The F-85 and the Cutlass variations that followed set record after record; production through 1968 exceeded that of each previous model year. This success was due to Oldsmobile's correct matching of customer tastes with new products: compact V8s for 1961-62; larger compacts with V6 option for 1964-65; and the high-performance 4-4-2 series from 1964 on. Every year, Oldsmobile's smallest series seemed to offer a package that was right on the money. Its standard-size cars also consistently sold well.

The F-85 was part of GM's "second-wave" compact program for 1961. Buick, Oldsmobile, and Pontiac each developed its own version of the same basic car using a shared bodyshell and dimensions. Pontiac's Tempest, with its curved driveshaft and rear transaxle, was very radical; Olds took a more conventional route. The

1961 F-85 Cutlass sport coupe

1962 F-85 Jetfire sport coupe

1964 Cutlass Holiday hardtop coupe

1966 4-4-2 Holiday hardtop coupe

1967 4-4-2 Holiday hardtop coupe

Oldsmobile

F-85's V8 was built by Buick and developed 155 bhp. It provided good performance (0 to 60 mph in 13 seconds) and reasonable economy (18 mpg). Styling was clean and less busy than the Buick Special's. It had sculptured bodysides, a crisp roofline, and a simple vertical-bar grille.

Naming the F-85 had been a small problem. Starfire had been the original choice, but that seemed to denote

1968 4-4-2 Holiday hardtop coupe

1970 Cutlass Supreme Holiday hardtop coupe

1970 4-4-2 Holiday hardtop coupe

1966 Toronado hardtop coupe

a big sporty car. Rockette was suggested, but was thought to project an unwanted image of the Radio City Music Hall dancers. The numerical designation was inspired by an Olds show car called F-88. The number 85 was chosen because it suggested a family relationship with that experimental, yet was different enough from "88" to avoid confusion with the full-size cars. Initially, F-85s were offered in standard and deluxe form as sedans, coupes, and wagons. The Deluxe coupe with bucket seats and luxury trim was called Cutlass—a name that would supplant the F-85 moniker later on.

For 1962, the Cutlass came standard with a 185-bhp Power-Pack version of Buick's little 215 V8. Also offered was a new model, the turbocharged Jetfire. The turbocharger increased output to 215 bhp—one horsepower per cubic inch—but the engine suffered problems, including carbon buildup with certain grades of gasoline. Olds resorted to the unorthodox technique of water injection (actually, a mixture of water and alcohol) to cure these maladies. The car was remarkably fast (0 to 60 mph in 8.5 seconds with a top speed of 107 mph), but the injection system proved unreliable. In 1964, Oldsmobile gave up on turbocharging and settled on a new 330-cid engine, a conventional V8 that provided 230 to 290 bhp. The 225-cid Buick V6 was added as an option, and continued unchanged until 1966 when it was replaced by an inline six with the same horsepower.

The F-85 grew larger through these years, as the public kept insisting on more impressive "compacts." Wheelbase went from 112 to 115 inches for 1964, and to 116 (112 for two-doors) for 1968. Bodies grew longer and wider, but styling actually improved as time went on. The truncated '61–'62 original was greatly cleaned up for 1963, and was even cleaner for '64 after a facelift that gave it a closer identity with the full-size Oldsmobiles. In 1966, the straight beltline yielded to a more flowing contour, incorporating a "Coke-bottle" hump over the rear wheels. After 1968, styling began to get cluttered again, with a busier grille and deck and clumsy-looking vinyl tops. This trend culminated in 1970 with the all-new Cutlass Supreme Holiday coupe with notchback roofline.

The F-85 that offered the best performance was the exciting 4-4-2. The designation stood for four speeds (or after 1965, 400 cubic inches), four-barrel carburetor, and dual exhausts. The first 1964 edition came with a hot 330-cid V8, heavy-duty suspension, and a four-speed manual gearbox. In 1965, it was hotter still with a 400-cid V8, an under-bored version of the big 425 engine used in the full-size models. The 4-4-2 option package with four-speed cost only about $250 in 1965. It included heavy-duty wheels, shocks, springs, rear axle, driveshaft, engine mounts, steering and frame; stabilizer bars front and rear; fat tires; special exterior and interior trim; 11-inch clutch; and a 70-amp battery. Performance was sensational: 0 to 60 in 7.5 seconds, the quarter-mile in 17 seconds at 85 mph, and a top speed of 125 mph. The 4-4-2 proved, as *Motor Trend*

magazine said, "that Detroit can build cars that perform, handle and stop, without sacrificing road comfort. . . ."

Each successive 4-4-2 was eagerly awaited. The 400-cid engine was never pushed much beyond 350 bhp, but the cars continued to be good-looking, fast, and great fun to drive. The 1969s had big 4-4-2 numerals on the center grille divider, front fenders, and deck; twin, black horizontal grilles; and a unique "two-plateau" hood with special stripes in contrasting paint. They'd become a bit outlandish, perhaps, but were no less the performance cars than they'd been in the beginning.

In 1966, though, Cutlass and 4-4-2 were overshadowed by the intriguing new front-wheel-drive Toronado. Offered only as a hardtop coupe, this car represented a clean break with the past (and a commitment to front-wheel-drive that would become corporate-wide by 1980). It marked a big turnabout for a company that had once panned the front-drive Cord, but GM planned well: the Toronado worked, and worked beautifully.

The goal for this front-wheel-drive exercise was to combine traditional American big-car power with outstanding handling and traction. Toronado's 425-cid V8 was shared with the conventional full-size models, but was teamed with its own new transmission divided into two parts. The torque converter was mounted behind the engine, the gearbox was located remotely under the left cylinder bank, and both were connected by a chain drive and sprocket. The chain drive, virtually unbreakable yet flexible, was developed to save weight and cut costs. It also resulted in a very compact engine and

1969 Toronado hardtop coupe

1970 Toronado hardtop coupe

drivetrain package. Most previous front-drive systems had put the engine behind a front-mounted transmission. Toronado's split transmission enabled the engine to be placed directly over the front wheels. The result was a front/rear weight distribution of 54/46, excellent for a front-wheel-drive car.

Toronado's styling was as sophisticated as its engi-

1967 Toronado hardtop coupe

1968 Toronado hardtop coupe

1960 Super 88 convertible

1961 Super 88 Starfire convertible

1962 Ninety Eight convertible

1963 Starfire hardtop coupe

1963 Ninety Eight convertible

1964 Jetstar 88 Celebrity four-door sedan

1965 Delta 88 Holiday hardtop sedan

1967 Ninety Eight Holiday hardtop coupe

1969 Ninety Eight Holiday hardtop coupe

1970 Delta 88 Custom Holiday hardtop sedan

neering. The C-pillars fell gently from the roof, there was no obvious beltline aft of the rear windows, and the roofline flowed down smoothly as a rakish fastback. The curved fuselage was set off by boldly flared wheel arches. The front and rear were clean and wrapped tightly underneath, as were the sides. Don Vorderman, then editor of *Automobile Quarterly* magazine, remarked: "A radically different look has been achieved with a minimum of fuss. There are no loose ends, no unresolved lines. . . The result is logical, imaginative, and totally unique."

The Toronado was a superb machine. It exhibited some understeer, but not much for a fwd car, and ran quietly even at 100 mph. It could do 135 mph when pressed, even with a "standard" rear axle ratio and automatic transmission. It was probably the most out-

standing single Olds model of the '60s. Although the 1968-70 versions were not as clean as the '66 and '67, the Toronado was a landmark creation.

While producing the interesting and exciting F-85, Cutlass, 4-2-2, and Toronado, Oldsmobile's mainstays were its conventional standard-size models. The 1960 lineup was traditional: Dynamic 88, the price leader; Super 88, the big-engined performance car of the group; and 98 (also called "Ninety Eight"), the luxury series. The lineup was expanded for 1964 when the Jetstar 88 arrived at the low end, along with the Jetstar I sports coupe (with concave backlight). To make room for the Jetstar, the Dynamic 88 moved up a notch on the price scale. In 1965, the Delta 88 replaced the Super; the Jetstar was replaced by the Delmont series, and its market territory was expanded by

eliminating the Dynamic series, too. For 1968, the line reverted to a three-series range of Delmont, Delta, and 98. Then in 1969, the Delmont was dropped and Delta 88s were offered in standard, Custom, and Royale.

The broad range of body styles offered through most of the '60s included hardtop coupes and sedans, convertibles, the Vista Cruiser wagon (with transparent roof windows), and Fiesta wagons. The design was clean in 1960, cleaner in '61, and spectacularly handsome ("Straightaway Styling") in '62. Though facelifts brought rounder, fatter bodies in 1965, the full-size cars retained visual similarity to their predecessors throughout the decade. In 1968-70 the wide, square 1962-64 grille reappeared. In between was an era of broad, pointed noses; single-bar grilles; and prominent quad headlights. Styling continuity was preserved through the use of just two wheelbases, 123 and 126 inches, from 1960 to 1968. An inch was added to each chassis in 1969.

Oldsmobile entered the '60s with two V8s: a 371 for the Dynamic 88, and a 394 for the Super 88 and 98. The latter was the only big Olds engine for 1962-63. The low-priced '64 Jetstar shared the F-85's 330 engine. In 1965, the 394 was stroked out to 425 cid, and power gradually rose to 385 bhp for the 1966-67 Toronado. Outputs decreased slightly across the board in 1968-70 with the advent of emission controls. The Delmont started out in '67 with the F-85's 330-cid V8, which was bored out to 350 cid (250 bhp) for 1968.

The Starfire of 1961-66 and the Jetstar I of 1964-65 were Oldsmobile's flings in the market of bucket-seated performance cars. The Starfire debuted as a limited-edition item, but production was boosted to over 40,000 cars for the 1962 model year. Equipped with Olds' most powerful engines, Starfire hardtops and coupes featured individual styling, with broad sweeps of brushed aluminum on early models; bucket seats with center console; and luxurious interiors. The Jetstar I was the same idea at a more popular price. But it didn't catch on; production totaled only about 22,600 units over two model years. Although neither Starfire nor Jetstar met the true definition of a sports car (as Oldsmobile often referred to them), they handled well for their size and offered distinctive transportation.

Like its sister GM divisions, Oldsmobile responded quickly and most often correctly to the tumultuous events of the 1970s. The Arab oil embargo of 1973-74 and the resulting energy crisis dramatically highlighted the need for smaller, thriftier cars in every size and price category, and Olds needed them as much as any medium-price make. The division's smallest models at the start of the decade were its two-door 112-inch wheelbase intermediates. By 1980 it had no fewer than three separate model lines on wheelbases of less than 110 inches, plus more sensibly sized versions of the full-size Ninety-Eight and Delta 88 and the personal-luxury Toronado. It's worth noting, however, that GM's decision to downsize its entire fleet, including Oldsmobile's, was actually made well in advance of the fuel shortage. That the first of the new

1971 Delta 88 Custom hardtop coupe

1971 Toronado hardtop coupe

1971 Cutlass S hardtop coupe

1972 Ninety-Eight hardtop coupe

1972 Cutlass Supreme hardtop coupe

1972 Toronado Custom hardtop coupe

1973 Omega three-door hatchback sedan

1973 Ninety-Eight Luxury hardtop coupe

1973 Toronado hardtop coupe

1973 Cutlass Supreme Colonnade hardtop coupe

breed appeared barely two years after the crisis had passed was merely happy coincidence.

Oldsmobile's high sales success in the '70s was *not* a coincidence but rather the outcome of canny marketing. In many years, Olds ranked number three among domestic producers, behind Ford and Chevrolet, which was remarkable considering its products in this period were basically corporate designs available under other nameplates for the same money—and usually less. What undoubtedly attracted buyers was the extra prestige of the Olds badge on more nicely trimmed cars astutely priced only a little upstream of comparable Chevy and Pontiac models and slightly below equivalent Buicks. The full-size B-body Delta 88 and the mid-size A-body Cutlass were far and away the division's biggest money spinners in these years.

The Cutlass became firmly established in the '70s as one of America's favorite cars, often sitting at the top of the individual model line sales charts. Although it remained essentially an upmarket version of the Chevy Chevelle/Malibu, it was offered in a broad range of body styles and trim levels at prices that were always competitively attractive. And it had a plus in wearing the more "important" Olds look. The posh, top-of-the line Supreme was the most popular edition of this popular series, the two-door accounting for nearly 220,000 sales in 1973 alone, greater than the combined total for other Cutlass models and Oldsmobile's compacts. Most buyers specified V8s, especially in the early '70s, though sixes were available beginning with the '75s, and coupes far outsold sedans and wagons in most years. With all this, the decision to downsize Cutlass for 1978 must have seemed very brave at the time, but buyers took to the new package as enthusiastically as before. The sole exception was the 1978-79 "aeroback" two- and four-door sedans, which were too dumpy and "foreign-looking" for the basically conservative tastes of most Olds buyers. Conventional notchback styling was applied to the four-door for 1980, and found immediate acceptance.

The enthusiast's Cutlass, the 4-4-2, fell on hard times in the '70s, along with every other Detroit muscle machine. The last of the traditional big-inch models appeared for 1971, packing the big 455 V8 and offered in convertible and Holiday hardtop form. Sales were slow. GM's redesigned "Colonnade" intermediates for 1973 saw the 4-4-2 reduced to a mere option package, while Oldsmobile tried a new approach with the Salon, an American-style European sports sedan somewhat equivalent to Pontiac's Grand Am. It failed to catch on, though the name kept popping up in later years in both the mid-size and compact lines. You could still get the 4-4-2 package as late 1978, but by then it was more strictly for show than go.

Like Buick, Oldsmobile returned to the compact-car segment in 1973—and with basically the same car. Called Omega, it was one of the badge-engineered derivatives of the 111-inch-wheelbase X-body platform introduced with the 1968 Chevy Nova. Though it sold a respectable 50,000 units in its first season, Omega was never a big winner. Sales actually fell for 1975 despite a handsome new outer skin and an improved chassis. When the X-

bodies were shrunk around more space-efficient front-drive mechanicals for 1980, Omega vied with Pontiac's Phoenix for low spot on the sales totem pole, though a raft of reliability problems and safety defects (both highly publicized) hardly helped.

A similar fate befell another "company car," the subcompact Starfire. Introduced for 1975, this was the Olds version of the Vega-based Chevrolet Monza, using the same 2+2 hatchback coupe body and powered by the same 231-cid V6 found in Buick's near-identical Skyhawk. Bearing a name once attached to the largest and most opulent Oldsmobiles, the Starfire was the smallest Olds in history and should have done well in the post-energy crisis market. But big-car sales were on the way back by then, and Starfire captured a mere six percent of division sales in its first season. It wouldn't do much better in later years.

Upper-middle-class luxury was still a big part of Oldsmobile's identity in the '70s, and the division's largest cars never strayed from it. What they *did* stray from, eventually,

1976 Starfire hatchback coupe with GT option

was needless bulk, which became an increasing liability in the more energy-conscious climate of the late-'70s. GM bowed its largest full-size cars in history for 1971, so Oldsmobile's B-body Delta 88 and C-body Ninety-Eight put on extra inches and pounds, even though wheelbases were unchanged from 1970. Big-block V8s prevailed, but

1974 Delta 88 Royale convertible

1976 Ninety-Eight Regency hardtop sedan

1974 Cutlass S Colonnade hardtop coupe

1977 Omega two-door sedan

1975 Cutlass Supreme Colonnade hardtop coupe

1977 Delta 88 Royale four-door Town Sedan

were progressively detuned as time went on in line with stricter emissions standards. Wagons in this design generation had an interesting touch in a "clamshell" liftgate and tailgate that retracted electrically into the body instead of opening outward. Olds shared it with the big Chevy, Pontiac, and Buick wagons. Unfortunately, it didn't always work well. As with the Cutlass, the full-size cars lost

nothing in popularity when they were downsized. If anything, the post-1976 models sold even better, no doubt due to the appeal of their improved fuel economy and maneuvering ease with no sacrifice in passenger room and ride comfort.

Much the same applies to the novel front-drive Toronado. For 1971, it too became as large as it would ever be,

1977 Cutlass S Colonnade hardtop coupe with 4-4-2 option

1977 Toronado XS coupe

1978 Delta 88 Royale Diesel four-door sedan

1978 Cutlass Supreme coupe

1979 Starfire hatchback coupe with Firenza option

1979 Toronado Brougham Diesel coupe

1979 Delta 88 Royale four-door sedan

1979 Cutlass Salon Brougham coupe

1980 Ninety-Eight Regency four-door sedan

1980 Toronado Diesel coupe

changing in character from mild sportiness to outright opulence in the process. Styling also changed—mostly for the worse—becoming more contrived and Cadillac-like through the end of this series in 1978. However, there were two appearance points that bear mentioning. One was a throwback to the early-postwar Studebaker Starlight coupes, a huge rear window that wrapped around to the sides in a near unbroken sweep, a feature included with the XS and XSR option packages of 1976-77. A more practical idea was a second set of brake lights mounted just

below the rear window, an item that has since been mandated by the government for all cars sold in the U.S. Toronado experience probably helped Olds and GM in the switch to front drive in the late '70s and early '80s, but the car would likely have been just as successful with rear drive. After 1973, when sales topped 50,000 for the model year, Toronado production was never exceptional, and 20,000 units was considered good. The new downsized generation arriving for 1979 was much closer to the original Toronado concept than its overblown predecessor.

Oldsmobile Specifications

1930

F-30 Standard Six (4 wood wheels) (wb 113.5)

	Wght	Price	Prod
covn rdstr 4P	2,665	995	822
w/5 wire wheels	2,735	1,050	364
phtn 5P	2,655	965	17
w/5 wire wheels	2,735	1,020	5
cpe 2P	2,755	895	3,726
w/5 wire wheels	2,835	950	343
spt cpe 4P	2,810	965	2,214
w/5 wire wheels	2,890	1,020	584
sdn 2d	2,840	895	9,295
w/5 wire wheels	2,920	950	1,357
sdn 4d	2,940	995	11,841
w/5 wire wheels	3,020	1,050	1,242
Patrician sdn 4d	2,945	1,060	1,015
w/5 wire wheels	3,025	1,140	303

F-30 Special Six (wb 113.5)

	Wght	Price	Prod
conv rdstr 4P	2,745	1,070	233
phtn 5P	2,730	1,040	5
cpe 2P	2,820	970	633
spt cpe 4P	2,895	1,040	478
sdn 2d	2,920	970	1,598
sdn 4d	3,020	1,070	3,031
Patrician sdn 4d	3,025	1,135	426

F-30 DeLuxe Six (wb 113.5)

	Wght	Price	Prod
conv rdstr 4P	2,815	1,125	1,560
phtn 5P	2,800	1,095	76
cpe 2P	2,900	1,025	306
spt cpe 4P	2,960	1,095	1,594
sdn 2d	2,990	1,025	615
sdn 4d	3,080	1,125	2,973
Patrician sdn 4d	3,090	1,190	2,525

Export Production:

	Wght	Price	Prod
conv rdstr 4P	—	—	27
phtn 5P	—	—	9
cpe 2P	—	—	5
sdn 2d	—	—	47
sdn 4d	—	—	95
Patrician sdn 4d	—	—	31

1930 Engine	bore×stroke	bhp	availability
L6, 197.5	3.19×4.13	62	S-all

1931

F-31 Standard Six (wb 113.5)

	Wght	Price	Prod
conv rdstr 4P	2,800	935	357
cpe 2P	2,750	845	2,423
spt cpe 2-4P	2,825	895	1,545
sdn 2d	2,855	845	5,323
sdn 4d	2,935	925	6,736
Patrician sdn 4d	2,950	960	958

F-31 DeLuxe Six (wb 113.5)

	Wght	Price	Prod
conv rdstr 4P	2,875	1,000	3,144
cpe 2P	2,815	910	1,277
spt cpe 2-4P	2,905	960	3,355
sdn 2d	2,925	910	3,833
sdn 4d	3,000	990	10,486

Oldsmobile

	Wght	Price	Prod
Patrician sdn 4d	3,020	1,025	7,840

Note: prices in both series were the same for either wire or wood wheels (five on Standards, six on DeLuxes). In addition, a few Standards were built with disc wheels: sdn 2d (1), sdn 4d (26), Patrician sdn (5). Distribution of wire and wood wheels was approximately equal.

1931 Engine	bore×stroke	bhp	availability
L6, 197.5	3.19×4.13	65	S-all

1932

F-32 Six (wb 116.5) (5 wheels)	Wght	Price	Prod
conv rdstr 2-4P	2,870	955	141
cpe 2P	2,845	875	760
spt cpe 2-4P	2,925	925	366
sdn 2d	2,960	875	1,829
sdn 4d	3,035	955	2,603
Patrician sdn 4d	3,040	990	236

F-32 Six (wb 116.5) (6 wheels)			
conv rdstr 2-4P	2,975	1,000	582
for export, RHD	—	—	21
spt cpe 2-4P	3,025	970	809
sdn 2d	3,060	920	975
sdn 4d	3,135	1,000	3,297
Patrician sdn 4d	3,155	1,035	1,878

D-32 Eight (wb 116.5) (5 wheels)			
conv rdstr 2-4P	2,995	1,055	47
cpe 2P	2,970	975	89
spt cpe 2-4P	3,045	1,025	84
sdn 2d	3,080	975	122
sdn 4d	3,165	1,055	525
Patrician sdn 4d	3,165	1,090	181

L-32 Eight (wb 116.5) (6 wheels)			
conv rdstr 2-4P	3,100	1,100	347
cpe 2P	3,075	1,020	127
spt cpe 2-4P	3,145	1,070	392
sdn 2d	3,180	1,020	149
sdn 4d	3,260	1,100	1,205
Patrician sdn 4d	3,275	1,135	2,081

1932 Engines	bore×stroke	bhp	availability
L6, 213.3	3.31×4.13	74	S-Six
L8, 240.0	3.00×4.25	87	S-Eight

1933

F-33 Six (wb 115.0)	Wght	Price	Prod
bus cpe 2P	2,945	745	1,547
spt cpe 2P	3,010	780	1,740
conv cpe 2P	2,970	825	317
cpe 5P	3,025	745	4,070
touring cpe 5P	3,090	775	5,464
sdn 4d	3,105	825	7,194
touring sdn 4d	3,165	855	5,720

L-33 Eight (wb 119.0)			
bus cpe 2P	3,090	845	396
spt cpe 2P	3,160	880	827
conv cpe 2P	3,110	925	267
cpe 5P	3,190	845	203
touring cpe 5P	3,230	875	1,901
sdn 4d	3,255	925	2,639
touring sdn 4d	3,305	955	4,357

1933 Engines	bore×stroke	bhp	availability
L6, 221.4	3.38×4.13	80	S-Six
L8, 240.3	3.00×4.25	90	S-Eight

1934

F-34 Six (wb 114.0)	Wght	Price	Prod
bus cpe 2P	2,970	650	3,934
spt cpe 2-4P	3,030	695	2,370
cpe 5P	3,040	695	4,679
touring cpe 5P	3,095	725	12,306
sdn 4d	3,100	755	7,014
sdn 4d T/B	3,160	785	20,781

L-34 Eight (wb 119.0)			
bus cpe 2P	3,320	885	900
spt cpe 2-4P	3,370	920	1,278
conv cpe 2-4P	3,325	975	915
cpe 5P	3,400	895	649
touring cpe 5P	3,440	925	4,291
sdn 4d	3,470	965	4,187
sdn 4d T/B	3,520	995	12,272

1934 Engines	bore×stroke	bhp	availability
L6, 213.3	3.31×4.13	84	S-Six
L8, 240.3	3.00×4.25	90	S-Eight

1935

F-35 Six (wb 115.0)	Wght	Price	Prod
bus cpe 2P	3,110	675	8,468
spt cpe 2-4P	3,150	725	2,905
conv cpe 2-4P	3,155	800	1,598
cpe 5P	3,225	725	12,785
touring cpe 5P T/B	3,225	755	18,821
sdn 4d	3,285	790	13,009
touring sdn 4d T/B	3,285	820	32,647

L-35 Eight (wb 121.0)			
bus cpe 2P	3,335	860	1,226
spt cpe 2-4P	3,380	895	959
conv cpe 2-4P	3,390	950	910
cpe 5P	3,480	870	870
touring cpe 5P	3,485	900	4,868
sdn 4d	3,530	940	2,976
touring sdn 4d T/B	3,530	970	18,058

1935 Engines	bore×stroke	bhp	availability
L6, 213.3	3.31×4.13	90	S-Six
L8, 240.3	3.00×4.25	100	S-Eight

1936

F-36 Six (wb 115.0)	Wght	Price	Prod
bus cpe 2P	3,019	665	19,346
spt cpe 2-4P	3,054	730	2,838
conv cpe 2-4P	3,109	805	2,136
cpe 5P	3,144	730	11,143
touring cpe 5P T/B	3,144	755	45,391
sdn 4d	3,179	795	4,082
touring sdn 4d T/B	3,194	820	66,714

L-36 Eight (wb 121.0)			
bus cpe 2P	3,231	810	2,181
spt cpe 2-4P	3,261	845	959
conv cpe 2-4P	3,321	935	931
cpe 5P	3,376	845	232
touring cpe 5P T/B	3,376	870	6,626
sdn 4d	3,401	910	395
touring sdn 4d T/B	3,421	935	28,373

1936 Engines	bore×stroke	bhp	availability
L6, 213.3	3.31×4.13	90	S-Six
L8, 240.3	3.00×4.25	100	S-Eight

1937

F-37 Six (wb 117.0)

	Wght	Price	Prod
bus cpe 2P	3,220	810	13,958
club cpe 2-4P	3,210	870	7,426
conv cpe 2-4P	3,350	965	1,619
sdn 2d	3,275	860	9,664
sdn 2d T/B	3,275	895	38,048
sdn 4d	3,310	920	4,020
sdn 4d T/B	3,295	945	62,933

L-37 Eight (wb 124.0)

	Wght	Price	Prod
bus cpe 2P	3,395	925	2,060
club cpe 2-4P	3,405	985	2,302
conv cpe 2-4P	3,530	1,080	728
sdn 2d	3,480	985	398
sdn 2d T/B	3,480	1,010	5,818
sdn 4d	3,510	1,035	496
sdn 4d T/B	3,495	1,060	30,365

1937 Engines	bore×stroke	bhp	availability
L6, 230.0	3.44×4.13	95	S-Six
L8, 257.0	3.25×3.88	110	S-Eight

1938

F-38 Six (wb 117.0)

	Wght	Price	Prod
bus cpe 2P	3,205	873	6,538
club cpe 2-4P	3,195	929	3,632
conv cpe 2-4P	3,360	1,046	1,184
sdn 2d	3,275	919	3,975
touring sdn 2d T/B	3,265	944	17,390
sdn 4d	3,285	970	1,477
touring sdn 4d T/B	3,290	995	30,914

L-38 (wb 124.0)

	Wght	Price	Prod
bus cpe 2P	3,400	989	1,098
club cpe 2-4P	3,385	1,035	1,136
conv cpe 2-4P	3,530	1,163	475
sdn 2d	3,475	1,030	137
touring sdn 2d T/B	3,465	1,056	1,950
sdn 4d	3,490	1,081	200
touring sdn 4d T/B	3,480	1,107	14,939

1938 Engines	bore×stroke	bhp	availability
L6, 230.0	3.44×4.13	95	S-Six
L8, 257.0	3.25×3.88	110	S-Eight

1939

F-39 Series 60 (wb 115.0)

	Wght	Price	Prod
bus cpe 2P	2,870	777	5,575
club cpe 2-4P	2,915	833	2,273
sdn 2d	2,965	838	16,910
sdn 4d	3,000	889	15,958

G-39 Series 70 (wb 120.0)

	Wght	Price	Prod
bus cpe 2P	3,040	840	5,211
club cpe 2-4P	3,080	891	4,795
conv cpe 2-4P	3,230	1,045	1,714
sdn 2d (incl. 17 Sun sdns)	3,140	901	19,442
sdn 4d (incl. 81 Sun sdns)	3,180	952	38,224

L-39 Series 80 (wb 120.0)

	Wght	Price	Prod
bus cpe 2P	3,190	920	738
club cpe 2-4P	3,230	971	1,147
conv cpe 2-4P	3,390	1,119	472
sdn 2d (incl. 7 Sun sdns)	3,290	992	1,571
sdn 4d (incl. 85 Sun sdns)	3,340	1,043	13,197

1939 Engines	bore×stroke	bhp	availability
L6, 229.7	3.44×4.13	90	S-60
L6, 229.7	3.44×4.13	95	S-70
L8, 257.1	3.25×3.78	110	S-90

1940

F-40 Series 60 (wb 116.0)

	Wght	Price	Prod
bus cpe	3,030	807	2,752
club cpe	3,015	848	7,664
conv cpe	3,110	1,021	1,347
sdn 2d	3,065	853	27,220
sdn 4d	3,100	899	24,422
wgn 4d	3,255	1,042	633

G-40 Series 70 (wb 120.0)

	Wght	Price	Prod
bus cpe	3,100	865	4,337
club cpe	3,105	901	8,505
conv cpe	3,240	1,045	1,070
sdn 2d	3,170	912	21,486
sdn 4d	3,220	963	41,467

L-40 Series 90 (wb 124.0)

	Wght	Price	Prod
club cpe	3,440	1,069	10,836
conv cpe	3,590	1,222	290
sdn 4d	3,555	1,131	33,075
conv phaeton 4d	3,750	1,570	50

1940 Engines	bore×stroke	bhp	availability
L6, 229.7	3.44×4.13	95	S-60, 70
L8, 257.1	3.25×3.88	110	S-90

1941

66 Special 6 (wb 119.0)

	Wght	Price	Prod
bus cpe	3,145	852	6,433
club cpe	3,185	893	23,796
conv cpe	3,355	1,048	2,814
sdn 2d	3,190	898	30,475
sdn 4d	3,230	945	25,899
Town Sedan 4d	3,220	945	11,921
wgn 4d	3,565	1,176	604

68 Special 8 (wb 119.0)

	Wght	Price	Prod
bus cpe	3,260	893	188
club cpe	3,300	935	2,684
conv cpe	3,455	1,089	776
sdn 2d	3,305	940	499
sdn 4d	3,360	987	3,831
Town Sedan 4d	3,345	987	2,188
wgn 4d	3,660	1,217	95

76 Dynamic Cruiser 6 (wb 125.0)

	Wght	Price	Prod
bus cpe	3,260	908	353
club sdn	3,325	954	46,885
sdn 4d	3,390	1,010	40,719

78 Dynamic Cruiser 8 (wb 125.0)

	Wght	Price	Prod
bus cpe	3,360	944	51
club sdn	3,420	989	13,598
sdn 4d	3,500	1,045	15,580

96 Custom Cruiser 6 (wb 125.0)

	Wght	Price	Prod
club cpe	3,320	1,043	2,196
conv cpe	3,525	1,191	325
sdn 4d	3,410	1,099	4,196

98 Custom Cruiser 8 (wb 125.0)

	Wght	Price	Prod
club cpe	3,430	1,079	6,305
conv cpe	3,620	1,227	1,263
conv phaeton 4d	3,790	1,575	119
sdn 4d	3,500	1,135	22,081

Oldsmobile

1941 Engines	bore × stroke	bhp	availability
L6, 238.1	3.50 × 4.13	100	S-66, 76, 96
L8, 257.1	3.25 × 3.88	110	S-68, 78, 98

1942

66 "Sixty" 6 (wb 119.0)

	Wght	Price	Prod
bus cpe	3,230	915	1,026*
club cpe	3,265	955	3,762*
conv cpe	3,560	1,185	746*
club sdn	3,270	970	9,744*
sdn 2d	3,280	960	3,245*
sdn 4d	3,315	1,005	7,086*
Town Sedan 4d	3,320	1,005	3,421*
wgn 4d	3,735	1,280	700*

68 "Sixty" 8 (wb 119.0)

	Wght	Price	Prod
bus cpe	3,365	955	140*
club cpe	3,405	995	501*
conv cpe	3,715	1,225	102*
club sdn	3,405	1,010	1,022*
sdn 2d	3,410	1,000	443*
sdn 4d	3,455	1,045	967*
Town Sedan 4d	3,445	1,045	467*
wgn 4d	3,890	1,320	95*

76 "Seventy" 6 (wb 125.0)

	Wght	Price	Prod
club sdn	3,395	1,010	7,481*
Deluxe club sdn	3,460	1,095	2,247*
sdn 4d	3,465	1,065	6,507*
Deluxe sdn 4d	3,510	1,150	2,414*

78 "Seventy" 8 (wb 125.0)

	Wght	Price	Prod
club sdn	3,520	1,050	3,055*
Deluxe club sdn	3,570	1,135	918*
sdn 4d	3,580	1,105	2,659*
Deluxe sdn 4d	3,640	1,190	986*

98 "Ninety" 8 (wb 127.0)

	Wght	Price	Prod
conv cpe	3,955	1,450	216
club sdn	3,635	1,220	1,771
sdn 4d	3,715	1,275	4,672

*Estimates based on percentage distribution of known production of 66 (30,219), 68 (4,089), 76 (19,013) and 78 (7,803).

1942 Engines	bore × stroke	bhp	availability
L6, 238.1	3.50 × 4.13	100	S-66, 76
L8, 257.1	3.25 × 3.88	110	S-68, 78, 98

1946

F-46 Special 66 (wb 119.0)

	Wght	Price	Prod
conv cpe	3,605	1,681	1,409
club cpe	3,315	1,407	4,537
club sdn 2d	3,330	1,433	11,721
sdn 4d	3,350	1,471	11,053
wgn 4d	3,750	2,089	140

G-46 Dynamic Cruiser 76 (wb 125.0)

	Wght	Price	Prod
club sdn 2d	3,460	1,497	30,929
Deluxe club sdn 2d	3,505	1,610	1,923
sdn 4d	3,510	1,568	18,425
Deluxe sdn 4d	3,555	1,678	2,179

J-46 Dynamic Cruiser 78 (wb 125.0)

	Wght	Price	Prod
club sdn 2d	3,600	1,554	8,723
Deluxe club sdn 2d	3,630	1,666	2,188
sdn 4d	3,640	1,624	7,103
Deluxe sdn 4d	3,670	1,733	2,929

L-46 Custom Cruiser 98 (wb 127.0)

	Wght	Price	Prod
club sdn 2d	3,680	1,762	2,459
conv cpe	4,025	2,040	874
sdn 4d	3,775	1,812	11,031

1946 Engines	bore × stroke	bhp	availability
L6, 238.1	3.50 × 4.13	100	S-66, 76
L8, 257.1	3.25 × 3.88	110	S-78, 98

1947

F-47 Special 66 (wb 119.0)

	Wght	Price	Prod
club sdn 2d	3,330	1,513	21,366*
club cpe	3,325	1,488	10,723*
conv cpe	3,605	1,845	3,949
sdn 4d	3,355	1,556	16,995*
wgn 4d	3,770	2,456	968

E-47 Special 68 (wb 119.0)

	Wght	Price	Prod
club sdn 2d	3,430	1,572	7,122*
club cpe	3,420	1,546	3,574*
conv cpe	3,710	1,903	2,579
sdn 4d	3,460	1,614	5,665*
wgn 4d	3,885	2,514	492

G-47 Dynamic Cruiser 76 (wb 125.0)

	Wght	Price	Prod
club sdn 2d	3,470	1,584	22,509*
Deluxe club sdn 2d	3,515	1,705	3,951*
sdn 4d	3,525	1,659	18,196*
Deluxe sdn 4d	3,590	1,773	4,710*

J-47 Dynamic Cruiser 78 (wb 125.0)

	Wght	Price	Prod
club sdn 2d	3,590	1,643	15,643*
Deluxe club sdn 2d	3,650	1,762	2,476*
sdn 4d	3,655	1,717	12,645*
Deluxe sdn 4d	3,705	1,830	3,184*

L-47 Custom Cruiser 98 (wb 127.0)

	Wght	Price	Prod
club sdn	3,715	1,865	8,475
conv cpe	4,075	2,307	3,940
sdn 4d	3,795	1,917	24,733

*Estimates based on percentage distribution of known production of 66 (55,610), 68 (17,956), 76 (49,711) and 78 (33,963).

1947 Engines	bore × stroke	bhp	availability
L6, 238.1	3.50 × 4.13	100	S-66, 76
L8, 257.1	3.25 × 3.88	110	S-68, 78, 98

1948

Dynamic 66 (wb 119.0)

	Wght	Price	Prod
club sdn 2d	3,285	1,634	15,071*
Deluxe club sdn 2d	3,300	1,776	2,016*
club cpe	3,240	1,609	5,923*
Deluxe club cpe	3,255	1,749	792*
conv cpe	3,550	2,003	1,801
sdn 4d	3,320	1,677	11,406*
Deluxe sdn 4d	3,335	1,818	1,656*
wgn 4d	3,620	2,614	840
Deluxe wgn 4d	3,635	2,739	553

Dynamic 68 (wb 119.0)

	Wght	Price	Prod
club sdn 2d	3,420	1,693	5,861*
Deluxe club sdn 2d	3,435	1,834	784*
club cpe	3,355	1,667	2,303*
Deluxe club cpe	3,370	1,808	308*
conv cpe	3,660	2,061	2,091
sdn 4d	3,445	1,735	4,436*
Deluxe sdn 4d	3,460	1,876	644*
wgn 4d	3,770	2,672	760
Deluxe wgn 4d	3,785	2,797	554

Dynamic 76 (wb 125.0)

	Wght	Price	Prod
club sdn 2d	3,425	1,726	9,984*
Deluxe club sdn 2d	3,445	1,873	4,866*
sdn 4d	3,500	1,801	7,342*
Deluxe sdn 4d	3,535	1,947	7,199*

Dynamic 78 (wb 125.0)	Wght	Price	Prod
club sdn 2d	3,545	1,785	6,939*
Deluxe club sdn 2d	3,590	1,931	3,383*
sdn 4d	3,625	1,859	5,102*
Deluxe sdn 4d	3,665	2,005	5,003*

Dynamic/Futuramic 98 (wb 127.0/125.0)**	Wght	Price	Prod
club sdn 2d	3,645	2,078	2,311
Deluxe club sdn 2d	3,685	2,182	11,949
sdn 4d	3,705	2,151	5,605
Deluxe sdn 4d	3,745	2,256	32,456
Deluxe conv cpe	4,035	2,624	12,914

*Estimates based on percentage distribution of known production of 66 (41,993), 68 (16,614), 76 (29,167) and 78 (20,651).
**Futuramic 98 introduced early 1948; weights and prices are for Futuramic, 98 production figures are for total Dynamic and Futuramic production.

1948 Engines	bore × stroke	bhp	availability
L6, 238.1	3.50 × 4.13	100	S-66, 76
L8, 257.1	3.25 × 3.88	110	S-68, 78
L8, 257.1	3.25 × 3.88	115	S-98

1949

Futuramic 76 (wb 119.5)	Wght	Price	Prod
club sdn 2d	3,290	1,758	23,059
Deluxe club sdn 2d	3,355	1,900	8,960
club cpe	3,260	1,732	9,403
Deluxe club cpe	3,315	1,873	3,280
conv cpe	3,580	2,148	5,338
Town Sedan 4d	3,335	1,821	3,741
Deluxe Town Sedan 4d	3,400	1,963	2,725
sdn 4d	3,340	1,832	23,631
Deluxe sdn 4d	3,375	1,974	13,874
Deluxe wgn 4d	3,680	2,895	1,545

Futuramic 88 (wb 119.5)	Wght	Price	Prod
club sdn 2d	3,585	2,170	16,887
Deluxe club sdn 2d	3,615	2,301	11,820
club cpe	3,550	2,143	6,562
Deluxe club cpe	3,590	2,274	4,999
conv cpe	3,845	2,559	5,434
Town Sedan 4d	3,625	2,233	2,859
Deluxe Town Sedan 4d	3,665	2,364	2,974
sdn 4d	3,615	2,244	23,342
Deluxe sdn 4d	3,645	2,375	23,044
Deluxe wgn 4d	3,945	3,296	1,355

Futuramic 98 (wb 125.0)	Wght	Price	Prod
club sdn	3,835	2,426	3,849
Deluxe club sdn	3,840	2,520	16,200
sdn 4d	3,890	2,500	8,820
Deluxe sdn 4d	3,925	2,594	49,001
Deluxe Holiday htp cpe	4,000	2,973	3,006
Deluxe conv cpe	4,200	2,973	12,602

1949 Engines	bore × stroke	bhp	availability
L6, 257.1	3.53 × 4.38	105	S-76
V8, 303.7	3.75 × 3.44	135	S-88, 98

1950

Futuramic 76 (wb 119.5)	Wght	Price	Prod
club sdn 2d	3,280	1,745	3,186
Deluxe club sdn 2d	3,285	1,813	1,919
club cpe	3,260	1,719	2,238
Deluxe club cpe	3,280	1,787	1,126
conv cpe	3,585	2,135	973
Holiday htp cpe	3,335	2,003	144
Deluxe Holiday htp cpe	3,385	2,108	394
sdn 4d	3,320	1,819	7,396
Deluxe sdn 4d	3,340	1,887	9,159
sdn 2d	3,290	1,761	3,865
Deluxe sdn 2d	3,295	1,829	2,489
wgn 4d	3,610	2,362	121
Deluxe wgn 4d	3,615	2,504	247

Futuramic 88 (wb 119.5)	Wght	Price	Prod
club sdn 2d	3,475	1,904	14,705
Deluxe club sdn 2d	3,486	1,982	16,388
club cpe	3,435	1,878	10,684
Deluxe club cpe	3,455	1,956	10,772
conv cpe	3,745	2,294	9,127
Holiday htp cpe	3,510	2,162	1,366
Deluxe Holiday htp cpe	3,565	2,267	11,316
sdn 4d	3,515	1,978	40,301
Deluxe sdn 4d	3,520	2,056	100,810
sdn 2d	3,485	1,920	23,889
Deluxe sdn 2d	3,500	1,998	26,672
wgn 4d	3,775	2,520	1,830
Deluxe wgn 4d	3,780	2,662	552

Futuramic 98 (wb 122.0)	Wght	Price	Prod
club sdn 2d	3,685	2,225	2,270
Deluxe club sdn 2d	3,705	2,319	9,719
Deluxe conv cpe	4,150	2,772	3,925
Holiday htp cpe	3,775	2,383	317
Deluxe Holiday htp cpe	3,840	2,641	7,946
Town Sedan 4d	3,710	2,267	255
Deluxe Town Sedan 4d	3,755	2,361	1,523
sdn 4d	3,765	2,299	7,499
Deluxe sdn 4d	3,775	2,393	72,766

1950 Engines	bore × stroke	bhp	availability
L6, 257.1	3.53 × 4.38	105	S-76
V8, 303.7	3.75 × 3.44	135	S-88, 98

1951

88 (wb 119.5)	Wght	Price	Prod
sdn 4d	3,542	2,111	22,848
sdn 2d	3,507	2,049	11,792

Super 88 (wb 120.0)	Wght	Price	Prod
club cpe	3,557	2,219	7,328
sdn 4d	3,636	2,328	90,131
sdn 2d	3,579	2,265	34,963
conv cpe	3,831	2,673	3,854
Holiday htp cpe	3,743	2,558	14,180

98 (wb 122.0)	Wght	Price	Prod
Deluxe sdn 4d	3,787	2,610	78,122
Holiday htp cpe	3,762	2,545	3,914
Deluxe Holiday htp cpe	3,857	2,882	14,012
Deluxe conv cpe	4,107	3,025	4,468

1951 Engine	bore × stroke	bhp	availability
V8, 303.7	3.75 × 3.44	135	S-all

1952

88 Deluxe (wb 120.0)	Wght	Price	Prod
sdn 4d	3,608	2,327	12,215
sdn 2d	3,565	2,262	6,402

Super 88 (wb 120.0)	Wght	Price	Prod
club cpe	3,597	2,345	2,050
sdn 4d	3,649	2,462	70,606
sdn 2d	3,603	2,395	24,963
conv cpe	3,867	2,853	5,162
Holiday htp cpe	3,640	2,673	15,777

Oldsmobile

98 (wb 124.0)		Wght	Price	Prod
	sdn 4d	3,765	2,786	58,550
	conv cpe	4,111	3,229	3,544
	Holiday htp cpe	3,874	3,022	14,150

1952 Engines	bore × stroke	bhp	availability
V8, 303.7	3.75 × 3.44	145	S-88
V8, 303.7	3.75 × 3.44	160	S-Super 88, 98

1953

88 Deluxe (wb 120.0)		Wght	Price	Prod
	sdn 4d	3,642	2,327	20,400
	sdn 2d	3,603	2,262	12,400

Super 88 (wb 120.0)		Wght	Price	Prod
	sdn 4d	3,673	2,462	119,317
	sdn 2d	3,628	2,395	36,824
	conv cpe	3,905	2,853	8,310
	Holiday htp cpe	3,661	2,673	36,881

98 (wb 124.0)		Wght	Price	Prod
	sdn 4d	3,779	2,786	64,431
	conv cpe	4,119	3,229	7,521
	Holiday htp cpe	3,893	3,022	27,920
	Fiesta conv cpe	4,450	5,717	450

1953 Engines	bore × stroke	bhp	availability
V8, 303.7	3.75 × 3.44	150	S-88
V8, 303.7	3.75 × 3.44	165	S-Super 88, 98

1954

88 (wb 122.0)		Wght	Price	Prod
	sdn 4d	3,719	2,337	29,028
	sdn 2d	3,699	2,272	18,013
	Holiday htp cpe	3,721	2,449	25,820

Super 88 (wb 122.0)		Wght	Price	Prod
	sdn 4d	3,780	2,477	111,326
	sdn 2d	3,729	2,410	27,882
	conv cpe	4,003	2,868	6,452
	Deluxe Holiday htp cpe	3,775	2,688	42,155

98 (wb 126.0)		Wght	Price	Prod
	Deluxe sdn 4d	3,895	2,806	47,972
	Holiday htp cpe	3,851	2,826	8,865
	Deluxe Holiday htp cpe	3,938	3,042	29,688
	Starfire conv cpe	4,193	3,249	6,800

1954 Engines	bore × stroke	bhp	availability
V8, 324.3	3.88 × 3.44	170	S-88
V8, 324.3	3.88 × 3.44	185	S-Super 88, 98

1955

88 (wb 122.0)		Wght	Price	Prod
	sdn 4d	3,707	2,362	57,777
	sdn 2d	3,688	2,297	37,507
	Holiday htp sdn	3,768	2,548	41,310
	Holiday htp cpe	3,707	2,474	85,767

Super 88 (wb 122.0)		Wght	Price	Prod
	sdn 4d	3,762	2,503	111,316
	sdn 2d	3,720	2,436	11,950
	conv cpe	3,983	2,894	9,007
	Deluxe Holiday htp sdn	3,825	2,788	47,385
	Deluxe Holiday htp cpe	3,765	2,714	62,534

98 (wb 126.0)		Wght	Price	Prod
	sdn 4d	3,864	2,833	39,847
	Starfire conv cpe	4,159	3,276	9,149
	Deluxe Holiday htp sdn	3,976	3,140	31,267
	Deluxe Holiday htp cpe	3,924	3,069	38,363

1955 Engines	bore × stroke	bhp	availability
V8, 324.3	3.88 × 3.44	185	S-88
V8, 324.3	3.88 × 3.44	202	S-Super 88, 98

1956

88 (wb 122.0)		Wght	Price	Prod
	sdn 4d	3,748	2,487	57,092
	sdn 2d	3,691	2,422	31,949
	Holiday htp sdn	3,797	2,671	52,239
	Holiday htp cpe	3,741	2,599	74,739

Super 88 (wb 122.0)		Wght	Price	Prod
	sdn 4d	3,768	2,640	59,728
	sdn 2d	3,717	2,574	5,465
	Holiday htp sdn	3,869	2,881	61,192
	Holiday htp cpe	3,771	2,808	43,054
	conv cpe	4,033	3,031	9,561

98 (wb 126.0)		Wght	Price	Prod
	sdn 4d	4,028	3,298	20,105
	Holiday htp sdn	4,167	3,551	42,320
	Holiday htp cpe	4,080	3,480	19,433
	Starfire conv cpe	4,325	3,740	8,581

1956 Engines	bore × stroke	bhp	availability
V8, 324.3	3.88 × 3.44	230	S-88
V8, 324.3	3.88 × 3.44	240	S-Super 88, 98

1957

Golden Rocket 88 (wb 122.0)		Wght	Price	Prod
3611	sdn 2d	3,942	2,733	18,477
3637	Holiday htp cpe	3,963	2,854	49,187
3639	Holiday htp sdn	4,052	2,932	33,830
3667TX	conv cpe	4,232	3,182	6,423
3669	sdn 4d	4,000	2,798	53,923
3693	Fiesta wgn 4d	4,281	3,202	5,052
3695	Fiesta htp wgn 4d	4,314	3,313	5,767

Golden Rocket Super 88 (wb 122.0)		Wght	Price	Prod
3637SD	Holiday htp cpe	4,010	3,180	31,155
3639SD	Holiday htp sdn	4,117	3,257	39,162
3667DTX	conv cpe	4,283	3,447	7,128
3669D	sdn 4d	4,044	3,030	42,629
3695SD	Fiesta htp wgn 4d	4,364	3,541	8,981
—	sdn 2d	4,001	2,968	2,983

Starfire 98 (wb 126.0)		Wght	Price	Prod
3037SDX	Holiday htp cpe	4,296	3,937	17,791
3039SDX	Holiday htp sdn	4,385	4,013	32,099
3067DX	conv cpe	4,572	4,217	8,278
3069D	sdn 4d	4,322	3,741	21,525

1957 Engine	bore × stroke	bhp	availability
V8, 371.1	4.00 × 3.69	277	S-all

1958

Dynamic 88 (wb 122.5)		Wght	Price	Prod
3611	sdn 2d	3,961	2,772	11,833
3637	Holiday htp cpe	3,972	2,893	53,036
3639	Holiday htp sdn	4,035	2,971	28,241
3667TX	conv cpe	3,987	3,221	4,456
3669	sdn 4d	3,985	2,837	60,429
3693	Fiesta wgn 4d	4,258	3,284	3,249
3695	Fiesta htp wgn 4d	4,297	3,395	3,323

Super 88 (wb 122.5)		Wght	Price	Prod
3637SD	Holiday htp cpe	4,000	3,262	18,653
3639SD	Holiday htp sdn	4,073	3,339	27,521
3667DTX	conv cpe	4,010	3,529	3,799
3669D	sdn 4d	4,008	3,112	33,844
3695SD	Fiesta htp wgn 4d	4,334	3,623	5,175

98 (wb 126.5)		Wght	Price	Prod
3037SDX	Holiday htp cpe	4,329	4,020	11,012
3039SDX	Holiday htp sdn	4,391	4,096	27,603
3067DX	conv cpe	4,318	4,300	5,605
3069D	sdn 4d	4,316	3,824	16,595

1958 Engines	bore × stroke	bhp	availability
V8, 371.1	4.00×3.69	265	S-88
V8, 371.1	4.00×3.69	305	S-Super 88, 98
V8, 371.1	4.00×3.69	312	O-Super 88, 98

1959

Dynamic 88 (wb 123.0)		Wght	Price	Prod
3211	sdn 4d	4,040	2,837	16,123
3219	Celebrity sdn 4d	4,130	2,902	70,995
3235	Fiesta wgn 4d	4,465	3,365	11,298
3237	Scenic htp cpe	4,085	2,958	38,488
3239	Holiday htp sdn	4,165	3,036	48,707
3267	conv cpe	4,120	3,286	8,491

Super 88 (wb 123.0)				
3519	Celebrity sdn 4d	4,135	3,178	37,024
3535	Fiesta wgn 4d	4,485	3,669	7,015
3537	Scenic htp cpe	4,090	3,328	20,259
3539	Holiday htp sdn	4,185	3,405	38,467
3567	conv cpe	4,135	3,595	4,895

98 (wb 126.3)				
3819	Celebrity sdn 4d	4,390	3,890	23,106
3837	Scenic htp cpe	4,360	4,086	13,669
3839	Holiday htp sdn	4,450	4,162	36,813
3867	conv cpe	4,360	4,366	7,514

1959 Engines	bore × stroke	bhp	availability
V8, 371.1	4.00×3.69	270	S-88
V8, 371.1	4.00×3.69	300	O-88
V8, 394.0	4.13×3.69	315	S-Super 88, 98

1960

Dynamic 88 (wb 123.0)		Wght	Price	Prod
3211	sdn 2d	4,026	2,835	13,545
3219	Celebrity sdn 4d	4,091	2,900	76,377
3235	Fiesta wgn 4d, 6P	4,449	3,363	8,835
3237	Sceni-Coupe htp	4,049	2,956	29,368
3239	Holiday htp sdn	4,139	3,034	43,761
3245	Fiesta wgn 4d, 8P	4,470	3,471	5,708
3267	conv cpe	4,101	3,284	12,271

Super 88 (wb 123.0)				
3519	Celebrity sdn 4d	4,128	3,176	35,094
3535	Fiesta wgn 4d, 6P	4,483	3,665	3,765
3537	Sceni-Coupe htp	4,086	3,325	16,464
3539	Holiday htp sdn	4,182	3,402	33,285
3545	Fiesta wgn 4d, 8P	4,506	3,773	3,475
3567	conv cpe	4,134	3,592	5,830

98 (wb 126.3)				
3819	Celebrity sdn 4d	4,360	3,887	17,188
3837	Sceni-Coupe htp	4,322	4,083	7,635
3839	Holiday htp sdn	4,431	4,159	27,257
3867	conv cpe	4,349	4,362	7,284

1960 Engines	bore × stroke	bhp	availability
V8, 371.1	4.00×3.69	240	S-88
V8, 371.1	4.00×3.69	260	O-88
V8, 394.0	4.13×3.69	315	S-Super 88, 98

1961

F-85 (wb 112.0)		Wght	Price	Prod
3019	sdn 4d	2,541	2,384	19,765

		Wght	Price	Prod
3027	club cpe	2,549	2,330	2,336
3035	wgn 4d, 6P	2,716	2,681	6,677
3045	wgn 4d, 8P	2,800	2,762	10,087

F-85 Deluxe (wb 112.0)				
3117	Cutlass spt cpe	2,664	2,621	9,935
3119	sdn 4d	2,547	2,519	26,311
3135	wgn 4d, 6P	2,731	2,816	526
3145	wgn 4d, 8P	2,822	2,897	757

Dynamic 88 (wb 123.0)				
3211	sdn 2d	3,966	2,835	4,920
3235	wgn 4d, 6P	4,354	3,363	5,374
3237	Holiday htp cpe	3,981	2,956	19,878
3239	Holiday htp sdn	4,074	3,034	51,562
3245	wgn 4d, 8P	4,428	3,471	4,013
3267	conv cpe	4,068	3,284	9,049
3269	Celebrity sdn 4d	4,031	2,900	42,584

Super 88 (wb 123.0)				
3535	wgn 4d, 6P	4,382	3,665	2,761
3537	Holiday htp cpe	4,024	3,325	7,009
3539	Holiday htp sdn	4,099	3,402	23,272
3545	wgn 4d, 8P	4,445	3,773	2,170
3567	conv cpe	4,099	3,592	2,624
3569	Celebrity sdn 4d	4,065	3,176	15,328
3667	Starfire conv cpe	4,330	4,647	7,600

98 (wb 126.3)				
3829	Holiday htp sdn	4,269	4,021	13,331
3837	Holiday htp cpe	4,187	4,083	4,445
3839	Sport Sedan (htp)	4,319	4,159	12,343
3867	conv cpe	4,225	4,362	3,804

1961 Engines	bore × stroke	bhp	availability
V8, 215.0	3.50×2.80	155	S-F-85
V8, 394.0	4.13×3.69	250	S-88
V8, 394.0	4,13×3.69	325	S-Super 88, 98; O-88

1962

F-85 (wb 112.0)		Wght	Price	Prod
3019	sdn 4d	2,599	2,457	8,074
3027	club cpe	2,607	2,403	7,909
3035	wgn 4d, 6P	2,780	2,754	3,204
3045	wgn 4d, 8P	2,852	2,835	1,887
3067	conv cpe	2,790	2,760	3,660

F-85 Deluxe (wb 112.0)				
3117	Cutlass spt cpe	2,651	2,694	32,461
3119	sdn 4d	2,634	2,592	18,736
3135	wgn 4d, 6P	2,812	2,889	4,974
3167	Cutlass conv cpe	2,830	2,971	9,893
3147	Jetfire spt cpe	2,739	3,049	3,765

Dynamic 88 (wb 123.0)				
3235	wgn 4d, 6P	4,392	3,460	8,527
3239	Holiday htp sdn	4,080	3,131	53,438
3245	wgn 4d, 8P	4,428	3,568	6,417
3247	Holiday htp cpe	3,992	3,054	39,676
3267	conv cpe	4,104	3,381	12,212
3269	Celebrity sdn 4d	4,038	2,997	68,467

Super 88 (wb 123.0)				
3535	Fiesta wgn 4d	4,412	3,762	3,837
3539	Holiday htp sdn	4,117	3,499	21,175
3547	Holiday htp cpe	4,022	3,422	9,010
3569	Celebrity sdn 4d	4,069	3,273	24,125

Starfire (wb 123.0)				
3647	htp cpe	4,213	4,131	34,839
3667	conv cpe	4,334	4,744	7,149

Oldsmobile

98 (wb 126.0)		Wght	Price	Prod
3819	Town Sedan 4d	4,258	3,984	12,167
3829	Holiday htp sdn	4,306	4,118	7,653
3839	Sport Sedan (htp)	4,337	4,256	33,095
3847	Holiday htp cpe	4,231	4,180	7,546
3867	conv cpe	4,298	4,459	3,693

1962 Engines	bore × stroke	bhp	availability
V8, 215.0	3.50×2.80	155	S-F-85 exc Cutlass/Jetfire
V8, 215.0	3.50×2.80	185	S-F-85 Cutlass; O-F-85
V8, 215.0	3.50×2.80	215	S-F-85 Jetfire
V8, 394.0	4.13×3.69	280	S-88
V8, 394.0	4.13×3.69	330	S-Super 88, 98
		345	S-Starfire

1963

F-85 (wb 112.0)		Wght	Price	Prod
3019	sdn 4d	2,629	2,457	8,937
3027	club cpe	2,599	2,403	11,276
3035	wgn 4d	2,812	2,754	3,348

F-85 Deluxe (wb 112.0)		Wght	Price	Prod
3117	Cutlass club cpe	2,679	2,694	41,343
3119	sdn 4d	2,659	2,592	29,269
3135	wgn 4d	2,833	2,889	6,647
3147	Jetfire htp cpe	2,774	3,048	5,842
3167	Cutlass conv cpe	2,858	2,971	12,149

Dynamic 88 (wb 123.0)		Wght	Price	Prod
3235	wgn 4d, 6P	4,322	3,459	9,615
3239	Holiday htp sdn	4,059	3,130	62,351
3245	wgn 4d, 8P	4,354	3,566	7,116
3247	Holiday htp cpe	3,839	3,052	39,071
3267	conv cpe	4,039	3,379	12,551
3269	Celebrity sdn 4d	3,998	2,995	68,611

Super 88 (wb 123.0)		Wght	Price	Prod
3535	Fiesta wgn 4d	4,347	3,748	3,878
3539	Holiday htp sdn	4,083	3,473	25,387
3547	Holiday htp cpe	3,966	3,408	8,930
3569	Celebrity sdn 4d	4,027	3,246	24,575

Starfire (wb 123.0)		Wght	Price	Prod
3657	htp cpe	4,172	4,129	21,148
3667	conv cpe	4,293	4,742	4,401

98 (wb 126.0)		Wght	Price	Prod
3819	Town Sedan 4d	4,240	3,982	11,053
3829	Luxury htp sdn	4,362	4,332	19,252
3839	Sport Sedan (htp)	4,347	4,258	23,330
3847	Holiday htp cpe	4,215	4,178	4,984
3867	conv cpe	4,272	4,457	4,267
3947	Custom htp cpe	4,285	4,381	7,422

1963 Engines	bore × stroke	bhp	availability
V8, 215.0	3.50×2.80	155	S-F-85 exc Cutlass/Jetfire
V8, 215.0	3.50×2.80	185	S-F-85 Cutlass; O-F-85
V8, 215.0	3.50×2.80	215	S-F-85 Jetfire
V8, 394.0	4.13×3.69	280	S-88
V8, 394.0	4.13×3.69	330	S-Super 88, 98 exc Custom
V8, 394.0	4.13×3.69	330	S-Starfire, 98 Custom

1964

F-85 (wb 115.0; Vista Crsr-120.0)		Wght	Price	Prod
3027	club cpe	2,980	2,343	16,298
3035	wgn 4d	3,274	2,689	4,047
3055	Vista Cruiser wgn 4d, 2S	3,652	2,938	1,305
3065	Vista Cruiser wgn 4d, 3S	3,729	3,072	2,089
3069	sdn 4d	3,025	2,397	12,106

		Wght	Price	Prod
3127	Del Sports Coupe	2,824	2,537	6,594
3135	Del wgn 4d	3,304	2,797	909
3169	Del sdn 4d	3,055	2,505	7,428

Cutlass (wb 115.0)		Wght	Price	Prod
3227	Sports Coupe	3,141	2,644	15,440
3237	Holiday htp cpe	3,180	2,784	36,153
3255	Custom wgn 4d 2S	3,714	3,146	3,320
3265	Custom Wgn 4d, 3S	3,781	3,270	7,286
3267	conv cpe	3,263	2,984	12,822

Jetstar 88 (wb 123.0)		Wght	Price	Prod
3339	Holiday htp sdn	3,783	3,069	19,325
3347	Holiday htp cpe	3,701	2,992	14,663
3367	conv cpe	3,754	3,318	3,903
3369	Celebrity sdn 4d	3,729	2,935	24,614

Dynamic 88 (123.0)		Wght	Price	Prod
3435	wgn 4d, 2S	4,286	3,468	10,747
3439	Holiday htp sdn	4,012	3,139	50,327
3445	wgn 4d, 3S	4,324	3,576	6,599
3447	Holiday htp cpe	3,924	3,062	32,369
3457	Jetstar I spt cpe	4,019	3,603	16,084
3467	conv cpe	3,996	3,389	10,042
3469	Celebrity sdn 4d	3,966	3,005	57,590

Super 88 (wb 123.0)		Wght	Price	Prod
3539	Holiday htp sdn	4,069	3,486	17,778
3569	Celebrity sdn 4d	4,009	3,256	19,736

Starfire (wb 123.0)		Wght	Price	Prod
3657	htp cpe	4,167	4,138	13,753
3667	conv cpe	4,253	4,753	2,410

98 (wb 126.0)		Wght	Price	Prod
3819	Town Sedan 4d	4,234	3,993	11,380
3829	Luxury sdn 4d	4,337	4,342	17,346
3839	Sport Sedan (htp)	4,323	4,265	24,791
3847	htp cpe	4,205	4,118	6,139
3867	conv cpe	4,255	4,468	4,004
3947	Custom htp cpe	4,271	4,391	4,594

1964 Engines	bore × stroke	bhp	availability
V6, 225.0	3.75×3.40	155	S-F-85
V8, 330.0	3.94×3.38	230	S-Vista Crsr; O-F-85, Jetstar 88
V8, 330.0	3.94×3.38	245	S-Jetstar 88
V8, 330.0	3.94×3.38	290	S-Cutlass; O-F-85, Jetstar 88
V8, 394.0	4.13×3.69	280	S-88
V8, 394.0	4.13×3.69	330	S-Super 88, 98; 0-88
V8, 394.0	4.13×3.69	345	S-Jetstar I, Starfire, 98 Custom; O-Super 88, 98

1965

F-85 (wb 115.0; Vista Crsr-120.0)		Wght	Price	Prod
3327	club cpe, V6	2,940	2,344	5,289
3335	wgn 4d, V6	3,252	2,689	714
3369	sdn 4d, V6	2,991	2,398	3,089
3427	club cpe, V8	3,146	2,415	7,720
3435	wgn 4d, V8	3,457	2,760	2,496
3455	Vista Crsr. wgn, 6P, V8	3,732	2,937	2,110
3465	Vista Crsr. wgn, 8P, V8	3,809	3,072	3,335
3469	sdn 4d, V8	3,174	2,469	5,661

F-85 Deluxe (wb 115.0; Cus-120.0)		Wght	Price	Prod
3527	Sports Coupe, V6	2,980	2,538	6,141
3535	wgn 4d, V6	3,262	2,797	659
3569	sdn 4d, V6	3,016	2,505	4,989
3635	wgn 4d, V8	3,459	2,868	10,365
3669	sdn 4d, V8	3,218	2,576	47,767
3855	Cus wgn 4d, 6P, V8	3,762	3,146	9,335
3865	Cus wgn 4d, 8P, V8	3,864	3,270	17,205

Cutlass (wb 115.0)		Wght	Price	Prod
3827	Sports Coupe, V8	3,221	2,643	26,441
3837	Holiday htp cpe, V8	3,245	2,784	46,138
3867	conv cpe, V8	3,338	2,983	12,628

Jetstar 88 (wb 123.0)		Wght	Price	Prod
5237	Holiday htp cpe	3,688	2,995	13,911
5239	Holiday htp sdn	3,775	3,072	15,922
5267	conv cpe	3,741	3,337	2,879
5269	Celebrity sdn 4d	3,726	2,938	22,725

Jetstar I (wb 123.0)		Wght	Price	Prod
5457	Sports Coupe	3,982	3,602	6,552

Dynamic 88 (wb 123.0)		Wght	Price	Prod
5637	Holiday htp cpe	3,873	3,065	24,746
5639	Holiday htp sdn	3,961	3,143	38,889
5667	conv cpe	3,946	3,408	8,832
5669	Celebrity sdn 4d	3,908	3,008	47,030

Delta 88 (wb 123.0)		Wght	Price	Prod
5837	htp cpe	3,924	3,253	23,194
5839	htp sdn	4,010	3,330	37,358
5869	Celebrity sdn 4d	3,940	3,158	29,915

Starfire (wb 123.0)		Wght	Price	Prod
6657	htp cpe	4,152	4,138	13,024
6667	conv cpe	4,247	4,778	2,236

98 (wb 126.0)		Wght	Price	Prod
8437	htp cpe	4,178	4,197	12,166
8439	htp sdn	4,286	4,273	28,480
8467	conv cpe	4,250	4,493	4,903
8469	Town Sedan 4d	4,186	4,001	13,266
8669	Luxury sdn 4d	4,285	4,351	33,591

1965 Engines	bore × stroke	bhp	availability
V6, 225.0	3.75 × 3.40	155	S-F-85 6
V8, 330.0	3.94 × 3.38	250/260	S-F-85 V8 exc Cutlass /Jetstar 88
V8, 330.0	3.94 × 3.38	315	S-Cutlass
V8, 400.0	4.00 × 3.98	320	O-Cutlass
V8, 425.0	4.13 × 3.98	310	S-Delta 88, Dynamic 88; 0-98
V8, 425.0	4.13 × 3.98	360	S-98; O-other full-size
V8, 425.0	4.13 × 3.98	370	S-Jetstar I, Starfire; O-full-size

1966

F-85 (wb 115.0)		Wght	Price	Prod
33307	cpe, L6	2,951	2,348	6,341
33335	wgn 4d, L6	3,246	2,695	508
33369	sdn 4d, L6	3,001	2,401	2,862
33407	cpe, V8	3,153	2,418	4,923*
33435	wgn 4d, V8	3,431	2,764	1,652
33469	sdn 4d, V8	3,187	2,471	3,754

F-85 Deluxe (wb 115.0)		Wght	Price	Prod
33517	Holiday htp cpe, L6	2,990	2,513	2,974
33535	wgn 4d, L6	3,273	2,793	434
33539	Holiday htp sdn, L6	3,077	2,629	1,002
33569	sdn 4d, L6	3,023	2,497	3,568
33617	Holiday htp cpe, V8	3,196	2,583	13,141*
33635	wgn 4d, V8	3,453	2,862	8,058
33639	Holiday htp sdn, V8	3,272	2,699	6,911
33669	sdn 4d, V8	3,210	2,567	27,452

Cutlass (wb 115.0)		Wght	Price	Prod
33807	Sports Coupe	3,219	2,633	13,518*
33817	Holiday htp cpe	3,243	2,770	34,580*
33839	Supreme htp sdn	3,296	2,846	30,871
33867	conv cpe	3,349	2,965	9,410*
33869	Celebrity sdn 4d	3,240	2,673	9,017

Vista Cruiser (wb 120.0)		Wght	Price	Prod
33455	wgn 4d, 2S	3,735	2,935	1,660
33465	wgn 4d, 3S	3,806	3,087	1,869
33855	Custom wgn 4d, 2S	3,765	3,137	8,910
33865	Custom wgn 4d, 3S	3,861	3,278	14,164

4-4-2 (wb 115.0)		Wght	Price	Prod
33407	cpe	3,454	2,604	1,430*
33617	htp cpe	3,502	2,769	3,827*
33807	spt cpe	3,506	2,786	3,937*
33817	Holiday htp cpe	3,523	2,923	10,053*
33867	conv cpe	3,629	3,118	2,750*

Jetstar 88 (wb 123.0)		Wght	Price	Prod
35237	Holiday htp cpe	3,727	2,983	8,575
35239	Holiday htp sdn	3,823	3,059	7,938
35269	Celebrity sdn 4d	3,776	2,927	13,734

Dynamic 88 (wb 123.0)		Wght	Price	Prod
35637	Holiday htp cpe	3,899	3,069	20,768
35639	Holiday htp sdn	3,982	3,144	30,784
35667	conv cpe	3,971	3,404	5,540
35669	Celebrity sdn 4d	3,930	3,013	38,742

Delta 88 (wb 123.0)		Wght	Price	Prod
35837	Holiday htp cpe	3,944	3,253	20,857
35839	Holiday htp sdn	4,026	3,328	33,326
35867	conv cpe	4,010	3,588	4,303
35869	Celebrity sdn 4d	3,963	3,160	30,140

Starfire (wb 123.0)		Wght	Price	Prod
35457	htp cpe	4,013	3,564	13,019

98 (wb 126.0)		Wght	Price	Prod
38437	Holiday htp cpe	4,165	4,158	11,488
38439	Holiday htp sdn	4,266	4,233	23,048
38467	conv cpe	4,233	4,443	4,568
38469	Town Sedan 4d	4,177	3,966	10,892
38669	Luxury Sedan 4d	4,271	4,308	30,123

Toronado (wb 119.0)		Wght	Price	Prod
39487	htp cpe	4,311	4,617	6,333
39687	Deluxe htp cpe	4,366	4,812	34,630

*Production combined; numbers given are proportional to production of same models in F-85 and Cutlass lines. Total 4-4-2 production: 21,997.

1966 Engines	bore × stroke	bhp	availability
L6, 250.0	3.88 × 3.53	155	S-F-85 6
V8, 330.0	3.94 × 3.38	250	S-F-85 V8, Vista Crsr; O-Jetstar 88
V8, 330.0	3.94 × 3.38	260	S-Jetstar 88
V8, 330.0	3.94 × 3.38	310	O-Cutlass, F-85, Vista Crsr
V8, 330.0	3.94 × 3.38	320	S-Cutlass; O-Jetstar 88, F-85, Vst. Crsr
V8, 400.0	4.00 × 3.98	350	S-442
V8, 425.0	4.13 × 3.98	300	O-Delta 88, Dynamic 88
V8, 425.0	4.13 × 3.98	310	S-Delta 88, Dynamic 88
V8, 425.0	4.13 × 3.98	365	S-98; O-Delta 88, Dynamic 88
V8, 425.0	4.13 × 3.98	375	S-Starfire; 0-98, Delta 88
V8, 425.0	4.13 × 3.98	385	S-Toronado

1967

F-85 (wb 115.0)		Wght	Price	Prod
33307	club cpe, L6	3,014	2,410	5,349
33335	wgn 4d, L6	3,295	2,749	2,749
33369	Town Sedan 4d, L6	3,031	2,457	2,458
33407	club cpe, V8	3,184	2,480	6,700
33435	wgn 4d, V8	3,463	2,818	1,625
33469	Town Sedan 4d, V8	3,469	2,527	5,126

Cutlass (wb 115.0)		Wght	Price	Prod
33517	Holiday htp cpe, L6	3,033	2,574	2,564
33535	wgn 4d, L6	3,308	2,848	365
33539	Holiday htp sdn, L6	3,125	2,683	644
33567	conv cpe, L6	3,125	2,770	567

		Wght	Price	Prod
33569	Town Sedan 4d, L6	3,055	2,552	2,219
33617	Holiday htp cpe, V8	3,216	2,644	29,799
33635	wgn 4d, V8	3,473	2,917	8,130
33639	Holiday htp sdn, V8	3,292	2,753	7,344
33667	conv cpe, V8	3,306	2,839	3,777
33669	Town Sedan 4d, V8	3,223	2,622	29,062

Cutlass Supreme (wb 115.0)

33807	Sports Coupe	3,238	2,694	13,041*
33817	Holiday htp cpe	3,262	2,831	41,344*
33839	Holiday htp sdn	3,346	2,900	22,571
33867	conv cpe	3,867	3,026	7,793*
33869	Town Sedan 4d	3,258	2,726	8,346

4-4-2 (wb 115.0)

33807	Sports Coupe	3,540	2,788	5,215*
33817	Holiday htp cpe	3,568	3,015	16,514*
33867	conv cpe	4,047	3,210	3,104*

Vista Cruiser (wb 120.0)

33465	wgn 4d, 3S	3,836	3,136	2,748
33855	Custom wgn 4d, 2S	3,796	3,228	9,513
33865	Custom wgn 4d, 3S	3,907	3,369	15,293

Delmont 88 "330" (wb 123.0)

05200	Holiday htp sdn	3,932	3,139	10,600
35269	Town Sedan 4d	3,867	3,008	15,076
35287	Holiday htp cpe	3,819	3,063	10,786

Delmont 88 "425" (wb 123.0)

35639	Holiday htp sdn	4,007	3,202	22,980
35667	conv cpe	4,010	3,462	3,525
35669	Town Sedan 4d	3,968	3,071	28,690
35687	Holiday htp cpe	3,914	3,126	16,699

Delta 88 (wb 123.0)

35839	Holiday htp sdn	4,053	3,386	21,909
35867	conv cpe	4,039	3,646	2,447
35869	Town Sedan 4d	3,986	3,218	22,770
35887	Holiday htp cpe	3,956	3,310	14,471

Delta 88 Custom (wb 123.0)

35439	Holiday htp sdn	4,081	3,582	14,306
35487	Holiday htp cpe	3,994	3,522	12,192

98 (wb 126.0)

38439	Holiday htp sdn	4,323	4,276	17,533
38457	Holiday htp cpe	4,221	4,214	10,476
38467	conv cpe	4,271	4,498	3,769
38469	Town Sedan 4d	4,242	4,009	8,900
38669	Luxury Sedan 4d	4,309	4,351	35,511

Toronado (wb 119.0)

39487	htp cpe	4,310	4,674	1,770
39687	Deluxe htp cpe	4,362	4,869	20,020

*Production combined; numbers given are proportional to production of same models in Cutlass Supreme line. Total 4-4-2 production: 24,833.

1967 Engines	bore × stroke	bhp	availability
L6, 250.0	3.88 × 3.53	155	S-F-85 6, Cutlass 6
V8, 330.0	3.94 × 3.38	250	S-F-85 V8, Cutlass V8, Vst. Crsr, Delm 88 man; O-Delm auto
V8, 330.0	3.94 × 3.38	260	S-Delmont 88 w/auto
V8, 330.0	3.94 × 3.38	310	O-Supreme, Cutls, F-85, VC
V8, 330.0	3.94 × 3.38	320	S-Sprme; O-Delm, VC, F-85,Cutls
V8, 400.0	4.00 × 3.98	300	O-Sprme cpe & conv
V8, 400.0	4.00 × 3.98	350	O-Sprme cpe & conv
V8, 425.0	4.13 × 3.98	300	S-all 88 man; O-all 88 auto
V8, 425.0	4.13 × 3.98	310	S-all 88 automatic
V8, 425.0	4.13 × 3.98	365	S-98; O-Delta 88, Delmont 425
V8, 425.0	4.13 × 3.98	375	O-98, Delta 88, Delmont 425
V8, 425.0	4.13 × 3.98	385	S-Toronado

1968

F-85 (wb 116.0; 2d-112.0)

		Wght	Price	Prod
33169	Town Sedan 4d, L6	3,108	2,560	1,847
33177	club cpe, L6	3,062	2,512	4,052
33269	Town Sedan 4d, V8	3,304	2,665	3,984
33277	club cpe, V8	3,255	2,618	5,426

Cutlass (wb 116.0; 2d-112.0)

33535	wgn 4d, 2S, L6	3,473	2,969	354
33539	Holiday htp sdn, L6	3,193	2,804	265
33567	conv cpe, L6	3,161	2,949	410
33569	Town Sedan 4d, L6	3,143	2,674	1,305
33577	Sports Coupe, L6	3,064	2,632	1,181
33587	Holiday htp cpe, L6	3,108	2,696	1,492
33635	wgn 4d, 2S, V8	3,649	3,075	9,291
33639	Holiday htp sdn, V8	3,374	2,910	7,839
33667	conv cpe, V8	3,342	3,055	13,667
33669	Town Sedan 4d, V8	3,325	2,779	25,994
33677	Sport Coupe, V8	3,271	2,738	14,586
33687	Holiday htp cpe, V8	3,282	2,801	59,577

Cutlass Supreme (wb 116.0; 2d-112.0)

34239	Holiday htp sdn	3,421	3,057	15,067
34269	Town Sedan 4d	3,372	2,884	5,524
34287	Holiday htp cpe	3,312	2,982	33,518

4-4-2 (wb 112.0)

34467	conv cpe	3,580	3,341	5,142
34477	Sports Coupe	3,502	3,087	4,282
34487	Holiday htp cpe	3,512	3,150	24,183

Vista Cruiser (wb 121.0)

34855	Custom wgn 4d, 2S	3,917	3,367	13,375
34865	Custom wgn 4d, 3S	4,027	3,508	22,768

Delmont 88 (wb 123.0)*

35439	Holiday htp sdn	3,928	3,278	21,056
35467	conv cpe	3,916	3,515	2,812
35469	Town Sedan 4d	3,873	3,146	24,365
35487	Holiday htp cpe	3,844	3,202	18,391

Delta 88 (wb 123.0)*

36439	Holiday htp sdn	4,038	3,525	30,048
36469	Town Sedan 4d	3,979	3,357	33,689
36487	Holiday htp cpe	3,950	3,449	18,501
36639	Custom Holiday htp sdn	4,059	3,721	10,727
36687	Custom Holiday htp cpe	3,982	3,661	9,540

98 (wb 126.0)

38439	Holiday htp sdn	4,278	4,422	21,147
38457	Holiday htp cpe	4,185	4,360	15,319
38467	conv cpe	4,264	4,618	3,942
38469	Town Sedan 4d	4,197	4,155	10,584
38669	Luxury Sedan 4d	4,273	4,497	40,755

Toronado (wb 119.0)

39487	htp cpe	4,322	4,750	3,957
39687	Custom htp cpe	4,374	4,945	22,497

*Factory records also indicate 54,794 Dynamic 88s, although other sources do not include these models.

1968 Engines	bore × stroke	bhp	availability
L6, 250.0	3.88 × 3.53	155	S-F-85 6, Cutlass 6
V8, 350.0	4.06 × 3.38	250	S-Vista Crsr; O-Cutls, F-85
V8, 350.0	4.06 × 3.38	310	S-Supreme; O-F-85, Cutls, Vista Cruiser, Delmont 88 auto
V8, 400.0	4.00 × 3.98	290	O-442 auto, Vista Cruiser auto
V8, 400.0	4.00 × 3.98	325	S-442 auto; O-Vista Cruiser auto
V8, 400.0	4.00 × 3.98	350	S-442 manual
V8, 400.0	4.00 × 3.98	360	O-442 all
V8, 455.0	4.13 × 4.25	310	S-Delta 88 & Custom; O-Delm
V8, 455.0	4.13 × 4.25	320	0-above models w/automatic
V8, 455.0	4.13 × 4.25	365	S-98; O-all 88 w/automatic

	bore × stroke	bhp	availability
V8, 455.0	4.13×4.25	375	S-Toronado
V8, 455.0	4.13×4.25	400	O-Toronado

1969

F-85 (wb 116.0; 2d-112.0)

		Wght	Price	Prod
33177	Sports Coupe, L6	3,082	2,561	2,899
33277	Sports Coupe, V8	3,281	2,672	5,541

Cutlass (wb 116.0; 2d-112.0)

		Wght	Price	Prod
33535	wgn 4d, 2S, L6	3,537	3,055	180
33539	Holiday htp sdn, L6	3,212	2,853	236
33567	S conv cpe, L6	3,188	2,998	236
33569	Town Sedan 4d, L6	3,155	2,722	137
33577	S Sports Coupe, L6	3,093	2,681	483
33587	S Holiday htp cpe, L6	3,118	2,745	566
33635	wgn 4d, 2S, V8	3,736	3,165	8,559
33639	Holiday htp sdn, V8	3,407	2,964	7,046
33667	S conv cpe, V8	3,386	3,109	13,498
33669	Town Sedan 4d, V8	3,356	2,833	24,521
33677	S Sports Coupe, V8	3,293	2,792	10,682
33687	S Holiday htp cpe, V8	3,316	2,855	66,495

Cutlass Supreme (wb 116; 2d-112.0)

		Wght	Price	Prod
34239	Holiday htp sdn	3,421	3,111	8,714
34269	Town Sedan 4d	3,361	2,938	4,522
34287	Holiday htp cpe	3,331	3,036	24,193

4-4-2 (wb 112.0)

		Wght	Price	Prod
34467	conv cpe	3,580	3,395	4,295
34477	Sports Coupe	3,502	3,141	2,475
34487	Holiday htp cpe	3,512	3,204	19,587

Vista Cruiser (wb 121.0)

		Wght	Price	Prod
34855	wgn 4d, 2S	3,952	3,457	11,879
34865	wgn 4d, 3S	4,052	3,600	21,508

Delta 88 (wb 124.0)

		Wght	Price	Prod
35437	Holiday htp cpe	3,812	3,277	41,947
35439	Holiday htp sdn	3,901	3,353	42,690
35467	conv cpe	3,892	3,590	5,294
35469	Town Sedan 4d	3,859	3,222	49,995
36437	Custom Holiday htp cpe	3,927	3,525	22,083
36439	Custom Holiday htp sdn	4,009	3,600	36,502
36469	Custom Town Sedan 4d	3,962	3,432	31,012
36647	Royale Holiday htp cpe	3,935	3,836	22,564

98 (wb 127.0)

		Wght	Price	Prod
38439	Holiday htp sdn	4,260	4,523	17,294
38457	Holiday htp cpe	4,150	4,461	27,041
38467	conv cpe	4,223	4,719	4,288
38469	Town Sedan 4d	4,150	4,255	11,169
38639	Luxury Sedan (htp)	4,288	4,692	25,973
38669	Luxury Sedan 4d	4,245	4,598	30,643

Toronado (wb 119.0)

		Wght	Price	Prod
39487	htp cpe	4,316	4,835	3,421
39687	Custom htp cpe	4,368	5,030	25,073

1969 Engines	bore × stroke	bhp	availability
L6, 250.0	3.88×3.53	155	S- F-85, Cutlass
V8, 350.0	4.06×3.38	250	S-Cutlass S/sdns/wgns, F-85, Delta 88, Vst Crsr; O-Supreme
V8, 350.0	4.06×3.38	310	S-Supreme; O-Cutlass, Vst Crsr, F-85
V8, 350.0	4.06×3.38	325	O-Cutlass S, F-85
V8, 400.0	4.00×3.98	325	S-442 auto, Vista Cruiser auto
V8, 400.0	4.00×3.98	350	S-442 manual
V8, 400.0	4.00×3.98	360	O-442
V8, 455.0	4.13×4.25	310	S-Dlta 88 Cus/Royale; O-Delta
V8, 455.0	4.13×4.25	365	S-98; O-all Delta 88
V8, 455.0	4.13×4.25	375	S-Toronado

	bore × stock	bhp	availability
V8, 455.0	4.13×4.25	390	O-all Delta 88
V8, 455.0	4.13×4.25	400	O-Toronado

1970

F-85 (wb 116.0; 2d-112.0)

		Wght	Price	Prod
33177	Sports Coupe, L6	3,190	2,676	2,836
33277	Sports Coupe, V8	3,401	2,787	8,274

Cutlass (wb 116.0; 2d-112.0)

		Wght	Price	Prod
33535	wgn 4d, 2S, L6	3,630	3,234	85
33539	Holiday htp sdn, L6	3,326	2,968	238
33569	Town Sedan 4d, L6	3,257	2,837	1,171
33577	S Sports Coupe, L6	3,201	2,796	484
33587	S Holiday htp cpe, L6	3,238	2,859	729
33635	wgn 4d, 2S, V8	3,837	3,344	7,686
33639	Holiday htp sdn, V8	3,523	3,079	9,427
33669	Town Sedan, V8	3,468	2,948	35,239
33677	S Sports Coupe, V8	3,416	2,907	10,677
33687	S Holiday htp cpe, V8	3,452	2,970	88,578

Cutlass Supreme (wb 116; 2d-112.0)

		Wght	Price	Prod
34239	Holiday htp sdn	3,558	3,226	10,762
34257	Holiday htp cpe	3,471	3,151	68,309
34267	conv cpe	3,510	3,335	11,354

4-4-2 (wb 112.0)

		Wght	Price	Prod
34467	conv cpe	3,740	3,567	2,933
34477	Sports Coupe	3,667	3,312	1,688
34487	Holiday htp cpe	3,713	3,376	14,709

Vista Cruiser (wb 121.0)

		Wght	Price	Prod
34855	wgn 4d, 2S	4,064	3,636	10,758
34865	wgn 4d, 3S	4,166	3,778	23,336

Delta 88 (wb 124.0)

		Wght	Price	Prod
35437	Holiday htp cpe	3,900	3,590	33,017
35439	Holiday htp sdn	3,986	3,666	37,695
35467	conv cpe	3,985	3,903	3,095
35469	Town Sedan 4d	3,944	3,534	47,067
36437	Custom Holiday htp cpe	3,999	3,848	16,149
36439	Custom Holiday htp sdn	4,087	3,924	28,432
36469	Custom Town Sedan 4d	4,040	3,755	24,727
36647	Royale Holiday htp cpe	4,002	4,159	13,249

98 (wb 127.0)

		Wght	Price	Prod
38439	Holiday htp sdn	4,329	4,582	14,098
38457	Holiday htp cpe	4,257	4,656	21,111
38467	conv cpe	4,289	4,914	3,161
38469	Town Sedan 4d	4,263	4,451	9,092
38639	Luxury htp sdn	4,400	4,888	19,377
38669	Luxury sdn 4d	4,356	4,793	29,005

Toronado (wb 119.0)

		Wght	Price	Prod
39487	htp cpe	4,331	5,023	2,351
39687	Custom htp cpe	4,386	5,216	23,082

1970 Engines	bore × stroke	bhp	availability
L6, 250.0	3.88×3.53	155	S- F-85, Cutlass
V8, 350.0	4.06×3.38	250	S- F-85/Cutlass V8, Vst Crsr; O-Supreme
V8, 350.0	4.06×3.38	310	S-Supreme; O-Vst Crsr, F-85, Cutlass
V8, 350.0	4.06×3.38	325	O-F-85, Cutlass S auto or 4 spd
V8, 455.0	4.13×4.25	310	S-Delta 88 manual
V8, 455.0	4.13×4.25	320	O-Cutlass w/automatic
V8, 455.0	4.13×4.25	365	S-442, 98; O-Supreme, 88/Vst Crsr manual
V8, 455.0	4.13×4.25	370	O-442 w/auto or close-ratio 4spd
V8, 455.0	4.13×4.25	375	S-Toronado
V8, 455.0	4.13×4.25	390	O-Delta 88
V8, 455.0	4.13×4.25	400	O-Toronado

Oldsmobile

1971

F-85 (wb 116.0)		Wght	Price	Prod
33169	Town sdn 4d L6	3,226	2,885	769
33269	Town sdn 4d V8	3,424	3,006	3,650

Cutlass (wb 116.0; 2d-112.0)				
33187	Holiday htp cpe L6	3,292	2,901	1,345
33536	wgn 4d 2S L6	3,732	3,454	47
33569	Town sdn 4d L6	3,252	2,999	618
33287	Holiday htp cpe V8	3,398	3,022	32,278
33636	wgn 4d 2S V8	3,927	3,575	6,742
33669	Town sdn 4d V8	3,438	3,120	31,904
33577	S spt cpe L6	3,196	2,958	113
33587	S Holiday htp cpe L6	3,228	3,021	169
33677	S spt cpe V8	3,392	3,079	4,339
33687	S Holiday htp cpe V8	3,398	3,142	63,145

Cutlass Supreme (wb 116.0; 2d-112.0)				
34239	Holiday htp sdn	3,541	3,398	10,458
34257	Holiday htp cpe	3,429	3,323	60,599
34267	conv	3,513	3,507	10,255

4-4-2 (wb 112.0)				
34467	conv cpe	3,731	3,743	1,304
34487	Holiday cpe	3,688	3,552	6,285

Vista Cruiser (wb 121.0)				
34856	wgn 4d 2S	4,163	3,866	5,980
34866	wgn 4d 3S	4,251	4,008	20,566

Delta 88 (wb 124.0; wgns-127.0)				
35439	Holiday sdn 4d	4,202	4,103	31,420
35457	Holiday htp cpe	4,122	4,041	27,031
35469	Town sdn 4d	4,150	3,985	38,298
36439	Custom Holiday htp sdn 4d	4,237	4,366	26,593
36457	Custom Holiday cpe	4,179	4,291	24,251
36469	Custom Town sdn 4d	4,202	4,198	22,209
36647	Royale Holiday htp cpe	4,221	4,549	8,397
36667	Royale conv	4,296	4,557	2,883
36835	Custom Cruiser wgn 4d 2S	4,880	4,776	4,049
36845	Custom Cruiser wgn 4d 3S	5,000	4,917	9,932

Ninety-Eight (wb 127.0)				
38437	Holiday htp cpe	4,382	4,790	8,335
38439	Holiday htp sdn	4,467	4,852	15,025
38637	Luxury htp cpe	4,418	5,065	14,876
38639	Luxury htp sdn	4,504	5,159	45,055

Toronado (wb 123.0)				
39657	htp cpe	4,522	5,457	28,980

1971 Engines	bore×stroke	bhp	availability	
L6, 250.0	3.88×3.53	145	S-F-85, Cutlass	
V8, 350.0	4.06×3.38	240	S-F-85, Cutlass, Delta, VC	
V8, 350.0	4.06×3.38	260	S-Supreme, O-F-85, Cutlass, VC	
V8, 455.0	4.13×4.25	280	O-Delta	
V8, 455.0	4.13×4.25	320	S-98; O-442,F-85,Ctls,VC, DLta	
V8, 455.0	4.13×4.25	340	S-442; O-F-85, Cutlass, VC	
V8, 455.0	4.13×4.25	350	S-Toronado	

1972

F-85 (wb 116.0)		Wght	Price	Prod
3D69	sdn 4d	3,420	2,958	3,792

Cutlass (wb 116.0; 2d-112.0)				
3F87	cpe	3,379	2,973	37,790
3G36	Cruiser wgn 4d 2S	3,919	3,498	7,979
3G69	Town sdn 4d	3,443	3,066	38,893
3G77	S spt cpe	3,387	3,027	4,141
3G87	S Holiday htp cpe	3,404	3,087	78,461

		Wght	Price	Prod
3J39	Supreme Holiday htp sdn	3,530	3,329	14,955
3J57	Supreme Holiday htp cpe	3,395	3,258	105,087
3J67	Supreme conv	3,528	3,433	11,571

Vista Cruiser (wb 121.0)				
3K56	wgn 4d 2S	4,150	3,774	10,573
3K66	wgn 4d 3S	4,241	3,908	21,340

Delta 88 (wb 124.0)				
3L39	Holiday sdn 4d	4,235	4,060	35,538
3L57	Holiday htp cpe	4,133	4,001	32,036
3L69	Town sdn 4d	4,187	3,948	46,092
3N39	Royale Holiday sdn 4d	4,263	4,238	42,606
3N57	Royale Holiday htp cpe	4,184	4,179	34,345
3N67	Royale conv	4,257	4,387	3,900
3N69	Royale Town sdn 4d	4,198	4,101	34,150
3R35	Custom Cruiser wgn 4d 2S	4,947	4,700	6,907
3R45	Custom Cruiser wgn 4d 3S	5,040	4,834	18,087

Ninety-Eight (wb 127.0)				
3U37	Holiday htp cpe	4,372	4,748	13,111
3U39	htp sdn	4,448	4,807	17,572
3V37	Luxury htp cpe	4,428	5,009	24,453
3V39	Luxury htp sdn	4,533	5,098	69,920

Toronado (wb 122.0)				
3Y57	Custom htp cpe	4,544	5,341	48,900

1972 Engines	bore×stroke	bhp	availability
V8, 350.0	4.06×3.38	160	S-F-85,Ctls,Dlta exc wgns
V8, 350.0	4.06×3.38	180	S-Supreme; O-Ctls,F-85, VC Delta exc wgn
V8, 455.0	4.13×4.25	225	S-Dlta exc wgn, 98; O-Dlta
V8, 455.0	4.13×4.25	250	S-Toro; O-Delta, 98

1973

Omega (wb 111.0)		Wght	Price	Prod
B17	htchbk cpe 3d	3,329	2,762	21,433
B27	cpe	3,217	2,613	26,126
B69	sdn 4d	3,280	2,641	12,804

Cutlass (wb 116.0; 2d-112.0)				
G29	Colonnade sdn 4d	3,786	3,137	35,578
F37	Colonnade sdn 2d	3,713	3,049	22,022
G37	Colonnade S sdn 2d	3,721	3,159	77,558
J29	Supreme Colonnade sdn 4d	3,808	3,395	26,099
J57	Supreme Colonnade sdn 2d	3,694	3,324	219,857

Vista Cruiser (wb 121.0)				
J35	wgn 5d 2S	4,240	3,789	10,894
J45	wgn 5d 3S	4,290	3,902	13,531

Delta 88 (wb 124.0)				
L39	htp sdn	4,270	4,108	27,986
L57	htp cpe	4,192	4,047	27,096
L69	Town sdn 4d	4,243	3,991	42,476
N39	Royale htp sdn	4,296	4,293	49,145
N57	Royale htp cpe	4,206	4,221	27,096
N67	Royale conv	4,298	4,442	7,088
N69	Royale Town sdn 4d	4,255	4,156	42,672
Q35	wgn 4d 2S	4,997	4,630	5,275
Q45	wgn 4d 3S	5,061	4,769	7,341
R35	Royale wgn 4d 2S	4,999	4,785	7,142
R45	Royale wgn 4d 3S	5,063	4,924	19,163

Ninety-Eight (wb 127.0)				
T37	htp cpe	4,435	4,799	7,850
T39	htp sdn	4,522	4,860	13,989
V37	Luxury htp cpe	4,471	5,071	26,925
V39	Luxury htp sdn	4,560	5,164	55,695
X39	Regency htp sdn	4,594	5,418	34,009

Toronado (wb 122.0)

		Wght	Price	Prod
Y57	htp cpe	4,654	5,441	55,921

1973 Engines	bore×stroke	bhp	availability
L6, 250.0	3.88×3.53	100	S-Omega
V8, 350.0	4.06×3.38	160	S-Delta exc wgns
V8, 350.0	4.06×3.38	180	S-Omega, Cutlass, VC
V8, 455.0	4.13×4.25	225	S-Dlta wgns; 98; O-Dlta
V8, 455.0	4.13×4.25	250	S-Toronado, O-Cutlass, VC

1974

Omega (wb 111.0)

		Wght	Price	Prod
B17	htchbk cpe 3d	3,423	3,166	12,449
B27	cpe	3,319	3,043	27,075
B69	sdn 4d	3,367	3,071	10,756

Cutlass (wb 116.0; 2d-112.0)

		Wght	Price	Prod
F37	Colonnade sdn 2d	3,868	3,793	16,063
G29	Colonnade sdn 4d	3,924	3,868	25,718
G37	Colonnade S sdn 2d	3,883	3,890	50,860
J29	Supreme Colonnade sdn 4d	3,969	4,142	12,525
J57	Supreme Colonnade sdn 2d	3,872	4,085	172,360
H35	Supreme Cruiser wgn 5d 2S	4,369	4,289	3,437
H45	Supreme Cruiser wgn 5d 3S	4,406	4,402	3,101

Vista Cruiser (wb 121.0)

		Wght	Price	Prod
J35	wgn 4d 2S	4,380	4,499	4,191
J45	wgn 4d 3S	4,417	4,612	7,013

Delta 88 (wb 124.0)

		Wght	Price	Prod
L39	htp sdn	4,428	4,490	11,941
L57	htp cpe	4,375	4,429	11,615
L69	Town sdn 4d	4,396	4,373	17,939
N39	Royale htp sdn	4,462	4,650	26,363
N57	Royale htp cpe	4,397	4,584	27,515
N67	Royale conv	4,454	4,799	3,716
N69	Royale Town sdn 4d	4,414	4,513	22,504
Q35	Custom Cruiser wgn 4d 2S	5,120	4,981	1,481
Q45	Custom Cruiser wgn 4d 3S	5,182	5,120	2,528
R35	Royale wgn 4d 2S	5,123	5,136	2,960
R45	Royale wgn 4d 3S	5,184	5,275	8,947

Ninety-Eight (wb 127.0)

		Wght	Price	Prod
T39	htp sdn	4,699	5,303	4,395
V37	Luxury cpe	4,638	5,514	9,236
V39	Luxury htp sdn 4d	4,730	5,607	21,896
X37	Regency cpe	4,664	5,776	10,719
X39	Regency htp sdn 4d	4,759	5,869	24,310

Toronado (wb 122.0)

		Wght	Price	Prod
Y57	htp cpe	4,698	5,933	27,582

1974 Engines	bore×stroke	bhp	availability
L6, 250.0	3.88×3.53	100	S-Omega
V8, 350.0	4.06×3.38	180	S-Omega, Ctls, VC, Delta exc wgns
V8, 350.0	4.06×3.38	200	O-Ctls, VC, Delta exc wgns
V8, 455.0	4.13×4.25	210	S-Delta wgns, 98; O-Delta
V8, 455.0	4.13×4.25	230	O-all exc Omega
V8, 455.0	4.13×4.25	275	O-Cutlass, VC

1975

Starfire (wb 97.0)

		Wght	Price	Prod
D37	htchbk cpe 3d	2,914	4,144	31,081
T07	htchbk cpe 3d	2,889	3,873	

Omega (wb 111.0)

		Wght	Price	Prod
S27	F-85 htchbk cpe 3d	3,250	3,203	15,979
B27	cpe	3,390	3,422	
B17	htchbk cpe	3,482	3,546	6,287
B69	sdn 4d	3,436	3,450	13,971

		Wght	Price	Prod
C17	Salon htchbk cpe 3d	3,566	4,298	1,694
C27	Salon cpe	3,476	4,148	2,176
C69	Salon sdn 4d	3,526	4,192	1,758

Cutlass (wb 116.0; 2d-112.0)

		Wght	Price	Prod
F37	Colonnade sdn 2d	3,684	3,742	12,797
G29	Colonnade sdn 4d	3,806	3,818	30,144
G37	Colonnade S sdn 2d	3,740	3,840	42,921
J29	Supreme Colonnade sdn 4d	3,852	4,092	15,517
J57	Supreme Colonnade sdn 2d	3,754	4,035	150,874
K29	Salon Colonnade sdn 4d V8	4,008	4,713	5,810
K57	Salon Colonnade sdn 2d V8	3,915	4,641	39,050
H35	Supreme Cruiser wgn 5d 2S V8	4,376	4,665	8,329
H45	Supreme Cruiser wgn 5d 3S V8	4,413	4,778	3,096
J35	Vista Cruiser wgn 5d 2S V8	4,380	4,875	7,089
J45	Vista Cruiser wgn 5d 3S V8	4,417	4,988	7,101

Delta 88 (wb 124.0)

		Wght	Price	Prod
L39	htp sdn	4,404	4,891	9,283
L57	htp cpe	4,343	4,830	8,522
L69	Town sdn 4d	4,356	4,778	16,112
N39	Royale htp sdn	4,454	5,051	32,481
N57	Royale htp cpe	4,386	4,985	23,465
N67	Royale conv	4,455	5,200	21,038
N69	Royale Town sdn 4d	4,385	4,914	7,181
Q35	Custom Cruiser wgn 4d 2S	5,095	5,413	6,008
R35	Royale wgn 4d 2S	5,107	5,568	
Q45	Custom Cruiser wgn 4d 3S	5,146	5,552	10,060
R45	Royale wgn 4d 3S	5,161	5,707	

Ninety-Eight (wb 127.0)

		Wght	Price	Prod
V37	Luxury cpe	4,591	5,950	8,798
V39	Luxury htp sdn 4d	4,743	6,091	18,091
X37	Regency cpe	4,621	6,212	16,697
X39	Regency htp sdn 4d	4,755	6,353	35,264

Toronado (wb 122.0)

		Wght	Price	Prod
Y57	Custom htp cpe	4,647	6,523	4,419
Z57	Brougham htp cpe	4,691	6,753	18,882

1975 Engines	bore×stroke	bhp	availability
V6, 231.0	3.80×3.40	110	S-Starfire
L6, 250.0	3.88×3.53	105	S-Omega, Ctls exc wgns
V8, 260.0	3.50×3.39	110	S-Omega, Ctls exc wgns
V8, 350.0	4.06×3.38	145	O-Omega
V8, 350.0	4.06×3.38	165	O-Omega
V8, 350.0	4.06×3.38	170	S-Ctls wgns; O-Ctls, Delta exc. Cust Crsr
V8, 400.0	4.12×3.75	185	O-Delta, 98
V8, 455.0	4.13×4.25	190	S-Delta Cus Crsr; O-Cutlass, other Delta
V8, 455.0	4.13×4.25	215	S-Toronado

1976

Starfire (wb 97.0)

		Wght	Price	Prod
D07	SX htchbk cpe 3d	2,864	4,062	20,854
T07	htchbk cpe 3d	2,857	3,882	8,305

Omega (wb 111.0)

		Wght	Price	Prod
S27	F-85 cpe	3,246	3,390	3,918
B17	htchbk cpe 3d	3,322	3,627	4,497
B27	cpe	3,248	3,485	15,347
B69	sdn 4d	3,270	3,514	20,221
E17	Brougham htchbk cpe 3d	3,332	3,817	1,235
E27	Brougham cpe	3,252	3,675	5,363
E69	Brougham sdn 4d	3,286	3,704	7,587

Cutlass (wb 116.0; 2d-112.0)

		Wght	Price	Prod
G29	S Colonnade sdn 4d	3,772	4,033	34,994
G37	S Colonnade sdn 2d	3,690	3,999	59,179
J29	Supreme Colonnade sdn 4d	3,812	4,415	37,112
J57	Supreme Colonnade cpe 2d	3,718	4,291	186,647

1976 Toronado coupe

		Wght	Price	Prod
M57	Supreme Brougham cpe	3,750	4,580	91,312
K29	Salon Colonnade sdn 4d V8	3,949	4,965	7,921
K57	Salon Colonnade cpe 2d V8	3,829	4,890	48,440
H35	Sprme Cruiser wgn 5d 2S V8	4,298	4,923	13,964
H35	Sprme Cruiser wgn 5d 3S V8	4,350	5,056	
J35	Vista Cruiser wgn 5d 2S V8	4,304	5,041	20,560
J35	Vista Cruiser wgn 5d 3S V8	4,350	5,174	

Delta 88 (wb 124.0; wgns 127.0)

L39	sdn 4d	4,000	5,030	9,759
L57	cpe 2d	4,243	4,975	7,204
L69	Town sdn 4d	4,279	4,918	17,115
N39	Royale sdn 4d	4,268	5,217	52,103
N57	Royale cpe 2d	4,263	5,146	33,364
N69	Royale Town sdn 4d	4,294	5,078	33,268
Q35	Custom Cruiser wgn 4d 2S	4,987	5,563	2,572
Q45	Custom Cruiser wgn 4d 3S	5,060	5,705	3,626
R35	Custom Cruiser wgn 4d 2S (woodgrain)	5,009	5,719	3,849
R45	Custom Cruiser wgn 4d 3S (woodgrain)	5,071	5,861	12,269

Ninety-Eight (wb 127.0)

V37	Luxury cpe 2d	4,501	6,271	6,056
V39	Luxury htp sdn 4d	4,633	6,419	16,802
X37	Regency cpe 2d	4,535	6,544	26,282
X39	Regency htp sdn 4d	4,673	6,691	55,339

Toronado (wb 122.0)

Y57	Custom htp cpe	4,694	6,891	2,555
Z57	Brougham htp cpe	4,729	7,137	21,749

1976 Engines	bore×stroke	bhp	availability
V6, 231.0	3.80×3.40	105	S-Starfire
L6, 250.0	3.88×3.53	105	S-Omega,Ctls exc Salon
V8, 260.0	3.50×3.39	110	S-Omega,Ctls Salon; O-Ctls
V8, 350.0	4.06×3.38	140/155	O-Omega
V8, 350.0	4.06×3.38	170	S-Ctls exc Salon; Delta exc wgn; O-Ctls, Salon
V8, 455.0	4.13×4.25	190	S-Delta wgn, 98; O-Ctls, other Delta
V8, 455.0	4.13×4.25	215	S-Toronado

1977

Starfire (wb 97.0)

		Wght	Price	Prod
D07	SX htchbk cpe 3d	2,836	4,140	14,181
T07	htchbk cpe 3d	2,808	3,942	4,910

Omega (wb 111.0)

S27	F-85 cpe	3,184	3,653	2,241
B17	htchbk cpe 3d	3,270	3,905	4,739
B27	cpe	3,202	3,740	18,611
B69	sdn 4d	3,236	3,797	21,723
E17	Brougham htchbk cpe 3d	3,302	4,105	1,189
E27	Brougham cpe	3,226	3,934	6,478
E67	Brougham sdn 4d	3,262	3,994	9,003

Cutlass (wb 116.0; 2d 112.0)

G29	S sdn 4d	3,690	4,387	42,993
G37	S cpe 2d	3,608	4,351	70,155
J29	Supreme sdn 4d	3,438	4,734	37,929
J57	Supreme cpe 2d	3,638	4,670	242,874
M29	Supreme Brougham sdn 4d	3,764	5,033	16,738
M57	Supreme Brougham cpe 2d	3,656	4,969	124,712
K57	Salon cpe 2d V8	3,787	5,269	56,757
H35	Supreme Cruiser wgn 5d V8	4,218	5,243	14,838
H35	Vista Cruiser wgn 5d V8	4,255	5,395	25,816

Delta (wb 116.0)

L37	cpe	3,496	5,145	8,788
L69	Town sdn 4d	3,537	5,205	26,084
N37	Royale cpe	3,505	5,363	61,138
N69	Royale Town sdn 4d	3,561	5,433	117,571
Q35	Custom Cruiser wgn 4d 2S V8	4,064	5,923	32,827
Q35	Custom Cruiser wgn 4d 3S V8	4,095	6,098	

Ninety-Eight (wb 119.0)

V37	Luxury cpe	3,753	6,609	5,058
V69	Luxury sdn 4d	3,807	6,786	14,323
X37	Regency cpe	3,767	6,949	32,072
X69	Regency sdn 4d	3,840	7,133	87,970

Toronado (wb 122.0)

W57	XSR htp cpe	4,688	11,132	2,714
Z57	Brougham htp cpe	4,634	8,134	31,371

1977 Engines	bore×stroke	bhp	availability
L4, 140.0	3.50×3.63	84	S-Starfire
V6, 231.0	3.80×3.40	105	S-Omega,Ctls,Delta; O-Strfre
V8, 260.0:	3.50×3.39	110	S-Ctls Salon; O-Omega, Cutlass, Delta
V8, 305.0	3.74×3.48	145	O-Omega
V8, 350.0	4.06×3.38	160	O-Delta
V8, 350.0	4.06×3.38	170	S-Omega,Ctls exc Salon, Delta, 98; O-Ctls Salon
V8, 403.0	4.35×3.38	185	O-Cutlass, Delta, 98
V8, 403.0	4.35×3.38	200	S-Toronado

1978

Starfire (wb 97.0)

		Wght	Price	Prod
D07	SX htchbk cpe 3d	2,790	4,306	9,265
T07	htchbk cpe 3d	2,786	4,095	8,056

Omega (wb 111.0)

B17	htchbk cpe 3d	3,250	4,173	4,084
B27	cpe	3,184	4,009	15,632
B69	sdn 4d	3,236	4,094	19,478
E27	Brougham cpe	3,204	4,215	3,798
E69	Brougham sdn 4d	3,246	4,300	7,125

Cutlass (wb 108.1)

G09	Salon sdn 4d	3,136	4,543	29,509
G87	Salon cpe	3,122	4,433	21,198
J09	Salon Brougham sdn 4d	3,186	4,828	21,902
J87	Salon Brougham cpe	3,082	4,717	10,741
R47	Supreme cpe	3,228	4,873	240,917
K47	Calais cpe	3,212	5,231	40,842
M47	Supreme Brougham cpe	3,204	5,287	117,880
H35	Cruiser wgn 4d 2S	3,308	5,287	44,617

Delta 88 (wb 116.0)

L37	cpe	3,496	5,549	17,469
L67	sdn 4d	3,541	5,634	25,322
N37	Royale cpe	3,507	5,778	68,469
N69	Royale sdn 4d	3,569	5,888	131,430
Q35	Custom Cruiser wgn 4d 2S V8	4,045	6,419	34,491
Q35	Custom Cruiser wgn 4d 3S V8	4,075	6,605	

Ninety-Eight (wb 119.0)

		Wght	Price	Prod
V37	Luxury cpe	3,753	7,170	2,956
V69	Luxury sdn 4d	3,805	7,351	9,136
X37	Regency cpe	3,767	7,538	28,573
X69	Regency sdn 4d	3,836	7,726	78,100

Toronado (wb 122.0)

		Wght	Price	Prod
Z57	Brougham cpe	4,624	9,412	22,362
W57	XSC cpe	—	—	2,453

1978 Engines	bore×stroke	bhp	availability
L4, 151.0	4.00×3.00	85	S-Starfire
V6, 231.0	3.80×3.40	105	S-Omega,Ctls,Delta; O-Starfre
V8, 260.0	3.50×3.39	110	S-Cutlass; O-Delta
V8, 305.0	3.74×3.48	145	O-Starfire,Omega,Cutlass
V8, 305.0	3.74×3.48	165	O-Cutlass
V8, 350.0dsl	4.06×3.38	120	O-Delta, 98
V8, 350.0	4.06×3.38	170	S-Delta, 98; O-Omega, Ctls
V8, 403.0	4.35×3.38	190	S-Toro; O-Delta, 98

1979

Starfire (wb 97.0)

		Wght	Price	Prod
D07	SX htchbk cpe 3d	2,703	4,475	7,155
T07	htchbk cpe 3d	2,690	4,275	13,144

Omega (wb 111.0)

B17	htchbk cpe 3d	3,222	4,345	956
B27	cpe	3,145	4,181	4,806
B69	sdn 4d	3,183	4,281	5,825
E27	Brougham cpe	3,156	4,387	1,078
E69	Brougham sdn 4d	3,214	4,487	2,145

Cutlass (wb 108.1)

G09	Salon sdn 4d	3,138	5,038	20,266
G87	Salon cpe	3,118	4,938	8,399
J09	Salon Brougham sdn 4d	3,185	5,352	18,714
J87	Salon Brougham cpe	3,158	5,227	3,617
R47	Supreme cpe	3,148	5,390	277,944
K47	Calais cpe	3,180	5,828	43,780
M47	Supreme Brougham cpe	3,174	5,829	137,323
G35	Cruiser wgn 4d 2S	3,281	5,223	10,755
H35	Cruiser B'ham wgn 4d 2S	3,325	5,775	42,953

Delta 88 (wb 116.0)

L37	cpe	3,550	6,112	16,202
L69	sdn 4d	3,576	6,212	25,424
N37	Royale cpe	3,560	6,399	60,687
N69	Royale sdn 4d	3,602	6,524	152,526
Q35	Custom Cruiser wgn 4d 2S V8	4,042	7,201	36,648
Q35	Custom Cruiser wgn 4d 3S V8	4,092	7,394	

Ninety-Eight (wb 119.0)

V37	Luxury cpe	3,806	8,614	2,104
V69	Luxury sdn 4d	3,850	8,795	6,720
X37	Regency cpe	3,810	9,236	26,965
X69	Regency sdn 4d	3,885	9,424	91,962

Toronado (wb 114.0)

Z57	Brougham cpe	3,731	10,709	50,056

1979 Engines	bore×stroke	bhp	availability
L4, 151.0	4.00×3.00	85	O-Starfire
L4, 151.0	4.00×3.00	90	S-Starfire
V6, 231.0	3.80×3.40	115	S-Omega,Ctls,Dlta; O-Strfre
V8D, 260.0	3.50×3.39	90	O-Cutlass
V8, 260.0	3.50×3.39	105	S-Ctls, Delta exc wgn
V8, 301.0	4.00×3.00	135	O-Delta exc wgn
V8, 305.0	3.74×3.48	130	S-Omega; O-Starfire
V8, 305.0	3.74×3.48	160	O-Cutlass
V8, 350.0	3.74×3.48	125	S-Delta wagons
V8D, 350.0	3.74×3.48	125	O-Ctls, 98, Toronado

			Wght	Price	Prod
V8, 350.0	3.74×3.48	160	S-98		
V8, 350.0	3.74×3.48	165	S-Toro; O-Omega, Ctls wgn		
V8, 403.0	4.35×3.38	175	O-Delta wgns, 98		

1980

Starfire (wb 97.0)

		Wght	Price	Prod
D07	SX htchbk cpe 3d	2,668	4,950	8,237
T07	htchbk cpe 3d	2,656	4,750	

Omega (wb 104.9)

B37	cpe	2,420	5,501	28,267
B69	sdn 4d	2,446	5,672	42,172
E37	Brougham cpe	2,452	5,858	21,595
E69	Brougham sdn 4d	2,478	6,013	42,289

Cutlass (wb 108.1)

G69	sdn 4d	3,144	6,124	36,923
G87	Salon cpe	3,140	5,764	3,429
J87	Salon Brougham cpe	3,140	6,054	965
R47	Supreme cpe	3,264	6,655	169,597
R69	LS sdn 4d	3,254	6,780	86,868
K47	Calais cpe	3,276	7,119	26,269
M47	Supreme Brougham cpe	3,276	7,094	77,875
M69	Supreme Brougham sdn 4d	3,280	7,219	52,462
G35	Cruiser wgn 4d 2S	3,343	6,572	7,815
H35	Cruiser Brougham wgn 4d 2S	3,380	6,809	22,791

Delta 88 (wb 116.0)

L37	cpe	3,395	6,808	6,845
L69	sdn 4d	3,428	6,905	15,285
N37	Royale cpe	3,403	7,076	39,303
N69	Royale sdn 4d	3,406	7,228	87,178
P35	Custom Cruiser wgn 4d 2S V8	3,910	7,820	17,067
P35	Custom Cruiser wgn 4d 3S V8	3,940	8,028	

Ninety-Eight (wb 119.0)

V69	Luxury sdn 4d	3,789	9,517	2,640
X37	Regency cpe	3,811	10,035	12,391
X69	Regency sdn 4d	3,832	10,159	58,603

Toronado (wb 114.0)

Z57	cpe	3,627	11,934	43,440

1980 Engines	bore×stroke	bhp	availability
L4, 151.0	4.00×3.00	85	O-Starfire
L4, 151.0	4.00×3.00	90	S-Starfire
V6, 173.0	3.50×3.00	115	S-Omega
V6, 231.0	3.80×3.40	110	S-Ctls,Delta exc wgns; O-Starfire
V8, 260.0	3.50×3.39	105	S-Cutlass
V8, 265.0	3.75×3.00	120	S-Delta exc wgns
V8, 305.0	3.74×3.48	155	O-Cutlass
V8, 307.0	3.80×3.38	150	S-Delta wgns, 98, Toro;O-Delta
V8, 350.0dsl	3.74×3.48	105	O-Ctls,Delta,98,Toro
V8, 350.0	3.75×3.48	160	O-Ctls,Delta,98,Toro

1980 Delta 88 four-door sedan

Packard

Packard Motor Car Co. Detroit, Michigan (to 1954);
Packard-Clipper Division, Studebaker-Packard Corp.
South Bend, Indiana (1954-58)

For many people, Packard was, in its heyday, "the supreme combination of all that is fine in motorcars." Technologically, it may not have been the "Standard of the World," but sociologically it was the Standard of America—even for the millions of would-be buyers who could never afford one. In 1929, more people owned stock in Packard than any other company save General Motors, and there were far more Packard stockholders than Packard owners.

Packard probably established its great renown with its 48-bhp Six of 1912. Then it leap-frogged Cadillac's new 1919 V8 with a V12, the fabled Twin Six. Shortly after that model was dropped in 1923, a new straight eight arrived. Packard did produce a less pretigious Six beginning in 1921, but that disappeared during the '20s and eight-cylinder engines maintained the Packard reputation from then on.

For a builder devoted singlemindedly to luxury cars, Packard compiled a remarkable production record. It had regularly outproduced Cadillac from 1925 on, even though its GM rival had help from the LaSalle beginning in 1927. With the exceptions of 1931, 1932, and 1934, Packard volume continued to exceed Cadillac/LaSalle output right through until World War II. But Packard's post-1934 production rested on middle-priced models rather than all-out luxury cars, especially the One Twenty, introduced for 1935. It literally saved the company from the Depression.

The 1930 line was continued from 1929 and was composed entirely of straight eights. Packard did not observe model years in this period, instead using a "series" number that dated from a practice begun in 1923. Historians have since applied model year designations to each series for ease of recognition, and 1930 coincides with the Seventh Series.

The Seventh Series hierarchy began with the Eight, which had the least pretentious bodies on a relatively short wheelbase. Next came the dashing Speedster Eight, offered as a lithe-looking boattail and standard roadster, as well as phaeton, victoria, and sedan. Speedsters cost the world ($5200 to $6000 in 1930), and only 150 were built, before the series disappeared the next year. A 385-cubic-inch engine powered the long-wheelbase Custom and De-luxe Eights, generally seen with closed bodies but also available in phaeton, roadster, and convertible styles from Packard and various custom coachbuilders. You can get a better idea of these cars' true cost by considering that $5000 would buy a rather nice house in those days.

The 1931 Eighth Series comprised two engines in three model lines, Standard, Custom, and Deluxe Eight. The Eight now included a range of "Individual Custom" models on a 134.5-inch wheelbase with a convertible sedan and victoria by Dietrich plus Packard's own cabriolets, land-aulets, and town cars. Mechanically, the Eighth Series gained an automatic Bijur chassis lubrication system and

1931 DeLuxe Eight sedan (for Alvin Macauley)

1932 Twin Six convertible sedan by Dietrich

1933 Super Eight coupe roadster

1934 Twelve sport sedan by Dietrich

1934 Twelve convertible runabout by Dietrich

1935 One Twenty four-door touring sedan

1935 Eight club sedan

1936 One Twenty four-door sedan

1937 Six eight-passenger wagon

1938 Eight business coupe

more power via modified intake and exhaust passages similar to those seen on the 1930 Speedster Eight. Packard also designed a quick-shift mechanism for its four-speed gearbox to reduce gearchanging effort, then switched to a three-speed all-synchromesh transmission for 1932.

Styling for 1932 was similar to 1930-31, except that bodies were lower for a more streamlined appearance. Two significant Ninth Series models were the Twin Six and Light Eight. The former bore no relationship to the 1916-23 cars. It had actually been designed for a front-wheel-drive layout that had been shelved before production. Though a fairly low numerical axle ratio was theoretically available, most of the V12 models had numerical ratios of 4.41:1 or higher, intended for smooth, relatively shift-free motoring rather than high performance. Packard claimed a sustained 100 mph was well within the capabilities of the Twin Six engine, but that was under test conditions, and the V12 usually ran out of breath at about 90 mph in stock tune. At 60 or 70 mph, however, it was whisper quiet and highly refined.

Twin Sixes and Twelves of 1932-34 shared bodies and wheelbases with the upper Eight series. Despite their prestige and billing as the ultimate Packards, the factory-bodied V12s were originally only $100-$200 more expensive than the DeLuxe Eights. The price gap grew wider as time went on, however, and custom-bodied Twelves cost considerably more. The 1932 Dietrich sport phaeton body listed for $6500 on the V12 chassis, compared to $5800 on the DeLuxe Eight platform. In 1935, when "senior model" production was consolidated to make space for the high-volume One Twenty, the Twelve shifted to 139- and 144-inch wheelbases. Super Eights were also offered in these sizes and a slightly smaller wheelbase, too, with the same general range of body styles. Custom offerings decreased as coachbuilders went out of business or were bought out by other companies.

As an independent, Packard didn't have the luxury of solid financial backing from a mighty parent like GM or Ford. Therefore, it had to introduce new products more suitable for the Depression-era market somewhat earlier than Cadillac or Lincoln. As a result, the Light Eight—Packard's first car in the medium-price field—arrived two years before Cadillac's smaller, cheaper LaSalle and four years before Lincoln's Zephyr. It used the Eight's 320-cid engine, rated for 1932 at 110 bhp, and had its own 127.6-inch-wheelbase chassis. The Light Eight was a quality product, built with the same meticulous care as other Packards. It was faster than the Eight, owing to its lighter chassis, but it was chunky looking because of its shorter wheelbase. Unfortunately, low prices made this line more minus than plus. It cost almost as much to make as the Eight yet sold for $500-$850 less, so the factory was lucky to break even on any Light Eight it sold. The range was dropped for 1933, and company president Alvan Macauley began searching the ranks of GM executives for someone wise in the ways of high-volume production who could help the firm develop a profitable middle-priced car.

Packard lost $7 million in 1932, much of it on the Light Eight, then realized a $500,000 profit in 1933. Its propor-

Packard

1938 Eight all-weather town car by Rollston

1939 One Twenty convertible coupe

tion of sales in the high-priced field that year was 38 percent, well above Cadillac's share. Trouble was, that there was hardly a field left. Macauley's recruiting campaign was vigorous. He ended up with Max Gilman, "that hardboiled guy in New York," who had started out as a Brooklyn truck salesman in 1919; and George T. Christopher, a production expert enticed out of retirement from General Motors. Gilman astutely built the image of a forthcoming new Packard, while Christopher overhauled most of the factory for high-volume production, modernizing it from end to end. The fruit of their efforts was announced on January 6, 1935: the Packard One Twenty.

The One Twenty was a dramatic departure from Packard tradition. A bit more than half as costly as the unmourned Light Eight, it was aimed precisely at all those people who had always wanted a Packard but had never been able to afford one. As such, it retained traditional Packard hallmarks, like the ox-yoke radiator/hood styling, red hexagon wheel hub emblems, and conservative body lines. The engine, designed largely by former GM people, was a straightforward L-head eight with five main bearings, a 2.75-inch crankshaft, counterweighted overlapping journals, a heavily ribbed block, ample water jacketing, and individual exhaust ports for each cylinder. It was easy on gas, a smooth performer, and granite strong. The 1936

and later One Twenty models had a longer stroke that yielded more power. Typical performance for these cars was 85 mph top speed and 0-60 mph in less than 20 seconds—pretty decent for any 3500-pound car in the prewar years. In 1936, a convertible sedan bearing "Dietrich" body plates was added to the One Twenty line. (Ray Dietrich personally had nothing to do with it, but his name had been owned by Murray since the early '30s.) A wagon, three DeLuxe closed models, and a long-wheelbase sedan and limousine appeared the next year.

Packard sold One Twentys like nickel hamburgers. The company soared to ninth place in production for calendar year 1935 with over 52,000 units. Output hit about 81,000 in 1936, and 110,000 in 1937. The 1938 recession slowed volume to about 50,000, but production picked up again and remained strong through World War II.

That 1937 production record was also due to the success of another, even less expensive offering, the One Ten, known as the Packard Six in 1938-39. This model had a One-Twenty-derived engine and initially rode a 115-inch wheelbase. Displacement was up to 245 cid and wheelbase to 122 inches for 1938-39, although horsepower remained unchanged. The lineup was similar to the One Twenty but prices were some $150 lower model for model, and the One Ten outsold the One Twenty by a ratio of

1939 Super Eight four-door sedan by Darrin

13 to 10 in 1937. Its six was not as smooth or powerful as the eight-cylinder One Twenty engine, but it did offer excellent gas mileage and adequate performance.

With the Fifteenth Series One Ten for 1937, Packard completed its transformation from a builder of exclusive, luxurious, virtually hand-made cars to a company with production volume in the industry's top ten. The development most responsible for this change—and the loss of Packard's prestige image—was probably the One Ten. The Light Eight wasn't around long enough to affect anybody's thinking much, and the One Twenty, though priced some $1200 less than a Standard Eight, was still very much a Packard in appearance and road behavior. Indeed, the Eight completely disappeared after 1936 and its 320-cid engine went into the Super Eight, with the 385-cid engine phased out. The One Twenty itself then became simply the Packard Eight. But the small, rather dumpy-looking One Ten/Packard Six was by no stretch of the imagination a Packard in the traditional sense. Perhaps the company had become too greedy for sales, too committed to George Christopher's philosophy of producing more and more cars. At any rate, Cadillac took over as the volume and prestige leader in the high-dollar market by the end of the decade. Many people who would not have been seen in one years before were now buying Cadillacs instead of the big Packards, which had been upstaged by the firm's own Sixes and One Twenty models that looked almost the same, at least from the front.

The 1940-41 cars were among the most interesting and beautiful in the company's long history. The Packard Six was now designated One Ten and sold in an attractive price range. Six body styles were offered including five-passenger coupe and convertible coupe. The One Twenty series included five deluxe-trim coupes and sedans. One exception to this competitive price structure was the custom-built Darrin Victoria, listed at $3819. An exquisite sporting soft-top with cutdown doors and raked windshield, it was the work of stylist Howard "Dutch" Darrin, and is one of the few One Twentys accorded "Classic" status by the Classic Car Club of America (CCCA). The One Ten was the smallest Packard in a generation, and rode a 122-inch wheelbase. Its 100-horsepower six displaced 245.3 cubic inches. The One Twenty sat on a 127-inch wheelbase and was powered by a 282-cid eight.

Packard dropped its 12-cylinder cars for 1940, but retained an impressive line of Super and Custom Eights. Wheelbases ranged from 127 to 148 inches. Styling remained traditional: an upright, slope-shouldered radiator and chiseled hood. The shortest chassis was reserved for coupes, convertibles, and sedans. A touring sedan rode a 138-inch wheelbase, and a long sedan and limousine used the 148. Custom coachwork was offered for the highest-priced models, two Darrins, a Custom Eight Victoria (priced only about $800 higher than the One Twenty Darrin), and a sleek, four-door convertible sedan priced at $6332, making it the most expensive of all. Other specials were the Rollston all-weather cabriolet, $4473, and town car, $4599. But such

exotic models accounted for only a fraction of total output. Of 98,000 cars, only 5662 were Super Eights and just 1900 were Customs. The rest were One Tens and One Twentys. Production was lower for 1941.

Packard's first big departure from traditional square-rigged styling came with the '41 Clipper. Designed by Darrin and modified by Packard's own Werner Gubitz, the Clipper had flowing fenders, hidden running boards, a tapered tail, and a narrow vertical grille. It came in only one body style, a four-door sedan priced at $1420—squarely between the One Twenty and One Sixty. The Clipper used a 127-inch wheelbase and 282-cid straight eight.

The same range of One Tens and One Twentys was placed at the lower end of the '41 line, while the Super Eight (now called One Sixty) and Custom Super (One Eighty) were the posher models. Again, Packard offered Darrin, Rollston, and LeBaron custom coachwork. LeBaron built long-wheelbase sedans and limousines and the beautifully formal Sport Brougham. An Electromatic Clutch, which eliminated the need to use the clutch pedal (but did require the driver to shift gears), was offered for only $37.50. Power for Supers and Customs came from a silky smooth straight eight, a 356-cid unit that developed 160 bhp at 3800 rpm. With nine main bearings and a crankshaft that weighed 105 pounds, the 356 was impressively quiet and powerful, capable of propelling some of the lighter models at well over 100 mph. It was used in Supers and Customs through 1947, in the Custom only through 1950, and was then dropped. Packard never built as large an engine again. The Clipper was popular, and over 16,000 sold in 1941. Accordingly, Packard converted almost entirely to Clipper styling for 1942. The only exceptions were some One Sixty and One Eighty models, plus commercial vehicles.

During the war, Packard built Rolls-Royce Merlin aircraft engines and other power units for military vehicles and PT boats. It was the only independent to emerge from the war completely free of debt. But then a significant decision was made—one that would adversely affect the company's future. Instead of reverting to luxury cars only, Packard continued to sell middle-price models in the One Twenty tradition. While such cars had been necessary before the war, they were not afterward and seriously damaged Packard's image. After 1945, Cadillac found it could sell anything on wheels, kept the cheaper LaSalle buried, and built high-priced cars only. Soon, it replaced Packard as the nation's premier luxury make.

The 1946 and '47 models were identical in all respects except for serial numbers. The low-priced '46 Clipper Six sedan and coupe looked exactly like the Clipper Eight series, which also included a DeLuxe sedan and club sedan. All used a 120-inch wheelbase. Clipper Supers and Customs—sedans and club sedans—rode the 127-inch wheelbase. The Custom series also offered a seven-passenger sedan and a limousine on the 148-inch wheelbase. Eights were

1940 Super Eight 160 club sedan

1941 One Eighty Sport Brougham by LeBaron

1942 Custom Super Clipper (180) club sedan

1946 Clipper Eight four-door sedan

1940 Custom Super Clipper limousine

1948 Eight Station Sedan (wagon)

equipped with the prewar 282 engine, while Supers and Customs used the 165-bhp 356. Overdrive and Electromatic clutch were available as options. Customs were trimmed with plush broadcloth and leather upholstery, special carpeting, and beautiful imitation wood paneling. Dashboards in these years were symmetrical, as they'd been before the war. The speedometer was located at the left, minor gauges at the far left, clock at the right, and the radio and heater controls in the center. Packard moved out over 30,000 cars in 1946, and over 50,000 in 1947.

But the Clipper design was growing old. Packard replaced it with an extensively facelifted model for '48, similar to a prewar show car known as the Phantom; the results were debatable. Management dictated heavy chunks of sheetmetal for a flow-through-fender effect, but this added about 200 extra pounds and made the new car look fat. ''Pregnant elephant'' was the term used by many to describe it. The styling wasn't helped by a short, squat grille—an eggcrate style on Customs and a bar-type on other models—that was far less elegant than the tall, narrow 1946-47 grille. Yet the 1948s sold well, and Packard produced some 92,000 of them.

In 1949 it did even better, building some 116,000 vehicles.

Chassis assignments were altered slightly for 1948, and the engine lineup was revised. Customs retained the 356 engine, but Supers were fitted with a new 327 straight eight with five main bearings. Standard Eights received a much squarer 288-cid engine. These powerplants were carried into 1949; horsepower on standards was raised to 135 bhp, Supers to 150.

The 1948 lineup included some familiar models: the standard and DeLuxe Eight in sedan and coupe form, and the sedan and coupe Super and Custom Eights. But some interesting additions were made: the novel Station Sedan in the standard Eight series, priced at $3425, and a pair of convertibles, one with the 127-inch wheelbase. The Station Sedan was made almost entirely of steel; its wooden body work was structural only at the tailgate. The Custom Eight convertible was the most luxurious standard-wheelbase American car and, at $4295, the most expensive. A 141-inch Super Eight wheelbase for two seven-passenger sedans and two limousines was also added, and a few long Custom chassis were created for commercial use. Packard built

1949 Custom Eight convertible

Scale model proposal for 1951 Packard styling

1951 Patrician 400 four-door sedan

1952 300 four-door sedan

Pan American show car by Henney, 1952

1953 Caribbean convertible

sixes only for taxi and export markets in 1948.

All Packard offerings were continued unchanged through May 1949, when a new series appeared. These were only slightly facelifted, mainly with a beltline spear. A new Super Deluxe series, using the Custom's eggcrate grille, was added to the lineup. The late '49s continued unchanged for 1950.

The big news was Ultramatic—the only automatic transmission developed by an independent without help from a transmission manufacturer. This shiftless drive combined a torque converter with multiple-disc and direct-drive clutches and forward/reverse bands. The car started from rest using the torque converter, then shifted into direct mechanical drive at about 15 miles an hour. Compared to Hydra-Matic, it was much smoother, but provided only leisurely acceleration. Frequent use of the low range for faster starts caused premature transmission wear.

Packard finally managed a total restyling for 1951, utilizing designer John Reinhart's praiseworthy shape on 122- and 127-inch wheelbases. But the firm per-

sisted with its less expensive models. Its 200 series even included a business coupe (the cheapest '51 Cadillac was $500 more expensive), plus two- and four-door sedans in basic and DeLuxe trim. The 200 really wasn't a Packard in the traditional sense of the word, and when the seller's market subsided it wasn't able to compete with established middle-priced rivals. Production was 71,000 cars in 1951, and less than 47,000 the following year.

The "real" Packard in 1951-52 was the 250, 300, and 400 line—all well-built, comfortable, high-speed road cars. The 250, on the shorter 122-inch wheelbase, included the Mayfair hardtop and 250 convertible, luxuriously trimmed, colorful, sporty cars that sold fairly well. The 300 and 400 were sedans, including the Patrician, Packard's highest-priced car in these years. The 356-cid straight eight was considered too expensive to build in light of potential sales, so the top engine for '51 was a 327 eight, also with nine bearings and almost the same output.

The '52 line was basically unchanged, though the 200

1953 Clipper DeLuxe four-door sedan

1955's Request show car

Balboa show car from 1953

1955 Clipper Custom Constellation hardtop coupe

1954 convertible (series 5431)

1956 Patrician four-door sedan

business coupe was dropped. Styling changes were minor: the most obvious was a different wing position on the pelican hood ornament. Colorful interiors in high-quality fabric and leather were done up by fashion designer Dorothy Draper. Power brakes were offered for the first time.

In May 1952, Packard's aging president, Hugh Ferry, announced the arrival of his successor, James J. Nance, and it was hoped that this market-wise promoter could invigorate the firm. By the time Nance arrived, the plant was working at only 50 percent of capacity. Incredibly, several long-time executives felt this was good enough. But Nance could see Packard was doomed at that level. Aggressively, he sought U.S. military business and laid out a vigorous new auto policy. Nance decreed the cheap 200 would henceforth be called Clipper and would eventually become a separate make. He also said Packard would go back to building nothing but luxury cars, returning to the long-wheelbase formal sedans and limousines it had neglected.

There was no time for a complete line-wide change for '53, but Nance did see to the inclusion of eight-passenger sedans and limousines. He even contracted with the Derham Body Company to build a few formal Patricians with leather-covered tops and tiny rear windows, priced at $6531 apiece. The glamorous Caribbean convertible was introduced, with handsome styling and a 180-bhp engine. Limited to 750 copies, it was well received and outsold Cadillac's comparable Eldorado. A colorful Clipper Sportster coupe was added at the bottom of the line.

Nance had hoped for all-new 1954 models, but time didn't permit this. Instead, a look-alike interim series was offered—outwardly distinguishable from the '53s by horn-rimmed headlamps and backup lights built into the taillight assemblies. The straight-eight Patrician engine was enlarged to 359 cid. Packard had been among the first to introduce air conditioning in 1940, and it was back in '54 for the first time since the war. But Packard had a terrible year, producing only about 30,000 cars. A revolutionary new model was on the way, but was de-

layed, partly because of the hubbub over the so-called Studebaker-Packard merger. Actually, Packard bought Studebaker. What Nance didn't know when he signed the papers was that Studebaker had huge productivity problems in its high-overhead South Bend plant, and that its break-even point was somewhere over 250,000 cars. Contrary to many accounts, Packard was still healthy at this time, but Studebaker was sinking and would drag Packard down with it.

As the '55s neared production, another smouldering problem burst into flame. Packard had given away its body business to Briggs in 1940. Briggs had sold out to Chrysler in 1954. Chrysler told Nance it would not continue Briggs' contract, and Packard had to settle for a cramped body plant on Conner Avenue in Detroit.

1957 Clipper four-door Country Sedan (wagon)

1957 Clipper four-door Town Sedan

1958 Hawk hardtop coupe

Never big enough, the plant caused big production line tie-ups and quality control problems. Though Packard built over 55,000 cars in prosperous 1955, the company would have done better to consign body building to its old but adequate main plant on Detroit's East Grand Boulevard.

Despite all these woes, the 1955 Packard was a technological wonder. Leading its list of features was Torsion-Level suspension, an interlinked torsion-bar setup operating on all four wheels. A complicated electrical system allowed the suspension to correct for load weight, and the interlinking of all four wheels provided truly extraordinary ride and handling. And there was more: the old-fashioned straight eights were superseded by powerful new V8s. These oversquare, very powerful engines displaced 320 cid on Clipper DeLuxe and Super, and 352 cid on Clipper Customs and Packards. Ultramatic was also improved to deal better with the engines' higher torque outputs. With the V8, Ultramatic, and Torsion-Level suspension, Packard had a fine chassis. Caribbeans, with four-barrel 352s belting out 275 bhp, were impressively fast and roadable cars—real Packards in every sense of the word. Styling also was impressive. A clever facelift of the old 1951 body produced "cathedral" taillights, peaked front fenders, and an ornate grille. The Clipper was given its own special grille and 1954-style taillights.

Some problems at the Conner plant were finally licked, but not in time to save the 1956 models. Studebaker's desperate struggle was scaring customers away. Also, many people refused to buy a '56 because of the notorious quality and service problems of the '55s. Ironically, the '56s were better built. Ultramatic was given new electronic pushbutton control, and horsepower increased. The Clipper, as a separate make, was given the 352; the Packard engine was bored out to 374 cid. There was a hardtop as well as a convertible Caribbean. Both had unique reversible seat cushions—fabric on one side, leather on the other. In mid-year, an Executive appeared on the 122-inch wheelbase in sedan and hardtop form, bridging the gap between Packard and Clipper. Executives wore the Clipper's pointed taillights and Packard grilles. But none of this product shuffling helped, and only about 10,000 Packards were built for model year 1956.

No financial backer was found for an all-new 1957 line, and in August 1956, Nance resigned. Studebaker-Packard was picked up by Curtiss-Wright Corporation as a dalliance and/or a tax write-off, and C-W's Roy Hurley began directing the firm's fortunes. Late in 1955, S-P decided to leave Detroit and to build Studebaker-based Packard cars in South Bend.

The 1957 Packard Clipper (or "Packardbaker," as detractors called it) was, despite it all, a very good Studebaker, though hardly in the image of the cars before it. A sedan and a station wagon were offered. A supercharged Studebaker 289 V8 provided 275 bhp, the same as some previous Packard V8s. Styling evoked Packard themes, and prices were higher than on com-

parable Studebakers. It was a charade, of course, and the public recognized it: only about 5000 '57 Clippers were built.

A big-Packard revival was still theoretically possible as the '58s were planned, so the firm again tried a holding action. This time, four Studebaker-based cars were marketed at prices up to $3995. On the shorter wheelbase came a two-door hardtop and wagon; a sedan and the Packard Hawk used the longer wheelbase. The latter, perhaps the most famous of this generation, was a more luxurious version of the Studebaker Golden Hawk. Featured were an all-leather interior and bizarre

styling. In defense of stylist Duncan McRae, the Packard Hawk was really built only because of Roy Hurley, who demanded the long, bolt-on fiberglass nose and gaudy, gold mylar tailfins. McRae, however, takes credit for the car's outside armrests. McRae was also forced to create the other three '58 Packards—garish, finned affairs with hastily contrived four-headlight systems designed to keep up with the competition. Only the Hawk retained the supercharged engine. After '58, Packard vanished from the automotive scene, although the name was continued in the corporation's title until 1962.

Packard Specifications

1930

726 Eight (wb 127.5)

		Wght	Price	Prod
403	sdn 4d	4,265	3,275	15,731

733 Eight (wb 134.5)—12,531 built

400	touring 7P	4,055	2,525	—
401	phtn 4P	3,935	2,425	—
402	rdstr 2-4P	3,945	2,425	—
404	sdn 7P	4,500	2,675	—
405	sdn limo 7P	4,555	2,775	—
406	club sdn 5P	4,325	2,675	—
407	cpe 5P	4,255	2,675	—
408	cpe 2-4P	4,180	2,525	—
409	conv cpe 2-4P	4,100	2,550	—
431	spt phtn 4P	4,130	2,725	—

734 Speedster Eight (wb 134.0)—113 built

422	boattail rdstr 2P	4,295	5,210	—
443	sdn 5P	4,660	6,000	—
445	phtn 4P	4,300	5,200	—
447	cpe victoria 5P	4,525	6,000	—
452	rdstr 2-4P	4,435	5,200	—

740 Custom Eight (wb 140.5)—6,200 built

410	touring 7P	4,345	3,325	—
411	phtn 4P	4,250	3,190	—
412	rdstr 2-4P	4,245	3,190	—
413	sdn 4d 5P	4,560	3,585	—
414	sdn 7P	4,765	3,785	—
415	sdn limo 7P	4,810	3,885	—
416	club sdn 5P	4,580	3,750	—
417	cpe 5P	4,555	3,650	—
418	cpe 2-4P	4,500	3,295	—
419	conv cpe 2-4P	4,425	3,350	—
441	spt phtn	4,450	3,490	—

745 DeLuxe Eight (wb 145.5)—1,789 built

420	touring 7P	4,745	4,585	—
421	phtn 4P	4,645	4,585	—
422	rdstr 2-4P	4,695	4,585	—
423	sdn 4d 5P	4,805	4,985	—
424	sdn 7P	5,095	5,185	—
425	sdn limo 7P	5,140	5,350	—
426	club sdn 5P	5,000	5,150	—
427	cpe 5P	4,995	5,100	—
428	cpe 2-4P	4,875	4,785	—
429	conv cpe 2-4P	4,665	4,885	—
451	spt phtn 4P	4,845	4,885	—

1930 Engines

1930 Engines	bore×stroke	bhp	availability
L8, 320.0	3.19×5.00	90	S-726,733
L0, 004.0	3.50×5.00	106	S-740,745
L8, 384.8	3.50×5.00	125-145	S-734

1931

826 Eight (wb 127.5)

		Wght	Price	Prod
463	sdn 4d 5P	4,479	2,385	6,009

833 Eight (wb 134.5)—6,096 built

460	touring 7P	4,256	2,525	—
461	phtn 4P	4,185	2,425	—
462	rdstr 2-4P	4,140	2,425	—
464	sdn 7P	4,665	2,785	—
465	sdn limo 7P	4,695	2,885	—
466	club sdn 5P	4,488	2,675	—
467	cpe 5P	4,308	2,675	—
468	cpe 2-4P	4,360	2,525	—
469	conv cpe 2-4P	4,290	2,550	—
481	spt phtn 4P	4,285	2,725	—
483	conv sdn 5P	4,555	3,465	—
	Individual custom:			
1879	Dietrich conv victoria 4P	4,186	4,275	—
1881	Dietrich conv sdn 4P	4,442	4,375	—
3000	A/W cab 7P	4,684	4,850	—
3001	A/W landaulet 7P	4,684	5,050	—
3002	A/W town car 7P	4,744	4,975	—
3003	A/W landaulet town car 7P	4,744	5,175	—
3004	sdn cab limo 6P	4,485	4,490	—
3008	A/W spt cab 7P	4,614	4,850	—
3009	A/W spt landaulet 7P	4,614	5,050	—

840 Custom Eight (wb 140.5)—2,035 built

470	touring 7P	4,507	3,595	—
471	phtn 4P	4,439	3,490	—
472	rdstr 2-4P	4,383	3,490	—
473	sdn 4d 5P	4,955	3,795	—
476	club sdn 5P	4,720	3,950	—
477	cpe 5P	4,673	3,850	—
478	cpe 2-4P	4,592	3,545	—
479	conv cpe 2-4P	4,523	3,595	—
491	spt phtn 4P	4,535	3,790	—
	Individual custom:			
1879	Dietrich conv victoria 4P	4,418	5,175	—
1881	Dietrich conv sdn 4P	4,674	5,275	—
3000	A/W cab 7P	4,916	5,750	—
3001	A/W landaulet 7P	4,976	5,950	—
3002	A/W town car 7P	4,976	5,875	—

		Wght	Price	Prod
3003	A/W landaulet town car 7P	4,976	6,075	—
3008	A/W spt cab 7P	4,846	5,750	—
3009	A/W spt landaulet 7P	4,846	5,950	—

845 DeLuxe Eight (wb 145.5)—1,310 built

		Wght	Price	Prod
474	sdn 7P	5,010	4,150	—
475	sdn limo 7P	5,080	4,285	—

1931 Engines	bore×stroke	bhp	availability
L8, 320.8	3.19×5.00	100	S-826,833
L8, 384.8	3.50×5.00	120	S-840,845

1932

900 Light Eight (wb 127.8)

		Wght	Price	Prod
553	sdn 4d	4,115	1,895	4,850*
558	cpe 2-4P	3,990	1,940	510*
559	cpe-rdstr 2-4P	3,930	1,940	1,060*
563	cpe-sdn 5P	4,060	1,940	330*

901 Eight (wb 129.5)

		Wght	Price	Prod
503	sdn 4d 5P	4,570	2,485	3,922

902 Eight (wb 136.5)—3,737 built

		Wght	Price	Prod
500	touring 7P	4,345	2,775	—
501	phtn 4P	4,300	2,650	—
504	sdn 7P	4,735	2,885	—
505	sdn limo 7P	4,770	2,985	—
506	club sdn 5P	4,555	2,775	—
507	cpe 5P	4,505	2,795	—
508	cpe 2-4P	4,475	2,675	—
509	cpe rdstr 2-4P	4,420	2,650	—
521	spt phtn 5P	4,400	2,950	—
523	conv sdn 5P	4,573	3,445	—
527	conv victoria 5P	4,317	3,395	—
543	sdn 4d 5P	4,590	3,685	—

903 DeLuxe Eight (wb 142.5)—955 built

		Wght	Price	Prod
510	touring 7P	4,760	3,795	—
511	phtn 4P	4,715	3,690	—
513	sdn 4d 5P	5,045	3,845	—
516	club sdn 5P	5,000	3,890	—
517	cpe 5P	4,985	3,850	—
518	cpe 2-4P	4,890	3,725	—
519	cpe rdstr 2-4P	4,825	3,750	—
531	spt phtn 4P	4,795	3,990	—
533	conv sdn 5P	4,985	4,550	—
537	conv victoria 5P	4,727	4,495	—

904 DeLuxe Eight (wb 147.5)—700 built

		Wght	Price	Prod
514	sdn 7P	5,195	4,150	—
515	sdn limo 7P	5,240	4,285	—
	Individual custom:			
2060	Dietrich stationary cpe 2-4P	5,000	5,900	—
2069	Dietrich spt phtn 4P	4,800	5,800	—
2070	Dietrich conv sdn 5P	5,100	6,250	—
2071	Dietrich conv cpe 2-4P	4,965	6,050	—
2072	Dietrich conv victoria 4P	4,815	6,150	—
4000	A/W cab 7P	5,250	6,850	—
4001	A/W landaulet 7P	5,250	7,250	—
4002	A/W town car 7P	5,310	6,850	—
4003	A/W landaulet town car 7P	5,310	7,250	—
4004	limo sdn cabriolet 6P	5,050	6,850	—
4005	spt sdn 4d 5P	5,030	6,850	—
4006	A/W brougham 7P	5,293	6,850	—
4007	Dietrich limo sdn 6P	5,075	6,850	—
4008	A/W spt cab 7P	5,180	6,850	—
4009	A/W spt landaulet 7P	5,180	7,250	—

905 Twin Six (wb 142.5)—311 built

		Wght	Price	Prod
570	touring 7P	5,315	3,895	—
571	phtn 4P	5,275	3,790	—
573	sdn 4d 5P	5,635	3,745	—
576	club sdn 5P	5,585	3,895	—
577	cpe 5P	5,485	3,850	—
578	cpe 2-4P	5,425	3,650	—
579	cpe rdstr 2-4P	5,350	3,750	—
581	spt phtn 4P	5,375	4,090	—
583	conv sdn 5P	5,255	4,395	—
587	conv victoria 5P	5,180	4,325	—

906 Twin Six (wb 147.5)—238 built

		Wght	Price	Prod
574	sdn 7P	5,765	3,995	—
575	sdn limo 7P	5,830	4,195	—
	Individual custom:			
2068	Dietrich cpe 2-4P	5,180	6,600	—
2069	Dietrich spt phtn 4P	4,980	6,500	—
2070	Dietrich conv sdn 5P	5,280	6,950	—
2071	Dietrich conv cpe 2-4P	5,145	6,750	—
2072	Dietrich conv victoria 4P	4,995	6,850	—
4000	A/W cabriolet 7P	5,430	7,550	—
4001	A/W landaulet 7P	5,430	7,950	—
4002	A/W town car 7P	5,490	7,550	—
4003	A/W town car landaulet 7P	5,490	7,950	—

*Estimates based on serial number analysis by Jack Triplett (*The Packard Cormorant,* Spring 1979).

1932 Engines	bore×stroke	bhp	availability
L8, 320.0	3.19×5.00	110	S-900,901,902
L8, 384.8	3.50×5.00	135	S-903,904
V12, 445.5	3.44×4.00	160	S-905,906

1933

1001 Eight (wb 127.5)

		Wght	Price	Prod
602	cpe sdn 5P	4,245	2,190	73*
603	sdn 4d 5P	4,335	2,150	1,465*
608	cpe 2-4P	4,200	2,160	120*
609	cpe rdstr 2-4P	4,150	2,250	215*
—	chassis	—	—	9*

1002 Eight (wb 136.0)—1,099 built

		Wght	Price	Prod
610	touring 7P	4,275	2,390	—
611	phtn 5P	4,270	2,370	—
613	sdn 4d 5P	4,590	2,385	—
614	sdn 7P	4,640	2,455	—
615	limo 7P	4,725	2,550	—
616	club sdn 5P	4,545	2,390	—
617	cpe 5P	4,500	2,440	—
618	cpe 2-4P	4,455	2,350	—
623	conv sdn 5P	4,515	2,890	—
627	conv victoria 5P	4,540	2,780	—
5633	formal sdn 4d 5P	4,900	3,085	—

1003 Super Eight (wb 135.0)

		Wght	Price	Prod
653	sdn 4d 5P	4,815	2,750	512

1004 Super Eight (wb 142.0)—788 built

		Wght	Price	Prod
650	touring 7P	4,610	2,980	—
651	phtn 5P	4,490	2,890	—
654	sdn 7P	4,965	3,090	—
655	limo 7P	5,025	3,280	—
656	club sdn 5P	4,795	2,975	—
657	cpe 5P	4,780	2,980	—
658	cpe 2-4P	4,670	2,780	—
659	cpe rdstr 2-4P	4,625	2,870	—
661	spt phtn 2-4P	4,690	3,150	—
663	conv sdn 5P	4,840	3,590	—
667	conv victoria 5P	4,795	3,440	—
673	formal sdn 4d 5P	5,155	3,600	—

1005 Twelve (wb 142.0)—244 built

		Wght	Price	Prod
631	phtn 5P	5,095	3,790	—

		Wght	Price	Prod
633	sdn 4d 5P	5,385	3,860	—
636	club sdn 5P	5,400	3,880	—
637	cpe 5P	5,300	3,890	—
638	cpe 2-4P	5,255	3,720	—
639	cpe rdstr 2-4P	5,160	3,850	—
641	spt phtn 5P	5,175	4,090	—
643	conv sdn 5P	5,405	4,650	—
647	conv victoria 5P	5,225	4,490	—
5633	formal sdn 5P	5,690	4,560	—

1006 (wb 147.0)—276 built

		Wght	Price	Prod
634	sdn 7P	5,600	4,085	—
635	limo 7P	5,650	4,285	—
	Individual custom:			
3068	Dietrich stationary cpe 2-4P	5,360	6,000	—
3069	Dietrich spt phtn 4P	5,160	5,875	—
3070	Dietrich conv sdn 5P	5,460	6,570	—
3071	Dietrich conv runabout 2-4P	5,325	6,085	—
3072	Dietrich conv victoria 4P	5,175	6,070	—
3182	Dietrich form sdn 7P	5,735	7,000	—
758	LeBaron A/W cab 7P	5,610	7,000	—
759	LeBaron A/W town car 7P	5,670	7,000	—
4000	A/W cab 7P	5,650	6,030	—
4001	A/W landaulet 7P	5,650	6,250	—
4002	A/W town car 7P	5,610	6,080	—
4003	landaulet town car 7P	5,610	6,250	—
4004	landaulet limo 7P	5,650	6,000	—
4005	spt sdn 4d 5P	5,330	6,000	—
4007	limo 7P	5,650	6,045	—

*Estimates based on serial number analysis by Jack Triplett (*The Packard Cormorant,* Spring 1979).

1933 Engines	bore×stroke	bhp	availability
L8, 320.0	3.19×5.00	120	S-1001,1002
L8, 384.8	3.50×5.00	145	S-1003,1004
V12, 445.5	3.44×4.00	160	S-1005,1006

1934

1100 Eight (wb 129.0)*

		Wght	Price	Prod
703	sdn 4d 5P	4,640	2,350	—

1101 Eight (wb 136.0)*

		Wght	Price	Prod
710	touring 7P	4,400	2,590	—
711	phtn 4P	4,359	2,570	—
712	formal sdn 5P	4,760	3,285	—
713	sdn 4d 5P	4,660	2,585	—
716	club sdn 5P	4,730	2,670	—
717	cpe 5P	4,580	2,640	—
718	cpe 2-4P	4,580	2,640	—
719	cpe rdstr 2-4P	4,430	2,580	—
721	spt phtn 4P	4,430	2,830	—
723	conv sdn 5P	4,680	3,090	—
727	conv victoria 5P	4,710	2,980	—

1102 Eight (wb 141.0)*

		Wght	Price	Prod
714	sdn 7P	4,945	2,655	—
715	limo sdn 7P	5,000	2,790	—

1103 Super Eight (wb 135.0)**

		Wght	Price	Prod
753	sdn 4d 5P	4,890	2,950	—

1104 Super Eight (wb 142.0)**

		Wght	Price	Prod
750	touring 7P	4,720	3,180	—
751	phtn 4P	4,645	3,090	—
752	formal sdn 5P	5,010	3,800	—
756	club sdn 5P	4,985	3,255	—
757	cpe 5P	4,885	3,180	—
758	cpe 2-4P	4,800	2,980	—
759	cpe rdstr 2-4P	4,680	3,070	—
761	spt phtn 4P	4,740	3,350	—
763	conv sdn 5P	4,930	3,790	—

		Wght	Price	Prod
767	conv victoria 5P	4,875	3,640	—
773	sdn 4d 5P	4,910	3,200	—

1105 Super Eight (wb 147.0)**

		Wght	Price	Prod
754	sdn 7P	5,245	3,290	—
755	sdn limo 7P	5,275	3,480	—
	Individual custom:			
280	LeBaron phtn 4P	4,755	7,065	—
858	LeBaron A/W cab 7P	5,205	5,450	—
859	LeBaron A/W town car 7P	5,265	5,450	—
4068	Dietrich stationary cpe 2-4P	4,955	5,445	—
4070	Dietrich conv sdn 5P	5,055	5,800	—
4071	Dietrich runabout conv 2-4P	4,920	5,365	—
4072	Dietrich conv victoria 4P	4,770	5,345	—
4182	Dietrich spot sdn 5P	5,380	6,295	—

1106 Twelve (wb 135.0)***

		Wght	Price	Prod
275	LeBaron spdstr runabout 2P	5,400	7,746	—

1107 Twelve (wb 142.0)***

		Wght	Price	Prod
730	touring 7P	5,415	3,980	—
731	phtn 4P	5,325	3,890	—
732	formal sdn 5P	5,630	4,660	—
733	sdn 4d 5P	5,530	3,960	—
736	club sdn 5P	5,660	4,060	—
737	cpe 5P	5,530	3,990	—
738	cpe 2-4P	5,585	3,820	—
739	cpe rdstr 2-4P	5,330	3,850	—
741	spt phtn 4P	5,400	4,190	—
743	conv sdn 5P	5,470	4,750	—
747	conv victoria 5P	5,440	4,590	—

1108 Twelve (wb 147.0)***

		Wght	Price	Prod
734	sdn 7P	5,700	4,185	—
735	sdn limo 7P	5,750	4,385	—
	Individual custom:			
280	LeBaron spt phtn 4P	5,130	7,065	—
858	LeBaron A/W cab 7P	5,655	6,155	—
859	LeBaron A/W town car 7P	5,655	6,155	—
4002	Dietrich A/W town car 7P	5,715	5,695	—
4068	Dietrich stationary cpe 2-4P	5,405	6,185	—
4069	Dietrich spt phtn 4P	5,400	5,180	—
4070	Dietrich conv sdn 5P	5,505	6,555	—
4071	Dietrich conv runabout 2-4P	5,370	6,100	—
4072	Dietrich conv victoria 4P	5,220	6,080	—
4182	Dietrich spt sdn 5P	5,130	7,060	—

*Total 1100/1101/1102 production: 5,120
**Total Super Eight production: 1,920
***Total Twelve production: 960

1934 Engines	bore×stroke	bhp	availability
L8, 320.0	3.19×5.00	120	S-Eight
L8, 384.8	3.50×5.00	145	S-Super Eight
V12, 445.5	3.44×4.00	160	S-Twelve

1935

120A One Twenty (wb 120.0)—24,995 built		Wght	Price	Prod
892	touring sdn 4d	3,550	1,095	—
893	sdn 4d	3,510	1,060	—
894	touring cpe 5P	3,455	1,025	—
895	spt cpe 2-4P	3,435	1,020	—
896	club sdn 5P	3,515	1,085	—
898	bus cpe 2P	3,400	980	—
899	conv cpe 2-4P	3,385	1,070	—

1200 Eight (wb 127.0)*

		Wght	Price	Prod
803	sdn 4d	4,780	2,385	—

1201 Eight (wb 134.0)*

		Wght	Price	Prod
195	LeBaron A/W cab 7P	5,185	5,240	—

		Wght	Price	Prod
807	conv victoria 5P	4,835	3,100	—
811	phtn 5P	4,475	2,670	—
812	formal sdn 4d 5P	5,035	3,285	—
813	sdn 4d 5P	4,935	2,585	—
816	club sdn 5P	4,845	2,580	—
817	cpe 5P	4,700	2,560	—
818	cpe 2-4P	4,625	2,475	—
819	conv cpe 2-4P	4,555	2,580	—

1202 Eight (wb 139.0)*

194	LeBaron A/W town car 7P	5,225	5,385	—
810	touring 7P	4,400	3,170	—
814	commcl sdn 8P	4,985	2,630	—
815	limo 7P	5,125	2,890	—
815	commcl limo 8P	5,150	2,765	—
863	conv sdn 5P	4,800	3,200	—

1203 Super Eight (wb 132.0)**

843	sdn 4d	4,985	2,990	—

1204 Super Eight (wb 139.0)**

195	LeBaron A/W cab 7P	5,300	5,670	—
841	spt phtn 5P	4,875	3,450	—
847	conv victoria 5P	5,000	3,760	—
851	phtn 5P	4,775	3,190	—
852	formal sdn 5P	5,150	3,800	—
856	club sdn 5P	5,100	3,170	—
857	cpe 5P	5,015	3,080	—
858	cpe 2-4P	4,920	2,880	—
859	conv cpe 2-4P	4,800	3,070	—

1205 Super Eight (wb 144.0)**

194	LeBaron A/W town car 7P	5,525	5,815	—
850	touring 7P	4,729	3,690	—
854	sdn 7P	5,375	3,390	—
854	comm sdn 8P	5,320	3,265	—
855	limo 7P	5,400	3,580	—
855	comm limo 8P	5,380	3,455	—
883	conv sdn 5P	5,050	3,910	—

1206 Twelve (wb 132.0)***

The "06" series of short-wheelbase Twelve sedans was omitted by Packard for this and subsequent years; there is some conjecture on whether minor production occurred, but this has not been confirmed to date.

1207 Twelve (wb 139.0)***

195	LeBaron A/W cab 7P	5,930	6,290	—
821	spt phtn 5P	5,550	4,290	—
827	conv victoria 5P	5,590	4,790	—
831	phtn 5P	5,470	3,990	—
832	formal sdn 7P	5,780	4,660	—
833	sdn 5P	5,700	3,960	—
836	club sdn 5P	5,800	4,060	—
837	cpe 5P	5,680	3,990	—
838	cpe 2-4P	5,635	3,820	—
839	conv cpe 2-4P	5,480	3,850	—

1208 Twelve (wb 144.0)***

194	LeBaron A/W town car 7P	5,950	6,535	—
830	touring 7P	5,415	4,490	—
834	sdn 7P	5,800	4,285	—
835	limo 7P	5,900	4,485	—
873	conv sdn 5P	5,620	4,950	—

*Total Eight production: 4,781
**Total Super Eight production: 1,392
***Total Twelve production: 721

1935 Engines	bore×stroke	bhp	availability
L8, 257.2	3.25×3.88	110	S-120A
L8, 320.0	3.19×5.00	130	S-1200,1201,1202
L8, 384.8	3.50×5.00	150	S-1203,1204,1205
V12, 473.0	3.44×4.25	175	S-1207,1208

1936

120B One Twenty (wb 120.0)—55,042 built		Wght	Price	Prod
992	touring sdn 5P	3,560	1,115	—
993	sdn 4d 5P	3,505	1,075	—
994	touring cpe 5P	3,575	1,040	—
995	spt cpe 2-4P	3,455	1,030	—
996	club sdn 5P	3,495	1,090	—
997	conv sdn 5P	3,660	1,395	—
998	bus cpe 2P	3,380	990	—
999	conv cpe 2-4P	3,525	1,110	—

1400 Eight (wb 127.0)*

903	sdn 4d 5P	4,815	2,385	—

1401 Eight (wb 134.0)*

294	LeBaron A/W cab 7P	5,185	5,240	—
907	conv victoria 5P	4,810	3,200	—
911	phtn 4P	4,890	3,020	—
912	formal sdn 7P	5,030	3,285	—
913	sdn 4d 5P	4,978	2,585	—
916	club sdn 5P	4,815	2,580	—
917	cpe 5P	4,745	2,560	—
918	cpe 2-4P	4,735	2,470	—
919	cpe rdstr 2-4P	4,740	2,730	—

1402 Eight (wb 139.0)*

295	LeBaron A/W town car 7P	5,225	5,385	—
910	touring 7P	5,060	3,270	—
914	sdn 7P	4,955	2,755	—
914	bus sdn 8P	4,985	2,630	—
915	limo 7P	5,045	2,890	—
915	bus limo 8P	5,150	2,765	—
963	conv sdn 5P	5,140	3,400	—

1403 Super Eight (wb 132.0)**

943	sdn 4d	5,080	2,990	—

1404 Super Eight (wb 139.0)**

294	LeBaron A/W cab 7P	5,300	5,670	—
941	spt phtn 5P	5,200	3,650	—
947	conv victoria 5P	5,122	3,860	—
951	phtn 5P	5,080	3,390	—
952	formal sdn 5P	5,245	3,800	—
956	club sdn 5P	5,178	3,170	—
957	cpe 5P	5,010	3,080	—
958	cpe 2-4P	4,933	2,880	—
959	cpe rdstr 2-4P	4,993	3,070	—

1405 Super Eight (wb 144.0)**

295	LeBaron A/W town car 7P	5,525	5,815	—
950	touring 7P	5,200	3,690	—
954	sdn 7P	5,300	3,390	—
954	bus sdn 8P	5,320	3,265	—
955	limo 7P	5,380	3,580	—
955	bus limo 8P	5,380	3,455	—
983	conv sdn 5P	5,390	4,010	—

1407 Twelve (wb 139.0)***

294	LeBaron A/W cab 7P	5,900	6,290	—
921	spt phtn 5P	5,785	4,490	—
927	conv victoria 5P	5,585	4,890	—
931	phtn 5P	5,480	4,190	—
932	formal sdn 5P	5,735	4,660	—
933	sdn 5P	5,695	3,960	—
936	club sdn 5P	5,640	4,060	—
937	cpe 5P	5,495	3,990	—
938	cpe 2-4P	5,495	3,820	—
939	cpe rdstr 2-4P	5,495	3,850	—

1408 Twelve (wb 144.0)

295	LeBaron A/W town car 7P	5,950	6,435	—
934	sdn 7P	5,790	4,285	—
935	limo 7P	5,890	4,483	—

Packard

		Wght	Price	Prod
930	touring 7P	5,460	4,490	—
973	conv sdn 5P	5,945	5,050	—

*Total Eight production: 3,973
**Total Super Eight production: 1,330
***Total Twelve production: 682

1936 Engines	bore×stroke	bhp	availability
L8, 282.0	3.25×4.25	120	S-120B
L8, 320.0	3.19×5.00	130	S-1400,1401,1402
L8, 384.8	3.50×5.00	150	S-1403,1404,1405
V12, 473.0	3.44×4.25	175	S-1407,1408

1937

115C Six (wb 115.0)—65,400 built		Wght	Price	Prod
1060	wgn 4d 8P	3,380	1,295	—
1082	touring sdn 5P	3,310	910	—
1083	sdn 4d 5P	3,265	895	—
1084	touring cpe 5P	3,235	860	—
1085	spt cpe 2-4P	3,215	840	—
1086	club sdn 5P	3,275	900	—
1088	bus cpe 2P	3,140	795	—
1089	conv cpe 2-4P	3,285	910	—

120C/CD One Twenty (wb 120.0)*				
1070	wgn 4d 8P	3,590	1,485	—
1092	touring sdn 5P	3,520	1,060	—
1093	sdn 4d 5P	3,465	1,045	—
1094	touring cpe 5P	3,435	1,010	—
1095	spt cpe 2-4P	3,415	990	—
1096	club sdn 5P	3,455	1,050	—
1097	conv sdn 5P	3,630	1,355	—
1098	bus cpe 2P	3,340	945	—
1099	conv cpe 2-4P	3,485	1,060	—
1094CD	touring cpe 5P	3,465	1,220	—
1096CD	club sdn 5P	3,485	1,260	—
1098CD	touring sdn 4d	3,550	1,270	—

138CD One Twenty (wb 138.0)*				
1090CD	touring limo 7P	3,900	1,840	—
1091CD	touring 7P	3,835	1,690	—

1500 Super Eight (wb 127.0)**				
1003	touring sdn 5P	4,530	2,335	—

1501 Super Eight (wb 134.0)**				
L394	LeBaron A/W cab 7P	4,965	4,850	—
1007	victoria 5P	4,650	3,150	—
1012	formal sdn 5P	4,795	3,235	—
1013	touring sdn 5P	4,670	2,535	—
1016	club sdn 5P	4,600	2,530	—
1017	cpe 5P	4,595	2,510	—
1018	cpe 2-4P	4,585	2,420	—
1019	conv cpe 2-4P	4,580	2,680	—

1502 Super Eight (wb 139.0)**				
L395	LeBaron A/W town car 7P	5,360	4,990	—
1014	touring sdn 7P	4,700	2,705	—
1014B	bus sdn 8P	4,755	2,580	—
1015	touring limo 7P	4,815	2,840	—
1015B	bus limo 8P	4,925	2,715	—
1063	conv sdn 5P	4,945	3,350	—

1506 Twelve (wb 132.0)***				
1023	touring sdn 5P	5,335	3,490	—

1507 Twelve (wb 139.0)***				
L394	LeBaron A/W cab 7P	5,740	5,700	—
1027	victoria 5P	5,345	4,490	—
1032	formal sdn 5P	5,550	4,260	—
1033	touring sdn 4d	5,525	3,560	—
1036	club sdn 5P	5,520	3,660	—
1037	cpe 5P	5,415	3,590	—

1937 Twelve four-door touring sedan

		Wght	Price	Prod
1038	cpe 2-4P	5,255	3,420	—
1039	conv cpe 2-4P	5,255	3,450	—

1508 Twelve (wb 144.0)***				
L395	LeBaron A/W town car 7P	5,790	5,900	—
1034	touring sdn 7P	5,600	3,885	—
1035	touring limo 7P	5,660	4,005	—
1073	conv sdn 5P	5,680	4,650	—

*Total One Twenty production: 50,100
**Total Super Eight production: 5,793
***Total Twelve production: 1,300

1937 Engines	bore×stroke	bhp	availability
L6, 237.0	3.44×4.25	100	S-Six
L8, 282.0	3.25×4.25	120	S-One Twenty
L8, 320.0	3.19×5.00	135	S-Super Eight
V12, 473.0	3.44×4.25	175	S-Twelve

1938

1600 Six (wb 122.0)—30,050 built		Wght	Price	Prod
1182	touring sdn 4d	3,525	1,175	—
1184	touring sdn 2d	3,475	1,145	—
1185	club cpe 2-4P	3,425	1,120	—
1188	bus cpe 2P	3,450	1,075	—
1189	conv cpe 2-4P	3,500	1,235	—

1601 Eight (wb 127.0)*				
1192	touring sdn 4d	3,650	1,525	—
1194	touring sdn 2d	3,600	1,295	—
1195	club cpe 2-4P	3,550	1,270	—
1197	conv sdn 5P	3,775	1,650	—
1198	bus cpe 2P	3,570	1,225	—
1199	conv cpe 2-4P	3,625	1,365	—
1172	Deluxe touring sdn 4d	3,685	1,540	—

1601 Eight (wb 139.0)*				
1665	Rollston A/W cabriolet 7P	—	4,810	—
1668	Rollston A/W brougham 4P	—	5,100	—
1669	Rollston A/W town car 7P	—	4,885	—

1602 Eight (wb 148.0)*				
1190	limo 7P	4,245	1,955	—
1191	touring sdn 7P	4,195	2,110	—

1603 Super Eight (wb 127.0)**				
1103	touring sdn 4d	4,530	2,790	—

1604 Super Eight (wb 134.0)**				
1107	victoria 5P	4,650	3,670	—
1112	formal sdn 5P	4,795	3,710	—
1113	touring sdn 4d	4,670	2,995	—
1116	club sdn 5P	4,600	2,990	—
1117	cpe 5P	4,595	2,965	—
1118	cpe 2-4P	4,585	2,925	—
1119	conv cpe 4P	4,580	3,210	—

1939 Twelve Victoria convertible coupe

1605 Super Eight (wb 139.0)**

		Wght	Price	Prod
494	Rollston A/W cab 7P	4,945	5,790	—
495	Rollston A/W town car 7P	4,940	5,890	—
1114	bus sdn 7P	4,815	3,165	—
1115	bus limo 7P	4,815	3,305	—
1143	conv sdn 5P	4,945	3,970	—
3086	Brunn touring cabriolet 7P	4,990	7,475	—
3087	Brunn A/W cabriolet 7P	4,995	7,475	—

1607 Twelve (wb 134.0)***

		Wght	Price	Prod
1127	victoria 5P	5,345	5,230	—
1132	formal sdn 5P	5,550	4,865	—
1133	touring sdn 4d	5,525	4,155	—
1136	club sdn 5P	5,520	4,255	—
1137	cpe 5P	5,415	4,185	—
1138	cpe 2-4P	5,255	4,135	—
1139	conv cpe 2-4P	5,255	4,370	—

1608 Twelve (wb 139.0)***

		Wght	Price	Prod
494	Rollston A/W cab 7P	5,740	6,730	—
495	Rollston A/W town car 7P	5,735	6,880	—
1134	touring sdn 7P	5,600	4,485	—
1135	touring limo 7P	5,600	4,485	—
1153	conv sdn 5P	5,680	5,390	—
3086	Brunn touring cabriolet 7P	5,725	8,510	—
3087	Brunn A/W cabriolet 7P	5,730	8,510	—

*Total Eight production: 22,624
**Total Super Eight production: 2,478
***Total Twelve production: 566

1938 Engines	bore×stroke	bhp	availability
L6, 245.0	3.50×4.25	100	S-Six
L8, 282.0	3.25×4.25	120	S-Eight
L8, 320.0	3.19×5.00	130	S-Super Eight
V12, 473.0	3.44×4.25	175	S-Twelve

1939

1700 Six (wb 122.0)—24,350 built

		Wght	Price	Prod
1282	touring sdn 4d	3,400	1,095	—
1283	wgn 4d 7P	3,652	1,404	—
1285	club cpe 2-4P	3,365	1,045	—
1284	touring sdn 2d	3,390	1,065	—
1285	club cpe 2-4P	3,365	1,045	—
1288	bus cpe 2P	3,295	1,000	—

1701 One Twenty (wb 127.0)*

		Wght	Price	Prod
1292	touring sdn 4d	3,605	1,295	—
1293	wgn 4d 7P	3,850	1,636	—
1294	touring sdn 2d	3,595	1,265	—
1295	club cpe 2-4P	3,535	1,245	—
1297	conv sdn 5P	3,780	1,700	—
1298	bus cpe 2P	3,490	1,200	—
1299	conv cpe 2-4P	3,545	1,390	—

1702 One Twenty (wb 148.0)*

		Wght	Price	Prod
1290	touring limo 7P	4,185	1,955	—

		Wght	Price	Prod
1291	touring sdn 7P	4,100	1,805	—

1703 Super Eight (wb 127.0)**

		Wght	Price	Prod
1272	touring sdn 4d	3,930	1,732	—
1275	club cpe 2-4P	3,860	1,650	—
1277	conv sdn 5P	4,005	2,130	—
1279	conv cpe 2-4P	3,870	1,875	—

1705 Super Eight (wb 148.0)**

		Wght	Price	Prod
1270	touring limo 7P	4,510	2,294	—
1271	touring sdn 7P	4,425	2,156	—

1707 Twelve (wb 134.0)

		Wght	Price	Prod
594	Rollston A/W cab 7P	4,950	6,730	—
1227	victoria 5P	5,570	5,230	—
1232	formal sdn 5P	5,745	4,865	—
1233	touring sdn 4d	5,670	4,155	—
1236	club cpe 5P	5,590	4,255	—
1237	cpe 5P	5,425	4,185	—
1238	cpe 2-4P	5,400	4,185	—
1239	conv cpe 2-4P	5,540	4,375	—

1708 Twelve (wb 139.0)***

		Wght	Price	Prod
595	Rollston A/W town car 7P	5,075	6,880	—
1234	touring sdn 7P	5,750	4,485	—
1235	touring limo 7P	5,825	4,690	—
1253	conv sdn 5P	5,890	5,395	—
4086	Brunn touring cabriolet 5P	5,845	8,355	—
4087	Brunn A/W cabriolet 6P	5,845	8,355	—

*Total One Twenty production: 17,647
**Total Super Eight production: 3,962
***Total Twelve production: 446

1939 Engines	bore×stroke	bhp	availability
L6, 245.0	3.50×4.25	100	S-Six
L8, 282.0	3.25×4.25	120	S-One Twenty
L8, 320.0	3.19×4.25	130	S-Super Eight
V12, 473.0	3.44×4.25	175	S-Twelve

1940

1800 One Ten (wb 122.0) — 62,300 built

		Wght	Price	Prod
1382	sdn 4d	3,200	996	—
1383	wgn 4d, 8P	3,380	1,200	—
1384	sdn 2d	3,190	964	—
1385	club cpe	3,165	940	—
1388	bus cpe	3,120	867	—
1389	conv cpe	3,200	1,104	—

1801 One Twenty (wb 127.0) — 28,138 built

		Wght	Price	Prod
700	conv vic by Darrin	3,826	3,819	—
1392	sdn 4d	3,520	1,166	—
1393	wgn 4d, 8P	3,590	1,404	—
1394	sdn 2d	3,510	1,135	—
1395	club cpe	3,450	1,111	—
1396	club sdn	3,520	1,239	—
1397	conv sdn	3,710	1,573	—
1398	bus cpe	3,340	1,038	—
1399	conv cpe	3,540	1,277	—
DE1392	Deluxe sdn 4d	3,495	1,246	—
DE1395	Deluxe club cpe	3,400	1,161	—
DE1396	Deluxe club sdn	3,480	1,314	—
DE1399	Deluxe conv cpe	3,470	1,318	—

1803 Super Eight One Sixty (wb 127.0) — 5,662 built
(includes all One Sixtys)

		Wght	Price	Prod
1372	sdn 4d	3,855	1,655	—
1375	club cpe	3,760	1,614	—
1376	club sdn	3,855	1,740	—
1377	conv sdn	4,000	2,075	—
1378	bus cpe	3,735	1,524	—
1379	conv cpe	3,825	1,797	—

1804 Super Eight One Sixty (wb 138.0)

		Wght	Price	Prod
1362	sdn 4d	4,165	1,919	—

1805 Super Eight One Sixty (wb 148.0)

1370	limo 7P	4,500	2,179	—
1371	sdn 4d, 7P	4,425	2,051	—

1806 Custom Super Eight One Eighty (wb 127.0) — 1,900 built (includes all One Eightys)

700	conv vic by Darrin	4,121	4,593	—
1356	club sdn	3,900	2,243	—

1807 Custom Super Eight One Eighty (wb 138.0)

694	A/W cabriolet by Rollston	4,050	4,473	—
710	conv sdn by Darrin	4,050	6,332	—
1332	form sdn	4,210	2,855	—
1342	sdn 4d	4,210	2,422	—

1808 Custom Super Eight One Eighty (wb 148.0)

695	A/W town car by Rollston	4,175	4,599	—
1350	limo 7P	4,585	2,683	—
1351	sdn 4d, 7P	4,510	2,554	—

1940 Engines

	bore × stroke	bhp	availability
L6, 245.3	3.50×4.25	100	S-One Ten
L8, 282.0	3.25×4.25	120	S-One Twenty
L8, 356.0	3.50×4.63	160	S-Super/Custom Super Eights

1941

1900 One Ten (wb 122.0) — 34,700 built

		Wght	Price	Prod
1482	sdn 4d	3,260	1,076	—
1483	wgn 4d, 8P	3,460	1,251	—
1484	sdn 2d	3,250	1,010	—
1485	club cpe	3,230	1,020	—
1488	bus cpe	3,190	927	—
1489	conv cpe	3,260	1,195	—
1463DE	Deluxe wgn 4d, 8P	3,470	1,236	—
1482DE	Deluxe sdn 4d	3,280	1,136	—
1484DE	Deluxe sdn 2d	3,270	1,070	—
1485DE	Deluxe club cpe	3,250	1,058	—
1489DE	Deluxe conv cpe	3,280	1,229	—

1901 One Twenty (wb 127.0) — 17,000 built

1473	Deluxe wgn 4d, 8P	3,730	1,541	—
1492	sdn 4d	3,535	1,291	—
1493	wgn 4d, 8P	3,720	1,466	—
1494	sdn 2d	3,525	1,260	—
1495	club cpe	3,470	1,235	—
1497	conv sdn	3,725	1,753	—
1498	bus cpe	3,360	1,142	—
1499	conv cpe	3,570	1,407	—

1951 Clipper (wb 127.0)

1401	sdn 4d	3,725	1,420	16,600

1903 Super Eight One Sixty (wb 127.0) — 3,525 built (includes all One Sixtys)

1472	sdn 4d	3,995	1,795	—
1475	club cpe	3,900	1,754	—
1477	conv sdn	4,140	2,225	—
1478	bus cpe	3,875	1,639	—
1479	conv cpe	3,965	1,937	—
1477DE	Deluxe conv sdn	4,160	2,450	—
1479DE	Deluxe conv cpe	3,985	2,112	—

1904 Super Eight One Sixty (wb 138.0)

1462	sdn 4d	4,305	2,054	—

1905 Super Eight One Sixty (wb 148.0)

1470	limo 7P	4,570	2,334	—
1471	sdn 4d 7P	4,495	2,206	—

1906 Custom Super Eight One Eighty (wb 127.0) — 930 built (inc all One Eightys)

		Wght	Price	Prod
1429	conv vic by Darrin	4,040	4,595	—

1907 Custom Super Eight One Eighty (wb 138.0)

794	A/W cabriolet by Rollston	4,075	4,695	—
1422	spt sdn by Darrin	4,490	4,795	—
1432	form sdn	4,350	3,090	—
1442	sdn 4d	4,350	2,632	—
1452	Sport Brougham by LeBaron	4,450	3,545	—

1908 Custom Super Eight One Eighty (wb 148.0)

795	A/W town car by Rollston	4,200	4,820	—
1420	limo 7P by LeBaron	4,850	5,595	—
1421	sdn 4d, 7P by LeBaron	4,740	5,345	—
1450	limo 7P	4,650	2,913	—
1451	sdn 4d, 7P	4,590	2,769	—

1941 Engines

	bore × stroke	bhp	availability
L6, 245.3	3.50×4.25	100	S-One Ten
L8, 282.0	3.25×4.25	120	S-One Twenty
L8, 282.0	3.25×4.25	125	S-Clipper
L8, 356.0	3.50×4.63	160	S-One Sixty, One Eighty

1942

2000 Clipper 110 Special (wb 120.0) — 11,325 built (includes all 110s)

		Wght	Price	Prod
1582	sdn 4d	3,435	1,232	—
1585	club sdn	3,415	1,199	—
1588	bus cpe	3,365	1,166	—

2010 Clipper 110 Custom (wb 120.0)

1502	sdn 4d	3,460	1,299	—
1505	club sdn	3,440	1,266	—

2020 Clipper 110 (wb 122.0)

1589	conv cpe	3,315	1,375	—

2001 Clipper 120 Special (wb 120.0) — 19,199 built (includes all 120s)

1592	sdn 4d	3,560	1,275	—
1595	club sdn	3,540	1,241	—
1598	bus cpe	3,490	1,208	—

2011 Clipper 120 Custom (wb 120.0)

1512	sdn 4d	3,585	1,341	—
1515	club sdn	3,565	1,308	—

2021 Clipper 120 (wb 127.0)

1599	conv cpe	3,585	1,469	—

2003 Clipper One Sixty (wb 127.0) — 2,580 built (includes all One Sixtys)

1572	sdn 4d	4,005	1,688	—
1575	club sdn	3,985	1,630	—

2023 Clipper One Sixty (wb 127.0)

1579	conv cpe	3,905	1,786	—

2004 Clipper One Sixty (wb 138.0)

1562	sdn 4d	4,090	1,893	—

2005 Clipper One Sixty (wb 148.0)

1570	limo 7P	4,445	2,156	—
1571	sdn 4d, 7P	4,325	2,034	—

2055 Clipper One Sixty (wb 148.0)

1590	bus limo 7P	4,435	2,010	—
1591	bus sdn 4d, 7P	4,315	1,888	—

2006 Clipper One Eighty (wb 127.0) — 672 built (includes all One Eightys)

1522	sdn 4d	4,030	2,196	—

		Wght	Price	Prod
1525	club sdn	4,010	2,099	—
1529	conv vic by Darrin	3,920	4,519	—

2007 Clipper One Eighty (wb 138.0)

		Wght	Price	Prod
894	A/W cabriolet by Rollston	4,075	4,792	—
1532	form sdn	4,390	3,011	—
1542	sdn 4d	4,280	2,440	—

2008 Clipper One Eighty (wb 148.0)

		Wght	Price	Prod
895	A/W town car by Rollston	4,200	4,889	—
1520	limo 7P by LeBaron	4,850	5,690	—
1521	sdn 4d, 7P by LeBaron	4,740	5,446	—
1550	limo 7P	4,540	2,645	—
1551	sdn 4d, 7P	4,525	2,523	—

1942 Engines	bore × stroke	bhp	availability
L6, 245.3	3.50 × 4.25	105	S-Clipper 110
L8, 282.0	3.25 × 4.25	125	S-Clipper 120
L8, 356.0	3.50 × 4.63	165	S-Clipper One Sixty, One Eighty

1946

2100 Clipper Six (wb 120.0) — 15,892 built

		Wght	Price	Prod
1682	sdn 4d	3,495	1,730	—
1685	club sdn	3,450	1,680	—

2101 Clipper Eight (wb 120.0)

1692	sdn 4d	3,630	1,802	1,500

2111 Clipper Deluxe Eight (wb 120.0) — 5,714 built

1612	sdn 4d	3,670	1,869	—
1615	club sdn	3,625	1,817	—

2103 Super Clipper (wb 127.0) — 4,924 built

1672	sdn 4d	3,995	2,290	—
1675	club sdn	3,950	2,241	—

2106 Custom Super Clipper (wb 127.0) — 3,081 built

1622	sdn 4d	4,060	3,047	—
1625	club sdn	4,000	2,913	—

2126 Custom Super Clipper (wb 148.0)

1650	limo 7P	4,900	4,496	1,291
1651	sdn 4d, 7P	4,870	4,332	1,790

1946 Engines	bore × stroke	bhp	availability
L6, 245.3	3.50 × 4.25	105	S-Clipper Six
L8, 282.0	3.25 × 4.25	125	S-Clipper Eight/DeLuxe Eight
L8, 356.0	3.50 × 4.63	165	S-Super/Custom Super Clipper

1947

2100 Clipper Six (wb 120.0) — 14,949 built

		Wght	Price	Prod
2182	sdn 4d	3,520	1,937	—
2185	club sdn	3,475	1,912	—

2111 Clipper DeLuxe Eight (wb 120.0) — 23,855 built

2112	sdn 4d	3,695	2,149	—
2115	club sdn	3,650	2,124	—

2103 Super Clipper (wb 127.0) — 4,802 built

2172	sdn 4d	4,025	2,772	—
2175	club sdn	3,980	2,747	—

2106 Custom Super Clipper (wb 127.0) — 7,480 built (includes 148 wb)

2122	sdn 4d	4,090	3,449	—
2125	club sdn	3,384	2,125	—

2126 Custom Super Clipper (wb 148.0)

2150	limo 7P	4,920	4,668	—
2151	sdn 4d, 7P	4,890	4,504	—

1947 Engines	bore × stroke	bhp	availability
L6, 245.3	3.50 × 4.25	105	S-Clipper Six
L8, 282.0	3.25 × 4.25	125	S-Clipper Eight/DeLuxe Eight
L8, 356.0	3.50 × 4.63	165	S-Super/Custom Super Clipper

1948

2201 Eight (wb 120.0) — 12,782* built

		Wght	Price	Prod
2292	sdn 4d	3,815	2,275	—
2293	Station Sedan wgn 4d	4,075	3,425	—
2295	club sdn	3,755	2,250	—

2211 DeLuxe Eight (wb 120.0) — 47,807 built

2262	sdn 4d	3,840	2,543	—
2265	club sdn	3,770	2,517	—

2202 Super Eight (wb 120.0) — 12,921 built

2272	sdn 4d	3,855	2,827	—
2275	club sdn	3,790	2,802	—

2222 Super Eight (wb 141.0) — 1,766 built

2270	DeLuxe limo 7P	4,610	4,000	—
2271	DeLuxe sdn 4d, 7P	4,590	3,850	—
2276	limo 7P	4,525	3,650	—
2277	sdn 4d, 7P	4,460	3,500	—

2232 Super Eight (wb 120.0)

2279	conv cpe	4,025	3,250	7,763

2206 Custom Eight (wb 127.0) — 5,936 built

2252	sdn 4d	4,175	3,750	—
2255	club sdn	4,110	3,700	—

2226 Custom Eight (wb 148.0) — 230 built

2250	limo 7P	4,880	4,868	—
2251	sdn 4d, 7P	4,860	4,704	—

2313 Custom Eight (wb 148.0)

—	chassis	—	—	1,941

2233 Custom Eight (wb 127.0)

2259	conv cpe	4,380	4,295	1,105

1948 Engines	bore × stroke	bhp	availability
L8, 288.0	3.50 × 3.75	130	S-Eight, DeLuxe Eight
L8, 327.0	3.50 × 4.25	145	S-Super Eight
L8, 356.0	3.50 × 4.63	160	S-Custom Eight

1949 First Series

2201 Eight (wb 120.0) — 13,553* built

		Wght	Price	Prod
2292-9	sdn 4d	3,815	2,275	—
2293-9	Station Sedan wgn 4d	4,075	3,425	—
2295-9	club sdn	3,755	2,250	—

2211 DeLuxe Eight (wb 120.0) — 27,422 built

2262-9	sdn 4d	3,840	2,543	—
2265-9	club sdn	3,770	2,517	—

2202 Super Eight (wb 120.0) — 5,879 built

2272-9	sdn 4d	3,855	2,827	—
2275-9	club sdn	3,790	2,802	—

2222 Super Eight (wb 141.0) — 867 built

2270-9	DeLuxe limo 7P	4,610	4,000	—
2271-9	DeLuxe sdn 4d, 7P	4,590	3,850	—
2276-9	limo 7P	4,525	3,650	—
2277-9	sdn 4d, 7P	4,460	3,500	—

2232 Super Eight (wb 120.0)

2279-9	conv cpe	4,025	3,250	1,237

Packard

2206 Custom Eight (wb 127.0) — 2,990 built		Wght	Price	Prod
2252-9	sdn 4d	4,175	3,750	—
2255-9	club sdn	4,110	3,700	—

2226 Custom Eight (wb 148.0) — 50 built		Wght	Price	Prod
2250-9	limo 7P	4,880	4,868	—
2251-9	sdn 4d, 7P	4,860	4,704	—

2213 Custom Eight (wb 148.0)				
—	chassis	—	—	220

2233 Custom Eight (wb 127.0)				
2259-9	conv cpe	4,380	4,295	213

1949 Second Series

2301 Eight (wb 120.0) — 53,168* built		Wght	Price	Prod
2362	DeLuxe sdn 4d	3,840	2,383	—
2365	DeLuxe club sdn	3,770	2,358	—
2392	sdn 4d	3,815	2,249	—
2393	Station Sedan wgn 4d	4,075	3,449	—
2395	club sdn	3,740	2,224	—

2302 Super Eight (wb 127.0) — 8,759 built				
2372	DeLuxe sdn 4d	3,925	2,919	—
2375	DeLuxe club sdn	3,855	2,894	—
2382	sdn 4d	3,870	2,633	—
2385	club sdn	3,800	2,608	—

2322 Super Eight (wb 141.0) — 4 built				
2370	DeLuxe limo 7P	4,620	4,100	—
2371	DeLuxe sdn 4d, 7P	4,600	3,950	—

2332 Super Eight (wb 127.0)				
2332	DeLuxe conv cpe	4,260	3,350	685

2306 Custom Eight (wb 127.0)				
2352	sdn 4d	4,310	3,750	973

2313 Custom Eight (wb 148.0)				
—	chassis	—	—	160

2333 Custom Eight (wb 127.0)				
2359	conv cpe	4,530	4,295	68

1949 Engines	bore × stroke	bhp	availability
L8, 288.0	3.50 × 3.75	135	S-Eight, DeLuxe Eight
L8, 327.0	3.50 × 4.25	150	S-Super/Super DeLuxe Eight
L8, 356.0	3.50 × 4.63	160	S-Custom Eight

1950

2301 Eight (wb 120.0) — 36,471* built		Wght	Price	Prod
2362-5	DeLuxe sdn 4d	3,840	2,383	—
2365-5	DeLuxe club sdn	3,770	2,358	—
2392-5	sdn 4d	3,815	2,249	—
2393-5	Station Sedan wgn 4d	4,075	3,449	—
2395-5	club sdn	3,740	2,224	—

2302 Super Eight (wb 127.0) — 4,528 built				
2372-5	DeLuxe sdn 4d	3,925	2,919	—
2375-5	club sdn	3,855	2,894	—
2382-5	sdn 4d	3,870	2,633	—
2385-5	club sdn	3,800	2,608	—

2332 Super Eight (wb 127.0)				
2379-5	conv cpe	4,110	3,350	600

2306 Custom Eight (wb 127.0)				
2352-5	sdn 4d	4,310	3,975	707

2313 Custom Eight (wb 148.0)				
—	chassis	—	—	244

2333 Custom Eight (wb 127.0)		Wght	Price	Prod
2359-5	conv cpe	4,530	4,520	77

1950 Engines	bore × stroke	bhp	availability
L8, 288.0	3.50 × 3.75	135	S-Eight, DeLuxe Eight
L8, 327.0	3.50 × 4.25	150	S-Super/Super DeLuxe Eight
L8, 356.0	3.50 × 4.63	160	S-Custom Eight

*Although Packard did not break down model year production by body style, some calendar year figures exist for the Station Sedan. These are: 126 in 1947, 3,266 in 1948, and 472 in 1949, for a total of 3,864. An estimated 75 percent were 1948 models.

1951

2401 200 (wb 122.0)		Wght	Price	Prod
2462	DeLuxe sdn 4d	3,660	2,616	47,052
2465	DeLuxe club sdn	3,605	2,563	
2492	sdn 4d	3,665	2,469	24,310
2495	club sdn	3,600	2,416	
2498	bus cpe	3,550	2,302	

2401 250 (wb 122.0) — 4,640 built				
2467	Mayfair htp cpe	3,820	3,234	—
2469	conv cpe	4,040	3,391	—

2402 300 (wb 127.0)				
2472	sdn 4d	3,875	3,034	15,309

2413 300 (wb 127.0)				
—	chassis	—	—	401

2406 Patrician 400 (wb 127.0)				
2452	sdn 4d	4,115	3,662	9,001

1951 Engines	bore × stroke	bhp	availability
L8, 288.0	3.50 × 3.75	135	S-Eight, DeLuxe Eight
L8, 327.0	3.50 × 4.25	150	S-250/300 manual
L8, 327.0	3.50 × 4.25	155	S-Patrician 400, 250/300 auto

1952

2501 200 (wb 122.0)—46,720 built		Wght	Price	Prod
2562	DeLuxe sdn 4d	3,685	2,695	—
2565	DeLuxe club sdn	3,660	2,641	—
2592	sdn 4d	3,680	2,548	—
2595	club sdn	3,640	2,494	—

2531 250 (wb 122.0)—5,201 built				
2577	Mayfair htp cpe	3,805	3,318	—
2579	conv cpe	4,000	3,476	—

2502 300 (wb 127.0)				
2572	sdn 4d	3,380	3,116	6,705

2513 300 (127.0)				
—	chassis	—	—	320

2506 Patrician 400 (wb 127.0)				
2552	sdn 4d	4,100	3,797	3,975

1952 Engines	bore × stroke	bhp	availability
L8, 288.0	3.50 × 3.75	135	S-Eight, DeLuxe Eight
L8, 327.0	3.50 × 4.25	150	S-250/300 manual
L8, 327.0	3.50 × 4.25	155	S-Patrician 400, 250/300 auto

1953

2601 Clipper (wb 122.0)		Wght	Price	Prod
2692	sdn 4d	3,730	2,598	23,126
2695	club sdn	3,700	2,544	6,370

continued on page 545

▲1969 Plymouth Road Runner coupe   ▼1969 Chevrolet Chevelle Malibu SS396 hardtop coupe

▲1969 Dodge Charger R/T hardtop coupe   ▼1969 Buick Riviera hardtop coupe

▲1969 Pontiac Firebird hardtop coupe   ▼1970 Buick LeSabre Custom convertible

▲1970 Ford Torino GT Sportsroof hardtop coupe ▼1970 Chevrolet Monte Carlo hardtop coupe

▲1970 Mercury Cougar hardtop coupe   ▼1970 Pontiac GTO hardtop coupe

▲1970 Dodge Coronet Super Bee hardtop coupe   ▼1971 Oldsmobile Cutlass Supreme 4-4-2 convertible

▲1970 Buick GSX convertible   ▼1970 Dodge Dart Swinger 340 hardtop coupe

▲1972 Oldsmobile Cutlass Supreme Holiday hardtop coupe   ▼1972 Plymouth Satellite Sebring hardtop coupe

▲1972 Ford Gran Torino hardtop coupe   ▼1971 Dodge Charger 500 hardtop coupe

▲1972 AMC Matador Brougham hardtop coupe ▼1972 Chevrolet Camaro SS Rallye Sport coupe

▲1973 Ford Thunderbird hardtop coupe ▼1974 Pontiac Firebird Trans Am coupe

▲1976 Dodge Aspen Special Edition coupe   ▼1977 Lincoln Versailles four-door sedan

▲1977 Pontiac Grand Safari four-door wagon　　▼1978 AMC Matador Barcelona coupe

▲1978 Buick Century Sport Coupe two-door sedan   ▼1979 Ford LTD Landau two-door and Country Squire wagon

▲1980 Dodge Diplomat Medallion coupe   ▼1979 Cadillac Seville Elegante four-door sedan

▲1980 Ford Thunderbird coupe   ▼1980 Buick Electra Limited coupe

continued from page 528

		Wght	Price	Prod
2697	Sportster cpe	3,720	2,805	3,672
—	chassis	—	—	1
2611 Clipper DeLuxe (wb 122.0)				
2662	sdn 4d	3,760	2,745	26,027
2665	club sdn	3,720	2,691	4,678
2633 Clipper commercial (wb 122.0)				
—	chassis (Henney bodies)	—	—	380
2631 (wb 122.0)				
2677	Mayfair htp cpe	3,905	3,278	5,150
2678	Caribbean conv cpe	4,265	5,210	750
2679	conv cpe	4,125	3,486	1,518
2602 Cavalier (wb 127.0)				
2672	sdn 4d	3,975	3,244	10,799
2613 Packard commercial (wb 127.0)				
—	chassis (Henney bodies)	—	—	166
2606 Patrician (wb 127.0)				
2652	sdn 4d	4,190	3,740	7,456
2653	form sdn by Derham	4,335	6,531	25*
2626 (wb 149.0)				
2650	Corporation limo 8P	4,720	7,100	50
2651	Executive sdn 4d, 8P	4,650	6,900	100
2602-2606-2631				
—	chassis	—	—	9

*Constructed from finished Patricians.

1953 Engines	bore × stroke	bhp	availability
L8, 288.0	3.50×3.75	150	S-2601
L8, 327.0	3.50×4.25	160	S-2611
L8, 327.0	3.50×4.25	180	S-2602, 2631 (5 main bearing)
L8, 327.0	3.50×4.25	180	S-2606, 2626 (9 main bearing)

1954

5400 Clipper Special (wb 122.0)		Wght	Price	Prod
5482	sdn 4d	3,650	2,594	970
5485	club sdn	3,585	2,544	912
5401 Clipper DeLuxe (wb 122.0)				
5492	sdn 4d	3,660	2,695	7,610
5495	club sdn	3,950	2,645	1,470
5497	Sportster cpe	3,595	2,830	1,336
5411 Clipper Super (wb 122.0)				
5462	sdn 4d	3,695	2,815	6,270
5465	club sdn	3,610	2,765	887
5467	Panama htp cpe	3,765	3,125	3,618
5433 Clipper commercial (wb 122.0)				
—	chassis (Henney bodies)	—	—	120
5402 Cavalier (wb 127.0)				
5472	sdn 4d	3,955	3,344	2,580
5413 Packard commercial (wb 127.0)				
—	chassis (Henney bodies)	—	—	205
5431 (wb 122.0)				
5477	Pacific htp cpe	4,065	3,827	1,189
5478	Caribbean conv cpe	4,660	6,100	400
5479	convertible cpe	4,290	3,935	863
—	chassis	—	—	1
5406 Patrician (wb 127.0)				
5452	sdn 4d	4,190	3,890	2,760

5426 (wb 149.0)		Wght	Price	Prod
5450	Corporation limo 8P	4,720	5,960	35
5451	Executive sdn 4d, 8P	4,650	5,610	65

1954 Engines	bore × stroke	bhp	availability
L8, 288.0	3.50×3.75	150	S-5400
L8, 327.0	3.50×4.25	165	S-5401, 5411
L8, 327.0	3.50×4.25	185	S-5402
L8, 359.0	3.56×4.50	212	S-5406, 5426, 5431 (9 mains)

1955

5540 Clipper (wb 122.0)		Wght	Price	Prod
5522	DeLuxe sdn 4d	3,680	2,586	8,039
5542	Super sdn 4d	3,670	2,686	7,979
5547	Super Panama htp cpe	3,700	2,776	7,016
5560 Clipper Custom (wb 122.0)				
5562	sdn 4d	3,885	2,926	8,708
5567	Constellation htp cpe	3,865	3,076	6,672
5580 (wb 127.0)				
5582	Patrician sdn 4d	4,275	3,890	9,127
5587	Four Hundred htp cpe	4,250	3,930	7,206
5588	Caribbean conv cpe	4,755	5,932	500*

*A very few 1955 Caribbean hardtops have been discovered.

1955 Engines	bore × stroke	bhp	availability
V8, 320.0	3.81×3.50	225	S-Clipper DeLuxe/Super
V8, 352.0	4.00×3.50	245	S-Clipper Custom
V8, 352.0	4.00×3.50	260	S-Packard exc Caribbean
V8, 352.0	4.00×3.50	275	S-Caribbean

1956

5670 Executive (wb 122.0)		Wght	Price	Prod
5672	sdn 4d	4,185	3,465	1,784
5677	htp cpe	4,185	3,560	1,031
5680 (wb 127.0)				
5682	Patrician sdn 4d	4,045	4,160	3,775
5687	Four Hundred htp cpe	4,080	4,190	3,224
5688 Caribbean (wb 127.0)				
5697	htp cpe	4,590	5,495	263
5699	conv cpe	4,960	5,995	276

1956 Engines	bore × stroke	bhp	availability
V8, 352.0	4.00×3.50	275	S-Executive
V8, 374.0	4.13×3.50	290	S-Patrician, Four Hundred
V8, 374.0	4.13×3.50	310	S-Caribbean

1957 Clipper

57L (wb 120.5; wgn-116.5)		Wght	Price	Prod
Y8	Town Sedan 4d	3,570	3,212	3,940
P8	Country Sedan wgn 4d	3,650	3,384	869

1957 Engine	bore × stroke	bhp	availability
V8, 289.0	3.56×3.63	275	S-all

1958

58L (wb 120.5; wgn/htp-116.5)		Wght	Price	Prod
J8	sdn 4d	3,505	3,212	1,200
J8	htp cpe	3,480	3,262	675
K9	Hawk htp cpe	3,470	3,995	588
P8	wgn 4d	3,555	3,384	159

1958 Engines	bore × stroke	bhp	availability
V8, 289.0	3.56×3.63	275	S-Hawk
V8. 289.0	3.56×3.63	210	S-Others

Pierce-Arrow

Pierce-Arrow Motor Car Company
Buffalo, New York

Pierce-Arrow lived in the golden age of American motoring greats: Cadillac, Duesenberg, LaSalle, Lincoln, Marmon, Packard, Peerless, Stutz, the Springfield Rolls-Royce. Peerless, like the American Rolls, was only a shadow of its former self by 1930, and of little importance as a competitor. Duesenberg, Marmon, and Stutz were still making magnificent motorcars that sold only in tiny numbers. Cadillac and Lincoln were bankrolled by big corporations and therefore had the best chance of survival among the prestige makes in the financially perilous years to come.

Pierce's closest rival in the '30s was Packard. They were the last of the great independents. Though each make had its own distinctive appearance, their engineering was remarkably similar. Pierce's Eight arrived in 1929, five years after Packard's, but it was technically superior and offered more performance. The 12-cylinder rivals were evenly matched. Packard, of course, was a stronger corporation, reflecting the inherent advantage of its Detroit location and a more forward-looking management team. By the time Pierce updated its cars from big sixes to straight-eight engines, Packard's lead was insurmountable, although Pierces of the early '30s showed the marque still had potential for greatness. In engineering, styling, quality, refinement, and prestige, Pierce-Arrow and Packard marked the summit of American classic-car achievement. They acknowledged few peers; they had no superiors.

Pierce-Arrow was acquired in 1928 by Studebaker under its accountant-turned-president, Albert R. Erskine. Pierce, which had been ailing for several years, was looking for a guardian angel, and Erskine wanted a prestige nameplate for the Studebaker empire he hoped to build. Pierce-Arrow continued as an independent entity under its own general manager, Arthur J. Chanter, though Erskine took over as president, and its own engineers, not Studebaker's, designed the 1929 Eight.

Both 1929-30 Pierce series shared the same nine-bearing engine. Distinctively Pierce-Arrow in design, they were enthusiastically received—and deserved to be. They were better looking, better handling, faster, lower slung, and lower priced than their six-cylinder predecessors. Sales in 1929 were more than double those of 1928, and even the stock market crash didn't immediately affect the situation as volume rose through the spring of 1930. By the second quarter, however, sales began falling off. There was no immediate concern in Buffalo, for 1930 would be the firm's second-best year ever. The market, which had been grim before the Studebaker takeover, was again viewed with Pierce's old combination of arrogance and naivete.

Cadillac's V16 sent Pierce chief engineer Karl M. Wise to work on a V12, which was introduced for 1932. It was initially offered in two sizes, but the smaller version was soon dropped because it didn't perform any better than Pierce's 385-cid eights. To keep up in the horsepower

1930 Model A seven-passenger sedan

1931 Model 41 town brougham

1932 Model 54 seven-passenger sedan

1932 Model 53 convertible roadster by LeBaron

race, the twelve was enlarged for 1933. Test driver Ab Jenkins took one to the Bonneville Salt Flats in September 1932, basically a standard car that had already seen 33,000 miles. Jenkins piled up 2710 miles at a 112.91-mph average over 24 hours. Fenders, windshield, and road equipment were then reinstalled, and the car was immedi-

1933 Model 1242 convertible sedan by Rollston

1934 DeLuxe Eight club sedan

1933 Silver Arrow four-door sedan

1936 Eight convertible roadster coupe

ately driven 2000 miles back across the continent to Buffalo. This run was followed by two more in 1933 and 1934, at 117.77 and 127 mph, respectively.

But as Marmon, Cadillac, Packard, and others were learning, multi-cylinder engines were not the key to survival in the luxury-car field of the early '30s, and Pierce-Arrow lost $3 million on sales of $8 million in 1932. Reflecting the optimism shared by its Studebaker owner, Pierce had underestimated the severity of the Depression. Extensive advertising hadn't helped, nor did raising prices about $500. In the first half of the year, the company sold 1523 cars compared to 2987 in 1931. A total of 2241 were sold for the full year, mostly to dealers and at retail through company sales outlets. Deliveries for the first six months of 1933 declined again, to 1020, but the company adapted to reduced demand and was able to cut operating costs.

Roy Faulkner, the dynamic former president of Auburn, took over as Pierce-Arrow sales manager in late 1932. His arrival lent credence to rumors of an impending merger with Auburn, but Pierce-Arrow went bankrupt in 1934, and Faulkner returned to Indiana a month later. His promotional efforts, the Silver Arrow show cars, and Jenkins' speed records were successful, but not for long. The fabulous Silver Arrow was an aesthetic success for those dark times. Radical and streamlined, it "gives you in 1933 the car of 1940," according to Pierce literature. It was a truly advanced design, though it did not inspire any of the firm's future styling.

Sales of the 12-cylinder models were up by 200 percent in January 1933, by 130 percent in February, and were 55 percent better than 1932 through October. But strikes at tool-and-die makers interfered with the fragile 1933 recovery, and 300-400 sales were lost late in the year. Studebaker bankrolled these losses, protecting the

company from the effects of the Depression. But Studebaker itself was overextended, and went bankrupt in the spring of 1933. Albert Erskine committed suicide the following July, and Pierce-Arrow was sold to a group of businessmen and bankers in August. The company was again an independent and, ironically, now more financially healthy than Studebaker. Its debts were cancelled and sales improved. The company hoped to break even at 3000 annual sales and make a million dollars profit at 4000 units. But sales reached only 2152 by the end of 1933, 89 less than the 1932 total. The new owners appointed former general manager Chanter, now 43, to succeed Erskine as president, and he and Faulkner laid plans to expand sales.

The 1934 models were restyled and became more streamlined. This basic look continued in 1935, the only external difference being rearranged hood louvers (from two groups of two in 1934 to a single line of three). Internally, there was a completely redone dashboard, with instruments grouped in two large dials flanking the steering column. One dial incorporated oil pressure, water temperature, ammeter, and fuel level gauges; the other housed a speedometer and odometer. Minor controls were in the center and a glovebox was on the right, with an electric clock mounted on its door.

Initial 1934 registrations were disappointing. Losses were $681,000 for the first six months of the year, and another $176,000 was lost in July. Pierce-Arrow filed for bankruptcy the very next month. Chanter sought funds from the Buffalo community and New York banks, and managed to raise about $1 million, but Pierce was forced to sell its retail sales branches. The reorganized company, named Pierce-Arrow Motor Corporation, began operations in May 1935.

Pierce-Arrow

The entire line was again redesigned for 1936 to keep in step with current ideas of style and streamlining. Body lines were fashionably rounded. A built-in trunk with top-hinged lid incorporated an interior light with mercury switch. Rear windows were one-piece full-pivoting types instead of half-fixed as previously. Mechanical changes included an additional cruciform frame member and moving the engine farther forward. The steering box was mounted ahead of the front axle with a trailing drag link, and the radiator was moved ahead several inches. Pierces had always been easy to drive, but the revised steering geometry, suspension, and weight distribution made the ride and handling of the 1936 models outstanding.

Briefly during 1936, it looked as if Pierce-Arrow had turned the corner. Registrations showed a 25 percent gain for the first third of the year, but sales soon tapered off to below the 1935 level. Production was suspended in 1937 except for the auto show models and spare parts.

A 1938 lineup was announced that October, but only 30 cars had been registered by the end of the following year.

The success of Packard and Lincoln with their medium-priced lines inspired another reorganization scheme in 1937. In August, the company announced plans to raise $10.7 million through a stock sale to produce 25,000 medium-priced cars, plus 4800 trailers and 1200 luxury models, and Pierce proposed turning over management duties to Postmaster General James A. Farley, then intending to leave the Roosevelt Administration. But none of this came to pass. Farley had received similar offers from Studebaker and Willys, which he also rejected because all three required him to use his influence with the government, presumably to obtain contract work or federal loans. Pierce declared bankruptcy again in December 1937 after losing nearly $250,000 in the 17 months from July 1936 through November 1937. Liquidation of the company's assets was ordered in 1938.

Pierce Arrow

1930*

Model A (144.0)—335 built

	Wght	Price	Prod
touring 7P	4,510	3,975	—
conv cpe 2P	4,540	3,975	—
sedan 7P	4,820	4,485	—
salon sdn 7P	4,900	4,835	—
salon town car 7P	5,040	5,035	—

Model B (wb 134.0; lwb-139.0)

	Wght	Price	Prod
rdstr 2P	4,290	3,125	
touring 4-5P	4,375	3,300	110
dual-cowl spt phtn 4-5P	4,470	3,600	
conv cpe 2-4P	4,420	3,350	
lwb victoria cpe 5P	4,590	3,475	
lwb sdn 4d	4,720	3,495	
lwb salon sdn 4d	4,780	3,795	
lwb salon club sdn 4d	4,770	3,795	
lwb salon club berline 5P	4,840	3,995	
lwb club sdn 5P	4,730	3,670	1,228
lwb club berline 7P	4,790	3,870	
lwb sdn 7P	4,790	3,625	
limo 7P (lwb)	4,820	3,825	
lwb salon sdn 7P	4,840	3,925	
lwb salon limo 7P	4,860	4,125	

Model C (wb 132.0)—1,082 built

	Wght	Price	Prod
cpe 2-4P	4,450	2,865	—
club brougham 5P	4,460	2,695	—
sdn 4d	4,525	2,875	—

*Production estimated where possible. Calendar year registrations: 6,795.

1930 Engines	bore×stroke	bhp	availability
L8, 340.0	3.38×4.75	115	S-C
L8, 366.0	3.50×4.75	125	S-133, 143, B
L8, 385.0	3.50×5.00	132	S-A

1931*

Model 41 (wb 147.0)

	Wght	Price	Prod
touring 7P	4,786	4,275	—
conv cpe 2-4P	4,740	4,275	—
sdn 7P	5,100	4,785	—
limo 7P	5,157	4,985	—
LeBaron cpe 2-4P	—	5,100	—
LeBaron victoria cpe 5P	—	5,100	—
LeBaron conv sdn 5P	—	5,200	—
LeBaron spt sdn 5P	—	5,375	—
LeBaron limo 7P	—	5,975	—
town brougham 7P	5,206	6,250	—
town car 7P	5,211	6,250	—
town landau 7P	—	6,400	—

Model 42 (wb 142.0)—700 built*

	Wght	Price	Prod
spt roadster 2-4P	4,565	3,450	—
touring 5P	4,605	3,450	—
dual-cowl spt phtn 4P	4,734	3,750	—
conv cpe 2-4P	4,698	3,650	—
sdn 4d	4,980	3,695	—
club sdn 5P	4,929	3,745	—
sdn 7P	5,046	3,825	—
club berline 5P	4,953	3,945	—
limo 7P	5,075	3,995	—

Model 43 (wb 134.0; lwb-137.0)—2,500 built*

	Wght	Price	Prod
rdstr 2-4P	4,332	2,895	—
touring 5P	4,372	2,895	—
cpe 2-4P	4,528	2,685	—
lwb sdn 4d	4,638	2,685	—
lwb club sdn 5P	4,654	2,835	—
lwb sdn 7P	4,717	2,995	—
limo (lwb) 7P	4,819	3,145	—
lwb conv sdn 5P	—	3,650	—

*Production estimated where possible. Calendar year registrations: 4,522.

1931 Engines	bore×stroke	bhp	availability
L8, 340.0	3.38×4.75	115	S-C
L8, 366.0	3.50×4.75	125	S-B, 43
L8, 385.0	3.50×5.00	132	S-A, 41, 42

1932*

Model 54 (wb 137.0; lwb-142.0)

	Wght	Price	Prod
conv rdstr 2-4P	4,650	3,100	
touring 4P	—	3,150	
spt phtn 4P	—	3,350	
cpe 2-4P	4,735	2,985	
club 5P brougham	4,745	2,850	1550
sdn 4d	4,819	2,985	
club sdn 5P	—	3,150	
conv sdn 5P	4,961	3,450	
club berline 5P	—	3,350	
lwb touring 7P	—	3,450	
lwb sdn 7P	5,024	3,185	237
limo (lwb) 7P	5,071	3,450	

Model 51/52 (wb 142.0; lwb-147.0)

		Wght	Price	Prod
52	sdn 4d	5,395	4,295	
52	club sdn 5P	—	4,400	61
52	club berline 5P	—	4,600	
51	lwb sdn 7P	5,465	4,535	138
51	limo 7P (lwb)	5,506	4,800	

Model 53 (wb 137.0; lwb-142.0)

	Wght	Price	Prod
conv rdstr 2-4P	—	3,900	
touring 4P	—	3,950	
spt phtn 4P	—	4,150	
cpe 2-4P	—	3,785	
club brougham 5P	5,042	3,650	187
sdn 4d	5,080	3,785	
club sdn 5P	5,244	3,950	
conv sdn 5P	—	4,250	
club berline 5P	—	4,150	
lwb touring 7P	—	4,250	
lwb sdn 7P	5,301	3,985	61
limo 7P (lwb)	5,366	4,250	

*Calendar year registrations: 2,481

1932 Engines	bore×stroke	bhp	availability
L8, 366.0	3.50×4.75	125	S-54
V12, 398.0	3.25×4.00	140	S-53
V12, 429.0	3.38×4.00	150	S-51/52

1933*

Model 836 (wb 136.0; lwb-139.0)

	Wght	Price	Prod
conv rdstr 2-4P	4,618	3,100	
cpe 2-4P	4,663	2,795	
club brougham 5P	4,622	2,385	
sdn 4d	4,660	2,575	
club sdn 5P	4,681	2,695	
conv sdn 5P	4,958	2,975	
lwb sdn 7P	4,780	2,850	
limo (lwb) 7P	4,819	2,975	swb: 1,268
salon conv rdstr 2-4P	4,643	3,265	lwb: 259
salon cpe 2-4P	4,688	2,960	
salon club brougham 5P	4,647	2,550	
salon sdn 4d	4,685	2,740	
salon club sdn 5P	4,706	2,860	
salon conv sdn 5P	4,983	3,140	
lwb salon sdn 7P	4,805	3,015	
salon limo lwb 7P	4,844	3,140	

Model 1236 (wb 136.0; lwb-139.0)

	Wght	Price	Prod
conv rdstr 2-4P	4,729	3,500	
cpe 2-4P	4,922	3,195	
club brougham 5P	4,854	2,785	
sdn 4d	4,892	2,975	
club sdn 5P	4,929	3,095	
conv sdn 5P	—	3,375	
lwb sdn 7P	5,027	3,250	
limo (lwb) 7P	5,088	3,375	swb: 361

	Wght	Price	Prod
salon conv rdstr 2-4P	4,754	3,665	lwb:144
salon cpe 2-4P	4,947	3,360	
salon club brougham 5P	4,879	2,950	
salon sdn 4d	4,917	3,140	
salon club sdn 5P	4,954	3,260	
salon conv sdn 5P	—	3,540	
lwb salon sdn 7P	5,052	3,415	
salon limo (lwb) 7P	5,113	3,540	

Model 1242 (wb 137.0; lwb-142.0)

	Wght	Price	Prod
conv cpe rdstr	5,107	3,900	
touring 5P	5,256	3,950	
spt phtn 5P	5,296	4,150	
cpe 2-4P	—	3,785	
club brougham 5P	5,198	3,650	45
sdn 4d	—	3,785	
club sdn 5P	5,361	3,950	
conv sdn 5P	5,438	4,250	
club berline 5P	—	4,150	
lwb touring 7P	—	4,250	
lwb sdn 7P	—	3,985	73
limo (lwb) 7P	5,507	4,250	

Model 1247 (wb 142.0; lwb-147.0)—143 built

	Wght	Price	Prod
sdn 4d	—	4,295	—
club sdn 5P	5,417	4,400	—
club berline 5P	5,421	4,600	—
lwb LeBaron cpe metal-back 2P	5,286	5,300	—
lwb LeBaron cpe leather-back 2P	5,286	5,600	—
lwb LeBaron conv vic 5P	5,198	5,200	—
lwb LeBaron conv sdn 5P	5,466	5,700	—
lwb LeBaron conv sdn/partition 5P	—	6,100	—
lwb LeBaron club sdn	5,391	5,700	—
lwb LeBaron sdn 7P	5,550	4,535	—
limo (lwb) 7P	5,550	4,800	—
LeBaron limo 7P (lwb)	5,778	6,200	—
lwb Brunn town brougham	—	6,700	—
lwb Brunn cab	—	7,200	—
lwb Brunn town car	5,768	6,700	—
lwb Brunn brougham	—	7,200	—

Silver Arrow (wb 139.0)

	Wght	Price	Prod
sdn 4d	5,729	10,000	5

*Calendar year registrations: 1,776.

1936 Engines	bore×stroke	bhp	availability
L8, 366.0	3.50×4.75	135	S-836
V12, 429.0	3.38×4.00	160	S-1236
V12, 462.0	3.50×4.00	175	S-1242,1247,S.Arrow

1934*

836A Eight (wb 136.0)

	Wght	Price	Prod
club brougham 5P	4,780	2,495	
club brougham salon 5P	4,797	2,595	700+
sdn 4d	4,923	2,595	
salon sdn 4d	4,940	2,695	

840A DeLuxe Eight (wb 139.0; lwb-144.0)

	Wght	Price	Prod
conv rdstr	4,817	2,995	
cpe 4P	4,913	2,895	
club brougham 5P	4,906	2,795	439
sdn 4d	4,964	2,895	
club sdn 5P	5,042	2,995	
Silver Arrow sdn 4d (lwb)	5,046	3,495	
lwb sdn 7P	5,107	3,200	
limo 7P (lwb)	5,183	3,350	219
Brunn metro town brougham 5P (lwb)	5,228	4,995	

1240A Salon Twelve (wb 139.0; lwb:144.0)

conv rdstr 4P	5,072	3,395	
cpe 4P	5,168	3,295	
club brougham 5P	5,152	3,195	167
sdn 4d	5,227	3,295	
club sdn 5P	5,315	3,395	
Silver Arrow sdn 4d (lwb)	5,347	3,895	
lwb sdn 7P	5,381	3,600	120
limo 7P (lwb)	5,442	3,750	
Brunn metro town brougham 7P (lwb)	5,529	5,395	

1248A Custom Twelve (wb 147.0)—90 built

sdn 7P	—	4,295	—
limo 7P	5,494	4,495	—
Brunn limo 7P	—	6,000	—
Brunn town brougham 7P	—	6,500	—
Brunn town cab 7P	—	7,000	—
Brunn town car 7P	—	6,500	—
Brunn brougham 7P	—	7,000	—

*Calendar year registrations: 1,740.

1934 Engines

	bore×stroke	bhp	availability
L8, 366.0	3.50×4.75	135	S-836A
L8, 385.0	3.50×5.00	140	S-840A
V12, 462.0	3.50×4.00	175	S-1240A, 1248A

1935*

845 Eight (wb 139.0; lwb-144.0)

	Wght	Price	Prod
conv rdstr 2-4P	—	2,995	
cpe 2-4P	—	2,895	
club brougham 5P	—	2,795	360
sdn 4d	4,964	2,895	
club sdn 5P	—	2,995	
Silver Arrow sdn 4d (lwb)	—	3,495	
lwb sdn 7P	—	3,200	163
limo 7P (lwb)	—	3,350	
Brunn metro town brougham 5P (lwb)	—	4,995	

1245 Twelve (wb 139.0; lwb-144.0)

	Wght	Price	Prod
conv rdstr 2-4P	—	3,395	
cpe 2-4P	—	3,295	
club brougham 5P	—	3,195	90
sdn 4d	5,433	3,295	
club sdn 5P	—	3,395	
lwb Silver Arrow sdn 4d	—	3,895	
lwb sdn 7P	—	3,600	
limo (lwb) 7P	—	3,750	54
lwb Brunn town brougham 5P	—	5,395	

1255 Twelve (wb 147.0)—60 built

sdn 7P	—	4,295	—
limo 7P	—	4,495	—

*Calendar year registrations: 875.

1935 Engines

	bore×stroke	bhp	availability
L8, 366.0	3.50×4.75	135	S-836A
L8, 385.0	3.50×5.00	140	S-845
V12, 462.0	3.50×4.00	175	S-1245, 1255

1936*

1601 Eight (wb 139.0, 144.0, 147.0)

		Wght	Price	Prod
438C	cpe 2P, 139″	—	3,115	
438E	club berline 5P, 139″	5,600	3,495	
438N	club sdn 5P, 139″	5,600	3,295	403
438P	conv rdstr cpe 2P, 139″	5,590	3,295	
438S	sdn 4d, 139″	—	3,195	
444L	limo 7P, 144″	—	3,650	207

		Wght	Price	Prod
444M	sdn 7P, 144″	—	3,500	
447L	limo 7P, 147″	—	—	26
447M	sdn 7P, 147″	—	—	

1602 Twelve (wb 139.0, lwb-144.0)—135 built**

		Wght	Price	Prod
538	sdn 4d	—	3,900	—
544	lwb sdn 7P*	—	4,050	—
538	conv rdstr cpe, 2P	5,800	3,695	—
538	club sdn 5P	5,850	3,795	—

1603 Twelve (wb 147.0)—71 built

		Wght	Price	Prod
sdn 7P		—	4,795	—
limo 7P		6,145	4,995	—
Brunn metro town car 7P		—	5,795	—

*Calendar year registrations: 787 **incl. additional styles as per 1601 "438" and "444".

1936 Engines

	bore×stroke	bhp	availability
L8, 385.0	3.50×5.00	150	S-Eight
V12, 462.0	3.50×4.00	185	S-Twelve

1937*

1701 (wb 139.0, 144.0, 147.0)

	Wght	Price	Prod
cpe 2P, 139″	—	3,195	
club berline 5P, 139″	5,600	3,495	
club sdn 5P, 139″	5,600	3,295	50
conv rdstr cpe 2P, 139″	5,590	3,295	
sdn 4d, 139″	—	3,195	
conv sdn 5P, 139″	—	—	
formal sdn 4d, 139″	—	—	
limo 7P, 144″	—	3,650	61
sdn 7P, 144″	—	3,500	
limo 7P, 147″	—	—	10
sdn 7P, 147″	—	—	

1702 Twelve (wb 139.0, lwb-144.0)

	Wght	Price	Prod
sdn 4d	—	3,900	
conv rdstr cpe 2P	5,800	3,695	
club sdn 5P	5,850	3,795	20
club berline 5P	5,850	3,945	
conv sdn 5P	5,920	4,650	
formal sdn 4d	—	—	
lwb sdn 7P	—	4,050	23

1703 Twelve (wb 147.0)—28 built

	Wght	Price	Prod
sdn 7P	6,065	4,845	—
limo 7P	6,145	4,995	—
town car 7P	6,100	6,500	—
Brunn metro town car 7P	6,085	5,795	—

*Calendar year registrations: 166

1937 Engines

	bore×stroke	bhp	availability
L8, 385.0	3.50×5.00	150	S-Eight
V12, 462.0	3.50×4.00	185	S-Twelve

1938

1801 Eight (wb 138.0, 144.0, 147.0)

	Wght	Price	Prod
Body Styles similar to 1937 "1701"			12*

1802 Twelve (wb 139.0, lwb-144.0)

Body styles similar to 1937 "1702"			12*

1803 Twelve (wb 147.0)

Body Styles similar to 1937 "1703"			12*

*estimated; actual model year production less than 40.

1938 Engines

	bore×stroke	bhp	availability
V8, 385.0	3.50×5.00	150	S-Eight
V12, 462.0	3.50×4.00	185	S-Twelve

Plymouth

Plymouth Division, Chrysler Corporation
Highland Park, Michigan

The name for Chrysler's low-priced make was suggested by company sales manager Joseph W. Frazer. It referred, of course, to Plymouth Rock, Massachusetts. Walter Chrysler wasn't sure whether people would make the connection, so Frazer reminded him of a well-known farm product. "Every Goddamn farmer in America's heard of Plymouth Binder Twine," ex-farmboy Chrysler replied—and Plymouth it was. The new line was a success from the day it debuted in 1928. At first it was available only from Chrysler dealers, but demand was high enough by 1930 for the company to give franchises to Dodge and DeSoto agents, too. It was an excellent strategy, insulating dealers for the more expensive lines from the Depression and vastly increasing the number of Plymouth outlets.

The 1930 Plymouth shared many of its styling features with other Chrysler makes, and offered an enlarged version of its familiar L-head four. The "New Finer Plymouth" cost more than Ford and Chevrolet, although Chrysler insisted buyers got more for their money. In an age of wood-framed bodies, for example, Plymouth followed company practice with all-steel construction. It also had four-wheel hydraulic brakes, while Ford and Chevrolet stayed with mechanical brakes for several more years. The Depression was definitely on by 1930, but because of its 68,000 unit sales and a record eighth-place finish, Walter Chrysler was satisfied with Plymouth's sales performance. In future years, he'd be even happier.

The first new Plymouth since the nameplate premiered arrived for 1931, the result of a development effort pegged at approximately $2.5 million. Though the four-cylinder engine was retained, its front and rear mounts were lined with heavy rubber to insulate it from the frame, an innovation dubbed "Floating Power." The engine was able to "float" on its mounts from side to side, which kept vibration in the passenger compartment to a minimum. Though it was a relatively small advance, its effect was astonishing in a low-priced car. Plymouth advertising made the most of it by claiming that its new PA had "the smoothness of an eight and the economy of a four." Plymouth finished third in production, the first time it had scored that well. It would

remain third for the next 23 years.

Plymouth was one of the few makes that actually scored a production increase in 1930-31. It even gained in 1932-33, two of the roughest Depression years for the industry as a whole. Output reached a record 527,177 units in 1936, then dropped a little the next year. The 1938 recession saw only about 300,000 cars, but a rally followed and production was again over the half-million mark by 1940. There was good reason for all this: these were good-looking, well-built, soundly engineered automobiles that offered outstanding value.

The 1932 Plymouth was introduced in February of that year, still with a four-cylinder engine but now packing more horsepower than many larger powerplants. A convertible sedan was offered for the first time, as Chrysler evidently felt comfortable enough to dabble with less popular body styles. Advertising asked the public to "Look at All Three," to compare Plymouth with its Ford and Chevy rivals. Many people apparently did just that, because Plymouth's market share grew appreciably. It was destined to do even better in 1933: a six-cylinder line was on the way.

The new six cost $9 million to develop, but was worth it in added sales, providing more horses for fewer cubic inches than the four. It was enlarged for 1934, and continued with that displacement for the rest of the decade. By 1936, it was spinning out 82 bhp, more than adequate for a car with a base price as low as $495. Performance was also improved by virtue of less weight compared to previous models. The '33 rode a two-inch shorter wheelbase than its predecessor, and the six-cylinder sedan weighed about 300 pounds less than its 1932 four-cylinder counterpart. The year also saw the appearance of a new winged-lady hood mascot and chrome-plated radiator shell; the latter was later painted body color.

The 1934 models had more streamlined styling, with skirted fenders and a new integral trunk. The millionth Plymouth rolled off the line on August 10, 1934, and Walter Chrysler raised his glass to a good idea. Independent coil-spring front suspension was first used on the '34s, which came in two series. DeLuxe models had safety glass and artillery-type steel wheels, the latter finding favor over wire wheels, which were starting to look distinctly out of date next to the more streamlined bodies of the middle '30s. The winged-lady hood ornament was replaced by the image of the good ship Mayflower, reminding buyers of the Plymouth Rock connection.

There was a complete restyle for 1935. High seatbacks were introduced for the first time, engines acquired full-length water jackets and the chassis got a stabilizer bar and better weight distribution. The '36 lineup had only minor styling changes, but bodies now rested on rubber insulators just as the engines did, another first for the low-price field. The instrument panel featured a large airplane-inspired speedometer dial in the center, and the vee'd radiator was now slightly curved at the top.

1931 PA two/four-passenger coupe

Plymouth

Plymouth was again restyled for 1937, this time with some consideration for safety, which was of growing interest to buyers and the industry by the late '30s. Safety glass was now standard equipment on all Chrysler Corporation cars, though the right-hand windshield wiper was still an optional accessory. All interior knobs and controls were recessed, the bottom of the dash was rounded, and the top of the front seat was padded. This was the last year for crank-operated windshields and the first for a concealed heater blower and defroster vents. It was also the first year when Plymouth prices topped $1000.

Plymouth entered its 10th year for 1938 with a number of firsts. The lineup now included the first station wagon listed as a regular catalog model, though wagons had been available to special order as early as 1934. Except for the long-wheelbase seven-passenger sedans, it was the most

1932 PB sport roadster

1933 PC two-door sedan

1934 PF Standard coupe

1935 DeLuxe Six convertible coupe

1936 DeLuxe seven-passenger sedan

1937 DeLuxe coupe

1938 DeLuxe Westchester wagon

1939 DeLuxe convertible sedan

expensive offering in the line. Its body was all-wood from the windshield back, and a lot of care was needed to keep it in sound condition: annual sanding and varnishing was mandatory. Glass windows all around were optional, although front door glass was standard. There was no rear bumper at all, but the tailgate-mounted spare tire acted as a sort of substitute. Bodies were built by the U.S. Body & Forge Company of New York and Indiana.

A new series for '38 was the Roadking, a lower-priced line comprising sedan, open, and coupe styles and lacking much of the bright decoration and creature comforts of the DeLuxe series. Styling was mostly a carryover from 1937, with a slight redo for grille, headlights, and hood ornament. The handbrake was moved from the middle of the floor to a position under the center of the dash.

It was hard to say much positive about Plymouth's lumpy 1937-38 styling, so ex-coachbuilder Raymond H. Dietrich came up with a completely new look for 1939. Its most noticeable feature was a strongly peaked prow-type front end, perhaps influenced by the Lincoln Zephyr, plus a vee'd two-piece windshield instead of the previous single pane. Headlights, now rectangular, were flush-mounted in the front fenders, and the gearshift was moved from the floor to the steering column. The canvas convertible top could be power-operated for the first time, a definite selling point for the low-price class. The last convertible sedan (revived for a 12-month stand) and the last rumble-seat convertible were run off this year. The '39s were the best-looking Plymouths in five years, a breath of fresh air from company design chief Dietrich.

The 1940 models offered an improved body with "speedline" fenders. Sealed-beam headlamps appeared for the first time that year, and prices were as low as $645, just a few dollars higher than that of an equivalent Ford V8/60. The line comprised two series: Roadking and DeLuxe, both on a 117-inch wheelbase. Six models were offered in the Roadking series. The DeLuxe line comprised two- and five-passenger coupes, sedans, a convertible, and a wood-bodied eight-passenger station wagon. In addition, there was a special 137-inch-wheelbase chassis for the DeLuxe seven-passenger sedan and limousine. Long-chassis cars were a Chrysler specialty in these years, even on its low-price makes, but the Plymouth versions did not sell well.

The four-main-bearing 1940 six developed 84 horsepower at 3600 rpm. In no way did it rival the performance of the Ford V8, but it did provide reliable cruising at over 65 mph and was well known for its economy. (The original design dated back to 1933.) For 1941, horsepower was boosted to 87 bhp at 3800 rpm. It was bored out the year after that for 95 bhp at 3400 rpm. With the same displacement, output was raised to 97 bhp at 3600 rpm for 1949.

Plymouth gave its cars a facelift for '41. Model year production increased to 546,000, thanks mainly to heavy output in the closing months of 1940. Actual calendar year figures reflected the turn toward defense production a year later, running some 50,000 units

behind Ford. The '41s were good-looking with a simple, almost heart-shaped horizontal grille. "speedline" fenders, and modest bright-metal side embellishments. Model lines increased to three: standard, Deluxe, and Special DeLuxe, the latter taking over from the 1940 DeLuxe. The longer wheelbase carried a seven-passenger sedan, but the slow-selling limousine was dropped after just 24 early-1941 examples were built. Other rarities among the '41s include the DeLuxe club coupe, the standard club coupe, utility sedan, and station wagon. New for all models was a Chrysler first, the Safety Rim wheel, designed to prevent tire loss during a blowout. The battery was moved under the hood for the first time, and Plymouth offered Powermatic shift, a vacuum transmission assist.

The 1942 line was revised with door sheetmetal extended to cover the running boards and a more massive horizontal grille. Plymouth retained its 117-inch standard wheelbase but dropped the 137. Only two lines

1940 DeLuxe four-door sedan

1941 DeLuxe club coupe

1942 Special DeLuxe convertible coupe

Plymouth

1946 DeLuxe club coupe

1947 Special DeLuxe four-door station wagon

1947 Special DeLuxe four-door sedan

Wartime proposal for postwar Plymouth

were fielded, DeLuxe and Special DeLuxe, and both used the more powerful engine. There were five DeLuxe models: three- and six-passenger coupes, two- and four-door sedans, and a two-door utility sedan. There were seven Special DeLuxe offerings: two coupes, two sedans, a convertible, a town sedan, and a station wagon. The town sedan was a new Chrysler style of the era, marked by a closed or "formal" rear roofline.

At the time World War II halted auto production, Ply-

mouth's 1942 output was slightly more than 152,000 units. As a result, many models are very scarce today. Only 80 utility sedans were built, for example, along with just 1136 wagons and 2806 convertibles.

Plymouth manufactured munitions and military engines during the war, while stylists like A. B. Grisinger, John Chika, and Herb Weissinger worked on postwar car ideas whenever they could. Their designs took the form of most Chrysler prototypes in this period: rounded shapes with smooth fenders, thin door pillars, and wraparound grilles blended into the bodysides. When production resumed in late 1945, Plymouth fielded its prewar styles, and continued to do so until midway into the 1949 model year. The all-new postwar models that arrived in March were much squarer and more upright than the wartime prototypes had suggested. Production took a while to build up after V-J Day. Plymouth built only 770 cars before December 31, 1945. Volume quickly rose, however, exceeding a quarter-million units for 1946 and surpassing half a million in 1949.

The 1946 facelift consisted of a new grille with alternating thick and thin horizontal bars, rectangular parking lights located under the headlamps, wide front fender moldings, a new hood ornament, and reworked rear fenders. DeLuxe and Special DeLuxe series returned, but body choices were fewer than in '42. For 1947, DeLuxe prices stayed where they'd been, but Special DeLuxes ran as much as $250 higher than the year before. The formula was repeated for 1948, and again prices rose, this time by as much as $300. There were no styling changes at all, so the cars are identifiable as to year only by serial numbers. The '48s were continued as 1949 models starting in December 1948, while Plymouth readied its all-new design for spring introduction. In the meantime, there were a few engineering changes from prewar Plymouths, including a switch in tire and wheel size around January from 6.00×16s to 6.70×15-inch tires. Other chassis modifications resulted in a weight reduction of about 50 pounds.

By the time the "real" '49s arrived, styling wizards like Grisinger and Weissinger had departed for Kaiser-Frazer, and a new design philosophy had been established, influenced by Chrysler Corporation chairman K. T. Keller. Keller, who took over as president after Walter Chrysler died in 1940, didn't like low, torpedo-like shapes. Instead, he preferred what stylists called "three-box styling—one box on top of two others." His reasoning was that practicality should take priority over beauty, saying: "Cars should accommodate people rather than the ideas of far-out designers." What he didn't realize was that after the war, people were *willing* to put up with cramped headroom and low ground clearance for the long, low look. In time, Keller's attitude would hurt Plymouth.

But in 1949 the seller's market was at its peak, and it didn't matter much what the cars looked like. Nonetheless, the new design was a very efficient package, comfortable and roomy with good visibility. Its chassis was

slightly longer than before. Plymouth also offered a shorter 111-inch wheelbase for a two-door sedan, three-passenger coupe, and the new all-steel Suburban wagon.

Plymouth liked to take credit for this first "modern" station wagon, though Oldsmobile and Pontiac had all-steel wagons at the same time. Still, the Suburban cost only $1840, well under the GM makes, and therefore sold well. Nearly 20,000 were registered, convincing buyers that wagons didn't have to be made of wood. Other Chrysler makes and the rest of the industry followed Plymouth's lead, and the "woody" soon vanished from the scene.

The longer-wheelbase models included the DeLuxe four-door sedan and coupe, priced in the $1500s; and the Special DeLuxe sedan, coupe, convertible, and wood-trimmed wagon, priced from about $1600 to $2400. The boxy body on all models carried a heavy grille extending under the headlamps, block letters spelling "Plymouth" on the hood, and an enlarged two-pane windshield. Quarter windows were eliminated for sedans, and both front and rear fenders continued as bolt-on units. Taillights were mounted high atop the rear fenders. A chrome nameplate and enameled crest were placed above the license plate on the decklid.

Plymouth's evolution in the '50s closely followed that of rival Chevrolet. It started the decade with economical, no-nonsense transportation, then fielded one of the industry's hot items in 1955. By the '60s, the division had an expanded line of increasingly luxurious and expensive models. Plymouths had no real style in 1950, but were among the best-looking cars in America after 1954.

The design and engineering revolutions of the '50s were prompted by Plymouth's declining fortunes in 1950-54. From 1931 up to that time, the division had never been challenged as the number-three producer behind Chevrolet and Ford, but Plymouth built fewer and fewer cars in the early '50s, dropping to fifth place in sales for calendar year 1954.

The 1950-54 models were well-engineered, solid and reliable—but not very fast and a little dull. All of them were powered by the same engine, Chrysler's smallest L-head six, which produced 97 bhp at 3800 rpm through 1952. Output was raised to 100 bhp for '53 (probably by the stroke of an ad writer's pen), and to 110 bhp the following season. This powerplant was capable of 20–23 miles per gallon and perhaps 80 mph if pressed hard enough. (Interestingly, the long-lived L-head lasted through 1959, after which it was replaced by the modern overhead-valve slant six, but not before it had been boosted up to 132 bhp.)

In 1950, there were two lines—DeLuxe and Special DeLuxe. The Special outsold its stablemate by about seven to five. Two important innovations for the low-priced field were automatic electric choke and the combination ignition/starter switch.

Plymouth had built about 500,000 units in 1949 and some 600,000 in 1950. For 1951, it built 611,000 of a

1949 DeLuxe Suburban two-door station wagon

1950 DeLuxe club coupe

1950 XX-500 show car by Ghia

1951 Cranbrook four-door sedan

slightly modified design that was a little less blunt at the front end. New model names helped make the line seem fresh. There were Concord two-door sedans, coupes, and wagons; Cambridge four-door sedans and coupes; and Cranbrook sedans, coupes, hardtops, and convertibles. The hardtop, christened Belvedere, was Plymouth's first true pillarless style, and arrived a year behind Chevrolet's. It was distinguished from other models by a two-tone paint scheme.

Like other Chrysler Corporation cars, Plymouth re-

1952 Cranbrook Belvedere hardtop coupe

1953 Cambridge two-door sedan

1953 Cranbrook club coupe

Ghia's "Explorer" show car of 1954

1954 Belvedere four-door sedan

1954 Belvedere hardtop coupe

1955 Belvedere V8 four-door sedan

1955 Belvedere V8 Sport Coupe hardtop

mained essentially unchanged for 1952. The easiest way to tell the '52s from the '51s is by looking at the rear. The '52s have the Plymouth name integrated with the trunk handle assembly; the '51s spell it out in a separate piece of script. One important improvement on all 1951-52 models was the Oriflow shock absorber—a Chrysler hydraulic type designed to improve ride and handling. About 200,000 fewer cars rolled out of the factory than the year before, but the rest of the industry

also cut back production because of the Korean War and Plymouth remained number three.

Flow-through fenderlines and a one-piece windshield arrived with the redesigned 1953 models. A 114-inch wheelbase replaced the two chassis previously used. The Concord was dropped and the Cambridge expanded to include business coupes and wagons. A mid-year introduction was Hy-Drive, a combination manual transmission and torque converter that made

second-to-third shifts unnecessary—but the driver still had to use the clutch for first-gear getaways. Hy-Drive was a follow-up to overdrive, introduced the year before. The '54s would offer two-speed PowerFlite automatic, which was to prove very popular.

Plymouth, and Chrysler in general, suffered in 1954 as a result of uninspired styling. Fewer than 500,000 Plymouths were built, despite a rearranged model lineup. Plaza, Savoy, and Belvedere covered the price spread between $1600 and $2300.

These series would be offered again in 1955, but with a dramatic difference: Virgil Exner's all-new styling. Suddenly, Plymouth looked exciting, and with a brand-new polyspherical-head V8 it had performance to match.

The 260-cid "Hy-Fire" V8 was an excellent engine in the small-displacement generation that began with Studebaker's 232 in 1951. With a bore and stroke of 3.56×3.25 inches, it produced 167 bhp "standard" or 177 bhp with four-barrel carb and dual exhausts. Its outstanding features included lightweight aluminum pistons, an aluminum carburetor, and chrome-plated top piston rings for longer life and better oil control.

Other new mechanical features for 1955 were dashboard-controlled PowerFlite automatic, suspended foot pedals, tubeless tires, and front shocks enclosed within the coil springs. For the first time, air conditioning, power windows, and power front seats joined the options list. Brisk new pointed-end styling and neat two-toning characterized the three-series lineup. The Belvedere included a sporty hardtop and convertible, the latter available with V8 only from '55 through the end of the decade. "A great new car for the young in heart," it was called—a total departure from the past. Model year figures for 1955 are misleading. For the calendar year, Plymouth built 742,991 cars, a record that would still stand in the '70s.

For 1956, Virgil Exner formally announced The Forward Look (which meant tailfins) and Plymouth rose to fourth. The engineering department simultaneously brought forth pushbutton PowerFlite, a 12-volt electrical system, and an optional Highway Hi-Fi record player that used special records and a tone arm designed to stay in the groove. A new Suburban line covered four different wagons, a four-door hardtop was added to the Belvedere series, and a two-door hardtop was added to the Savoy.

The hottest performance news for '56 was the limited-production Fury—an attractive hardtop painted white with gold anodized body appliqués. It featured a 303-cid version of the V8 with a 9.25:1 compression ratio, solid lifters, stronger valve springs, dual exhausts, and Carter four-barrel carburetor. With its 240 bhp at 4800 rpm, the Fury approached 145 mph on test at Daytona Beach, and would do 0 to 60 mph in 10 seconds. Top speed in standard form was 111 mph. The Fury contributed greatly to Plymouth's growing performance image, and 4485 were sold—not bad for a car priced $600 higher than the Belvedere hardtop.

If 1955 had seen a victory with record production, 1957 was a second triumph. Over 655,000 cars were built during the calendar year. Exner's fresh new design prompted ad men to exclaim, "Suddenly it's 1960," and indeed, compared to the competition, Plymouth probably *was* three full years ahead. It had the lowest beltline, the most glass, the cleanest lines, and the highest tailfins in the field. It rode a 118-inch wheelbase (wagons were 122 inches) and was more powerful than ever. The old L-head six now ground out 132 bhp, the

1956 Fury hardtop coupe

1957 Belvedere convertible

1957 Fury hardtop coupe

1957 Belvedere four-door sedan

Hy-Fire V8 delivered up to 235 bhp, and the Fury's new 318 delivered 290 bhp. Like other Chrysler cars that year, torsion-bar front suspension was featured, with revised geometry that made for the best-handling Plymouth in history.

It's hard to remember how truly revolutionary the '57 Plymouths were at the time. The hardtop roofline, for example, was so clean and delicate-looking that it did not appear to serve any structural purpose. The grille, usually a large ornate object in those days, was slim

1958 Fury hardtop coupe

1958 Belvedere hardtop sedan

1959 Sport Fury hardtop coupe

1960 Fury hardtop sedan

and graceful. Grille height was reduced by a raised bumper that rode over a separate stone shield. At a time when rival cars were often garishly two-toned, Plymouth settled for a slim contrasting color spear along the sides painted to match the roof. Solid colors were also offered, or sometimes only the roof was done in a different hue. Traditional pillar sedans had huge glass areas; the convertible's windshield curved around at the top as well as the sides. By mid-year, there was a four-door hardtop in the Savoy as well as the Belvedere line. All hardtops had beautiful interiors trimmed in jacquard and vinyl. Dashboards grouped all instruments in a bolt-upright pod directly in front of the driver, with control knobs located safely out of the way. Suburbans saved load space by placing the spare tire vertically in the right rear fender—an idea first seen on the Plymouth Plainsman show car of 1956. The '57s were indeed memorable, but their tendency to rust (the design's major flaw) has made them rare finds today.

Plymouth's 1958 line was mostly a carryover, except for four headlamps and a new front stone shield without the vertical slots. The V8's output was up to at least 225 bhp, and as much as 315 in the high-performance Fury. Instant recognition at the rear was provided by round taillights, with the space above them filled by a piece of bright metal. Because of the recession, Plymouth built fewer '58s, but everyone else was affected, too. The division remained third overall in production.

Tailfins grew as big as they'd ever get in 1959 and were not very pretty. Front ends received a more garish eggcrate grille and a flatter hood, while the more expensive models used anodized silver panels for side decoration. The Plaza line vanished, and other model names moved down a notch in price as Fury became a separate series offering four-door sedan and hardtop as well as two-door hardtop and convertible. Moving in as the new high-performance entry was the Sport Fury. Priced at around $3000-3200, this two-door hardtop and convertible was the top of the '59 line, equipped with a standard 260-bhp version of the 318 V8. For $87 extra, buyers could get a new 361 Golden Commando V8 with 305 bhp at 4600 rpm.

Plymouth show cars of the '50s were unique and interesting. The XX-500 of 1951 was a Ghia exercise—a very pretty sedan that won Exner's patronage for the Italian coachworks to build various show cars and limousines that followed. Ghia also did the Plymouth Explorer of 1954, a fast, smoothly styled grand tourer. A Briggs project was the 1954 Belmont, suggesting there might be a Plymouth two-seater (built by Briggs) to compete with Corvette and Thunderbird. Limited sales of the two American sports cars in '55 caused Plymouth to drop the idea. Two dream cars lending new features to production models were both wagons: Plainsman in 1956, Cabana in 1958. The Plainsman was marked by lots of glass like Chevrolet's Nomad, and donated the aforementioned concealed spare-tire compartment to the '57s. The Cabana sported even more glass and four-door hardtop styling. Neither saw production.

1960 Fury hardtop coupe

1960 Valiant V100 four-door station wagon

1960 Valiant V200 four-door sedan

1961 Fury hardtop coupe

1962 Valiant V200 four-door sedan

1962 Fury (Suburban) four-door station wagon

1963 Valiant Signet 200 hardtop coupe

1963 Fury hardtop sedan

Like the '50s, the '60s would be years of ups and downs for Plymouth. The division had barely recovered third place in production when it was knocked out by Rambler and Oldsmobile. A line of slow-selling intermediates and no standard-sized alternative dropped Plymouth to as low as eighth place in the early '60s. It recovered in 1963, but could not dislodge Pontiac from third place. These problems were of Plymouth's own doing. Time and again, management failed to gauge the market correctly. Plymouth had the right cars, but at the wrong time.

The difficulties began at the top of the line, with a garish, tailfinned line of Savoy, Belvedere, Fury, and Suburban models for 1960. Although Plymouth's new

225-cid slant-six engine was a good one, Rambler campaigned with conservative styling and more economical sixes, outproducing Plymouth by 2000 units for the calendar year. For 1961, Exner's drastically restyled bodyshell was marked by a strange, pinched grille and ponderous pod-like taillights, and was totally devoid of fins. The result was a fourth-place finish as Rambler swept by on the strength of its successful new compacts.

In 1962 came Plymouth's worst mistake of the decade. Anticipating a strong demand for compact "standard" cars, the company shaved up to eight inches from the wheelbase and 550 pounds from curb weight. The same model lineup was fielded on a shrunken 116-

1963 Fury convertible

Satellite II show car from 1964

1965 Fury I two-door sedan

1966 Satellite hardtop coupe

wheelbase (121 inches for station wagons). This new Fury line was offered in four series: Fury I, II, III, and Sport Fury. The largest Plymouths ever offered, they were greater in wheelbase, overall length, and width than the 1964 models, with greatly increased interior dimensions. Like all Plymouths since 1960, they used unitized body/chassis construction, but also had a bolt-on subframe to carry the engine and front suspension.

Plymouth had retained its 116-inch-wheelbase for its 1965 intermediate line, which was more in tune with buyer tastes. Designated Belvedere, it was styled to resemble the Fury with a squared-off roofline, clean sides, and a stamped grille. There were Belvedere I and II sixes and V8s, a Belvedere I Super Stock hardtop, and a top-line Satellite V8 hardtop and convertible. Standard on the Super Stock (and optional for other Belvederes and Furys) was a 426-cid wedge-head engine that developed 365 bhp and 470 pounds-feet of torque. The Super Stock had a special 115-inch wheelbase and weighed just 3170 pounds. Its mighty engine provided terrific performance: 120-mph top speed and 0 to 60 mph in eight seconds. Not cheap at a $4671 base price, the S/S was intended primarily for racing, and could be ordered with a hemi-head 426 as well as the wedge-head.

For 1966, the incredible 425-bhp Hemi was made available as an option on Belvedere II and Satellite. The result was the electrifying "Street Hemi," equipped as standard with heavy-duty suspension and oversize brakes. It was first offered with a four-speed gearbox, later with optional TorqueFlite automatic. Since the '66 Belvedere was as short and light as the '65, the Street Hemi could be a docile tourer at low speeds and a demon when stirred up. Equipped with the proper tires and axle ratio, and correctly tuned, it could reach 120 mph in 12 or 13 seconds. Right off the floor it was ready for drag-race competition in A/Stock or AA/Stock classes, and along with Dodge's Coronet was allowed to run on NASCAR's shorter circuits in 1966—with predictable results. David Pearson won the '66 NASCAR championship for Dodge; Richard Petty won in '67 for Plymouth. Petty also won the 1964 Daytona 500 in a Plymouth. These were major breakups of Ford's otherwise tight stranglehold on NASCAR between 1965 and 1970.

The Satellites and Belvedere IIs were elegant-looking cars. When equipped with smaller V8s of 273, 318, and 361 cubic-inch displacement, they were among the best all-around Plymouths. Their crisp, chiseled styling was retained for 1967. In that year, the Hemi option was offered on the new Belvedere GTX, in addition to a 440-cid wedge-head V8 of 375 bhp. GTXs looked the part, with a silver-and-black grille and rear deck appliqués, simulated hood air intakes, sport striping, and dual exhausts.

In 1968, Plymouth restyled its intermediates with more rounded lines than before that looked just as pretty. The hottest model was ingenuously named Road Runner, available as a hardtop or coupe. The coupe was a European-looking machine with narrow pillars

inch wheelbase with Valiant-like styling. Plymouth's engines provided fine performance in these light cars, but that didn't make any difference. A public still hungry for large cars shunned Plymouth and looked to Ford or Chevrolet instead. Hasty facelifts took place. A more conventional grille, razor-edged fenders, and squared-off roof styling were devised for 1963; a Chevy-like grille and increased side decoration appeared for '64. These changes didn't help much, either. Plymouth's rebound to fourth place in 1963 was largely due to the success of its compact Valiant rather than any increased demand for its revamped standard models.

Plymouth's renaissance really began in 1965 when the division returned to the big-car fold with a 119-inch

and flip-out rear quarter windows. Road Runner name-plates and cartoon birds on the sides and rear, plus simulated hood scoops and racy wheels, identified it. Squeezed under the hood was either a 383-cid engine with a 440 intake manifold and heads, or a 426 Hemi. The GTX's beefy suspension and four-speed transmission options were also available for the Road Runner. On street or track, the car was dynamite. Extraordinary as it seems, this finely tuned package of power and performance was available for only about $2800 to $3100.

In addition to the Road Runner, the GTX continued in hardtop and convertible form for 1968, along with the more mundane Belvedere, Satellite, and Sport Satellite sedans, coupes, and wagons. The lineup stayed mostly like this through 1970, but a Road Runner convertible was added for '69.

Full-size Plymouths continued on the 119-inch wheelbase through 1968 (wagons rode slightly longer spans). Fury I, II, and III models were offered with sixes and V8s. Sport Fury hardtops, convertibles, and fastbacks came with V8s in 1967-68. The top-of-the-line model in 1966 was the VIP, which had a "formal" roofline and conservative trim, in hardtop coupe or sedan form. Power options in 1965 included 361, 383, and 426 hemi engines. In 1966, a 440 wedge-head replaced the Hemi. From 1967 on, the optional big-blocks were the 383 and 440.

Plymouth's salvation in its poorer years of the '60s was the compact Valiant. The early 1960-62 models were ruggedly built, unit-body cars. Virgil Exner's styling included pronounced fenderlines, short decks, and square grilles, all on a 106-inch wheelbase. Elwood Engel's clean, square styling was featured on the same wheelbase for 1963-66. The line was completely redesigned again for '67, adopting a 108-inch wheelbase and four-square lines reminiscent of some middle-size European sedans. Valiant remained in this form, the top seller among Detroit compacts, until it was replaced by the Volaré in the mid-'70s.

One of Valiant's strong points was its robust slant-six engine. This powerplant was developed to give a low hoodline, but engineers also claimed certain manufacturing and operational efficiencies for the configuration. In stock form, the 170-cid version produced 101 bhp, though a four-barrel carburetor option for 1960-61 called Hyper-Pack raised output to 148 bhp. A larger, 225-cid unit was standard on larger Plymouths in 1960-61. From 1962 on, the 225 was optional for Valiant as well. A long-lived design of great durability, the 225 was still being used in the early '80s on some Plymouth models.

Valiant was straightforward in design with a conventional suspension. It was offered initially in two series—the V100 and V200, with sedans and wagons only in 1960. A hardtop was added the following year, and a bucket-seat Signet version answered the sporty compact challenge from Falcon and Corvair in '62. When Engel's styling took over for 1963, a Signet convertible was added.

1966 Barracuda fastback hardtop coupe

1967 Belvedere GTX hardtop coupe

1967 Barracuda hardtop coupe

1967 Valiant Signet four-door sedan

1967 VIP hardtop sedan

The success of the Corvair Monza and the imminent arrival of Ford's Mustang prompted Plymouth to refocus its sights on the sporty-compact market. Accordingly, the Barracuda was launched in mid-1964 for the '65 model year. A hasty tooling revision carried out on the Valiant's upper body structure, it was a fastback coupe with a huge piece of curved glass forming part of a rakish roofline. Barracuda came standard with the 225

slant six, but a new V8 was optional, and desirable. A derivation of the Plymouth 318, it was a strong rival for Ford's excellent 260/289. It displaced 273 cubic inches and was oversquare (bore and stroke 3.62×3.31

1968 Barracuda fastback hardtop coupe

I968 GTX hardtop coupe

1968 Sport Fury convertible

1969 Valiant Signet four-door sedan

1969 Road Runner convertible

inches). In base form, horsepower was 180, but a high-performance 235-bhp version was also offered. The 235 had a high-lift, high-overlap camshaft; dome-shaped pistons; solid lifters; dual-contact breaker points; an unsilenced air cleaner; and a sweet-sounding, low-back-pressure exhaust system. With Rallye Suspension (heavy-duty torsion bars and anti-sway bars up front, plus stiff rear leaf springs), Firm-Ride shocks, and a four-speed gearbox, the 235-bhp Barracuda would do 0 to 60 mph in eight seconds flat and the quarter-mile in 16 seconds.

Barracuda offered a combination of sporty looks, high performance, good handling, utility, and room for four.

For 1966, Barracuda was facelifted with an eggcrate grille, then handsomely redesigned for '67: wheelbase was lengthened by two inches, overall length increased five inches. A sleek hardtop coupe and convertible joined the fastback. Plymouth's 383-cid V8 with four-barrel carb, detuned to 280 bhp, was now available. Although it gave better straightline performance, the 383 added up to 300 extra pounds, mostly over the front wheels, to the detriment of handling. The 273 was a better choice. Either V8 could be ordered with a Formula S package, which included heavy-duty suspension, tachometer, Goodyear Wide-Oval tires, and special identification.

Happily, Barracuda was not drastically changed for a few years. A vertical-bar grille appeared in 1968, and a checkered grille and redesigned taillights came along in '69. In both years beefy, big-block models, the 'Cuda 340 and 383, were offered. The former had 275 bhp; the latter 300 bhp in '68 and 330 bhp in 1969. Then came the completely redesigned 1970 model, sharing an all-new bodyshell with a Dodge double, the Challenger. Compared to previous models, the new Barracuda was shorter, wider, and somehow less distinctive. One of the more interesting variations was the mid-year AAR (All-American Racer) 'Cuda 340, quickly identifiable by its bold "strobe" tape stripes. Standard were a 340 V8 with Edelbrock intake manifold, special heads, and a modified block and valve train; heavy-duty suspension; wide tires; matte-black fiberglass hood with functional scoop; and functional rear spoiler. Only about 2800 were built.

Valiant underwent another of its periodic revivals with the 1970 debut of the semi-fastback Duster coupe, a pleasantly named little car of good quality that ran up nearly 200,000 sales. Among these were several thousand Gold Dusters, an option package consisting of gold trim on grille, body, and interior, plus bucket seats, whitewall tires, and special wheel covers. A racy derivation, the Duster 340, used a mechanical package similar to that of the AAR 'Cuda, which turned the inoffensive Valiant into a tiger. Equipment included a 275-bhp engine, three-speed floorshift, front disc brakes, wide-tread tires, and tuned suspension.

Among Plymouth's intermediates, 1970's most startling newcomer was the Superbird (part of the Road

1969 'Cuda 383 fastback hardtop coupe

1970 Sport Fury S/23 hardtop coupe

1970 Valiant Duster coupe

1970 'Cuda hardtop coupe

Runner series), an evolution of Dodge's 1969 Charger Daytona. With a special "droop-snoot" front end, slippery bodywork, and huge tailfins carrying a stabilizer wing high above the rear deck, the Superbird looked fast—and it was. Over 220 mph was recorded by racing versions. The standard street drivetrain was the four-barrel 440 with TorqueFlite automatic, but a six-barrel 440, a racing 426 Hemi, and four-speed manual transmission were on the options list. After Dodge effortlessly built about 500 Charger Daytonas to qualify it as a "production" model for NASCAR events, the organization increased its minimum count to 1500. That was no problem for Plymouth, and 1920 Superbirds were built.

The Superbird's great moment came at Daytona when Pete Hamilton romped to victory at a near-150 mph average—ahead of every Dodge and every Ford. Of Chrysler's 38 Grand National wins in 1970, 21 were Superbird victories. NASCAR changed its regulations again in 1971, thus ending the Superbird's dominance on the high-speed ovals, but the aerodynamic lessons learned from this car would later be applied in developing the fuel-efficient, ultra-slippery Plymouth Horizon TC3 coupe of 1979.

Even Plymouth's full-size cars were given the performance treatment in 1970. Most notable was the Sport Fury GT, with standard 440 engine, heavy-duty suspension, and long-legged rear axle ratios (as high as 2.76:1). Another Sport Fury package was the S/23, though it was not in the GT's league. Standard engine here was the 318 V8. Equipment also included a tuned suspension and "strobe tape." The luxury VIP was dropped that year, but in the spring Plymouth released the plush Gran Coupe, which offered almost every comfort and convenience feature except air conditioning for $3833, and included "air" for $4216.

Plymouth had all but disappeared by 1980, as improbable as that may seem. The consolidation of Chrysler Corporation's traditional five divisions to two (Dodge and Chrysler-Plymouth) during the 1960s was the root cause. Once Chrysler and Plymouth were wrapped up together, there was no need to put both nameplates on each of the firm's major platforms and, time and again, "glamour" assignments like Cordoba went to Chrysler.

However, this diminished role was nowhere in sight at the beginning of the decade, when Plymouth met its Big Three competition head-on with five separate model lines spanning 44 individual models and about 70 basic varia-

1971 Duster 340 fastback coupe

1971 Road Runner hardtop coupe

Plymouth

1971 'Cuda 340 hardtop coupe

1972 Fury Gran Coupe hardtop

1973 Satellite Sebring Plus hardtop coupe

1973 Valiant four-door sedan

1973 Fury Gran Sedan hardtop

tions, counting trim levels and engines. The compact Valiant, the longest-running survivor among the Big Three's original compacts, dominated its market in its last six years. A key factor was the popular Duster coupe, which chalked up well over a quarter-million sales for model year 1974 all by itself. The basic Duster was conventional and uncomplicated, well-engineered, and at least as well built as comparable GM and Ford products. And Plymouth kept sales moving with a continuing stream of extra-cost packages. The "Twister" option for 1971 included flat-black hood paint, bodyside tape striping, Rallye wheels, and Duster 340-type flat-black grille. Another special was the 1971-75 "Gold Duster," with color keyed pebble-grain vinyl roof, paint, and trim, plus special identificaiton. The "Space Duster" was Plymouth's equivalent of Dodge's Dart Sport "Convertriple," with a wagon-style fold-down rear seatback and a carpeted cargo area 6½ feet long. In Valiant's last season, 1976, there was a "Silver Duster" in handsome combinations of silver, red and black, and a "Feather Duster" (a reply to Ford's "MPG" models) featuring an economy-tuned 225 six with aluminum intake manifold and lightened hood and deck with aluminum instead of steel inner panels. With stickshift/overdrive transmission, which had an aluminum case, the Feather Duster was surprisingly frugal for its size, and a prudent driver could nurse one up to 30 mpg.

Also bolstering the Valiant line was the performance-oriented Duster 340/360 with standard V8, and the Brougham, a 1974-76 luxury trim option for sedans and two-door hardtops, with a level of opulence not usually found in the compact field. Finally, there was the Scamp hardtop, which filled the price gap between the economy and high-line offerings. Altogether, the Valiant line (and the Dodge Dart) was an impressive seller in its class, and gave Chrysler the lead in compact sales over Ford and Chevy in some years.

Plymouth unveiled the Volaré at mid-model year 1976, a more upscale compact that would supercede the Valiant entirely the following year. Though only marginally larger outside, the Volaré (and its Dodge Aspen cousin) had been carefully designed to take advantage of its available interior space, and was quite good in this regard. Workmanship, however, was anything but, although the problems didn't seem to have any damaging effect on sales, perhaps because they didn't surface for a few years. As with Valiant, there was a high-line series offering unexpected luxury, the Premier, initially priced at about $4500. And there was a new wagon body style in addition to the expected coupe and sedan, Plymouth's first compact wagon since 1966. The Volaré seemed right on target for the economy-conscious '70s, and racked up almost 400,000 model year sales in 1977. Most examples left the factory with the 225-cid slant six or 318 V8, both able veterans with a history dating back almost two decades. Not unorthodox in any way, the Volaré appealed primarily for its restrained styling and decent performance/economy balance, plus a modicum of luxury in the upper-priced models.

While Plymouth remained strong in the compact field throughout the '70s, its intermediate and full-size cars fared

x

OK

564

poorly. So, too, did the Barracuda, which was of no significance at all in the steadily declining ponycar market. The 1971 edition, basically a continuation of the all-new 1970 design, came in a choice of six different variations. Sales were meager for all except the base coupe, so the line was pared the following year to standard and 'Cuda V8 coupes, convertibles being scrubbed at the same time. Plymouth carried on with it for two more seasons before giving up after 1974. It was too bad, because the Barracudas had been quite handsome cars since 1967, and could be impressive performers, thanks to a broad range of V8s from the 340 small-block up to the legendary 426 hemi and the huge 440-cid wedge-head.

The mid-size Plymouths were completely revamped for 1971, shedding their boxy contours for more radically sculptured sheetmetal and large loop bumper/grilles. As was then the rage in Detroit, coupes rode a shorter wheelbase than sedans and wagons, and convertibles vanished. However, the Road Runner and GTX were still around, and there was smart new sporty-luxury hardtop called Sebring

Plus. Unfortunately, these cars suffered the same fate as most '70s intermediates, becoming progressively more ponderous, thirsty, and ugly. The GTX was dumped for '72 due to lack of interest, and the Road Runner, still ostensibly a separate model, wasn't nearly as fast on its feet as before. An attempt to regroup for 1975 brought the "small Fury," basically the existing design with heavily revised outer sheetmetal and a new name, but sales continued to languish. The last of these cars rolled out the door in 1978.

The big Plymouths didn't even last that long, being retired after 1977. The full-size Fury continued through 1973 with the basic "fuselage" body/chassis design first seen for 1969, and the same four-series lineup consisting of the top-drawer Sport Fury and three lower trim levels designated by Roman numerals. C-P began whittling away at this group for '72, with Gran Fury taking over at the top and the economy Fury I offerings cut from four to one. Meanwhile, Chrysler Corporation was preparing a brand-new design for all its full-size lines, scheduled well in

1974 Fury Gran Sedan hardtop

1976 Valiant Feather Duster fastback coupe

1974 Barracuda coupe

1976 Volare Premier coupe

1975 Fury Sport hardtop coupe

1977 Volare coupe with Road Runner option

advance of the Middle East oil crisis. Nevertheless, the arrival of the bulkier new Fury for 1974 (and the corresponding Dodge Monaco and Chrysler Newport/New Yorker) seemed incredibly ill-timed. And significantly, sales didn't improve even after gas supplies eased and a general recovery in the big-car segment was underway. The line was called Gran Fury beginning with model year 1975 to avoid confusion with the newly renamed intermediates, but Chrysler never seemed to understand that badge shifting seldom (if ever) makes any difference in sales. Except for the midrange Custom sedan, not a single Gran Fury saw more than 10,000 copies in 1976, and production of some of the Brougham and wagon models was laughably low for a traditionally high-volume make. Plainly, there was no longer much place for such cars, and the lineup was trimmed for '76 and again for '77 in hopes of cutting losses, mainly by deleting hardtop sedans and some trim variations. It was all to no avail, and Plymouth temporarily abandoned the full-size market. It returned half-heartedly for 1980 with a bargain-basement version of the downsized

R-body Chrysler Newport, again bearing the Gran Fury name and intended mainly for the fleet market. It's doubtful Plymouth will ever try a car of even this size again, let alone a "traditional" mid-'70s biggie.

The shape of Plymouth's future arrived for 1978 in the form of the new front-drive subcompact Horizon. It was virtually identical with Dodge's Omni except for grille, taillights, and badges, and shared the distinction of being the first domestically produced front-drive small car. The Horizon undoubtedly saved Plymouth's hide, selling briskly right from the start despite some unfortunate, ill-founded claims by a well-known consumer magazine that handling wasn't all it should be. As a matter of fact, roadability was one of the Horizon's strong points, along with a versatile and roomy hatchback body and fine economy (courtesy of a Volkswagen-derived four-cylinder engine). A sleeker 2+2 hatchback coupe dubbed TC3 arrived for 1979 to add some spice to the recipe. Although few people knew it at the time, the advent of the Horizon/TC3 signalled the eventual demise of the Volaré, as Chrysler was pushing ahead

1977 Gran Fury Brougham coupe

1977 Fury Salon four-door sedan

1978 Fury Sport hardtop coupe

1978 Horizon five-door hatchback sedan

1978 Volare Premier four-door sedan

1979 Volare coupe with Road Runner option

1979 Horizon TC3 hatchback coupe

1980 Horizon TC3 hatchback coupe

1980 Volare Premier coupe

1980 Gran Fury four-door sedan

with plans to convert most or all its cars to front-wheel drive by the mid-'80s.

That was also the year Plymouth's model line began to shrivel dramatically. The big Gran Fury was gone, and the mid-size Fury woudn't be replaced by anything after it departed. The only domestically built models left by 1980 were the Horizon/TC3, the revived Gran Fury on a 118.5-inch wheelbase, and the compact Volaré, which was in its final season. Management tried to maintain the illusion of Plymouth as a full-line make by slapping the nameplate on several captive imports supplied by Mitsubishi of Japan. Smaller than anything Plymouth had previously offered, they included the little Arrow hatchback coupe (from 1976), the more luxurious Sapporo (introduced for 1978 with a Dodge double called Challenger), and the front-drive

Champ economy hatchback (also duplicated as the Dodge Colt). It was a good move, providing vital sales support at a time when Plymouth most needed it, but only served to downgrade a once-prominent marque even further. Curiously, there was never a Plymouth equivalent to the personal-luxury Chrysler Cordoba coupe. There was a Plymouth version of the successful mid-size Chrysler LeBaron/Dodge Diplomat, but it didn't appear until 1982 and by then it was looking very long in the tooth. (However, Canadian buyers loyal to Plymouth could get the Caravelle, a badge-engineered Diplomat, before this.) The front-drive Reliant K-car would mark a revival of sorts for Plymouth in the '80s, but the make continues to play second fiddle at this writing, and the company's most interesting newer products are still reserved for Chrysler and/or Dodge.

Plymouth Specifications

1930

Model U (wb 109.0)

	Wght	Price	Prod*
rdstr 2-4P	2,265	610	—
phaeton 5P	2,355	625	—
cpe 2P	2,380	590	—
Deluxe cpe 2-4P	2,415	625	—
sdn 2d	2,475	610	—
sdn 4d	2,555	625	—
Deluxe sdn 4d	2,590	675	—

Model 30U (wb 109.0)

spt rdstr 2-4P	2,280	610	—
phaeton 5P	2,340	625	—
cpe 2P	2,420	590	—
cpe 2-4P	2,510	625	—
sdn 4d	2,595	625	—
Deluxe sdn 4d	2,590	745	—
conv cpe 2-4P	2,450	695	—
chassis	—	—	—

1930 Engines	bore×stroke	bhp	availability
L4, 175.4	3.63×4.25	45	S-Model U
L4, 196.0	3.63×4.75	48	S-Model 30U

Plymouth

*1930 model year production was confused by the overlapping of the Model U into 1929 and the Model 30U into 1931.

For the Model U, no serial number spans are recorded for 1929 or 1930, but 1929 calendar year production was 93,592, and total 1929-30 Model U production was 108,350.

For the 1930-31 Model 30U, total production was 76,950. The 1930-model 30U carried serial numbers 1500001 to 1530244 (30,244 cars), while 1931 models carried serial numbers 1530245 to 1570300 (40,055 cars). This does not add up to the 76,950 total figure, but may serve to provide an approximate breakdown between the two model years. Individual factory production figures for Model 30U body styles are given under 1931. Note that the business roadster and both two-door sedans were not offered during model year 1930.

1931

Model 30U (wb 109.0)

	Wght	Price	Prod
bus rdstr 2P	2,245	535	1,609
sdn 2d	2,497	565	7,980
commercial sdn 2d	2,450	750	80
spt rdstr 2-4P	2,280	610	2,884*
spt phaeton 5P	2,340	625	632*
cpe 2P	2,420	565	9,189*
cpe 2-4P	2,510	625	5,850*
sdn 4d	2,595	625	47,152*
conv cpe 2-4P	2,450	695	1,272*
chassis	—	—	302*

*Combined production for 1930-31 models. For approximate breakdown, take 57% of total shown for 1931, 43% for 1930. See also production notes under 1930.

1931 Engine	bore×stroke	bhp	availability
L4, 196.0	3.63×4.75	48	S-all

1932

Model PA (wb 109.0)

	Wght	Price	Prod
bus rdstr 2P	2,440	535	2,000
spt rdstr 2-4P	2,470	595	2,680
spt phaeton 5P	2,545	595	528
cpe 2P	2,600	565	1,279
cpe 2-4P	2,645	610	9,696
conv cpe 2-4P	2,615	645	2,783
sdn 2d	2,650	575	23,038
sdn 4d	2,730	635	49,465
Deluxe sdn 4d	2,795	690	4,384
Thrift sdn 2d	2,690	495	*
Thrift sdn 4d	2,745	575	*
chassis and taxicabs	—	—	243

Model PB (wb 112.0; lwb-121.0)

	Wght	Price	Prod
bus rdstr 2P	2,550	495	3,225
spt rdstr 2-4P	2,600	595	2,163
spt phaeton 5P	2,660	595	259
cpe 2P	2,700	565	11,126
cpe 2-4P	2,755	610	8,159
conv cpe 2-4P	2,735	645	4,853
sdn 2d	2,830	575	13,031
sdn 4d	2,875	635	38,066
conv sdn 5P	2,925	785	690
lwb sdn 7P	3,075	725	2,179
chassis and taxicabs	—	—	159

*Production included with 2d and 4d sedans. Total production of Thrift models was 4,894.

1932 Engines	bore×stroke	bhp	availability
L4, 196.1	3.63×4.75	56	S-PA
L4, 196.1	3.63×4.75	65	S-PB

1933

PC Six (wb 107.0/108.0)

	Wght	Price	Prod
cpe 2P	2,418	495	10,853
cpe 2-4P	2,473	525	8,894

	Wght	Price	Prod
conv cpe 2-4P	2,483	565	2,034
sdn 2d	2,498	505	4,008
sdn 4d	2,553	545	33,815
chassis	—	—	396

PCXX Standard Six (wb 108.0)

	Wght	Price	Prod
bus cpe 2P	2,353	445	9,200
cpe 2-4P	2,423	485	2,497
sdn 2d	2,443	464	17,736
sdn 4d	2,523	510	13,661
chassis	—	—	309

PD DeLuxe Six (wb 112.0)

	Wght	Price	Prod
cpe 2P	2,485	495	30,728
cpe 2-4P	2,545	545	20,821
conv cpe 2-4P	2,530	595	4,596
sdn 2d	2,560	525	49,826
sdn 4d	2,645	575	88,404
chassis	—	—	779

1933 Engine	bore×stroke	bhp	availability
L6, 189.8	3.13×4.14	70	S-all

1934

PE DeLuxe (wb 114.0)

	Wght	Price	Prod
bus cpe 2P	2,668	595	28,433
cpe 2-4P	2,733	630	15,658
conv cpe 2-4P	2,698	685	4,482
sdn 2d	2,773	610	58,535
sdn 4d	2,848	660	108,407
town sdn 4d 5P	2,898	695	7,049
sdn 7P	—	—	891
chassis	—	—	2,362

PF Standard (wb 108.0)

	Wght	Price	Prod
bus cpe 2P	2,513	540	6,980
cpe 2-4P	2,573	570	2,061
sdn 2d	2,603	560	12,562
sdn 4d	2,693	600	16,789
chassis	—	—	1,152

PFXX Special (wb 108.0)

	Wght	Price	Prod
bus cpe 2P	2,563	560	3,721
cpe 2-4P	2,608	590	1,746
sdn 2d	2,658	580	12,497
sdn 4d	2,708	620	16,760
town sdn 4d 5P	2,783	655	574

PG Standard (wb 108.0)

	Wght	Price	Prod
bus cpe 2P	2,438	485	7,844
sdn 2d	2,538	510	12,603
sdn 4d	—	—	62
chassis	—	—	3

1934 Engine	bore×stroke	bhp	availability
L6, 201.3	3.13×4.38	77	S-all

1935

PJ Six (wb 113.0)

	Wght	Price	Prod
Business cpe 2P (Jan 1935-)	2,625	510	16,691
Business sdn 2d (Jan 1935-)	2,670	535	29,942
Business sdn 4d (Jan 1935-)	2,720	570	15,761
cpe 2P(Dec 1934-Jan 1935)	2,665	565	6,664
sdn 2d (Dec 1945-Jan 1935)	2,685	615	7,284

PJ DeLuxe Six (wb 113.0; lwb-128.0)

	Wght	Price	Prod
bus cpe 2P	2,675	575	29,190
cpe 2-4P	2,730	630	12,118
conv cpe 2-4P	2,830	695	2,308
sdn 2d	2,720	625	12,424
touring sdn 2d T/B	2,780	650	45,203

	Wght	Price	Prod
sdn 4d	2,790	660	66,083
touring sdn 4d T/B	2,815	685	82,068
Traveler lwb sdn 5P	—	895	77
lwb sdn 7P	3,130	895	350
comcl sdn 4d	2,735	635	1,142
Westchester suburban wgn 4d	—	765	119
chassis (lwb)	—	—	24

1935 Engine	bore×stroke	bhp	availability
L6, 201.3	3.13×4.13	82	S-all

1936

P1 Business Series (wb 113.0)

	Wght	Price	Prod
cpe 2P	2,650	510	26,856
sdn 2d	2,720	545	39,516
sdn 4d	2,750	590	19,104
wgn 4d	2,920	765	309
comcl sdn 2d	—	605	3,527
touring sdn 4d T/B	—	—	1,544
touring sdn 2d T/B	—	—	768
chassis	—	—	1,211

P2 DeLuxe Series (wb 113.0; lwb-125.0)

	Wght	Price	Prod
cpe 2P	2,705	580	54,601
cpe 2-4P	2,775	620	9,663
conv cpe 2-4P	2,830	725	3,297
sdn 2d	2,785	625	6,149
touring sdn 2d T/B	2,815	645	99,373
sdn 4d	2,820	660	10,001
touring sdn 4d T/B	2,850	680	240,136
touring sdn 7P T/B (lwb)	3,155	895	1,504
chassis	—	—	2,775

1936 Engine	bore×stroke	bhp	availability
L6, 201.3	3.13×4.38	82	S-all

1937

P3 Business Series (wb 112.0)

	Wght	Price	Prod
cpe 2P	2,771	580	18,202
cpe 2-4P	2,841	620	540
sdn 2d	2,841	620	28,685
touring sdn 2d T/B	2,871	640	1,350
sdn 4d	2,841	665	16,000
touring sdn 4d T/B	2,871	685	7,842
chassis	—	—	1,025

P4 DeLuxe Series (wb 112.0; lwb-132.0)

	Wght	Price	Prod
cpe 2P	2,839	650	67,144
cpe 2-4P	2,884	700	6,877
conv cpe 2-4P	2,994	830	3,110
sdn 2d	2,899	715	7,926
touring sdn 2d T/B	2,914	725	111,099
sdn 4d	2,914	745	9,000
touring sdn 4d T/B	2,944	755	269,062
lwb sdn 7P	3,333	995	1,840
sdn limo 7P (lwb)	3,400	1,095	63
chassis and taxicabs	—	—	2,229

1937 Engine	bore×stroke	bhp	availability
L6, 201.3	3.13×4.38	82	S-all

1938

P5 Business/Roadking* (wb 112.0)

	Wght	Price	Prod
cpe 2P	2,739	645	15,932
sdn 2d	2,764	685	15,393
sdn 4d	2,809	730	6,459
touring sdn 2d T/B	2,779	701	16,413
touring sdn 4d T/B	2,824	746	18,664
cpe 2-4P	2,809	695	338
chassis	—	—	1,586

*Name changed to Roadking March 31, 1938, and touring sdns introduced.

P6 DeLuxe (wb 112.0; lwb-132.0)

	Wght	Price	Prod
cpe 2P	2,804	730	27,181
cpe 2-4P	2,864	770	2,000
conv cpe 2-4P	3,009	850	1,900
sdn 2d	2,874	773	1,222
touring sdn 2d T/B	2,864	785	46,669
sdn 4d	2,894	803	1,446
touring sdn 4d T/B	2,874	815	119,669
Suburban wgn 4d 8P	3,039	880	555
lwb sdn 7P T/B	3,289	1,005	1,824
sdn limo 7P (lwb)	3,300	1,095	75
chassis and taxicabs	—	—	2,062

1938 Engine	bore×stroke	bhp	availability
L6, 201.3	3.13×4.38	82	S-all

1939

P7 Roadking (wb 114.0)

	Wght	Price	Prod
cpe 2P	2,724	645	22,537
cpe 2-4P	2,784	695	222
sdn 2d	2,824	685	7,499
touring sdn 2d T/B	2,824	699	42,186
sdn 4d	2,839	726	2,553
touring sdn 4d T/B	2,829	740	23,047
util sdn 2d	2,844	685	341
commercial sdn	—	—	2,270
Suburban wgn 4d	—	—	97
chassis	—	—	1,616

P8 DeLuxe (wb 114.0; lwb-134.0)

	Wght	Price	Prod
cpe 2P	2,789	725	41,924
cpe 2-4P	2,874	755	1,332
conv cpe 2-4P	3,044	895	5,976
sdn 2d	2,889	761	2,653
touring sdn 2d T/B	2,894	775	80,981
sdn 4d	2,909	791	2,279
touring sdn 4d T/B	2,919	885	175,054
Suburban wgn 4d 8P (side curtains)	3,089	930	1,680
Suburban wgn 4d 8P (glass encl.)	3,189	970	
util sd 2d	—	—	13
lwb sdn 7P T/B	3,374	1,005	1,837
sdn limo 7P (lwb)	3,440	1,095	98
chassis and taxicabs	—	—	947

P8 DeLuxe (wb 117.0)

	Wght	Price	Prod
conv sdn T/B 5P	3,209	1,150	387

1939 Engine	bore×stroke	bhp	availability
L6, 201.3	3.13×4.38	82	S-all

1940

P9 Roadking (wb 117.0)

	Wght	Price	Prod
bus cpe	2,769	645	26,745
sdn 2d	2,834	699	55,092
sdn 4d	2,869	740	20,076
util sdn	2,769	699	589
club cpe	2,814	699	360
wgn 4d	3,089	925	80
chassis	—	—	907

P10 DeLuxe (wb 117.0; 7P-137.0)

	Wght	Price	Prod
bus cpe	2,804	725	32,244
sdn 2d	2,889	775	76,781
sdn 4d	2,924	805	173,351
util sdn	2,824	775	4
club cpe	2,849	770	22,174
conv cpe	3,049	950	6,986
wgn 4d	3,144	970	3,126

Plymouth

P10 DeLuxe (wb 117.0; 7P-137.0)	Wght	Price	Prod
sdn 4d 7P	3,359	1,005	1,179
limo 7P	3,409	1,080	68
chassis	—	—	503

1940 Engine	bore×stroke	bhp	availability
L6, 201.3	3.13×4.38	84	S-all

1941

P11 DeLuxe (wb 117.0)	Wght	Price	Prod
bus cpe	2,809	720	23,754
sdn 2d	2,859	769	46,646
sdn 4d	2,889	800	21,175
util sdn	2,794	760	468
club cpe	2,819	764	994
wgn 4d	3,139	1,006	217
DeLuxe bus cpe	2,839	760	15,862
DeLuxe sdn 2d	2,899	809	46,138
DeLuxe sdn 4d	2,924	845	32,336
DeLuxe club cpe	2,859	804	204
DeLuxe util sdn	—	proto	1
chassis	—	—	676

P12 Special DeLuxe (wb 117.0; 7P-137.0)	Wght	Price	Prod
bus cpe	2,860	795	23,851
sdn 2d	2,934	845	84,810
sdn 4d	2,959	877	190,513
util sdn	—	proto	2
club cpe	2,934	842	37,352
conv cpe	3,166	1,007	10,545
wgn 4d	3,194	1,031	5,594
sdn 4d, 7P	3,379	1,078	1,127
limo, 7P	3,429	1,153	24
chassis	—	—	321

1941 Engine	bore×stroke	bhp	availability
L6, 201.3	3.13×4.38	87	S-all

1942

P14S DeLuxe (wb 117.0)	Wght	Price	Prod
bus cpe	2,906	812	3,783
sdn 2d	2,961	850	9,350
sdn 4d	3,001	889	11,973
util sdn	2,906	842	80
club cpe	2,966	885	2,458
chassis	—	—	1

P14C Special DeLuxe (wb 117.0)	Wght	Price	Prod
bus cpe	2,931	855	7,258
sdn 2d	2,996	895	24,142
sdn 4d	3,036	935	68,924
Town Sedan	3,061	980	5,821
club cpe	3,011	928	14,685
conv cpe	3,231	1,078	2,806
wgn 4d	3,371	1,145	1,136
chassis	—	—	10

1942 Engine	bore×stroke	bhp	availability
L6, 217.8	3.25×4.38	95	S-all

1946*

P15S DeLuxe (wb 117.0)	Wght	Price	Prod
bus cpe	2,977	1,089	—
sdn 2d	3,047	1,124	—
sdn 4d	3,082	1,164	—
club cpe	3,037	1,159	—
chassis	—	—	—

P15C Special DeLuxe (wb 117.0)	Wght	Price	Prod
bus cpe	2,982	1,159	—

	Wght	Price	Prod
sdn 2d	3,062	1,199	—
sdn 4d	3,107	1,239	—
club cpe	3,057	1,234	—
conv cpe	3,282	1,439	—
wgn 4d	3,402	1,539	—
chassis	—	—	—

1946 Engine	bore×stroke	bhp	availability
L6, 217.8	3.25×4.38	95	S-all

1947*

P15S DeLuxe (wb 117.0)	Wght	Price	Prod
bus cpe	2,977	1,139	—
sdn 2d	3,047	1,164	—
sdn 4d	3,082	1,214	—
club cpe	3,037	1,189	—
chassis	—	—	—

P15C Special DeLuxe (wb 117.0)	Wght	Price	Prod
bus cpe	2,982	1,209	—
sdn 2d	3,062	1,239	—
sdn 4d	3,107	1,289	—
club cpe	3,057	1,264	—
conv cpe	3,282	1,565	—
wgn 4d	3,402	1,765	—
chassis	—	—	—

1947 Engine	bore×stroke	bhp	availability
L6, 217.8	3.25×4.38	95	S-all

1948*

P15S DeLuxe (wb 117.0)	Wght	Price	Prod
bus cpe	2,955	1,346	—
sdn 2d	2,995	1,383	—
sdn 4d	3,030	1,441	—
club cpe	3,005	1,409	—
chassis	—	—	—

P15C Special DeLuxe (wb 117.0)	Wght	Price	Prod
bus cpe	2,950	1,440	—
sdn 2d	3,030	1,471	—
sdn 4d	3,045	1,529	—
club cpe	3,020	1,503	—
conv cpe	3,225	1,857	—
wgn 4d	3,320	2,068	—
chassis	—	—	—

1948 Engine	bore×stroke	bhp	availability
L6, 217.8	3.25×4.38	95	S-all

1949 First Series*

P15S DeLuxe (wb 117.0)	Wght	Price	Prod
bus cpe	2,955	1,346	—
sdn 2d	2,995	1,383	—
sdn 4d	3,030	1,441	—
club cpe	3,005	1,409	—
chassis	—	—	—

P15C Special DeLuxe (wb 117.0)	Wght	Price	Prod
bus cpe	2,950	1,440	—
sdn 2d	3,030	1,471	—
sdn 4d	3,045	1,529	—
club cpe	3,020	1,503	—
conv cpe	3,225	1,857	—
wgn 4d	3,320	2,068	—
chassis	—	—	—

1949(1) Engine	bore×stroke	bhp	availability
L6, 217.8	3.25×4.38	95	S-all

*Factory combined production figures for 1946 through 1949 First Series.

Combined 1946–1949 First Series Production:

P15S DeLuxe (wb 117.0)

	Prod
bus cpe	16,117
sdn 2d	49,918
sdn 4d	120,757
club cpe	10,400
chassis	10

P15C Special DeLuxe (wb 117.0)

	Prod
bus cpe	31,399
sdn 2d	125,704
sdn 4d	514,986
club cpe	156,629
conv cpe	15,295
wgn 4d	12,913
chassis	5,361

1949 Second Series

P17 DeLuxe (wb 111.0)

	Wght	Price	Prod
bus cpe	2,825	1,371	15,715
sdn 2d	2,951	1,492	28,516
Suburban wgn 2d	3,105	1,840	19,220
chassis	—	—	4

P18 DeLuxe (wb 118.5)

	Wght	Price	Prod
sdn 4d	3,059	1,551	61,021
club cpe	3,034	1,519	25,687

P18 Special DeLuxe (wb 118.5)

	Wght	Price	Prod
sdn 4d	3,079	1,629	252,878
club cpe	3,046	1,603	99,680
conv cpe	3,323	1,982	15,240
wgn 4d	3,341	2,372	3,443
chassis	—	—	981

1949(2) Engine	bore×stroke	bhp	availability
L6, 217.8	3.25×4.38	97	S-all

1950

P19 DeLuxe (wb 111.0)

	Wght	Price	Prod
bus cpe	2,872	1,371	16,861
sdn 2d	2,946	1,492	67,584
Suburban wgn 2d	3,116	1,840	34,457
Suburban Special wgn 2d	3,155	1,946	
chassis	—	—	1

P20 DeLuxe (wb 118.5)

	Wght	Price	Prod
sdn 4d	3,068	1,551	87,871
club cpe	3,040	1,519	53,890

P20 Special DeLuxe (wb 118.5)

	Wght	Price	Prod
sdn 4d	3,072	1,629	234,084
club cpe	3,041	1,603	99,361
conv cpe	3,295	1,982	12,697
wgn 4d	3,353	2,372	2,059
chassis	—	—	2,091

1950 Engine	bore×stroke	bhp	availability
L6, 217.8	3.25×4.38	97	S-all

1951*

P22 Concord (wb 111.0)

	Wght	Price	Prod
bus cpe	2,919	1,537	—
sdn 2d	2,969	1,673	—
Savoy wgn 2d	3,184	2,182	—
Suburban wgn 2d	3,124	2,064	—

P23 Cambridge (wb 118.5)

	Wght	Price	Prod
sdn 4d	3,104	1,739	—
club cpe	3,059	1,703	—

P23 Cranbrook (wb 118.5)

	Wght	Price	Prod
sdn 4d	3,109	1,826	—
club cpe	3,074	1,796	—
conv cpe	3,294	2,222	—
Belvedere htp cpe	3,182	2,114	—

1951 Engine	bore×stroke	bhp	availability
L6, 217.8	3.25×4.38	97	S-all

1952*

P22 Concord (wb 111.0)

	Wght	Price	Prod
bus cpe	2,893	1,610	—
sdn 2d	2,959	1,753	—
Savoy wgn 2d	3,165	2,287	—
Suburban wgn 2d	3,145	2,163	—

P23 Cambridge (wb 118.5)

	Wght	Price	Prod
sdn 4d	3,068	1,822	—
club cpe	3,030	1,784	—

P23 Cranbrook (wb 118.5)

	Wght	Price	Prod
sdn 4d	3,088	1,914	—
club cpe	3,046	1,883	—
conv cpe	3,256	2,329	—
Belvedere htp cpe	3,105	2,216	—

1952 Engine	bore×stroke	bhp	availability
L6, 217.8	3.25×4.38	97	S-all

*Factory combined 1951 and 1952 production figures.

Combined 1951–1952 Production:

P22 Concord (wb 111.0)

	Prod
bus cpe	14,255
sdn 2d	49,139
Savoy/Suburban wgn 2d	76,520

P23 Cambridge (wb 118.5)

	Prod
sdn 4d	179,417
club cpe	101,784

P23 Cranbrook (wb 118.5)

	Prod
sdn 4d	388,785
club cpe	126,725
Belvedere htp cpe	51,266
conv cpe	15,650
chassis	4,171

1953

P24-1 Cambridge (wb 114.0)

	Wght	Price	Prod
bus cpe	2,888	1,618	6,975
sdn 2d	2,943	1,727	56,800
sdn 4d	2,983	1,765	93,585
club cpe	2,950	1,725	1,050
Suburban wgn 2d	3,129	2,064	43,545

P24-2 Cranbrook (wb 114.0)

	Wght	Price	Prod
sdn 4d	3,023	1,873	298,976
club cpe	2,971	1,843	92,102
Belvedere htp cpe	3,027	2,064	35,185
conv cpe	3,193	2,220	6,301
Savoy wgn 2d	3,170	2,207	12,089
chassis	—	—	843

1953 Engine	bore×stroke	bhp	availability
L6, 217.8	3.25×4.38	100	S-all

1954

P25-1 Plaza (wb 114.0)

	Wght	Price	Prod
bus cpe	2,889	1,618	5,000
club cpe	2,950*	1,700*	1,275
sdn 4d	3,004	1,765	43,077
sdn 2d	2,943	1,727	27,976

	Wght	Price	Prod
Suburban wgn 2d	3,122	2,064	35,937
chassis	—	—	1

P25-2 Savoy (wb 114.0)

	Wght	Price	Prod
club cpe	2,982	1,843	30,700
sdn 4d	3,036	1,873	139,383
sdn 2d	2,986	1,835	25,396
Suburban wgn 2d	3,165*	2,172*	450
chassis	—	—	3,588

P25-3 Belvedere (wb 114.0)

	Wght	Price	Prod
sdn 4d	3,050	1,953	106,601
Sport Coupe htp	3,038	2,145	25,592
conv cpe	3,273	2,301	6,900
Suburban wgn 2d	3,186	2,288	9,241
chassis	—	—	2,031

*Estimated.

1954 Engines	bore×stroke	bhp	availability
L6, 217.8	3.25×4.38	100	S-all to engine #P25-243000
L6, 230.2	3.25×4.63	110	S-all from engine #P25-243001

1955

P26-1 Plaza, L6 (wb 115.0)

	Wght	Price	Prod
sdn 4d	3,129	1,781	68,826
club cpe	3,089	1,738	45,561
Suburban wgn 2d	3,261	2,077	23,319
Suburban wgn 4d	3,282	2,158	10,594
bus cpe	3,025	1,639	4,882

P27-1 Plaza, V8 (wb 115.0)

	Wght	Price	Prod
sdn 4d	3,246	1,884	15,330
club cpe	3,202	1,841	8,049
Suburban wgn 2d	3,389	2,180	8,469
Suburban wgn 4d	3,408	2,262	4,828

P26-3 Savoy, L6 (wb 115.0)

	Wght	Price	Prod
sdn 4d	3,154	1,880	93,716
club cpe	3,109	1,837	45,438
chassis	—	—	1

P27-3 Savoy, V8 (wb 115.0)

	Wght	Price	Prod
sdn 4d	3,265	1,983	69,025
club cpe	3,224	1,940	29,442

P26-2 Belvedere, L6 (wb 115.0)

	Wght	Price	Prod
sdn 4d	3,159	1,979	69,128
club cpe	3,129	1,936	19,471
Sport Coupe htp	3,330	2,113	13,942
Suburban wgn 4d	3,312	2,322	6,197

P27-2 Belvedere V8 (wb 115.0)

	Wght	Price	Prod
sdn 4d	3,262	2,082	91,856
club cpe	3,228	2,039	22,174
Sport Coupe htp	3,261	2,217	33,433
conv cpe	3,409	2,351	8,473
Suburban wgn 4d	3,475	2,425	12,291

1955 Engines	bore×stroke	bhp	availability
L6, 230.2	3.25×4.63	117	S-all Sixes
V8, 241.0	3.44×3.25	157	O-all V8
V8, 260.0	3.56×3.25	167	S-all V8
V8, 260.0	3.56×3.25	177	O-all V8

1956

P28/29-1 Plaza (wb 115.0)

	Wght	Price	Prod
bus cpe	3,100	1,784	3,728
sdn 4d	3,210	1,926	60,197
club sdn	3,175	1,883	43,022

P28/29-2 Savoy (wb 115.0)

	Wght	Price	Prod
sdn 4d	3,228	2,025	151,762
club sdn	3,190	1,982	57,927
Sport Coupe htp	3,200	2,130	16,473

P28/29-3 Belvedere (wb 115.0)

	Wght	Price	Prod
sdn 4d	3,248	2,109	84,218
Sport Sedan htp	3,343	2,281	17,515
Sport Coupe htp	3,243	2,214	24,723
conv cpe	3,435	2,478	6,735

P28/29 Suburban (wb 115.0)

	Wght	Price	Prod
DeLuxe wgn 2d	3,373	2,196	23,866
Custom wgn 2d	3,418	2,267	9,489
Custom wgn 4d	3,470	2,314	33,333
Sport wgn 4d	3,513	2,484	15,104

P29-3 Fury (wb 115.0)

	Wght	Price	Prod
htp cpe	3,650	2,866	4,485

1956 Engines	bore×stroke	bhp	availability
L6, 230.2	3.25×4.38	125	S-all exc Fury, Belv conv
L6, 230.2	3.25×4.38	131	O-all exc Fury, Belv conv
V8, 270.0	3.63×3.26	180	O-Plaza, Savoy, Belvedere
V8, 277.0	3.75×3.13	187	S-Belv conv; O-DeLuxe, Savoy, Plaza
V8, 277.0	3.75×3.13	200	O-all exc Fury
V8, 303.0	3.82×3.31	240	S-Fury

1957

P30/31-1 Plaza (wb 118.0)

	Wght	Price	Prod
bus cpe	3,235	1,899	2,874
sdn 4d	3,333	2,050	70,248
sdn 2d	3,245	2,009	49,137

P30/31-2 Savoy (wb 118.0)

	Wght	Price	Prod
sdn 4d	3,340	2,194	153,093
Sport Sedan htp	3,428	2,317	7,601
sdn 2d	3,263	2,147	55,590
Sport Coupe htp	3,335	2,229	31,373

P30/31-3 Belvedere (wb 118.0)

	Wght	Price	Prod
sdn 4d	3,373	2,310	110,414
Sport Sedan htp	3,428	2,419	37,446
sdn 2d	3,288	2,264	55,590
Sport Coupe htp	3,348	2,349	67,268
conv cpe	3,585	2,638	9,866

P30/31 Suburban (wb 122.0)

	Wght	Price	Prod
DeLuxe wgn 2d	3,620	2,330	20,111
Custom wgn 2d	3,668	2,440	11,196
Custom wgn 4d, 6P	3,753	2,494	40,227
Custom wgn 4d, 9P	3,800	2,649	9,357
Sport wgn 4d, 6P	3,748	2,622	15,414
Sport wgn 4d, 9P	3,795	2,777	7,988

P31 Fury (wb 118.0)

	Wght	Price	Prod
htp cpe	3,595	2,925	7,438

1957 Engines	bore×stroke	bhp	availability
L6, 230.2	3.25×4.63	132	S-all exc Fury, Belv conv
V8, 277.0	3.75×3.13	197	S-Plaza
V8, 277.0	3.75×3.13	235	O-Plaza
V8, 301.0	3.91×3.13	215	O-all exc Fury
V8, 301.0	3.91×3.13	235	O-all exc Fury
V8, 318.0	3.91×3.31	290	S-Fury

1958

LP1/2-L Plaza (wb 118.0)

		Wght	Price	Prod
21	club sdn	3,253	2,118	39,062
22	bus cpe	3,245	2,028	1,472

		Wght	Price	Prod
41	sdn 4d	3,335	2,169	54,194

LP1/2-M Savoy (wb 118.0)

		Wght	Price	Prod
21	club sdn	3,290	2,254	17,624
23	Sport Coupe htp	3,320	2,329	19,500
41	sdn 4d	3,310	2,305	67,933
43	Sport Sedan htp	3,393	2,400	5,060

LP1/2-H Belvedere (wb 118.0)

		Wght	Price	Prod
21	club sdn	3,305	2,389	4,229
23	Sport Coupe htp	3,325	2,457	36,043
27	conv cpe	3,545	2,762	9,941
41	sdn 4d	3,343	2,440	49,124
43	Sport Sedan htp	3,425	2,528	18,194

LP1/2 Suburban (wb 122.0)

		Wght	Price	Prod
—	Deluxe wgn 4d	3,660	2,486	15,535
25	DeLuxe wgn 2d	3,560	2,432	15,625
25	Custom wgn 2d	3,630	2,553	5,925
45A	Custom wgn 4d, 6P	3,665	2,607	38,707
45B	Custom wgn 4d, 9P	3,763	2,747	17,158
45A	Sport wgn 4d, 6P	3,680	2,760	10,785
45B	Sport wgn 4d, 9P	3,758	2,900	12,385

LP2-H Fury (wb 118.0)

		Wght	Price	Prod
23	htp cpe	3,510	3,067	5,303

1958 Engines	bore×stroke	bhp	availability
L6, 230.2	3.25×4.63	132	S-all exc Fury, Belv conv
V8, 318.0	3.91×3.31	225	O-all exc Fury
V8, 318.0	3.91×3.31	250	O-all exc Fury
V8, 318.0	3.91×3.31	290	S-Fury
V8, 350.0	4.06×3.38	305	O-all
V8, 350.0	4.06×3.38	315	O-all (fuel injection)

1959

MP1/2-L Savoy (wb 118.0)

		Wght	Price	Prod
21	club sdn	3,333	2,222	46,979
22	bus cpe	3,130	2,143	1,051
41	sdn 4d	3,333	2,283	84,272

MP1/2-M Belvedere (wb 118.0)

		Wght	Price	Prod
21	club sdn	3,310	2,389	13,816
23	htp cpe	3,318	2,461	23,469
27	conv cpe	3,580	2,814	5,063
41	sdn 4d	3,353	2,440	67,980
43	htp sdn 4d	3,335	2,525	5,713

MP2-H Fury (wb 118.0)

		Wght	Price	Prod
23	htp cpe	3,435	2,714	21,494
41	sdn 4d	3,455	2,691	30,149
43	htp sdn	3,505	2,771	13,614

MP2-P Sport Fury (wb 118.0)

		Wght	Price	Prod
23	htp cpe	3,475	2,927	17,867
27	conv cpe	3,670	3,125	5,990

MP1/2 Suburban (wb 122.0)

		Wght	Price	Prod
25	DeLuxe wgn 2d	3,625	2,694	15,074
25	Custom wgn 2d, 6P	3,690	2,814	1,852
45A	DeLuxe wgn 4d	3,675	2,761	35,086
45A	Custom wgn 4d, 6P	3,678	3,881	35,024
45B	Custom wgn 4d, 9P	3,775	2,991	16,993
45A	Sport wgn 4d, 6P	3,760	3,021	7,224
45B	Sport wgn 4d, 9P	3,805	3,131	9,549

1959 Engines	bore×stroke	bhp	availability
L6, 230.2	3.25×4.63	132	S-Savoy, Belvedere, Suburb exc Cus 9P, Sports
V8, 318.0	3.91×3.31	230	S-Fury; O-other exc Sport Fury
V8, 318.0	3.91×3.31	260	S-Sport Fury; O-others

	bore×stroke	bhp	availability
V8, 361.0	4.12×3.38	305	O-all

1960

V100 Valiant (wb 106.5)

		Wght	Price	Prod
110	sdn 4d	2,635	2,053	52,788
140	wgn 4d, 6P	2,815	2,365	12,018
—	wgn 4d, 9P	2,845	2,488	1,928

V200 Valiant (wb 106.5)

		Wght	Price	Prod
130	sdn 4d	2,655	2,130	106,515
170	wgn 4d, 6P	2,855	2,443	16,368
—	wgn 4d, 9P	2,860	2,566	4,675

PP1/2-L Savoy (wb 118.0)

		Wght	Price	Prod
21	club sdn	3,410	2,260	26,820
41	sdn 4d	3,433	2,310	51,384

PP1/2-M Belvedere (wb 118.0)

		Wght	Price	Prod
21	club sdn	3,423	2,389	6,529
23	htp cpe	3,438	2,641	14,085
41	sdn 4d	3,448	2,439	42,130

PP1/2-H Fury (wb 118.0)

		Wght	Price	Prod
23	htp cpe	3,465	2,599	18,079
27	conv cpe	3,630	2,967	7,080
41	sdn 4d	3,475	2,575	21,292
43	htp sdn	3,528	2,656	9,036

PP1/2 Suburban (wb 122.0)

		Wght	Price	Prod
25	DeLuxe wgn 2d	3,375	2,721	5,503
45	DeLuxe wgn 4d	3,815	2,787	18,484
45	Custom wgn 4d, 6P	3,890	2,880	17,308
45	Custom wgn 4d, 9P	3,875	2,990	8,116
45	Sport wgn 4d, 6P	3,895	3,024	3,333
45	Sport wgn 4d, 9P	4,020	3,134	4,253

1960 Engines	bore×stroke	bhp	availability
L6, 170.0	3.40×3.13	101	S-Valiant
L6, 170.0	3.40×3.13	148	O-Valiant only
L6, 225.0	3.40×4.13	145	S-full-size only
V8, 318.0	3.91×3.31	230	S-full-size V8 (PP2)
V8, 361.0	4.12×3.38	305	O-all full-size

1961

V100 Valiant (wb 106.5)

		Wght	Price	Prod
111	sdn 4d	2,590	2,014	25,695
156	wgn 4d	2,745	2,327	6,717

V200 Valiant (wb 106.5)

		Wght	Price	Prod
132	htp cpe	2,605	2,137	18,586
133	sdn 4d	2,600	2,110	59,056
176	wgn 4d	2,770	2,423	10,794

RP1/2-L Savoy (2b 118.0)

		Wght	Price	Prod
211	sdn 2d, L6	3,300	2,260	⎤ 18,729
311	sdn 2d, V8	3,440	2,379	⎦
213	sdn 4d, L6	3,310	2,310	⎤ 44,913
313	sdn 4d, V8	3,465	2,430	⎦

RP1/2-M Belvedere (wb 118.0)

		Wght	Price	Prod
221	sdn 2d, L6	3,300	2,389	⎤ 4,740
321	sdn 2d, V8	3,450	2,508	⎦
222	htp cpe, L6	3,320	2,461	⎤ 9,591
322	htp cpe, V8	3,460	2,580	⎦
223	sdn 4d, L6	3,315	2,439	⎤ 40,090
323	sdn 4d, V8	3,470	2,559	⎦

RP1/2-H Fury (wb 118.0)

		Wght	Price	Prod
232	htp cpe, L6	3,330	2,599	⎤ 16,141
332	htp cpe, V8	3,520	2,718	⎦

Plymouth

		Wght	Price	Prod
233	sdn 4d, L6	3,350	2,575	⎤ 22,619
333	sdn 4d, V8	3,515	2,694	⎦
234	htp sdn, L6	3,390	2,656	⎤ 8,507
334	htp sdn, V8	3,555	2,775	⎦
335	conv cpe, V8	3,535	2,967	6,948

RP1/2 Suburban (wb 122.0)

		Wght	Price	Prod
255	DeLuxe wgn 2d, L6	3,675	2,602	⎤ 2,464
355	DeLuxe wgn 2d, V8	3,845	2,721	⎦
256	DeLuxe wgn 4d, L6	3,715	2,668	⎤ 12,980
356	DeLuxe wgn 4d, V8	3,885	2,788	⎦
266	Custom wgn 4d, L6	3,730	2,761	⎤
366	Custom wgn 4d, V8	3,885	2,880	⎥ 13,553
367	Custom wgn 4d, 9P, V8	3,985	2,990	⎦
376	Sport wgn 4d, 6P, V8	3,890	3,024	2,844
377	Sport wgn 4d, 9P, V8	3,995	3,134	3,088

1961 Engines	bore×stroke	bhp	availability
L6, 170.0	3.40×3.13	101	S-Valiant
L6, 170.0	3.40×3.13	148	O-Valiant only
L6, 225.0	3.40×4.13	145	S-full-size only
V8, 318.0	3.91×3.31	230	S-full-size eights (RP2)
V8, 318.0	3.91×3.31	260	O-full-size with TorqueFlite
V8, 361.0	4.12×3.38	305	O-full-size exc PowerFlite or air cond
V8, 383.0	4.25×3.38	330	O-full-size exc PowerFlite or air cond

1962

SV1-L Valiant V100 (wb 106.5)

		Wght	Price	Prod
111	sdn 2d	2,480	1,930	19,679
113	sdn 4d	2,500	1,991	33,769
156	wgn 4d	2,660	2,285	5,932

SV1-H Valiant V200 (wb 106.5)

131	sdn 2d	2,500	2,026	8,484
133	sdn 4d	2,510	2,087	55,789
176	wgn 4d	2,690	2,381	8,055

SV1-P Valiant Signet (wb 106.5)

142	htp cpe	2,515	2,230	25,586

SP1/2-L Savoy (wb 115.0)

211	sdn 2d, L6	2,930	2,206	⎤ 18,825
311	sdn 2d, V8	3,080	2,313	⎦
213	sdn 4d, L6	2,960	2,262	⎤ 49,777
313	sdn 4d, V8	3,115	2,369	⎦

SP1/2-M Belvedere (wb 116.0)

221	sdn 2d, L6	2,930	2,342	⎤ 3,128
321	sdn 2d, V8	3,070	2,450	⎦
222	htp cpe, L6	2,945	2,431	⎤ 5,086
322	htp cpe, V8	3,075	2,538	⎦
223	sdn 4d, L6	2,960	2,399	⎤ 31,263
323	sdn 4d, V8	3,095	2,507	⎦

SP1/2-H Fury (wb 116.0)

232	htp cpe, L6	2,960	2,585	⎤ 9,589
332	htp cpe, V8	3,105	2,693	⎦
233	sdn 4d, L6	2,990	2,563	⎤ 17,531
333	sdn 4d, V8	3,125	2,670	⎦
334	htp sdn, V8	3,190	2,742	5,995
335	conv cpe, V8	3,210	2,924	4,349

SP2-P Sport Fury (wb 116.0)

342	htp cpe, V8	3,195	2,851	4,039
345	conv cpe, V8	3,295	3,082	1,516

SP1/2 Suburban (wb 116.0)*

256	Savoy wgn 4d, L6	3,225	2,609	⎤ 12,710
356	Savoy wgn 4d, V8	3,390	2,717	⎦

		Wght	Price	Prod
266	Belvedere wgn 4d, 6P, L6	3,245	2,708	⎤ 9,781
366	Belvedere wgn 4d, 6P, V8	3,390	2,815	⎦
367	Belvedere wgn 4d, 9P, V8	3,440	2,917	4,168
376	Fury wgn 4d, 6P, V8	3,395	2,968	2,352
377	Fury wgn 4d, 9P, V8	3,455	3,071	2,411

*Due to factory numbering in 1962, model names such as "Savoy" were listed as body style names. This practice occurred in 1962 only.

1962 Engines	bore×stroke	bhp	availability
L6, 170.0	3.40×3.13	101	S-Valiant
L6, 225.0	3.40×4.13	145	S-SP1; O-Valiant
V8, 318.0	3.91×3.31	230	S-all SP2 exc Sport Fury
V8, 318.0	3.91×3.31	260	O-all SP2 exc Sport Fury
V8, 361.0	4.12×3.38	305	S-Sport Fury; O-other SP2 exc w/PowerFlite or AC

1963

TV1-L Valiant V100 (wb 106.0)

		Wght	Price	Prod
111	sdn 2d	2,515	1,910	32,761
113	sdn 4d	2,535	1,973	54,617
156	wgn 4d	2,700	2,268	11,864

TV1-H Valiant V200 (wb 106.0)

131	sdn 2d	2,515	2,026	10,605
133	sdn 4d	2,555	2,097	57,029
135	conv cpe	2,640	2,340	7,122
176	wgn 4d	2,715	2,392	11,147

TV1-P Valiant Signet 200 (wb 106.0)

142	htp cpe	2,570	2,230	30,857
145	conv cpe	2,675	2,454	9,154

TP1/2-L Savoy (wb 116.0)

211	sdn 2d, L6	2,980	2,206	⎤ 20,281
311	sdn 2d, V8	3,200	2,313	⎦
213	sdn 4d, L6	3,020	2,262	⎤ 56,313
313	sdn 4d, V8	3,220	2,369	⎦
256	wgn 4d, 6P, L6	3,325	2,609	⎤ 12,874
356	wgn 4d, 6P, V8	3,475	2,717	⎦
257	wgn 4d, 9P, L6	3,375	2,710	⎤ 4,342
357	wgn 4d, 9P, V8	3,560	2,818	⎦

TP1/2-M Belvedere (wb 116.0)

221	sdn 2d, L6	3,000	2,342	⎤ 6,218
321	sdn 2d, V8	3,215	2,450	⎦
222	htp cpe, L6	3,025	2,431	⎤ 9,204
322	htp cpe, V8	3,190	2,538	⎦
223	sdn 4d, L6	3,020	2,399	⎤ 54,929
323	sdn 4d, V8	3,235	2,507	⎦
366	wgn 4d, 6P, V8	3,490	2,815	10,297
367	wgn 4d, 9P, V8	3,585	2,917	4,012

TP1/2-H Fury (wb 116.0)

232	htp cpe, L6	3,030	2,585	⎤ 13,832
332	htp cpe, V8	3,215	2,693	⎦
233	sdn 4d, L6	3,075	2,563	⎤ 31,891
333	sdn 4d, V8	3,265	2,670	⎦
334	htp sdn, V8	3,295	2,742	11,887
335	conv cpe, V8	3,340	2,924	5,221
376	wgn 4d, 6P, V8	3,545	2,968	3,304
377	wgn 4d, 9P, V8	3,590	3,071	3,368

TP2-P Sport Fury (wb 116.0)

342	htp cpe, V8	3,235	2,851	11,483
345	conv cpe, V8	3,385	3,082	3,836

1963 Engines	bore×stroke	bhp	availability
L6, 170.0	3.40×3.13	101	S-Valiant
L6, 225.0	3.40×4.13	145	S-all TP1; O-Valiant
V8, 318.0	3.91×3.31	230	S-all TP2
V8, 361.0	4.12×3.38	265	O-all TP2
V8, 383.0	4.25×3.38	330	O-all TP2

1964

VV1-L Valiant V100 (wb 106.0)	Wght	Price	Prod
111 sdn 2d	2,540	1,921	35,403
113 sdn 4d	2,575	1,992	44,208
156 wgn 4d	2,725	2,273	10,759

VV1-H Valiant V200 (wb 106.0)			
131 sdn 2d	2,545	2,044	11,013
133 sdn 4d	2,570	2,112	63,828
135 conv cpe	2,670	2,349	5,856
176 wgn 4d	2,730	2,388	11,146

VV1-P Valiant Signet 200 (wb 106.0)			
142 htp cpe	2,600	2,256	37,736
145 conv cpe	2,690	2,473	7,636
149 Barracuda htp cpe	2,740	2,365	23,443

VP1/2-L Savoy (wb 116.0)	Wght	Price	Prod
211 sdn 2d, L6	2,990	2,224	⎤ 21,326
311 sdn 2d, V8	3,205	2,332	⎦
213 sdn 4d, L6	3,040	2,280	⎤ 51,024
313 sdn 4d, V8	3,210	2,388	⎦
256 wgn 4d, 6P, L6	3,345	2,620	⎤ 12,401
356 wgn 4d, 6P, V8	3,495	2,728	⎦
257 wgn 4d, 9P, L6	3,400	2,721	⎤ 3,242
357 wgn 4d, 9P, V8	3,600	2,829	⎦

VP1/2-M Belvedere (wb 116.0)			
221 sdn 2d, L6	3,000	2,359	⎤ 5,364
321 sdn 2d, V8	3,210	2,466	⎦
222 htp cpe, L6	3,010	2,444	⎤ 16,334
322 htp cpe, V8	3,190	2,551	⎦
223 sdn 4d, L6	3,065	2,417	⎤ 57,307
323 sdn 4d, V8	3,225	2,524	⎦
366 wgn 4d, 6P, V8	3,510	2,826	10,317
367 wgn 4d, 9P, V8	3,605	2,928	42,107

VP1/2-H Fury (wb 116.0)			
232 htp cpe, L6	3,040	2,598	⎤ 36,303
332 htp cpe, V8	3,212	2,706	⎦
233 sdn 4d, L6	3,045	2,573	⎤ 34,901
333 sdn 4d, V8	3,230	2,680	⎦
334 htp sdn, V8	3,300	2,752	13,713
335 conv cpe, V8	3,345	2,937	5,173
376 wgn 4d, 6P, V8	3,530	2,981	3,646
377 wgn 4d, 9P, V8	3,630	3,084	4,482

VP2-P Sport Fury (wb 116.0)			
342 htp cpe, V8	3,270	2,864	23,695
345 conv cpe, V8	3,405	3,095	3,858

1964 Engines	bore×stroke	bhp	availability
L6, 170.0	3.40×3.13	101	S-Valiant
L6, 225.0	3.40×4.13	145	S-VP1; O-Valiant
V8, 273.0	3.62×3.31	180	O-Valiant
V8, 318.0	3.91×3.31	230	S-all VP2
V8, 361.0	4.12×3.38	265	O-all exc Valiant
V8, 383.0	4.25×3.38	330	O-all exc Valiant
V8, 426.0	4.25×3.75	365	O-all exc Valiant

1965

AV1-L Valiant 100 (wb 106.0)*	Wght	Price	Prod
V11 sdn 2d	2,560	2,004	40,434
V13 sdn 4d	2,590	2,075	42,857
V56 wgn 4d	2,750	2,361	10,822

AV1-H Valiant 200 (wb 106.0)*			
V31 sdn 2d	2,570	2,127	8,919
V33 sdn 4d	2,605	2,195	41,642

	Wght	Price	Prod
V35 conv cpe	2,695	2,437	2,769
V78 wgn 4d	2,755	2,476	6,133

AV-1P Valiant Signet (wb 106.0)*			
V42 htp cpe	2,620	2,340	10,999
V45 conv cpe	2,725	2,561	2,578

AV1-P Barracuda (wb 106.0)*			
V89 htp cpe	2,725	2,487	64,596

Belvedere I (wb 116.0; SS-115.0)			
R01 Super Stock htp cpe	3,170	4,671	—
R11 sdn 2d	3,088	2,226	12,536
R13 sdn 4d	3,153	2,265	35,968
R56 wgn 4d	3,423	2,562	8,338

Belvedere II (wb 116.0)			
R32 htp cpe	3,123	2,378	24,924
R33 sdn 4d	3,128	2,352	41,445
R35 conv cpe	3,230	2,597	1,921
R76 wgn 4d, 6P	3,425	2,649	5,908
R77 wgn 4d, 9P	3,488	2,747	3,294

Satellite (wb 116.0)			
R42 htp cpe	3,220	2,649	23,341
R45 conv cpe	3,325	2,869	1,860

Fury I (wb 119.0; wgns-121.0)			
P11 sdn 2d	3,518	2,376	17,294
P13 sdn 4d	3,573	2,430	48,575
P56 wgn 4d	4,030	2,776	13,360

Fury II (wb 119.0; wgn-121.0)			
P21 sdn 2d	3,525	2,478	4,109
P23 sdn 4d	3,573	2,532	43,350
P66 wgn 4d, 6P	4,135	2,948	12,853
P67 wgn 4d, 9P	4,160	3,051	6,445

Fury III (wb 119.0; wgns-121.0)			
P32 htp cpe	3,563	2,691	43,251
P33 sdn 4d	3,595	2,684	50,725
P34 htp sdn	3,690	2,863	21,367
P35 conv cpe	3,710	3,048	5,524
P76 wgn 4d, 6P	4,140	3,090	8,931
P77 wgn 4d, 9P	4,200	3,193	9,546

Sport Fury (wb 119.0)			
P42 htp cpe	3,715	2,960	38,348
P45 conv cpe	3,755	3,209	6,272

*Factory quoted only V8 Valiant prices this year, which are given along with V8 weights. For sixes, deduct approximately $128.

1965 Engines	bore×stroke	bhp	availability
L6, 170.0	3.40×3.13	101	S-Valiant
L6, 225.0	3.40×4.13	145	S-Barracuda, Furys, Belv; O-Valiant
V8, 273.0	3.62×3.31	180	S-Satellite; O-Valiant, Barracuda, Belvedere
V8, 273.0	3.62×3.31	235	O-Valiant, Barracuda
V8, 318.0	3.91×3.31	230	S-Furys; O-Belvedere, Satellite
V8, 361.0	4.12×3.38	265	O-Belvedere, Satellite
V8, 383.0	4.25×3.38	270	O-Belv, Satellite, Furys
V8, 383.0	4.25×3.38	330	O-Belv, Satellite, Furys
V8, 426.0	4.25×3.75	365	S-Belv I SS; O-Belvedere, Satellite, Furys
V8, 426.0	4.25×3.75	425	O-Belvedere I Super Stock

1966

BV1/2-L Valiant 100 (wb 106.0)	Wght	Price	Prod
21 sdn 2d	2,700	2,025	35,787

		Wght	Price	Prod
41	sdn 4d	2,725	2,095	36,031
45	wgn 4d	2,648	2,387	6,838

BV1/2-H Valiant 200 (wb 106.0)

41	sdn 4d	2,728	2,226	39,392
45	wgn 4d	2,883	2,502	4,537

BV1/2-H Valiant Signet (wb 106.0)

23	htp cpe	2,735	2,261	13,045
27	conv cpe	2,830	2,527	2,507

BV1/2-P Barracuda (wb 106.0)

29	htp cpe	2,865	2,556	38,029

BR1/2-L Belvedere I (wb 116.0; wgn-117.0)

21	sdn 2d	3,095	2,277	9,381
41	sdn 4d	3,125	2,315	31,063
45	wgn 4d	3,523	2,605	8,200

BR1/2-H Belvedere II (wb 116.0; wgn-117.0)

23	htp cpe	3,123	2,430	36,644
27	conv cpe	3,200	2,644	2,502
41	sdn 4d	3,115	2,405	49,941
45	wgn 4d, 6P	3,525	2,695	8,667
46	wgn 4d, 9P	3,618	2,804	1,720

BR2-P Satellite (wb 116.0)

23	htp cpe	3,255	2,695	35,399
27	conv cpe	3,320	2,910	2,759

BP1/2-L Fury I (wb 119.0; wgn-121.0)

21	sdn 2d	3,518	2,426	12,538
41	sdn 4d	3,570	2,479	39,698
45	wgn 4d	4,048	2,836	9,690

BP1/2-M Fury II (wb 119.0; wgn-121.0)

21	sdn 2d	3,530	2,526	2,503
41	sdn 4d	3,573	2,579	55,016
45	wgn 4d, 6P	4,145	2,986	10,718
46	wgn 4d, 9P	4,175	3,087	5,580

BP1/2-H Fury III (wb 119.0; wgn-121.0)

23	htp cpe	3,578	2,724	41,869
27	conv cpe	3,720	3,074	4,326
41	sdn 4d	3,217	2,718	46,505
43	htp sdn	3,730	2,893	33,922
45	wgn 4d, 6P	4,155	3,115	9,239
46	wgn 4d, 9P	4,165	3,216	10,886

BP2-P Sport Fury (wb 119.0)

23	htp cpe	3,730	3,006	32,523
27	conv cpe	3,755	3,251	3,418

VP2-H VIP (wb 119.0)*

23	htp cpe	3,700	3,069	—
43	htp sdn	3,780	3,133	—

*Included with Fury III.

1966 Engines	bore×stroke	bhp	availability
L6, 170.0	3.40×3.13	101	S-Valiant
L6, 225.0	3.40×4.13	145	S-Brcda, Belv exc Satellite, Fury sdns/wgns, Fury III 43; O-Val
V8, 273.0	3.62×3.31	180	S-Sat; O-Belv, Brcda, Val
V8, 273.0	3.62×3.31	235	O-Brcda, Valiant exc wgns
V8, 318.0	3.91×3.31	230	S-VIP, Spt Fury, Fury II wgns, Fury III conv/htp/wgn; O-Fury, Belv
V8, 361.0	4.12×3.38	265	O-Belvedere, Satellite
V8, 383.0	4.25×3.38	325	O-VIP, Furys, Belv, Sat
V8, 426.0	4.25×3.75	425	O-Belv, Sat exc wgns
V8, 440.0	4.32×3.75	365	O-VIP, Furys

1967

CV1/2-L Valiant 100 (wb 108.0)

		Wght	Price	Prod
21	sdn 2d	2,738	2,117	29,093
41	sdn 4d	2,753	2,163	46,638

CV1/2-H Valiant Signet (wb 108.0)

21	sdn 2d	2,765	2,262	6,843
41	sdn 4d	2,750	2,308	26,395

CV1/2-P Barracuda (wb 108.0)

23	htp cpe	2,793	2,449	28,196
27	conv cpe	2,903	2,779	4,228
29	fstbk cpe	2,878	2,639	30,110

CR1/2-E Belvedere (wb 117.0)

45	wgn 4d	3,543	2,579	5,477

CR1/2-L Belvedere I (wb 116.0; wgn-117.0)

21	sdn 2d	3,095	2,318	4,718
41	sdn 4d	3,125	2,356	13,988
45	wgn 4d	3,553	2,652	3,172

CR1/2-H Belvedere II (wb 116.0; wgn-117.0)

23	htp cpe	3,130	2,457	34,550
27	conv cpe	3,205	2,695	1,552
41	sdn 4d	3,118	2,434	42,694
45	wgn 4d, 6P	3,553	2,729	5,583
46	wgn 4d, 9P	3,595	2,836	3,968

CR2-P Satellite (wb 116.0)

23	htp cpe	3,265	2,747	30,328
27	conv cpe	3,335	2,986	2,050

CR2-P Belvedere GTX (wb 116.0)*

23	htp cpe	3,545	3,178	—
27	conv cpe	3,615	3,418	—

CP1/2-E Fury I (wb 119.0; wgn-122.0)

21	sdn 2d	3,493	2,473	6,647
41	sdn 4d	3,533	2,517	29,354
45	wgn 4d	4,000	2,884	6,067

CP1/2-L Fury II (wb 119.0; wgn-122.0)

21	sdn 2d	3,490	2,571	2,783
41	sdn 4d	3,526	2,614	45,673
45	wgn 4d, 6P	4,045	3,021	10,736
46	wgn 4d, 9P	4,110	3,122	5,649

CP1/2-M Fury III (wb 119.0; wgn-122.0)

23	htp cpe	3,535	2,872	37,448
27	conv cpe	3,670	3,118	4,523
41	sdn 4d	3,555	2,746	52,690
43	htp sdn	3,650	2,922	43,614
45	wgn 4d, 6P	4,080	3,144	9,270
46	wgn 4d, 9P	4,135	3,245	12,533

CP2-H Sport Fury (wb 119.0)

23	htp cpe	3,630	3,033	28,448
23	fstbk htp cpe	3,705	3,062	28,448
27	conv cpe	3,645	3,279	3,133

CP2-P VIP (wb 119.0)

23	htp cpe	3,705	3,182	7,912
43	htp sdn	3,660	3,117	10,830

*Included with Satellite.

1967 Engines	bore×stroke	bhp	availability
L6, 170.0	3.40×3.13	115	S-Valiant
L6, 225.0	3.40×4.13	145	S-CR2 exc Sat/GTX, Fury sdns, Fury I wgn, Fury III htp, Brcda; O-Val
V8, 273.0	3.62×3.31	180	S-CR2 exc GTX, Brcda, Val
V8, 273.0	3.62×3.31	235	O-Valiant, Barracuda

	bore×stroke	bhp	availability
V8, 318.0	3.91×3.31	230	S-Furys; O-Belv exc GTX
V8, 383.0	4.25×3.38	270	O-Furys; Belv exc GTX
V8, 383.0	4.25×3.38	280	O-Barracuda
V8, 383.0	4.25×3.38	325	O-Brcda, Furys, Belv exc GTX
V8, 426.0	4.25×3.75	425	O-Belvedere GTX
V8, 440.0	4.32×3.75	350	O-Fury wgns
V8, 440.0	4.32×3.75	375	S-GTX; O-Furys exc wgns

1968

VL Valiant 100 (wb 108.0)*

		Wght	Price	Prod
21	sdn 2d	2,733	2,254	31,178
41	sdn 4d	2,763	2,301	49,446

VH Valiant Signet (wb 108.0)

21	sdn 2d	2,745	2,400	6,265
41	sdn 4d	2,768	2,447	23,906

VH Barracuda (wb 108.0)

23	htp cpe	2,810	2,605	19,997
27	conv cpe	2,923	2,907	2,840
29	fstbk cpe	2,895	2,762	22,575

RL Belvedere (wb 116.0; wgn-117.0)

21	cpe	3,050	2,444	15,702
41	sdn 4d	3,080	2,483	17,214
45	wgn 4d	3,553	2,773	8,982

RH Satellite (wb 116.0; wgn-117.0)

23	htp cpe	3,070	2,594	46,539
27	conv cpe	3,188	2,824	1,771
41	sdn 4d	3,080	2,572	42,309
45	wgn 4d, 6P	3,605	2,891	12,097
46	wgn 4d, 9P	3,625	2,998	10,883

RP Sport Satellite (wb 116.0; wgn-117.0)

23	htp cpe	3,155	2,822	21,014
27	conv cpe	3,285	3,036	1,523
45	wgn 4d, 6P	3,610	3,131	**
46	wgn 4d, 9P	3,685	3,239	**

RM Road Runner (wb 116.0)

21	cpe	3,440	2,896	29,240
23	htp cpe	3,455	3,034	15,359

RS GTX (wb 116.0)

23	htp cpe	3,470	3,355	17,914
27	conv cpe	3,595	3,590	1,026

PE Fury I (wb 119.0)

21	sdn 2d	3,480	2,617	5,788
41	sdn 4d	3,653	2,660	23,208

PL Fury II (wb 119.0)

21	sdn 2d	3,488	2,715	3,112
41	sdn 4d	3,533	2,757	49,423

PM Fury III (wb 119.0)

23	htp cpe	3,538	2,912	60,472
23	fstbk htp cpe "PX"	3,528	2,932	
27	conv cpe	3,680	3,236	4,483
41	sdn 4d	3,545	2,890	57,899
43	htp sdn	3,635	3,067	45,147

PH Sport Fury (wb 119.0)

23	htp cpe	3,620	3,206	6,642
23	fstbk htp cpe "PS"	3,615	3,225	17,073
27	conv cpe	3,710	3,425	2,489

PP VIP (wb 119.0)

23	fstbk htp cpe	3,615	3,260	6,768
43	htp sdn	3,655	3,326	10,745

DP Suburban (wb 122.0)

		Wght	Price	Prod
45	wgn 4d	3,990	3,048	6,749
45	Custom wgn 4d, 6P	4,045	3,252	17,078
46	Custom wgn 4d, 9P	4,090	3,353	9,954
45	Sport wgn 4d, 6P	4,055	3,442	9,203
46	Sport wgn 4d, 9P	4,100	3,543	13,224

*Includes "Valiant 200" trim option.
**Sport Satellite wagon included with Satellite wagon.

1968 Engines	bore×stroke	bhp	availability
L6, 170.0	3.40×3.13	115	S-Valiant
L6, 225.0	3.40×4.13	145	S-Brcda, Belv, Sat, FI/II, FIII sdn, htps, Suburban; O-Val
V8, 273.0	3.62×3.31	190	O-Val, Belv, Sat, Spt Sat wgn
V8, 318.0	3.91×3.31	230	S-Spt Sat, Fury III; O-Val, Brcda, Belv, Sat, Spt Sat wgn
V8, 340.0	4.04×3.31	275	S-Barracuda Formula S
V8, 383.0	4.25×3.38	290	O-Belv, Sat, Spt Sat, Furys
V8, 383.0	4.25×3.38	300	O-Barracuda Formula S
V8, 383.0	4.25×3.38	330	O-Belv, Satellite, Furys, Suburbans
V8, 383.0	4.25×3.38	335	S-Road Runner
V8, 426.0	4.25×3.75	425	O-Road Runner, GTX
V8, 440.0	4.32×3.75	375	S-GTX; O-Fury exc DP
V8, 440.0	4.32×3.75	350	O-Suburban

1969

VL Valiant 100 (wb 108.0)*

		Wght	Price	Prod
21	sdn 2d	2,740	2,094	29,672
41	sdn 4d	2,760	2,154	49,409

VH Valiant Signet (wb 108.0)

21	sdn 2d	2,740	2,253	6,645
41	sdn 4d	2,760	2,313	21,492

VH Barracuda (wb 108.0)

23	htp cpe	2,815	2,780	12,757
27	conv cpe	2,940	3,082	1,442
29	fstbk htp cpe	2,902	2,813	17,788

RL Belvedere (wb 116.0; wgn-117.0)

21	cpe	3,052	2,509	7,063
41	sdn rd	3,082	2,548	12,914
45	wgn 4d	3,540	2,879	7,038

RH Satellite (wb 116.0; wgn-117.0)

23	htp cpe	3,080	2,659	38,323
27	conv cpe	3,200	2,875	1,137
41	sdn 4d	3,087	2,635	35,296
45	wgn 4d, 6P	3,540	2,997	5,837
46	wgn 4d, 9P	3,612	3,106	4,730

RP Sport Satellite (wb 116.0; wgn-117.0)

23	htp cpe	3,156	2,883	15,807
27	conv cpe	3,276	3,081	818
41	sdn 4d	3,196	2,911	5,836
45	wgn 4d, 6P	3,596	3,241	3,221
45	wgn 4d, 9P	3,666	3,350	3,152

RM Road Runner (wb 116.0)

21	cpe	3,435	2,945	33,743
23	htp cpe	3,450	3,083	48,549
27	conv cpe	3,790	3,313	2,128

RS GTX (wb 116.0)

23	htp cpe	3,465	3,416	14,902
27	conv cpe	3,590	3,635	700

PE Fury I (wb 120.0)

21	sdn 2d	3,501	2,701	4,971
41	sdn 4d	3,533	2,744	18,771

Plymouth

PL Fury II (wb 120.0)		Wght	Price	Prod
21	sdn 2d	3,506	2,813	3,268
41	sdn 4d	3,536	2,841	41,047

PM Fury III (wb 120.0)		Wght	Price	Prod
23	htp cpe	3,516	3,000	44,168
27	conv cpe	3,704	3,324	4,129
29	form htp cpe	3,601	3,020	22,738
41	sdn 4d	3,541	2,979	72,747
43	htp sdn	3,643	3,155	68,818

PH Sport Fury (wb 120.0)		Wght	Price	Prod
23	htp cpe	3,603	3,283	14,120
27	conv cpe	3,729	3,502	1,579
29	form htp cpe	3,678	3,303	2,169

PP VIP (wb 120.0)		Wght	Price	Prod
23	htp cpe	3,583	3,382	4,740
29	form htp cpe	3,668	3,382	1,059
43	htp sdn	3,663	3,433	7,982

EP Suburban (wb 122.0)		Wght	Price	Prod
45	wgn 4d	4,056	3,231	6,424
45	Custom wgn 4d, 6P	4,103	3,436	15,976
46	Custom wgn 4d, 9P	4,148	3,527	10,216
45	Sport wgn 4d, 6P	4,123	3,651	8,201
46	Sport wgn 4d, 9P	4,173	3,718	13,502

*Includes "Valiant 200" trim option.

1969 Engines	bore×stroke	bhp	availability
L6, 170.0	3.40×3.13	115	S-Valiant
L6, 225.0	3.40×4.13	145	S-Brcda, Belv, Sat, Fury I/II; O-Valiant
V8, 273.0	3.62×3.31	190	O-Valiant
V8, 318.0	3.91×3.31	230	S-Spt Sat, Fury III, Spt Fury, VIP, Suburban
V8, 340.0	4.04×3.31	275	O-Barracuda
V8, 383.0	4.25×3.38	290	O-Belv, Sat, Spt Sat, Furys, VIP
V8, 383.0	4.25×3.38	330	O-Brcda, Belv, Sat, Spt Sat, Furys, VIP
V8, 383.0	4.25×3.38	335	S-Road Runner
V8, 426.0	4.25×3.75	425	O-Road Runner, GTX
V8, 440.0	4.32×3.75	375	S-GTX; O-Furys exc EP
V8, 440.0	4.32×3.75	350	O-Suburban

1970

VL Valiant (wb 108.0)		Wght	Price	Prod
29	Duster fstbk cpe	2,830	2,172	192,375
41	sdn 4d	2,835	2,250	50,810

VS Valiant Duster 340 (wb 108.0)		Wght	Price	Prod
29	htp cpe	3,110	2,547	24,817

BH Barracuda (wb 108.0)		Wght	Price	Prod
23	htp cpe	2,905	2,764	25,651
27	conv cpe	3,071	3,034	1,554

BP Barracuda Gran Coupe (wb 108.0)		Wght	Price	Prod
23	htp cpe	3,015	2,934	8,183
27	conv cpe	3,090	3,160	596

BS 'Cuda (wb 108.0)		Wght	Price	Prod
23	htp cpe	3,395	3,164	18,180
27	conv cpe	3,480	3,433	635

RL Belvedere (wb 116.0; wgn-117.0)		Wght	Price	Prod
21	cpe	3,095	2,603	4,717
41	sdn 4d	3,130	2,641	13,945
45	wgn 4d	3,655	3,075	5,584

RH Satellite (wb 116.0; wgn-117.0)		Wght	Price	Prod
23	htp cpe	3,105	2,765	28,200
27	conv cpe	3,225	3,006	701
41	sdn 4d	3,125	2,741	30,377
45	wgn 4d, 6P	3,637	3,101	4,204
46	wgn 4d, 9P	3,747	3,211	3,277

RP Sport Satellite (wb 116.0; wgn-117.0)		Wght	Price	Prod
23	htp cpe	3,170	2,988	8,749
41	sdn 4d	3,205	3,017	3,010
45	wgn 4d, 6P	3,675	3,345	1,975
46	wgn 4d, 9P	3,750	3,455	2,161

RM Road Runner (wb 116.0)		Wght	Price	Prod
21	cpe	3,450	2,896	15,716
23	htp cpe	3,475	3,034	24,944
23	Superbird htp cpe	3,785	4,298	1,920
27	conv cpe	3,550	3,289	824

RS GTX (wb 116.0)		Wght	Price	Prod
23	htp cpe	3,515	3,535	7,748

PE Fury I (wb 120.0)		Wght	Price	Prod
21	sdn 2d	3,603	2,790	2,353
41	sdn 4d	3,640	2,825	14,813

PL Fury II (wb 120.0)		Wght	Price	Prod
21	sdn 2d	3,583	2,903	21,316
41	sdn 4d	3,643	2,922	27,694

PM Fury III (wb 120.0)		Wght	Price	Prod
23	htp cpe	3,610	3,091	21,373
27	conv cpe	3,770	3,415	1,952
29	form htp cpe	3,645	3,333	12,367
41	sdn 4d	3,645	3,069	50,876

PH Sport Fury (wb 120.0)		Wght	Price	Prod
23	htp cpe	3,630	3,313	⎤
23	S/23 htp cpe "PS"	3,660	3,379	⎬ 8,018
23	GT htp cpe "PP"	3,925	3,898	⎦
29	form htp cpe	3,645	3,333	5,688
41	sdn 4d	3,680	3,291	5,135
43	htp sdn	3,705	3,363	6,854

PL Fury Gran Coupe (wb 120.0)		Wght	Price	Prod
21	cpe	3,864	3,833	*

FP Suburban (wb 122.0)		Wght	Price	Prod
45	wgn 4d, 6P	4,125	3,303	5,300
46	wgn 4d, 9P	4,205	3,518	2,250
45	Custom wgn 4d, 6P	4,155	3,527	8,898
46	Custom wgn 4d, 9P	4,215	3,603	6,792
45	Sport wgn 4d, 6P	4,200	3,725	4,403
46	Sport wgn 4d, 9P	4,260	3,804	9,170

*Included with Fury II sdn 2d.

1970 Engines	bore×stroke	bhp	availability
L6, 198.0	3.40×3.64	125	S-Valiant, Duster
L6, 225.0	3.40×4.13	145	S-Brcda, Belv, Sat, Fury I/II; O-Valiant, Duster
V8, 318.0	3.91×3.31	230	S-Spt Sat, Fury III, Spt Fury, Gran Coupe, Suburban
V8, 340.0	4.04×3.31	275	S-Duster 340; O-'Cuda
V8, 383.0	4.25×3.38	290	O-all exc Valiant
V8, 383.0	4.25×3.38	330	O-all exc Valiant
V8, 383.0	4.25×3.38	335	S-Road Runner, 'Cuda
V8, 426.0	4.25×3.75	425	O-RR, 'Cuda, GTX
V8, 440.0	4.32×3.75	350	S-Spt Fury GT; O-other Fury
V8, 440.0	4.32×3.75	375	S-GTX; O-'Cuda
V8, 440.0	4.32×3.75	390	O-'Cuda, RR, GTX, PH23

1971

Valiant (wb 108.0; Scamp-111.0)		Wght	Price	Prod
VL29	Duster fstbk cpe	2,825	2,313	173,592
VL41	sdn 4d	2,831	2,392	42,660
VH23	Scamp htp cpe	2,900	2,561	48,253
VS29	Duster 340 fstbk cpe	3,140	2,703	12,886

Barracuda (wb 108.0)		Wght	Price	Prod
VH21	cpe 2d	3,040	2,654	} 9,459
VH23	htp cpe	3,075	2,766	
VH27	conv	3,145	3,023	1,014
VP23	Gran Coupe htp cpe V8	3,105	3,029	1,615
VS23	'Cuda htp cpe V8	3,475	3,155	6,228
VS27	'Cuda conv cpe V8	3,550	3,412	374

Satellite (wb 117.0; 2d-115.0)		Wght	Price	Prod
RL41	sdn 4d	3,294	2,734	11,059
RL21	cpe	3,230	2,663	} 46,807
RH23	Sebring htp cpe	3,256	2,931	
RL45	wgn 4d 2S	3,770	3,058	7,138
RH41	Custom sdn 4d	3,286	2,908	30,773
RH45	Custom wgn 4d 2S	3,776	3,235	5,045
RH46	Custom wgn 4d 3S	3,846	3,315	4,626
RM23	Road Runner htp cpe V8	3,640	3,147	14,218
RP23	Sebring Plus htp cpe V8	3,300	3,179	16,253
RP41	Brougham sdn 4d V8	3,330	3,189	3,020
RP45	Regent wgn 4d 2S V8	3,815	3,558	2,161
RP46	Regent wgn 4d 3S V8	3,885	3,638	2,985
RS23	GTX htp cpe V8	3,675	3,733	2,942

Fury (wb 120.0; wgn-122.0)		Wght	Price	Prod
PE41	I sdn 4d	3,742	3,163	} 16,395
PE41	I Custom sdn 4d	3,742	3,241	
PE21	I sdn 2d	3,708	3,113	} 5,152
PE21	I Custom sdn 2d	3,708	3,208	
PL23	II htp cpe	3,710	3,283	7,859
PL41	II sdn 4d	3,746	3,262	20,098
PL45	II Suburban wgn 4d 2S V8	4,245	3,758	4,877
PL46	II Suburban wgn 4d 3S V8	4,290	3,869	2,662
PM23	III htp cpe	3,716	3,458	21,319
PM41	III sdn 4d	3,752	3,437	44,244
PM29	III formal htp cpe V8	3,750	3,600	24,465
PM43	III htp sdn V8	3,820	3,612	55,356
PM45	III Cus Suburban wgn 4d 2S V8	4,240	3,854	10,874
PM46	III Cus Suburban wgn 4d 3S V8	4,300	3,930	11,702

Sport Fury (wb 120.0; wgn-122.0)		Wght	Price	Prod
PH23	htp cpe V8	3,805	3,677	3,912
PH29	formal htp cpe V8	3,810	3,710	3,957
PH41	sdn 4d V8	3,845	3,656	2,823
PH43	htp sdn V8	3,865	3,724	4,813
PH45	Sport Suburban wgn 4d 2S V8	4,290	4,071	5,103
PH46	Sport Suburban wgn 4d 3S V8	4,370	4,146	13,021
PP23	GT htp cpe V8	4,090	4,111	375

1971 Engines	bore×stroke	bhp	availability
L6, 198.0	3.40×3.64	125	S-Val,Brcda cpe
L6, 225.0	3.40×4.13	145	S-Brcda exc cpe, Sat,Fury; O-Val,Brcda cpe
V8, 318.0	3.91×3.31	230	S-Sat,Fury; O-Val,Brcda
V8, 340.0	4.04×3.31	275	S-Dstr 340,Cuda; O-Brcda
V8, 360.0	4.00×3.58	255	O-Fury
V8, 383.0	4.25×3.38	275	O-Brcda,Rd Runner,Fury
V8, 383.0	4.25×3.38	300	S-Cuda,Rd Runner; O-Barracuda,Fury
V8, 426.0	4.25×3.75	425	O-Barracuda
V8, 440.0	4.32×3.75	335	O-Fury
V8, 440.0	4.32×3.75	370	S-Fury GT; O-Fury
V8, 440.0	4.32×3.75	385	O-Barracuda

1972

Valiant (wb 108.0; Scamp-111.0)		Wght	Price	Prod
VL29	Duster fstbk cpe	2,780	2,287	212,331
VL41	sdn 4d	2,800	2,363	52,911
VH23	Scamp htp cpe	2,825	2,528	49,470
VS29	Duster 340 fstbk cpe	3,100	2,742	15,681

Barracuda (wb 108.0)		Wght	Price	Prod
VH23	htp cpe	3,185	2,710	10,622
VS23	'Cuda htp cpe V8	3,195	3,029	7,828

Satellite (wb 117.0; 2d-115.0)		Wght	Price	Prod
RL21	cpe	3,272	2,609	10,507
RL41	sdn 4d	3,312	2,678	12,794
RL45	wgn 4d 2S V8	3,785	3,167	7,377
RH23	Sebring htp cpe	3,282	2,871	34,353
RH41	Custom sdn 4d	3,318	2,848	34,973
RH45	Custom wgn 4d 2S V8	3,825	3,340	5,485
RH46	Custom wgn 4d 3S V8	3,780	3,418	5,637
RP23	Sebring Plus htp cpe V8	3,320	3,127	21,399
RP45	Regent wgn 4d 2S V8	3,790	3,562	1,893
RP46	Regent wgn 4d 3S V8	3,830	3,640	2,907
RM23	Road Runner htp cpe V8	3,495	3,095	7,628

Fury (wb 120.0; wgn-122.0)		Wght	Price	Prod
PL41	I sdn 4d	3,840	3,464	14,006
PM23	II htp cpe	3,790	3,605	7,515
PM41	II sdn 4d	3,830	3,583	20,051
PM45	II Suburban wgn 4d 2S	4,315	4,024	5,268
PM46	II Suburban wgn 4d 3S	4,360	4,139	2,773
PH23	III htp cpe	3,790	3,785	21,204
PH29	III formal htp cpe	3,790	3,818	9,036
PH41	III sdn 4d	3,830	3,763	46,731
PH43	III htp sdn	3,855	3,829	48,618
PH45	III Cus Suburban wgn 4d 2S	4,315	4,123	11,067
PH46	III Cus Suburban wgn 4d 3S	4,365	4,201	14,041
PP23	Gran Fury htp cpe	3,735	3,941	15,840
PP29	Gran Fury formal htp cpe	3,805	3,974	8,509
PP43	Gran Fury htp sdn	3,865	3,987	17,551
PP45	Sport Suburban wgn 4d 2S	4,335	4,389	4,971
PP46	Sport Suburban wgn 4d 3S	4,395	4,466	15,628

1972 Engines	bore×stroke	bhp	availability
L6, 198.0	3.40×3.64	100	S-Valiant
L6, 225.0	3.40×4.13	110	S-Brcda,Sat; O-Valiant
V8, 318.0	3.91×3.31	150	S-Sat,Fury; O-Val,Brcda
V8, 340.0	4.04×3.31	240	S-Duster 340,Cuda, Rd Runner; O-Barracuda
V8, 360.0	4.00×3.58	170	O-Fury
V8, 400.0	4.34×3.38	190/250	O-Fury
V8, 440.0	4.32×3.75	230/285	O-Fury

1973

Valiant (wb 108.0; Scamp-111.0)		Wght	Price	Prod
VL29	Duster fstbk cpe	2,830	2,376	249,243
VL41	sdn 4d	2,865	2,447	61,826
VH23	Scamp htp cpe	2,885	2,617	53,792
VS29	Duster 340 fstbk cpe	3,175	2,822	15,731

Barracuda (wb 108.0)		Wght	Price	Prod
VH23	htp cpe	3,140	2,935	11,587
VS23	'Cuda htp cpe	3,235	3,120	10,626

Satellite (wb 117.0; 2d-115.0)		Wght	Price	Prod
RL21	cpe	3,408	2,755	13,570
RL41	sdn 4d	3,482	2,824	14,716
RL45	wgn 4d 2S V8	3,950	3,272	6,906
RH23	Sebring htp cpe	3,425	2,997	51,575
RH41	Custom sdn 4d	3,478	2,974	46,748
RH45	Custom wgn 4d 2S V8	3,945	3,400	6,733
RH46	Custom wgn 4d 3S V8	3,990	3,518	7,705
RP23	Sebring Plus htp cpe V8	3,455	3,258	43,628
RP45	Regent wgn 4d 2S V8	3,950	3,621	2,781
RP46	Regent wgn 4d 3S V8	4,010	3,740	4,786
RM21	Road Runner cpe V8	3,525	3,115	19,056

Fury (wb 120.0; wgn-122.0)

PL41	I sdn 4d	3,865	3,575	17,365
PM41	II sdn 4d	3,845	3,694	21,646
PM45	II Suburban wgn 4d 2S	4,410	4,150	5,206
PH23	III htp cpe	3,815	3,883	34,963
PH41	III sdn 4d	3,860	3,866	51,742
PH43	III htp sdn	3,880	3,932	51,215
PH45	III Cus Suburban wgn 4d 2S	4,420	4,246	9,888
PH46	III Cus Suburban wgn 4d 3S	4,465	4,354	15,671
PP23	Gran Fury htp cpe	3,845	4,064	18,127
PP43	Gran Fury htp sdn	3,890	4,110	14,852
PP45	Sport Suburban wgn 4d 2S	4,435	4,497	4,832
PP46	Sport Suburban wgn 4d 3S	4,495	4,599	15,680

1973 Engines	bore×stroke	bhp	availability	
L6, 198.0	3.40×3.64	100	S-Valiant	
L6, 225.0	3.40×4.13	110	S-Brcda,Sat; O-Valiant	
V8, 318.0	3.91×3.31	150	S-Sat,Fury; O-Val,Brcda	
V8, 340.0	4.04×3.31	240	S-Duster 340,Cuda,Rd Runner; O-Barracuda	
V8, 360.0	4.00×3.58	175	O-Fury	
V8, 400.0	4.34×3.38	190/250	O-Fury	
V8, 440.0	4.32×3.75	230/285	O-Fury	

1974

Valiant (wb 111.0; fstbk 100.0)

		Wght	Price	Prod
VL29	Duster fstbk cpe	2,975	2,829	277,409
VS29	Duster 360 fstbk cpe	3,315	3,288	
VL41	sdn 4d	3,035	2,942	127,430
VP41	Brougham sdn 4d	3,195	3,819	
VP23	Brougham htp cpe	3,180	3,794	2,545
VH23	Scamp htp cpe	3,010	3,077	51,699

Barracuda (wb 108.0)

VH23	htp cpe	3,210	3,067	6,745
VS23	'Cuda htp cpe	3,300	3,252	4,989

Satellite (wb 117.0; 2d-115.0)

RL21	cpe	3,470	3,155	10,634
RL41	sdn 4d	3,555	3,226	12,726
RL45	wgn 4d 2S V8	4,065	3,654	4,622
RH23	Sebring htp cpe	3,490	3,353	31,980
RH41	Custom sdn 4d	3,550	3,329	45,863
RH45	Custom wgn 4d 2S V8	4,065	3,839	4,354
RH46	Custom wgn 4d 3S V8	4,110	4,152	5,591
RP23	Sebring Plus htp cpe V8	3,555	3,621	18,480
RM21	Road Runner cpe V8	3,615	3,545	11,555

Fury (wb 120.0; wgn-124.0)

PL41	I sdn 4d	4,185	4,101	8,162
PM41	II sdn 4d	4,165	4,223	11,649
PM45	II Suburban wgn 4d 2S	4,745	4,669	2,490
PH23	III htp cpe	4,125	4,418	14,167
PH41	III sdn 4d	4,180	4,400	27,965
PH43	III htp sdn	4,205	4,268	18,778
PH45	III Cus Suburban wgn 4d 2S	4,755	4,767	3,877
PH46	III Cus Suburban wgn 4d 3S	4,800	4,878	5,628
PP23	Gran Fury htp cpe	4,300	4,627	9,617
PP43	Gran Fury htp sdn	4,370	4,675	8,191
PP45	Sport Suburban wgn 4d 2S	4,795	5,025	1,712
PP46	Sport Suburban wgn 4d 3S	4,850	5,130	6,047

1974 Engines	bore×stroke	bhp	availability
L6, 198.0	3.40×3.64	95	S-Valiant exc B'ham
L6, 225.0	3.40×4.13	105	S-Val,B'ham,Sat; O-Val
V8, 318.0	3.91×3.31	150	S-Brcda,Sat; O-Valiant
V8, 318.0	3.91×3.31	170	S-Road Runner
V8, 360.0	4.00×3.58	180	S-Fury exc wgn/Gran Fury
V8, 360.0	4.00×3.58	200	O-Sat, Fury exc wgn/G.Fury
V8, 360.0	4.00×3.58	245	S-Duster 360; O-Valiant
V8, 400.0	4.34×3.38	185	S-G.Fury,Fury wgns; O-Fury
V8, 400.0	4.34×3.38	205	O-Satellite, Fury

V8, 400.0	4.34×3.38	240	O-Fury
V8, 400.0	4.34×3.38	250	O-Satellite
V8, 440.0	4.32×3.75	230/250	O-Fury
V8, 440.0	4.32×3.75	275	O-Satellite

1975

Valiant (wb 111.0; fstbk-108.0)

		Wght	Price	Prod
VL29	fstbk cpe	2,970	3,243	79,384
VH29	Duster Custom fstbk cpe	2,970	3,418	38,826
VL41	sdn 4d	3,040	3,247	44,471
VH41	Custom sdn 4d	3,040	3,422	56,258
VH23	Scamp htp cpe	3,020	3,518	23,581
VS29	Duster 360 fstbk cpe V8	3,315	3,979	1,421
VP23	Brougham htp cpe	3,240	4,232	5,781
VP41	Brougham sdn 4d	3,250	4,139	17,803

Fury (wb 117.5; 2d-115.0)

RL21	cpe	3,612	3,542	8,398
RL41	sdn 4d	3,642	3,591	11,432
RL45	wgn 4d V8	4,180	4,309	4,468
RH23	Custom cpe	3,692	3,711	27,486
RH41	Custom sdn 4d	3,692	3,704	31,080
RH45	Custom wgn 4d 2S V8	4,230	4,512	3,890
RH46	Custom wgn 4d 3S V8	4,285	4,632	4,285
RP23	Sport htp cpe V8	3,790	4,105	17,782
RP45	Sport Suburban wgn 4d 2S V8	4,230	4,770	1,851
RP46	Sport Suburban wgn 4d 3S V8	4,295	4,867	3,107

Gran Fury (wb 121.5; wgn-124.0)

PM41	sdn 4d	4,260	4,565	8,185
PM45	wgn 4d 2S	4,855	5,067	2,295
PH23	Custom htp cpe	4,205	4,781	6,041
PH41	Custom sdn 4d	4,260	4,761	19,043
PH43	Custom htp sdn	4,290	4,837	11,292
PH45	Custom wgn 4d 2S	4,870	5,176	3,155
PH46	Custom wgn 4d 3S	4,915	5,294	4,500
PP29	Brougham htp cpe	4,310	5,146	6,521
PP43	Brougham htp sdn	4,400	5,067	5,521
PP45	Sport Suburban wgn 4d 2S	4,885	5,455	1,508
PP46	Sport Suburban wgn 4d 3S	4,930	5,573	4,740

1975 Engines	bore×stroke	bhp	availability
L6, 225.0	3.40×4.13	90	S-Valiant
L6, 225.0	3.40×4.13	95	S-Fury
V8, 318.0	3.91×3.31	135	S-Fury
V8, 318.0	3.91×3.31	150	O-Fury,G.Fury exc wgn/B'ham
V8, 360.0	4.00×3.58	180	S-G.F. exc wgn/B'ham; O-Fury, G.F. wgn/B'ham
V8, 360.0	4.00×3.58	190	O-Fury, Gran Fury
V8, 400.0	4.34×3.38	165/185	O-Fury
V8, 400.0	4.34×3.38	175	S-G.F. B'ham wgn; O-other
V8, 400.0	4.34×3.38	190/235	O-Fury
V8, 400.0	4.34×3.38	195	O-Gran Fury
V8, 440.0	4.32×3.75	215	O-Gran Fury

1976

Valiant (wb 111.0; fstbk-108.0)

		Wght	Price	Prod
VL23	Scamp Special htp cpe	3,020	3,337	4,018
VL29	Duster fstbk cpe	2,975	3,241	34,681
VL41	sdn 4d	3,050	3,276	40,079
VH23	Scamp htp cpe	3,020	3,510	6,908

Volare (wb 112.5; cpe-108.5)

HL29	spt cpe	3,222	3,324	37,024
HL41	sdn 4d	3,252	3,359	23,058
HL45	wgn 5d	3,622	3,646	46,065
HH29	Custom spt cpe	3,232	3,506	31,252
HH41	Custom sdn 4d	3,262	3,541	36,407
HP29	Premier cpe	3,438	4,402	31,475
HP41	Premier sdn 4d	3,472	4,389	37,131

		Wght	Price	Prod
HH45	Premier wgn 5d	3,628	3,976	49,507

Fury (wb 117.5; 2d-115.0)

		Wght	Price	Prod
RL23	htp cpe	3,708	3,699	16,415
RL41	sdn 4d	3,742	3,733	22,654
RL45	wgn 4d 2S V8	4,285	4,597	4,624
RL46	wgn 4d 3S V8	4,350	4,739	4,412
RH23	Sport htp cpe	3,712	3,988	28,851
RH41	Salon sdn 4d	3,762	4,022	20,234
RH45	Sport Suburban wgn 2S V8	4,285	4,986	2,175
RH46	Sport Suburban wgn 3S V8	4,360	5,128	3,482

Gran Fury (wb 121.5; wgn-124.0)

		Wght	Price	Prod
PM41	sdn 4d	4,140	4,349	8,928
PM45	wgn 4d 2S	4,880	4,909	1,587
PH23	Custom htp cpe	4,265	4,730	2,733
PH41	Custom sdn 4d	4,305	4,715	14,738
PH45	Custom Suburban wgn 4d 2S	4,895	5,193	1,433
PH46	Custom Suburban wgn 4d 3S	4,940	5,316	1,998
PP29	Brougham htp cpe	4,400	5,334	2,619
PP41	Brougham sdn 4d	4,435	5,162	2,990
PP46	Sport Suburban wgn 4d 3S	4,975	5,761	2,484

1976 Engines	bore×stroke	bhp	availability
L6, 225.0	3.40×4.13	100	S-Val,Vol,Fury exc wgn
V8, 318.0	3.91×3.31	150	S-Vol,Fury exc wgn, GF sdn; O-Valiant
V8, 360.0	4.00×3.58	170	S-Fury wgn, G.Fury Cus; O-Val,Vol,Fury, G.F. exc Cus/ B'ham
V8, 400.0	4.34×3.38	175	S-G.F.wgn/B'ham; O-Fury
V8, 400.0	4.34×3.38	200/210	O-Gran Fury

1977

Volare (wb 112.7; cpe-108.7)

		Wght	Price	Prod
HL29	spt cpe	3,235	3,570	42,455
HL41	sdn 4d	3,290	3,619	44,550
HL45	wgn 4d	3,500	3,941	80,180
HH29	Custom spt cpe	3,240	3,752	34,196
HH41	Custom sdn 4d	3,295	3,801	50,859
HP29	Premier spt cpe	3,430	4,305	21,979
HP41	Premier sdn 5d	3,496	4,354	31,443
HH45	Premier wgn 5d	3,505	4,271	76,756

Fury (wb 117.5; 2d-115.0)

		Wght	Price	Prod
RL23	htp cpe	3,742	3,893	16,410
RL41	sdn 4d	3,772	3,944	25,172
RL45	Suburban wgn 4d 2S V8	4,335	4,687	6,765
RL46	Suburban wgn 4d 3S V8	4,390	4,830	5,556
RH23	Sport htp cpe	3,748	4,132	30,075
RH41	Salon sdn 4d	3,782	4,185	25,617
RH45	Sport Suburban wgn 4d 2S V8	4,330	5,192	2,502
RH46	Sport Suburban wgn 4d 3S V8	4,400	5,335	4,065

Gran Fury (wb 121.5; wgn-124.0)

		Wght	Price	Prod
PM23	cpe	4,070	4,692	2,772
PM41	sdn 4d	4,145	4,677	14,242
PM45	Suburban wgn 4d 2S	4,885	5,315	2,055
PH23	Brougham cpe	4,190	4,963	4,846
PH41	Brougham sdn 4d	4,250	4,948	17,687
PH45	Sport Suburban wgn 4d 2S	4,880	5,558	1,631
PH46	Sport Suburban wgn 4d 3S	4,925	5,681	4,319

1977 Engines	bore×stroke	bhp	availability
L6, 225.0	3.40×4.13	100	S-Volare exc wgns
L6, 225.0	3.40×4.13	110	S-Vol wgns; Fury exc wgns
V8, 318.0	3.91×3.31	145	S-Vol,Fury exc wgns, Gran Fury exc B'ham wgn
V8, 360.0	4.00×3.58	155	S-Fury wgns, GF B'ham; O-Volare,Fury, Gran Fury
V8, 360.0	4.00×3.58	170	O-Fury, Gran Fury
V8, 400.0	4.34×3.38	190	S-GF wgns; O-Fury, GF
V8, 440.0	4.32×3.75	185/195	O-Gran Fury

1978

Horizon (wb 99.2)

		Wght	Price	Prod
ML44	htchbk sdn 5d	2,145	3,976	106,772

Volare (wb 112.7; cpe-108.7)

		Wght	Price	Prod
HL29	spt cpe	3,200	3,771	74,818
HL41	sdn 4d	3,235	3,899	100,718
HL45	wgn 5d	3,465	4,241	81,242

Fury (wb 117.5; 2d-115.0)

		Wght	Price	Prod
RL23	htp cpe	3,725	4,236	13,276
RL41	sdn 4d	3,760	4,326	83,649
RL45	Suburban wgn 4d 2S V8	4,310	5,084	4,522
RL46	Suburban wgn 4d 3S V8	4,370	5,227	3,889
RH23	Sport htp cpe	3,735	4,483	13,031
RH41	Salon sdn 4d	3,770	4,568	14,964
RH45	Sport Suburban wgn 4d 2S V8	4,300	5,545	1,720
RH46	Sport Suburban wgn 4d 3S V8	4,375	5,688	2,528

1978 Engines	bore×stroke	bhp	availability
L4, 104.7	3.13×3.40	70	S-Horizon
L6, 225.0	3.40×4.13	90	O-Volare exc wgn
L6, 225.0	3.40×4.13	100	S-Volare exc wgn
L6, 225.0	3.40×4.13	110	S-Volare wgn, Fury
V8, 318.0	3.91×3.31	140	S-Volare, Fury exc wgns
V8, 318.0	3.91×3.31	155	O-Volare, Fury exc wgns
V8, 360.0	4.00×3.58	155	S-Fury wgns; O-Vol, Fury
V8, 360.0	4.00×3.58	165/175	O-Volare
V8, 360.0	4.00×3.58	170	O-Fury
V8, 400.0	4.34×3.38	190	O-Fury

1979

Horizon (wb 99.2; TC3-96.7)

		Wght	Price	Prod
ML24	TC3 htchbk cpe 3d	2,195	4,864	63,715
ML44	htchbk sdn 5d	2,135	4,469	99,048

Volare (wb 112.7; cpe-108.7)

		Wght	Price	Prod
HL29	spt cpe	3,110	4,387	63,620
HL41	sdn 4d	3,175	4,504	95,383
HL45	wgn 5d 2S	3,435	5,110	50,683

1979 Engines	bore×stroke	bhp	availability
L4, 104.7	3.13×3.40	70	S-Horizon
L6, 225.0	3.40×4.13	100	S-Volare
L6, 225.0	3.40×4.13	110	O-Volare
V8, 318.0	3.91×3.31	135	S-Volare
V8, 360.0	4.00×3.58	195	O-Volare

1980

Horizon (wb 99.2; TC3-96.7)

		Wght	Price	Prod
ML24	TC3 htchbk cpe 3d	2,135	5,681	67,738
ML44	htchbk sdn 5d	2,095	5,526	94,740

Volare (wb 112.7; cpes 108.7)

		Wght	Price	Prod
HE29	Special cpe L6	3,155	5,151	16,475
HE41	Special sdn 4d L6	3,210	5,151	25,509
HL29	cpe	3,170	5,033	17,781
HL41	sdn 4d	3,225	5,150	30,097
HL45	wgn 5d 2S	3,540	5,022	19,910

Gran Fury (wb 118.5)

		Wght	Price	Prod
JL42	sdn 4d	3,562	6,741	15,469
JH42	Salon sdn 4d	3,438	7,116	3,255

1980 Engines	bore×stroke	bhp	availability
L4, 104.7	3.13×3.40	65	S-Horizon
L6, 225.0	3.40×4.13	90	S-Volare, Gran Fury
V8, 318.0	3.91×3.31	120	S-Volare exc Spcl, G. Fury
V8, 360.0	4.00×3.58	130	O-Gran Fury

Pontiac

Pontiac Division of General Motors Corp.
Pontiac, Michigan

Pontiac remains the only General Motors nameplate introduced after the company's founding in 1908 to survive past 1940. It's also the only survivor among GM's four original companion makes, which appeared beginning in the mid-1920s. But Pontiac's future was far from secure in the early Depression years. The first car to bear the name, the Pontiac Six of 1926, quickly proved far more popular than parent Oakland (see entry), and pushed total division sales to over 200,000 units by 1929. Then came the Great Crash and, as everywhere else in the industry, Pontiac sales plummeted, hitting rock-bottom in 1932 at less than 47,000 units. What saved the make was the calm, confident policies of GM president Alfred Sloan, who combined Pontiac and Chevrolet manufacturing facilities in early 1933, thus saving vast amounts in tooling expenses through greater use of shared components. At the same time, he consolidated Buick, Oldsmobile, and Pontiac sales operations, with existing dealers for each make now required to sell the other two as well. These belt-tightening measures were in force through mid-1934 and, in effect, reduced GM to three divisions: Cadillac, Chevrolet, and B-O-P.

The well-styled Pontiac Eight for 1933 turned the marque's fortunes around completely. The division was back over the 200,000 mark by 1937, and would continue as one of the top five or six industry producers through the end of the 1940s. A group of highly competent leaders contributed mightily to this recovery. Among the more notable were former Ford executive William S. "Big Bill" Knudsen; chief engineer Benjamin H. Anibal, father of the Pontiac eight; and studio stylist Frank Hershey, creator of the handsome '33 and subsequent models.

Pontiac continued to capture the majority of division sales through the Oakland's demise in 1931. The 1930-31 line was all six-cylinder, with a conventional inline L-head engine and the usual open and closed body types; sedans and coupes were the most popular. For 1932, the old Oakland and its rough-running V8 became a Pontiac but met with no more success, being outsold by the Sixes by a ratio of over six to one. A major turning point came the following year when the six was replaced by Anibal's newly designed straight eight, which was far more powerful and much smoother than the V8 and thus far more saleable. Initially sized at 223 cubic inches, it was enlarged to 249 cid for 1937, where it would remain through model year 1949. It proved highly reliable, too, and would be the backbone of Pontiac power until the division's first modern high-compression V8 appeared for 1955.

Pontiac left sixes to Chevrolet in 1933-34, but would return to them for 1935. Because of Sloan's corporate consolidation, these cars shared many body panels with Chevrolet yet managed to look distinctly different, thanks largely to the efforts of Hershey and chief body engineer Roy Milner. Hershey convinced company styling director Harley Earl of the need for a more streamlined ap-

1930 Big Six two/four-passenger roadster

1931 Six two-door sedan

1932 V-8 convertible coupe

1933 Eight two-door sedan

1933 Eight convertible coupe

1935 DeLuxe Six four-door sedan

1938 DeLuxe Six two-door trunkback sedan

1937 DeLuxe Eight four-door trunkback sedan

1939 DeLuxe Eight touring sedan

pearance, and accordingly designed a Bentley-type radiator as well as skirted front fenders with little "speed streaks." Milner gave the open models a smooth deck and made their beltline moldings different from Chevrolet's. Combined with the firm's new "Knee-Action" independent front suspension and the new straight eight, the 1933 model was a pleasing package. In performance, a Pontiac Eight wouldn't quite keep up with a Ford or Terraplane, but the difference was insignificant. Pontiac's future was now assured.

With the economy looking up, a broader model line was tried for 1935, and sixes returned on a new 112-inch wheelbase in Standard and Deluxe guise. For 1937-39, the six was enlarged to 222.8 cid and 85 bhp. The price difference between Sixes and the Eights in 1935 was about $100, which was a lot in those days. The Sixes outsold the Eights by a wide margin through the remainder of the decade.

Pontiac styling followed industry trends throughout the period. The 1930-32 models were boxy, upright, and undistinguished. The 1933-34s were among the prettiest medium-price cars of the era. For 1935, the division inherited GM's all-steel "Turret Top" closed body construction and introduced its distinctive "Silver Streak" trim, which started at the cowl and ran straight forward right over the hood and down the grille. It was originated by young designer Virgil Exner, who would later contribute to the early postwar Studebakers and Chrysler's "Forward Look" of the '50s. Exner liked chrome ornamentation, and his Silver Streak hallmark lasted more than 20 years. The 1936-38 models had massive horizontal grilles, yet the vertical streaks continued, resulting in a confused front-

end look. That was cured for 1939 with Harley Earl's "twin catwalk" grilles, located between the fenders and main grille. With all-vertical frontal lines, the '39 Pontiac looked much better than previous models. By this time, smoother pontoon fenders and lower overall height had come in, too.

Pontiac sales kept increasing through 1937. The national

1938 DeLuxe Six sport coupe

1939 Quality DeLuxe Six two-door touring sedan

recession in 1938 cut output, and Pontiac dropped behind Dodge. But the next year, it built almost twice as many cars. Production in 1940 surged up to a quarter-million for the first time, and Pontiac moved back into fifth place, a position it had not held since 1933.

Bill Knudsen decided on a two-series line for 1937-38, and wheelbases were lengthened. Except for a woody wagon on the six-cylinder chassis, body styles were identical for both series: business and sport coupes, cabriolet, two- and four-door sedans and touring sedans, and convertible sedans. The last, eliminated after 1938, was the nicest-looking Pontiac of these years, as well as the most expensive, selling in 1938 for $1310 as a Six and $1358 as an Eight. It's also the rarest body style of this period, so these are naturally among the most sought-after Pontiacs today.

As the recession eased in late 1938, Pontiac brought out a restyled 1939 line with three attractive series. Wheelbases were reduced again and model names altered. A hybrid offering was the Deluxe 120, which used the six-cylinder engine in the 120-inch-wheelbase Deluxe Eight chassis. Both these series shared the same body styles: coupes, sedans, and a convertible. The Quality Deluxe, priced about $50 less than the 120, offered coupes, sedans, and a wagon. There were no engine changes this year and none appeared necessary. The six was reliable and economical; the eight was smoother, perhaps a bit thirstier, but certainly quite powerful. An English road test of a 1938 Eight suggested the car "might be borne along by the wind," so impressive were its quietness and smoothness.

In 1940 there were two lines for each engine: the six-cylinder Special and DeLuxe, and the eight-cylinder DeLuxe and Torpedo. Each series offered four-passenger coupes and four-door sedans. The lineup also included the Special six-cylinder business coupe and wagon, the DeLuxe six-cylinder "cabriolet" convertible, and the DeLuxe eight-cylinder cabriolet and business coupe. Pontiac engines were sturdy, smooth-running units delivering modest performance with reasonable economy.

In keeping with a corporate-wide restyle for 1941, Pontiac adopted higher, crisper fenders embellished with additional silver streaks. A new body style that year was a fastback sedan. Six separate series were offered: DeLuxe, Streamliner, and Custom Torpedos with six- or eight-cylinder engines. The DeLuxe Torpedo comprised the widest range of body styles, including a Metropolitan sedan with blind rear roof quarters that gave a formal appearance. The convertible was appealing, having clean, sleek lines and a soft top uninterrupted by rear side windows, a treatment reminiscent of earlier custom-bodied Packards.

Pontiac sales were good in 1940—217,000 for the model year. Sales were better yet the following year. The DeLuxe series, offering a wide range of body styles, accounted for 150,000 sales. Pontiac was seen as the next step up from Chevy, but was far less luxurious than Oldsmobile or Buick. Trimmed conservatively, it lacked exotic body styles, and was carefully

built to a price. But that price was a competitive one: under $800 for the cheapest model in 1940 and just a little more than that in '41. The highest price in those two years was $1250 for the wood-bodied Custom Torpedo station wagon.

For 1942, Pontiac built about 84,000 cars, all except 15,000 produced in the closing months of 1941. Again Pontiac followed GM styling practice: long front fenders blending into the front doors, rounded "drop-off"

1940 Torpedo Eight four-door sedan

1940 Torpedo Eight sport coupe

1941 Custom Torpedo Eight four-door sedan

1941 Custom Torpedo Eight Deluxe station wagon

rear fenders, and a gaudy grille. Considerable model shuffling occurred. The '42 line included only the Torpedo on the 119-inch wheelbase and Streamliner on the 122-inch wheelbase. Each was available with either a six- or eight-cylinder engine. Streamliner was broken down into standard and Chieftain sub-series, each of which offered a coupe, sedan, and wagon. Chieftains cost $50 more than the standard Streamliner, which was priced higher than the Torpedo. The eight-cylinder option cost only $25 more than the six. Production split about 50/50 between sixes and eights.

While marking time with prewar body styles for 1946-48, Pontiac stylists made each succeeding edition look a little different. The 1946s, which began rolling out of the plant in September 1945, were distinguished by triple chrome fender strips and a massive, full-width grille composed of vertical and horizontal bars. The grille was simplified for 1947, but became busy again for '48: vertical grille bars returned, and a small upper grille carried the Pontiac name. The 1948 was the first Pontiac to bear the Silver Streak nameplate, though the term had been used earlier in reference to styling. Despite name changes and minor appearance alterations, however, these early postwar models were entirely prewar in design and specifications. They used the same engines, the same conventional ladder chassis, the same suspension. Inexplicably, the eight was listed at 104 bhp in 1948 instead of 103, the only change from 1942 specifications.

Pontiac offered just four series in '46: the 119-inch wheelbase Torpedo and the 122-inch wheelbase Streamliner, each available with six- or eight-cylinder engines. There was no Chieftain sub-series as in '42, but body styles were the same as before. The eight cost $30 more than the six throughout the range. Torpedo styles included two- and four-door sedans, business and sport coupes, and the coupe sedan, a five-passenger fastback. Wagons had wooden bodies and were costly to build. All models came only with three-speed manual transmissions as Pontiac had decided to stay away from GM's popular Hydra-Matic for the time being.

All body styles were carried over for '47 except for a deluxe convertible added to the Torpedo line. For the 1948 model year, there was a model realignment. Without altering engine or chassis specifications, Pontiac offered most of its body styles with a choice of "standard" or "deluxe" trim. A deluxe sold for $90 to $120 extra. Chrome fender moldings, gravel guards, and wheel discs were part of the package. All models were available with either six or eight cylinders for a record 30 separate body/engine combinations. The division finally added Hydra-Matic as a $185 option in 1948, and this undoubtedly contributed to Pontiac's 235,000 sales that year. Hydra-Matic was especially important to eight-cylinder buyers who were gradually coming to dominate the ranks of Pontiac customers. Eight-cylinder sales surpassed the sixes in 1947, and were far ahead in '48. Only 50 percent of the sixes were

equipped with Hydra-Matic, compared with 80 percent of the eights.

The increasing sales of Pontiac Eights indicated the division was moving away from the "big Chevy" class and toward the upper-medium-price bracket. In those days, strict market placement was still the rule: each GM make carved out its own price territory. Although Pontiac continued to build sixes until 1955, its eight-cylinder models had become the top sellers long before that. When the division switched to a new overhead-

1941 Custom Torpedo Eight three-passenger coupe

1942 Torpedo Eight four-door sedan

1946 Torpedo Eight convertible

1946 Streamliner Eight Deluxe station wagon

1947 Torpedo Six four-door sedan

1948 Torpedo Eight coupe sedan

1949 Streamliner Eight Deluxe coupe sedan

1950 Chieftain Eight Deluxe Catalina hardtop coupe

1950 Streamliner Eight coupe sedan

1951 Chieftain Eight Super Catalina hardtop coupe

valve V8 in 1955, it simultaneously dropped its six-cylinder engine.

In the corporate-wide restyling of 1949 Pontiac fared extremely well. For the new 120-inch-wheelbase chassis, GM styling chief Harley Earl developed a smooth body for the Silver Streak Six and Silver Streak Eight, each offered in standard and deluxe form as Streamliners or Chieftains. The latter had notchback instead of fastback styling. Deluxe models had extra chrome, including side moldings, rear fender gravel guards, chrome wheel discs, chrome vent wings, and bright windshield trim. Engine displacement remained unchanged from 1948, but a new high-compression head boosted horsepower to 93 bhp for the six and 106 for the eight.

Styling was attractive. A full-width grille was bisected by a single bar and a row of little vertical teeth, a conservative "face" in the automotive world that year. Tradition dictated Exner's silver streaks would continue to adorn the deck and hood. However, the old pontoon-style fenders were replaced by free-flowing front fenders integral with the bodysides. Beltline and roofline were lower than those of any Pontiac that had gone before. Though the '49s looked lighter than the '48s,

they actually weighed a bit more. Performance stayed about the same, despite the small horsepower increase.

Inflation was an economic reality in the late '40s, and Pontiac prices rose considerably in 1949. The most expensive convertible model increased by nearly $200 over 1948. The woody wagon now exceeded $2600. The new metal-bodied station wagon was more practical than the woody though, and outsold it. Pontiac was a pioneer of this body style, along with Plymouth and Oldsmobile, and dropped its wood-bodied wagons after '49.

During the '50s, Pontiac usually built the right cars at the right time. When buyers began passing up six-cylinder medium-priced cars, Pontiac wisely switched to V8s only; at the height of the horsepower race, Pontiac brought out the Bonneville. For most of the decade, the division maintained competitive prices, which helped win sales, especially from Plymouth and Dodge.

Pontiacs of the early '50s still offered six- or eight-cylinder engines in the usual wide array of body styles. For 1950 there were two- and four-door sedans, business and club coupes, all-steel wagons, hardtops, convertibles, and two- and four-door Streamliner fastbacks. Styling was a facelift of the all-new '49

1952 Chieftain Eight Deluxe four-door sedan

1953 Chieftain Eight Custom Catalina hardtop coupe

1954 Star Chief Custom Catalina hardtop coupe

design. The illuminated countenance of Chief Pontiac was continued as a hood mascot. Optional Hydra-Matic drive was offered at $158. This was also the first year for a Pontiac hardtop, the Catalina, offered in four varieties. By the end of the year, Catalinas were accounting for some nine percent of total production.

Although 1951 proved less successful in sales volume, it was by no means disappointing to Pontiac. Output that year was the second-best in the division's history. (On August 11, the four-millionth Pontiac was built.) The Streamliner fastback two-door sedan, the sole holdover of that style from 1950, was dropped in the spring of '51. Other models were altered little from those of the year before, except for a new "V" grille motif.

Pontiac dropped its coupe bodies for 1952, reducing both Six and Eight series to sedans, four-door wagons, Catalinas, and convertibles. Within each line there were still three separate trim levels, standard, DeLuxe, and Super DeLuxe. This was the last year for the 1949 design, which would be replaced by a new Chieftain Six and Eight on a 122-inch wheelbase. Korean War restrictions and a nationwide steel strike slowed 1952 production to 271,000 cars, but Pontiac remained in fifth place.

Buying trends were clear as the 1953 models made their debut. Catalina hardtops, for example, were accounting for over 20 percent of volume, and Hydra-Matic installations had climbed to 84 percent. As a result, the '53s bore a distinct resemblance to earlier styles, but were larger in almost every dimension. New features were a kick-up rear fender line (Pontiac fenders had tapered downward in the past), a lower and more streamlined grille, upright-winged "chief" hood ornament, and a one-piece windshield. Mechanical improvements included optional power steering. Hydra-Matic models had an especially low rear axle ratio of 3.03:1, which gave smooth top-range performance. A fire in the Hydra-Matic plant in mid-1953 shortened supplies, however, so about 18,500 Pontiacs were fitted with Chevrolet's Powerglide in '53 and '54. Pontiac did extremely well for model year 1953, producing nearly 419,000 cars.

The 1954 models were facelifted '53s, with revised side moldings and a narrow scoop built into the central grille bar. The new top-line series that year was the luxury Star Chief in sedans, hardtop, and convertible form.

A big change was hinted at in early 1954: Pontiac's first modern overhead-valve V8. Known as the Strato Streak, it produced 180 bhp, or 200 bhp with optional four-barrel carburetor. Original displacement was 287.2 cubic inches, but it was capable of more and soon grew to over 300 cid. A lively, strong, conventional design with five main bearings, it was up to date, oversquare, and ran on regular gas.

Of course, there was more for 1955 besides a new engine. Pontiac claimed 109 new features altogether, including extensively revised styling and an improved chassis. The lineup consisted of Chieftain and Star Chief series; both featured a wraparound windshield, cowl ventilation, new colors and two-tone combinations, tubeless tires, and a 12-volt electrical system. The 122-inch-wheelbase Chieftain comprised an 860 series of sedans and wagons, and an 870 line of sedans, wagons, and Catalina hardtop. Chieftains included an exotic new hardtop-styled Safari two-door wagon based on the Chevrolet Nomad. Carl Renner, Chevrolet stylist said: "When Pontiac saw [the Nomad] they felt they could do something with it . . . Management wanted it for the Pontiac line—so it worked out." Safaris retained this styling through 1957. They were priced higher than equivalent Nomads, of course, and sold in fewer numbers.

On balance, 1955 rated as a vintage year for Pontiac. The division built a record 553,000 cars. The lineup was a solid hit with both public and dealers. But Pontiac had some rough times in the later 1950s. The division didn't equal this volume again until 1963, after which it began setting new sales records. The reason was a change in the market. Buick's Special and Oldsmobile's standard 88 were more competitively priced than they'd been before, and demand for lower-medium-price cars was shrinking as import sales steadily increased. Pontiac did not tend to capture the enthusiasm of buyers in the

Pontiac

1956-58 period, even though its cars were certainly competitive in these years, and faster than ever.

A mild facelift and the addition of four-door hardtops marked 1956. Styling was less distinctive (Tom McCahill said the '56 looked like "it had been born on its nose"). Though the V8 had grown to 316.6 cid, it didn't pack an extraordinary amount of power—only 227 bhp maximum in the Star Chief. Unfortunately, too, the cars had picked up a reputation for a hard ride.

GM appointed Semon E. "Bunky" Knudsen as Pontiac general manager, told him to do what he could with the '55–'56 engineering, and hoped for the best in '57. Knudsen hustled. Though sticking with the same wheelbase, the '57s had very long rear springs mounted in rubber shackles. Ball-joint front suspension, adopted by other GM divisions, was not used, however. New 14-inch tires replaced the previous 15-inchers, and a foot pedal parking brake was instituted, along with an op-

1955 Star Chief convertible

1956 Star Chief Custom Safari station wagon

1957 Bonneville convertible

1957 Star Chief Custom four-door sedan

1958 Bonneville hardtop coupe

1959 Catalina Vista hardtop sedan

1959 Catalina Sport hardtop coupe

Bonneville Special show car of 1954

tional automatic antenna. The massive buck-toothed grille was revised, two-toning switched from its half-a-car 1956 pattern to a simpler sweep-spear motif, and Silver Streak exterior trim was banished. There was a new 347 V8—and Bunky had his day by creating the fast and flashy Bonneville.

Providing 300 bhp by way of fuel injection, hydraulic lifters, and racing cam, this $5782 convertible was the fastest Pontiac in history. It was even faster with optional Tri-Power (three two-barrel carbs). A fuel-injected Bonneville was timed at 18 seconds for the standing quarter-mile; one with Tri-Power did the same leap in 16.8. Though fuel injection never proved popular, Bonneville wasn't a hot seller mainly because of its price—only 630 were sold. But it did give the division a whole new performance image. Corporate racing was being played down, however. A few '57 Pontiacs raced with distinction in NASCAR, but were strictly private entries. Yet lack of race victories didn't affect sales. Chevy, Olds, and Buick all suffered downturns from 1956 (as Chrysler products filled the gap), but Pontiac built about 333,000 of its '57 cars and moved to within 51,000 units of Olds.

An all-new body should have brought added success in '58, but a recession set in and held the division's production to only 217,000 units. Compared to most GM products that year, Pontiac was really well-styled. A simpler, full-width grille was adopted, quad headlights appeared, and the side spear was wider and now concave. Bodies were lower, but not much longer or wider; wheelbases were unchanged. No fewer than seven Catalina hardtops were offered with two or four doors. Bonneville became a regular series with about 12,000 convertibles and hardtops sold.

For 1959, Pontiac shared inner body panels with Chevrolet, Buick, and Olds—and built some of the best-looking cars around. The first of the famous split grilles was introduced, along with modest twin-fin rear fenders and minimal side trim—plus the new Wide-Track chassis. The V8 was puffed up to 389 cid and delivered 315 bhp with Tri-Power. Pontiac also made a new Tempest 420E unit for economy-minded buyers, an engine that could deliver 20 miles per gallon if driven prudently. The old Chieftain and Super Chief were discontinued, replaced by the Catalina series on the 122 wheelbase; Star Chief and Bonneville shared a 124-inch chassis. Bonneville was a real hit, and some 82,000 were sold in '59.

During the '50s, Pontiac produced a number of interesting one-offs. The smooth-looking Strato Streak of 1954 was a harbinger of pillarless four-doors to come for '56. Also shown in '54 was the first Bonneville, a Corvette-like two-seater with a canopy-type cockpit and a 100-inch wheelbase. Both of these cars were fitted with straight eights. The Strato-Star of 1955 was a two-door, four-seat hardtop that previewed '56 styling. Metallic silver paint and a red leather and brushed aluminum interior were featured, as was flow-through ventilation and the new ohv V8. The wildest show car was the 1956 Club de Mer with "twin pod" seating and dual bubble windshields. Standing only 38.4 inches high, its anodized-aluminum body was painted Cerulean blue (Harley Earl's favorite color).

After being honored for its '59 line, Pontiac was named Car of the Year three more times by *Motor Trend* magazine in the 1960s. Some say that award is often breathlessly bestowed on ordinary cars or worse, but Pontiac truly deserved the title. Piloted by engineering-oriented general managers like Knudsen and Elliot M. (Pete) Estes (later to become GM president), Pontiac Division became the home of high performance. The early-'50s image of staid family cars vanished. Again and again, Pontiac introduced exciting automobiles: the unique '61 Tempest, the personal-luxury '62 Grand Prix, the swift and nimble '64 GTO, the singular '66 Tempest Sprint with its overhead-cam six, and the sporty '67 Firebird. All were interesting cars; some were great cars.

Most of Pontiac's revolutionary news was made by the compact Tempest, and the intermediate into which it later evolved. The original '61 version won the Car of the Year award for three reasons: GM's first postwar four-cylinder engine, a radical and unprecedented flexible driveshaft, and a transaxle (rear-mounted transmission and independent link-type rear suspension). *Motor Trend* said the new Tempest "sets many new trends and unquestionably is a prototype of the American car for the Sixties," a summary that was wrong on at least one count. Nobody copied its driveshaft or transaxle (unless we count the Porsche 928 of 18 years later), and not until the late 1970s was there a strong shift in Detroit to four-cylinder engines. The public bought many 1961-63 Tempests, but their more conventional successors did far better. The 195-cid four, created by chopping one cylinder bank from the 389 V8, was abandoned in '64 for an inline six—practical, but hardly innovative.

The Tempest's driveshaft could be likened to a speedometer cable in that it transmitted rotary action through a bend, or at least a slight curve. It was a long torsion bar bent in an arc under the floor—thin, but lightly stressed. Mounted on bearings, it was permanently lubricated inside a steel case. The bent shaft eliminated the floor hump in the front, but not in the rear. It also eliminated universal joints and allowed for softer engine mounts giving better isolation of vibration from the interior.

The Tempest transaxle was a first for Detroit (if not the world). Aside from allowing for an ostensibly superior independent rear suspension, it made the Tempest less nose-heavy than its corporate cousins, the Olds F-85 or Buick Special. At the same time, the suspension made the car prone to oversteer, which could be especially alarming on wet roads. Yet the Tempest handled well generally, and tracked safely in mud and snow. Its unit body/chassis had a 112-inch wheelbase that was the standard B-O-P compact platform for 1961-63.

The four-cylinder engine came in several stages of

tune (regular or premium gas) and was available with manual and automatic transmission. Over its three-year-period, horsepower ranged from 110 to 166 bhp. The 1961-62 models were also offered with Buick's 155/185-bhp, 215 V8 as an option. A 260-bhp 326 debuted for '63, making Tempest a quick car, capable of 0–60 mph times of 9.5 seconds and a top speed of 115 mph. At first, there was only one series of two-door and four-door sedans and a Safari wagon. A coupe and convertible were added for '62 in deluxe and LeMans versions. A separate LeMans series was fielded for '63 with a bucket-seat coupe and convertible offering plusher interiors. Styling didn't change much during Tempest's early years. A twin semi-oval grille was used for 1961, a full-width three-section design for '62. The twin grille returned for 1963 along with squarer body lines. For '64, GM lengthened its compact wheelbase to 115 inches, and Pontiac redesigned the Tempest, using taut, geo-

metric lines. Good styling and numerous high-performance models won Pontiac its second Car of the Year award in 1965.

Destined for greatness was a mid-1964 introduction, the Tempest GTO, the first of what soon became known as the "muscle cars." The nickname was well taken. Equipped with the proper options, a GTO could deliver unprecedented performance for a six-passenger automobile. Of course, it could be ordered in relatively mild-mannered form with automatic transmission, a 335-bhp engine, and so on. Enthusiasts, however, learned to use the option book wisely. The base was a Tempest LeMans coupe priced at $2500. The GTO package—floorshift, 389-cid engine, quick steering, stiff shocks, dual exhaust, and premium tires—cost about $300. The four-speed gearbox was $188 more. Another $75 bought a package comprising metallic brake linings, heavy-duty radiator, and limited-slip differential. And

1961 Tempest LeMans sport coupe (prototype)

1964 Tempest GTO sport coupe

1966 LeMans sport coupe

1968 LeMans hardtop sedan

1969 GTO hardtop coupe

1970 GTO hardtop coupe

an additional $115 would buy a 360-bhp engine. At that point, all you needed was a lead foot and lots of gasoline.

Sports-car folk took umbrage at Pontiac's use of GTO (gran turismo omologato), an international term for production-class racing cars. *Car and Driver* magazine brazenly took issue with the critics by comparing Pontiac's GTO with Ferrari's. A good Pontiac, they said, would trim the Ferrari in a drag race and lose on a road course. But "with the addition of NASCAR road racing suspension, the Pontiac will take the measure of any Ferrari other than prototype racing cars . . . The Ferrari costs $20,000. With every conceivable option on a GTO, it would be difficult to spend more than $3800. That's a bargain."

The 115-inch-wheelbase LeMans and Tempest changed little in ensuing years. Vertical headlights and crisp styling for a three-inch-longer body appeared for 1966. "Coke-bottle" rear fenders and a divided vertical-bar grille were featured for '67. In 1968, the cars adopted GM's dual wheelbases of 116 inches for four-doors and 112 inches for two-doors, and borrowed styling themes from the big Pontiacs such as a large bumper/grille. The GTO's standard engine that year was a 400-cid V8 pumping out 350 bhp. It could also be ordered with 360 bhp by way of a Ram-Air hood scoop. The GTO featured an energy-absorbing front bumper made of Endura rubber that was neatly blended into the front-end styling. For performance mainly, Pontiac won its fourth Car of the Year award in 1968. Its 1969 intermediates were facelifted and cleaner than the '68s. The hottest GTO was now "The Judge" with a 366-bhp Ram-Air V8 and three-speed manual gearbox with Hurst shifter. The 1970s had all-new styling with changes at the front and rear, plus new bumpers and doors. The end result was a curvy, heavier-looking Tempest, GTO, LeMans, and LeMans Sport. Collectors have since tended to prefer the tidier 1964-69 models.

The 1964-65 Tempest's 140-bhp Oldsmobile six gave way to a surprise engine for '66: an overhead-cam six. The first performance six since the Hudson Hornet, and not in a league with hairier GTOs, the ohc was nevertheless satisfying. Typical acceleration for the Sprint version was 0 to 60 in 10 seconds flat and a top speed of 115 mph. With a capacity of 230 cid, it developed either 165 bhp standard or 207 in Sprint form (with Rochester Quadra-Jet carburetor, hotter valve timing, and double valve springs). The crankshaft had seven main bearings; the camshaft was driven by a fiberglass-reinforced notched belt rather than conventional chain or gear drive. The optional four-speed transmission, clean styling, and an interior that featured bucket seats and console gave the Sprint the look and feel of a true grand touring car. But its life span was short. By 1968, the Tempest had grown bulky, and by 1970, the engine had been emasculated by emission controls and detuning and was soon discontinued.

Since Pontiac had such a good reputation for performance and handling, division managers knew that

1967 Firebird hardtop coupe

1968 Firebird H.O. hardtop coupe

1969 Firebird convertible

1970 Firebird Formula 400 hardtop coupe

the Firebird "ponycar," based on the Chevrolet Camaro, had to be something special. Although it used the Camaro's bodyshell and 108-inch wheelbase, Firebird had its own divided grille and an optional 400-cid V8. Optional engines included the ohc six, which made it a sprightly yet economical performer. Changes were

1960 Catalina Vista hardtop sedan

1962 Catalina Vista hardtop sedan

1963 Bonneville convertible

1965 Bonneville convertible

1965 Catalina 2+2 convertible

1967 Catalina hardtop sedan

slight in subsequent model years. Side marker lights were added in 1968. The lower body and grille were revised, and a host of government-ordered safety features were added in '69. Convertibles continued to be offered until Firebird was redesigned with coupe-only bodywork for 1970. That styling, timeless and lovely, was still around 10 years later—albeit with much tamer performance than a decade before. In the 1967-70 period, before federal regulations took serious performance tolls, Firebirds rarely sold for more than $3500. They were performance cars designed to be enjoyed by good drivers.

Despite the publicity won by Pontiac's smaller models, its full-size cars were among the better-styled, better-handling standard-size cars of the decade. The public responded enthusiastically. Model year production for 1960 had been about 400,000. By 1969, the division

was building close to half a million full-size sedans, hardtops, convertibles, and wagons. In model year output, Pontiac ran third to Chevrolet and Ford from 1962 through 1970, and the big cars had a lot to do with this success.

Pontiac originally had a four-model lineup. The 1960-61 entries, from bottom to top, consisted of Catalina, Ventura, Star Chief, and Bonneville. In 1962, the Ventura was dropped; its place was taken by the bucket-seated, limited-edition Grand Prix. This elegantly tailored hardtop coupe, with crisp styling and svelte good looks, rapidly gained in popularity. By 1969, it was outselling all large Pontiac models except Catalina—with a single body style. (A convertible, offered in 1967 only, is now a collector's item since only 5,856 were built.)

Design of the standard-size cars kept improving, at

1968 Grand Prix hardtop coupe

1968 Catalina hardtop coupe

1969 Grand Prix Model J hardtop coupe

1969 Bonneville convertible

1970 Bonneville hardtop sedan

1970 Grand Prix Model SJ hardtop coupe

least through 1966. The distinctive split grille, first introduced in '59 and dropped for '60, was reintroduced in 1961. Clean machines with narrow, split grilles were the rule for 1963-64. The '65s were equally well executed, but had a prominent, bulging grille that was toned down slightly in 1966. Bulkier designs with heavy, curved rear fenders arrived in '67, and a huge bumper/grille was used in '68. The front end was greatly improved for 1969-70. Catalina and Grand Prix always rode the smaller Pontiac wheelbase. Bonnevilles, Star Chiefs, and Executives rode the longer one. Each model, separated from the others by a few hundred dollars, offered a comprehensive range of body styles.

Pontiac's big-car engines, though offered with numerous horsepower ratings, came in just two sizes throughout the '60s. The smaller was a 389-cid V8 (400 cid after 1966). Standard on all models, its horsepower ranged from 215 on up to 350, the latter version being standard on the 1967-70 Grand Prix. The larger engine, optional on most large Pontiacs, was a 421-cid unit in

1963-66, and 428 until 1970 when it was replaced by a 455. It began with 353 bhp in '63 and reached 376 by '67. A 421-cid, 427-bhp monster was offered in 1963-64 for a special drag racing Catalina with aluminum body panels, plastic side windows, and a drilled-out frame.

Unfortunately, the ensuing decade would prove to be one of the most difficult in division history. An attempt to outproduce and outprice Chevy (a decision some insiders have credited to the DeLorean regime of the late '60s) while simultaneously reaching up into Buick and Oldsmobile territory caused quality control to slip badly. It also resulted in a confusing succession of models that left many buyers wondering just what a Pontiac was. Even worse than a blurred image, sales sagged. For example, Olds nosed out Pontiac in 1973 model year registrations by a little more than 1300 units, the first time that had happened since 1958. By 1975, even Buick was a threat to Pontiac's traditional number-three spot. At the end of the decade, Pontiac trailed Buick by 95,000 units; the gap with Oldsmobile was 195,000.

The Firebird was one of the least changed U.S. cars of

the '70s. The brilliant second-generation design launched for "1970½" was successfully—and handsomely—updated just three times during the decade: 1974, 1977, and 1979. Like Chevy's Camaro, it almost died at one point due to corporate doubts about the future of performance cars, aggravated by a factory strike in 1972 that severely cut volume. But Pontiac kept the faith not only in the Firebird itself but in the all-out high-performance Trans Am, and reaped just rewards. While the hottest Camaro, the Z 28, was temporarily dropped for 1975-76, the T/A lived on—a factory hot rod that refused to die. As the most serious entry in the Pontiac line, it kept interest alive in performance cars, an interest that would begin to blossom again in the late '70s and early '80s. It was a feat that only added to the T/A's growing mystique. It also added to sales, and this model moved from being a peripheral seller (only 2116 units for '71) to the most popular Firebird of all (over 93,000 for '78). We should also not forget that Pontiac fielded the same four-model lineup each year—base coupe, luxury Esprit, roadworthy Formula, and T/A—while Chevy fiddled with Camaro offerings. The later Formula and T/A went on a horsepower diet out of deference to the government's corporate average fuel economy (CAFE) mandates, but they never relinquished their V8s and never failed to provide lively motoring. For 1980, a turbocharged 301 V8 was issued, offering only a bit less go than the big-blocks of old while being somewhat easier on gasoline.

Higher-than-ever fuel prices were only one legacy of the Arab oil embargo, but gas had been getting more expensive for a long time. In fact, one small sign of the energy crisis to come was renewed buyer interest for smaller, thriftier cars in the early '70s. At that time, Pontiac had nothing below the intermediate LeMans in size, so it drafted Chevrolet's compact Nova, grafted on a different nose, and called it Ventura II. Most of the comments made about the Nova in these years (see "Chevrolet") apply equally to this corporate cousin (which wasn't launched until March 1971 and therefore had a relatively slow start in sales).For 1974, the hallowed GTO was based on the Ventura platform instead of the mid-size LeMans—and you could almost hear the hollering from Hoboken to Pasadena. This was a GTO in name only, basically a Sprint with hood scoop, different grille, and standard 350 V8, priced $195 higher. Interestingly enough, Pontiac moved a bit more than 7000 of these pretenders, then rang down the curtain on a great performance tradition—a year too late.

Along with GM's other X-body compacts, Ventura adopted a more European look for 1975—and promptly withered on the vine. Inept marketing tactics and mediocre build quality were probably as much to blame here as competition from within the Pontiac line and elsewhere. An upmarket version called Phoenix arrived at mid-model year 1977, with plusher interiors and a busier front end, and the Ventura name vanished the following year. Unhappily, Phoenix was also an also-ran, and remained so even when it was switched to GM's sprightly new front-drive X-body platform for 1980.

Another "lend-lease" deal with Chevrolet Motor Division produced the subcompact Astre, introduced to the U.S.

1971 Firebird Trans Am sport coupe

1971 Catalina hardtop coupe

1971 Ventura II two-door sedan

1972 Grand Ville hardtop sedan

1972 LeMans hardtop coupe with GTO option

1972 Grand Prix SJ hardtop coupe

1973 Luxury LeMans Colonnade hardtop coupe

1973 Ventura Custom two-door sedan with Sprint option

1973 Grand Prix SJ coupe

1974 Grand Am Colonnade hardtop coupe

1974 Firebird Esprit sport coupe

1974 Ventura two-door sedan with GTO option

1975 Grand Prix SJ coupe

for 1975 (although it had been sold in Canada per GM practice for a few years before it came here). It was little more than a badge-engineered version of the ill-starred Chevy Vega and, predictably, shared most of its many faults. Pontiac varied the model program a bit with price-leader S and semi-sporty SJ models. There was also a GT package option, combining the low-line interior with the SJ's performance and handling mods. In its final season, 1977, the Astre was treated to Pontiac's then-new

"Iron Duke" four, a nickname chosen partly to overcome the horrendous durability reputation of the all-aluminum Vega unit.

Chevy had introduced its Vega-based Monza sporty coupe for 1975, and it was only a matter of time before Pontiac got in on this act. The time came with model year 1976. However, unlike other versions of the corporate H-special platform, the new Sunbird was offered initially only as the notchback two-door known at Chevy as the Monza

1975 Astre hatchback coupe with GT option

1976 Sunbird coupe

1976 Grand LeMans coupe

1976 Grand Prix LJ coupe

1976 Bonneville coupe with Landau option

1976 Firebird Limited Edition (50th Anniversary) Trans Am

1977 Bonneville coupe

1978 Phoenix LJ four-door sedan

Towne Coupe. The 2+2 fastback body was added for 1978 as the Sunbird Sport Hatch, along with the pretty little three-door wagon from the now-discontinued Vega/ Astre line. Bolstered by various option groups, including a sporty Formula package, the Sunbird sold respectably, but it was not the big sales success the division had hoped for. It carried on with few changes through model year 1981, the final cars sold actually being 1980 leftovers.

The history of Pontiac's intermediates and standard-size cars of the '70s reads with about as much excitement as a dictionary. In basic design, all of these were neither better nor worse than their GM counterparts, except possibly for more contrived styling and workmanship that always seemed a half-notch below that of other divisions. However, the more sensible late-'70s offerings were definitely more attractive and better suited to the times than comparable Ford and Chrysler products. It was here that Pontiac seemed to forget performance in its eagerness to play

1978 Firebird Trans Am coupe

1980 Phoenix LJ coupe

1978 Grand Prix coupe

1980 Bonneville Brougham four-door sedan

1979 Phoenix LJ coupe with Landau option

1980 Firebird Trans Am Turbo coupe

1979 LeMans Grand Am coupe

1980 Grand LeMans four-door sedan

up luxury and convenience.

There was one interesting exception, however: the Grand Am. Introduced in 1973, it was billed as combining Grand Prix luxury with Trans Am performance, hence the name. It was largely the creation of assistant chief engineer Bill Collins, who had been heavily involved with the early GTO, and chassis wizard John Seaton. The idea was to turn the ordinary LeMans into a close approximation of European sports sedans like the Mercedes-Benz 250/280 and the BMW Bavaria, but selling at a third to one-half less. While some features strained at mimickry (the Mercedes-style jumbo-hub steering wheel, for instance), the "G/A" was on balance, one of the most impressive big Detroit cars of the entire decade. Of course, it failed to make any real impression in a market where most buyers were interested in either everyday transportation or as much glitz as their money would buy. The Grand Am scored only about 43,000 sales (most of them

two-doors) in its debut year. That plummeted to 17,000 the next year, then to 11,000 or so for '75. To no one's surprise, Pontiac dropped this model like a hot potato. Curiously, the name reappeared in the downsized LeMans line for '78, but this Grand Am was nowhere nearly as "special" and would prove similarly short-lived.

One of Pontiac's more notable successes in the '70s was the personal-luxury Grand Prix, which in some years led the line in individual model sales. The handsome 1969-70 design was carried on through 1972. Although horsepower went down a little in the last two years, these cars could still be surprising performers when equipped with the big-block V8s. The GP continued as essentially a stretched-wheelbase derivative of the corporate A-body intermediate through the 1973-77 "Colonnade" generation, similar in this respect to Chevy's Monte Carlo. A vertical grille and a more formal roofline always set it apart from the ordinary LeMans, as did more standard amenities and higher prices. Interestingly, the Grand Prix set a new all-time sales record in the final year for this design, 1977, with close to 288,500 deliveries. Even more interestingly, downsizing had only a minor effect on the car's appeal, the 1978 models finding 228,000 buyers. Clearly, the GP succeeded in a way that the gussied-up LeMans series didn't. Without it, Pontiac wouldn't have weathered the decade's economic ups and downs nearly as well.

Pontiac

1930

6-29 Big Six (wb 110.0)	Wght	Price	Prod*
rdstr 4P	2,394	775	—
phaeton 5P	2,407	825	—
std cpe 2P	2,532	745	—
sdn 2d	2,595	745	—
sdn 4d	2,717	845	—

6-30 Big Six (wb 110.0)			
rdstr 2-4P	2,410	665	—
phaeton 5P	2,475	695	—
std cpe 2P	2,580	665	—
spt cpe 2-4P	2,655	725	—
sdn 2d	2,695	665	—
sdn 4d	2,745	725	—
Custom sdn 4d	2,785	785	—

*Total production: 62,888. Pontiac does not state whether this is model or calendar year.

1930 Engine	bore×stroke	bhp	availability
L6, 200.0	3.31×3.88	60	S-all

1931

401 Six (wb 112.0)	Wght	Price	Prod*
cpe 2P	2,670	675	—
spt cpe 2-4P	2,730	715	—
conv cpe 2-4P	2,710	745	—
sdn 2d	2,765	675	—
sdn 4d	2,845	745	—
Custom sdn 4d	2,855	785	—

*Total production: 84,708. Pontiac does not state whether this is model or calendar year.

1931 Engine	bore×stroke	bhp	availability
L6, 200.0	3.31×3.88	60	S-all

1932

402 Six (wb 114.0)—39,059 built	Wght	Price	Prod
std cpe 2P	2,765	635	—
spt cpe 2-4P	2,810	715	—
conv cpe 2-4P	2,770	765	—
sdn 2d	2,870	645	—
sdn 4d	2,960	725	—
Custom sdn 4d	2,965	795	—

302 V-8 (wb 117.0)—6,281 built			
std cpe 2P	3,145	845	—
spt cpe 2-4P	3,205	925	—
conv cpe 2-4P	3,165	945	—
sdn 2d	3,225	845	—
sdn 4d	3,310	945	—
Custom sdn 4d	3,335	1,025	—

1932 Engines	bore×stroke	bhp	availability
L6, 200.0	3.31×3.88	65	S-402
V8, 251.0	3.44×3.38	85	S-302

1933—90,198 built

601 Eight (wb 115.0)	Wght	Price	Prod
rdstr 2-4P	2,675	585	—
cpe 2P	2,865	635	—
spt cpe 2-4P	2,930	670	—
conv cpe 2-4P	2,905	695	—
touring sdn 4d	2,995	675	—
sdn 2d	2,945	635	—
sdn 4d	3,020	695	—

1933 Engine	bore×stroke	bhp	availability
L8, 223.4	3.19×3.50	77	S-all

1934—78,859 built

603 Eight (wb 117.5)	Wght	Price	Prod
cpe 2P	3,185	675	—
spt cpe 2-4P	3,260	725	—
cabriolet 2-4P	3,225	765	—
sdn 2d	3,280	705	—
sdn 2d T/B	3,300	745	—
sdn 4d	3,350	765	—
sdn 4d T/B	3,405	805	—

1934 Engine	bore×stroke	bhp	availability
L8, 223.4	3.19×3.50	84	S-all

1935

701 Standard Six (wb 112.0)—48,302 built	Wght	Price	Prod
cpe 2P	3,065	615	—
sdn 2d T/B	3,195	695	—
sdn 2d	3,195	665	—
touring sdn 4d T/B	3,245	745	—
sdn 4d	3,245	715	—

701 DeLuxe Six (wb 112.0)—36,032 built			
cpe 2P	3,125	675	—
spt cpe 2-4P	3,150	725	—
cabriolet 2-4P	3,180	775	—
sdn 2d T/B	3,245	745	—
sdn 2d	3,245	715	—
touring sdn 4d T/B	3,300	795	—
sdn 4d	3,300	765	—

605 Eight (wb 116.6)—44,134 built			
cpe 2P	3,260	730	—
spt cpe 2-4P	3,290	780	—
cabriolet 2-4P	3,305	840	—
sdn 2d T/B	3,400	805	—
sdn 2d	3,400	775	—
touring sdn 4d T/B	3,450	860	—
sdn 4d	3,450	830	—

1935 Engines	bore×stroke	bhp	availability
L6, 208.0	3.38×3.88	80	S-701
L8, 223.4	3.19×3.50	84	S-605

1936

6BB Master Silver Streak (wb 112.0)—93,475 built	Wght	Price	Prod
cpe 2P	3,085	615	—
spt cpe 2-4P	3,120	675	—
cabriolet 2-4P	3,125	760	—
sdn 2d	3,195	675	—
touring sdn 2d T/B	3,195	700	—
sdn 4d	3,235	720	—
touring sdn 4d T/B	3,245	745	—

6BA DeLuxe Silver Streak (wb 112.0)—44,040 built			
cpe 2P	3,130	665	—
spt cpe 2-4P	3,165	720	—
cabriolet 2-4P	3,200	810	—
sdn 2d	3,265	720	—
touring sdn 2d T/B	3,270	745	—
sdn 4d	3,300	770	—
touring sdn 4d T/B	3,300	795	—

8BA DeLuxe Eight Silver Streak (wb 116.0)—38,755 built			
cpe 2P	3,250	730	—
cpt cpe 2-4P	3,285	785	—
cabriolet 2-4P	3,335	855	—
sdn 2d	3,390	770	—
touring sdn 2d T/B	3,390	795	—
sdn 4d	3,415	815	—
touring sdn 4d T/B	3,420	840	—

1936 Engines	bore×stroke	bhp	availability
L6, 208.0	3.38×3.88	80	S-6BA,6BB
L8, 232.3	3.25×3.50	87	S-Eight

1937

6CA DeLuxe Six (wb 117.0)—179,244 built	Wght	Price	Prod
cpe 2P	3,165	781	—
spt cpe 2-4P	3,165	853	—
cabriolet 2-4P	3,250	945	—
sdn 2d	3,240	830	—
touring sdn 2d T/B	3,240	855	—
sdn 4d	3,265	881	—
touring sdn 4d T/B	3,275	906	—
conv sdn 5P	3,375	1,197	—
wgn 4d	3,340	992	—

8CA DeLuxe Eight (wb 122.0)—56,945 built			
cpe 2P	3,305	857	—
spt cpe 2-4P	3,305	913	—
cabriolet 2-4P	3,360	985	—
sdn 2d	3,385	893	—
touring sdn 2d T/B	3,380	919	—
sdn 4d	3,410	939	—
touring sdn 4d T/B	3,400	965	—
conv sdn 5P	3,505	1,235	—

1937 Engines	bore×stroke	bhp	availability
L6, 222.7	3.44×4.00	85	S-Six
L8, 248.9	3.25×3.75	100	S-Eight

1938

6DA DeLuxe Six (wb 117.0)—77,713 built	Wght	Price	Prod
cpe 2P	3,190	835	—
spt cpe 2-4P	3,200	891	—
cabriolet 2-4P	3,285	993	—
sdn 2d	3,265	865	—
touring sdn 2d T/B	3,265	891	—
sdn 4d	3,295	916	—
touring sdn 4d T/B	3,280	942	—
conv sdn 5P	3,410	1,310	—
wgn 4d	3,420	1,110	—

8DA DeLuxe Eight (wb 122.0)—19,426 built			
cpe 2P	3,320	898	—
spt cpe 2-4P	3,325	955	—
cabriolet 2-4P	3,390	1,057	—
sdn 2d	3,395	934	—
touring sdn 2d T/B	3,385	960	—
sdn 4d	3,415	980	—
touring sdn 4d T/B	3,410	1,006	—
conv sdn 5P	3,530	1,353	—

1938 Engines	bore×stroke	bhp	availability
L6, 222.7	3.44×4.00	85	S-Six
L8, 248.9	3.25×3.75	100	S-Eight

1939

6EA Quality DeLuxe (wb 115.0)—55,736 built	Wght	Price	Prod
cpe 3P	2,875	758	—
spt cpe 5P	2,920	809	—
touring sdn 2d T/B	2,965	820	—
touring sdn 4d T/B	3,000	866	—
wgn 4d	3,175	990	—

6EB DeLuxe 120 (wb 120.0)—53,830 built			
cpe 3P	3,020	814	—
spt cpe 5P	3,055	865	—
conv cpe 5P	3,155	993	—
touring sdn 2d T/B	3,115	871	—
touring sdn 4d T/B	3,165	922	—

8EA DeLuxe Eight (wb 120.0)—34,774 built			
cpe 3P	3,105	862	—
spt cpe 5P	3,165	913	—
conv cpe 5P	3,250	1,046	—
touring sdn 2d T/B	3,225	919	—
touring sdn 4d T/B	3,265	970	—

1939 Engines	bore×stroke	bhp	availability
L6, 222.7	3.44×4.00	85	S-6EA,6EB
L8, 248.9	3.25×3.75	100	S-Eight

Pontiac Specifications

1940

25HA Special Six (wb 117.0)—106,892 built

	Wght	Price	Prod
cpe 3P	3,060	783	—
spt cpe 4P	3,045	819	—
sdn 2d	3,095	830	—
wgn 4d, 8P	3,295	1,015	—
sdn 4d	3,125	876	—

26HB DeLuxe Six (wb 120.0)—58,452 built

	Wght	Price	Prod
cpe 3P	3,115	835	—
spt cpe 4P	3,105	876	—
cabriolet (conv)	3,190	1,003	—
sdn 2d	3,170	881	—
sdn 4d	3,210	932	—

28HA DeLuxe Eight (wb 120.0)—20,433 built

	Wght	Price	Prod
cpe 3P	3,180	875	—
spt cpe 4P	3,195	913	—
cabriolet (conv)	3,280	1,046	—
sdn 2d	3,250	919	—
sdn 4d	3,300	970	—

29HB Torpedo Eight (wb 122.0)—31,224 built

	Wght	Price	Prod
spt cpe 4P	3,390	1,016	—
sdn 4d	3,475	1,072	—

1940 Engines	bore×stroke	bhp	availability
L6, 222.7	3.44×4.00	87	S-Six
L8, 248.9	3.25×3.75	100	S-Eight

1941

25JA DeLuxe Torpedo Six (wb 119.0)—117,976 built

	Wght	Price	Prod
cpe 3P	3,145	828	—
sdn cpe	3,180	864	—
conv cpe	3,335	1,023	—
sdn 2d	3,190	874	—
sdn 4d	3,235	921	—
Metropolitan sdn 4d	3,230	921	—

26JB Streamliner Torpedo Six (wb 122.0)—82,527 built

	Wght	Price	Prod
sdn cpe	3,305	923	—
Super sdn cpe	3,320	969	—
sdn 4d	3,365	980	—
Super sdn 4d	3,400	1,026	—

24JC Custom Torpedo Six (wb 122.0)—8,257 built

	Wght	Price	Prod
sdn cpe	3,260	995	—
sdn 4d	3,355	1,052	—
wgn 4d, 8P	3,650	1,175	—
DeLuxe wgn 4d, 8P	3,665	1,225	—

27JA DeLuxe Torpedo Eight (wb 119.0)—37,823 built

	Wght	Price	Prod
cpe 3P	3,220	853	—
sdn cpe	3,250	889	—
conv cpe	3,390	1,048	—
sdn 2d	3,250	899	—
sdn 4d	3,285	946	—
Metropolitan sdn 4d	3,295	946	—

28JB Streamliner Torpedo Eight (wb 122.0)—66,287 built

	Wght	Price	Prod
sdn cpe	3,370	948	—
Super sdn cpe	3,385	994	—
sdn 4d	3,425	1,005	—
Super sdn 4d	3,460	1,051	—

29JC Custom Torpedo Eight (wb 122.0)—17,191 built

	Wght	Price	Prod
sdn cpe	3,325	1,020	—

	Wght	Price	Prod
sdn 4d	3,430	1,077	—
wgn 4d, 8P	3,715	1,200	—
DeLuxe wgn 4d, 8P	3,730	1,250	—

1941 Engines	bore×stroke	bhp	availability
L6, 239.2	3.56×4.00	90	S-Six
L8, 248.9	3.25×3.75	103	S-Eight

1942

25KA Torpedo Six (wb 119.0)—29,886 built

	Wght	Price	Prod
cpe 3P	3,210	895	—
sdn cpe	3,255	950	—
spt cpe	3,260	935	—
conv cpe	3,535	1,165	—
sdn 2d	3,265	940	—
sdn 4d	3,305	985	—
Metropolitan sdn 4d	3,295	985	—

26KB Streamliner Six (wb 122.0)

	Wght	Price	Prod
sdn cpe	3,355	980	10,284
sdn 4d	3,415	1,035	
wgn 4d, 8P	3,810	1,265	
Chieftain sdn cpe	3,400	1,030	2,458
Chieftain sdn 4d	3,460	1,085	
Chieftain wgn 4d, 6P	3,785	1,315	

27KA Torpedo Eight (wb 119.0)—14,421 built

	Wght	Price	Prod
cpe dP	3,270	920	—
sdn cpe	3,320	975	—
spt cpe	3,320	960	—
conv cpe	3,605	1,190	—
sdn 2d	3,325	965	—
sdn 4d	3,360	1,010	—
Metropolitan sdn 4d	3,355	1,010	—

28KB Streamliner Eight (wb 122.0)

	Wght	Price	Prod
sdn cpe	3,430	1,005	15,465
sdn 4d	3,485	1,060	
wgn 4d, 8P	3,885	1,290	
Chieftain sdn cpe	3,460	1,055	11,041
Chieftain sdn 4d	3,515	1,110	
Chieftain wgn 4d, 6P	3,865	1,340	

1942 Engines	bore×stroke	bhp	availability
L6, 239.2	3.56×4.00	90	S-Six
L8, 248.9	3.25×3.75	103	S-Eight

1946

25LA Torpedo Six (wb 119.0)—26,636 built

	Wght	Price	Prod
sdn 4d	3,361	1,427	—
sdn 2d	3,326	1,368	—
cpe sdn	3,326	1,399	—
spt cpe	3,311	1,353	—
cpe 3P	3,261	1,307	—
conv cpe	3,591	1,631	—

26LB Streamliner Six (wb 122.0)—43,430 built

	Wght	Price	Prod
sdn 4d	3,490	1,510	—
cpe sdn	3,435	1,438	—
wgn 4d, 8P	3,790	1,942	—
DeLuxe wgn 4d, 8P	3,735	2,019	—

27LA Torpedo Eight (wb 119.0)—18,273 built

	Wght	Price	Prod
sdn 4d	3,436	1,455	—
sdn 2d	3,396	1,395	—
cpe sdn	3,391	1,428	—

	Wght	Price	Prod
spt cpe	3,376	1,381	—
cpe 3P	3,331	1,335	—
conv cpe	3,651	1,658	—

28LB Streamliner Eight (wb 122.0)—49,301 built

	Wght	Price	Prod
sdn 4d	3,550	1,538	—
cpe sdn	3,495	1,468	—
wgn 4d, 8P	3,870	1,970	—
DeLuxe wgn 4d, 8P	3,850	2,047	—

1946 Engines	bore×stroke	bhp	availability
L6, 239.2	3.56×4.00	90	S-Six
L8, 248.9	3.25×3.75	103	S-Eight

1947

6MA Torpedo Six (wb 119.0)—67,125 built

	Wght	Price	Prod
sdn 4d	3,320	1,512	—
sdn 2d	3,295	1,453	—
cpe sdn	3,300	1,484	—
spt cpe	3,295	1,438	—
cpe 3P	3,245	1,387	—
conv cpe	3,560	1,811	—
DeLuxe conv cpe	3,560	1,853	—

6MB Streamliner Six (wb 122.0)—42,336 built

	Wght	Price	Prod
sdn 4d	3,450	1,598	—
cpe sdn	3,400	1,547	—
wgn 4d, 8P	3,775	2,235	—
DeLuxe wgn 4d, 8P	3,715	2,312	—

8MA Torpedo Eight (wb 119.0)—34,815 built

	Wght	Price	Prod
sdn 4d	3,405	1,559	—
sdn 2d	3,370	1,500	—
cpe sdn	3,370	1,531	—
spt cpe	3,360	1,485	—
cpe 3P	3,310	1,434	—
conv cpe	3,635	1,854	—
DeLuxe conv cpe	3,635	1,900	—

8MB Streamliner Eight (wb 122.0)—86,324 built

	Wght	Price	Prod
sdn 4d	3,515	1,645	—
cpe sdn	3,455	1,595	—
wgn 4d, 8P	3,845	2,282	—
DeLuxe wgn 4d, 8P	3,790	2,359	—

1947 Engines	bore×stroke	bhp	availability
L6, 239.2	3.56×4.00	90	S-Six
L8, 248.9	3.25×3.75	103	S-Eight

1948

6PA Torpedo Six (wb 119.0)—39,262 built

	Wght	Price	Prod
sdn 4d	3,320	1,641	—
sdn 2d	3,280	1,583	—
cpe sdn	3,275	1,614	—
spt cpe	3,220	1,552	—
bus cpe	3,230	1,500	—
DeLuxe sdn 4d	3,340	1,731	—
DeLuxe cpe sdn	3,275	1,704	—
DeLuxe spt cpe	3,230	1,641	—
DeLuxe conv cpe	3,525	2,025	—

6PB Streamliner Six (wb 122.0)—37,742 built

	Wght	Price	Prod
sdn 4d	3,450	1,727	—
cpe sdn	3,365	1,677	—
wgn 4d, 8P	3,755	2,364	—
DeLuxe sdn 4d	3,455	1,817	—
DeLuxe cpe sdn	3,370	1,766	—
DeLuxe wgn 4d, 6P	3,695	2,442	—

8PA Torpedo Eight (wb 119.0)— 35,300 built

	Wght	Price	Prod
sdn 4d	3,395	1,689	—
sdn 2d	3,360	1,630	—
cpe scn	3,340	1,661	—
spt cpe	3,295	1,599	—
bus cpe	3,295	1,548	—
DeLuxe sdn 4d	3,395	1,778	—
DeLuxe cpe sdn	3,340	1,751	—
DeLuxe spt cpe	3,305	1,689	—
DeLuxe conv cpe	3,600	2,072	—

8PB Streamliner Eight (wb 122.0)—123,115 built

	Wght	Price	Prod
sdn 4d	3,525	1,775	—
cpe sdn	3,425	1,724	—
wgn 4d, 8P	3,820	2,412	—
DeLuxe sdn 4d	3,530	1,864	—
DeLuxe cpe sdn	3,455	1,814	—
DeLuxe wgn 4d, 6P	3,765	2,490	—

1948 Engines	bore×stroke	bhp	availability
L6, 239.2	3.56×4.00	90	S-Six
L8, 248.9	3.25×3.75	104	S-Eight

1949

6R Streamliner Six (wb 120.0)— 69,654 built (includes 6R Chieftain)

	Wght	Price	Prod
sdn 4d	3,385	1,740	—
cpe sdn	3,360	1,689	—
wgn 4d, 8P wood body	3,745	2,543	—
wgn 4d, 8P metal body	3,650	2,543	—
DeLuxe sdn 4d	3,415	1,835	—
DeLuxe cpe sdn	3,375	1,784	—
DeLuxe wgn 4d, 6P wood body	3,730	2,622	—
DeLuxe wgn 4d, 6P metal body	3,580	2,622	—

6R Chieftain Six (wb 120.0)

	Wght	Price	Prod
sdn 4d	3,385	1,761	—
sdn 2d	3,355	1,710	—
cpe sdn	3,330	1,710	—
bus cpe	3,280	1,587	—
DeLuxe sdn 4d	3,415	1,856	—
DeLuxe sdn 2d	3,360	1,805	—
DeLuxe cpe sdn	3,345	1,805	—
DeLuxe conv cpe	3,600	2,138	—

8R Streamliner Eight (wb 120.0)—235,165 built (inc 8R Chieftain)

	Wght	Price	Prod
sdn 4d	3,470	1,808	—
cpe sdn	3,435	1,758	—
wgn 4d, 8P wood body	3,835	2,611	—
wgn 4d, 8P metal body	3,690	2,611	—
DeLuxe sdn 4d	3,500	1,903	—
DeLuxe cpe sdn	3,445	1,853	—
DeLuxe wgn 4d, 6P wood body	3,800	2,690	—
DeLuxe wgn 4d, 6P metal body	3,640	2,690	—

8R Chieftain Eight (wb 120.0)

	Wght	Price	Prod
sdn 4d	3,475	1,829	—
sdn 2d	3,430	1,779	—
cpe sdn	3,390	1,779	—
bus cpe	3,355	1,656	—
DeLuxe sdn 4d	3,480	1,924	—
DeLuxe sdn 2d	3,430	1,874	—
DeLuxe cpe sdn	3,415	1,874	—
DeLuxe conv cpe	3,670	2,206	—

1949 Engines	bore×stroke	bhp	availability
L6, 239.2	3.56×4.00	90	S-Six
L6, 239.2	3.56×4.00	93	O-Six
L8, 248.9	3.25×3.75	104	S-Eight
L8, 248.9	3.25×3.75	106	O-Eight

Pontiac

1950

6T Streamliner Six (wb 120.0)—
115,542 built (includes 6T Chieftain)

	Wght	Price	Prod
fstbk sdn 4d	3,414	1,724	—
fstbk cpe sdn	3,379	1,673	—
wgn 4d, 8P	3,714	2,264	—
DeLuxe fstbk sdn 4d	3,419	1,819	—
DeLuxe fstbk cpe sdn	3,399	1,768	—
DeLuxe wgn 4d, 6P	3,649	2,343	—

6T Chieftain Six (wb 120.0)

	Wght	Price	Prod
sdn 4d	3,409	1,745	—
sdn 2d	3,384	1,694	—
cpe sdn	3,359	1,694	—
bus cpe	3,319	1,571	—
DeLuxe sdn 4d	3,414	1,840	—
DeLuxe sdn 2d	3,389	1,789	—
DeLuxe cpe sdn	3,364	1,789	—
DeLuxe Catalina htp cpe	3,469	2,000	—
DeLuxe conv cpe	3,624	2,122	—
Super Catalina htp cpe	3,469	2,058	—

8T Streamliner Eight (wb 120.0)—330,887 built (inc 8T Chieftain)

	Wght	Price	Prod
fstbk sdn 4d	3,499	1,792	—
fstbk cpe sdn	3,464	1,742	—
wgn 4d, 8P	3,799	2,332	—
DeLuxe fstbk sdn 4d	3,509	1,887	—
DeLuxe fstbk cpe sdn	3,469	1,837	—
DeLuxe wgn 4d, 6P	3,739	2,411	—

8T Chieftain Eight (wb 120.0)

	Wght	Price	Prod
sdn 4d	3,494	1,813	—
sdn 2d	3,454	1,763	—
cpe sdn	3,444	1,763	—
bus cpe	3,399	1,640	—
DeLuxe sdn 4d	3,499	1,908	—
DeLuxe sdn 2d	3,464	1,858	—
DeLuxe cpe sdn	3,454	1,858	—
DeLuxe Catalina htp cpe	3,549	2,069	—
DeLuxe conv cpe	3,704	2,190	—
Super Catalina htp cpe	3,549	2,127	—

1950 Engines	bore×stroke	bhp	availability
L6, 239.2	3.56×4.00	90	S-Six
L8, 268.4	3.38×3.75	108	S-Eight

1951

6U Streamliner Six (wb 120.0)—
53,748 built (includes 6U Chieftain)

	Wght	Price	Prod
fstbk cpe sdn	3,363	1,824	—
wgn 4d, 8P	3,718	2,470	—
DeLuxe fstbk cpe sdn	3,378	1,927	—
DeLuxe wgn 4d, 6P	3,638	2,556	—

6U Chieftain Six (wb 120.0)

	Wght	Price	Prod
sdn 4d	3,388	1,903	—
sdn 2d	3,358	1,848	—
cpe sdn	3,338	1,848	—
bus cpe	3,308	1,713	—
DeLuxe sdn 4d	3,388	2,006	—
DeLuxe sdn 2d	3,358	1,951	—
DeLuxe cpe sdn	3,343	1,951	—
DeLuxe Catalina htp cpe	3,458	2,182	—
DeLuxe conv cpe	3,603	2,314	—
Super Catalina htp cpe	3,468	2,244	—

8U Streamliner Eight (wb 120.0)—316,411 built (inc 8U Chieftain)

	Wght	Price	Prod
fstbk cpe sdn	3,458	1,900	—
wgn 4d, 8P	3,813	2,544	—
DeLuxe fstbk cpe sdn	3,463	2,003	—
DeLuxe wgn 4d, 6P	3,743	2,629	—

8U Chieftain Eight (wb 120.0)

	Wght	Price	Prod
sdn 4d	3,478	1,977	—
sdn 2d	3,443	1,922	—
cpe sdn	3,418	1,922	—
bus cpe	3,388	1,787	—
DeLuxe sdn 4d	3,488	2,081	—
DeLuxe sdn 2d	3,448	2,026	—
DeLuxe cpe sdn	3,433	2,026	—
DeLuxe Catalina htp cpe	3,543	2,257	—
DeLuxe conv cpe	3,683	2,388	—
Super Catalina htp cpe	3,548	2,320	—

1951 Engines	bore×stroke	bhp	availability
L6, 239.2	3.56×4.00	102	S-Six
L8, 268.4	3.38×3.75	122	S-Eight

1952

6W Chieftain Six (wb 120.0)—19,809 built

	Wght	Price	Prod
sdn 4d	3,403	2,014	—
sdn 2d	3,378	1,956	—
wgn 4d, 8P	3,718	2,615	—
DeLuxe sdn 4d	3,403	2,119	—
DeLuxe sdn 2d	3,378	2,060	—
DeLuxe Catalina htp cpe	3,483	2,304	—
DeLuxe conv cpe	3,603	2,444	—
DeLuxe wgn 4d, 6P	3,653	2,699	—
Super Catalina htp cpe	3,493	2,370	—

8W Chieftain Eight (wb 120.0)—251,564 built

	Wght	Price	Prod
sdn 4d	3,503	2,090	—
sdn 2d	3,458	2,031	—
wgn 4d, 8P	3,813	2,689	—
DeLuxe sdn 4d	3,503	2,194	—
DeLuxe sdn 2d	3,458	2,136	—
DeLuxe Catalina htp cpe	3,568	2,380	—
DeLuxe conv cpe	3,683	2,518	—
DeLuxe wgn 4d, 6P	3,758	2,772	—
Super Catalina htp cpe	3,573	2,446	—

1952 Engines	bore×stroke	bhp	availability
L6, 239.2	3.56×4.00	102	S-Six
L8, 268.4	3.38×3.75	122	S-Eight

1953

6X Chieftain Six (wb 122.0)—38,914 built

	Wght	Price	Prod
sdn 4d	3,506	2,015	—
sdn 2d	3,466	1,956	—
wgn 4d, 6P	3,713	2,450	—
wgn 4d, 6P (woodgrain)	3,713	2,530	—
wgn 4d, 8P	3,791	2,505	—
wgn 4d, 8P (woodgrain)	3,791	2,585	—
DeLuxe sdn 4d	3,521	2,119	—
DeLuxe sdn 2d	3,481	2,060	—
DeLuxe Catalina htp cpe	3,546	2,304	—
DeLuxe conv cpe	3,696	2,444	—
DeLuxe wgn 4d, 6P	3,751	2,590	—
DeLuxe wgn 4d, 6P (woodgrain)	3,751	2,670	—
Custom Catalina htp cpe	3,546	2,370	—

8X Chieftain Eight (wb 122.0)—379,705 built

	Wght	Price	Prod
sdn 4d	3,581	2,090	—
sdn 2d	3,546	2,031	—
wgn 4d, 6P	3,811	2,525	—
wgn 4d, 6P (woodgrain)	3,811	2,605	—
wgn 4d, 8P	3,881	2,580	—
wgn 4d, 8P (woodgrain)	3,881	2,660	—
DeLuxe sdn 4d	3,596	2,194	—
DeLuxe sdn 2d	3,561	2,136	—
DeLuxe Catalina htp cpe	3,621	2,380	—
DeLuxe conv cpe	3,751	2,518	—
DeLuxe wgn 4d, 6P	3,841	2,664	—
DeLuxe wgn 4d, 6P (woodgrain)	3,841	2,744	—
Custom Catalina htp cpe	3,621	2,446	—

1953 Engines	bore×stroke	bhp	availability
L6, 239.2	3.56×4.00	115	S-Six man
L6, 239.2	3.56×4.00	118	S-Six auto
L8, 268.4	3.38×3.75	118	S-Eight man
L8, 268.4	3.38×3.75	122	S-Eight auto

1954

6Z Chieftain Six (wb 122.0)—22,670 built

	Wght	Price	Prod
Special sdn 4d	3,391	2,027	—
Special sdn 2d	3,331	1,968	—
Special wgn 4d, 8P	3,691	2,419	—
Special wgn 4d, 6P	3,601	2,364	—
DeLuxe sdn 4d	3,406	2,131	—
DeLuxe sdn 2d	3,351	2,072	—
DeLuxe Catalina htp cpe	3,421	2,316	—
DeLuxe wgn 4d, 6P	3,646	2,504	—
Custom Catalina htp cpe	3,421	2,382	—

8Z Chieftain Eight (wb 122.0)—149,986 built

	Wght	Price	Prod
Special sdn 4d	3,451	2,102	—
Special sdn 2d	3,396	2,043	—
Special wgn 4d, 8P	3,771	2,494	—
Special wgn 4d, 6P	3,676	2,439	—
DeLuxe sdn 4d	3,466	2,206	—
DeLuxe Catalina htp cpe	3,491	2,392	—
DeLuxe wgn 4d, 6P	3,716	2,579	—
Custom Catalina htp cpe	3,491	2,458	—

8Z Star Chief (wb 124.0)—115,088 built

	Wght	Price	Prod
DeLuxe sdn 4d	3,536	2,301	—
DeLuxe conv cpe	3,776	2,630	—
Custom sdn 4d	3,536	2,394	—
Custom Catalina htp cpe	3,551	2,557	—

1954 Engines	bore×stroke	bhp	availability
L6, 239.2	3.56×4.00	115	S-Chieftain Six man
L6, 239.2	3.56×4.00	118	S-Chieftain Six auto
L8, 268.4	3.38×3.75	122	S-Chftn 8/Star Chief man
L8, 268.4	3.38×3.75	127	S-Chftn 8/Star Chief auto

1955

860 Chieftain (wb 122.0)

	Wght	Price	Prod
sdn 4d	3,511	2,164	65,155
sdn 2d	3,476	2,105	58,654
wgn 4d, 8P	3,686	2,518	6,091
wgn 2d, 6P	3,626	2,434	8,620

870 Chieftain (wb 122.0)

	Wght	Price	Prod
sdn 4d	3,511	2,268	91,187
sdn 2d	3,476	2,209	28,950
Catalina htp cpe	3,521	2,335	72,608
wgn 4d, 6P	3,676	2,603	19,439
Custom Safari wgn 2d, 6P	3,636	2,962	3,760

Star Chief (wb 124.0)

	Wght	Price	Prod
sdn 4d	3,556	2,362	44,800
conv cpe	3,791	2,691	19,762
Custom sdn 4d	3,557	2,455	35,153
Custom Catalina htp cpe	3,566	2,499	99,629

1955 Engine	bore×stroke	bhp	availability
V8, 287.2	3.75×3.25	180	S-all

1956

860 Chieftain (wb 122.0)

	Wght	Price	Prod
sdn 4d	3,512	2,298	41,987
Catalina htp sdn	3,577	2,443	35,201
sdn 2d	3,452	2,240	41,908
Catalina htp cpe	3,512	2,370	46,335
wgn 4d, 9P	3,707	2,653	12,702
wgn 2d, 6P	3,612	2,569	6,099

870 Chieftain (wb 122.0)

	Wght	Price	Prod
sdn 4d	3,512	2,413	22,082
Catalina htp sdn	3,577	2,534	25,372
Catalina htp cpe	3,512	2,840	24,744
wgn 4d, 6P	3,657	2,749	21,674
Custom Safari wgn 2d, 6P	3,642	3,129	4,042

Star Chief (wb 124.0)

	Wght	Price	Prod
sdn 4d	3,577	2,527	18,346
conv cpe	3,797	2,857	13,510
Custom Catalina htp sdn	3,647	2,735	48,035
Custom Catalina htp cpe	3,567	2,665	43,392

1956 Engines	bore×stroke	bhp	availability
V8, 316.6	3.94×3.25	205	S-Chieftains
V8, 316.6	3.94×3.25	227	S-Star Chief

1957

Chieftain (wb 122.0)

	Wght	Price	Prod
sdn 4d	3,560	2,527	35,671
Catalina htp sdn	3,635	2,614	40,074
sdn 2d	3,515	2,463	21,343
Catalina htp cpe	3,555	2,529	51,017
Safari wgn 4d, 9P	3,835	2,898	11,536
Safari wgn 2d, 6P	3,690	2,841	2,934

Super Chief (wb 122.0)

	Wght	Price	Prod
sdn 4d	3,585	2,664	15,153
Catalina htp sdn	3,640	2,793	19,758
Catalina htp cpe	3,570	2,735	15,494
Safari wgn 4d, 6P	3,765	3,021	14,095
Custom Safari wgn 2d, 6P*	3,750	3,481	1,292

Star Chief (wb 124.0; wgn-122.0)

	Wght	Price	Prod
sdn 4d	3,630	2,839	3,774
conv cpe	3,860	3,105	12,789
Custom sdn 4d	3,645	2,896	8,874
Custom Catalina htp sdn	3,710	2,975	44,283
Custom Catalina htp cpe	3,640	2,901	32,864
Custom Safari wgn 4d, 6P	3,810	3,636	1,894

Bonneville (wb 124.0)

	Wght	Price	Prod
conv cpe	4,285	5,782	630

*All Pontiac wagons were called Safaris in 1957. The model indicated is the hardtop-styled Safari, first offered in 1955 and discontinued after 1957.

1957 Engines	bore×stroke	bhp	availability
V8, 347.0	3.94×3.56	252	S-Chieftain
V8, 347.0	3.94×3.56	270	S-Super Chief, Star Chief
V8, 347.0	3.94×3.56	290	O-all exc Bonneville
V8, 370.0	4.06×3.56	300+	S-Bonneville (fuel injection)

1958

Chieftain (wb 122.0)

		Wght	Price	Prod
2567	conv cpe	3,850	3,019	7,359
2731	Catalina htp cpe	3,650	2,707	26,003
2739	Catalina htp sdn	3,785	2,792	17,946
2741	sdn 2d	3,640	2,573	17,394
2749	sdn 4d	3,735	2,638	44,999
2793	Safari wgn 4d, 6P	4,025	3,019	9,701
2794	Safari wgn 4d, 9P	4,070	3,088	5,417

Super Chief (wb 124.0)

		Wght	Price	Prod
2831D	Catalina htp cpe	3,690	2,880	7,236
2839D	Catalina htp sdn	3,810	2,961	7,886
2849D	sdn 4d	3,770	2,834	12,006

Star Chief Custom (wb 124.0)

		Wght	Price	Prod
2793SC	Safari wgn 4d, 6P	4,065	3,350	2,905
2831SD	Catalina htp cpe	3,735	3,122	13,888
2839SD	Catalina htp sdn	3,850	3,210	21,455
2849SD	sdn 4d	3,825	3,071	10,547

Pontiac

Bonneville Custom (wb 122.0)		Wght	Price	Prod
2547SD	htp cpe	3,710	3,481	9,144
2567SD	conv cpe	3,925	3,586	3,096

1958 Engines	bore×stroke	bhp	availability
V8, 370.0	4.06×3.56	240	S-Chieftain/Super Chief man
V8, 370.0	4.06×3.56	255	S-Star Chief/Bonneville man
V8, 370.0	4.06×3.56	270	S-Chieftain/Super Chief auto
V8, 370.0	4.06×3.56	285	S-Star Chief/Bonneville auto
V8, 370.0	4.06×3.56	300	O-all (Tri-Power)
V8, 370.0	4.06×3.56	310	O-all (fuel injection)

1959

Catalina (wb 122.0)		Wght	Price	Prod
2111	Sport sdn 2d	3,870	2,633	26,102
2119	sdn 4d	3,955	2,704	72,377
2135	Safari wgn 4d, 6P	4,345	3,101	21,162
2137	Sport htp cpe	3,900	2,768	38,309
2139	Vista htp sdn	4,005	2,844	45,012
2145	Safari wgn 4d, 9P	4,405	3,209	14,084
2167	conv cpe	3,970	3,080	14,515

Star Chief (wb 124.0)		Wght	Price	Prod
2411	Sport sdn 2d	3,930	2,934	10,254
2419	sdn 4d	4,005	3,006	27,072
2439	Vista htp sdn	4,055	3,138	30,689

Bonneville (wb 124.0; wgn-122.0)		Wght	Price	Prod
2735	Custom Safari wgn 4d, 6P	4,370	3,532	4,673
2837	Sport htp cpe	3,985	3,257	27,769
2839	Vista htp sdn	4,085	3,333	38,696
2867	conv cpe	4,070	3,478	11,426

1959 Engines	bore×stroke	bhp	availability
V8, 389.0	4.06×3.75	215	O-all auto
V8, 389.0	4.06×3.75	245	S-Catalina/Star Chief man
V8, 389.0	4.06×3.75	260	S-Bonneville auto
V8, 389.0	4.06×3.75	280	S-Catalina/Star Chief auto
V8, 389.0	4.06×3.75	300	S-Bonneville auto
V8, 389.0	4.06×3.75	—	O-all (4bbl)
V8, 389.0	4.06×3.75	310	O-all (Tri-Power)

1960

Catalina (wb 122.0)		Wght	Price	Prod
2111	Sport sdn 2d	3,835	2,631	25,504
2119	sdn 4d	3,935	2,702	72,650
2135	Safari wgn 4d, 6P	4,310	3,099	21,253
2137	Sport htp cpe	3,850	2,766	27,496
2139	Vista htp sdn	3,990	2,842	32,710
2145	Safari wgn 4d, 9P	4,365	3,207	14,149
2167	conv cpe	3,940	3,078	17,172

Ventura (wb 122.0)		Wght	Price	Prod
2337	Sport htp cpe	3,865	2,971	27,577
2339	Vista htp sdn	3,990	3,047	28,700

Star Chief (wb 124.0)		Wght	Price	Prod
2411	Sport sdn 2d	3,910	2,932	5,797
2419	sdn 4d	3,995	3,003	23,038
2439	Vista htp sdn	4,040	3,136	14,856

Bonneville (wb 124.0; wgn-122.0)		Wght	Price	Prod
2735	Custom Safari wgn 4d, 6P	4,360	3,530	5,163
2837	Sport htp cpe	3,965	3,255	24,015
2839	Vista htp sdn	4,065	3,331	39,037
2867	conv cpe	4,030	3,476	17,062

1960 Engines	bore×stroke	bhp	availability
V8, 389.0	4.06×3.75	215	O-all auto
V8, 389.0	4.06×3.75	245	S-Star Chief/Cat/Vent man
V8, 389.0	4.06×3.75	260	S-Bonneville man

	bore×stroke	bhp	availability
V8, 389.0	4.06×3.75	283	S-Star Chief/Cat/Vent auto
V8, 389.0	4.06×3.75	303	S-Bonneville auto
V8, 389.0	4.06×3.75	318	O-all (Tri-Power)

1961

Tempest (wb 112.0)		Wght	Price	Prod
2117	Custom spt cpe	2,795	2,297	7,455
2119	sdn 4d	2,800	2,167	22,557
2120	Custom sdn 4d	2,810	2,351	40,082
2127	spt cpe	2,785	2,113	7,432
2135	wgn 4d	2,980	2,438	7,404
2136	Custom wgn 4d	2,990	2,622	15,853

Catalina (wb 119.0)		Wght	Price	Prod
2311	Sport sdn 2d	3,650	2,631	9,846
2335	Safari wgn 4d, 6P	4,135	3,099	12,595
2337	Sport htp cpe	3,680	2,766	14,524
2339	Vista htp sdn	3,785	2,842	17,589
2345	Safari wgn 4d, 9P	4,175	3,207	7,783
2367	conv cpe	3,805	3,078	12,379
2369	sdn 4d	3,725	2,702	38,638

Ventura (wb 119.0)		Wght	Price	Prod
2537	Sport htp cpe	3,665	2,971	13,297
2539	Vista htp sdn	3,795	3,047	13,912

Star Chief (wb 123.0)		Wght	Price	Prod
2639	Vista htp sdn	3,870	3,136	13,559
2669	sdn 4d	3,840	3,003	16,024

Bonneville (wb 123.0)		Wght	Price	Prod
2735	Custom Safari wgn 4d	4,185	3,530	3,323
2837	Sport htp cpe	3,810	3,255	16,906
2839	Vista htp sdn	3,895	3,331	30,830
2867	conv cpe	3,905	3,476	18,264

1961 Engines	bore×stroke	bhp	availability
L4, 194.5	4.06×3.75	110	S-Tempest man
L4, 194.5	4.06×3.75	130	S-Tempest auto
V8, 215.0	3.50×2.80	155	O-Tempest
V8, 389.0	4.06×3.75	215	S-Star Chief/Cat/Vent man
V8, 389.0	4.06×3.75	230	O-all auto exc Tempest
V8, 389.0	4.06×3.75	235	S-Bonneville man; O-other man
V8, 389.0	4.06×3.75	267	S-Catalina/Ventura auto
V8, 389.0	4.06×3.75	283	S-Star Chief auto
V8, 389.0	4.06×3.75	287	O-Catalina/Ventura auto
V8, 389.0	4.06×3.75	303	S-Bonneville auto; O-Star Chief auto
V8, 389.0	4.06×3.75	318	O-all exc Tempest (Tri-Power)

1962

Tempest (wb 112.0)*		Wght	Price	Prod
2117	spt cpe	2,800	2,294	51,981
2119	sdn 4d	2,815	2,240	37,430
2127	cpe	2,785	2,186	15,473
2135	Safari wgn 4d	2,995	2,511	17,674
2167	conv cpe	2,955	2,564	20,635

Catalina (wb 120.0; wgn-119.0)		Wght	Price	Prod
2311	Sport sdn 2d	3,705	2,725	14,263
2335	Safari wgn 4d, 6P	4,180	3,193	19,399
2339	Vista htp sdn	3,825	2,936	29,251
2345	Safari wgn 4d, 9P	4,220	3,301	10,716
2347	Sport htp cpe	3,730	2,860	46,024
2367	conv cpe	3,855	3,172	16,877
2369	sdn 4d	3,765	2,796	68,124

Star Chief (wb 123.0)		Wght	Price	Prod
2639	Vista htp sdn	3,925	3,230	13,882
2669	sdn 4d	3,875	3,097	27,760

	Bonneville (wb 123.0)	Wght	Price	Prod
2735	Custom Safari wgn 4d	4,255	3,624	4,527
2839	Vista htp sdn	4,005	3,425	44,015
2847	Sport htp cpe	3,900	3,349	31,629
2867	conv cpe	4,005	3,570	21,582

	Grand Prix (wb 120.0)			
2947	Sport htp cpe	3,835	3,490	30,195

*Tempest includes DeLuxe and LeMans trim options. Factory records include the following production breakdowns:

	std	DeLuxe	LeMans
cpe	15,473	—	—
spt cpe	—	12,319	39,662
sdn 4d	16,057	21,373	—
wgn 4d	6,504	11,170	—
conv cpe	—	5,076	15,559

1962 Engines	bore×stroke	bhp	availability
L4, 194.5	4.06×3.75	110	S-Tempest man
L4, 194.5	4.06×3.75	115	S-Tempest auto
V8, 215.0	3.50×2.80	185	O-Tempest
V8, 389.0	4.06×3.75	215	S-Catalina/Star Chief man
V8, 389.0	4.06×3.75	230	O-all full-size
V8, 389.0	4.06×3.75	235	S-Bonn man; O-Cat/S Chf man
V8, 389.0	4.06×3.75	267	S-Catalina auto
V8, 389.0	4.06×3.75	283	S-Star Chief auto
V8, 389.0	4.06×3.75	303	S-Bonn auto, GP; O-others
V8, 389.0	4.06×3.75	318	O-all full-size (Tri-Power)
V8, 389.0	4.06×3.75	333	O-all full-size (4bbl)
V8, 389.0	4.06×3.75	348	O-all full-size (Tri-Power)

1963

	Tempest (wb 112.0)	Wght	Price	Prod
2117	DeLuxe spt cpe	2,820	2,294	13,157
2119	sdn 4d (incl DeLuxe)	2,835	2,241	28,221
2127	cpe	2,810	2,188	13,307
2135	wgn 4d (incl DeLuxe)	2,995	2,512	10,135
2167	DeLuxe conv cpe	2,980	2,564	5,012

	Tempest LeMans (wb 112.0)			
2217	spt cpe	2,865	2,418	45,701
2267	conv cpe	3,035	2,742	15,957

	Catalina (wb 120.0, wgn-119.0)			
2311	Sport sdn 2d	3,685	2,725	14,091
2335	Safari wgn 4d, 6P	4,175	3,193	18,446
2339	Vista htp sdn	3,815	2,934	31,256
2345	Safari wgn 4d, 9P	4,230	3,300	11,751
2347	Sport htp cpe	3,725	2,859	60,795
2367	conv cpe	3,835	3,179	18,249
2369	sdn 4d	3,755	2,795	79,961

	Star Chief (wb 123.0)			
2639	Vista htp sdn	3,915	3,229	12,448
2669	sdn 4d	3,885	3,096	28,309

	Bonneville (wb 123.0; wgn-119.0)			
2835	Safari wgn 4d, 6P	4,245	3,623	5,156
2839	Vista htp sdn	3,985	3,423	49,929
2847	Sport htp cpe	3,895	3,348	30,995
2865	conv cpe	3,970	3,568	23,459

	Grand Prix (wb 120.0)			
2957	Sport htp cpe	3,915	3,489	72,959

1963 Engines	bore×stroke	bhp	availability
L4, 194.5	4.06×3.75	115	S-Tempest
L4, 194.5	4.06×3.75	120	O-Tempest man
L4, 194.5	4.06×3.75	140	O-Tempest auto
L4, 194.5	4.06×3.75	166	O-Tempest

	bore×stroke	bhp	availability
V8, 326.0	3.72×3.75	260	O-Tempest
V8, 389.0	4.06×3.75	215	S-Catalina/Star Chief man
V8, 389.0	4.06×3.75	230	O-all full-size auto
V8, 389.0	4.06×3.75	235	S-Bonn man; O-Cat/Star Chief man
V8, 389.0	4.06×3.75	267	S-Catalina man
V8, 389.0	4.06×3.75	283	S-Star Chief man
V8, 389.0	4.06×3.75	303	S-GP, Bonn auto; O-SC/Cat auto
V8, 389.0	4.06×3.75	318	O-all full-size (Tri-Power)
V8, 421.0	4.09×4.00	353	O-all full-size
V8, 421.0	4.09×4.00	370	O-all full-size

1964

	Tempest (wb 115.0)	Wght	Price	Prod
2027	spt cpe	2,930	2,259	6,365
2035	Safari wgn 4d	3,245	2,605	6,834
2069	sdn 4d	2,970	2,313	19,427
2127	Custom spt cpe	2,955	2,345	25,833
2135	Custom Safari wgn 4d	3,260	2,691	10,696
2167	Custom conv cpe	3,075	2,641	7,987
2169	Custom sdn 4d	2,990	2,399	29,948
2227	LeMans spt cpe	2,975	2,491	31,317
2237	LeMans htp cpe	2,995	2,556	31,310
2267	LeMans conv cpe	3,125	2,796	17,559

	Tempest G.T.O. (wb 115.0)			
2227	spt cpe	3,000	3,200	7,384
2237	htp cpe	3,020	3,250	18,422
2267	conv cpe	3,150	3,500	6,644

	Catalina (wb 120.0; wgn-119.0)*			
2311	sdn 2d	3,695	2,735	12,480
2335	Safari wgn 4d, 6P	4,190	3,203	20,356
2339	Vista htp sdn	3,835	2,945	33,849
2345	Safari wgn 4d, 9P	4,235	3,311	13,140
2347	Sport htp cpe	3,750	2,869	74,793
2367	conv cpe	3,825	3,181	18,693
2369	sdn 4d	3,770	2,806	84,457

	Star Chief (wb 123.0)			
2639	Vista htp sdn	3,945	3,239	11,200
2669	sdn 4d	3,885	3,107	26,453

	Bonneville (wb 120.0; wgn-119.0)			
2835	Safari wgn 4d	4,275	3,633	5,844
2839	htp sdn	3,995	3,433	57,630
2847	htp cpe	3,920	3,358	34,769
2867	conv cpe	3,985	3,578	22,016

	Grand Prix (wb 120.0)			
2957	Sport htp cpe	3,930	3,499	63,810

*Includes models equipped with 2+2 option package.

1964 Engines	bore×stroke	bhp	availability
L6, 215.0	3.75×3.25	140	S-Tempest exc GTO
V8, 326.0	3.72×3.75	250	O-Tempest
V8, 326.0	3.72×3.75	280	O-Tempest
V8, 389.0	4.06×3.75	230	O-all full-size auto
V8, 389.0	4.06×3.75	235	S-Catalina/Star Chf man
V8, 389.0	4.06×3.75	267	S-Catalina/Star Chf auto
V8, 389.0	4.06×3.75	283	S-Cat 2+2 option; O-Cat/SC auto
V8, 389.0	4.06×3.75	303	S-GP/Bonn auto; O-Cat/SC auto
V8, 389.0	4.06×3.75	306	S-GP/Bonn man; O-Cat/SC man
V8, 389.0	4.06×3.75	325	S-GTO; O-Tempest
V8, 389.0	4.06×3.75	330	O-full-size
V8, 389.0	4.06×3.75	348	O-GTO
V8, 421.0	4.09×4.00	350	O-full-size
V8, 421.0	4.09×4.00	370	O-full-size

Pontiac

1965

233 Tempest (wb 115.0)

		Wght	Price	Prod
27	spt cpe	2,930	2,260	18,198
35	Safari wgn 4d	3,220	2,605	5,622
69	sdn 4d	2,975	2,313	15,705

235 Tempest Custom (wb 115.0)

27	spt cpe	2,975	2,346	18,367
35	Safari wgn 4d	3,215	2,619	10,792
37	htp cpe	2,975	2,411	29,906
67	conv cpe	3,080	2,641	8,346
69	sdn 4d	2,980	2,400	25,242

237 Tempest LeMans (wb 115.0)

27	spt cpe	3,020	2,491	18,881
27	G.T.O. spt cpe	3,468	2,751	8,319
37	htp cpe	3,030	2,556	60,548
37	G.T.O. htp cpe	3,478	2,816	55,722
67	conv cpe	3,115	2,797	13,897
67	G.T.O. conv cpe	3,563	3,057	11,311
69	sdn 4d	3,020	2,551	14,227

252 Catalina (wb 121.0)*

11	sdn 2d	3,695	2,734	9,526
35	Safari wgn 4d, 6P	4,165	3,202	22,399
37	Sport htp cpe	3,750	2,860	92,009
39	Vista htp sdn	3,855	2,945	38,814
45	Safari wgn 4d, 9P	4,210	3,309	15,110
67	conv cpe	3,815	3,196	18,347
69	sdn 4d	3,750	2,805	78,853

256 Star Chief (wb 124.0)

39	htp sdn	3,925	3,238	9,132
69	sdn 4d	3,860	3,106	22,183

262 Bonneville (wb 124.0; wgn-121.0)

35	Safari wgn 4d	4,310	3,632	6,460
37	Sport htp cpe	3,890	3,357	44,030
39	htp sdn	3,990	3,433	62,480
67	conv cpe	3,950	3,594	21,050

266 Grand Prix (wb 121.0)

57	Sport htp cpe	3,940	3,498	57,881

*Includes models equipped with 2+2 option package.

1965 Engines	bore×stroke	bhp	availability
L6, 215.0	3.75×3.25	140	S-Tempest exc GTO
V8, 326.0	3.72×3.75	250	O-Tempest
V8, 326.0	3.72×3.75	285	O-Tempest
V8, 389.0	4.06×3.75	256	S-Cat/SC man; O-other full-size
V8, 389.0	4.06×3.75	290	S-Catalina/Star Chf auto
V8, 389.0	4.06×3.75	325	S-Bonn/Grand Prix auto
V8, 389.0	4.06×3.75	333	S-Bonn/Grand Prix man
V8, 389.0	4.06×3.75	335	S-GTO
V8, 389.0	4.06×3.75	360	O-GTO
V8, 421.0	4.09×4.00	338	S-Cat 2+2; O-other full-size
V8, 421.0	4.09×4.00	356	O-all full-size
V8, 421.0	4.09×4.00	376	O-all full-size

1966

233 Tempest (wb 115.0)

		Wght	Price	Prod
07	spt cpe	3,040	2,278	22,266
35	wgn 4d	3,340	2,624	40,095
69	sdn 4d	3,075	2,331	17,392

235 Tempest Custom (wb 115.0)

07	spt cpe	3,060	2,362	17,182
17	htp cpe	3,075	2,426	31,322
35	wgn 4d	3,355	2,709	7,614
39	htp sdn	3,195	2,547	10,996
67	conv cpe	3,170	2,665	5,557
69	sdn 4d	3,100	2,415	23,988

237 LeMans (wb 115.0)

		Wght	Price	Prod
07	spt cpe	3,090	2,505	16,654
17	htp cpe	3,125	2,568	78,109
39	htp sdn	3,195	2,701	13,897
67	conv cpe	3,220	2,806	13,080

242 Tempest G.T.O. (wb 115.0)

07	spt cpe	3,445	2,783	10,363
17	htp cpe	3,465	2,847	73,785
67	conv cpe	3,555	3,082	12,798

252 Catalina (wb 121.0)

11	sdn 2d	3,715	2,762	7,925
35	wgn 4d, 6P	4,250	3,217	21,082
37	htp cpe	3,835	2,893	79,013
39	htp sdn	3,910	2,968	38,005
45	wgn 4d, 9P	4,315	3,338	12,965
67	conv cpe	3,860	3,219	14,837
69	sdn 4d	3,785	2,831	80,483

254 2+2 (wb 121.0)*

37	htp cpe	4,005	3,298	—
67	conv cpe	4,030	3,602	—

256 Star Chief Executive (wb 124.0)

07	htp cpe	3,920	3,170	10,140
39	htp sdn	3,980	3,244	10,583
69	sdn 4d	3,920	3,114	24,489

262 Bonneville (wb 124.0; wgn-121.0)

37	htp cpe	4,020	3,354	42,004
39	htp sdn	4,070	3,428	68,646
45	wgn 4d, 3S	4,390	3,747	8,452
67	conv cpe	4,015	3,586	16,299

266 Grand Prix (wb 121.0)

57	htp cpe	4,015	3,492	36,757

*Included in Catalina production figures.

1966 Engines	bore×stroke	bhp	availability
L6, 230.0	3.88×3.26	165	S-Tempest, LeMans
L6, 230.0	3.88×3.26	207	O-Tempest, LeMans
V8, 326.0	3.72×3.75	250	O-Tempest, LeMans
V8, 326.0	3.72×3.75	285	O-Tempest, LeMans
V8, 389.0	4.06×3.75	256	S-Cat/SC man O-other full-size
V8, 389.0	4.06×3.75	290	O-Catalina, Star Chief
V8, 389.0	4.06×3.75	325	S-Bonn/GP auto; O-Cat, Star Chief
V8, 389.0	4.06×3.75	333	S-Bonn/GP man, GTO
V8, 389.0	4.06×3.75	360	O-GTO
V8, 421.0	4.09×4.00	338	S-2+2; O-other full-size
V8, 421.0	4.09×4.00	356	O-all full-size
V8, 421.0	4.09×4.00	376	O-all full-size

1967

223 Firebird (wb 108.1)

		Wght	Price	Prod
37	htp cpe	2,955	2,666	67,032
67	conv cpe	3,247	2,903	15,526

233 Tempest (wb 115.0)

07	cpe	3,110	2,341	17,978
35	wgn 4d	3,370	2,666	3,495
69	sdn 4d	3,140	2,388	13,136

235 Tempest Custom (wb 115.0)

07	cpe	3,130	2,437	12,469
17	htp cpe	3,140	2,494	30,512
35	wgn 4d	3,370	2,760	5,324
39	htp sdn	3,240	2,608	5,493
67	conv cpe	3,240	2,723	4,082
69	sdn 4d	3,145	2,482	17,445

237 LeMans (wb 115.0)		Wght	Price	Prod
07	cpe	3,155	2,586	10,693
17	htp cpe	3,155	2,648	75,965
39	htp sdn	3,265	2,771	8,424
67	conv cpe	3,250	2,881	9,820

239 Tempest Safari (wb 115.0)				
35	wgn 4d	3,390	2,936	4,511

242 Tempest G.T.O. (wb 115.0)				
07	cpe	3,425	2,871	7,029
17	htp cpe	3,430	2,935	65,176
67	conv cpe	3,515	3,165	9,517

252 Catalina (wb 121.0)*				
11	sdn 2d	3,735	2,807	5,633
35	wgn 4d, 6P	4,275	3,252	18,305
39	htp sdn	3,960	3,020	37,256
45	wgn 4d, 9P	4,340	3,374	11,040
67	conv cpe	3,910	3,276	10,033
69	sdn 4d	3,825	2,866	80,551
87	htp cpe	3,860	2,951	77,932

256 Executive (wb 124.0; wgn-121.0)				
35	wgn 4d, 6P	4,290	3,600	5,903
39	htp sdn	4,020	3,296	8,699
45	wgn 4d, 9P	4,370	3,722	5,593
69	sdn 4d	3,955	3,165	19,861
87	htp cpe	3,925	3,227	6,931

262 Bonneville (wb 124.0; wgn-121.0)				
39	htp sdn	4,110	3,517	56,307
45	wgn 4d, 9P	4,415	3,819	6,771
67	conv cpe	4,010	3,680	8,902
87	htp cpe	3,975	3,448	31,016

266 Grand Prix (wb 121.0)				
57	htp cpe	4,005	3,549	37,125
67	conv cpe	4,040	3,813	5,856

*Includes models equipped with 2+2 option package.

1967 Engines	bore×stroke	bhp	availability
L6, 230.0	3.88×3.26	165	S-Firebird, LeMans,Temp exc GTO
L6, 230.0	3.88×3.26	215	O-Firebird, LeMans, Temp exc GTO
V8, 326.0	3.72×3.75	250	O-Firebird, LeMans, Temp exc GTO
V8, 326.0	3.72×3.75	285	O-Firebird, LeMans, Temp exc Tempest Safari wgn
V8, 400.0	4.12×3.75	255	O-GTO auto
V8, 400.0	4.12×3.75	265	S-Cat/Vent/Exec man; O-auto
V8, 400.0	4.12×3.75	290	S-Cat/Vent/Exec auto
V8, 400.0	4.12×3.75	325	S-Bonn auto, Firebird 400 O-Catalina, Ventura, Exec
V8, 400.0	4.12×3.75	333	S-Bonn man; O-Cat, Vent, Exec
V8, 400.0	4.12×3.75	335	S-GTO
V8, 400.0	4.12×3.75	350	S-Grand Prix
V8, 400.0	4.12×3.75	360	O-GTO
V8, 428.0	4.12×4.00	360	S-2+2; O-Cat, Exec, Bonn, Grand Prix
V8, 428.0	4.12×4.00	376	O-Catalina, Exec, Bonn, Grand Prix

1968

223 Firebird (wb 108.1)		Wght	Price	Prod
37	htp cpe	3,061	2,781	90,152
67	conv cpe	3,346	2,996	16,960

233 Tempest (wb 116.0; 2d-112.0)				
27	spt cpe	3,242	2,461	19,991

233 Tempest (wb 116.0; 2d-112.0)		Wght	Price	Prod
69	sdn 4d	3,309	2,509	11,590

235 Tempest Custom (wb 116.0; 2d-112.0)				
27	spt cpe	3,252	2,554	10,634
35	wgn 4d	3,667	2,906	8,253
37	htp cpe	3,277	2,614	40,574
39	htp sdn	3,384	2,728	6,147
67	conv cpe	3,337	2,839	3,518
69	sdn 4d	3,297	2,602	17,304

237 LeMans (wb 116.0; 2d-112.0)				
27	spt cpe	3,287	2,724	8,439
37	htp cpe	3,302	2,786	110,036
39	htp sdn	3,407	2,916	9,002
67	conv cpe	3,377	3,015	8,820

239 Tempest Safari (wb 116.0)				
35	wgn 4d	3,677	3,107	4,414

242 Tempest G.T.O. (wb 112.0)				
37	htp cpe	3,506	3,101	77,704
67	conv cpe	3,590	3,227	9,980

252 Catalina (wb 121.0)				
11	sdn 2d	3,839	2,945	5,247
35	wgn 4d, 6P	4,327	3,390	21,848
39	htp sdn	4,012	3,158	41,727
45	wgn 4d, 9P	4,408	3,537	13,363
67	conv cpe	3,980	3,391	7,339
69	sdn 4d	3,888	3,004	94,441
87	htp cpe	3,943	3,089	92,217

256 Executive (wb 124.0; wgn-121.0)				
35	wgn 4d, 6P	4,378	3,744	6,195
39	htp sdn	4,077	3,439	7,848
45	wgn 4d, 9P	4,453	3,890	5,843
69	sdn 4d	4,022	3,309	18,869
87	htp cpe	3,975	3,371	5,880

262 Bonneville (wb 124.0; wgn-121.0)				
39	htp sdn	4,171	3,660	57,055
45	wgn 4d, 9P	4,485	3,987	6,926
67	conv cpe	4,090	3,800	7,358
69	sdn 4d	4,122	3,530	3,499
87	htp cpe	4,054	3,592	29,598

266 Grand Prix (wb 121.0)				
57	htp cpe	4,075	3,697	31,701

1968 Engines	bore×stroke	bhp	availability
L6, 250.0	3.88×3.53	175	S-Firebird, LeMans, Tempest exc GTO
L6, 250.0	3.88×3.53	215	S-Frbrd Sprint; O-as above exc wgns
V8, 350.0	3.88×3.75	265	S-Frbrd 350; O-Tempest exc GTO, LeMans
V8, 350.0	3.88×3.75	320	S-Frbrd HO; O-Temp, LeM exc wgns
V8, 400.0	4.12×3.75	265	O-GTO, all full-size
V8, 400.0	4.12×3.75	290	S-Catalina, Ventura, Exec
V8, 400.0	4.12×3.75	330	S-Firebird 400
V8, 400.0	4.12×3.75	335	O-Firebird 400 (Ram-Air)
V8, 400.0	4.12×3.75	340	S-Bonn; O-Cat, Vent, Exec
V8, 400.0	4.12×3.75	350	S-Grand Prix, GTO
V8, 400.0	4.12×3.75	360	O-GTO
V8, 428.0	4.12×4.00	375	O-Cat, Vent, Exec, Bonn, GP
V8, 428.0	4.12×4.00	390	O-Cat, Vent, Exec, Bonn, GP

1969

223 Firebird (wb 108.0)		Wght	Price	Prod
37	htp cpe	3,080	2,821	76,059
67	conv cpe	3,330	3,045	11,649

Pontiac

233 Tempest (wb 116.0; 2d-112.0)	Wght	Price	Prod
27 spt cpe	3,180	2,510	17,181
69 sdn 4d	3,250	2,557	9,741

235 Tempest Custom (wb 116.0; 2d-112.0)			
27 spt cpe	3,210	2,603	7,912
35 wgn 4d	3,595	2,956	6,963
37 htp cpe	3,220	2,663	46,886
39 htp sdn	3,315	2,777	3,918
67 conv cpe	3,265	2,888	2,379
69 sdn 4d	3,235	2,651	16,532

237 LeMans (wb 116.0; 2d-112.0)			
27 spt cpe	3,225	2,773	5,033
37 htp cpe	3,245	2,835	82,817
67 conv cpe	3,290	3,064	5,676
69 htp sdn	3,360	2,965	6,475

239 Tempest Safari (wb 116.0)			
36 wgn 4d	3,690	3,198	4,115

242 Tempest G.T.O. (wb 112.0)			
37 htp cpe	3,503	3,156	64,851
67 conv cpe	3,553	3,382	7,436

252 Catalina (wb 122.0)			
36 wgn 4d, 6P	4,455	3,519	20,352
37 htp cpe	3,925	3,174	84,006
39 htp sdn	4,005	3,244	38,814
46 wgn 4d, 9P	4,520	3,664	13,393
67 conv cpe	3,985	3,476	5,436
69 sdn 4d	3,945	3,090	84,590

256 Executive (wb 125.0; wgn-122.0)			
36 wgn 4d, 6P	4,475	3,872	6,411
37 htp cpe	3,970	3,456	4,492
39 htp sdn	4,065	3,525	6,522
46 wgn 4d, 9P	4,545	4,017	6,805
69 sdn 4d	4,045	3,394	14,831

262 Bonneville (wb 125.0; wgn-122.0)			
37 htp cpe	4,080	3,688	27,773
39 htp sdn	4,180	3,756	50,817
46 wgn 4d, 9P	4,600	4,104	7,428
67 conv cpe	4,130	3,896	5,438
69 sdn 4d	4,180	3,626	4,859

276 Grand Prix (wb 118.0)			
57 htp cpe	3,715	3,866	112,486

1969 Engines	bore×stroke	bhp	availability
L6, 250.0	3.88×3.53	175	S-Frbrd, LeMans, Tempest exc GTO
L6, 250.0	3.88×3.53	230	S-Frbrd Sprint; O-LeMans, Tempest exc GTO
V8, 350.0	3.88×3.75	265	S-Frbrd 350; O-Tempest, LeMans
V8, 350.0	3.88×3.75	325	S-Firebird 350 HO
V8, 350.0	3.88×3.75	330	O-Frbrd, Tpst, LeMans exc wgns/GTO
V8, 400.0	4.12×3.75	265	O-GTO/full-size auto
V8, 400.0	4.12×3.75	290	S-Catalina, Ventura, Exec
V8, 400.0	4.12×3.75	330	S-Firebird 400
V8, 400.0	4.12×3.75	335	O-Firebird 400 (Ram Air)
V8, 400.0	4.12×3.75	345	O-Firebird 400 (Ram Air)
V8, 400.0	4.12×3.75	350	S-GTO, Grand Prix
V8, 400.0	4.12×3.75	366	O-GTO (Ram Air)
V8, 400.0	4.12×3.75	370	O-GTO (Ram Air)

1970

223 Firebird (wb 108.0)	Wght	Price	Prod
87 htp cpe	3,140	2,875	18,874
87 Formula 400 htp cpe	3,470	3,370	7,708

	Wght	Price	Prod
87 Trans Am htp cpe	3,550	4,305	3,196
87 Esprit htp	3,435	3,241	18,961

233 Tempest (wb 116.0; 2d-112.0)			
27 cpe	3,225	2,623	11,977
37 htp cpe	3,250	2,683	20,883
69 sdn 4d	3,295	2,670	9,187

235 LeMans (wb 116.0, 2d-112.0)			
27 cpe	3,240	2,735	5,656
35 wgn 4d	3,585	3,092	7,165
37 htp cpe	3,265	2,795	52,304
39 htp sdn	3,385	2,921	3,872
69 sdn 4d	3,315	2,782	15,255

237 LeMans Sport (wb 116.0; 2d-112.0)			
27 cpe	3,265	2,891	1,673
36 wgn 4d	3,775	3,328	3,823
37 htp cpe	3,290	2,953	58,356
39 htp sdn	3,405	3,083	3,657
67 conv cpe	3,330	3,182	4,670

242 G.T.O. (112.0)*			
37 htp cpe	3,641	3,267	36,366
67 conv cpe	3,691	3,492	3,783

252 Catalina (wb 122.0)			
36 wgn 4d, 6P	4,517	3,646	16,944
37 htp cpe	3,952	3,249	70,350
39 htp sdn	4,042	3,319	35,155
46 wgn 4d, 9P	4,607	3,791	12,450
67 conv cpe	4,027	3,604	3,686
69 sdn 4d	3,997	3,164	84,795

256 Executive (wb 125.0; wgn-122.0)			
36 wgn 4d, 6P	4,552	4,015	4,861
37 htp cpe	4,042	3,600	3,499
39 htp sdn	4,132	3,669	5,376
46 wgn 4d, 9P	4,632	4,160	5,629
69 sdn 4d	4,087	3,538	13,061

262 Bonneville (wb 125.0; wgn-122.0)			
37 htp cpe	4,111	3,832	23,418
39 htp sdn	4,226	3,900	44,241
46 wgn 4d, 9P	4,686	4,247	7,033
67 conv cpe	4,161	4,040	3,537
69 sdn 4d	4,181	3,770	3,802

276 Grand Prix (wb 118.0)			
57 htp cpe	3,784	3,985	65,750

*Includes models equipped with "The Judge" option.

1970 Engines	bore×stroke	bhp	availability
L6, 250.0	3.88×3.53	155	S-Tempest, LeMans, Firebird
V8, 350.0	3.88×3.75	255	S-Firebird Esprit; O-above models, Cat exc conv and wgns
V8, 400.0	4.12×3.75	265	O-all auto exc GTO, Bonn
V8, 400.0	4.12×3.75	290	S-Cat conv/wgn, Exec; O-other Cat
V8, 400.0	4.12×3.75	330	S-Frbrd 400; O-Tpst/LeM/Cat/Exec auto
V8, 400.0	4.12×3.75	345	S-Frbrd Trans Am; O-Tpst/LeMans man
V8, 400.0	4.12×3.75	350	S-GTO, Grand Prix
V8, 400.0	4.12×3.75	366	S-GTO Judge; O-GTO (Ram Air)
V8, 400.0	4.12×3.75	370	O-GTO (Ram Air); O-GTO Judge
V8, 455.0	4.15×4.21	360	S-Bonn; O-Cat, Exec, GTO
V8, 455.0	4.15×4.21	370	S-Grand Prix SJ; O-GP J, Cat, Exec, Bonn

1971

21327	cpe	Wght	Price	Prod
Ventura II (wb 111.0)		**Wght**	**Price**	**Prod**
21327	cpe	3,010	2,458	34,681
21369	sdn 4d	3,050	2,488	13,803
Firebird (wb 108.0)				
22387	cpe	3,292	3,047	23,021
22487	Esprit cpe V8	3,423	3,416	20,185
22687	Formula 400 cpe V8	3,473	3,445	7,802
22887	Trans Am cpe V8	3,578	4,595	2,116
LeMans (wb 116.0; 2d 112.0)				
23327	T-37 cpe	3,317	2,747	7,184
23337	T-37 htp cpe	3,322	2,807	29,466
23369	T-37 sdn 4d	3,347	2,795	8,336
23527	cpe	3,327	2,877	2,374
23536	wgn 4d 2S	3,867	3,353	6,311
23537	htp cpe	3,327	2,938	40,966
23539	htp sdn	3,442	3,064	3,186
23546	wgn 4d 3S	3,917	3,465	4,363
23569	sdn 4d	3,357	2,925	11,979
23737	Sport htp cpe	3,327	3,125	34,625
23739	Sport htp sdn	3,442	3,255	2,451
23767	Sport conv	3,417	3,359	3,865
24237	GTO htp cpe V8	3,619	3,446	9,497
24237	GTO Judge htp cpe	3,650	3,840	357
24267	GTO conv	3,664	3,676	661
24267	GTO Judge conv	3,700	4,070	17
Catalina (wb 124.0; wgn-127.0)				
25235	Safari wgn 4d 2S	4,815	4,315	10,332
25239	htp sdn	4,107	3,939	22,333
25245	Safari wgn 4d 3S	4,905	4,462	9,283
25257	htp cpe	4,042	3,870	46,257
25267	conv	4,081	4,156	2,036
25269	sdn 4d	4,077	3,770	59,355
25839	Brougham htp sdn	4,179	4,154	9,001
25857	Brougham htp cpe	4,119	4,084	8,823
25869	Brougham sdn 4d	4,149	4,000	6,069
Bonneville (wb 126.0; wgn-127.0)				
26235	Grand Safari wgn 4d 2S	4,843	4,643	3,613
26239	htp sdn	4,273	4,340	16,393
26245	Grand Safari wgn 4d 3S	4,913	4,790	5,972
26257	htp cpe	4,188	4,272	8,778
26269	sdn 4d	4,213	4,210	6,513
Grand Ville (wb 126.0)				
26847	htp cpe	4,223	4,497	14,017
26849	htp sdn	4,303	4,566	30,524
26867	conv cpe	4,266	4,706	1,789
	chassis	—	—	194
Grand Prix (wb 118.0)				
27657	htp cpe	3,863	4,557	58,325

1971 Engines	bore×stroke	bhp	availability
L6, 250.0	3.88×3.53	145	S-LeM exc GTO; Fbd exc Formula & T/A
L6, 250.0	3.88×3.53	185	S-Ventura
V8, 307.0	3.88×3.25	235	S-Ventura
V8, 350.0	3.88×3.75	250	S-LeM exc GTP, Fbd exc T/A, Cat exc Br/Saf
V8, 400.0	4.12×3.75	265	S-Cat Br/Saf; O-Fbd exc Frmla & T/A, Catalina
V8, 400.0	4.12×3.75	300	S-GTO, Fbd Frmla, GP O-LeMans, Fbd Esprit
V8, 455.0	4.15×4.21	280	S-Bonn; O-Catalina
V8, 455.0	4.15×4.21	325	S-GV; O-LeM, Fbd T/A, Catalina, GP
V8, 455.0	4.15×4.21	335	S-Trans Am; O-LeMans

1972

2Y27	cpe	Wght	Price	Prod
Ventura II (wb 110.0)		**Wght**	**Price**	**Prod**
2Y27	cpe	3,019	2,426	51,203
2Y69	sdn 4d	3,054	2,454	21,584
Firebird (wb 108.0)				
2S87	cpe	3,263	2,828	12,000
2T87	Esprit cpe V8	3,359	3,194	11,415
2U87	Formula cpe V8	3,424	3,221	5,250
2V87	Trans Am cpe V8	3,564	4,256	1,286
LeMans (wb 116.0; 2d-112.0)*				
2D27	cpe	3,402	2,722	6,855
2D36	wgn 4d 2S	3,907	3,271	8,332
2D37	htp cpe	3,342	2,851	80,383
2D46	wgn 4d 3S	3,947	3,378	5,266
2D67	conv	3,392	3,228	3,438
2D69	sdn 4d	3,377	2,814	19,463
2G37	Luxury htp cpe V8	3,488	3,196	37,615
2G39	Luxury htp sdn V8	3,638	3,319	8,641
Catalina (wb 123.5; wgns 127.0)				
2L35	Safari wgn 4d 2S	4,743	4,232	14,536
2L39	htp sdn	4,879	3,874	28,010
2L45	Safari wgn 4d 3S	4,818	4,372	12,766
2L57	htp cpe	4,129	3,808	60,233
2L67	conv	4,204	4,080	2,399
2L69	sdn 4d	4,154	3,713	83,004
2M39	Brougham htp sdn	4,238	4,062	8,762
2M57	Brougham htp cpe	4,158	3,996	10,545
2M69	Brougham sdn 4d	4,188	3,916	8,007
Bonneville (wb 126.0; wgns 127.0)				
2N35	Grand Safari wgn 4d 2S	4,918	4,581	5,675
2N39	htp sdn	4,338	4,293	15,806
2N45	Grand Safari wgn 4d 3S	4,938	4,721	8,540
2N57	htp cpe	4,238	4,228	10,568
2N69	sdn 4d	4,288	4,169	9,704
Grand Ville (wb 126.0)				
2P47	htp cpe	4,262	4,442	19,852
2P49	htp sdn	4,378	4,507	41,346
2P67	conv cpe	4,333	4,640	2,213
	chassis	—	—	320
Grand Prix (wb 118.0)				
2K57	htp cpe	3,898	4,472	91,961

*Note: Sport ($164), GTO ($344) and GT ($231) were option packages. GTO production: 5,807.

1972 Engines	bore×stroke	bhp	availability
L6, 250.0	3.88×3.53	110	S-Vntra,LeM,Fbd exc T/A
V8, 307.0	3.88×3.25	130	S-Ventura exc Calif.
V8, 350.0	3.88×3.75	160	S-Vntra (Cal.), LeM, Fbd exc T/A, Cat exc Saf,Br
V8, 400.0	4.12×3.75	175	S-Cat Saf, Br; O-LeM,Cat,Firebird exc T/A
V8, 400.0	4.12×3.75	250	S-GP; O-Fbd exc T/A
V8, 455.0	4.15×4.21	185	S-Bonn, GV,GSaf; O-Cat
V8, 455.0	4.15×4.21	220	O-Bonn,GV,GSaf,Cat
V8, 455.0	4.15×4.21	230	O-LeMans
V8, 455.0	4.15×4.21	250	O-LeMans, Grand Prix
V8, 455.0	4.15×4.21	300	S-Fbd T/A; O-LeM, Fbd

1973

		Wght	Price	Prod
Ventura (wb 111.0)		**Wght**	**Price**	**Prod**
Y17	htchbk cpe 3d	3,276	2,603	26,335
Z17	Custom htchbk cpe 3d	3,309	2,759	
Y27	cpe	3,170	2,452	49,153
Z27	Custom cpe	3,203	2,609	
Y69	sdn 4d	3,230	2,481	21,012
Z69	Custom sdn 4d	3,263	2,638	

Firebird (wb 108.0)

S87	cpe	3,270	2,895	14,096
T87	Esprit cpe V8	3,309	3,249	17,249
U87	Formula cpe V8	3,318	3,276	10,166
V87	Trans Am cpe V8	3,504	4,204	4,802

LeMans (wb 116.0; 2d-112.0)

D29	Colonnade sdn 4d	3,713	2,918	26,554
D35	Safari wgn 5d 2S	4,064	3,296	10,446
D37	Colonnade sdn 2d	3,687	2,920	68,230
D45	Safari wgn 5d 3S	4,101	3,429	6,127
F37	Sport Colonnade sdn 2d	3,702	3,008	50,999
G29	Luxury Colonnade sdn 4d V8	3,867	3,344	9,377
G37	Luxury Colonnade sdn 2d V8	3,799	3,274	33,916

Grand Am (wb 116.0; 2d-112.0)

H29	Colonnade sdn 4d V8	4,018	4,353	8,691
H37	Colonnade sdn 2d V8	3,992	4,264	34,443

Catalina (wb 124.0; wgn-127.0)

L35	Safari wgn 4d 2S	4,791	4,311	15,762
L39	htp sdn	4,270	3,938	31,663
L45	Safari wgn 4d 3S	4,873	4,457	14,654
L57	htp cpe	4,190	3,869	74,394
L69	sdn 4d	4,234	3,770	100,592

Bonneville (wb 124.0)

N39	htp sdn	4,369	4,292	17,202
N57	htp cpe	4,292	4,225	13,866
N69	sdn 4d	4,333	4,163	15,830

Grand Ville/Grand Safari (wb 126.0/127.0)

P35	Grand Safari wgn 4d 2S	4,823	4,674	6,894
P45	Grand Safari wgn 4d 3S	4,925	4,821	10,776
P47	Grand Ville htp cpe	4,321	4,524	23,963
P49	Grand Ville htp sdn	4,376	4,592	44,092
P67	Grand Ville conv	4,339	4,766	4,447
	chassis	—	—	240

Grand Prix (wb 116.0)

K57	htp cpe	4,025	4,583	153,899

Note: GT ($246) and GTO ($368) were option packages. GTO production: 4,806.

1973 Engines	bore×stroke	bhp	availability
L6, 250.0	3.88×3.53	100	S-Vntra,LeM,Fbd exc T/A
V8, 350.0	3.88×3.75	150	S-Vntra,LeM,Fbd exc T/A,Cat exc wgn
V8, 350.0	3.88×3.75	175	O-Vntra,LeM,Fbd exc T/A
V8, 400.0	4.12×3.75	170	S-GA,Bonn,Cat wgn; O-LeMans, Catalina
V8, 400.0	4.12×3.75	185	O-GA,LeM,Bon,Cat
V8, 400.0	4.12×3.75	200	S-Grand Saf
V8, 400.0	4.12×3.75	230	S-GA,LeM,Fbd exc T/A, GSaf,Cat, Bonn
V8, 400.0	4.12×3.75	250	S-Grand Prix
V8, 455.0	4.15×4.21	215	S-GV; O-GSaf,Cat,Bonn
V8, 455.0	4.15×4.21	250	S-Fbd T/A; O-Fbd,GSaf,GV,Bonn,GP
V8, 455.0	4.15×4.21	310	O-Firebird

1974

Ventura (wb 111.1)

		Wght	Price	Prod
Y17	htchbk cpe 3d	3,372	3,018	}16,694
Z17	Custom htchbk cpe 3d	3,376	3,176	
Y27	cpe	3,262	2,892	}47,782
Z27	Custom cpe	3,298	3,051	
Y69	sdn 4d	3,284	2,921	}17,323
Z69	Custom sdn 4d	3,332	3,080	

Firebird (wb 108.0)

S87	cpe	3,394	3,335	26,372
T87	Esprit cpe V8	3,540	3,687	22,583

1974 Catalina hardtop coupe

		Wght	Price	Prod
U87	Formula cpe V8	3,548	3,659	14,519
V87	Trans Am cpe V8	3,655	4,446	10,255

LeMans (wb 116.0; 2d-112.0)

D29	Colonnade sdn 4d	3,736	3,236	17,266
D37	Colonnade sdn 2d	3,660	3,216	37,061
D35	Safari wgn 5d 2S V8	4,333	4,052	4,743
D45	Safari wgn 5d 3S V8	4,371	4,186	3,004
F37	Sport Colonnade sdn 2d	3,688	3,300	37,955
G35	Luxury Safari wgn 5d 2S V8	4,363	4,326	952
G29	Luxury Colonnade sdn 4d V8	3,904	3,759	4,513
G37	Luxury Colonnade sdn 2d V8	3,808	3,703	25,882
G45	Luxury Safari wgn 5d 3S V8	4,401	4,459	1,178

Grand Am (wb 116.0; 2d-112.0)

H29	Colonnade sdn 4d	4,073	4,623	3,122
H37	Colonnade sdn 2d	3,992	4,534	13,961

Catalina (wb 124.0; wgn-127.0)

L35	Safari wgn 4d 2S	4,973	4,692	5,662
L39	htp sdn	4,352	4,347	11,769
L45	Safari wgn 4d 3S	5,037	4,834	6,486
L57	htp cpe	4,279	4,278	40,654
L69	sdn 4d	4,294	4,190	46,025

Bonneville (wb 124.0)

N39	htp sdn	4,444	4,639	6,151
N57	htp cpe	4,356	4,572	7,639
N69	sdn 4d	4,384	4,510	6,770

Grand Ville/Safari (wb 124.0/127.0)

P35	Grand Safari wgn 4d 2S	5,011	5,099	2,894
P45	Grand Safari wgn 4d 3S	5,112	5,256	5,255
P47	Grand Ville htp cpe	4,432	4,871	11,631
P49	Grand Ville htp sdn	4,515	4,939	21,714
P67	Grand Ville conv	4,476	5,113	3,000
	chassis	—	—	113

Grand Prix (wb 116.0)

K57	htp cpe	4,096	4,936	99,117

Note: GTO ($195) was an option package for Ventura coupe only. GTO production: 7,058

1974 Engines	bore×stroke	bhp	availability
L6, 250.0	3.88×3.53	100	S-Vntra,LeM,Fbd S87
V8, 350.0	3.88×3.75	155	S-Vntra,LeM,Fbd S87/T87
V8, 350.0	3.88×3.75	170	S-Fbd U87; O-LeMans
V8, 350.0	3.88×3.75	200	O-LeMans
V8, 400.0	4.12×3.75	175	S-GA,Cat,Bonn,GSaf,GV
V8, 400.0	4.12×3.75	190	O-Grand Am
V8, 400.0	4.12×3.75	200	O-Cat,Bon,GSaf,GV
V8, 400.0	4.12×3.75	225	S-Fbd T/A; O-GA,Fbd
V8, 455.0	4.15×4.21	215	S-GV; O-GA,Cat,Bonn
V8, 455.0	4.15×4.21	225	S-Grand Prix
V8, 455.0	4.15×4.21	250	O-GA,Fbd T/A,GP

		Wght	Price	Prod
L69	sdn 4d	4,347	4,612	40,398

Bonneville (wb 124.0; wgns 127.0)

		Wght	Price	Prod
P35	Grand Safari wgn 4d 2S	5,035	5,433	2,568
P45	Grand Safari wgn 4d 3S	5,090	5,580	4,752
P47	cpe	4,370	5,085	7,854
P49	htp sdn	4,503	5,153	12,641

Grand Ville Brougham (wb 126.0)

		Wght	Price	Prod
R47	cpe	4,404	5,729	7,477
R49	htp sdn	4,558	5,896	15,686
R67	conv	4,520	5,858	4,519
	chassis	—	—	60

Grand Prix (wb 116.0)

		Wght	Price	Prod
K57	cpe	4,032	5,296	86,582

1975 Engines	bore×stroke	bhp	availability
L4, 140.0	3.50×3.63	78	S-Astre exc SJ
L4, 140.0	3.50×3.63	87	S-Astre SJ; O-Astre
L6, 250.0	3.88×3.53	105	S-Vntra,LeM exc Saf, GA, Fbd S87/T87
V8, 260.0	3.50×3.39	110	S-Ventura
V8, 350.0	3.88×3.75	145/165	O-Ventura
V8, 350.0	3.88×3.75	155	S-LeM exc Saf; Fbd S87/T87
V8, 350.0	3.88×3.75	175	S-Fbd U87; O-LeM exc Saf
V8, 400.0	4.12×3.75	170	S-LeM Saf, GA, Bon, Cat exc wgn; O-LeM,GP
V8, 400.0	4.12×3.75	185	S-T/A,Cat wgn; GSaf, GV; O-LeM,GA,U87
V8, 455.0	4.15×4.21	200	O-all exc Astre

1976

Astre (wb 97.0)

		Wght	Price	Prod
C11	sdn 2d	2,439	3,064	18,143
C15	Safari wgn 3d	2,545	3,306	13,125
C77	htchbk cpe 3d	2,505	3,179	19,116

Sunbird (wb 97.0)

		Wght	Price	Prod
M27	htchbk cpe 3d	2,653	3,431	52,031

Ventura (wb 111.1)

		Wght	Price	Prod
Y17	htchbk cpe 3d	3,428	3,503	8,251
Z17	SJ htchbk cpe 3d	3,460	3,775	
Y27	cpe	3,358	3,326	33,288
Z27	SJ cpe	3,370	3,612	
Y69	sdn 4d	3,350	3,361	32,577
Z69	SJ sdn 4d	3,406	3,637	

Firebird (wb 108.0)

		Wght	Price	Prod
S87	cpe	3,473	3,906	21,209
T87	Esprit cpe	3,521	4,162	22,252
U87	Formula cpe V8	3,625	4,566	20,613
W87	Trans Am cpe V8	3,640	4,987	46,701

LeMans (wb 116.0; 2d-112.0)

		Wght	Price	Prod
D29	sdn 4d	3,848	3,813	22,199
D37	sdn 2d	3,738	3,768	21,130
D35	Safari wgn 4d 2S V8	4,336	4,687	3,988
D45	Safari wgn 4d 3S V8	4,374	4,820	2,393
F37	Sport cpe	3,756	3,916	15,582
G29	Grand LeMans sdn 4d	3,948	4,433	8,411
G37	Grand LeMans sdn 2d	3,834	4,330	14,757
G35	Gd. LeM. Safari wgn 5d 2S V8	4,389	4,928	1,393
G45	Gd. LeM. Safari wgn 5d 3S V8	4,427	5,061	3,964

Catalina (wb 124.0; wgns-127.0)

		Wght	Price	Prod
L35	Safari wgn 4d 2S	4,944	5,324	4,735
L45	Safari wgn 4d 3S	5,000	5,473	5,513
L57	cpe	4,256	4,844	15,262
L69	sdn 4d	4,276	4,767	47,235

1975 Ventura three-door hatchback sedan

				Wght	Price	Prod
V8, 455.0	4.15×4.21	255		O-all full-size LNP		
V8, 455.0	4.15×4.21	290		O-Fbd Formula/Trans Am		

1975

Astre (wb 97.0)

		Wght	Price	Prod
C11	S sdn 2d	2,416	2,841	8,339
C15	S Safari wgn 3d	2,519	3,071	
V15	Safari wgn 3d	2,545	3,175	15,332
X15	SJ Safari wgn 3d	2,602	3,686	
C77	S htchbk cpe 3d	2,487	2,954	
V77	htchbk cpe 3d	2,499	3,079	40,809
X77	SJ htchbk cpe 3d	2,558	3,610	

Ventura (wb 111.1)

		Wght	Price	Prod
E27	S cpe	3,360	3,162	
Y27	cpe	3,382	3,293	34,023
Z27	Custom cpe	3,442	3,449	
B27	SJ cpe	3,424	3,829	
Y17	htchbk cpe	3,466	3,432	
Z17	Custom htchbk cpe 3d	3,482	3,593	10,463
B17	SJ htchbk cpe 3d	3,484	3,961	
Y69	sdn 4d	3,418	3,304	
Z69	Custom sdn 4d	3,462	3,464	22,068
B69	SJ sdn 4d	3,454	3,846	

Firebird (wb 108.0)

		Wght	Price	Prod
S87	cpe	3,498	3,713	22,293
T87	Esprit cpe	3,543	3,958	20,826
U87	Formula cpe V8	3,631	4,349	13,670
W87	Trans Am cpe V8	3,716	4,740	27,274

LeMans (wb 116.0; 2d-112.0)

		Wght	Price	Prod
D29	Colonnade sdn 4d	3,838	3,612	15,065
D35	wgn 5d 2S V8	4,401	4,555	3,988
D37	Colonnade sdn 2d	3,766	3,590	20,636
D45	wgn 5d 3S V8	4,439	4,688	2,393
F37	Sport cpe	3,798	3,708	23,817
G35	Grand wgn 5d 2S V8	4,462	4,749	1,393
G29	Grand Colonnade sdn 4d	3,896	4,157	4,906
G37	Grand Colonnade sdn 2d	3,832	4,101	19,310
G45	Grand wgn 5d 3S V8	4,500	4,882	1,501

Grand Am (wb 116.0; 2d 112.0)

		Wght	Price	Prod
H29	Colonnade sdn 4d	4,055	4,976	1,893
H37	Colonnade sdn 2d	4,008	4,887	8,786

Catalina (wb 124.0; wgns 127.0)

		Wght	Price	Prod
L35	Safari wgn 4d 2S	4,933	5,149	3,964
L45	Safari wgn 4d 3S	5,000	5,295	4,992
L57	htp cpe	4,334	4,700	21,644

Bonneville (wb 124.0; wgns-127.0)

P35	Grand Safari wgn 4d 2S	5,035	5,746	3,462
P45	Grand Safari wgn 4d 3S	5,091	5,895	6,176
P47	cpe	4,308	5,246	9,189
P49	sdn 4d	4,460	5,312	14,942
R47	Brougham cpe	4,341	5,734	10,466
R49	Brougham sdn 4d	4,514	5,906	20,236

Grand Prix (wb 116.0)—228,091 built

J57	cpe	4,048	4,798	—
K57	SJ cpe	4,052	5,223	—

1976 Engines	bore×stroke	bhp	availability
L4, 140.0	3.50×3.63	70	S-Astre,Sunbird
L4, 140.0	3.50×3.63	84	O-Astre,Sunbird
V6, 231.0	3.80×3.40	105	O-Sunbird
L6, 250.0	3.88×3.53	110	S-Vntra,LeM,Fbd exc T/A
V8, 260.0	3.50×3.39	110	S-Ventura; O-LeMans
V8, 350.0	3.88×3.75	140/155	O-Ventura
V8, 350.0	3.88×3.75	160	S-LeM,Fbd exc T/A,GP exc SJ
V8, 350.0	3.88×3.75	165	O-LeM,Fbd exc T/A,GP exc SJ
V8, 400.0	4.12×3.75	170	S-GLem,Glem Saf,Cat,Bonn
V8, 400.0	4.12×3.75	185	S-Fbd T/A, GP SJ; O-LeM, Fbd,Cat,Bon,GP
V8, 455.0	4.15×4.21	200	S-Cat/Bonn wgns; O-LeM,Fbd T/A,Cat,Bonn,GP

1977

Astre (wb 97.0)

		Wght	Price	Prod
C11	sdn 2d	2,480	3,305	10,327
C15	Safari wgn 3d	2,608	3,595	10,341
C77	htchbk cpe 3d	2,573	3,430	12,120

Sunbird (wb 97.0)

M07	htchbk cpe 3d	2,693	3,784	⎤
M27	htchbk cpe 3d	2,662	3,659	⎦ 55,398

Phoenix (wb 111.1)

X27	cpe	3,283	4,075	10,489
X69	sdn 4d	3,331	4,122	13,639

Ventura (wb 111.1)

Y17	htchbk cpe 3d	3,292	3,792	4,015
Y27	cpe	3,170	3,596	26,675
Y69	sdn 4d	3,210	3,650	27,089
Z17	SJ htchbk cpe 3d	3,336	4,165	1,100
Z27	SJ cpe	3,248	3,985	3,418
Z69	SJ sdn 4d	3,278	4,012	4,339

Firebird (wb 108.0)

S87	cpe	3,306	4,270	30,642
T87	Esprit cpe	3,354	4,551	34,548
U87	Formula cpe V8	3,411	4,977	21,801
W87	Trans Am cpe V8	3,526	5,456	68,745

LeMans (wb 116.0; 2d-112.0)

D29	sdn 4d	3,680	4,105	23,060
D37	cpe	3,592	4,057	16,038
D35	wgn 4d 2S V8	4,135	4,889	⎤
D35	wgn 4d 3S V8	4,167	5,041	⎦ 10,081
F37	Sport cpe	3,600	4,216	12,277
G29	Grand LeMans sdn 4d	3,782	4,742	5,584
G37	Grand LeMans cpe	3,630	4,614	7,851
G35	Grand LeMans wgn 4d 2S V8	4,179	5,144	⎤
G35	Grand LeMans wgn 4d 3S V8	4,211	5,296	⎦ 5,393

Catalina (wb 124.0; wgns-127.0)

L37	cpe	3,521	5,053	14,752
L69	sdn 4d	3,555	5,050	46,926
L35	Safari wgn 4d 2S V8	4,024	5,492	⎤
L35	Safari wgn 4d 3S V8	4,056	5,657	⎦ 13,058

Bonneville (wb 124.0; wgns 127.0)

N35	Grand Safari wgn 4d 2S	4,066	5,772	⎤
N35	Grand Safari wgn 4d 3S	4,098	5,937	⎦ 18,304
N37	cpe	3,579	5,411	37,117
N69	sdn 4d	3,616	5,457	13,697
Q37	Brougham cpe	3,617	5,897	15,901
Q69	Brougham sdn 4d	3,680	5,992	47,465

Grand Prix (wb 116.0)—228,430 built

J57	cpe	3,804	5,120	—
K57	LJ cpe	3,815	5,483	—
H57	SJ cpe	3,976	5,753	—

1977 Engines	bore×stroke	bhp	availability
L4, 140.0	3.50×3.63	84	O-Astre
L4, 151.0	4.00×3.00	87	S-Ast,Sbd; O-Phnx,Vntra
V6, 231.0	3.80×3.40	105	S-Phnx,Vntra,LeM,Fbd exc T/A, Cat; O-Sunbird
V8, 301.0	4.00×3.00	135	S-Vntra,LeM,Fbd exc T/A, Cat,Bon,GP exc SJ
V8, 305.0	3.70×3.48	145	S-Phnx; O-Vntra, Fbd exc T/A
V8, 350.0	3.88×3.75	170	O-Phnx, Vntra,LeM,Fbd exc T/A,GP
V8, 350.0	3.88×3.75	180	O-Cat,Bonn
V8, 400.0	4.12×3.75	180	S-Fbd T/A,GP SJ; O-LeM, Fbd,GP
V8, 403.0	4.36×3.39	185	O-Fbd,Cat,Bonn

1978

Sunbird (wb 97.0)—86,789 built

		Wght	Price	Prod
E27	htchbk cpe 3d	2,662	3,590	—
M07	htchbk cpe 3d	2,694	3,962	—
M15	Safari spt wgn 3d	2,610	3,741	—
M27	htchbk spt cpe	2,662	3,823	—

Phoenix (wb 111.1)

Y17	htchbk cpe 3d	3,250	4,103	3,252
Y27	cpe	3,167	3,907	26,143
Y69	sdn 4d	3,217	3,992	32,529
Z27	LJ cpe	3,276	4,399	6,210
Z69	LJ sdn 4d	3,325	4,484	8,393

Firebird (wb 108.0)

S87	cpe	3,316	4,593	32,672
T87	Esprit cpe	3,346	4,897	36,926
U87	Formula cpe V8	3,452	5,533	24,346
W87	Trans Am cpe V8	3,511	5,889	93,341

LeMans (wb 116.0; 2d-112.0)

D19	sdn 4d	3,108	4,512	22,728
D27	cpe	3,098	4,427	20,581
D35	Safari wgn 4d	3,298	4,980	15,714
F19	Grand LeMans sdn 4d	3,158	4,915	21,252
F27	Grand LeMans cpe	3,130	4,801	18,433
F35	G. LeM Safari wgn 5d	3,316	5,310	11,125
G19	Grand Am sdn 4d V8	3,239	5,634	2,841
G27	Grand Am cpe V8	3,209	5,520	7,767

Catalina (wb 116.0)

L35	Safari wgn 4d 2S V8	3,976	6,011	12,819
L37	cpe	3,498	5,439	9,224
L69	sdn 4d	3,530	5,484	39,707

Bonneville (116.0)

N35	Grand Safari wgn 4d 2S	4,002	6,319	13,847
N37	cpe	3,581	5,913	22,510
N69	sdn 4d	3,637	6,023	48,647
Q37	Brougham cpe	3,611	6,674	17,948
Q69	Brougham sdn 4d	3,667	6,784	36,192

Grand Prix (wb 108.1)—228,444 built

J37	cpe V6/V8	3,162	4,880	—
K37	LJ cpe V8	3,216	5,815	—
H37	SJ cpe V8	3,229	6,088	—

1978 Engines	bore×stroke	bhp	availability
L4, 151.0	4.00×3.00	85	S-Snbd; O-Phnx
V6, 231.0	3.80×3.40	105	S-Phnx,LeM exc GA, Fbd S87/T87, Cat,GP, exc SJ O-Snbd
V8, 301.0	4.00×3.00	140	S-LeM GA,Cat,Bonn,GP exc SJ
V8, 301.0	4.00×3.00	150	O-LeM GA, GP SJ
V8, 305.0	3.70×3.48	145	S-Phnx,LeM,Fbd exc U/W87; O-Snbd LeM GA, GP
V8, 350.0	3.88×3.75	160	O-Phoenix,Firebird
V8, 350.0	3.88×3.75	155/170	O-Catalina, Bonn
V8, 400.0	4.12×3.75	180	S-Fbd T/A; O-Fbd Fmla Cat, Bonn
V8, 403.0	4.36×3.38	185	O-Fbd,Cat,Bonn

	bore×stroke	bhp	availability
V8, 301.0	4.00×3.00	150	O-LeM GA, GP SJ
V8, 305.0	3.70×3.48	145	S-Phnx,LeM,Fbd S/T87; O-Sunbd, Lem GA, GP
V8, 350.0	3.88×3.75	160	O-Phnx, Fbd
V8, 350.0	3.88×3.75	155/170	O-Catalina, Bonn
V8, 400.0	4.12×3.75	180	S-Fbd T/A; O-Fbd Fml, Cat, Bonn
V8, 403.0	4.36×3.38	185	O-Fbd,Cat,Bonn

1979

Sunbird (wb 97.0)

		Wght	Price	Prod
M07	cpe	2,642	4,379	24,221
M15	Safari spt wgn 3d	2,651	4,321	2,902
M27	spt cpe	2,593	4,274	70,647
E27	htchbk cpe 3d	2,593	4,016	—

Phoenix (wb 111.1)

		Wght	Price	Prod
Y17	htchbk cpe 3d	3,319	4,239	923
Y27	cpe	3,236	4,089	9,233
Y69	sdn 4d	3,286	4,189	10,565
Z27	LJ cpe	3,345	4,589	1,826
Z69	LJ sdn 4d	3,394	4,689	2,353

Firebird (wb 108.0)

		Wght	Price	Prod
S87	cpe	3,294	5,260	38,642
T87	Esprit cpe	3,324	5,638	30,853
U87	Formula cpe V8	3,460	6,564	24,850
W87	Trans Am cpe V8	3,551	6,883	109,609
X87	T/A Limited Edition	3,551	10,620	7,500

LeMans (wb 116.0; 2d-112.0)

		Wght	Price	Prod
D19	sdn 4d	3,082	5,134	26,958
D27	cpe	3,076	5,031	14,197
D35	Safari wgn	3,240	5,587	27,517
F19	Grand LeMans sdn 4d	3,126	5,430	28,599
F27	Grand LeMans cpe	3,098	5,302	13,020
F35	Grand LeM Safari wgn	3,274	5,931	20,783
G19	Grand Am sdn 4d	3,124	5,529	1,865
G27	Grand Am cpe	3,120	5,530	4,021

Catalina (wb 116.0)

		Wght	Price	Prod
L35	wgn 4d 2S V8	3,997	6,681	⎤ 13,353
L35	wgn 4d 3S V8	4,029	6,864	⎦
L37	cpe	3,534	6,020	5,410
L69	sdn 4d	3,566	6,076	28,121

Bonneville (wb 116.0)

		Wght	Price	Prod
N35	Safari wgn 4d 2S	4,022	7,050	⎤ 16,925
N35	Safari wgn 4d 3S	4,054	7,233	⎦
N37	cpe	3,616	6,593	51,491
Q37	Brougham cpe	3,659	7,395	⎤
N69	sdn 4d	3,672	6,718	⎥ 111,000
Q69	Brougham sdn 4d	3,726	7,584	⎦

Grand Prix (wb 108.1)—210,050 built

		Wght	Price	Prod
J37	cpe	3,166	5,454	—
K37	LJ cpe V8	3,285	6,555	—
H37	SJ cpe V8	3,349	6,814	—

1979 Engines	bore×stroke	bhp	availability
L4, 151.0	4.00×3.00	85	S-Sunbd; O-Phnx
V6, 231.0	3.80×3.40	115	S-all 6s; O-Sunbd
V8, 301.0	4.00×3.00	140	S-Phnx,LeM exc GA, Fbd,GP exc SJ

1980

Sunbird (wb 97.0)

		Wght	Price	Prod
E07	htchbk cpe 3d	2,651	4,808	52,952
M07	spt cpe	2,657	4,996	⎤
E27	htchbk cpe 3d	2,603	4,623	⎥ 135,027
M27	spt cpe	2,609	4,885	⎦

Phoenix (wb 104.9)

		Wght	Price	Prod
Y37	cpe	2,516	5,465	49,485
Y67	htchbk sdn 5d	2,558	5,656	72,875
Z37	LJ cpe	2,550	5,936	23,674
Z68	LJ htchbk sdn 5d	2,610	6,127	32,256

Firebird (wb 108.0)

		Wght	Price	Prod
S87	cpe	3,306	5,948	29,811
T87	Esprit cpe	3,360	6,311	17,277
V87	Formula cpe V8	3,410	7,256	9,356
W87	Trans Am cpe V8	3,429	7,480	50,896

LeMans (wb 108.0)

		Wght	Price	Prod
D19	sdn 4d	3,080	5,758	20,484
D27	cpe	3,064	5,652	9,109
D35	Safari wgn 4d	3,296	6,257	12,912
F19	Grand LeMans sdn 4d	3,129	6,120	18,561
F27	Grand LeMans cpe	3,090	5,947	6,477
F35	Grand LeMans Safari wgn 4d	3,328	6,682	14,832
G27	Grand Am cpe V8	3,299	7,504	1,647

Catalina (wb 116.0)

		Wght	Price	Prod
L35	Safari wgn 4d 2S V8	3,929	7,362	⎤ 2,930
L35	Safari wgn 4d 3S V8	3,961	7,561	⎦
L37	cpe	3,448	6,703	3,319
L69	sdn 4d	3,474	6,761	10,408

Bonneville (wb 116.0)

		Wght	Price	Prod
N35	Safari wgn 4d 2S V8	3,939	7,958	⎤ 5,309
N35	Safari wgn 4d 3S V8	3,981	8,157	⎦
N37	cpe	3,486	7,034	⎤ 29,144
R37	Brougham cpe	3,525	7,968	⎦
N69	sdn 4d	3,532	7,167	⎤ 47,359
R69	Brougham sdn 4d	3,610	8,160	⎦

Grand Prix (wb 108.1)—114,000 built

		Wght	Price	Prod
J37	cpe V6/V8	3,201	6,621	—
K37	LJ cpe V6/V8	3,342	7,000	—
H37	SJ cpe V8	3,291	7,597	—

1980 Engines	bore×stroke	bhp	availability
L4, 151.0	4.00×3.00	86	S-Sunbird
L4, 151.0	4.00×3.00	90	S-Phoenix
V6, 173.0	3.50×3.00	115	S-Phoenix
V6, 231.0	3.80×3.40	110	S-LeMans
V6, 231.0	3.80×3.40	115	S-Fbd,Cat,Bon,GP; O-Sbd
V8, 265.0	3.75×3.00	120	S-LeM,Fbd S/T, Cat, Bonn exc wgn, GP exc SJ
V8, 301.0	4.00×3.00	140	S-GA,Fbd V/W,Cat,Bonn wgn, GP SJ; O-LeM, Fbd, Cat,Bonn, GP
V8, 301.0 turbo	4.00×3.00	210	O-Fbd V/W
V8, 305.0	3.70×3.48	150	O-LeM, Fbd, GP
V8, 350.0 dsl	3.88×3.75	105	O-Cat,Bonn wgn/B'ham
V8, 350.0	3.88×3.75	155/160	O-Catalina, Bonn

Rambler

**American Motors Corp.
Kenosha, Wisconsin**

When George Romney succeeded George Mason as president of American Motors, he turned his full attention to the Rambler and soon forgot about Mason's merger plans (see Nash), including a link-up with Studebaker-Packard. The Rambler was AMC's most successful car, and developed a whole new market.

Retaining the 108-inch wheelbase unit body/chassis introduced in '56, AMC removed ostensible Nash and Hudson parentage to make Rambler a separate nameplate for the 1957 model year. The car was solidly built, reliable, and perfectly attuned to the burgeoning market for economy cars. By 1961, its successors had brought Rambler to third place in the industry.

All but forgotten today is the fact that AMC introduced the industry's first four-door hardtop wagon: the 1956 (Nash and Hudson) Rambler Cross Country. This neat, airy, roomy wagon featured a 33 percent increase in cargo space over that of the '55s, and a roll-down tailgate window that eliminated the clumsy upper hatch. "We just rolled with those cars," said former AMC Board Chairman Roy D. Chapin, Jr. "We couldn't get enough." There was nothing like the luxurious little Cross Country, and the public responded accordingly.

In 1957, with the big Hudson and Nash destined for oblivion, American Motors built 118,990 cars; 114,084

of them were Ramblers. The overhead-valve six was raised in horsepower, while a lively new oversquare V8 was offered with 190 hp at 4900 rpm. It was available only on the upper-priced cars—Custom and Super sedan and wagon. An interesting new Custom model was the specially trimmed Rebel, a four-door hardtop announced at mid-year with an even larger V8, the new AMC 327. The Rebel had Gabriel shocks, an anti-roll bar, heavy-duty springs, power steering, and power brakes. All that and 255 bhp from the V8's 9.5:1 compression ratio transformed Rambler's image. During tests at Daytona Beach, a Rebel flew from 0 to 60 mph (and 50 to 80) in scarcely more than seven seconds. Unfortunately, it just didn't appeal to the Rambler market, and only 1500 were built. Rebel was the most expensive '57 offering, and that may have contributed to its low sales.

Economy cars were continuing to set sales records, so AMC brought back its old 100-inch '55 models for 1958. Called Rambler American and fitted with a new mesh-type grille, it was priced very low. It couldn't help but sell, and over 42,000 Americans were registered for the 12 months. Larger Ramblers received more than 100 changes for '58, and were outwardly quite different from their predecessors. The grille was made more massive

1957 Custom hardtop sedan

1957 DeLuxe four-door sedan

1957 Custom Cross Country hardtop wagon

1957 Rebel Custom hardtop sedan

and square, dual headlamps were used, fashionable little fins appeared at the rear, and a pedal-type parking brake was adopted. The six-cylinder Super Cross Country wagon was the top seller that year. The Rebel name was retained for top-line models powered by the 250-cid V8. But Rambler did not revive its fancy, limited-edition Rebel hardtop. Instead, it created a new 117-inch wheelbase for a separate line powered by the 327 V8 and named Ambassador.

Actually, Ambassador styling had been predicted in mid-1957, when it was thought that these cars would bear separate Nash and Hudson identification. In essence, they were stretched versions of the roomy, squarish Rambler unit body/chassis, available as four-door sedans and wagons, with or without roof pillars. The Ambassador hardtop wagon was the only one of its type in the '58 line, and only 294 were sold. In fact, sales overall were quite disappointing—just 1340 for the model year. Ambassador was entering a field of heavy competition and decreasing demand, and AMC did much better with its smaller Ramblers. Registrations of all 1958 models climbed in a year that was generally a disaster for other manufacturers. After four years of losses, AMC turned the corner, making a profit of $26 million on sales of $470 million.

For 1959, it was the same formula again. This time, the company netted $60 million in profits and built nearly 364,000 cars for an all-time record. The same models and powertrains were fielded, but horsepower wasn't raised. Unlike its competitors, AMC had apparently decided enough was enough.

A two-door wagon was revived for the Rambler American DeLuxe and Super lines, helping rack up 90,000 sales for the '59 junior series. The 108-inch-wheelbase cars were mildly facelifted with thin "color sweep" side moldings and simplified grilles. As in 1958, Rambler V8s were called Rebels and used the 250-cid engine. The Ambassador Super and Custom continued as before on the longer wheelbase and with a more ornate grille.

At the beginning of the '60s, everything looked rosy. Led by hard-driving president Romney, Rambler could do no wrong. In 1960 it almost beat Plymouth for third place in production, with nearly half a million cars, and did in 1961. This was the highest sales volume ever recorded for an independent. But Rambler's success triggered an avalanche of compacts from the Big Three—and formidable new competition. A downward slide began in 1962, when Rambler was passed by Pontiac. By 1967, AMC as a whole was in 12th place.

Perhaps Romney saw the handwriting on the wall, because he left the company in 1962. Replacing him was Roy Abernethy, who began a program of product diversification that tried to meet the opposition on every front. It didn't work, and Abernethy was succeeded by Roy D. Chapin, Jr. in 1966. Chapin became AMC board chairman in 1967, and William V. Luneberg became president. The Chapin-Luneberg administration ordered new makes like the Javelin, and dropped

the Rambler name completely after 1969.

For 1960, the 108-inch-wheelbase unibody Rambler acquired less cluttered lines, little tailfins, and a full-width grille. Facelifts occurred in 1961 and '62 as the cars became known as Rambler Classics. A lower hoodline for '61 was accompanied by an eggcrate

1958 Rebel Custom four-door sedan

1958 Rebel Custom Cross Country station wagon

1959 Rebel Custom Country Club hardtop sedan

1959 American Super two-door sedan

1960 American Super two-door station wagon

1961 Classic Custom four-door station wagon

1961 Ambassador Custom four-door sedan

1961 American Custom convertible

grille. In 1962, the crate held larger eggs, the fins were cropped, and the side sweep-spear was moved higher. An interesting option was the E-stick, a combination automatic and clutch transmission that cost $60. But it was too complex to sell really well. It was similar in concept to the twin-stick manual gearbox of the 1979 Dodge Colt FF and Plymouth Champ made by Mitsubishi of Japan.

Richard A. Teague joined the American Motors design staff in 1961, and the first cars he was able to influence were the '63 Classic and Ambassador. Teague used a longer (112-inch) wheelbase, a lower silhouette than before, a concave grille, sculptured body panels, and curved side glass to create a smooth new shape. Although still chunky, the new Rambler was at least cleanly styled. The Classic retained this basic body shape throughout its life span. Teague made further refinements to the design over the next few years. The 1964s had a new flush grille and stainless-steel-trimmed rocker panels. Two hardtop coupes were added to the line, which until then had consisted of two- and four-door sedans and four-door Cross Country station wagons. The 1965s received a new grille, a squared-off hood, and wraparound taillights. The '66s featured a new roof with convertible-like accents, a revised roof and tailgate for station wagons, and more sharply creased lines from front to rear.

For 1967, the Classic was renamed Rebel. From 1968 on, Rebel was listed as a separate make (see the American Motors chapter), the Rambler name reserved only for the smaller American line. The '67 Rebel had a two-inch longer wheelbase. Its all-new styling comprised a floating rectangular grille flanked by horizontal dual

headlamps and squarish front fenders that flowed into a curved rear fenderline. The rear end displayed large, canted taillights blended into the fenders.

Rambler started the '60s with two engines, a six and a V8. The six, a holdover from Nash days, developed 127 or 138 bhp, and was standard on Classics through 1964. The V8 had been designed for use by Hudson and Nash in the mid-1950s. In its 1960-61 form, it developed either 200 or 215 bhp.

The '61 Classic V8 scored well for both performance and economy. When equipped with the optional Flash-omatic (Borg-Warner) automatc transmission, it could spring from 0 to 60 mph in ten seconds, and delivered 16 to 20 miles per gallon. But the V8 was heavier than the six, so that no less than 57 percent of the car's curb weight was over the front wheels. Sales were not high. When the Ambassador was made smaller for 1962-63, the V8 Classic was temporarily dropped.

In 1964, it returned with 198 bhp. For 1965, a 270-bhp version was available. For the 1967 Rebel, the engine was stroked for 200 bhp. A larger V8, the Ambassador 327, was also offered for the '66 Classic. For the 1967 Rebel, it was enlarged by boring and stroking to 343 cid, which gave 235 or 280 bhp depending on tune.

As an option to the Classic's standard six, Rambler brought out a new oversquare engine for 1964, the Torque Command or Typhoon six, which yielded 145 bhp. About 2500 special Typhoon hardtops, painted yellow and black, were released to celebrate the occasion.

At the lower end of the size and price scale was the Rambler American. In 1960 form, it was an anachronism with its old Pininfarina styling and an ancient Nash L-

head six. Convinced that the American was marketable, AMC restyled it for 1961. The new model also got a new overhead-valve engine that had actually appeared in mid-1960 on the larger Ramblers. Available with either 90 or 125 bhp, it gave the American fuel mileage in the middle 20s, plus adequate performance. The styling, created by Edmund Anderson, was something else again: boxy and truncated, with odd, concave side sculpturing. Sedans, business coupes, two- and four-door wagons, and a convertible were offered in three series. Although they were genuine economy cars and provided a fair amount of interior room, they were anything but beautiful. Teague decided to change them at all costs for 1964.

The revamped design sat on a longer 106-inch wheelbase, as the Classic had already gone from 108 to 112. It was a clean car with curved glass and modest brightwork—quite in keeping with its function. The styling was so good, in fact, that it wasn't significantly altered for the rest of the decade. By 1968, the American had a specially trimmed hardtop derivative, the Rogue. In 1969, the base American was still listed under $2000. A post-introduction decision was to offer AMC's new 290-cid V8 as an option. This led to a limited-edition Rogue, equipped with an even larger 315-bhp 390 engine and Hurst shifter, called the SC/Rambler. "Scramblers" were sold to a handful of buyers. Though hardly in keeping with the traditional Rambler image, they were impressive performers.

Teague hastily conjured up a bucket-seat fastback for 1965 to do battle with Mustang and Barracuda. The result was the Marlin, a Rambler model in 1965 and a make in its own right thereafter. The Marlin was basically a Rambler Classic reworked above the beltline with a sweeping glassed-in greenhouse. When equipped with the 327 V8, a Marlin would do 0 to 60 mph in 12 seconds and the standing quarter-mile in 18 seconds at 76 mph—not earthshaking, but performance of a sort. And that was the goal: to turn Rambler's image around by making cars that appeared sporty and fun to drive, instead of just dull and economical.

The 1960-61 Ambassador was a continuation of the '58 original, with increasingly luxurious interiors and slightly excessive ornamentation. The price leader in both years was the Deluxe four-door sedan. In addition, there were Super and Custom four-doors, and wagons with either six or eight seats. In 1961, a posh Custom 400 sedan with the highest-quality trim and standard automatic was added. The 327 V8 was standard power. But before the end of the '50s, AMC managers had decided the large Ambassador V8s were not salable. For 1962, therefore, the 117-inch wheelbase was dropped, and Ambassador shared the Classic body and chassis. The V8 was dropped from the Classic's option list and was restricted to Ambassador only.

For 1963, Teague planned to restyle the Classic, which, of course, meant a restyled Ambassador as well. Again, both cars shared the same wheelbase. From a distance, Classics and Ambassadors looked almost

1966 American 440 convertible

1967 Rebel SST hardtop coupe

1969 Rogue hardtop coupe

identical—and they *were* similar, except for power-plants. For 1964, Classic was offered with an optional small V8. Ambassador was then restricted to one 327-powered 990 series. There was a sedan, a Cross Country wagon, and two hardtop coupes called the 990 and 990H. The 990H was the only Ambassador with the 270-bhp engine standard.

The 1964 lineup wasn't particularly successful, so the game plan was changed again for '65. Ambassador now returned its own (116-inch) wheelbase (the Classic stayed with the 112), and in standard form had the 232-cid six. There were almost no changes for '66, except that the name was registered as a separate make.

The styling of the '65 Rambler Ambassador was probably the best it had ever been. Teague's four-square design resulted in an intermediate comparable in size to the Ford Fairlane, but with distinctive looks and more interior space.

AMC made a play for the soft-top market in 1965: there was a convertible in every line—American, Classic, and Ambassador. Unhappily, they tended to leak because of the curved side windows, and did not sell well. Soft-top production in '65 consisted of 3882 Americans, 4953 Classics, and 3499 Ambassadors. The Ambassador convertible was dropped after 1967.

Rambler

Rambler Specifications

1957*

Six (wb 108.0)		Wght	Price	Prod
5715	DeLuxe sdn 4d	2,911	1.961	—
5715-1	Super sdn 4d	2,914	2,123	—
5715-2	Custom sdn 4d	2,938	2,213	—
5718-1	Super Crss Cntry wgn 4d	3,042	2,410	—
5718-2	Custom Crss Cntry wgn 4d	3,076	2,500	—
5719-1	Super htp sdn	2,936	2,208	—

V8 (wb 108.0)				
5723-2	Custom Crss Cntry htp wgn 4d	3,409	2,715	—
5725-1	Super sdn 4d	3,223	2,253	—
5725-2	Custom sdn 4d	3,259	2,343	—
5728-1	Super Crss Cntry wgn 4d	3,359	2,540	—
5728-2	Custom Crss Cntry wgn 4d	3,392	2,630	—
5729-2	Custom htp sdn	3,269	2,428	—
5739-2	Custom Rebel htp sdn	3,353	2,786	1,500

*Total model year registrations: 91,409.

1957 Engines	bore×stroke	bhp	availability
L6, 195.6	3.13×4.25	135	S-Six
V8, 250.0	3.50×3.25	190	S-V8 exc Rebel
V8, 327.0	4.00×3.25	255	S-Rebel

1958*

American (wb 100.0)		Wght	Price	Prod
5802	bus sdn 3P	2,439	1,775	—
5806	DeLuxe sdn 2d	2,463	1,789	—
5806-1	Super sdn 2d	2,475	1,874	—

Six (wb 108.0)				
5815	DeLuxe sdn 4d	2,947	2,047	—
5815-1	Super sdn 4d	2,960	2,212	—
5815-2	Custom sdn 4d	2,968	2,327	—
5818	DeLuxe wgn 4d	3,050	2,370	—
5818-1	Super Crss Cntry wgn 4d	3,069	2,506	—
5818-2	Custom Crss Cntry wgn 4d	3,079	2,621	—
5819-1	Super Ctry Club htp cpe	2,983	2,287	—

Rebel V8 (wb 108.0)				
5825	DeLuxe sdn 4d	3,287	2,177	—
5825-1	Super sdn 4d	3,300	2,342	—
5825-2	Custom sdn 4d	3,313	2,457	—
5828-1	Super Crss Cntry wgn 4d	3,410	2,636	—
5828-2	Custom Crss Cntry wgn 4d	3,418	2,751	—
5829-2	Custom Ctry Club htp cpe	3,328	2,532	—

Ambassador (wb 117.0)—1,340 built (inc 294 model 5883-2)				
5883-2	Custom Crss Cntry htp wgn 4d	3,586	3,116	—
5885-1	Super sdn 4d	3,456	2,587	—
5885-2	Custom sdn 4d	3,462	2,732	—
5888-1	Super Crss Cntry wgn 4d	3,544	2,881	—
5888-2	Custom Crss Cntry wgn 4d	3,568	3,026	—
5889-2	Custom Ctry Club htp sdn	3,475	2,822	—

*Total model year registrations: 186,227.

1958 Engines	bore×stroke	bhp	availability
L6, 195.6	3.13×4.25	90	S-American
L6, 195.6	3.13×4.25	127	S-Six
L6, 195.6	3.13×4.25	138	O-Six
V8, 250.0	3.50×3.25	215	S-Rebel
V8, 327.0	4.00×3.25	270	S-Ambassador

1959*

American (wb 100.0)—90,000 built		Wght	Price	Prod
5902	bux scn 3P	2,435	1,821	—
5904	DeLuxe wgn 2d	2,554	2,060	—
5904-1	Super wgn 2d	2,554	2,145	—
5906	DeLuxe sdn 2d	2,476	1,835	—
5906-1	Super sdn 2d	2,492	1,920	—

Six (wb 108.0)				
5915	DeLuxe sdn 4d	2,934	2,098	—
5915-1	Super sdn 4d	2,951	2,268	—
5915-2	Custom sdn 4d	2,956	2,383	—
5918	DeLuxe Crss Cntry wgn 4d	3,047	2,427	—
5918-1	Super Crss Cntry wgn 4d	3,082	2,562	—
5918-2	Custom Crss Cntry wgn 4d	3,097	2,677	—
5919-1	Super Ctry Club htp sdn	2,961	2,343	—

Rebel V8 (wb 108.0)				
5925	DeLuxe sdn 4d	3,283	2,228	—
5925-1	Super sdn 4d	3,287	2,398	—
5925-2	Custom sdn 4d	3,295	2,513	—
5928-1	Super Crss Cntry wgn 4d	3,398	2,692	—
5928-2	Custom Crss Cntry wgn 4d	3,407	2,807	—
5929-2	Custom Ctry Club htp sdn	3,338	2,600	—

Ambassador (wb 117.0)				
5983-2	Custom htp wgn 4d	3,591	3,116	—
5985-1	Super sdn 4d	3,428	2,587	—
5985-2	Custom sdn 4d	3,437	2,732	—
5988-1	Super Crss Cntry wgn 4d	3,546	2,881	—
5988-2	Custom Crss Cntry wgn 4d	3,562	3,026	—
5989-2	Custom Ctry Club htp sdn	3,483	2,822	—

*Total model year registrations: 363,372.

1959 Engines	bore×stroke	bhp	availability
L6, 195.6	3.13×4.25	90	S-American
L6, 195.6	3.13×4.25	127	S-Six
L6, 195.6	3.13×4.25	138	O-Six
V8, 250.0	3.50×3.25	215	S-Rebel
V8, 327.0	4.00×3.25	270	S-Ambassador

1960*

American (wb 100.0)		Wght	Price	Prod
6002	DeLuxe bus sdn 3P	2,428	1,781	—
6004	DeLuxe wgn 2d	2,527	2,020	—
6004-1	Super wgn 2d	2,549	2,185	—
6004-2	Custom wgn 2d	2,606	2,235	—
6005	DeLuxe sdn 4d	2,474	1,844	—
6005-1	Super sdn 4d	2,490	1,929	—
6005-2	Custom sdn 4d	2,551	2,059	—
6006	DeLuxe sdn 2d	2,451	1,795	—
6006-1	Super sdn 2d	2,462	1,880	—
6006-2	Custom sdn 2d	2,523	2,010	—

Six (wb 108.0)				
6015	DeLuxe sdn 4d	2,912	2,098	—
6015-1	Super sdn 4d	2,930	2,268	—
6015-2	Custom sdn 4d	2,929	2,383	—
6018	DeLuxe wgn 4d	3,051	2,427	—
6018-1	Super wgn 4d, 6P	3,054	2,562	—
6018-2	Custom wgn 4d, 6P	3,057	2,677	—
6018-3	Super wgn 4d, 8P	3,117	2,687	—
6018-4	Custom wgn 4d, 8P	3,137	2,802	—
6019-2	Custom htp sdn	2,981	2,458	—

Rebel V8 (wb 108.0)				
6025	DeLuxe sdn 4d	3,252	2,217	—
6025-1	Super sdn 4d	3,270	2,387	—
6025-2	Custom sdn 4d	3,278	2,502	—

		Wght	Price	Prod
6028-1	Super wgn 4d, 6P	3,391	2,681	—
6028-2	Custom wgn 4d, 6P	3,395	2,796	—
6028-3	Super wgn 4d, 8P	3,446	2,806	—
6028-4	Custom wgn 4d, 8P	3,447	2,921	—
6029-2	Custom htp sdn	3,319	2,577	—

Ambassador (wb 117.0)

		Wght	Price	Prod
6083-2	Custom htp wgn 4d	3,583	3,116	—
6085	DeLuxe sdn 4d	3,384	2,395	—
6085-1	Super sdn 4d	3,395	2,587	—
6085-2	Custom sdn 4d	3,408	2,732	—
6088-1	Super wgn 4d, 6P	3,521	2,881	—
6088-2	Custom wgn 4d, 6P	3,538	3,026	—
6088-3	Super wgn 4d, 8P	3,581	3,006	—
6088-4	Custom wgn 4d, 8P	3,592	3,151	—
6089-2	Custom htp sdn	3,465	2,822	—

*Total model year registrations: 422,273.

1960 Engines	bore×stroke	bhp	availability
L6, 195.6	3.13×4.25	90	S-American
L6, 195.6	3.13×4.25	127	S-Six
L6, 195.6	3.13×4.25	138	O-Six
V8, 250.0	3.50×3.25	200	S-Rebel
V8, 250.0	3.50×3.25	215	O-Rebel
V8, 327.0	4.00×3.25	250	S-Ambassador
V8, 327.0	4.00×3.25	270	O-Ambassador

1961*

American (wb 100.00)

		Wght	Price	Prod
6102	DeLuxe bus sdn 2d	2,454	1,831	—
6104	DeLuxe wgn 2d	2,549	2,080	—
6104-1	Super wgn 2d	2,556	2,165	—
6104-2	Custom wgn 2d	2,617	2,295	—
6105	DeLuxe sdn 4d	2,523	1,894	—
6105-1	Super sdn 4d	2,530	1,979	—
6105-2	Custom sdn 2d	2,557	2,060	—
6106	DeLuxe sdn 2d	2,490	1,845	—
6106-1	Super sdn 2d	2,499	1,930	—
6106-2	Custom sdn 2d	2,557	2,060	—
6107-2	Custom conv cpe	2,712	2,369	—
6108	DeLuxe wgn 4d	2,595	2,129	—
6108-1	Super wgn 4d	2,602	2,214	—
6108-2	Custom wgn 4d	2,660	2,344	—

Classic Six (wb 108.0)

		Wght	Price	Prod
6115	DeLuxe sdn 4d	2,905	2,098	—
6115-1	Super sdn 4d	2,923	2,268	—
6115-2	Custom sdn 4d	2,863	2,413	—
6118	DeLuxe wgn 4d	3,037	2,437	—
6118-1	Super wgn 4d, 6P	3,046	2,572	—
6118-2	Custom wgn 4d, 6P	2,984	2,717	—
6118-3	Super wgn 4d, 8P	3,087	2,697	—
6118-4	Custom wgn 4d, 8P	3,023	2,842	—

Classic V8 (wb 108.0)

		Wght	Price	Prod
6125	DeLuxe sdn 4d	3,237	2,227	—
6125-1	Super sdn 4d	3,255	2,397	—
6125-2	Custom sdn 4d	3,262	2,512	—
6128-1	Super wgn 4d, 6P	3,372	2,701	—
6128-2	Custom wgn 4d, 6P	3,378	2,816	—
6128-3	Super wgn 4d, 8P	3,408	2,826	—
6128-4	Custom wgn 4d, 8P	3,420	2,941	—

Ambassador (wb 117.0)

		Wght	Price	Prod
6185	DeLuxe sdn 4d	3,343	2,395	—
6185-1	Super sdn 4d	3,361	2,537	—
6185-2	Custom sdn 4d	3,380	2,682	—
6188-1	Super wgn 4d, 6P	3,493	2,841	—
6188-2	Custom wgn 4d, 6P	3,495	2,986	—
6188-3	Super wgn 4d, 8P	3,560	2,966	—
6188-4	Custom wgn 4d, 8P	3,566	3,111	—

*Total model year registrations: 370,685.

1961 Engines	bore×stroke	bhp	availability
L6, 195.6	3.13×4.25	90	S-American exc Custom
L6, 195.6	3.13×4.25	125	S-American Custom
L6, 195.6	3.13×4.25	127	S-Classic Six
L6, 195.6	3.13×4.25	138	O-Classic Six
V8, 250.0	3.50×3.25	200	S-Classic V8
V8, 250.0	3.50×3.25	215	O-Classic V8
V8, 327.0	4.00×3.25	250	S-Ambassador
V8, 327.0	4.00×3.25	270	O-Ambassador

1962*

American (wb 100.0)

		Wght	Price	Prod
6202	DeLuxe bus sdn 2d	2,454	1,832	—
6204	DeLuxe wgn 2d	2,555	2,081	—
6204-2	Custom wgn 2d	2,565	2,141	—
6205	DeLuxe sdn 4d	2,500	1,895	—
6205-2	Custom sdn 4d	2,512	1,958	—
6205-5	400 sdn 4d	2,585	2,089	—
6206	DeLuxe sdn 2d	2,480	1,846	—
6206-2	Custom sdn 2d	2,492	1,909	—
6206-5	400 sdn 2d	2,558	2,040	—
6207-5	400 conv cpe	2,735	2,344	—
6208	DeLuxe wgn 4d	2,573	2,130	—
6208-2	Custom wgn 4d	2,600	2,190	—
6208-5	400 wgn 4d	2,692	2,320	—

Classic (wb 108.0)

		Wght	Price	Prod
6215	DeLuxe sdn 4d	2,888	2,050	—
6215-2	Custom sdn 4d	2,898	2,200	—
6215-5	400 sdn 4d	2,853	2,349	—
6216	DeLuxe sdn 4d	2,866	2,000	—
6216-2	Custom sdn 2d	2,876	2,150	—
6216-5	400 sdn 2d	2,841	2,299	—
6218	DeLuxe wgn 4d, 6P	3,014	2,380	—
6218-2	Custom wgn 4d, 6P	3,024	2,492	—
6218-4	Custom wgn 4d, 8P	3,094	2,614	—
6218-5	400 wgn 4d	2,985	2,640	—

Ambassador (wb 108.0)

		Wght	Price	Prod
6285	DeLuxe sdn 4d	3,249	2,336	—
6285-2	Custom sdn 4d	3,259	2,464	—
6285-5	400 sdn 4d	3,283	2,605	—
6286	DeLuxe sdn 2d	3,227	2,282	—
6286-2	Custom sdn 2d	3,237	2,410	—
6286-5	400 sdn 2d	3,261	2,551	—
6288	DeLuxe wgn 4d	3,375	2,648	—
6288-2	Custom wgn 4d	3,385	2,760	—
6288-5	400 wgn 4d, 6P	3,408	2,901	—
6288-6	400 wgn 4d, 8P	3,471	3,023	—

*Total model year registrations: 423,104.

1962 Engines	bore×stroke	bhp	availability
L6, 195.6	3.13×4.25	90	S-American
L6, 195.6	3.13×4.25	125	O-American
L6, 195.6	3.13×4.25	127	S-Classic
L6, 195.6	3.13×4.25	138	O-Classic
V8, 327.0	4.00×3.25	250	S-Ambassador
V8, 327.0	4.00×3.25	270	O-Ambassador

1963*

American (wb 100.0)

		Wght	Price	Prod
6302	220 bus sdn 2d	2,446	1,832	—

		Wght	Price	Prod
6304	220 wgn 2d	2,528	2,081	—
6304-2	330 wgn 2d	2,539	2,141	—
6305	220 sdn 4d	2,485	1,895	—
6305-2	330 sdn 4d	2,500	1,958	—
6305-5	440 sdn 4d	2,575	2,089	—
6306	220 sdn 2d	2,472	1,846	—
6306-2	330 sdn 2d	2,484	1,909	—
6306-5	440 sdn 2d	2,556	2,040	—
6307-5	440 conv cpe	2,743	2,344	—
6308	220 wgn 4d	2,549	2,130	—
6308-2	330 wgn 4d	2,561	2,190	—
6308-5	440 wgn 4d	2,638	2,320	—
6309-5	440 htp cpe	2,550	2,136	—
6309-7	440H htp cpe 4P	2,567	2,281	—

Classic (wb 112.0)

		Wght	Price	Prod
6315	550 sdn 4d	2,729	2,105	—
6315-2	660 sdn 4d	2,740	2,245	—
6315-5	770 sdn 4d	2,686	2,349	—
6316	550 sdn 2d	2,720	2,055	—
6316-2	660 sdn 2d	2,725	2,195	—
6316-5	770 sdn 2d	2,663	2,299	—
6318	550 wgn 4d	2,893	2,435	—
6318-2	660 wgn 4d, 6P	2,890	2,537	—
6318-4	660 wgn 4d, 9P	2,005	2,609	—
6318-5	770 wgn 4d	2,828	2,640	—

Ambassador (wb 112.0)

		Wght	Price	Prod
6385	800 sdn 4d	3,140	2,391	—
6385-2	880 sdn 4d	3,145	2,519	—
6385-5	990 sdn 4d	3,158	2,660	—
6386	800 sdn 2d	3,110	2,337	—
6386-2	880 sdn 2d	3,116	2,465	—
6386-5	990 sdn 2d	3,132	2,606	—
6388	800 wgn 4d	3,270	2,703	—
6388-2	880 wgn 4d	3,275	2,815	—
6388-5	990 wgn 4d, 6P	3,298	2,956	—
6388-6	990 wgn 4d, 9P	3,305	3,018	—

*Total model year registrations: 428,346.

1963 Engines	bore×stroke	bhp	availability
L6, 195.6	3.13×4.25	90	S-American 220/330; 0-440
L6, 195.6	3.13×4.25	125	S-American 440; 0-220/330
L6, 195.6	3.13×4.25	127	S-Classic
L6, 195.6	3.13×4.25	138	S-American 440H; O-Classic
V8, 327.0	4.00×3.25	250	S-Ambassador
V8, 327.0	4.00×3.25	270	O-Ambassador

1964*

American (wb 106.0)

		Wght	Price	Prod
6405	220 sdn 4d	2,527	1,964	—
6405-2	330 sdn 4d	2,526	2,057	—
6405-5	440 sdn 4d	2,572	2,150	—
6406	220 sdn 2d	2,506	1,907	—
6406-2	330 sdn 2d	2,504	2,000	—
6407-5	440 conv cpe	2,752	2,346	—
6408	220 wgn 4d	2,661	2,240	—
6408-2	330 wgn 4d	2,675	2,324	—
6409-5	440 htp cpe	2,596	2,133	—
6409-7	440H htp cpe 5P	2,617	2,292	—

Classic (wb 112.0)

		Wght	Price	Prod
6415	550 sdn 4d	2,755	2,116	—
6415-2	660 sdn 4d	2,758	2,256	—
6415-5	770 sdn 4d	2,763	2,360	—
6416	550 sdn 2d	2,732	2,066	—
6416-2	660 sdn 2d	2,736	2,206	—

		Wght	Price	Prod
6416-5	770 sdn 2d	2,740	2,310	—
6418	550 wgn 4d	2,915	2,446	—
6418-2	660 wgn 4d	2,916	2,548	—
6418-5	770 wgn 4d	2,921	2,651	—
6419-5	770 htp cpe	2,789	2,397	—
6419-7	Typhoon htp cpe	2,818	2,509	—

Ambassador 990 (wb 112.0)

		Wght	Price	Prod
6485-5	sdn 4d	3,204	2,671	—
6488-5	wgn 4d	3,350	2,985	—
6489-5	htp cpe	3,213	2,736	—
6489-7	990H htp cpe	3,255	2,917	—

*Total model year registrations: 379,412.

1964 Engines	bore×stroke	bhp	availability
L6, 195.6	3.13×4.25	90	S-American 220/330; 0-440
L6, 195.6	3.13×4.25	125	S-American 440; 0-220/330
L6, 195.6	3.13×4.25	127	S-Classic
L6, 195.6	3.13×4.25	138	S-American 440H; O-Classic exc Typhoon
L6, 232.0	3.75×3.50	145	S-Typhoon; O-other Classic
V8, 287.0	3.75×3.25	198	O-Classic
V8, 327.0	4.00×3.25	250	S-Ambassador exc 990H
V8, 327.0	4.00×3.25	270	S-Amb 990H; O-Other Amb

1965*

American (wb 106.0)

		Wght	Price	Prod
6505	220 sdn 4d	2,518	2,036	—
6505-2	330 sdn 4d	2,522	2,129	—
6505-5	440 sdn 4d	2,580	2,222	—
6506	220 sdn 2d	2,492	1,979	—
6506-2	330 sdn 2d	2,490	2,072	—
6507-5	440 conv cpe	2,747	2,418	3,882
6508	220 wgn 4d	2,684	2,312	—
6508-2	330 wgn 4d	2,682	2,396	—
6509-5	440 htp cpe	2,596	2,205	—
6509-7	440H htp cpe	2,622	2,327	—

Classic (wb 112.0)

		Wght	Price	Prod
6515	550 sdn 4d	2,987	2,192	—
6515-2	660 sdn 4d	—	—	—

Classic 550 (wb 112.0)

		Wght	Price	Prod
6515	sdn 4d	2,987	2,192	—
6516	sdn 2d	2,963	2,142	—
6518	wgn 4d	3,134	2,522	—

Classic 660 (wb 112.0)

		Wght	Price	Prod
6515-2	sdn 4d	3,016	2,332	—
6516-2	sdn 2d	2,991	2,282	—
6518-2	wgn 4d	3,155	2,624	—

Classic 770 (wb 112.0)

		Wght	Price	Prod
6515-5	sdn 4d	3,029	2,436	—
6517-5	conv cpe	3,169	2,696	4,953
6518-5	wgn 4d	3,180	2,727	—
6519-5	htp cpe	3,063	2,436	—
6519-7	770H htp cpe	3,089	2,548	—

Marlin (wb 112.0)

		Wght	Price	Prod
6559-7	htp cpe	3,234	3,100	10,327

Ambassador (wb 116.0)

		Wght	Price	Prod
6585-2	880 sdn 4d	3,120	2,565	—
6585-5	990 sdn 4d	3,151	2,656	—
6586-2	880 sdn 2d	3,087	2,512	—
6587-5	990 conv cpe	3,265	2,955	3,499
6588-2	880 wgn 4d	3,247	2,879	—
6588-5	990 wgn 4d	3,268	2,970	—

		Wght	Price	Prod
6589-5	990 htp cpe	3,168	2,669	—
6589-7	990H htp cpe	3,198	2,837	—

*Total model year registrations: 324,669.

1965 Engines	bore×stroke	bhp	availability
L6, 195.6	3.13×4.25	90	S-American 220/330
L6, 195.6	3.13×4.25	125	S-American 440/440H
L6, 199.0	3.75×3.00	128	S-Classic 550
L6, 232.0	3.75×3.25	145	S-Classic 660/770/770H, Marlin; O-Amb, American
L6, 232.0	3.75×3.25	155	S-Amb; O-Classic
V8, 287.0	3.75×3.25	198	O-Classic, Marlin, Amb
V8, 327.0	4.00×3.25	270	O-Classic, Marlin, Amb

1966*

American 220 (wb 106.0)

		Wght	Price	Prod
6605	sdn 4d	2,574	2,086	—
6606	sdn 2d	2,554	2,017	—
6608	wgn 4d	2,740	2,369	—

American 440 (wb 106.0)

		Wght	Price	Prod
6605-5	sdn 4d	2,582	2,203	—
6606-5	sdn 2d	2,562	2,134	—
6607-5	conv cpe	2,782	2,486	—
6608-5	wgn 4d	2,745	2,477	—
6609-5	htp cpe	2,610	2,227	—

Rogue (wb 106.0)

		Wght	Price	Prod
6609-7	htp cpe	2,630	2,370	—

Classic 550 (wb 112.0)

		Wght	Price	Prod
6615	sdn 4d	2,885	2,238	—
6616	sdn 2d	2,860	2,189	—
6618	wgn 4d	3,070	2,542	—

Classic 770 (wb 112.0)

		Wght	Price	Prod
6615-5	sdn 4d	2,905	2,337	—
6617-5	conv cpe	3,070	2,616	—
6618-5	wgn 4d	3,071	2,629	—
6619-5	htp cpe	2,935	2,363	—

Rebel (wb 112.0)

		Wght	Price	Prod
6619-7	htp cpe	2,950	2,523	—

*Total model year registrations: 265,712.

1966 Engines	bore×stroke	bhp	availability
L6, 199.0	3.75×3.00	128	S-American, Rogue
L6, 232.0	3.75×3.50	145	S-Classic, Rebel
L6, 232.0	3.75×3.50	155	O-all
V8, 287.0	3.75×3.25	198	O-Classic, Rebel
V8, 327.0	4.00×3.25	250	O-Classic, Rebel
V8, 327.0	4.00×3.25	270	O-Classic, Rebel

1967*

American 220 (wb 106.0)

		Wght	Price	Prod
6705	sdn 4d	2,621	2,142	—
6706	sdn 2d	2,591	2,073	—
6708	wgn 4d	2,767	2,425	—

American 440 (wb 106.0)

		Wght	Price	Prod
6705-5	sdn 4d	2,613	2,259	—
6706-5	sdn 2d	2,586	2,191	—
6708-5	wgn 4d	2,769	2,533	—
6709-5	htp cpe	2,643	2,283	—

American Rogue (wb 106.0)

		Wght	Price	Prod
6707-7	conv cpe	2,821	2,611	—
6709-7	htp cpe	2,663	2,426	—

Rebel 550 (wb 114.0)

		Wght	Price	Prod
6715	sdn 4d	3,055	2,319	—
6716	sdn 2d	3,089	2,294	—
6718	wgn 4d	3,287	2,623	—

Rebel 770 (wb 114.0)

		Wght	Price	Prod
6715-5	sdn 4d	3,053	2,418	—
6718-5	wgn 4d	3,288	2,710	—
6719-5	htp cpe	3,092	2,443	—

Rebel SST (wb 114.0)

		Wght	Price	Prod
6717-7	conv cpe	3,180	2,872	—
6719-7	htp cpe	3,109	2,604	—

*Total model year registrations: 237,785.

1967 Engines	bore×stroke	bhp	availability
L6, 199.0	3.75×3.00	128	S-American
L6, 232.0	3.75×3.25	145	S-Rebel; O-American
L6, 232.0	3.75×3.25	155	O-American, Rebel
V8, 290.0	3.75×3.28	200	O-American, Rebel
V8, 290.0	3.75×3.28	225	O-American
V8, 343.0	4.08×3.28	235	O-Rebel
V8, 343.0	4.08×3.28	280	O-Rebel

1968*

American (wb 106.0)

		Wght	Price	Prod
6805	sdn 4d	2,638	2,024	—
6806	sdn 2d	2,604	1,946	—

American 440 (wb 106.0)

		Wght	Price	Prod
6805-5	sdn 4d	2,643	2,166	—
6808-5	wgn 4d	2,800	2,426	—

Rogue (wb 106.0)

		Wght	Price	Prod
6809-7	htp cpe	2,678	2,244	—

*Total model year registrations: 259,346

1968 Engines	bore×stroke	bhp	availability
L6, 199.0	3.75×3.00	128	S-American
L6, 232.0	3.75×3.50	145	S-Rogue; O-American
V8, 290.0	3.75×3.28	225	O-American, Rogue

1969*

American (wb 106.0)

		Wght	Price	Prod
6905	sdn 4d	2,638	2,076	—
6906	sdn 2d	2,604	1,998	—

American 440 (wb 106.0)

		Wght	Price	Prod
6905-5	sdn 4d	2,643	2,218	—
6908-5	wgn 4d	2,800	2,478	—

Rogue (wb 106.0)

		Wght	Price	Prod
6909-7	htp cpe	2,678	2,296	—

SC/Rambler-Hurst (wb 106.0)

		Wght	Price	Prod
6909-7	htp cpe	3,160	2,998	1,512

*Total model year registrations: 239,937.

1969 Engines	bore×stroke	bhp	availability
L6, 199.0	3.75×3.00	128	S-American
L6, 232.0	3.75×3.50	145	S-Rogue; O-American
V8, 290.0	3.75×3.28	200	O-Rogue, American 440
V8, 290.0	3.75×3.28	225	O-Rogue
V8, 390.0	4.17×3.57	315	S-SC/Rambler-Hurst

Reo

Reo Motor Car Company
Lansing, Michigan

A difference of opinion at Olds Motor Works in 1904 led to the formation of a new car company bearing the initials of Oldsmobile's founder. While his colleagues wanted to build more substantial four- and six-cylinder models, Ransom Eli Olds would have nothing to do with it. For him, it was the single-cylinder curved-dash Oldsmobile or nothing. Olds duly quit, and set up a rival concern in the same Michigan town. The upshot of this affair was that his new Reo Motor Car Company outproduced his original firm through 1917.

The first Reos were single-cylinder runabouts in the image of Ransom's cherished "Merry Oldsmobile." But gas was a dime a gallon at the time, and the trend was toward more powerful and much larger cars. Reo did offer four-cylinder models through 1919 and sixes beginning the following year. It even managed to field a companion make in 1928-29, the Wolverine. By that time, however, Reo was far down the industry production ranks, though it had been as high as third in 1907, behind Ford and Buick.

The Depression finished off Reo. The firm never built more than 5000 cars annually after 1931—but what it did build was memorable, for these were among the most classically beautifully automobiles ever created.

The 1930 Reos were powered exclusively by L-head sixes, two burly powerplants sharing the same bore and using different strokes. Prices were in the upper-middle bracket, ranging from a low of $1175 to a high of $1870. Styling, the work of designer Amos Northup, was classic and formal. All models through mid-1931 bore the name Flying Cloud, and displayed a fine sense of proportion as well as splendid workmanship and quality interior furnishings.

The two sixes were joined by a pair of straight eights for 1931. The smaller unit, which had about the same power and displacement as the larger six, powered a new Flying Cloud Eight, available on three different wheelbases. The larger eight powered the magnificent new Royale, with pioneering streamlined bodywork (again by Northup) featuring fashionable skirted fenders. For 1932, an immense 152-inch-wheelbase chassis was added to the Royale family, along with enormous seven-passenger sedan and limousine body styles of substantial appearance. With their big nine-main-bearing engine, the Royales had effortless performance, but they were hardly the kind of cars appropriate for an age of hard times, and Reo sales fell by 50 percent in 1931-32.

In response, management tried hard to economize, and

1930 Model 25 Flying Cloud Standard four-door sedan

1932 Model 8-31 Royale coupe

1931 Model 21 Flying Cloud Eight coupe

1934 S-4 Flying Cloud Six DeLuxe four-door sedan

model offerings were drastically cut beginning in January 1932. A new 230-cubic-inch six with 80 horsepower appeared for the 117-inch-wheelbase Model 6-S Flying Cloud. Available in a choice of nine open and closed body styles in Standard and DeLuxe trim, priced at $1000-1200, this was the firm's price leader, its attempt to win back some of its lost business. Completing the line were the Royale and Royale Custom, powered by the big 358-cid eight and mounted on wheelbases of 131, 135, and 152 inches. This lineup returned for 1933, with the 6-S engine now at 268 cid and 85 bhp. The company continued its practice of issuing revised, mid-year models in January, but the changes this time were slight. The 152-inch chassis was eliminated from the eight-cylinder line, which now comprised Royale Standard, Elite, and Custom. Prices were cut at the same time, though the reductions weren't large enough to matter much. Registrations amounted to only 3623 this year, the firm's lowest total on record.

Most of Reo's 1934 offerings appeared in July and September of 1933. The S-2/S-3 Flying Cloud, the N-2 Royale Eight, and the N-2 Custom Royale were all essentially carryovers from the previous year, though there were minor changes. A "genuine" '34 didn't arrive until April of that year, the Model S-4 Flying Cloud, with lovely, streamlined styling marked by a new hood and grille, hood side louvers, more deeply skirted fenders, and an optional built-in trunk for four-door sedans. Wheelbase, engine, and basic body types were all retained from the previous year's Flying Cloud. Unfortunately, the S-4 was no more successful, and Reo production for calendar 1934 was just 4460 cars, plus 11,222 trucks.

The debut of the S-4 was overshadowed by internal company quarrels that had been erupting sporadically since the stock market crash. Ransom E. Olds, who was still involved in the firm's affairs up to this point, suddenly resigned in December 1933, touching off a management shakeup. Donald E. Bates was elected president in April 1934 and Olds briefly returned to the board. Meantime, the S-4 was continued for 1935 as the Model S-5.

A brand-new Flying Cloud marked the "1935½" season, announced on January 2nd of that year. Featuring an ambitious restyle, the new A-6 offered fastback two- and four-door sedans on a 115-inch wheelbase and powered by a 90-bhp 228-cid six. Front-end styling was somewhat reminiscent of the 1935 Auburn, with flared fenders and a V-shaped bumper. Ransom Olds was against the new model, claiming its $450,000 tooling was a waste of money. In his mind, the '34 was fine as it was. But, as had happened long before at Oldsmobile, his colleagues disagreed, and pushed ahead with even bigger changes for 1936.

The result was more substantial styling and the shortest model list in many a year. Appearance was marked by fuller fenders, a reworked hood and grille, vertical grille bands extending up into the radiator shell, rubber-tipped bumper guards, and optional "Zeppelin-style" fender lamps. There was no self-shifter option, but an optional overdrive transmission was announced in May. By this time, however, cars had dwindled to a sideline, and trucks were far more profitable for Reo. Production of the 1936 Flying Clouds was a mere 3206 units, versus 4692 the previous year.

On May 18, 1936, the Reo board approved moving truck assembly into the main plant. The firm officially left the car business on September 3rd. Losses on the 1936 models ran to nearly $1.4 million, though the company was able to write off $604,000 of that for terminating its automotive operations. Reo then continued as a truck builder, and would survive for the next 40 or so years.

Reo Specifications

1930

Model C Master Flying Cloud (wb 121.0)*	Wght	Price	Prod
rdstr 2-4P	3,380	1,685	—
cpe 2P	3,465	1,625	—
spt cpe 2-4P	3,615	1,750	—
victoria 4P	3,550	1,695	—
spt victoria 4P	3,715	1,820	—
brougham 2d	3,540	1,595	—
spt brougham 2d	3,675	1,720	—
sdn 4d	3,665	1,745	—
Deluxe sdn 4d	3,800	1,870	—
spt rdstr 2-4P	3,570	1,810	—
Model B-2 Flying Cloud (wb 115.0)*			
phtn 5P	—	1,395	—
spt phtn 5P 6W	—	1,595	—
Standard cpe 2P	3,170	1,375	—
Standard cpe 2P 5W	3,180	1,435	—
Standard cpe 2-4P	3,220	1,395	—

	Wght	Price	Prod
Standard cpe 2-4P 6W	3,230	1,455	—
spt cpe 2-4P	3,325	1,495	—
Standard sdn 4d 5W	3,280	1,395	—
Standard sdn 4d 6W	3,300	1,455	—
spt sdn 4d	3,390	1,495	—
Model 20 Flying Cloud (wb 120.0)—2,189 built			
Standard cpe 2-4P	3,635	1,595	—
spt cpe 2-4P	3,720	1,705	—
Standard sdn 4d	3,700	1,595	—
spt sdn 4d	3,785	1,705	—
Model 25 Flying Cloud (wb 124.0)—2,128 built			
Standard sdn 4d	3,795	1,795	—
spt sdn 4d	3,945	1,905	—
Model 15 Flying Cloud (wb 115.0)—1,789 built			
Standard phtn 5P	3,050	1,195	—
spt phtn 5P	3,140	1,238	—
Standard cpe 2P	3,110	1,175	—
spt cpe 2P	3,200	1,218	—

			Wght	Price	Prod
	Standard cpe 2-4P		3,170	1,195	—
	spt cpe 2-4P		3,260	1,238	—
	Standard sdn 4d		3,300	1,295	—
	spt sdn 4d		3,370	1,338	—

*Production not available

1930 Engines	bore×stroke	bhp	availability
L6, 214.7	3.38×4.00	60	S-B-2,15
L6, 268.3	3.38×5.00	80	S-C,20,25

1931

Model 15 Flying Cloud (wb 115.0)—858 built

		Wght	Price	Prod
	Standard phtn 5P	3,050	1,195	—
	spt phtn 5P	3,140	1,238	—
	Standard cpe 2P	3,110	1,175	—
	spt cpe 2P	3,200	1,218	—
	Standard cpe 2-4P	3,170	1,195	—
	spt cpe 2-4P	3,260	1,238	—
	Standard sdn 4d	3,300	1,295	—
	spt sdn 4d	3,370	1,338	—

Model 20 Flying Cloud (wb 120.0)—1,782 built

		Wght	Price	Prod
	Standard cpe 2-4P	0,033	1,595	—
	spt cpe 2-4P	3,720	1,705	—
	Standard sdn 4d	3,700	1,595	—
	spt sdn 4d	3,785	1,705	—

Model 25 Flying Cloud (wb 124.0)—895 built

		Wght	Price	Prod
	Standard sdn 4d	3,795	1,795	—
	spt sdn 4d	3,945	1,905	—

Model 21 Flying Cloud Six (wb 121.0)—703 built

		Wght	Price	Prod
	cpe 2P	3,645	1,295	—
	Custom spt cpe 2-4P	3,800	1,410	—
	sdn 4d	3,495	1,295	—
	Custom spt sdn 4d	3,630	1,410	—

Model 21 Flying Cloud Eight (wb 121.0)—743 built

		Wght	Price	Prod
	cpe 2P	3,740	1,395	—
	Custom spt cpe 2-4P	3,845	1,510	—
	sdn 4d	3,685	1,395	—
	Custom spt sdn 4d	3,725	1,510	—

Model 25 Flying Cloud Six (wb 124.0/125.0)—898 built

		Wght	Price	Prod
	cpe 2-4P	3,895	1,695	—
	victoria 4P	3,880	1,695	—
	sdn 4d	3,950	1,695	—

Model 25 Flying Cloud Eight (wb 125.0)—73 built

		Wght	Price	Prod
	cpe 2-4P	3,841	1,745	—
	victoria 5P	3,904	1,745	—
	sdn 4d	4,050	1,745	—

Model 830 Flying Cloud Eight (wb 130.0)—926 built

		Wght	Price	Prod
	cpe 2-4P	4,380	1,995	—
	victoria 4P	4,400	1,995	—
	sdn 4d	4,500	1,995	—

Model 831 Royale (wb 131.0)—707 built

		Wght	Price	Prod
	cpe 2-4P	4,310	2,145	—
	victoria 4P	4,320	2,145	—
	sdn 4d	4,375	2,145	—

Model 835 Royale (wb 135.0)—2,711 built

		Wght	Price	Prod
	cpe 2-4P	4,500	2,745	—
	victoria 4P	4,475	2,745	—
	sdn 4d	4,650	2,745	—

1931 Engines	bore×stroke	bhp	availability
L6, 214.7	3.38×4.00	60	S-15
L6, 268.3	3.38×5.00	80	S-20,25

			Wght	Price	Prod
L6, 268.3	3.38×5.00	85	S-21		
L8, 358.0	3.38×5.00	125	S-30,31,35		
L8, 268.6	3.00×4.75	90	S-21,25		

1932

Model 6-21 Flying Cloud (wb 121.0)—1,352 built

		Wght	Price	Prod
	cpe 2-4P	3,495	995	—
	spt cpe 2-4P	3,630	1,110	—
	sdn 4d	3,.645	995	—
	spt sdn 4d	3,800	1,110	—

Model 6-25 Flying Cloud (wb 125.0)—27 built

		Wght	Price	Prod
	victoria 5P	3,880	1,565	—
	sdn 4d	3,950	1,565	—
	cpe 2-4P	3,895	1,565	—

Model 6-S Flying Cloud (wb 117.0) (from 4/32)—1,509 built

		Wght	Price	Prod
	Standard cpe 2-4P	3,300	995	—
	Standard conv cpe 2-4P	3,220	1,045	—
	Standard sdn 4d	3,403	995	—
	spt cpe 2-4P	3,445	1,070	—
	spt conv cpe 2-4P	3,360	1,120	—
	spt sdn 4d	3,510	1,070	—
	DeLuxe spt cpe 2-4P	—	1,155	—
	DeLuxe spt conv cpe 2-4P	—	1,205	—
	DeLuxe spt sdn 4d	—	1,155	—

Model 8-21 Flying Cloud (wb 121.0)—323 built

		Wght	Price	Prod
	cpe 2-4P	3,685	1,195	—
	spt cpe 2-4P	3,725	1,310	—
	sdn 4d	3,740	1,195	—
	spt sdn 4d	3,845	1,310	—

Model 8-25 Flying Cloud (wb 125.0)—421 built

		Wght	Price	Prod
	cpe 2-4P	3,841	1,565	—
	victoria 5P	3,904	1,565	—
	sdn 4d	4,050	1,565	—

Model 8-31 Royale (wb 131.0)—126 built

		Wght	Price	Prod
	cpe 2-4P	4,310	1,985	—
	victoria 4P	4,320	1,985	—
	sdn 4d	4,375	1,985	—

Model 8-35-52 Royale (wb 135.0; lwb-152.0)

		Wght	Price	Prod
	cpe 2-4P	4,500	2,445	
	victoria 5P	4,475	2,445	164
	sdn 4d	4,650	2,445	
	lwb sdn 7P	5,010	3,695	
	lwb sdn 7P partition	5,075	3,895	12

Model RYL Royale (131.0) began 4/32—6,654 built

		Wght	Price	Prod
	cpe 2-4P	4,310	1,785	—
	victoria 4P	4,320	1,785	—
	sdn 4d	4,375	1,785	—

Royale Custom (wb 135.0; lwb-152.0) (from 4/32)

		Wght	Price	Prod
	cpe 2-4P	4,500	2,445	
	victoria 5P	4,475	2,445	
	conv cpe 2-4P	4,440	2,995	5,124
	sdn 4d	4,650	2,445	
	lwb sdn 7P	5,010	3,695	
	lwb berline 7P	5,075	3,895	4

1932 Engines	bore×stroke	bhp	availability
L6, 230.0	3.13×5.00	80	S-6-S
L6, 268.3	3.38×5.00	80	S-6-25
L6, 268.3	3.38×5.00	85	S-6-21
L8, 268.6	3.00×4.75	90	S-8-21,8-25
L8, 358.0	3.38×5.00	125	S-all Royale

1933

Model 6-S Flying Cloud (wb 117.0)—615 built

	Wght	Price	Prod
cpe 2-4P	3,300	995	—
conv cpe 2-4P	3,220	1,045	—
sdn 4d	3,405	995	—
spt cpe 2-4P	3,445	1,070	—
spt conv cpe 2-4P	—	1,120	—
spt sdn 4d	3,510	1,070	—
DeLuxe spt cpe 2-4P	—	1,155	—
DeLuxe spt conv cpe 2-4P	—	1,205	—
DeLuxe spt sdn 4d	—	1,155	—
cabriolet 2-4P	3,710	1,250	—

Model S-2 Flying Cloud Six (wb 118.0)

	Wght	Price	Prod
cpe 2-4P	3,450	995	
Elite cpe 2-4P	3,515	1,090	
conv cpe 2-4P	3,390	1,045	2,099*
Elite conv cpe 2-4P	3,490	1,140	
sdn 4d	3,540	995	
Elite sdn 4d	3,645	1,090	

Royale (wb 131.0)—121 built

	Wght	Price	Prod
cpe 2-4P	4,310	1,785	—
victoria 5P	4,320	1,785	—
sdn 4d	4,375	1,785	—

Royale Eight (wb 131.0; lwb-135.0)

		Wght	Price	Prod
N-2	Standard cpe 2-4P	—	1,745	
N-2	Standard victoria 5P	4,500	1,745	
N-2	Standard sdn 4d	4,725	1,745	
N-2	Elite cpe 2-4P	—	1,845	1,150
N-2	Elite victoria 5P	4,625	1,845	
N-2	Elite sdn 4d	4,850	1,845	
N-1	Custom lwb cpe 2-4P	4,540	2,445	
N-1	Custom lwb victoria 5P	4,515	2,445	NA
N-1	Custom lwb sdn 4d	4,690	2,445	

Royale Custom Eight (wb 135.0; lwb-152.0)—127 built

	Wght	Price	Prod
cpe 2-4P	4,500	2,445	—
conv cpe 2-4P	4,440	2,995	—
victoria 5P	4,475	2,445	—
sdn 4d	4,650	2,445	—
lwb sdn 7P	5,010	3,695	—
lwb sdn brougham 7P	5,075	3,895	—

*incl. 1934 S-2

1933 Engines	bore×stroke	bhp	availability
L6, 268.3	3.38×5.00	85	S-sixes
L8, 358.0	3.38×5.00	125	S-eights

1934

S-2 Flying Cloud Six (wb 118.0)

	Wght	Price	Prod
cpe 2-4P	3,500	845	
Elite cpe 2-4P	3,563	920	
conv cpe 2-4P	3,440	1,045	2,099*
Elite conv cpe 2-4P	3,540	1,140	
sdn 4d	3,590	845	
Elite sdn 4d	3,695	920	

S-3 Flying Cloud Six (wb 118.0)**

	Wght	Price	Prod
cpe 2-4P	3,500	795	—
sdn 4d	3,590	795	—

S-4 Flying Cloud Six (wb 118.0) (from April 1934)**

	Wght	Price	Prod
bus cpe 2P	—	795	—
cpe 2-4P	3,510	895	—
conv cpe 2-4P	—	925	—
sdn 4d	3,630	895	—
DeL cpe 2-4P	3,530	945	—
DeL conv cpe 2-4P	—	975	—
DeL sdn 4d	3,650	945	—
DeL cpe 2-4P 6W	3,605	995	—

	Wght	Price	Prod
DeL sdn 4d 6W	3,725	995	—

N-2 Royale Eight (wb 131.0)**

	Wght	Price	Prod
cpe 2-4P	4,640	1,500	—
Elite cpe 2-4P	4,790	1,600	—
victoria 5P	4,730	1,500	—
Elite victoria 5P	4,815	1,600	—
sdn 4d	4,765	1,500	—
Elite sdn 4d	4,955	1,600	—

N-1 Royale Custom Eight (wb 135.0)**

	Wght	Price	Prod
Elite cpe 2-4P	4,825	1,700	—
Elite victoria 5P	4,915	1,700	—
Elite sdn 4d	5,015	1,700	—

*incl. 1933 S-2
**Production not available.

1934 Engines	bore×stroke	bhp	availability
L6, 268.3	3.38×5.00	85	S-sixes
L8, 358.0	3.38×5.00	125	S-eights

1935*

S-5 Flying Cloud Six (wb 118.0)

	Wght	Price	Prod
bus cpe 2P	3,445	795	—
Standard cpe 2-4P	3,510	895	—
DeLuxe cpe 2-4P 5W	3,530	945	—
DeLuxe cpe 2-4P 6W	3,605	995	—
Standard conv cpe 2-4P	3,495	895	—
DeLuxe conv cpe 2-4P 5W	3,515	975	—
DeLuxe conv cpe 2-4P 6W	3,590	1,025	—
Standard sdn 4d	3,630	895	—
DeLuxe sdn 4d 5W	3,650	945	—
DeLuxe sdn 4d 6W	3,725	995	—

A-6 Flying Cloud Six (wb 115.0)—(from Jan. 1935)

		Wght	Price	Prod
6AB	sdn 2d	3,190	795	—
6AS	sdn 4d	3,220	845	—

S-7 Royale Six (wb 118.0)

		Wght	Price	Prod
7SC	cpe 3-5P	3,550	985	—
7SS	sdn 4d	3,595	985	—

*Production not available

1935 Engines	bore×stroke	bhp	availability
L6, 228.0	3.38×4.25	90	S-A-6
L6, 268.3	3.38×5.00	85	S-S-5
L6, 268.3	3.38×5.00	95	S-S-7

1936*

Flying Cloud Six (wb 115.0)

	Wght	Price	Prod
sdn 2d	3,270	795	—
sdn 4d	3,300	845	—

6-75 Flying Cloud DeLuxe (wb 118.0)

	Wght	Price	Prod
brougham 2d	3,560	845	—
sdn 4d	3,595	985	—
touring sdn 4d T/B	3,625	895	—

*Production not available

1936 Engines	bore×stroke	bhp	availability
L6, 228.0	3.38×4.25	90	S-Six
L6, 268.3	3.38×5.00	95	S-6-75

Reo Calendar Year Production 1930-1936

1930	11,450
1931	6,762
1932	3,870
1933	3,623
1934	4,460
1935	4,692
1936	3.206

Shelby

Shelby Automotive, Ionia, Michigan
Ford Motor Co., Dearborn, Michigan

Carroll Shelby, who retired from racing for health reasons in 1960, settled down to become America's most charismatic manufacturer of specialty cars. Between 1962 and 1970 he built or contributed to many blindingly fast, raceworthy classics: the AC Cobra, Sunbeam Tiger, Cobra 427, Ford GT40, and Ford Mark IV. He helped bring Ford to its racing pinnacle, the winning of Le Mans.

Shelby's most popular project from the standpoint of sales was the GT-350, a super-tuned version of the Ford Mustang. Built by Shelby American in 1965-66, it was an uncompromising, potent grand touring car equally at home on road or track. Later models, built by Ford from 1967 through 1970, were not quite what their predecessors had been, but were good examples of what talented specialists could do with a stock package like the Mustang.

The 1965 GT-350 was aimed primarily at the B-Production racing class of the Sports Car Club of America

(SCCA). (It was B-Production champion in 1965-67.) Shelby began with a blue-striped white Mustang fastback powered by the high-performance version of Ford's 289 cubic-inch V8. He added a high-rise manifold, a big four-barrel carburetor, and free-flow exhaust headers. This brought horsepower up to 306 at 6000 rpm. All Shelbys came with a Borg-Warner T-10 four-speed gearbox, a regular Mustang option. Instead of the Mustang's Falcon-based rear axle, GT-350s used a stronger unit from the Fairlane station wagon. Other significant component revisions included metallic-lined rear brakes, Koni shock absorbers, and extra-heavy-duty front disc brakes with metallic pads. Steering was made quicker by relocating the front suspension mounting points. Connecting the tops of the front shock absorbers to each other with a length of steel tubing prevented shock flex under hard cornering. Shelby used its own 15-inch cast-aluminum road wheels shod with high-performance Goodyear bias-ply

1965 GT-350 fastback coupe

1968 GT-500 convertible

1968 GT-500 convertible

1968 GT-500 fastback coupe

1968 GT-500KR fastback coupe

1968 GT-500KR fastback coupe

tires. The result of all this chassis tuning was nearly neutral handling instead of the stock Mustang's strong understeer.

Externally, the stock Mustang's steel hood was replaced with a fiberglass one containing a prominent scoop and held down by NASCAR hood pins. The galloping horse emblem was removed from the grille, and the simulated side scoops were opened up to admit cool air to the rear brakes. For 1966, the fastback's stock rear-quarter air extractor vents were replaced by plastic windows. Internally, the only changes consisted of competition-style three-inch seatbelts and a mahogany-rimmed steering wheel. GT-350s also came without the stock Mustang's rear seat, with the spare tire lashed down in the vacated space. Shelby offered a kit so the buyer could put the spare back in the trunk and install a new rear seat. The stock front seats were left alone, and all interiors were solid black.

For the racing version of the GT-350, Shelby achieved 350 bhp—an astounding 1.21 horsepower per cubic inch. This engine was basically the same one used in the racing Cobra 289. Its four-speed gearbox had an aluminum case to save weight. The interior was stripped and a racing seat was installed along with a roll bar and safety harness. Competition tires and an extra-heavy-duty suspension were fitted. A special fiberglass nose eliminated the front bumper and provided a rudimentary air dam with a central slot as an additional air intake. The ultimate racing GT-350 had four-wheel disc brakes, a 400-bhp engine, and wide tires under flared fenders.

Hertz Rent-A-Car got into the act in 1966 when it ordered 936 Shelbys painted black with gold stripes. Hertz called it the GT-350H, and would rent one for $17 a day and 17 cents a mile. It was a stock GT-350, aside from the special paint job and a three-speed automatic transmission instead of the stock four-speed manual. Hertz inevitably rented some of these to weekend racers, and a few of them performed successfully on SCCA tracks.

In 1967, when Ford Motor Company offered Mustang with a 390-cid V8, Shelby went one better and tossed in a huge 428. The result was the GT-500, sold as a linemate to the GT-350. Its advertised horsepower was 335, but the real figure was probably closer to 400. The GT-350 was advertised at its usual 306 bhp, but the ac-

1969 GT-500 fastback coupe

1969 GT-500 convertible

1969 GT-500 fastback coupe

1969 GT-500 convertible

1969 GT-500 fastback coupe

1969 GT-500 convertible

tual rating was below 300 because the '67 did not have steel-tube exhaust headers like the '66 model.

The '67 Shelby now had its own fiberglass front end to distinguish it from production Mustangs, plus other styling modifications and minor chassis refinements. It also bore a new emblem: a coiled cobra in anodized gold. The interior featured a huge, black-painted roll bar, to which were affixed inertia-reel seatbelts instead of the three-inch harness. Over 3000 cars were built, and they were priced lower than the 1965-66 models.

In 1968, the 350 and 500 were again offered with only a wider hood scoop for identification. Interiors were lifted from the stock Mustang with few alterations. A Stewart Warner oil pressure gauge and ammeter were mounted on the central console. A convertible was added to each line, priced about $100 higher than the fast-back. Also new was the GT-500KR ("King of the Road"), which had Ford's Cobra Jet 428 block, extra-large heads and intake manifold, and a Holley 735-cfm four-barrel carburetor. The KR sold for $4473 as a fastback and $4594 as a convertible.

Mechanically, the 1969 GT-350 and GT-500 were more closely related to the production Mustang than their predecessors had been (the Mustang was all-new that year). There were now air scoops in the fiberglass front fenders, and side stripes were relocated midway up the bodysides. Although a few 1969s were reserialed for 1970, Shelby production effectively ended in '69. A combination of government regulations and spiraling insurance rates (the cars' accident record was staggering) prompted Carroll Shelby to ask the then-president of Ford, Lee Iacocca, to cancel the program.

Shelby Specifications

1965

GT-350 (wb 108.0)

	Wght	Price	Prod
fstbk cpe	2,800	4,547	562

1965 Engine	bore×stroke	bhp	availability
V8, 289.0	4.00×2.87	306	S-all

1966

GT-350 (wb 108.0)

	Wght	Price	Prod
fstbk cpe	2,800	4,600	2,378

1966 Engine	bore×stroke	bhp	availability
V8, 289.0	4.00×2.87	306	S-all

1967

GT-350 (wb 108.0)

	Wght	Price	Prod
fstbk cpe	2,800	3,995	1,175

GT500 (wb 108.0)

	Wght	Price	Prod
fstbk cpe	3,000	4,195	2,050

1967 Engines	bore×stroke	bhp	availability
V8, 289.0	4.00×2.87	290	S-GT350
V8, 428.0	4.13×3.98	400*	S-GT500

*Estimated; advertised bhp lower.

1968

GT-350 (wb 108.0)

	Wght	Price	Prod
fstbk cpe	3,000	4,117	1,253
conv cpe	3,100	4,238	404

GT-500 (wb 108.0)

	Wght	Price	Prod
fstbk cpe	3,100	4,317	1,140
conv cpe	3,200	4,439	402

GT-500KR (wb 108.0)

	Wght	Price	Prod
fstbk cpe	3,200	4,473	933
conv cpe	3,300	4,594	318

1968 Engines	bore×stroke	bhp	availability
V8, 302.0	4.00×3.00	250	S-GT350
V8, 302.0	4.00×3.00	350	O-GT350 (supercharged)
V8, 390.0	4.05×3.78	335	S-GT500
V8, 428.0	4.13×3.98	360	S-GT500
V8, 428.0	4.13×3.98	400*	S-GT500KR

*Estimated; advertised bhp lower.

1969

GT-350 (wb 108.0)

	Wght	Price	Prod
fstbk cpe	3,000	4,434	1,085
conv cpe	3,100	4,753	194

GT-500 (wb 108.0)

	Wght	Price	Prod
fstbk cpe	3,100	4,709	1,536
conv cpe	3,200	5,027	335

1969 Engines	bore×stroke	bhp	availability
V8, 351.0	4.00×3.50	290	S-GT350
V8, 428.0	4.13×3.98	400*	S-GT500

*Estimated; advertised bhp lower.

1970

GT-350 (wb 108.0)

	Wght	Price	Prod
fstbk cpe	3,000	4,500*	315
conv cpe	3,100	4,800*	

GT-500 (wb 108.0)

	Wght	Price	Prod
fstbk cpe	3,100	4,800*	286
conv cpe	3,200	5,100*	

*Estimated.

1970 Engines	bore×stroke	bhp	availability
V8, 351.0	4.00×3.50	290	S-GT350
V8, 428.0	4.13×3.98	375*	S-GT500

*Estimated; advertised bhp lower.

Studebaker

Studebaker Corp. (Studebaker-Packard Corp., 1954-62)
South Bend, Indiana and Hamilton, Ontario, Canada

America's oldest manufacturer of wheeled vehicles had been around since 1852, when Henry and Clem Studebaker built three covered wagons together. Actually there were five Studebaker brothers, all as bearded as the Brothers Smith, and all participated in the firm's affairs over the years. J.M. "Wheelbarrow Johnny" Studebaker was running the company when it began building automobiles in 1902. At first, these were confined to electrics, as "Mr. J.M." hated gasoline-powered cars, calling them "clumsy, dangerous noisy brutes [that] stink to high heaven, break down at the worst possible moment, and are a public nuisance." But even he was forced to bow to the inevitable, and gas-engine Studebakers appeared beginning in 1911.

J.M. Studebaker relinquished his presidency to Albert Erskine Russell in 1919, and it was this former accountant who took the firm into the '30s. Erskine made a series of serious mistakes, beginning with the car he named after himself (see entry), followed by the ill-timed acquisition of Pierce-Arrow in 1928. In the depths of the Depression, he put the company's smallest six-cylinder engine into the Rockne (see entry), another short-lived junior make. Dictator, another bizarre moniker of the Erskine regime, was a name that seemed downright un-American, with Hitler and Mussolini in power. Yet incredibly, Studebaker stayed with it through 1937.

Not counting the Erskine, there were no fewer than six different engines and seven different series available for 1930. Six- and eight-cylinder inline powerplants of similar size and power were featured in the 115-inch-wheelbase Dictator and 120-inch-wheelbase Commander lines. Bracketing these were the short-chassis, low-priced Studebaker Six and the magnificent top-line President Eight. The latter were truly memorable cars, the finest automobiles South Bend offered in this decade and perhaps the finest ever. Powered through 1933 by a potent 337-cubic-inch straight eight, the President "finds a parallel in sustained speed only in the light of comets, meteors, and other heavenly bodies," according to company propaganda. Such unabashed hyperbole was hardly unusual, but it did have a basis in fact: two totally stock President Eight roadsters had each run over 30,000 miles in less than 27,000 minutes back in 1928.

The President of these years sported a pedigree as impressive as its immense proportions. The engineer behind it was the hard-driving Delmar G. "Barney" Roos, formerly of Locomobile, Marmon, and Pierce-Arrow, who designed the model's short-stroke engine with integrally cast block and crankcase. Geared to turn only 2800 rpm at 60 mph, this straight eight was rated at 115 horsepower for 1930. The next year it was given nine (versus the previous five) main bearings, a coated-steel crankshaft, and higher compression, all of which boosted output to 122 bhp, rising to 132 bhp for 1933. The crank was derived from that used in the Liberty aircraft engine, and was largely responsi-

1931 President Eight "Four-Season" roadster

1932 Commander Eight Regal convertible sedan

1934 Dictator Regal convertible roadster

ble for the engine's tremendous low-end stamina.

Economic misfortunes spelled the demise of the big-inch Presidents after 1933, but not before they had written a great competition story. Racers based on this platform competed with distinction at Indianapolis, for example, where Russel Snowberger drove to eighth and fifth place finishes in 1930-31, respectively, averaging over 90 mph. The factory sent its own team to Indy in 1932, and Cliff Bergere finished third with an average of 102.66 mph, the first time a semi-stock car had exceeded the magic century mark. Tony Gulotta ended the factory's Indy campaign in 1933 by finishing seventh in the 500 at 99 mph.

1934 Commander Eight four-door sedan

1938 State President convertible sedan

1938 Commander Six Custom coupe

1939 President two-door club sedan

Studebaker cut its offerings for 1931, though there were still Dictator, Commander, and President models ranging in output from 70 to 122 bhp and in wheelbase from 114 to 136 inches. The same lineup returned for 1932-33, when the 205-cid six went into the Rockne. Studebaker also retained a six for its senior line, a 230-cid 80-bhp unit for a new 117-inch-wheelbase Dictator chassis. The 205 came back in 1934 for Standard, Special, and Deluxe Dictator models.

Most auto companies suffered greatly in the early Depression years, but Studebaker suffered more than most. One reason was that the successive failures of Erskine, Pierce-Arrow, and Rockne were aggravated by spendthrift financial practices. For instance, the firm continued to pay dividends through 1931, even though they had to come from capital reserves, and a planned merger with White Motors fell through. Meanwhile, sales slowly dwindled. Studebaker went into receivership in 1933 and Erskine resigned; shortly afterwards, he committed suicide.

What saved Studebaker at this point was production vice-president Harold S. Vance and sales vice-president Paul G. Hoffman, who would jointly guide the company's destiny through 1949. They first got rid of Pierce-Arrow, then got South Bend's idle production lines going again. The firm realized a small profit in mid-1934, but it was enough to secure a line of credit. The worst was over, and

production began inching up: 46,000 units in 1934, 49,000 the next year, and over 80,000 in 1936-37. Part of this success reflected a reversal of Erskine's full-line market approach. Only three series—Dictator Six, Commander Eight, and President Eight—were fielded for 1935, and the firm concentrated on the medium-priced, cleanly styled Dictators and Presidents for 1936-37, both with longer wheelbases and more powerful engines.

Studebaker styling in the '30s was usually good and sometimes exceptional. The formal lines of the early years gave way in 1933 to graceful skirted fenders and radiators that curved forward at the bottom. As the streamlining craze got going at mid-decade, Studebaker adopted pontoon fenders and rounded grilles like most other makes, but retained a crisp, individual appearance. And there was considerable technical progress. Along with Warner overdrive for 1935 came Roos' novel "planar" independent front suspension, a successful innovation consisting of a transverse leaf spring with upper and lower links, and rotary (later, telescopic) shocks. The next year, Studebaker trumpeted its new "Hill Holder," a coupling between clutch and brake system that prevented the car from rolling backward down a hill when the clutch was engaged. Other new features in this period were automatic choke, vacuum-powered brakes, rotary door latches, and all-steel bodies. Most of these can be credited to Roos, who left

for Britain's Rootes Group in 1936. He later returned to America and Willys-Overland, where he had a hand in designing the World War II Jeep. His post at Studebaker was taken by W.S. James, but the real engineering power after his departure was engineering vice-president Roy Cole.

Hoffmann brought in Raymond Loewy, the brilliant industrial designer who had created the handsome 1932-34 Hupmobiles, to restyle the 1938 models. He instituted a prow-front motif with flush-mounted headlights a year before most competitors had something similar. The 1939 front end imitated the streamlined nose of the Lincoln-Zephyr, but it was pretty and distinctive. Production faltered in 1938 due to the national recession, but it improved markedly the next year, hitting 106,470 units, a record for the decade and the company's best performance since 1928.

A big reason for this gain was the cleanly styled Champion, a new economy series priced about even with Chevy and Ford and below most Plymouths. It was powered by an L-head six that was smaller and less powerful than the "Big Three" engines, but the car weighed 500-700 pounds less than its rivals and thus delivered comparable performance plus fantastic gas mileage—up to 22 mpg. The Champion was no match for the 85-bhp Ford V8, but it would run up to 78 mph, equal to or better than Chevy, Plymouth and the 60-bhp Ford.

Champions came in four body styles for 1940; three- and five-passenger coupes and two- and four-door sedans. Standard and DeLuxe trim were offered. The Champion's price range of $660 to $785 made it a formidable competitor for the Big Three makes, and 1940 volume rose to more than 66,000 units.

The middle-priced 1940 Studebaker was Commander, offered in three body styles on a 116.5-inch wheelbase: a three-passenger coupe, and two- and four-door sedans. Commanders used a 226-cid six with 90 bhp at 3400 rpm, and differed from the Champion in styling. The Commander had a sharply creased nose and a latticework grille, more like Ford's than the Champion's rounded lines.

The company continued to offer the President, equipped with a smooth, nine-main-bearing straight eight delivering 110 bhp at 3600 rpm. Prices were roughly $125 higher than for the equivalent Commander. Presidents rode a 122-inch wheelbase, were offered in the same three body styles as Commander, and had similar styling.

Raymond Loewy had earned his high standing at Studebaker on the strength of the Champion. For 1941, he reworked the entire line with more formal, elegant styling. A new body style, the Land Cruiser (with closed rear roof quarters), was developed for the Commander and President. Loewy pioneered the first bodyside two-toning, consisting of a color sweep just below the beltline. Engines were reworked. The Champion unit was stroked out to four inches for 169.6 cid and 80 bhp. The Commander powerplant was raised to 94 bhp, while the President's silky straight eight was increased to 117.

The 1941 facelift brought additional trim levels to all three lines. For the Champion, these were Custom, Custom DeLuxe, and Delux-Tone trims available for all body styles. Commanders were offered in Custom, DeLux-Tone, and Skyway versions. The Skyway was a very richly trimmed, fender-skirted series that went into production in March 1941. There was also a Skyway President. South Bend had another excellent year in '41. Nearly 85,000 Champions were built; Commander

1939 Champion Custom coupe (with Judy Garland)

1940 President convertible sedan by Derham

1940 President four-door Cruising Sedan

1941 Commander Skyway Land Cruiser four-door sedan

production reached nearly 42,000 units. (Presidents traditionally sold in much smaller quantities.)

Before the war put an end to civilian auto production in 1942, Studebaker built about 50,000 units—sufficient to keep the company in eighth place. Then the factory turned to defense work, building trucks, airplane engines, and Weasel personnel carriers. Styling generally ground to a halt at most auto companies during wartime as skeleton design crews could spend only a fraction of their time on civilian projects. But Studebaker was different. Its car styling was being handled by Loewy As-

1942 President Skyway sedan-coupe

1946 Champion Skyway five-passenger coupe

1947 Commander Regal DeLuxe five-passenger coupe

sociates, an outside consultant firm not entirely occupied with defense contracts. As a result, Studebaker was able to introduce an all-new postwar design in the spring of 1946—well ahead of everyone else.

Earlier that year, the company offered a handful of Skyway Champions, slightly facelifted versions of the 1942 model. The alterations were indeed modest: the upper grille molding was extended under the headlamps, the side hood moldings were eliminated, and optional lamps appeared atop the fenders. The usual four body styles—three- and five-passenger coupes, two- and four-door sedans—were offered. Only 19,275 were built before production changed over.

The appealing new 1947 Studebaker was mainly the product of the Loewy Studios. Virgil M. Exner, who had left Pontiac to join Loewy before the war, had directed the '47 design at first, but split with Loewy before introduction time. Engineer Roy Cole supported Exner with staff and equipment for a home studio outside South Bend. His design was based on shapes that Loewy had developed earlier, and was officially accepted over Loewy's own proposal. Exner's influence on it was mostly from the cowl forward—a shorter hood and a more blunt, very ornate front end. This basic look was retained, except for detail changes, through 1949, followed by Loewy Studio's novel "bullet-nose" facelift for 1950-51.

The Commander and Champion series returned for '47, but the Skyway designation didn't. A special 123-inch wheelbase carried the Commander Land Cruiser, Studebaker's luxury sedan. Among standard-wheelbase Commanders, the usual four closed body styles were offered in DeLuxe and Regal DeLuxe trim, the latter priced about $120 higher. A new Regal convertible also debuted. The Champion followed the same pattern on a 112-inch wheelbase, and was nearly identical mechanically with its prewar counterpart.

One reason Studebaker styling didn't change much from 1947 to '52 was because the Loewy/Exner design—low profile, large glass area, and flow-through fenders—was so far ahead of the competition. Instant recognition of the '48s was provided by a winged hood medallion. The 1949 Commander was a continuation of the '48, while that year's Champion had a new grille composed of horizontal and vertical louvers forming three rows of rectangular openings. The most significant change in 1947-49 was mechanical. The Commander engine's stroke was lengthened to 4.75 inches for a displacement of 245.6 cubic inches and an even 100 bhp.

Studebaker's model offerings remained the same in 1948-49 as in '47. Commander coupes and sedans in DeLuxe and Regal DeLuxe trim, a Regal DeLuxe convertible, and long-wheelbase Land Cruiser; plus a similar Champion lineup minus the Land Cruiser. The big selling point continued to be styling, despite certain jokes ("Which way is it going?"). The design was an innovation, eliminating the bolt-on fenders of prewar models. The envelope body allowed for an increase of

six inches in front seat width and 10 in the rear, providing excellent interior room, too. Even after the major manufacturers restyled in 1949, Studebaker's shape remained one of the most advanced on the road.

The company enjoyed its best year ever in 1950, and many grand predictions were made about its upcoming "second century." But United States operations came to an end some 14 years later, and the Hamilton, Ontario branch built the last Studebaker automobile two years after that.

The story of how this happened is complex, but it can be summarized as follows: (1) Studebaker's productivity was lower than the rest of the industry, even though its work force was highly paid; (2) the firm's old South Bend plant suffered from high overhead and was more isolated from component suppliers than Detroit factories; and (3) the Big Three, competing with each other, caused casualties among the independents (an example is the Ford and Chevrolet price wars, which Studebaker dealers could not match because of their lower volume).

The product itself probably had less to do with the firm's failures than these commercial factors. Though Studebaker styling was controversial, it usually featured ideas adopted later by other manufacturers. Although the bullet-nose front end of 1950-51 wasn't really copied by anyone else, it did suggest the strong central grille styling that would appear later in different form on Edsels and Pontiacs. The 1950 models also offered Studebaker's excellent automatic transmission, designed in cooperation with the Detroit Gear Division of Borg-Warner.

Studebaker fielded a short-wheelbase Champion in three trim variations for 1950. Commanders rode a longer wheelbase and continued to offer a larger six-cylinder engine. The long-wheelbase Land Cruiser was still part of this series, available as a four-door sedan only. The Champion engine was continued for 1951, while the Commander received Studebaker's first V8.

Displacing 232.6 cubic inches, this new powerplant developed 120 bhp at 4000 rpm. Its engineering was fairly conventional, though overhead cams and hemispherical combustion chambers had been considered. The 232 and its successors have been called heavy for their size, but such statements were made on the basis of comparisons with engines developed much later. In fact, Studebaker's V8 was the first in a long line of robust, efficient small-blocks of less than 300 cid. Those that followed from Dodge, Ford, Chevrolet, and Plymouth certainly benefited from its technology. The 232's greatest contribution, perhaps, was that it closed the power gap between popular-priced cars and luxury machines. As a result, the V8 would become the engine design favored by automakers and buyers alike.

The '51 Studebaker line was essentially the same as in 1950. The main difference was body size: Commanders now shared the 115-inch wheelbase with Champions, while the Land Cruiser shrank from 124 to 119 inches. Prices went up slightly, but buyers seemed

1947 Champion Regal DeLuxe convertible

1949 Champion Regal DeLuxe convertible

1950 Champion DeLuxe four-door sedan

1951 Commander State five-passenger coupe

happy to pay the difference for the lively V8, which increased Commander sales considerably. The 232 was no powerhouse, but it did give 90-mph performance. As time would tell, it was capable of considerably more displacement and horsepower.

Styling changes for '51 were slight. The bullet-nose was refined with a second chrome ring, the prominent air vents above the grille were deleted, and model names were spelled out on the leading edges of the hood. Whatever can be said about its styling now, the bullet-nose Studebaker was popular when new.

With 222,000 unit sales for calendar 1951, Studebaker fell far below its 1950 record, though this was more a result of Korean War restrictions than decreased demand. The firm's market share actually increased, from 4.02 to 4.17 percent.

The company's centenary was marked in 1952. Though all-new styles weren't ready, that year's facelift was acceptably different. The bullet-nose was replaced by a low, toothy grille that some stylists called the "clam digger." The model lineup stayed the same, with the addition of a new hardtop, the Starliner. But production was much lower throughout the industry, and Studebaker built fewer cars. Optimistically, management looked on the upcoming '53s with more enthusiasm

The now-legendary "Loewy coupes"—Commander and Champion Starliner hardtop and Starlight pillar coupe—were actually designed by Robert E. Bourke, chief of the Loewy Studios at South Bend. Originally envisioned only as a special show car, Loewy sold the design as a production model to Studebaker's management. These coupes were truly magnificent. Mounted on the new 120.5-inch Land Cruiser wheelbase rather than the sedans' 116.5-inch span, they were perfect from every angle. Not a line or a detail was out of place. They were hailed at the time as the "new European look." Today, they're considered by many as the finest American automotive styling of the entire decade.

Sadly, the changeover to the new design delayed production, which was disappointly low. Further problems surfaced when demand for coupes began running four times higher than for the sedans (which had the same general lines but were shorter, higher, and more ungainly). Management had planned just the reverse, and time was lost in switching around.

The same lineup was offered for 1954 (an eggcrate grille was the most obvious change), but production was even lower. By now, the company's weaknesses were becoming apparent: the cost of building each car was frightening. As an experiment, Bourke "priced out" a Commander Starliner using the General Motors cost structure, and found Chevrolet could have sold it for about $1900. Meanwhile, the Ford Blitz was on, as Dearborn waged a price war with GM. Neither giant damaged the other, but both wreaked havoc on the independents. Just when things looked blackest, Packard bought Studebaker and announced a bold new effort to create "the industry's Big Four."

Unable to justify new styling so soon, Studebaker hung a lot of chrome on the old bodies for '55 and adopted a wraparound windshield in mid-year. The model line was shaken up, with Champions (excluding the coupes) still placed on the shorter wheelbase. The

longer chassis now served a separate series, the revived President. The Champion six was raised to 101 bhp. For more economy, the firm shrank the Commander V8 to 224.3 cid, which resulted in 140 bhp. Presidents, in turn, used a larger V8: 259.2 cid and 175 bhp. The top of the line was the wildly two-toned President Speedster hardtop, with special "quilted" leather seats, tooled metal dash, and color combinations like pink and black or "lemon and lime." At $3253, the Speedster was not a big seller, and neither were its linemates. In a year when nearly every company was setting new sales records, Studebaker produced only about 116,000 cars. Soon it was determined the company needed to sell about 250,000 cars a year just to break even.

While Studebaker-Packard president James Nance shopped for financing (eventually leading to a takeover by Curtiss-Wright), the firm gamely restyled for 1956. Retaining the old wheelbases and bodyshells, styling became more upright and squared off, with larger, mesh-type grilles. A cheap two-door called the sedanet was offered in the Commander and Champion series. The long-wheelbase chassis was now reserved for the top-line President Classic sedan and the sporty new Hawks.

The Hawks were the last Studebakers of the '50s designed by Loewy's team, and were good-looking, exciting to drive, competent on the curves, and impressive on the straightaways. There were four altogether. The Power (V8) and Flight (six) Hawks were descendents of the pillar-type Starlight coupe. Based on the old Starliner hardtop were the Sky Hawk and Golden Hawk, the latter with the 352-cid Packard engine. Styling was keyed to a square classic-style grille, freestanding parking lights, and deluxe interiors with engine-turned dash like the '55 Speedster's. The Flight Hawk was priced under $2000, while the Golden Hawk listed at only $3061, so they were good buys. Unfortunately, they were all peripheral models that appeared mainly to enthusiasts, while the bread-and-butter family cars continued to sell slowly. Only 70,000 vehicles were turned out at South Bend in 1956, and things would continue to get worse. In 1957 and '58, Studebaker and Packard combined couldn't produce more than 70,000 cars a year.

This was the period when none of the plant's employees knew from one day to the next whether they were working their last shift. With so little money to alter the '56 design, there was nothing else to do but try a facelift. Accordingly, a full-width grille appeared for 1957, and grew more massive in 1958, when Studebakers also got hastily developed quad headlight systems and ungainly tailfins. The Scotsman—a naked, bargain-priced line of sedans and a station wagon—did not spark sales. Neither did the nice-looking Starlight hardtop with its DeSoto-like roof.

Mechanical changes were beneficial, however. The '56 Golden Hawk's huge Packard engine had made it embarrassingly front-heavy, so the 1957-58 edition

1952 Commander State Starliner hardtop coupe

1953 Commander Regal Starliner hardtop coupe

1954 Commander Regal Conestoga station wagon

1955 President Speedster hardtop coupe

1956 President Classic four-door sedan

1956 Golden Hawk hardtop coupe

1956 Sky Hawk hardtop coupe

1957 President Classic four-door sedan

used a 289 V8 with Paxton supercharger. This arrangement developed the same 275 bhp, but in a more efficient way: the blower freewheeled economically until the accelerator was floored. The other Hawks were replaced by a single fixed-pillar Silver Hawk with plainer trim and an unblown 289 developing 210 bhp. The Golden Hawk and Silver Hawk were fine road machines, capable of carrying four people comfortably over long distances at high speed in true *gran turismo* style. As "personal cars," their appeal was limited, however, especially in 1958 when Studebaker hit bot-

tom. Fewer than 45,000 cars were built that year.

The end might have come right there had not the firm succeeded with the compact 1959 Lark. Though the Lark used many body panels and mechanical components from earlier '53–'58 models, stylist Duncan McRae had done enough to the exterior to make it look considerably different. The boxy, practical styling found a market among compact-conscious buyers, and people flocked to Studebaker dealerships in droves. The turnaround was astounding. Compared to 18,850 four-door sedans built for '58, a total of 48,459 four-door

'59 Larks rolled off the lines. The Lark was also offered as a two-door sedan, two-door wagon, and two-door hardtop, all on a 108.5-inch wheelbase. Six-cylinder models still used the old 169.6-cid L-head, detuned to 90 bhp. The V8 versions were fitted with the 259, rated at 180 bhp, or 195 with four-barrel carburetor. In V8 form, the Lark was lively yet surprisingly easy on gas. The Hawk was also continued for '59, but only the Silver Hawk was issued. As a result of all this, Studebaker made its first profit in six years, building over 126,000 cars. But the Lark would provide only a temporary reprieve.

For 1960, Lark was changed only mildly from the introductory model, receiving a new grille composed of thick and thin horizontal bars, and small alterations in script and medallions. The Hawk was carried over virtually unaltered. It sold for $2650 and was worth it. Equipped with functional white-on-black instruments and semi-bucket seats, it was a unique "family sports car" offering good performance. But scant advertising plus emphasis on the Lark hampered its sales.

For 1961, Lark was modestly facelifted. The six-cylinder engine was converted to overhead-valve design, yielding 112 bhp. One new model was the Lark Cruiser, outfitted with rich upholstery and riding the wagon wheelbase for extra rear seat room. It could be ordered with the Hawk's 289 V8, available with a power pack consisting of four-barrel carburetor and dual exhausts that raised output to 225 bhp. The Hawk itself was slightly revised for 1961, receiving two-tone color panels just below the fins and an optional four-speed gearbox.

When Sherwood Egbert became company president in early 1961, he asked Milwaukee stylist Brooks Stevens to help redesign the Lark and Hawk on a six-month crash basis. Randall Faurot, Studebaker's head of styling, willingly stepped back. Stevens adopted the longer 113-inch wheelbase for all four-door models, then developed elongated rear quarters, large round taillights, and a Mercedes-like rectangular grille (Studebaker was distributing Mercedes-Benz cars at the time). A new entry with either six or V8 power was the sporty Lark Daytona, which had bucket seats, bright new interiors, and an optional 289 engine.

In reworking the Hawk, Stevens reskinned the old Loewy-styled coupe to create a true hardtop with a Thunderbird-like rear roofline. He eliminated the large tailfins, which had become dated by 1960, and restyled the dashboard, which retained its full complement of purposeful gauges. Christened Gran Turismo, the result was a remarkable piece of expeditious redesign. The GT's optional 225-bhp engine provided a 120-mph top speed and a 0-60 sprint of less than 10 seconds. Although heavy, the 289 V8 was incredibly strong, capable of performance far greater than its displacement suggested. Sales picked up in 1962, when about 8400 Gran Turismos were built.

For 1963, Stevens reworked the Lark's body above the beltline. He improved visibility by using more glass

1957 Golden Hawk hardtop coupe

1958 President Starlight hardtop coupe

1960 Lark Regal convertible

and thinner upper door frames. The grille was revised slightly. The dashboard was completely new, fitted with needle gauges, rocker-type control switches, and a "vanity" style glove compartment containing a makeup case and pop-up mirror. For utility-car buyers, Stevens came up with a great innovation: the Wagonaire, with a sliding rear roof panel.

Stevens gave the 1963 GT Hawk a new grille similar to the Lark's, round amber parking lights, a wood-like dash, and pleated vinyl seats. Both Lark and Hawk were available by mid-year with the R1 (240 bhp) and R2 (290 bhp) Avanti engines, priced at $210 and $372 respectively. The R2 Super Hawk exceeded 140 mph at Bonneville, and an R2 Super Lark did over 132 mph.

Studebaker's greatest achievement of the decade was undoubtedly the Avanti, introduced for 1963. This brilliantly conceived grand touring car was created by

Raymond Loewy and a team of talented designers—John Ebstein, Robert Andrews, and Tom Kellogg. Like Stevens, Loewy had been hired by Sherwood Egbert. While Stevens attended to emergency restyling, Egbert asked Loewy for an exotic sports-type car that would revitalize the company's image. It was the first assignment Loewy had been given by Studebaker since his old contract lapsed following completion of the 1956 Hawks. In haste and in complete secrecy, he gathered his team at a rented house in Palm Springs, California.

The car they developed had a Coke-bottle shape, a large rear window, and a built-in roll bar. Front fenders were razor-edged, and swept back into curved rear fenders, then flowed into a jacked-up tail. Avoiding a conventional grille, Loewy designed an air scoop under a thin front bumper. An asymmetrical hump in the hood directed the driver's vision forward and added character to the front-end shape. Inside, ample crash padding was combined with four slim-section vinyl bucket seats and an aircraft-style control panel. The whole design was accepted for production with very little change from Loewy's original small scale model.

Fiberglass was chosen as the body material for reasons of cost and time, and chief engineer Eugene Harding chose a Lark convertible frame, shortened and highly modified, fitted with front and rear anti-sway bars and rear radius rods. The Bendix disc brakes used on the Avanti (as well as on some Larks and Hawks) were the first caliper discs in domestic production. The engine was, of course, the 289 V8. In standard (R1) form, it developed 240 bhp, thanks to a Paxton supercharger, ¾-race high-lift cam, dual-breaker distributor, four-barrel carburetor, and dual exhausts. Andy Granatelli and Paxton also developed a supercharged R2 version with 290 bhp, followed by a bored-out 304.5-cid version in three higher states of tune, the R3, R4, and R5. The experimental R5 had two Paxton superchargers, one for each cylinder bank, along with magneto ignition and Bendix fuel injection. It developed an incredible 575 horsepower, but was not a production option.

The Avanti had a remarkably slippery shape, even though Loewy had not had time for wind tunnel tests—he'd just guessed. In late 1962, Granatelli broke 29 Bonneville speed records with an R3, traveling faster than anyone ever had in an American stock car.

Unfortunately, Studebaker failed to get Avanti production going immediately after announcement. Unexpected distortion during fiberglass curing accounted partly for the delay. As a result, the firm was forced to add its own fiberglass body facility. By the time all the bugs were out, most of the customers who'd placed advance orders had given up on the Avanti and bought Corvettes. Fewer than 4600 were produced during 1963 and 1964. Production had already ceased by the time Studebaker stopped building Larks in December 1963.

The car was revived, however, by a pair of South Bend dealers. Equipped with a Corvette engine, it was still being produced in the 1980s (see Avanti II).

1961 Hawk coupe

1962 Gran Turismo Hawk hardtop coupe (prototype)

1963 Lark Daytona hardtop coupe

Despite the Avanti's obvious showroom appeal, Studebaker sales plunged in 1963. Model year output fell short of 70,000 units. The company ranked 12th in production, ahead of only Lincoln and Imperial among the major makes. Egbert, who'd been hospitalized repeatedly, entered the hospital again in November 1963 and did not return to the company. (He died of cancer in 1969.) Byers Burlingame replaced him as president. A month later, after desperate last-ditch attempts to obtain backing for future models, Burlingame announced the closure of the South Bend factory. Operations were transferred to the assembly plant in Hamilton, Ontario, where management hoped to continue production at the rate of 20,000 a year. After '64, all Studebakers were Canadian-built.

The 1964 models were the most attractive of the decade. Brooks Stevens had created more new styling for the Cruiser, Daytona, and Lark: a crisp, squared-off body, six inches longer than the 1963 version; a broad, horizontal grille integrated with the headlights; and a pointed upper tail section housing backup lights and taillamps. A stripped Challenger line was added at around $2100, and a still more powerful R3 engine was

1964 Avanti sport coupe

1966 Daytona two-door sedan

announced for the Super Lark and Super Hawk. (The Super Lark could do 0 to 60 mph in 7.3 seconds.) The '64 GT Hawk had a landau-style roof with partial vinyl top (optional), a smoothed-off deck, and a matte-black dash. A test driver pushed an R2 Hawk to 90 mph in 13.8 seconds and estimated its top speed at 150-plus mph. All the high-performance specials were dropped after the move to Canada.

The 1965 models were unchanged in appearance. However, without the South Bend engine plant, Hamilton had to find another powerplant. Ultimately, the source was Chevrolet, which provided its solid 120-bhp, 194-cid six and its excellent 283-cid V8 with 195 bhp. A six-cylinder Cruiser was available along with

Commander two- and four-door sedans and a four-door Wagonaire (with or without sliding roof). The V8 was offered for Commander sedans and wagon, the Daytona Sport sedan and wagon, and the Cruiser.

The Hamilton plant almost met its 20,000-unit quota for 1965. But the lack of facilities for advanced research and development meant production simply couldn't last. The last Studebaker—the '66—had new front-end styling with two dual-beam headlights instead of quads, a revised grille with rectangular panels, new bodyside moldings, and air-extraction ports in the rear panel. But production numbered only 8947 units. Despite rescue attempts by Stevens and others, Studebaker was doomed.

Studebaker Specifications

1930

53 Six (wb 114.0)—built Nov/29-Nov/30

	Wght	Price	Prod
touring 5P	2,840	965	
Regal touring 5P	2,900	1,065	
bus cpe 2P	2,835	895	
cpe 2-4P	2,890	985	
club sdn 5P	2,875	935	22,371*
sdn 4d	2,950	985	
Regal sdn 4d	3,100	1,085	
landau sdn 4d	3,110	1,125	

GJ Commander Six (wb 120.0)—built Dec/28-Apr/30

Regal rdstr 2-4P	3,000	1,495	
touring 5P	3,070	1,395	
touring 7P	3,095	1,360	
Regal touring 5P	3,200	1,495	
Regal touring 7P	3,225	1,460	
cpe 2P	3,105	1,345	
cpe 2-4P	3,160	1,425	16,019*
victoria 4P	3,130	1,425	
conv cab 4P	3,215	1,545	
sdn 4d	3,235	1,425	
Regal sdn 4d	3,335	1,545	
brougham (mohair uph.) 5P	3,415	1,575	
brougham (broadcloth) 5P	3,390	1,575	

GL Dictator Six (wb 115.0)—built Jun/29-May/30

touring 5P	2,955	1,145	
Regal touring 5P	3,075	1,265	
cpe 2P	2,915	1,135	
cpe 2-4P	2,980	1,195	
brougham 5P	3,250	1,295	17,561*
club sdn 5P	2,970	1,095	
sdn 4d	3,080	1,195	
Regal sdn 4d	3,200	1,295	

FC Dictator Eight (wb 115.0)—built May/29-Aug/30

touring 5P	2,980	1,285	
Regal touring 5P	3,100	1,385	
cpe 2P	2,950	1,255	
cpe 2-4P	3,010	1,315	
brougham 5P	3,275	1,415	16,359*
club sdn 5P	2,990	1,195	
sdn 4d	3,095	1,295	
Regal sdn 4d	3,230	1,415	

FD Commander Eight (wb 120.0)—built Dec/28-Jun/30

Regal rdstr 2-4P	3,040	1,595	
touring 5P	3,100	1,495	
Regal touring 5P	3,250	1,595	
cpe 2P	3,150	1,495	
cpe 2-4P	3,235	1,545	24,639*
victoria 4P	3,200	1,515	
conv cab 4P	3,345	1,695	
sdn 4d	3,310	1,515	

	Wght	Price	Prod
Regal sdn 4d	3,435	1,695	
sdn 7P	3,355	1,695	
Regal sdn 7P	3,480	1,845	
brougham (mohair uph.) 5P	3,540	1,695	
brougham (broadcloth) 5P	3,520	1,695	

FH President Eight (wb 125.0)—built Dec/28–Jun/30

	Wght	Price	Prod
rdstr 2-4P	3,810	1,795	
conv cab 4P	4,000	1,995	
State victoria 4P	4,050	1,995	
sdn 4d	4,110	1,795	17,527*
State sdn 4d (mohair uph.)	4,235	1,995	
State sdn 4d (broadcloth)	4,225	1,995	

FE President Eight (wb 135.0)—built Dec/28–Jun/30

	Wght	Price	Prod
touring 7P	4,020	1,845	
State touring 7P	4,175	2,145	
brougham (mohair uph.) 5P	4,440	2,395	
brougham (broadcloth) 5P	4,425	2,345	
sdn 7P	4,035	2,095	
State sdn (mohair uph.) 7P	4,435	2,295	8,740*
State sdn (broadcloth) 7P	4,435	2,295	
limo 7P	4,205	2,295	
State limo 7P	4,445	2,595	
State victoria 5P	4,230	2,295	

*incl. 1929 production; FC also includes 1931.

1930 Engines	bore×stroke	bhp	availability
L6, 205.3	3.25×4.13	70	S-53
L6, 221.0	3.38×4.13	68	S-GL
L6, 248.3	3.38×4.63	75	S-GJ
L8, 221.0	3.06×3.75	70	S-FC
L8, 250.4	3.06×4.25	80	S-FD
L8, 337.0	3.50×4.38	115	S-FH,FE

1931

53 Six (wb 114.0)—built Nov/29–Nov/30

	Wght	Price	Prod
rdstr 2P	2,720	795	
touring 5P	2,840	895	
Regal touring 5P	2,990	995	
bus cpe 2P	2,785	845	
cpe 2-4P	2,840	895	22,371*
club sdn 5P	2,830	845	
sdn 4d	2,900	895	
Regal sdn 4d	3,030	995	
landau sdn 4d	3,110	995	

54 Six (wb 114.0)—built Dec/30–Sep/31

	Wght	Price	Prod
rdstr 2P	2,700	895	
bus cpe 2P	2,790	845	
cpe 2-4P	2,840	895	
sdn 4d	2,930	895	23,917*
Regal sdn 4d	3,075	970	
touring 5P	2,805	895	
Regal touring 5P	2,960	970	

FC Dictator Eight (wb 115.0)—built May/29–Aug/30

	Wght	Price	Prod
touring 5P	2,980	1,285	
Regal touring 5P	3,100	1,385	
cpe 2P	2,950	1,255	
cpe 2-4P	3,010	1,315	16,359*
brougham 5P	3,275	1,415	
club sdn 5P	2,990	1,195	
sdn 4d	3,095	1,295	
Regal sdn 4d	3,230	1,415	

61 Dictator Eight (wb 114.0)—built Aug/30–Sep/31

	Wght	Price	Prod
cpe 2P	2,905	1,095	
cpe 2-4P	2,955	1,150	14,141*
sdn 4d	3,055	1,150	
Regal sdn 4d	3,195	1,225	

70 Commander Eight (wb 124.0)—built Jun/30–Sep/31

	Wght	Price	Prod
victoria 4P	3,390	1,585	
cpe 4P	3,400	1,585	
Regal b'ham (mohair uph.) 5P	3,660	1,685	
Regal b'ham (broadcloth) 5P	3,655	1,685	10,823*
sdn 4d	3,520	1,585	
Regal sdn 4d	3,660	1,685	

80 President Eight (wb 130.0)—built Jun/30–Sep/31

	Wght	Price	Prod
rdstr 4P	4,130	1,900	
cpe 2P	3,995	1,850	
State cpe 4P	4,200	1,950	6,340*
sdn 4d	4,230	1,850	
State sdn (mohair uph.) 4d	4,385	1,950	
State sdn (broadcloth) 4d	4,380	1,950	

90 President Eight (wb 136.0)—built Jun/30–Sep/31

	Wght	Price	Prod
State victoria 5P	4,275	2,250	
State b'ham (moahir uph.) 5P	4,460	2,250	
State b'ham (broadcloth) 5P	4,450	2,250	
sdn 7P	4,360	2,150	2,762*
State sdn 7P	4,520	2,250	
touring 7P	4,125	1,850	
State touring 7P	4,265	2,050	
State limo 7P	4,580	2,550	

*incl. 1930; FC includes 1929-30.

1931 Engines	bore×stroke	bhp	availability
L6, 205.3	3.25×4.13	70	S-53,54
L8, 221.0	3.06×3.75	70	S-FC
L8, 221.0	3.06×3.75	81	S-61
L8, 250.4	3.06×4.25	101	S-70
L8, 337.0	3.50×4.38	122	S-80,90

1932

55 Six (wb 117.0)—13,647 built

	Wght	Price	Prod
conv rdstr 2-4P	3,035	915	—
Regal conv rdstr 2-4P	3,135	1,020	—
cpe 2P	3,025	840	—
Regal cpe 2P	3,125	945	—
cpe 2-4P	3,080	890	—
Regal cpe 2-4P	3,165	995	—
St. Regis brougham 5P	3,130	915	—
St. Regis Regal brougham 5P	3,215	1,020	—
sdn 4d	3,170	915	—
Regal sdn 4d	3,260	1,020	—
conv sdn 5P	—	985	—
Regal conv sdn 5P	—	1,090	—

62 Dictator Eight (wb 117.0)—6,021 built

	Wght	Price	Prod
conv rdstr 2-4P	3,115	1,060	—
Regal conv rdstr 2-4P	3,190	1,155	—
cpe 2P	3,085	980	—
Regal cpe 2P	3,170	1,085	—
cpe 2-4P	3,160	1,030	—
Regal cpe 2-4P	3,225	1,135	—
St. Regis brougham 5P	3,225	1,050	—
St. Regis Regal b'ham 5P	3,280	1,155	—
sdn 4d	3,240	1,050	—
Regal sdn 4d	3,330	1,155	—
conv sdn 5P	3,285	1,125	—
Regal conv sdn 5P	3,370	1,230	—

71 Commander Eight (wb 125.0)—3,551 built

	Wght	Price	Prod
conv rdstr 2-4P	3,380	1,445	—
Regal conv rdstr 2-4P	3,480	1,550	—
cpe 2P	3,400	1,295	—
Regal cpe 2P	3,475	1,400	—
cpe 2-4P	3,465	1,350	—
Regal cpe 2-4P	3,530	1,455	—
St. Regis brougham 5P	3,530	1,445	—
St. Regis Regal brougham 5P	3,585	1,550	—
sdn 4d	3,545	1,445	—

	Wght	Price	Prod
Regal sdn 4d	3,645	1,550	—
conv sdn 5P	3,690	1,560	—
Regal conv sdn 5P	3,775	1,665	—

91 President Eight (wb 135.0)—2,399 built

	Wght	Price	Prod
conv rdstr 2-4P	4,100	1,750	—
State conv rdstr	4,200	1,855	—
cpe 2P	4,120	1,595	—
State cpe 2P	4,220	1,700	—
cpe 2-4P	4,265	1,690	—
State cpe 2-4P	4,365	1,795	—
St. Regis brougham 5P	4,200	1,750	—
St. Regis State brougham 5P	4,300	1,855	—
sdn 4d	4,260	1,750	—
State sdn 4d	4,390	1,855	—
conv sdn 5P	4,335	1,880	—
State conv sdn 5P	4,445	1,985	—
sdn 7P	4,365	1,890	—
State sdn 7P	4,475	1,995	—
limo 7P	4,415	1,990	—
State limo 7P	4,525	2,095	—

1932 Engines	bore×stroke	bhp	availability
L6, 230.0	3.25×4.63	80	S-55
L8, 221.0	3.06×3.75	85	S-62
L8, 250.4	3.06×4.25	101	S-71
L8, 337.0	3.50×4.38	122	S-91

1933

56 Six (wb 117.0)—6,861 built

	Wght	Price	Prod
rdstr 2-4P	3,165	915	—
Regal rdstr 2-4P	3,260	1,020	—
cpe 2P	3,160	840	—
Regal cpe 2P	3,245	945	—
cpe 2-4P	3,210	890	—
Regal cpe 2-4P	3,300	995	—
St. Regis brougham 5P	3,300	915	—
St. Regis Regal brougham 5P	3,375	1,020	—
sdn 4d	3,310	915	—
Regal sdn 4d	3,435	1,020	—
conv sdn 5P	3,380	1,015	—
Regal conv sdn 5P	3,460	1,120	—

73 Commander Eight (wb 117.0)—3,841 built

	Wght	Price	Prod
conv rdstr 2-4P	3,245	1,095	—
Regal conv rdstr 2-4P	3,335	1,200	—
cpe 2P	3,220	1,000	—
Regal cpe 2P	3,345	1,105	—
cpe 2-4P	3,275	1,050	—
Regal cpe 2-4P	3,405	1,155	—
St. Regis brougham 5P	3,375	1,075	—
St. Regis Regal brougham 5P	3,475	1,180	—
sdn 4d	3,385	1,075	—
Regal sdn 4d	3,500	1,180	—
conv sdn 5P	3,475	1,195	—
Regal conv sdn 5P	3,545	1,300	—

82 President Eight (wb 125.0)—1,194 built

	Wght	Price	Prod
conv rdstr 2-4P	3,480	1,385	—
State conv rdstr 2-4P	3,560	1,490	—
cpe 2-4P	3,520	1,325	—
State cpe 2-4P	3,600	1,430	—
St. Regis brougham 5P	3,605	1,385	—
St. Regis State brougham 5P	3,670	1,490	—
sdn 4d	3,640	1,385	—
State sdn 4d	3,720	1,490	—
State conv sdn 5P	3,745	1,650	—

92 President Eight (wb 135.0)—635 built

	Wght	Price	Prod
conv rdstr 2-4P	4,205	1,685	—
State conv rdstr 2-4P	4,285	1,790	—
cpe 2-4P	4,255	1,625	—

	Wght	Price	Prod
State cpe 2-4P	4,335	1,730	—
St. Regis State brougham 5P	4,400	1,790	—
sdn 4d	4,380	1,685	—
State sdn 4d	4,465	1,790	—
State conv sdn 5P	4,470	1,960	—
sdn 7P	4,470	1,835	—
State sdn 7P	4,565	1,940	—
State limo 7P	4,605	2,040	—

1933 Engines	bore×stroke	bhp	availability
L6, 230.0	3.25×4.63	85	S-56
L8, 235.0	3.06×4.00	100	S-73
L8, 250.0	3.06×4.25	110	S-82
L8, 337.0	3.50×4.38	132	S-92

1934

A Dictator Six (wb 113.0)—45,851 built

	Wght	Price	Prod
conv rdstr 2-4P	2,860	790	—
Regal conv rdstr 2-4P	2,935	820	—
cpe 2P	2,795	740	—
Regal cpe 2P	2,860	770	—
cpe 2-4P	2,865	790	—
Regal cpe 2-4P	2,950	820	—
St. Regis brougham 5P	2,840	760	—
St. Regis Regal brougham 5P	2,935	810	—
St. Regis Custom brougham 5P	2,890	810	—
sdn 4d	2,910	790	—
Regal sdn 4d	3,005	840	—
Custom sdn 4d	2,950	840	—
Special series:			
cpe 2P	2,780	685	—
Regal cpe 2P	2,845	720	—
cpe 2-4P	2,850	740	—
Regal cpe 2-4P	2,935	770	—
St. Regis brougham 5P	2,825	710	—
St. Regis Regal brougham 5P	2,920	760	—
St. Regis Custom brougham 5P	2,875	760	—
sdn 4d	2,895	740	—
Regal sdn 4d	2,990	790	—
Custom sdn 4d	2,935	790	—
"Year Ahead" series (from Jul/34):			
cpe 3P	2,800	695	—
Regal cpe 3P	2,885	730	—
cpe 5P	2,880	750	—
Regal cpe 5P	2,980	780	—
St. Regis sdn 4d	2,850	720	—
St. Regis Custom sdn 4d	2,910	755	—
St. Regis Regal sdn 4d	2,970	770	—
sdn 4d	2,915	750	—
Custom sdn 4d	2,960	785	—
Regal sdn 4d	3,020	800	—
Deluxe sub-series:			
rdstr 3-5P	2,900	800	—
Regal rdstr 3-5P	2,970	800	—
cpe 3P	2,830	750	—
Regal cpe 3P	2,920	780	—
cpe 3-5P	2,900	800	—
Regal cpe 3-5P	3,020	830	—
St. Regis sdn 4d	2,895	770	—
St. Regis Regal sdn 4d	2,985	820	—
St. Regis Custom sdn 4d	2,945	805	—
sdn 4d	2,945	800	—
Regal sdn 4d	3,055	850	—
Custom sdn 4d	2,990	835	—
Land Cruiser sd 4d	3,015	995	—
Regal Land Cruiser sdn 4d	3,110	995	—

B Commander Eight (wb 119.0)—10,315 built

	Wght	Price	Prod
conv rdstr 2-4P	3,255	970	—
Regal conv rdstr 2-4P	3,335	1,000	—
cpe 2P	3,205	920	—

	Wght	Price	Prod
Regal cpe 2P	3,290	950	—
cpe 2-4P	3,280	970	—
Regal cpe 2-4P	3,350	1,000	—
St. Regis brougham 5P	3,235	940	—
St. Regis Regal brougham 5P	3,355	990	—
St. Regis Custom brougham 5P	3,295	990	—
sdn 4d	3,310	970	—
Regal sdn 4d	3,435	1,020	—
Custom sdn 4d	3,360	1,020	—
Land Cruiser sdn 4d	3,385	1,165	—
Regal Land Cruiser sdn 4d	3,480	1,165	—
"Year Ahead" series (began Jul/34):			
rdstr 3-5P	3,290	915	—
Regal rdstr 3-5P	3,355	945	—
cpe 3P	3,215	865	—
Regal cpe 3P	3,300	895	—
cpe 3-5P	3,295	915	—
Regal cpe 3-5P	3,375	945	—
St. Regis Regal sdn 4d	3,385	935	—
St. Regis Custom sdn 4d	3,340	920	—
Regal sdn 4d	3,435	965	—
Custom sdn 4d	3,395	950	—
Land Cruiser sdn 4d	3,410	1,135	—
Regal Land Cruiser sdn 4d	3,500	1,135	—

C President Eight (wb 123.0)—3,698 built

	Wght	Price	Prod
conv rdstr 2-4P	3,435	1,220	—
Regal conv rdstr 2-4P	3,510	1,250	—
cpe 2P	3,370	1,170	—
Regal cpe 2P	3,470	1,200	—
cpe 2-4P	3,410	1,220	—
Regal cpe 2-4P	3,510	1,250	—
sdn 4d	3,490	1,220	—
Regal sdn 4d	3,620	1,270	—
Custom sdn 4d	3,550	1,270	—
Land Cruiser sdn 4d	3,565	1,445	—
Regal Land Cruiser sdn 4d	3,655	1,445	—
Custom berline 5P	—	1,420	—
Regal berline 5P	—	1,420	—
"Year Ahead" series (began Jul/34)			
rdstr 3-5P	3,460	1,220	—
Regal rdstr 3-5P	3,520	1,250	—
cpe 3P	3,395	1,170	—
Regal cpe 3P	3,495	1,200	—
cpe 3-5P	3,465	1,220	—
Regal cpe 3-5P	3,535	1,250	—
Regal sdn 4d	3,630	1,270	—
Custom sdn 4d	3,560	1,255	—
Regal berline 6P	3,720	1,420	—
Custom berline 6P	3,660	1,405	—
Land Cruiser sdn 4d	3,595	1,445	—
Regal Land Cruiser sdn 4d	3,710	1,445	—

1934 Engines	bore×stroke	bhp	availability
L6, 205.3	3.25×4.13	88	S-Dictator
L8, 221.0	3.06×3.75	103	S-Commander
L8, 250.0	3.06×4.25	110	S-President

1935

1A Dictator Six* (wb 114.0)—11,742 built

	Wght	Price	Prod
rdstr 3-5P	2,985	745	—
Regal rdstr 3-5P	3,070	775	—
cpe 3P	2,895	695	—
Regal cpe 3P	3,005	725	—
cpe 3-5P	2,995	745	—
Regal cpe 3-5P	3,070	775	—
St. Regis sdn 4d	2,965	715	—
St. Regis Regal sdn 4d	3,085	755	—
St. Regis Custom sdn 4d	3,035	740	—
sdn 4d	3,030	745	—
Regal sdn 4d	3,160	785	—

	Wght	Price	Prod
Custom sdn 4d	3,085	770	—
Land Cruiser sdn 4d	3,100	880	—
Regal Land Cruiser sdn 4d	3,220	895	—

2A Dictator Six (wb 114.0)—23,550 built**

	Wght	Price	Prod
rdstr 3-5P	3,040	780	—
Regal rdstr 3-5P	3,140	810	—
cpe 3P	2,975	720	—
Regal cpe 3P	3,075	760	—
cpe 3-5P	3,065	780	—
Regal cpe 3-5P	3,135	810	—
St. Regis sdn 4d	3,035	750	—
St. Regis Regal sdn 4d	3,170	790	—
St. Regis Custom sdn 4d	3,105	775	—
sdn 4d	3,095	780	—
Regal sdn 4d	3,230	820	—
Custom sdn 4d	3,155	805	—
Land Cruiser sdn 4d	3,170	915	—
Regal Land Cruiser sdn 4d	3,285	930	—

1B Commander Eight (wb 120.0)—6,085 built

	Wght	Price	Prod
rdstr 3-5P	3,510	980	—
Regal rdstr 3-5P	3,570	1,010	—
cpe 3P	3,420	925	—
Regal cpe 3P	3,510	960	—
cpe 3-5P	3,520	980	—
Regal cpe 3-5P	3,570	1,010	—
St. Regis Regal sdn 4d	3,620	1,000	—
St. Regis Custom sdn 4d	3,550	985	—
Regal sdn 4d	3,685	1,030	—
Custom sdn 4d	3,600	1,015	—
Land Cruiser sdn 4d	3,692	1,115	—
Regal Land Cruiser sdn 4d	3,720	1,130	—

1C President Eight (wb 124.0)—2,305 built

	Wght	Price	Prod
rdstr 3-5P	3,645	1,295	—
Regal rdstr 3-5P	3,740	1,325	—
cpe 3P	3,600	1,245	—
Regal cpe 3P	3,685	1,275	—
cpe 3-5P	3,660	1,295	—
Regal cpe 3-5P	3,740	1,325	—
Regal sdn 4d	3,900	1,345	—
Custom sdn 4d	3,790	1,330	—
Land Cruiser sdn 4d	3,820	1,430	—
Regal Land Cruiser sdn 4d	3,900	1,445	—
Custom berline 5P	3,900	1,430	—
Regal berline 5P	3,970	1,445	—

*conventional front suspension **planar front suspension
Note: DeLuxe version of all Sixes also offered at $40 higher, 15 pounds more weight, and included free-wheeling, Startix, dual windshield wipers, sunvisor, taillamp, robe rail, ash receivers. All Regal models equipped with trunks and six wire wheels all series.

1935 Engines	bore×stroke	bhp	availability
L6, 205.3	3.25×4.13	88	S-1A,2A
L8, 250.0	3.06×4.25	107	S-1B
L8, 250.0	3.06×4.25	110	S-1C

1936

3A Dictator Six* (wb 116.0)—26,634 built

	Wght	Price	Prod
bus cpe 3P	2,910	665	—
Custom cpe 3P	2,965	695	—
Custom cpe 5P	3,020	720	—
St. Regis Custom sdn 4d	3,075	725	—
St. Regis Cruising sdn 4d T/B	3,080	745	—
Custom sdn 4d	3,110	755	—
Cruising sdn 4d T/B	3,120	775	—

4A Dictator Six (wb 116.0)—22,029 built**

	Wght	Price	Prod
bus cpe 3P	2,980	685	—
Custom cpe 3P	3,035	705	—
Custom cpe 5P	3,090	740	—

	Wght	Price	Prod
St. Regis Custom sdn 4d	3,145	745	—
St. Regis Cruising sdn 4d T/B	3,150	765	—
Custom sdn 4d	3,180	775	—
Cruising sdn 4d T/B	3,190	795	—

2C President Eight (wb 125.0)—7,297 built

Custom cpe 3P	3,460	965	—
Custom cpe 5P	3,515	995	—
St. Regis Custom sdn 4d	3,560	1,015	—
St. Regis Cruising sdn 4d T/B	3,570	1,035	—
Custom sdn 4d	3,600	1,045	—
Cruising sdn 4d T/B	3,615	1,065	—

*conventional front suspension **planar front suspension

1936 Engines	bore×stroke	bhp	availability
L6, 218.0	3.25×4.38	90	S-Dictator
L8, 250.0	3.06×4.25	115	S-President

1937

5A Dictator Six* (wb 116.0)—50,000 built*

	Wght	Price	Prod
bus cpe 3P	2,695	765	—
Custom cpe 3P	3,005	820	—
Custom cpe 5P	3,045	845	—
St. Regis Custom sdn 4d	3,100	850	—
St. Regis Cruising sdn 4d T/B	3,100	830	—
Custom sdn 4d	3,130	880	—
Cruising sdn 4d T/B	3,140	900	—

6A Dictator Six (wb 116.0)—79,000 built***

bus cpe 3P	2,765	785	—
Custom cpe 3P	3,075	840	—
Custom cpe 5P	3,115	865	—
St. Regis Custom sdn 4d	3,170	870	—
St. Regis Cruising sdn 4d T/B	3,170	890	—
Custom sdn 4d	3,200	900	—
Cruising sdn 4d T/B	3,210	920	—

3C President Eight (wb 125.0)—9,000 built*

Custom cpe 3P	3,510	1,087	—
Custom cpe 5P	3,540	1,115	—
St. Regis Custom sdn 4d	3,600	1,135	—
St. Regis Cruising sdn 4d T/B	3,610	1,155	—
Custom sdn 4d	3,620	1,165	—
Cruising sdn 4d T/B	3,635	1,185	—

*conventional front suspension **planar front suspension ***estimated
Note: President State trim option $30 higher

1937 Engines	bore×stroke	bhp	availability
L6, 218.0	3.25×4.38	90	S-Dictator
L8, 250.0	3.06×4.25	115	S-President

1938

7A Commander Six (wb 116.5)—19,260 built

	Wght	Price	Prod
bus cpe 3P	3,045	875	—
Custom cpe 3P	3,060	900	—
Club sdn 2d 6P	3,140	955	—
Cruising sdn 4d	3,140	960	—
conv sdn 6P	3,390	1,315	—

8A State Commander (wb 116.5)—22,053 built

Custom cpe 3P	3,095	965	—
Club sdn 2d 6P	3,160	1,030	—
Cruising sdn 4d 6P	3,215	1,040	—
conv sdn 6P	3,400	1,365	—

4C State President (wb 122.0)—5,474 built

cpe 3P	3,315	1,130	—
club sdn 2d 6P	3,400	1,195	—
Cruising sdn 4d 6P	3,455	1,205	—
conv sdn 6P	3,640	1,555	—

1938 Engines	bore×stroke	bhp	availability
L6, 226.2	3.31×4.38	90	S-Commander
L8, 250.0	3.06×4.25	110	S-President

1939

G Champion (wb 110.0)—33,905 built

	Wght	Price	Prod
Custom cpe 3P	2,260	660	—
Custom club sdn 2d 5P	2,330	700	—
Custom Cruising sdn 4d	2,360	740	—
DeLuxe cpe 3P	2,275	720	—
DeLuxe club sdn 2d 5P	2,345	760	—
DeLuxe Cruising sdn 4d	2,375	800	—

9A Commander (wb 116.5)—43,724 built

bus cpe 3P	3,045	875	—
Custom cpe 3P	3,080	900	—
club sdn 2d 6P	3,160	955	—
Cruising sdn 4d	3,200	965	—
conv sdn 6P	3,400	1,290	—

5C President (wb 122.0)—8,205 built

Custom cpe 3P	3,300	1,035	—
club sdn 2d 6P	3,390	1,100	—
Cruising sdn 4d	3,440	1,110	—
conv sdn 6P	3,640	1,460	—

1939 Engines	bore×stroke	bhp	availability
L6, 164.3	3.00×3.88	78	S-Champion
L6, 226.2	3.31×4.38	90	S-Commander
L8, 250.0	3.06×4.25	110	S-President

Note: Some station wagons were built on Commander chassis by Hercules Body Company in 1939. Production figures include chassis.

1940

2G Champion (wb 110.0)—66,264 built

	Wght	Price	Prod
cpe 3P	2,290	660	—
cpe 5P	2,335	696	—
club sdn	2,360	700	—
Cruising Sedan 4d	2,390	740	—
DeLuxe cpe 3P	2,315	705	—
DeLuxe cpe 5P	2,360	740	—
DeLuxe club sdn	2,385	745	—
DeLuxe Cruising Sedan 4d	2,415	785	—

LOA Commander (wb 116.5)—34,477 built

Custom cpe 3P	3,055	895	—
club sdn	3,135	925	—
Cruising Sedan 4d	3,180	965	—

6C President (wb 122.0)—6,444

	Wght	Price	Prod
cpe 3P	3,280	1,025	—
club sdn	3,370	1,055	—
Cruising Sedan 4d	3,420	1,095	—

1940 Engines	bore×stroke	bhp	availability
L6, 164.3	3.00×3.88	78	S-Champion
L6, 226.2	3.31×4.38	90	S-Commander
L8, 250.4	3.06×4.25	110	S-President

1941

3G Champion (wb 110.0)—84,910 built

	Wght	Price	Prod
Custom cpe 3P	2,370	710	—
Custom Opera cpe	2,410	750	—
Custom club sdn	2,450	755	—
Custom Cruising Sedan 4d	2,480	795	—
Custom DeLuxe cpe 3P	2,395	745	—
Custom DeLuxe Opera cpe	2,425	780	—
Custom DeLuxe club sdn	2,470	785	—
Custom DeLuxe Cruising Sdn 4d	2,500	825	—
DeLux-Tone cpe 3P	2,400	780	—
DeLux-Tone Opera cpe	2,430	815	—

	Wght	Price	Prod
DeLux-Tone club sdn	2,470	820	—
DeLux-Tone Cruising Sedan 4d	2,500	860	—

11A Commander (wb 119.0)—41,996 built

	Wght	Price	Prod
Custom sdn cpe	3,160	990	—
Custom Cruising Sedan 4d	3,210	1,010	—
Custom Land Cruiser sdn 4d	3,230	1,055	—
DeLux-Tone Cruising Sedan 4d	3,225	1,075	—
DeLux-Tone Land Cruiser sdn 4d	3,245	1,120	—
Skyway sdn cpe	3,200	1,080	—
Skyway Cruising Sedan 4d	3,240	1,100	—
Skyway Land Cruiser sdn 4d	3,260	1,130	—

7C President (wb 124.5)—6,994 built

	Wght	Price	Prod
Custom Cruising Sedan 4d	3,450	1,140	—
Custom Land Cruiser sdn 4d	3,475	1,185	—
DeLux-Tone Cruising Sedan 4d	3,475	1,205	—
DeLux-Tone Land Cruiser sdn 4d	3,500	1,250	—
Skyway sdn cpe	3,440	1,210	—
Skyway Cruising Sedan 4d	3,500	1,230	—
Skyway Land Cruiser sdn 4d	3,520	1,260	—

1941 Engines	bore×stroke	bhp	availability
L6, 169.6	3.00×4.00	80	S-Champion
L6, 226.2	3.31×4.38	94	S-Commander
L8, 250.4	3.06×4.25	117	S-President

1942

4G Champion (wb 110.0)—29,678 built

	Wght	Price	Prod
Custom cpe 3P	2,415	744	—
Custom Double Dater cpe 5P	2,455	769	—
Custom club sdn	2,495	774	—
Custom Cruising Sedan 4d	2,520	804	—
DeLuxstyle cpe 3P	2,435	779	—
DeLuxstyle Double Dater cpe 5P	2,470	804	—
DeLuxstyle club sdn	2,520	809	—
DeLuxstyle Cruising Sedan 4d	2,545	839	—

12A Commander (wb 119.0)—17,500 built

	Wght	Price	Prod
Custom sdn cpe	3,195	1,025	—
Custom Cruising Sedan 4d	3,265	1,045	—
Custom Land Cruiser sdn 4d	3,290	1,080	—
DeLuxstyle sdn cpe	3,210	1,070	—
DeLuxstyle Cruising Sedan 4d	3,280	1,090	—
DeLuxstyle Land Cruiser sdn 4d	3,305	1,125	—
Skyway sdn cpe	3,240	1,105	—
Skyway Cruising Sedan 4d	3,300	1,125	—
Skyway Land Cruiser sdn 4d	3,315	1,160	—

8C President (wb 124.5)—3,500 built

	Wght	Price	Prod
Custom sdn cpe	3,440	1,141	—
Custom Cruising Sedan 4d	3,485	1,161	—
Custom Land Cruiser sdn 4d	3,510	1,196	—
DeLuxstyle sdn cpe	3,455	1,186	—
DeLuxstyle Cruising Sedan 4d	3,500	1,206	—
DeLuxstyle Land Cruiser sdn 4d	3,515	1,241	—
Skyway sdn cpe	3,470	1,221	—
Skyway Cruising Sedan 4d	3,540	1,241	—
Skyway Land Cruiser sdn 4d	3,540	1,276	—

1942 Engines	bore×stroke	bhp	availability
L6, 169.6	3.00×4.00	80	S-Champion
L6, 226.2	3.31×4.38	94	S-Commander
L8, 250.4	3.06×4.25	117	S-President

1946

5G Skyway Champion (wb 110.0)

	Wght	Price	Prod
cpe 3P	2,456	1,002	2,465
cpe 5P	2,491	1,044	1,285
club sdn	2,541	1,046	5,000
Cruising Sedan 4d	2,566	1,097	10,525

1946 Engine	bore×stroke	bhp	availability
L6, 169.6	3.00×4.00	80	S-all

1947

6G Champion (wb 112.0)—105,097 built

	Wght	Price	Prod
DeLuxe sdn 4d	2,735	1,478	—
DeLuxe sdn 2d	2,685	1,446	—
DeLuxe cpe 5P	2,670	1,472	—
DeLuxe cpe 3P	2,600	1,378	—
Regal DeLuxe sdn 4d	2,760	1,551	—
Regal DeLuxe sdn 2d	2,710	1,520	—
Regal DeLuxe cpe 5P	2,690	1,546	—
Regal DeLuxe cpe 3P	2,620	1,451	—
Regal DeLuxe conv cpe	2,875	1,902	—

15A Commander (wb 119.0; LC-123.0)—56,399 built

	Wght	Price	Prod
DeLuxe sdn 4d	3,265	1,761	—
DeLuxe sdn 2d	3,230	1,729	—
DeLuxe cpe 5P	3,210	1,755	—
DeLuxe cpe 3P	3,140	1,661	—
Regal DeLuxe sdn 4d	3,280	1,882	—
Regal DeLuxe sdn 2d	3,245	1,850	—
Regal DeLuxe cpe 5P	3,225	1,877	—
Regal DeLuxe cpe 3P	3,155	1,782	—
Regal DeLuxe conv cpe	3,420	2,236	—
Land Cruiser sdn 4d	3,340	2,043	—

1947 Engines	bore×stroke	bhp	availability
L6, 169.6	3.00×4.00	80	S-Champion
L6, 226.2	3.31×4.38	94	S-Commander

1948

7G Champion (wb 112.0)—99,282 built

	Wght	Price	Prod
Deluxe sdn 4d	2,720	1,636	—
Deluxe sdn 2d	2,675	1,604	—
Deluxe cpe 5P	2,670	1,630	—
Deluxe cpe 3P	2,590	1,535	—
Regal DeLuxe sdn 4d	2,725	1,709	—
Regal DeLuxe sdn 2d	2,685	1,678	—
Regal DeLuxe cpe 5P	2,690	1,704	—
Regal DeLuxe cpe 3P	2,615	1,609	—
Regal DeLuxe conv cpe	2,865	2,060	—

15A Commander (wb 119.0; LC-123.0)—85,711 built

	Wght	Price	Prod
DeLuxe sdn 4d	3,195	1,956	—
DeLuxe sdn 2d	3,165	1,925	—
DeLuxe cpe 5P	3,150	1,951	—
DeLuxe cpe 3P	3,080	1,856	—
Regal DeLuxe sdn 4d	3,215	2,078	—
Regal DeLuxe sdn 2d	3,175	2,046	—
Regal DeLuxe cpe 5P	3,165	2,072	—
Regal DeLuxe cpe 3P	3,095	1,978	—
Regal DeLuxe conv cpe	3,385	2,431	—
Land Cruiser sdn 4d	3,280	2,265	—

1948 Engines	bore×stroke	bhp	availability
L6, 169.6	3.00×4.00	80	S-Champion
L6, 226.2	3.31×4.38	94	S-Commander

1949

8G Champion (wb 112.0)—85,604 built

	Wght	Price	Prod
DeLuxe sdn 4d	2,745	1,689	—
DeLuxe sdn 2d	2,720	1,657	—
DeLuxe cpe 5P	2,705	1,683	—
DeLuxe cpe 3P	2,645	1,588	—
Regal DeLuxe sdn 4d	2,750	1,762	—
Regal DeLuxe sdn 2d	2,725	1,731	—
Regal DeLuxe cpe 5P	2,725	1,757	—
Regal DeLuxe cpe 3P	2,650	1,652	—
Regal DeLuxe conv cpe	2,895	2,086	—

Studebaker

16A Commander (wb 119.0; LC-123.0)—43,694 built

	Wght	Price	Prod
DeLuxe sdn 4d	3,240	2,019	—
DeLuxe sdn 2d	3,215	1,988	—
DeLuxe cpe 5P	3,200	2,014	—
DeLuxe cpe 3P	3,130	1,919	—
Regal DeLuxe sdn 4d	3,245	2,141	—
Regal DeLuxe sdn 2d	3,220	2,109	—
Regal DeLuxe cpe 5P	3,205	2,135	—
Regal DeLuxe cpe 3P	3,135	2,041	—
Regal DeLuxe conv cpe	3,415	2,468	—
Land Cruiser sdn 4d	3,325	2,328	—

1949 Engines	bore×stroke	bhp	availability
L6, 169.6	3.00×4.00	80	S-Champion
L6, 245.6	3.31×4.75	100	S-Commander

1950

9G Champion (wb 113.0)—270,604 built

	Wght	Price	Prod
Custom sdn 4d	2,730	1,519	—
Custom sdn 2d	2,695	1,487	—
Custom cpe, 5P	2,690	1,514	—
Custom cpe 3P	2,620	1,419	—
DeLuxe sdn 4d	2,750	1,597	—
DeLuxe sdn 2d	2,720	1,565	—
DeLuxe cpe 5P	2,705	1,592	—
DeLuxe cpe 3P	2,635	1,497	—
Regal DeLuxe sdn 4d	2,755	1,676	—
Regal DeLuxe sdn 2d	2,725	1,644	—
Regal DeLuxe cpe 5P	2,715	1,671	—
Regal DeLuxe cpe 3P	2,640	1,576	—
Regal DeLuxe conv cpe	2,900	1,981	—

17A Commander (wb 120.0; LC-124.0)—72,562 built

	Wght	Price	Prod
DeLuxe sdn 4d	3,255	1,902	—
DeLuxe sdn 2d	3,215	1,871	—
DeLuxe cpe 5P	3,215	1,897	—
Regal DeLuxe sdn 4d	3,265	2,024	—
Regal DeLuxe sdn 2d	3,220	1,992	—
Regal DeLuxe cpe 5P	3,220	2,018	—
Regal DeLuxe conv cpe	3,375	2,328	—
Land Cruiser sdn 4d	3,355	2,187	—

1950 Engines	bore×stroke	bhp	availability
L6, 169.6	3.00×4.00	85	S-Champion
L6, 245.6	3.31×4.75	102	S-Commander

1951

10G Champion (wb 115.0)—144,286 built

	Wght	Price	Prod
Custom sdn 4d	2,690	1,667	—
Custom sdn 2d	2,670	1,634	—
Custom cpe 5P	2,650	1,662	—
Custom cpe 3P	2,585	1,561	—
DeLuxe sdn 4d	2,715	1,759	—
DeLuxe sdn 2d	2,690	1,716	—
DeLuxe cpe 5P	2,675	1,744	—
DeLuxe cpe 3P	2,610	1,643	—
Regal sdn 4d	2,720	1,833	—
Regal sdn 2d	2,690	1,800	—
Regal cpe 5P	2,675	1,828	—
Regal cpe 3P	2,615	1,727	—
Regal conv cpe	2,890	2,157	—

H Commander (wb 115,0; LC-119.0)—124,280 built

	Wght	Price	Prod
Regal sdn 4d	3,065	2,032	—
Regal sdn 2d	3,045	1,997	—
Regal cpe 5P	3,030	2,026	—
State sdn 4d	3,070	2,143	—
State sdn 2d	3,045	2,108	—
State cpe 5P	3,030	2,137	—
State conv cpe	3,240	2,381	—
Land Cruiser sdn 4d	3,165	2,289	—

1951 Engines	bore×stroke	bhp	availability
L6, 169.6	3.00×4.00	85	S-Champion
V8, 232.6	3.38×3.25	120	S-Commander

1952

12G Champion (wb 115.0)—101,390 built

	Wght	Price	Prod
Custom sdn 4d	2,695	1,769	—
Custom sdn 2d	2,655	1,735	—
Custom cpe 5P	2,660	1,763	—
DeLuxe sdn 4d	2,720	1,862	—
DeLuxe sdn 2d	2,685	1,828	—
DeLuxe cpe 5P	2,675	1,856	—
Regal sdn 4d	2,725	1,946	—
Regal sdn 2d	2,690	1,913	—
Regal cpe 5P	2,695	1,941	—
Regal Starliner htp cpe	2,860	2,220	—
Regal conv cpe	2,870	2,273	—

3H Commander (wb 115.0; LC-119.0)—84,849 built

	Wght	Price	Prod
Regal sdn 4d	3,085	2,121	—
Regal sdn 2d	3,040	2,086	—
Regal cpe 5P	3,030	2,115	—
State sdn 4d	3,075	2,208	—
State sdn 2d	3,055	2,172	—
State cpe 5P	3,025	2,202	—
State Starliner htp cpe	3,220	2,488	—
State conv cpe	3,230	2,548	—
Land Cruiser sdn 4d	3,155	2,365	—

1952 Engines	bore×stroke	bhp	availability
L6, 169.6	3.00×4.00	85	S-Champion
V8, 232.6	3.38×3.25	120	S-Commander

1953

14G Champion (wb 116.5; cpes-120.5)—93,807 built

	Wght	Price	Prod
Custom sdn 4d	2,710	1,767	—
Custom sdn 2d	2,690	1,735	—
DeLuxe sdn 4d	2,735	1,863	—
DeLuxe sdn 2d	2,700	1,831	—
DeLuxe Starlight cpe	2,695	1,868	—
Regal sdn 4d	2,745	1,949	—
Regal sdn 2d	2,715	1,917	—
Regal Starlight cpe	2,700	1,955	—
Regal Starliner htp cpe	2,760	2,116	—

4H Commander (wb 116.5; LC/cpes-120.5)—76,092 built

	Wght	Price	Prod
DeLuxe sdn 4d	3,075	2,121	—
DeLuxe DeLuxe sdn 2d	3,055	2,089	—
DeLuxe Starlight cpe	3,040	2,127	—
Regal sdn 4d	3,095	2,208	—
Regal Starlight cpe	3,040	2,213	—
Regal Starliner htp cpe	3,120	2,374	—
Land Cruiser sdn 4d	3,180	2,316	—

1953 Engines	bore×stroke	bhp	availability
L6, 169.6	3.00×4.00	85	S-Champion
V8, 232.6	3.38×3.25	120	S-Commander

1954

15G Champion Six (wb 116.5; cpes-120.5)—51,431 built

	Wght	Price	Prod
Custom sdn 4d	2,735	1,801	—
Custom sdn 2d	2,705	1,758	—
DeLuxe sdn 4d	2,765	1,918	—
DeLuxe sdn 2d	2,730	1,875	—
DeLuxe Starlight cpe	2,740	1,972	—
DeLuxe Conestoga wgn 2d	2,930	2,187	—
Regal sdn 4d	2,780	2,026	—
Regal sdn 2d	2,745	1,983	—
Regal Starlight cpe	2,750	2,080	—

	Wght	Price	Prod
Regal Starliner htp cpe	2,825	2,241	—
Regal Conestoga wgn 2d	2,950	2,295	—

5H Commander (wb 116.5; LC/cpes-120.5)—30,499 built

	Wght	Price	Prod
DeLuxe sdn 4d	3,105	2,179	—
DeLuxe sdn 2d	3,075	2,136	—
DeLuxe Starlight cpe	3,085	2,233	—
DeLuxe Conestoga wgn 2d	3,265	2,448	—
Regal sdn 4d	3,120	2,287	—
Regal Starlight cpe	3,095	2,341	—
Regal Starliner htp cpe	3,175	2,502	—
Regal Conestoga wgn 2d	3,265	2,556	—
Land Cruiser sdn 4d	3,180	2,438	—

1954 Engines	bore×stroke	bhp	availability
L6, 169.6	3.00×4.00	85	S-Champion
V8, 232.6	3.38×3.25	120	S-Commander

1955

16G Champion (wb 116.5; cpes-120.5)—50,368 built

	Wght	Price	Prod
Custom sdn 4d	2,790	1,783	—
Custom sdn 2d	2,740	1,741	—
DeLuxe sdn 4d	2,805	1,885	—
DeLuxe sdn 2d	2,780	1,841	—
DeLuxe cpe	2,790	1,875	—
DeLuxe wgn 2d	2,980	2,141	—
Regal sdn 4d	2,815	1,993	—
Regal cpe	2,795	1,975	—
Regal htp cpe	2,865	2,125	—
Regal wgn 2d	2,985	2,312	—

6G Commander (wb 116.5; cpes-120.5)—58,792 built

	Wght	Price	Prod
Custom sdn 4d	3,065	1,919	—
Custom sdn 2d	3,105	1,873	—
DeLuxe sdn 4d	3,075	2,014	—
DeLuxe sdn 2d	3,045	1,969	—
DeLuxe cpe	3,065	1,989	—
DeLuxe wgn 2d	3,265	2,274	—
Regal sdn 4d	3,080	2,127	—
Regal cpe	3,065	2,094	—
Regal htp cpe	3,150	2,282	—
Regal Conestoga wgn 2d	3,274	2,445	—

6H President (wb 120.5)

	Wght	Price	Prod
DeLuxe sdn 4d	3,165	2,311	22,451
State sdn 4d	3,220	2,381	
State cpe	3,210	2,270	
State htp cpe	3,175	2,456	
Speedster htp cpe	3,301	3,253	2,215

1955 Engines	bore×stroke	bhp	availability
L6, 185.6	3.00×4.38	101	S-Champion
V8, 224.3	3.56×2.81	140	S-early Commander
V8, 259.2	3.56×3.25	162	S-late Commander
V8, 259.2	3.56×3.25	175	S-President
V8, 259.2	3.56×3.25	185	S-early Spdstr; O-late Pres

1956

56G Six (wb 116.5; Hawk-120.5)—28,918* built

	Wght	Price	Prod
Champion sdn 4d	2,835	1,996	—
Champion sdn 2d	2,800	1,946	—
Champion sedanet	2,780	1,844	—
Pelham wgn 2d	3,000	2,232	—
Flight Hawk cpe	2,780	1,986	—

56B V8, 259 (wb 116.5; Hawk-120.5)—30,654* built

	Wght	Price	Prod
Commander sdn 4d	3,140	2,125	—
Commander sdn 2d	3,110	2,076	—
Commander sedanet	3,085	1,974	—
Parkview wgn 2d	3,300	2,354	—
Power Hawk cpe	3,095	2,101	—

56H V8, 289 (wb 116.5; Classic/Hawk-120.5)

	Wght	Price	Prod
President sdn 4d	3,210	2,235	18,209
President sdn 2d	3,180	2,188	
President Classic sdn 4d	3,295	2,489	
Pinehurst wgn 2d	3,395	2,529	
Sky Hawk htp cpe	3,215	2,477	3,610

56J V8, 352 (wb 120.5)

	Wght	Price	Prod
Golden Hawk htp cpe	3,360	3,061	4,071

*Includes 11,484 Flight Hawks and Power Hawks.

1956 Engines	bore×stroke	bhp	availability
L6, 185.6	3.00×4.38	101	S-Champion, Flight Hawk, Pelham
V8, 259.2	3.56×3.25	170	S-Commander, Power Hawk, Parkview
V8, 259.2	3.56×3.25	185	O-Champ, Comm, Power/Flight Hawk, Wgns
V8, 289.0	3.56×3.63	195	S-President, Pinehurst
V8, 289.0	3.56×3.63	210	Classic, Sky Hawk
V8, 289.0	3.56×3.63	225	O-Pres,Pinehurst,Sky Hawk
V8, 352.0	4.00×3.50	275	S-Golden Hawk

1957*

57G Six (wb 116.5; Hawk-120.5)

	Wght	Price	Prod
Scotsman sdn 4d	2,725	1,826	—
Scotsman club sdn	2,680	1,776	—
Scotsman wgn 2d	2,875	1,995	—
Champion Custom sdn 4d	2,785	2,049	—
Champion Custom club sdn	2,755	2,001	—
Champion DeLuxe sdn 4d	2,810	2,171	—
Champion DeLuxe club sdn	2,780	2,123	—
Pelham wgn 2d	3,015	2,382	—
Silver Hawk cpe	2,790	2,142	**

57B V8, 259 (wb 116.5)

	Wght	Price	Prod
Commander Custom sdn 4d	3,105	2,173	—
Commander Custom club sdn	3,075	2,124	—
Commander DeLuxe sdn 4d	3,140	2,295	—
Commander DeLuxe club sdn	3,100	2,246	—
Provincial wgn 4d	3,355	2,561	—
Parkview wgn 2d	3,310	2,505	—

57H V8, 289 (wb 116.5; Classic/Hawks-120.5)

	Wght	Price	Prod
President Classic sdn 4d	3,270	2,539	—
President sdn 4d	3,205	2,407	—
President club sdn	3,170	2,358	—
Broadmoor wgn 4d	3,415	2,666	—
Silver Hawk cpe	3,185	2,263	**
Golden Hawk htp cpe	3,185	3,182	4,356

*Total 1957 production: 74,738.
**Silver Hawk only: 15,318.

1957 Engines	bore×stroke	bhp	availability
L6, 185.6	3.00×4.38	101	S-Scotsman, Champ, Silver Hawk, Pelham
V8, 259.2	3.56×3.25	180	S-Commander & 57B Wagons
V8, 259.2	3.56×3.25	195	O-Commander & 57B Wagons
V8, 289.0	3.56×3.63	210	S-President, Silver Hawk, 57H Wagons
V8, 289.0	3.56×3.63	225	S-President Classic; O-Silver Hawk, 57H Wgn
V8, 289.0	3.56×3.63	275	S-Golden Hawk

1958

58G Six (wb 116.5; Hawk-120.5)

	Wght	Price	Prod
Silver Hawk cpe	2,810	2,291	*

Studebaker

	Wght	Price	Prod
Scotsman sdn 4d	2,740	1,874	
Scotsman sdn 2d	2,695	1,795	20,870
Scotsman wgn 2d	2,870	2,055	
Champion sdn 4d	2,835	2,253	10,325
Champion sdn 2d	2,795	2,189	

58B V8, 259 (wb 116.5)—12,249 built

	Wght	Price	Prod
Commander sdn 4d	3,185	2,378	—
Commander Starlight htp cpe	3,270	2,493	—
Provincial wgn 4d	3,420	2,664	—

58H V8, 289 (wb 120.5; Starlight htp-116.5)

	Wght	Price	Prod
President sdn 4d	3,365	2,639	
President Starlight htp cpe	3,355	2,695	10,442
Silver Hawk cpe	3,210	2,352	*
Golden Hawk htp cpe	3,470	3,282	878

*Total Silver Hawk: 7,350.

1958 Engines	bore×stroke	bhp	availability
L6, 185.6	3.00×4.38	101	S-Scotsman, Champion, Silver Hawk
V8, 259.2	3.56×3.25	180	S-Commander, Provincial
V8, 289.0	3.56×3.63	210	O-Silver Hawk
V8, 289.0	3.56×3.63	225	S-President; O-Silver Hawk
V8, 289.0	3.56×3.63	275	S-Golden Hawk

1959

59S Lark VI (wb 108.5; Regal wgn-113.0)— 98,744 built

	Wght	Price	Prod
DeLuxe sdn 4d	2,605	1,995	—
DeLuxe sdn 2d	2,577	1,925	—
DeLuxe wgn 2d	2,805	2,295	—
Regal sdn 4d	2,600	2,175	—
Regal htp cpe	2,710	2,275	—
Regal wgn 2d	2,815	2,455	—

59V Lark VIII (wb 108.5; wgn-113.0)—32,334 built

	Wght	Price	Prod
Regal sdn 4d	2,924	2,310	—
Regal htp cpe	3,034	2,411	—
Regal wgn 2d	3,148	2,590	—

59S/59V Silver Hawk (wb 120.5)

	Wght	Price	Prod
cpe, L6	2,795	2,360	2,417
cpe, V8	3,140	2,495	5,371

1959 Engines	bore×stroke	bhp	availability
L6, 169.6	3.00×4.00	90	S-Lark VI, Silver Hawk 6
V8, 259.2	3.56×3.25	180	S-Lark VIII, Silver Hawk 8
V8, 259.2	3.56×3.25	195	O-Lark VIII, Silver Hawk 8

1960

60S Lark VI (wb 108.5; wgns-113.0)— 70,153 built

	Wght	Price	Prod
DeLuxe sdn 4d	2,592	2,046	—
DeLuxe sdn 2d	2,588	1,976	—
DeLuxe wgn 4d	2,792	2,441	—
DeLuxe wgn 2d	2,763	2,366	—
Regal sdn 4d	2,619	2,196	—
Regal htp cpe	2,697	2,296	—
Regal conv cpe	2,961	2,621	—
Regal wgn 4d	2,836	2,591	—

60V Lark VIII (wb 108.5; wgns-113.0)—57,562 built

	Wght	Price	Prod
DeLuxe sdn 4d	2,941	2,181	—
DeLuxe sdn 2d	2,921	2,111	—
DeLuxe wgn 4d	3,161	2,576	—
DeLuxe wgn 2d	3,138	2,501	—
Regal sdn 4d	2,966	2,331	—
Regal htp cpe	3,033	2,431	—
Regal conv cpe	3,315	2,756	—
Regal wgn 4d	3,183	2,726	—

60V Hawk (wb 120.5)

	Wght	Price	Prod
cpe	3,207	2,650	3,939

1960 Engines	bore×stroke	bhp	availability
L6, 169.6	3.00×4.00	90	S-Lark VI
V8, 259.2	3.56×3.25	180	S-Lark VIII
V8, 259.2	3.56×3.25	195	O-Lark VIII
V8, 289.0	3.56×3.63	210	S-Hawk
V8, 289.0	3.56×3.63	225	O-Hawk

1961

61S Lark VI (wb 108.5; wgns-113.0)— 41,035 built

	Wght	Price	Prod
DeLuxe sdn 4d	2,665	1,935	—
DeLuxe sdn 2d	2,661	2,005	—
DeLuxe wgn 4d	2,865	2,370	—
DeLuxe wgn 2d	2,836	2,290	—
Regal sdn 4d	2,692	2,155	—
Regal htp cpe	2,770	2,243	—
Regal conv cpe	3,034	2,554	—
Regal wgn 4d	2,836	2,520	—

61V Lark VIII (wb 108.5; Crsr/wgns-113.0)—25,934 built

	Wght	Price	Prod
DeLuxe sdn 4d	2,941	2,140	—
DeLuxe sdn 2d	2,921	2,070	—
DeLuxe wgn 4d	3,183	2,505	—
DeLuxe wgn 2d	3,112	2,425	—
Regal sdn 4d	2,956	2,290	—
Regal htp cpe	3,074	2,378	—
Regal conv cpe	3,315	2,689	—
Regal wgn 4d	3,183	2,655	—
Cruiser sdn 4d	3,001	2,458	—

61V Hawk (wb 120.5)

	Wght	Price	Prod
cpe	3,205	2,650	3,340

1961 Engines	bore×stroke	bhp	availability
L6, 169.6	3.00×4.00	112	S-Lark VI
V8, 259.2	3.56×3.25	180	S-Lark VIII
V8, 259.2	3.56×3.25	195	O-Lark VIII
V8, 289.0	3.56×3.63	210	S-Hawk
V8, 289.0	3.56×3.63	225	O-Hawk

1962

62S Lark Six (wb 113.0; 2d-109.0)— 54,397 built

	Wght	Price	Prod
DeLuxe sdn 4d	2,760	2,040	—
DeLuxe sdn 2d	2,655	1,935	—
DeLuxe wgn 4d	2,845	2,405	—
Regal sdn 4d	2,770	2,190	—
Regal wgn 4d	2,875	2,555	—
Regal htp cpe	2,765	2,218	—
Regal conv cpe	3,075	2,589	—
Daytona htp cpe	2,765	2,308	—
Daytona conv cpe	3,075	2,679	—

62V Lark Eight (wb 113.0; 2d-109.0)—38,607 built

	Wght	Price	Prod
DeLuxe sdn 4d	3,015	2,175	—
DeLuxe sdn 2d	2,925	2,070	—
DeLuxe wgn 4d	3,115	2,540	—
Regal sdn 4d	3,025	2,325	—
Regal wgn 4d	3,145	2,690	—
Regal htp cpe	3,015	2,353	—
Regal conv cpe	3,305	2,724	—
Daytona htp cpe	3,015	2,443	—
Daytona conv cpe	3,305	2,814	—
Cruiser sdn 4d	3,030	2,493	—

62V Gran Turismo Hawk (wb 120.5)

	Wght	Price	Prod
htp cpe	3,230	3,095	8,388

1962 Engines	bore×stroke	bhp	availability
L6, 169.6	3.00×4.00	112	S-Lark Six
V8, 259.2	3.56×3.25	180	S-Lark Eight
V8, 259.2	3.56×3.25	195	O-Lark Eight
V8, 289.0	3.56×3.63	210	S-GT Hawk; O-Lark Cruiser
V8, 289.0	3.56×3.63	225	O-GT Hawk, Lark Cruiser

1963

63S Lark Six (wb 113.0; 2d-109.0)—74,201 built (includes 63V)

	Wght	Price	Prod
Standard sdn 4d	2,775	2,040	—
Standard sdn 2d	2,650	1,935	—
Standard wgn 4d	3,285	2,430	—
Regal sdn 4d	2,790	2,160	—
Regal sdn 2d	2,665	2,055	—
Regal wgn 4d	3,200	2,550	—
Custom sdn 4d	2,800	2,285	—
Custom sdn 2d	2,680	2,180	—
Daytona wgn 4d	3,245	2,700	—
Daytona htp cpe	2,795	2,308	—
Daytona conv cpe	3,045	2,679	—

63V Lark Eight (wb 113.0; 2d-109.0)

	Wght	Price	Prod
Standard sdn 4d	2,985	2,175	—
Standard sdn 2d	2,910	2,070	—
Standard wgn 4d	3,435	2,565	—
Regal sdn 4d	3,000	2,295	—
Regal sdn 2d	2,925	2,190	—
Regal wgn 4d	3,450	2,685	—
Custom sdn 4d	3,010	2,420	—
Custom sdn 2d	2,940	2,315	—
Daytona wgn 4d	3,490	2,835	—
Daytona htp cpe	3,035	2,443	—
Daytona conv cpe	3,265	2,814	—
Cruiser sdn 4d	3,065	2,595	—

63V Gran Turismo Hawk (wb 120.5)

	Wght	Price	Prod
htp cpe	3,280	3,095	4,634

63R Avanti (wb 109.0)

	Wght	Price	Prod
spt cpe	3,140	4,445	3,834

1963 Engines	bore×stroke	bhp	availability
L6, 169.6	3.00×4.00	112	S-Lark 6
V8, 259.2	3.56×3.25	180	S-Lark V8
V8, 259.2	3.56×3.25	195	O-Lark V8
V8, 289.0	3.56×3.63	210	S-Hawk, Cruiser; O-Lark V8
V8, 289.0	3.56×3.63	225	O-Hawk, Lark V8, Cruiser
V8, 289.0	3.56×3.63	240	S-Avanti; O-Hawk, Lark V8 (R1)
V8, 289.0	3.56×3.63	290	O-Avanti, Hawk, Lark V8 (R2)

1964

64S Lark Six (wb 113.0; 2d-109.0)—44,184 built (includes 64V)

	Wght	Price	Prod
Challenger sdn 4d	2,780	2,048	—
Challenger sdn 2d	2,660	1,943	—
Challenger wgn 4d	3,230	2,438	—
Commander sdn 4d	2,815	2,168	—
Commander sdn 2d	2,695	2,063	—
Commander Special sdn 2d	2,725	2,193	—
Commander wgn 4d	3,265	2,558	—
Daytona sdn 4d	2,790	2,318	—
Daytona conv cpe	3,040	2,670	—
Daytona wgn 4d	3,240	2,708	—

64V Lark Eight (wb 113.0; 2d-109.0)

	Wght	Price	Prod
Challenger sdn 4d	3,010	2,183	—
Challenger sdn 2d	2,910	2,078	—
Challenger wgn 4d	3,480	2,573	—
Commander sdn 4d	3,045	2,303	—
Commander sdn 2d	2,945	2,198	—
Commander Special sdn 2d	2,975	2,328	—
Daytona sdn 4d	3,055	2,453	—
Daytona htp cpe	3,060	2,451	—
Daytona conv cpe	3,320	2,805	—
Daytona wgn 4d	3,555	2,843	—
Cruiser sdn 4d	3,120	2,603	—

64V Gran Turismo Hawk (wb 120.5)

	Wght	Price	Prod
htp cpe	3,120	2,966	1,767

64R Avanti (wb 109.0)

	Wght	Price	Prod
spt cpe	3,195	4,445	809

1964 Engines	bore×stroke	bhp	availability
L6, 169.6	3.00×4.00	112	S-Challenger/Commander/Daytona 6
V8, 259.2	3.56×3.25	180	S-Challenger/Commander/Daytona 8
V8, 259.2	3.56×3.25	195	O-Challenger/Commander/Daytona 8
V8, 289.0	3.56×3.63	210	S-Hawk, Cruiser; O-other V8
V8, 289.0	3.56×3.63	225	O-all V8 exc Avanti
V8, 289.0	3.56×3.63	240	S-Avanti; O-other V8 (R1)
V8, 289.0	3.56×3.63	290	O-all (R2)
V8, 304.5	3.65×3.63	335	O-all exc. Challenger (R3)
V8, 304.5	3.65×3.63	280	O-all exc. Challenger (R4)

1965—19,435 built

C-1 Six (wb 113.0; 2d-109.0)

	Wght	Price	Prod
Commander sdn 4d	2,815	2,230	—
Commander sdn 2d	2,695	2,125	—
Commander wgn 4d	3,265	2,620	—
Cruiser sdn 4d	2,820	2,470	—

C-5 Eight (wb 113.0; 2d-109.0)

	Wght	Price	Prod
Commander sdn 4d	2,995	2,370	—
Commander sdn 2d	2,895	2,265	—
Commander wgn 4d	3,465	2,760	—
Daytona Sport sdn 2d	2,970	2,565	—
Daytona wgn 4d	3,505	2,890	—
Cruiser sdn 4d	3,070	2,610	—

1965 Engines	bore×stroke	bhp	availability
L6, 194.0	3.56×3.25	120	S-Commander 6, Cruiser 6
V8, 283.0	3.88×3.00	195	S-Commander/Cruiser V8, Daytona

1966—8,947 built

Six (wb 113.0; 2d-109.0)

	Wght	Price	Prod
Commander sdn 4d	2,815	2,165	—
Commander sdn 2d	2,695	2,060	—
Wagonaire wgn 2d	3,246	2,555	—
Daytona sdn 2d	2,755	2,405	—
Cruiser sdn 4d	2,815	2,405	—

Eight (wb 113.0; 2d-109.0)

	Wght	Price	Prod
Commander sdn 4d	2,991	2,305	—
Commander sdn 2d	2,891	2,200	—
Wagonaire wgn 2d	3,501	2,695	—
Daytona sdn 2d	3,006	2,500	—
Cruiser sdn 4d	3,066	2,545	—

1966 Engines	bore×stroke	bhp	availability
L6, 194.0	3.56×3.25	120	S-Commander/Cruiser/Daytona 6
V8, 283.0	3.88×3.00	195	S-Commander/Cruiser/Daytona V8

Postwar Studebaker production includes cars manufactured in South Bend and Hamilton, Ontario for U.S., Canadian, and export sale.

Stutz

Stutz Motor Car Company
Indianapolis, Indiana

Mention Stutz, and most people immediately conjure up an image of the fabulous Bearcat, typically piloted at breathtaking speeds along a country lane by a racoon-coated playboy. Or they think of a founder Harry K. Stutz and his "car that made good in a day." There were Stutz Bearcats in the '30s, but they were rather different from the dashing speedsters of the Teens, the products of a different genius. Though Frederick E. Moskovics left the firm in 1929, the Stutzes of the 1930s were very much his own. European-born, brilliantly educated, and financially comfortable, he was socially at ease in any company. Round faced, amply proportioned, and usually found smoking an expensive cigar, he looked every inch the genial tycoon he was, especially when dressed in plus-fours and golfing cap. Moskovics was typically American in his fascination with the march of progress, and delighted in the finer European sporting machines. But he scorned the idea that such cars had to be slowly and expensively hand-built, seeing that technical know-how could be harnessed to produce a thoroughbred at reasonable cost. Fred Moskovics was not interested in or given to compromise. There was only one right way, and he found it every time.

The Depression era saw the end of this great marque, and there were no major mechanical changes at Stutz from 1930 through the last of the line in 1936. The Vertical Eight engine was the basis for all models except the notorious 1929-30 Blackhawk, which had a Continental L-head eight. Though Stutz died mainly because of the crippled national economy, a sporting image didn't help. It was handily outsold by Cadillac, Packard, Lincoln, and Pierce-Arrow in a market where buyers demanded silence, riding comfort, mechanical simplicity, reliability, and ease of maintenance, all of which were hard to achieve in a machine that could be successfully raced right from the showroom floor.

A Stutz speedster could outrun every other American car save the Model J Duesenberg. Yet the sedans were buzz boxes below 50 mph, thanks to relatively low rear axle ratios. Lack of crankshaft counterweights was questionable in the high-revving engine, though they would have further increased its already complex servicing requirements. The 1930 Model M was blessed with outstanding specific output and an rpm capability higher than that of rivals with similarly sized engines, yet its power-to-weight ratio was mediocre. More displacement would have compensated for the high weight and a higher final drive would have increased engine life and fuel economy, but 322 cubic inches was as large as this powerplant would ever get, and it was simply outclassed by the multi-cylinder giants from Cadillac, Marmon, and others.

Stutz couldn't afford to retool for a 12- or 16-cylinder engine, but the company did experiment with a supercharger, which boosted horsepower from 113 to 143. The blower was a huge affair, mounted low in front of the

1932 DV32 Continental Coupe by Waterhouse

1931 DV32 convertible sedan by Waterhouse

radiator and driven directly from the crankshaft. It did the job, but it was noisy, and carburetion was a problem. For 1931, Stutz followed Duesenberg's approach and designed a new 32-valve head with dual overhead camshafts. The dual ignition system of the previous SV16 unit was lost in the process (there was no room for it), but improved breathing gave the new DV32 engine some 161 bhp at 3900 rpm.

A major factor in Stutz's demise was high prices. The chassis alone cost $3200, and there were about 30 body styles available from such high-buck coachbuilders as LeBaron, Fleetwood, Rollston, Weymann, Brunn, Waterhouse, and Derham. Weymann's unusual fabric bodies (actually padded leatherette) were light, strong, safe, elastic, quiet, and durable. Compared to steel construction, they soaked up road shock and noise better, lasted longer, and were easier to repair. Color was impregnated in the lacquer-coated cloth, so these bodies never faded or needed repainting, but many people disliked their dull, pebbled finish and dowdy looks. Stutz also offered an aluminum bodied model, the novel Monte Carlo sedan.

For 1931, the lineup was broadened with the six-cylinder Model LA, designated LAA for 1932-33. An attempt to cut prices against the deepening Depression, the LA listed for only $2245 in sedan form; the 1932 LAA cost even less.

Power for these cars was supplied by what was really a Vertical Eight less two cylinders and, at over 4300 pounds, they were hardly noted for their performance. Fewer than 50 of the LAA models were sold.

The new DV32 Series debuted in chassis form at the New York Auto Show in the winter of 1930-31. The factory issued prices by the end of March 1931, and production was underway by July. At about the same time, Stutz announced it had netted $20,000 on a gross profit of $100,000, a pitifully meager income that, nevertheless, was preferable to the red ink that had been flowing since 1929. The DV32 was demonstrated in dramatic fashion by three groups of cars that toured the nation as "flying circuses," led by a new model with an old name: Bearcat. A late addition to the line, it was calculated to stir up nostalgic feelings among potential customers. There was also a Super Bearcat on a special 116-inch wheelbase and initially fitted with Weymann bodywork done in artificial leather. With 4.1:1 rear axle ratio, the standard models were capable of 90 mph, while the Super Bearcat was guaranteed to do 100-plus mph. The DV32 sedans could cruise at up to 70 mph and reach 25 mph in first gear, 48 in second, and 70 in third. First gear was actually an emergency ratio, actuated by lifting a lockout device on the lever of the four-speed gearbox, which had been introduced in 1929 along with the 322-cid engine. Brakes were hydraulic with servo-vacuum assist, and could be adjusted from the instrument panel. A one-shot central lubrication system meant that only three points required lubrication, the water pump bearings and the distributor. Semi-elliptic springs and hydraulic shock absorbers were employed, and final drive was by worm gear, which had originally appeared on the "Safety Stutz" chassis of 1926.

Stutz announced several changes for 1932. The four-speed transmission was replaced with a very rugged, Muncie three-speed synchronized unit, and freewheeling was now an option. The hot-air manifold was replaced with a hot-water heating system, and an oil cooler was provided. A new trunk rack and dust valance were installed at the rear, the body dropped in a curving line to cover the straight frame, and single-bar bumpers replaced the previous double bars.

When regulations for the Indianapolis 500 were relaxed to allow stock-based entries, Stutz made a point of running *strictly* stock to add a touch of drama to its track appearances. Thus, the 1930 Indianapolis "Jones Special" was powered by the 322 engine and used the highest optional gear ratio available (3.6:1). As the only stock contender, it weighed 1500 pounds more than the next heaviest car, but it still managed to finish 10th at an average speed of 85.36 mph, one of the great performances of all time.

Stutz lost $315,000 in 1932, but continued to stumble on. It lost close to a half-million dollars the next year, then a quarter-million in 1934. While not huge amounts by the standards of the day, these were tremendous drains considering the company's meager resources. Management sought refuge by agreeing to build a line of small trucks called Pak-Age-Cars, and George H. Freers was appointed chief engineer in charge of this effort. The first 28 vehicles out of a total order of 340 were completed in the summer of 1936. But this wasn't nearly enough to keep things going, and the firm filed a bankruptcy petition in April 1937. By this time, total assets were $1.2 million and liabilities only $733,000, but Stutz still couldn't meet its debts. Since creditors could not agree on a reorganization plan a federal judge ordered liquidation of all assets in April 1938. It was completed that summer, and the Pak-Age-Car program was taken over by the Diamond T Truck Company.

Stutz Specifications

1930

Model M (wb 134.5; lwb 145.0)—649 built*

		Wght	Price	Prod
	Torpedo speedster 2P	4,595	3,450	—
	cpe 2P	4,850	3,295	—
	sdn 4d	4,918	3,695	—
	Weymann Versailles sdn 4d	—	3,945	—
	phaeton 5P	—	3,945	—
	lwb sdn 7P	5,210	3,895	—
	lwb Weymann Monte Carlo spt sdn 5P	—	4,495	—
	chassis (both wbs, various coachbldrs)	—	—	—

*incl. some 1929 production

1930 Engine	bore×stroke	bhp	availability
L8, 322.0	3.38×4.50	113	S-all

1931*

Model LA (wb 127.5)

		Wght	Price	Prod
	sdn 4d	4,320	2,245	—
	cpe 2P	4,275	1,995	—
	five other body styles	—	—	—

Model MA/MB (wb 134.5; MB-145.0)

			Wght	Price	Prod
21	sdn 4d		4,918	3,195	—
23	cpe 2P		4,850	2,995	—
24	speedster 2P		4,595	3,495	—
40	sdn 7P (MB)		5,210	3,895	—
	dual-cowl phaeton (MB)		—	4,495	—
	Fleetwood transformable town car 7P (MB)		—	7,495	—
	chassis (both wbs, various coachbldrs)		—	—	—

Model DV32 (wb 134.5; lwb-145.0)

		Wght	Price	Prod
21	sdn 4d	5,035	4,995	—

Stutz

		Wght	Price	Prod
23	cpe 2P	4,909	4,995	—
24	Bearcat speedster 2P	4,678	4,995	—
40	lwb sdn 7P	5,270	5,395	—
	chassis (both wbs, various coachbldrs)	—	—	—

*Production not available

1931 Engines	bore×stroke	bhp	availability
L6, 241.5	3.38×4.50	85	S-LA
L8, 322.0	3.38×4.50	113	S-MA,MB
L8, 322.0	3.38×4.50	161	S-DV32

1932*

Model LAA (wb 127.5)**		Wght	Price	Prod
	sdn 4d	4,385	1,620	—
	cpe 2P	4,315	1,620	—
	five other body styles	—	—	—

Model SV16 (wb 134.5; lwb-145.0)				
21	sdn 4d	4,985	2,995	—
23	cpe 2P	4,859	2,995	—
24	Bearcat speedster 2P	4,628	3,495	—
40	lwb sdn 7P	5,220	3,895	—
	chassis (both wbs, various coachbldrs)	—	—	—

Model DV32 (wb 134.5; lwb-145.0)				
21	sdn 4d	5,185	3,995	—
23	cpe 2P	5,059	3,995	—
24	Bearcat speedster 2P	4,828	4,495	—
40	lwb sdn 7P	5,420	4,895	—
	Super Bearcat spdstr 2P (wb 116.0)	—	5,895	—
	chassis (both wbs, various coachbldrs)	—	—	—

*Production not available
**under 50 built 1932-33

1933*

Model LAA (wb 127.5)**		Wght	Price	Prod
	sdn 4d	4,243	1,895	—
	cabriolet cpe 5P	—	2,185	—
	three other body styles ($1900-2200)	—	—	—

Model SV16 (wb 134.5; lwb-145.0)				
21	sdn 4d	4,845	3,095	—
23	cpe 2P	4,719	3,095	—
24	Bearcat speedster 2P	4,488	3,195	—
40	lwb sdn 7P	5,080	3,560	—
	Super Bearcat speedster 2P (wb 116.0)	—	5,095	—
	chassis (both wbs, various coachbldrs)	—	—	—

Model DV32 (wb 134.5; lwb-145.0)				
21	sdn 4d	5,045	3,795	—
23	cpe 2P	4,919	3,795	—
24	Bearcat speedster 2P	4,688	3,895	—
40	lwb sdn 7P	5,280	4,260	—
	Super Bearcat speedster 2P (wb 116.0)	—	5,795	—
	Weymann Monte Carlo spt sdn 5P (lwb)	5,120	4,895	—
64	LeBaron lwb sdn 4d 6P	5,346	3,410	—
	chassis (both wbs, various coachbldrs)	—	—	—

*Production not available
**under 50 built 1932-33

1933 Engines	bore×stroke	bhp	availability
L6, 241.5	3.38×4.50	85	S-LAA
L8, 322.0	3.38×4.50	113	S-SV16
L8, 322.0	3.38×4.50	161	S-DV32

1934*

SV16 (wb 134.5; lwb 145.0)		Wght	Price	Prod
21	sdn 4d	4,845	3,095	—
23	cpe 2P	4,719	3,095	—
24	Bearcat speedster 2P	4,488	3,195	—
40	lwb sdn 7P	5,080	3,560	—
	chassis (both wbs, 10 custom bodies)	—	—	—

DV32 (wb 134.5; lwb-145.0)				
21	sdn 4d	5,045	3,795	—
23	cpe 2P	4,919	3,795	—
24	Bearcat speedster 2P	4,688	3,895	—
40	lwb sdn 7P	5,280	4,260	—
	chassis (both wbs, 10 custom bodies)	—	—	—

*Production not available

1934 Engines	bore×stroke	bhp	availability
L8, 322.0	3.38×4.50	113	S-SV16
L8, 322.0	3.38×4.50	156	S-DV32

1935*

SV16 (wb 134.5; lwb-145.0)		Wght	Price	Prod
21	sdn 4d	4,745	3,095	—
23	cpe 2-4P	4,619	3,095	—
24	Bearcat speedster 2-4P	4,488	3,195	—
40	lwb sdn 7P	4,980	3,560	—
	chassis (both wbs, various coachbldrs)	—	—	—

DV32 (wb 134.5; lwb-145.0)				
21	sdn 4d	4,895	3,795	—
23	cpe 2-4P	4,769	3,795	—
24	Bearcat speedster 2-4P	4,538	3,895	—
40	lwb sdn 7P	5,130	4,260	—
	chassis (both wbs, various coachbldrs)	—	—	—

*Production not available

1935 Engines	bore×stroke	bhp	availability
L8, 322.0	3.38×4.50	113	S-SV16
L8, 322.0	3.38×4.50	156	S-DV32

1936*

SV16 (wb 134.5; lwb-145.0)		Wght	Price	Prod
21	sdn 4d	4,745	3,095	—
23	cpe 2-4P	4,619	3,095	—
24	Bearcat speedster 2-4P	4,488	3,195	—
40	lwb sdn 7P	4,980	3,560	—
	chassis (both wbs, various coachbldrs)	—	—	—

DV32 (wb 134.5; lwb-145.0)				
21	sdn 4d	4,895	3,795	—
23	cpe 2-4P	4,769	3,795	—
24	Bearcat speedster 2-4P	4,538	3,895	—
40	lwb sdn 7P	5,130	4,260	—
	chassis (both wbs, various coachbldrs)	—	—	—

*Production not available

1936 Engines	bore×stroke	bhp	availability
L8, 322.0	3.38×4.50	113	S-SV16
L8, 322.0	3.38×4.50	156	S-DV32

Terraplane

Hudson Motor Car Company
Detroit, Michigan

The abundant success of the Essex Terraplane (see Essex) prompted Hudson president Roy Chapin Sr. to list Terraplane as a separate make for 1934, replacing Essex. The eight-cylinder engine used in the Essex model was replaced by a new, larger six with 80-85 bhp, upped to 88 bhp for 1935-36. Terraplane reverted to a series in the standard Hudson line for 1938, but in the critical middle years of the decade it saved the company.

While the 1932 Essex Terraplane sold for as little as $425, the 1935-37 Terraplane was more expensive, as well as more rakishly styled and available in a wider variety of models. Unlike most rivals of the period, it avoided design excesses, except for the debatable 1936-37 water-

fall grille. Terraplane grew larger in these years, moving from a 106-inch wheelbase in its original Essex guise to as much as 116 inches, but all these cars were fine performers. A British road test of a 1936 sedan recorded 0-60 mph acceleration of 26.6 seconds and a top speed of 82 mph—highly creditable for a car of that era weighing nearly 2800 pounds. "The six-cylinder engine gives plenty of power and has that suppleness and quietness in its running that are characteristic of American design," wrote the editors. "The speed at which this car travels on the open road is almost wholly a matter of the driver's choice . . . Even at 70 there is no special fuss from the mechanism. It can thus be a decidedly swift car for journeying over long

1934 Major Six four-door sedan

1936 Deluxe Six touring brougham

1934 Special Six coupe

1937 Super four-door sedan

1935 DeLuxe Six five-passenger coach

1937 Super wagon by U.S. Body & Forging Co.

distances, and is an easy one to handle, too. . . The Terraplane gives, and does, much for its price."

During its four years as a separate make, Terraplane accounted for over 300,000 sales, thus taking the lion's share of Hudson Motor Car Company's production each year, and built up to a peak of over 93,000 units in calendar 1936. The model lineup expanded also, ultimately comprising 16 separate offerings (plus chassis) in DeLuxe and Super trim. No roadsters or phaetons were listed, bu

there were sedans and broughams in regular and "touring" (trunkback) form and, for the 1936 season, even a woody station wagon.

Unfortunately, Terraplane sales began trending downward in 1937, and this convinced Hudson that separate-make status was no longer necessary. Terraplane vanished a year after it was incorporated within the Hudson line. Its direct successor was the 1939-model Hudson Series 91 Pacemaker and Series 92 Six.

Terraplane Specifications

Note: production figures based on serial number spans and other calculations; may exceed actual production.

1934

K Special Six (wb 112.0)—23,726 built

	Wght	Price	Prod
cpe 2P	2,600	600	—
cpe 2-4P	2,605	645	—
conv cpe 2-4P	2,625	695	—
victoria 5P T/B	2,655	655	—
coach 5P	2,630	615	—
sdn 4d	2,710	675	—
sdn 4d T/B	2,735	715	—

KS Challenger Six (wb 112.0)—20,265 built

	Wght	Price	Prod
cpe 2P	2,540	565	—
cpe 2-4P	2,590	610	—
coach 5P	2,600	575	—
sdn 4d	2,670	635	—

KU Major Six (wb 116.0)—7,093 built

	Wght	Price	Prod
cpe 2P	2,650	665	—
cpe 2-4P	2,700	710	—
conv cpe 2-4P	2,695	750	—
victoria 5P T/B	2,755	720	—
coach 5P	2,730	680	—
sdn 4d	2,780	740	—
sdn 4d T/B	2,805	780	—

1934 Engines

	bore×stroke	bhp	availability
L6, 212.0	3.00×5.00	80	S-KS,K
L6, 212.0	3.00×5.00	85	S-KU

1935

G Special Six (wb 112.0)—37,772 built

	Wght	Price	Prod
cpe 2P	2,505	585	—
cpe 2-4P	2,555	625	—
touring brougham 5P T/B	2,610	625	—
coach 5P	2,595	595	—
sdn 4d	2,655	655	—
Suburban sdn 4d T/B	2,670	685	—

GU DeLuxe Six (wb 112.0)—13,362 built

	Wght	Price	Prod
cpe 2P	2,565	635	—
cpe 2-4P	2,635	675	—
conv cpe 2-4P	2,590	725	—
touring brougham 5P T/B	2,680	675	—
coach 5P	2,665	645	—
sdn 4d	2,710	705	—
Suburban sdn 4d T/B	2,725	735	—

1935 Engine

	bore×stroke	bhp	availability
L6, 212.0	3.00×5.00	88	S-all

1936

61 DeLuxe Six (wb 115.0)—69,750 built

	Wght	Price	Prod
cpe 2P	2,620	595	—
cpe 2-4P	2,690	640	—
conv sdn 2-4P	—	—	—
brougham 5P	2,745	615	—
touring brougham 5P T/B	2,760	635	—
sdn 4d	2,805	670	—
touring sdn 4d T/B	2,820	690	—
wgn 4d	—	700	—

62 Custom Six (wb 115.0)—17,041 built

	Wght	Price	Prod
cpe 2P	2,675	650	—
cpe 2-4P	2,745	690	—
conv cpe 2-4P	—	—	—
brougham 5P	2,800	665	—
touring brougham 5P T/B	2,815	685	—
sdn 4d	2,860	720	—
touring sdn 4d T/B	2,875	740	—

1936 Engine

	bore×stroke	bhp	availability
L6, 212.0	3.00×5.00	88	S-all

1937

71 DeLuxe (wb 117.0)—70,346 built

	Wght	Price	Prod
bus cpe 3P	2,370	595	—
cpe 3P	2,715	605	—
victoria 4P	2,765	850	—
conv cpe 3P	2,765	725	—
brougham 6P	2,830	625	—
conv brougham 6P	2,780	800	—
sdn 4d	2,865	675	—
touring sdn 4d T/B	2,865	695	—
chassis	—	—	—

72 Super (wb 117.0)—19,907 built

	Wght	Price	Prod
cpe 3P	2,755	880	—
touring sdn 4d T/B	2,905	745	—
victoria 4P	2,795	700	—
conv cpe 3P	2,825	770	—
conv brougham 6P	2,915	845	—
brougham 6P	2,875	680	—
touring brougham 6P	2,875	700	—
sdn 4d	2,905	725	—
chassis	—	—	—

1937 Engine

	bore×stroke	bhp	availability
L6, 212.0	3.00×5.00	96	S-71
L6, 212.0	3.00×5.00	102	S-72

Willys
Willys-Overland Motors (Kaiser-Willys Sales Division 1954-55),
Toledo, Ohio

John North Willys was a car dealer in Elmira, New York with a yen to do more than just sell the things. In 1907 he bought the ailing Overland Company of Indianapolis. A year later he renamed it Willys-Overland, moved into the old Pope plant in Toledo, Ohio, and began rebuilding the firm's fortunes. For most of the Teens, the four-cylinder Overland was second in sales only to the Model T Ford and by 1918, J. N. Willys owned the second largest auto company in the world. The post-World War I recession slowed production, but sales soared with the 1926 introduction of the low-priced Whippet (see entry). The all-time record came in 1928, when the company built 315,000 cars and rocketed to third place behind Chevrolet and Ford. Then came the Depression, and Willys-Overland declined to the point of declaring bankruptcy in 1933. It resumed production after reorganization, but built only about 8000 units in calendar 1934.

The Toledo-built cars entered the '30s with a name change, as the Overland badge was dropped in favor of the Willys nameplate. Besides a group of conventionally engined models, the company continued its line of sleeve-valve Willys-Knight offerings through 1933. This engine employed that interesting valve arrangement patented by brilliant inventor Charles Yale Knight. Replacing the usual cam-and-spring actuated poppet valves was a double sliding sleeve that let the fuel/air mixture directly into the cylinders. Many makes used sleeve-valve engines in the Teens, but Willys built more of them than anybody else and continued them longer. Though the Knight system was very advanced compared to its early contemporaries, it was also more complicated than the simple, efficient side-valve layout that found favor even on luxury makes like Cadillac. The Willys-Knights of the early '30s were six-cylinder cars offered in two engine and wheelbase sizes. The larger series used a 255-cid six with 72-87 horsepower and 120- or 121-inch wheelbases. The '33 Streamline Six, a sedan priced at $1420, was the last sleeve-valve car built in America.

The rest of the Willys line in this period, comprising conventional L-head sixes and eights, featured attractive styling and competitive prices, which ranged from $500 to $800. The Eight, which rode a longer wheelbase than the Six, was introduced in 1931—an inopportune time for big-engine cars. Bankruptcy finished off both in early 1933.

The reorganization that followed ushered in bespectacled Ward Canaday to take over the helm. A pillar of the Toledo business community with a great sense of loyalty to his employees, Canaday ached to get the corporation back on its feet. Under his management, all of Willys-Overland's resources were put into a new small car built on a 100-inch wheelbase, the Willys 77, which continued with little change as the firm's only model from early 1933 through 1936. Powered by an ultra-economical four-cylinder engine developing 48 bhp, the 77 was unique and unmistakable. The radiator was hidden under the hood,

1930 Series 87 Knight four-door sedan

1931 Model 97 Six two-door sedan

1932 Series 66D Knight four-door sedan

and the vertical-bar grille was rounded at the top and tapered at the bottom to a sharp point. This design earned the nickname "potato digger," and the car lived up to that title by digging a financial hole in the ground. The best annual production total it could manage was about 30,000 units. Today, the 77 looks refreshing compared to most of the lumpy cars of this era. But back then—and despite low prices—it just wouldn't sell.

Canaday had another idea for 1937. Retaining the "potato digger" engine and wheelbase, he ordained a complete restyle. The result was, again, less than ideal: a rounded body with pontoon fenders and a wild front not unlike that of the sharknose Graham. Model offerings were expanded with Standard and Deluxe versions of the basic

coupe and sedan. This car was designated Model 37, then Model 38, and finally 38 and 48 for 1939. While this styling was no less bizarre than the 77's, it met with some success, and Willys sales shot up to 63,467 in 1937. But this was a recovery year for the industry as a whole and, despite twice the production, Willys was only able to move from 15th to 14th place in the standings. The 1938 reces-

sion put output back to 16,173, and Willys again had to settle for 15th.

For 1939, Toledo fielded the same weird-looking line as it had the previous two years, and it sold just a little better than the '38. Some help was provided by a revived Overland nameplate for a new 102-inch-wheelbase entry, the Model 39. Styled differently than the Willys, it also had

1933 Model 77 four-door sedan

1937 Model 37 DeLuxe four-door sedan

1939 Overland Model 39 Deluxe two-door sedan

1938 Model 38 Clipper two-door sedan

1939 Overland Model 39 Deluxe coupe

a Graham-like front end, but with the headlamps carried in fender pods instead of being flush-mounted. Prices were a little higher than for the Willys 38, but the extra money bought significantly better performance, thanks to a compression increase and a fixed-jet carburetor that coaxed 62 bhp out of the little four. Calendar year production moved up to 25,383 units.

Joseph W. Frazer left Chrysler Corporation to become president and general manager of Willys-Overland in 1939, while Canaday remained board chairman. Frazer knew how to cut his losses, and decreed much more conventional styling for 1940. However, it's doubtful even he could have saved Willys passenger cars, and the company's ultimate salavation was the wartime Jeep.

The new line, designated Series 440 (four cylinders, 1940) was powered by the firm's 61-bhp L-head four, which displaced 134.2 cubic inches and delivered 25 miles per gallon. It remained the standard Willys powerplant through the decade, though horsepower increased (to 63) in 1941. In 1949 it was converted by engineer Barney Roos to F-head, overhead-valve configuration. The chassis was a conventional ladder design with an X-braced center and a 102-inch wheelbase. There were five body styles in two series. Model year production was up to nearly 27,000 for 1940.

For the '41 Series 441, Frazer and his team made further improvements. The new line was named American, providing patriotic appeal, and got more horsepower

and a longer wheelbase. It came in three series: the Speedway coupe and sedan; the DeLuxe coupe, sedan, and wagon; and the top-line Plainsman coupe and sedan. Styling was Ford-like, with faired-in headlamps on the front fenders and a sharply pointed nose over a small vertical-bar grille.

Production for 1942 was cut short earlier than for most automakers since Willys had begun building Jeeps for the Army. The '42 Americars were the same as the '41s—three models and seven body styles. Prices rose slightly, ranging from $695 to $978. The original Jeep was conceived mainly by American Bantam, but Willys-Overland produced a similar design in vast quantities through 1945.

During the war, Frazer left to take over Graham-Paige, while chairman Ward Canaday planned postwar activities around Jeep-like vehicles.

A truck-type all-steel station wagon using the L-head four and the 104-inch wheelbase was announced for 1946-47. It was significant in that it was the first true all-steel wagon, though for purposes of the industry and this book it was considered more of a truck than a car. It was Willys' main civilian product in those two years, priced at $1495 in 1946 and $1625 in '47.

For 1948, Willys-Overland continued the wagon (now listed at $1645) and added two new vehicles: the four-cylinder Jeepster "phaeton" priced at $1765, and the six-cylinder Station Sedan, which went for $1890. The

1941 Series 440 DeLuxe station wagon

1948 Jeepster phaeton convertible

1943 Army Jeep

1950 Jeepster phaeton convertible

1955 Bermuda hardtop coupe

Jeepster was a pleasant little touring car designed during the war by Brooks Stevens, who borrowed its lines from the Jeep. It had a big open compartment behind the cowl and a mechanically operated soft top. The six-cylinder Station Sedan was a luxury version of the four-cylinder wagon, with a larger body and wider seats. Together with the Jeepster, it helped keep Willys-Overland alive.

For 1949, Willys offered a new 104.5 inch-wheelbase wagon priced at $1895, plus the regular wagon and two Jeepsters in its four-cylinder lineup. The second series Jeepster appeared in January, powered by the firm's first F-head engine. The company continued to sell the six-cylinder Station Sedan and wagon, and debuted a six-cylinder Jeepster at $1530. Conversion to overhead-valve engines was completed for all models by 1950. Over 10,000 Jeepsters were sold for 1948. In 1950, however, only 4066 fours and 1778 sixes were sold. Some leftovers were registered as 1951s.

The 1952 Aero-Willys was a unit-body car styled by Phil Wright and engineered by Clyde Paton. Returning Willys to the passenger-car field, it was a clean design, providing good comfort and handling. Four separate models were offered. The Aero-Lark used the older 161-cid, 75-bhp L-head six; the Wing, Ace, and Eagle hardtop used the overhead-valve version. The 161 was small but a good performer, providing economy on the order of 25 mpg. The biggest problem for these cars was their list prices. The Eagle hardtop, for example, carried a $2155 price tag; a Chevrolet Bel Air hardtop cost $150 less. Willys-Overland dealers were hard pressed—not only to explain how builders of Jeeps could produce a smooth, comfortable family car, but also why they had to charge so much for it. Production was good, but not great. For the '52 model year, about 31,000 Aeros were built. About 23 percent were base-line Larks, while seven percent were Eagle hardtops.

Willys expanded the Aero line for 1953 and made only minor appearance changes, including red-painted wheel cover emblems and a gold-plated "W" in the grille to symbolize the firm's 50th anniversary. About 500 Larks were fitted with an F-head four-cylinder engine. The Aero-Wing was replaced by the Aero-Falcon, and a new four-door sedan was developed for the Lark, Falcon, and Ace. Again, the hardtop Eagle was

priced on the high side. Willys-Overland had another modestly good year, selling about 42,000 units.

In 1954, Willys-Overland was purchased by Henry Kaiser, who combined it with his ailing Kaiser-Frazer Corporation to form the Toledo-based Kaiser-Willys Sales Corporation. The K-F plant at Willow Run was sold to General Motors, and Kaiser production was shifted to the old Willys plant.

At first, the new '54 Aero appeared to be the same as the '53 with larger taillights and revised interiors. But in March 1954, the company made the 226-cid L-head six available as an option for the Ace and Eagle. To further complicate matters, there were Ace and Eagle Customs—the designation merely indicating the presence of a "continental" spare tire. With the Kaiser 226, the Aero was relatively fast. Though its 85-mph top speed was little higher than the Willys-engine models, it was geared for good acceleration: a typical 0-60 mph time was 14 seconds. As an experiment, a few cars were fitted with the 140-bhp supercharged Manhattan engine, which engineers say gave pickup comparable to that of contemporary V8s.

The 1954 Aero also handled much better than before. A new front end was adopted using threaded trunions adjustable for wear. The kingpins and coil springs were longer, shocks and A-arms were stronger, and the steering idler arm was lengthened. A cross member connected left and right front suspension assemblies to eliminate lateral torque and reduce tow-in variations. The Aero-Willys was thus one of the best combinations of ride and handling offered by a domestic manufacturer in the '50s. The Eagle hardtop in particular was an attractive car, though price was still a problem: the '54 version sold for close to $2600 with Hydra-Matic. Sales dropped to around 12,000 units.

By early 1955, Kaiser-Willys had decided to abandon passenger cars, but not before selling some 6500 of the '55 models. No longer called Aeros, the line was divided into the Custom two- or four-door sedans and the Bermuda hardtop (plus a handful of Ace sedans). Engine options included 161- and 226-cid sixes. Prices were cut drastically in an effort to spark sales, and the Bermuda was advertised as the nation's lowest-priced hardtop. But only 2215 were built, most powered by the 226 engine.

Styling for '55 was much busier than before, and no designer takes credit for it. A clumsy attempt at two-toning involved complicated side trim; the grille was no longer a simple bar, but a garish expanse of concave, vertical bars. In contrast to this glitter, a neat hardtop-wagon had been planned for '55 and a very sleek face-lift was scheduled for 1956. Neither materialized.

The Aero did get a new lease on life in South America. Its dies were eventually shipped to the former Kaiser subsidiary, Willys do Brasil, where a cleaned-up '55 model without the busy side molding was built with F-head Willys power through 1962. In all, the Aero actually lasted over 10 years—which attests to its basically good design.

Willys Specifications

Note: production figures based on serial number spans; may exceed actual production

1930

98B Six (wb 110.0)—27,870 built*	Wght	Price	Prod
rdstr 2-4P	2,497	725	—
sdn 4d	2,641	795	—
rdstr 2P	—	695	—
DeLuxe sdn 4d	2,650	850	—
cpe 2P	—	745	—
DeLuxe cpe 5P	—	800	—
DeLuxe rdstr 2P	—	750	—
DeLuxe rdstr 2-4P	—	780	—

8-80 Eight (wb 120.0)—1,901 built (from Jan/30)			
cpe 2P	—	875	—
rdstr 2-4P	—	855	—
sdn 4d	—	895	—
rdstr 2P	—	825	—
DeLuxe cpe 5P	—	900	—
DeLuxe rdstr 2-4P	—	910	—
DeLuxe sdn 4d	—	950	—
DeLuxe rdstr 2P	—	910	—

87-Knight (wb 112.5; sdn-115.0)—3,627 built (from Jun/30)			
rdstr 2-4P	2,718	975	—
cpe 2-4P	2,922	1,075	—
sdn 4d	2,989	1,075	—

70B-Knight (wb 112.5; sdn 115.0)—10,723 built			
rdstr 2-4P	2,748	1,045	—
DeLuxe cpe 2-4P	2,916	1,145	—
sdn 4d	3,015	1,145	—

66B-Knight (wb 120.0)—5,820 built			
rdstr 2-4P	3,592	1,895	—
cpe 2-4P	3,815	1,895	—
sdn 4d	3,934	1,895	—

*incl. 1931 Model 97.

1930 Engines	bore×stroke	bhp	availability
L6, 177.9	2.94×4.38	53	S-70B
L6, 177.9	2.94×4.38	55	S-87
L6, 193.0	3.25×3.88	65	S-98B
L6, 255.0	3.38×4.75	72	S-66B
L8, 245.4	3.13×4.00	75	S-Eight

1931

97 Six (wb 110.0)—37,678 built*	Wght	Price	Prod
rdstr 2P	2,407	495	—
cpe 2P	2,528	565	—
sdn 4d	2,670	675	—

98B Six (wb 110.0)—27,870 built*			
rdstr 2-4P	2,430	725	—
sdn 4d	2,623	795	—

98D Six (wb 113.0)—3,653 built			
victoria cpe 5P	2,656	795	—
sdn 4d	2,706	795	—

8-80D Eight (wb 120.0; lwb-121.0)—1,686 built				
80	cpe 2-4P	3,061	1,245	—
80	sdn 4d	3,076	1,295	—
80D	lwb victoria cpe 5P (from Jan/31)	3,063	995	—
80D	lwb sdn 4d (from Jan/31)	3,131	995	—

66B-Knight (wb 120.0)—2,189 built			
rdstr 2-4P	3,515	1,795	—
cpe 2-4P	3,745	1,795	—
sdn 4d	3,868	1,795	—

66D-Knight (wb 121.0)—4,982 built (from Jan/31)			
victoria cpe 5P	3,336	1,095	—
sdn 4d	3,400	1,095	—

87-Knight (wb 112.5; lwb-115.0)—2,541 built			
rdstr 2-4P	2,739	975	—
cpe 2-4P	2,882	1,075	—
sdn 4d	3,001	1,075	—

*incl. 1930 Model 98B.

1931 Engines	bore×stroke	bhp	availability
L6, 177.9	2.94×4.38	55	S-87
L6, 193.0	3.25×3.88	65	S-97,98B,98D
L6, 255.0	3.38×4.75	87	S-66B,66D
L8, 245.4	3.13×4.00	80	S-Eight

1932

6-90-Overland Six (wb 113.0)—13,148 built	Wght	Price	Prod
rdstr 2P	2,570	415	—
cpe 2P	2,749	530	—
sdn 4d	2,814	610	—

97 Six (wb 110.0)—9,754 built			
rdstr 2P	2,407	495	—
cpe 5P 2W	2,648	595	—
sdn 4d	2,670	675	—

98D Six (wb 113.0)—245 built			
victoria cpe 4P	2,656	795	—
sdn 4d	2,706	795	—

8-80D Eight (wb 121.0)—452 built			
victoria cpe 4P	3,100	995	—
sdn 4d	3,131	995	—

8-88-Overland Eight (wb 121.0)—1,296 built			
rdstr 2P	2,981	730	—
cpe 2P	3,148	780	—
Custom victoria 4P	3,337	1,030	—
sdn 4d	3,250	830	—

95-Knight (wb 113.0)—1,300 built (est.)			
Silver Ann. cpe 2P	2,915	745	—
Silver Ann. cpe 2-4P	2,994	775	—
Silver Ann. coach 5P	2,982	745	—
Silver Ann. sdn 4d	3,031	795	—

66D-Knight (wb 121.0)			
victoria cpe 5P	3,360	1,095	718
sdn 4d	3,400	1,095	
Silver Ann. Custom victoria 5P	3,664	1,145	900
Silver Ann. Custom sdn 4d	3,775	1,295	

1932 Engines	bore×stroke	bhp	availability
L6, 177.9	2.94×4.38	60	S-95
L6, 193.0	3.25×3.88	65	S-97,98D,6-90
L6, 255.0	3.38×4.75	87	S-66D
L8, 245.4	3.13×4.00	80	S-8-80D, 8-88

1933

6-90A-Overland Streamlined Six (wb 113.0)—6,775 built	Wght	Price	Prod
rdstr 2P	2,569	535	—
cpe 2P	2,781	650	—
sdn 4d	2,913	740	—

8-88A-Overland Streamlined Eight (wb 121.0)—1,022 built			
cpe 2P	3,217	955	—

		Wght	Price	Prod
	sdn 4d	3,368	995	—

77 (wb 100.0)—12,820 built

		Wght	Price	Prod
	cpe 2P	2,058	395	—
	Custom cpe 2P	2,072	415	—
	cpe 2-4P	2,072	425	—
	Custom cpe 2-4P	2,105	445	—
	sdn 4d	2,136	445	—
	Custom sdn 4d	2,156	475	—

66E-Knight Streamlined Six (wb 121.0)

		Wght	Price	Prod
	Custom sdn 4d	3,830	1,420	574

1933 Engines	bore×stroke	bhp	availability
L4, 134.2	3.13×4.38	48	S-77
L6, 193.0	3.25×3.88	65	S-6-90A
L6, 255.0	3.38×4.75	87	S-66E
L8, 245.4	3.13×4.00	80	S-8-88A

1934—13,235 built

77 (wb 100.0)

		Wght	Price	Prod
	cpe 2P	2,058	395	—
	Custom cpe 2P	2,072	415	—
	cpe 2-4P	2,072	425	—
	Custom cpe 2-4P	2,105	445	—
	sdn 4d	2,131	445	—
	Custom sdn 4d	2,156	475	—
	Second Series (from Jan/34):			
	cpe 2P	2,058	430	—
	sdn 4d	2,131	450	—

1934 Engine	bore×stroke	bhp	availability
L4, 134.2	3.13×4.38	48	S-all

1935

77 (wb 100.0)—10,715 built

		Wght	Price	Prod
	cpe 2P	2,034	475	—
	sdn 4d	2,111	495	—

1935 Engine	bore×stroke	bhp	availability
L4, 134.2	3.13×4.38	48	S-all

1936

77 (wb 100.0)—30,826 built

		Wght	Price	Prod
	cpe 2P	2,034	395	—
	sdn 4d	2,131	415	—

1936 Engine	bore×stroke	bhp	availability
L4, 134.2	3.13×4.38	48	S-all

1937

37 (wb 100.0)—63,467 built

		Wght	Price	Prod
	cpe 2P	2,146	499	—
	DeLuxe cpe 2P	2,146	579	—
	sdn 4d	2,200	538	—
	DeLuxe sdn 4d	2,306	589	—

1937 Engine	bore×stroke	bhp	availability
L4, 134.2	3.13×4.38	48	S-all

1938—26,691 built*

38 (wb 100.0)

		Wght	Price	Prod
	Standard cpe 2P	2,145	499	—
	Deluxe cpe 2P	2,155	574	—
	Clipper sdn 2d	2,258	539	—
	Standard sdn 4d	2,247	563	—
	Deluxe Clipper sdn 2d	2,258	575	—
	Deluxe sdn 4d	2,263	614	—
	Custom sdn 4d	2,336	700	—

*incl. 1939 Model 38 production

1938 Engine	bore×stroke	bhp	availability
L4, 134.2	3.13×4.38	48	S-all

1939

38 (wb 100.0)*

		Wght	Price	Prod
	Standard cpe 2P	2,181	499	—
	Standard sdn 2d	2,258	539	—
	Standard sdn 4d	2,300	563	—
	Deluxe cpe 2P	2,181	574	—
	Deluxe sdn 2d	2,258	575	—
	Deluxe sdn 4d	2,306	614	—

39 Overland (wb 102.0)—15,214 built

		Wght	Price	Prod
	Standard Speedway cpe 2P	2,137	596	—
	Standard Speedway sdn 2d	2,217	616	—
	Standard Speedway sdn 4d	2,249	631	—
	Deluxe cpe 2P	2,193	646	—
	Deluxe sdn 2d	2,262	667	—
	Deluxe sdn 4d	2,306	689	—
	Speedway Special cpe 2P	2,193	610	—
	Speedway Special sdn 2d	2,262	631	—
	Speedway Special sdn 4d	2,306	646	—

48 (wb 100.0)—2,625 built

		Wght	Price	Prod
	cpe 2P	2,181	524	—
	sdn 2d	2,258	565	—
	sdn 4d	2,300	586	—

*incl. 1938 Model 38 production

1939 Engines	bore×stroke	bhp	availability
L4, 134.2	3.13×4.38	48	S-38,48
L4, 134.2	3.13×4.38	62	S-39

1940

440 (wb 102.0)—26,698 built

		Wght	Price	Prod
	Speedway cpe	2,146	529	—
	Speedway sdn 4d	2,238	596	—
	DeLuxe cpe	2,190	641	—
	DeLuxe sdn 4d	2,255	672	—
	DeLuxe wgn 4d	2,124	830	—

1940 Engine	bore×stroke	bhp	availability
L4, 134.2	3.13×4.38	61	S-all

1941

441 Americar (wb 104.0)*

		Wght	Price	Prod
	Speedway cpe	2,116	634	—
	Speedway sdn 4d	2,230	674	—
	DeLuxe cpe	2,135	685	—
	Deluxe sdn 4d	2,265	720	—
	DeLuxe wgn 4d	2,483	916	—
	Plainsman cpe	2,175	740	—
	Plainsman sdn 4d	2,305	771	—

1941 Engine	bore×stroke	bhp	availability
L4, 134.2	3.13×4.38	63	S-all

1942

442 Americar (wb 104.0)*

		Wght	Price	Prod
	Speedway cpe	2,142	695	—
	Speedway sdn 4d	2,261	745	—
	DeLuxe cpe	2,184	769	—
	DeLuxe sdn 4d	2,295	795	—
	DeLuxe wgn 4d	2,512	978	—
	Plainsman cpe	2,242	819	—
	Plainsman sdn 4d	2,353	845	—

1942 Engine	bore×stroke	bhp	availability
L4, 134.2	3.13×4.38	63	S-all

*Total 1941-1942 Americar production: 28,935.

1948

463 Four (wb 104.0)		Wght	Price	Prod
Jeepster phtn conv		2,468	1,765	10,326

1948 Engine	bore×stroke	bhp	availability
L4, 134.3	3.13×4.38	63	S-all

1949

463 Four (wb 104.0)—2,307 built (includes VJ-3 Four)		Wght	Price	Prod
Jeepster phtn conv		2,468	1,495	—

VJ-3 Four (wb 104.5)		Wght	Price	Prod
Jeepster phtn conv		2,468	1,495	—

VJ-3 Six (wb 104.0)		Wght	Price	Prod
Jeepster phtn conv		2,392	1,530	653

1949 Engines	bore×stroke	bhp	availability
L4, 134.3	3.13×4.38	63	S-463 Four
L4, 134.3	3.13×4.38	72	S-VJ3 Four (F-head)
L6, 148.5	3.00×3.50	72	S-Six

1950

473 Four (wb 104.0)—4,066 built (includes VJ-3)		Wght	Price	Prod
Jeepster phtn conv		2,459	1,390	—

VJ-3 Four (wb 104.0)		Wght	Price	Prod
Jeepster phtn conv		2,468	1,495	—

673VJ Six (wb 104.0)		Wght	Price	Prod
Jeepster phtn conv		2,485	1,490	1,778

1950 Engines	bore×stroke	bhp	availability
L4, 134.2	3.13×4.38	63	S-Four, 1st series, L-head
L4, 134.2	3.13×4.38	72	S-Four, 2nd series, F-head
L6, 148.5	3.00×3.50	72	S-Six, 1st series, L-head
L6, 161.0	3.13×4.38	75	S-Six, 2nd series, F-head

1951

473-VJ Four (wb 104.0)*		Wght	Price	Prod
Jeepster phtn conv		2,459	1,426	—

673-VJ Six (wb 104.0)*		Wght	Price	Prod
Jeepster phtn conv		2,485	1,529	—

*Combined with 1950 totals; includes 1950 leftovers sold as '51s.

1951 Engines	bore×stroke	bhp	availability
L4, 134.2	3.13×4.38	72	S-Four
L6, 161.0	3.13×4.38	75	S-Six

1952

652-K Aero-Lark (wb 108.0)		Wght	Price	Prod
KA2-675 sdn 2d		2,487	1,731	7,474

652-L Aero-Wing (wb 108.0)		Wght	Price	Prod
LA1-685 sdn 2d		2,570	1,989	12,819

652-M Aero- (wb 108.0)				
MA1-685 Ace sdn 2d		2,584	2,074	8,706
MC1-685 Eagle htp cpe		2,575	2,155	2,364

1952 Engines	bore×stroke	bhp	availability
L6, 161.0	3.13×4.38	75	S-Lark
L6, 161.0	3.13×4.38	90	S-Wing, Ace, Eagle

1953

653-K Aero-Lark (wb 108.0)		Wght	Price	Prod
KA1-675 sdn 2d		2,487	1,646	8,205
KB1-675 sdn 4d		2,509	1,732	7,692

653-M Aero- (wb 108.0)				
MA1-685 Ace sdn 2d		2,584	1,963	4,988
MB1-685 Ace sdn 4d		2,735	2,038	7,475
MC1-685 Eagle htp cpe		2,575	2,157	7,018

653-P Aero-Falcon (wb 108.0)				
PA1-675 sdn 2d		2,507	1,760	3,054
PB1-675 sdn 4d		2,529	1,861	3,117

1953 Engines	bore×stroke	bhp	availability
L4, 134.2	3.13×4.38	72	S-Lark 4
L6, 161.0	3.13×4.38	75	S-Lark 6, Falcon
L6, 161.0	3.13×4.38	90	S-Ace, Eagle

1954

654-K Aero-Lark (wb 108.0)		Wght	Price	Prod
KA2 sdn 2d, (226)		2,740	—	59
KB2 sdn 4d, (226)		2,730	—	282
KA3-685 sdn 2d		2,623	1,737	1,370
KA3-685 Custom sdn 2d		2,678	1,798	1,132
KB3-685 sdn 4d		2,661	1,823	1,482
KB3-685 Custom sdn 4d		2,722	1,878	548

654-M Aero- (wb 108.0)				
MA1 Ace DeLuxe sdn 2d (226)		2,751	—	1,195
MA1 Ace DeLuxe Custom sdn 2d (226)		2,806	—	7
MB1 Ace DeLuxe sdn 4d (226)		2,778	—	1,498
MB1 Ace DeLuxe Custom sdn 4d (226)		2,833	—	9
MA2-685 Ace sdn 2d		2,682	1,892	2
MA2-685 Ace Custom sdn 2d		2,737	1,947	586
MB2-685 Ace sdn 4d		2,709	1,968	1,380
MB2-685 Ace Custom sdn 4d		2,764	2,023	611
MC1 Eagle htp cpe (226)		2,847	—	660
MC1 Eagle Custom htp cpe (226)		2,904	—	11
MC2 Eagle Special htp cpe (226)		—	—	302
MC3-685 Eagle DeLuxe htp cpe		—	2,222	84
MC3-685 Eagle DeLuxe Custom htp cpe		—	2,411	499

1954 Engines	bore×stroke	bhp	availability
L4, 134.2	3.13×4.38	72	S-Lark 4
L6, 161.0	3.13×4.38	90	S-Lark 6, Ace, Eagle
L6, 226.2	3.31×4.38	115	O-Lark 6, Ace, Eagle

1955

522/6 Ace (wb 108.0)		Wght	Price	Prod
52367 sdn 4d (226)		—	—	659

523/4 Custom (wb 108.0)				
52367 sdn 4d (226)		2,778	1,795	2,822
52462 sdn 2d (161)		—	—	2
52467 sdn 2d (226)		2,751	1,725	288

525 Bermuda (wb 108.0)				
52527 htp cpe (161)		—	—	59
52567 htp cpe (226)		2,831	1,997	2,156

1955 Engines	bore×stroke	bhp	availability
L6, 161.0	3.13×4.38	90	S-Custom, Bermuda
L6, 226.2	3.31×4.38	115	S-Ace; O-Custom, Bermuda

Willys production does not include steel-bodied station wagons manufactured from 1946 through 1961, or Wagoneers (wagons) manufactured from 1960 onward. Aero production does not include export or taxi models.

Model Year Production 1930-1980

(1,000 or more units)
(*calculated or estimated)

(**calendar year production)

1930

1. Ford	1,140,710
2. Chevrolet	640,980
3. Buick	181,743
4. Studebaker	123,216
5. Dodge	90,755
6. Chrysler	77,881
7. Plymouth	76,950
8. Essex	68,593
9. Nash	63,265
10. Pontiac	62,888
11. Oldsmobile	49,395
12. Hudson	36,674**
13. Packard	36,334
14. Graham	33,560
15. DeSoto	32,091
16. Whippet	30,000*
17. Willys	29,650*
18. Hupmobile	22,183**
19. Oakland	21,943
20. Cadillac	17,117*
21. Rockne	16,150
22. LaSalle	14,986
23. Auburn	14,380
24. Reo	11,450**
25. Pierce-Arrow	9,865
26. American Austin	8,558
27. Franklin	5,744
28. Marmon	4,681***
29. Lincoln	3,212
30. Cord	1,700
31. Viking	1,390

1931

1. Chevrolet	619,554
2. Ford	615,455
3. Buick	138,965
4. Plymouth	106,986
5. Studebaker	96,173**
6. Pontiac	84,708
7. Willys	65,800*
8. Chrysler	65,500
9. Dodge	52,364
10. Essex	47,418
11. Oldsmobile	47,277
12. Nash	37,386
13. Auburn	36,148
14. DeSoto	32,580
15. Graham	28,428
16. Hudson	22,246
17. Hupmobile	17,451
18. Packard	15,450
19. Cadillac	15,196*
20. Oakland	13,408
21. Whippet	13,400*
22. LaSalle	10,095
23. Reo	6,762**
24. Marmon	5,687***
25. Pierce-Arrow	4,500*
26. Lincoln	3,556
27. Franklin	2,851
28. Cord	1,433
29. American Austin	1,279

1932

1. Chevrolet	313,404
2. Ford	210,824
3. Plymouth	83,910
4. Buick	56,790
5. Pontiac	45,340
6. Essex	32,285
7. Nash	30,834
8. Willys	27,800*
9. Dodge	27,555
10. Chrysler	25,699
11. Studebaker	25,618
12. DeSoto	24,896
13. Rockne	22,715
14. Oldsmobile	18,846
15. Packard	16,613
16. Reo	15,716
17. Graham	12,967**
18. Auburn	11,646
19. Hupmobile	10,476
20. Hudson	7,777**
21. Cadillac	4,698
22. American Austin	3,846
23. Lincoln	3,749
24. LaSalle	3,386
25. Pierce-Arrow	2,234
26. Franklin	1,900*

1933

1. Chevrolet	486,261
2. Ford	334,969**
3. Plymouth	298,557
4. Dodge	106,103
5. Pontiac	90,198
6. Buick	46,924
7. Essex	38,150**
8. Oldsmobile	36,648
9. Chrysler	32,241
10. DeSoto	22,736
11. Willys	21,191
12. Nash	14,973**
13. Rockne	13,326
14. Studebaker	12,531
15. Graham	10,970**
16. Auburn	8,027
17. Hupmobile	7,313
18. Packard	4,803
19. American Austin	4,726
20. Reo	4,112
21. LaSalle	3,482
22. Cadillac	3,173
23. Hudson	2,852
24. Pierce-Arrow	2,298
25. Lincoln	1,703
26. Franklin	1,487

1934

1. Ford	563,921**
2. Chevrolet	551,191
3. Plymouth	321,171
4. Dodge	95,011
5. Pontiac	78,859
6. Oldsmobile	75,574
7. Buick	71,009
8. Studebaker	59,864
9. Terraplane	51,084
10. Chrysler	36,091
11. Hudson	27,054
12. Nash	23,616***
13. DeSoto	13,940
14. Willys	13,235
15. Graham	11,430**
16. Hupmobile	9,420**
17. Packard	8,000
18. LaSalle	7,195
19. Cadillac	5,819
20. Auburn	5,536
21. LaFayette	5,000*
22. Reo	4,460**
23. Lincoln	2,431
24. Pierce-Arrow	1,735

1935

1. Ford	820,253
2. Chevrolet	548,215
3. Plymouth	327,448
4. Pontiac	178,770
5. Dodge	158,999
6. Oldsmobile	120,374
7. Buick	53,249
8. Terraplane	51,134
9. Studebaker	43,682
10. Chrysler	38,533
11. Nash	35,184***

1936

12. Packard	31,889
13. DeSoto	26,800
14. Hudson	21,020
15. Graham	15,965**
16. Hupmobile	10,781
17. Willys	10,715
18. LaFayette	9,400*
19. LaSalle	8,651
20. Reo	4,692**
21. Cadillac	4,236
22. Lincoln	1,434

1. Ford	930,778
2. Chevrolet	918,278
3. Plymouth	520,334
4. Dodge	263,647
5. Oldsmobile	191,357
6. Pontiac	176,270
7. Buick	168,596
8. Terraplane	86,791
9. Packard	61,027
10. Chrysler	59,258
11. Studebaker	55,960
12. Nash	43,070***
13. DeSoto	40,299
14. Willys	30,826
15. LaFayette	27,860
16. Hudson	26,347
17. Graham	19,225
18. Lincoln	16,528
19. LaSalle	13,004
20. Cadillac	12,880
21. Reo	3,206**
22. Hupp	2,171
23. Auburn	1,848

1937

1. Ford	942,005
2. Chevrolet	815,375
3. Plymouth	551,994
4. Dodge	295,047
5. Pontiac	236,189
6. Buick	220,346
7. Oldsmobile	179,830
8. Packard	122,593
9. Chrysler	106,120
10. Studebaker	98,000*
11. Terraplane	90,253
12. DeSoto	81,775
13. Nash	77,000
14. Willys	63,467
15. LaSalle	32,000
16. Lincoln	30,875
17. Hudson	20,464
18. Graham	18,219
19. Cadillac	14,152

1938

1. Chevrolet	465,158
2. Ford	410,263
3. Plymouth	279,338
4. Buick	168,689
5. Dodge	114,529
6. Pontiac	97,139
7. Oldsmobile	85,045
8. Packard	55,718
9. Chrysler	52,949
10. Hudson	50,270
11. Studebaker	46,787
12. Nash	41,542
13. DeSoto	38,831
14. Lincoln	19,626
15. LaSalle	14,635
16. Willys	13,500*
17. Cadillac	9,268
18. Graham	5,020
19. Hupmobile	2,001
20. American Bantam	2,000*

1939

1. Chevrolet	577,278
2. Ford	487,031
3. Plymouth	417,529
4. Buick	208,259
5. Pontiac	144,340
6. Oldsmobile	127,227
7. Studebaker	85,834
8. Hudson	81,521**
9. Dodge	79,600
10. Mercury	75,000*
11. Chrysler	72,443
12. Nash	62,854
13. DeSoto	54,449
14. Packard	46,405
15. Lincoln	21,134
16. LaSalle	21,127
17. Cadillac	13,581
18. Graham	5,392
19. Crosley	2,017
20. American Bantam	1,200*
21. Hupmobile	1,035

1940

1. Chevrolet	764,616
2. Ford	541,896
3. Plymouth	423,155
4. Buick	278,784
5. Pontiac	217,001
6. Dodge	195,505
7. Oldsmobile	185,154
8. Studebaker	107,185
9. Packard	98,020
10. Chrysler	92,419
11. Hudson	87,915
12. Mercury	81,128*
13. DeSoto	65,467
14. Nash	62,131
15. LaSalle	24,130
16. Lincoln	21,765
17. Willys	21,418*
18. Cadillac	13,043
19. Graham	2,000*

1941

1. Chevrolet	1,008,976
2. Ford	691,455
3. Plymouth	545,811
4. Buick	374,196
5. Pontiac	330,061
6. Oldsmobile	265,864
7. Dodge	237,002
8. Chrysler	161,704
9. Studebaker	133,900
10. DeSoto	97,497
11. Hudson	91,769
12. Nash	84,007
13. Mercury	82,391*
14. Packard	72,855
15. Cadillac	66,130
16. Willys	22,102*
17. Lincoln	18,244
18. Crosley	2,289

1942

1. Chevrolet	254,885
2. Ford	160,432
3. Plymouth	152,427
4. Buick	92,573
5. Pontiac	83,555
6. Dodge	68,522
7. Oldsmobile	67,783
8. Studebaker	50,678
9. Hudson	40,661
10. Chrysler	36,586
11. Packard	33,776
12. Nash	31,780
13. DeSoto	24,015
14. Mercury	22,816
15. Cadillac	16,511

(continued)

16. Lincoln	6,547
17. Crosley	1,029

1946

1. Ford	468,022
2. Chevrolet	398,028
3. Plymouth	264,660*
4. Dodge	163,490*
5. Buick	153,627
6. Pontiac	137,640
7. Oldsmobile	117,623
8. Nash	94,000*
9. Hudson	91,039
10. Mercury	86,608
11. Chrysler	83,310*
12. DeSoto	66,900*
13. Packard	30,793
14. Cadillac	29,214
15. Studebaker	19,275
16. Lincoln	16,645
17. Crosley	4,999

1947

1. Chevrolet	671,546
2. Ford	429,674
3. Plymouth	382,290*
4. Buick	272,827
5. Dodge	243,160*
6. Pontiac	230,600
7. Oldsmobile	193,895
8. Studebaker	161,496
9. Chrysler	119,260*
10. Nash	101,000*
11. Hudson	92,038
12. DeSoto	87,000*
13. Mercury	85,383
14. Kaiser	70,474
15. Frazer	68,775
16. Cadillac	61,926
17. Packard	51,086
18. Lincoln	21,460
19. Crosley	19,344

1948

1. Chevrolet	696,449
2. Ford	430,198
3. Plymouth	412,540*
(+ '49 First Series)	
4. Dodge	243,340*
(+ '49 First Series)	
5. Pontiac	235,419
6. Buick	213,599
7. Studebaker	184,993
8. Oldsmobile	172,852
9. Chrysler	130,110*
(+ '49 First Series)	
10. Hudson	117,200
11. Nash	110,000*
12. DeSoto	98,890*
(+ '49 First Series)	
13. Packard	92,251
14. Kaiser	91,851
15. Cadillac	52,706
16. Mercury	50,268
17. Frazer	48,071
18. Crosley	26,239
19. Lincoln	7,769

1949

1. Ford	1,118,308
2. Chevrolet	1,010,013
3. Plymouth	520,385
(+ '49 Second Series)	
4. Buick	324,276
5. Pontiac	304,819
6. Mercury	301,319
7. Oldsmobile	288,310
8. Dodge	256,857
(+ '49 Second Series)	

*** calendar year registrations   *** calendar year registrations

9.	Hudson	159,100
10.	Nash	135,328*
11.	Studebaker	129,298
12.	Chrysler	124,218
	(+ '49 Second Series)	
13.	Packard	116,248
14.	DeSoto	94,201
	(+ '49 Second Series)	
15.	Cadillac	92,554
16.	Kaiser	79,947*
17.	Lincoln	73,507
18.	Frazer	21,223*
19.	Crosley	7,431

1950

1.	Chevrolet	1,498,590
2.	Ford	1,208,912
3.	Buick	667,826
4.	Plymouth	610,954
5.	Pontiac	466,429
6.	Oldsmobile	407,889
7.	Dodge	341,797
8.	Studebaker (US)	320,884
9.	Mercury	293,658
10.	Chrysler	179,299
11.	Nash	171,782
12.	DeSoto	133,854
13.	Hudson	121,408
14.	Cadillac	103,857
15.	Packard	42,627
16.	Lincoln	28,190
17.	Kaiser	15,228*
18.	Crosley	6,792
19.	Frazer	3,700*

1951

1.	Chevrolet	1,229,986
2.	Ford	1,013,381
3.	Plymouth	611,000*
4.	Buick	592,511
5.	Pontiac	370,159
6.	Mercury	310,387
7.	Dodge	290,000*
8.	Oldsmobile	285,612
9.	Studebaker (US)	246,195
10.	Nash	205,307
11.	Chrysler	163,613
12.	Kaiser	139,452*
13.	Hudson	131,915
14.	Cadillac	110,340
15.	DeSoto	106,000*
16.	Packard	100,713
17.	Henry J	81,942
18.	Lincoln	32,574
19.	Frazer	10,214
20.	Crosley	6,614

1952

1.	Chevrolet	818,142
2.	Ford	671,733
3.	Plymouth	396,000*
4.	Buick	367,760
5.	Pontiac	271,373
6.	Oldsmobile	213,419
7.	Dodge	206,000*
8.	Mercury	172,087
9.	Studebaker (US)	167,662
10.	Nash	154,291
11.	Cadillac	90,259
12.	Chrysler	87,470*
13.	DeSoto	88,000*
14.	Hudson	70,000
15.	Packard	62,921
16.	Kaiser	32,131
17.	Willys	31,363
18.	Henry J	30,585
19.	Lincoln	27,271
20.	Crosley	2,075
21.	Allstate	1,566

1953

1.	Chevrolet	1,346,475
2.	Ford	1,247,542

3.	Plymouth	650,451
4.	Buick	486,812
5.	Pontiac	418,619
6.	Oldsmobile	334,462
7.	Dodge	320,008
8.	Mercury	305,863
9.	Chrysler	170,006
10.	Studebaker (US)	151,576
11.	DeSoto	130,404
12.	Nash	121,793
13.	Cadillac	109,651
14.	Packard	90,252
15.	Hudson	66,143
16.	Willys	42,057
17.	Lincoln	40,762
18.	Kaiser	27,652*
19.	Henry J	16,672

1954

1.	Ford	1,165,942
2.	Chevrolet	1,143,561
3.	Plymouth	463,148
4.	Buick	442,903
5.	Oldsmobile	354,001
6.	Pontiac	287,744
7.	Mercury	259,305
8.	Dodge	154,648
9.	Chrysler	105,030
10.	Cadillac	96,680
11.	Nash	91,121
12.	DeSoto	76,580
13.	Studebaker (US)	68,708
14.	Hudson	50,670
15.	Lincoln	36,993
16.	Packard	31,291
17.	Willys	11,856
18.	Kaiser	8,539
19.	Henry J	1,123*

1955

1.	Chevrolet	1,704,667
2.	Ford	1,451,157
3.	Buick	737,035
4.	Oldsmobile	583,179
5.	Pontiac	553,808
6.	Plymouth	401,075
7.	Mercury	329,808
8.	Dodge	276,936
9.	Chrysler	152,777
10.	Cadillac	140,777
11.	Nash	126,000*
12.	Studebaker (US)	116,333
13.	DeSoto	114,765
14.	Packard	55,247
15.	Hudson	46,000*
16.	Lincoln	27,222
17.	Imperial	11,432
18.	Willys	6,565
19.	Kaiser	1,291

1956

1.	Chevrolet	1,567,117
2.	Ford	1,408,478
3.	Buick	635,158
4.	Plymouth	552,577
5.	Oldsmobile	485,458
6.	Pontiac	405,429
7.	Mercury	327,943
8.	Dodge	240,686
9.	Cadillac	154,577
10.	Chrysler	128,322
11.	DeSoto	110,418
12.	Nash	83,420
13.	Studebaker (US)	69,593
14.	Lincoln	50,322
15.	Hudson	35,671*
16.	Clipper	18,482
17.	Imperial	10,684
18.	Packard	10,353
19.	Continental	1,325

1957

1.	Ford	1,676,449

2.	Chevrolet	1,505,910
3.	Plymouth	762,231
4.	Buick	404,049
5.	Oldsmobile	384,390
6.	Pontiac	333,473
7.	Dodge	287,608
8.	Mercury	286,163
9.	Cadillac	146,841
10.	Chrysler	124,675
11.	DeSoto	117,514
12.	Rambler	91,469
13.	Studebaker (US)	63,101
14.	Lincoln	41,123
15.	Imperial	37,593
16.	Nash	20,317
17.	Packard	4,809
18.	Hudson	3,876

1958

1.	Chevrolet	1,142,460
2.	Ford	987,945
3.	Plymouth	443,799
4.	Oldsmobile	314,374
5.	Buick	240,659
6.	Pontiac	216,982
7.	Rambler	186,227*
8.	Mercury	153,271
9.	Dodge	137,861
10.	Cadillac	121,778
11.	Chrysler	63,681
12.	Edsel	63,110
13.	DeSoto	49,445
14.	Studebaker (US)	44,759
15.	Lincoln	17,134
16.	Imperial	16,133
17.	Metropolitan	13,128
18.	Continental	12,550
19.	Packard	2,622

1959

1.	Chevrolet	1,462,140
2.	Ford	1,450,953
3.	Plymouth	458,259
4.	Pontiac	382,940
5.	Oldsmobile	382,864
6.	Rambler	363,372*
7.	Buick	284,248
8.	Dodge	156,385
9.	Mercury	149,987
10.	Cadillac	142,272
11.	Studebaker (US)	126,156
12.	Chrysler	69,970
13.	DeSoto	45,724
14.	Edsel	44,891
15.	Metropolitan	22,309
16.	Imperial	17,269
17.	Lincoln	15,780
18.	Continental	11,126

1960

1.	Chevrolet	1,653,168
2.	Ford	1,439,370
3.	Plymouth	447,724
4.	Rambler	422,273*
5.	Pontiac	396,179
6.	Dodge	367,804
7.	Oldsmobile	347,142
8.	Mercury	271,331
9.	Buick	253,807
10.	Cadillac	142,184
11.	Studebaker (US)	120,465
12.	Chrysler	77,285
13.	DeSoto	25,581
14.	Imperial	17,719
15.	Lincoln	13,734
16.	Metropolitan	13,103
17.	Continental	11,086
18.	Checker	6,980*
19.	Edsel	3,008

1961

1.	Ford	1,338,790
2.	Chevrolet	1,318,014

3.	Rambler	370,685*
4.	Plymouth	350,285
5.	Pontiac	340,248
6.	Oldsmobile	317,548
7.	Mercury	317,351
8.	Buick	276,754
9.	Dodge	269,367
10.	Cadillac	138,379
11.	Chrysler	96,454
12.	Studebaker (US)	59,713
13.	Lincoln	25,164
14.	Imperial	12,258
15.	Checker	5,683
16.	DeSoto	3,034

1962

1.	Chevrolet	2,072,000*
2.	Ford	1,476,031
3.	Pontiac	521,437
4.	Oldsmobile	428,853
5.	Rambler	423,104
6.	Buick	399,526
7.	Mercury	341,366
8.	Plymouth	339,814
9.	Dodge	240,484
10.	Cadillac	160,840
11.	Chrysler	128,921
12.	Studebaker (US)	89,318
13.	Lincoln	31,061
14.	Imperial	14,337
15.	Checker	8,173

1963

1.	Chevrolet	2,148,000*
2.	Ford	1,525,404
3.	Pontiac	589,294
4.	Plymouth	488,448
5.	Oldsmobile	476,753
6.	Buick	457,818
7.	Dodge	446,129
8.	Rambler	428,346*
9.	Mercury	301,581
10.	Cadillac	163,174
11.	Chrysler	128,937
12.	Studebaker (US)	69,555
13.	Lincoln	31,233
14.	Imperial	14,121
15.	Checker	7,050

1964

1.	Chevrolet	2,308,700*
2.	Ford	1,594,053
3.	Pontiac	738,317
4.	Plymouth	596,221
5.	Buick	510,490
6.	Dodge	501,781
7.	Oldsmobile	493,991
8.	Rambler	379,412*
9.	Mercury	298,609
10.	Cadillac	165,909
11.	Chrysler	153,319
12.	Studebaker (US/Canada)	36,697
13.	Lincoln	36,297
14.	Imperial	23,295
15.	Checker	6,310

1965

1.	Chevrolet	2,372,900*
2.	Ford	2,170,795
3.	Pontiac	801,357
4.	Plymouth	721,234
5.	Buick	600,145
6.	Oldsmobile	591,701
7.	Dodge	489,065
8.	Mercury	346,751
9.	Rambler	324,669*
10.	Chrysler	206,089
11.	Cadillac	182,435
12.	Lincoln	40,180
13.	Studebaker (Canada)	19,435
14.	Imperial	18,409
15.	Checker	6,136

1966

1.	Ford	2,212,415
2.	Chevrolet	2,206,200*
3.	Pontiac	830,778
4.	Plymouth	683,879
5.	Dodge	632,658
6.	Oldsmobile	578,385
7.	Buick	553,870
8.	Mercury	343,149
9.	Rambler	265,712*
10.	Chrysler	264,848
11.	Cadillac	196,685
12.	AMC	76,239
13.	Lincoln	54,755
14.	Imperial	13,742
15.	Studebaker (Canada)	8,947
16.	Checker	5,761
17.	Shelby	2,378

1967

1.	Chevrolet	2,193,100*
2.	Ford	1,730,224
3.	Pontiac	782,734
4.	Plymouth	636,893
5.	Buick	562,507
6.	Oldsmobile	548,390
7.	Dodge	465,732
8.	Mercury	354,923
9.	Rambler	237,785*
10.	Chrysler	218,742
11.	Cadillac	200,000
12.	AMC	65,160
13.	Lincoln	45,667
14.	Imperial	17,620
15.	Checker	5,822
16.	Shelby	3,225

1968

1.	Chevrolet	2,131,200*
2.	Ford	1,753,334
3.	Pontiac	910,482
4.	Plymouth	747,237
5.	Buick	651,823
6.	Dodge	627,533
7.	Oldsmobile	562,459
8.	Mercury	360,467
9.	Chrysler	264,853
10.	Rambler	259,346*
11.	Cadillac	230,003
12.	AMC	187,435
13.	Lincoln	39,134
14.	Imperial	15,367
15.	Continental	7,770
16.	Checker	5,477
17.	Shelby	4,451

1969

1.	Chevrolet	2,106,500*
2.	Ford	1,826,777
3.	Pontiac	870,081
4.	Plymouth	720,209
5.	Buick	665,422
6.	Oldsmobile	635,241
7.	Dodge	611,645
8.	Mercury	398,262
9.	Chrysler	260,773
10.	Rambler	239,937*
11.	Cadillac	223,237
12.	AMC	173,106
13.	Lincoln	38,290
14.	Continental	23,088
15.	Imperial	22,103
16.	Checker	5,417
17.	Shelby	3,150

1970

1.	Ford	2,096,184
2.	Chevrolet	1,456,574
3.	Pontiac	690,953
4.	Plymouth	684,975
5.	Buick	666,501
6.	Oldsmobile	633,981

Model Year Production

7. Dodge	543,019
8. Mercury	324,716
9. AMC	276,000*
10. Cadillac	238,744
11. Chrysler	180,777
12. Lincoln	37,695
13. Continental	21,432
14. Imperial	11,822
15. Checker	5,500*

1971

1. Ford	2,054,351
2. Chevrolet	1,830,319
3. Plymouth	702,115
4. Pontiac	586,853
5. Oldsmobile	567,891
6. Dodge	551,386
7. Buick	551,188
8. Mercury	365,310
9. AMC	244,758
10. Cadillac	188,537
11. Chrysler	175,118
12. Lincoln	62,642
13. Imperial	11,558

1972

1. Chevrolet	2,420,564
2. Ford	2,246,563
3. Oldsmobile	762,199
4. Plymouth	756,605
5. Pontiac	706,978
6. Buick	679,921
7. Dodge	7,870
8. Mercury	441,964
9. Cadillac	267,787
10. AMC	258,134
11. Chrysler	204,704
12. Lincoln	94,560
13. Imperial	15,804

1973

1. Chevrolet	2,579,509
2. Ford	2,349,815
3. Oldsmobile	922,771
4. Pontiac	919,870
5. Plymouth	882,196
6. Buick	821,165
7. Dodge	665,536
8. Mercury	486,470
9. AMC	392,105***
10. Cadillac	304,839
11. Chrysler	234,223
12. Lincoln	128,073
13. Imperial	16,729

*** calendar year registrations

1974

1. Chevrolet	2,333,839
2. Ford	2,179,791
3. Plymouth	739,894
4. Oldsmobile	581,195
5. Pontiac	580,045
6. Buick	495,063
7. Dodge	477,728
8. AMC	431,798
9. Mercury	403,977
10. Cadillac	242,330
11. Chrysler	117,373
12. Lincoln	93,983
13. Imperial	14,426

1975

1. Chevrolet	1,755,773
2. Ford	1,569,608
3. Oldsmobile	631,795
4. Pontiac	531,922
5. Buick	481,768
6. Plymouth	454,105
7. Mercury	404,650
8. Dodge	377,462
9. Cadillac	264,732
10. Chrysler	251,549
11. AMC	241,501
12. Lincoln	101,843
13. Imperial	8,830

1976

1. Chevrolet	2,103,862
2. Ford	1,861,537
3. Oldsmobile	891,368
4. Pontiac	746,430
5. Buick	737,466
6. Plymouth	519,962
7. Mercury	480,361
8. Dodge	430,641
9. Cadillac	309,139
10. AMC	283,577
11. Chrysler	222,153
12. Lincoln	124,756

1977

1. Chevrolet	2,543,153
2. Ford	1,840,427
3. Oldsmobile	1,135,803
4. Pontiac	850,620
5. Buick	845,234
6. Plymouth	546,132
7. Dodge	526,254
8. Mercury	521,909
9. Chrysler	399,297
10. Cadillac	358,488
11. Lincoln	191,355
12. AMC	182,005

1978

1. Chevrolet	2,375,436
2. Ford	1,923,655
3. Oldsmobile	1,015,805
4. Pontiac	900,380
5. Buick	803,187
6. Mercury	635,051
7. Plymouth	501,129
8. Dodge	467,720
9. Chrysler	354,029
10. Cadillac	349,684
11. Lincoln	169,620
12. AMC	137,860

1979

1. Chevrolet	2,284,749
2. Ford	1,835,937
3. Oldsmobile	1,068,154
4. Pontiac	907,434
5. Buick	727,275
6. Mercury	669,138
7. Dodge	404,266
8. Cadillac	383,138
9. Plymouth	372,449
10. Chrysler	349,450
11. Lincoln	189,546
12. AMC	169,439

1980

1. Chevrolet	2,288,745
2. Ford	1,162,275
3. Oldsmobile	910,306
4. Buick	854,011
5. Pontiac	770,100
6. Mercury	347,711
7. Dodge	308,638
8. Plymouth	290,974
9. Cadillac	230,028
10. AMC	199,613
11. Chrysler	164,510
12. Lincoln	74,908

Minor Makes

NOTES TO THE READER

What follows is a compilation of all American-built automobiles in the 1940-1970 period not listed in the preceding "Major Makes" section. The vast majority of these saw very limited production; some never proceeded beyond the prototype stage; a rare few were sold for several years. The facts about some of them are, unfortunately, completely elusive or, at best, sketchy.

Several rules were adopted in compiling this section. To keep the list within the scope of the book, all unsubstantiated, experimental, racing, and Canadian cars were omitted, as were products designed only for children. Though a number of prototypes are included, they fall within this primary qualification adopted: evidence of *serious intent to manufacture in complete form*. Vehicles sold as kits ("kit cars") are included only where fully assembled models were also available from the manufacturer or a dealer.

Each entry is dated as accurately as possible, and builder or factory locations are stated where known. Where only one year is shown (1965-?) the editors were unable to determine exactly when "production" ceased. When "c." (circa) is shown, it was not possible to determine the precise date promotion started and/or terminated.

Aerocar

Aerocar Inc., Longview, WA
Years built: 1948-c.1970
Production: 7

Developed by Moulton P. Taylor, this car/plane was powered by a 100-bhp Franklin engine and first sold in late 1954 for $7500. The main section was 124 inches long on a 78-inch wheelbase, and the wings and propeller assembly were carried in a 14-foot trailer for road use. An Aerocar International Corp. of Fort Worth, Texas reportedly planned production in 1961, but it's not known whether this firm completed any vehicles.

Aircar

Advanced Vehicle Engineers, Van Nuys, CA
Years built: 1970-c.1973
Production: NA

The Aircar was a car/plane conversion based on Cessna Skymaster control surfaces. Contemporary Pontiac Firebirds were commonly used as the starting point, although one Ford Pinto-based model was test flown around 1973 as the Mizar. The effort seems to have evaporated at that point.

Airphibian

Continental, Inc., Danbury, CT
Years built: 1946-52
Production: NA

Robert E. Fulton, Jr. was one of many who saw possibilities for a car/plane in the postwar market. His Airphibian, first shown in 1946, had a passenger compartment made of aluminum, and could be converted from plane to two-passenger car be detaching wings, propeller, and fuselage, a five-minute exercise. A six-cylinder, 150-bhp engine produced a top speed on the highway of 45 mph. Fulton was still trying to get production started as late as 1952.

Airscoot

Aircraft Products Company, Wichita, KS
Year built: 1947
Production: NA

The three-wheel, two-passenger Airscoot was made of lightweight tubing, and had a 2.6-bhp single-cylinder engine. Overall length was just 60 inches on this toteable car, which weighed just 72 pounds and could be folded up for easy carrying. Unfolded, it had a top speed of 25 mph. Fuel milage of 60 mpg was promised. This unique auto apparently never reached production.

Airway

Airway Motors, Inc., San Diego, CA
Years built: 1948-50
Production: 2

At least two prototypes for this "vicinity car" were built. A 1948-49 trial had a very plain, two-door fastback sedan body; a 1950 effort was a notchback-style coupe. Both used a 10-bhp air-cooled aluminum engine, with power taken through a fluid drive. Weight was in the 600-700-pound range; top speed was 45-50 mph. Series production is doubtful.

American Buckboard

American Buckboard Corp., Los Angeles, CA
Year built: 1955
Production: NA

This was a tiny roadster powered by an air-cooled motorcycle twin, mounted at the rear and driving a fifth wheel. It also had four normal wheels, 70-inch wheelbase, 10-foot overall length, and a projected price of around $750. Production under this name is unknown, but the basic design was built in 1956 as the Bearcat.

Apache

Interco Development Corporation, New York City, NY
Years built: 1966-?
Production: NA

The Apache was similar to European economy cars in overall size, engine displacement, and seating, but little else is known about it. However, it did have an unusual collapsible roof, which transformed it from a fastback coupe to an open convertible.

Apollo

International Motor Cars, Inc., Oakland, CA
Years built: 1962-1965
Production: 88

This high-performance sports car featured Italian coachwork, a 215-cid Buick aluminum V8, and a ladder-type frame with Buick Special suspension. Total production included 77 coupes, 11 convertibles and one experimental 2 + 2. Entrepreneurs Newt Davis and Milt Brown were serious about the project, but the Apollo was never advertised nationally, and the firm lacked a sufficient dealer network. The initial GT models had claimed 0-60 mph acceleration of 8 seconds. In 1964, a 5000 GT appeared with a 300-cid Buick V8, offering 7.5-second 0-60 mph go and a top speed of over 150 mph. Some bodies (built by Carrozzeria Intermeccanica of Turin to a Ron Plescia design modified by Scaglione) were later sold to a Dallas, Texas firm and assembled as the Vetta Ventura (see entry).

Argonaut

Argonaut Motor Machine Company, Cleveland, OH
Years built: 1959-63
Production: NA

A very ambitious luxury-car effort in the Pierce-Arrow/Duesenberg mold, the Argonaut was announced in a choice of seven models, ranging from the "Steed" two-seat sports coupe on a 126.5-inch wheelbase to a huge 154-inch-wheelbase limousine. Styling for the aluminum bodies (slated to be built in both the U.S. and Italy) was flowing and low-slung, aided by vast overall length of

218-258 inches. Engineering envisioned an air-cooled, overhead-cam aluminum V12, reported to develop an astonishing 1020 horsepower and good for a claimed top speed in excess of 240 mph. Prices were targeted at $25,150 to $36,000 and factory-direct sales were planned, with servicing done either at factory depots or an owner's home. No finished examples are known to survive, and production is doubtful in any case.

Arnolt

S.H. Arnolt, Inc., Chicago, IL
Years built: 1952-c.1958
Production: 65 (MG), 142 (Bristol)

Industrialist and import-car magnate S.H. "Wacky" Arnolt offered two sports cars under his name, both with specially designed bodywork supplied by Bertone of Italy. The initial Arnolt-MG was a pleasant-looking, square-cut two-seater, but it was saddled by the anemic four-cylinder engine from the contemporary TD and a lofty price of $3195. Predictably it found few takers and disappeared after about 1954. However, it led to a much more memorable machine, the Arnolt-Bristol. Rounded and low-slung, this car was powered by a 2.0-liter, 130-bhp six, built by Bristol in England as the BSI Mark II and derived from BMW's famous prewar engine. Offered in three models (closed coupe and roadsters with or without top) at $4000-$6000, the A-B was light (about 2100 pounds) and thus quite quick. Typical performance was 8.7 seconds 0-60 mph, 17 seconds at 82 mph in the standing quarter-mile, and 110 mph maximum. Though production reportedly continued through Arnolt's death in 1963, few if any cars were likely completed after about 1958. A warehouse fire destroyed 12 of the 142 Bristol-engine machines; of the remaining 130, only three were coupes.

Arrowbile

Waldo D. Waterman,
Santa Monica, CA
Years built: c.1937-c.1958
Production: 8 (est.)

Initially known as Arrowbile, later Aerobile, this series of flying autos was perhaps the earliest serious attempt in the U.S. to produce such a vehicle for commercial sale. The first examples used Studebaker Commander six-cylinder engines. In fact, Studebaker intended to sell the Arrowbile through selected dealers, but backed out because of a downturn in the economy. The final Aerobile, powered by a horizontally opposed, water-cooled Franklin six, was apparently

put together in San Diego during the '50s.

Asardo

American Special Automotive Research and Design Organization, North Bergen, NJ
Year built: 1959
Production: NA

The Asardo had a fiberglass sport coupe body, an 88-inch wheelbase, overall length of 150 inches, and total weight of 1350 pounds. It was powered by a 91.3-cid Alfa Romeo four, tuned to develop 135 bhp. With a four-speed transmission, the Asardo (the name was the acronym of its builder) did 0-60 mph in 6.4 seconds and had a top speed of 135 mph. Price was slated at $5875.

Ascot

Glasspar Co., Santa Ana, CA
Year built: 1955
Production: NA

The body for this 1700-pound, 94-inch-wheelbase roadster was made of fiberglass, no surprise considering the car's builder. Styling highlights included butterfly-type fenders, freestanding headlights, a square grille, external deck-mounted spare tire, and a 48-inch overall height (with top up). Originally, a 172-cid Ford industrial engine was envisioned, but various other units were tried.

Auburn

Glenn Pray Co., Auburn, IN
Years built: 1967-81
Production: NA

The second replicar effort by the creator of the mid-'60s Cord 8/10 was a surprisingly accurate copy of the 1935-36 Auburn 851/852 Speedster. Designated 866, it was built on a modified Ford Galaxie frame with the same 127-inch wheelbase as the original. The fiberglass body, authentic enough to fool many vintage-car enthusiasts, reduced curb weight from the 851's 3800 pounds to around 3100, and a standard 365-bhp 428-cid Thunderbird V8 yielded a top speed in the neighborhood of 130 mph. Price was $8450, and the only options were the owner's choice of paint colors and upholstery materials. The 866 was later joined by the model 874, a dual-cowl phaeton that had no 1930s counterpart.

Aurora

Father Alfred A. Juliano,
Branford, CT
Year built: 1954
Production: 1

This one-off safety prototype was built at a cost of $30,000 on a 1954 Buick Roadmaster chassis, and featured a fiberglass body with transparent plastic roof and forward-raked bubble windshield. Profits from planned sales were to

have been used to further research in car safety.

Auto Cub

Randall Products,
Hampton, NH
Year built: 1956
Production: NA

Just 51 inches long, this 115-pound, single-passenger runabout had tiller steering and a 1.6-bhp Briggs & Stratton or Clinton engine mounted at the rear. Fuel consumption was 75 mpg, and top speed 15 mph for this $169.50 mite, which appears to be an economy running mate to the Daytona (see entry).

Autoette

Autoette Electric Car Co.,
Long Beach, CA
Years built: 1952-1957
Production: NA

A small, electric shopping-type car for two passengers, this was a three-wheeler with a single wheel at the front and steel bodywork. A set of four heavy-duty six-volt batteries supplied power to a 24-volt DC motor. Prices in 1954 ranged from $775 to $950, and three versions were available.

Bassons Star

Bassons Industries
Corporation, Bronx, NY
Year built: 1956
Production: NA

The three-wheeled Bassons Star was an open, two-passenger fiberglass car intended for short-haul delivery service. Its German J.L.O. engine, a single-cylinder, two-cycle unit with 10 bhp, was mounted between the passengers and a small rear storage area. Measuring 33 inches high, 49 inches wide, and 125 inches long, the vehicle weighed but 400 pounds, and could cruise at 40 mph. Top speed was 70 mph. Advertised price was $1000. Bassons also showed an enclosed fiberglass bodied delivery van called the Stationette, a 1955 update of an earlier wood-body model designed by James V. Martin (see Martinette).

Baymont

Baymont Company,
Redwood City, CA
Year built: 1955
Production: NA

The Baymont Suburban Model 240 was basically an electric golf cart modified for local running on city streets. It had room for two passengers, plus several bags of groceries in the rear. It could reach 20 mph, and had a range of 60 miles.

Beechcraft Plainsman

Beech Aircraft Co.,
Wichita, KS
Year built: 1948
Production: 1

A prototype for a possible venture into the automobile busi-

ness by Beech Aircraft, this car had a quite unorthodox drive system. A four-cylinder Franklin air-cooled engine was used to drive an electric generator that, in turn, drove four electric motors, one at each wheel. The very large six-passenger body concealed an all-independent air suspension and air-filled shock absorbers at each wheel. With all this, the Plainsman would likely have cost more to build than the $5000 price optimistically set for it.

Bergermobile

Berger Air-Turbine Car Co.,
Mount Vernon, NY
Year built: 1948
Production: 1

This converted Chevrolet was actually a test bed for a proposed engine swap. It featured a 30-gallon air tank and an Ingersoll-Rand air turbine engine. A 24-volt storage battery supplied electrical power to drive the compressed-air turbine and also ran the car's electrical equipment.

Blackhawk

Stutz Motor Car Company,
Indianapolis, IN
Years built: 1929-30
Production: 1,310 (1929), 280 (1930)

Stutz's companion make was derived from the 1928 Model BB and was built on a 127½-inch wheelbase. An array of open and closed body styles was offered, with the four-door sedan selling at $2395. An 85-bhp overhead-cam six was initially available along with a 90-bhp Continental L-head eight, but only the latter is listed by contemporary sources for 1930. Curb weight was near two tons even on closed models, so performance was leisurely.

B.M.C.

British Motor Car Co.,
San Francisco, CA
Year built: 1952
Production: NA

Despite plans to produce 400 units a year, this sports car venture was terminated after only a few months. It had no connection with British Motor Corporation. In fact, the fiberglass-bodied two-seater was designed around the engine and chassis of the Singer 1500 from the Rootes Group in England.

Bocar

Bocar Racing Cars, Inc.,
Denver, CO
Years built: 1958-60
Production: less than 100

The first production sports car from Bob Carnes (hence the marque name) was the XP-4 of 1958, built on a 90-inch-wheelbase tubular frame. Power was supplied by either a Pontiac 370 or Chevrolet 283

V8. The latter was coaxed up to an alleged 350 bhp in 1959, when it was used on the $11,000 XP-5, a further development bearing sleek, aerodynamic lines. The 1960 XP-6, which sold alongside the XP-5 at $700 more, packed a claimed 400 bhp from a 283 supercharged via a GMC blower. It weighed 2300 pounds, had a 104-inch wheelbase, and was capable of over 135 mph. All Bocars were built primarily for racing, though they were occasionally seen on the street.

Bobbi-Kar

Bobbi Motor Car Corporation,
San Diego, CA
Years built: 1945-1947
Production: NA

The Bobbi-Kar was a two-passenger roadster with a four-cylinder, 25-horsepower engine, an overall length of 132 inches, and a wheelbase of 80 inches. Projected price was around $500. Other models were proposed but never built.

Brewster

Springfield Manufacturing
Company, Springfield,
Massachusetts
Years built: 1934-1936
Production: approx. 300

This attempt to salvage business for what was left of the Brewster coachbuilding company involved special bodies (both open and closed, usually the latter) on contemporary Ford, Buick, and other chassis. High prices ($3000 and up) led the venture to close after two years.

Bricklin

Bricklin Vehicle Corp.,
St. John, New Brunswick,
Canada
Years built: 1974-75
Production: 2,897

Millionaire hardware and motor scooter merchant Malcolm Bricklin was the force behind this "safety sports car." Designated SV-1, it was a two-seat fiberglass-bodied coupe with gullwing doors, a large impact-resistant front bumper, and ungainly, high-waisted styling. Paint color was impregnated in the outer acrylic shell, which seemed like a useful idea but made for a grainy finish. Power initially came from a 175-bhp (SAE net) AMC 360 V8, changed for 1975 to a 162-bhp Ford 351. Suspension was basically that of the AMC Javelin, and a number of other proprietary parts were used. Though the Bricklin listed at $7490 ($9775 in its second year), news stories suggested it cost at least $15,000 to build.

Brogan

B & B Specialty Co.,
Rossmoyne, OH
Years built: 1946-c.1952
Production: NA

The first vehicle marketed by

this firm was a two-seat three-wheeler, with the single wheel in front. Power was provided by a 10-hbp rear-mounted air-cooled twin, and total weight was 450 pounds. Mileage of 65-70 mpg was claimed, and top speed was 45 mph. There was also a smaller model called the Broganette, which scored up to 85 mpg but could barely reach 40 mph. The Brogan name was phased out in 1951, and the lone wheel was moved to the rear for a revised Broganette, which measured about 10 feet long and 52 inches wide. Top speed was now 50 mph, mileage was 55-60 mpg, and price stood at $550. Some 1947 models were apparently sold under the name B & B Three Wheel, but no more than 30 were built.

Buckaroo
Cleveland, OH
(manufacturer unknown)
Year built: 1957
Production: NA

The Buckaroo was a very small $400 car with a top speed of only 18 mph. Nothing else is known about it.

Buckboard
Don Bruce, Bronx, NY
Year built: 1956
Production: 1

An Ariel "Square-4" motorcycle engine, mounted amidships on a Renault 4CV frame, powered this modern cycle car. Construction plans were available for do-it-yourselfers. The unusual wood body was constructed on a 94-inch wheelbase and measured 143 inches long overall. Curb weight was 738 pounds, and top speed was in excess of 90 mph. Production beyond a single show car is unlikely.

Bugetta
Bugetta, Inc., Costa Mesa, CA
Years built: c.1968-?
Production: NA

A two/four-passenger open design with fiberglass body, the mid-engine Bugetta employed a Ford 302 V8, and was offered with both fiberglass and fabric tops at a $3695 starting price. This firm also made some off-road vehicles, but no design information on them survives.

Californian
Californian Motor Car Company, Los Angeles, CA
Years built: 1945-46
Production: NA

The predecessor of the Davis, this three-wheel convertible utilized a 58-bhp engine that enabled it to reach 100 mph and up to 40 mpg. The prototype was built by former race driver Frank Kurtis. The Californian differed from the Davis in having separate instead of flush rear fenders and a grille

with headlights mounted behind instead of hidden lamps and no grille.

Chadwick
Chadwick Engineering Works, Pottstown, PA
Year built: 1960
Production: NA

This open car was only 87 inches long and weighed 680 pounds. A 58-inch-wheelbase tubular chasis with independent front suspension, quarter-elliptic rear leaf springs, and four-wheel hydraulic brakes was featured. The single-cylinder 13-bhp air-cooled motorcycle engine came from BMW, and was connected to a four-speed BMW transmission with enclosed chain drive.

Charles Town-About
Stinson Aircraft Tool & Engineering Corporation, San Diego, CA
Years built: 1958-1960
Production: NA

Essentially an electric conversion of a VW Karmann-Ghia with DeSoto fins and taillights grafted on, this hybrid was designed by Dr. Charles H. Graves. Top speed was 58 mph, and a 77-mile range was claimed between charges of the 48-volt electrical system. A 3.2-bhp motor was used at each rear wheel. Van-About was the name for the utility model, which had a protruding cargo box like the coupe-pickups of the 1930s.

Chicagoan
Triplex Industries Ltd., Blue Island, IL
Years built: 1952-1954
Production: 15 (est.)

This two-passenger fiberglass sports car used a six-cylinder Willys engine. The name was probably changed to Triplex around 1954.

CitiCar
Sebring Vanguard Corp., Sebring, FL
Years built: 1974-date
Production: 1000-3000 annually

One of the few American-made electrics to survive more than a handful of years, this small, two-seat runabout features an almost triangular-shape body made of Cycolac ABS plastic. Overall length is 94 inches on a 65½-inch wheelbase. Eight General Electric 6-volt batteries wired in series provide 6 net horsepower and approximately 500 miles between charges. Initial price at the factory was $2988.

Colt
Colt Manufacturing Company, Milwaukee, WI or Colt Motors Corporation, Boston, MA
Year built: 1958
Production: NA

A change in location and

manufacturer might explain the discrepancy above. The Colt was a 700-pound two-passenger economy model with fiberglass body. Its single-cylinder four-cycle engine was a 23-cid Wisconsin air-cooled unit capable of returning 60 mpg with the standard automatic transmission. The Colt had a top speed of 50 mph, and its price was $995.

Comet (i)
General Developing Company, Ridgewood, NY
Years built: c.1946-1948
Production: NA

A three-wheeler with a tubular frame and plastic body, this Comet measured only 114 inches in length. The single wheel was mounted at the front and the 4.5-bhp engine was located at the rear. Claimed fuel economy was a startling 100 mpg.

Comet (ii)
Comet Manufacturing Company, Sacramento, CA
Years built: 1951-1955
Production: NA

Micro-midget race cars were the mainstay of this company in the early '50s. In 1951, however, it advertised a special two-seat roadster, available as a kit or fully assembled. Billed as the world's lowest-priced transportation (claimed running costs were 50 cents a week), it came with a 6-horsepower engine, automatic transmission, heavy-duty brakes, and oversize balloon tires. Performance of 40 mph and 60 mpg was touted.

Continental (ii)
Continental Automobile Company, Detroit, MI
Years built: 1933-1934
Production: NA

The famous independent engine company fielded four and six-cylinder cars under its own name in 1933, based on the uninspiring body styles of DeVaux, which was out of business by then. The Fours sold for as little as $335 and used a 101.5-inch wheelbase; the Light Six and Ace Big Six had 65- and 85-bhp engines and used 107- and 114-inch wheelbases. Only the Fours were offered in 1934, the make's second and last year.

Convaircar
Consolidated-Vultee Aircraft Corporation, San Diego, CA
Years built: 1941-1948
Production: NA

This car/plane got its road power from a 26.5-horsepower Crosley engine and for flying from a 190-bhp Lycoming. The four-seat fiberglass body had a long sloping back and considerable rear overhang. The airframe, with its 34½-foot wing span, was attached to the roof at three points. The

Convaircar had made three successful trial flights before it ran out of fuel and crashed in late 1947. Development work continued, however, and by 1950 it had become the Hall Flying Auto with a price tag of $20,000.

Cord (ii)
Cord Automobile Company, Tulsa, OK
Years built: 1964-1966; 1968-1970
Production: approx. 100

This mid-'60s replicar revived one of the all-time greats, the 1936-37 Cord 810/812, and was built under the aegis of Glenn Pray. Gordon Buehrig, who designed the original, styled the replica too. It was about 80 percent of the original's size, and was thus designated the Cord 8/10. Its front-wheel drivetrain was taken from the rear-engine Corvair. In 1968, the car was taken over and redesigned by the Sports Automobile Manufacturing Company of Mannford, Oklahoma. A Ford 302 V8 became standard, a Chrysler 440-cid Magnum V8 was optional, and front drive gave way to rear drive.

Cortez
North American Motors, Dallas, TX
Years built: c.1947-c.1950
Production: NA

Though it does not appear to have reached production, this full-size car was intended for volume sale at $1000 a copy. Well-known automotive designer John Tjaarda (of Lincoln-Zephyr fame) was involved, but not much else is known about this project.

Crofton
Crofton Marine Engine Company, San Diego, CA
Years built: 1959-1961
Production: approx. 200

This Jeep-style vehicle used a Crosley engine and had a wheelbase of 63 inches and overall length of 111 inches. Base price was $1350, but a "Brawny Kit" was available for an extra $450. This consisted for a six-speed transmission, limited-slip differential, crash pan, 9.00 x 10 tires (5.30 x 12s were standard), and deluxe seats.

Cubster
Osborn Wheel Company, Doylestown, PA
Year built: 1949
Production: NA

Osborn sold a racing chassis, complete with a 6.6-horse-power engine, for $299.50, with the body needed to make a Cubster available at extra cost. This was a two-passenger roadster of modern fenderless design. A top speed of 35 mph was claimed.

Cunningham (i)
B.S. Cunningham Co., West Palm Beach, FL
Years built: 1953-1955
Production: 27 (C-3)

Wealthy sportsman Briggs Cunningham built the fastest sports machines in America from 1951 through 1955. The prototype was the 1951 C-1, a beautifully styled and finished car on a 105-inch wheelbase. The C-2R series followed, using both open and closed body styles. Both were powered by Chrysler hemi-head V8s, modified for greater performance. The C-3 of 1953-55 was a grand touring $10,000 "production" car. Cunningham raced his cars at LeMans and did well in several outings. He retired from both racing and automaking after 1955.

Cunningham (ii)
James Cunningham and Sons Company, Rochester, NY
Years built: 1930-33
Production: NA, but limited

This 100-year-old firm built some of America's most expensive luxury automobiles. Its last cars were powered by a 355-cid V8, rated at 110 bhp in 1930 and 140 bhp in 1932. The posh open and closed bodies were built mostly by Cunningham itself, which also supplied coachwork to other manufacturers. But there were few buyers in the Depression for cars priced up to $9000, and after 1933 the firm concentrated on coachbuilding.

Curtis-Wright Air-Car
Curtis-Wright Corporation, South Bend, IN
Years built: 1959-1960
Production: NA

The Air-Car had no wheels but travelled on a cushion of low-pressure, low-velocity air at a height of 6-12 inches over land, water, swamps or mud. The odd-looking four-passenger vehicle was said to have a top speed of about 60 mph. Other versions planned included an Air-Bus and Air-Car pickups and trucks.

Cushman
Cushman Motor Works, Lincoln, NE
Years built: 1945-date
Production: NA

Built by a company best known for its motor scooters and golf carts, this shopper car uses a low-power, one-cylinder air-cooled engine. Electric models have been occasionally available. The Town & Fairway model, offered around 1969, could be converted from a four-passenger minicar to a golf car or carry-all.

Custer
Custer Specialty Company, Dayton, Ohio
Years built: 1959-1960
Production: NA

Custer had built an electric car in 1898 or 1899. It again offered cars from 1920 to 1946, and made another try at the business in 1959. This effort involved a two-passenger "buckboard" vehicle, with either a Custer Special electric motor or a 6-horsepower four-cylinder gasoline engine. The electric had a top speed of 18 mph and the gas model could reach 40 mph. Custer left the automobile business permanently in 1960.

Darrin
Howard A. "Dutch" Darrin
Years built: 1946-1947
Production: 1

The noted designer of prewar custom coachwork made a bid for the volume market with an intriguing 115-inch-wheelbase convertible in 1946. One of the first cars designed expressly for fiberglass construction, it was a five-seater with an elaborate hydraulic system to power the top and front seat as well as jacking and hood-raising mechanisms. Power was from the 100-bhp 226-cid Kaiser six. Darrin had hoped to build up to 30,000 a year, but was unable to secure financial backing.

Davis
Davis Motor Co.,
Van Nuys, CA
Years built: 1947-1949
Production: 17

The Davis is perhaps the best-known postwar three-wheeler made in the U.S. It was the brainchild of Glen Gordon "Gary" Davis, who is said to have obtained his idea for a "tricycle" car from none other than Howard Hughes. A seven-passenger sedan and an 11-passenger station wagon were planned, but only a four-place, single-seat coupe was actually built. A Continental engine was used in the first few years, but most had a 113-cid 60-bhp Hercules four. But the enterprise collapsed, and Gary Davis was convicted of fraud, though he claimed innocence.

Daytona
Randall Products,
Hampton, NH
Year built: 1956
Production: NA

Priced at $495, this was the rich man's version of the Auto Cub, bigger, heavier, and more substantial. It was 72 inches long and weighed 235 pounds. A steel chassis was used for this two-passenger runabout, but body panels were made of Formica. A rear-mounted 2-horsepower Briggs & Stratton engine gave a top speed of 18 mph and fuel economy of 75 mpg.

Debonnaire
Replac Corporation,
Euclid, OH

Year built: 1955
Production: NA

Although contemporary accounts of the Debonnaire indicated it was available with top for about $1800, it is unclear whether this was a complete car or just a kit. It is clear, however, that the fiberglass body was designed for the 1941-48 Ford platform.

Delcar
American Motors Inc., Troy, NY
Years built: 1947-1949
Production: NA

Most Delcars were small delivery trucks, but at least one station wagon was built. It was a very boxy vehicle with no hood, because the four-cylinder engine was situated under the front floor. The wagon was roomy enough for six people, yet it had a short 60-inch wheelbase and 102-inch overall length.

Del Mar
Del Mar Motors, Inc.,
San Diego, CA
Year built: 1949
Production: less than 10 (est.)

Only a few prototypes for this neat-looking, early postwar subcompact were completed on wheelbases of 100-104 inches. The drivetrain comprised a 160-cid 63-bhp Continental four and Warner three-speed gearbox, said to deliver 80 mph top speed and up to 30 mpg. Ford transverse leaf springs made up the front and rear suspension, though some cars had more modern semi-elliptic rear springs. The body was a combination of aluminum, plastic, and steel, with styling not unlike that of the British Hillman introduced at about the same time. Production never materialized, but the planned 600 daily rate would have allowed prices as low as $1200.

Detroiter
Detroit Accessories Company,
St. Clair Shores, Michigan
Year built: 1953
Production: NA

This fiberglass-bodied convertible was conceived by Raymond Russell, who was also responsible for the Gadabout and Russell cars (see entries). Built on a 115-inch-wheelbase chassis (Ford or shortened Cadillac), it employed a Ford drivetrain, with a 110-bhp 239.4-cid flathead V8. Production was miniscule.

DeVaux
DeVaux-Hall Motor Corp.,
Grand Rapids, Michigan
Years built: 1931-32
Production: 4,315 (1931),
1,239 (1933)

This was a short-lived attempt at a volume model by Norman DeVaux, president of Durant of California. The initial 113-inch-

wheelbase Model 6-75 was powered by a 70-bhp, 214.7-cid Continental L-head six and was priced at $645-$885. Its 1932 successor was the slightly more expensive Model 6-80, marketed by the engine maker as the "Continental DeVaux" in 1932-33.

Devin
Devin Motors, Inc.,
El Monte, CA
Years built: 1958-64
Production: 15 (SS model)

Exotic-car dealer Bill Devin teamed with Irish engineer Malcolm MacGregor for a series of high-performance sports cars sold both as kits and fully assembled. The mold for the fiberglass body was pulled from an aluminum Scaglietti body originally used on an Ermini 1100 chassis. Devin later modified it to fit MacGregor's state-of-the-art steel-tube frame, with deDion rear suspension and all-disc brakes. A stock Corvette 283 V8 with low-profile manifold was bolted in along with Borg-Warner T-10 four-speed manual transmission. The resulting Devin SS could hit 60 mph from rest in 4.8 seconds and do 0-100 mph in 12 seconds. A similar approach was tried beginning in 1959 with power-trains from the VW Beetle (Devin D) and Chevy Corvair (Devin C) in the same body. Hundreds were sold as kits, but few were built at the factory before Devin got out of the car business completely.

Diehlmobile
H.L. Diehl Co.,
South Willington, CT
Years built: 1962-64
Production: NA

The unusual thing about this tiny three-wheeler was that it could be folded up and carried in the trunk of a normal car. With wire wheels and 3-bhp Briggs & Stratton engine, it weighed only 225 pounds. Price was $299.50.

Die Valkyrie
Brooks Stevens Design Associates, Milwaukee, WI and Spohn Carosserie, Ravensburg, West Germany
Years built: 1952
Production: 1

Commissioned by a Cleveland syndicate as a low-volume, special-order car on a contemporary Cadillac chassis, this distinctively styled coupe created some interest at the 1952 Paris Salon, but production did not materialize beyond the show prototype.

Doble
Doble Steam Motors Corp.,
Emeryville, CA
Years built: 1924-31
Production: NA

The world's most practical and

powerful steam car saw only very limited production in its last two years. The final Model F, launched in 1929, was sold through 1931 amidst corporate misfortune, and differed little from Abner Doble's initial 1924 Model E. The 125-bhp, 213-cid four-cylinder engine provided a 75-mph cruising speed and a 100-mph top speed in these luxurious cars, which sold for up to $12,000. Bodies spanned a broad array of styles and were most often supplied by Murphy. The Doble's claim to fame was its automatic boiler ignition system, which gave it the best of both steam and internal-combustion engines. But although the product had long been perfected by 1930, the company had been on the brink of bankruptcy since 1926. The Great Crash merely provided the final push into the financial abyss.

Doray
Doray, Inc., Miami Springs, FL
Year built: 1950
Production: NA

Based on the contemporary Willys Jeepster chassis, this three-seat roadster had a steel body with a Cord-like coffin-nose front made of fiberglass. The rest of the car also aped Cord 810/812 styling, especially the pontoon front fenders that left insufficient wheel turning clearance and had to be partly hinged to achieve the necessary arc. The rock-hard Jeepster suspension made for a rugged ride, and performance was mediocre with both the F-head or L-head Willys engines fitted. Whether production went beyond the prototype stage is questionable, though that seems to have been the intent.

Dow Electric
Dow Testing Laboratory, Inc.,
Detroit, Michigan
Year built: 1960
Production: none

Douglas Dow, former research chief at Detroit Edison, designed this two-passenger electric car powered by a pair of 0.3-horsepower motors driven by three 12-volt and four 24-volt batteries. Top speed was 15-20 mph; range was 30 miles between charges. Dow tried to get his 447-pound, 74-inch-long minicar into production, but couldn't find a backer willing to underwrite the cost. Had things been different, the projected price was $500-$800.

Dual-Ghia
Dual Motors Corp., Detroit, MI
Years built: 1956-63
Production: 117 (1956-58),
26 (1961-63)

Bankrolled by Eugene Casaroll, owner of a Detroit trucking firm called Automobile Ship-

pers, this Italo-American was inspired by the D Firearrow, a 1952 show styled by Chrysler design Virgil Exner and built by (in Turin. Initially priced $7650, the first produc model was similar to the sh car in appearance. Power w provided by the 315-cid Dod Red Ram V8 in 230-, 260 and 285-bhp tune teamed wi floorshift PowerFlite automati The chassis was basicall stock Dodge, modified by Ghi chief engineer Giovanni Savo nuzzi with a Hudson-like step-down floor. Delays and high build costs limited production to only 102 units, all four-seat convertibles, plus 13 proto-types. Casaroll regrouped, then introduced a successor model in August 1960. Called L6.4, this sleek, glassy semi-fastback coupe used far fewer stock Chrysler components than the earlier D-G, and sat on a purpose-designed chassis with the same 115-inch wheelbase. Overall length was up seven inches to 210. Powered by the Chrysler 325-bhp wedge-head 383, the L6.4 listed at $13,000 in Italy and $15,000 f.o.b. Detroit, which severely limited demand. Dual Motors soon collapsed, and Casaroll's death in the late '60s left a planned third-generation model stillborn.

Duesenberg (ii)
Duesenberg Corporation,
Indianapolis, IN
Year built: 1966
Production: 1

This attempt to revive the hallowed 1930s nameplate was headed by "Fritz" Duesenberg, son of the late Fred. Its design was inspired by Virgil Exner's ideas on how several great classics might have looked had their makers not gone out of business. Plans envisioned a massive brougham sedan with center-opening doors and a combination of modern and traditional styling elements, plus every conceivable luxury as standard equipment. The one prototype shown was built by Ghia on a 137.5-inch wheelbase and stretched out to 245 inches overall. Under the long hood was a Chrysler 440 V8, sufficient to propel the 5700-pound curb weight. A limousine and convertible sedan were planned also. Price was announced at $19,500, but financial backing evaporated.

Duesenberg (iii)
Duesenberg Company,
Gardena and Inglewood, CA
Years built: 1970-75
Production: NA

Yet another revival effort, this time a $24,500 replica of the original two-seat SSJ roadster. Wheelbase was 128 inches,

665

overall length 116.5 inches, weight 3600 pounds. A supercharged Chrysler 383 V8 said to develop 500 bhp was fitted along with automatic transmission, though a four-speed gearbox was optional, as was air conditioning. In 1974, the company moved to Inglewood, raised price to $41,500, and substituted a detoxed, normally aspirated 440 V8 with 215 net bhp.

Duesenberg (iv)
Duesenberg Brothers Company, Mundelein and Evanston, IL
Year built: 1979
Production: 1

A much less ambitious revival attempt than Duesenberg (ii), this effort was headed by Harlan and Kenneth Duesenberg, nephews of the famous brothers, and Robert Peterson of the Lehmann-Peterson coachworks in Chicago. Again the idea was a modern Duesenberg with classic styling "cues" and sybaritic luxury, but the one prototype built was little more than an ineptly disguised Cadillac Fleetwood Brougham, with the same 133-inch wheelbase and 195-bhp (net) fuel-injected 425 V8. Price was pegged at an astronomical $100,000. Lack of funds precluded development.

duPont
duPont Motors, Inc., Moore, PA
Years built: 1930-32
Production: less than 100

Doomed to extinction by the Depression, the cars built by the firm founded by E. Paul duPont were among America's finest expressions of luxury in the 1920s. The main 1930 offering was the 144-inch-wheelbase Model G, powered by a 140-bhp Continental side-valve straight eight and clothed in bodywork by Merrimac (a few Waterhouse and Derham bodies were also mounted on this chassis). Also in 1930, duPont sold a score of Model Es, which had a smaller supercharged engine. The mammoth 146-inch-wheelbase Model G followed in 1931, but only three were built, and duPont elected to give up on the car business shortly after that rather than try to survive on inferior products.

Durant
Durant Motors of America, Detroit, Michigan
Years built: 1930-32
Production: 21,440 (1930), 7,229 (1931), 1,135 (1932)

William Crapo Durant, the brash and daring founder of General Motors, was shunted out of that firm in the late Teens, so he decided to build a rival empire. Established in 1921, Durant Motors produced a legion of makes, but only the Durant itself survived past 1930. That year's line consisted of six models on a 112-inch wheelbase, with undistinguished styling, a 58-70-bhp Continental six, and mechanical brakes. The 1931 lineup shrank to four models selling at $695-$775. Sales dried up to a trickle for 1932, when the Models 621 and 622 were offered with a 71-bhp Continental engine at a starting price of $700. The company closed its American operations in early 1932, though its Canadian branch sold cars under the Frontenac name through 1933.

Edwards
Edwards Engineering Co., South San Francisco, CA
Years built: 1953-55
Production: 6

Though wealthy industrialist Sterling H. Edwards had built a couple of race-and-ride sports cars as early as 1949, his first "production" model didn't appear until late 1953. Called the America, it was a good-looking, slab-sided convertible with a large, rectangular eggcrate grille and built on a Mercury station wagon chassis. One car ran a 303.7-cid Olds V8, two had 205-bhp Lincoln units, and the remaining three carried 210-bhp Cadillac V8s. Volume production was never in the cards, mainly due to high prices ($7800 by 1955) and factory setup costs that were beyond Edwards' means.

Elcar
Elcar Motor Company, Elkhart, IN
Years built: 1930-31
Production: NA

Though this well-established automaker was on the ropes by 1930, its lineup that year consisted of no fewer than 32 models in four series with three engines and three chassis. The least expensive was the 117-inch-wheelbase Model 75, powered by a 61-bhp Lycoming six. The Model 95 and 96 shared a 90-bhp Lycoming eight and a 123-inch wheelbase. Top of the line was the 130-inch-wheelbase Model 130, priced up to $2500 and mounting a 140-bhp Lycoming straight eight, the industry's third most powerful engine at the time. The 95 was dropped for 1931, but the even more luxurious Model 140 appeared on a 135-inch wheelbase. These Elcars were finely proportioned, fleet, and appealing, but they were doomed to extinction by the Depression. The firm spent its last days trying to revive the legendary Mercer before going out of business in 1932.

Electra
Die Mesh Corp., Pelham, NY
Years built: 1974-76
Production: NA

The Electra was essentially a Fiat 850 Sport Spyder converted to electric operation via triple motors producing a total of 10 horsepower. Range between charges was limited to only about 40 miles, a major drawback, and the heavy batteries increased weight from about 1620 pounds for the rear-engine Fiat to over 3000 pounds.

Electra King
B & Z Electric Car Co., Long Beach, CA
Years built: 1961-c. 1981
Production: NA

A tall two-passenger car only 88 inches long, this electric was available with either three or four wheels (with the single wheel in front on the tricycle model). Body and removeable top were made of fiberglass, resulting in an all-up weight of only 675 pounds. A variety of power packs were offered over the years, usually five 6-volt batteries in series, but some examples had 24-, 30-, and 36-volt systems. A choice of four motors producing 1 to 3.5 horsepower was available in the 1970s, with performance and range depending on the motor/battery pack combination. Speeds ran from 16 to 29 mph maximum; range was 18-36 miles.

Electricar
Boulevard Machine Works, North Hollywood, CA
Years built: 1950-c. 1966
Production: NA

This small electric was offered in three versions, all open runabouts. The two-seat Boulevard was 106 inches long and had four 1/6-horsepower electric motors, one to drive each wheel. The single-seat Cutie had two such motors, one in front and one in back, and a 25-mph top speed. The Cutie Junior had just one motor, and could reach only 10 mph. How long production continued is uncertain.

Electric Shopper
Electric Car Co., Long Beach, CA
Years built: 1956-?
Production: NA

The lifespan of this battery-powered shopping car is open to question. One source says it's 1960-73, another 1956-62. However, all seem to agree that this was a fiberglass three-wheeler, 86 inches long on a 61-inch wheelbase and priced at $945. A metal-body model was also sold at about $750. Power was supplied by a 1.5-bhp 24-volt DC series-wound motor. Top speed was

18 mph and range was only 30-35 miles between charges.

Electrobile
Manufacturer unknown
Year built: 1951
Production: NA, but doubtful

A three-wheel, fiberglass-body runabout, this 300-pound electric was the brainchild of two enterprising Chicagoans. A high-speed DC motor and built-in charger were included in the proposed $350 selling price, and a range of 25-35 miles between recharges was expected. The body was made up of several molded sections over an aluminum framework. Only sketches of this car were shown, and it's doubtful even a prototype was built.

Electro Master
Nepa Manufacturing Co., Pasadena, CA
Years built: 1962-?
Production: NA

This 680-pound electric shopping car had a fiberglass body and a 2-horsepower motor connected to six 6-volt batteries. Top speed was 20 mph, range 40 miles. Production reportedly ended in 1964, but may have continued longer.

Electronic
Electronic Motor Car Corp., Salt Lake City, UT
Year built: 1955
Production: NA

Sedan, station wagon, panel truck, and sports car body styles were proposed for this 110-inch-wheelbase hybrid-power model. A gasoline or diesel engine charged an 80-cell battery pack connected to a "Dual-Torque" electric motor located within the rear axle housing. An "Electro-Magnetic Differential" was also provided, an electric device that was supposed to have some limited-slip effect. Only a prototype was built. Production was planned for either Detroit or Oxford, Michigan, but never materialized.

El Morocco
Rueben Allenden, Detroit, MI
Years built: 1956-57
Production: approx. 30

An attempt to make a 1956-57 Chevy look more like a Cadillac Eldorado, this styling conversion consisted of alterations to grille, bumpers, side trim, and fins. Available on convertible and two- and four-door hardtop body styles, the conversion didn't add that much to the standard Chevy price despite the considerable work involved.

Erskine
Studebaker Corporation, South Bend, IN
Year built: 1930
Production: 22,371

Named for company president Albert R. Erskine, Stude-

baker's first try at a companion make expired after 1930. Originally conceived for the European market, this pretty little six-cylinder car was launched in 1927 as a sort of Studebaker reply to Hudson's Essex, but inept development and prices high for the class conspired to limit sales. The final 1930 Model 53 was offered in nine variations, all powered by a 205.3-cid L-head six with 70 bhp and an unfashionably long stroke.

Fergus
Fergus Motors, Inc., New York, NY
Year built: 1949
Production: NA

The second attempt by this firm to become an automaker in its own right (the first came in 1915-22) was essentially an Austin A40 with a restyled body patterned after that of the relatively uncommon Austin A40 Sports. Development did not proceed beyond the prototype stage.

Ferrer
Ferrer Motors Corp., Miami, FL
Year built: 1966
Production: NA

Similar in appearance to Ford's GT endurance racers of the mid-'60s, the Ferrer GT consisted of a sleek, steel-reinforced fiberglass body and Volkswagen Beetle chassis and running gear. Overall length was 158 inches, width 60 inches, height 42 inches. Sold as a basic or deluxe kit at $990 and $1750, respectively, it was also offered fully assembled at $2950 with 50-bhp engine, or at $3800 with a reworked 70-bhp version of the VW flat four. The standard model was claimed to cruise at its 90-mph top speed, reach 60 mph from rest in 12.5 seconds, and return 29 mpg at a steady 68 mph.

Fibersport
Fibersport, Inc., Bloomington, IL
Years built: 1953-54
Production: NA

A fiberglass sports roadster based on the Crosley Hot Shot platform (see Crosley), this was another kit car that was also sold fully assembled ($2850 versus $650-$750). The claimed 100-mph top speed seems reasonable in view of the light 1150-pound curb weight. Crosley's demise forced the firm to design its own new tubular frame and adopt Morris Minor gearboxes. Unlike most of this ilk, these were well-engineered, smooth-looking cars—and desirable today, if you can find one.

Fina
Fina, Inc., New York, NY
Years built: 1953-c. 1955
Production: NA

Based on a 115-inch-wheelbase Ford chassis, the Fina Sport was backed by European car dealer and connoisseur Perry Fina. Convertible or hardtop bodies were offered, built by Vignale of Italy and measuring 188 inches long. Though almost any Detroit V8 could be ordered, the standard engine was the 210-bhp Cadillac unit; a 300-bhp version was available at extra cost. GM's Dual-Range Hydra-Matic was the only transmission fitted. Prices ran around $10,000.

Fitch (i)
Sports and Utility Motors, Inc.
White Plains, NY
Year built: 1949
Production: NA

Named for its originator, race driver John Fitch, this was a race-and-ride sports car with the emphasis on racing. Only one prototype, designated Type A, was built. A proposed Type B model used the 96-inch-wheelbase Fiat 1100 chassis mounting a souped-version of the flathead Ford V8/60 with 105 bhp and wrapped up in a modified Crosley Hot Shot body. Dry weight was estimated at only 1250 pounds, and predicted top speed was 120 mph.

Fitch (ii)
John Fitch and Co., Inc.
Falls Village, CT
Years built: 1961-69
Production: NA

John Fitch's second manufacturing venture initially involved performance, handling, and appearance modifications for the contemporary Chevrolet Corvair (see entry). Marketed as the Fitch GT, they could be made to an existing car or to a brand-new one ordered through Fitch, and were offered as separate packages. For example, there was a $29 engine kit that raised output to 155 bhp, good for 9.5-second 0-60 mph acceleration. The appearance package for 1965 and later Corvairs included add-on "flying buttresses" for the roof. The more amibitious Fitch Phoenix, shown in 1966, was a 2150-pound targa-top two-seater based on Corvair running gear. Illustrator Coby Whitmore helped style the long-nose body (which had twin sidemount spares), built by Intermeccanica in Italy. A modified 170-bhp Corvair engine produced a 0-60 mph time of 7.5 seconds and a top speed of 130 mph. A planned 500-unit run never materialized owing to the expense of meeting federal safety standards, and the only Phoenix built was the prototype.

Fletcher
Fletcher Aviation Corp.,
Rosemead, CA
Year built: 1954
Production: NA

A four-wheel-drive Jeep-type vehicle, the Fletcher Flair had an unlikely powerplant: a 1500cc Porsche flat four. Wheelbase was 78 inches and overall length was 115-126 inches.

Flintridge-Darrin
Flintridge Motor Manufacturing Corp.,
Los Angeles, CA
Year built: 1957
Production: 15 (est.)

A contemporary German DKW sedan with a low-slung roadster body, this hybrid is sometimes known as the Flintridge, Darrin-DKW, or Flintridge-DKW. Howard "Dutch" Darrin of Kaiser-Frazer fame did the styling, marked by a concave rear deck with scalloped trailing edge. The fiberglass body, supplied by Woodill (see entry), was 10 inches longer and 6.5 inches lower than the sedan body. Price for the 1870-pound sports tourer was $3195, compared to $2275 for the DKW. Problems at Woodill and with the unusual two-stroke engine limited both sales appeal and production.

Ford 1901
Horseless Carriage Corp.,
Ft. Lauderdale, FL
Year built: 1968
Production: NA, but limited

This new/old "antique" was billed as a "¾-scale replica of the 1901 Ford," though Henry's first production car, the Model A, wasn't built until 1903. Specifications have been lost to historians, but production lasted only a few months.

France Jet
France Jet Motors, Ltd.,
New York, NY
Year built: 1961
Production: NA, but limited

Fuel economy of 65 mpg was claimed for this $1595 fiberglass-body two-seater, powered by a 17-cid four-cycle one-cylinder engine. An optional 66-cid 40-bhp twin was available for hot rodders at $250 extra.

Frazen
Ray Green Company,
Toledo, OH
Years built: 1951-62
Production: NA, but limited

This fiberglass sports roadster was supposedly available in the early '60s, though its Henry J chassis and running gear were long gone by then. It's possible some cars were assembled up to that point, as they sold in tiny numbers. The Frazen was offered in both kit form and fully assembled. All examples appear to have had the 161-cid Henry J flathead

six, not the four. The fully assembled price in 1952 was $2795, fairly heady territory for this odd-looking car.

Frick
Bill Frick Motors,
Rockville Centre, NY
Year built: 1955
Production: NA

Engine-swap expert Frick tried to become an automaker with this Ferrari-like coupe, bodied by Vignale of Italy and based on Cadillac running gear. The 110-inch-wheelbase chassis was Frick's own box-channel design, with conventional independent front suspension and live-axle/leaf-spring rear suspension. All-up weight was 3000 pounds. Production beyond a single prototype is unlikely.

Gadabout
Ray Russell,
Grosse Pointe, MI
Year built: 1945
Production: none

Literally a home workshop project for industrial designer Russell, this 80-inch-wheelbase three-seat roadster mounted a flush-fender body made of duraluminum over an MG chassis and running gear. An unobtrusive steel perimeter tube at bumper height provided crash protection, and the 1100-pound weight contributed to claimed 50-mpg fuel economy, though top speed was only about 50 mph. Had Russell found a backer, production models were to have been offered with both front and rear engine placement at the customer's option.

Gardner
Gardner Motor Car Company,
St. Louis, MO
Years built: 1930-31
Production: NA

Established by Russell E. Gardner, this firm had been building four-cylinder cars since 1916. Like so many other automakers, however, it would not survive the Depression. The 1930 Models 136 and 140 used a 70-bhp six and 90-bhp eight, respectively, while the 150 had a 126-bhp eight. All engines were supplied by Lycoming, and all the last Gardners had hydraulic brakes. A desperation move to save the flagging company was the Gardner Front-Drive, appearing in early 1930 and accurately billed as "the only front-drive car in the $2000 field." Riding low on a 133-inch wheelbase, it bore clean, classic lines, but had to get around with only an 80-bhp Lycoming six. It didn't catch on. After a weak sales effort in 1931, the firm tried making hearses and ambulances, then went bankrupt the following year.

Gaslight
Gaslight Motors Corp.,
Detroit, MI
Years built: 1960-61
Production: NA

Priced at $1495, this 640-pound replica of the 1902 Rambler was built on a 77-inch wheelbase and carried a 4-bhp air-cooled single-cylinder engine. It may have been a continuation of the Rambler 1902 Replica.

Gaylord
Gaylord Cars Ltd.,
Chicago, IL
Years built: 1955-57
Production: 3

Named for brothers Edward and Jim Gaylord, this exclusive luxury two-seater was a retractable hardtop convertible styled by Brooks Stevens and executed by the Spohn coachworks in Ravensburg, West Germany. The purpose-built chassis employed conventional suspension heavily isolated in rubber and a Chrysler hemi-head V8. Though it weighed almost two tons, the Gaylord was quick, with an easy 120-mph top end and 0-60 mph acceleration averaging 8 seconds. Stevens' ingenious retractable top mechanism was much simpler than that of the later Ford Skyliner, and his styling was bold and unmistakable. The target production price was $17,500, but perfectionist Jim Gaylord drove himself to a nervous breakdown during the engineering phase and the company got into a dispute over quality with the body contractor. The project was abandoned after only three production chassis were completed.

Glassic
Glassic Industries, Inc. (1966-72) and Glassic Motor Car Company (1972-75),
West Palm Beach, FL
Years built: 1966-72
Production: NA

Founded by Jack Faircloth and his son Joel, this firm specialized in Model A Ford-style fiberglass bodywork for the humble International Scout chassis and running gear. Sold only in fully assembled form, the Glassic listed initially at $3800, rising to some $10,000 by 1972 (a special 1967 version was retailed by Abercrombie & Fitch at $5200). Fred Pro bought the business, changed its name, moved to larger facilities, and switched from the Scout's 94-bhp four to a 210-bhp Ford 302 V8. Sometime in 1976-77, the firm again changed hands, and continued operations under the name Replicar.

Glasspar
Glasspar, Inc.,
Santa Ana, CA

Years built: 1950-54
Production: 200 (est.)

The company set up by Bill Tritt to produce fiberglass boat hulls was also a pioneer in automotive applications for fiberglass. Though most of Tritt's sleek two-seat roadsters were sold as body kits for popular production chassis, a few were sold fully assembled for $3000 and up through 1954, when Glasspar concentrated on kits only. The best-known of these was the G-2, initially fitted with Ford and Mercury flathead V8s, ohv units from the same company on later examples. Wheelbase was usually 100 inches. The production estimate seems high for assembled cars only; it may include some kits also.

Goff
Charles Goff,
Texarkana, TX
Year built: 1956
Production: NA

Offered as a $600 kit or a $1500 fully built car, this five-passenger sports model was conceived around the 1939 Ford chassis and running gear, though other engines could be installed at extra charge. The fiberglass body was made up of five separate pieces, and a matching top was available at extra cost. Production was only a handful at most.

Gordon
H. Gordon Hansen,
San Lorenzo, CA
Years built: c.1947-48
Production: NA

This one-off powered by a 100-bhp Ford truck engine was called the "Diamond" because of its unusual wheel placement: a diamond pattern with one wheel in front, one in back, and one on either side. The end wheels stood 156 inches apart, with the side wheels halfway between. Construction envisioned a tubular steel cage for rollover protection. The 95-mph top speed was good for a 3750-pound car—and undoubtedly exciting on bumpier roads.

Griffith
Griffith Motors,
Syoset, NY and Griffith Motor Car Co.,
Plainview, NY
Years built: 1964-66
Production: 285

A true hybrid, Jack Griffith's closed sports car was built around his own tubular chassis design fitted with a Ford 289 V8 and topped by a modified fiberglass body from the British TVR. Dubbed Series 200, this car could fly from 0 to 60 mph in less than four seconds. The 138-inch-long two-seater sold initially at $3995, later raised to at least

$4800. After TVR body supplies were cut off, the firm acquired manufacturing rights to the Vetta Ventura (see entry and Apollo), and introduced a new, sleeker GT model, with body by Intermeccanica of Italy and power by Plymouth's hot 235-bhp 273 V8. A four-speed manual gearbox was an optional alternative to standard TorqueFlite automatic. Base price was $6095. With further engine swaps, this car was continued after 1966 as the Omega (see entry) and, later, as the Intermeccanica.

Henney
Henney Motor Co.,
Canastota, NY
Years built: 1960-c. 1964
Production: 100 maximum

This electric conversion of the French-built Renault Dauphine was the brainchild of C. Russell Feldman, board chairman and president of National Union Electric Corporation, which had acquired the famous Henney coachworks and also made Exide batteries. Outfitted with 12 6-volt batteries and a 7-bhp motor, the aptly named Henney Kilowatt could run up to 40 mph, though 30 mph was recommended to extend charge intervals to 40 miles. Curb weight was 2250 pounds, some 750 pounds heavier than the Dauphine. Though Henney ordered 100 Renault bodies, it sold only 47 Kilowatts through the end of 1961.

Honey Bee
Swift Manufacturing Company, El Cajon, CA
Year built: 1959
Production: NA

Priced at $195 and advertised as "designed for kids between 7 and 77," this tiny, fiberglass-body open three-wheeler had a teardrop shape and a low, rounded nose. The solo wheel was up front, and a four-cycle Briggs & Stratton 1.5-bhp engine was at the rear. This company also made several mini-replicars under the name Swift (see entry).

Hoppenstand
Hoppenstand Motors, Inc.,
Greenville, PA
Years built: 1948-49
Production: NA

The Hoppenstand was a rather odd-looking two-passenger open economy model powered by an 8.5-bhp, 21.4-cid air-cooled flat twin, which was mounted at the rear of a 90-inch-wheelbase chassis. The aluminum body measured 162 inches long overall and kept weight to just 684 pounds. All-independent suspension and standard automatic torque converter were included in the $1000 base price. Top speed was 50 mph.

Fuel consumption was said to be about 35 mpg.

Hydramotive
Hydramotive Corp.,
Charlotte, NC
Year built: c.1960
Production: 1

Designed by Durward Willis, this small diesel-engine car was unusual in having no transmission, universal joints, driveshaft, differential, axles, or brakes. It was also the crux of a 1961 stock fraud investigation by the Securities and Exchange Commission, which turned up a prototype in the process. The intended selling price was $1200.

Imp
International Motor Products,
Glendale, CA
Years built: 1949-51
Production: NA

Several ideas for a midget convertible were tried by this firm over a four year span. The original 1949 prototype had a rear-mounted 7.5-bhp Gladden 75 engine and a doorless, fiberglass-laminate body on a 63-inch wheelbase. Weighing just 475 pounds and only 120 inches long, it was capable of 35 mph and could go 180-240 miles on a 3-gallon tank of gas. A 1951 experiment was only 108 inches long. Though priced at a low $500, the Imp disappeared after seeing limited production in 1950.

Jetmobile
Richard Harp, Frederick, MD
Year built: 1952
Production: NA

This eye-catching three-wheel open car was a missle-shaped single-seater made out of an aircraft fuel tank. The odd wheel was at the front and the engine was at the rear, originally a 75-bhp Lycoming unit, later a 60-bhp Ford flathead V8. The builder had plans to add folding rotors to turn this into a car/plane, but that idea—and the entire project—never got off the ground.

Jomar
Saidell Sports Racing Cars,
Manchester, NH
Years built: c.1954-60
Production: NA

The outcome of an effort headed by racing enthusiast Ray Saidell, this was basically the British-made TVR chassis mated to a specially designed aluminum body instead of the original fiberglass one. The standard engine was the 71.5-cid British Ford Anglia four, and various optional alternatives were envisioned, including a supercharged version and at least three Coventry-Climax units. Prices ranged from $2995 to $4595 depending on engine.

Jordan
Jordan Motor Car Company,
Inc., Cleveland, OH
Years built: 1930-31
Production: 2,851

The make named for Edward S. "Ned" Jordan went out in style in the early 1930s after pioneering the romantic approach to auto advertising in the '20s ("somewhere west of Laramie"). The 1930 range consisted of the 120-inch-wheelbase Great Line 80 and 125-inch-wheelbase Great Line 90, powered by 80-85-bhp straight eights and offered in a wide array of body styles starting at $1495 and $2295, respectively. Series 90 roadsters and touring cars rode a special 131-inch-wheelbase chassis shared with a seven-seat limousine and sedan. These models were repeated for 1931, when Jordan introduced its greatest triumph, the Model Z Speedway. Magnificent in every way, it rode a 145-inch wheelbase chassis mounting a 125-bhp 318-cid Continental straight eight, and boasted aircraft-type instrumentation. Custom-built Coburn aluminum bodywork was a feature of the Sportsman sedan and Ace roadster, both capable of an easy 100 mph and selling at $5500 a copy.

Keen Steamliner
Charles F. Keen,
Madison, WI and Thermal Kinetics Corp., Rochester, NY
Years built: c.1955-c.1968
Production: NA

The original Keen Steamliner was a shortened, vintage 1946-48 Plymouth converted to steam power. Sometime between 1955 and 1968, designer Keen produced a second car, a modern fiberglass-bodied convertible based on the Victress shell also used for the Williams steamer (see entry), which had a front engine and rear boiler, just the reverse of the Keen. Conflicting reports mentioned top speeds of 60 and 100 mph for the Keen, which used a V4 engine of unknown origin that reportedly operated on any distillate fuel such as kerosene. Thermal Kinetics acquired Keen's interests by 1968, but likely did not produce any additional cars. Series production of the earlier models is doubtful.

Keller
Keller Motors Corp.,
Huntsville, AL
Years built: 1948-50
Production: 18 (est.)

Headed by George D. Keller, this firm was an outgrowth of the Bobbi Motor Car Corporation. Its renamed product was a slightly longer and more powerful version of the Bobbi-

Kar, with the same front-end styling, "Torsilastic" suspension, and wagon and convertible body styles in two series. Chief models were powered by a 47-bhp 133-cid Hercules engine; the costlier Super Chief had a 162-cid, 58-bhp Continental unit. The 2400-pound three-seat convertible was available either front- or rear-engined; the two-door wagon weighed 300 pounds less. Prices started at $895. The company claimed to have an 1150-strong dealer network in 1948, and annual production volume was supposed to reach 150,000, almost as high as Mercury's at the time. But all this was mostly wishful thinking, and the firm went bankrupt in early 1950.

King Midget
Midget Motors Supply Co. and Midget Motors Corp.,
Athens, OH
Years built: 1946-c. 1969
Production: approx. 5000

Developed by Claud Dry and Dale Orcutt, this tiny buckboard-type vehicle was first available only as a kit, but was also sold fully assembled from about 1949 on. A more car-like replacement arrived in 1951 and lasted through 1957, when an even more conventional-looking third-generation design appeared. Engines, all rear-mounted, comprised 7.3-8.5-bhp single-cylinder Wisconsin units through 1966, after which 9.3-12-bhp Kohler engines were used. Fuel economy of up to 60 mpg was the King Midget's strongest selling point over the years. Overall length grew from the initial 96 inches to 117 inches, but all models rode a 76.5-inch wheelbase. Weight also went up over time, from 400 to 700 pounds, and prices kept pace, running from a low of near $350 to over $1000 in later years.

Kissel
Kissel Motor Company,
Hartford, WI
Year built: 1930
Production: 93

The year 1930 saw the last of these finely crafted, almost custom-built machines, and the firm that considered 2500 units good annual production even in its heyday. Even so, the last Kissels were as pleasing as their forebears. The lineup began with the 117-inch-wheelbase Model 6-73, powered by a 70-bhp six. Next came the 125-inch-wheelbase Model 95 with 246 cid and 95 bhp. The 8-126 White Eagle, long a certified Classic, offered a 126-bhp, 298-cid eight and wheelbases of up to 139 inches at prices well above $3000. There was also a sports roadster with the

romantic Gold Bug name. After token output, the company reorganized in 1931 as Kissel Industries, and went on to the more profitable business of producing outboard motors.

Krim-Ghia
Krim Car Import Co.,
Detroit, MI and Carrozzeria Ghia, Turin, Italy
Year built: 1966
Production: NA, but limited

Two different models appeared under this badge, both with bodywork supplied by the famous Italian design house named in it. The 1500 GT was a sports coupe powered by an 86-bhp Fiat four-cylinder engine. The second, better known offering was a roadster on the Plymouth Barracuda chassis and using its 245-bhp V8. Both models were in production only a few months.

Kurtis
Kurtis-Craft, Glendale, CA
Years built: 1948-1949
Production: under 50

Racing-car builder Frank Kurtis designed this postwar sports car, using mostly stock production car pieces. The Kurtis was 169 inches long and weighed only 2300 pounds. Into this light body, Kurtis installed a supercharged Studebaker Champion engine. The small L-head wasn't quick enough, so future cars were fitted with either Ford flathead V8s or 160-bhp Cadillac V8s. Only a handful of cars were built before Kurtis sold out to Earl "Madman" Muntz for $200,000. In later years, Kurtis concentrated on all-out competition machines.

LaFayette
Nash Motors, Kenosha, WI
Years built: 1934-36
Production: 5,000 (1934), 9,400 (1935), 27,860 (1936)

Nash's lower-priced "junior" make was planned during the depths of the Depression, but arrived just as the economy was beginning to recover. It was thus ill-timed and not a big success. Unlike their luxurious V8-powered forbears of the 1920s, these cars were built down to a price, which ranged from $585 to $715, and bore very ordinary styling on a 113-inch wheelbase, used in all three years. The only powerplant available was the 217.8-cid six from the company's low-end 1930-33 offerings and rated at 75-83 bhp. LaFayette became the lowest-priced Nash series for 1937, and continued as such through model year 1940.

La Saetta
Testaguzza Brothers,
Detroit, MI
Year built: 1955
Production: aprox. 15

These fiberglass-bodied two-

passenger roadsters used several different engines (primarily Olds 88 and Hudson) and no two were alike. Wheelbase was around 110 inches; overall length ranged from 200 to 210 inches. Late in 1955 a linkup was formed with Electronic Motor Corporation of Salt Lake City. The result was a turbo-electric called Electronic.

Lawler
James H. Lawler,
Huntington Park, CA
Years built: 1948-1950
Production: NA

A steam-powered conversion of a 1938 Terraplane. There is some indication he carried out similar conversions of other cars at nearby South Gate. Whatever base was used, all conversions were dubbed Lawler Steamobile.

MK III
Auto Craft Northwest,
Portland, OR
Year built: 1968
Production: NA

The mid-engined model of this car used either a 327 or 427-cubic-inch Chevrolet V8 engine. The rear-engine version used the 164-cid Corvair flat six. The MK III was offered as a limited-production sports car built to owner specifications. It was also available in kit form.

Marketour
Marketour Electric Cars,
Long Beach, CA
Year built: 1964
Production: NA

This was a two-passenger, three-wheel electric with the single wheel at the front. Six heavy-duty batteries provided power for its 36-volt motor. The car had four forward speeds and one reverse. Operating range was 35-40 miles on a single charge. This boxy vehicle had a steel body with a removable leatherette-covered top. A ¼-ton pickup model was also built.

Markette
Westinghouse Electric Corp.
Years built: 1967-1968
Production: 1

This boxy electric was 116-inches long and had a 45-horsepower motor. Twelve 6-volt batteries accounted for about half the 1730-pound curb weight. Although this was a prototype, production cars were planned to sell for under $2000. Production did not get under way, probably due to lack of buyer interest.

Marquis
Plasticar, Doylestown, PA
Year built: 1954
Production: NA

The chassis of this two-door fastback sports coupe was a Renault, presumably the 4CV

model. Marquis was to be a rather luxurious small car with a proposed selling price of $3100. The prototype's body was made of aluminum, but production models were to be of "plastic," perhaps fiberglass.

Marquette
Buick Motor Division,
General Motors Corp.,
Flint, MI
Year built: 1930
Production: 35,007

Except for Pontiac, all of GM's "companion" makes launched in the '20s would ultimately fail to endure. Buick's junior edition was no exception, introduced in 1929 and discontinued after only about a year. The 1930 lineup comprised six body styles on a 114-inch wheelbase, with prices running around $1000. All were powered by a 213-cid enlargement of the contemporary Oldsmobile L-head six, rated at 67.5 bhp.

Mars II
Electric Fuel Propulsion Inc.,
Ferndale, MI
Years built: 1966-c.1970
Production: NA

This was an electric car based on the Renault 10 body. Power was provided by four 3-volt battery packs, each consisting of five lead-cobalt batteries. The battery packs alone weighed 1900 pounds, accounting for almost half the car's 4160-pound weight. Five-year or 50,000-mile battery life was claimed. This electric had a top speed of 68 mph, and took just 12 seconds to accelerate from 0 to 40 mph.

Martinette
Martin Development
Laboratories,
Rochelle Park, NY
Year built: 1954
Production: NA

James Vernon Martin, an innovative designer, sketched out a three-wheeler in 1932. After many experiments, false-starts, and revisions, a prototype was completed in 1948. By 1954, Martin's company had been reorganized as the Commonwealth Research Corporation of New York City. Under Commonwealth's auspices, a few cars were built. Like the prototype, they were two- or three-passenger cars of teardrop shape, all three-wheelers with the single wheel at the rear. The rear-mounted engine was a 24-horsepower Hercules. An unknown number were sold for $1000 each. One was a panel delivery produced in 1955 and based on Martin's design. The designer sold his business to Bassons Industries Corp., sometime around 1955 or 1956 and his car was renamed the Bassons Star (see entry).

Maverick
Maverick Motors,
Mountain View, CA
Years built: 1953-1955
Production: approx. 7

For a three-passenger car, the Maverick was quite large. Mounted on a Cadillac chassis, it had a wheelbase of 122 to 128 inches, and its length was 16 feet. The sleek fiberglass body was available with one, two or three doors. A Cadillac engine with Borg-Warner overdrive was used.

Mighty Mite
Mid-America Research
Corporation, Wheatland, PA
Year built: 1953
Production: NA

This full-time four-wheel-drive vehicle was designed by Ben F. Gregory. A Jeep-like machine, it could be fitted with a wide range of body styles. The prototype's air-cooled Porsche engine was to be replaced in production versions by a modified Lycoming 65-horsepower aircraft engine.

Minicar
Minicars, Inc., Goleta, CA
Year built: 1969
Production: 1

This small three-passenger machine was designed with big car features like automatic transmission and air conditioning. Overall length was a modest 108 inches and a Corvair six-cylinder engine was used. The anticipated price of $2500 was based on production volume of 25,000 units annually, but it's doubtful the project ever went beyond the 1969 prototype.

Mohs
Bruce Baldwin Mohs,
Madison, WI
Years built: 1967-1978
Production: NA

The first Mohs car was not built until 1967, though the company dates to 1948. The monstrous Ostentatienne Opera Coupe tipped the scales at 5740 pounds, and measured 246 inches long. Wheelbase was only 119 inches. International Harvester supplied the chassis to Mohs specifications, as well as a 304-cubic-inch V8 with 193 horsepower. A 549-cid V8 was optional. Equipment included a water-cooled automatic transmission, removable skylight, butane furnace-heater, 24-karat gold inlaid walnut-covered instrument panel, ¾-inch Ming Dynasty-style carpeting and velvet upholstery. All this cost $19,600 in the late '60s, with the 549 V8 priced at $25,600. Demand for such an expensive, unorthodox car was limited and production ran to three or four cars a year.

Mota
Banning Electric Products
Corp., New York City, NY
Year built: 1953
Production: NA

This gas-electric hybrid had a fiberglass body. No other information is available.

Multiplex
Multiplex Manufacturing Co.,
Berwick, PA
Years built: 1952-1954
Production: 3

From 1912 to 1915, this firm built a very good car, but production was limited to scarcely more than a dozen units. The postwar Multiplex was a two-passenger sports car made from proprietary components. Willys F-head four- and six-cylinder engines were used, modified to develop 87 and 124 horsepower, respectively. The car's frame was a tubular truss-type.

Muntz
The Muntz Car Company,
Evanston, IL
Years built: 1949-1954
Production: 394

Earl "Madman" Muntz had been a promoter since the age of 12, when he bought old Model T's, fixed them up, and sold them at a profit. He opened a used-car lot in his hometown of Elgin, Illinois in the early '30s. Later he began selling car radios. When Frank Kurtis decided to quit the auto business, the Madman bought him out. The Muntz Car Company built 28 Muntz Jets in Glendale before moving to Evanston, Illinois. There another 366 Jets were built. Muntz switched body construction from aluminum to steel, which was not only more durable but cheaper. The Jet sold for $5000-6000. Early cars used a Cadillac V8 and Lincoln motors were installed later. According to Muntz, a Jet would do 128 mph.

Mustang (ii)
Mustang Engineering Corp.,
Seattle, WA
Year built: 1948
Production: NA

The Mustang was designed by Roy C. McCarty, formerly service manager of the Ford Motor Company's Lincoln-Mercury Division. The Mustang had room for six people, two in the front and four in the back. A tubular-steel frame was used and the body was aluminum. The 59-horsepower rear-mounted Hercules four was accessible by a door on the left side. It was expected that this unusual car would sell for $1235, but volume production was not achieved.

Nash-Healey
Nash-Kelvinator Corporation,
Kenosha, WI
Years built: 1950-1955
Production: 512

George Mason, president of Nash-Kelvinator, met English rally driver and car designer Donald Healey in 1949. Soon, an idea hatched: why not build a Nash-based two-seater, powered by the big 235 cubic-inch Nash six? The result was one of the first Anglo-American hybrids. Healey went to work, and the result was a Nash-Healey that was competitive at LeMans. With performance and durability established, the cars went into production with bodies by Panelcraft of England. For '52, the cars were restyled by Pininfarina. Hundreds were sold, in both hardtop and convertible form, but in the end volume was not enough to sustain the project.

Navajo
Navajo Motor Car Co.,
New York City, NY
Year built: c.1954
Production: NA

The Navajo was a three-passenger sports car. A Mercury flathead V8 tweaked up to 130 horsepower was used. A 0-60 mph acceleration time of 7.8 seconds was quoted. The car's most striking feature was its styling, a close copy of the Jaguar XK-120.

Nu-Klea
Nu-Klea Automobile Corp.,
Lansing, MI
Years built: 1959-1960
Production: NA

Despite its name, this was a small electric and not an atomic-powered car. Each rear wheel was driven by a separate motor. The steel chassis carried a fiberglass body in either convertible or hardtop style. A range of 75-85 miles per charge was claimed. This two-passenger car was suspended by leaf springs at the rear and coil springs in front.

Oakland
Oakland-Pontiac Division,
General Motors Corp.,
Pontiac, MI
Years built: 1930-31
Production: 21,943 (1930),
13,408 (1931)

This pioneer automaker was founded in 1907 and acquired the next year by William C. Durant, who made it one of the keystones in his new General Motors enterprise. Oakland prospered for a time, then experienced falling sales in the early '20s, which led to a less expensive but more refined companion model, the Pontiac Six, introduced in 1926. It proved such a success that it soon rendered its "parent" superfluous. The final Oaklands of 1930-31 rode a 117-inch wheelbase and were offered in a variety of open and closed body types spanning an $895-$1055 price spread. All were powered by an 85-bhp 250-cid V8 with uncommonly

oversquare cylinder dimensions and a 180-degree crankshaft that made it a very rough runner.

Olds 1901 Replica
Horseless Carriage Corp.,
Fort Lauderdale, FL
Year built: 1968
Production: NA

This was a ¾-scale replica of the early curved-dash Olds runabout.

Omega
Suspensions International Corporation, Manhasset, NY
Years built: 1967-1968
Production: NA

The stillborn 1966 Griffith GT was given new life in 1967 as the Omega. The car was taken over by Suspensions International though actual construction was carried out by Holman and Moody of Charlotte, North Carolina. The only major change made by the new firm was a switch from the Griffith's Plymouth V8 to a Ford 289 engine and driveline. Base price was $8950. As before, the steel bodies were made by Intermeccanica of Turin, Italy. After this point, the car continued in production for several years as the Torino, Italia, and IMX. All were presumably assembled by Intermeccanica.

Panda
Small Cars Inc.,
Kansas City, KS
Years built: 1955-1956
Production: NA

The Panda was a $1000, two-passenger car built on a 70-inch wheelbase. A fiberglass roadster body was styled like a child's pedal car and was mounted on a frame of the manufacturer's own design. A choice of a 44-cubic-inch Aerojet four-cylinder engine or a 67-cid Kohler flat twin was announced for 1956 (the 1955 prototype sported a Crosley engine).

Panther
Panther Automobile Co.,
Bedford Hills, NY
Years built: 1962-c.1963
Production: NA

This two-passenger fiberglass sports car used a Daimler V8 engine. Coil springs were used for the independent front suspension, while semi-elliptic leaf springs and radius rods were employed at the rear. A 94-inch wheelbase was used.

Paxton
Paxton Engineering Co.,
Los Angeles, CA
Years built: 1951-1954
Production: NA

Sometimes known as the Paxton Phoenix, this was a five-passenger car with styling by Brooks Stevens. A fiberglass body, a "torque-box" frame, and an electronically-operated top were features. At least two

possible engines were considered. The more interesting of these was a 120-horsepower three-cylinder steamer. A compound six-cylinder steam engine was also under development. Much of the engine work was done by none other than Abner Doble, who had created the advanced Doble steam cars of 1914-1931. Ultimately, a rear-mounted Porsche 1500 engine was fitted instead. High production costs ended the venture in 1954.

Peerless
Peerless Motor Car Corp.,
Cleveland, OH
Years built: 1900-1932
Production: NA

"All that the name implies" was the Peerless slogan, and in earlier years it was just that: one of the finer American cars. Through the early '20s, Peerless ranked with Packard and Pierce Arrow the vaunted "Three Ps" of the American industry. When Peerless started to seek higher sales volume in the mid-'20s with cheaper cars using proprietary engines, it lost its earlier quality reputation. In 1932 Peerless made one last-ditch effort to restore its luxury image with a Murphy-bodied V16. It was a beautiful aluminum-bodied sedan, but only one was completed. The Peerless company entered the brewing business after cancelling car operations.

Pioneer
Nic-L-Silver Battery Co.,
Santa Ana, CA
Years built: 1959-c.1960
Production: NA

Pioneer, Lippencott Pioneer and Nic-L-Silver are names that have been applied to this electric car. The design featured twin motors to drive the rear wheels. By flipping a toggle switch, the driver could put the car in forward or reverse. Depending on conditions, range was 40-100 miles between charges. The Pioneer used fiberglass body construction. Overall length was 157 inches and curb weight was 1800 pounds.

Playboy
Playboy Motor Car Corp.,
Buffalo, NY
Years built: 1947-1951
Production: approx. 90

This much-publicized minicar was a three-passenger convertible, with a folding steel top. A Hercules 40-horsepower four was used in most Playboys, although some had a Continental engine of similar displacement. Two of the car's more noteworthy features were a three-speed Warner Gear automatic transmission and self-adjusting brakes. On a 90-inch wheelbase, the 2035-

pound Playboy had an overall length of 155 inches.

Powell
Powell Manufacturing Company, Compton, CA
Years built: 1954-1956
Production: approx. 2400

The Powell Sport Wagon was unusual in several ways. Although registered and sold as new, it incorporated remanufactured Plymouth parts. It was a full-size model, selling initially for only $998. The body was steel, except for a fiberglass nose panel. The rebuilt chassis and 90-horsepower engine were from Plymouths from the '40s and '50s. A pickup truck was styled along similar lines.

Publix
Publix Motor Car Co.,
Buffalo, NY
Years built: 1947-1948
Production: NA

This was a two-passenger three-wheeler with a choice of fabric or plexiglass top. The single wheel was at the front. An aluminum tube frame was used, along with an aluminum body and an aluminum engine. A feather-light vehicle, the Publix weighed only 150 to 200 pounds. Speeds of 40 to 60 mph were attainable. Fuel economy of 70-90 mpg was claimed.

Pup
Pup Motor Car Company,
Spencer, WI
Years built: 1948-1949
Production: NA

Two quite different cars were proposed under the Pup nameplate. One was a very basic open two-seat roadster with four separate fenders and no doors or top. The other, presumably a later design, was an enclosed coupe with slab-sided styling. The bodies were of wood and both models were available with a choice of 7.5-horsepower single-cylinder Briggs & Stratton engine, or a 10-bhp two-cylinder unit. Fuel consumption was in the 50-60 mpg range, top speed was 35-40 mph, and prices were $500-600.

Quantum
Quantum Corporation,
Rockland, MA
Years built: 1962-1963
Production: NA

This rebodied Saab was a light 900 pounds, and shorter than a standard Saab. It was distributed through individual Saab dealers in the U.S.

Rambler 1902 Replica
American Air Products,
Fort Lauderdale, FL
Years built: c.1959-1960
Production: NA

The Rambler 1902 Replica was taken over by Gas-

light Motors Corp. of Lethrup Village, Michigan. In view of this, it seems reasonable to assume that the Rambler Replica was a predecessor of the 1960 Gaslight.

Roadable
Portable Products Corp.,
Garland, TX
Year built: 1946
Production: 1

This three-wheeled car/plane had its single wheel mounted at the front. The two rear wheels and the propeller aided in take-off. When airborne, the wheels disengaged from the drive, and ailerons and elevators were controlled by the steering wheel. A Franklin 130-horsepower engine powered this machine, which could cruise at about 110 mph in the air with a range of 600 miles. Only five minutes were required to remove the wings, twin-boom tail section, and propeller in converting the vehicle for road use. On the highway, the Roadable was good for 60 mph.

Rockefeller Yankee
Rockefeller Sports Car Corp.,
Rockville Centre, NY
Year built: 1953
Production: NA

A tough, durable body of fiberglass and Vibrin was the main feature of this four-passenger sports car. The engine and driveline was all-Ford. The car had a 100-inch wheelbase, a 66-inch width and an overall length of 14 feet. A top speed of 100 mph was claimed.

Rocket
Hewson Pacific Corp.,
Los Angeles, CA
Year built: 1948
Production: NA

The Rocket was a three-passenger car riding a 106-inch wheelbase, with a 161-inch overall length. Two engines were available, either a 65-horsepower four or a 95-bhp six. With either engine, a torque-converter automatic transmission was standard. The body consisted of ten aluminum panels, and the styling was simple and attractive. Price was around $1500. Very few Rockets were made.

Rockne
Studebaker Corporation,
South Bend, IN
Years built: 1932-33
Production: 22,715 (1932), 13,326 (1933)

Named for a local favorite, Notre Dame football coach Knute Rockne, this was another of those Depression-era gambits to preserve a company in trouble with a smaller, lower-priced car line. Introduced for 1932, the Rockne was offered in two series at prices ranging from $585 to no higher than $735. The base

offering was the 110-inch-wheelbase Model 65, powered by a 66-bhp, 190-cid flathead six. The costlier Model 75 had a 114-inch chassis and a 205-cid six with 72 bhp. The cheaper line was redesignated Model 10 for 1933 and got slightly higher compression for an extra four horsepower, though none of these cars were known for performance.

Rollsmobile
Starts Manufacturing Co.,
Fort Lauderdale, FL
Years built: 1958-c.1961
Production: NA

Two replicas were offered, one based on the 1901 Olds and the other on the "1901" Ford. Since the first Ford appeared in 1903, the latter designation is incorrect. Power came from an air-cooled 3-horsepower Continental engine, and top speed was 30 mph. Gas mileage was over 100 mpg.

Roosevelt
Marmon Motor Car Company,
Indianapolis, IN
Years built: 1930-31
Production: 4,132

Introduced in 1929 and named after President Theodore Roosevelt, this was Marmon's "companion" make, the brainchild of George M. Williams, who had been hired by Howard Marmon in 1924 to improve his firm's fiscal health. Bearing handsome lines, the Roosevelt rode a 113-inch wheelbase and was powered by a 202-cid straight eight with 77 bhp. Two coupes and a sedan were offered in all years; a convertible was listed for 1931. The 1929 models bore the image of "T.R.," removed the following year, when the line officially became Marmon-Roosevelt. Prices spanned a narrow $950-$995 range. The Depression severely reduced demand for cars like this, and the Roosevelt expired three years before the Marmon itself.

Rowan
Rowan Controller Co.,
Westminster, MD
Years built: 1967-1969
Production: NA

The tiny Rowan electric was built by Rowan Controller Co. of Westminster, Maryland, and/or Oceanport, New York. It was a closed electric runabout with a pleasant-looking Ghia body. Some of its mechanical parts were from DeTomaso. The car used the dynamic-braking method of generating power during coasting and deceleration. Its range was 200 miles between charges.

Ruger
Sturm Ruger & Co. Inc.,
Southport, CT
Years built: 1969-c.1972

Production: NA

Built by the famous gun maker, and inspired by the 4.5-liter Bentley tourer, the Ruger used fiberglass body panels covered with nauga-hyde. The engine was a 427 cubic-inch Ford V8, which gave 7.7-second 0-60 times—very good for a 3500-pound car. The price was $13,000, and production continued into the early 1970s.

Ruxton
New Era Motors Inc.,
New York, NY
Year built: 1930
Production: approx. 500

Here was one of the most interesting and beautiful cars of the '30s. Its creator was the controversial Archie Andrews, hot-shot promoter and erstwhile Hupp director. The Ruxton used an 85-bhp straight eight to power its ground-hugging front-wheel-drive chassis. The car looked revolutionary with its ultra-low hood and fenders, optional Woodlite headlamps, and absence of running boards. The Ruxton's announcement coincided with the beginning of the Depression, and production ended in November, 1930.

Saviano
Saviano Vehicles Inc.,
Warren, MI
Year built: 1960
Production: NA

The Saviano Scat was a go-anywhere two-door, four-passenger Jeep-type car. The rear seats could be folded down for additional cargo space. The frame was made of welded rectangular tubing. The body used 16-gauge steel, twice the thickness of that commonly used. The engine was an air-cooled 25-horsepower Kohler unit teamed to a Borg-Warner transmission. The 1700-pound vehicle had an 80-inch wheelbase and was priced at $1395.

Scooter Car
Manufacturer unknown
Year built: 1947
Production: NA

The Scooter Car was a two-passenger vehicle available in several forms. One 5-horse-power model lacked a conventional body and was fitted only with angular mud guards. Production lasted only a few months.

Scootmobile
Years built: c.1946-1952
Production: NA

Scootmobile was the result of efforts by three Corunna, Michigan men: Norman Anderson, Vernon Servoss, and Lester Sworthwood. Their car made use of many aircraft parts. The body was a modified auxiliary fuel tank that rolled

on airplane wheels, two in front and one at the rear. Top speed was a moderate 40 mph, although 70 mph was claimed. Production plans for this $350 car, which included an automatic transmission, never materialized.

Seagrave
Seagrave Fire Apparatus Co.,
Columbus, OH
Year built: 1960
Production: 3

This compact sat on a 93-inch wheelbase, and used a four-cylinder Continental engine. Two of the cars had fiberglass bodies, while the third was made of aluminum. Seagrave hoped to sell it for under $3000, but the car never saw production.

Skorpion
Wilro Co., Pasadena, CA
Years built: 1952-1954
Production: NA

This low-priced, fiberglass sports car received rather wide publicity in its day. It was sold as a kit for $445, or fully assembled for $1200. The Skorpion was designed to accept several different chassis and engines. The best combination was the Crosley Hot Shot chassis and the Ford flathead V8.

Skyline
Skyline Inc., Jamaica, NY
Year built: c.1953
Production: NA

The Skyline was a two-passenger hardtop-convertible that shared its L-head six-cylinder engine, its chassis and most of its lower body panels with the Henry J. At the push of a button, the top swung completely out of sight. Many safety features were incorporated, including seat belts, shoulder harness, padded instrument panel and recessed knobs. The Skyline was intended to sell for less than $3000.

Spook Electric
Dynamic Development,
Pasadena, CA
Year built: 1968
Production: NA

The Spook featured a 36-volt DC ball-bearing motor connected to the rear wheels by a chain drive. Six 6-volt batteries completed the power package. The steel-and-fiberglass body rested on a steel-channel frame. The car weighed only 750 pounds, and was 99 inches long and 41 inches high.

Star Dust
Grantham Motor Car Co.,
Los Angeles, CA
Year built: 1953
Production: NA

Star Dust used an altered Ford chassis with a 110-inch wheelbase. The engine was also Ford, but located five inches

lower and 19 inches farther back in the chassis than normal. Weight was 2650 pounds. Estimated price was $3750.

Starlite
Kish Industries Inc.,
Lansing, MI
Years built: c.1959-?
Production: NA

This was an electric sports model, with an 82-inch wheel-base and an overall length of 148 inches. A soft-top version was produced, and a clear-plastic hardtop model was planned. Prices were around $3000.

Stearns-Knight
F.B. Stearns Company,
Cleveland, OH
Years built: 1899-1930
Production: NA

The Stearns Company was founded in 1899, and built nothing but luxury cars. The sleeve-valve Stearns-Knight engine displaced 385 cubic inches and developed 127 bhp in this final model year. Eight body styles were offered in the stratospheric price heights of $5000 and up. Most were sedans, though a swank cabriolet roadster was also available. Stearns' three wheelbases were 126, 134, and 145 inches.

Storm
Sports Car Development
Corp., Detroit, MI
Year built: 1954
Production: NA

The Storm had a two-passenger Bertone body and a 250-bhp Dodge V8, but little other information about it is available.

Stout Project Y
Kaiser-Frazer Corporation,
Detroit, MI
Year built: 1946
Production: 1

Beginning in 1936, the brilliant inventor/engineer William B. Stout produced unique streamlined cars called Scarabs in his Detroit factory. After World War II, Stout teamed up with Kaiser-Frazer to build a revolutionary postwar car with a fiberglass body, Mercury V8, a 74-inch wide rear seat and sleek styling. K-F abandoned this effort, called Project Y, in the summer of 1946 because it was too radical and too expensive. The price was also forbidding: Stout estimated that a production version might cost $10,000. Project Y was saved, and may be seen today at the Detroit Historical Museum.

Stuart
Stuart Motors, Kalamazoo, MI
Year built: 1962
Production: 1

The Stuart was a two-passenger fiberglass-bodied electric. Overall length was 115 in-

ches, width 64 inches, height 56 inches. Eight 6-volt batteries supplied current to the 4-horsepower motor. The Stuart had a 40-mile range when driven at 35 mph. The 1200-pound vehicle was available in a passenger version for $1600, or as a commercial for $1500.

Studillac
Bill Frick Motors,
Rockville Centre, NY
Years built: 1953-1955
Production: NA

Around 1953, Bill Frick began installing Cadillac engines in Studebaker hardtops. This was a great combination: a production body of outstanding beauty coupled with a high-performance Cadillac V8. Acceleration from 0 to 60 miles per hour took just 8.5 seconds, and top speed was 125 mph. The Studillac conversion added some $1500 to the Studebaker's cost, so the total package price in 1954 was $3695 with three-speed manual transmission, or $4195 with Dual-Range Hydra-Matic.

Stutz
Stutz Motor Car of America
Inc., New York City, NY
Years built: 1969-date
Production: NA

This was a revival in name only. The car itself was modern, quite similar in appearance to the 1966 Duesenberg. Indeed, Virgil Exner styled both cars. Based on the Pontiac Grand Prix chassis with a 116-inch wheelbase, Stutz offered two-door hardtop, convertible, and limousine body styles, and, briefly, a ceremonial parade car. The bodies were supplied by Carrozzeria Padana of Italy. Prices, depending on model, have ranged from $22,500 to over $110,000.

Super Station Wagon
Henney Motor Co.,
Freeport, IL
Year built: 1954
Production: NA

This conversion was based on the contemporary 1954 Packard Cavalier sedan. A 12-passenger station wagon, it featured an observation lounge arrangement with a three-passenger curved rear seat and a table. Packard's straight-eight engine was retained. Though production was intended, the car's price of around $7500 precluded many orders.

Surrey
E.W. Bliss Co.,
Canton, OH
Year built: c.1960
Production: NA

This antique replica duplicated the appearance of the curved-dash Olds. The standard engine was rated at 4.8

horsepower, but an 8-bhp air-cooled Cushman unit was optional. The car rode on 12-spoke wooden wheels. Top speed was 35 mph and mileage was a claimed 65 mpg. The base model was priced at $1045; the DeLuxe was $100 more. The Surrey was also available in kit form for $895.

Swift
Swift Manufacturing Co.,
El Cajon, CA
Year built: 1959
Production: NA

The Swift was first built by Swift Manufacturing, then by W.M. Manufacturing Co. in San Diego. Three different 5/8-scale replica models were offered. All used the same basics—a single-cylinder air-cooled Clinton engine and belt drive. The Swift-T looked like a 1910 Model T Ford. The Stutz Bearcat was mirrored by the Swift-Cat, while the Swifter was similar to the first 1903 Cadillac. Top speed was hardly swift at 27 mph. Prices were in the vicinity of $795.

Tasco
Derham Body Co.,
Rosemont, PA
Year built: 1948
Production: NA

Tasco is an acronym for The American Sports Car Company of Hartford, Connecticut, organized by members of the SCCA to build an American sports car. The Tasco was designed by Gordon Buehrig and featured removeable plastic roof panels. The front fenders turned with the wheels as the car was steered. The engine was a modified Mercury V8. Had it been produced, the Tasco would have cost $7500, too high to attract many buyers in 1948.

Taylor-Dunn
Taylor-Dunn Manufacturing
Co., Anaheim, CA
Years built: 1948-1968
Production: NA

This electric was built in car and truck form. The cars were built with three or four wheels. The three-wheelers had a 98-inch wheelbase, while four-wheelers had an inch-longer wheelbase and were three inches longer overall. Passenger capacity varied from two to four, depending on model. These electrics could reach a speed of 12 mph and had a range of 30 miles between charges.

Thrif-T
Tri-Wheel Motor Corp.,
Oxford, NC
Years built: 1947-55
Production: NA

The most notable feature of this $800 three-wheeler was a 62.6-cid Onan flat twin mounted on a detachable cradle that

could be detached and rolled away in about 30 minutes. Pickup, closed delivery, and open utility body types were offered on an 85-inch wheelbase and 126-inch overall length. Curb weight was about 900 pounds, payload about 500 pounds, top speed 35-40 mph. The company optimistically expected to build 500 vehicles monthly, but startup was delayed several years and it's doubtful the rate was even 50 per month.

Towne Shopper
International Motor Car Company, San Diego, CA
Year built: 1948
Production: NA

This 116-inch-long two-seat open car sat on a 63-inch wheelbase and weighed but 600 pounds, thanks to extensive use of aluminum in its construction. A combination starter/generator/flywheel was employed along with a 10.5-bhp Onan twin, giving a 50-mph top speed and 50-mpg fuel economy. Announced price was $595 and planned volume was 100 units per day. In September 1948, shortly after the builder went out of business, a Carter Motor Corporation announced its "Town Shopper," with a 79-inch wheelbase, 130-inch overall length, 1000-pound curb weight, and steel body and frame. It's not known whether this was a revised design by a reorganized company or a new model by a different firm.

Tri-Car
Lycoming Division, Avco Corp., Williamsport, PA or Tri-Car Co., Wheatland, PA
Year built: 1955
Production: NA

Though sources disagree on who built it, they do agree that this was a small, rear-engine three-wheeler, with the single wheel at the rear. The closed, three-passenger fiberglass body was mounted on a Goodrich rubber suspension system, and a Lycoming vertical twin drove the rear wheel via torque converter. A top speed of 65 mph and fuel consumption of 41.5 mpg were reported for this 117-inch-long vehicle.

Triplex
Ketchem's Automotive Corp., Chicago, IL
Years built: c.1954-1955
Production: NA

Sometimes referred to as the Lightning, this two-place sports model with one-piece fiberglass body was derived from the earlier Chicagoan

(see entry). Almost any engine could be fitted, but the box-section chassis was intended primarily to accept a contemporary Ford V8.

Tucker
Tucker Corporation, Chicago, IL
Years built: 1948-50
Production: 51

One of the most controversial cars ever built, the Tucker 48 was a rear-engine, fastback four-door sedan on a 128-inch wheelbase. Styling, from the pen of the respected Alex Tremulis, was marked by pontoon fenders and a unique "cyclop's eye" third headlight in front. Power was supplied by a 335-cid air-cooled flat six made of aluminum alloy, basically a Franklin engine modified by Aircooled Motors of Syracuse, New York. All-independent suspension and a safety-inspired interior were featured. With 166 bhp and the highest power-to-weight ratio yet seen on a U.S. car, the Tucker was capable of 0-60 mph in 10 seconds and 120 mph maximum. The enterprising Preston Tucker sold $15 million worth of stock and planned production in a leased Dodge aircraft plant in Chicago, but the venture collapsed due to a highly publicized Securities and Exchange Commission fraud investigation

U.S. Mark II
U.S. Fiberglass Company, Norwood, NJ
Year built: 1956
Production: NA

A fiberglass convertible on wheelbases of 110 to 118 inches, this car was sold in both kit and fully assembled form. No other information about it survives today.

Valkyrie
Fiberfab, Inc., Los Angeles, CA
Years built: 1967-69
Production: NA

This well-known kit-car company briefly became a manufacturer of sorts by putting its familiar Valkyrie body on a special ladder-type frame with a rear-mounted 450-bhp 427 Chevy V8 and five-speed ZF transaxle. The rather outlandish $12,500 asking price bought you claimed 3.9-second 0-60 mph acceleration and a top speed in excess of 180 mph. A conspicuous drag chute was provided as an aid to high-speed braking.

Vetta Ventura
Vanguard Motors Corp., Dallas, TX

Years built: 1964-66
Production: NA

The Vetta Ventura was identical with the Apollo (see entry) in everything but name, and it appears both were produced simultaneously for a time. The Apollo seems to have been phased out during 1965, while the Vetta was still to be sold in May 1966. Coupe and convertible models were listed at that time at $6897 and $7237, respectively. Bodies were built by Intermeccanica in Turin, and shipped to Texas for final assembly.

Viking
Oldsmobile Motor Division, General Motors Corp., Lansing, MI
Year built: 1930
Production: 1,390

Born in the optimism of 1929, the Viking died in the pessimism and uncertainty of the early Depression. Unlike GM's other companion makes, this was not a cheaper "junior edition" but an upmarket extension of its parent, offering more deluxe coachwork, better trim, and an eight-cylinder engine for about $500 more than a comparable six-cylinder Olds. More closely resembling LaSalle in overall design, the Viking was powered by an 81-bhp 260-cid V8 with nearly square cylinder dimensions and a row of horizontal valves, actuated by a chain-driven camshaft. Three body styles were offered for 1930, and there were few changes from the 1929 versions, which saw production of just 6612 units.

Voltra
Voltra, Inc., New York, NY
Year built: c.1962
Production: NA

As the name suggests, this was a compact electric car. Powered by a General Electric DC motor, it rode a 106-inch wheelbase, was 170 inches long, weighted 1600 pounds, and could reach a maximum speed of 45 mph.

Warrior
Vanguard Products, Inc., Dallas, TX
Year built: 1964
Production: NA

Mounted on a 94-inch-wheelbase chassis made of rectangular steel tubing, this two-seat targa-roof sports car was powered by a Ford Germany V4 engine mounted at the rear. It had an unlikely orginator: an air conditioner manufacturer.

Westcoaster
Manufacturer unknown

Year built: 1960
Production: NA

An electric from the "first" compact-car era, the Westcoaster used a 36-volt GE system that differed from most other designs in having a built-in battery charger with automatic voltage relay. Strictly a golf cart or very light-duty shopper, it was a three-wheeler with a rudimentary fiberglass body and no doors; a snap-on fiberglass hardtop was optional. Production apparently did not continue beyond the introductory year.

Whippet
Willys-Overland Motors, Toledo, OH
Years built: 1930-31
Production: 43,422 (est.)

Introduced with a fanfare in 1926, the Whippet sent Willys-Overland sales soaring to a peak of 315,000 units in 1928. It continued as the "price leader" in the lengthy 1930 Willys line and came in two versions: the 103.3-inch-wheelbase Model 96A with a 40-bhp, 136-cid four, and the 112.5-inch-wheelbase Model 98A, powered by a 50-bhp 179-cid six. Coupe, sedan, and roadster were offered in each series. Prices started at an attractively low $505 for the fours, but the sixes ran a considerable $180 higher.

Williams
Williams Engine Co., Ambler, PA
Years built: 1957-68
Production: NA

Calvin Williams and his sons labored on a practical, modern steam-driven automobile since the 1940s. When they entered the market in the mid-'50s, it was with mostly conventional gasoline engines converted to steam operation. A 1963 model used the fiberglass S-4 body from Victress, the kit car manufacturer, and sold for $7000. A later effort was a converted '66 Chevrolet Chevelle priced at $10,250. The high costs of maintaining low-volume production ultimately forced the firm to abandon the auto business entirely.

Woodill
Woodill Motor Company, Downey, CA
Years built: 1952-56
Production: 15

This company gets credit for launching America's first fiberglass-bodied production sports car. Called the Wildfire, it was conceived by Dodge/Willys dealer B.R. "Woody" Woodill mainly as a kit, but a

few fully assembled cars were sold at prices ranging from an initial $2900 to a final $4500. The low-silhouette bodywork, supplied by Glasspar (see entry), was mated to a 101-inch-wheelbase frame designed by engineer and ex-hot rodder Shorty Post around the Willys 90-bhp F-head six and three-speed overdrive manual transmission. The Wildfire was quick despite its pedestrian mechanicals, and might have seen volume production had not Willys-Overland been purchased by Kaiser-Frazer.

Yank
Custom Auto Works, San Diego, CA
Year built: 1950
Production: NA

This two-seat aluminum-bodied sports car was built on a 100-inch wheelbase and could run up to 78 mph with its Willys four-cylinder engine. The price was $1000.

Yankee Clipper
Strassberger Motor Company, Menlo Park, CA
Years built: 1953-54
Production: NA

A lightweight, purpose-designed 101-inch-wheelbase chassis topped by a Glasspar G-2 body (see Glasspar) made up this completely assembled car, which stood just 37 inches high and weighed 1900 pounds. Many 1954 Ford components were fitted, including a 130-bhp V8. Early plans called for production of 40 units a month and a selling price of $3400, but actual output was likely limited at best.

Yenko
Yenko Sportscars, Inc., Cannonsburg, PA
Years built: 1965-71?
Production: 185

Operated by Chevrolet dealer Don Yenko, this firm initially offered five modified versions of the Corvair Corsa coupe, packing 160 to 240 horsepower and intended mainly for competition. All versions were called Stinger, and all used the 164-cid Corvair flat six except for the most powerful model, which had a slightly overbored 176-cid powerplant. A Stinger won the SCCA's 1967 national D-production road racing championship. Two Camaro-based Yenko models were listed for 1969, with engines of 435 and 450 bhp. In 1971, Yenko announced a Turbo Stinger, a blown version of the subcompact Vega to be available through selected Chevy dealers. How many of these were built is not known.